The Dramatic Experience

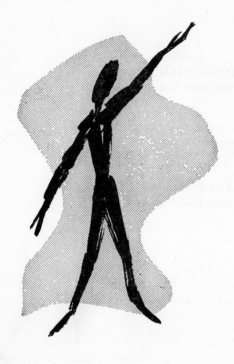

JUDAH BIERMAN
JAMES HART
STANLEY JOHNSON

1958
PRENTICE-HALL, INC.
Englewood Cliffs, N.J.

PRENTICE-HALL ENGLISH LITERATURE SERIES

Maynard Mack *editor*

© 1958 BY

PRENTICE-HALL, INC.
ENGLEWOOD CLIFFS, N.J.

Table of

One — The Elements of Drama

Oregon Shakespearean Festival Association, Ashland, Oregon (Angus L. Bowmer, director; William W. Patton, general manager), for permission to use photographs from their productions of *Twelfth Night* (1951) and *Othello* (1957).

Stratford Shakespearean Festival, Ontario, Canada, for a photograph from their production of *Oedipus* (1954), directed by Tyrone Guthrie, with James Mason as Oedipus, Robert Goodier as Creon, Eleanor Stuart as Jocasta.

Acknowledgments

The editors wish to make the following acknowledgments for permission to use the material included in this book:

Random House, Inc., for *The Desperate Hours* (play) and for excerpts from *The Desperate Hours* (novel), both by Joseph Hayes. *The Desperate Hours* (novel) by Joseph Hayes, copyright 1954 by Marijane and Joseph Hayes. Reprinted by permission of Random House, Inc. *The Desperate Hours* (play), copyright 1955 by Joseph Hayes. Reprinted by permission of Random House, Inc.

Charles Scribner's Sons for *Abe Lincoln in Illinois* by Robert E. Sherwood. Copyright 1939 by Robert E. Sherwood and reprinted by permission of Charles Scribner's Sons.

Harcourt, Brace and Company, Inc., for *The Time of Your Life* by William Saroyan. Copyright 1939 by Harcourt, Brace and Company, Inc., and reprinted with their permission.

Dodd, Mead & Co., Inc., for *Caesar and Cleopatra* by Bernard Shaw. Copyright 1900 by Herbert S. Stone & Co. Copyright 1928 by George Bernard Shaw. By arrangement with Dodd, Mead & Co., Inc.

Harcourt, Brace and Company, Inc., for *The Oedipus Rex of Sophocles:* An English Version by Dudley Fitts and Robert Fitzgerald. Copyright 1949 by Harcourt, Brace and Company, Inc., and reprinted with their permission.

iii

New Directions for *Blood Wedding* by Federico Garcia Lorca, translated by Richard L. O'Connell and James Graham-Luján. Copyright 1947 by New Directions.

Viking Press for *Death of a Salesman* by Arthur Miller. Copyright 1949 by Arthur Miller. Reprinted by permission of The Viking Press, Inc.

We are also indebted to the following for permission to quote excerpts from other works:

Rinehart and Co., Inc., for permission to reprint an excerpt from *You Can't Take It With You* by Moss Hart and George S. Kaufman.

Random House for permission to quote from *The Hairy Ape* by Eugene O'Neill. Copyright 1922 by Eugene O'Neill. Published by Random House, Inc.

New Directions for permission to quote a paragraph from the essay, "The Timeless World of a Play," by Tennessee Williams. Copyright 1950 by Tennessee Williams. Reprinted by permission of New Directions Books.

Cambridge University Press for permission to quote from the Jebb translation of *Oedipus Tyrannus*, published by the Cambridge University Press.

Methuen and Co., Ltd., London, for permission to quote from *Greek Tragedy* by H. D. F. Kitto.

The editors also wish to acknowledge their indebtedness to Professor Hoyt C. Franchere, Chairman of the Division of Humanities, Portland State College, for making available funds for editorial assistants, and for continued support and encouragement.

Valuable assistance was given by *Theatre Arts* magazine and the Theatre Arts Librarian, New York Public Library, in obtaining photographs used in this book. For individual photographs, we are indebted to the following:

New York Public Library for photographs of productions of *Everyman, Blood Wedding, The Desperate Hours,* and *Caesar and Cleopatra.*

British Information Services, 45 Rockefeller Plaza, New York 20, for permission to use a photograph from the Laurence Olivier-Vivien Leigh production of *Caesar and Cleopatra.*

Contents

Two — The Major Modes of Drama

Part
One

The Elements
of
Drama

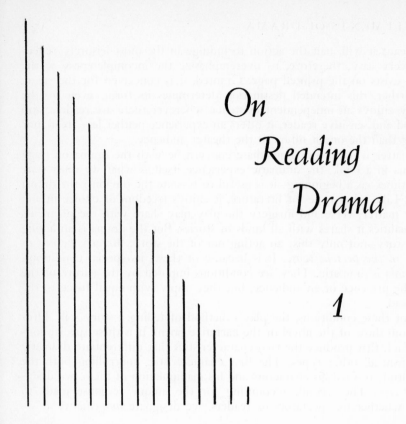

On Reading Drama

1

THE DRAMATIC EXPERIENCE

Partisans of the legitimate theater have a way of telling us that no play can exist apart from the stage for which it was written. Divorce the dramatist from his theater collaborators, they contend, and you find yourself with nothing but bare bones: lifeless words on the printed page. Leave out of account the actor, you sacrifice both his vital physical presence and the countless vocal inflexions he can bring to his speaking of the printed dialogue; leave out of account setting and costume, you sacrifice spectacle—dimension, proportion, color; leave out of account the audience, you deprive yourself of one of the distinctive satisfactions the drama offers—subtle, perhaps, but very real: your awareness of a shared experience.

At first sight, claims such as these may seem unanswerable. And this much is true: it is certainly valid to distinguish between the play as seen and the play as read. No less valid is the parallel distinction between spectator and reader, and beyond question the latter must do without the peculiar vividness of the live performance. Yet such losses as he incurs are not, finally, irreparable; minimal acquaintance with the special responsibilities of actor, designer, and producer will work toward the making good of these losses. Nor should we overlook the reader's freedom to exercise a prerogative that is his and not the spectator's: he can, at will, halt the action to indulge in the most leisurely reflection. It is very easy, therefore, to overemphasize the incompleteness of the drama as it exists on the printed page. Granted, it is conceived for the stage; granted, further, this intended destination determines its form: even so, the printed play enjoys an independent existence wherever there are readers, and to the skilled and sensitive reader, it offers an experience neither less "real" nor less exciting than the one it offers to the theater audience.

But no matter whether our immediate concern be with the drama on stage or the drama in a book, the dramatic experience itself is what we must start with. Sometimes—as a beginning—it is useful to re-state the obvious: the drama is dramatic. Like other types of literature, it enjoys freedom of choice in aim and subject matter; verse and imagery the play may share with the poem; its narrative qualities it shares with all kinds of stories. But the drama is an *acting out* of the story—not only this: an acting out of the story, *directly before us and always in the present tense*. It is because of these, its special conditions, that the drama is dramatic. They are conditions imposed by the nature of the stage and the presence of an audience, but they apply with equal force to the drama as read.

Because of these conditions, the play's method of telling a story will differ radically from those of the novel or the narrative poem. It is these special conditions, in fact, that produce the two characteristics that differentiate dramatic literature from all other types. The first characteristic, controlling both the author's attitude toward his characters and his manipulation of them, we designate *objectivity*. The second, accounting for the unique response made to the drama, whether by spectators or readers, we designate *immediacy*.

Objectivity

We soon discover that, even in our reading of a play, we never move outside the circumscribing orbit of the characters' world. Our attention never shifts from the characters themselves, who, once they are set in motion, must seem from that moment forth to be moving independently of their creator, to be working out their own destinies without assistance from the author. We stand directly in the presence of these created human beings, at the very moment when they move and speak. If the author is to succeed in enlisting our belief, he must ensure that we remain conscious *only* of his characters; he must never allow us for an instant to become conscious of his manipulating hand. Indeed, just as soon as, and just so far as, we do become aware of the author's imminence, we cease to credit his invention. He must therefore make certain that his own voice is at all times inaudible; he remains *objective*, altogether "outside" the story his characters are unfolding for him. His ideas can be articulated only through the voices of his characters, his created human beings; on stage, the dramatist has no voice of his own.

Because dialogue is the primary medium of the play, the credibility of the characters as human beings is necessarily measured by their speech. The dramatist, knowing that every individual possesses his own distinctive personality, knows also that that personality finds expression in an individualized tone of voice and in idiosyncrasies of vocabulary. In creating a character, therefore, he is bound to honor the principle of objectivity in two related ways: He must not intrude himself into the life of his character, and he must maintain that character's self-consistency. In the drama, as in life, tone of voice and vocabulary are products of environmental factors, of climate and geography, of economic status and education, as well as of the emotional situation of the moment. Hence the dramatist will put into each character's mouth only such words as may arise readily and naturally from a distinctive personality. In the first play in this book, *The Desperate Hours,* the heavy, thick voice of the escaped convict, Robish, is easily distinguishable both from the high-pitched, nervously edged sound of Griffin's speech and the rather dull, then exasperated, and finally desperate tones of Daniel Hilliard. Moreover, Hilliard speaks to his wife on a level of reference not available to Griffin and Robish. And like all young people, the Hilliard boy has a language—vocabulary, tone, delivery—all his own. The dramatist thus finds it necessary to create a great variety of voices, but in no case may the tone of voice or the language be recognizable as his own. For the sound of the dramatist's own voice destroys the characters' integrity and with it the reality of their created, self-consistent world.

The central importance of dialogue in the drama raises a second problem in regard to objectivity. Unlike the novelist, the playwright cannot interrupt the progress of his story for the sake of explication; that is, he is not free to walk on stage, interrupt his characters' conversation, and then stride to the footlights to disentangle for us, in direct speech, a skein of complex motives. And yet, like all writers, he often wishes to penetrate beneath the surface of things; the broader his aims, the deeper he will need to penetrate in order to project his vision of life. No aspect of experience lies outside his range; he may rightfully concern himself even with what Eugene O'Neill called "the behind-life," the life of the subconscious. Yet it is just when the dramatist enters this area of subtle motivation, of psychological and moral complexity, that the principle of objectivity creates for him a problem from which the novelist is free. Both kinds of writers are at liberty to search the minds of the human beings they create; they enjoy the same omniscience. But only the novelist may publish his discoveries directly; whenever he chooses he may be his own spokesman. The dramatist has no voice of his own, and so cannot insist on the prerogatives of (for example) Dickens, who, in the novel, *Dombey and Son,* interrupts the conversation of a pair of his characters to explain:

These [remembrances] were associated with a woman who hated him deeply, and who knew him, and who mistrusted him because she knew him, and because he knew her; but who fed her resentment by suffering him to draw nearer and yet nearer to her every day, in spite of the hate she cherished for him. In spite of it! For that very reason; since in its very depths, too far down for her threatening eye to pierce, though she could see into them dimly, lay the dark retaliation, whose faintest shadow, seen once and shuddered at, and never seen again, would have been sufficient stain upon her soul.

How is the dramatist to communicate such information as this? Dickens is here addressing us, his readers, directly, and to do so is an advantage not allowed to the dramatist, who has but one spokesman, the character upon the stage. And because the actions of the character often fail to explain themselves visually to our observing eye, the dramatist must depend on the character's heard speech to complete our understanding. He does not enjoy the freedom to alternate between passages of dialogue and passages of explication which characterizes the fictional narrative. What we need to learn, he must allow us to overhear. We have but one verbal source of information, and this is the dialogue which the author puts into the mouths of his characters.

Immediacy: the audience

From what has been said of the problem of objectivity, it is clear that the dramatist is subject to limiting rules and conventions unknown to the novelist. He cannot speak in his own voice; neither can he halt the forward movement of his story to offer analytical or descriptive comment. Nevertheless, these seeming limitations conspire to produce what is assuredly his most conspicuous advantage, namely, the fact that those for whom he ultimately writes will be people seated before a stage, in the company of actors who are like themselves in form and speech, who move and talk, who respond emotionally and intellectually in clearly apprehensible ways. Though his characters may be citizens of medieval Verona or Napoleon's France, they yet inhabit, in the theater, a three-dimensional stage setting where for their hour they live their lives as fellow human beings of palpable presence. All the physical properties of the theater combine to lead us into that "willing suspension of disbelief" described by Coleridge. They lead us beyond the point of passively giving credence to the author's creation, and enlist our minds and emotions as co-participants with the characters in the developing story.

The dramatist knows that in the theater there exists between his characters —in the persons of the actors—and the audience a special relationship, the essence of which is its unique directness. Here nothing intervenes between the author's words and the auditors for whom he intended them. Equally important, however, is the special relationship between audience and action, for this is not action *described* but action *witnessed*, and the difference between the two is as great as the difference, let us say, between witnessing a violent highway accident and reading about it, twenty-four hours later, in a newspaper report. As a consequence of such relationships, immediacy becomes the distinguishing feature of "live" drama. Thus the experience of watching a play unfold on the stage, always in the present tense, is distinct from the experience of reading a story, which is essentially a "report" of a past action.

Immediacy: the reader

If immediacy is the special distinction of the drama in the theater, it is also, with certain qualifications we must frankly recognize, the special distinction of the drama as read. Obviously we miss, on the printed page, the three-dimensional attractions which the theater supplies. We cannot actually hear the differentiated voices of the live actors. We do not see movement or gesture or costume. These are, to be sure, significant losses. Yet, as readers we can learn to train our imaginations to supply what is sacrificed when the play is taken away from the stage. Moreover, what still remains, even after the physical properties of the theater are subtracted, will suffice to provide the immediate impact that makes drama so unusual an experience.

For example, the reader accustomed to the novel or short story will be surprised, on his first encounter with the printed drama, at the rapidity with which things happen. This swiftness of action, carrying us from one event to the next, is the consequence, simply, of the continuity of movement essential to drama. Once the imaginary curtain is up, the action can never be arrested until the immediate segment or "chapter" of the total story has been completed and the curtain falls again.

Rapidity and continuity of movement, then, make immediacy a distinguishing feature of the *printed* drama, too. And this rapidity and continuity are consequences of the special kind of time the drama keeps. The reader of drama is always in the presence of the dramatist's characters at the very moment when they speak and move. The writer of a short story or novel conventionally identifies the voices of his characters by adding to the words they speak such phrases as *he said* or *she asked;* but in the drama, even as read, the present tense always takes the place of the past, for what we "hear" are the characters themselves *speaking.* Again, when we give our belief to story or novel, we tend to feel that we *were* "there" at the time of the events described, for the action in such literature usually takes place in some sort of indefinite past, either remote or immediate. But in the drama, whether on stage or printed page, we *are* "there." The same time-present engulfs both character and reader. This present-ness of the drama is not duplicated in any other type of literature; it enables us to participate in a play, emotionally and intellectually, to a degree unknown in our reading of non-dramatic narratives. We may therefore say that under all circumstances, and wherever encountered, the drama offers, as its unique distinction, the impact of immediacy.

Reading the play

This sense of immediacy produces a certain dramatic tension. When you are inside a warm and darkened theater, your attention is focused on the lighted stage, where people like you are moving and conversing. Because all the rushing, crowding, distracting irrelevancies of life are excluded for the moment, life on the stage, as opposed to life on the street or in the school, is a life in which every moment is meaningful; devoid of daydreaming, of drifting, of brief periods of aimlessness, it is a life of more constant awareness than that we experience from day to day. Even when the dramatist's story demands a day-dreaming character, the daydreaming the character indulges in has specific dramatic purpose; it is never merely digressive, but is part of a controlled creation.

In the final analysis this tension is the result of the two-fold nature of time in the drama. Time in the drama is both accelerated, in the sense that events appear to move with unusual rapidity, and controlled, in such a way that time is allotted only to those actions and speeches which point to the conclusion the author wishes to reach. In a play, as Tennessee Williams has noted,

. . . time is arrested in the sense of being confined. By a sort of legerdemain, events are made to remain *events*, rather than being reduced so quickly to *occurrences*. The audience can sit back in a comforting dusk to watch a world which is flooded with light and in which emotion and action have a dimension and dignity that they would likewise have in real existence, if only the shattering intrusion of time could be locked out.[1]

To understand how we, as readers, can share in the experience Williams describes, we need to look more closely at the nature of a printed play. Such a play consists wholly of the dialogue and the author's directions for scene design and stage movement. In the play as seen, these stage directions are translated into setting, action, gesture, costume, and tone of voice. But in the play as read, one is apt to be so absorbed in the rapidly developing story and shifting exchanges of dialogue that these significant elements are overlooked. There is no question about the centrality of dialogue in the drama, seen or read; but any reading of the play must be incomplete that does not include the closest attention to the playwright's stage directions. This aspect of the printed drama therefore requires special emphasis.

The play you read is to the play you see as an architect's blueprint is to the finished house. The house is there on the blueprint, the play there on the page; but just as a whole corps of workmen are needed to raise and finish the house, in order to realize the architect's intentions, so too the dramatist must turn over the staging of his play to a director, to the actors, to the scene designer and the whole backstage crew. Each man has a function to perform; and only after all have been molded into a working unit, only when all their individual contributions have been forged into the final joint-creation, will the audience be able to see what the dramatist intended.

The play you see must therefore be either that live performance by the playwright's fellow workers, or—and this is the present concern—the imagined performance that you create in the mind's eye and ear. This imagined presentation, which the reader "stages" as he reads, is not without compensations for the loss of visual and aural impact inside the theater, for the dramatist's professional collaborators are, after all, limited by a full share of human fallibility. A poorly designed setting, the wooden behavior of a single inept actor, a miscalculated or badly timed gesture—any one of these may call attention to itself, and, in so doing, prove fatal both to the audience's illusion and the author's intention. But obviously the reader of a play is not subject to distractions of this kind. While he reads, his imagination produces for him his own performance of a play, and this will be as nearly ideal as his own experience will allow.

But although the dramatist is powerless to bring his play unaided into the theater, he does conceive of his work, as he writes, in terms of its ultimate staging. Writing thus for the stage, he knows that his own creative capacities will be augmented by those of his collaborators—designer, actor, director. For these fellow workers are more than mere conduits through which the playwright's vision comes to you. They, too, are creators whose task is to bring to life his idea in three dimensions, in color, in voice, and in gesture. The author writes always with the knowledge that a word or phrase of direction can be translated into a complex movement. Consider something so simple as Ibsen's directions to the actors playing Gregers and Hialmar in his drama, *The Wild Duck:*

[1] "The Timeless World of a Play," preface to *The Rose Tattoo* (Norfolk, Conn.: New Directions, 1951), pp. viii-ix.

Gregers [*softly*]: You must join in, Hialmar.
Hialmar [*writhing*]: What am I to talk about?

The single words in brackets actually suggest the facial expressions of the two characters (one troubled and solicitous, the other insecure and frightened), their tone of voice, and their postures. More than this, the dramatist depends upon the actor playing Gregers to use a quality of softness in this exchange which will be clearly differentiated from the kind of softness he uses later in the interview with his father. Thus the dramatist writes for, and so makes use of, his fellow workers.

The contrast in this respect between playwright and novelist is important. The novelist has no professional collaborators; he lacks all of the special resources implicit in the immediate contact between character and audience. He must therefore bend all his efforts toward making his reader, while he reads, create imaginatively the elements of setting, costume, gesture, and tone of voice. His reader's participation in action and emotional current is wholly dependent on the functioning of his inner responses.

In this sense of visualizing or imagining the action, reading a play is much like reading a novel. But there is, for the reader, this highly significant difference: While the novelist may describe or comment as he will, the dramatist is limited, save for the actual dialogue, to his stage directions. How important these directions are, we may best see by contrasting two versions of the same climactic moment in an unhappy love affair. The first consists exclusively of dialogue:

Mme. de Cintré: Something very grave has happened. I can't marry you.
Newman: Why not?
Mme. de Cintré: You must ask my mother. You must ask my brother.
Newman: Why can't she marry me?
Marquis de Bellegarde: It's impossible!
Mme. de Bellegarde: It is improper.
Newman: Oh, you're fooling!
Marquis de Bellegarde: My sister, you've no time; you're losing your train.
Newman: Come, is he mad?
Mme. de Cintré: No; don't think that. But I'm going away.
Newman: Where are you going?
Mme. de Cintré: To the country . . . to be alone.
Newman: To leave *me* alone?
Mme. de Cintré: I can't see you now.
Newman: "Now"—why not?
Mme. de Cintré: I'm ashamed.
Newman: What have you done to her? What does it mean?
Mme. de Cintré: It means that I've given you up. It means that.

Even taken from its proper context in this way, and without stage directions, this dialogue reports something about an event that is occurring; the meaning of the words, as words, is clear and significant. We learn that Newman (either an Englishman or an American, but probably the latter, since in his exasperation he exclaims, "Oh, you're fooling!") has received a promise of marriage from a titled Frenchwoman, and that, for reasons not explicitly stated, her mother and brother have persuaded her to break the engagement. However, this is almost literally the maximum information which the passage conveys as it stands. It offers the merest skeleton of a situation, the merest suggestion of a presumably complex relationship involving four human beings.

But so far as it interests us at all, the incident revealed in this exchange raises a series of questions which it leaves altogether unanswered. Some are quite obvious: Where is this scene taking place? What is its setting—a Parisian drawing room or a New York apartment? Other questions point to more complicated relationships: What does the heroine do during the encounter? What are her feelings, and how, aside from her relatively impersonal and cold words, does she reveal them? What are Newman's feelings? Is Mme. de Cintré genuinely ashamed? Is Newman angry, or puzzled, or both? Still another kind of question arises: Why does the Marquis speak so suddenly and (it would seem) irrelevantly about the train?

Reprinting the scene as Henry James actually conceived it[2] will answer these questions for us; but, more important, it will allow the reader, first, to grasp the relationship between stage directions and the novelist's freely injected explanatory comments, and, second, to arrive at an appreciation of the value of such stage directions to the dramatist. This is the passage in the novel:

In the middle of the room stood Mme. de Cintré; her face was flushed and marked and she was dressed for traveling. Behind her, before the fireplace, stood [the Marquis] de Bellegarde and looked at his fingernails; near the Marquis sat his mother, buried in an armchair and with her eyes fixing themselves on the invader, as he felt them pronounce him. He knew himself, as he entered, in the presence of something evil. . . . His heart rose into his throat and he was on the point of turning to [Mme. de Cintré's] companions with an angry challenge; but she checked him, pressing the hand of which she had possessed herself.

"Something very grave has happened," she brought out. "I can't marry you."

Newman dropped her hand—as if, suddenly and unnaturally acting with the others, she had planted a knife in his side. He stood staring, first at her, and then at them. "Why not?" he asked as quietly as his quick gasp permitted.

Mme. de Cintré almost smiled, but the attempt was strange. "You must ask my mother. You must ask my brother."

"Why can't she marry me?"—and he looked all at them.

Madame de Bellegarde never moved in her seat, but her consciousness had paled her face. The Marquis hovered protectingly. She said nothing for some moments, but she kept her clear eyes on their visitor. The Marquis drew himself up and considered the ceiling. "It's impossible," he finely articulated.

"It's improper," said Madame de Bellegarde.

Newman began to laugh. "Oh, you're fooling!" he exclaimed.

"My sister, you've no time; you're losing your train," the Marquis went on.

"Come, is he mad?" Newman asked.

"No; don't think that," said Mme. de Cintré. "But I'm going away."

"Where are you going?"

"To the country . . . to be alone."

"To leave *me* alone?" Newman put it.

"I can't see you now," she simply answered.

" 'Now'—why not?"

"I'm ashamed," she still more simply confessed.

Newman turned to the Marquis. "What have you done to her—what does it mean?" he asked with the same effort at calmness, the fruit of his constant practice of taking

2 The passage is from his novel, *The American*.

things easily. He was excited, but excitement with him was only an intenser deliber-
ateness . . .

"It means that I've given you up," said Mme. de Cintré. "It means that."

Her appearance was too charged with tragic expression not fully to confirm her
words.

The significant difference between the two versions of this love scene is that
the second—James's original in *The American*—answers satisfactorily the questions raised by the emasculated dialogic transcription. We know, now, where
this crisis is taking place. James has in fact been previously at great pains to
elaborate the surroundings. More important, Mme. de Cintré and Newman
now come to life, and no longer strike us merely as names that speak. We see
and respond to their attempt and their pathetic failure, under the circumstances,
to communicate. We see, too, the icy contempt of the mother and brother for
the American suitor; and we recognize how, in the Marquis's reminder of train
time, both that contempt and his uneasiness—a tacit confession of treachery—
are revealed; having mentioned the impossibility of the marriage, he is obviously eager to conclude a most embarrassing interview.

The reader can now visualize the scene. He can now in some measure "see"
these four characters as they sit or stand in relation to one another within a
certain spatial area. He can "see" them turn toward or away from each other.
What has been added to the bare dialogue is dramatic action—a term embracing
everything from a just perceptible, subtle gesture to the violence of a battle
scene; for the drama is a paradigm of actions whose meaning is conveyed by a
series of concrete images. In a printed play the dramatic action is indicated by
means of the stage directions. They bring not only all the suggestions for movement and gesture noted here, but also—and this is especially important—what
James suggests in phrases like "as quietly as his quick gasp permitted" and "he
finely articulated." In such phrases, the novelist attempts, as Ibsen did with the
one-word direction, "writhing," to deepen his reader's insight into the scene by
letting him "hear" the *tone of voice* of each speaker, both as an individual differentiated from other speakers, and as an individual whose voice undergoes
marked changes in response to particular emotional stimuli. The novelist's version thus offers a scene enriched by setting, by movement, and by the scrupulously individualized voices of the participants (or "actors"), as they respond
severally to the flow of emotional currents.

And, just as the freely given explanatory comment functions for the novelist, so the stage-direction functions for the playwright. The latter outlines the
total effect he desires, and his co-workers in the theater—actors, scene designer,
director, and others—will then bring their own specialized skills to the realization of the author's blueprinted intentions. Thus if the first, skeletal version of
James's crisis scene quoted above were to appear as part of a printed play, it
would necessarily be preceded by full directions, addressed to the designer, for
the construction of the de Bellegarde drawing room and for its decoration in
such a way as to highlight Newman's oppressive awareness that he was "in the
presence of something evil." In a similar way, movement, voice, gesture, and
even costume are, in our own day, fully outlined in the stage directions to help
the actor objectify the individual personality the writer has created. This is

why the stage directions, though often brief and unobtrusive, must never be overlooked. Apart from the dialogue, they are the dramatist's only tools.[3]

The reader in three roles: designer, actor, director

The reader must learn to do what the workers in the theater do each time they pick up a fresh playscript—erect imaginatively, as he reads, the total experience for which the printed page is but the initial design. He must, in fact, learn to "read" much that actually does not appear on the page in front of him. He must make a conscious attempt not only to hear the words spoken by each character, but to hear them *in context*—to hear what intent lies behind them, how they sound to other characters, and how their meaning is affected by the time and place in which they are spoken. And then, further, if he is to get the full meaning of a play, the reader must *visualize the total experience* it offers. He must become his own designer, creating a picture of the stage setting from the author's description; his own acting troupe, creating each role; and his own director, molding all a play's elements into a coherent whole.

As a designer

It is easy to underestimate the psychological significance of a play's setting, of the physical environment in which words are spoken and deeds done. But the setting of a play does more than offer background for the action. It helps to characterize the persons in the play, just as physical appearance tells us much about the people we meet in real life. We learn almost as much about our friends from their rooms and the clothes they wear as from their words and actions, for man is not only a social and political animal, but also a clothes-wearing and housekeeping one. All of man's proclivities help to reveal his character. But while in life the clothes a man wears and the furnishings of his home may mislead us as to his character, circumstances sometimes forcing him to accept choices actually displeasing to him, in a play the settings and costumes, being part of a created and controlled experience, are specifically designed to reveal the truth about the characters. The reader, therefore, should note with care all stage directions which deal with the stage-picture, in order to visualize the scene both in its detail and as a whole. Each lamp, each rug, each landscape or portrait on the wall, the size of the room as well as its furnishings, are there to communicate something about the characters in the play. The physical setting and all the objects in it assist in framing the action and the actor, limiting him to a place and time and all that that particular place and time may suggest.

As an actor

It is the function of an actor, guided by the director, to create a unified concept of a given character, and then, by using his own skills and the theatrical

[3] Detailed stage directions are actually a somewhat recent development in drama. Earlier dramatists (Shakespeare, for example) included many of their directions, both as to setting and action, in the dialogue itself. Thus Roderigo, in *Othello*, I, 1, 74, says to Iago: "Here is her father's house, I'll call aloud."

devices available to him, to project that character to the audience. It often happens that different actors see the same character in different lights, as do different readers. For example, Tennessee Williams's heroine, Blanche, in *A Streetcar Named Desire*, has been played in as many different ways as there have been actresses to interpret the role. One actress played Blanche as if she were insane from the beginning of the play, thus leading the audience to pity her, but not to feel genuinely drawn to her; another saw her in a more sympathetic light, making her a deeply troubled but basically sane young woman until the brutality of Kowalski at the end of the play drove her into helpless insanity. Whether one interpretation is closer than the other to the author's intention is of secondary interest to us at the moment; what is significant in this variety of interpretive views is the realization that no actor may simply mouth words, nor merely recite the lines the author has written for him. He must "see" the character in his own mind and make every speech, gesture, and movement conform to the view he has developed of that character as a total personality.

The reader of a play must make a similar attempt. Like the actor, he must decide what the lines "mean" in addition to what they "say." He must learn not to take all the dialogue at its face value, remembering that much of what a person says—on stage as in life—is not to be taken literally. He himself sometimes says the opposite of what he means, perhaps to deceive someone else, or simply because he is moved to speak playfully, sarcastically, or ironically. In reading, he must therefore keep always in mind the situation out of which the lines grow, for the intended meaning resides not alone in the words spoken, but, significantly, in the tone of voice as well. As Bernard Shaw once wrote, "There are fifty ways of saying Yes, and five hundred of saying No, but only one way of writing them down."

The beginner cannot of course be expected to create unaided what ordinarily requires the sustained efforts of several trained actors, but he will soon become more and more sensitive to distinctions between characters beyond the obvious ones of male and female, old and young, good and evil, happy and unhappy. His first step toward recognition of the distinguishing complexities of the individual must be close attention to the actions and words of each character. A second will lead him to listen with special care to what is said of one character by others in the course of conflict. For example, in *Othello* we learn something of the forthrightness of Othello's nature when we hear him explain to the Duke how he has won Desdemona's love—by telling her the story of his adventurous life:

> She wish'd she had not heard it, yet she wish'd
> That heaven had made her such a man. She thank'd me,
> And bade me, if I had a friend that lov'd her,
> I should but teach him how to tell my story,
> And that would woo her. Upon this hint I spake.
> She lov'd me for the dangers I had pass'd,
> And I lov'd her that she did pity them.
> This only is the witchcraft I have us'd.

A related light is thrown on his character when Desdemona herself, testifying to her own feelings, says:

> That I did love the Moor to live with him,
> My downright violence and storm of fortunes
> May trumpet to the world. My heart's subdu'd
> Even to the very quality of my lord.
> I saw Othello's visage in his mind,
> And to his honors and his valiant parts
> Did I my soul and fortunes consecrate.

These affirmations of Othello's goodness and nobility are endorsed, seemingly, by Iago:

> The Moor (howbeit that I endure him not)
> Is of a constant, noble, loving nature;
> And I dare think he'll prove to Desdemona
> A most dear husband.

Yet what Iago intends by this seeming praise becomes clear in a soliloquy that follows:

> His soul is so enfetter'd to her love,
> That she may make, unmake, do what she list,
> Even as her appetite shall play the god
> With his weak function.

In other words, Iago sees the openness of Othello not as nobility, but as over-trustfulness, and whatever our sympathies we cannot without danger ignore this other side of the Moor.

These statements by and about Shakespeare's protagonist illustrate the necessity of reading any drama with one eye on the words spoken, and the other on the context in which the words appear. The latter will often suggest the tone of voice to be employed, and so help us to understand the true motives of the characters.

All those contributions made in the theater by the actor, the reader must himself make if he would see the play whole. It may not be possible for the novice to "see" all the characters when he reads his first play, or his second, or his third; that ability will develop gradually and perhaps slowly at first. He should begin by trying to bring the major characters to life; he will soon discover that, through close attention to the stage directions and dialogue, he can (stopping the play when necessary) create any character in whatever image seems most consistent with the total design of the play. With improved skill he will realize an increasing number of characters, as individuals and as contributors to a complex web of relationships, and will watch these persons develop as the action moves forward.

As a director

The task of imagining the characters in action is made simpler by the reader's third role—that of the director. In the staged play the director moves the characters about and controls the timing of their actions. Further, since each individual actor undoubtedly sees the over-all play initially from his own point of view, or from that of the person he is portraying, the director, in order to create a group with a single interpretive purpose, must reconcile the varying concepts of his several actors. He must decide what to emphasize and what to subordinate. In short, he is responsible for the unity of his production. So, too, the reader. He must never permit himself to be sidetracked into following minor characters and subplots, no matter how fascinating they may be. As his own director, he must center his attention on the major conflict and so achieve for his imaginary production the same unity the director in the theater strives for.

Again there are reliable guides: the structure of the play itself and the author's directions. The play, particularly its exposition, will soon make clear what it is "about," what its central conflict is, the direction in which its action is tending. To the reader, as to the director, the stage directions for placement and movement of characters are instructions to help in creating the play's visual images. These will allow him to reinforce what the play says in its dialogue with the appropriate appeals to the mind's eye. Functioning as director, the reader will therefore give careful attention to details of movement and gesture and to such suggestions as are provided for expression and tone of voice, but he will at the same time take care to see the details, always, in relation to the total impression which the drama makes.

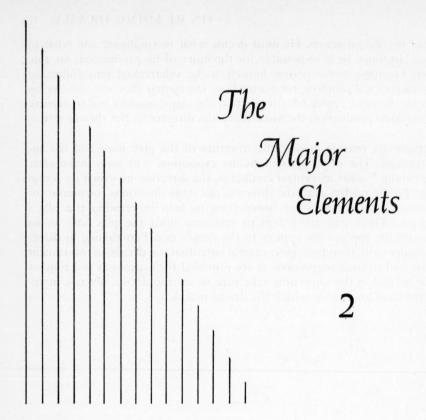

The Major Elements

2

THE ELEMENT OF ACTION: *THE DESPERATE HOURS*

A literary work is composed of a number of elements in different proportions, and the final result depends upon both the nature of the ingredients and the quantitative relationship they bear to each other. It is of course possible for stories and plays, like pre-cooked dinners in this age of the can-opener, to be mass-produced—witness the constant stream of stories that fill the romance and western magazines, and the soap operas on radio and television. Such fictions have little more distinction or separate identity than cans of spaghetti on your grocer's shelf. Any work, however, that pretends to offer fresh insights into human nature or to enlarge the reader's experience, any work of enough interest to merit our serious consideration, will be a unique and individually designed product; it must have an identity and a vitality of its own. Yet, despite this uniqueness, the *ingredients* it contains may well be standard; indeed, to achieve any communication, its elements must be recognizable and bear some stamp of familiarity. One of the pleasures literature provides is the continuing discovery of the new within the old, and such discovery is often made possible by a fresh use of the customary elements.

Certain of these elements in a play—or in any literary work—are obvious at once: action, characters, setting, and theme. That is, something happens to somebody, and it has to happen somewhere, and to some purpose. These elements are not all of equal importance, of course: *What* happens, for example, is usually more significant than *where* it happens; it is very probable that the story of *The Desperate Hours* could be shifted from Indianapolis to, say, Naples or Marseilles, and its human beings "translated" into Italians or Frenchmen, without important modifications. But apart from setting, which generally assumes a role in support of action, character, and theme, the major elements may each, in a given drama, receive the writer's primary attention. Either action, or theme, or character, may be the dominant ingredient of a play; and the structure of a play, the quality of its appeal, and its over-all accomplishment may be determined by the author's decision as to which element to emphasize, which to subordinate.

The first three plays in this collection have been chosen as illustrations of emphasis on each of the three major components of drama in turn. The first play—*The Desperate Hours*—is a straightforward contemporary melodrama with an emphasis on *story;* it has a high degree of interest primarily because of its skillful use of narrative elements, its suspense, its fast-moving action. The second drama, *Everyman*, is a medieval Morality Play with a primary emphasis on theme. The third, *Abe Lincoln in Illinois*, illustrates the emphasis on character as a unifying and motivating force in drama. (These first three plays will be followed—to anticipate for a moment—by Henrik Ibsen's *The Wild Duck*, which shows how all of these various primary elements can be combined and balanced in a single work.)

The emphasis on story, on action alone—the emphasis found in our first play—occurs in a good many literary works. Such works usually so engross the reader in fast-moving action and keep his faculties so absorbed that he may never stop to question the motivation of the action, its results, or its meaning. The action that engages his attention may be like the toy that swings in front of a child and holds him enraptured, merely attention-getting movement that exists for its own sake. On the other hand, it may be logical and meaningful, pointing to something beyond itself. Such action provides an old and honorable path to enjoyment; the great writers of the past have been skilled at keeping a good story going, while commenting meaningfully on experience. Indeed, when we ask about a book, play, or movie the customary question, "What's it about?" indicates our interest in *story;* and we usually receive an answer that summarizes the incidents that make up the action of the work.

Such is the case with *The Desperate Hours*, the story of the invasion of an ordinary American household by a trio of escaping criminals, and their terrorizing of its members. Our interest as readers of the play is captured and sustained not so much by the character of the protagonist (Dan Hilliard, the head of the victimized family) or by any thematic implications in the action, as by the swiftly-developing story itself. This emphasis makes *The Desperate Hours* a melodrama and gives it some characteristics in common with the routine crime thrillers that occupy the television screens every night. Full of violent action, the story moves forward with such great rapidity that one is lulled into temporary forgetfulness of the actual complexity of life; one forgets that, in life, most situations present a choice among a perplexing range of grays rather than between the blacks and whites, the obvious goods and bads, of the world of melodrama. The conflict in *The Desperate Hours* seems, as we read or view the play, to be real enough, in the sense of being immediate and overpowering; but because it forces on our attention no choice meaningful in our own lives, what we remember most about the play is the sense of excitement it engenders.

Calculated, like much radio and television drama, to keep the audience in suspense, Joseph Hayes's play tries not only to make us feel involved in the resolution of the action but also in doubt about its outcome. On reflection we may wonder whether we ever believed it likely that Griffin, the leader of the convicts, could succeed in his plan to escape, but as we read we are so caught up in the succession of events that, like Dan Hilliard, we believe that Griffin is real, and the danger present and pressing. It is this quality of suspense—the desire to know what happens next to hero and villain—that keeps us turning the pages of this play breathlessly.

But although *The Desperate Hours* is a melodrama, it is an unusually convincing one, superior to most, because it also possesses the other basic ingredients of drama in sufficient quantity to give the play substance and body that action alone cannot bring. Hayes's creation of several minor conflicts—one between the girl and her father with respect to her marriage, another between the sheriff and the state trooper, another between Griffin and his father—adds the dimension of depth to the central struggle, at the same time increasing and varying our interest. In addition, *The Desperate Hours* presents a set of characters "real" enough to enlist sympathetic belief; around Daniel Hilliard, Hayes has created a family group whose reality we accept without serious question, for their activities and relationships have an air of familiarity and probability. Finally, our acceptance of these characters leads us to see that the terror they face could also have meaning for us. This melodrama thus has a theme—actually a two-fold one. It speaks in the first place of the unsuspected strengths called forth in us by emergencies; and it also forcefully reminds us that beneath the surface of complacent middle-class life in well-protected American cities there is yet danger in the form of the irrational elements in our society, and that this danger may, at any moment and without warning, confront and overwhelm us.

While, therefore, *The Desperate Hours* is a melodrama with an emphasis on violent action and thus well illustrates the first basic element of drama, it also takes into account the other two fundamental sources of dramatic interest: theme and character.

The problem of what elements to use, and in what proportion, is not the only one confronting the dramatist. He must also make certain decisions regarding the organization and structure of his material. Many of his problems are too technical or too specialized to delay us here; we are, after all, more concerned with the final effect he produces in the theater or on the printed page than with the means whereby he attains that effect. But some awareness of his special problems, some knowledge of why the dramatist does what he does, will assuredly quicken our enjoyment of his finished product.[1]

---

[1] Joseph Hayes's essay following *The Desperate Hours* in this book will give further insight into some of the opportunities offered and limits imposed by the dramatic form. As author both of the original novel and of the play adapted from it, Mr. Hayes is in a position to offer some unique and valuable comments on the problems he faced in dramatizing his own novel.

There is, for example, the problem of getting a story told on the stage within a reasonable time, and the concomitant problem of determining where it should begin and end. Established tradition in the modern theater generally limits the playing time of a drama to approximately two hours. This limitation imposes some significant restrictions on both structure and subject matter. Most stories, considered as totalities, are too long and too full of incident to be enacted, without omissions, inside the established two hours. For this reason, one of the dramatist's chief tasks at the outset is to decide where in the total action to begin his play. Suppose, for example, he wishes to write a play about Lincoln. With only two hours at his disposal in the theater, he must decide whether to begin with the log cabin of Lincoln's childhood, with the tension of the Lincoln-Douglas debates, with the entry into the White House, with the outbreak of the Civil War, or even, conceivably, with the dawn of the last day of the President's life.

There are several possible solutions to this problem. Among them is the one exemplified by Shakespeare's practice in *Julius Caesar*. This play begins almost literally at the beginning of the complete story. But, having begun thus, the author is able to reach the prescribed end—with the death of Brutus and the triumph of Antony—because he telescopes the succeeding events of the story, giving us (essentially) only its highlights: the developing conspiracy, the death of Caesar, the incendiary funeral oration, and the final scenes of battle and defeat. Having begun his drama so early in the over-all chain of events connected with Caesar's death, Shakespeare is forced to select only those incidents which have major significance. One effect of this procedure, common to many historical dramas, is that the play so developed—*Abe Lincoln in Illinois* is another example—is by nature episodic, its various scenes striking us as so many beads strung on a thread of familiar history.

A second possible solution (one of the oldest and most common) is to begin the play, not at the beginning of the total story, but at a point well along in its action. When a drama is begun thus in the midst of things, its remaining action will unfold to its appointed end, incident following incident in a closely consecutive order. And here the effect is likely to be, not that of a series of episodes, but that of a series of actions each growing out of the other in an immediately apprehensible cause-and-effect relationship, as in *The Desperate Hours*. To secure this latter effect, Mr. Hayes, in dramatizing his own novel, does not begin with the convicts' escape from prison, nor their wild ride to Indianapolis, but rather with the tense reaction of the sheriff to the news of that escape. He does so because the center of his story is the impact of the escapees on an average, "safe" community, and he has no time to waste in getting to the point. The leisurely pace that Hayes as a novelist could use is not available to him as a dramatist; in his play, he has to fasten his attention relentlessly on the most critical moments of the total situation, and rigorously prune away the earlier incidents.

Where, actually, does Hayes's story begin? At first glance it would appear to begin with the convicts' initial plan to escape from prison, motivated by Griffin's desire for freedom and his determination to avenge himself for the sheriff's earlier brutality. But if we consider motivation in our search for the true beginning, we are carried back to Griffin's childhood, specifically to the nature of his relationship with his father; from this relationship, presumably, spring many actions that occurred before the section of the story the author chose to dramatize. Among these antecedent actions are early crimes committed by Griffin, his earlier beating at the hands of the sheriff, the prison break, the theft of a car, and the birth of the shrewd idea to use the home of a respectable middle-class family as a hideout and center of operations. But even in Hayes's original novel, this part of the action was of secondary interest; not in any sense irrelevant, it yet merely prepared the way for the critical action to come, and the latter began only with the entry of the convicts into the Hilliard home.

To designate these early happenings as preparatory events, however, is not to describe them as unimportant. Without them, much of the novel's later, more significant action would be incomprehensible. The dramatist, like the novelist, must make such information about his characters' past available to reader and audience, but, unlike the novelist, he does not have time to go back and begin at the beginning; he must find some way of incorporating into the present action of his play all we need to know about the previous behavior of his characters. In doing so he encounters the problem, special to his craft, of *dramatic exposition*, of presenting necessary background information unobtrusively at the same time he is getting his story started and keeping it moving forward. The problem is a special one for the dramatist because—again unlike the novelist—he is not free to interpolate anywhere a straightforward account of antecedent actions; dialogue is his essential medium of communication, and his story is always acted out in time-present. On stage when the curtain rises are two or more characters whom the author has placed there, and whom the audience discovers at some point in a continuing action. What is their situation now? What has happened in the past—yesterday or a year ago—to account for their situation? What, specifically, is their relationship? The printed program may identify them as father and son, or husband and wife. But this description conveys little enough, for many degrees of intimacy, of love, of hate and dislike, may exist within such relationships. We need to know more, and the playwright has to rely primarily on dialogue to give it to us. His problem therefore is to create circumstances in which the explanatory lines can be spoken, and yet seem to come forth naturally.

A common solution to this problem is to situate at least one of the characters on stage so that he, like the audience, requires some information about the past. His questions eliciting such information, and the answers to them, must be plausible, for if they are not the audience will come to feel that the spoken lines are intended, not for the other characters on the stage, but simply and obviously for the audience itself. Our illusion of reality can be perilously disturbed when the characters behind the footlights exchange, merely *for our benefit*, information which common sense tells us they themselves would already have. We then recognize that such "voices" are no longer the characters' but the author's, saying, in effect, "Pay attention! Here is knowledge you will need later in the play, but I've got to give it to you now, this way." If this intrusive voice of the author is such as to call attention to itself, it may cause an irreparable breakdown in the communication between character and audience.

In *The Desperate Hours*, Mr. Hayes, beginning his enacted story after the prison break, solves this crucial problem with considerable success. The first scene of Act I offers characters to whom the necessary information is quite naturally of the greatest professional and (in at least one instance) personal interest. Further, the use of the telephone necessitates the relaying of this information to the rest of the characters on the stage and so, simultaneously, to the audience. At the start of Scene 2, on the other hand, no such device as the dramatic telephone call is suitable, and here the lines exchanged by the four Hilliards seem somewhat strained; since the purpose of the quiet opening is to establish these characters in their unquestioning, routine existence, Hayes can reveal their relationships only through an ordinary, unexciting exchange of dialogue. The things we need to know about the Hilliards must be conveyed without forcing the Hilliards to tell us more than they would naturally tell each other.

In most plays, as in *The Desperate Hours*, the exposition of the existing situation is confined to the opening scenes, although the extent of the exposition will, of course, depend in large part on the author's choice of a beginning point. In a play like *Abe Lincoln in Illinois*, which begins very nearly at the beginning of the over-all action, exposition will be brief; in others, beginning more nearly at the middle of the total action, exposition is of necessity more extensive. The relative complexity of the dramatist's situation and characters, the urgency of his need to engross his audience in significant action as early as possible, are the governing factors. (In one sense, of course, exposition may extend to the very end of a play, as the characters continue to develop and unfold; but normally the essential expository information is given early in the play and has usually been supplied by the end of the first act.)

But if there is no prescribed length for dramatic exposition, there is at least a point in the forward movement of the play when exposition is normally terminated. This point is marked by the emergence of what is called the "exciting force"—in *The Desperate Hours*, clearly, the violent entry of the three convicts into Mrs. Hilliard's suburban living room. Conflict is now joined, and the author leaves exposition behind. His problem changes. His concern shifts to the process of deliberate entanglement known as dramatic *complication;* he becomes engaged now in weaving the various strands of his conflict into a rising action. From this moment forward, his story will mount, through a complex interweaving of motives and actions, and through successive stages of tension, to the point of greatest emotional intensity. This point, the *crisis,* is that stage in the plot where, because of a decisive step by the protagonist, the play's resolution or outcome becomes inevitable. Hayes's crisis scene, for example, occurs in the attic of the house next door, where Hilliard makes his fateful decision to return to his own home with the unloaded revolver. Then a culminating point known as the *climax* is reached, usually somewhere between the middle and end of a play. In a melodrama like Hayes's, it frequently comes just before the final curtain, so that suspense may be maintained and augmented to the last. In plays of another sort—*Julius Caesar* and *Oedipus* are examples—the climax may come early, but other factors keep author and audience alike as interested in what follows as in what precedes the climax. When Teiresias in the latter drama makes his final, devastating revelations to Oedipus, the play in which they figure has reached its climax; but what follows—the falling action, or *dénouement*—involves us still more deeply in the protagonist's fate.

The term *dénouement*, borrowed from the French and translatable as "untying," derives from a favorite dramatic concept of the ancients, one which may serve to sum up a discussion of the structural elements of a play. A play, they believed, was to be thought of as a complex knot, in which many strands were entangled. The author of such a work is engaged, first, in picking up the strands of his story (in the *exposition*), then in tying his knot (by means of rising action or *complication*), and finally, after coming to a *crisis* and the ensuing *climax*, in untying it once more (by means of falling action or *dénouement*). The drama has undergone many radical changes between Sophocles' age and our own; but its basic elements and its fundamental concepts are as apparent in *The Desperate Hours* as they are in *Oedipus Rex*.

The Desperate Hours

by

Joseph Hayes

Characters

TOM WINSTON
JESSE BARD
HARRY CARSON
ELEANOR HILLIARD
RALPHIE HILLIARD
DAN HILLIARD
CINDY HILLIARD
GLENN GRIFFIN
HANK GRIFFIN
ROBISH
CHUCK WRIGHT
MR. PATTERSON
LT. CARL FREDERICKS
MISS SWIFT

TIME: *The present*
SCENE: *The City of Indianapolis*
ACT ONE: *A day in autumn*
ACT TWO: *Later*
ACT THREE: *Later*

SCENE

The action throughout the play alternates between two sets on stage. In the first two acts, the Hilliard home is at stage-right and the Sheriff's office is at stage-left. In ACT THREE, the Hilliard home is at stage-right, and at stage-left is a corner of an attic room. The action shifts back and forth between the two sets by the use of blackouts and sliding black curtains which mask the set that is not in focus.

The Hilliard home is the principal set. This consists of various rooms, all blended together by fluid action; lights focus the attention in the various rooms, as the action of the play requires.

On the ground-floor level of the house, there are two rooms in view at all times: the living room and a back hall or pantry. In the living room, there is an outside door in the rear wall; next to this door are stairs rising to the upstairs level. At right a door gives access to a den or library, off-stage. At left, facing downstage, there is another door; this door, presumably, leads into a dining room; the dining room is adjacent to a kitchen; the kitchen door opens into the pantry or back hall. In this manner, a character leaving the living room exits through the dining-room door and in a moment reappears in the pantry. This pantry is a small room in itself. In addition to the kitchen door, there is an exterior side door of the house itself opening off the pantry at stage-left. Back stairs descend along the exterior wall at left: a narrow passageway gives access to the upper floor. The entire ground floor, then, consists of a living room with front stairs curving up, a front door, a door to the den and a door to the dining room; a pantry with a door to the kitchen, an exterior side door, shelves, and a narrow stairway going up. In addition, a portion of the side yard is visible at left.

The upper level—constructed above the ground-floor level described above— consists of two bedrooms and an upstairs hall between; this hall gives access to the downward flow of the front stairway. The bedroom at stage-right is the master bedroom, containing twin beds, windows right and up-center, and a bureau. The bedroom at stage-left is a boy's bedroom, with a bunk, various shelves with toys, and a window overlooking the side yard. Between the two bedrooms is a small hall: downstage is a small table with a telephone.

23

At far left stage, during the first two acts, is the Sheriff's office on ground level, a bare sort of room with a wall-clock, a desk, various files, and radio and intercom apparatus. In the last act, a corner of an attic appears at stage-left; this is constructed above the Sheriff's office, and in ACT THREE the office is completely masked.

ACT ONE

SHERIFF'S OFFICE: The curtain rises, morning light fades in on the Sheriff's office. WINSTON, a deputy sheriff inclined to matter-of-fact laziness, sits at desk, speaking on the telephone. On the desk are an intercom, radio apparatus, sheafs of papers, and so forth. The wall-clock reads 8:10.

WINSTON. [*Plaintively.*] Baby . . . didn't I just tell you? I can't leave till Bard gets here. [*He listens.*] Listen, baby —this night shift gets my goat as much as it does yours. You think I wouldn't like to be in that nice warm bed? [*There is a buzz from the intercom on the desk.*] Hold it. [*He speaks into the intercom.*] Yeah, Dutch?

DUTCH'S VOICE. Winston . . . Bard's going to want those Terre Haute reports right away.

WINSTON. [*Irascibly, into intercom.*] What do you think I'm gonna do with 'em . . . eat 'em for breakfast? [*He flips off the intercom, returns to the phone.*] Hello, baby . . . [*Listens.*] Yeah, that's what I said, isn't it? In that nice warm bed *with you.* Who'd you think I . . . [*Listens.*] Okay, okay, baby . . . go back to sleep and wait for Papa. [*Hangs up, shakes head, pleased; speaks with gusto.*] Give me a jealous woman every time! [BARD *enters.* WINSTON *is sleepy and glad to be relieved.* BARD *takes off jacket, removes gun from shoulder-holster through the following. All very casual and commonplace at first.*]

BARD. [*As he enters.*] Morning, Tom.

WINSTON. [*Stretching.*] Well! About time.

BARD. [*Stows gun in drawer of file.*] Overslept. Sorry.

WINSTON. [*Rising slowly.*] You got a lovely excuse.

BARD. I'll tell her you think so. [*Above desk, riffles reports.*] Quiet night?

WINSTON. [*Preparing to go.*] If kids'd stay out of cars and off motorcycles, we'd soon be out of jobs around here.

BARD. Not another burglary in Speedway City? [*Laughs.*] This guy's getting tiresome.

WINSTON. A real sex-nut, that one. Same old story . . . all he took was diamonds and women's panties. What the hell's the connection.

BARD. You figure it out, Tom. [*Then tensing . . . so that from now on the pace and tone change.*] What's this?

WINSTON. [*Yawns, looking over* BARD'S *shoulder.*] Federal prison break . . . Terre Haute. None of our concern.

BARD. When'd it come in?

WINSTON. [*Ready to leave.*] Hours ago. The three of 'em busted out some time before dawn. . . .

BARD. [*Sits at desk, snaps button on intercom.*] Why didn't you call me?

WINSTON. Call you? Why?

DUTCH'S VOICE. Yes, Jesse?

BARD. [*Into intercom.*] Dutch . . . get me Lieutenant Fredericks, State Police.

WINSTON. Jesse . . . remember what your Irish wife threatened last time I routed you out of the nest. . . .

BARD. Terre Haute's only seventy miles away. They could've *walked* here by now!

FREDERICKS' VOICE. [*On intercom—crisp, middle-aged, cynical.*] I wondered when you'd start yipping, Bard.

BARD. [*Quickly.*] Fredericks . . . anybody sitting on anything?

FREDERICKS' VOICE. I'm sitting on just what you're sitting on, Deputy. Only mine ain't sweatin'.

BARD. Griffin's woman . . . Helen Laski . . . any dope on her?

FREDERICKS' VOICE. Not a trace. Chicago . . . Cleveland . . . St. Louie. All we know is she was here in town three weeks ago.

BARD. Just don't let any cop touch her.

She's the beacon'll lead us straight . . .

FREDERICKS' VOICE. Bard . . . it's an FBI case anyway. The city police've ripped whole buildings apart. We got the highways blocked. We're working through all the dives. . . .

BARD. If Glenn Griffin wants to come here, no roadblock's gonna stop him. And he's too sharp to hole up any place you'd think of looking.

FREDERICKS' VOICE. Look, lad . . . get that chip off your shoulder. [*Shortly.*] You want Griffin so bad, go get him! [BARD *flips off the intercom.* WINSTON *reluctantly removes his coat.*]

WINSTON. Glenn Griffin . . . is he the one you . . . ?

BARD. [*Thoughtfully.*] Yeah . . . he's the one. [*Studying reports.*] Glenn Griffin . . . his brother, Hank . . . and . . . who's this third one? Samuel Robish.

WINSTON. Life-termer. A three-time loser. And nasty. [*As* BARD *picks up the phone and dials,* WINSTON *returns his coat to the hanger.*] You're not going to get any sleep today, are you, Winston? No, I'm not going to get any sleep today. I'm going to sit on the teletype machine like a good little boy scout. . . . [BARD *smiles a bit as* WINSTON *exits. Then he speaks into the telephone in contrasting gentle tones.*]

BARD. Hello, Katie. Did I wake you? . . . I've just had an idea . . . why don't you go over to my mother's for the day? [*Laughs—but the urgency comes through.*] Oh, stop groaning . . . how often do I ask you to *let* her talk your arm and leg off? . . . No, not this afternoon. *Now!* . . . And Katie . . . don't mention where you're going, huh? . . . To the neighbors, anyone . . . Good. . . . Right away. Take a taxi. . . . Sure, splurge. [BARD *hangs up, sits thinking, with the smile fading.* WINSTON *enters, with* CARSON, *who is youthful, business-like, rather studious-looking.* WINSTON *places a teletype message on desk before* BARD.]

WINSTON. It had to break, Jesse. [*Then with a touch of sarcasm as* BARD *reads.*] Oh—this is Mr. Carson, FBI.

BARD. [*Briskly.*] How are you? Look, it says they beat up a farmer south of the prison before daybreak. How come we're just getting it?

CARSON. They left him in his barn, out cold . . . ripped out his phone. He just staggered into a general store and reported his car stolen. . . . [*With a touch of good-natured irony.*] How are *you?*

BARD. Have you put this on the air?

CARSON. Deputy, I've been in touch with Sheriff Masters by telephone.

BARD. I hope he's enjoying his extended vacation . . . he sure picked a fine time to leave me in charge here. . . .

CARSON. The way I understand it, you know this Glenn Griffin fellow better than any police officer in the area. How about your taking over this section? [*Pause. The whole weight falls on* BARD. *He accepts it . . . slowly. Then:*]

BARD. Okay . . . *Okay* . . . Let's find that car! [*He goes into action—hands teletype to* WINSTON.] Tom, put this description on the air. Tell 'em to repeat it every half hour.

WINSTON. [*Protesting.*] We'll be flooded with calls. Every crackpot in five states . . .

BARD. [*Sitting at desk.*] We'll follow up every tip!

WINSTON. [*To* CARSON—*groaning.*] I hope you know what you just did! [WINSTON *exits.* CARSON *moves to desk and offers* BARD *a cigarette.*]

CARSON. Any ideas where they might dig in?

BARD. [*Shaking his head.*] All I know is . . . just as long's Glenn Griffin's running around free and safe—with that prison guard's .38 in his paw—well, it's not free or safe for anyone else. No decent people anywhere—whether they've ever . . . [*The lights begin to dim.*] heard of Glenn Griffin or not . . .

HILLIARD HOME: *Lights rise slowly. We see the complete outline of a typical house in the suburbs: pleasant, comfortable, undistinguished.* ELEANOR HILLIARD, *an attractive woman in her early forties, enters from the dining room, moves to front door, opens it and looks out. The morning light outside is bright and cheerful. Not finding the morning paper, she closes the door as* RALPHIE *enters from dining room.* RALPHIE, *aged ten, is dressed for school and carries a half-empty glass of milk, which he stares at balefully as he sits.* ELEANOR, *who is extremely neat, is arranging pillows on the sofa.*]

ELEANOR. [*Gently.*] Ralphie, you left your bike outside all night again.

RALPHIE. [*As though this answers her.*] It didn't rain.

ELEANOR. Well, it's not going to rain today, either. But you're going to put it in the garage before you go to school. [DAN HILLIARD *enters from dining room and crosses to front door to look out. He is a typical, undistinguished but immediately likable man in his forties.*]

DAN. [*Calling up the stairs as he passes.*] Cindy! It's eight-thirty.

CINDY. [*Off, in her room upstairs.*] Can't a girl straighten her girdle in peace?

DAN. [*Surprised.*] Girdle? . . . Girdle! [*Goes to* ELEANOR.] Ellie, can a twenty-year-old child with a figure like Cindy's . . .

ELEANOR. [*Smiling.*] It's a joke, Dan.

DAN. Oh. Thank the Lord. She has to have a solid hour for primping and then she complains all the way downtown because we don't live in the city limits.

RALPHIE. Ain't love disgusting?

ELEANOR. Don't say "ain't."

DAN. [*To* RALPHIE—*firmly.*] Don't say "love," either. [*There is a thud of a newspaper thrown against the front door.* DAN *steps swiftly to the door. He and* ELEANOR *have a slight collision. She moves downstage and he opens the door and goes off onto the porch.*] Hey! Hey!

ELEANOR. [*Teasing.*] Try holding your nose and gulping it, Ralphie.

RALPHIE. It tastes sour.

ELEANOR. [*Picking up her small pad and pencil from coffee table.*] Yesterday it tasted like chalk. [*She sits and starts making her shopping list.* DAN *returns, picks up the* Indianapolis Star, *and enters the room, closing the door.*]

DAN. [*A suggestion of grouchiness.*] Some day I'm going to catch up with that paper boy and we're going to have a lawsuit on our hands.

ELEANOR. Dan, you have time for a second cup of coffee.

DAN. [*Glances at his watch and then up the stairs.*] In half a minute she'll come prancing down those stairs and start urging *me* to hurry. [DAN *exits into the dining room.* RALPHIE *takes a long drink of the milk but cannot finish it.* CINDY *comes down the stairs in time to see him.*]

CINDY. Well, *today* you are a man! [*She goes to the closet, gets her coat and bag.*]

RALPHIE. If cows only knew how I hated 'em!

ELEANOR. What would they do?

CINDY. [*To* ELEANOR.] Where's Dad? What was he shouting at me?

ELEANOR. What does he shout every morning at eight-thirty?

CINDY. He shouts it's eight-thirty.

ELEANOR. You win the kewpie-doll. [CINDY *moves swiftly toward the dining room as* DAN *appears in the door with a cup of coffee.*]

CINDY. [*To* DAN *as she swings past him.*] Say, you'd better hurry!

DAN. [*Looks after* CINDY, *then to* ELEANOR *as he sits on sofa.*] What'd I tell you? [DAN *sets his cup of coffee on the table and picks up the newspaper and reads.*]

RALPHIE. Dad . . . Why did the moron lock his father in the refrigerator?

DAN. [*His attention on the newspaper.*] Ralphie, do I have to answer that one?

RALPHIE. [*Brightly.*] Because he liked cold pop! [*There is an escape of breath from* DAN *which might or might not pass for a laugh.*] Well, why don't you laugh?

DAN. I laughed. What do you want me to do . . . roll on the floor?

RALPHIE. You *almost* rolled on the floor last night when I told you why the moron ate dynamite.

ELEANOR. [*Shakes her head warningly but continues writing.*] Ralphie . . .

RALPHIE. My name is Ralph. R-a-l-p-h. There's no Y on the end of it. I looked up my birth certificate.

ELEANOR. Sorry. [*Through the following,* RALPHIE *rises and, with glass in hand, moves to the chair by front door to pick up his jacket and football; he rather elaborately manages to conceal the half-glass of milk on the floor out of sight in the process.*]

RALPHIE. Big game after school today. Fourth grade versus fifth grade. [*Having achieved his purpose; with a sigh of relief.*] We'll slaughter 'em! [*Kisses* ELEANOR.]

ELEANOR. 'Bye, darling. [DAN *leans back to be kissed, but* RALPHIE *brushes past him and goes to dining-room door, where* DAN's *voice stops him.*]

DAN. Hey! Aren't you forgetting something?

RALPHIE. [*Embarrassed and uncertain.*] Oh. [*He then returns to* DAN, *who leans for a kiss; instead,* RALPHIE *extends his hand and shakes* DAN's *hand with grave formality.*] So long, Dad. I hope you have a very pleasant day at the office. [*He turns and goes into the dining room, leaving* DAN *staring after him, then reappears in the pantry on his way to the side door.*] So long, dream-witch. I hope Chuck Wright doesn't even notice your new dress.

CINDY. [*Steps into pantry with glass of orange juice in her hand.*] 'Bye. Flunk geography, will you, pest?

RALPHIE. [*As he goes out the side door.*] *Mister* Pest to you.

ELEANOR. [*Calling from living room.*] Ralphie! Your bicycle!

DAN. What do you suppose that was all about?

ELEANOR. [*Toying with her pad and pencil.*] Our son Ralph . . . spelled R-a-l-p-h . . . considers himself too old to kiss a man . . . that's you . . . good-bye or good-night.

DAN. [*Covering his hurt.*] Oh.

ELEANOR. He said last night he hoped you'd understand.

DAN. [*With an empty smile.*] I was hoping maybe he just didn't like my shave-lotion. [*As* ELEANOR *unconsciously touches his hair.*] Ellie, what's happening to both of them lately? This . . . this young lawyer Cindy works for . . . she can't be *serious,* can she?

ELEANOR. [*Sits.*] She hasn't confided in me, Dan . . . which could mean she is.

DAN. She's only twenty years old!

ELEANOR. I was nineteen.

DAN. You had some sense.

ELEANOR. Sure. I married you.

DAN. [*As though he has proved a point.*] Well, I didn't drive a Jaguar! [CINDY *enters from the dining room and goes to put on her coat.*]

CINDY. Chuck and I find his Jaguar a very comfortable little surrey. Come climb into my Ford coupé, Dad . . . and don't whisper when I'm in the next room. It's not polite.

DAN. [*As he rises and moves to closet.*] Now she'll speed.

ELEANOR. [*Automatically.*] Careful now, Dan.

CINDY. [*Satirically—chidingly.*] Mother . . . you say that every morning of the world. What could possibly happen to a man in the personnel office of a department store? [*She exits, closing the door.*]

DAN. [*Pointing at closed door.*] That's what I mean! That's not Cindy. Those are Chuck Wright's ideas. Last night on the way home, she asked me point-blank if I didn't think I led a pretty dull life.

ELEANOR. What'd you say?

DAN. [*Firmly.*] I said I didn't like Chuck Wright, either. [DAN *goes to the door, and* ELEANOR *follows him.*]

ELEANOR. Dan . . . at Chuck's age . . . you were going to be another Richard Halliburton, remember? Climb the Matterhorn . . . swim at midnight in the Taj Mahal. My father threatened to throw you . . . [*Outside,* CINDY *taps horn impatiently.*]

DAN. I'm going to be late. [*They kiss: casual, without meaning, habit.*] If you're going to use the car today, buy some gas first. *Before* you have to walk a mile for it this time. [DAN *exits.* ELEANOR *closes the door.* ELEANOR *leans against the door a second, utters an almost silent "Whew," puts her shopping list and pencil on the telephone table, pushes her hair back from her forehead, pushes up her sleeves and prepares to begin the day. She moves to sofa, folds the newspaper and straightens the cushions. Then she goes upstairs, casually humming, and into* RALPHIE's *room. She shakes her head and begins to gather up the soiled clothes. She flips on a small portable radio and takes the clothes down the hall, presumably to the bathroom, disappears.*]

NEWSCASTER'S VOICE. . . . five-state alarm. Police authorities have requested all citizens to be on the lookout for a 1941 Dodge sedan . . . gray . . . mud-spattered . . . bearing Indiana license plates number HL6827 . . . that is HL6827. . . . One of the convicts is wearing a pair of faded blue farmer's overalls which were . . . [ELEANOR *has returned and flips the radio to music. The music plays through the scene.* ELEA-NOR *starts to make* RALPHIE'S *bed. The door chimes sound.*]

ELEANOR. Wouldn't you know it . . . every time . . . [*The chimes sound again, insistently. She comes down the stairs, but before she reaches the last step the chimes are heard for the third time. She crosses to the door and opens it.*] Yes? [*The young man who stands there . . . still out of sight . . . is in his mid-twenties and wears faded blue farmer's overalls. He is tall with—at the moment —a rather appealing boyish expression on his handsome face.*]

GLENN. Sorry to bother you, ma'am, but it looks like I lost my way. [*As he speaks,* ROBISH *and* HANK GRIFFIN *appear outside and enter the house by the side door, stealthily.*] Could you kindly direct me to the Bowden Dairy? I know it's somewhere in the neighborhood, but I must have the wrong . . . [HANK GRIF-FIN—*who is younger than* GLENN, *shorter, not so handsome, with a confused, hard but somehow rather sensitive face—remains in the pantry, looking out the window of the side door.* ROBISH *is large, bull-like, slow, with a huge head sunk between two bulky upthrust shoulders. He goes into the kitchen at once and reappears in the dining-room door. Both wear prison garb. The following action has a cold, machine-like precision about it.*]

ELEANOR. [*Her back to the room.*] Let me see. I've seen that sign. But there are no dairies very close. You see, this is a residential . . . [ROBISH *now stands in the room.* ELEANOR *becomes conscious of his presence. She breaks off and turns. In that moment* GLENN *whips out the gun,*

forces his way into the room, pushing ELEANOR. *He slams the door and locks it, then moves down to* ELEANOR.]

GLENN. Take it easy, lady. [*As her mouth trembles open.*] Easy, I said. You scream, the kid owns that bike out there'll come home an' find you in a pool of blood. [GLENN *only nods to* RO-BISH, *who stumps up the stairs and through the following looks into* CINDY'S *room,* RALPHIE'S *room, then enters the master bedroom and searches.*] You there, Hank?

HANK. [*Speaking as he moves into the living room.*] All clear out back. Lincoln in garage . . . almost new. Garage lock broken. [ELEANOR *looks at* HANK, *who returns her stare boldly. A shudder goes through her. Through the following,* GLENN'S *swagger suggests a deep insecurity. Above,* ROBISH *is examining and discarding various of* DAN'S *clothes in the bedroom . . . creating havoc.* GLENN *steps to* ELEANOR.]

GLENN. I'll take the keys to the Lincoln now, lady . . .

ELEANOR. Keys? . . . [*Conquering shudders.*] Keys? . . .

GLENN. Lady, when I talk, you snap. Snap fast!

ELEANOR. Top of . . . top of refrigerator . . . I think . . . I always misplace the . . . [*As* GLENN *nods to* HANK, *who goes into dining room then into pantry with the keys and out the side door and off.*] Take it . . . you only want the car . . . take it and go. . . .

GLENN. [*Shouts toward the stairs.*] What're you doin' up there, Robish— takin' a bath?

ROBISH. Nobody home but the missus. [*He goes into upstairs hall, with* DAN'S *clothes.*]

GLENN. I figured it. [*He examines the house . . . looks into the den.*] Good-lookin' family you got, lady. I seen 'em leavin'. [*As* ROBISH *descends.*] How many bedrooms up there, Robish?

ROBISH. Four. An' two complete cans, for Chrissake. . . . [*The sound of a car door being slammed startles* ELEANOR.]

GLENN. Don't be so jumpy, lady. Only the kid brother takin' care of the cars.

ROBISH. [*Holding up* DAN'S *suit.*] Th'

sonofabitch's got five suits up there. [*He tosses the suit over the back of chair and goes into the dining room . . . to reappear a few moments later searching the shelves in the pantry.*]

GLENN. Class, all the way. . . . [*To* ELEANOR.] I guess you're tumbling to the idea, ain't you, lady?

ELEANOR. [*Picks up her purse from sofa.*] You want money . . . here . . . take it . . . anything . . .

GLENN. [*Takes purse and dumps contents on sofa.*] Pretty. [*Holds up a locket.*] Gold? [*As* ELEANOR *nods wordlessly, he slips it into his pocket.*] I got a gal with a yen for gold a mile wide. [*Picks up the money.*] This all the dough you got in the house?

ELEANOR. [*With difficulty.*] Yes . . . yes . . . my husband always says . . . too much cash in . . .

GLENN. [*Grins.*] Old man's right. Ain't ever safe to have too much cash layin' around. [*He pockets the money.*] Gives people ideas. [ROBISH *returns, disgruntled.*]

ROBISH. [*To* GLENN.] My gut's growlin'.

GLENN. We heard it.

ROBISH. [*To* ELEANOR.] Missus, where you keep th' liquor?

ELEANOR. [*Backing away from him to chair, sits.*] We don't have . . . I don't think we . . . [HANK *enters the side door, locks it.*]

GLENN. [*Gesturing to den.*] Robish . . . park your butt'n there'n keep your eyes peeled that side-a th' house.

ROBISH. [*Aggressively; to* ELEANOR.] I ain't had me a drink'n eighteen years.

GLENN. Robish, you don't hear so good. It's a kinda library. Improve your mind. [HANK *enters from dining room.*]

HANK. Gray job's in the garage, outta sight. Lincoln's ready in the driveway . . . headin' out. But she's low on gas. [*He hands the car keys to* GLENN, *who pockets them.*]

ROBISH. [*Stolidly.*] I need me a gun. [GLENN *nods to* HANK, *who turns and runs upstairs. Through the following, he looks into* CINDY'S *room,* RALPHIE'S *room, and enters the master bedroom, where he searches through the top bureau drawer, tossing out handkerchiefs and other odds and ends of clothing.*] I don't like none of it.

GLENN. [*Calling up the stairs.*] Hey, Hank, Robish don't like it. After them hard bunks . . . them concrete floors!

HANK. Tell 'im to lump it.

GLENN. Lump it. Robish. [*Gestures to den.*] In there.

ROBISH. I don't feel right without a gun.

GLENN. Tell you what, Robish . . . Let's you'n me go out an' stick up a hardware store!

ROBISH. Now you're talkin'!

GLENN. [*Sardonically.*] Sure . . . Come'n, Robish. Every copper'n the state's waitin' for us to pull a job like that! [*Moves to door.*] What're you stallin' for? [HANK *finds an automatic in the drawer and pockets it and starts back downstairs.*] Come on!

ROBISH. [*Turning away—growling, inwardly seething.*] Awwww . . . don't do me no favors. [*For the first time,* GLENN *laughs.* HANK, *watching* ROBISH, *joins in.* ELEANOR *stares.* ROBISH'S *face hardens and, scowling, he makes a sudden movement toward* HANK.] What're you yakkin' at, yuh . . . [*But* GLENN *moves. The laughter dies. He grabs* ROBISH, *whips him about.*]

GLENN. [*In low hard tones.*] Lissen! How many times I gotta tell you? Keep your mitts off the kid, you don't wanna get your skull laid open. [*Pause.* ROBISH *and* GLENN *face each other. Then* ROBISH *turns sullenly and grabs suit of clothes, growling.* GLENN, *having asserted his total control, laughs, takes cigar from humidor on coffee table and tosses it to* ROBISH.] Here . . . make yourself sick on a good cigar. [ROBISH, *seething, doesn't attempt to catch it; it falls to the floor. Then, defiantly,* ROBISH *steps on it, grinding it into the carpet.*]

GLENN. Robish, you gonna give the lady the idea we ain't neat.

ROBISH. [*He picks up the humidor.*] Coupla brothers! Shoulda knowed better. Ain't neither one dry back-a the ears yet. [ROBISH *exits into the den.*]

ELEANOR. [*Who has been watching in horror.*] What . . . what do you . . . ?

GLENN. [*Ignoring her, crosses to* HANK.] What'd you find? [HANK, *keeping his eyes on* ELEANOR, *takes the automatic out of his pocket and hands it to* GLENN, *who examines it.* GLENN, *to* ELEANOR.] Lady, now I ask you . . . is that a nice thing to keep aroun' the house? [*He hands the automatic to* HANK, *whispering.*] Put it in your pocket and keep it there. Family secret, huh? What Robish don't know, don't hurt nobody . . . okay? [GLENN *laughs, gives* HANK *a playful push and goes to chair in high spirits.*] Let 'em comb the dives!

HANK. [*Sits on sofa; jubilantly.*] You foxed 'em good, Glenn.

GLENN. Came aroun' their roadblocks like we was flyin' a airplane! Everything's chimin'! [*He sits in the armchair, becomes conscious of the comfort. He raises himself by the arms and sinks again into the chair, delighted.*] Foam rubber, I betcha. Foam rubber, lady? [ELEANOR *nods.*] I seen the ads. [*He squirms in the seat, enjoying it.*] Melts right into your tail!

HANK. [*Takes a cigarette from the box on the coffee table, lights it with the table lighter and, rising, hands it to* GLENN.] Christ, what a place to take the stir-taste outta your mouth! Freezer full-a meat! Carpet makes you want to take your shoes off!

ELEANOR. How long do you intend to . . .

GLENN. [*Casually.*] Be outta here by midnight, lady.

HANK. Midnight? I thought you said Helen was waiting . . .

GLENN. Not in town, Hank. We don't make it so easy for 'em. She left three weeks ago.

HANK. [*Laughs, rises, grabs a fistful of cigarettes from the box on the coffee table, picks up the lighter, and flips it several times in her face.*] I don't care if we never leave. [*He exits into the dining room and reappears in the pantry, where he stands looking out the window of the side door.*]

GLENN. [*Rises.*] Now, lady . . . you think you can talk on the phone without bustin' into tears?

ELEANOR. [*Rises with great difficulty, takes a feeble step, then gets control of herself, straightens, and walks with dig-nity and determination to the phone table, turns to face* GLENN.] Whom do you want me to call? [GLENN *laughs.*]

GLENN. I always go for a gal with guts! That's *whom* we're gonna call—a gal with real guts. Person to person . . . Mr. James calling Mrs. James . . . Atlantic 6-3389 . . . in Pittsburgh. Pittsburgh, P. A. [*Blackout.*]

SHERIFF'S OFFICE: *Lights rise swiftly.* CARSON *sits near desk, writing on small note-pad. The clock reads 5:32.* BARD *is finishing a telephone conversation, a note of exultation in his voice.*

BARD. [*Into phone.*] Yeah . . . okay . . . good deal! [*He replaces the phone.*] Pittsburgh! They've located Helen Laski. Avalon Hotel, Pittsburgh. We'll have a record of any calls to or from . . . in a few minutes now.

CARSON. Bard . . . stop me if I'm out of line . . . but what's this thing to you? You, personally?

BARD. [*Slowly rubbing his chin.*] You've heard of that first law of the jungle . . . haven't you, Carson? [*The light on the radio flashes.* BARD *presses the button, snaps.*] Deputy Bard!

WINSTON'S VOICE. Jess . . . this is Winston. Car three.

BARD. What've you got, Tom?

WINSTON'S VOICE. That hardware store holdup on the south side . . .

BARD. [*Eagerly.*] Yeah? Yeah?

WINSTON'S VOICE. [*Wearily.*] No guns stolen. All they took was fishing rods. [BARD *presses the button and looks at* CARSON.]

CARSON. They'd be too shrewd to pull a stunt like that.

BARD. Look, Carson . . . do me a favor. It's almost time for supper. All I've heard since morning is how damn wise those rats are. I'm up to here with it.

CARSON. Where're they getting their clothes?

BARD. My theory is they're running around naked so nobody'll notice 'em. [*The telephone rings.* BARD *picks it up.*] Deputy Bard . . . Yeah . . . [*Disappointment.*] Yeah. Okay. [*Hangs up.*] Helen Laski checked out of the Avalon Hotel last night. No phone calls, no messages of any kind received today. . . . [CARSON *rises and with a look at* BARD *goes to the window.* BARD *bursts out.*] I know! I know! They'd be too smart to make a call to a hotel. They used somebody in between!

CARSON. [*At the window.*] I didn't say a word.

BARD. You know where that leaves us, don't you? Beating our tails ragged over nothing around here.

CARSON. Only you don't believe it.

BARD. Sure I believe it. I'm a trained police officer. I go by the facts, not crazy hunches. I reckon they're not here.

CARSON. [*Turns.*] Why don't you put some more patrol cars on the streets, anyway? Just in case?

BARD. [*Rises and paces.*] That damn jalopy's been reported in every state in the union . . . sixty times in Indiana alone! The earth won't open up and swallow it! Okay, let's try anything! [*He picks up phone, dials . . . as the lights dim.*] Where is that beat-up gray car?

HILLIARD HOME: *It is dark outside and dim throughout the house, except for the living room which is brilliantly lighted.* ELEANOR *sits on the sofa, staring ahead.* HANK *is in the pantry sitting in a chair which is obviously from the breakfast nook; he holds the portable radio from* RALPHIE'S *room in his lap with the music playing—a loud jazzy tune, in contrast to the soft gentleness of the morning music.* HANK *wears a dark red shirt with a cardigan sweater over it and the prison trousers. He smokes fairly steadily.*

The ravages of the afternoon are everywhere apparent; the atmosphere of invasion hangs over the entire house. There is an open box of cigars on the coffee table with some of the cigars scattered on the table. There is a carton of cigarettes, with the top ripped back, on the table. A coffee cup is also on the table and another is on the table beside the armchair. There are odds and ends of food. The ashtrays are filled to overflowing.

In the living room, GLENN, *at window, is filled with a sense of triumph; he is almost gay, and his enjoyment of what follows is clear.* GLENN *wears a pair of* DAN'S *slacks and a sport shirt.* ELEANOR, *alert in every fiber, is pale, haggard, stiff.* ROBISH *is entering from the den; he is wearing a full suit including shirt and tie—*DAN'S *best, and it does not quite fit. A cigar is jammed in the corner of his mouth.*

ROBISH. What if this joker gets suspicious . . . that gray car parked right in his own garage?

GLENN. [*Casually.*] Can it, Robish.

ROBISH. [*To* ELEANOR.] Why ain't he here? You said quarter to six.

ELEANOR. The traffic may be heavy . . . or Cindy may have had to work late . . . or . . . anything . . . *anything!* [HANK *suddenly rises and looks out the window in the side door. He moves up toward the kitchen door and calls:*]

HANK. Glenn! Black coop just turned in the driveway.

GLENN. Turn off the clatter back there, Hank. [HANK *turns off the radio and places it on the back stairs.*]

HANK. [*Looking out the side door.*] You want me to grab 'em?

GLENN. Not with all them cars goin' by out there.

HANK. Woman comin' around to the front door, Glenn. [ELEANOR *places her hand at her mouth.* GLENN *unlocks the door.*]

GLENN. [*To* ELEANOR.] You don't have to do nothin' but keep your trap shut. [*He turns the gun to cover the front door. There is a brief pause. The front door opens and* CINDY *enters, casually, swiftly, a trifle breathless. She stops dead when she sees* GLENN.] Come right in, redhead. [CINDY *backs away, pulling the door closed, but she suddenly stops, frozen in the door. The reason she stops is simply that* GLENN *has turned the gun toward* ELEANOR'S *head.*] We still got the old lady, Sis. [ROBISH *is standing at den door . . . dull, brutish . . . with his little eyes roving over* CINDY. CINDY *closes the door and stands in front of it.* GLENN *grins.*] That's bein' real sensible.

CINDY. [*Planting her feet slightly.*] Mother . . . how long have these animals been here? [ELEANOR *starts, as though she would warn* CINDY. GLENN's *grin flickers, fades and a hardness comes into his face . . . but not into his tone.*]

GLENN. Spitfire, too. You watch out, redhead.

HANK. [*At side door, calls.*] Glenn! He's lookin' in the garage.

GLENN. [*Calling to* HANK—*confident, knowing.*] He'll come in. [*He grabs* CINDY *and pushes her toward chair.*] Sit down now, sweetie . . . and no talking. Not a goddam word.

HANK. [*In pantry.*] He's coming around now—fast. [GLENN *moves into position near front door. Pause. Then the door opens, and* DAN *enters, evening paper in hand.*]

DAN. Ellie, whose car is that in the . . . [GLENN *slams door shut behind* DAN, *and* DAN *breaks off, staring in bewilderment at* GLENN, *then at the gun.*]

GLENN. [*In flat cold tones.*] It's loaded. Now lock the door. . . . [*Sardonically.*] Please. [*Unable to speak yet, his eyes on* GLENN, DAN *turns and locks the door. Then:*]

DAN. [*Baffled; softly.*] What're you . . . why . . . I don't . . .

GLENN. You never know what's comin', do you, Pop? [DAN *then turns to* ELEANOR.]

DAN. Ellie? . . .

ELEANOR. I'm all right, Dan.

DAN. [*Looking about the room, glances toward stairs.*] Where's Ralphie?

ELEANOR. Not home yet.

HANK. [*Calls from pantry.*] Driveway ain't blocked, Glenn.

CINDY. The house is crawling with them, Dad.

GLENN. [*Sizing her up.*] Don't get me jumpy, redhead, this thing's liable to explode.

DAN. [*Flatly, glancing at newspaper in his hand.*] Glenn Griffin.

GLENN. [*Laughs, takes paper.*] Lotsa people heard-a me, didn't they? [*In satisfaction.*] Front page. [*Disgusted.*] They always gotta use the same goddam picture. [*He tosses the paper to the floor.*]

DAN. Griffin . . . you fire that thing . . . and you'll have the whole neighborhood in here in two minutes.

GLENN. I don't want to take that

chance, Hilliard . . . any more'n you want me to.

ROBISH. You dumb, mister?

GLENN. [*Sizing up* DAN.] Naw, he ain't dumb, Robish. He's a smart-eyed bastard, this guy. . . .

DAN. What're you . . . I don't understand . . . what do you *want?*

GLENN. Take it easy, Pop.

DAN. [*Controlling himself with effort.*] What do you want here?

GLENN. [*Takes a step toward* DAN.] I don't want nobody to get hurt. . . . What do *you* want, Pop?

DAN. That's . . . what I want, too. [*Then, shrewdly.*] That's what you're depending on, isn't it?

GLENN. You got it, Buster. First try.

DAN. But . . . why *here?* Why *my* house?

GLENN. Your break, Pop. I like the location. Those empty lots'n both sides. The bike parked on the nice lawn. I like suckers with kids . . . they don't take no chances.

DAN. Anyone who could think up a scheme like that is . . .

GLENN. [*Cutting in.*] . . . is smart, Pop.

ELEANOR. [*Quickly.*] Dan! They've done nothing.

GLENN. Now I'm gonna explain the facts-a-life to you, Hilliard. You listen, too, redhead . . . listen good. You can get brave . . . any one of you . . . just about any time you feel up to it. Might even get away with it. *But* . . . that ain't sayin' what'll happen to the others . . . the old lady here . . . the redhead . . . the little guy owns the bike. . . . [*Slight pause.*] Okay, Pop, you got it all the way now. [*Another pause.* DAN *moves to sofa and drops his hat on it.* ELEANOR's *hand and his meet, briefly clasping.* DAN *turns to* GLENN.]

DAN. [*Taking a deep breath.*] How long?

GLENN. [*Grinning.*] Now that's the kinda sensible talk a guy likes to hear.

DAN. [*Firmly.*] How long?

GLENN. Matter of hours . . . before midnight . . . maybe sooner. Meantime, everything goes on just like normal.

DAN. Why midnight?

GLENN. [*Almost politely.*] None-a your goddam business.

ELEANOR. They have a friend coming . . . with money.

DAN. What if . . .

GLENN. [*Speaking at the same time; stops* DAN] Lady, you speak when I tell you.

DAN. The police are looking everywhere for you. What if . . .

GLENN. They ain't looking here, Pop. They show here, it ain't gonna be pretty.

DAN. They could trail your friend . . .

GLENN. Let's get one thing straight, Pop. [*Gesturing to the window.*] Any red lights show out there . . . you folks get it first. [*There is a slight pause.* DAN *crosses to the window and peeks out between the drawn curtains.* GLENN *laughs.*] Gives you a funny feelin', don't it? You don't know what's happenin' . . . or where . . . or what it adds up to . . . for you. Ever had that feelin' before, Pop? Me, I get it all the time. Even kinda like it. But you and me . . . we ain't much alike, are we, Pop?

CINDY. [*A breath.*] Thank God.

DAN. [*Turns from window.*] Griffin . . . if you . . . what if I could get you the same amount of money you're waiting for? Now. Before midnight.

ROBISH. Hey, that don't sound like a bad . . .

GLENN. Hilliard, you maybe think you're a big shot . . . fifteen thousand a year. But I had me a look at your bankbooks. Two hundred lousy bucks in the kitty. Hell, I had more'n fifteen grand in my hands at one time, Pop . . . and I ain't twenty-five yet.

CINDY. I hope it helped pass your time in jail . . . counting it.

DAN. I could raise more. I could . . .

ROBISH. What about that? We could blow outta here right away! This joker's usin' his brain.

GLENN. [*Sharply.*] Use yours, Robish. Helen's on her way *here.*

ROBISH. To hell with that! Why should me and the kid risk our necks . . . just so you can get some copper knocked off.

GLENN. [*Dangerously now—low and intense.*] Go spill your guts somewhere else!

ROBISH. [*Shouting.*] What do I care who busted your goddam jawbone?

GLENN. [*Topping him.*] I'll bust yours if . . . [*They are now shouting at each other across* DAN.]

ROBISH. This guy talks sense! Don't I have nothin' to say? . . .

GLENN. NO! You ain't got a goddam stinkin' thing to say! [ROBISH *retreats slightly.* GLENN *turns on* DAN *more quietly but with force.*] You, Hilliard . . . I seen what you been up to. Robish here, he ain't got a brain. *But* . . . he ain't got a gun, either. Don't try to get in between, you smart-eyed sonofabitch. Clickety-clickety-click. [*He makes a gesture at* DAN's *temple.*] I can see them wheels goin' around in there, Pop. *Don't ever try that again!* [*He backs away, eyes on* DAN; *speaks softly now—to* ELEANOR.] Now, lady . . . serve us up that chicken you been thawin' out.

DAN. My wife's not your servant.

GLENN. [*Thinly . . . daring* DAN *to protest.*] I always wanted me a servant. . . .

ELEANOR. [*Begins to rise.*] I don't mind, Dan.

DAN. [*Firmly.*] I do. Sit down, Ellie.

GLENN. [*Exploding wildly.*] Lissen, Hilliard! I . . . [*Then he stops; sizing* DAN *up, forcing control . . . almost quietly at first, building in intensity.*] I had a old man like you. Always callin' the tune. Outside his house, nobody. Inside, Mister God! Little punk went to church every Sunday . . . took it from everybody . . . licked their shoes . . . tried to beat it into Hank'n me . . . be a punk, be a nobody . . . take it from you shiny-shoed, down-your-noses sonsabitches with white handkerchiefs in your pockets! [*He snatches the handkerchief from* DAN's *breast pocket, spits into it, and throws it on the floor.*] You remember, Pop . . . I could kill you just for kicks. [*Pause. Without taking his eyes off* DAN *he again gestures to* ELEANOR, *speaks coldly again.*] Now, lady . . . get out there'n cook it. [ELEANOR *starts to rise, but* HANK's *voice stops her.*]

HANK. [*Turning from window in side door.*] Kid comin' up the driveway . . .

walkin' . . . [GLENN *starts for the front door.*]

DAN. Griffin . . . you've got to let me explain to Ralphie first. . . . [ROBISH *grabs* DAN *by the shoulders and shoves him against the window.*]

GLENN. I don't got to do nothin'. You pull anything now, you can sit'n watch me kick the kid's face in.

HANK. [*Calling again from the side door.*] Comin' to the front door . . .

GLENN. [*At front door, unlocks it.*] You got to learn to take orders from other people now, Pop. . . . [*The front door opens and* RALPHIE *enters, whistling.* GLENN *slams the door behind him and locks it.* RALPHIE *stops.*]

RALPHIE. [*Bewildered.*] Hey . . . what is . . . [ROBISH *takes a single step.*] Who are you? [*He turns to the door, sees* GLENN. *A split second. Then he turns and runs to the dining room . . . as* HANK *appears in the dining-room door.*] Get out of . . . [RALPHIE *whirls and dashes to the front door, evading* GLENN.]

DAN. [*Quickly.*] Ralphie, it's all right! It's . . . [ROBISH *grabs* RALPHIE *at the door. He shakes him by the shoulders roughly, venting on the child the spleen that* GLENN *has stirred in him.*]

ROBISH. Where ya think you're goin? Don't you know who's boss 'roun' here? Ya gotta take orders from Griffin. Griffin's the big shot 'roun' here. . . . [*As* RALPHIE's *head snaps back and forth,* DAN *moves. He grabs* ROBISH, *whips him around.* RALPHIE *breaks away and runs, fighting tears, to* ELEANOR *on the sofa. She takes him in her arms as he sits, clutching her.* DAN *slams* ROBISH *against the window and draws back for a blow, his mind gone blank; he is propelled blindly by jungle atavistic urges beyond his control. But* GLENN *steps in.*]

GLENN. It ain't gonna be like this! Not like this, see! [*In the scuffle the table near the chair is overturned.* ELEANOR *stifles a scream as* GLENN *brings the gun down on* DAN's *shoulder.* DAN *goes down.* ROBISH *recovers and starts toward* DAN, *but* GLENN *steps in between.*] You hear me, Robish? *Nothin's gonna screw this up!*

ROBISH. [*Blinking owlishly at the gun*

in GLENN's *hand.*] You think I'm gonna let that . . .

GLENN [*An order—low, intense.*] Get outta here!

ROBISH [*Glaring, goes to dining-room door.*] My gut's growlin' again. [ROBISH *kicks open the dining-room door and exits.* DAN, *his tie askew, manages to sit in chair, holding his shoulder.* GLENN *regains his familiar swagger.*]

GLENN. Give the old lady a hand, redhead. Out there . . . if you please. [CINDY *and* ELEANOR *rise,* ELEANOR *going into dining room.*]

CINDY. Where do we keep the rat poison? [*As* CINDY *follows* ELEANOR, HANK *steps into her path, blocking her way.* GLENN *laughs and crosses to foot of stairs;* CINDY *is trapped between them.*]

GLENN. [*Goading* DAN.] She's a honey, ain't she, Hank?

HANK. [*Arrogantly.*] I don't go for redheads.

DAN. [*Sensing danger for* CINDY.] Griffin . . .

CINDY. [*With a sharpness, to* HANK.] For God's small favors, make me eternally grateful. [HANK *drops his arm and* CINDY *exits into the dining room.* HANK *follows her with his eyes and gives a low whistle.* GLENN *turns to* DAN.]

GLENN. Kid's been in stir for three years, Pop. Don't cost nothin' to look.

DAN. [*His eyes still on* HANK.] Just don't try changing your mind, young fellow.

GLENN. Hilliard, you're a funny gink. You don't know when you're licked, do you? . . . Now just one thing—you got a gun in the house?

RALPHIE. [*Too quickly, as he kneels on sofa.*] No . . . we don't.

GLENN. [*Enjoying himself.*] Well, Pop?

DAN. You heard the boy. I don't have a gun.

GLENN. That's right. You don't. Show him, Hank. [*After* HANK *displays the automatic.*] There for a minute I thought you was gonna lie to me, Pop.

DAN. Griffin . . . listen to me . . .

GLENN. I'll do the talkin'. You listen, Hilliard! That dough's halfway here now and nothin's gonna foul this up, see. You pull any of that muscle-stuff again . . .

DAN. That won't happen again . . .

GLENN. . . . and I'm gonna let Robish work you over . . .

DAN. . . . I went blank there for a . . .

GLENN. . . . after that, you ain't gonna know what happens to the others. That the way you want it?

DAN. *Griffin* . . . [*Very softly . . . with strength now.*] *hands off.*

GLENN. I don't go for threats. . . .

DAN. Hands off, that's all I know! If one of you touches one of us again . . .

GLENN. Don't talk tough to me, Hilliard. . . .

DAN. . . . I can't promise what'll happen. . . . I can't promise *anything* . . . if one of you touches one of us again. I don't *know* what I'll do. Can't you understand that, you half-baked squirt? I'll make you use that gun, Griffin. So help me. We're done for then, but so are you. [*Drops voice.*] It won't matter then whether your friend gets here or not. . . . [*Blackout.*]

SHERIFF'S OFFICE: *The clock reads 7:03.* WINSTON, *his feet propped up on desk, is trying to sleep. The radio signal is flickering.* BARD *flips on radio.*

CARSON'S VOICE. Bard . . . this is Carson.

BARD. [*Wearily.*] I'm still here, Carson.

CARSON'S VOICE. Helen Laski's been spotted.

BARD. [*Changing—alert and eager.*] Where?

CARSON'S VOICE. She's heading west from Pittsburgh. On U.S. 40. Driving very slow and careful. Approaching Columbus, Ohio. Heading west!

BARD. [*With satisfaction.*] West!

CARSON'S VOICE. Ought to be here about eleven or twelve tonight.

BARD. [*An excited throb in his voice.*] Okay. Now listen. Don't let anyone tail her. I don't want her picked up, or alerted. But I want her clocked. Every town she goes through . . . every village. I want to know every time she stops to get gas, go to the can, anything.

CARSON'S VOICE. Looks like your hunch is paying off, Bard.

BARD. Could be, Carson. *Could be!*

[BARD *flips off the radio and slaps* WIN-STON'S *feet off the desk.*] I told you they were homing pigeons, Tom! They do it every time . . . right back to the womb that spewed 'em.

WINSTON. Okay, they're pigeons. You're an owl. I'm sleepy.

BARD. They're layin' low here now . . . thinkin' how clever they been . . . getting Laski out of town so she could backtrack to 'em. Clever! *Not so damned!*

WINSTON. Jess, you're raving. How long since you ate solid food?

DUTCH'S VOICE. [*On intercom.*] Jess . . .

BARD. [*Flips intercom button.*] Yeah, Dutch?

DUTCH'S VOICE. Your wife called again. She says she's still at your mother's but drowning in a sea of words . . . whatever that means.

BARD. [*With a laugh.*] Tell her to stay there all night, Dutch. Tell her I said it's . . . uh . . . Be-Kind-to-Talkative-Mothers-Week. [*He flips off the intercom, turns to* WINSTON *exultantly.*] About twenty miles out of town, we'll put a real tag on Miss Helen Laski and she'll breeze right in and lead us straight to the hole! How many hours till midnight, Tom?

WINSTON. By my watch . . . [*The lights begin to dim.*] too god-damned-many. [*Blackout.*]

HILLIARD HOME: *The living room lights are on; the rest of the house is in dimness.* HANK *is in the chair in the pantry, smoking. In the living room the family is arranged in a pattern within view of the windows. The curtains are slightly open.* ROBISH *is sitting on the stairs.* GLENN *is lounging in a chair near the windows.* DAN *looks at his watch.*

GLENN. Pop, that's a good-looking timepiece you got there. [*He extends his hand.*] I'll take it. [DAN *rises, pauses . . . then slips the wrist-watch band off his wrist. He crosses and hands the watch to* GLENN, *who examines it.*] Fancy. [*He slips it on his own wrist.*] D'you snitch this from that department store, Pop?

DAN [*Quietly . . . with dignity.*] My

wife gave it to me . . . on our twentieth anniversary. [*He returns to sit.*]

GLENN. [*Winding the watch.*] Now ain't that real touchin'? [*To* RALPHIE.] Hey, Buster . . . ain't it time for you to hit the sack? You want to grow up, be a big man like Pop here, don't you? [RALPHIE *kisses* ELEANOR *good-night, then crosses directly to* GLENN.]

RALPHIE. Half-baked squirt! [ROBISH *laughs.* GLENN *grabs the front of* RALPHIE'S *shirt but releases him after a moment with a laugh.* RALPHIE *turns and goes upstairs and into his own room and sits on the bed.*]

GLENN. [*As* RALPHIE *goes.*] Some brat you got there, missus. Some day he's gonna get his head knocked off. [DAN *rises and crosses to the stairs.* ROBISH *stands up and blocks his way.*]

ROBISH. What you think you're gonna do . . . go to the toilet for him?

GLENN. It's his house, Robish. Hilliard don't want that kid hollering out a window up there any more'n we do. [ROBISH *steps down from the stairs and* DAN *goes up to* RALPHIE'S *room.* ROBISH *moves toward the window.* GLENN *flips off the livingroom lights and jumps up, closing the window curtains.*] How many times I gotta tell you—stay outta the way-a them windows! [*He motions* ROBISH *toward the den.*] Get in there and turn on the television.

ROBISH. [*Protesting.*] Listen, Griffin . . .

GLENN. And keep it lit so it looks natural from out front. [ROBISH *stomps angrily into the den. The living room is now in dimness.* DAN *turns on light in* RALPHIE'S *room, stands a moment without speaking.* RALPHIE *studies his father a second.*]

RALPHIE. Dad . . . they're not so tough.

DAN. [*Still facing the door, abstracted.*] Don't you fool yourself, Ralphie.

RALPHIE. You could've licked the big guy if that Griffin hadn't . . .

DAN [*Turning to the boy.*] Ralphie, we can't lick them . . . at least not that way. I lost my temper, that's all. I . . . can't let that happen again.

RALPHIE [*Not daring to believe it.*] Dad . . . are you scared?

DAN. Of course not. Why, you ought to know . . . [*He suddenly sits on the bed, facing the boy.*] Ralphie, listen to me. Those two guns they have down there . . . they're loaded. Those are real bullets. When a gun goes off, it doesn't only make a sound. Those bullets can kill people. Do you understand that, son?

RALPHIE. I've been thinking . . . I could climb out Cindy's window . . . out across the porch roof. . . . I could get to the Wallings. Get help . . .

DAN. [*Patience running thin.*] Ralphie . . .

RALPHIE. The porch isn't much higher'n the garage roof. I've jumped off the garage roof a lot of times.

DAN. Ralphie, how many times have I told you to stay off the garage roof?

RALPHIE. *You* could, though. I'll *bet* you could.

DAN. Look, Ralphie . . . Listen, Ralph . . . Ralph. You want me to call you Ralph, don't you? You want to be considered a grown-up boy in this house? Then you've got to behave like one . . . *think* like one . . . beginning right now!

RALPHIE. I've got a better idea. I could wait till that young one goes into the living room, sometime, then sneak down the back stairs. . . .

DAN. [*Anger rising.*] Ralphie, didn't you hear them? If you got out of here . . . even if you brought the police . . . do you know what would happen? They would shoot your mother and your sister . . . and *you* . . . *you'd* be the reason they did it.

RALPHIE. You *are* scared.

DAN. No, no, of course not . . . It's only . . . [*Suddenly changes.*] Yes, son . . . yes, I'm scared. But I'm not ashamed of being scared. . . . Sometimes it's better to be scared. . . . You think about that now. You think hard about that, hear?

RALPHIE. Well, I'm not. And Cindy's not either.

DAN. [*Rising, urgently.*] You'd better . . . [*The telephone in the house rings.* DAN *stops. Immediate tension . . . there is a pause until the second ring starts.* GLENN *rises and turns on the living-room lights.* HANK *runs up the back stairs and to the phone extension in the upstairs hall.* ROBISH *appears in the door of the den.*]

GLENN. Hank! [*To* CINDY.] Okay, red-head . . .you get the pleasure. [CINDY *rises from the sofa and crosses toward telephone.*] If it's for Mr. James, I'll take it. Anyone else, let 'em talk . . . except the brat. [*The telephone continues to ring—insistently, mechanically.* HANK *picks up the phone in the upstairs hall with his hand on the circuit breaker in the cradle until he hears* CINDY *speak. Then he opens the circuit and listens.* DAN *stands behind the door to* RALPHIE'S *room . . . alert, waiting.*]

HANK. [*When he is ready at the phone.*] Okay, Glenn.

GLENN. [*Beside* CINDY *at the phone table.*] Like any other night, see. Normal. [CINDY *picks up the phone with her left hand.* GLENN *grabs the instrument and puts it in her right hand so he can try to listen, too.*]

CINDY. [*Into phone.*] Hello? . . . Oh . . . No, I can't . . . not tonight . . . I simply can't, that's all. . . . Nothing's the matter, I . . . [*She slowly replaces the phone. Upstairs,* HANK *replaces the extension and starts down the stairs into the living room.* DAN *opens the door of* RALPHIE'S *room and comes down a few steps on the stairs.*]

GLENN. [*To* CINDY—*impatiently.*] Well? Well?

CINDY. [*Bleakly.*] I flunked.

GLENN. Who was it?

HANK [*Descending stairs.*] His name's Chuck. And he's coming, anyway. For a date. [*Pause . . .* HANK'S *eyes on* CINDY. GLENN *takes a few steps, thinking furiously.*]

GLENN. You ain't 's wise's I thought you was, spitfire.

HANK. She couldn't help it. He was in a drug store around the corner. Wouldn't even listen. Wants her to go dancing.

GLENN. [*Turns to* CINDY.] Okay. You be ready, cutie. When boy friend stops out front, you duck out. . . . [*Pause: general amazement.*]

ROBISH. Griffin . . . you off your rocker?

GLENN. [*Calling.*] Hilliard . . . get down here. [*To* ELEANOR.] You stick with the brat, he don't get ideas. [ELEANOR *rises and starts up the stairs, passing* DAN *as he descends.*]

DAN. [*To* ELEANOR, *in a low voice.*] Lock the door. [GLENN *flips on radio, then crosses to* CINDY *as the music rises.*]

GLENN. You wanna dance, redhead? You should-a told Hank. [*To* HANK.] C'mon, kid, you want a dance, take a dance. [*To* CINDY, *who moves slightly away.*] Give the kid a break, spitfire. [DAN *watches tensely . . . as* HANK *looks* CINDY *over, with arrogance, but the longing clear in his face. Then* HANK *moves, crossing toward* CINDY, *passing her, flipping off the radio. In silence, he walks with dignity, inwardly disturbed, toward the dining-room door, exits. A moment—while* GLENN *stares after* HANK, *amazed, frowning. Above,* ELEANOR *enters* RALPHIE'S *bedroom, closes and locks door, turns off bedroom light.*]

GLENN [*Baffled, almost to himself.*] Oughta see Hank dance. Has all the babes groggy. [HANK *appears in pantry, oddly shaken.*]

HANK. [*In whisper.*] Dammitohell . . .

GLENN. [*Recovering, turning to* DAN.] Hilliard . . . the gas is low in that fancy buggy of yours. Fill'er up'n check the battery'n oil.

ROBISH. You ain't lettin' 'em *both* out? [*In the pantry,* HANK *sinks into the chair, sits quietly.*]

GLENN. The kid'n the missus stay. Him or the redhead pull something, they know what'll happen here. Pop here's a smart cookie. He don't want no coppers settin' up machine guns on his nice smooth lawn . . . throwin' tear gas through his windows. [*Moves closer to* DAN, *threateningly.*] Cause that happens, you know who's gonna get it, don't you, Hilliard? Not you. [*He gestures upstairs.*] *Them.* I'm gonna see to it personal. [*Slowly.*] An' you're gonna stay alive to remember it the rest of your life. [*There is a pause. Then* DAN *steps toward* CINDY.]

DAN. You hear that, Cindy? [DAN *crosses to closet and gets his coat and* CINDY'S.]

CINDY. I'll do *anything* to get away from that voice.

ROBISH. Okay, everybody's gone nuts. Gimme some liquor.

DAN. No, no liquor.

GLENN. This time the old man's right, Robish.

ROBISH. [*Shrewdly—striking the weak spot.*] You lettin' this joker give the orders?

GLENN. [*Tricked.*] Nobody gives me orders. Not ever again! [*To* DAN.] Make it bourbon, Pop. Bonded. [*To* CINDY.] You . . . bring back some late-edition papers. [*He sits.*]

CINDY. [*Getting into her coat—scathingly.*] Would you like a scrapbook and a jar of paste? [HANK, *suddenly alert in pantry, looks out window of side door.*]

HANK. [*Calling.*] Car stoppin' at the curb. Little low-slung job. Foreign make, some kind.

CINDY. [*To* GLENN.] It's a Jaguar. You should know what a jaguar is . . . it's a fierce jungle animal . . . very brave against smaller, less ferocious animals. But it's a snarling coward when trapped. [*She goes to the door.* DAN *follows, stops her.*]

DAN. Cindy! [*She turns to him; slight pause; then gently.*] You . . . you be careful, hear? [*As* DAN *opens the door,* GLENN *rises quickly and steps to the dining-room door, out of sight of the front door.* CINDY *goes out and* DAN *closes the door.* HANK *watches out the window of the side door.*]

GLENN. If that spitfire tries anything!

DAN. Griffin . . . what if the police track you down? Sooner or later . . . through no fault of ours . . . what if . . .

GLEN. [*Smugly—in control.*] I'd never know who done it, Pop.

DAN. But you couldn't blame *us!*

GLENN. [*Slowly.*] Hilliard, I got news for you. I—can—do—anything—I—want. Nice family you got here, Pop. You love that woman of yours, you ain't gonna reach for no phone in that filling station. Them coppers're after *me*, y'know. They don't give a hoot in hell about you. *Or* your family. [*He crosses to the door.*] Clickety-clickety-click . . . give you

something to think about, Pop. [GLENN *opens the door and gestures* DAN *to go.* DAN *goes out, setting his shoulders. Above,* ELEANOR *watches out* RALPHIE'S *window.*]

ROBISH. [*As* GLENN *closes and locks the door.*] Jeez, I'm gettin' up a thirst all of a sudden. [*He exits into den.* GLENN, *after a short pause, turns out the living-room lights and goes through the dining-room door and into the pantry where he joins* HANK, *who stares moodily out the window of the side door.*]

GLENN. Kid, everythin's chimin'! Told you I'd shack you up in style, didn't I?

HANK. [*Noncommital.*] Yeah . . .

GLENN. Hey . . . what's eatin' you, anyway?

HANK. Y'know something, Glenn? I never had a "date" in my life.

GLENN. Date? Hell, you laid enough babes to . . .

HANK. Naw, I mean a *date.* Y'know . . . ordinary things like that.

GLENN. [*Scornfully.*] Malted milks? Hot dogs at a drive-in?

HANK. Maybe . . .

GLENN. You got it comin', kid . . . all the babes you can handle and still walk straight up.

HANK. Babes like Helen?

GLENN. [*Astonished.*] Yeah. . . . What's the matter with Helen?

HANK. She's a tramp. [HANK *goes to the kitchen door and disappears.* GLENN *stares after him, puzzled. Blackout.*]

SHERIFF'S OFFICE: BARD *is at the desk, working over various reports.* CARSON *enters briskly. Clock: 8:56.*

CARSON. Bard . . . hold onto your hat. She's not coming.

BARD. What're you talking about . . . not coming? She's halfway . . .

CARSON. [*Shaking his head.*] Helen Laski's not coming. She made one simple mistake. She ran a red light on the outskirts of Columbus. A patrol car gave chase.

BARD. [*Rising, outraged.*] Carson . . . are you telling me they arrested Helen Laski for a traffic violation? Good God, they had orders! It's been on every teletype for hours . . . *do not arrest!*

CARSON. They didn't arrest her. She gave them the slip . . . in downtown Columbus. Abandoned the convertible. Swallowed up. Presto! [*He shrugs.*] These mistakes are bound to happen.

BARD. You can't afford mistakes against a mind like Glenn Griffin's! [*He sits at the desk and flips the button on the intercom.*] Dutch! I want every long distance telephone call and a record of every telegram from Columbus, Ohio, to Indianapolis from . . . [*He looks at* CARSON.]

CARSON. Eight.

BARD. From eight o'clock to now . . . and straight through the night. As fast as they get 'em. Any number to any number. Names, addresses, the works. [*Flips off the intercom, sits back.*] Imagine those greedy sonsabitches in Columbus trying to pick her off for a lousy fifteen-buck fine!

CARSON. [*Sits and picks up the deck of cards on the desk.*] She has to contact him . . . wherever he is. All we can do is wait. How about a game of double solitaire?

BARD. [*Rising and pacing.*] Wait . . . wait . . . wait. [*Dimout.*]

HILLIARD HOME: *The lights are dim throughout the house.* ELEANOR *is moving from the window to the door in* RALPHIE'S *room.* RALPHIE *is asleep on his bed.* HANK *is in the pantry watching out the window of the side door.* ROBISH *is turning from the window in the living room.* GLENN *is leaving the pantry to appear in the living room.*

ROBISH. Tired-awaitin'. I been thinkin' about a snort of whisky for eighteen years.

GLENN. [*As he enters from the dining room.*] Shut up, he's comin' in. [*He gestures for* ROBISH *to turn on the living-room lights.* ROBISH *turns on the lights and unlocks and opens the front door.* DAN *enters, the fury and frustration packed solid through his whole frame. A new fear has taken root in him now, and he speaks flatly, quietly.* GLENN *says:*] C'mere, Pop. [*As* DAN *crosses and* ROBISH *closes and locks the front door.*] You mind takin' your hands outta your pockets? [DAN *obliges.*] Thank you kindly. . . .

ROBISH. Where the hell you been? [DAN *faces* ROBISH. GLENN *frisks him expertly.*]

DAN. The service stations close early in this neighborhood. . . . [GLENN *is circling* DAN.] I don't have a gun, Griffin. [GLENN *brings the whisky bottle out of* DAN'S *coat pocket. It is in a paper bag which he removes and drops on the floor.*]

ROBISH. [*Outraged, seeing the bottle.*] Chrissake, a pint!

DAN. You didn't specify any particular amount.

GLENN. [*Laughs, looking at the bottle.*] Kentucky Tavern . . . nothing but the best for Pop! [*As* ROBISH *snatches the bottle.*] Robish, go'n out'n check the car over. [*He sits on the sofa, putting his feet up.*]

ROBISH. [*Working with the bottle.*] Maybe he's got coppers stashed in the back seat. Let Hank check it.

GLENN. [*Dismissing it—lifts voice.*] Hank! Check the car.

HANK. [*Bitterly.*] Yeh . . . me. [*He rises from the chair and opens the door as he calls.*] Okay, Glenn. [*He exits through the side door, closing it.* DAN *goes to the stairs, begins to mount.*]

GLENN. You didn't get any ideas out there, did you, Hilliard?

ROBISH. [*Struggling with bottle.*] Kee-rist . . . eighteen years an' then you can't get it open! [*Succeeds, takes a long swig from bottle.*]

DAN. [*On second step of stairs, calls.*] Ellie . . .

ELEANOR. [*Comes out of the room to the head of the stairs.*] We're all right, Dan. Cindy's not back yet.

GLENN. Pop, when I ask you a question, you answer!

DAN. [*Turns, flatly.*] No. No ideas. [*Above,* ELEANOR *returns to* RALPHIE'S *room and closes the door.* HANK *re-enters the pantry and speaks as he crosses toward the living room.*]

HANK. Car's okay. [*He enters the living room through the dining-room door.*] I didn't try the motor. [*A glance at* DAN.] Looks like the whole street's gone to sleep.

GLENN. See, Robish. Hank ain't yellow. Taught him how not to be yellow, didn't I, Hank?

HANK. You taught me everything. [*The strange twist of bitterness in his tone causes* GLENN *to look at him sharply.*]

DAN. [*Haunted by his new fear.*] Griffin . . .

GLENN. [*Briskly; unpleasantly now.*] Your woman's waitin'. Go to bed.

DAN. [*Firmly.*] Griffin . . . when you do leave tonight, we're staying in this house. My family. All of us.

GLENN. [*Eyes on* HANK.] Yeh, yeh. You give me a fair shake, I give you a fair shake. [*Pause.* DAN *stands, thinking.* HANK *crosses to take the bottle from* ROBISH; *drinks.* GLENN *rises, glaring at* DAN. DAN *turns and goes upstairs.* GLENN *stops* HANK *as he returns the bottle to* ROBISH *and turns to leave the room.* GLENN *presses on, puzzled.*] I did teach you everything, didn't I, Hank?

HANK. [*Meeting his brother's gaze: levelly.*] Yeh. Everything . . . except maybe how to live in a house like this. [HANK *goes swiftly to dining-room door and exits. He enters the pantry and sits in the chair. Above,* DAN *enters the master bedroom, takes off topcoat, and sits in the dimness on the bed, facing the door, alone.* GLENN, *after a pause, follows* HANK *into the pantry.*]

ROBISH. Ahhh . . . my gut's beginnin' to burn good! [ROBISH *turns off the living-room lights, then sits, drinking.*]

GLENN. [*In the pantry; baffled.*] Live here? We ain't gonna *live* here.

HANK. No. Or any place like it. Ever.

GLENN. Hank, what the hell's . . .

HANK. When Helen gets here, we gonna give Hilliard a fair shake?

GLENN. [*Angrily.*] Anybody ever give *you* a fair shake?

HANK. Who the hell ever had a chance?

GLENN. [*An idea.*] The redhead! She got you goin', kid? [*Laughs and kneels facing* HANK; *with warm comradeship.*] Tell you what, kid . . . when we leave, we'll take her along. Just for you.

HANK. [*After a pause—bitterly.*] Fair shake!

GLENN. [*Anger again.*] What you think I'm gonna do? [*Trying to sell*

HANK *the idea.*] Nobody's gonna be suspicious if we got two women'n the car. We'll take 'em both. [*He gives* HANK *a playful punch.*] You give me the idea yourself! [GLENN *rises and leaves the pantry through the kitchen door. He appears in the living room, pauses for a moment, looking back, and then crosses and exits into the den. Above,* ELEANOR *rises and leaves* RALPHIE'S *room, leaving the door ajar. She crosses the hall and enters the master bedroom, turns on the lights. She gazes a moment at* DAN.]

ELEANOR. [*Not quite a question.*] Dan . . .

DAN. [*Still sitting on the bed.*] I did what they told me. I saw the Wallings coming home from the movies. I could've . . . [*Bursting out rebelliously.*] What should I have done, Ellie?

ELEANOR. Nothing. If the police come, Dan . . . it could be worse.

DAN. And if they don't? . . . You can't deal with boys like that. With guns in their hands. Stone walls! If you could just *talk* to them . . . *reason* . . . be sure he means what he . . .

ELEANOR. Dan . . . it won't be long now . . .

DAN. [*Rises.*] It makes no sense! You open a door . . . a door you've opened thousands of times . . . and wham, all of a sudden the whole world makes no sense!

ELEANOR. [*Moves to him, puts her hand on his shoulder.*] Dan, some day we'll look back on these hours and . . .

DAN. [*Quietly.*] Ellie, there is no *some day.* They've all been smashed now . . . [*He sinks into chair.*] broken off . . .

ELEANOR. They can't do this to you! I won't allow them to . . .

DAN. My brain's like a stone in my head. All this must've started months ago . . . maybe years . . . when that kid down there started hatching this scheme in his cell . . . before we ever even heard his name. . . .

ELEANOR. Dan, it's such a short, *short* time. Any minute now. All they'll have is the car. Even that's insured . . . isn't it silly, the things you think of? As soon as they've gone, you'll pick up the phone . . . [*The expression on* DAN'S *face stops her. Across the hall,* RALPHIE *rises from his bed and stands at his door, listening.*]

DAN. [*Turning away—flatly.*] Just like that . . .

ELEANOR. [*Sitting on bed, facing* DAN.] Dan . . . what are you thinking?

DAN. I'm thinking a man could be haunted forever . . . afterwards . . . by the thought that if he'd done just this at just the right time . . . or that at just the proper moment . . . he might have prevented it all.

ELEANOR. No, no, something else. When they leave you'll pick up the phone and . . . [*Stops; realizing.*] They won't let you do that, will they?

DAN. [*Rising; speaks reassuringly now.*] Of course they will, darling. . . .

ELEANOR. No!

DAN. Shh . . .

ELEANOR. How can they stop it?

DAN. They can't. There's no way to . . .

ELEANOR. [*Finally.*] I know, Dan. I know.

DAN. Don't imagine things, Ellie!

ELEANOR. [*Hollowly.*] They'll have to take someone along. . . .

DAN. [*Turned away.*] No, Ellie, no. The thought never occurred to me. . . . I . . . I hope Cindy doesn't stay out too late, that's all.

ELEANOR. She won't take any chances, Dan.

DAN. [*Turning, sees* RALPHIE, *who has crossed into the room and stands at the door.*] Hey, skipper . . . what're you doing up this late? [*He knows* RALPHIE *has heard, stops.* ELEANOR *rises and goes to* RALPHIE.]

RALPHIE. [*To* DAN, *their eyes locked.*] Are you going to let them . . . what you just said? . . .

DAN. Ralphie, I just explained to your mother . . .

ELEANOR. [*Her arms around* RALPHIE'S *shoulders.*] Dear, your mother had a wild idea, that's all. Those men haven't even thought of that.

RALPHIE. I don't want them to take me along with them.

DAN. [*Kneeling across the bed, takes* RALPHIE'S *shoulders.*] I wouldn't let them

do that, Ralphie. You ought to *know* I wouldn't let them do that!

RALPHIE. [*Backs away, turns and goes to the door.*] How are you going to stop them? [RALPHIE *turns away and goes to his door. He looks back at* DAN *and* ELEANOR, *then goes into his room and closes the door and sinks onto the bed.* DAN *and* ELEANOR *look at each other, helplessly. The sound of an approaching motorcar is heard. There is immediate tension.* DAN *steps to the window. Below,* HANK *leaps to the side door, looks out the window, gun ready.*]

ELEANOR. Cindy?

DAN. Yes, dear . . . Cindy. [ELEANOR *turns off the bedroom lights and she and* DAN *sit in the darkness on the bed. The car motor stops and two car doors slam. In pantry,* HANK *steps back from the side door. In the headlight beams from the car,* CINDY *appears outside, followed by* CHUCK, *who is a rather ordinary-appearing young man in his mid-twenties. He wears a sports coat and an expression of amazed bewilderment.*]

CHUCK. [*Catching up with her.*] Cindy . . . are you going in like this?

CINDY. [*At the step.*] Please, Chuck!

CHUCK. Look, I know I bowled you over. I've bowled myself over, too. But when a fellah proposes to a girl, he kind of expects an answer . . . like yes or no . . . not: "Take me home, Chuck!"

CINDY. [*Her mind elsewhere.*] Was . . . was that a proposal?

CHUCK. Well, it wasn't much of one, but it was the best I could manage . . . with you off on another planet somewhere. I don't mind admitting you've got me so balled-up tonight, I . . . [*Shakes his head as* CINDY *fumbles in her pocket for her keys. He touches her arm.*] Look . . . redhead . . .

CINDY. [*Whirling on him; sharply.*] Don't call me that!

CHUCK. But I always call you . . . All *right!* One minute you act like you hate me . . .

CINDY. Oh, no . . .

CHUCK. . . . and the next . . .

CINDY. Chuck . . .

CHUCK. [*Hopefully.*] Yes? . . .

CINDY. Chuck . . . listen.

CHUCK. Well? . . .

CINDY. [*Abruptly changing her mind.*] I'll tell you tomorrow . . . at the office.

CHUCK. You'll tell me one thing right now . . .

CINDY. [*Tensely, turns away.*] It doesn't concern you, Chuck.

CHUCK. [*Turns her around, takes her hands.*] If it concerns you, it concerns me. There. That's all I've been trying to say all evening. You've done something to me, Cindy. I've known a lot of girls . . . but . . . but you've opened doors . . . in me . . . in the world. So I've got to know . . . now . . . have I been kidding myself? Are you closing the doors? [*Suddenly,* CINDY *throws her arms around his neck and kisses him, in desperation, deeply touched, clinging to him. He slips his arms around her waist. Inside,* HANK *is watching . . . turns away. They break the kiss slowly and* CINDY *lays her head against his chest.*] Cindy . . . you're trembling all over. [*He lifts her chin.*] You'd better tell me.

CINDY. Yes . . .

CHUCK. Your family? . . . [*She nods.*] Cindy, you can't fret about it. If it's them. Because . . . look . . . it's *you.* *You're* the one I want to take care of now. *Only* you. [*She stares, realizing that she cannot tell him.*] Well, Cindy? [CINDY *shakes her head. She turns to the door, taking out her keys.*]

CINDY. [*With finality.*] No! Good night, Chuck.

CHUCK. [*Off on another tangent.*] Your father doesn't like me. He thinks I've helled around too much, maybe. . . .

CINDY. Please, Chuck . . .

CHUCK. Let's go in and talk it over with him. I . . .

CINDY. [*Turning on him—in desperation.*] Please . . . please . . . *please!* [CHUCK, *with mingled disgust and defeat, takes the keys from her hand and unlocks the door.* HANK, *in the pantry, holds the automatic in readiness.* CINDY *pushes past* CHUCK *and blocks the door as he lets it swing open, the keys still in the lock.*]

CHUCK. All right, Cindy. I'm not coming in. . . . [CINDY *closes the door in his face and leans limply against it, facing*

HANK. CHUCK *stands for a moment staring at the door. Then, he turns away; suddenly he turns back and takes the keys from the lock and is about to call to* CINDY. *He thinks better of it, looks at the keys, then at the house, and turns and walks away, putting the keys in his pocket. There is the sound of one car door slam and the motor starts and the car drives away . . . the headlights dimming out quickly. Inside,* CINDY *moves toward the back stairs.*]

HANK. [*His voice sardonic, aping* GLENN'S *manner.*] Use the other stairs, redhead. Glenn'll want to know you're home. [CINDY *turns and leaves the pantry through the kitchen door. Above,* DAN *leaves the bedroom and goes to the head of the stairs. In the living room* ROBISH *turns on the lights. He is now quite drunk, his voice heavier and louder than before. As* CINDY *enters from the dining room, he leans across the stairs with his hand against the wall, blocking her way.*]

ROBISH. Have fun, sweetie? Parkin' with the boy friend. [HANK *appears in the dining-room door, the gun out of view.*] He gettin' any, that guy? [*Above,* DAN *turns on the light in the upstairs hall.* ELEANOR *comes to the door of the bedroom.*]

DAN. Cindy? . . .

HANK. [*Eyes on* ROBISH.] Get on upstairs, miss. [DAN *descends the stairs and* ELEANOR *comes to the head of the stairs, leaning over the railing.*]

ROBISH. [*Voice blurred.*] Aw naw, aw naw. Ain't been searched yet. Got to search her first.

DAN. [*Taking in the situation swiftly . . . barks.*] Griffin!

ROBISH. Searched the ol' man, didn't we?

HANK. Get out of her way, Robish. [GLENN *appears in the door of the den, immediately alert, throwing off sleep.*]

DAN. Griffin, if you intend to let him get away with this . . .

GLENN. [*Revolver in hand now.*] Stay where you are, Hilliard!

ROBISH. Pretty little gal might try to sneak a gun in. . . .

DAN. Griffin, you don't want to have to use that gun of yours, do you?

GLENN. [*Grabs* ROBISH.] You goddam lunkhead . . .

ROBISH. [*With one swing of his arm throws* GLENN *back.*] Everybody givin' me orders! [*Steps toward* CINDY.] Lift your arms, baby.

DAN. [*Coming down between* ROBISH *and* CINDY.] A shot'll be heard, Griffin. . . . [*But* HANK *steps in with the automatic drawn on* ROBISH *and pushes* DAN *back onto the stairs. There is a pause.* ROBISH *stands blinking owlishly at the automatic.*]

GLENN. [*A breath.*] Hank . . . you damn fool.

ROBISH. [*Incredulously.*] Where'd ya get that?

HANK. [*Still covering* ROBISH.] You going up to bed now, miss?

ROBISH. [*Bawling.*] *Where'd yuh get that gun?*

GLENN. [*Shoves* ROBISH *toward dining room.*] Go sleep it off, Robish.

ROBISH. [*Turns at the dining-room door.*] Turnin' on me, huh? All of yuh. [*Drunkenly maudlin.*] Turnin' on your ol' pal Robish. Okay. Ya wait. Ya-*all* wait. . . . [*He goes into the dining room. Above, for the first time,* RALPHIE *moves: cautiously he opens the door of his room.* ROBISH *appears in the pantry, staggering.*]

GLENN. What's it to you, Hank?

HANK. [*Muttering defensively.*] It ain't safe to touch the women.

GLENN. Yeah? . . .

CINDY. Thank you . . . Hank. . . .

HANK. [*After the briefest sort of pause.*] Get the hell to bed.

GLENN. [*Crosses toward* CINDY.] Don't get the idea you ain't gonna be searched, redhead! [*At this point* ROBISH *goes out the side door, slamming it behind him. The significance of* ROBISH's *exit reaches* GLENN *in the living room. He springs into action.*]

GLENN. Christ! [*He runs through the dining-room door as he speaks.*] Cover 'em, Hank. Let 'em have it if you have to! [*He goes through the pantry and out the side door, slamming it as he goes.* DAN *turns to* CINDY; *then both turn to*

HANK. *Gun pointed,* HANK *is tense all through . . . and uncertain.*]

HANK. Don't get the idea I won't . . .

ELEANOR. [*On stairs above.*] Dan?

DAN. Stay up there, Ellie . . . hear?

HANK. [*A warning.*] Don't get any ideas now. . . .

DAN. [*To* CINDY.] Cindy! You look . . . [*He glances at* HANK, *then back to* CINDY.] Are you sick?

CINDY. No, I . . . [CINDY *turns to* DAN. *Their eyes meet. Pause. And then* CINDY *collapses.* DAN *takes a step toward her. She holds onto the back of the chair and sinks into it.*]

ELEANOR. Cindy!

HANK. Don't move, mister!

DAN. Dammit, this child's sick. If there's any decency in you at all . . . [RALPHIE *appears in the pantry, coming down the back stairs. He listens a moment, then goes to the side door and opens it.*]

HANK. If you're trying to . . . [RALPHIE *slams the side door as he goes out into the darkness.*] Glenn? . . . [*There is no reply.* HANK, *utterly bewildered, motions* DAN *into the corner and moves cautiously to* CINDY.] She's just scared, I guess. . . . [*He bends over* CINDY.] Miss . . . no need to be . . . [CINDY *moves with animal swiftness. She grasps* HANK's *arm and sinks her teeth into his wrist, hard.* HANK *drops the automatic on the floor in front of* CINDY. *He utters a cry of pain and surprise and straightens up, holding his wrist.* DAN *moves in with his right arm encircling* HANK's *shoulders, pinning his hands to his chest.* CINDY *picks up the automatic and stands ready.* DAN *drags* HANK *to the front door and opens it.* HANK *calls for "Glenn," but* DAN *succeeds in pushing him out the door.* DAN *closes and locks the door as* CINDY *runs across the room to the light switch. She turns off the living-room lights. There is only the light flooding down the stairs from the upstairs hall.*]

DAN. Ellie! Get on the phone up there! [CINDY *crosses to hand* DAN *the automatic.*] Cindy . . . lock the back door! [*Above,* ELEANOR *goes down the hall and notices the door to* RALPHIE's *room open.*

She steps in and calls. Then she goes into the master bedroom and calls.]

ELEANOR. Ralphie! . . . Ralphie! [CINDY *goes through the dining room on the run and into the pantry, where she locks the side door and returns to the living room.*]

DAN. Ellie, for God's sake, get on the phone! Stay away from the windows, hear! [*He impatiently picks up the phone and dials the operator.*]

ELEANOR. [*In master bedroom.*] Dan! [*She runs to the head of the stairs.*]

DAN. Operator. *Operator!* [CINDY *returns to the living room and starts up the front stairs.*]

ELEANOR. Don't, Dan . . . for God's sake! [*Screams.*] Dan, don't! *Ralphie's not in the house!* [CINDY *freezes on the stairs, looks at* DAN. DAN *stands with the phone in his hand.*]

OPERATOR. [*On phone.*] Operator. Operator. This is your operator. Your call, please? Your call, please? . . . [DAN *replaces the phone.*]

DAN. [*A whisper.*] God Almighty.

CINDY. Maybe he got away. [*Another pause, shorter; then* GLENN *appears outside at the side door with* RALPHIE. GLENN *has* RALPHIE'S *arm pinned behind him and holds the boy as a shield. They move to the steps, out of sight of the door.*]

GLENN. Hilliard! Can you hear me in there, Hilliard?

RALPHIE. [*Plaintively.*] Dad! Dad, he's hurting my arm.

ELEANOR. [*In terror.*] Dan, was that Ralphie? *Was that Ralphie?*

DAN. Stay up there, Ellie! [*Calling slightly louder.*] Don't shout out there, Griffin! [*Then, lower.*] Cindy, take your mother to her room. If you hear a shot . . . make the call! [DAN *goes through the dining-room door and on into the pantry.* CINDY *goes up the front stairs.* ELEANOR *goes into the master bedroom and stands near the door.* CINDY *picks up the extension phone in the upstairs hall, but keeps her hand on the circuit breaker. She is tense, waiting, her attention turned toward the stairs.* DAN *is in the pantry.*]

GLENN. [*A loud whisper.*] We go now,

Hilliard . . . they find the brat in a ditch. [DAN *unlocks and opens the side door.*] Turn on the light. And toss out the automatic.

DAN. Let the boy come in, Griffin.

GLENN. Lights first. Then the gun. [DAN *turns on the pantry light. Then he tosses the automatic out.* GLENN *pushes* RALPHIE *up the steps and into the pantry before him.*] You're both covered, Pop.

RALPHIE. [*Still defiant.*] I . . . I tried.

DAN. [*Gently.*] So did I. Go up to your mother now. [RALPHIE *slips behind the open door and mounts the rear stairs.* HANK *appears outside and picks up the automatic.*]

GLENN. [*Casually, to* HANK.] Get the lunkhead inside. [GLENN *faces* DAN.]

HANK. [*Off-stage.*] On your feet, Robish.

GLENN. Couldn't wait, could you, Pop? Less'n a hour an' you couldn't wait. [HANK *appears, the gun in hand, urging a staggering* ROBISH, *who is groggy, holding his head.* HANK *guides him through the pantry and into the living room.*]

ROBISH. [*As he passes through the pantry.*] Wha' happened? What . . .

HANK. Shut up! [ROBISH *and* HANK *appear in the living room.* ROBISH *flops on the sofa.* HANK *stands at the foot of the stairs.* GLENN *closes the side door.*]

GLENN. I hadda put Robish on ice for a while, Pop . . . cause he couldn't learn who was runnin' things aroun' here. I guess I gotta learn you, too. [GLENN *strikes* DAN'S *left shoulder with his left fist, violently. Then* GLENN *strikes him a stomach blow with the pistol in his right hand.* DAN *crumples and falls.* GLENN *kneels over him and strikes three violent blows with the pistol.* DAN *doesn't move. All this is very silent.* GLENN *rises, turns and locks the side door . . . and steps over* DAN'S *body, goes through the kitchen door and into the living room through the dining-room door.* HANK *follows him with his eyes as* GLENN *crosses slowly to sit in the chair at the window. He looks up at* HANK. *Their eyes meet.* HANK *sits slowly on the stairs. The lights begin to dim slowly.*]

VERY SLOW CURTAIN

ACT TWO

SHERIFF'S OFFICE: Outside the window, night. The clock reads 12:04. CARSON, seated at desk, plays solitaire. WINSTON sits curled up awkwardly on chair. BARD leans against files, thumbing through telephone-reports. A long pause. CARSON glances at his watch.

CARSON. It's another day . . . in case anyone's interested.

BARD. There's a full moon, too. So what? [*Holding up the reports.*] Collect calls . . . person-to-person . . . pay stations. Would you believe this many people sit up talking on the telephone at night? Why the hell don't they go to bed? [*Drops the reports on the desk.*]

WINSTON. Why don't we?

CARSON. [*Picking up the reports.*] You've got all the reasons right here. . . . Sickness . . . impulse . . . birth . . . death . . . drunkenness . . . love . . . hate . . .

BARD. What the hell're you . . . a poet or something?

CARSON. It'll break, Bard. You can stretch a wire just so tight.

DUTCH'S VOICE. [*On intercom.*] Jess . . . that 11:02 person-to-person from Columbus to Blackstone 2726 . . .

BARD. [*Flipping intercom button.*] Yeah, yeah?

DUTCH'S VOICE. It was the daughter calling to say the honeymoon was already a huge success.

BARD. Great!

DUTCH'S VOICE. My theory is this Helen Laski found another guy and climbed in the hay. [BARD *flips off the intercom.* WINSTON *rises sleepily.*]

WINSTON. I'll be in the file room, flat on my face. *My* theory is this Helen Laski don't believe in telephones. Uses carrier pigeons. Has a secret compartment in her brassière. [WINSTON *exits. Outside, a police siren is heard fading in and coming to a stop.*]

CARSON. [*Shuffling cards.*] You'd find double solitaire kind of restful.

BARD. Carson, you deal me just one of those cards and I'm gonna report you to J. Edgar Hoover. [*Shaking head but smiling faintly.*] Isn't it just my luck to meet up with a character like you on a night like this?

CARSON. You're not such hot company yourself. . . . Ten bucks says they're in Denver . . . or New Orleans . . . or Nome, Alaska, by now.

BARD. They're here.

CARSON. Who told you . . . that monkey on your back?

BARD. I say they're here, Carson, because Glenn Griffin's got all kinds of dark pockets in his mind . . . all kinds of weird twists. [*Pacing.*] He's always acting, for one thing . . . trying to live up to some phony picture he carries around in that snarled-up brain of his . . . some stupid, childish image of what a really clever criminal should be.

CARSON. [*Shrugs.*] Well, that's a good reason. It doesn't explain why he's in town, but it's a good reason. Any others?

BARD. [*Sits.*] Carson, did you ever look into the eyes of one of those crazy kids . . . and hear him say, "You got yours coming, copper"? Between his teeth . . . with his broken jaw wired up tight . . . "I'll get you." *That's* why I know he's here and that's why *I'm* going to get to him before he gets to *me.* [*Rises.*] Any objections, Carson?

CARSON. No objections, Bard. But if we catch up with him . . . our job's to arrest, if possible.

BARD. You remindin' me who's actually in charge here, Carson?

CARSON. Something like that. My friends call me Harry. [*He goes back to his cards.*]

BARD. Well, I'll tell you right now . . . I'm making no promises . . . Harry. [*Dimout.*]

HILLIARD HOME: *Dimness over all the house.* GLENN *is at the living-room window, smoking. The window curtains are parted slightly.* HANK *is in the pantry, sitting on the back stairs.* CINDY *sits in*

RALPHIE's *bedroom.* RALPHIE *is on the bed asleep. In the master bedroom,* DAN *is stretched out on the bed with a damp towel folded and placed over his forehead.* ELEANOR *sits on the twin bed, facing him, with a dry towel in her hands.*

ELEANOR. [*Softly.*] Darling . . . can you hear me? I want you to promise . . .

DAN. What? Oh . . . I must've dozed off. Isn't that . . . remarkable?

ELEANOR. You needed it. I slipped off myself several times . . . but I heard every sound . . . every car that went by. [DAN *stirs.*]

DAN. What time is it? [ELEANOR *reaches out and turns on the lamp on the night table between the beds. She looks at the clock on the table.*]

ELEANOR. After one . . .

DAN. [*Trying to sit up.*] Midnight. He said mid . . .

ELEANOR. Shhh. Don't move. Listen. What you did—what you tried—that was a foolish and terrible and wonderful thing . . . [*Shakes her head as though trying to clear it.*] No, no, that's not what I meant to say. Dan, you must never do anything like that again. Ever. You . . . you might have been killed. I want you to promise me now. Dan, are you listening?

DAN. What're they doing down there? Why haven't they gone?

ELEANOR. Dan, please. Nobody knows anything about what's happening here. Nobody in the world. We're all alone in this. Dan, I'm pleading with you. . . .

DAN. Ellie . . . how long has it been since I said I love you?

ELEANOR. Dan . . .

DAN. Why shouldn't a man say it? Why didn't I say it all the time . . . over and over?

ELEANOR. You didn't need . . .

DAN. Ellie, why'm I so grouchy in the mornings? No, that's not what I mean . . . I mean . . . what's the matter, people don't laugh more? Waking up . . . seeing the sun . . . That . . . that was a funny joke Ralphie told . . . about the moron and the icebox.

ELEANOR. [*Smiling wanly.*] Not very . . .

DAN. All right, it was lousy. Is that any reason not to laugh? [*In awe.*] God . . . this morning. How many hours ago? It's . . . it's like looking back on something that happened . . . a whole lifetime ago. [*Reaches out his right hand to her face.*] Your face . . . darling, you're beautiful. Do you know that? I must've been deaf, dumb and blind. For years.

ELEANOR. [*Takes his hand in hers.*] Dan . . . you haven't promised. [DAN *sits up with difficulty.*]

DAN. Ellie . . . I can't. I'm feeling along a blank wall. In the dark. If I find a hole . . . or even a crack . . . I've got to explore it. There's light behind that wall, Ellie. I never knew how much. There was light there once and there's got to be light again!

ELEANOR. Dan, look at yourself. Your head. Next time . . . you don't know. *You don't know.* He'll kill you.

DAN. [*Grimly.*] He won't kill me as long as he needs me. [*Suddenly.*] You look so *tired.* Damn them! [*Gently.*] When this is over, we're going to have a maid here. A full-time maid.

ELEANOR. You wouldn't really like it, Dan. None of us like having strangers in the . . . [*She breaks off, realizing what she is saying. Their eyes meet. Pause. Then, there is the sound of a branch cracking off a tree and brushing down the side of the house. She starts and crumples.* DAN *holds her. Below,* GLENN *looks out the living-room window.* HANK *rises and looks out the window in the side door.*]

DAN. It's all right, dear. It's all right. Only one of those dead branches off the oak. [*He takes her into his arms.*] My God, Ellie . . . it's a jungle. We jump at nothing. That's how you slept, isn't it . . . like an animal in the . . . [*The telephone rings, cutting him off. In the living room,* GLENN *quickly steps to the phone and turns on the hall light.* HANK *runs up the back stairs to the extension phone in the upstairs hall.* CINDY *rises and opens the door of* RALPHIE's *room.* RALPHIE *doesn't stir.* DAN *opens the bedroom door.*]

GLENN. I'll take it, Hank.

HANK. [*Ready at the phone upstairs.*] I'm here, Glenn. [HANK *takes up the phone after* GLENN *answers and stands staring at* CINDY *in the door of* RALPHIE'S *room as he listens.*]

GLENN. [*Picks up the phone downstairs.*] Hello? . . . Put her on. . . . Yeah, this is Mr. James. *Put her on!* . . . Hi, doll, what's up? . . . Where are you? . . . Mmm—okay, get this. That stuff you're carrying . . . put it in a envelope . . . an' take down this address . . . Daniel C. Hilliard . . . [GLENN *continues, but his voice is* under *the following dialogue so that the address is not heard.*]

HANK. [*To* CINDY, *harshly.*] Stay inside an' shut the door, redhead. [CINDY, *in defiance, doesn't move.*]

ELEANOR. Dan, what is it?

DAN. Shhh . . .

GLENN. [*Under above dialogue.*] . . . 243 North Central Avenue. . . . Soon's I get it, we'll make tracks, doll. . . . See you Louisville. You know where. [GLENN *hangs up.* HANK *replaces the extension phone and comes down the front stairs and is about to go into the dining room. He stops in door when* DAN *comes downstairs.* DAN *follows* HANK *down the hall and comes near the bottom of the stairs.*]

ELEANOR. [*Follows* DAN *to the bedroom door.*] Dan!

DAN. [*As he comes down the stairs.*] Griffin! Who was that? What's happening?

GLENN. [*Casually.*] Tell you in the morning, Pop . . . after breakfast.

DAN. [*Shocked.*] After break— You'll tell me now!

GLENN. [*Angry.*] What's another day, Pop? Get some shuteye. You're gonna need it. [GLENN *turns his back on* DAN *and walks toward the window.* DAN *starts toward* GLENN.]

HANK. Glenn! Watch it! [GLENN *whirls.* DAN *stops, looks at* HANK, *then at* GLENN, *and turns and goes up the stairs.* ELEANOR *moves into bedroom and stands waiting for* DAN. CINDY, *who has been waiting at the head of the stairs, goes into her room and closes the door.* GLENN *goes to the window, picks up the road map from the table, and stands in the window, studying it.* HANK *goes into the pantry*

and stands looking out the window of the side door.]

ELEANOR. [*As* DAN *comes into the bedroom.*] Well? . . .

DAN. [*Flatly . . . low.*] They're not going.

ELEANOR. Oh Dan, no!

DAN. [*Suddenly the violence in him mounts to a determined grimness.*] They're going! [DAN *turns to the door.* ELEANOR *stops him. The following builds in intensity until they are almost snarling at each other.*]

ELEANOR. Dan, you promised, you promised!

DAN. [*Erupting slightly.*] Ellie, don't tie my hands! I'm tied up enough already!

ELEANOR. [*Desperately.*] If you go down there now, something terrible is going to happen. I know it. I *feel* it.

DAN. How long can we go on sitting on top of a volcano?

ELEANOR. [*Takes his hand, tugging at him.*] Dan, you're going to lie down now! I'm telling you!

DAN. [*Shouting, throws her off.*] You're not telling me what to do! [*Pause. They are appalled. They stand looking at each other for a moment. Then they go into each other's arms.* DAN *says, almost whispering.*] Ellie, what're we doing? What're we *doing?* [*Slight pause.*] How can he know, that scum down there . . . how can he know how to do this? A boy who never loved anyone in his life. [ELEANOR *turns out the bed lamp and sits on the bed.* DAN *sits beside her and puts his arms around her. Below,* GLENN *flicks the map with his fingers and exits; goes into the pantry.* HANK *turns away from the door.*]

HANK. Glenn . . . we gotta get outta here. What if they trace that call?

GLENN. [*Grinning.*] You ever hear of a burg called Circleville, Ohio? It's nineteen miles south-a Columbus. Them dumb coppers might be tracin' calls outta Columbus, Hank, but not outta no jerktown like Circleville.

HANK. [*Turns back to the window.*] We'd be better off anywhere but here.

GLENN. It can't be nowhere else but

here. With that much dough . . . in this town . . . I can have that copper put on ice for good.

HANK. [*Shaking his head.*] That one idea . . .

GLENN. Yeah, that one idea. Kid, you gotta stick with me on this. You're . . . Hank, you're all I got. You know that. It's you'n me against 'em all!

HANK. [*Trapped: conflicting emotions. He turns to the window.*] I know, I know . . . [GLENN *grabs him, turns him around.*]

GLENN. You know . . . you know! You don't know nothin'! I gotta get this outta my brain. I gotta sleep again. You didn't lay in that bed . . . pain twistin' down in your gut . . . months . . . jaw clamped up in a vise . . . eatin' that slop through a tube . . . *months* . . . till pretty soon there ain't nothin' in your mind but the face-a the guy that done it. Me with my hands up . . . tossin' out my gun . . . and that bastard walkin' up'n cloutin' me. I can still hear the way the bone cracked. . . . *An' me with my hands up!* [*Blackout.*]

SHERIFF'S OFFICE: *Clock: 6:15. Early morning.* CARSON *is seated.* BARD *is rising from behind the desk.*

BARD. Yeah, he had his hands up. Trying to surrender. *After* he'd plugged one of the best damn cops ever walked. While Jerry was laying there twisting and screaming in the gutter . . . with a bullet in a nerve . . . *then* Griffin throws out his empty gun and steps out of the doorway of that hotel, big as life. Only I didn't let him get away with it. I let him have it. One crack . . . right in that grinning face of his. [*Rubbing his fist.*] If I'd only arrested him . . . or shot him before he gave up . . . he'd probably've forgotten it. But according to *his* warped code, *I* double-crossed *him*.

CARSON. [*Quietly.*] Under the circumstances . . . police code, too.

BARD. [*Leans over desk.*] Listen! That kid's as ruthless as they come! He'd as soon kill a human being as step on a bug.

CARSON. All right . . . so civilization didn't take. In his case. But we've climbed a long way out of the slime, Jess. Maybe

that slime still clings to some of us. *Them.* But you're a police officer, Jess . . . and civilized men can't let the slime on *them* drag *us* back down. If we don't live by the rules, the rules will soon disappear. Then . . . [*Shrugs.*] we're all right back where we started.

BARD. Rules! He was sentenced to ten years. He'd have been out again anyway inside of three more.

CARSON. Which only proves it's a pretty ramshackle system. But it's all we've got. You had no right to break his jaw. And if we find him, you've no right to kill him unless it's the only way to stop him.

BARD. [*Sits on edge of desk; bitterly.*] Sure, send him back to that cardboard prison . . . so he can start all over again.

CARSON. No choice, Jess. Unless you want to become just like him. In that case, he wins, anyway. [*Rises.*] I'm ready for breakfast. How about you? [BARD, *thoughtful for a moment, looks at* CARSON, *rises.*]

BARD. Yeah. [*Dimout.*]

HILLIARD HOME: *It is morning.* ELEANOR *is seated on the sofa,* RALPHIE *beside her.* HANK *stands at the window, smoking.* DAN *is entering from the dining room, followed by* GLENN. GLENN *picks his teeth with finger and wipes hand on sofa.*]

GLENN. Lady, that 'as a goddam good breakfast. [*Takes* HANK's *cigarette, turns to* DAN.] Hilliard, you ever broke, your woman can support you good. Cookin'. [*Takes a drag on the cigarette and returns it to* HANK.]

DAN. [*Sitting in chair.*] How much longer, Griffin?

GLENN. Hell, you don't have any worse headache'n Robish 'n there . . . [*Gestures into the den.*] and he's nursin' a hangover to boot.

DAN. [*Level and insistent.*] How long?

GLENN. Till I get a certain envelope in the mail. Meantime . . . everything goes on just like before aroun' here. You'n the redhead go to work.

HANK. Glenn, if he's gonna be gone all day outta the house . . .

GLENN. You don't trust Hilliard, Hank?

Now me—I trust the old gink. You know why? I got him where the hair's short, that's why. Junior here gets a break. He misses a day of school. [CINDY *comes out of her room and down the stairs.*] Won't hurt you none, kid. Missed a few myself.

CINDY. [*At foot of stairs; scornfully.*] And look at you.

RALPHIE. [*Kneeling on sofa.*] I'd just as soon go. . . .

GLENN. [*Crosses to* CINDY.] Yeah, you're lookin', Sis. Pass you on the street, you'd look right through us both. You're seein' us now, redhead.

CINDY. No comment.

GLENN. [*To* DAN.] Now, get the lead outta your . . . [*The thud of the newspaper is heard against the front door. The* HILLIARDS *are not startled but* GLENN *and* HANK *jump into action.* HANK, *drawing the automatic, moves up to the door.* GLENN, *with the .38 ready, covers the family.* HANK *unlocks and opens the door a crack. He kneels down and reaches out with his left hand to bring in the paper.* HANK *rises, closing the door, and hands the paper to* GLENN. GLENN *unfolds the paper.* HANK *locks the door.* RALPHIE, *who has been watching it all, snickers. After a split-second pause.*] Get your kicks young, kid. [*To* DAN.] You don't want to be late for that time-clock, Pop. [ELEANOR *rises and crosses to* GLENN, *fire in her eyes.*]

ELEANOR. Why do you want to go on torturing my husband? You know what he'll be thinking . . . wondering . . . imagining . . . in that office! You take pleasure in torturing him, don't you?

GLENN. [*Easily.*] Lady, I take pleasure in looking out for my own skin . . . and Hank's.

DAN. [*In warning.*] Ellie . . .

ELEANOR. No, no, it's some sort of cruel, inhuman, sadistic game with you. You're playing a *game!* [*Abruptly, she explodes into violence; slaps* GLENN *full across the face.* DAN *steps in, grabs her and swings her around to the far end of the sofa, then turns to look at* GLENN. *The family is in a small group, defiant. Long pause, while* GLENN *rubs his jaw.*]

GLENN. [*Quietly, sitting.*] Whole fam-

ily gettin' tough this morning. Nothin' personal, ma'am.

DAN. [*Grimly—knowing.*] It's personal all right. In some strange mixed-up way.

GLENN. Clickety-click. Don't get ulcers tryin' to dope it, Pop. [*To* CINDY.] You, redhead. Keep that pretty mouth shut today, see. Or that boy friend of yours ain't gonna want to take you on no more rides. Not after Robish gets done with you. [*Pause.*]

DAN. [*Deciding—a step.*] I'm not leaving this house today.

GLENN. [*Hardening.*] You ain't learned yet who's runnin' it?

HANK. [*Steps near* GLENN.] Glenn, I think . . .

GLENN. [*Rising; exploding.*] You think! With what? I'm lookin' out for you, you slobberin' pukin' little bastard. Now get in there and turn on the news reports! [GLENN *turns to* DAN.] You ain't had nothin', Pop. Nothin' like what you deserve.

DAN. Deserve? . . .

GLENN. Yeah . . . deserve! You'n your fancy carpet and your big lawn'n your goddam snazzy car!

DAN. [*Takes a step toward* GLENN.] Griffin . . . [ELEANOR *touches* DAN's *arm to restrain him but he pulls away and continues.*] you're not going to take it out on me and my family because you hate the world! I've worked for every cent I ever made . . . worked hard . . . for this house, that car . . . and I'm proud of it. That table you've scarred with your whisky . . . the furniture you've wiped your filthy hands on . . . the carpet you've burnt holes in. Proud because I *did* work for it!

GLENN. [*Spits on carpet with contempt.*] Sucker! Just like our old man, ain't he, Hank?

DAN. I pity the poor man!

GLENN. Don't waste your time. He kicked off while we was in reform school. He was a *proud* bastard, too. Now get outta here!

DAN. I'm staying right here!

GLENN. [*Violent.*] Hilliard, I told you . . . [*Changes—shrugs.*] Okay . . . [*Sits.*] Okay . . . You stay . . . an' we stay. 'Cause we ain't gonna beat it outta here till we get that dough. An' that dough's in a letter . . . addressed to you . . . at your office. [*Pause. The fight goes out of* DAN.] We don't want no Federal men tracin' anything up to your front door here, do we? . . . See, Pop, I'm thinkin' of you. [ELEANOR *takes* DAN's *arm.*]

ELEANOR. He'll go. He's going. [*As* CINDY *moves to closet and gets her own coat and brings* DAN's *coat to him.*] Dan, I'll be upstairs with Ralphie. If one of them starts up the stairs, I'll scream so loud they'll *have* to use their guns. That'll be the end of it. For them too. Now I'll get your coat. It's getting colder every minute. . . . [CINDY *already stands waiting with* DAN's *coat.*]

DAN. I . . . I can hold my own coat, Cindy.

CINDY. Maybe I'd *like* to hold your coat. [DAN *climbs into coat, then turns to* ELEANOR.]

ELEANOR. Careful now, Dan . . . I know, I say that every morning of the world, don't I? [DAN *takes* ELEANOR *in his arms. They kiss . . . with great meaning and tenderness, in sharp contrast to yesterday morning's casual good-bye.* GLENN *makes a kissing sound with his mouth, then makes a pop with his finger in his mouth.* HANK *takes a step down as* GLENN *laughs mockingly.*]

HANK. What's so funny? [*As* GLENN *frowns, the laughter dying.*] I don't see nothin' so funny, you should break your neck laughin'.

GLENN. I laugh when I feel like it. You don't have a goddam thing to say about it. That right? .ˑ . . That right, Hank?

HANK. I never had nothin' to say about anything. [HANK *turns on his heel and goes through the dining-room door and into the pantry.* CINDY *steps down to* RALPHIE, *and tousles his hair.*]

CINDY. [*Softly.*] *Mister* pest to you.

GLENN. You, Hilliard. That nick on your head—you got a story ready? 'Cause it wouldn't take much of a slip today, Pop. Just a little one and . . . you're gonna wish you never come back through that door.

DAN. [*Quietly . . . with dignity and force.*] Griffin . . . you're staying here now for only one reason. To get a man killed. A man who did something to you. I couldn't understand that before. Now I can. I understand it because I'm more like you now than you know. If any harm comes to anyone in this house, Griffin, I'm going to kill you. Me. No matter what it takes . . . whether the police capture you first or not . . . if it takes my whole life, Griffin, I'll find you and I'll kill you. Do you understand that?

GLENN. [*Impressed but attempting swagger.*] Pop . . . you're a regular comedian.

DAN. *Do you understand that?*

GLENN. Sure, Pop . . . I got you. All the way.

DAN. And if not you, Griffin . . . your brother.

GLENN. [*Immediately tense, violent; leaps up.*] You come near Hank and . . .

DAN. [*Firmly.*] That's the deal, Griffin. That's the deal. You've turned me into your kind of animal now. [GLENN *does not move.* DAN *turns, takes a long look at* RALPHIE, *then* ELEANOR. CINDY *opens the door.* DAN *follows* CINDY *out, closing the door behind him.*]

GLENN. [*Moving up to the door.*] Lady . . . you didn't know what a tough old bird you married, did you?

ELEANOR. [*Softly.*] No. No, I didn't. [*She sits quietly.*]

GLENN. [*Calls.*] Robish! [*As* GLENN *moves into the dining room,* ROBISH *enters from the den and sits. He is suffering from a hangover and from last night's violence.* GLENN *appears in the pantry.* HANK *is now standing at the window of the side door, watching* DAN *and* CINDY *drive away.* GLENN *stands for a moment, looks down at the radio, bends down and turns it on. Music rises.*] You ain't interested in the news?

HANK. Same old stuff. That car. That's all they got. [*Faces* GLENN *suddenly.*] Glenn . . . why're you crowdin' it? Why go on takin' these chances?

GLENN. You don't take chances, you might as well be dead. [*The sound of an old truck approaching fades in.*]

HANK. That's what we're gonna be . . . all of us . . . this keeps up.

GLENN. You start yammerin' again, I'm gonna give you a belt across the . . . [*They hear the truck. Immediate tension.* GLENN *tries to see out the window of the side door, then rushes into the living room.* ELEANOR *has risen and crossed up to the window.* HANK *stays looking out the window of the side door.*] Who is it, lady?

ELEANOR. Only Mr. Patterson. He . . . he hauls away the trash.

GLENN. Okay, let him get it and clear out.

ELEANOR. Only . . . he'll . . . this is the end of the month. He'll come to the door to collect.

GLENN. [*Calls.*] Hank! [HANK *leaves the pantry and comes into living room.*] Okay, pay him. [ELEANOR *goes to pick up her checkbook from sofa.* GLENN *turns to* RALPHIE.] Upstairs, kid. And not a squeak. [RALPHIE, *on sofa, folds arms, doesn't move.*] Take him up, Hank, and keep his mouth shut. [HANK *lifts* RALPHIE *off the sofa, sets him on his feet and pushes him upstairs.* ELEANOR *goes into the pantry.* MR. PATTERSON *appears outside and knocks at the side door. Above,* HANK *stands at the door of* RALPHIE'S *room, listening.* RALPHIE *sits on the bed.*]

ROBISH. [*Miserable.*] My gut's growling.

GLENN. Knock off.

ROBISH. Jeez, I forgot what a headache feels like. . . .

GLENN. Shut up! [ELEANOR *opens the side door and admits* MR. PATTERSON *to the pantry.*]

ELEANOR. Just a minute. Mr. Patterson, while I . . . You stay here, please. . . .

PATTERSON. [*Pushes right in.*] Don't mind if I do. . . . [ELEANOR *returns to the living room.*] Wind always puts a nasty nip in the air . . . raises merry . . . [*He sees that* ELEANOR *has gone, raises his voice.*] raises merry cain with my arthritis. [PATTERSON, *through the following, notices with interest the small radio, the stacked cigarette butts, the chair. He gathers up the newspapers and places them on the chair, glancing with some interest at the headlines. In the liv-ing room* ELEANOR *sits on the sofa and writes the check on the coffee table.* GLENN *leans over the back of the sofa, watching her.*]

GLENN. [*Whisper.*] You always pay the old gink with a check?

ROBISH. Who the hell is it? [GLENN *silences* ROBISH *with a gesture.*]

ELEANOR. Yes, yes, my husband . . . [*Then firmly.*] my husband thinks it's not safe to have cash in the house. [*Signs.*] That's *funny*, isn't it?

PATTERSON. You speaking to me, Mrs. Hilliard?

ELEANOR. [*Rises.*] No, Mr. Patterson, I'm coming. [GLENN *stops* ELEANOR, *takes the check and examines it.*]

GLENN. Hank's upstairs with the brat. Be careful. [*He returns the check to* ELEANOR, *who goes into the pantry.*]

ROBISH. [*Rises.*] Who is that out . . .

GLENN. [*At dining-room door, listening.*] Shut up! [ROBISH *and* GLENN *listen,* GLENN *holding the dining-room door slightly open.*]

PATTERSON. [*As* ELEANOR *enters the pantry.*] You . . . uh . . . got company, Mrs. Hilliard?

ELEANOR. Company?

PATTERSON. Well . . . I notice things, y'know. Always have. [*Takes the check from* ELEANOR'S *hand.*] Thank you, thank you! [*Peering.*] You feelin' yourself, Mrs. Hilliard?

ELEANOR. [*Desperate to get him out.*] Only . . . I've got a slight cold. Nothing . . .

PATTERSON. [*Turns and opens the door.*] We-ell, lotta colds around. Flu, too. Bad year for the flu, y'know. [*In the doorway, he turns back.*] Your daughter buy herself another one of them second-hand cars?

ELEANOR. [*Holding the door open for him.*] No. No! [*In panic, she closes the door in his face, leans against it.* GLENN *rushes into the pantry, followed by* RO-BISH. HANK *looks out the window of* RALPHIE'S *room.* PATTERSON, *after a look back at the house, disappears.* GLENN *pushes* ELEANOR *upstage and looks out the window of the side door.*]

ROBISH. He's snoopin' around the garage.

ELEANOR. Oh, no, he's only taking the trash from the containers alongside.

ROBISH. Up on his toes lookin' in the windows!

ELEANOR. On Thursday mornings he always . . .

HANK. [*Leaving* RALPHIE's *room to run down back stairs.*] Glenn! He wrote something down.

ROBISH. Griffin, that joker wrote down the license. I seen him! Fork over the gun.

ELEANOR. I'm sure he . . .

GLENN. [*Locked in indecision.*] Dry up, both-a-you, I'm thinkin'.

ROBISH. He's climbin' in the cab of the truck. *Gimme the gun!* I can hop on the back.

HANK. [*At foot of back stairs.*] Glenn . . . we don't want a murder rap ridin' us! [GLENN *meets* HANK's *eyes, then, with a smile of defiance and revenge, hands the gun to* ROBISH. *The truck door is heard being slammed. Then, the motor starting and failing . . . starting and failing under the following.*]

GLENN. [*To* ROBISH.] You call me on the phone. An' stay outta sight till it's dark, see. I'll have Hilliard bring you back. Use your head for a change!

ROBISH. [*Going out the side door on the run.*] My head feels better already. [*As Robish disappears, the truck motor catches and we hear it start up, shift, and drive away.* HANK *looks pale and sick.* ELEANOR, *stunned, moves dazedly toward the living room.*]

ELEANOR. He . . . he knew nothing. [*Corrects self.*] *Knows* nothing. [*She goes into the living room and sinks onto the sofa slowly, beginning to weep.*]

HANK. Glenn, are you crazy? Hilliard won't bring Robish back in here.

GLENN. He will when I'm done with him on the phone. Pop don't want Robish picked up any more'n we do . . . an' tippin' the cops this address. [*Suddenly grabs* HANK, *pushes him against wall of the pantry.*] What's the matter with you anyway, kid? You got a weak stomach after all? [HANK *turns his head*

away.] What're you stewin' about? You're free, ain't you?

HANK. [*Wrenches himself loose, starts for kitchen door.*] I was free-er in that cell! [HANK *goes into the living room. After a second* GLENN *follows him.* HANK *ignores* GLENN *and goes to the den door with a side glance at* ELEANOR; *he slams the door.* GLENN *is baffled and angry.*]

GLENN. [*To* ELEANOR.] Lady! Shut up that wailin'! Go some place elsen'n cry! [ELEANOR *rises slowly and, with difficulty, mounts the stairs.*]

ELEANOR. Poor man . . . that poor old man . . . he wouldn't hurt a fly. [*Dimout.*]

SHERIFF'S OFFICE: *Darkness outside.* WINSTON *is seated,* BARD *is pacing.*

BARD. Who'd want to pump three slugs in the back of an innocent old guy like that?

WINSTON. Who can say? Somebody settling an old score . . . old crony he cheated at cards. . . .

BARD. Sixty-three years old, half-crippled with arthritis . . . wouldn't harm a fly. [BARD *looks up as* FREDERICKS *enters.* LT. FREDERICKS *is an older man, crisp and efficient, with a weathered face. He wears a State Police uniform.*] Fredericks, are we going to get that stuff from the state's attorney's office or aren't we?

FREDERICKS. Carson's prying it out of them. Bard, why make so much of an old garbage man gettin' bumped?

BARD. He was killed by a .38. The prison guard at Terre Haute . . .

FREDERICKS. Sure, there's only one .38 in the state! Deputy, you got a obsession. You can't tie in every crime in the area with those three.

BARD. I reckon not, Lieutenant. Only *you* tell *me* why anybody'd . . . [*Breaks off as* CARSON *enters.*] Well, Carson?

CARSON. [*Tearing the top off large manila envelope which he has brought in, emptying the contents on the desk during the following.*] Claude Patterson died at the hands of person or persons unknown. All I've got is the junk the old man was carrying in his pockets when they found the body. [*Handling the items.*] Checks

. . . Seventeen one-dollar bills . . . Ballpoint pen . . . A snuff box . . . Wallet . . . Usual stuff. Driver's license . . . Photograph of a young girl, taken forty years ago, at least.

BARD. [*Examining checks.*] Checks made out to Claude Patterson, some to cash. Thirteen for three dollars, two for six bucks.

WINSTON. The guy made more'n I do.

CARSON. Some scraps of paper . . . [BARD *smoothes them out during the following.*]

WINSTON. [*To* CARSON.] How long ago do they figure it happened?

CARSON. Before noon, coroner said. Old man must've run into the woods from the truck. A hunter came across the body just before dusk. City police found the truck parked alongside a service station other side of . . .

BARD. [*Very, very quietly.*] Hold it. [*Low whistle of amazement between teeth.*] God. Look't this . . . [*As others examine the scrap of paper.*] State's attorney's office examined this stuff?

CARSON. [*As he looks at paper.*] That was my impression. [*Then softly, too.*] Good Lord!

WINSTON. [*An excited whisper.*] Patterson might've got just a quick glance. In a hurry, y'know . . .

FREDERICKS [*Cynically.*] He heard it on the radio . . . jotted it down just in case.

WINSTON. But if you change that 3 to a 8, you got it. Maybe his eyes . . . a old man like that . . .

BARD. [*Thoughtfully.*] Or there was mud on the plate.

WINSTON. Jesse, if you change that 3 to a 8, you got it!

BARD. [*With throb in voice.*] Just for a while . . . just for a little while now . . . we're *going* to change that 3 to an 8. We'll just kinda pretend Mr. Patterson didn't *own* a radio. We're gonna pretend he saw that license. Tom . . . these checks. Start working backwards! [*As* WINSTON *rises.*] Names, addresses, telephone numbers, where they work. Everything!

FREDERICKS. Sure, let's go on a wild-

goose chase . . . break the monotony.

BARD. Those were the last people saw him alive. These and whatever other customers live in that neighborhood. Let's find that neighborhood and let's scour it down with a wire brush.

WINSTON. Go ahead, Jess, say it.

BARD. I don't like to say it, Tom . . .

WINSTON. Say it, Jess. [*To* CARSON *as he exits.*] He was right. . . . This is it!

BARD. God, it might be. Right here in town!

FREDERICKS. You want any more troopers on it, lemme know. My men got nothing else to do. [*He exits.*]

BARD. [*Sitting at the desk.*] Any bets now, Carson? Any bets that beat-up gray car isn't in that neighborhood somewhere? Any bets, Harry?

CARSON. No bets, Jess.

BARD. [*Flips intercom, speaks into it.*] Dutch. Get me a city map in here. And a city directory! [*Flips off intercom. To* CARSON.] Now. If only we can get to 'em before some other innocent citizen stumbles across their path . . . [*Blackout.*]

HILLIARD HOME: *Evening. Living-room lights are on. Light in* RALPHIE'S *room is on. The door chimes sound.* ELEANOR *stands facing the door.* GLENN *is moving from the window to the stairs.* HANK *is in the door of den, automatic ready. Above,* RALPHIE *sits on his bed with a small toy. The door chime is heard a second time.*

GLENN. Okay, lady, answer it. But careful. [*He goes up the stairs until he is out of sight of the front door.* ELEANOR *looks at* HANK, *then goes to the front door and unlocks and opens it slightly.* MISS SWIFT *barges right in and* HANK *ducks into the den and closes the door, leaving it open enough to hear and also cover the people in the room.* GLENN *moves around the bend of the landing and stands near the head of the stairs, listening.* MISS SWIFT *is youngish, pert.*]

MISS SWIFT. [*As she pushes into the room.*] Good evening, Mrs. Hilliard, I've come to see Ralph.

ELEANOR. [*Standing with the door open wide.*] Oh . . . yes. [*Glances nervously upstairs.*] Yes . . . [*Speaks for* GLENN's *benefit.*] Ralphie, it's your teacher. Miss Swift. [ELEANOR *closes the door. Upstairs,* RALPHIE *opens the door of his room and starts down the hall; but, seeing* GLENN, *he returns to his room and stands listening at the door.*]

MISS SWIFT. [*As she moves down.*] You see, Ralph so rarely misses a day at school that I thought I'd drop by to . . . [*She stops, looking at the disordered room; her manner changes.*] I . . . I daresay I should have telephoned first.

ELEANOR. [*Nervously.*] Oh, no, no, that's perfectly all . . . [*Abruptly.*] Please sit down.

MISS SWIFT. [*Sits on sofa.*] I do hope that Ralph isn't seriously ill . . . [*She realizes that she is sitting on an uncomfortable object, reaches back and brings out the empty whisky bottle, which she places on the coffee table.*]

ELEANOR. [*With a valiant effort at control.*] Only . . . just a cold. But we thought it best not to expose the other children. [*Above,* RALPHIE *turns from the door of his room, picks up a composition book and a pencil from the bookshelves beside the bed. He sits in the chair writing in the composition book through the following.*]

MISS SWIFT. My dear Mrs. Hilliard, there is no such thing as a cold. Have you had a doctor's opinion?

ELEANOR. No. That is, we thought we could doctor it ourselves. . . .

MISS SWIFT. Mrs. Hilliard, how could you *possibly* doctor it yourself if you're convinced it's a *cold?* One member of a class stays home one day, and whoosh, it goes through the entire room. Not the germs, you understand, but the *idea* of the germs. [*She rises and moves quickly to stairs.*] Perhaps I'd better have a look at him myself. [GLENN *quickly ducks out of sight and down the back stairs.* ELEANOR *moves fast and stops* MISS SWIFT *on the third step.*]

ELEANOR. No, you can't!

RALPHIE. [*Calling from his room.*] I'll be down in a minute, Miss Swift!

MISS SWIFT. Well, of course, if I've come . . .

RALPHIE. I'm just finishing my composition!

MISS SWIFT. [*Smiling.*] Your son, Mrs. Hilliard, is going to be a brilliant author some day. . . . [CINDY *enters through front door, followed by* DAN *and* ROBISH.] You mark my . . . [*She breaks off as she sees* DAN.] Mr. Hilliard? [CINDY *stops.* ROBISH, *after one glance at* MISS SWIFT, *closes the door and stands against the frame with his back to her.*]

ELEANOR. Dan, you . . . uh . . . remember Miss Swift. Ralphie's *teacher!* [DAN *glances from den to rear hall, immediately alert.*] Ralphie, are you *coming?*

DAN. Sure I remember. How're you, Miss Swift?

ELEANOR. Miss Swift . . . dropped in to see how Ralphie was feeling. [*As* MISS SWIFT *stares at* DAN, *he makes his decision. He is drunk! He immediately goes into a muted drunk act, turns to* ROBISH.]

DAN. She did, did she? What do you think of that . . . Johnny? That's what I call a nice little old PTA practice. [*Ushering* ROBISH *toward the dining room.*] You know where I keep it, Johnny. Help yourself. [MISS SWIFT *stares at* ROBISH *as he, keeping his face turned away from her, moves into the dining room. He turns, when out of her line of vision, and draws the .38 from his pocket as the dining-room door closes.* DAN *grabs* MISS SWIFT *by the arm, turning her away from* ROBISH.] Miss Swift! Met old pal Johnny at a . . . [*Turns to* CINDY.] Cindy, say hello to Miss Swift. [CINDY *and* MISS SWIFT *exchange nods.* DAN *sits on sofa.*] Whew, has Cindy been laying it to me! Leave it to Cindy to know where to find her old man. [ROBISH *appears in pantry, speaks to* GLENN, *who is listening. Above,* RALPHIE *starts down the stairs.*]

ROBISH. She seen me!

GLENN. *Clam up!*

DAN. [*Picks up whisky bottle from coffee table and upends it into coffee cup.*] Where does the stuff go in this house? [*He lays the bottle flat on the coffee table.*]

RALPHIE. [*On stair, one step above* MISS

SWIFT.] I . . . I finished my composition for this week, Miss Swift.

MISS SWIFT. [*Nonplused, takes composition book.*] I'll . . . I'll see that you get full credit, Ralph. [*She turns and steps down one step, but* DAN *stops her.*]

DAN. [*In a commanding tone.*] Miss Swift! [*He rises and goes to foot of stairs.*] I'll take that, please. [*He takes the composition book from her hands rudely, opens it and reads, then looks up at* RALPHIE, *who turns and runs up the stairs and into his own room, where he stands listening at the partly closed door.*] So . . . so this is what they call a composition nowadays. You . . . you encourage such drivel, Miss Swift?

MISS SWIFT. Mr. Hilliard . . . in all fairness . . . I don't think you're in any condition to discuss *any*thing tonight.

DAN. In that case, I'll read it in the morning. [MISS SWIFT *glances upstairs, then comes down and crosses to* ELEANOR, *places a hand on her arm.*]

MISS SWIFT. Mrs. Hilliard, let me assure you that what I've seen here tonight will in no way affect my belief in Ralph. [*After a glance back at* DAN, *she goes quickly to the front door, opens it, and marches out, closing the door. Immediately,* HANK *rushes in from the den and up to the front door and locks it, then moves to the window and stands looking out.* ELEANOR *crosses toward* DAN, *who sinks into the chair.* ROBISH *enters from the dining room, followed by* GLENN.]

ELEANOR. Oh, Dan . . . Dan, how did you ever? . . .

ROBISH. Griffin, we gotta stop that dame!

HANK. Sure, Robish . . . shoot up the whole town!

ROBISH. She seen *me!*

DAN. She wasn't looking at you!

GLENN. Old guy's right, Robish. Hilliard took her mind offa you. Stand up, Pop! [DAN *rises and* GLENN *frisks him.*] Gotta hand it to you, Hilliard. You had that dame in a real stew. You'd of made a great con man. [*To* ELEANOR.] Get up there with that smart brat. [ELEANOR *turns and goes up the stairs.*]

HANK. Glenn . . . this is goin' on too long.

GLENN. [*Ignoring* HANK.] Robish, did you get that piece of paper outta the old guy's pocket?

ROBISH. Couldn't. He jumped outta the truck.

GLENN. You dumb goddam . . .

ROBISH. [*Displaying the pistol.*] He didn't get far.

GLENN. [*Reaching for it.*] I'll take the .38 now, Robish.

ROBISH. [*Holds it away.*] I kinda like th' feel of it. [*Pause . . . a silent duel.*]

GLENN. [*An effort to hold his command.*] Get on the back door.

ROBISH. Get on the back door yourself, Griffin. Stuff it! [ROBISH *laughs defiantly, pockets the gun and sits.*]

DAN. Griffin . . . the money didn't come to the office today.

GLENN. [*His mind on* ROBISH *and the gun.*] Dope it yourself, Pop, you're so smart.

DAN. You didn't really expect it.

GLENN. Mail takes time. You should-a thought of that. It wasn't mailed till early this mornin. [*Grinning, turns to* DAN.] Ought to get here some time tomorrow. [*Pause. General shock.*]

HANK. [*Bleakly.*] Tomorrow?

DAN. [*To* GLENN—*angrily.*] Why, you young . . .

GLENN. Take it easy, Pop . . . 'n stay healthy. [*To* HANK.] Yeah . . . tomorrow. What's one more night?

HANK. [*Low.*] Christ!

DAN. Griffin, I've played your filthy game up to now . . . but by bringing that ape back here after he killed a man . . .

ROBISH. [*Threatening, under his breath.*] Who you callin' an ape?

DAN. . . . we're accessories now.

GLENN. That's right, Hilliard. You're on our side now. [*To* HANK.] I'll take the automatic, kid.

HANK. [*Takes a backward step away from* GLENN.] I'm hanging onto it. [HANK *turns and exits through the dining-room door and goes into the pantry, where he stands looking out the window of the side door.* GLENN *steps to the dining-room door, stops, and turns back to* DAN.]

GLENN. How you like that, Pop? They both got the guns. [*Raises his voice so*

HANK *can hear in the pantry.*] Only they ain't got half a brain between 'em. Without me, they're cooked . . . an' they know it. [GLENN *turns on* CINDY, *moving toward her.*] You didn't feel like blabberin' to the boy friend, did you, sweetie?

CINDY. [*Holding her ground.*] I felt like it. But I didn't. I'll explain it the night you take your walk to the electric chair. [GLENN's *tension has been growing. He explodes.* HANK *turns from the pantry window and rushes into the living room.*]

GLENN. [*Threateningly, to* CINDY, *who backs away.*] There're ways of shuttin' that pretty face of yours, redhead!

HANK. [*As he enters the living room.*] What's the boy friend doin' drivin' past the house out there . . . slow?

GLENN. [*Pushing her shoulder, forces her against window.*] If you pulled a fast one, spitfire . . .

HANK. [*In panic.*] Glenn, listen!

GLENN. [*Turning back into room.*] Lemme think, willya?

HANK. Glenn! They're not gonna stop comin' to the door!

GLENN. [*Crossing to him.*] Yellow, Hank?

HANK. Yeah . . . okay . . . yellow! *They're not gonna stop coming to the door!* [*Blackout.*]

SHERIFF'S OFFICE: *Clock: 8:25. There is a map of Indianapolis on the wall and an area has been marked off with heavy crayon.* FREDERICKS *is studying the map.* BARD *is speaking over the radio.*

BARD. I'm looking at a map of the neighborhood, Tom. Where are you?

WINSTON'S VOICE. Parked behind a service station. Corner of Kessler Boulevard and Keystone. [*As* BARD *marks an X on the map location.*] The main roads are covered. The other cars're just where you put 'em. It's a high-toned sort of neighborhood, Jess.

BARD. Okay. Now. Let's start knocking on a few high-toned doors!

FREDERICKS. Bard . . . there're over two hundred houses in that area. It'll take all night and part of tomorrow. . . .

BARD. [*Ignoring* FREDERICKS.] Every one

of the trashman's customers. Begin with those. And Tom . . . especially the garages, you got me? [CARSON *enters.*]

WINSTON'S VOICE. We're on it, Jess. . . . [BARD *switches off the radio.*]

CARSON. [*Holding out letter.*] This, my friend, was brought into the city police station during the noon hour.

BARD. [*Taking the letter.*] Noon!

CARSON. A bellhop's given six different descriptions of the man who tipped him five bucks to deliver it. All we know for sure is the man had two arms, two legs and presumably one head.

BARD. [*Takes letter out of envelope, glances at it.*] It's not signed.

CARSON. Go ahead, read it . . . you'll understand why.

BARD. [*Begins to read briskly . . . and tone changes to a hushed whisper.*] "To the Police . . . innocent people will be in the house or automobile with the three fugitives you want. If you shoot, you will be responsible for taking the lives of people who have done no harm. Any attempt to trace this letter will only endanger my family. . . ." [*Pause.* BARD *holds letter up to light.*] Handwriting disguised . . . no watermarks.

FREDERICKS. It's a blind.

BARD. [*Whisper . . . touched.*] The idiot.

CARSON. That letter's no blind.

BARD. But he ought to *know!* God, doesn't he know? Carson, isn't there some way to get word to this guy, whoever he is, that you can't play ball with savages like that?

CARSON. How? Without tipping them he wrote that?

BARD. *You* take a shot in the dark, Federal man! They'll tear that poor guy to ribbons, inside and out, before they're done. You can't co-operate with scum like that!

CARSON. No? . . . What would *you* do, Jesse? I'd say he was smart to write that. Might keep some itchy-fingered officer from shooting his wife or child.

BARD. Itchy-fingered like me, Carson?

CARSON. You got more sense. That's what's eating you, friend. You know what a spot the man's on. What *would* you do, Jesse . . . under the circumstances?

BARD. [*After a moment.*] I'd play ball. [BARD *flips on intercom and speaks into it.*] Dutch, get me car nine . . . Deputy Winston. [*Flips off the intercom. Quietly.*] Yeah, I reckon I'd do just that. An' maybe pray a little. [BARD *switches on radio circuit light.*]

WINSTON'S VOICE. Car nine . . .

BARD. Tom . . . stop 'em up there.

WINSTON'S VOICE. [*Incredulously.*] Stop 'em . . . ?

BARD. You heard me. I'm countermanding the orders. Bury those prowl cars, *bury* 'em.

FREDERICKS. You can't put off a showdown, lad.

BARD. Nobody wants a showdown any more'n I do . . . but not if it means getting some poor slob's family massacred! [*Into mike.*] You hear me, Tom? Keep those patrols off the streets! Stash 'em!

WINSTON'S VOICE. You're callin' it, Jess. . . . Listen—that sporty little foreign car I reported a while ago . . . he just went by the corner again.

BARD. [*Considers a moment.*] Okay. Bring him in, Tom. Who knows? But quiet up there! No sirens, no red lights.

WINSTON'S VOICE. It'll be a pleasure to arrest *anybody*! [BARD *switches off the radio.*]

FREDERICKS. You call that police work?

BARD. What do you propose . . . alert 'em, force their hand?

FREDERICKS. That letter pretty well establishes they're in that neighborhood. I'll tell you what I propose—tear gas.

BARD. Anybody wonder why this guy didn't sign his name? Why he doesn't trust the police to help him?

FREDERICKS. Tear gas and riot guns. I'll have some moved up there . . . just in case you begin to see the light! [FREDERICKS *exits. Pause.*]

CARSON. [*Quietly.*] Changing your tune, Jess? . . . [BARD *moves to the desk, puzzled at himself and his feelings, ignores* CARSON. *He rereads the letter in silence.*]

BARD. Those guys wouldn't try to use a sports car for a getaway. Probably some fresh kid out trying to pick up a girl. . . . [*Blackout.*]

HILLIARD HOME: *The living-room lights are on, the rest of the house dim.* ELEANOR *is with* RALPHIE *in his room.* DAN *is seated in the living room.* ROBISH *is at door of den.* CINDY *is on the second step of the stairs.* HANK *is at the window.* GLENN *is at the front door, which is very slightly ajar so that he can look out through the crack.*

HANK. He knows somethin's up. . . .

CINDY. Chuck knows nothing. Naturally, he's puzzled . . . he . . .

GLENN. [*Closes and locks the door.*] Knock off, I'm thinkin'.

HANK. Glenn . . .

GLENN. [*Abstracted.*] Don't let it get you, kid.

HANK. Glenn . . . I've had it.

GLENN. What're you talkin' about?

HANK. The old man with the trash . . . the teacher . . . now this guy goin' by out there . . . over'n over. I've had it. [*He goes into the dining room and to the pantry, where he stands looking out the window of the side door.*]

GLENN. [*Moving fast to the dining room.*] Robish, cover 'em! [ROBISH *rises and glances out window.*]

GLENN. [*Enters the pantry, grabs* HANK's *arm.*] What the hell does that mean? "I've had it"?

HANK. What're we waitin' for, Glenn?

GLENN. Don't start that again! I gotta dope this . . .

HANK. We're accessories now. [DAN *rises and leaves the living room by the dining-room door.* CINDY *moves to the dining-room door, listening.*]

GLENN. You're learnin' big words aroun' this house, ain't you?

HANK. Glenn . . . I ain't going to the chair 'cause that ape in there got trigger happy.

GLENN. We're pullin' stakes tomorrow . . . *after* we get the dough. [DAN *appears in the pantry.*]

HANK. [*Shouting.*] What good's the dough gonna do you in the death house?

GLENN. [*Intensely.*] I gotta pay Flick to take care of Bard, don't I? [*Turns, following* HANK's *gaze, sees* DAN.] What're you gapin' at?

HANK. I'm goin', Glenn. By myself.

GLENN. [*Whirling on him.*] You leave here without me, they'll have you back'n stir'n less'n a hour.

HANK. I can take care of myself.

GLENN. Since when?

HANK. [*Firmly.*] Since right now! [GLENN *is baffled, angry, frightened, unable to cope.*]

GLENN. *Listen*, you yellow little punk . . . you're gonna do what I tell you!

HANK. Not any more, Glenn.

DAN. Hank, I don't advise your leaving here alone. . . .

HANK. They won't catch me, Mr. Hilliard. Don't worry about that.

GLENN. [*Between them.*] Look who's tellin' who not to worry! You're talkin' like Hilliard was our old man. [*Faces* DAN.] If Hilliard was our old man, he'd have something coming to him from way back! [HANK *unlocks the door and* GLENN *whips about . . . changing: pleading now, helpless, slightly pathetic.*] Listen, Hank . . . you can't duck out on me. Christ, kid . . . it's always been *us*. You'n me. Listen . . . without you . . . without you . . .

GLENN. Come along, Glenn?

GLENN. [*Wildly.*] Goddammit, I'm callin' the tune! You're gonna listen to me, I took care of you, I . . . [GLENN *breaks off because* HANK *has taken the automatic from his pocket.* GLENN *stares.*]

HANK. You ain't stoppin' me . . . either one of you. [*Pause.*] I'll take the girl's coop. [CINDY, *who has been standing at the dining-room door, now slips out, heading for the pantry.*]

DAN. [*Quickly.*] They could trace that license in ten minutes.

HANK. Okay, Mr. Hilliard . . . I can pick up a car anywhere.

ROBISH. [*Calls to* GLENN.] Griffin . . . redhead's gettin' nosy! [CINDY *appears in the pantry.* HANK *sees her, and on his face is the naked longing.* GLENN *turns, frowning . . . he sees* CINDY. *He taps his forehead with the heel of his hand, smiling.*]

GLENN. I get it. Christ, kid, I get it now! [*He grabs* CINDY *and pulls her toward*

HANK. DAN *puts his arm around her, holding* GLENN *off.*] Ain't I always learned you? You want something *take* it!

DAN. Your brother knows it's not that simple, Griffin!

GLENN. [*Fiercely.*] I'll *make* it that simple! *Hank gets what he wants!* [*Pause . . . while* HANK *looks at* CINDY.]

HANK. [*In choked tones.*] I doubt it, Glenn. I doubt if I ever will. [HANK *suddenly opens the door, turns and goes out, slamming the door behind him. He quickly disappears.* GLENN *springs to the door and looks out the window. Stunned, muttering almost to himself, he sags in door.*]

GLENN. You be careful, kid. . . . Take care of yourself, see . . . You . . . [*He turns and sees* CINDY *in* DAN's *arms, pulls up the swagger.*] Good riddance. He was beginnin' to get on my nerves. [*Then, abruptly.*] You satisfied, redhead?

DAN. Cindy had nothing to do with . . .

GLENN. *Satisfied?*

DAN. Go to your room, Cindy. [CINDY *slips up the back stairs.* DAN *turns to* GLENN, *who goes toward the living room, seething, growing more and more violent.* DAN *follows* GLENN.] Griffin, you'd better get hold of yourself. [*Above,* ELEANOR *has left* RALPHIE *and is now at the head of the stairs.*]

ELEANOR. Dan, what is it? What . . .

GLENN. [*As he enters the living room.*] All of you. All of you! [*Turns on* DAN.] You satisfied now, you smart-eyed bastard? Clickety-click, you got at him, didn't you? [*Above,* RALPHIE *joins* ELEANOR *at head of stairs.*]

DAN. God, boy, you'd better . . .

GLENN. *Shut up, Pop!* . . . Pop! If you was our pop . . .

DAN. Griffin, I don't know how much reason you've got left in that head of yours, but you can't turn this on . . .

GLENN. [*Pacing like a maddened caged animal.*] *I can do anything I want!* You and your goddam house!

ROBISH. [*At window.*] Stir-crazy!

GLENN. That goddam spitfire'n her fancy skirts swishin'!

DAN. I'd advise you to let loose of that idea!

GLENN. [*Grabs composition book from table and sweeps ash tray to the floor.*] That brat an' his "composition"!

DAN. [*Still at foot of stairs.*] If you don't get hold . . . [ELEANOR *comes down the stairs a few steps.*]

GLENN. I got hold! I got hold good! [*Twisting the composition book in his hands.*] Now I'm gonna "advise" you, Pop. You're gonna go up there now an' you're gonna learn that kid we ain't playin' cowboys-an'-Indians aroun' here. [*Taking pleasure in it.*] You're gonna give that brat a real old-fashioned lacin'.

DAN. We don't do things that way in this house!

GLENN. This house, this house! I got my gut-full-a this house! [*Eyes on* DAN.] Robish! How'd *you* like to show Hilliard how it's done?

ROBISH. Yeah . . . I ain't got nothin' else to do. [*Above,* RALPHIE *returns to his own room, stands by bed.*]

GLENN. [*Sadistically.*] Okay, Robish . . . whale the tar outta that brat! [RO-BISH *starts to the stairs.* DAN *moves up the stairs slowly.* ROBISH *stops at foot of stairs.*]

ELEANOR. [*Leaning on stair rail. To* GLENN.] I hope they get your brother! I hope they kill him!

GLENN. [*Calls up to* DAN.] Let's hear him bawlin', Pop! Loud. My old man used a belt! [DAN *enters* RALPHIE'S *room, closes the door and turns on the light.* ELEANOR *mounts the stairs and goes into the master bedroom, where she stands listening behind the closed door.* DAN *faces* RALPHIE.]

DAN. [*Breathlessly.*] Ralphie . . .

RALPHIE. Did Hank take your gun? Then there's only one gun now. . . .

DAN. [*Gently, but urgently.*] Son . . . you've got to help. . . .

ROBISH. [*Starts up the stairs.*] We don't hear nothin', Hilliard!

DAN. [*Swiftly, softly, suffering.*] Ralphie . . . listen to me. No matter what you think now . . . no matter what you think of me . . . what names you give it . . . you've got to do what I tell you.

ROBISH. [*Rounding the landing.*] What's goin' on in there?

DAN. Ralphie, listen! I want you to cry.

ROBISH [*Coming down the hall.*] What's the stall?

DAN. [*Almost a whisper.*] Do you hear me? Ralphie . . . son . . . please . . . for God's sake do what I say now.

RALPHIE. I . . . I can't.

ROBISH. [*Outside the door.*] You want some help, Hilliard? [*Trapped,* DAN *lifts his hand and brings down, in desperation, open-palmed: a stinging blow across the boy's face.* RALPHIE, *stunned, stands staring at his father.* DAN *goes sick and empty clear through. Then* DAN *sinks to bed, gathers* RALPHIE *in his arms, and* RALPHIE *begins to cry. He cries softly at first, then louder and louder. Below,* GLENN *hears the sounds and drops the composition book to the floor, as though he has found some small release inside. Dimout.*]

SHERIFF'S OFFICE: *Clock reads 8:59.* WINSTON *stands to one side of* CHUCK, *who, bewildered, faces* BARD *across the desk.* BARD *is examining* CHUCK'S *driver's license.*

BARD. What's your business, Mr. . . . [*Glances at license.*] Wright?

CHUCK. Attorney, Swisshelm and Edwards. Circle Tower Building. . . . What's this all about?

BARD. Your firm handle criminal cases?

CHUCK. We're strictly corporation law. You haven't answered my question, Deputy.

WINSTON. Don't get fresh.

BARD. Empty out your pockets, Wright.

CHUCK. You've no right to . . .

BARD. Look, Wright . . . you're not in court! Empty out your pockets! [*As* CHUCK *complies.*] What you been up to, last hour or so . . . in that . . . [*Consults* CHUCK'S *registration.*] Jaguar of yours? Cruising round in circles?

WINSTON. You scoutin' for those rats, Wright?

CHUCK. What rats?

BARD. Let's not be cagey, kid . . . it makes me suspicious. [*Picks up newspaper from top of radio and hands it to* CHUCK, *who reads the headlines and begins to realize . . .*] We know they're up there somewhere . . . holed up in one of those nice houses . . . so . . .

[*Stops, frowning . . . studying expression on* CHUCK's *face.*] What's up, boy?

CHUCK. Nothing . . .

BARD. You know something? [*When* CHUCK *shakes his head.*] Suspect something?

CHUCK. No . . .

BARD. [*Rising.*] Dammit, don't lie to to me! Your face looks like I just kicked you.

CHUCK. Well . . . it's just that . . . my girl lives . . . there.

BARD. Name?

CHUCK. Her name's . . . Allen [*Firmly.*] Constance Allen.

WINSTON. [*Consulting the list.*] No Allens on the list, Jess.

BARD. [*Picks up* DAN's *letter, hands it to* CHUCK.] Here . . . read this. [BARD *sits as* CHUCK *reads.*] Now. Let's have it, kid. What's the girl's name?

CHUCK. I . . . don't know.

BARD. [*Gently probing now.*] She's in there . . . with those three. What's the address?

CHUCK. If . . . if he'd wanted you to know . . . [*Tosses letter to the desk.*] he'd have signed his name.

BARD. [*Changing.*] Wright, that guy ought to know he can't cribbage aroun' with the police like this. If he doesn't, you should!

CHUCK. What do you expect him to do? He's doing all he can! He's quite a guy!

BARD. [*Rising.*] Kid . . . I honestly don't know what I'd do if I was in your shoes . . . but I'm in mine . . . and I want that name. Now spit it out or I'll slap you in the pokey so fast . . .

CHUCK. You've got no charges!

BARD. I've got sixty of 'em. Aidin' and abettin' . . . withholding evidence . . . accessory to murder! Or didn't you know they murdered a man this afternoon? Yeah, that's the kind of scum you're lettin' your girl spend the evening with. [*Pause.* CHUCK *sinks into chair.* BARD *sits on edge of desk.* CHUCK *swallows.*]

CHUCK. I . . . I can't make that decision. For them. You'd better slap on one of those charges, Deputy. Because I don't know the name. I never said I did.

BARD. [*Rising.*] Why, you young . . .

[*He is interrupted by the intercom.*]

DUTCH'S VOICE. Special Agent Carson, Jesse.

BARD. [*Switches on radio.*] Yes, Carson?

CARSON'S VOICE. Deputy . . . it just blew wide open!

BARD. What? . . . What've you got?

CARSON'S VOICE. City policemen just caught Hank Griffin trying to steal a car. He decided to shoot it out. . . .

BARD. Killed?

CARSON'S VOICE. Killed.

BARD. [*In a different tone . . . very quietly.*] Anything else?

CARSON'S VOICE. Plenty . . . The gun the boy was carrying—it was registered. [*As* BARD's *eyes meet* CHUCK's.] In the name of Hilliard . . . Daniel C. Hilliard. [BARD *glances at* WINSTON, *who glances at list, looks up, nods.*]

BARD. Just like that. Eleanor Hilliard wrote a check to Claude Patterson this morning.

WINSTON. [*Reading from list.*] Hilliard, Daniel C. Wife, Eleanor. One son age ten, Ralph. One daughter age twenty, Cynthia . . . called Cindy. [CHUCK *has turned in the chair, watching* WINSTON. *Their eyes now meet.*]

BARD. [*After a slight pause.*] Okay. Carson . . . throw a cordon around the Hilliard house. Let no one in or out of that block. Only keep everything out of sight of the windows. I'll be up there in ten minutes. And Carson . . . have the newsboys got this?

CARSON'S VOICE. Not yet. Not even the death.

BARD. Well, for god's sake, keep 'em off it!

CARSON'S VOICE. We'll try, Jess. [BARD *flips off the radio circuit light.*]

WINSTON. [*Gets coat.*] You call it, Jess.

CHUCK. [*Rising.*] You can't move in! You read Mr. Hilliard's letter.

BARD. [*Taking his revolver out of desk drawer, checks it. Abstracted.*] Get out of here now, kid.

CHUCK. [*Demanding.*] What're you going to do?

BARD. What the sweet hell do you think I'm going to do . . . blow up the house? [BARD *takes his jacket from back of chair and starts putting it on.*]

CHUCK. [*Earnestly.*] Deputy . . . what if you could sneak someone inside? With a gun. There are only two of them in there now.

WINSTON. [*Putting on coat.*] This is police work, son. Stay out of it.

CHUCK. If somebody was in there . . . between them and the family . . . and if he could get 'em both at one crack . . .

BARD. [*Ignoring* CHUCK, *flips on intercom.*] Dutch . . . get an ambulance up to Kessler and Keystone. Keep it out of sight. [*Flips off intercom. Turns to* CHUCK.] You're out of it, Wright. Stay out!

CHUCK. I'm not out of it! Those're my people in there! [*To* BARD, *urgently.*] You read the letter. There can't be any shooting when they come out, either. . . . *What are you going to do?*

BARD. [*Annoyed at the question.*] Look! Will you get out of here!

CHUCK. May I have my things?

BARD. [*Shoving items across the desk.*] Take 'em.

CHUCK. [*Picking up his things, putting them in pockets.*] May I have those keys, Deputy?

BARD. [*Looks at keys, which he has unconsciously been holding in his hand since he went through* CHUCK'S *belongings.*] Here. [*He hands the keys to* CHUCK.]

CHUCK. Thanks. [CHUCK *goes out, as* WINSTON *returns with rifle.*]

WINSTON. The boy's got a good question, Jess.

BARD. [*Thoughtfully; quietly.*] A damn good question . . . . I wish I had the answer. [*As they start out.*] Well, let's get on it now. Let's get up there! [*Dimout.*]

CURTAIN

ACT THREE

HILLIARD HOME: DAN is at the window of the master bedroom. ELEANOR is sitting on the bed. Across the hall, RALPHIE is asleep on his bed. CINDY is out of sight in her room. ROBISH is at the window in the living room. GLENN is in the pantry. As the lights dim up he is leaving the pantry and appears in the living room. Living-room lights are on; the rest of the house is dim.

ROBISH. [*Turning from the window as* GLENN *enters.*] Griffin . . . somethin' funny goin' on. There ain't been no cars goin' by out there for a long time. [*Steps toward* GLENN.] Griffin, you deef?

GLENN. [*Who has been pacing, stops.*] Robish . . . let's grab the two women'n blow.

ROBISH. With no dough?

GLENN. [*Vacantly.*] With no dough.

ROBISH. Okay. Ya wanna go . . . go. Wind up like the kid brother. In the morgue.

GLENN. Lay off, Robish.

ROBISH. On a slab. By this time they got 'im or shot 'im. [*Above,* DAN *goes to other window in the bedroom.*]

GLENN. [*Wildly.*] Nothin' happens to Hank!

ROBISH. [*Chuckles heavily.*] That's po'try, Griffin. Got 'im or shot 'im.

GLENN. [*Starting toward* ROBISH.] You don't know nothin'! Goddam you, Robish . . . [ROBISH *lifts the gun, almost casually. In this moment, the telephone shrills.* GLENN *stops.*]

ROBISH. [*Shouting.*] Hilliard! Answer that! [DAN *turns on the bedroom lights, opens the door, and picks up the phone in the upstairs hall at the time that* GLENN, *below, is already answering it.* CINDY *has come out of her room and stands near the door to* RALPHIE'S *room,* DAN, *undecided as to what to do with the phone, looks at* CINDY.]

GLENN. [*Leaping to the phone almost before the first ring is over.*] Hank! [*Into instrument.*] Hello! [*Then, sagging in disappointment, snarls.*] Who? . . . [*He replaces the phone angrily.*]

ROBISH. [*Approaching* GLENN.] Christ, who is it?

GLENN. [*Vacantly, going through din-*

ing-room door.] Something about . . . a night watchman . . .

ROBISH. [*Calling.*] Hilliard!

DAN. [*Speaks into the extension.*] Hello . . . this is Mr. Hilliard speaking. [*Suddenly alert.*] Yes, Carl? . . . I'll be right down. [DAN *replaces the phone and turns to the stairs.*]

ROBISH. [*At foot of stairs.*] Who was that? What's going on?

DAN. [*On stairs, calls down.*] The money's here. It arrived special delivery at the store. I'll go get it. [DAN *turns back up the stairs and enters the bedroom, where he faces* ELEANOR, *who is sitting on the bed.* CINDY *returns to her own room.* GLENN *has returned from the dining room during* DAN's *last speech.* ROBISH *turns to him.*]

ROBISH. [*Trying to penetrate* GLENN's *preoccupation.*] Griffin . . . the dough's here.

GLENN. [*Stands for a moment at foot of stairs.*] How come that wasn't Hank on the phone?

ROBISH. You better snap out of it. [*As* GLENN *goes into the den.*] Jeez, you're givin' me the willies. . . . [*He stands looking after* GLENN. *In the bedroom above,* DAN *picks up his coat from over the back of the chair and paces with the coat in his hands.* ELEANOR *follows him with her eyes as she speaks.*]

ELEANOR. I can't believe it. Now. Tonight! No more waiting. In an hour now . . . *Less* than an hour! [*Slight pause.* DAN *puts on his coat.*] Dan . . . look at me. . . . [*Rises, fighting alarm.*] Dan!

ROBISH. [*Shouting up the stairs.*] Hilliard! That dough's waiting!

ELEANOR. Tell me. What are you planning, Dan? [*Pause.* DAN *turns to face her.*]

DAN. I can't wait any longer for the opportune moment, that's all.

ELEANOR. What do you mean?

DAN. I've got to . . . make the moment . . . for myself.

ELEANOR. [*Sinks down at foot of bed.*] Dan, tell me. My blood's stopped. Dan . . .

DAN. There are only three bullets left in that gun down there.

ELEANOR. I'm going to scream!

DAN. No you're not, you're going to listen.

ELEANOR. My heart's pushing up out of . . . Dan, *what do you mean?*

DAN. I'm going to force Robish to use those bullets.

ELEANOR. [*Whispers.*] Use them . . . How?

DAN. [*Quietly.*] On me.

ROBISH. Hilliard, what's the stall?

ELEANOR. [*Rising, to him.*] Dan, this isn't you. They've driven you . . . Oh, God, *Dan!*

DAN. I've tried every other way, haven't I? *Haven't* I?

ELEANOR. [*Swiftly . . . in a whisper.*] We know, we're not asking for more, we know what you've done. Even Ralphie . . .

DAN. If I can get Griffin out of the way before Robish even knows what's happening . . . [*Grimly; murderously.*] And I *can.*

ELEANOR. Dan, no matter how much you want to kill Griffin . . .

DAN. There's no other way!

ELEANOR. There is. There has to be!

DAN. [*Gently, urgently.*] Darling, you've got to face this with me. Griffin hates me. He hated me before he even saw me. I can't explain it. Every hour some new black hole appears in him. He's cracking up, Ellie. God knows what a mind like that will turn to . . . which one of us . . . Now. Do you see? We're no better off when I get the money. Do you see?

ELEANOR. All I see is one thing. One thing . . . *We're* not saved if *you* die.

DAN. Please, Ellie, don't make it so . . .

ELEANOR. All right . . . go down there. Kill Griffin. Make Robish shoot you. Do you imagine a man like that has to have *bullets* to . . . [DAN *turns to her.*] against Ralphie? . . . or Cindy? . . . or me? *Do* you?

DAN. [*Realizing that it was only panic, softly.*] All right, Ellie.

ELEANOR. We're not saved if you die.

DAN. All *right,* Ellie!

ELEANOR. [*Sits on bed.*] Oh, God, darling. [DAN *sinks into chair.*] Dan . . . you're the hub . . . it all revolves around you. If anything . . .

DAN. Everything's blurred again. One minute it all looks sharp . . . clear . . .

ELEANOR. [*Places her hand on* DAN's.]

Dan. [*He looks at her.*] We can't let them panic us now. [*There is a moment of understanding between them.*]

ROBISH. Hilliard! Get th' lead out! [DAN *and* ELEANOR *break. He rises and opens the door, starting downstairs.* ELEANOR *rises and stands at the door.*]

GLENN. [*Entering from den.*] Ask 'em where they get the news on that damn thing. [DAN *is coming down the stairs.* CINDY *comes out of her room and follows.* GLENN *sinks to chair.*]

ROBISH. Goddam you, Hilliard, you don't get down here, I'm gonna . . . [*He sees* DAN *on the stairs.*] We ain't gonna blow till we get that dough, Hilliard.

GLENN. Where's the redhead? [DAN, *moving to the closet, turns to* CINDY *on stairs.*]

DAN. Cindy, go to your room. Lock the door.

GLENN. Redhead goes along! [CINDY *remains on the stairs.*]

ROBISH. [*Turning to* GLENN.] The gal stays right here.

GLENN. [*Ignoring* ROBISH—*a grotesque caricature of his old self.*] Open the letter . . . take out two thousand dollars . . .

ROBISH. To hell with that!

GLENN. Redhead takes it to Lombardi's Grille . . .

DAN. [*Putting on coat.*] Cindy is not going to deliver any . . .

GLENN. [*Turns in chair to face* DAN.] Lombardi Grille. South Illinois Street.

ROBISH. To hell with that. Ain't got time now!

GLENN. She sits'n has a drink. A man sits down with her. Then . . .

ROBISH. Then nothin'! Yuh lissen to me. . . .

GLENN. [*Vaguely.*] Then . . .

DAN. What then, Griffin?

GLENN. She gives him the dough. Two G's.

ROBISH. Yuh bring all that dough here, Hilliard . . . soon's yuh lay your mitts on it. [DAN *goes to open the door.*]

GLENN. We don't get outta here till I hear from Flick he's got his money. [DAN, *with door open, now nods to* CINDY, *who comes down the stairs and goes out.* DAN *follows and closes the door.*]

ROBISH. Wastin' time, wastin' time. I tell yuh the redhead stays. We gotta have . . . [*He hears the door close. Turns.*] Now, how we gonna get two dames in the car? [*He locks the door as* GLENN *goes to the phone, dials.*] Loco. Christ! Loco. [ROBISH *goes into pantry, locks the back door.*]

GLENN. [*On phone.*] What? . . . Oh . . . Mr. Flick. Room . . . uh . . . 202. [ROBISH *returns to the living room.*]

ROBISH. [*In dining-room door.*] I lay my hands'n that dough, yuh can rot'n here, Griffin. . . . [*Blackout.*]

THE WALLINGS' ATTIC: *The corner of an attic room that seems to be suspended in darkness. The room has a cluttered look: discarded furniture, an old iron bedframe leaning against the wall. A single small window overlooks the Hilliard house in the distance.* CARSON *is looking out the window through binoculars.* BARD *behind him, wearing hat.* FREDERICKS *is seated on an old trunk. On an old box is radio apparatus. A rifle with a telescopic sight leans against the wall near the window.*

CARSON. [*Reporting, without lowering binoculars.*] Jesse . . . a man and a girl just came out the front door of the Hilliard house.

BARD. That'll be Hilliard and his daughter.

CARSON. They're getting into the black coupé in the driveway. [*He hands the glasses to* BARD, *who looks through the window.*] Cocky, aren't they? Letting them both out of there even now.

BARD. Yeah . . . gettin' real cocksure.

FREDERICKS. [*Crisply.*] Why not? They know they got us hog-tied . . . 's long as we sit up here in the attic of the house next door.

BARD. [*Hands glasses back to* CARSON *and turns to* FREDERICKS.] Don't start riding me again, Fredericks. [*There is a buzz from the radio apparatus.* BARD *flips a switch and picks up the microphone.*]

WINSTON'S VOICE. [*On radio.*] Car nine —Winston.

BARD. [*Into mike.*] Yeah, Tom?

WINSTON'S VOICE. Jesse . . . Hilliard and his daughter just turned south on Keystone. You want me to pick 'em up?

BARD. No.

FREDERICKS. What the hell're we waitin' for? We got the phone tap. We know where he's going.

BARD. [*Annoyed—into mike.*] Tom . . . let them get downtown to that store. Then . . . when he's got his mail, whatever it is . . . pick him up and bring him here to the Wallings' house. Come in here from the north, though . . . and careful nobody in the Hilliard windows can see you.

WINSTON'S VOICE. What'll I tell the guy?

BARD. Nothing. [*Flips off radio, puts down mike.*]

FREDERICKS. Bard, this is stupid as hell! I tell you, we got no choice now. Move in.

BARD. And I tell you I've got an animal gnawing away inside me tonight, Fredericks, and I don't need this crap from you! I'm aware of the alternatives. We could bust in there now . . . or try to bluff 'em out . . . or try to sneak in and flush 'em . . . but . . .

FREDERICKS. [*Rising.*] Let's get one thing straight. There's going to be blood. There're only two people in that house now.

BARD. Two human beings.

FREDERICKS. Okay! Measure them against the just as innocent people those two can knock off if they bluff their way out of this trap.

BARD. The guy's wife and kid!

FREDERICKS. Lad, you're putting a weapon in the hands of every felon in the country, you let . . .

BARD. [*Overriding.*] I didn't invent the scheme, dammit! I'm doing all I can. We've got sixty officers in those woods now . . . the streets are blocked off. . . .

FREDERICKS. Bastards like them're wily.

BARD. [*Turning to* CARSON.] Carson! Those're escapees from a Federal prison in there. You call it!

CARSON. [*Turns from window slightly.*] I'll string along with you, Deputy . . . at least until we speak to Hilliard.

FREDERICKS. O-kay, lads. It's your baby. I'm just a sour old man hates to see frisky young slobs make fools of theirselves. [*Harshly.*] But pity's a luxury your

badge don't afford! [*The radio buzzes.* BARD *flips switch, picks up mike.*]

BARD. [*Into mike.*] Deputy Bard . . .

DUTCH'S VOICE. We just got another telephone report, Jess. A man's voice, unidentified, *inside* the house called a downtown hotel . . . spoke to a man named Flick . . . told him to meet a redheaded girl at Lombardi Grille . . . South Illinois Street.

BARD. [*Lowers mike.*] God Almighty, that's the daughter. [*Into mike.*] Dutch . . . put a city detective in the Lombardi Grille. Have him pick up the man and the girl.

DUTCH'S VOICE. There's more. The one called Flick is supposed to call back to the Hilliard house . . . let the telephone ring three times, then hang up. Some sort of hanky-panky.

BARD. Thanks, Dutch. [*Flips off radio. Puts down mike.*] Wonder what the devil that's all about.

CARSON. [*Quietly—looking through the glasses.*] Bard . . . there's some sort of activity behind the Hilliard garage. You can barely make it out in the light from the window.

BARD. [*Takes glasses, looks.*] Looks to me like somebody stretched out on the ground. [*Blackout.*]

HILLIARD HOME: *The lights are on in the living room and in the master bedroom. The rest of the house is dim.* ELEANOR *and* RALPHIE *stand at the window of the master bedroom.* ROBISH *is in the window in the pantry, looking out the window of the side door.* GLENN *sits on the arm of the sofa in the living room, listening to the newscaster on the radio. Though* ROBISH *begins speaking as soon as the lights are up, the radio newscaster is heard all through the beginning of the scene until* GLENN *turns the radio off.*

RADIO NEWSCASTER. [*On speaker, under scene.*] . . . see what the weather man has in store for us. Clear skies tomorrow, much colder, with brisk winds tomorrow and Sunday. No more rain is predicted for the Indianapolis area . . . but better dig out that overcoat because winter is almost here! This has been Kyle McGreevey, your ten-o'clock newscaster, now saying . . . good-night and good cheer!

ROBISH. [*As the lights come up.*] Griffin! [GLENN *does not answer, his attention on radio.*] Griffin, can yuh hear me? I seen somethin' out by the garage! [*Still no answer.* ROBISH *takes an uncertain step toward the kitchen, suddenly whirls and unlocks the side door, opens it a crack, hiding behind it, gun ready, speaks in low, cautious growl.*] Hey, out there? [*Turns and calls into house . . . a plea for help, lost without his "leader."*] Griffin! [*Out the door . . . slightly louder.*] Listen . . . anybody out there . . . coppers . . . we'll blast the woman'n kid in here! [*Pause. The silence works on him; the uncertainty becomes turbulent.*] Christ. What am I gonna . . . *Christ!* [ROBISH *closes and locks the side door, turns and goes through the kitchen door to appear in the living room.* GLENN *rises from sofa and turns off the radio. There is a growing wildness in him. Convinced now, deluding himself into thinking what he wants to believe, he enters another phase . . . in which nothing can touch him. This is in sharp contrast to the stunned glassy fear of the last scenes. He is gay, refusing reality, like a man with too many drinks.* ROBISH, *entering the living room, cannot reach him through the following.*] Griffin, yuh hear me?

GLENN. [*In soft disbelief.*] He's okay.

ROBISH. I seen . . .

GLENN. [*Mounting joy.*] Hank's okay, Robish.

ROBISH. To hell with the kid. He's in the clink. Lissen . . . [*During the following,* CHUCK *appears at the side door outside. He lets himself in with* CINDY's *key and closes the door. He stands for a while in the pantry, listening. He moves to the pantry wall and stands with an ear against it. Then he goes up the back stairs and appears in the upstairs hall. He looks around cautiously, listens down the front stairs and then steps cautiously into* RALPHIE's *room and closes the door, leaving it slightly ajar.*]

GLENN. [*With violent relief.*] They'd have had it on the news, wouldn't they? Nothing. They're still lookin' for all of us. Not a goddam word about Hank!

ROBISH. Lissen . . . we gotta change our ideas.

GLENN. [*At the stairs.*] Ideas perkin' fine. Everythin's chimin'. *Hank made it!* He's on his way to Helen!

ROBISH. [*Disgusted.*] Who yuh tryin' to con? I tell yuh, I seen somethin' move out by the garage.

GLENN. [*High spirits. Laughs.*] Goblins, Robish. Like on Halloween when we was kids. God, how Hank used to go for that Halloween crap! Dress up . . . burnt cork'n his face . . .

ROBISH. [*Looks out window.*] Any coppers out there . . .

GLENN. We're snug, we're snug. Two hours now, we'll be in Louisville. Hank's with Helen.

ROBISH. They put that on the radio, did they? Any cops stick their necks'n here, I blow up the whole goddam house. [CHUCK *is now in* RALPHIE's *bedroom, his gun ready. Blackout.*]

THE WALLINGS' ATTIC: FREDERICKS *is still seated on the trunk.* BARD *has the glasses and is looking out the window.* CARSON *stands by.*

FREDERICKS. If there's any shooting over there . . .

BARD. [*Hands glasses to* CARSON, *turns.*] I'll give the signal to close in. Satisfied, Lieutenant?

FREDERICKS. [*Rises as* CARSON *takes up the watch through the window.*] No, I'm not. There's another gun in that house now . . . 'cause we waited.

BARD. [*Turning toward the window.*] What I'd like to know is how that kid got through the police lines.

FREDERICKS. Plenty of ways . . . you know the neighborhood well enough.

CARSON. [*His first show of emotion.*] A reckless muddlehead like that could botch up everything if he startles them in there!

FREDERICKS. Why shouldn't he take it in his own hands?

CARSON. If only his gun's between those two and the family somehow . . .

BARD. My hunch is the boy's layin' low . . . not knowin' where everybody is . . . waitin' for someone to make a move . . . us or them.

FREDERICKS. Lads, you're up a creek.

CARSON. The boy's smart enough to know he's done for if he doesn't get them both at the same time . . . and fast!

FREDERICKS. Lads, you're up a long, long creek and no paddles. [*The radio buzzes.* BARD *flips switch, picks up mike.*]

BARD. [*Into mike.*] Deputy Bard . . .

WINSTON'S VOICE. [*On radio.*] Jess . . . Hilliard's on his way upstairs. Tread easy now, you guys. This gentleman's had it. [BARD *flips off radio, puts down mike. They all wait, looking at the stairs.*]

FREDERICKS. [*As he turns.*] Man plays with dynamite, he's going to get it. [DAN *enters up the stairs, looks around, quietly terrified but determined.*]

BARD. Evening, Mr. Hilliard. My name's Bard. Deputy Sheriff, Marion County . . . I received your letter, Mr. Hilliard.

DAN. I didn't write you any letter.

BARD. [*Taking letter out of his pocket.*] Look, Mr. Hilliard . . . we wouldn't be here if we didn't have it all pretty straight. So let's not waste . . . [*Stops, staring into* DAN's *face; then, very gently.*] Sorry. You want to sit down, Mr. Hilliard? [BARD *helps* DAN *to box where he sits beside the radio equipment, back to audience.*]

DAN. [*Flatly.*] Where'd I slip up?

BARD. You didn't. Young Griffin's dead. He had your gun.

DAN. [*The name sinking in . . . recognition.*] Bard . . . Bard . . . do you know a man named Flick?

BARD. I've heard the name.

DAN. My daughter's paying Flick two thousand dollars to kill you.

BARD. So . . . [*In wonder.*] So that's the way he was going to do it. [*Briskly.*] Well, Mr. Flick's being arrested, right about now . . . Lombardi Grille . . .

DAN. [*Rises, steps threateningly toward* BARD.] You fool! You damned clumsy . . .

BARD. Okay, Hilliard. Let off steam. Take a swing. How'd I know what they'd send your girl into? I swear . . .

DAN. Swear? What can you swear to? That when I'm not back in there in time . . . when Flick doesn't call . . . they won't jump to the conclusion that . . . [*Breaks off.*] What can anyone swear to?

BARD. Don't worry about Flick's call, Mr. Hilliard. We know the signal. We can handle it.

DAN. [*Picks up rifle with telescopic sight.*] Are you planning to use this?

FREDERICKS. They both still in there?

DAN. Yes.

BARD. [*Takes rifle from* DAN, *replaces it.*] How many guns?

DAN. [*Looks out window toward his own house.*] One. With three bullets.

FREDERICKS. That helps!

DAN. [*Turns from window. Slowly.*] Also . . . my wife and son.

FREDERICKS. Mr. Hilliard—if these two convicts get away with this scheme . . .

DAN. I don't care about that now. I don't want them . . . or you . . . to kill my wife or boy. That's first. *First.* God help me, that comes first.

BARD. Nobody's blaming you, Mr. Hilliard. Nobody in his right mind can raise a voice against what you've done . . . But I can't let you go back in there. [*Pause. Then, slowly,* DAN *takes the special delivery envelope containing money from his inside topcoat pocket. He hands it to* BARD, *who examines the contents.*]

DAN. Until they get that . . . they're not coming out.

FREDERICKS. [*Crisply.*] Then we move in.

DAN. [*Erupting.*] What'm I supposed to do . . . *sit up here and watch it happen?*

FREDERICKS. It's plain suicide for you to go back in there now!

DAN. [*A look at the window.*] That may be. There comes a time when that fact just doesn't enter in . . . You don't give a hang about a life or two . . . what's one more?

BARD. [*Drops envelope with money on box; he is having an inner struggle.*] Mr. Hilliard . . . we're trying to help you.

DAN. [*Pleading forcefully, hopelessly.*] Then clear out! Get away. Take your men . . . your rifles . . . your floodlights . . . and *get away!* [CARSON *steps in, picks up the envelope with the money and holds it out to* DAN.]

CARSON. We can't do that, Mr. Hilliard.

I'll give you ten minutes . . . from the time you walk through that door over there. Shortly after you're inside, we'll give them the telephone signal they're waiting for. If you need us, flicker a light. You've got ten minutes. It's on your shoulders. [*Pause.* DAN *takes the envelope.* CARSON *steps back.*]

BARD. Mr. Hilliard, you'd better have the whole picture. Charles Wright is in the house.

DAN. [*Amazed. Turns to* BARD.] Chuck?

BARD. And he's armed. We couldn't prevent it. [*Slight pause.*] Do you want a gun, Mr. Hilliard?

DAN. [*Quietly.*] No . . . thanks. [*He puts the envelope into his inside topcoat pocket.*]

BARD. They search you when you come in? [DAN *nods slowly.*] Good luck . . . sir. [DAN *turns to the stairs . . . then stops . . . turns.*]

DAN. I've changed my mind.

BARD. You want a gun?

DAN. Please. [BARD *takes his own revolver from his holster and hands it to* DAN.]

BARD. You know how to use it? [DAN *looks at revolver, nods, breaks it and shakes the bullets into his hand, examines the empty chamber.*]

FREDERICKS. [*Shocked.*] Are you crazy?

DAN. Maybe. Only a crazy man'd go in there with an empty gun. Griffin doesn't think I'm crazy.

BARD. That's a pretty long shot, isn't it?

DAN. I don't have any short ones in sight. Do you? [DAN *firmly puts the bullets into* BARD'S *hand. Then, he turns and goes down the stairs. Pause. Then* BARD *flips the switch on the radio, picks up mike.*]

BARD. [*Into mike.*] Car nine . . . Winston.

WINSTON'S VOICE. Parked in side drive, Jess.

BARD. Tom . . . take Mr. Hilliard back to his car. [BARD *puts down the mike, flips off the radio; thoughtfully.*] How'd you like to be riding up to *your* door like that, Fredericks?

FREDERICKS. Just luck I'm not. Or you.

BARD. Yeah. They didn't happen to pick on us, that's all. [BARD *picks up binoculars from window sill.* CARSON *looks at his watch. Blackout.*]

HILLIARD HOME: *The lights are on in the living room; the rest of the house is dim.* ELEANOR *and* RALPHIE *are in the master bedroom at the window.* CHUCK *still stands in* RALPHIE'S *room with the door open, listening, waiting.* GLENN *is at the window in the living room.* ROBISH *is turning from the window in the side door in the pantry.*

ROBISH. [*Calling as he moves toward living room.*] Here he comes, Griffin!

GLENN. [*Exhilarated.*] Only two hours now, Robish. Two lousy hours! I'll do the drivin', make it in less!

ROBISH. [*As he enters the living room.*] The little gal ain't with him. [*Above,* CHUCK *steps into the upstairs hall, listening.*]

GLENN. Who cares? Who gives a damn? [GLENN *steps to the door, unlocks and opens it.* DAN *stands in the doorway, his hands in his topcoat pockets.* DAN *comes into the room.* GLENN *closes and locks the door and moves to* DAN. GLENN'S *mood is almost a travesty on his previous behavior.* DAN'S *manner is profoundly quiet, as he sizes up the situation, frowning at the strange change in* GLENN.]

ROBISH. [*At foot of stairs.*] Hand over the dough, Hilliard.

DAN. [*Ignores this, lifts voice.*] Stay up there, Ellie. Keep the door locked.

ROBISH. Yuh hear me?

DAN. [*Flatly—almost a challenge.*] I don't have it.

ROBISH. [*Roaring.*] What?

GLENN. Now, Pop . . . who you kiddin'? Take your hands outta your pockets . . . please. [*This is what* DAN *wants. He does so, facing* GLENN. GLENN *frisks him, feels the gun in the pocket, reaches in.*]

ROBISH. I'll take the cash, Griffin. [GLENN *takes the gun out of* DAN'S *pocket with his right hand, looking into* DAN'S *eyes.*]

GLENN. What'd you say, Robish? [*He whips the gun out, points it at* ROBISH *and pushes* DAN *around behind him.*] I didn't hear you, Robish! [ROBISH *stares at the gun, lowering his own.*]

ROBISH. [*Steps toward* DAN.] You lousy sonofa . . .

GLENN. [*Laughs.*] Had it all doped, didn't you? [*He reaches with his left hand across his own body, keeping the aim on* ROBISH, *into* DAN's *inside coat pocket . . . brings out the envelope.*] This what you had in mind, Robish?

ROBISH. [*To* DAN.] You bastard!

GLENN. [*Stepping toward* ROBISH, *who backs away.*] Not Pop. Not my old pal Pops! [*Pockets the money.*] Any objections, Robish?

ROBISH. Let's get outta here. [*The telephone rings.* ROBISH *makes a move to answer it.*]

GLENN. Stay away from it, Robish. [*They all stand and listen in frozen silence while the phone rings three times: spaced, automatic.* GLENN *waits after the third ring until he's sure that there won't be a fourth. He laughs.*] Well, that takes care of Bard! Time to break up housekeeping. [*Above,* ELEANOR *moves to bedroom door, switches on the bedroom lights and opens the door. She sees* CHUCK *in the hall, gasps. He turns to her and signals her to silence. She closes and locks the door and stands with* RALPHIE, *who has come to her side.*]

ROBISH. [*As action takes place above.*] Let's get movin'.

DAN. Griffin . . . you'd better take me along. *Only* me!

ROBISH. Like hell. We gotta have a dame in the car. [GLENN *has stopped on the stair, looks at* DAN.]

DAN. Griffin . . . I'm the only one who knows you hired a man named Flick to kill Bard.

GLENN. [*Makes the "clickety-click" gesture.*] Right up to the very end!

DAN. You'd better take me along.

GLENN. Nothin' can touch me now, Hilliard! Everythin's goin' my way!

ROBISH. Come on. Them woods out there could be full-a Feds, all we know.

GLENN. And you . . . you, Hilliard, can come along, too. 'Cause it's like this, see—Hank's waitin'.

DAN. Waiting?

ROBISH. You're off your rocker!

GLENN. So I'm in a kinda hurry! [*He goes to the stairs and up.* CHUCK *steps into* RALPHIE's *room and closes the door.*] Hey, missus, get the brat ready. We're goin' on a little picnic. [*He reaches the door of the bedroom.* ELEANOR *and* RALPHIE *move away from the door.*]

ROBISH. [*Covers* DAN *with pistol.*] He's gettin' some sense back. [GLENN *tries the bedroom door.*]

GLENN. Hey, folks, you don' wanna miss the fun. The ice cream'll be all et up! [*He knocks on the door.*] Lady, you don' want me to have to kick in this nice shiny door, do you? [GLENN *steps back, lifts his leg and kicks the door; it splinters. At the same moment,* CHUCK *opens the door of* RALPHIE's *bedroom and steps behind* GLENN, *lifting his gun. He brings it down with great force on* GLENN's *head behind the ear;* GLENN *spins and falls backward into* RALPHIE's *bedroom.* CHUCK *plunges down the stairs.*]

ROBISH. No racket up there! No noise! [DAN *sees* CHUCK *descending the stairs, gun in hand;* DAN *ducks into dining-room door, as* ROBISH *catches sight of* CHUCK. ROBISH *fires, hitting* CHUCK, *whose gun explodes toward the floor.* CHUCK, *clutching his shoulder, falls across living-room floor.* ROBISH, *out of control, unthinking now, throws open the front door. Above,* ELEANOR—*hearing the shots—runs out of the bedroom and comes down the stairs wildly, leaving* RALPHIE *alone in the bedroom. Outside, floodlights illuminate the whole house in a harsh cold light.*]

ELEANOR. Dan? . . .

DAN. [*Shouting.*] Stay there, Ellie!

ROBISH. [*In open door, shouting.*) Hey, out there! You hear me out there, coppers? [*As* DAN *moves cautiously toward* ROBISH's *back.*] I got one of yuh! Who wants it next? [DAN *moves fast now, driving his shoulder into* ROBISH's *back, sending him catapulting out the front door.* DAN *slams, locks door, as* ELEANOR *comes plunging down the stairs, heedless.*]

ELEANOR. Dan, Dan . . . [DAN *grabs* ELEANOR, *swings her across the room, out of line of the front door. Above,* RALPHIE *starts out of master bedroom just as* GLENN *lifts himself to his feet in* RALPHIE's *bedroom, regaining consciousness.* GLENN *and* RALPHIE *meet at door of master bed-room.* GLENN, *rubbing his head, turns the gun on* RALPHIE *and backs him into the bedroom as: Blackout.*]

THE WALLINGS' ATTIC: CARSON *is kneel-ing in the window with the binoculars, looking out.* BARD *stands behind him with the rifle pointed out, looking through the telescopic sight.*

BARD. It's Robish . . .

CARSON. Get him, Jesse. I'll give the sig-nal to close in.

BARD. [*Lowering the rifle.*] Somebody pushed him out that door.

CARSON. He's heading for the car. Get him, Jesse!

BARD. Five minutes, Carson. Give Hil-liard five more minutes!

CARSON. Hilliard might be dead!

BARD. Harry, I'm pleading with you. *Somebody shoved that big guy out the door. Five minutes!* [*Slight pause.* CARSON *turns, still kneeling, switches on radio, picks up mike.*]

CARSON. All right, Jesse. [*Into mike.*] Fredericks . . . Robish is in the Hilliard car. He's armed. Stop him. [BARD *picks up the PA mike and speaks into it.*]

BARD. [*His voice sounding in distance over PA.*] Hilliard. Do you need us? *Hil-liard.* [*Blackout.*]

HILLIARD HOME: *Outside, the floodlights remain on. There is light in living room and in master bedroom.* GLENN, *still groggy from the blow, is in bedroom, gun on* RALPHIE, *who is against the wall. In the living room,* DAN *and* ELEANOR *are helping* CHUCK *toward front door; he can-not stand without support.*

BARD'S VOICE. [*The hollow sound of PA system.*] Hilliard, can you hear me?

DAN. Get him out of here! [DAN *un-locks and opens front door.*]

CHUCK. I flubbed it, didn't I?

DAN. [*Stepping out, waves off.*] Hold fire out there!

RALPHIE. [*In bedroom above—as* GLENN *grabs him and holds him in front of him-self as a shield.*] Dad! Dad!

DAN. [*As he and* ELEANOR *get* CHUCK *to door.*] Get this boy some help.

CHUCK. [*Faintly.*] I . . . I couldn't do anything else, I . . .

DAN. [*Taking the pistol from his hand.*] You won't need this, son.

ELEANOR. [*Urgently, as she goes out with* CHUCK.] Ralphie!

DAN. [*Firmly.*] Ralphie's all right! [ELEANOR *and* CHUCK *go out door.* DAN *turns, looking at pistol he has taken from* CHUCK. *He leaves the front door open wide.*]

GLENN. [*Calling.*] I'm with him, Hil-liard.

RALPHIE. Dad . . . are you coming?

DAN. [*Puts pistol in his pocket, turns to stairs; speaks with grim determina-tion.*] I'm coming, son!

GLENN. In here, Hilliard. [*As* DAN *en-ters bedroom.*] I'm still gonna make it . . . still gonna pull it off. [*As* DAN *stops.*] You're gonna get me outta this.

DAN. [*Firmly, tonelessly.*] Let go of the boy, Griffin.

GLENN. Fat chance, them coppers out there!

BARD'S VOICE. [*Over PA.*] Griffin . . . Come out with your hands up . . . No gun! [DAN *steps to window, opens it, calls out.*]

DAN. Stay out of here. Turn off the light! [*The floodlights go out.* DAN *turns to* GLENN.] Now. Take your hands off him. [GLENN *does so, but places the gun at back of* RALPHIE'S *neck.*]

GLENN. You move, kid, I'll blow your head off.

DAN. [*Gently, urgently.*] Ralph . . . listen to me. That man is not going to hurt you.

GLENN. Try budgin', kid, you'll find out.

DAN. He's not going to hurt you at all because . . .

GLENN. Lay off, my head's bustin', Hank's waitin', lay off . . .

DAN. Ralph . . . have I ever lied to you? [RALPHIE *shakes his head.*]

GLENN. [*Gun against* RALPHIE'S *neck.*] Feel that? . . .

DAN. [*To* RALPHIE.] Now—I want you to do exactly as I tell you. Because that gun is not loaded.

GLENN. Stop bluffin', Hilliard, and let's get . . .

DAN. It has no bullets in it, Ralph. Do you understand that? [RALPHIE *nods.*]

GLENN. You're lyin'! You wouldn't've brung it in here if . . .

DAN. [*Stepping slightly, to clear the way; shouts.*] Run! [*Without hesitation,* RALPHIE *obeys. He runs . . . fast. He goes out of the bedroom, down the stairs and out the front door. As he starts,* GLENN *pulls the trigger of the revolver. There is a click.* GLENN *is astonished. Then, he tries again and again. A dazed bleak horror mounts* GLENN'S *face. He starts for* DAN, *raising the gun to strike him. The sound of an ambulance siren is heard starting up and fading in the distance.* DAN *brings out* CHUCK'S *pistol and holds it pointed at* GLENN.]

GLENN. [*As he starts to strike* DAN.] You goddam . . . [*He breaks off, staring at the pistol in* DAN'S *hand, incredulous. Long pause.*]

DAN. Why don't you say something, Griffin? Clickety-clickety-click. [*Steps closer.*] You're not talking. Where's your voice now? *Call me Pop.* Say something, *damn you!*

GLENN. It ain't gonna be like this . . . Hank's waitin' . . .

DAN. [*Almost brutally.*] Griffin . . . your brother's not waiting anywhere. He's dead! [GLENN *is glassy-eyed, stunned.*] Full of police bullets. *Dead!*

GLENN. [*Suddenly wild.*] You're lyin', I don't believe . . . you're lyin'!!

DAN. You did that, too, damn you. . . . *Damn you!* [*The life goes out of* GLENN. *He swings full circle now . . . back to the stunned, depressed, lifeless phase of earlier in the evening. Despair . . . and worse. From now on he has no desire to survive. What follows is the death-wish all the way . . . finally erupting in his attempt to goad* DAN *into killing.*]

DAN. It's your turn, Griffin . . . how do you like it?

GLENN. [*Bleakly.*] Go ahead . . . [*Lifelessly.*] Get it over with. . . .

DAN. You don't like waiting? I've waited for hours . . . all of us . . . like years . . . all night . . . two days . . .

GLENN. Get it over with! [*He senses the hesitation in* DAN, *changes his tactics shrewdly.*] You ain't got it in you!

DAN. [*Low, hard.*] I've got it in me. *You* put it there!

GLENN. [*Goading.*] Then go ahead!

BARD'S VOICE. [*On the PA.*] Hilliard, can you hear me? . . . Your wife's here. And the boy. They're both safe! [*Pause.* GLENN *and* DAN *are both staring.*]

GLENN. You ain't got it in you! [DAN *tenses with the revolver pointed at* GLENN. *Then, suddenly realizing what he has almost done, he lowers the gun, relieved.*]

DAN. [*Quietly.*] You're right. [*Low— with disgust.*] Thank God, you're right! [*Quietly—with great dignity.*] Get out of my house. [*Then he steps to* GLENN *and slaps him a resounding, violent blow across the face.*] Get out of my house! [GLENN *is staggered by the blow. He recoils. There is a pause while* GLENN *cowers, rubbing his jaw. Then,* GLENN *begins muttering, dazed.*]

GLENN. [*His voice whining . . . self-pity . . . a boy again.*] I'm gettin' out, Pop . . . I'm goin'. Only I'm takin' Hank along. You hit me for the last goddam time. . . . You ain't ever gonna hit Hank or me again. [*He moves toward the bedroom door as* DAN *steps out of his way.*] I'm takin' Hank along and you ain't gonna see either one of us ever again! [*He turns in the upstairs hall and shouts back at* DAN *in the bedroom.*] You can sit here'n rot in your stinkin' house, Mister God! I hated this crummy joint the day I was born! [GLENN *turns and starts down the stairs as* DAN *follows him to the bedroom door.*]

DAN. [*In amazement; weary disgust.*] Get out.

GLENN. [*On his way downstairs.*] You ain't gonna beat it into Hank'n me! Hank'n me's gonna be right on top! [GLENN, *now at the foot of the stairs, pauses, looks around, still dazed.* DAN *follows him down the stairs, pauses on lower step.* GLENN *turns toward the open door, beckoning to an imaginary* HANK.] C'mon, Hank . . . we'll show 'em! [*The floodlights come on outside as* GLENN *steps in the doorway brandishing the gun. He goes out of sight, shouting.*]

We'll show 'em, Hank, we'll show 'em, Hank, we'll . . . [*A rifle shot is heard, echoing down the quiet street.* DAN *stands quietly on the stairs. . . . Lights remain on in Hilliard home.*]

THE WALLINGS' ATTIC: *Lights rise on the attic.* BARD *is lowering the rifle. He looks at* CARSON *a moment, a strange expression on his face.*

CARSON. [*Almost reassuringly.*] He asked for it, Jess. He . . . he acted like he was begging for it. [BARD *looks at the rifle, then places it against the wall; slowly sits on the box.*]

CARSON. You going over there?

BARD. [*Softly.*] In a little while.

CARSON. You feel all right, Jess?

BARD. Just . . . maybe a little disgusted with the human race.

CARSON. Mmmm. Including Hilliard?

BARD. [*Looks up at him, smiles wanly.*] Thanks, Harry. . . . No, *not* including Hilliard.

CARSON. World's full of Hilliards. [CARSON *turns and goes down the attic stairs.* BARD *sits quietly, thinking . . . as the lights fade slowly on the attic scene. In the Hilliard home,* DAN *still stands unmoving on the stairs.* ELEANOR *appears at front door; she looks stunned, worn. She gazes at the havoc that was her home. She moves slowly to the sofa, almost helplessly rearranges a pillow.* RALPHIE *enters behind her; he crosses to* DAN, *whose head is down;* RALPHIE *stands gazing at his father. . . . Outside,* CINDY *appears and enters the pantry, disappears into kitchen a moment. As* CINDY *enters the living room from dining room,* DAN *lifts his head, looks at her; then, slowly, he turns his gaze on* ELEANOR. *Their eyes meet, hold. They stand looking at each other as though cognizant of the miracle . . . as though seeing in each other, and perhaps in the world, more than words could convey. Dimout.*]

SLOW CURTAIN

SEVERAL ASPECTS OF A COMPLEX PROBLEM

Joseph Hayes

Because of the limitations of space, it is impossible to discuss here all of the complex aspects of converting a narrative into a drama. For the sake of discussion, then, let us limit ourselves to the manner in which a dramatist takes some of the materials of a novel and converts them into the dynamic terms of the theatre.

The basic concept of the novel, *The Desperate Hours*—on which it depends for a large portion of its effect—is counterpoint action. What occurs on the street of the town, let's say, affects what will happen in the house, and only the reader, not the involved characters, realizes this; therefore, the reader's sense of suspension, the onward rush of his emotional suspense, is heightened. Since the novel was written as novel and with no intention of its becoming a stage play, the author was faced with a staggering technical problem: how to allow the theatre audience to share in this anxious uncertainty by revealing to him dynamically all that occurs outside the invaded home? To solve this problem it was necessary to create an unusual stage set which would allow audience focus to shift from house to sheriff's office, so that the facts and emotions revealed in the one (the sheriff's office) would intensify the suspense of what might happen next in the house. Having accomplished this, in concept at least, the author was then faced with the problem of revealing, in dialog and action, within the limits of a small stage-set, all of the important action that occurred all over the city in the novel: the killing of the trashman, the finding of the license-number, the narrowing down to a neighborhood, the death of Hank and its consequences, etc. What's more, these revelations must take place in a dynamic scene, not as simple exposition. It would be interesting to trace here all of the outside events which are revealed in the sheriff's office and the manner of their revelation, and to discuss the ways in which these scenes build the audience's tension in regard to the plight of the trapped family. (If anyone should care to do this, he might also be interested in analyzing the character of Jesse Bard and the manner in which his personality, his own fears, and his earlier involvement with Glenn Griffin, all enter into the state of uncertainty as to what will happen if and when the police get to the house.)

The problem of "exposition" in the theatre is a complex one, and certain rules apply. For instance, it is not permissible to state to a character something which that character would ordinarily know simply because it is necessary to give this information to an audience. Further, all information must be couched in dialog-terms, words and sentences that the character would normally speak; if possible, these words should have an *intrinsic* character interest because character as well as information is being absorbed by an audience in those first minutes of a play. A chemical blending, so complete that an audience is not aware of absorbing any "exposition" as such, is the ideal—so that the audience will settle back, but not relax, in a mood which allows the unconscious inner voice of each spectator to murmur, "Yes, I see; this is the way it is. The set, the people—they are all true. I am interested." This comes first. In other words, by the time the first few minutes have elapsed, each member of the audience should forget technicalities, make-up, lights, set, "actors," and should give himself over to the *events* occurring on the stage as though he were witnessing and taking part in something actual and spontaneous that is occurring for the first time in the history of man. In a realistic play, this then is the ideal.

The novel opens with the three escapees emerging from the woods, approaching a farmhouse, knocking out a farmer, stealing his car. We have only a hint at the personalities of the three, but we get a visual picture and a mood has been created. The next scene in the novel reveals Deputy Sheriff Jesse Webb (his name was changed in the play to Bard) being awakened in his home; he receives word of the escape and he tells his wife what has happened while he urgently dresses to leave. The revenge motive is hinted at, and at the same time certain "expository" information is given:

> Jesse Webb, of the Marion County Sheriff's office, himself in charge this entire week because his superior, Sheriff Masters, had gone to South Carolina on a combined extradition case and hunting trip, turned to his wife in the doorway and explained why he thought, or hoped, that Glenn Griffin would come to Indianapolis. In the first place, he said, you had to bank on the homing-pigeon instinct in the criminal mind: a familiar town, even if their faces are known in it, gives them the illusion of security. They always think they know where to hide, although today all such rat holes would be turned inside out by nightfall. Then, too, there was the woman, name of Helen Lamar; she was thirty-five at least, ten years older than Glenn Griffin himself, but important to him. And Jesse had a hunch she had the money.

The information packed into this brief scene in the novel is spread throughout the early section of the play. Jesse's urgency, revealed previous to the quoted paragraph, erupts definitely and dynamically throughout the first scene of the play—not only in dialog ("Why didn't you call me?" and "Yeah, he's the one—") but also in action: the telephone call to Lt. Fredericks, the barked orders, all climaxed in theatrical terms by the FBI turning the conduct of the case over to Jesse. The fact that Sheriff Masters is away is revealed in the play in "expository" dialog that loses the "expository" ring due to the fact that, naturally, the FBI man has contacted the superior and also due to Jesse's bitter reply, which reveals as much about Jesse and his personality as it does about the situation, "He sure picked a fine time to leave me in charge here." In later scenes of the play, Jesse's conviction that Glenn Griffin will come to Indianapolis—only a thought in the exposition paragraph of the novel—has been intensified into a driving force, until (page 110 of the published play) Lt. Fredericks says, "Deputy, you got a obsession." The fact that the woman (Helen Lamar in the novel, Helen Laski in the play) would be the "beacon that'll lead us straight" becomes a dynamic factor in the play, and in the same exchange of dialog Lt. Fredericks reveals that already the search has begun. The restrained "today all such rat holes would be turned inside out by nightfall" (in the novel) becomes (in the play) the laconic but much more visual and dramatic "The city police've ripped whole buildings apart. We got the highways blocked. We're working through all the dives." Then, Jesse's reply, revealing the crafty intelligence of Glenn Griffin, is a compact statement of the information that comes, in the novel, in the following scene.

In this scene Robish, Hank, and Glenn are cruising along in the stolen gray sedan, which plays such an important part in the later sections of the play. In the novel this scene serves to reveal Glenn's shrewdness, which comes out in the scene in the play *after* they have entered the house and have established themselves. (In that scene Glenn says, "Came aroun' their roadblocks like we was flyin' a airplane"— proving Jesse's point that no roadblock'll stop Glenn. But in the play it was necessary to establish the threat of Glenn's intelligence *before* this—which explains why Jesse was given the attitude of respect for Glenn's intelligence in his dialog.) The cruising scene in the novel reads, in part:

"You're going south," Robish was complaining in a heavy but querulous voice. "Indianapolis is northeast."

"I'm going southeast now," Glenn Griffin said easily, and the words leaped and flickered in that laughter that now colored every word he spoke and filled the car with an exultancy that moved like warmth over Hank in the back seat.

"Didn't you say Lamar was in Indianapolis? With the dough."

"She moved away last week. To Pittsburgh. If they can't locate her in Indianapolis, it'll take the heat off. They won't locate her."

"Where the hell we heading then?"

"Indianapolis," Glenn said quietly, mocking the man beside him, with the laughter still in his tone. "I got some business there, remember? But we're not walking into a roadblock from the west, pal. We'll circle all the way around and come in from the northeast some time this afternoon."

"Then what?"

"Then we'll find us a cozy spot. And I'll contact Helen."

"A cozy spot—like where?"

"You name it, Robish. Only no hangouts, see. They'll be watching all of them. No hotels, either. Pick a nice quiet house on a nice quiet street on the edge of town, say, with no other houses close by. Make it a big place, though, with soft furniture. Comfortable, scared people—a sucker who goes to work every day, maybe a kid in the family. Some place to take the stir-taste out of our mouths."

"Then what?"

"We wait."

"How long?"

"Till Helen gets there from Pittsburgh, P.A. Now shut up, Robish, let a guy enjoy his freedom."

In the back seat Hank heard Robish swear under his breath. Hank had to hand it to Glenn: he could certainly handle Robish. First, Robish had growled that they had to ditch the prison clothes; Glenn wouldn't listen. He'd get him clothes when he needed them—good clothes. Meanwhile, stay down. And then Robish had complained about not carrying a gun: it made him feel helpless. What if they ran into a roadblock? They wouldn't, Glenn had said, because nobody ever heard of these roads. As for the gun, they couldn't afford to pull a job and tip off their whereabouts; besides, Glenn had one, didn't he? A .38 revolver, taken from the guard who was now in the prison infirmary with a bump on his head, if nothing worse. Relax, Robish, and enjoy yourself.

But Hank was not relaxed. He was looking ahead. And he was picturing a house such as Glenn had described. After the clank of locks, the smooth mechanical sound of cell doors closing, the hard stiffness of concrete floors and metal bunks, he was imagining sinking down again into a deep soft chair, his feet planted on deep-tufted carpet, the warm and intimate reality of ordinary walls with framed pictures on them. As yet even the crisp, cold air that penetrated the closed windows of the sedan had not reached the valleys of memory where the harsh iron-tasting odor of the last two years still lingered like stench from a swamp. But in a house like that, he said to himself . . .

Now this scene firmly established what they are going to do, so that when we move from it into the Hilliard home in the novel we already have a sense of anticipation, knowing that this is the house which they will take over. In the play version much of the information in this novel scene emerges *after* they have established themselves in the house. Still, it is necessary to form a bridge between their intent and the Hilliard family when we are introduced to the Hilliard family in the play. So it is that Jesse half-glimpses the awful potentialities in his transition line, "Just as long's Glenn Griffin's running around free and safe—with that prison guard's .38 in his paw—well, it's not free or safe for anyone else. No decent people anywhere—whether they've ever heard of Glenn Griffin or not."

(The novel scene quoted above also contains many other elements essential to understanding the complex situation: Hank's dependence on Glenn, the fact that only Glenn has a gun, the sluggish but menacing mind of a rebellious Robish, and Hank's attitude toward such a house as the Hilliards'. In the stage version we *see* Hank sinking into a comfortable chair; we *hear* him comment on the carpet. "I don't care if we never leave," he says. The quoted novel scene contains the basic information about the plot revolving around Helen Lamar (Laski). Presumably, in life, Glenn would have told Hank this scheme in prison. For the purposes of the novel, he tells him in the car; for the purposes of the play, he explains in the house after they have arrived. In either case, the time at which this information is revealed to Hank does not cause the audience to question the probability of it simply because, in both instances, the audience is too caught up in the action and emotion by then to ask such a question and also because the audience has learned, even that early, to accept *character:* the kind of person Glenn is and Hank's dependence on him, so that Glenn does not feel obliged to explain to him until he, Glenn, wishes to do so. . . . There are other elements in the scene quoted from the novel which emerge in different context in the play, but space does not permit a thorough analysis.)

When we move into the Hilliard home, in both the novel and play, we know that this house is to be invaded. This emotional awareness overlies the scene. In the novel we see, first, the house and its location, an important element. Then we meet the family as they come downstairs for breakfast:

As Dan came down the stairs at 7:40 on this particular Wednesday morning, he was trying to look ahead to the complicated problems of the day at the office rather than give in to the nagging uncertainty, almost anxiety, he had begun to feel about his daughter, Cindy. Not that he had anything personal or in particular against Charles Wright. Perhaps, he chided himself, only a banked-down sort of envy. Dan had had to work for everything he had ever made, every cent. This house itself was evidence of how long and how hard. Without an education past the second year in high school, he had come to this. And he was proud—a hard pride that was compounded of a personal sense of accomplishment and of gratitude. Charles Wright, on the other hand, was not the sort of young man with whom Dan could ever feel comfortable. Chuck —as Cindy had come to call him after going to work as secretary in the law office where young Wright was already a junior partner—had had it all handed to him, everything easy. Fine. He was lucky. But he was also, Dan knew from hearsay and from certain knowledge, an irresponsible young man, more interested in fast sports cars, beautiful girls, and long, wine-drenched parties than in finding a solid place for himself in the life of the community. Very well, then, Dan was acting like a typical father, or as Cindy had chided, "a conservative old fogy."

In the kitchen the day's routine had begun almost an hour before. Ralphie, who dawdled over breakfast as though it were some sort of punishment for past crimes, was glaring at a half-full glass of milk. He looked up when Dan doubled up a huge freckled fist and placed the knuckles lightly against the soft ten-year-old cheek. Eleanor, whose face was rounded like her son's and who had passed along to him also her light-colored hair, smiled and placed Dan's steaming ham and eggs before him, then sat down across from him, at the kitchen table. Without make-up, she looked like a child herself, small and still slender.

"Lucille is sick," she announced, explaining the absence of the maid who usually came on Wednesdays and Saturdays.

"Again?" Dan said. "Any gin missing?"

Eleanor frowned and shook her head in swift wifely warning, nodding to Ralphie, who lifted his eyes from the milk and grinned knowingly. "She's probably blotto," he said sagely.

"Where does he learn his language?" Dan inquired.

"Comic books," Eleanor said, buttering toast. "Television. Do you know what blotto means, Ralphie?"

"My name," Ralphie announced, punctuating each word with a click of his glass on the table, "is Ralph. R-a-l-p-h. There's no y on the end of it."

"Sorry, old fellow," Dan said.

"And blotto means tight. Tight means drunk. Have I drunk enough milk?"

Eleanor was laughing, behind her napkin, and nodding. Ralphie was up, jarring the table, kissing his mother's hair swiftly; then he turned grave eyes on Dan and gave him a swift salute, half defiance and half apology, and turned on his heel.

"I'll ride my bike. I've got a whole half-hour, almost." He disappeared onto the rear porch, clumped down the three steps and was gone. Dan heard the garage door sliding up and was reminded again that he had to oil the runner mechanism soon.

Eleanor said, "Our son Ralph, spelled R-a-l-p-h, is too old to kiss a man—that's you —good-bye or good night."

"Well," Dan said wryly, but feeling a pinch somewhere inside, "that seems to be that."

"A milepost," Eleanor said, her eyes on him steadily now, studying him.

"We seem to be flying past mileposts darned fast, old girl," he said.

What Eleanor saw was a man of average height with heavy shoulders, the bulk of his body fitting finely under the double-breasted suit; she looked into the familiar deep blue eyes and was conscious of the mahogany-red hair above and the freckles climbing over and across the rather broad nose and the deep fine lines that added, she thought, so much character to an otherwise very ordinary but very appealing face.

Reading his mind, she said, "Cindy'd like to ask him for Thanksgiving dinner, Dan."

Dan downed the last swallow of coffee, stood up, yanked at his suit coat like a boy dressed for a party and determined to impress.

"Should she?" Eleanor asked.

Dan shrugged, but not successfully. "Ellie, I don't want to jump in and start opposing this thing and get Cindy's back up. But—well, Thanksgiving's a sort of family day."

Eleanor lifted her face for his kiss, then walked to the kitchen window while Dan went out the rear door, his topcoat thrown over his arm instead of over his shoulders.

When she opened the window, the gusty warning of winter swept through the kitchen. She watched from an angle as Dan backed the blue car out of the garage, maneuvering it around Cindy's black coupe in the driveway. Then, for absolutely no reason at all except that it was a ritual between them, meaning at the same time more and less than the word itself, she called, "Careful. And I mean it."

His hat pulled at its usual not quite proper angle, Dan shouted back, "Close the window," and swept out of her line of vision.

Eleanor complied, as she did every morning, five days a week. She never caught colds, and Dan knew this, just as she knew that there was no particular reason for him to be careful. Careful of what?

As she set a fresh place for Cindy, Eleanor decided against mentioning Chuck Wright this morning, especially in view of Dan's unspoken rejection of the Thanks-giving-dinner idea. All the words that occurred to her seemed stereotyped and flat, anyway—that Chuck Wright had a reputation for being wild, that he was the type that would never settle down. Cindy would only reply again, from the summit of nineteen years, that you could blame the war for that, hinting at some great tragedy and dramatic feat that, if known, would explain Charles Wright completely and utterly and make him totally acceptable in every far corner of the land.

Eleanor flipped on the radio, punching the buttons one after the other, finally set-tling for a news report as she prepared to drink her second cup of coffee.

After listening for perhaps five minutes—her attention not caught by the report of three escaped convicts in Terre Haute or attracted by the warning that these men were armed and dangerous—she heard Cindy descending the uncarpeted back stairs that only the family used, her heels a quick tattoo. Eleanor turned off the radio and set down her cup. As soon as Cindy was out of the house, Eleanor's own day would really begin.

In the play version of the corresponding scene, it becomes necessary to create, in dialog, a certain mood, revealing the characters in a completely dif-ferent manner, really. The information conveyed in this scene—that Cindy is in love with a young lawyer of whom her father does not approve and that Dan is a self-made, hard-working executive—is really not important. What is important in the theatre version is that this family create a "typical" morning, so that an audience can smile and *identify*. This sense of identification is the essential key to the scene: the dramatist in this case must engage the audience's complete sympathy. What better way than to concentrate on the seemingly trivial little universal things that occur in most households on an ordinary morning? To do this, it is good to add a touch of humor here and there, re-membering here that *the audience knows that a certain fate awaits these people*. Unless, in this scene, the dramatist and the actors succeed in engaging the sympathy of the audience for these people, the total emotional balance of the play that follows is destroyed, and therefore the desired effect. A study of the scene in the play, relative to the above quoted scene from the novel, should be interesting in terms less of "exposition" than in terms of audience-sympathy.

No brief discussion of this sort could possibly cover the complex detailed elements which enter into the dramatization of a novel. For instance, "exposi-tion" in terms of the revelation of character continues to the final curtain; the necessary elimination of incidents imposes the necessity for exploring and exploiting new values, some only hinted at in the novel (the relationship of Glenn and his own father, for instance, and the deepened character conflict between Glenn and Dan Hilliard, and many others); interior struggles have to be externalized, dramatized (within Dan, within Hank, within Jesse, whose determined personal revenge motive changes into human pity and understanding). All of these—and many other—problems face the "adaptor" of a novel, whether or not he has written the original novel. And in the case of *The Desperate Hours*, both the play and the novel were later converted into screenplay form by the author, another adaptation of the material which imposes its own laws and restrictions. But the samples quoted above should give some small indication of the technical challenges and the manner of their solution.

THE ELEMENT OF THEME: *EVERYMAN*

During the course of his day, the dramatist comes into contact with a variety of forces—with other men, individually and collectively; with his environment, physical and social; with his gods, fates and fortunes, however conceived. These contacts, the pressures exerted on the dramatist by his society, determine his choice of a theme to illuminate his vision of life. Although this vision (if the dramatist be a great one) will finally transcend the particularities of his immediate world, it is clearly conditioned by that world, and the pressures his society brings to bear on him will further suggest a specific *conflict* to embody both vision and theme. Conflict is often said to be the very essence of drama because it operates so centrally in two important areas— one of them fundamental, the other secondary. To begin with the less important, conflict produces those tensions and actions which command and sustain our interest throughout the unfolding of the story. Far more important, conflict dictates the dramatist's arrangement of structural elements—exposition, complication, and climax, for example—in the play of which it is the essential feature.

When we speak, in any context, of "the dramatic," we refer in fact to what is tense and exciting because it involves human clash and struggle; we refer to conflict. With respect to drama (as to life at large), such struggle is not always so simple and uncomplicated as that between Hilliard and Griffin in *The Desperate Hours*. Further, it is generally inaccurate to think of a play as containing only a single conflict; for most dramas, ancient and modern, involve several minor conflicts in addition to the central one; for example (as we have seen), the struggle between Griffin and the sheriff complements, and comments on, that between the convict and Hilliard. But conflict of some sort— between persons antipathetic, between warring ideas, or, again, between an individual and his society—lies at the base of all drama; even the broadest farce is based finally on a clash of opposed persons, and every serious play can be considered as an objectification of its author's view of life as revealed in human struggle.

The presentation of the author's chosen conflict is the primary function of dramatic structure. Structure serves as an architectural framework, and all its elements will be deliberately and thoughtfully arranged to accommodate the particular forces of conflict in each drama. The arrangement of these elements, then, will vary, not only from author to author, but from play to play. The proportions of exposition and complication, the placement of crisis and climax, the complexity of the *dénouement*—these problems can be solved only in the light of each drama's specific demands, and these demands are determined by the nature of the conflict which the author has selected to represent his view of man's condition.

The view of life in *Everyman* is readily definable; it is doubtful if any dramatist's has ever been more so. In this nameless medieval writer's vision, life is a journey to the grave, and his play reveals to us how central to fifteenth century man was the search for the pathway to salvation. Its very centrality as a universal concern presented the author with his theme—salvation as the only thinkable goal of man's life; such a theme then demanded a particular conflict—between the idea of the good life and the idea of the evil life; and this choice, in turn—once made—dictated the drama's structure. The progress which has just been traced, however, from the general to the more particular, from social pressure to the dramatist's vision, to theme, conflict, and structure, is actually a reconstruction possible to us because of our familiarity with historical information and with this particular drama. As we increase our skill in the reading of plays we will see that this same process must often be turned about, for structure is one of the keys to an interpretation of the dramatist's vision. *Everyman*'s "journey-structure" leads us to understand the play's conflict, and this understanding, in turn, will lead us finally to the author's theme and vision.

Because it focuses attention on forces familiar and easy to understand, the kind of conflict most readily apprehended is that between two individuals: wary of complication, humanity is generally happy to see life's problems reduced to a clash between recognizable personalities, for problems so seen are likely to appear both comprehensible and manageable. *The Desperate Hours* presents this simple kind of conflict, between a "good" protagonist (Daniel Hilliard) and an "evil" antagonist (Glenn Griffin). That is, the play offers a main character whose motives and actions provide a center of interest in the story, and a second character with whom he comes into active conflict. But why is it that we call Hilliard, and not Griffin, the "main character"? To be sure, in so simple a contest between good and evil, we instinctively identify ourselves with the "good" character. But instinct is not always trustworthy in answering such questions. As Hayes has plotted his story, Griffin is important *only because* his aims come into violent conflict with Hilliard's. The threat he represents has no intrinsic value in this particular structure; it has significance only in relation to its possible effects on the Hilliard family. Hence, in a consideration of the structure (or the plotting) of this play, our abhorrence of Griffin and our sympathy with Hilliard are virtually irrelevant matters. It is not Hilliard's "goodness" that defines him as Hayes's protagonist, but rather his centrality in the play's structure. This structure frames his motives and actions in such a way as to place him, and keep him, in the center of the picture; and it forces into subsidiary positions all other motives and actions, including Griffin's, allowing them significance only as they relate to those of the central figure. Obviously Hayes might have told a different story in which Griffin, for all his evil, would have been the protagonist; but such a story would also evolve from a different concept of society, would call for a different conflict, and therefore a different structure.

Though *The Desperate Hours* takes into account all three of the fundamental sources of dramatic interest—theme and character, as well as action—it is nevertheless a melodrama, owing to its emphasis on violent action. There is no doubt where Hayes's chief interest lies. His concern *centers*, clearly enough, not in subtle characterization or a message of universal applicability, but in a story of mounting tension. In the drama that follows—*Everyman*—the author's interest (and our own) no longer resides in action, but in the *meaning of action*. This medieval Morality Play testifies that an author's emphasis may fall on elements other than story. And when the emphasis falls on theme, as it does in *Everyman*, it is clear that the conflict employed will have to be developed on somewhat different grounds. Dominant concern for thematic values indicates a dominant interest in ideas, and *The Summoning of Everyman* (to give this drama its full title) dramatizes the clash, not between characters, but between two ways of life: between the road to salvation and the road to damnation, between the life of righteousness and holy seeking and the life of sinfulness and vice. And because the conflict is between ideas, or attitudes, or ways of life, rather than between individuals, our response to *The Summoning of Everyman* differs inevitably from our response to Hayes's melodrama.

For example, the fact that the outcome is here immediately foreseeable does not, surprisingly, cause us to lose interest in reading this medieval play. For our interest is quickened and sustained, in *Everyman*, by quite different stimuli. Suspense plays no real part here. Nor are the dramatist's characters so compellingly individualized that we are drawn to them by interest or sympathy. A glance at their names indicates how completely lacking they are in particularized personalities: Death, Good Deeds, Knowledge, Fellowship. Even the protagonist is, after all, only Every Man. The reader's interest is captured, not by rousing events or compelling characters, but by the meaning of the events, and by the intensity with which the play unfolds that meaning. It is the *theme* of *Everyman* which quickens and finally focuses our attention. And that theme is most forcefully conveyed to us in the final climactic scene before Everyman's grave, since the author's dramatic structure reproduces his vision of life as a journey toward Death.

Again, however, the reader will be mistaken if he assumes, because of this obvious didactic emphasis and thematically dominated structure, that there is neither characterization nor action in the play. He should notice, for example, the careful delineation of the protagonist as he develops from libertine to penitent; or the variety of differentiating excuses—some of them comic—offered by Everyman's companions for their abandonment of him; or, again, the differences in character implicit in the final speeches of Beauty, Strength, Discretion, and Five Wits. And with regard to action, the reader should recognize that the incidents have been arranged to provide a series of climaxes and periods of mounting and diminishing tension.

In sum, although the dramatist's vision looks beyond the immediate limits of his own society, it arises inevitably out of the tensions and problems and conflicting values of that society. Feeling himself compelled to communicate his interpretation of man's condition, he discovers a particular conflict, of men or ideas, to embody his vision, for he tends to see life as conflict. His choice of a conflict, then, determines the structure of his drama, and simultaneously, the center of the audience's response: various types of conflict engender varying sorts of interest. But it is evident that, whatever the dramatist's emphasis, he must give attention ultimately to all the elements fundamental to his medium, the drama.

Still another point needs to be made, with specific reference to the drama that follows. A play in which emphasis falls on theme demands more of both audience and reader than one emphasizing action, for here the conflict cannot be revealed so simply nor the interest held by obvious theatrical devices. And yet there are at least four good reasons why *The Summoning of Everyman*, which surpasses all other English Morality Plays, remains today a stirring drama. The first of these is that its theme transcends its origins in the troubled heart of medieval man; its concern for the right choice of a way of life is eternally relevant. A second reason is that the nameless author is a far sounder dramatist than his fellows in this genre, and his soundness shows conspicuously in his rejection of certain generally accepted conventions: for example, though *Everyman*, like other Moralities, centers on the journey toward Death, its author repudiates the convention of showing us that journey complete from cradle to grave. His choice of a starting point at the moment of crisis—with the approach of Death—insures both tension and concentration. Thirdly, the author has resisted a second convention, the inclusion of low-comedy episodes popular with the medieval audience but distractingly irrelevant and prevailingly vulgar,[1] and the rejection of this second convention contributes likewise to the drama's concentration, while it also guarantees the dignity appropriate to so great a theme. And finally, *Everyman* surpasses other plays of its kind because the author, employing familiar abstractions as his characters, nevertheless invests those abstractions with enough warmth of humanity to make them distinct from one another; because of his success in this respect, he brings his great theme down from its high level of abstraction and underscores its human relevance to every reader or spectator. Throughout the Western world, *Everyman* continues to be performed in the middle of the twentieth century; what more conclusive evidence could one ask of its enduring power to move?

A good rousing melodrama may hold us spellbound—while it lasts; but its hold, like its excitement, is of the moment and hardly survives a first reading. But no-one is likely to forget the heartwarming salutation that Knowledge proffers to the distressed medieval hero: "Everyman, I will go with thee and be thy guide." For Knowledge here is not mere knowledge of books and the world; this is the knowledge that answers, in the name of Christianity, the ultimate question of life: inevitable but unaccountable Death. Whether *Everyman*'s answer squares in all particulars with our own, it yet affords us immediate contact with man's central experience.

[1] A clear and readily available example of catering to this medieval taste is to be found in the *Second Shepherd's Play*.

Everyman

HERE BEGINNETH *a treatise how the high father of heaven sendeth death to summon every creature to come and give account of their lives in this world, and is in manner of a moral play.*

Characters

GOD
MESSENGER
DEATH
EVERYMAN
FELLOWSHIP
KINDRED
COUSIN
GOODS
GOOD DEEDS
KNOWLEDGE
CONFESSION
BEAUTY
STRENGTH
DISCRETION
FIVE WITS
ANGEL
DOCTOR

MESSENGER. I pray you all give your audience,
And hear this matter with reverence,
By figure a moral play:
The *Summoning of Everyman* called it is,
That of our lives and ending shows
How transitory we be all day.
This matter is wondrous precious,
But the intent of it is more gracious,
And sweet to bear away.
The story saith: Man, in the beginning
Look well, and take good heed to the ending,
Be you never so gay!
Ye think sin in the beginning full sweet,
Which in the end causeth the soul to weep,
When the body lieth in clay.
Here shall you see how Fellowship and Jollity,
Both Strength, Pleasure, and Beauty,
Will fade from thee as flower in May;
For ye shall hear how our Heaven King
Calleth Everyman to a general reckoning:
Give audience, and hear what he doth say. [*Exit.*]

[GOD *speaketh.*]

GOD. I perceive, here in my majesty,
How that all creatures be to me unkind,
Living without dread in worldly prosperity:
Of ghostly sight the people be so blind,
Drowned in sin, they know me not for their God;
In worldly riches is all their mind,
They fear not my righteousness, the sharp rod.
My law that I showed, when I for them died,
They forget clean, and shedding of my blood red;
I hanged between two, it cannot be denied;
To get them life I suffered to be dead;
I healed their feet, with thorns hurt was my head.
I could do no more than I did, truly;
And now I see the people do clean forsake me:
They use the seven deadly sins damnable,
As pride, covetise, wrath, and lechery
Now in the world be made commendable;

83

And thus they leave of angels the heavenly company.
Every man liveth so after his own pleasure,
And yet of their life they be nothing sure:
I see the more that I them forbear
The worse they be from year to year.
All that liveth appaireth fast;
Therefore I will, in all the haste,
Have a reckoning of every man's person;
For, and I leave the people thus alone
In their life and wicked tempests,
Verily they will become much worse than beasts;
For now one would by envy another up eat;
Charity they do all clean forget.
I hoped well that every man
In my glory should make his mansion,
And thereto I had them all elect;
But now I see, like traitors deject,
They thank me not for the pleasure that I to them meant,
Nor yet for their being that I them have lent.
I proffered the people great multitude of mercy,
And few there be that asketh it heartily.
They be so cumbered with worldly riches
That needs on them I must do justice,
On every man living without fear.
Where art thou, Death, thou mighty messenger?

[Enter DEATH.]

  DEATH. Almighty God, I am here at your will,
Your commandment to fulfil.
  GOD. Go thou to Everyman,
And show him, in my name,
A pilgrimage he must on him take,
Which he in no wise may escape;
And that he bring with him a sure reckoning
Without delay or any tarrying. [GOD *withdraws.*]
  DEATH. Lord, I will in the world go run overall,

And cruelly outsearch both great and small;
Every man will I beset that liveth beastly
Out of God's laws, and dreadeth not folly.
He that loveth riches I will strike with my dart,
His sight to blind, and from heaven to depart—
Except that alms be his good friend—
In hell for to dwell, world without end.
Lo, yonder I see Everyman walking.
Full little he thinketh on my coming;
His mind is on fleshly lusts and his treasure,
And great pain it shall cause him to endure
Before the Lord, Heaven King.

[Enter EVERYMAN.]

Everyman, stand still! Whither art thou going
Thus gaily? Hast thou thy Maker forget?
  EVERYMAN. Why askest thou?
Wouldest thou wit?
  DEATH. Yea, sir; I will show you:
In great haste I am sent to thee
From God out of his majesty.
  EVERYMAN. What, sent to me?
  DEATH. Yea, certainly.
Though thou have forget him here,
He thinketh on thee in the heavenly sphere,
As, ere we depart, thou shalt know.
  EVERYMAN. What desireth God of me?
  DEATH. That shall I show thee:
A reckoning he will needs have
Without any longer respite.
  EVERYMAN. To give a reckoning longer leisure I crave;
This blind matter troubleth my wit.
  DEATH. On thee thou must take a long journey;
Therefore thy book of count with thee thou bring,
For turn again thou cannot by no way.
And look thou be sure of thy reckoning,
For before God thou shalt answer, and show

Thy many bad deeds, and good but a
few;
How thou hast spent thy life, and in
what wise,
Before the chief Lord of paradise.
Have ado that we were in that way,
For, wit thou well, thou shalt make none
attorney.
EVERYMAN. Full unready I am such
reckoning to give.
I know thee not. What messenger art
thou?
DEATH. I am Death, that no man
dreadeth,
For every man I rest, and no man spar-
eth;
For it is God's commandment
That all to me should be obedient.
EVERYMAN. O Death, thou comest
when I had thee least in mind!
In thy power it lieth me to save;
Yet of my good will I give thee, if thou
will be kind:
Yea, a thousand pound shalt thou have,
And defer this matter till another day.
DEATH. Everyman, it may not be, by
no way.
I set not by gold, silver, nor riches,
Ne by pope, emperor, king, duke, ne
princes;
For, and I would receive gifts great,
All the world I might get;
But my custom is clean contrary.
I give thee no respite. Come hence, and
not tarry.
EVERYMAN. Alas, shall I have no longer
respite?
I may say Death giveth no warning!
To think on thee, it maketh my heart
sick,
For all unready is my book of reckon-
ing.
But twelve year and I might have abid-
ing,
My counting-book I would make so
clear
That my reckoning I should not need to
fear.
Wherefore, Death, I pray thee, for God's
mercy,
Spare me till I be provided of remedy.

DEATH. Thee availeth not to cry, weep,
and pray;
But haste thee lightly that thou were
gone that journey,
And prove thy friends if thou can;
For, wit thou well, the tide abideth no
man,
And in the world each living creature
For Adam's sin must die of nature.
EVERYMAN. Death, if I should this pil-
grimage take,
And my reckoning surely make,
Show me, for saint charity,
Should I not come again shortly?
DEATH. No, Everyman; and thou be
once there,
Thou mayst never more come here,
Trust me verily.
EVERYMAN. O gracious God in the
high seat celestial,
Have mercy on me in this most need!
Shall I have no company from this vale
terrestrial
Of mine acquaintance, that way me to
lead?
DEATH. Yea, if any be so hardy
That would go with thee and bear thee
company.
Hie thee that thou were gone to God's
magnificence,
Thy reckoning to give before his pres-
ence.
What, weenest thou thy life is given
thee,
And thy worldly goods also?
EVERYMAN. I had wend so, verily.
DEATH. Nay, nay; it was but lent thee;
For as soon as thou art go,
Another a while shall have it, and then
go therefro,
Even as thou hast done.
Everyman, thou art mad! Thou hast thy
wits five,
And here on earth will not amend thy
life;
For suddenly I do come.
EVERYMAN. O wretched caitiff, whither
shall I flee,
That I might scape this endless sorrow?
Now, gentle Death, spare me till to-
morrow,

That I may amend me
With good advisement.

DEATH. Nay, thereto I will not consent,
Nor no man will I respite;
But to the heart suddenly I shall smite
Without any advisement.
And now out of thy sight I will me hie;
See thou make thee ready shortly,
For thou mayst say this is the day
That no man living may scape away.
[*Exit* DEATH.]

EVERYMAN. Alas, I may well weep
with sighs deep!
Now have I no manner of company
To help me in my journey, and me to
keep;
And also my writing is full unready.
How shall I do now for to excuse me?
I would to God I had never be get!
To my soul a full great profit it had be;
For now I fear pains huge and great.
The time passeth. Lord, help, that all
wrought!
For though I mourn it availeth nought.
The day passeth, and is almost ago;
I wot not well what for to do.
To whom were I best my complaint to
make?
What and I to Fellowship thereof spake,
And showed him of this sudden chance?
For in him is all mine affiance;
We have in the world so many a day
Be good friends in sport and play.
I see him yonder, certainly.
I trust that he will bear me company;
Therefore to him will I speak to ease
my sorrow.
Well met, good Fellowship, and good
morrow!

[FELLOWSHIP *speaketh*.]

FELLOWSHIP. Everyman, good morrow,
by this day!
Sir, why lookest thou so piteously?
If any thing be amiss, I pray thee me say,
That I may help to remedy.

EVERYMAN. Yea, good Fellowship, yea;
I am in great jeopardy.

FELLOWSHIP. My true friend, show to
me your mind;

I will not forsake thee to my life's end,
In the way of good company.

EVERYMAN. That was well spoken, and
lovingly.

FELLOWSHIP. Sir, I must needs know
your heaviness;
I have pity to see you in any distress.
If any have you wronged, ye shall revenged be,
Though I on the ground be slain for
thee—
Though that I know before that I
should die.

EVERYMAN. Verily, Fellowship, gramercy.

FELLOWSHIP. Tush! by thy thanks I set
not a straw.
Show me your grief, and say no more.

EVERYMAN. If I my heart should to you
break,
And then you to turn your mind from
me,
And would not me comfort when ye
hear me speak,
Then should I ten times sorrier be.

FELLOWSHIP. Sir, I say as I will do
indeed.

EVERYMAN. Then be you a good friend
at need:
I have found you true herebefore.

FELLOWSHIP. And so ye shall evermore;
For, in faith, and thou go to hell,
I will not forsake thee by the way.

EVERYMAN. Ye speak like a good
friend; I believe you well.
I shall deserve it, and I may.

FELLOWSHIP. I speak of no deserving,
by this day!
For he that will say, and nothing do,
Is not worthy with good company to go;
Therefore show me the grief of your
mind,
As to your friend most loving and kind.

EVERYMAN. I shall show you how it is:
Commanded I am to go a journey,
A long way, hard and dangerous,
And give a strait count, without delay,
Before the high Judge, Adonai.
Wherefore, I pray you, bear me com-
pany,
As ye have promised, in this journey.

FELLOWSHIP. That is matter indeed.
Promise is duty;
But, and I should take such a voyage on
me,
I know it well, it should be to my pain;
Also it maketh me afeard, certain.
But let us take counsel here as well as
we can,
For your words would fear a strong
man.
EVERYMAN. Why, ye said if I had need
Ye would me never forsake, quick ne
dead,
Though it were to hell, truly.
FELLOWSHIP. So I said, certainly,
But such pleasures be set aside, the sooth
to say;
And also, if we took such a journey,
When should we come again?
EVERYMAN. Nay, never again, till the
day of doom.
FELLOWSHIP. In faith, then will not I
come there! Who hath you these
tidings brought?
EVERYMAN. Indeed, Death was with
me here.
FELLOWSHIP. Now, by God that all
hath bought,
If Death were the messenger,
For no man that is living to-day
I will not go that loath journey—
Not for the father that begat me!
EVERYMAN. Ye promised otherwise,
pardie.
FELLOWSHIP. I wot well I said so, truly;
And yet if thou wilt eat, and drink, and
make good cheer,
Or haunt to women the lusty company,
I would not forsake you while the day
is clear,
Trust me verily.
EVERYMAN. Yea, thereto ye would be
ready!
To go to mirth, solace, and play,
Your mind will sooner apply,
Than to bear me company in my long
journey.
FELLOWSHIP. Now, in good faith, I will
not that way.
But and thou will murder, or any man
kill,

In that I will help thee with a good will.
EVERYMAN. O, that is a simple advice
indeed.
Gentle fellow, help me in my necessity!
We have loved long, and now I need;
And now, gentle Fellowship, remember
me.
FELLOWSHIP. Whether ye have loved
me or no,
By Saint John, I will not with thee go.
EVERYMAN. Yet, I pray thee, take the
labour, and do so much for me
To bring me forward, for saint charity,
And comfort me till I come without the
town.
FELLOWSHIP. Nay, and thou would give
me a new gown,
I will not a foot with thee go;
But, and thou had tarried, I would not
have left thee so.
And as now God speed thee in thy
journey,
For from thee I will depart as fast as I
may.
EVERYMAN. Whither away, Fellowship?
Will thou forsake me?
FELLOWSHIP. Yea, by my fay! To God I
betake thee.
EVERYMAN. Farewell, good Fellowship;
for thee my heart is sore.
Adieu for ever! I shall see thee no more.
FELLOWSHIP. In faith, Everyman, fare-
well now at the ending;
For you I will remember that parting is
mourning. [*Exit* FELLOWSHIP.]
EVERYMAN. Alack! shall we thus depart
indeed—
Ah, Lady, help!—without any more com-
fort?
Lo, Fellowship forsaketh me in my most
need.
For help in this world whither shall I re-
sort?
Fellowship herebefore with me would
merry make,
And now little sorrow for me doth he
take.
It is said, 'In prosperity men friends may
find,
Which in adversity be full unkind.'
Now whither for succour shall I flee,

Sith that Fellowship hath forsaken me?
To my kinsmen I will, truly,
Praying them to help me in my necessity;
I believe that they will do so,
For kind will creep where it may not
go.
I will go say, for yonder I see them.
Where be ye now, my friends and kins-
men?

[*Enter* KINDRED *and* COUSIN.]

KINDRED. Here be we now at your
commandment.
Cousin, I pray you show us your intent
In any wise, and do not spare.
COUSIN. Yea, Everyman, and to us de-
clare
If ye be disposed to go anywhither;
For, wit you well, we will live and die
together.
KINDRED. In wealth and woe we will
with you hold,
For over his kin a man may be bold.
EVERYMAN. Gramercy, my friends and
kinsmen kind.
Now shall I show you the grief of my
mind:
I was commanded by a messenger,
That is a high king's chief officer;
He bade me go a pilgrimage, to my
pain,
And I know well I shall never come
again;
Also I must give a reckoning strait,
For I have a great enemy that hath me in
wait,
Which intendeth me for to hinder.
KINDRED. What account is that which
ye must render?
That would I know.
EVERYMAN. Of all my works I must
show
How I have lived and my days spent;
Also of ill deeds that I have used
In my time, sith life was me lent;
And of all virtues that I have refused.
Therefore, I pray you, go thither with
me
To help to make mine account, for saint
charity.

COUSIN. What, to go thither? Is that the
matter?
Nay, Everyman, I had liefer fast bread
and water
All this five year and more.
EVERYMAN. Alas, that ever I was bore!
For now shall I never be merry,
If that you forsake me.
KINDRED. Ah, sir, what ye be a merry
man!
Take good heart to you, and make no
moan.
But one thing I warn you, by Saint
Anne—
As for me, ye shall go alone.
EVERYMAN. My Cousin, will you not
with me go?
COUSIN. No, by our Lady! I have the
cramp in my toe.
Trust not to me, for, so God me speed,
I will deceive you in your most need.
KINDRED. It availeth not us to tice.
Ye shall have my maid with all my heart;
She loveth to go to feasts, there to be
nice,
And to dance, and abroad to start:
I will give her leave to help you in that
journey,
If that you and she may agree.
EVERYMAN. Now show me the very ef-
fect of your mind:
Will you go with me, or abide behind?
KINDRED. Abide behind? Yea, that will
I, and I may!
Therefore farewell till another day. [*Exit*
KINDRED.]
EVERYMAN. How should I be merry or
glad?
For fair promises men to me make,
But when I have most need they me for-
sake.
I am deceived; that maketh me sad.
COUSIN. Cousin Everyman, farewell
now,
For verily I will not go with you.
Also of mine own an unready reckoning
I have to account; therefore I make
tarrying.
Now God keep thee, for now I go. [*Exit*
COUSIN.]

EVERYMAN. Ah, Jesus, is all come
hereto?
Lo, fair words maketh fools fain;
They promise, and nothing will do, cer-
tain.
My kinsmen promised me faithfully
For to abide with me steadfastly,
And now fast away do they flee:
Even so Fellowship promised me.
What friend were best me of to pro-
vide?
I lose my time here longer to abide.
Yet in my mind a thing there is:
All my life I have loved riches;
If that my Good now help me might,
He would make my heart full light.
I will speak to him in this distress—
Where art thou, my Goods and riches?

[GOODS *speaks from a corner.*]

GOODS. Who calleth me? Everyman?
What! hast thou haste?
I lie here in corners, trussed and piled so
high,
And in chests I am locked so fast,
Also sacked in bags. Thou mayst see with
thine eye
I cannot stir; in packs low I lie.
What would ye have? Lightly me say.
EVERYMAN. Come hither, Goods, in all
the haste thou may,
For of counsel I must desire thee.
GOODS. Sir, and ye in the world have
sorrow or adversity,
That can I help you to remedy shortly.
EVERYMAN. It is another disease that
grieveth me;
In this world it is not, I tell thee so.
I am sent for, another way to go,
To give a strait count general
Before the highest Jupiter of all;
And all my life I have had joy and pleas-
ure in thee,
Therefore, I pray thee, go with me;
For, peradventure, thou mayst before
God Almighty
My reckoning help to clean and purify;
For it is said ever among
That money maketh all right that is
wrong.

GOODS. Nay, Everyman, I sing another
song.
I follow no man in such voyages;
For, and I went with thee,
Thou shouldst fare much the worse for
me;
For because on me thou did set thy mind,
Thy reckoning I have made blotted and
blind,
That thine account thou cannot make
truly;
And that hast thou for the love of me.
EVERYMAN. That would grieve me full
sore,
When I should come to that fearful an-
swer.
Up, let us go thither together.
GOODS. Nay, not so! I am too brittle, I
may not endure;
I will follow no man one foot, be ye sure.
EVERYMAN. Alas, I have thee loved, and
had great pleasure
All my life-days on good and treasure.
GOODS. That is to thy damnation,
without leasing,
For my love is contrary to the love ever-
lasting;
But if thou had me loved moderately
during,
As to the poor to give part of me,
Then shouldst thou not in this dolour be,
Nor in this great sorrow and care.
EVERYMAN. Lo, now was I deceived ere
I was ware,
And all I may wite misspending of
time.
GOODS. What, weenest thou that I am
thine?
EVERYMAN. I had wend so.
GOODS. Nay, Everyman, I say no.
As for a while I was lent thee;
A season thou hast had me in prosperity.
My condition is man's soul to kill;
If I save one, a thousand I do spill.
Weenest thou that I will follow thee?
Nay, not from this world, verily.
EVERYMAN. I had wend otherwise.
GOODS. Therefore to thy soul Goods is
a thief;
For when thou art dead, this is my
guise—

Another to deceive in this same wise
As I have done thee, and all to his soul's
    reprief.
EVERYMAN. O false Goods, cursed may
    thou be,
Thou traitor to God, that hast deceived
    me
And caught me in thy snare!
GOODS. Marry, thou brought thyself in
    care,
Whereof I am glad;
I must needs laugh, I cannot be sad.
EVERYMAN. Ah, Goods, thou hast had
    long my heartly love;
I gave thee that which should be the
    Lord's above.
But wilt thou not go with me indeed?
    I pray thee truth to say.
GOODS. No, so God me speed!
Therefore farewell, and have good day.
    [*Exit* GOODS.]
EVERYMAN. O, to whom shall I make
    my moan
For to go with me in that heavy journey?
First Fellowship said he would with me
    gone;
His words were very pleasant and gay,
But afterward he left me alone.
Then spake I to my kinsmen, all in de-
    spair,
And also they gave me words fair;
They lacked no fair speaking,
But all forsook me in the ending.
Then went I to my Goods, that I loved
    best,
In hope to have comfort, but there had I
    least;
For my Goods sharply did me tell
That he bringeth many into hell.
Then of myself I was ashamed,
And so I am worthy to be blamed;
Thus may I will myself hate.
Of whom shall I now counsel take?
I think that I shall never speed
Till that I go to my Good Deed.
But, alas, she is so weak
That she can neither go nor speak;
Yet will I venture on her now.
My Good Deeds, where be you?

[GOOD DEEDS *speaks from the ground.*]

GOOD DEEDS. Here I lie, cold in the
    ground;
Thy sins hath me sore bound,
That I cannot stir.
EVERYMAN. O Good Deeds, I stand in
    fear!
I must you pray of counsel,
For help now should come right well.
GOOD DEEDS. Everyman, I have under-
    standing
That ye be summoned account to make
Before Messias, of Jerusalem King;
And you do by me, that journey with
    you will I take.
EVERYMAN. Therefore I come to you,
    my moan to make;
I pray you that ye will go with me.
GOOD DEEDS. I would full fain, but I
    cannot stand, verily.
EVERYMAN. Why, is there anything on
    you fall?
GOOD DEEDS. Yea, sir, I may thank you
    of all;
If ye had perfectly cheered me,
Your book of count full ready had be.
Look, the books of your works and deeds
    eke!
Behold how they lie under the feet,
To your soul's heaviness.
EVERYMAN. Our Lord Jesus help me!
For one letter here I cannot see.
GOOD DEEDS. There is a blind reckon-
    ing in time of distress.
EVERYMAN. Good Deeds, I pray you
    help me in this need,
Or else I am for ever damned indeed;
Therefore help me to make reckoning
Before the Redeemer of all thing,
That King is, and was, and ever shall.
GOOD DEEDS. Everyman, I am sorry of
    your fall,
And fain would I help you, and I were
    able.
EVERYMAN. Good Deeds, your counsel
    I pray you give me.
GOOD DEEDS. That shall I do verily;
Though that on my feet I may not go,
I have a sister that shall with you also,

Called Knowledge, which shall with you
abide,
To help you to make that dreadful reckoning.

[*Enter* KNOWLEDGE.]

KNOWLEDGE. Everyman, I will go with
thee, and be thy guide,
In thy most need to go by thy side.
EVERYMAN. In good condition I am
now in every thing,
And am wholly content with this good
thing,
Thanked be God my creator.
GOOD DEEDS. And when she hath
brought you there
Where thou shalt heal thee of thy smart,
Then go you with your reckoning and
your Good Deeds together,
For to make you joyful at heart
Before the blessed Trinity.
EVERYMAN. My Good Deeds, gram-
ercy!
I am well content, certainly,
With your words sweet.
KNOWLEDGE. Now go we together lov-
ingly
To Confession, that cleansing river.
EVERYMAN. For joy I weep; I would we
were there!
But, I pray you, give me cognition
Where dwelleth that holy man, Confes-
sion.
KNOWLEDGE. In the house of salvation.
We shall find him in that place,
That shall us comfort, by God's grace.

[KNOWLEDGE *takes* EVERYMAN *to* CONFES-
SION.]

Lo, this is Confession. Kneel down and
ask mercy,
For he is in good conceit with God Al-
mighty.
EVERYMAN. O glorious fountain, that all
uncleanness doth clarify,
Wash from me the spots of vice unclean,
That on me no sin may be seen.
I come with Knowledge for my redemp-
tion,
Redempt with heart and full contrition;

For I am commanded a pilgrimage to
take,
And great accounts before God to make.
Now I pray you, Shrift, mother of salva-
tion,
Help my Good Deeds for my piteous ex-
clamation.
CONFESSION. I know your sorrow well,
Everyman.
Because with Knowledge ye come to me,
I will you comfort as well as I can,
And a precious jewel I will give thee,
Called penance, voider of adversity;
Therewith shall your body chastised be,
With abstinence and perseverance in
God's service.
Here shall you receive that scourge of
me,
Which is penance strong that ye must
endure,
To remember thy Saviour was scourged
for thee
With sharp scourges, and suffered it pa-
tiently;
So must thou, ere thou scape that painful
pilgrimage.
Knowledge, keep him in this voyage,
And by that time Good Deeds will be
with thee.
But in any wise be siker of mercy,
For your time draweth fast, and ye will
saved be,
Ask God mercy, and he will grant truly.
When with the scourge of penance man
doth him bind,
The oil of forgiveness then shall he find.
EVERYMAN. Thanked be God for his
gracious work!
For now I will my penance begin;
This hath rejoiced and lighted my heart,
Though the knots be painful and hard
within.
KNOWLEDGE. Everyman, look your pen-
ance that ye fulfil,
What pain that ever it to you be;
And Knowledge shall give you counsel
at will
How your account ye shall make clearly.
EVERYMAN. O eternal God, O heavenly
figure,

O way of righteousness, O goodly vision,
Which descended down in a virgin pure
Because he would every man redeem,
Which Adam forfeited by his disobedi-
ence:
O blessed Godhead, elect and high divine,
Forgive my grievous offence;
Here I cry thee mercy in this presence.[41]
O ghostly treasure, O ransomer and re-
deemer,
Of all the world hope and conductor,
Mirror of joy, and founder of mercy,
Which enlumineth heaven and earth
thereby,
Hear my clamorous complaint, though it
late be;
Receive my prayers, of thy benignity;
Though I be a sinner most abominable,
Yet let my name be written in Moses'
table.
O Mary, pray to the Maker of all thing,
Me for to help at my ending;
And save me from the power of my
enemy,
For Death assaileth me strongly.
And, Lady, that I may by mean of thy
prayer
Of your Son's glory to be partner,
By the means of his passion, I it crave;
I beseech you help my soul to save.
Knowledge, give me the scourge of pen-
ance;
My flesh therewith shall give acquit-
tance:
I will now begin, if God give me grace.
  KNOWLEDGE. Everyman, God give you
  time and space!
Thus I bequeath you in the hands of our
Saviour;
Now may you make your reckoning sure.
  EVERYMAN. In the name of the Holy
  Trinity,
My body sore punished shall be:
Take this, body, for the sin of the flesh!
[*Scourges himself.*]
Also thou delightest to go gay and fresh,
And in the way of damnation thou did
me bring,
Therefore suffer now strokes and punish-
ing.

Now of penance I will wade the water
clear,
To save me from purgatory, that sharp
fire.

[GOOD DEEDS *rises from the ground.*]

  GOOD DEEDS. I thank God, now I can
  walk and go,
And am delivered of my sickness and
woe.
Therefore with Everyman I will go,
and not spare;
His good works I will help him to de-
clare.
  KNOWLEDGE. Now, Everyman, be merry
  and glad!
Your Good Deeds cometh now; ye may
not be sad.
Now is your Good Deeds whole and
sound,
Going upright upon the ground.
  EVERYMAN. My heart is light, and shall
  be evermore;
Now will I smite faster than I did before.
  GOOD DEEDS. Everyman, pilgrim, my
  special friend,
Blessed be thou without end;
For thee is preparate the eternal glory.
Ye have me made whole and sound,
Therefore I will bide by thee in every
stound.
  EVERYMAN. Welcome, my Good Deeds;
  now I hear thy voice,
I weep for very sweetness of love.
  KNOWLEDGE. Be no more sad, but ever
  rejoice;
God seeth thy living in his throne above.
Put on this garment to thy behoof,
Which is wet with your tears,
Or else before God you may it miss,
When ye to your journey's end come
shall.
  EVERYMAN. Gentle Knowledge, what
  do ye it call?
  KNOWLEDGE. It is a garment of sorrow:
From pain it will you borrow;
Contrition it is,
That geteth forgiveness;
It pleaseth God passing well.

GOOD DEEDS. Everyman, will you wear
it for your heal?
EVERYMAN. Now blessed be Jesu,
Mary's Son,
For now have I on true contrition.
And let us go now without tarrying;
Good Deeds, have we clear our reckon-
ing?
GOOD DEEDS. Yea, indeed, I have it here.
EVERYMAN. Then I trust we need not
fear;
Now, friends, let us not part in twain.
KNOWLEDGE. Nay, Everyman, that will
we not, certain.
GOOD DEEDS. Yet must thou lead with
thee
Three persons of great might.
EVERYMAN. Who should they be?
GOOD DEEDS. Discretion and Strength
they hight,
And thy Beauty may not abide behind.
KNOWLEDGE. Also ye must call to mind
Your Five Wits as for your counsellors.
GOOD DEEDS. You must have them ready
at all hours.
EVERYMAN. How shall I get them
hither?
KNOWLEDGE. You must call them all
together,
And they will hear you incontinent.
EVERYMAN. My friends, come hither
and be present,
Discretion, Strength, my Five Wits, and
Beauty.

[*Enter* BEAUTY, STRENGTH, DISCRETION, *and*
FIVE WITS.]

BEAUTY. Here at your will we be all
ready.
What will ye that we should do?
GOOD DEEDS. That ye would with Every-
man go,
And help him in his pilgrimage.
Advise you, will ye with him or not in
that voyage?
STRENGTH. We will bring him all
thither,
To his help and comfort, ye may believe
me.

DISCRETION. So will we go with him all
together.
EVERYMAN. Almighty God, lofed may
thou be!
I give thee laud that I have hither brought
Strength, Discretion, Beauty, and Five
Wits. Lack I nought.
And my Good Deeds, with Knowledge
clear,
All be in my company at my will here;
I desire no more to my business.
STRENGTH. And I, Strength, will by you
stand in distress,
Though thou would in battle fight on
the ground.
FIVE WITS. And though it were through
the world round,
We will not depart for sweet ne sour.
BEAUTY. No more will I unto death's
hour,
Whatsoever thereof befall.
DISCRETION. Everyman, advise you first
of all;
Go with a good advisement and delibera-
tion.
We all give you virtuous monition
That all shall be well.
EVERYMAN. My friends, harken what I
will tell:
I pray God reward you in his heavenly
sphere.
Now harken, all that be here,
For I will make my testament
Here before you all present:
In alms half my good I will give with my
hands twain
In the way of charity, with good intent,
And the other half still shall remain
In queth, to be returned there it ought
to be.
This I do in despite of the fiend of hell,
To go quit out of his peril
Ever after and this day.
KNOWLEDGE. Everyman, harken what I
say:
Go to priesthood, I you advise,
And receive of him in any wise
The holy sacrament and ointment to-
gether.
Then shortly see ye turn again hither;

We will all abide you here.

FIVE WITS. Yea, Everyman, hie you that ye ready were.

There is no emperor, king, duke, ne baron,

That of God hath commission

As hath the least priest in the world being;

For of the blessed sacraments pure and benign

He beareth the keys, and thereof hath the cure

For man's redemption—it is ever sure—

Which God for our soul's medicine

Gave us out of his heart with great pine.

Here in this transitory life, for thee and me,

The blessed sacraments seven there be:

Baptism, confirmation, with priesthood good,

And the sacrament of God's precious flesh and blood,

Marriage, the holy extreme unction, and penance;

These seven be good to have in remembrance,

Gracious sacraments of high divinity.

EVERYMAN. Fain would I receive that holy body,

And meekly to my ghostly father I will go.

FIVE WITS. Everyman, that is the best that ye can do.

God will you to salvation bring,

For priesthood exceedeth all other thing:

To us Holy Scripture they do teach,

And converteth man from sin heaven to reach;

God hath to them more power given

Than to any angel that is in heaven.

With five words he may consecrate,

God's body in flesh and blood to make,

And handleth his Maker between his hands.

The priest bindeth and unbindeth all bands,

Both in earth and in heaven.

Thou ministers all the sacraments seven;

Though we kissed thy feet, thou were worthy;

Thou art surgeon that cureth sin deadly:

No remedy we find under God

But all only priesthood.

Everyman, God gave priests that dignity,

And setteth them in his stead among us to be;

Thus be they above angels in degree.

[EVERYMAN *goes to the priest to receive the last sacraments.*]

KNOWLEDGE. If priests be good, it is so, surely.

But when Jesus hanged on the cross with great smart,

There he gave out of his blessed heart

The same sacrament in great torment:

He sold them not to us, that Lord omnipotent.

Therefore Saint Peter the apostle doth say

That Jesu's curse hath all they

Which God their Saviour do buy or sell,

Or they for any money do take or tell.

Sinful priests giveth the sinners example bad;

Their children sitteth by other men's fires, I have heard;

And some haunteth women's company

With unclean life, as lusts of lechery:

These be with sin made blind.

FIVE WITS. I trust to God no such may we find;

Therefore let us priesthood honour,

And follow their doctrine for our souls' succour.

We be their sheep, and they shepherds be

By whom we all be kept in surety.

Peace, for yonder I see Everyman come,

Which hath made true satisfaction.

GOOD DEEDS. Methink it is he indeed.

[*Re-enter* EVERYMAN.]

EVERYMAN. Now Jesu be your alder speed!

I have received the sacrament for my redemption,

And then mine extreme unction:

Blessed be all they that counselled me to take it!

And now, friends, let us go without longer respite;

I thank God that ye have tarried so long.
Now set each of you on this rood your
hand,
And shortly follow me:
I go before there I would be; God be
our guide!
STRENGTH. Everyman, we will not from
you go
Till ye have done this voyage long.
DISCRETION. I, Discretion, will bide by
you also.
KNOWLEDGE. And though this pilgrim-
age be never so strong,
I will never part you fro.
STRENGTH. Everyman, I will be as sure
by thee
As ever I did by Judas Maccabee.

[EVERYMAN *comes to his grave.*]

EVERYMAN. Alas, I am so faint I may
not stand;
My limbs under me doth fold.
Friends, let us not turn again to this
land,
Not for all the world's gold;
For into this cave must I creep
And turn to earth, and there to sleep.
BEAUTY. What, into this grave? Alas!
EVERYMAN. Yea, there shall ye con-
sume, more and less.
BEAUTY. And what, should I smother
here?
EVERYMAN. Yea, by my faith, and never
more appear.
In this world live no more we shall,
But in heaven before the highest Lord
of all.
BEAUTY. I cross out all this; adieu, by
Saint John!
I take my cap in my lap, and am gone.
EVERYMAN. What, Beauty, whither will
ye?
BEAUTY. Peace, I am deaf; I look not
behind me,
Not and thou wouldest give me all the
gold in thy chest. [*Exit* BEAUTY.]
EVERYMAN. Alas, whereto may I trust?
Beauty goeth fast away from me;
She promised with me to live and die.
STRENGTH. Everyman, I will thee also
forsake and deny;

Thy game liketh me not at all.
EVERYMAN. Why, then, ye will forsake
me all?
Sweet Strength, tarry a little space.
STRENGTH. Nay, sir, by the rood of
grace!
I will hie me from thee fast,
Though thou weep till thy heart to-brast.
EVERYMAN. Ye would ever bide by me,
ye said.
STRENGTH. Yea, I have you far enough
conveyed.
Ye be old enough, I understand,
Your pilgrimage to take on hand;
I repent me that I hither came.
EVERYMAN. Strength, you to displease
I am to blame;
Yet promise is debt, this ye well wot.
STRENGTH. In faith, I care not.
Thou art but a fool to complain;
You spend your speech and waste your
brain.
Go thrust thee into the ground! [*Exit*
STRENGTH.]
EVERYMAN. I had wend surer I should
you have found.
He that trusteth in his Strength
She him deceiveth at the length.
Both Strength and Beauty forsaketh me;
Yet they promised me fair and lovingly.
DISCRETION. Everyman, I will after
Strength be gone;
As for me, I will leave you alone.
EVERYMAN. Why, Discretion, will ye
forsake me?
DISCRETION. Yea, in faith, I will go from
thee,
For when Strength goeth before
I follow after evermore.
EVERYMAN. Yet, I pray thee, for the
love of the Trinity,
Look in my grave once piteously.
DISCRETION. Nay, so nigh will I not
come;
Farewell, every one! [*Exit* DISCRETION.]
EVERYMAN. O, all thing faileth, save
God alone—
Beauty, Strength, and Discretion;
For when Death bloweth his blast,
They all run from me full fast.
FIVE WITS. Everyman, my leave now of
thee I take;

I will follow the other, for here I thee forsake.

EVERYMAN. Alas, then may I wail and weep,

For I took you for my best friend.

FIVE WITS. I will no longer thee keep;

Now farewell, and there an end. [*Exit* FIVE WITS.]

EVERYMAN. O Jesu, help! All hath forsaken me.

GOOD DEEDS. Nay, Everyman; I will bide with thee.

I will not forsake thee indeed;

Thou shalt find me a good friend at need.

EVERYMAN. Gramercy, Good Deeds! Now may I true friends see.

They have forsaken me, every one;

I loved them better than my Good Deeds alone.

Knowledge, will ye forsake me also?

KNOWLEDGE. Yea, Everyman, when ye to Death shall go;

But not yet, for no manner of danger.

EVERYMAN. Gramercy, Knowledge, with all my heart.

KNOWLEDGE. Nay, yet I will not from hence depart

Till I see where ye shall become.

EVERYMAN. Methink, alas, that I must be gone

To make my reckoning and my debts pay,

For I see my time is nigh spent away.

Take example, all ye that this do hear or see,

How they that I loved best do forsake me,

Except my Good Deeds that bideth truly.

GOOD DEEDS. All earthly things is but vanity:

Beauty, Strength, and Discretion do man forsake,

Foolish friends, and kinsmen, that fair spake—

All fleeth save Good Deeds, and that am I.

EVERYMAN. Have mercy on me, God most mighty;

And stand by me, thou mother and maid, holy Mary.

GOOD DEEDS. Fear not; I will speak for thee.

EVERYMAN. Here I cry God mercy.

GOOD DEEDS. Short our end, and minish our pain;

Let us go and never come again.

EVERYMAN. Into thy hands, Lord, my soul I commend;

Receive it, Lord, that it be not lost.

As thou me boughtest, so me defend,

And save me from the fiend's boast,

That I may appear with that blessed host

That shall be saved at the day of doom.

In manus tuas, of mights most

For ever, *commendo spiritum meum*. [*He sinks into his grave.*]

KNOWLEDGE. Now hath he suffered that we all shall endure;

The Good Deeds shall make all sure.

Now hath he made ending;

Methinketh that I hear angels sing,

And make great joy and melody

Where Everyman's soul received shall be.

ANGEL. Come, excellent elect spouse, to Jesu!

Hereabove thou shalt go

Because of thy singular virtue.

Now the soul is taken the body fro,

Thy reckoning is crystal-clear.

Now shalt thou into the heavenly sphere,

Unto the which all ye shall come

That liveth well before the day of doom.

[*Enter* DOCTOR.]

DOCTOR. This moral men may have in mind.

Ye hearers, take it of worth, old and young,

And forsake Pride, for he deceiveth you in the end;

And remember Beauty, Five Wits, Strength, and Discretion,

They all at the last do every man forsake,

Save his Good Deeds there doth he take.

But beware, for and they be small

Before God, he hath no help at all;

None excuse may be there for every man.

Alas, how shall he do then?

For after death amends may no man make,

For then mercy and pity doth him forsake.
If his reckoning be not clear when he
doth come,
God will say: '*Ite, maledicti, in ignem
eternum.*'
And he that hath his account whole and
sound,

High in heaven he shall be crowned;
Unto which place God brings us all
thither,
That we may live body and soul together.
Thereto help the Trinity!
Amen, say ye, for saint charity.

THUS ENDETH THIS MORAL PLAY
OF EVERYMAN

THE ELEMENT OF CHARACTER: *ABE LINCOLN IN ILLINOIS*

What a play says is most directly revealed in the outcome of its central conflict. Thus, *The Desperate Hours,* through Hilliard's triumph, reaffirms our faith in the enduring strength of the average man, particularly when his family is threatened. And *Everyman* recalls us to the good life, reminding us that inevitable death must be a doorway to either eternal bliss or eternal hellfire. Part of the excellence of these two very different dramas, one dominated by action and the other by the tolling of its somber theme, lies in the directness with which the conflict is embodied and then resolved. But not all conflicts lie so openly in view or can be so easily settled. In some plays the emphasis centers not on action or theme but in character, the third major element of drama; and in such plays the conflict is usually internal, not external

Because we normally think of conflict as an external clash of opposing forces, an increased emphasis on character portrayal involves the dramatist in new and yet more complex problems. Such emphasis on character means usually that the scene of the principal conflict shifts from an external area to the mind and soul of the protagonist. Yet, as we have seen, the dramatist is apparently obligated by the very nature of his medium—its objectivity, its exclusion of the voice of the author—to deal only with externals, only with what a person does and says, and not with what he thinks and feels. On the other hand, the story and the people who act it out are, obviously, inseparable. We know people by their actions, and we measure the significance of actions by their effect on people. No play can lay claim to greatness, or even effectiveness, which does not reveal in some measure a meaningful development of human character. This is a primary requirement. Thus, even in the Hayes melodrama, after the comfortable routine of existence is shattered by the intrusion of the gangsters, Daniel Hilliard reveals the kind of courage which enables him to withstand their attacks, and eventually to conquer, without sacrificing the human standards which are his strength.

Nor—and this is a second requirement the dramatist must meet in character portrayal—is any play likely to prove effective if its characters are not easily approachable. As Mr. Hayes points out in his essay, much time is spent in the first scene in the Hilliard home creating characters with whom we can easily identify. And it is similarly true that no matter how frequently the theme is repeated in *Everyman,* no matter how sternly the audience is addressed, the reader develops a strong empathy with the character of Everyman as he searches futilely for external support in his journey toward eternity.

It is sometimes said that the interest of the modern reader in the motivation of character is owing partly to the influence of psychology, with its emphasis on explaining the external actions of man in terms of his hidden inner life. But literature, and drama in particular, has always been concerned with examining and portraying human beings as they "really" are or as they would like to be; present-day psychology is only re-emphasizing the need for looking beyond surface actions. It merely reinforces what the literary artist knew all the time, that human nature is deep, complex, and endlessly fascinating, that character of and by itself is a subject deserving profound study and speculation. We have always known that "the proper study of mankind is man." Modern psychology is but giving us new and valuable tools to help us understand ourselves, as modern physics has given us new tools to help us understand the world we live in.

The play here chosen to illustrate the emphasis on character growing out of a special type of conflict, on character as the focal point and the unifying element of a drama, is Robert E. Sherwood's *Abe Lincoln in Illinois*. This drama centers on an "inner" conflict, a struggle that takes place largely within the central character himself, and is resolved only in the protagonist's hardwon decision to accept social responsibility. What is shown in this play, specifically, is the portrait of a young, likable, and good-humored, but unambitious lawyer who is pushed into public life not because he has demonstrated any aptitude for leadership, but simply because most of his neighbors like him. Some, to be sure, think him lazy and shiftless, and others wonder how far he can be trusted when he gets away from home; but all admit to his good nature. Whatever his neighbors' opinions, however, the young man himself is deeply insecure; there is a profound streak of pessimism in him, and he is troubled and unsure of his own future course.

Wanting to remain out of the limelight, trying to compromise in order to avoid committing himself to any positive course of action, this young man nevertheless grows into the Lincoln of fame and legend; he becomes, by slow stages, the liberal statesman, the man of conviction and action, the teacher and the conscience of his country. This inspiring growth, this picture of a man of doubt rising to the greatest moral heights, is the real subject matter of the play. Sherwood's own times, his involvement in the New Deal crusade of Franklin D. Roosevelt, drove him to see the spiritual significance of such a commitment; and his artistic, his dramatic sense prompted his choice of the early life of Lincoln as an effective embodiment of this vision.

In approaching this play, the reader may be inclined to ask by what authority the dramatist takes a "real" person and manipulates him for his own purpose. Is not a historical play obligated to tell the "truth" about its subject? Yes; the difficulty, however, as even a cursory reading of biography or history reveals, is that the "facts" surrounding a historical personage are often contradictory and difficult to learn. But the important point at the moment is that a figure in a biographical or historical play is, like all other created characters, a fiction; he is real in the theater only as any created character is real: by virtue of his probability and plausibility in human terms. Only by making the character's problems our problems can the dramatist convince us that his character is living and breathing, that his struggles are being undertaken at that very moment and in our presence. It follows, then, that plays based on incidents in the life of a historical personage are therefore usually plays involving political or social attitudes significant in the lives of the audience. Every time the dramatist creates such a character in such a play, as Sherwood creates Lincoln in this play, he does in effect interpret history.

But though *Abe Lincoln in Illinois* shows how a dilemma faced and solved by a historical personage in past time may be used in the theater by a modern dramatist desirous of making a pertinent and provocative comment on the present, Sherwood's success as a creative artist depends on something more than the historical and political importance of Lincoln. It depends also on his clear vision of the conflict *within* the historical personage, a conflict successfully transferred to the stage figure he has created. In the simplest melodrama, the conflict—the clash or struggle between opposing persons or forces—is physical and the combatants are clearly labeled as "good" and "bad," thus offering the spectator no choice as to where his sympathy must go, and obviating the troublesome complications that arise when one realizes that a "bad" man may be partly right and a "good" one partly wrong. But when we observe that the struggle is between two traits within the protagonist himself, we realize that no such easy decision is possible, either for him or for us. Moreover, the situation is further complicated, and hence dramatically more interesting, when we recognize that though we can sometimes solve our problems satisfactorily by recourse to reason and sometimes by following our emotions, still other situations arise, often involving life's most critical decisions, when opposing desires of equal strength so confuse and torment us as to make the problems seem unsolvable.

In these cases, the individual, we say, is caught in a *dilemma;* faced with two equally repugnant alternatives, he must nevertheless choose one. Sherwood portrays Lincoln as facing such a choice, one requiring him to decide which of various competing elements in his basic makeup shall dominate him. Scene Six of the play, for example, reveals Lincoln facing a dilemma in his personal life, weighing the problem of seeking his release from Mary Todd on the day of his intended marriage. The scene culminates in Lincoln's tortured admission of near madness, as he says:

I just feel that I've got to the end of my rope, and I must let go, and drop—and where I'll land, I don't know, and whether I'll survive the fall, I don't know that either . . . But this I *do* know: I've got to get out of this thing—I can't go through with it—I've got to have my release.

Sherwood skillfully translates this personal dilemma into its relevant political terms when at the end of that scene Billy Herndon accuses Lincoln of forsaking his destiny when he forsakes Mary Todd, for Herndon recognizes Mary Todd as a force that will push Lincoln to the Presidency. Lincoln too has seen in Mary Todd what he calls "her infernal ambition," and he dislikes it. "If her poor soul craves importance in life," he says of her, "then let her marry Stephen Douglas. He's ambitious, too." As for Lincoln himself, "I only want to be left alone!" he exclaims. It is then that Billy Herndon enters the conversation, taunting Lincoln in such a way as to force him to recognize the dual public and private nature of his dilemma. (See pp. 128–129.)

The intensity of the struggle exemplified in this scene, culminating in the picture of a man won to the right course almost in spite of himself, is what gives meaning to the play and makes it far more than merely a chronicle of the highlights of Lincoln's life.

The fact that Sherwood's play ends with the legendary Lincoln we "know" may obscure some of the art of the play. We may be led to believe that we accept this character because the portrait corresponds to a knowledge of Lincoln gained otherwise, but the text of the drama will reveal that Sherwood makes Lincoln "real," that is, humanly plausible, not on the basis of familiarity but by creating an internally consistent, well-motivated character. From the very opening scene presenting Mentor Graham and his discourse on the moods, with its obvious foreshadowing in the examples he gives the young Lincoln to read, Sherwood is engaged in *motivating* the Lincoln we "know," in showing us the torment and the struggle out of which the great man grew. His theme, his revelation of what Lincoln came finally to understand, we of the audience also come to understand, but in terms applicable to our own times. We have come to know this Lincoln largely because Sherwood has motivated him; he has presented Lincoln as a plausible flesh-and-blood man, not as a legend; he has made us understand that Lincoln's assumption of social responsibility was the result of a human struggle such as we ourselves endure, here and now.

A consistent, well-motivated character like Sherwood's Lincoln is called a rounded character. The responsibility of the dramatist to create rounded rather than flat characters is perhaps best seen in light of the analogy between drama and life. In life, we often wonder about the hidden thoughts and motives of people we meet casually. But, except on rare occasions, we do not need to know what motivates them; we can live in peace without that knowledge. Of the people we live with more intimately, however, people whose lives are enmeshed with ours, whose actions call forth our reactions, of such people we must have more knowledge if we are to survive, let alone thrive. We try to learn their "character"; that is, we try to predict the pattern of action they are likely to follow from what we have observed of their past actions and from what we know of them by report. So too in the drama. But not all the characters we meet will be rounded and fully motivated. Some will be two-dimensional characters, lacking any depth. Like the scenery flats, they always face one way; we never see behind them. If the dramatist manipulates such characters as though they were puppets, pulls them this way and that into actions which are never explained, they become a liability to his play. For one thing, if many of the characters are insufficiently motivated, the action will appear implausible. But, more important, if many of the characters have none of the depth and complexity we have come to expect in "real" people, as distinct from those we meet casually here and there, the dramatic conflict we came to witness is likely to be still-born.

Sometimes, however, as in *Everyman*, the author intentionally creates personified abstractions, mere speaking names, for what he desires is not to give independent existence, but merely a body and a voice to certain traits and qualities he needs for the moment. It is worth noting that many of the characters in *Abe Lincoln* are not far removed in function from the personified abstractions of *Everyman*. Mentor Graham, Josh Speed, Bowling Green, Ninian Edwards, Ann Rutledge have life only as they are warmed by the personality of Lincoln. They represent certain traits in Lincoln which have been objectified in the people who helped Lincoln to realize them in himself. But we would not accept these characters today as "Good Teacher," "Strong Friend," "Shallow Politician," or "Young Love" because our ways of thought have changed. Unlike the people of medieval times who saw the real in the idea or essence which lay behind the thing or person, we tend to believe in the real only as it is embodied in actual things and people. Thus, to objectify the conflict within Lincoln, Sherwood had to do more than show Lincoln in various moods.

He had to create characters not only plausible in themselves, but also representative of the many sides of Lincoln's character. It is only through these externalized conflicts that we can come to know the inner Lincoln.

This distinction between flat and rounded characters is based on depth of motivation and consistency of action, not on the quality of the stage figure as a man. Thus a shallow, vain, immature person like Hialmar in *The Wild Duck*, though certainly not a well-rounded man, is, dramatically speaking, a well-rounded character. On the other hand, Robish and the FBI agent in *The Desperate Hours* are both flat. Neither develops at all during his stage life; each remains essentially as we first know him, our first view being the only side of him we ever come to know. But Robish is the kind of flat character we call a type or stock character, in this case the low-grade criminal type. The stock character is defined by the fact that the dramatist has available, out of past drama as well as out of life, a whole series of stereotypes. He has them in stock, on the shelf; he can pull one down at will, counting on the fact that his audience has been conditioned to react automatically to certain types. So long as he breathes some life into them, they serve him and us well. In fact, one mark of the competent dramatist is the quality of his stock characters. Without obvious effort, he makes them live, and they leave him free to concentrate on the major persons in his play.

All characters—major and minor, flat, rounded, or stock—are realized in the same way. Most obviously, we see them in their actions and we hear them speak. Somewhat less obviously, we hear others talk about them, see others react to them. Still other devices help bring them to life. Their costumes and their homes are distinctive external garments; and their speech patterns and their diction, if properly differentiated, can be made to reflect other differences of their environment or their basic natures. One mark of a poor play is that all characters speak in the same voice—usually the author's. But the practiced dramatist will strive to create men who seem to live independently of him, while at the same time he so moves them about that we learn all we need to know to help us live with such people. Character drawing above all else takes the measure of the dramatist. It may be impossible for story and theme to be new, but the study of character, in its infinite variety and its endless combinations, will always challenge the dramatist and engross the reader.

Abe Lincoln in Illinois

by

ROBERT EMMET SHERWOOD

Characters

MENTOR GRAHAM
ABE LINCOLN
ANN RUTLEDGE
BEN MATTLING
JUDGE BOWLING GREEN
NINIAN EDWARDS
JOSHUA SPEED
TRUM COGDAL
JACK ARMSTRONG
BAB
FEARGUS
JASP
SETH GALE
NANCY GREEN
WILLIAM HERNDON
ELIZABETH EDWARDS
MARY TODD
THE EDWARDS' MAID
JIMMY GALE
AGGIE GALE
GOBEY
STEPHEN A. DOUGLAS
WILLIE LINCOLN
TAD LINCOLN
ROBERT LINCOLN
THE LINCOLNS' MAID
CRIMMIN
BARRICK
STURVESON
JED
KAVANAGH
MAJOR
SOLDIERS, RAILROAD MEN, TOWNSPEOPLE

ACT ONE

1

MENTOR GRAHAM's cabin near New Salem, Illinois. Late at night. There is one rude table, piled with books and papers. Over it hangs an oil lamp, the only source of light.

At one side of the table sits MENTOR GRAHAM, a sharp but patient schoolteacher. Across from him is ABE LINCOLN —young, gaunt, tired but intent, dressed in the ragged clothes of a backwoodsman.

He speaks with the drawl of southern Indiana—an accent which is more Kentuckian than Middle-Western. MENTOR is leaning on the table. ABE's chair is tilted back, so that his face is out of the light. MENTOR turns a page in a grammar book.

MENTOR. The Moods. [MENTOR *closes the book and looks at* ABE.] Every one of us has many moods. You yourself have more than your share of them, Abe.

103

They express the various aspects of your character. So it is with the English language—and you must try to consider this language as if it were a living person, who may be awkward and stumbling, or pompous and pretentious, or simple and direct. Name me the five moods.

ABE. The Indicative, Imperative, Potential, Subjunctive, and Infinitive.

MENTOR. And what do they signify?

ABE. The Indicative Mood is the easy one. It just indicates a thing—like "He loves," "He is loved"—or, when you put it in the form of a question, "Does he love?" or "Is he loved?" The Imperative Mood is used for commanding, like "Get out and be damned to you."

MENTOR. [Smiling.] Is that the best example you can think of?

ABE. Well—you can put it in the Bible way—"Go thou in peace." But it's still imperative.

MENTOR. The mood derives its name from the implication of command. But you can use it in a very different sense—in the form of the humblest supplication.

ABE. Like "Give us this day our daily bread and forgive us our trespasses."

MENTOR. [Reaching for a newspaper in mess on the table.] I want you to read this—it's a speech delivered by Mr. Webster before the United States Senate. A fine document, and a perfect usage of the Imperative Mood in its hortatory sense. Here it is. Read this—down here. [He leans back to listen.]

ABE. [Takes paper, leans forward into the lights and reads.] "Sir," the Senator continued, in the rich deep tones of the historic church bells of his native Boston, "Sir—I have not allowed myself to look beyond the Union, to see what might be hidden in the dark recess behind. While the Union lasts . . ." [ABE has been reading in a monotone, without inflection.]

MENTOR. [Testily.] Don't read it off as if it were an inventory of Denton Offut's groceries. Imagine that you're making the speech before the Senate, with the fate of your country at stake. Put your own life into it!

ABE. I couldn't use words as long as Dan'l Webster.

MENTOR. That's what you're here for—to learn! Go ahead.

ABE. [Reading slowly, gravely.] "While the Union lasts, we have high prospects spread out before us, for us and our children. Beyond that, I seek not to penetrate the veil. God grant that in my day, at least, the curtain may not rise."

MENTOR. Notice the use of verbs from here on.

ABE. [Reads.] "When my eyes shall be turned to behold for the last time the sun in heaven, may I not see him shining on the broken and dishonored fragments of a once glorious Union; on States dissevered, discordant, belligerent; on a land rent with civil feuds, or drenched, it may be, in fraternal blood! Let their last feeble glance rather behold the glorious ensign of the republic, now known and honored throughout the earth, not a single star of it obscured, bearing for its motto no such miserable interrogatory . . ." [He stumbles over the pronunciation.]

MENTOR. Interrogatory.

ABE. [Continuing.] ". . . interrogatory as 'What is all this worth?' Nor, those other words of delusion and folly, 'Liberty first and Union afterwards'; but everywhere, spread all over in characters of living light, that other sentiment, dear to every true American heart—Liberty and Union . . ."

MENTOR. Emphasize the "and."

ABE. "Liberty and Union, now and forever, one and inseparable!" [He puts the paper back on the table.] He must have had 'em up on their feet cheering with that, all right.

MENTOR. Some cheered, and some spat, depending on which section they came from.

ABE. What was he talking about?

MENTOR. It was in the debate over the right of any state to secede from the Union. Hayne had pleaded South Carolina's cause—pleaded it ably. He said that just as we have liberty as individuals—so have we liberty as states—to go as we please. Which means, if we don't like the Union, as expressed by the will of its majority, then we can leave it, and set up a new nation, or many nations—so that this continent might be as divided as Europe. But Webster answered him all right. He proved that without Union, we'd have precious little liberty left. Now—go on with the Potential Mood.

ABE. That signifies possibility—usually of an unpleasant nature. Like, "If I ever get out of debt, I will probably get right back in again."

MENTOR. [*Smiles.*] Why did you select that example, Abe?

ABE. Well—it just happens to be the thought that's always heaviest on my mind.

MENTOR. Is the store in trouble again?

ABE. [*Calmly.*] Yes. Berry's drunk all the whiskey we ought to have sold, and we're going to have to shut up any day now. I guess I'm my father's own son. Give me a steady job, and I'll fail at it.

MENTOR. You haven't been a failure here, Abe. There isn't a manjack in this community that isn't fond of you and anxious to help you get ahead.

ABE. [*With some bitterness.*] I know—just like you, Mentor, sitting up late nights, to give me learning, out of the goodness of your heart. And now, Josh Speed and Judge Green and some of the others I owe money to want to get me the job of post-master, thinking that maybe I can handle *that*, since there's only one mail comes in a week. I've got friends, all right—the best friends. But they can't change my luck, or maybe it's just my nature.

MENTOR. What you want to do is get out of New Salem. This poor little forgotten town will never give any one any opportunity.

ABE. Yes—I've thought about moving, think about it all the time. My family have always been movers, shifting about, never knowing what they were looking for, and whatever it was, never finding it. My old father ambled from Virginia, to one place after another in Kentucky, where I was born, and then into Indiana, and then here in Illinois. About all I can remember of when I was a boy was hitching up, and then unhitching, and then hitching up again.

MENTOR. Then get up and go, Abe.

Make a new place for yourself in a new world.

ABE. As a matter of fact, Seth Gale and me have been talking a lot about moving—out to Kansas or Nebraska territory. But—wherever I go—it'll be the same story—more friends, more debts.

MENTOR. Well, Abe—just bear in mind that there are always two professions open to people who fail at everything else: there's school-teaching, and there's politics.

ABE. Then I'll choose school-teaching. You go into politics, and you may get elected.

MENTOR. Yes—there's always that possibility.

ABE. And if you get elected, you've got to go to the city. I don't want none of that.

MENTOR. What did I say about two negatives?

ABE. I meant, any of that.

MENTOR. What's your objection to cities, Abe? Have you ever seen one?

ABE. Sure. I've been down river twice to New Orleans. And, do you know, every minute of the time I was there, I was scared?

MENTOR. Scared of what, Abe?

ABE. Well—it sounds kind of foolish—I was scared of people.

MENTOR. [*Laughs.*] Did you imagine they'd rob you of all your gold and jewels?

ABE. [*Serious.*] No. I was scared they'd kill me.

MENTOR. [*Also serious.*] Why? Why should they want to kill you?

ABE. I don't know.

MENTOR. [*After a moment.*] You think a lot about death, don't you?

ABE. I've had to, because it has always seemed to be so close to me—always—as far back as I can remember. When I was no higher than this table, we buried my mother. The milksick got her, poor creature. I helped Paw make the coffin—whittled the pegs for it with my own jackknife. We buried her in a timber clearing beside my grandmother, old Betsy Sparrow. I used to go there often and look at the place—used to watch the deer running over her grave with their little feet. I never could kill a deer after that. One time I catched hell from Paw because when he was taking aim I knocked his gun up. And I always compare the looks of those deer with the looks of men—like the men in New Orleans—that you could see had murder in their hearts.

MENTOR. [*After a moment.*] You're a hopeless mess of inconsistency, Abe Lincoln.

ABE. How do you mean, Mentor?

MENTOR. I've never seen any one who is so friendly and at the same time so misanthropic.

ABE. What's that?

MENTOR. A misanthrope is one who distrusts men and avoids their society.

ABE. Well—maybe that's how I am. Oh —I like people, well enough—when you consider 'em one by one. But they seem to look different when they're put into crowds, or mobs, or armies. But I came here to listen to you, and then I do all the talking.

MENTOR. Go right on, Abe. I'll correct you when you say things like "catched hell."

ABE. [*Grins.*] I know. Whenever I get talking about Paw, I sort of fall back into his language. But—you've got your own school to teach tomorrow. I'll get along. [*He stands up.*]

MENTOR. Wait a minute. . . . [*He is fishing about among the papers. He takes out a copy of an English magazine.*] There's just one more thing I want to show you. It's a poem. [*He finds the place in the magazine.*] Here it is. You read it, Abe. [*He hands* ABE *the magazine.* ABE *seats himself on the edge of the table, and holds the magazine under the light.*]

ABE. [*Reads.*] " 'On Death,' written at the age of nineteen by the late John Keats:

'Can death be sleep, when life is but a dream,
And scenes of bliss pass as a phantom by?
The transient [*He hesitates on that word.*] pleasures as a vision seem,
And yet we think the greatest pain's to die. [*He moves closer to the light.*]

How strange it is that man on earth should roam,
And lead a life of woe, but not forsake
His rugged path—nor dare he view alone
His future doom—which is but to awake.' " [*He looks at* MENTOR.] That sure is good, Mentor. It's *fine!* [*He is reading it again, to himself, when the lights fade.*]

2

The Rutledge Tavern, New Salem. Noon on the Fourth of July. It is a large room, with log walls, but with curtains on the windows and pictures on the walls to give it an air of dressiness. The pictures include likenesses of all the Presidents from Washington to Jackson, and there is also a picture (evidently used for campaign purposes) of Henry Clay. At the left is a door leading to the kitchen. At the back, toward the right, is the main entrance, which is open. The sun is shining brightly. The furniture of the room consists of two tables, two benches, and various chairs and stools.

BEN MATTLING is seated on a bench at the rear of the room. He is an ancient, paunchy, watery-eyed veteran of the Revolution, and he wears a cocked hat and the tattered but absurd semblance of a Colonial uniform. JUDGE BOWLING GREEN and NINIAN EDWARDS come in, followed by JOSHUA SPEED. BOWLING is elderly, fat, gentle. NINIAN is young, tall, handsome, prosperous. JOSH is quiet, mild, solid, thoughtful, well-dressed.

BOWLING. [*As they come in.*] This is the Rutledge Tavern, Mr. Edwards. It's not precisely a gilded palace of refreshment.

NINIAN. Make no apologies, Judge Green. As long as the whiskey is wet. [JOSH *has crossed to the door at the left. He calls off-stage.*]

JOSH. Miss Rutledge.

ANN. [*Appearing at the door.*] Yes, Mr. Speed?

JOSH. Have you seen Abe Lincoln?

ANN. No. He's probably down at the

foot races. [*She goes back into the kitchen.* JOSH *turns to* BOWLING.]

JOSH. I'll find Abe and bring him here.

NINIAN. Remember, Josh, we've got to be back in Springfield before sundown. [JOSH *has gone out.*]

BOWLING. [*To* MATTLING.] Ah, good day, Uncle Ben. Have a seat, Mr. Edwards. [*They cross to the table at the right.*]

BEN. Good day to you, Bowling. [ANN *comes in from the kitchen.*]

ANN. Hello, Judge Green.

BOWLING. Good morning, Ann. We'd be grateful for a bottle of your father's best whiskey.

ANN. Yes, Judge. [*She starts to go off.*]

BEN. [*Stopping her.*] And git me another mug of that Barbadoes rum.

ANN. I'm sorry, Mr. Mattling, but I've given you one already and you know my father said you weren't to have any more till you paid for . . .

BEN. Yes, wench—I know what your father said. But if a veteran of the Revolutionary War is to be denied so much as credit, then this country has forgot its gratitude to them that made it.

BOWLING. Bring him the rum, Ann. I'll be happy to pay for it. [TRUM COGDAL *comes in. He is elderly, pernicketty.*]

BEN. [*Reluctantly.*] I have to say thank you, Judge.

TRUM. Ann, bring me a pot of Sebago tea.

ANN. Mr. Cogdal. [*She goes out at the left.* TRUM *sits down at the table.*]

BOWLING. Don't say a word, Ben.

TRUM. Well, Mr. Edwards—what's your impression of our great and enterprising metropolis?

NINIAN. Distinctly favorable, Mr. Cogdal. I could not fail to be impressed by the beauty of your location, here on this hilltop, in the midst of the prairie land.

TRUM. Well, we're on the highroad to the West—and when we get the rag, tag, and bobtail cleaned out of here, we'll grow. Yes, sir—we'll grow!

NINIAN. [*Politely.*] I'm sure of it. [ANN *has returned with the whiskey, rum and tea.*]

BOWLING. Thank you, Ann.

ANN. Has the mud-wagon come in yet?

TRUM. No. I been waiting for it.

BOWLING. Not by any chance expecting a letter, are you, Ann?

ANN. Oh, no—who'd be writing to *me*, I'd like to know?

BOWLING. Well—you never can tell what might happen on the Fourth of July. [*He and* NINIAN *lift their glasses.*] But I beg to wish you all happiness, my dear. And let me tell you that Mr. Edwards here is a married man, so you can keep those lively eyes to yourself.

ANN. [*Giggles.*] Oh, Judge Green—you're just joking me! [*She goes to the kitchen.*]

NINIAN. A mighty pretty girl.

TRUM. Comes of good stock, too.

NINIAN. With the scarcity of females in these parts, it's a wonder some one hasn't snapped her up. Some one has. The poor girl promised herself to a man who called himself McNiel—it turned out his real name's McNamar. Made some money out here and then left town, saying he'd return soon. She's still waiting for him. But your time is short, Mr. Edwards; so if you tell us just what it is you want in New Salem, we'll do our utmost to . . .

NINIAN. I'm sure you gentlemen know what I want.

TRUM. Naturally, you want votes. Well you've got mine. Anything to frustrate that tyrant, Andy Jackson. [*He shakes a finger at the picture of Andrew Jackson.*]

NINIAN. I assure you that I yield to none in my admiration for the character of our venerable president, but when he goes to the extent of ruining our banking structure, destroying faith in our currency and even driving sovereign states to the point of secession—then, gentlemen, it is time to call a halt.

BOWLING. We got two more years of him—if the old man lives that long. You can't make headway against his popularity.

NINIAN. But we can start now to drive out his minions here in the government of the state of Illinois. We have a great battle cry: "End the reign of Andrew

Jackson." [JACK ARMSTRONG *and three others of the Clary's Grove boys have come in during this speech. The others are named* BAB, FEARGUS *and* JASP. *They are the town bullies—boisterous, good-natured but tough.*]

JACK. [*Going to the door at the left.*] Miss Rutledge!

ANN. [*Appearing in the doorway.*] What do *you* want, Jack Armstrong?

JACK. Your humble pardon, Miss Rutledge, and we will trouble you for a keg of liquor.

BAB. And we'll be glad to have it quick, because we're powerful dry.

ANN. You get out of here—you get out of here right now—you low *scum!*

JACK. I believe I said a keg of liquor. Did you hear me say it, boys?

FEARGUS. That's how it sounded to me, Jack.

JASP. Come along with it, Annie——

ANN. If my father were here, he'd take a gun to you, just as he would to a pack of prairie wolves.

JACK. If your Paw was here, he'd be scareder than you. 'Cause he knows we're the wildcats of Clary's Grove, worse'n any old wolves, and we're a-howlin', and a-spittin' for drink. So get the whiskey, Miss Annie, and save your poor old Paw a lot of expenses for damages to his property. [*Ann goes.*]

TRUM. [*In an undertone to* NINIAN.] That's the rag, tag, and bobtail I was . . .

JACK. And what are you mumblin' about, old measely-weasely Trum Cogdal —with your cup of tea on the Fourth of July?

BAB. He's a cotton-mouthed traitor and I think we'd better whip him for it.

FEARGUS. [*At the same time.*] Squeeze that air tea outen him, Jack.

JASP. [*Shouting.*] Come on you, Annie, with that liquor!

JACK. And you, too, old fat-pot Judge Bowling Green that sends honest men to prison—and who's the stranger? Looks kind of damn elegant for New Salem.

BOWLING. This is Mr. Ninian Edwards of Springfield, Jack—and for the Lord's sake, shut up, and sit down, and behave yourselves.

JACK. Ninian Edwards, eh! The Governor's son, I presume. Well—well!

NINIAN. [*Amiably.*] You've placed me.

JACK. No wonder you've got a New Orleans suit of clothes and a gold fob and a silver-headed cane. I reckon you can buy the best of everything with that steamin' old pirate land-grabber for a Paw. I guess them fancy pockets of yourn are pretty well stuffed with the money your Paw stole from us taxpayers —eh, Mr. Edwards?

BAB. Let's take it offen him, Jack.

FEARGUS. Let's give him a lickin', Jack.

JACK. [*Still to* NINIAN.] What you come here for anyway? Lookin' for a fight? Because if that's what you're a-cravin', I'm your man—wrasslin', clawin', bitin', and tearin'.

ANN. [*Coming in.*] Jack Armstrong, here's your liquor! Drink it and go away. [ANN *carries four mugs.*]

JASP. He told you to bring a keg!

JACK. [*Contemplating the mugs.*] One little noggin apiece? Why—that ain't enough to fill a hollow tooth! Get the keg, Annie.

FEARGUS. Perhaps she can't tote it. I'll get it, Jack. [*He goes out into the kitchen.*]

ANN. [*Desperately.*] Aren't there any of you men can do anything to protect decent people from these ruffians?

NINIAN. I'll be glad to do whatever I . . . [*He starts to rise.*]

BOWLING. [*Restraining him.*] I'd be rather careful, Mr. Edwards.

JACK. That's right, Mr. Edwards. You be careful. Listen to the old Squire. He's got a round pot but a level head. He's seen the Clary's Grove boys in action, and he can tell you you might get that silver-headed cane rammed down your gullet. Hey, Bab—you tell him what we did to Hank Spears and Gus Hocheimer. Just tell him!

BAB. Jack nailed the two of 'em up in a barr'l and sent 'em rollin' down Salem hill and it jumped the bank and fotched up in the river and when we opened up the barr'l they wasn't inclined to move much.

JACK. Of course, it'd take a bigger barr'l to hold you and your friend here,

Squire, but I'd do it for you and I'd do it for any by God rapscallions and sons of thieves that come here a-preachin' treachery and disunion and pisenin' the name of Old Hickory, the people's friend. [FEARGUS *returns with the keg.*]

BEN. Kill him, boys! You're the only *real* Americans we got left!

NINIAN. [*Rising.*] If you gentlemen will step outside, I'll be glad to accommodate you with the fight you seem to be spoiling for.

TRUM. You're committing suicide, Mr. Edwards.

JACK. Oh, no—he ain't. We ain't killers —we're just bone crushers. After a few months, you'll be as good as new, which ain't saying much. You bring that keg, Feargus. [*They are about to go when* ABE *appears in the door. He now is slightly more respectably dressed, wearing a battered claw-hammer coat and pants that have been "foxed" with buckskin. He carries the mail. Behind him is* JOSH SPEED.]

ABE. The mud-wagon's in! Hello, Jack. Hello, boys. Ain't you fellers drunk yet? Hello, Miss Ann. Got a letter for you. [*There is a marked shyness in his attitude toward* ANN.]

ANN. Thank you, Abe. [*She snatches the letter and runs out with it.*]

BEN. Abe, there's goin' to be a fight!

NINIAN. [*To* JACK.] Well—come on, if you're coming.

JACK. All right, boys.

ABE. Fight? Who—and why?

JACK. This is the son of Ninian Edwards, Abe. Come from Springfield lookin' for a little crotch hoist and I'm aimin' to oblige. [ABE *looks* NINIAN *over.*]

BOWLING. Put a stop to it, Abe. It'd be next door to murder.

JACK. You shut your trap, Pot Green. Murder's too good for any goose-livered enemy of Andy Jackson. Come on, boys!

ABE. Wait a minute, boys. Jack, have you forgotten what day it is?

JACK. No, I ain't! But I reckon the Fourth is as good a day as any to whip a politician!

ABE. [*Amiably.*] Well, if you've just got to fight, Jack, you shouldn't give preference to strangers. Being postmaster of this thriving town, I can rate as a politician, myself, so you'd better try a fall with me—[*He thrusts* JACK *aside and turns to* NINIAN.] And as for you, sir, I haven't the pleasure of your acquaintance; but my name's Lincoln, and I'd like to shake hands with a brave man.

NINIAN. [*Shaking hands with* ABE.] I'm greatly pleased to know you, Mr. Lincoln.

ABE. You should be. Because I come here just in time to save you quite some embarrassment, not to mention injury. Oh, got a couple of letters for you, Bowling, and here's your *Cincinnati Journal*, Trum.

JACK. Look here, Abe—you're steppin' into something that ain't none of your business. This is a private matter of patriotic honor . . .

ABE. Everything in this town is my business, Jack. It's the only kind of business I've got. And besides—I saw Hannah down by the grove and she says to tell you to come on to the picnic and that means *now* or she'll give the cake away to the Straders children and you and the boys'll go hungry. So get moving.

FEARGUS. [*To* JACK.] Are you goin' to let Abe talk you out of it?

ABE. Sure he is. [*He turns to* TRUM.] Say, Trum—if you ain't using that *Journal* for a while, would you let me have a read?

TRUM. By all means, Abe. Here you are. [*He tosses the paper to* ABE.]

ABE. Thanks. [*He turns again to* JACK.] You'd better hurry, Jack, or *you'll* get a beating from Hannah. [*He starts to take the wrapper off, as he goes over to a chair at the left.* JACK *looks at* ABE *for a moment, then laughs.*]

JACK. [*To* NINIAN.] All right! Abe Lincoln's saved your hide. I'll consent to callin' off the fight just because he's a friend of mine.

ABE. [*As he sits.*] And also because I'm the only one around here you can't lick.

JACK. But I just want to tell you, Mr. Ninian Edwards, Junior, that the next time you come around here a-spreadin' pisen and . . .

ABE. Go on, Jack. Hannah's waiting.

JACK. [*Walking over to* ABE.] I'm going, Abe. But I warn you—you'd better stop this foolishness of readin'—readin'—readin', mornin', noon, and night, or you'll be gettin' soft and you won't be the same fightin' man you are now—and it would break my heart to see you licked by anybody, includin' me! [*He laughs, slaps* ABE *on the back, then turns to go.*] Glad to have met you, Mr. Edwards. [*He goes out, followed by* BAB *and* JASP. FEARGUS *picks up the keg and starts after them.*]

NINIAN. [*To Jack.*] It's been a pleasure.

ABE. Where'd you get that keg, Feargus?

FEARGUS. [*Nervously.*] Jack told me to take it outen Mis' Rutledge's kitchen and I . . .

ABE. Well—put it down. . . . If you see Seth Gale, tell him I've got a letter for him.

FEARGUS. I'll tell him, Abe. [FEARGUS *puts down the keg and goes.* JOSH SPEED *laughs and comes up to the table.*]

JOSH. Congratulations, Ninian. I shouldn't have enjoyed taking you home to Mrs. Edwards after those boys had done with you.

NINIAN. [*Grinning.*] I was aware of the certain consequences, Josh. [*He turns to* ABE.] I'm deeply in your debt, Mr. Lincoln.

ABE. Never mind any thanks, Mr. Edwards. Jack Armstrong talks big but he means well.

NINIAN. Won't you join us in a drink?

ABE. No, thank you. [*He's reading the paper.* BOWLING *fills the glasses.*]

BOWLING. *I'm* going to have another! I don't mind telling you, I'm still trembling. [*He hands a glass to* NINIAN, *then drinks himself.*]

TRUM. You see, Mr. Edwards. It's that very kind of lawlessness that's holding our town back.

NINIAN. You'll find the same element in the capital of our nation, and everywhere else, these days. [*He sits down and drinks.*]

ABE. Say, Bowling! It says here that there was a riot in Lyons, France. [*He reads.*] "A mob of men, deprived of employment when textile factories installed the new sewing machines, re-enacted scenes of the Reign of Terror in the streets of this prosperous industrial center. The mobs were suppressed only when the military forces of His French Majesty took a firm hand. The rioters carried banners inscribed with the incendiary words, 'We will live working or die fighting!' " [ABE *looks at the group at the right.*] That's Revolution!

BOWLING. Maybe, but it's a long way off from New Salem.

JOSH. Put the paper down, Abe. We want to talk to you.

ABE. Me? What about? [*He looks curiously at* JOSH, BOWLING, *and* NINIAN.]

JOSH. I brought Mr. Edwards here for the sole purpose of meeting you—and with his permission, I shall tell you why.

NINIAN. Go right ahead, Josh. [*All are looking intently at* ABE.]

JOSH. Abe—how would you like to run for the State Assembly?

ABE. When?

JOSH. Now—for the election in the fall.

ABE. Why?

NINIAN. Mr. Lincoln, I've known you for only a few minutes, but that's long enough to make me agree with Josh Speed that you're precisely the type of man we want. The whole Whig organization will support your candidacy.

ABE. This was all your idea, Josh?

JOSH. [*Smiling.*] Oh, no, Abe—you're the people's choice!

TRUM. What do *you* think of it, Bowling?

BOWLING. [*Heartily.*] I think it's as fine a notion as I ever heard. Why, Abe—I can hear you making speeches, right and left, taking your stand on all the issues—secession, Texas, the National Bank crisis, abolitionism—it'll be more fun than we ever had in our lives!

ABE. [*Rising.*] Isn't anybody going to ask what *I* think?

JOSH. [*Laughs.*] All right, Abe—*I'll* ask you.

ABE. [*After a moment's pause.*] It's a comical notion, all right—and I don't know if I can give you an answer to it offhand. But my first, hasty impression is that I don't think much of it.

BOWLING. Don't overlook the fact that,

if elected, your salary would be three whole dollars a day.

ABE. That's fine money. No doubt of that. And I see what you have in mind, Bowling. I owe you a considerable sum of money; and if I stayed in the legislature for, say, twenty years I'd be able to pay off—let me see—two dollars and a half a day. . . . [*He is figuring it up on his fingers.*]

BOWLING. I'm not thinking about the debts, Abe.

ABE. I know you ain't, Bowling. But I've got to. And so should you, Mr. Edwards. The Whig party is the party of sound money and God save the National Bank, ain't it?

NINIAN. Why, yes—among other things. . . .

ABE. Well, then—how would it look if you put forward a candidate who has demonstrated no earning power but who has run up the impressive total of fifteen hundred dollars of debts?

BOWLING. [*To* NINIAN.] I can tell you something about those debts. Abe started a grocery store in partnership with an unfortunate young man named Berry. Their stock included whiskey, and Berry started tapping the keg until he had consumed all the liquid assets. So the store went bankrupt—and Abe voluntarily assumed all the obligations. That may help to explain to you, Mr. Edwards, why we think pretty highly of him around here.

NINIAN. It's a sentiment with which I concur most heartily.

ABE. I thank you one and all for your kind tributes, but don't overdo them, or I'll begin to think that three dollars a day ain't enough!

JOSH. What's the one thing that you want most, Abe? You want to learn. This will give you your chance to get at a good library, to associate with the finest lawyers in the State.

ABE. I've got a copy of Blackstone already. Found it in an old junk barrel. And how can I tell you that the finest lawyers would welcome association with *me?*

NINIAN. You needn't worry about that. I saw how you dealt with those ruffians.

You quite obviously know how to handle men.

ABE. I can handle the Clary's Grove boys because I can outwrassle them—but I can't go around Sangamon County throwing *all* the voters.

BOWLING. [*Laughing.*] I'll take a chance on that, Abe.

ABE. [*To* NINIAN.] Besides—how do you know that my political views would agree with yours? How do you know I wouldn't say the wrong thing?

NINIAN. What *are* your political leanings, Mr. Lincoln?

ABE. They're all toward staying out. . . . What sort of leanings did you want?

NINIAN. We have a need for good conservative men to counteract all the radical firebrands that have swept over this country in the wake of Andrew Jackson. We've got to get this country back to first principles!

ABE. Well—I'm conservative, all right. If I got into the legislature you'd never catch me starting any movements for reform or progress. I'm pretty certain I wouldn't even have the nerve to open my mouth.

JOSH. [*Laughs.*] I told you, Ninian—he's just the type of candidate you're looking for. [NINIAN *laughs too, and rises.*]

NINIAN. [*Crossing toward* ABE.] The fact is, Mr. Lincoln, we want to spike the rumor that ours is the party of the more privileged classes. That is why we seek men of the plain people for candidates. As postmaster, you're in an excellent position to establish contacts. While delivering letters, you can also deliver speeches and campaign literature, with which our headquarters will keep you supplied.

ABE. Would you supply me with a suit of store clothes? A candidate mustn't look *too* plain.

NINIAN. [*Smiling.*] I think even that could be arranged, eh, Judge?

BOWLING. I think so.

NINIAN. [*Pompously.*] So—think it over, Mr. Lincoln, and realize that this is opportunity unlimited in scope. Just consider what it means to be starting up the ladder in a nation which is now expanding southward, across the vast area of Texas; and westward, to the Empire of the Californias on the Pacific Ocean. We're becoming a continent, Mr. Lincoln—and all that we need is men! [*He looks at his watch.*] And now, gentlemen, if you will excuse me—I must put in an appearance at the torch-light procession in Springfield this evening, so I shall have to be moving on. Good-by, Mr. Lincoln. This meeting has been a happy one for me.

ABE. [*Shaking hands.*] Good-by, Mr. Edwards. Good luck in the campaign.

NINIAN. And the same to you. [*All at the right have risen and are starting to go, except* BEN MATTLING, *who is still sitting at the back, drinking.*]

ABE. Here's your paper, Trum.

TRUM. Go ahead and finish it, Abe. I won't be looking at it yet awhile.

ABE. Thanks, Trum, I'll leave it at your house. [TRUM *and* NINIAN *have gone.*]

BOWLING. I'll see you later, Abe. Tell Ann I'll be back to pay for the liquor.

ABE. I'll tell her, Bowling. [BOWLING *goes.* JOSH *is looking at* ABE, *who, after a moment, turns to him.*] I'm surprised at you, Josh. I thought you were my friend.

JOSH. I know, Abe. But Ninian Edwards asked me is there anybody in that God-forsaken town of New Salem that stands a chance of getting votes, and the only one I could think of was you. I can see you're embarrassed by this—and you're annoyed. But—whether you like it or not—you've got to grow; and here's your chance to get a little scrap of importance.

ABE. Am I the kind that wants importance?

JOSH. You'll deny it, Abe—but you've got a funny kind of vanity—which is the same as saying you've got some pride—and it's badly in need of nourishment. So, if you'll agree to this—I don't think you'll be sorry for it or feel that I've betrayed you.

ABE. [*Grins.*] Oh—I won't hold it against you, Josh. [*He walks away and looks out the door.*] But that Mr. Ninian Edwards—he's rich and he's prominent and he's got a high-class education. Poli-

tics to him is just a kind of game. And maybe I'd like it if I could play it *his* way. [*He turns to* JOSH.] But when you get to reading Blackstone, not to mention the Bible, you can't help feeling maybe there's some serious responsibility in the giving of laws—and maybe there's something more important in the business of government than just getting the Whig Party back into power. [SETH GALE *comes in. He is a young, husky frontiersman, with flashes of the sun of Western empire in his eyes.*]

SETH. Hey, Abe—Feargus said you've got a letter for me.

ABE. [*Fishing in his mail pouch.*] Yes.

SETH. Hello, Mr. Speed.

JOSH. How are you, Mr. Gale?

ABE. Here you are, Seth. [*He hands him a letter.* SETH *takes it to the right, sits down and starts to read.*]

JOSH. I've got to get home to Springfield, Abe, but I'll be down again in a week or so.

ABE. I'll be here, Josh. [JOSH *goes.* ABE *sits down again at the right, picks up his paper, but doesn't read it.* BEN *stands up and comes down a bit unsteadily.*]

BEN. [*Angrily.*] Are you going to do it, Abe? Are you goin' to let them make you into a *candidate?*

ABE. I ain't had time to think about it yet.

BEN. Well—I tell you to stop thinkin' before it's too late. Don't let 'em get you. Don't let 'em put you in a store suit that's the uniform of degradation in this miserable country. You're an honest man, Abe Lincoln. You're a good-for-nothin', debt-ridden loafer—but you're an honest man. And you have no place in that den of thieves that's called gov'ment. They'll corrupt you as they've corrupted the whole damn United States. Look at Washington, look at Jefferson, and John Adams—[*He points grandly to the pictures.*]—where are they today? Dead! And everything they stood for and fought for and *won*—that's dead too. [ANN *comes in to collect the mugs from the table at the left.* ABE *looks at her.*] Why—we'd be better off if we was all black niggers held in the bonds of slavery. *They* get fed—*they* get looked after when they're old and sick. [ANN *goes.*] But *you* don't care—you ain't listenin' to me, neither . . . [*He starts slowly toward the door.*]

ABE. Of course I'm listening, Ben.

BEN. No, you ain't. *I* know. You're goin' to the assembly and join the wolves who're feedin' off the carcass of Liberty. [*He goes out.*]

ABE. You needn't worry. I'm not going. [ANN *comes in. She crosses to the right to pick up the glasses. She seems extremely subdued.* ABE *looks at her, curiously.*]

ABE. Bowling Green said to tell you he'd be back later, to pay you what he owes.

ANN. [*Curtly.*] That's all right. [ANN *puts the glasses and bottle on a tray and picks it up.* ABE *jumps to his feet.*]

ABE. Here, Ann. Let me take that.

ANN. [*Irritably.*] No—leave it alone! I can carry it! [*She starts across to the left.*]

ABE. Excuse me, Ann. . . .

ANN. [*Stopping.*] Well?

ABE. Would you come back after you're finished with that? I—I'd like to talk to you. [SETH *has finished the letter. Its contents seem to have depressed him.*]

ANN. All right. I'll talk to you—if you want. [*She goes out.* SETH *crosses toward* ABE, *who, during the subsequent dialogue, is continually looking toward the kitchen.*]

SETH. Abe . . . Abe—I got a letter from my folks back in Maryland. It means—I guess I've got to give up the dream we had of moving out into Nebraska territory.

ABE. What's happened, Seth?

SETH. [*Despondently.*] Well—for one thing, the old man's took sick, and he's pretty feeble.

ABE. I'm sorry to hear that.

SETH. So am I. They've sent for me to come back and work the farm. Measly little thirty-six acres—sandy soil. I tell you, Abe, it's a bitter disappointment to me, when I had my heart all set on going out into the West. And the worst of it is —I'm letting *you* down on it, too.

ABE. [*With a glance toward the kitchen.*] Don't think about that, Seth.

Maybe I won't be able to move for a while myself. And when your father gets to feeling better, you'll come back . . .

SETH. He won't get to feeling better. Not at his age. I'll be stuck there, just like he was. I'll be pushed in and cramped all the rest of my life, till the malaria gets me, too. . . . Well—there's no use crying about it. If I've got to go back East, I've got to go. [ANN *comes back.*] I'll tell you good-by, Abe, before I leave. [*He goes.* ABE *turns and looks at* ANN, *and she at him.*]

ANN. Well—what is it, Abe?

ABE. [*Rising.*] I just thought—you might like to talk to me.

ANN. [*Sharply.*] What about?

ABE. That letter you got from New York State.

ANN. What do *you* know about that letter?

ABE. I'm the postmaster. I know more than I ought to about people's private affairs. I couldn't help seeing that that was the handwriting of Mr. McNiel. And I couldn't help seeing, from the look on your face, that the bad news you've been afraid of has come. [ANN *looks at him with surprise. He is a lot more observant than she had thought.*]

ANN. Whatever the letter said it's no concern of yours, Abe.

ABE. I know that, Ann. But—it appears to me that you've been crying—and it makes me sad to think that something could have hurt you. The thing is—I think quite a lot of you—always have—ever since I first came here, and met you. I wouldn't mention it, only when you're distressed about something it's a comfort sometimes to find a pair of ears to pour your troubles into—and the Lord knows my ears are big enough to hold a lot. [*Her attitude of hostility softens and she rewards him with a tender smile.*]

ANN. You're a Christian gentleman, Abe Lincoln. [*She sits down.*]

ABE. No, I ain't. I'm a plain, common sucker with a shirt-tail so short I can't sit on it.

ANN. [*Laughs.*] Well—sit down, anyway, Abe—here, by me.

ABE. Why—it'd be a pleasure. [*He crosses and sits near her.*]

ANN. You can always say something to make a person laugh, can't you?

ABE. Well—I don't even have to *say* anything. A person just has to *look* at me.

ANN. You're right about that letter, Abe. It's the first I've heard from him in months—and now he says he's delayed by family troubles and doesn't know when he'll be able to get to New Salem again. By which he probably means— never.

ABE. I wouldn't say that, Ann.

ANN. I would. [*She looks at him.*] I reckon you think I'm a silly fool for ever having promised myself to Mr. McNiel.

ABE. I think no such thing. I liked him myself, and still do, and whatever reasons he had for changing his name I'm sure were honorable. He's a smart man, and a handsome one—and I—I wouldn't blame any girl for—loving him.

ANN. [*Too emphatically.*] I guess I don't love him, Abe. I guess I couldn't love anybody that was as—as faithless as that.

ABE. [*Trying to appear unconcerned.*] Well, then. There's nothing to fret about. Now—poor Seth Gale—he got some *really* bad news. His father's sick and he has to give up his dream which was to go and settle out West.

ANN. [*Looks at him.*] I don't believe you know much about females, Abe.

ABE. Probably I don't—although I certainly spend enough time thinking about 'em.

ANN. You're a big man, and you can lick anybody, and you can't understand the feelings of somebody who is weak. But—I'm a female, and I can't help thinking what they'll be saying about me—all the old gossips, all over town. They'll make it out that he deserted me; I'm a rejected woman. They'll give me their sympathy to my face, but they'll snigger at me behind my back. [*She rises and crosses toward the right.*]

ABE. Yes—that's just about what they would do. But—would you let *them* disturb you?

ANN. [*Rising.*] I told you—it's just weakness—it's just vanity. It's something you couldn't understand, Abe. [*She has*

crossed to the window and is staring out. ABE *twists in his chair to look at her.*]

ABE. Maybe I can understand it, Ann. I've got a kind of vanity myself. Josh Speed said so, and he's right. . . . It's— it's nothing but vanity that's kept me from declaring my inclinations toward you. [*She turns, amazed, and looks at him.*] You see, I don't like to be sniggered at, either. I know what I am—and I know what I look like—and I know that I've got nothing to offer any girl that I'd be in love with.

ANN. Are you saying that you're in love with me, Abe?

ABE. [*With deep earnestness.*] Yes—I am saying that. [*He stands up, facing her. She looks intently into his eyes.*] I've been loving you—a long time—with all my heart. You see, Ann—you're a particularly fine girl. You've got sense, and you've got bravery—those are two things that I admire particularly. And you're powerful good to look at, too. So—it's only natural I should have a great regard for you. But—I don't mean to worry you about it, Ann. I only mentioned it because—if you would do me the honor of keeping company with me for a while, it might shut the old gossips' mouths. They'd figure you'd chucked McNiel for —for someone else. Even me.

ANN. [*Going to him.*] I thought I knew you pretty well, Abe. But I didn't.

ABE. [*Worried.*] Why do you say that? Do you consider I was too forward, in speaking out as I did?

ANN. [*Gravely.*] No, Abe. . . . I've always thought a lot of you—the way I thought you were. But—the idea of love between you and me—I can't say how I feel about that, because now you're like some other person, that I'm meeting for the first time.

ABE. [*Quietly.*] I'm not expecting you to feel anything for me. I'd never dream of expecting such a thing.

ANN. I know that, Abe. You'd be willing to give everything you have and never expect anything in return. Maybe you're different in that way from any man I've ever heard of. And I can tell you this much—now, and truthfully—if I ever do love you, I'll be happy about it—

and lucky, to be loving a good, decent man. . . . If you just give me time—to think about it. . . .

ABE. [*Unable to believe his eyes and ears.*] You mean—if you took time—you might get in your heart something like the feeling I have for you?

ANN. [*With great tenderness.*] I don't know, Abe. [*She clutches his lapel.*] But I do know that you're a man who could fill any one's heart—yes, fill it and warm it and make it glad to be living. [ABE *covers her hand with his.*]

ABE. Ann—I've always tried hard to believe what the orators tell us—that this is a land of equal opportunity for all. But I've never been able to credit it, any more than I could agree that God made all men in his own image. But—if I could win you, Ann—I'd be willing to disbelieve everything I've ever seen with my own eyes, and have faith in everything wonderful that I've ever read in poetry books. [*Both are silent for a moment. Then* ANN *turns away.*] But—I'm not asking you to say anything now. And I won't ask you until the day comes when I know I've got a right to. [*He turns and walks quickly toward the door, picking up his mail pouch.*]

ANN. Abe! Where are you going?

ABE. I'm going to find Bowling Green and tell him a good joke. [*He grins. He is standing in the doorway.*]

ANN. A *joke?* What about?

ABE. I'm going to tell him that I'm a candidate for the assembly of the State of Illinois. [*He goes. The light fades.*]

3

BOWLING GREEN'S house near New Salem. It is a small room, but the walls are lined with books and family pictures. In the center is a table with a lamp on it. Another light—a candle in a glass globe —is on a bureau at the right. There are comfortable chairs on either side of the table, and a sofa at the left. At the back, toward the left, is the front door. A rifle is leaning against the wall by the door. There is another door in the right wall. Toward the right, at the back, is a lad-der fixed against the wall leading up through an opening to the attic. It is late in the evening, a year or so after Scene II. A storm is raging outside.

BOWLING is reading aloud from a sort of pamphlet. His comfortable wife, NANCY, is listening and sewing.

BOWLING. "And how much more interesting did the spectacle become when, starting into full life and animation, as a simultaneous call for 'Pickwick' burst from his followers, that illustrious man slowly mounted into the Windsor chair, on which he had been previously seated, and addressed the club himself had founded." [BOWLING *chuckles.* NANCY *laughs.*]

NANCY. He sounds precisely like *you,* Bowling. [*There is a knock at the door.*]

NANCY. [*Nervous.*] That's not Abe's knock. Who can it be?

BOWLING. [*Rising.*] We don't know yet, my dear.

NANCY. It's a strange hour for any one to be calling. You'd better have that gun ready. [BOWLING *unbolts and opens the door. It is* JOSH SPEED.]

BOWLING. Why—Josh Speed!

JOSH. Good evening, Bowling.

BOWLING. We haven't seen you in a coon's age.

NANCY. Good evening, Mr. Speed.

JOSH. Good evening, Mrs. Green. And I beg you to forgive me for this untimely intrusion.

NANCY. We're delighted to see you. Take your wrap off.

JOSH. Thank you. I've just come down from Springfield. I heard Abe Lincoln was in town and I was told I might find him here.

BOWLING. He's been sleeping here, up in the attic.

NANCY. But he's out at the Rutledge Farm, tending poor little Ann.

JOSH. Miss Rutledge? What's the matter with her?

NANCY. She's been taken with the brain sickness. It's the most shocking thing. People have been dying from it right and left.

BOWLING. But Ann's young. She'll pull through, all right. Sit down, Josh.

JOSH. Thank you. [*He sits.* BOWLING *places the pamphlet on the top of the bookcase and stands there, filling his pipe.*]

NANCY. I suppose you know that Abe came rushing down from Vandalia the moment he heard she was taken. He's deeply in love with her.

BOWLING. Now, Nancy—don't exaggerate. [JOSH *is listening to all this, intently.*]

JOSH. So Abe is in love. I wondered what has been the matter with him lately.

NANCY. Why, it's written all over his poor, homely face.

JOSH. The last time I saw him, he seemed pretty moody. But when I asked him what was wrong, he said it was his liver.

BOWLING. [*Laughing.*] That sounds more likely. Has he been getting on well in the Assembly?

JOSH. No. He has just been sitting there —drawing his three dollars a day—and taking no apparent interest in the proceedings. Do you fancy that Miss Rutledge cares anything for him?

NANCY. Indeed she does! She broke her promise to that Mr. McNiel because of her feelings for Abe!

JOSH. Has he any notion of marrying her?

NANCY. It's the only notion of his life right now. And the sooner they are married, the better for both of them.

BOWLING. [*Seating himself.*] Better for her, perhaps—but the worse for him.

NANCY. [*Finishing her sewing.*] And why? The Rutledges are fine people, superior in every way to those riff-raff Hankses and Lincolns that are Abe's family!

BOWLING. I think you feel as I do, Josh. Abe has his own way to go and—sweet and pretty as Ann undoubtedly is—she'd only be a hindrance to him.

JOSH. I guess it wouldn't matter much if she could give him a little of the happiness he's never had.

NANCY. [*Rising.*] That's just it! I think as much of Abe as you do, Bowling. But we can't deny that he's a poor man, and he's failed in trade, and he's been in the legislature for a year without accomplishing a blessed thing . . . [*She goes to the bookcase to put her sewing-basket away.*]

BOWLING. He could go to Springfield and set up a law practice and make a good thing of it. Ninian Edwards would help him to get started. And he'd soon forget little Ann. He has just happened to fasten on her his own romantic ideal of what's beautiful and unattainable. Let him ever attain her, and she'd break his heart.

NANCY. [*Seating herself.*] Do you agree with Bowling on that, Mr. Speed?

JOSH. [*Sadly.*] I can't say, Mrs. Green. I've abandoned the attempt to predict anything about Abe Lincoln. The first time I ever saw him was when he was piloting that steamboat, the *Talisman.* You remember how she ran into trouble at the dam. I had a valuable load of goods aboard for my father's store, and I was sure that steamboat, goods, and all were a total loss. But Abe got her through. It was a great piece of work. I thought, "Here is a reliable man." So I cultivated his acquaintance, believing, in my conceit, that I could help him to fame and fortune. I soon learned differently. I found out that he has plenty of strength and courage in his body—but in his mind he's a hopeless hypochondriac. He can split rails, push a plough, crack jokes, all day —and then sit up all night reading "Hamlet" and brooding over his own fancied resemblance to that melancholy prince. Maybe he's a great philosopher—maybe he's a great fool. I don't know what he is.

BOWLING. [*Laughs.*] Well—if only Ann had sense enough to see all the things *you* saw, Josh, she'd be so terrified of him she'd run all the way back to York State and find McNiel. At least, *he's* not complicated.

NANCY. [*With deeper emotion.*] You're talking about Abe Lincoln as if he were some problem that you found in a book, and it's interesting to try to figure it out. Well—maybe he is a problem—but he's also a man, and a miserable one. And what do you do for his misery? You laugh at his comical jokes and you vote for him on election day and give him board and lodging when he needs it. But all that doesn't give a scrap of satisfaction to Abe's soul—and never will. Because the one thing he needs is a woman with the will to face life for him.

BOWLING. You think he's afraid to face it himself?

NANCY. He is! He listens too much to the whispers that he heard in the forest where he grew up, and where he always goes now when he wants to be alone. They're the whispers of the women behind him—his dead mother—and *her* mother, who was no better than she should be. He's got that awful fear on him, of not knowing what the whispers mean, or where they're directing him. And none of your back-slapping will knock that fear out of him. Only a woman can free him—a woman who loves him truly, and believes in him . . . [*There is a knock on the door.*]

BOWLING. That's Abe now. [*He gets up and opens it.* ABE *is there, bareheaded, wet by the storm. He now wears a fairly respectable dark suit of clothes. He looks older and grimmer.*]

BOWLING. Why, hello, Abe! We've been sitting up waiting for you. Come on in out of the wet! [ABE *comes in.* BOWLING *shuts the door behind him.*]

NANCY. We were reading "The Posthumous Papers of the Pickwick Club" when Mr. Speed came in.

ABE. Hello, Josh. Glad to see you.

JOSH. Hello, Abe. [ABE *turns to* NANCY.]

ABE. Nancy . . .

NANCY. Yes, Abe?

ABE. She's dead.

BOWLING. Ann? She's dead?

ABE. Yes. Tonight the fever suddenly got worse. They couldn't seem to do anything for it. [NANCY *gives* BOWLING *a swift look, then goes quickly to* ABE *and takes his hand.*]

NANCY. Oh, Abe—I'm so sorry. She was such a dear little girl. Every one who knew her will join in mourning for her.

ABE. I know they will. But it won't do any good. She's dead.

BOWLING. Sit down, Abe, and rest yourself.

ABE. No—I'm not fit company for anybody. I'd better be going. [*He turns toward the door.*]

JOSH. [*Stopping him.*] No, you don't,

Abe. You'll stay right here.

BOWLING. You better do what Josh tells you.

NANCY. Come here, Abe. Please sit down. [ABE *looks from one to the other, then obediently goes to a chair and sits.*] Your bed is ready for you upstairs when you want it.

ABE. [*Dully.*] You're the best friends I've got in the world, and it seems a pretty poor way to reward you for all that you've given me, to come here now, and inflict you with a corpse.

BOWLING. This is your home, Abe. This is where you're loved.

ABE. Yes, that's right. And I love you, Bowling and Nancy. But I loved her more than everything else that I've ever known.

NANCY. I know you did, Abe. I know it.

ABE. I used to think it was better to be alone. I was always most contented when I was alone. I had queer notions that if you got too close to people, you could see the truth about them, that behind the surface they're all insane, and they could see the same in you. And then—when I saw her, I knew there could be beauty and purity in people—like the purity you sometimes see in the sky at night. When I took hold of her hand and held it, all fear, all doubt, went out of me. I believed in God. I'd have been glad to work for her until I die, to get for her everything out of life that she wanted. If she thought I could do it, then I could. That was my belief. . . . And then I had to stand there, as helpless as a twig in a whirlpool; I had to stand there and watch her die. And her father and mother were there, too, praying to God for her soul. "The Lord giveth, and the Lord taketh away, blessed be the name of the Lord!" That's what they kept on saying. But I couldn't pray with them. I couldn't give any devotion to one who has the power of death, and uses it. [*He has stood up, and is speaking with more passion.*] I'm making a poor exhibition of myself—and I'm sorry—but—I can't stand it. I can't live with myself any longer. I've got to die and be with her again, or I'll go crazy! [*He goes to the door and opens it. The storm continues.*] I can't bear to think of her out there alone! [NANCY *looks at* BOWLING *with frantic appeal. He goes to* ABE, *who is standing in the doorway, looking out.*]

BOWLING. [*With great tenderness.*] Abe . . . I want you to go upstairs and see if you can't get some sleep. . . . Please, Abe —as a special favor to Nancy and me.

ABE. [*After a moment.*] All right, Bowling. [*He turns and goes to the ladder.*]

NANCY. Here's a light for you, dear Abe. [*She hands him the candle.*]

ABE. Thank you, Nancy. . . . Good night. [*He goes up the ladder into the attic. They all look up after him.*]

NANCY. [*Tearful.*] Poor, lonely soul. [BOWLING *cautions her to be quiet.*]

JOSH. Keep him here with you, Mrs. Green. Don't let him out of your sight.

BOWLING. We won't, Josh.

JOSH. Good night. [*He picks up his hat and cloak and goes.*]

BOWLING. Good night, Josh. [*He closes and bolts the door, then comes down to the table and picks up the lamp.* NANCY *looks up once more, then goes out at the right.* BOWLING *follows her out, carrying the lamp with him. He closes the door behind him, so that the only light on the stage is the beam from the attic.*]

CURTAIN

ACT TWO

4

Law office of Stuart and Lincoln on the second floor of the Court House in Springfield, Illinois. A sunny summer's afternoon, some five years after the preceding scene. The room is small, with two windows and one door, upstage, which leads to the hall and staircase. At the right is a table and chair, at the left an old desk, littered with papers. At the back is a ramshackle bed, with a buffalo robe thrown over it. Below the windows are some rough shelves, sagging with law books. There is an old wood stove. On the wall above the desk is hung an American flag, with 26 stars. Between the windows is an election poster, for Harrison and Tyler, with a list of Electors, the last of whom is Ab'm Lincoln, of Sangamon.

BILLY HERNDON is working at the table. He is young, slight, serious-minded, smouldering. He looks up as ABE comes in. ABE wears a battered plug hat, a light alpaca coat, and carries an ancient, threadbare carpet-bag. He is evidently not in a talkative mood. His boots are caked in mud. He is only thirty-one years old, but his youth was buried with Ann Rutledge. He leaves the office door open, and lettered on it we see the number 4,

and the firm's name—Stuart & Lincoln, Attorneys & Counsellors at Law.

BILLY. How de do, Mr. Lincoln? Glad to see you back.

ABE. Good day, Billy. [*He sets down the carpet-bag, takes off his hat and puts it on his desk.*]

BILLY. How was it on the circuit, Mr. Lincoln?

ABE. About as usual.

BILLY. Have you been keeping in good health?

ABE. Not particularly. But Doc Henry dosed me enough to keep me going. [*He sits down at the desk and starts looking at letters and papers that have accumulated during his absence. He takes little interest in them, pigeonholing some letters unopened.*]

BILLY. Did you have occasion to make any political speeches?

ABE. Oh—they got me up on the stump a couple of times. Ran into Stephen Douglas—he was out campaigning, of course—and we had some argument in public.

BILLY. [*Greatly interested.*] That's good! What issues did you and Mr. Douglas discuss?

ABE. Now—don't get excited, Billy. We

weren't taking it serious. There was no blood shed. . . . What's the news here?

BILLY. Judge Stuart wrote that he arrived safely in Washington and the campaign there is getting almost as hot as the weather. Mrs. Fraim stopped in to say she couldn't possibly pay your fee for a while.

ABE. I should hope not. I ought to be paying her, seeing as I defended her poor husband and he hanged. [BILLY *hands him a letter and watches him intently while he reads it.*]

BILLY. That was left here by hand, and I promised to call it especially to your attention. It's from the Elijah P. Lovejoy League of Freemen. They want you to speak at an Abolitionist rally next Thursday evening. It'll be a very important affair.

ABE. [*Reflectively.*] It's funny, Billy—I was thinking about Lovejoy the other day—trying to figure what it is in a man that makes him glad to be a martyr. I was on the boat coming from Quincy to Alton, and there was a gentleman on board with twelve Negroes. He was shipping them down to Vicksburg for sale—had 'em chained six and six together. Each of them had a small iron clevis around his wrist, and this was chained to the main chain, so that those Negroes were strung together precisely like fish on a trotline. I gathered they were being separated forever from their homes—mothers, fathers, wives, children—whatever families the poor creatures had got—going to be whipped into perpetual slavery, and no questions asked. It was quite a shocking sight.

BILLY. [*Excited.*] Then you will give a speech at the Lovejoy rally?

ABE. [*Wearily.*] I doubt it. That Freemen's League is a pack of hell-roaring fanatics. Talk reason to them and they scorn you for being a mealy-mouth. Let 'em make their own noise. [ABE *has opened a letter. He starts to read it.* BILLY *looks at him with resentful disappointment, but he knows too well that any argument would be futile. He resumes his work. After a moment,* BOWLING GREEN *comes in, followed by* JOSH SPEED.]

BOWLING. Are we interrupting the majesty of the Law?

ABE. [*Heartily.*] Bowling! [*He jumps up and grasps* BOWLING's *hand.*] How are you, Bowling?

BOWLING. Tolerably well, Abe—and glad to see you.

ABE. This is Billy Herndon—Squire Green, of New Salem. Hello, Josh.

JOSH. Hello, Abe.

BILLY. [*Shaking hands with* BOWLING.] I'm proud to know you, sir. Mr. Lincoln speaks of you constantly.

BOWLING. Thank you, Mr. Herndon. Are you a lawyer, too?

BILLY. [*Seriously.*] I hope to be, sir. I'm serving here as a clerk in Judge Stuart's absence.

BOWLING. So now you're teaching others, Abe?

ABE. Just providing a bad example.

BOWLING. I can believe it. Look at the mess on that desk. Shameful!

ABE. Give me another year of law practice and I'll need a warehouse for the overflow. . . . But—sit yourself down, Bowling, and tell me what brings you to Springfield. [BOWLING *sits.* JOSH *has sat on the couch, smoking his pipe.* BILLY *is again at the table.*]

BOWLING. I've been up to Lake Michigan—fishing—came in today on the steamcars—scared me out of a year's growth. But how are you doing, Abe? Josh says you're still broke, but you're a great social success.

ABE. True—on both counts. I'm greatly in demand at all the more elegant functions. You remember Ninian Edwards?

BOWLING. Of course.

ABE. Well, sir—I'm a guest at his mansion regularly. He's got a house so big you could race horses in the parlor. And his wife is one of the Todd family from Kentucky. Very high-grade people. They spell their name with two D's—which is pretty impressive when you consider that one was enough for God.

JOSH. Tell Bowling whom you met over in Rochester.

ABE. The President of the United States!

BOWLING. You don't tell me so!

ABE. Do you see that hand? [*He holds out his right hand, palm upward.*]

BOWLING. Yes—I see it.

ABE. It has shaken the hand of Martin Van Buren!

BOWLING. [*Laughing.*] Was the President properly respectful to you, Abe?

ABE. Indeed he was! He said to me, "We've been hearing great things of you in Washington." I found out later he'd said the same thing to every other crossroads politician he'd met. [*He laughs.*] But Billy Herndon there is pretty disgusted with me for associating with the wrong kind of people. Billy's a firebrand —a real, radical abolitionist—and he can't stand anybody who keeps his mouth shut and abides by the Constitution. If he had his way, the whole Union would be set on fire and we'd all be burned to a crisp. Eh, Billy?

BILLY. [*Grimly.*] Yes, Mr. Lincoln. And if you'll permit me to say so, I think you'd be of more use to your fellowmen if you allowed some of the same incendiary impulses to come out in you.

ABE. You see, Bowling? He wants me to get down into the blood-soaked arena and grapple with all the lions of injustice and oppression.

BOWLING. Mr. Herndon—my profound compliments.

BILLY. [*Rising and taking his hat.*] Thank you, sir. [*He shakes hands with* BOWLING, *then turns to* ABE.] I have the writ prepared in the Willcox case. I'll take it down to the Clerk of Court to be attested.

ABE. All right, Billy.

BILLY. [*To* BOWLING.] Squire Green— Mr. Lincoln regards you and Mr. Speed as the best friends he has on earth, and I should like to beg you, in his presence, for God's sake drag him out of this stagnant pool in which he's rapidly drowning himself. Good day, sir—good day, Mr. Speed.

JOSH. Good day, Billy. [BILLY *has gone.*]

BOWLING. That's a bright young man, Abe. Seems to have a good grasp of things.

ABE. [*Looking after* BILLY.] He's going downstairs to the Clerk's office, but he

took his hat. Which means that before he comes back to work, he'll have paid a little visit to the Chenery House saloon.

BOWLING. Does the boy drink?

ABE. Yes. He's got great fires in him, but he's putting 'em out fast. . . . Now— tell me about New Salem. [*He leans against the wall near the window.*]

BOWLING. Practically nothing of it left.

ABE. How's that blessed wife of yours?

BOWLING. Nancy's busier than ever, and more than ever concerned about your innermost thoughts and yearnings. In fact, she instructed me expressly to ask what on earth is the matter with you?

ABE. [*Laughs.*] You can tell her there's nothing the matter. I've been able to pay off my debts to the extent of some seven cents on the dollar, and I'm sound of skin and skeleton.

BOWLING. But why don't we hear more from you and of you?

ABE. Josh can tell you. I've been busy.

BOWLING. What at?

ABE. I'm a candidate.

JOSH. [*Pointing to the poster.*] Haven't you noticed his name? It's here—at the bottom of the list of Electors on the Whig ticket.

ABE. Yes, sir—if old Tippecanoe wins next fall, I'll be a member of the Electoral College.

BOWLING. The Electoral College! And is that the best you can do?

ABE. Yes—in the limited time at my disposal. I had a letter from Seth Gale—remember—he used to live in New Salem and was always aiming to move West. He's settled down in Maryland now and has a wife and a son. He says that back East they're powerful worried about the annexation of Texas.

BOWLING. They have reason to be. It would probably mean extending slavery through all the territories, from Kansas and Nebraska right out to Oregon and California. That would give the South absolute rule of the country—and God help the rest of us in the free states.

JOSH. It's an ugly situation, all right. It's got the seeds in it of nothing more nor less than civil war.

ABE. Well, if so, it'll be the abolitionists' own fault. They know where this trouble might lead, and yet they go right on agitating. They ought to be locked up for disturbing the peace, all of them.

BOWLING. I thought you were opposed to slavery, Abe. Have you changed your mind about it?

ABE. [*Ambles over to the couch and sprawls on it.*] No. I am opposed to slavery. But I'm even more opposed to going to war. And, on top of that, I know what you're getting at, both of you. [*He speaks to them with the utmost good nature.*] You're following Billy Herndon's lead—troubling your kind hearts with concerns about me and when am I going to amount to something. Is that it?

BOWLING. Oh, no, Abe. Far be it from me to interfere in your life.

JOSH. Or me, either. If we happen to feel that, so far, you've been a big disappointment to us, we'll surely keep it to ourselves.

ABE. [*Laughs.*] I'm afraid you'll have to do what I've had to do—which is, learn to accept me for what I am. I'm no fighting man. I found that out when I went through the Black Hawk War, and was terrified that I might have to fire a shot at an Indian. Fortunately, the Indians felt the same way, so I never saw one of them. Now, I know plenty of men who like to fight; they're willing to kill, and not scared of being killed. All right. Let them attend to the battles that have to be fought.

BOWLING. Peaceable men have sometimes been of service to their country.

ABE. They may have been peaceable when they started, but they didn't remain so long after they'd become mixed in the great brawl of politics. [*He sits up.*] Suppose I ran for Congress and got elected. I'd be right in the thick of that ugly situation you were speaking of. One day I might have to cast my vote on the terrible issue of war or peace. It might be war with Mexico over Texas; or war with England over Oregon; or even war with our own people across the Ohio River. What attitude would I take in deciding which way to vote? "The Liberal attitude," of course. And what is the Liberal attitude? To go to war, for a tract of land, or a moral principle? Or to avoid

war at all costs? No, sir. The place for me is in the Electoral College, where all I have to do is vote for the President whom everybody else elected four months previous.

BOWLING. Well, Abe—you were always an artful dodger—and maybe you'll be able to go on to the end of your days avoiding the clutch of your own conscience. [NINIAN EDWARDS *comes in. He is a little stouter and more prosperous.*]

ABE—JOSH. Hello, Ninian.

NINIAN. Hello. I saw Billy Herndon at the Chenery House and he said you were back from the circuit. [*He sees* BOWLING.] Why—it's my good friend Squire Green. How de do?—and welcome to Springfield. [*He shakes hands with* BOWLING.]

BOWLING. Thank you, Mr. Edwards.

NINIAN. I just called in, Abe, to tell you you must dine with us. And, Squire, Mrs. Edwards would be honored to receive you, if your engagements will permit—and you, too, Josh.

JOSH. Delighted!

NINIAN. We're proudly exhibiting my sister-in-law, Miss Mary Todd, who has just come from Kentucky to grace our home. She's a very gay young lady—speaks French like a native, recites poetry at the drop of a hat, and knows the names and habits of all the flowers. I've asked Steve Douglas and some of the other eligibles to meet her, so you boys had better get in early.

BOWLING. My compliments to Mrs. Edwards, but my own poor wife awaits me impatiently, I hope.

NINIAN. I appreciate your motives, Squire, and applaud them. You'll be along presently, Abe?

ABE. I wouldn't be surprised.

NINIAN. Good. You'll meet a delightful young lady. And I'd better warn you she's going to survey the whole field of matrimonial prospects and select the one who promises the most. So you'd better be on your guard, Abe, unless you're prepared to lose your standing as a free man.

ABE. I thank you for the warning, Ninian.

NINIAN. Good day to you, Squire. See you later, Josh. [*He goes out.*]

ABE. There, Bowling—you see how things are with me. Hardly a day goes by but what I'm invited to meet some eager young female who has all the graces, including an ability to speak the language of diplomacy.

BOWLING. I'm sorry, Abe, that I shan't be able to hear you carrying on a flirtation in French. [ABE *looks at him, curiously.*]

ABE. I'm not pretending with you, Bowling—or you, Josh. I couldn't fool you any better than I can fool myself. I know what you're thinking about me, and I think so, too. Only I'm not so merciful in considering my own shortcomings, or so ready to forgive them, as you are. But—you talk about civil war—there seems to be one going on inside me all the time. Both sides are right and both are wrong and equal in strength. I'd like to be able to rise superior to the struggle—but—it says in the Bible that a house divided against itself cannot stand, so I reckon there's not much hope. One of these days, I'll just split asunder, and part company with myself—and it'll be a good riddance from both points of view. However—come on. [*He takes his hat.*] You've got to get back to Nancy, and Josh and I have got to make a good impression upon Miss Mary Todd, of Kentucky. [*He waves them to the door. As they go out, the light fades.*]

5

Parlor of the Edwards house in Springfield. An evening in November, some six months after the preceding scene. There is a fireplace at the right, a heavily curtained bay window at the left, a door at the back leading into the front hall. At the right, by the fireplace, are a small couch and an easy chair. There is another couch at the left, and a table and chairs at the back. There are family portraits on the walls. It is all moderately elegant.

NINIAN is standing before the fire, in conversation with ELIZABETH, his wife. She is high-bred, ladylike—excessively

so. She is, at the moment, in a state of some agitation.

ELIZABETH. I cannot believe it! It is an outrageous reflection on my sister's good sense.

NINIAN. I'm not so sure of that. Mary has known Abe for several months, and she has had plenty of chance to observe him closely.

ELIZABETH. She has been entertained by him, as we all have. But she has been far more attentive to Edwin Webb and Stephen Douglas and many others who are distinctly eligible.

NINIAN. Isn't it remotely possible that she sees more in Abe than you do?

ELIZABETH. Nonsense! Mr. Lincoln's chief virtue is that he hides no part of his simple soul from any one. He's a most amiable creature, to be sure; but as the husband of a high-bred, high-spirited young lady . . .

NINIAN. Quite so, Elizabeth. Mary *is* high-spirited! That is just why she set her cap for him. [ELIZABETH *looks at him sharply, then laughs.*]

ELIZABETH. You're making fun of me, Ninian. You're deliberately provoking me into becoming excited about nothing.

NINIAN. No, Elizabeth—I am merely trying to prepare you for a rude shock. You think Abe Lincoln would be overjoyed to capture an elegant, cultivated girl, daughter of the President of the Bank of Kentucky, descendant of a long line of English gentlemen. Well, you are mistaken . . . [MARY TODD *comes in. She is twenty-two—short, pretty, remarkably sharp. She stops short in the doorway, and her suspecting eyes dart from* ELIZABETH *to* NINIAN.]

MARY. What were you two talking about?

NINIAN. I was telling your sister about the new song the boys are singing:
"What is the great commotion, motion,
Our country through?
It is the ball a-rolling on
For Tippecanoe and Tyler, too—for Tippecanoe . . ."

MARY. [*With a rather grim smile.*] I compliment you for thinking quickly, Ninian. But you were talking about *me!*

[*She looks at* ELIZABETH, *who quails a little before her sister's determination.*] Weren't you?

ELIZABETH. Yes, Mary, we were.

MARY. And quite seriously, I gather.

NINIAN. I'm afraid that our dear Elizabeth has become unduly alarmed . . .

ELIZABETH. [*Snapping at him.*] Let me say what I have to say! [*She turns to* MARY.] Mary—you must tell me the truth. Are you—have you ever given one moment's serious thought to the possibility of marriage with Abraham Lincoln? [MARY *looks at each of them, her eyes flashing.*] I promise you, Mary, that to me such a notion is too far beyond the bounds of credibility to be . . .

MARY. But Ninian has raised the horrid subject, hasn't he? He has brought the evil scandal out into the open, and we must face it, fearlessly. Let us do so at once, by all means. I shall answer you, Elizabeth: I have given more than one moment's thought to the possibility you mentioned—and I have decided that I shall be Mrs. Lincoln. [*She seats herself on the couch.* NINIAN *is about to say, "I told you so," but thinks better of it.* ELIZABETH *can only gasp and gape.*] I have examined, carefully, the qualifications of all the young gentlemen, and some of the old ones, in this neighborhood. Those of Mr. Lincoln seem to me superior to all others, and he is my choice.

ELIZABETH. Do you expect me to congratulate you upon this amazing selection?

MARY. No! I ask for no congratulations, nor condolences, either.

ELIZABETH. [*Turning away.*] Then I shall offer none.

NINIAN. Forgive me for prying, Mary—but have you as yet communicated your decision to the gentleman himself?

MARY. [*With a slight smile at* NINIAN.] Not yet. But he is coming to call this evening, and he will ask humbly for my hand in marriage; and, after I have displayed the proper amount of surprise and confusion, I shall murmur, timidly, "Yes!"

ELIZABETH. [*Pitiful.*] You make a brave jest of it, Mary. But as for me, I am deeply and painfully shocked. I don't know what to say to you. But I urge you,

I beg you, as your elder sister, responsible to our father and our dead mother for your welfare . . .

MARY. [*With a certain tenderness.*] I can assure you, Elizabeth—it is useless to beg or command. I have made up my mind.

NINIAN. I admire your courage, Mary, but I should like . . .

ELIZABETH. I think, Ninian, that that is a matter for discussion solely between my sister and myself!

MARY. No! I want to hear what Ninian has to say. [*To* NINIAN.] What is it?

NINIAN. I only wondered if I might ask you another question.

MARY. [*Calmly.*] You may.

NINIAN. Understand, my dear—I'm not quarreling with you. My affection for Abe is eternal—but—I'm curious to know —what is it about him that makes you choose him for a husband?

MARY. [*Betraying her first sign of uncertainty.*] I should like to give you a plain, simple answer, Ninian. But I cannot.

ELIZABETH. [*Jumping at this.*] Of course you cannot! You're rushing blindly into this. You have no conception of what it will mean to your future.

MARY. You're wrong about that, Elizabeth. This is not the result of wild, tempestuous infatuation. I have not been swept off my feet. Mr. Lincoln is a Westerner, but that is his only point of resemblance to Young Lochinvar. I simply feel that of all the men I've ever known, he is the one whose life and destiny I want most to share.

ELIZABETH. Haven't you sense enough to know you could never be happy with him? His breeding—his background—his manner—his whole point of view . . .?

MARY. [*Gravely.*] I could not be content with a "happy" marriage in the accepted sense of the word. I have no craving for comfort and security.

ELIZABETH. And have you a craving for the kind of life you would lead? A miserable cabin, without a servant, without a stitch of clothing that is fit for exhibition in decent society?

MARY. [*Raising her voice.*] I have not yet tried poverty, so I cannot say how I should take to it. But I might well prefer it to anything I have previously known—so long as there is forever before me the chance for high adventure—so long as I can know that I am always going forward, with my husband, along a road that leads across the horizon. [*This last is said with a sort of mad intensity.*]

ELIZABETH. And how far do you think you will go with any one like Abe Lincoln, who is lazy and shiftless and prefers to stop constantly along the way to tell jokes?

MARY. [*Rising; furious.*] He will *not* stop, if I am strong enough to make him go on! And I am strong! I know what *you* expect of me. You want me to do precisely as you have done—and marry a man like Ninian—and I know many, that are *just* like him! But with all due respect to my dear brother-in-law—I don't want that—and I won't have it! Never! You live in a house with a fence around it—presumably to prevent the common herd from gaining access to your sacred precincts—but really to prevent you, yourselves, from escaping from your own narrow lives. In Abraham Lincoln I see a man who has split rails for other men's fences, but who will never build one around himself!

ELIZABETH. What are you *saying,* Mary? You are talking with a degree of irresponsibility that is not far from sheer madness . . .

MARY. [*Scornfully.*] I imagine it does seem like insanity to you! You married a man who was settled and established in the world, with a comfortable inheritance, and no problems to face. And you've never made a move to change your condition, or improve it. You consider it couldn't be improved. To you, all this represents perfection. But it doesn't to me! I want the chance to *shape* a new life, for myself, and for my husband. Is that irresponsibility? [*A* MAID *appears.*]

MAID. Mr. Lincoln, ma'am.

ELIZABETH. He's here.

MARY. [*Firmly.*] I shall see him!

MAID. Will you step in, Mr. Lincoln? [ABE *comes in, wearing a new suit, his hair nearly neat.*]

ABE. Good evening, Mrs. Edwards. Good evening, Miss Todd. Ninian, good evening.

ELIZABETH. Good evening.

MARY. Good evening, Mr. Lincoln. [*She sits on the couch at the left.*]

NINIAN. Glad to see you, Abe. [ABE *sees that there is electricity in the atmosphere of this parlor. He tries hard to be affably casual.*]

ABE. I'm afraid I'm a little late in arriving, but I ran into an old friend of mine, wife of Jack Armstrong, the champion rowdy of New Salem. I believe you have some recollection of him, Ninian.

NINIAN. [*Smiling.*] I most certainly have. What's he been up to now?

ABE. [*Stands in front of the fireplace.*] Oh, he's all right, but Hannah, his wife, is in fearful trouble because her son Duff is up for murder and she wants me to defend him. I went over to the jail to interview the boy and he looks pretty tolerably guilty to me. But I used to give him lessons in the game of marbles while his mother foxed my pants for me. [*He turns to* ELIZABETH.] That means, she sewed buckskin around the legs of my pants so I wouldn't tear 'em to shreds going through underbrush when I was surveying. Well—in view of old times, I felt I had to take the case and do what I can to obstruct the orderly processes of justice.

NINIAN. [*Laughs, with some relief.*] And the boy will be acquitted. I tell you, Abe—this country would be law-abiding and peaceful if it weren't for you lawyers. But—if you will excuse Elizabeth and me, we must hear the children's prayers and see them safely abed.

ABE. Why—I'd be glad to hear their prayers, too.

NINIAN. Oh, no! You'd only keep them up till all hours with your stories. Come along, Elizabeth. [ELIZABETH *doesn't want to go, but doesn't know what to do to prevent it.*]

ABE. [*To* ELIZABETH.] Kiss them good night, for me.

NINIAN. We'd better not tell them you're in the house, or they'll be furious.

ELIZABETH. [*Making one last attempt.*]

Mary! Won't you come with us and say good night to the children?

NINIAN. No, my dear. Leave Mary here —to keep Abe entertained. [*He guides* ELIZABETH *out, following her.*]

MARY. [*With a little laugh.*] I don't blame Ninian for keeping you away from those children. They all adore you.

ABE. Well—I always seemed to get along well with children. Probably it's because they never want to take me seriously.

MARY. You understand them—that's the important thing . . . But—do sit down, Mr. Lincoln. [*She indicates that he is to sit next to her.*]

ABE. Thank you—I will. [*He starts to cross to the couch to sit beside* MARY. *She looks at him with melting eyes. The lights fade.*]

6

Again the Law Office. It is afternoon of New Year's Day, a few weeks after the preceding scene.

ABE is sitting, slumped in his chair, staring at his desk. He has his hat and overcoat on. A muffler is hanging about his neck, untied. JOSH SPEED is half-sitting on the table at the right. He is reading a long letter, with most serious attention. At length he finishes it, refolds it very carefully, stares at the floor.

ABE. Have you finished it, Josh?

JOSH. Yes.

ABE. Well—do you think it's all right?

JOSH. No, Abe—I don't. [ABE *turns slowly and looks at him.*] I think the sending of this letter would be a most grave mistake—and that is putting it mildly and charitably.

ABE. Have I stated the case too crudely? [ABE *is evidently in a serious state of distress, although he is making a tremendous effort to disguise it by speaking in what he intends to be a coldly impersonal tone. He is struggling mightily to hold himself back from the brink of nervous collapse.*]

JOSH. No—I have no quarrel with your choice of words. None whatever. If anything, the phraseology is too correct. But

your method of doing it, Abe! It's brutal, it's heartless, it's so unworthy of you that I—I'm at a loss to understand how you ever thought you could do it this way.

ABE. I've done the same thing before with a woman to whom I seemed to have become attached. She approved of my action.

JOSH. This is a different woman. [*He walks over to the window, then turns again toward* ABE.] You cannot seem to accept the fact that women are human beings, too, as variable as we are. You act on the assumption that they're all the same one—and that one is a completely unearthly being of your own conception. This letter isn't written to Mary Todd— it's written to yourself. Every line of it is intended to provide salve for your own conscience.

ABE. [*Rising; coldly.*] Do I understand that you will not deliver it for me?

JOSH. No, Abe—I shall not.

ABE. [*Angrily.*] Then some one else will!

JOSH. [*Scornfully.*] Yes. You could give it to the minister, to hand to the bride when he arrives for the ceremony. But—I hope, Abe, you won't send it till you're feeling a little calmer in your mind. . . .

ABE. [*Vehemently, turning to* JOSH.] How can I ever be calm in my mind until this thing is settled, and out of the way, once and for all? Have you got eyes in your head, Josh? Can't you see that I'm desperate?

JOSH. I can see that plainly, Abe. I think your situation is more desperate even than you imagine, and I believe you should have the benefit of some really intelligent medical advice.

ABE. [*Seating himself at* BILLY's *table.*] The trouble with me isn't anything that a doctor can cure.

JOSH. There's a good man named Dr. Drake, who makes a specialty of treating people who get into a state of mind like yours, Abe . . .

ABE. [*Utterly miserable.*] So that's how you've figured it! I've done what I've threatened to do many times before: I've gone crazy. Well—you know me better than most men, Josh—and perhaps you're not far off right. I just feel that I've got to the end of my rope, and I must let go, and drop—and where I'll land, I don't know, and whether I'll survive the fall, I don't know that either. . . . But—this I *do* know: I've got to get out of this thing —I can't go through with it—I've got to have my release! [JOSH *has turned to the window. Suddenly he turns back, toward* ABE.]

JOSH. Ninian Edwards is coming up. Why not show this letter to him and ask for his opinion. . . .

ABE. [*Interrupting, with desperation.*] No, no! Don't say a word of any of this to him! Put that letter in your pocket. I can't bear to discuss this business with him, now. [JOSH *puts the letter in his pocket and crosses to the couch.*]

JOSH. Hello, Ninian.

NINIAN. [*Heartily, from off.*] Hello, Josh! Happy New Year! [NINIAN *comes in. He wears a handsome, fur-trimmed great-coat, and carries two silver-headed canes, one of them in a baize bag, which he lays down on the table at the right.*]

NINIAN. And Happy New Year, Abe— in fact, the happiest of your whole life!

ABE. Thank you, Ninian. And Happy New Year to you.

NINIAN. [*Opening his coat.*] That didn't sound much as if you meant it. [*He goes to the stove to warm his hands.*] However, you can be forgiven today, Abe. I suppose you're inclined to be just a wee bit nervous. [*He chuckles and winks at* JOSH.] God—but it's cold in here! Don't you ever light this stove?

ABE. The fire's all laid. Go ahead and light it, if you want.

NINIAN. [*Striking a match.*] You certainly are in one of your less amiable moods today. [*He lights the stove.*]

JOSH. Abe's been feeling a little under the weather.

NINIAN. So it seems. He looks to me as if he'd been to a funeral.

ABE. That's where I have been.

NINIAN. [*Disbelieving.*] What? A funeral on your wedding day?

JOSH. They buried Abe's oldest friend, Bowling Green, this morning.

NINIAN. [*Shocked.*] Oh—I'm mighty sorry to hear that, Abe. And—I hope you'll forgive me for—not having known about it.

ABE. Of course, Ninian.

NINIAN. But I'm glad you were there, Abe, at the funeral. It must have been a great comfort to his family.

ABE. I wasn't any comfort to any one. They asked me to deliver an oration, a eulogy of the deceased—and I tried—and I couldn't say a thing. Why do they expect you to strew a lot of flowery phrases over anything so horrible as a dead body? Do they think that Bowling Green's soul needs quotations to give it peace? All that mattered to me was that he was a good, just man—and I loved him —and he's dead.

NINIAN. Why didn't you say that, Abe?

ABE. [*Rising.*] I told you—they wanted an oration.

NINIAN. Well, Abe—I think Bowling himself would be the first to ask you to put your sadness aside in the prospect of your own happiness, and Mary's—and I'm only sorry that our old friend didn't live to see you two fine people married. [*He is making a gallant attempt to assume a more cheerily nuptial tone.*] I've made all the arrangements with the Reverend Dresser, and Elizabeth is preparing a bang-up dinner—so you can be sure the whole affair will be carried off handsomely *and* painlessly. [BILLY HERNDON *comes in. He carries a bottle in his coat pocket, and is already more than a little drunk and sullen, but abnormally articulate.*] Ah, Billy—Happy New Year!

BILLY. The same to you, Mr. Edwards. [*He puts the bottle down on the table and takes his coat off.*]

NINIAN. I brought you a wedding present, Abe. Thought you'd like to make a brave show when you first walk out with your bride. It came from the same place in Louisville where I bought mine. [*He picks up one of the canes and hands it proudly to* ABE, *who takes it and inspects it gravely.*]

ABE. It's very fine, Ninian. And I thank you. [*He takes the cane over to his desk and seats himself.*]

NINIAN. Well—I'll frankly confess that in getting it for you, I was influenced somewhat by consideration for Mary and her desire for keeping up appearances. And in that connection—I know you'll forgive me, Josh, and you, too, Billy, if I say something of a somewhat personal nature.

BILLY. [*Truculent.*] If you want me to leave you, I shall be glad to. . . .

NINIAN. No, please, Billy—I merely want to speak a word or two as another of Abe's friends; it's my last chance before the ceremony. Of course, the fact that the bride is my sister-in-law gives me a little added responsibility in wishing to promote the success of this marriage. [*He crosses to* ABE.] And a success it will me, Abe . . . if only you will bear in mind one thing: you must keep a tight rein on her ambition. My wife tells me that even as a child, she had delusions of grandeur—she predicted to one and all that the man she would marry would be President of the United States. [*He turns to* JOSH.] You know how it is—every boy in the country plans some day to be President, and every little girl plans to marry him. [*Again to* ABE.] But Mary is one who hasn't entirely lost those youthful delusions. So I urge you to beware. Don't let her talk you into any gallant crusades or wild goose chases. Let her learn to be satisfied with the estate to which God hath brought her. With which, I shall conclude my pre-nuptial sermon. [*He buttons his coat.*] I shall see you all at the house at five o'clock, and I want you to make sure that Abe is looking his prettiest.

JOSH. Good-by, Ninian. [NINIAN *goes out.* ABE *turns again to the desk and stares at nothing.* BILLY *takes the bottle and a cup from his desk and pours himself a stiff drink. He raises the cup toward* ABE.]

BILLY. [*Huskily.*] Mr. Lincoln, I beg leave to drink to your health and happiness . . . and to that of the lady who will become your wife. [ABE *makes no response.* BILLY *drinks it down, then puts the cup back on the table.*] You don't want to accept my toast because you think it wasn't sincere. And I'll admit I've made it plain that I've regretted the step you've taken. I thought that in this marriage, you were lowering yourself—you were trading your honor for some exalted family connections. . . . I wish to apologize for so thinking. . . .

ABE. No apologies required, Billy.

BILLY. I doubt that Miss Todd and I will ever get along well together. But I'm now convinced that our aims are the same—particularly since I've heard the warnings delivered by her brother-in-law. [*A note of scorn colors his allusion to* NINIAN.] If she really is ambitious for you—if she will never stop driving you, goading you—then I say, God bless her, and give her strength! [*He has said all this with* ABE's *back to him.* BILLY *pours himself another drink, nearly emptying the large bottle.* ABE *turns and looks at him.*]

ABE. Have you had all of that bottle today?

BILLY. This bottle? Yes—I have.

JOSH. And why not? It's New Year's Day!

BILLY. [*Looking at* JOSH.] Thank you, Mr. Speed. Thank you for the defense. And I hope you will permit me to propose one more toast. [*He takes a step toward* ABE.] To the President of the United States, and Mrs. Lincoln! [*He drinks.*]

ABE. [*Grimly.*] I think we can do without any more toasts, Billy.

BILLY. Very well! That's the last one—until after the wedding. And then, no doubt, the Edwards will serve us with the costliest champagne. And, in case you're apprehensive, I shall be on my best behavior in that distinguished gathering!

ABE. There is not going to be a wedding. [BILLY *stares at him, and then looks at* JOSH, *and then again at* ABE.] I have a letter that I want you to deliver to Miss Todd.

BILLY. What letter? What is it?

ABE. Give it to him, Josh. [JOSH *takes the letter out of his pocket, and puts it in the stove.* ABE *jumps up.*] You have no right to do that!

JOSH. I know I haven't! But it's done. [ABE *is staring at* JOSH.] And don't look at me as if you were planning to break my neck. Of course you could do it, Abe —but you won't. [JOSH *turns to* BILLY.] In that letter, Mr. Lincoln asked Miss Todd for his release. He told her that he had made a mistake in his previous protestations of affection for her, and so he couldn't go through with a marriage which could only lead to endless pain and misery for them both.

ABE. [*Deeply distressed.*] If that isn't the truth, what is?

JOSH. I'm not disputing the truth of it. I'm only asking you to tell her so, to her face, in the manner of a man.

ABE. It would be a more cruel way. It would hurt her more deeply. For I couldn't help blurting it *all* out—all the terrible things I didn't say in that letter. [*He is speaking with passion.*] I'd have to tell her that I have hatred for her infernal ambition—that I don't want to be ridden and driven, upward and onward through life, with her whip lashing me, and her spurs digging into me! If her poor soul craves importance in life, then let her marry Stephen Douglas. He's ambitious, too. . . . I want only to be left alone! [*He sits down again and leans on the table.*]

JOSH. [*Bitterly.*] Very well, then—tell her all that! It will be more gracious to admit that you're afraid of her, instead of letting her down flat with the statement that your ardor, such as it was, has cooled. [BILLY *has been seething with a desire to get into this conversation. Now, with a momentary silence, he plunges.*]

BILLY. May I say something?

ABE. I doubt that you're in much of a condition to contribute. . . .

JOSH. What is it, Billy?

BILLY. [*Hotly.*] It's just this. Mr. Lincoln, you're not abandoning Miss Mary Todd. No! You're only using her as a living sacrifice, offering her up, in the hope that you will thus gain forgiveness of the gods for your failure to do your own great duty!

ABE. [*Smouldering.*] Yes! My own great duty. Every one feels called upon to remind me of it, but no one can tell me what it is.

BILLY. [*Almost tearful.*] I can tell you! I can tell you what is the duty of every man who calls himself an American! It is

to perpetuate those truths which were once held to be self-evident: that all men are created equal—that they are endowed with certain inalienable rights—that among these are the right to life, liberty, and the pursuit of happiness.

ABE. [*Angrily.*] And are those rights denied to *me?*

BILLY. Could you ever enjoy them while your mind is full of the awful knowledge that two million of your fellow beings in this country are slaves? Can you take any satisfaction from looking at that flag above your desk, when you know that ten of its stars represent states which are willing to destroy the Union—rather than yield their property rights in the flesh and blood of those slaves? And what of all the States of the future? All the territories of the West—clear out to the Pacific Ocean? Will they be the homes of free men? Are you answering *that* question to your own satisfaction? That is your flag, Mr. Lincoln, and you're proud of it. But what are you doing to save it from being ripped into shreds? [ABE *jumps to his feet, towers over* BILLY *and speaks with temper restrained, but with great passion.*]

ABE. I'm minding my own business—that's what I'm doing! And there'd be no threat to the Union if others would do the same. And as to slavery—I'm sick and tired of this righteous talk about it. When you know more about law, you'll know that those property rights you mentioned are guaranteed by the Constitution. And if the Union can't stand on the Constitution, then let it fall!

BILLY. The hell with the Constitution! This is a matter of the rights of living men to freedom—and those came before the Constitution! When the Law denies those rights, then the Law is wrong, and it must be changed, if not by moral protest, then by force! There's no course of action that isn't justified in the defense of freedom! And don't dare to tell me that any one in the world knows that better than you do, Mr. Lincoln. You, who honor the memory of Elijah Lovejoy and every other man who ever died for that very ideal!

ABE. [*Turning away from him.*] Yes—I honor them—and envy them—because they could believe that their ideals are *worth* dying for. [*He turns to* JOSH *and speaks with infinite weariness.*] All right, Josh—I'll go up now and talk to Mary—and then I'm going away. . . .

JOSH. Where, Abe?

ABE. [*Dully.*] I don't know. [*He goes out and closes the door after him. After a moment,* BILLY *rushes to the door, opens it, and shouts after* ABE.]

BILLY. You're quitting, Mr. Lincoln! As surely as there's a God in Heaven, He knows that you're running away from your obligations to Him, and to your fellow-men, and your own immortal soul!

JOSH. [*Drawing* BILLY *away from the door.*] Billy—Billy—leave him alone. He's a sick man.

BILLY. [*Sitting down at the table.*] What can we do for him, Mr. Speed? What can we do? [BILLY *is now actually in tears.*]

JOSH. I don't know, Billy. [*He goes to the window and looks out.*] He'll be in such a state of emotional upheaval, he'll want to go away by himself, for a long time. Just as he did after the death of poor little Ann Rutledge. He'll go out and wander on the prairies, trying to grope his way back into the wilderness from which he came. There's nothing we can do for him, Billy. He'll have to do it for himself.

BILLY. [*Fervently.*] May God be with him! [*The lights fade.*]

7

On the prairie, near New Salem. It is a clear, cool, moonlit evening, nearly two years after the preceding scene. In the foreground is a campfire. Around it are packing cases, blanket rolls and one ancient trunk. In the background is a covered wagon, standing at an angle, so that the opening at the back of it is visible to the audience.

SETH GALE is standing by the fire, holding his seven-year-old son, JIMMY, in his arms. The boy is wrapped up in a blanket.

JIMMY. I don't want to be near the fire, Paw. I'm burning up. Won't you take the blanket offen me, Paw?

SETH. No, son. You're better off if you keep yourself covered.

JIMMY. I want some water, Paw. Can't I have some water?

SETH. Yes! Keep quiet, Jimmy! Gobey's getting the water for you now. [*He looks off to the right, and sees* JACK ARMSTRONG *coming.*] Hello, Jack, I was afraid you'd got lost.

JACK. [*Coming in.*] I couldn't get lost anywheres around New Salem. How's the boy?

SETH. [*With a cautionary look at* JACK.] He—he's a little bit thirsty. Did you find Abe?

JACK. Yes—it took me some time because he'd wandered off—went out to the old cemetery across the river to visit Ann Rutledge's grave.

SETH. Is he coming here?

JACK. He said he'd better go get Doc Chandler who lives on the Winchester Road. He'll be along in a while. [*He comes up to* JIMMY.] How you feelin', Jimmy?

JIMMY. I'm burning . . . [AGGIE *appears, sees* JACK.]

AGGIE. Oh—I'm glad you're back, Mr. Armstrong.

JACK. There'll be a doctor here soon, Mrs. Gale.

AGGIE. Thank God for that! Bring him into the wagon, Seth. I got a nice, soft bed all ready for him.

SETH. You hear that, Jimmy? Your ma's fixed a place where you can rest comfortable. [AGGIE *retreats into the wagon.*]

JIMMY. When'll Gobey come back? I'm thirsty. When'll he bring the water?

SETH. Right away, son. You can trust Gobey to get your water. [*He hands* JIMMY *into the wagon.*]

JACK. He's worse, ain't he?

SETH. [*In a despairing tone.*] Yes. The fever's been raging something fierce since you left. It'll sure be a relief when Abe gets here. He can always do something to put confidence in you.

JACK. How long since you've seen Abe, Seth?

SETH. Haven't laid eyes on him since I

left here—eight—nine years ago. We've corresponded some.

JACK. Well—you may be surprised when you see him. He's changed plenty since he went to Springfield. He climbed up pretty high in the world, but he appears to have slipped down lately. He ain't much like his old comical self.

SETH. Well, I guess we all got to change. [*He starts up, hearing* GOBEY *return.*] Aggie! [GOBEY, *a Negro, comes in from the left, carrying a bucket of water.* AGGIE *appears from the wagon.*] Here's Gobey with the water.

GOBEY. Yes, Miss Aggie. Here you are. [*He hands it up.*]

AGGIE. Thanks, Gobey. [*She goes back into the wagon.*]

GOBEY. How's Jimmy now, Mr. Seth?

SETH. About the same.

GOBEY. [*Shaking his head.*] I'll get some more water for the cooking. [*He picks up a kettle and a pot and goes.*]

SETH. [*To* JACK.] It was a bad thing to have happen, all right—the boy getting sick—when we were on an expedition like this. No doctor—no way of caring for him.

JACK. How long you been on the road, Seth?

SETH. More than three months. Had a terrible time in the Pennsylvania Mountains, fearful rains and every stream flooded. I can tell you, there was more than one occasion when I wanted to turn back and give up the whole idea. But—when you get started—you just can't turn . . . [*He is looking off right.*] Say! Is that Abe coming now?

JACK. [*Rising.*] Yep. That's him.

SETH. [*Delighted.*] My God, look at him! Store clothes and a plug hat! Hello —Abe!

ABE. Hello, Seth. [*He comes on and shakes hands, warmly.*] I'm awful glad to see you again, Seth.

SETH. And me, too, Abe.

ABE. It did my heart good when I heard you were on your way West. Where's your boy?

SETH. He's in there—in the wagon. . . . [AGGIE *has appeared from the wagon.*]

AGGIE. Is that the doctor?

SETH. No, Aggie—this is the man I was telling you about I wanted so much to see. This is Mr. Abe Lincoln—my wife, Mrs. Gale.

ABE. Pleased to meet you, Mrs. Gale.

AGGIE. Pleased to meet you, Mr. Lincoln.

ABE. Doc Chandler wasn't home. They said he was expected over at the Boger farm at midnight. I'll go there then and fetch him.

SETH. It'll be a friendly act, Abe.

AGGIE. We'll be in your debt, Mr. Lincoln.

ABE. In the meantime, Mrs. Gale, I'd like to do whatever I can. . . .

SETH. There's nothing to do, Abe. The boy's got the swamp fever, and we're just trying to keep him quiet.

AGGIE. [*Desperately.*] There's just one thing I would wish—is—is there any kind of a preacher around this God-forsaken place?

SETH. [*Worried.*] Preacher?

ABE. Do you know of any, Jack?

JACK. No. There ain't a preacher within twenty miles of New Salem now.

AGGIE. Well—I only thought if there was, we might get him here to say a prayer for Jimmy. [*She goes back into the wagon.* SETH *looks after her with great alarm.*]

SETH. She wants a preacher. That looks as if she'd given up, don't it?

JACK. It'd probably just comfort her.

ABE. Is your boy very sick, Seth?

SETH. Yes—he is.

JACK. Why don't *you* speak a prayer, Abe? You could always think of somethin' to say.

ABE. I'm afraid I'm not much of a hand at praying. I couldn't think of a blessed thing that would be of any comfort.

SETH. Never mind. It's just a—a religious idea of Aggie's. Sit down, Abe.

ABE. [*Looking at the wagon.*] So you've got your dream at last, Seth. You're doing what you and I used to talk about—you're moving.

SETH. Yes, Abe. We got crowded out of Maryland. The city grew up right over our farm. So—we're headed for a place where there's more room. I wrote you—about four months back—to tell you we were starting out, and I'd like to meet up with you here. I thought it was possible you might consider joining in this trip.

ABE. It took a long time for your letter to catch up with me, Seth. I've just been drifting—down around Indiana and Kentucky where I used to live. [*He sits down on a box.*] Do you aim to settle in Nebraska?

SETH. No, we're not going to stop there. We're going right across the continent—all the way to Oregon.

ABE. [*Deeply impressed.*] Oregon?

JACK. Sure. That's where they're all headin' for now.

SETH. We're making first for a place called Westport Landing—that's in Kansas right on the frontier—where they outfit the wagon trains for the far West. You join up there with a lot of others who are like-minded, so you've got company when you're crossing the plains and the mountains.

ABE. It's staggering—to think of the distance you're going. And you'll be taking the frontier along with you.

SETH. It may seem like a fool-hardy thing to do—but we heard too many tales of the black earth out there, and the balance of rainfall and sunshine.

JACK. Why don't you go with them, Abe? That country out west is gettin' settled fast. Why—last week alone, I counted more than two hundred wagons went past here—people from all over—Pennsylvania, Connecticut, Vermont—all full of jubilation at the notion of gettin' land. By God, I'm goin' too, soon as I can get me a wagon. They'll need men like me to fight the Indians for 'em—and they'll need men with brains, like you, Abe, to tell 'em how to keep the peace.

ABE. [*Looking off.*] It's a temptation to go, I can't deny that.

JACK. Then what's stoppin' you from doin' it? You said yourself you've just been driftin'.

ABE. Maybe that's it—maybe I've been drifting too long. . . . [*He changes the subject.*] Is it just the three of you, Seth?

SETH. That's all. The three of us and Gobey, the nigger.

ABE. Is he your slave?

SETH. Gobey? Hell, no! He's a free man! My father freed his father twenty years ago. But we've had to be mighty careful about Gobey. You see, where we come from, folks are pretty uncertain how they feel about the slave question, and lots of good free niggers get snaked over the line into Virginia and then sold down river before you know it. And when you try to go to court and assert their legal rights, you're beaten at every turn by the damned, dirty shyster lawyers. That's why we've been keeping well up in free territory on this trip.

ABE. Do you think it will be free in Oregon?

SETH. Of course it will! It's got to . . .

ABE. [*Bitterly.*] Oh no, it hasn't, Seth. Not with the politicians in Washington selling out the whole West piece by piece to the slave traders.

SETH. [*Vehemently.*] That territory has got to be free! If this country ain't strong enough to protect its citizens from slavery, then we'll cut loose from it and join with Canada. Or, better yet, we'll make a *new* country out there in the far west.

ABE. [*Gravely.*] A new country?

SETH. Why not?

ABE. I was just thinking—old Mentor Graham once said to me that some day the United States might be divided up into many hostile countries, like Europe.

SETH. Well—let it be! Understand—I love this country and I'd fight for it. And I guess George Washington and the rest of them loved England and fought for it when they were young—but they didn't hesitate to cut loose when the government failed to play fair and square with 'em. . . .

JACK. By God, if Andy Jackson was back in the White House, he'd run out them traitors with a horsewhip!

ABE. It'd be a bad day for us Americans, Seth, if we lost you, and your wife, and your son.

SETH. [*Breaking.*] My son!—Oh—I've been talking big—but it's empty talk. If he dies—there won't be enough spirit left in us to push on any further. What's the use of working for a future when you know there won't be anybody growing up to enjoy it. Excuse me, Abe—but I'm feeling pretty scared.

ABE. [*Suddenly rises.*] You mustn't be scared, Seth. I know I'm a poor one to be telling you that—because I've been scared all my life. But—seeing you now—and thinking of the big things you've set out to do—well, it's made me feel pretty small. It's made me feel that I've got to do something, too, to keep you and your kind in the United States of America. You mustn't quit, Seth! Don't let anything beat you—don't you ever give up! [AGGIE *comes out of the wagon. She is very frightened.*]

AGGIE. Seth!

SETH. What is it, Aggie?

AGGIE. He's worse, Seth! He's moaning in his sleep, and he's gasping for breath. . . . [*She is crying.* SETH *takes her in his arms.*]

SETH. Never mind, honey. Never mind. When the doctor gets here, he'll fix him up in no time. It's all right, honey. He'll get well.

ABE. If you wish me to, Mrs. Gale—I'll try to speak a prayer. [*They look at him.*]

JACK. That's the way to talk, Abe!

SETH. We'd be grateful for anything you might say, Abe. [ABE *takes his hat off. As he starts speaking,* GOBEY *comes in from the left and stops reverently to listen.*]

ABE. Oh God, the father of all living, I ask you to look with gentle mercy upon this little boy who is here, lying sick in this covered wagon. His people are travelling far, to seek a new home in the wilderness, to do your work, God, to make this earth a good place for your children to live in. They can see clearly where they're going, and they're not afraid to face all the perils that lie along the way. I humbly beg you not to take their child from them. Grant him the freedom of life. Do not condemn him to the imprisonment of death. Do not deny him his birthright. Let him know the sight of great plains and high mountains, of green valleys and wide rivers. For this little boy is an American, and these things belong to him, and he to them. Spare him, that he too may strive for the ideal

for which his fathers have labored, so faithfully and for so long. Spare him and give him his fathers' strength—give us all strength, Oh God, to do the work that is before us. I ask you this favor, in the name of *your* son, Jesus Christ, who died upon the Cross to set men free. Amen.

GOBEY. [*With fervor.*] Amen!

SETH AND AGGIE. [*Murmuring.*] Amen! [ABE *puts his hat on.*]

ABE. It's getting near midnight. I'll go over to the Boger farm and get the doctor. [*He goes out.*]

SETH. Thank you, Abe.

AGGIE. Thank you—thank you, Mr. Lincoln.

GOBEY. God bless you, Mr. Lincoln! [*The lights fade quickly.*]

8

Again the parlor of the Edwards house. A few days after preceding scene.

MARY *is seated, reading a book. After a moment, the* MAID *enters.*

MAID. Miss Mary—Mr. Lincoln is here.

MARY. Mr. Lincoln! [*She sits still a moment in an effort to control her emotions, then sharply closes the book and rises.*]

MAID. Will you see him, Miss Mary?

MARY. Yes—in one moment. [*The* MAID *goes off.* MARY *turns, drops her book on the sofa, then moves over toward the right, struggling desperately to compose herself. At the fireplace, she stops and turns to face* ABE *as he enters.*] I'm glad to see you again, Mr. Lincoln. [*There is considerable constraint between them. He is grimly determined to come to the point with the fewest possible words; she is making a gallant, well-bred attempt to observe the social amenities.*]

ABE. Thank you, Mary. You may well wonder why I have thrust myself on your mercy in this manner.

MARY. [*Quickly.*] I'm sure you're always welcome in Ninian's house.

ABE. After my behavior at our last meeting here, I have not been welcome company for myself.

MARY. You've been through a severe

illness. Joshua Speed has kept us informed of it. We've been greatly concerned.

ABE. It is most kind of you.

MARY. But you're restored to health now—you'll return to your work, and no doubt you'll be running for the assembly again—or perhaps you have larger plans?

ABE. I have no plans, Mary. [*He seems to brace himself.*] But I wish to tell you that I am sorry for the things that I said on that unhappy occasion which was to have been our wedding day.

MARY. You need not say anything about that, Mr. Lincoln. Whatever happened then, it was my own fault.

ABE. [*Disturbed by this unforeseen avowal.*] *Your* fault! It was my miserable cowardice . . .

MARY. I was blinded by my own self-confidence! I—I loved you. [*For a moment her firm voice falters, but she immediately masters that tendency toward weakness.*] And I believed I could make you love me. I believed we might achieve a real communion of spirit, and the fire of my determination would burn in you. You would become a man and a leader of men! But you didn't wish that. [*She turns away.*] I knew you had strength—but I did not know you would use it, all of it, to resist your own magnificent destiny.

ABE. [*Deliberately.*] It is true, Mary—you once had faith in me which I was far from deserving. But the time has come, at last, when I wish to strive to deserve it. [MARY *looks at him sharply.*] When I behaved in that shameful manner toward you, I did so because I thought that our ways were separate and could never be otherwise. I've come to the conclusion that I was wrong. I believe that our destinies are together, for better or for worse, and I again presume to ask you to be my wife. I fully realize, Mary, that taking me back now would involve humiliation for you.

MARY. [*Flaring.*] I am not afraid of humiliation, if I know it will be wiped out by ultimate triumph! But there can be no triumph unless you yourself are sure. What was it that brought you to this change of heart and mind?

ABE. On the prairie, I met an old friend of mine who was moving West, with his wife and child, in a covered wagon. He asked me to go with him, and I was strongly tempted to do so. [*There is great sadness in his tone—but he seems to collect himself, and turns to her again, speaking with a sort of resignation.*] But then I knew that was not my direction. The way I must go is the way you have always wanted me to go.

MARY. And you will promise that never again will you falter, or turn to run away?

ABE. I promise, Mary—if you will have me—I shall devote myself for the rest of my days to trying—to do what is right —as God gives me power to see what is right. [*She looks at him, trying to search him. She would like to torment him, for a while, with artful indecision. But she can not do it.*]

MARY. Very well, then—I shall be your wife. I shall fight by your side—till death do us part. [*She runs to him and clutches him.*] Abe! I love you—oh, I love you! Whatever becomes of the two of us, I'll die loving you! [*She is sobbing wildly on his shoulder. Awkwardly, he lifts his hands and takes hold of her in a loose embrace. He is staring down at the carpet, over her shoulder.*]

CURTAIN

ACT THREE

9

A speakers' platform in an Illinois town. It is a summer evening in the year 1858. A light shines down on the speaker at the front of the platform.

At the back of the platform are three chairs. At the right sits JUDGE STEPHEN A. DOUGLAS—at the left, ABE, who has his plug hat on and makes occasional notes on a piece of paper on his knee. The chair in the middle is for NINIAN, acting as Moderator, who is now at the front of the platform.

NINIAN. We have now heard the leading arguments from the two candidates for the high office of United States Senator from Illinois—Judge Stephen A. Douglas and Mr. Abraham Lincoln. A series of debates between these two eminent citizens of Illinois has focused upon our state the attention of the entire nation, for here are being discussed the vital issues which now affect the lives of all Americans and the whole future history of our beloved country. According to the usual custom of debate, each of the candidates will now speak in rebuttal. . . . Judge Douglas. [NINIAN *retires and sits, as* DOUGLAS *comes forward. He is a brief but magnetic man, confident of his powers.*]

DOUGLAS. My fellow citizens: My good friend, Mr. Lincoln, has addressed you with his usual artless sincerity, his pure, homely charm, his perennial native humor. He has even devoted a generously large portion of his address to most amiable remarks upon my fine qualities as a man, if not as a statesman. For which I express deepest gratitude. But—at the same time—I most earnestly beg you not to be deceived by his seeming innocence, his carefully cultivated spirit of good will. For in each of his little homilies lurk concealed weapons. Like Brutus, in Shakespeare's immortal tragedy, Mr. Lincoln is an honorable man. But, also like Brutus, he is an adept at the art of inserting daggers between an opponent's ribs, just when said opponent least expects it. Behold me, gentlemen—I am covered with scars. And yet—somehow or other—I am still upright. Perhaps because I am supported by that sturdy prop called "Truth." Truth —which, crushed to earth by the assassin's blades, doth rise again! Mr. Lincoln makes you laugh with his pungent anecdotes. Then he draws tears from your eyes with his dramatic pictures of the plight of the black slave labor in the South. Always, he guides you skilfully to the threshold of truth, but then, as you are about to cross it, diverts your attention elsewhere. For one thing—he never, by any mischance, makes reference to the condition of labor here in the North! Oh, no! Perhaps New England is so far beyond the bounds of his parochial ken that he does not know that tens of thousands of working men and women in the textile industry are now on STRIKE! And why are they on strike? Because from early morning to dark of night—fourteen hours a day— those "free" citizens must toil at shattering looms in soulless factories and never see the sun; and then, when their fearful day's work at last comes to its exhausted end, these ill-clad and undernourished laborers must trudge home to their foul abodes in tenements that are not fit habitations for rats! What kind of Liberty is this? And if Mr. Lincoln has not heard of conditions in Massachusetts—how has it escaped his attention that here in our own great state no wheels are now turning on that mighty railroad, the Illinois Central? Because its oppressed workers are also on STRIKE! Because they too demand a living wage! So it is throughout the North. Hungry men, marching through the streets in ragged order, promoting riots, because they are not paid enough to keep the flesh upon the bones of their babies! What kind of Liberty is *this?* And what kind of equality? Mr. Lincoln harps constantly on this subject of equality. He repeats over and over the argument used by Lovejoy and other abolitionists: to wit, that the Declaration of Independence having declared all men free and equal, by divine law, thus Negro equality is an inalienable right. Contrary to this absurd assumption stands the verdict of the Supreme Court, as it was clearly stated by Chief Justice Taney in the case of Dred Scott. The Negroes are established by this decision as an inferior race of beings, subjugated by the dominant race, enslaved and, therefore, *property*—like all over property! But Mr. Lincoln is inclined to dispute the constitutional authority of the Supreme Court. He has implied, if he did not say so outright, that the Dred Scott decision was a prejudiced one, which must be overruled by the voice of the people. Mr. Lincoln is a lawyer, and I presume, therefore, that he knows that when he seeks to destroy public confidence in the integrity, the inviolability of the Supreme Court, he is preaching *revolution!* He is attempting to stir up odium and rebellion in this country against the constituted authorities; he is stimulating the passions of men to resort to violence and to mobs, instead of to the law. He is setting brother against brother! There can be but one consequence of such inflammatory persuasion—and that is *Civil War!* He asks me to state my opinion of the Dred Scott decision, and I answer him unequivocally by saying, "I take the decisions of the Supreme Court as the law of the land, and I intend to obey them as such!" Nor will I be swayed from that position by all the rantings of all the fanatics who preach "racial equality," who ask us to vote, and eat, and sleep, and marry with Negroes! And I say further—Let each State mind its own business and leave its neighbors alone. If we will stand by that principle, then Mr. Lincoln will find that this great republic can exist forever divided into free and slave states. We can go on as we have done, increasing in wealth, in population, in power, until we shall be the admiration and the terror of the world! [*He glares at the audience, then turns, mopping his brow, and resumes his seat.*]

NINIAN. [*Rising.*] Mr. Lincoln. [ABE *glances at his notes, takes his hat off, puts the notes in it, then rises slowly and comes forward. He speaks quietly, reasonably. His words come from an emotion so profound that it needs no advertisement.*]

ABE. Judge Douglas has paid tribute to my skill with the dagger. I thank him for that, but I must also admit that he can do more with that weapon than I can. He can keep ten daggers flashing in the air at one time. Fortunately, he's so good at it that none of the knives ever falls and hurts anybody. The Judge can condone slavery in the South and protest hotly against its extension to the North. He can crowd loyalty to the Union and defense of states' sovereignty into the same

breath. Which reminds me—and I hope the Judge will allow me one more homely little anecdote, because I'd like to tell about a woman down in Kentucky. She came out of her cabin one day and found her husband grappling with a ferocious bear. It was a fight to the death, and the bear was winning. The struggling husband called to his wife, "For heaven's sake, *help* me!" The wife asked what could *she* do? Said the husband, "You could at least *say* something encouraging." But the wife didn't want to seem to be taking sides in this combat, so she just hollered, "Go it, husband—go it, bear!" Now, you heard the Judge make allusion to those who advocate voting and eating and marrying and sleeping with Negroes. Whether he meant me specifically, I do not know. If he did, I can say that just because I do not want a colored woman for a slave, I don't necessarily want her for a wife. I need not have her for either. I can just leave her alone. In some respects, she certainly is not my equal, any more than I am the Judge's equal, in some respects; but in her natural right to eat the bread she earns with her own hands without asking leave of some one else, she is my equal, and the equal of all others. And as to sleeping with Negroes—the Judge may be interested to know that the slave states have produced more than four hundred thousand mulattoes—and I don't think many of them are the children of abolitionists. That word "abolitionists" brings to mind New England, which also has been mentioned. I assure Judge Douglas that I have been there, and I have seen those cheerless brick prisons called factories, and the workers trudging silently home through the darkness. In those factories, cotton that was picked by black slaves is woven into cloth by white people who are separated from slavery by no more than fifty cents a day. As an American, I cannot be proud that such conditions exist. But—as an American—I can ask: would any of those striking workers in the North elect to change places with the slaves in the South? Will they not rather say, "The remedy is in *our* hands!" And, still as an American, I can say—thank God we live under a system by which men have the *right* to strike! I am not preaching rebellion. I don't have to. This country, with its institutions, belongs to the people who inhabit it. Whenever they shall grow weary of the existing government, they can exercise their constitutional right of amending it, or their revolutionary right to dismember or overthrow it. If the founding fathers gave us anything, they gave us that. And I am not preaching disrespect for the Supreme Court. I am only saying that the decisions of mortal men are often influenced by unjudicial bias —and the Supreme Court is composed of mortal men, most of whom, it so happens, come from the privileged class in the South. There is an old saying that judges are just as honest as other men, and not more so; and in case some of you are wondering who said that, it was Thomas Jefferson. [*He has half turned to* DOUGLAS.] The purpose of the Dred Scott decision is to make property, and nothing but property, of the Negro in all states of the Union. It is the old issue of property rights versus human rights —an issue that will continue in this country when these poor tongues of Judge Douglas and myself shall long have been silent. It is the eternal struggle between two principles. The one is the common right of humanity, and the other the divine right of kings. It is the same spirit that says, "You toil and work and earn bread, and I'll eat it." Whether those words come from the mouth of a king who bestrides his people and lives by the fruit of their labor, or from one race of men who seek to enslave another race, it is the same tyrannical principle. As a nation, we began by declaring, "All men are created equal." There was no mention of any exceptions to the rule in the Declaration of Independence. But we now practically read it, "All men are created equal except Negroes." If we accept this doctrine of race or class discrimination, what is to stop us from decreeing in the future that "All men are created equal except Negroes, foreigners, Catholics, Jews, or—just poor people?" That is the conclusion toward which the advocates of slavery are driving us. Many good citizens, North and South, agree with the Judge that we should accept that conclusion—don't stir up trouble— "Let each State mind its own business." That's the safer course, for the time being. But—I advise you to watch out! When you have enslaved any of your fellow beings, dehumanized him, denied him all claim to the dignity of manhood, placed him among the beasts, among the damned, are you quite sure that the demon you have thus created will not turn and rend *you?* When you begin qualifying freedom, watch out for the consequences to *you!* And I am not preaching civil war. All I am trying to do—now, and as long as I live—is to state and restate the fundamental virtues of our democracy, which have made us great, and which can make us greater. I believe most seriously that the perpetuation of those virtues is now endangered, not only by the honest proponents of slavery, but even more by those who echo Judge Douglas in shouting, "Leave it alone!" This is the complacent policy of indifference to evil, and that policy I cannot but hate. I hate it because of the monstrous injustice of slavery itself. I hate it because it deprives our republic of its just influence in the world; enables the enemies of free institutions everywhere to taunt us as hypocrites; causes the real friends of freedom to doubt our sincerity; and especially because it forces so many good men among ourselves into an open war with the very fundamentals of civil liberty, denying the good faith of the Declaration of Independence, and insisting that there is no right principle of action but *self-interest.* . . . In his final words tonight, the Judge said that we may be "the terror of the world." I don't think we want to be that. I think we would prefer to be the encouragement of the world, the proof that man is at last worthy to be free. But—we shall provide no such encouragement, unless we can establish our ability as a nation to live and grow. And we shall surely do neither if these states fail to remain *united.* There can be no distinction in the definitions of liberty as between one section and another, one race and another, one class and another. "A house divided against itself cannot stand." This government can not endure permanently, half slave and half free! [*He turns and goes back to his seat. The lights fade.*]

10

Parlor of the Edwards home, now being used by the Lincolns. Afternoon of a day in the early Spring of 1860.

ABE is sitting on the couch at the right, with his seven-year-old son, TAD, on his lap. Sitting beside them is another son, WILLIE, aged nine. The eldest son, ROBERT, a young Harvard student of seventeen, is sitting by the window, importantly smoking a pipe and listening to the story ABE has been telling the children. JOSHUA SPEED is sitting at the left.

ABE. You must remember, Tad, the roads weren't much good then—mostly nothing more than trails—and it was hard to find my way in the darkness. . . .

WILLIE. Were you scared?

ABE. Yes—I was scared.

WILLIE. Of Indians?

ABE. No—there weren't any of them left around here. I was afraid I'd get lost, and the boy would die, and it would be all my fault. But, finally, I found the doctor. He was very tired, and wanted to go to bed, and he grumbled a lot, but I made him come along with me then and there.

WILLIE. Was the boy dead?

ABE. No, Willie. He wasn't dead. But he was pretty sick. The doctor gave him a lot of medicine.

TAD. Did it taste bad, Pa?

ABE. I presume it did. But it worked. I never saw those nice people again, but I've heard from them every so often. That little boy was your age, Tad, but now he's a grown man with a son almost as big as you are. He lives on a great big farm, in a valley with a river that runs right down from the tops of the snow mountains. . . . [MARY *comes in.*]

MARY. Robert! You are smoking in my parlor!

ROBERT. [*Wearily.*] Yes, Mother. [*He rises.*]

MARY. I have told you that I shall not tolerate tobacco smoke in my parlor or, indeed, in any part of my house, and I mean to . . .

ABE. Come, come, Mary—you must be respectful to a Harvard man. Take it out to the woodshed, Bob.

ROBERT. Yes, Father.

MARY. And this will not happen again!

ROBERT. No, Mother. [*He goes out.*]

ABE. I was telling the boys a story about some pioneers I knew once.

MARY. It's time for you children to make ready for your supper. [*The* CHILDREN *promptly get up to go.*]

WILLIE. But what happened after that, Pa?

ABE. Nothing. Everybody lived happily ever after. Now run along. [WILLIE *and* TAD *run out.*]

JOSH. What time *is* it, Mary?

MARY. It's nearly half past four. [*She is shaking the smoke out of the curtains.*]

JOSH. Half past four, Abe. Those men will be here any minute.

ABE. [*Rising.*] Good Lord!

MARY. [*Turning sharply to* ABE.] What men?

ABE. Some men from the East. One of them's a political leader named Crimmin—and there's a Mr. Sturveson—he's a manufacturer—and . . .

MARY. [*Impressed.*] Henry D. Sturveson?

ABE. That's the one—and also the Reverend Dr. Barrick from Boston.

MARY. [*Sharply.*] What are they coming here for?

ABE. I don't precisely know—but I suspect that it's to see if I'm fit to be a candidate for President of the United States. [MARY *is, for the moment, speechless.*] I suppose they want to find out if we still live in a log cabin and keep pigs under the bed. . . .

MARY. [*In a fury.*] And you didn't *tell* me!

ABE. I'm sorry, Mary—the matter just slipped my . . .

MARY. You forgot to tell me that we're having the most important guests who ever crossed the threshold of my house!

ABE. They're not guests. They're only here on business.

MARY. [*Bitterly.*] Yes! Rather important business, it seems to me. They want to see us as we *are*—crude, sloppy, vulgar Western barbarians, living in a house that reeks of foul tobacco smoke.

ABE. We can explain about having a son at Harvard.

MARY. If I'd only *known!* If you had only given me a little time to prepare for them. Why didn't you put on your best suit? And those filthy old boots!

ABE. Well, Mary, I clean forgot. . . .

MARY. I declare, Abraham Lincoln, I believe you would have treated me with much more consideration if I had been your slave, instead of your wife! You have never, for one moment, stopped to think that perhaps I have some interests, some concerns, in the life we lead together. . . .

ABE. I'll try to clean up my boots a little, Mary. [*He goes out, glad to escape from this painful scene.* MARY *looks after him. Her lip is quivering. She wants to avoid tears.*]

MARY. [*Seating herself; bitterly.*] You've seen it all, Joshua Speed. Every bit of it—courtship, if you could call it that, change of heart, change back again, and marriage, eighteen years of it. And you probably think just as all the others do—that I'm a bitter, nagging woman, and I've tried to kill his spirit, and drag him down to my level. . . . [JOSH *rises and goes over to her.*]

JOSH. [*Quietly.*] No, Mary. I think no such thing. Remember, I know Abe, too.

MARY. There never could have been another man such as he is! I've read about many that have gone up in the world, and all of them seemed to have to fight to assert themselves every inch of the way, against the opposition of their enemies and the lack of understanding in their own friends. But he's never had any of that. He's never had an enemy, and every one of his friends has always been completely confident in him. Even before I met him, I was told that he had a glorious future, and after I'd known him a day, I was sure of it myself. But he didn't believe it—or, if he did,

secretly, he was so afraid of the prospect that he did all in his power to avoid it. He had some poem in his mind, about a life of woe, along a rugged path, that leads to some future doom, and it has been an obsession with him. All these years, I've tried and tried to stir him out of it, but all my efforts have been like so many puny waves, dashing against the Rock of Ages. And now, opportunity, the greatest opportunity, is coming here, to him, right into his own house. And what can I do about it? He *must* take it! He *must* see that this is what he was meant for! But I can't persuade him of it! I'm tired—I'm tired to death! [*The tears now come.*] I thought I could help to shape him, as I knew he should be, and I've succeeded in nothing—but in breaking myself. . . . [*She sobs bitterly.* JOSH *sits down beside her and pats her hand.*]

JOSH. [*Tenderly.*] I know, Mary. But —there's no reason in heaven and earth for you to reproach yourself. Whatever becomes of Abe Lincoln is in the hands of a God who controls the destinies of all of us, including lunatics, and saints. [ABE *comes back.*]

ABE. [*Looking down at his boots.*] I think they look all right now, Mary. [*He looks at* MARY, *who is now trying hard to control her emotion.*]

MARY. You can receive the gentlemen in here. I'll try to prepare some refreshment for them in the dining-room. [*She goes out.* ABE *looks after her, miserably. There are a few moments of silence. At length,* ABE *speaks, in an off-hand manner.*]

ABE. I presume these men *are* pretty influential.

JOSH. They'll have quite a say in the delegations of three states that may swing the nomination away from Seward.

ABE. Suppose, by some miracle, or fluke, they did nominate me; do you think I'd stand a chance of winning the election?

JOSH. An excellent chance, in my opinion. There'll be four candidates in the field, bumping each other, and opening up the track for a dark horse.

ABE. But the dark horse might run in the wrong direction.

JOSH. Yes—you can always do that, Abe. I know *I* wouldn't care to bet two cents on you.

ABE. [*Grinning.*] It seems funny to be comparing it to a horse-race, with an old, spavined hack like me. But I've had some mighty energetic jockeys—Mentor Graham, Bowling Green, Bill Herndon, you, and Mary—most of all, Mary.

JOSH. [*Looking at* ABE.] They don't count now, Abe. You threw 'em all, long ago. When you finally found yourself running against poor little Douglas, you got the bit between your teeth and went like greased lightning. You'd do the same thing to him again, if you could only decide to get started, which you probably won't . . . [*The doorbell jangles,* JOSH *gets up.*]

ABE. I expect that's them now.

JOSH. I'll go see if I can help Mary. [*He starts for the door but turns and looks at* ABE, *and speaks quietly.*] I'd just like to remind you, Abe—there are pretty nearly thirty million people in this country; most of 'em are common people, like you. They're in serious trouble, and they need somebody who understands 'em, as you do. So—when these gentlemen come in—try to be a *little* bit polite to them. [ABE *grins.* JOSH *looks off.*] However—you won't listen to any advice from me. [JOSH *goes. The door is opened by a* MAID *and* STURVESON, BARRICK, *and* CRIMMIN *come in.* STURVESON *is elderly, wealthy, and bland.* BARRICK *is a soft Episcopalian dignitary.* CRIMMIN *is a shrewd, humorous fixer.*]

ABE. Come right in, gentlemen. Glad to see you again, Mr. Crimmin. [*They shake hands.*]

CRIMMIN. How de do, Mr. Lincoln? This is Dr. Barrick of Boston, and Mr. Sturveson, of Philadelphia.

DR. BARRICK. Mr. Lincoln.

STURVESON. I'm honored, Mr. Lincoln.

LINCOLN. Thank you, sir. Pray sit down, gentlemen.

STURVESON. Thank you. [*They sit.*]

CRIMMIN. Will Mrs. Lincoln seriously object if I light a seegar?

LINCOLN. Go right ahead! I regret that Mrs. Lincoln is not here to receive you, but she will join us presently. [*He sits down.*]

BARRICK. [*With great benignity.*] I am particularly anxious to meet Mrs. Lincoln, for I believe, with Mr. Longfellow, that "as unto the bow the cord is, so unto the man is woman."

STURVESON. [*Very graciously.*] And we are here dealing with a bow that is stout indeed. [ABE *bows slightly in acknowledgment of the compliment.*] And one with a reputation for shooting straight. So you'll forgive us, Mr. Lincoln, for coming directly to the point.

ABE. Yes, sir. I understand that you wish to inspect the prairie politician in his native lair, and here I am.

STURVESON. It is no secret that we are desperately in need of a candidate—one who is sound, conservative, safe—and clever enough to skate over the thin ice of the forthcoming campaign. Your friends—and there's an increasingly large number of them throughout the country —believe that you are the man.

ABE. Well, Mr. Sturveson, I can tell you that when first I was considered for political office—that was in New Salem, twenty-five years ago—I assured my sponsors of my conservatism. I have subsequently proved it, by never progressing anywhere.

BARRICK. [*Smiling.*] Then you agree that you are the man we want?

ABE. I'm afraid I can't go quite that far in self-esteem, Dr. Barrick, especially when you have available a statesman and gentleman as eminent as Mr. Seward, who, I believe, is both ready and willing.

STURVESON. That's as may be. But please understand that this is not an inquisition. We merely wish to know you better, to gain a clearer idea of your theories on economics, religion, and national affairs, in general. To begin with—in one of your memorable debates with Senator Douglas, your opponent indulged in some of his usual demagoguery about industrial conditions in the North, and you replied shrewdly that whereas the slaves in the South . . .

ABE. Yes, I remember the occasion. I replied that I was thankful that laborers in free states have the right to strike. But that wasn't shrewdness, Mr. Sturveson. It was just the truth.

STURVESON. It has gained for you substantial support from the laboring classes, which is all to the good. But it has also caused a certain amount of alarm among business men, like myself.

ABE. I cannot enlarge on the subject. It seems obvious to me that this nation was founded on the supposition that men have the right to protest, violently if need be, against authority, that is unjust or oppressive. [*He turns to* BARRICK.] The Boston Tea Party was a kind of strike. So was the Revolution itself. [*Again to* STURVESON.] So was Nicholas Biddle's attempt to organize the banks against the Jackson administration.

STURVESON. Which is all perfectly true —but—the days of anarchy are over. We face an unprecedented era of industrial expansion—mass production of every conceivable kind of goods—railroads and telegraph lines across the continent—all promoted and developed by private enterprise. In this great work, we must have a free hand, and a firm one, Mr. Lincoln. To put it bluntly, would you, if elected, place the interests of labor above those of capital?

ABE. I cannot answer that, bluntly, or any other way; because I cannot tell what I should do, if elected.

STURVESON. But you must have inclinations toward one side or the other. . . .

ABE. I think you know, Mr. Sturveson, that I am opposed to slavery.

BARRICK. And we of New England applaud your sentiments! We deplore the inhumanity of our Southern friends in . . .

ABE. [*To* BARRICK.] There are more forms of slavery than that which is inflicted upon the Negroes in the South. I am opposed to all of them. [*He turns again to* STURVESON.] I believe in our democratic system—the just and generous system which opens the way to all —gives hope to all, and consequent energy and progress and improvement of condition to all, including employer and employee alike.

BARRICK. We support your purpose,

Mr. Lincoln, in steadfastly proclaiming the rights of men to resist unjust authority. But I am most anxious to know whether you admit One Authority to whom devotion is unquestioned?

ABE. I presume you refer to the Almighty?

BARRICK. I do.

ABE. I think there has never been any doubt of my submission to His will.

BARRICK. I'm afraid there is a great deal of doubt as to your devotion to His church.

ABE. I realize that, Doctor. They say I'm an atheist, because I've always refused to become a church member.

BARRICK. What have been the grounds of your refusal?

ABE. I have found no churches suitable for my own form of worship. I could not give assent without mental reservations to the long, complicated statements of Christian doctrine which characterize their Articles of Belief and Confessions of Faith. But I can promise you, Dr. Barrick—I shall gladly join any church at any time if its sole qualification for membership is obedience to the Saviour's statement of Law and Gospel: "Thou shalt love the Lord thy God with all thy heart and with all thy soul and with all thy mind, and thou shalt love thy neighbor as thyself." . . . But—I beg you gentlemen to excuse me for a moment. I believe Mrs. Lincoln is preparing a slight collation, and I must see if I can help with it. . . .

CRIMMIN. Certainly, Mr. Lincoln. [ABE *goes, closing the door behind him.* CRIMMIN *looks at the door, then turns to the others.*] Well?

BARRICK. The man is unquestionably an infidel. An idealist—in his curious, primitive way—but an infidel!

STURVESON. And a radical!

CRIMMIN. A radical? Forgive me, gentlemen, if I enjoy a quiet laugh at that.

STURVESON. Go ahead and enjoy yourself, Crimmin—but I did not like the way he evaded my direct question. I tell you he's as unscrupulous a demagogue as Douglas. He's a rabble rouser!

CRIMMIN. Of course he is! As a dealer

in humbug, he puts Barnum himself to shame.

STURVESON. Quite possibly—but he is not *safe!*

CRIMMIN. Not safe, eh? And what do you mean by that?

STURVESON. Just what I say. A man who devotes himself so whole-heartedly to currying favor with the mob develops the mob mentality. He becomes a preacher of discontent, of mass unrest. . . .

CRIMMIN. And what about Seward? If we put him up, he'll start right in demanding liberation of the slaves—and then there *will* be discontent and unrest! I ask you to believe me when I tell you that this Lincoln *is* safe—in economics and theology and everything else. After all—what is the essential qualification that we demand of the candidate of our party? It is simply this: that he be able to get himself elected! And there is the man who can do that. [*He points off-stage.*]

STURVESON. [*Smiling.*] I should like to believe you!

BARRICK. So say we all of us!

CRIMMIN. Then just keep faith in the eternal stupidity of the voters, which is what *he* will appeal to. In that uncouth rail splitter you may observe one of the smoothest, slickest politicians that ever hoodwinked a yokel mob! You complain that he evaded your questions. Of course he did, and did it perfectly! Ask him about the labor problem, and he replies, "I believe in democracy." Ask his views on religion, and he says, "Love thy neighbor as thyself." Now—you know you couldn't argue with that, either of you. I tell you, gentlemen, he's a vote-getter if I ever saw one. His very name is right —Abraham Lincoln! Honest Old Abe! He'll play the game with us now, and he'll go right on playing it when we get him into the White House. He'll do just what we tell him. . . .

BARRICK. [*Cautioning him.*] Careful, Mr. Crimmin. . . . [ABE *returns.*]

ABE. If you gentlemen will step into the dining-room, Mrs. Lincoln would be pleased to serve you with a cup of tea.

BARRICK. Thank you.

STURVESON. This is most gracious. [*He*

and BARRICK *move off toward the door.*]

ABE. Or perhaps something stronger for those who prefer it. [STURVESON *and* BARRICK *go.* CRIMMIN *is looking for a place to throw his cigar.*]

ABE. [*Heartily.*] Bring your seegar with you, Mr. Crimmin!

CRIMMIN. Thank you—thank you. [*He smiles at* ABE, *gives him a slap on the arm, and goes out,* ABE *following. The lights fade.*]

11

Lincoln campaign headquarters in the Illinois State House. The evening of Election Day November 6th, 1860. It is a large room with a tall window opening out on to a wide balcony. There are doors upper right and upper left. At the left is a table littered with newspapers and clippings. There are many chairs about, and a liberal supply of spittoons. At the back is a huge chart of the thirty-three states, with their electoral votes, and a space opposite each side for the posting of bulletins. A short ladder gives access to Alabama and Arkansas at the top of the list. On the wall at the left is an American flag. At the right is a map of the United States, on which each state is marked with a red, white, or blue flag.

ABE is sitting at the table, with his back to the audience, reading newspaper clippings. He wears his hat and has spectacles on. MRS. LINCOLN is sitting at the right of the table, her eyes darting nervously from ABE, to the chart, to the map. She wears her bonnet, tippet and muff. ROBERT LINCOLN is standing near her, studying the map. NINIAN EDWARDS is sitting at the left of the table and JOSH SPEED is standing near the chart. They are both smoking cigars and watching the chart. The door at the left is open, and through it the clatter of telegraph instruments can be heard. The window is partly open, and we can hear band music from the square below, and frequent cheers from the assembled mob, who are watching the election returns flashed from a magic lantern on the State House balcony. Every now and then, a telegraph operator named JED comes in from the left and tacks a new bulletin up on the chart. Another man named PHIL is out on the balcony taking bulletins from JED.

ROBERT. What do those little flags mean, stuck into the map?

JOSH. Red means the state is sure for us. White means doubtful. Blue means hopeless. [ABE *tosses the clipping he has been reading on the table and picks up another.* JED *comes in and goes up to pin bulletins opposite Illinois, Maryland, and New York.*]

NINIAN. [*Rising to look.*] Lincoln and Douglas neck and neck in Illinois. [JOSH *and* ROBERT *crowd around the chart.*]

JOSH. Maryland is going all for Breckenridge and Bell. Abe—you're nowhere in Maryland.

MARY. [*With intense anxiety.*] What of New York?

JED. [*Crossing to the window.*] Say, Phil—when you're not getting bulletins, keep that window closed. We can't hear ourselves think.

PHIL. All right. Only have to open 'er up again. [*He closes the window.*]

MARY. What does it say about New York? [JED *goes.*]

NINIAN. Douglas a hundred and seventeen thousand—Lincoln a hundred and six thousand.

MARY. [*Desperately, to* ABE.] He's winning from you in New York, Abe!

JOSH. Not yet, Mary. These returns so far are mostly from the city, where Douglas is bound to run the strongest.

ABE. [*Interested in a clipping.*] I see the New York *Herald* says I've got the soul of a Uriah Heep encased in the body of a baboon. [*He puts the clipping aside and starts to read another.*]

NINIAN. [*Who has resumed his seat.*] You'd better change that flag on Rhode Island from red to white, Bob. It looks doubtful to me. [ROBERT, *glad of something to do, changes the flag as directed.*]

MARY. What does it look like in Pennsylvania, Ninian?

NINIAN. There's nothing to worry about there, Mary. It's safe for Abe. In fact, you needn't worry at all.

MARY. [*Very tense.*] Yes. You've been

saying that over and over again all evening. There's no need to worry. But how can we help worrying when every new bulletin shows Douglas ahead?

JOSH. But every one of them shows Abe gaining.

NINIAN. [*Mollifying.*] Just give them time to count all the votes in New York and then you'll be on your way to the White House.

MARY. Oh, why don't they hurry with it? Why don't those returns come in?

ABE. [*Preoccupied.*] They'll come in, soon enough. [BILLY HERNDON *comes in from the right. He has been doing a lot of drinking but has hold of himself.*]

BILLY. That mob down there is sickening! They cheer every bulletin that's flashed on the wall, whether the news is good or bad. And they cheer every picture of every candidate, including George Washington, with the same, fine, ignorant enthusiasm.

JOSH. That's logical. They can't tell 'em apart.

BILLY. [*To* ABE.] There are a whole lot of reporters down there. They want to know what will be your first official action after you're elected.

NINIAN. What do you want us to tell 'em, Abe?

ABE. [*Still reading.*] Tell 'em I'm thinking of growing a beard.

JOSH. A beard?

NINIAN. [*Amused.*] Whatever put that idea into your mind?

ABE. [*Picking up another clipping.*] I had a letter the other day from some little girl. She said I ought to have whiskers, to give me more dignity. And I'll need it—if elected. [JED *arrives with new bulletins.* BILLY, NINIAN, JOSH, *and* ROBERT *huddle around* JED, *watching him post the bulletins.*]

MARY. What do they say now? [JED *goes to the window and gives some bulletins to* PHIL.]

MARY. Is there anything new from New York?

NINIAN. Connecticut—Abe far in the lead. That's eleven safe electoral votes anyway. Missouri—Douglas thirty-five thousand—Bell thirty-three—Breckenridge sixteen—Lincoln eight. . . . [*Cheers from the crowd outside until* PHIL *closes the window.* JED *returns to the office at the left.*]

MARY. What are they cheering for?

BILLY. They don't know!

ABE. [*With another clipping.*] The Chicago *Times* says, "Lincoln breaks down! Lincoln's heart fails him! His tongue fails him! His legs fail him! He fails all over! The people refuse to support him! They laugh at him! Douglas is champion of the people! Douglas skins the living dog!" [*He tosses the clipping aside.* MARY *stands up.*]

MARY. [*Her voice is trembling.*] I can't stand it any longer!

ABE. Yes, my dear—I think you'd better go home. I'll be back before long.

MARY. [*Hysterical.*] I won't go home! You only want to be rid of me. That's what you've wanted ever since the day we were married—and before that. Anything to get me out of your sight, because you hate me! [*Turning to* JOSH, NINIAN, *and* BILLY.] And it's the same with all of you—all of his friends—you hate me—you wish I'd never come into his life.

JOSH. No, Mary. [ABE *has stood up, quickly, at the first storm signal. He himself is in a fearful state of nervous tension—in no mood to treat* MARY *with patient indulgence. He looks sharply at* NINIAN *and at the others.*]

ABE. Will you please step out for a moment?

NINIAN. Certainly, Abe. [*He and the others go into the telegraph office.* JOSH *gestures to* ROBERT *to go with them.* ROBERT *casts a black look at his mother and goes. . . .* ABE *turns on* MARY *with strange savagery.*]

ABE. Damn you! Damn you for taking every opportunity you can to make a public fool of me—and yourself! It's bad enough, God knows, when you act like that in the privacy of our own home. But here—in front of people! You're not to do that again. Do you hear me? You're never to do that again! [MARY *is so aghast at this outburst that her hysterical temper vanishes, giving way to blank terror.*]

MARY. [*In a faint, strained voice.*] Abe!

You cursed at me. Do you realize what you did? You cursed at me. [ABE *has the impulse to curse at her again, but with considerable effort, he controls it.*]

ABE. [*In a strained voice.*] I lost my temper, Mary. And I'm sorry for it. But I still think you should go home rather than endure the strain of this—this Death Watch. [*She stares at him, uncomprehendingly, then turns and goes to the door.*]

MARY. [*At the door.*] This is the night I dreamed about, when I was a child, when I was an excited young girl, and all the gay young gentlemen of Springfield were courting me, and I fell in love with the least likely of them. This is the night when I'm waiting to hear that my husband has become President of the United States. And even if he does—it's ruined, for me. It's too late. . . . [*She opens the door and goes out.* ABE *looks after her, anguished, then turns quickly, crosses to the door at the left and opens it.*]

ABE. [*Calling off.*] Bob! [ROBERT *comes in.*] Go with your mother.

ROBERT. Do I have to?

ABE. Yes! Hurry! Keep right with her till I get home. [ROBERT *has gone.* ABE *turns to the window.* PHIL *opens it.*]

PHIL. Do you think you're going to make it, Mr. Lincoln?

ABE. Oh—there's nothing to worry about.

CROWD OUTSIDE. [*Singing.*]
Old Abe Lincoln came out of the wilderness
Out of the wilderness
Out of the wilderness
Old Abe Lincoln came out of the wilderness
Down in Illinois!

[NINIAN, JOSH, BILLY, *and* JED *come in, the latter to post new bulletins. After* JED *has communicated these,* PHIL *again closes the window.* JED *goes.*]

NINIAN. It looks like seventy-four electoral votes sure for you. Twenty-seven more probable. New York's will give you the election. [ABE *walks around the room.* JOSH *has been looking at* ABE.]

JOSH. Abe, could I get you a cup of coffee?

ABE. No, thanks, Josh.

NINIAN. Getting nervous, Abe?

ABE. No. I'm just thinking what a blow it would be to Mrs. Lincoln if I should lose.

NINIAN. And what about me? I have ten thousand dollars bet on you.

BILLY. [*Scornfully.*] I'm afraid that the loss to the nation would be somewhat more serious than that.

JOSH. How would you feel, Abe?

ABE. [*Sitting on the chair near the window.*] I guess I'd feel the greatest sense of relief of my life. [JED *comes in with a news despatch.*]

JED. Here's a news despatch. [*He hands it over and goes.*]

NINIAN. [*Reads.*] "Shortly after nine o'clock this evening, Mr. August Belmont stated that Stephen A. Douglas has piled up a majority of fifty thousand votes in New York City and carried the state."

BILLY. Mr. Belmont be damned! [CRIMMIN *comes in, smoking a cigar, looking contented.*]

CRIMMIN. Good evening, Mr. Lincoln. Good evening, gentlemen—and how are you feeling *now*? [*They all greet him.*]

NINIAN. Look at this, Crimmin. [*He hands the despatch to* CRIMMIN.]

CRIMMIN. [*Smiles.*] Well—Belmont is going to fight to the last ditch, which is just what he's lying in now. I've been in Chicago and the outlook there is cloudless. In fact, Mr. Lincoln, I came down tonight to protect you from the office-seekers. They're lining up downstairs already. On the way in I counted four Ministers to Great Britain and eleven Secretaries of State. [JED *has come in with more bulletins to put on the chart and then goes to the window to give* PHIL *the bulletins.*]

BILLY. [*At the chart.*] There's a bulletin from New York! Douglas a hundred and eighty-three thousand—Lincoln a hundred and eighty-*one* thousand! [JED *goes.*]

JOSH. Look out, Abe! You're catching up!

CRIMMIN. The next bulletin from New York will show you winning. Mark my words, Mr. Lincoln, this election is all wrapped up tightly in a neat bundle, ready for delivery on your doorstep tonight. We've fought the good fight, and we've won!

ABE. [*Pacing up and down the room.*] Yes—we've fought the good fight—in the dirtiest campaign in the history of corrupt politics. And if I have won, then I must cheerfully pay my political debts. All those who helped to nominate and elect me must be paid off. I have been gambled all around, bought and sold a hundred times. And now I must fill all the dishonest pledges made in my name.

NINIAN. We realize all that, Abe—but the fact remains that you're winning. Why, you're even beating the coalition in Rhode Island!

ABE. I've got to step out for a moment. [*He goes out at the right.*]

NINIAN. [*Cheerfully.*] Poor Abe.

CRIMMIN. You gentlemen have all been close friends of our Candidate for a long time, so perhaps you could answer a question that's been puzzling me considerably. Can I possibly be correct in supposing that he doesn't want to win?

JOSH. The answer is—yes.

CRIMMIN. [*Looking toward the right.*] Well—I can only say that, for me, this is all a refreshingly new experience.

BILLY. [*Belligerently.*] Would *you* want to become President of the United States at this time? Haven't you been reading the newspapers lately?

CRIMMIN. Why, yes—I try to follow the events of the day.

BILLY. [*In a rage.*] Don't you realize that they've raised ten thousand volunteers in South Carolina? They're arming them! The Governor has issued a proclamation saying that if Mr. Lincoln is elected, the State will secede tomorrow, and every other state south of the Dixon line will go with it. Can you see what that means? War! Civil War! And *he'll* have the whole terrible responsibility for it—a man who has never wanted anything in his life but to be let alone, in peace!

NINIAN. Calm down, Billy. Go get yourself another drink. [JED *rushes in.*]

JED. Mr. Edwards, here it is! [*He hands a news despatch to* NINIAN, *then rushes to the window to attract* PHIL's *attention and communicate the big news.*]

NINIAN. [*Reads.*] "At 10:30 tonight the New York *Herald* conceded that Mr. Lincoln has carried the state by a majority of at least twenty-five thousand and has won the election!" [*He tosses the despatch in the air.*] He's won! He's won! Hurrah! [*All on the stage shout, cheer, embrace, and slap each other.*]

BILLY. God be praised! God be praised!

CRIMMIN. I knew it! I never had a doubt of it! [JED *is on the balcony, shouting through a megaphone.*]

JED. Lincoln is elected! Honest Old Abe is our next President! [*A terrific cheer ascends from the crowd below.* ABE *returns. They rush at him.* BILLY *shakes hands with him, too deeply moved to speak.*]

NINIAN. You've carried New York, Abe! You've won! Congratulations!

CRIMMIN. My congratulations, Mr. President. This is a mighty achievement for all of us. [JED *comes in and goes to* ABE.]

JED. My very best, Mr. Lincoln!

ABE. [*Solemnly.*] Thank you—thank you all very much. [*He comes to the left.* JOSH *is the last to shake his hand.*]

JOSH. I congratulate you, Abe.

ABE. Thanks, Josh.

NINIAN. Listen to them, Abe. Listen to that crazy, howling mob down there.

CRIMMIN. It's all for you, Mr. Lincoln.

NINIAN. Abe, get out there and let 'em see you!

ABE. No. I don't want to go out there. I —I guess I'll be going on home, to tell Mary. [*He starts toward the door. A short, stocky officer named* KAVANAGH *comes in from the right. He is followed by two* SOLDIERS.]

CRIMMIN. This is Captain Kavanagh, Mr. *President.*

KAVANAGH. [*Salutes.*] I've been detailed to accompany you, Mr. Lincoln, in the event of your election.

ABE. I'm grateful, Captain. But I don't need you.

KAVANAGH. I'm afraid you've got to have us, Mr. Lincoln. I don't like to be alarming, but I guess you know as well as I do what threats have been made.

ABE. [*Wearily.*] I see . . . Well— Good night, Josh—Ninian—Mr. Crimmin—Billy. Thank you for your good wishes. [*He starts for the door. The others bid him good night, quietly.*]

KAVANAGH. One moment, Sir. With your permission, I'll go first. [*He goes out,* ABE *after him, the two other* SOLDIERS *follow. The light fades.*]

12

The yards of the railroad station at Springfield. The date is February 11, 1861. At the right, at an angle toward the audience, is the back of a railroad car. From behind this, off to the upper left, runs a ramp. Flags and bunting are draped above. In a row downstage are SOLDIERS, with rifles and bayonets fixed, and packs on their backs, standing at ease. Off to the left is a large CROWD, whose excited murmuring can be heard.

KAVANAGH is in the foreground. A BRAKEMAN with a lantern is inspecting the wheels of the car, at the left. A WORKMAN is at the right, polishing the rails of the car. KAVANAGH is pacing up and down, chewing a dead cigar. He looks at his watch. A swaggering MAJOR of militia comes down the ramp from the left.

MAJOR. I want you men to form up against this ramp. [*To* KAVANAGH, *with a trace of scorn.*] You seem nervous, Mr. Kavanagh.

KAVANAGH. Well—I am nervous. For three months I've been guarding the life of a man who doesn't give a damn what happens to him. I heard today that they're betting two to one in Richmond that he won't be alive to take the oath of office on March the 4th.

MAJOR. I'd like to take some of that money. The State Militia is competent to protect the person of our Commander-in-Chief.

KAVANAGH. I hope the United States Army is competent to help. But those Southerners are mighty good shots. And I strongly suggest that your men be commanded to keep watch through every window of every car, especially whenever the train stops—at a town, or a tank, or anywhere. And if any alarm is sounded, at any point along the line . . .

MAJOR. [*A trifle haughty.*] There's no need to command my men to show courage in an emergency.

KAVANAGH. No slur was intended, Major—but we must be prepared in advance for everything. [*A brass band off to the left strikes up the campaign song, "Old Abe Lincoln came out of the wilderness." The crowd starts to sing it, more and more voices taking it up. A* CONDUCTOR *comes out of the car and looks at his watch. There is a commotion at the left as* NINIAN *and* ELIZABETH EDWARDS, *and* JOSH, BILLY, *and* CRIMMIN *come in and are stopped by the* SOLDIERS. *The* MAJOR *goes forward, bristling with importance.*]

MAJOR. Stand back, there! Keep the crowd back there, you men!

NINIAN. I'm Mr. Lincoln's brother-in-law.

MAJOR. What's your name?

KAVANAGH. I know him, Major. That's Mr. and Mrs. Edwards, and Mr. Speed and Mr. Herndon with them. I know them all. You can let them through.

MAJOR. Very well. You can pass. [*They come down to the right. The* MAJOR *goes off at the left.*]

CRIMMIN. How is the President feeling today? Happy?

NINIAN. Just as gloomy as ever.

BILLY. [*Emotionally.*] He came down to the office, and when I asked him what I should do about the sign, "Lincoln and Herndon," he said, "Let it hang there. Let our clients understand that this election makes no difference to the firm. If I live I'll be back some time, and then we'll go right on practising just as if nothing had happened."

ELIZABETH. He's always saying that— "If I live" . . . [*A tremendous cheer starts and swells offstage at the left. The* MAJOR *comes on briskly.*]

MAJOR. [*To* KAVANAGH.] The President has arrived! [*To his men.*] Attention! [*The* MAJOR *strides down the platform and takes his position by the car, looking off to the left.*]

KAVANAGH. [*To* NINIAN *and the others.*] Would you mind stepping back there?

We want to keep this space clear for the President's party. [*They move upstage, at the right. The cheering is now very loud.*]

MAJOR. Present—Arms! [*The* SOLDIERS *come to the Present. The* MAJOR *salutes. Preceded by* SOLDIERS *who are looking sharply to the right and left,* ABE *comes in from the left, along the platform. He will be fifty-two years old tomorrow. He wears a beard. Over his shoulders is his plaid shawl. In his right hand, he carries his carpetbag; his left hand is leading* TAD. *Behind him are* MARY, ROBERT, *and* WILLIE, *and the* MAID. *All, except* MARY, *are also carrying bags. She carries a bunch of flowers. When they come to the car,* ABE *hands his bag up to the* CONDUCTOR, *then lifts* TAD *up.* MARY, ROBERT, WILLIE, *and the* MAID *get on board, while* ABE *steps over to talk to* NINIAN *and the others. During this, there is considerable commotion at the left, as the* CROWD *tries to surge forward.*]

MAJOR. [*Rushing forward.*] Keep 'em back! Keep 'em back, men! [*The* SOLDIERS *have broken their file on the platform and are in line, facing the* CROWD. KAVANAGH *and his* MEN *are close to* ABE. *Each of them has his hand on his revolver, and is keeping a sharp lookout.*]

KAVANAGH. Better get on board, Mr. President. [ABE *climbs up on to the car's back platform. There is a great increase in the cheering when the* CROWD *sees him. They shout: "Speech! Speech! Give us a speech, Abe! Speech, Mr. President! Hurray for Old Abe!" etc. . . .* ABE *turns to the* CROWD, *takes his hat off and waves it with a half-hearted gesture. The cheering dies down.*]

NINIAN. They want you to say something, Abe. [*For a moment,* ABE *stands still, looking off to the left.*]

ABE. My dear friends—I have to say good-by to you. I am going now to Washington, with my new whiskers—of which I hope you approve. [*The* CROWD *roars with laughter at that. More shouts of "Good Old Abe!" In its exuberant enthusiasm, the* CROWD *again surges forward, at and around the* SOLDIERS, *who shout, "Get back, there! Stand back, you!"*]

ABE. [*To the* MAJOR.] It's all right—let them come on. They're all old friends of mine. [*The* MAJOR *allows his* MEN *to retreat so that they form a ring about the back of the car.* KAVANAGH *and his* MEN *are on the car's steps, watching. The* CROWD—*an assortment of townspeople, including some Negroes—fills the stage.*]

ABE. No one, not in my situation, can appreciate my feelings of sadness at this parting. To this place, and the kindness of you people, I owe everything. I have lived here a quarter of a century, and passed from a young to an old man. Here my children have been born and one is buried. I now leave, not knowing when or whether ever I may return. I am called upon to assume the Presidency at a time when eleven of our sovereign states have announced their intention to secede from the Union, when threats of war increase in fierceness from day to day. It is a grave duty which I now face. In preparing for it, I have tried to enquire: what great principle or ideal is it that has kept this Union so long together? And I believe that it was not the mere matter of separation of the colonies from the motherland, but that sentiment in the Declaration of Independence which gave liberty to the people of this country and hope to all the world. This sentiment was the fulfillment of an ancient dream, which men have held through all time, that they might one day shake off their chains and find freedom in the brotherhood of life. We gained democracy, and now there is the question whether it is fit to survive. Perhaps we have come to the dreadful day of awakening, and the dream is ended. If so, I am afraid it must be ended forever. I cannot believe that ever again will men have the opportunity we have had. Perhaps we should admit that, and concede that our ideals of liberty and equality are decadent and doomed. I have heard of an eastern monarch who once charged his wise men to invent him a sentence which would be true and appropriate in all times and situations. They presented him the words, "And this too shall pass away." That is a comforting thought in time of affliction—"And this too shall pass away." And yet—[*Suddenly he speaks with quiet but urgent authority.*] —let us believe that it is not true! Let us live to prove that we can cultivate the natural world that is about us, and the intellectual and moral world that is within us, so that we may secure an individual, social, and political prosperity, whose course shall be forward, and which, while the earth endures, shall not pass away. . . . I commend you to the care of the Almighty, as I hope that in your prayers you will remember me. . . . Good-by, my friends and neighbors. [*He leans over the railing of the car platform to say good-by to* NINIAN, ELIZABETH, JOSH, BILLY, *and* CRIMMIN, *shaking each by the hand. The band offstage strikes up "John Brown's Body." The cheering swells. The* CONDUCTOR *looks at his watch and speaks to the* MAJOR, *who gets on board the train. The* CROWD *on stage is shouting "Good-by, Abe," "Good-by, Mr. Lincoln," "Good luck, Abe," "We trust you, Mr. Lincoln." As the band swings into the refrain, "Glory, Glory Hallelujah," the* CROWD *starts to sing, the number of voices increasing with each word.* KAVANAGH *tries to speak to* ABE *but can't be heard. He touches* ABE'S *arm, and* ABE *turns on him quickly.*]

KAVANAGH. Time to pull out, Mr. President. Better get inside the car. [*These words cannot be heard by the audience in the general uproar of singing.* NINIAN, ELIZABETH, JOSH *and* BILLY *are up on the station platform. The* SOLDIERS *are starting to climb up on to the train.* ABE *gives one last wistful wave of his hat to the* CROWD, *then turns and goes into the car, followed by* KAVANAGH, *the* MAJOR, *and the* SOLDIERS. *The band reaches the last line of the song.*]

ALL. [*Singing.*] "His soul goes marching on." [*The* BRAKEMAN, *downstage, is waving his lantern. The* CONDUCTOR *swings aboard. The* CROWD *is cheering, waving hats and handkerchiefs. The shrill screech of the engine whistle sounds from the right.*]

CURTAIN

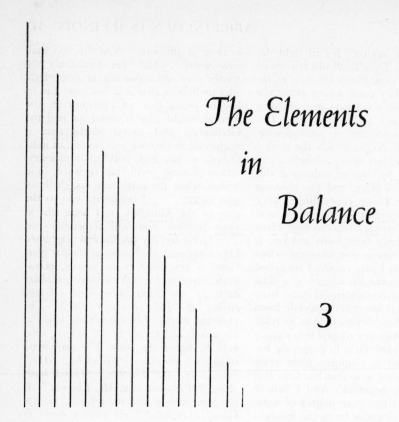

The Elements
in
Balance

3

THE WILD DUCK

It answered the purposes of the authors of *The Desperate Hours*, *Everyman*, and *Abe Lincoln in Illinois* to emphasize, in turn, one of the three major elements of the drama: action, theme, character. But the question in each case is one of emphasis only. While the Hayes melodrama concentrates on swift action, it is not without some character development and thematic significance; *Everyman*, engaged chiefly in expounding a message vital to its audience and its age, does not overlook the elements of character and action; and *Abe Lincoln in Illinois*, while drawing a portrait that fills the center of the stage, also offers action as a means of illustrating character, and presents a currently relevant theme embodied in Lincoln's development. Indeed, while it is convenient to distinguish these three elements for purposes of analysis—especially in considering dramas where one of the three is emphasized more than the others—they remain, in actual practice, inseparable.

These same elements are found again in the work that follows, Henrik Ibsen's *The Wild Duck*, but the dramatist's aims are such that we find a shift from emphasis on a single element to a balance of all three in an organic whole, within which each of the three is of approximately equal importance. And the point should be made that Ibsen's play shares with a majority of the world's great dramas a common structural goal: the integration, on equal terms, of action, theme, and character. It will be seen presently that varying approaches to this problem of integration have been developed whenever fresh aims have pointed the way to technical innovation. The experimental temper has been particularly evident in our own century, when the demand for maximum realism within established conventions of the theater has been relaxed. Our immediate concern, however, lies with a drama that is fundamentally realistic, in ways and to a degree that will become clear in the course of discussion.

We should look first at the elements themselves, and ask how close they come to answering the particular aims Ibsen set himself in this play. To begin with, there is a story in *The Wild Duck*. Stated with utmost brevity, it relates the efforts of Gregers Werle to rescue Hialmar Ekdal and his family from the lake-bottom of illusions that supports their existence. But even this bare statement about Ibsen's *story* points the way to Ibsen's *characters*, and it suggests several things about them. The fact that they carry obviously individualized names—Gregers, Hialmar, Hedvig, Gina—implies that they are far removed from the personifications of the medieval Morality Play. These persons will be individuals, and (again in the light of our bare account of the action) individuals with a high degree of self-consciousness; in all probability, they will be more concerned to find solutions to present problems than to discover the road to ultimate salvation. Moreover, the nature of their problem, implied in the description of Gregers' rescue-mission, suggests that we will need to know much more about them than was the case with, say, the Hilliards of *The Desperate Hours*. Choosing to dramatize this species of problem, Ibsen commits himself to a less superficial treatment of character; he must make us intimately acquainted with the internal life of his people. Yet, brief as our description of the action was, it also points to a conflict between two persons—between Gregers and Hialmar; since the opposed forces are nearly equally matched, and since the conflict between them is dramatized externally, Ibsen's approach to character will inevitably differ somewhat from Sherwood's in *Abe Lincoln in Illinois*.

The Wild Duck, then, tells a story, culminating in a pathetic suicide, about a group of highly individualized persons. The play has a theme as well: calling in question the assumed moral superiority of people who face up to reality, it asks what right any man has to destroy the illusions of a fellow human being. Forcing father and daughter to abandon the illusions that sustain them so precariously, the high-minded Gregers thrusts them violently to the surface of reality, and his "idealism" (*meddling* reflects the author's view more accurately) brings in its wake destruction and death. This theme is the ideological center of Ibsen's play; as such, it is fully as important to his over-all aim as the action and the characters that invest it with dramatic life.

It is just at this point that we must pause for a moment. The elements are here kept in balance; no one of them receives exclusive or even primary attention. Yet Ibsen's theme, and the plot and characters by means of which he dramatizes it, introduce us to a fresh problem. What of illusions as the subject of a story that must be communicated in dialogue? Surely there are few experiences more private by nature, more subjective, than our illusory pictures of ourselves—few idealizations we are more reluctant to divulge to others than our hopes of the way we appear to those around us. If deep-seated feelings such as these are themselves the subject of the drama, how are they to be made objective on the stage? If the dramatist wishes to reveal to us those kinds of experience which do not normally rise to the surface of conversation, how is he to proceed, inasmuch as the essential medium of the drama is, after all, conversation? Shakespeare and his contemporaries enjoyed the advantage of the *soliloquy*, and of a stage constructed to help make this device acceptable; thus Hamlet could reveal in direct speech, at a moment of intense inner questioning, his doubts about the admissibility of suicide. But despite an occasional revival, as in Eugene O'Neill's *Strange Interlude*, the soliloquy has not been adapted to the modern proscenium-stage; it has proved generally unacceptable to audiences since the decline of Jacobean drama. Why not, then (one may ask), simply allow a pair of characters to talk things out behind the footlights, just as they do in real life? Surely, if the criterion here is likeness to life, this procedure is valid.

The modern dramatist does rely on this revelatory kind of conversation often enough (notice, as an example, the scene in *The Wild Duck* during which Gregers discloses his sense of mission), but he is limited in his use of the prolonged revelatory exchange by a further consideration he can never afford to lose sight of: having chosen to work in the drama, he must abide by the unchanging basic requirements of that type, and these entail a responsibility to tell his story through a series of related *actions*. In itself insufficient to constitute a play, action is yet that element which keeps the play constant in its forward movement. Any interruption of this movement for the sake of a dialogic confessional risks a slackening of the drama's *tempo*, and this, by chain-reaction, will breed in the audience a restlessness fatal to the play. In life (or in a novel) we can be patient while an acquaintance or a character describes his feelings at length, either directly to us, or to a third person whose responses we overhear; we are prepared in these instances to adapt ourselves to a shift in tempo from *presto* to *largo*. With a play we are less patient. The conventions of the medium, dependent in the first place on the psychological responses of the audience, demand that the tempo, though it may begin at *largo*, shall gradually accelerate to *presto*. And, once this faster tempo has been gained, the play can never thereafter afford to slacken for long its pace. This does not mean, of course, that the tempo must be handled with metronomic rigidity; but it does mean that any prolonged hiatus in the forward movement will incur a perilous risk. For this reason, no matter how vital the feelings of an individual character may be, those feelings must commonly find some immediate issue in significant action.

By the start of the twentieth century, the playwright, inevitably affected by discoveries in psychology and psychiatry, and intent therefore on probing deeply beneath the conversational surfaces of life, found himself face to face with a challenging problem: the dramatic objectification of inner states of being. He was denied the soliloquy, denied direct revelation; yet the drama as it existed at the close of the nineteenth century suggested no alternative solutions. New and more complex aims apparently called for new methods; the expressive limits of dialogue, setting, movement, costume, and gesture—as these materials had been traditionally conceived—now seemed to have been reached. As a consequence, the theater of the present day has been notable for experiment. Skeptical of accepted methods, it has shown a continuing interest in new techniques, and the result has been an enlargement of the theater's capacity to display our increased knowledge of the complexity of human character.

The Wild Duck exemplifies one of the solutions discovered for this problem of objectifying on the modern stage the internal life of man: the extended use of symbolism. A second solution, expressionism, will be discussed briefly at the end of the present chapter.

Symbolism is very nearly as old as man himself. From the first he has given it an important place in his religious observances; but almost as early he discovered its usefulness in his arts—for art, like religion, represents an attempt by man to organize his experience in such a way as to show universal meanings and to express the unseen.

The object which stands at the peak of most Christian church steeples has, we all recognize, a purely objective existence as two pieces of wood or other material, joined in a certain fixed position. Yet to see this object only in this way is to miss its significance altogether. For this particular arrangement in wood *symbolizes*, by agreement that is really universal since it overrides individual religious sympathies, the climactic moment in the life of Christ. Behind the obvious identity of the cross as a wooden object, then, stands its symbolic significance.

Symbolism involves this use of a real object as a two-way pointer. When the object is used symbolically, it points to something beyond itself—as does the Christian cross. But it is the special usefulness of symbols that, once recognized, they lead us to further recognitions. We initially grasp the meaning "beyond" the object: in our example, the crucifixion is the meaning that lies "beyond" the cross. Secondly, however, we come to see that that meaning "beyond" *points back to the object*, and in doing so adds to our total understanding, by redefining both the object and the context in which it is found. Thus, in our example, the high-arched edifice with stained-glass windows (the architectural "context" of our object) must be a building connected with Christ, in all probability, a Christian temple. The symbols in Ibsen's drama operate precisely this way.

Employed in dramatic literature, the symbol functions as a means of extending, or commenting upon, the meaning of the primary elements of action, theme, and character. It amplifies the author's list of usable materials; dialogue, setting, movement, costume and gesture are supplemented by the symbol. The more conventional materials satisfied the more conventional dramatic aims of Hayes and Sherwood. But Ibsen is concerned, in the play that represents him here, with people whose intensely-lived inner lives are of central importance, but who are, nevertheless, quite inarticulate. By resorting to symbolism, the dramatist manages to convey to audience and reader what his characters are ill-equipped to express for themselves.

The wild duck of Ibsen's title is one of the two key symbols in the play; the other is the bird-dog described by Gregers Werle, that self-righteous missionary for reality whose mission precipitates the play's catastrophe. Between them, these two symbols sum up the whole action and meaning of the drama. But the responsibility with which symbols are here charged involves far more than the mere telling of a story by a kind of short-hand; they must also comment revealingly on the characters to whom they refer, and, through them, on Ibsen's theme. Our understanding of the girl Hedvig, for example, is significantly extended through her identification with the duck, which, the moment it is wounded, dives instinctively for the lake-bottom, and there entangles itself in the weeds and mud. Similarly, in Werle's identification of himself with the bird-dog, we read Ibsen's comment on well-intentioned meddlers; in attempting to "save" Hialmar and Hedvig from the lake-bottom of their sustaining illusions, Werle is, in fact, merely gratifying the demands of his own ego. He is acting blindly, compulsively, and altogether without reference to the actual needs of those whom he presumes to rescue.

Hence Ibsen's use of symbols broadens and deepens our insight into character in a situation where the characters themselves are incapable of full self-expression; it contributes, further, to the successful articulation of the play's theme. But in addition, since theme and conflict determine the drama's structure, it is clear that wherever symbolism is used, it fulfills an important structural function as well. Ibsen's use of the make-believe "forest" in Ekdal's garret is central to the development of his plot. Finally, by means of symbols like the duck and the would-be retriever, the dramatist can objectify and illuminate a moral dilemma which could otherwise reach the surface of conversation only through recourse to excessively "loaded" and hence artificial dialogue.

The author's examination of the inner life of his characters and his decision to challenge the accepted views of his time in regard to reality and illusion are perhaps the most striking aspects of *The Wild Duck*. The choice of such a theme, and of such people to embody it, is a choice that grows naturally if not inevitably out of Ibsen's own period. His nineteenth-century outlook on life differs necessarily from that of the fifteenth-century author of our Morality Play, and this divergence, for one thing, goes far to account for the radical difference in their treatment of character. But it accounts for a second difference as well. The *structure* of a drama (it has already been said) depends on the particular conflict with which the playwright chooses to deal; and the choice of that conflict by the dramatist will be affected, ultimately, by the society in which he lives. His theme evolves out of his response to his society, and the means he discovers for objectifying his theme will determine his structure. Therefore it is clear that any differences in outlook like those that set the fifteenth century apart from the nineteenth must inevitably have produced changes of the utmost importance in the development of drama. One such change we have already discussed: the alteration from an early acceptance of frank personifications to a demand for three-dimensional characters. But the drama has seen a parallel change from the simple structure dictated by Everyman's graveward journey to one that reflects the multifold complexity of more modern interests and motives. The unquestioning acceptance by its contemporaries of *Everyman's* straightforward "journey"-structure is implicit evidence that the drama's early audiences recognized in the play a reflection of their own society. And this was a society in which an encompassing faith cradled man, at once helping him to keep in perspective the lesser obstacles on the road to his ultimate destination, and giving him, since the faith he shared was a universal one, a sense of identification with all men. *The Wild Duck,* on the other hand, offers us a group of characters who are "modern" in their conspicuous self-consciousness, in their awareness of their essential isolation as individuals. They belong to a prevalently materialistic society for which the earlier encompassing faith has lost its directive force. The City of God has long since been supplanted by the City of Man, and the citizens of Ibsen's world direct their eyes, not toward the illimitable future, but toward the complexities of the immediate present.

The pervasive belief of fifteenth-century English society—that age's preoccupation with the question of salvation—in a sense permits, even compels, the simple structure of the medieval drama. Conversely, the very multiplicity of Ibsen's late nineteenth-century society, its lack of a center, its "atomistic" nature, seems to impose on him the necessity to take into account, within the scope of this single play, persons so variously motivated that they display only one common characteristic: self-centeredness. The dramatist, consequently, must so plot his story as to accommodate all the subsidiary conflicts that arise inescapably in a group composed of such marked individuals. This is a major responsibility. But he must also reveal, finally, just how these minor conflicts contribute to the central struggle of *The Wild Duck*, between Hialmar's determination to escape from reality and Gregers' equal—and ultimately overbearing—determination to force reality upon him.

In summary, there are two aspects of Ibsen's play that have special interest for us. There is, first, the fact that in *The Wild Duck* neither action nor theme nor character is allowed finally to dominate. When the contributions of all three to the total play are assayed, they will be found to be roughly equal. The elements are here in balance, even though we can hardly expect as readers or spectators to be equally conscious of all three at the same moment. It is very often the case that action and character force themselves to our immediate attention, the thematic content of a play requires a period of contemplation to emerge. Its emergence, however, is a central part of the total experience the play offers us, and in this total experience each element has an equal share. Second, Ibsen's choice of theme resulted in a special set of difficulties, since it led him to create characters markedly sensitive but not fully articulate. Hence the author's use of symbols to comment on his characters, and to enlarge the meaning of the actions in which he has engaged them.

Yet, despite its employment of symbolism, *The Wild Duck* is essentially a realistic play. Its stage-setting—often a direct clue to the author's technical methods—is designed to arouse in us immediate recognitions. Those are "real" windows and walls we see, real chairs, rugs, and tables; and their dimensions and proportions and textures are commensurate with what we find outside the theater. So it is with the postures and movements of the characters, their costumes, the use they make of their voices.

Symbolism, after all, is not a pervasive dramatic technique. Rather, it is one of the tested means for man's contemplation of his own experience. Analogy, metaphor, symbol, though they operate differently, are alike in that they aid man in expressing his relationship to the universe at large. He turns to these means because, even in the throes of particular experiences, he remains a generalizing creature.

The complex of ideas we loosely identify as nineteenth-century Romanticism fostered, among other phenomena, an unprecedented interest in the recesses of the human mind. This interest, inevitably reflected in the literature of the century, has deepened and expanded in the work of those more recent writers who have come under the influence of Sigmund Freud. Wherever the interest in psychology has entered literature it has effected innovations in method; but nowhere have such innovations been more conspicuous than in contemporary drama, and this is because the drama, hedged in as it has always been by its own special conditions, lacks the flexibility of its sister-types. Within the basically narrative structures of the novel, for example (different as these may be in particular instances), there is abundant freedom to accommodate various points of view—even shifting points of view—from omniscience to stream-of-consciousness. The drama, as we have seen, offers no such freedom; it must remain, after all, dramatic. As a consequence, no matter how subtle or sensitive his psychological insights may be, the dramatist has had to discover means for employing them that will not do violence to the dual characteristics of the drama itself: its objectivity and its immediacy. These are its fixed conditions, without which the drama ceases to be dramatic. So it is that the combination of fixed conditions with exploratory aims has produced a crucial problem.

A sharp distinction should be made, however, between basic conditions and temporal conventions. All drama is dependent on the acceptance of certain conventions, on the willingness of audience (or reader) to join the author in an act of make-believe. We *know* that the man behind the footlights is not Macbeth, but an actor named Jones or Smith; yet it rarely occurs to us to question his pretending (assuming the actor's performance is an adequate one) because, enjoying make-believe, we willingly embrace the conventions that dramatic story-telling imposes on us.[1] We accept as real what we *know* is a mere appearance of reality. Nevertheless, what we are willing to accept as real is subject to change. It has changed from period to period, as we have already seen: the fifteenth-century spectator apparently accepted Five Wits as unquestioningly as we can accept Daniel Hilliard. Further, this acceptance applies not only to character but to other materials the dramatist uses. *Julius Caesar* was originally played on a bare stage, and in broad daylight, and the Roman characters were clothed in doublet and hose; the carrying of a lighted torch on stage was enough to ensure the acceptance of the scene as nocturnal, and the sounding of contrasting, off-stage trumpet-alarums enough to represent the general currents of a large-scale battle. The area of acceptance, then, has never been confined by rigid boundaries, and the experimental dramatist of the twentieth century has asked us to join him in exploring new areas of acceptance. Yet his problem has been a real one, because the conventions that prevailed at the end of the nineteenth century—still manifest today in a drama like Hayes's—were those of realism, were of a sort that made only minimal demands on our capacity to make believe. It was these conventions he had to break through in order to make his psychological insights employable in a medium whose inescapable characteristics are objectivity and immediacy. He has been driven to an attempt to free himself from the bonds of everyday actuality in order to make objective and immediate certain kinds of experience not heretofore recognized as dramatic. The results have frequently looked more like revolution than evolution.

[1] A more extreme case in point is that of opera, where we must accept not only the fact of impersonation but the further fact that all the characters sing, instead of speak, the dialogue.

Of the many experiments our theater has witnessed, one of the most conspicuous, and one of the most successful, has been *expressionism*. This method, a second solution to the problem of objectifying (in O'Neill's phrase) the "behind-life" of a character, is not, like symbolism, merely a way of perceiving the analogies inherent in man's experience. Rather, it is a dramatic technique that pervades the drama employing it. Though there is certainly an intimate relationship between symbolism and expressionism, the terms refer to different areas of usage. As *The Wild Duck* reveals, symbolism may be quite at home in a realistic setting. Wherever it appears, it serves chiefly to facilitate the clarification of individual points of importance, usually with respect to complexities of character or theme; its function is, in the fullest sense, illustrative. But expressionism is a way of governing the author's over-all attitude toward, and development of, his materials. It assigns symbolic value to *all* the conventional materials he works with—dialogue, setting, movement, character, costume—with the consequence that, instead of functioning illustratively at critical points in the drama's unfolding, symbolism becomes the very climate we live in for the duration of the play. Expressionism may therefore be defined as an extension of symbolism, a conscious development of it into a controlling technique of the drama. A specific example of its use should make this point clear.

Impatient with the failure of nineteenth-century realistic drama to dig deep enough below surface realities, Eugene O'Neill made an uneven career of experimentation, and tested repeatedly the utility of expressionism in a theater influenced by Freud. Many of his expressionistic devices have become famous: the slow acceleration and crescendo of the jungle drums in *The Emperor Jones*, for example, or the distorting masks of *The Great God Brown*, or the protagonist's inner-life double in *Days Without End*. His most successful and most sustained expressionist drama, however, is *The Hairy Ape*, and here his method reveals itself with the initial description, in the stage directions, of Yank, the "Ape" of O'Neill's title.

Yank is a stoker aboard a transatlantic liner. He is inarticulate, and yet O'Neill wishes him to function as the voice of his fellow-workers. For Yank is a symbol himself, a symbol of all modern men who are beset with doubts about the dignity of the work they do. In the eyes of the other stokers, he is "the last word in what they are, their most highly developed individual."[2] Such a description of him of course warns us that we must be ready at all times to see Yank in two ways: as an individual, and as a symbol. He is a human, a real individual made pathetic by his bewilderment; he enlists our compassion by his desire to belong to a society which has so little respect for him that it relegates him to a position just short of the bestial, and confines him in an industrial cage. He cannot belong to a humanity which thus rejects him; nor can he identify himself with the animal world. This latter identification he desperately attempts in the play's final (and expressionistic) scene; he releases a real ape from its cage and is at once crushed to death. Wherever Yank turns, that is, he faces probable destruction but certain denial, and perhaps there is no more urgent human problem in modern society than his. If he is a forsaken individual, however, Yank is also a not-quite-human symbol of the outcasts misbegotten and then irresponsibly disowned by that same society.

Setting as well as character is used in *The Hairy Ape* symbolically; it re-

2 Eugene O'Neill, *The Hairy Ape*. By permission of Random House, Inc., publishers.

veals an attitude, not an actuality. The stage-set for Scene 1, O'Neill tells us, is to be so constructed that none of the stokers can stand upright; the ceiling is "crushed down upon the men's heads." This is not realistic, but a symbolic (or expressionistic) use of the stage to disclose a state of mind of which the men are only dimly aware themselves. Similarly, the lines of bunks, with cross-work of steel beams and uprights, are so designed as to suggest a row of cages to accommodate all of these essentially identical hairy apes.

Even movement itself is used expressionistically. Mention has been made of O'Neill's last scene; no one on reflection will take the release of the ape for reality, since Yank accomplishes this feat by bending the bars with his bare hands. Equally divorced from realism is the action in Scene 5. Here the protagonist lurches angrily into the pedestrians on Fifth Avenue, but the violent collisions with this huge man have no effect on them. They continue on their way, totally unaware of his existence, until at last the clapping of a gentleman's hands brings down on Yank's back a whole battalion of police. Realism, no; but effective symbolism, yes, since it shows us—objectively—Yank's inarticulate but passionate need to "belong," to establish some communication, even an angry one, with a society that excludes him.

O'Neill's expressionism in *The Hairy Ape* performs the double service of illuminating character and commenting on theme, thus uniting and balancing the elements of drama in yet another way. Without the assisting symbols, Yank would remain inarticulate, unable even to define the longing that destroys him. At the same time, Yank's dilemma is one that O'Neill interprets as an inescapable consequence of the Industrial Revolution everywhere: the separation, in our modern society, of the worker from any work in which he can take a personal pride. Profoundly influenced, like so many of his contemporaries, by Freudian psychology, O'Neill employed the devices of dramatic expressionism to reveal in the theater the "behind-life" of his characters. But he was also in *The Hairy Ape* a social critic, and such expressionistic stage directions as those that refer to the metallic clang of the firemen's voices as they speak in unison, or those that refer to the cage-like settings of the early scenes (culminating in the actual cage of the drama's close) help the author to dramatize his vision of a society driven by mechanical perfections it has not learned to master.

To recapitulate, the difference between symbolism and expressionism is fundamentally one of degree. The wooden cross, the wild duck, the clang of the firemen's voices all serve the same interpretive function. But the expressionistic drama multiplies its symbols, or, rather, makes subject to symbolic treatment all of the materials at the dramatist's disposal.

The Wild Duck

by

HENRIK IBSEN

translated by

Frances E. Archer

THE FIRST ACT PASSES IN WERLE'S HOUSE,
THE REMAINING ACTS AT HIALMAR EKDAL'S.

PRONUNCIATION OF NAMES:
GREGERS WERLE, *Grayghers Verlë*
HIALMAR EKDAL, *Yalmar Aykdal*
GINA, *Cheena*
GRABERG, *Groberg*
JENSEN, *Yensen*

Characters

WERLE, *merchant, manufacturer, etc.*
GREGERS WERLE, *his son*
OLD EKDAL
HIALMAR EKDAL, *his son, a photographer*
GINA EKDAL, *Hialmar's wife*
HEDVIG, *their daughter, fourteen*
MRS. SÖRBY, *Werle's housekeeper*
RELLING, *a doctor*
MOLVIK, *student of theology*
GRABERG, *Werle's bookkeeper*
PETTERSEN, *Werle's servant*
JENSEN, *a hired waiter*
A FLABBY GENTLEMAN
A THIN-HAIRED GENTLEMAN
A SHORT-SIGHTED GENTLEMAN
SIX OTHER GENTLEMEN
SEVERAL HIRED WAITERS

ACT ONE

At WERLE's house. A richly and comfortably furnished study; bookcases and upholstered furniture; a writing-table, with papers and documents, in the centre of the room; lighted lamps with green shades, giving a subdued light. At the back, open folding-doors with curtains drawn back. Within is seen a large and handsome room, brilliantly lighted with lamps and branching candlesticks. In front, on the right (in the study), a small baize door leads into WERLE's office. On the left, in front, a fireplace with a glowing coal fire, and farther back a double door leading into the dining-room.

WERLE's servant, PETTERSEN, in livery, and JENSEN, the hired waiter, in black, are putting the study in order. In the large room, two or three other hired waiters are moving about, arranging things and lighting more candles. From the dining-room, the hum of conversation and laughter of many voices are heard; a glass is tapped with a knife; silence follows, and a toast is proposed; shouts of "Bravo!" and then again a buzz of conversation.

PETTERSEN. [*Lights a lamp on the chimney-place and places a shade over it.*] Hark to them, Jensen! now the old man's on his legs holding a long palaver about Mrs. Sörby.

JENSEN. [*Pushing forward an armchair.*] Is it true, what folks say, that they're—very good friends, eh?

PETTERSEN. Lord knows.

JENSEN. I've heard tell as he's been a lively customer in his day.

PETTERSEN. May be.

JENSEN. And he's giving this spread in honour of his son, they say.

PETTERSEN. Yes. His son came home yesterday.

JENSEN. This is the first time I ever heard as Mr. Werle had a son.

PETTERSEN. Oh, yes, he has a son, right enough. But he's a fixture, as you might say, up at the Höidal works. He's never once come to town all the years I've been in service here.

A WAITER. [*In the doorway of the other room.*] Pettersen, here's an old fellow wanting . . .

PETTERSEN. [*Mutters.*] The devil—

who's this now? [OLD EKDAL *appears from
the right, in the inner room. He is dressed
in a threadbare overcoat with a high collar; he wears woollen mittens and carries
in his hand a stick and a fur cap. Under
his arm, a brown paper parcel. Dirty red-
brown wig and small grey moustache.*]

PETTERSEN. [*Goes towards him.*] Good
Lord—what do you want here?

EKDAL. [*In the doorway.*] Must get into
the office, Pettersen.

PETTERSEN. The office was closed an
hour ago, and . . .

EKDAL. So they told me at the front
door. But Graberg's in there still. Let me
slip in this way, Pettersen; there's a good
fellow. [*Points towards the baize door.*]
It's not the first time I've come this way.

PETTERSEN. Well, you may pass. [*Opens
the door.*] But mind you go out again the
proper way, for we've got company.

EKDAL. I know, I know—h'm! Thanks,
Pettersen, good old friend! Thanks!
[*Mutters softly.*] Ass! [*He goes into the
office; PETTERSEN shuts the door after
him.*]

JENSEN. Is he one of the office people?

PETTERSEN. No, he's only an outside
hand that does odd jobs of copying. But
he's been a tip-topper in his day, has old
Ekdal.

JENSEN. You can see he's been through
a lot.

PETTERSEN. Yes; he was an army officer,
you know.

JENSEN. You don't say so?

PETTERSEN. No mistake about it. But
then he went into the timber trade or
something of the sort. They say he once
played Mr. Werle a very nasty trick.
They were partners in the Höidal works
at the time. Oh, I know old Ekdal well, I
do. Many a nip of bitters and bottle of
ale we two have drunk at Madam Eriksen's.

JENSEN. He don't look as if he'd much
to stand treat with.

PETTERSEN. Why, bless you, Jensen, it's
me that stands treat. I always think
there's no harm in being a bit civil to
folks that have seen better days.

JENSEN. Did he go bankrupt, then?

PETTERSEN. Worse than that. He went
to prison.

JENSEN. To prison!

PETTERSEN. Or perhaps it was the Peni-
tentiary. [*Listens.*] Sh! They're leaving
the table. [*The dining-room door is
thrown open from within by a couple of
waiters.* MRS. SÖRBY *comes out conversing
with two gentlemen. Gradually the
whole company follows, amongst them*
WERLE. *Last come* HIALMAR EKDAL *and*
GREGERS WERLE.]

MRS. SÖRBY. [*In passing, to the servant.*] Tell them to serve the coffee in the
music-room, Pettersen.

PETTERSEN. Very well, Madam. [*She
goes with the two gentlemen into the inner room and thence out to the right.*
PETTERSEN *and* JENSEN *go out the same
way.*]

A FLABBY GENTLEMAN. [*To a* THIN-
HAIRED GENTLEMAN.] Whew! What a
dinner!—It was no joke to do it justice!

THE THIN-HAIRED GENTLEMAN. Oh, with
a little good-will one can get through a
lot in three hours.

THE FLABBY GENTLEMAN. Yes, but afterwards, afterwards, my dear Chamberlain!

A THIRD GENTLEMAN. I hear the coffee
and maraschino are to be served in the
music-room.

THE FLABBY GENTLEMAN. Bravo! Then
perhaps Mrs. Sörby will play us something.

THE THIN-HAIRED GENTLEMAN. [*In a low
voice.*] I hope Mrs. Sörby mayn't play us
a tune we don't like, one of these days!

THE FLABBY GENTLEMAN. Oh, no, not
she! Bertha will never turn against her
old friends. [*They laugh and pass into
the inner room.*]

WERLE. [*In a low voice, dejectedly.*] I
don't think anybody noticed it, Gregers.

GREGERS. [*Looks at him.*] Noticed
what?

WERLE. Did you not notice it either?

GREGERS. What do you mean?

WERLE. We were thirteen at table.

GREGERS. Indeed? Were there thirteen
of us?

WERLE. [*Glances towards* HIALMAR
EKDAL.] Our usual party is twelve. [*To
the others.*] This way, gentlemen! [WERLE
and the others, all except HIALMAR *and*
GREGERS, *go out by the back, to the right.*]

HIALMAR. [*Who has overheard the*

conversation.] You ought not to have invited me, Gregers.

GREGERS. What! Not ask my best and only friend to a party supposed to be in my honour . . . ?

HIALMAR. But I don't think your father likes it. You see I am quite outside his circle.

GREGERS. So I hear. But I wanted to see you and have a talk with you, and I certainly shan't be staying long.—Ah, we two old schoolfellows have drifted far apart from each other. It must be sixteen or seventeen years since we met.

HIALMAR. Is it so long?

GREGERS. It is indeed. Well, how goes it with you? You look well. You have put on flesh and grown almost stout.

HIALMAR. Well, "stout" is scarcely the word; but I daresay I look a little more of a man than I used to.

GREGERS. Yes, you do; your outer man is in first-rate condition.

HIALMAR. [*In a tone of gloom.*] Ah, but the inner man! That is a very different matter, I can tell you! Of course you know of the terrible catastrophe that has befallen me and mine since last we met.

GREGERS. [*More softly.*] How are things going with your father now?

HIALMAR. Don't let us talk of it, old fellow. Of course my poor unhappy father lives with me. He hasn't another soul in the world to care for him. But you can understand that this is a miserable subject for me.—Tell me, rather, how you have been getting on up at the works.

GREGERS. I have had a delightfully lonely time of it—plenty of leisure to think and think about things. Come over here; we may as well make ourselves comfortable. [*He seats himself in an armchair by the fire and draws* HIALMAR *down into another alongside of it.*]

HIALMAR. [*Sentimentally.*] After all, Gregers, I thank you for inviting me to your father's table; for I take it as a sign that you have got over your feeling against me.

GREGERS. [*Surprised.*] How could you imagine I had any feeling against you?

HIALMAR. You had at first, you know.

GREGERS. How at first?

HIALMAR. After the great misfortune.

It was natural enough that you should. Your father was within an ace of being drawn into that—well, that terrible business.

GREGERS. Why should that give me any feeling against you? Who can have put that into your head?

HIALMAR. I know it did, Gregers; your father told me so himself.

GREGERS. [*Starts.*] My father! Oh, indeed. H'm.—Was that why you never let me hear from you?—not a single word.

HIALMAR. Yes.

GREGERS. Not even when you made up your mind to become a photographer?

HIALMAR. Your father said I had better not write to you at all, about anything.

GREGERS. [*Looking straight before him.*] Well, well, perhaps he was right.—But tell me now, Hialmar: are you pretty well satisfied with your present position?

HIALMAR. [*With a little sigh.*] Oh, yes, I am; I have really no cause to complain. At first, as you may guess, I felt it a little strange. It was such a totally new state of things for me. But of course my whole circumstances were totally changed. Father's utter, irretrievable ruin,—the shame and disgrace of it, Gregers . . .

GREGERS. [*Affected.*] Yes, yes; I understand.

HIALMAR. I couldn't think of remaining at college; there wasn't a shilling to spare; on the contrary, there were debts —mainly to your father, I believe . . .

GREGERS. H'm . . .

HIALMAR. In short, I thought it best to break, once for all, with my old surroundings and associations. It was your father that specially urged me to it; and since he interested himself so much in me . . .

GREGERS. My father did?

HIALMAR. Yes, you surely knew that, didn't you? Where do you suppose I found the money to learn photography, and to furnish a studio and make a start? All that cost a pretty penny, I can tell you.

GREGERS. And my father provided the money?

HIALMAR. Yes, my dear fellow, didn't you know? I understood him to say he had written to you about it.

GREGERS. Not a word about his part in the business. He must have forgotten it. Our correspondence has always been purely a business one. So it was my father that . . . !

HIALMAR. Yes, certainly. He didn't wish it to be generally known; but he it was. And of course it was he, too, that put me in a position to marry. Don't you —don't you know about that either?

GREGERS. No, I haven't heard a word of it. [*Shakes him by the arm.*] But, my dear Hialmar, I can't tell you what pleasure all this gives me—pleasure, and self-reproach. I have perhaps done my father injustice after all—in some things. This proves that he has a heart. It shows a sort of compunction . . .

HIALMAR. Compunction . . . ?

GREGERS. Yes, yes—whatever you like to call it. Oh, I can't tell you how glad I am to hear this of father.—So you are a married man, Hialmar! That is further than I shall ever get. Well, I hope you are happy in your married life?

HIALMAR. Yes, thoroughly happy. She is as good and capable a wife as any man could wish for. And she is by no means without culture.

GREGERS. [*Rather surprised.*] No, of course not.

HIALMAR. You see, life is itself an education. Her daily intercourse with me . . . And then we know one or two rather remarkable men, who come a good deal about us. I assure you, you would hardly know Gina again.

GREGERS. Gina?

HIALMAR. Yes; had you forgotten that her name was Gina?

GREGERS. Whose name? I haven't the slightest idea . . .

HIALMAR. Don't you remember that she used to be in service here?

GREGERS. [*Looks at him.*] Is it Gina Hansen . . . ?

HIALMAR. Yes, of course it is Gina Hansen.

GREGERS. . . . who kept house for us during the last year of my mother's illness?

HIALMAR. Yes, exactly. But, my dear friend, I'm quite sure your father told you that I was married.

GREGERS. [*Who has risen.*] Oh, yes, he mentioned it; but not that . . . [*Walking about the room.*] Stay—perhaps he did—now that I think of it. My father always writes such short letters. [*Half seats himself on the arm of the chair.*] Now tell me, Hialmar—this is interesting—how did you come to know Gina—your wife?

HIALMAR. The simplest thing in the world. You know Gina did not stay here long; everything was so much upset at that time, owing to your mother's illness and so forth, that Gina was not equal to it all; so she gave notice and left. That was the year before your mother died—or it may have been the same year.

GREGERS. It was the same year. I was up at the works then. But afterward . . . ?

HIALMAR. Well, Gina lived at home with her mother, Madam Hansen, an excellent hard-working woman, who kept a little eating-house. She had a room to let, too; a very nice comfortable room.

GREGERS. And I suppose you were lucky enough to secure it?

HIALMAR. Yes; in fact, it was your father that recommended it to me. So it was there, you see, that I really came to know Gina.

GREGERS. And then you got engaged?

HIALMAR. Yes. It doesn't take young people long to fall in love . . . ; h'm . . .

GREGERS. [*Rises and moves about a little.*] Tell me: was it after your engagement—was it then that my father—I mean was it then that you began to take up photography?

HIALMAR. Yes, precisely. I wanted to make a start and to set up house as soon as possible; and your father and I agreed that this photography business was the readiest way. Gina thought so, too. Oh, and there was another thing in its favour, by-the-bye; it happened, luckily, that Gina had learnt to retouch.

GREGERS. That chimed in marvellously.

HIALMAR. [*Pleased, rises.*] Yes, didn't it? Don't you think it was a marvellous piece of luck?

GREGERS. Oh, unquestionably. My father seems to have been almost a kind of providence for you.

HIALMAR. [*With emotion.*] He did not

forsake his old friend's son in the hour of his need. For he has a heart, you see.

MRS. SÖRBY. [Enters, arm-in-arm with WERLE.] Nonsense, my dear Mr. Werle; you mustn't stop there any longer staring at all the lights. It's very bad for you.

WERLE. [Lets go her arm and passes his hand over his eyes.] I daresay you are right. [PETTERSEN and JENSEN carry round refreshment trays.]

MRS. SÖRBY. [To the guests in the other room.] This way, if you please, gentlemen. Whoever wants a glass of punch must be so good as to come in here.

THE FLABBY GENTLEMAN. [Comes up to MRS. SÖRBY.] Surely, it isn't possible that you have suspended our cherished right to smoke?

MRS. SÖRBY. Yes. No smoking here, in Mr. Werle's sanctum, Chamberlain.

THE THIN-HAIRED GENTLEMAN. When did you enact these stringent amendments on the cigar law, Mrs. Sörby?

MRS. SÖRBY. After the last dinner, Chamberlain, when certain persons permitted themselves to overstep the mark.

THE THIN-HAIRED GENTLEMAN. And may one never overstep the mark a little bit, Madame Bertha? Not the least little bit?

MRS. SÖRBY. Not in any respect whatsoever, Mr. Balle. [Most of the guests have assembled in the study; servants hand round glasses of punch.]

WERLE. [To HIALMAR, who is standing beside a table.] What are you studying so intensely, Ekdal?

HIALMAR. Only an album, Mr. Werle.

THE THIN-HAIRED GENTLEMAN. [Who is wandering about.] Ah, photographs! They are quite in your line, of course.

THE FLABBY GENTLEMAN. [In an armchair.] Haven't you brought any of your own with you?

HIALMAR. No, I haven't.

THE FLABBY GENTLEMAN. You ought to have; it's very good for the digestion to sit and look at pictures.

THE THIN-HAIRED GENTLEMAN. And it contributes to the entertainment, you know.

THE SHORT-SIGHTED GENTLEMAN. And all contributions are thankfully received.

MRS. SÖRBY. The Chamberlains think

that when one is invited out to dinner, one ought to exert oneself a little in return, Mr. Ekdal.

THE FLABBY GENTLEMAN. Where one dines so well, that duty becomes a pleasure.

THE THIN-HAIRED GENTLEMAN. And when it's a case of the struggle for existence, you know . . .

MRS. SÖRBY. I quite agree with you! [They continue the conversation, with laughter and joking.]

GREGERS. [Softly.] You must join in, Hialmar.

HIALMAR. [Writhing.] What am I to talk about?

THE FLABBY GENTLEMAN. Don't you think, Mr. Werle, that Tokay may be considered one of the more wholesome sorts of wine?

WERLE. [By the fire.] I can answer for the Tokay you had today, at any rate; it's one of the very finest seasons. Of course you would notice that.

THE FLABBY GENTLEMAN. Yes, it had a remarkably delicate flavour.

HIALMAR. [Shyly.] Is there any difference between the seasons?

THE FLABBY GENTLEMAN. [Laughs.] Come! That's good!

WERLE. [Smiles.] It really doesn't pay to set fine wine before you.

THE THIN-HAIRED GENTLEMAN. Tokay is like photographs, Mr. Ekdal: they both need sunshine. Am I not right?

HIALMAR. Yes, light is important no doubt.

MRS. SÖRBY. And it's exactly the same with Chamberlains—they, too, depend very much on sunshine,[1] as the saying is.

THE THIN-HAIRED GENTLEMAN. Oh, fie! That's a very threadbare sarcasm!

THE SHORT-SIGHTED GENTLEMAN. Mrs. Sörby is coming out . . .

THE FLABBY GENTLEMAN. . . . and at our expense, too. [Holds up his finger reprovingly.] Oh, Madame Bertha, Madame Bertha!

MRS. SÖRBY. Yes, and there's not the least doubt that the seasons differ greatly. The old vintages are the finest.

THE SHORT-SIGHTED GENTLEMAN. Do you reckon me among the old vintages?

_____
[1] The "sunshine" of court favour.

MRS. SÖRBY. Oh, far from it.

THE THIN-HAIRED GENTLEMAN. There now! But me, dear Mrs. Sörby . . . ?

THE FLABBY GENTLEMAN. Yes, and me? What vintage should you say that we belong to?

MRS. SÖRBY. Why, to the sweet vintage, gentlemen. [*She sips a glass of punch. The gentlemen laugh and flirt with her.*]

WERLE. Mrs. Sörby can always find a loop-hole—when she wants to. Fill your glasses, gentlemen! Pettersen, will you see to it . . . ! Gregers, suppose we have a glass together. [GREGERS *does not move.*] Won't you join us, Ekdal? I found no opportunity of drinking with you at table. [GRABERG, *the bookkeeper, looks in at the baize door.*]

GRABERG. Excuse me, sir, but I can't get out.

WERLE. Have you been locked in again?

GRABERG. Yes, and Flakstad has carried off the keys.

WERLE. Well, you can pass out this way.

GRABERG. But there's some one else . . .

WERLE. All right; come through, both of you. Don't be afraid. [GRABERG *and* OLD EKDAL *come out of the office.*]

WERLE. [*Involuntarily.*] Ugh! [*The laughter and talk among the guests cease.* HIALMAR *starts at the sight of his father, puts down his glass and turns towards the fireplace.*]

EKDAL. [*Does not look up, but makes little bows to both sides as he passes, murmuring.*] Beg pardon, come the wrong way. Door locked—door locked. Beg pardon. [*He and* GRABERG *go out by the back, to the right.*]

WERLE. [*Between his teeth.*] That idiot Graberg.

GREGERS. [*Open-mouthed and staring, to* HIALMAR.] Why surely that wasn't . . . !

THE FLABBY GENTLEMAN. What's the matter? Who was it?

GREGERS. Oh, nobody, only the book-keeper and some one with him.

THE SHORT-SIGHTED GENTLEMAN. [*To* HIALMAR.] Did you know that man?

HIALMAR. I don't know—I didn't notice . . .

THE FLABBY GENTLEMAN. What the deuce has come over every one? [*He joins another group who are talking softly.*]

MRS. SÖRBY. [*Whispers to the servant.*] Give him something to take with him;—something good, mind.

PETTERSEN. [*Nods.*] I'll see to it. [*Goes out.*]

GREGERS. [*Softly and with emotion, to* HIALMAR.] So that was really he!

HIALMAR. Yes.

GREGERS. And you could stand there and deny that you knew him!

HIALMAR. [*Whispers vehemently.*] But how could I . . . !

GREGERS. . . . acknowledge your own father?

HIALMAR. [*With pain.*] Oh, if you were in my place . . . [*The conversation amongst the guests, which has been carried on in a low tone, now swells into constrained joviality.*]

THE THIN-HAIRED GENTLEMAN. [*Approaching* HIALMAR *and* GREGERS *in a friendly manner.*] Aha! Reviving old college memories, eh? Don't you smoke, Mr. Ekdal? May I give you a light? Oh, by-the-bye, we mustn't . . .

HIALMAR. No, thank you, I won't . . .

THE FLABBY GENTLEMAN. Haven't you a nice little poem you could recite to us, Mr. Ekdal? You used to recite so charmingly.

HIALMAR. I am sorry I can't remember anything.

THE FLABBY GENTLEMAN. Oh, that's a pity. Well, what shall we do, Balle? [*Both gentlemen move away and pass into the other room.*]

HIALMAR. [*Gloomily.*] Gregers—I am going! When a man has felt the crushing hand of Fate, you see . . . Say good-bye to your father for me.

GREGERS. Yes, yes. Are you going straight home?

HIALMAR. Yes. Why?

GREGERS. Oh, because I may perhaps look in on you later.

HIALMAR. No, you mustn't do that. You must not come to my home. Mine is a melancholy abode, Gregers; especially after a splendid banquet like this. We can always arrange to meet somewhere in the town.

MRS. SÖRBY. [*Who has quietly approached.*] Are you going, Ekdal?

HIALMAR. Yes.

MRS. SÖRBY. Remember me to Gina.

HIALMAR. Thanks.

MRS. SÖRBY. And say I am coming up to see her one of these days.

HIALMAR. Yes, thank you. [*To* GREGERS.] Stay here; I will slip out unobserved. [*He saunters away, then into the other room, and so out to the right.*]

MRS. SÖRBY. [*Softly to the servant, who has come back.*] Well, did you give the old man something?

PETTERSEN. Yes; I sent him off with a bottle of cognac.

MRS. SÖRBY. Oh, you might have thought of something better than that.

PETTERSEN. Oh, no, Mrs. Sörby; cognac is what he likes best in the world.

THE FLABBY GENTLEMAN. [*In the doorway with a sheet of music in his hand.*] Shall we play a duet, Mrs. Sörby?

MRS. SÖRBY. Yes, suppose we do.

THE GUESTS. Bravo, bravo! [*She goes with all the guests through the back room, out to the right.* GREGERS *remains standing by the fire.* WERLE *is looking for something on the writing-table and appears to wish that* GREGERS *would go; as* GREGERS *does not move,* WERLE *goes towards the door.*]

GREGERS. Father, won't you stay a moment?

WERLE. [*Stops.*] What is it?

GREGERS. I must have a word with you.

WERLE. Can it not wait till we are alone?

GREGERS. No, it cannot; for perhaps we shall never be alone together.

WERLE. [*Drawing nearer.*] What do you mean by that? [*During what follows, the pianoforte is faintly heard from the distant music-room.*]

GREGERS. How has that family been allowed to go so miserably to the wall?

WERLE. You mean the Ekdals, I suppose.

GREGERS. Yes, I mean the Ekdals. Lieutenant Ekdal was once so closely associated with you.

WERLE. Much too closely; I have felt that to my cost for many a year. It is thanks to him that I—yes *I*—have had a kind of slur cast upon my reputation.

GREGERS. [*Softly.*] Are you sure that he alone was to blame?

WERLE. Who else do you suppose . . . ?

GREGERS. You and he acted together in that affair of the forests . . .

WERLE. But was it not Ekdal that drew the map of the tracts we had bought—that fraudulent map! It was he who felled all that timber illegally on Government ground. In fact, the whole management was in his hands. I was quite in the dark as to what Lieutenant Ekdal was doing.

GREGERS. Lieutenant Ekdal himself seems to have been very much in the dark as to what he was doing.

WERLE. That may be. But the fact remains that he was found guilty and I acquitted.

GREGERS. Yes, I know that nothing was proved against you.

WERLE. Acquittal is acquittal. Why do you rake up these old miseries that turned my hair grey before its time? Is that the sort of thing you have been brooding over up there, all these years? I can assure you, Gregers, here in the town the whole story has been forgotten long ago—so far as *I* am concerned.

GREGERS. But that unhappy Ekdal family . . .

WERLE. What would you have had me do for the people? When Ekdal came out of prison he was a broken-down being, past all help. There are people in the world who dive to the bottom the moment they get a couple of slugs in their body and never come to the surface again. You may take my word for it, Gregers, I have done all I could without positively laying myself open to all sorts of suspicion and gossip . . .

GREGERS. Suspicion . . . ? Oh, I see.

WERLE. I have given Ekdal copying to do for the office, and I pay him far, far more for it than his work is worth . . .

GREGERS. [*Without looking at him.*] H'm; that I don't doubt.

WERLE. You laugh? Do you think I am not telling you the truth? Well, I certainly can't refer you to my books, for I never enter payments of that sort.

GREGERS. [*Smiles coldly.*] No, there are certain payments it is best to keep no account of.

WERLE. [*Taken aback.*] What do you mean by that?

GREGERS. [*Mustering up courage.*] Have you entered what it cost you to have Hialmar Ekdal taught photography?

WERLE. I? How "entered" it?

GREGERS. I have learnt that it was you who paid for his training. And I have learnt, too, that it was you who enabled him to set up house so comfortably.

WERLE. Well, and yet you talk as though I had done nothing for the Ekdals! I can assure you these people have cost me enough in all conscience.

GREGERS. Have you entered any of these expenses in your books?

WERLE. Why do you ask?

GREGERS. Oh, I have my reasons. Now tell me: when you interested yourself so warmly in your old friend's son—it was just before his marriage, was it not?

WERLE. Why, deuce take it—after all these years, how can I . . . ?

GREGERS. You wrote me a letter about that time—a business letter, of course; and in a postscript you mentioned—quite briefly—that Hialmar Ekdal had married a Miss Hansen.

WERLE. Yes, that was quite right. That was her name.

GREGERS. But you did not mention that this Miss Hansen was Gina Hansen—our former housekeeper.

WERLE. [*With a forced laugh of derision.*] No; to tell the truth, it didn't occur to me that you were so particularly interested in our former housekeeper.

GREGERS. No more I was. But [*Lowers his voice.*] there were others in this house who were particularly interested in her.

WERLE. What do you mean by that? [*Flaring up.*] You are not alluding to me, I hope?

GREGERS. [*Softly but firmly.*] Yes, I am alluding to you.

WERLE. And you dare . . . ! You presume to . . . ! How can that ungrateful hound—that photographer fellow—how dare he go making such insinuations!

GREGERS. Hialmar has never breathed a word about this. I don't believe he has the faintest suspicion of such a thing.

WERLE. Then where have you got it from? Who can have put such notions in your head?

GREGERS. My poor unhappy mother told me; and that the very last time I saw her.

WERLE. Your mother! I might have known as much! You and she—you always held together. It was she who turned you against me, from the first.

GREGERS. No, it was all that she had to suffer and submit to, until she broke down and came to such a pitiful end.

WERLE. Oh, she had nothing to suffer or submit to; not more than most people, at all events. But there's no getting on with morbid, overstrained creatures—that I have learnt to my cost.—And you could go on nursing such a suspicion—burrowing into all sorts of old rumours and slanders against your own father! I must say, Gregers, I really think that at your age you might find something more useful to do.

GREGERS. Yes, it is high time.

WERLE. Then perhaps your mind would be easier than it seems to be now. What can be your object in remaining up at the works, year out and year in, drudging away like a common clerk, and not drawing a farthing more than the ordinary monthly wage? It is downright folly.

GREGERS. Ah, if I were only sure of that.

WERLE. I understand you well enough. You want to be independent; you won't be beholden to me for anything. Well, now there happens to be an opportunity for you to become independent, your own master in everything.

GREGERS. Indeed? In what way . . . ?

WERLE. When I wrote you insisting on your coming to town at once—h'm . . .

GREGERS. Yes, what is it you really want of me? I have been waiting all day to know.

WERLE. I want to propose that you should enter the firm, as partner.

GREGERS. I! Join your firm? As partner?

WERLE. Yes. It would not involve our being constantly together. You could take over the business here in town, and I should move up to the works.

GREGERS. You would?

WERLE. The fact is, I am not so fit for work as I once was. I am obliged to spare my eyes, Gregers; they have begun to trouble me.

GREGERS. They have always been weak.

WERLE. Not as they are now. And besides, circumstances might possibly make it desirable for me to live up there—for a time, at any rate.

GREGERS. That is certainly quite a new idea to me.

WERLE. Listen, Gregers: there are many things that stand between us; but we are father and son after all. We ought surely to be able to come to some sort of understanding with each other.

GREGERS. Outwardly, you mean, of course?

WERLE. Well, even that would be something. Think it over, Gregers. Don't you think it ought to be possible? Eh?

GREGERS. [*Looking at him coldly.*] There is something behind all this.

WERLE. How so?

GREGERS. You want to make use of me in some way.

WERLE. In such a close relationship as ours, the one can always be useful to the other.

GREGERS. Yes, so people say.

WERLE. I want very much to have you at home with me for a time. I am a lonely man, Gregers; I have always felt lonely, all my life through; but most of all now that I am getting up in years. I feel the need of some one about me . . .

GREGERS. You have Mrs. Sörby.

WERLE. Yes, I have her; and she has become, I may say, almost indispensable to me. She is lively and even-tempered; she brightens up the house; and that is a very great thing for me.

GREGERS. Well, then, you have everything just as you wish it.

WERLE. Yes, but I am afraid it can't last. A woman so situated may easily find herself in a false position, in the eyes of the world. For that matter it does a man no good, either.

GREGERS. Oh, when a man gives such dinners as you give, he can risk a great deal.

WERLE. Yes, but how about the woman, Gregers? I fear she won't accept the situation much longer; and even if she did—even if, out of attachment to me, she were to take her chance of gossip and scandal and all that . . . ? Do you think, Gregers—you with your strong sense of justice . . .

GREGERS. [*Interrupts him.*] Tell me in one word: are you thinking of marrying her?

WERLE. Suppose I were thinking of it? What then?

GREGERS. That's what I say: what then?

WERLE. Should you be inflexibly opposed to it!

GREGERS. Not at all. Not by any means.

WERLE. I was not sure whether your devotion to your mother's memory . . .

GREGERS. I am not overstrained.

WERLE. Well, whatever you may or may not be, at all events you have lifted a great weight from my mind. I am extremely pleased that I can reckon on your concurrence in this matter.

GREGERS. [*Looking intently at him.*] Now I see the use you want to put me to.

WERLE. Use to put you to? What an expression!

GREGERS. Oh, don't let us be nice in our choice of words—not when we are alone together, at any rate. [*With a short laugh.*] Well, well! So this is what made it absolutely essential that I should come to town in person. For the sake of Mrs. Sörby, we are to get up a pretence at family life in the house—a tableau of filial affection! That will be something new indeed.

WERLE. How dare you speak in that tone!

GREGERS. Was there ever any family life here? Never since I can remember. But now, forsooth, your plans demand something of the sort. No doubt it will have an excellent effect when it is reported that the son has hastened home, on the wings of filial piety, to the grey-haired father's wedding-feast. What will then remain of all the rumours as to the wrongs the poor dead mother had to submit to? Not a vestige. Her son annihilates them at one stroke.

WERLE. Gregers—I believe there is no one in the world you detest as you do me.

GREGERS. [*Softly.*] I have seen you at too close quarters.

WERLE. You have seen me with your mother's eyes. [*Lowers his voice a little.*] But you should remember that her eyes were—clouded now and then.

GREGERS. [*Quivering.*] I see what you are hinting at. But who was to blame for mother's unfortunate weakness? Why you, and all those . . . ! The last of them was this woman that you palmed off upon Hialmar Ekdal, when you were . . . Ugh!

WERLE. [*Shrugs his shoulders.*] Word for word as if it were your mother speaking!

GREGERS. [*Without heeding.*] And there he is now, with his great, confiding, childlike mind, compassed about with all this treachery—living under the same roof with such a creature and never dreaming that what he calls his home is built upon a lie! [*Comes a step nearer.*] When I look back upon your past, I seem to see a battle-field with shattered lives on every hand.

WERLE. I begin to think the chasm that divides us is too wide.

GREGERS. [*Bowing, with self-command.*] So I have observed; and therefore I take my hat and go.

WERLE. You are going! Out of the house?

GREGERS. Yes. For at last I see my mission in life.

WERLE. What mission?

GREGERS. You would only laugh if I told you.

WERLE. A lonely man doesn't laugh so easily, Gregers.

GREGERS. [*Pointing towards the background.*] Look, father,—the Chamberlains are playing blind-man's-buff with Mrs. Sörby.— Good-night and good-bye. [*He goes out by the back to the right. Sounds of laughter and merriment from the company, who are now visible in the outer room.*]

WERLE. [*Muttering contemptuously after* GREGERS.] Ha . . . ! Poor wretch— and he says he is not overstrained!

THE CURTAIN FALLS

ACT TWO

HIALMAR EKDAL's studio, a good-sized room, evidently in the top story of the building. On the right, a sloping roof of large panes of glass, half-covered by a blue curtain. In the right-hand corner, at the back, the entrance door; farther forward, on the same side, a door leading to the sitting-room. Two doors on the opposite side, and between them an iron stove. At the back, a wide double sliding-door. The studio is plainly but comfortably fitted up and furnished. Between the doors on the right, standing out a little from the wall, a sofa with a table and some chairs; on the table a lighted lamp with a shade; beside the stove an old armchair. Photographic instruments and apparatus of different kinds lying about the room. Against the back wall, to the left of the double door, stands a bookcase containing a few books, boxes, and bottles of chemicals, instruments, tools, and other objects. Photographs and small articles, such as camel's-hair pencils, paper, and so forth, lie on the table.

GINA EKDAL sits on a chair by the table, sewing. HEDVIG is sitting on the sofa, with her hands shading her eyes and her thumbs in her ears, reading a book.

GINA. [*Glances once or twice at* HEDVIG, *as if with secret anxiety; then says.*] Hedvig! [HEDVIG *does not hear.* GINA *repeats more loudly.*] Hedvig!

HEDVIG. [*Takes away her hands and looks up.*] Yes, mother?

GINA. Hedvig dear, you mustn't sit reading any longer now.

HEDVIG. Oh, mother, mayn't I read a little more? Just a little bit?

GINA. No, no, you must put away your book now. Father doesn't like it; he never reads hisself in the evening.

HEDVIG. [*Shuts the book.*] No, father doesn't care much about reading.

GINA. [*Puts aside her sewing and takes up a lead pencil and a little account-book from the table.*] Can you remember how much we paid for the butter today?

HEDVIG. It was one crown sixty-five.

GINA. That's right. [*Puts it down.*] It's terrible what a lot of butter we get through in this house. Then there was the smoked sausage, and the cheese—let me see—[*Writes.*]—and the ham—[*Adds up.*] Yes, that makes just . . .

HEDVIG. And then the beer.

GINA. Yes, to be sure. [*Writes.*] How it do mount up! But we can't manage with no less.

HEDVIG. And then you and I didn't need anything hot for dinner, as father was out.

GINA. No; that was so much to the good. And then I took eight crowns fifty for the photographs.

HEDVIG. Really! So much as that?

GINA. Exactly eight crowns fifty. [*Silence.* GINA *takes up her sewing again,* HEDVIG *takes paper and pencil and begins to draw, shading her eyes with her left hand.*]

HEDVIG. Isn't it jolly to think that father is at Mr. Werle's big dinner-party?

GINA. You know he's not really Mr. Werle's guest. It was the son invited him. [*After a pause.*] We have nothing to do with that Mr. Werle.

HEDVIG. I'm longing for father to come home. He promised to ask Mrs. Sörby for something nice for me.

GINA. Yes, there's plenty of good things going in that house, I can tell you.

HEDVIG. [*Goes on drawing.*] And I believe I'm a little hungry, too. [OLD EKDAL, *with the paper parcel under his arm and another parcel in his coat pocket, comes in by the entrance door.*]

GINA. How late you are today, grandfather!

EKDAL. They had locked the office door. Had to wait in Graberg's room. And then they let me through—h'm.

HEDVIG. Did you get some more copying to do, grandfather?

EKDAL. This whole packet. Just look.

GINA. That's capital.

HEDVIG. And you have another parcel in your pocket.

EKDAL. Eh? Oh, never mind, that's nothing. [*Puts his stick away in a corner.*] This work will keep me going a long time, Gina. [*Opens one of the sliding-doors in the back wall a little.*] Hush! [*Peeps into the room for a moment, then pushes the door carefully to again.*] Hee-hee! They're fast asleep, all the lot of them. And she's gone into the basket herself. Hee-hee!

HEDVIG. Are you sure she isn't cold in that basket, grandfather?

EKDAL. Not a bit of it! Cold? With all that straw? [*Goes towards the farther door on the left.*] There are matches in here, I suppose.

GINA. The matches is on the drawers. [EKDAL *goes into his room.*]

HEDVIG. It's nice that grandfather has got all that copying.

GINA. Yes, poor old father; it means a bit of pocket-money for him.

HEDVIG. And he won't be able to sit the whole forenoon down at that horrid Madam Eriksen's.

GINA. No more he won't. [*Short silence.*]

HEDVIG. Do you suppose they are all still at the dinner-table?

GINA. Goodness knows; as like as not.

HEDVIG. Think of all the delicious things father is having to eat! I'm certain he'll be in splendid spirits when he comes. Don't you think so, mother?

GINA. Yes: and if only we could tell him that we'd got the room let . . .

HEDVIG. But we don't need that this evening.

GINA. Oh, we'd be none the worse of it, I can tell you. It's no use to us as it is.

HEDVIG. I mean we don't need it this evening, for father will be in a good humour at any rate. It is best to keep the letting of the room for another time.

GINA. [*Looks across at her.*] You like having some good news to tell father when he comes home in the evening?

HEDVIG. Yes; for then things are pleasanter somehow.

GINA. [*Thinking to herself.*] Yes, yes, there's something in that. [OLD EKDAL *comes in again and is going out by the foremost door to the left.*]

GINA. [*Half turning in her chair.*] Do you want something out of the kitchen, grandfather?

EKDAL. Yes, yes, I do. Don't you trouble. [*Goes out.*]

GINA. He's not poking away at the fire, is he? [*Waits a moment.*] Hedvig, go and see what he's about. [EKDAL *comes in again with a small jug of steaming hot water.*]

HEDVIG. Have you been getting some hot water, grandfather?

EKDAL. Yes, hot water. Want it for something. Want to write, and the ink has got as thick as porridge—h'm.

GINA. But you'd best have your supper first, grandfather. It's laid in there.

EKDAL. Can't be bothered with supper, Gina. Very busy, I tell you. No one's to come to my room. No one—h'm. [*He goes into his room;* GINA *and* HEDVIG *look at each other.*]

GINA. [*Softly.*] Can you imagine where he's got money from?

HEDVIG. From Graberg, perhaps.

GINA. Not a bit of it. Graberg always sends the money to me.

HEDVIG. Then he must have got a bottle on credit somewhere.

GINA. Poor grandfather, who'd give him credit? [HIALMAR EKDAL, *in an overcoat and grey felt hat, comes in from the right.*]

GINA. [*Throws down her sewing and rises.*] Why, Ekdal, is that you already?

HEDVIG. [*At the same time jumping up.*] Fancy your coming so soon, father!

HIALMAR. [*Taking off his hat.*] Yes, most of the people were coming away.

HEDVIG. So early?

HIALMAR. Yes, it was a dinner-party, you know. [*Is taking off his overcoat.*]

GINA. Let me help you.

HEDVIG. Me, too. [*They draw off his coat;* GINA *hangs it up on the back wall.*]

HEDVIG. Were there many people there, father?

HIALMAR. Oh, no, not many. We were about twelve or fourteen at table.

GINA. And you had some talk with them all?

HIALMAR. Oh, yes, a little; but Gregers took me up most of the time.

GINA. Is Gregers as ugly as ever?

HIALMAR. Well, he's not very much to look at. Hasn't the old man come home?

HEDVIG. Yes, grandfather is in his room, writing.

HIALMAR. Did he say anything?

GINA. No, what should he say?

HIALMAR. Didn't he say anything about . . . ? I heard something about his having been with Graberg. I'll go in and see him for a moment.

GINA. No, no, better not.

HIALMAR. Why not? Did he say he didn't want me to go in?

GINA. I don't think he wants to see nobody this evening . . .

HEDVIG. [*Making signs.*] H'm—h'm!

GINA. [*Not noticing.*] . . . he has been in to fetch hot water . . .

HIALMAR. Aha! Then he's . . .

GINA. Yes, I suppose so.

HIALMAR. Oh, God! my poor old white-haired father! . . . Well, well; there let him sit and get all the enjoyment he can. [OLD EKDAL, *in an indoor coat and with a lighted pipe, comes from his room.*]

EKDAL. Got home? Thought it was you I heard talking.

HIALMAR. Yes, I have just come.

EKDAL. You didn't see me, did you?

HIALMAR. No, but they told me you had passed through—so I thought I would follow you.

EKDAL. H'm, good of you, Hialmar.—Who were they, all those fellows?

HIALMAR. Oh, all sorts of people. There was Chamberlain Flor, and Chamberlain Balle, and Chamberlain Kaspersen and Chamberlain—this, that, and the other—I don't know who all . . .

EKDAL. [*Nodding.*] Hear that, Gina! Chamberlains every one of them!

GINA. Yes, I hear as they're terrible genteel in that house nowadays.

HEDVIG. Did the Chamberlains sing, father? Or did they read aloud?

HIALMAR. No, they only talked nonsense. They wanted me to recite something for them; but I knew better than that.

EKDAL. You weren't to be persuaded, eh?

GINA. Oh, you might have done it.

HIALMAR. No; one mustn't be at everybody's beck and call. [*Walks about the room.*] That's not my way, at any rate.

EKDAL. No, no; Hialmar's not to be had for the asking, he isn't.

HIALMAR. I don't see why *I* should bother myself to entertain people on the rare occasions when I go into society. Let the others exert themselves. These fellows go from one great dinner-table to the next and gorge and guzzle day out and day in. It's for them to bestir themselves and do something in return for all the good feeding they get.

GINA. But you didn't say that?

HIALMAR. [*Humming.*] Ho-ho-ho . . . ; faith, I gave them a bit of my mind.

EKDAL. Not the Chamberlains?

HIALMAR. Oh, why not? [*Lightly.*] After that, we had a little discussion about Tokay.

EKDAL. Tokay! There's a fine wine for you!

HIALMAR. [*Comes to a standstill.*] It may be a fine wine. But of course you know the vintages differ; it all depends on how much sunshine the grapes have had.

GINA. Why, you know everything, Ekdal.

EKDAL. And did they dispute that?

HIALMAR. They tried to; but they were requested to observe that it was just the same with Chamberlains—that with them, too, different batches were of different qualities.

GINA. What things you do think of!

EKDAL. Hee-hee! So they got that in their pipes, too?

HIALMAR. Right in their teeth.

EKDAL. Do you hear that, Gina? He said it right in the very teeth of all the Chamberlains.

GINA. Fancy . . . ! Right in their teeth!

HIALMAR. Yes, but I don't want it talked about. One doesn't speak of such things. The whole affair passed off quite amicably of course. They were nice, genial fellows; I didn't want to wound them—not I!

EKDAL. Right in their teeth, though . . . !

HEDVIG. [*Caressingly.*] How nice it is to see you in a dress-coat! It suits you so well, father.

HIALMAR. Yes, don't you think so? And this one really fits to perfection. It fits almost as if it had been made for me;—a little tight in the arm-holes perhaps;—help me, Hedvig. [*Takes off the coat.*] I think I'll put on my jacket. Where is my jacket, Gina?

GINA. Here it is. [*Brings the jacket and helps him.*]

HIALMAR. That's it! Don't forget to send the coat back to Molvik first thing tomorrow morning.

GINA. [*Laying it away.*] I'll be sure and see to it.

HIALMAR. [*Stretching himself.*] After all, there's a more homely feeling about this. A free-and-easy indoor costume suits my whole personality better. Don't you think so, Hedvig?

HEDVIG. Yes, father.

HIALMAR. When I loosen my necktie into a pair of flowing ends—like this—eh?

HEDVIG. Yes, that goes so well with your moustache and the sweep of your curls.

HIALMAR. I should not call them curls exactly; I should rather say locks.

HEDVIG. Yes, they are too big for curls.

HIALMAR. Locks describes them better.

HEDVIG. [*After a pause, twitching his jacket.*] Father.

HIALMAR. Well, what is it?

HEDVIG. Oh, you know very well.

HIALMAR. No, really I don't . . .

HEDVIG. [*Half laughing, half whimpering.*] Oh, yes, father; now don't tease me any longer!

HIALMAR. Why, what do you mean?

HEDVIG. [*Shaking him.*] Oh, what nonsense; come, where are they, father? All the good things you promised me, you know?

HIALMAR. Oh—if I haven't forgotten all about them!

HEDVIG. Now you're only teasing me, father! Oh, it's too bad of you! Where have you put them?

HIALMAR. No, I positively forgot to get anything. But wait a little! I have something else for you, Hedvig. [*Goes and searches in the pockets of the coat.*]

HEDVIG. [*Skipping and clapping her hands.*] Oh, mother, mother!

GINA. There, you see; if you only give him time . . .

HIALMAR. [*With a paper.*] Look, here it is.

HEDVIG. That? Why, that's only a paper.

HIALMAR. That is the bill of fare, my dear; the whole bill of fare. Here you see: "Menu"—that means bill of fare.

HEDVIG. Haven't you anything else?

HIALMAR. I forgot the other things, I tell you. But you may take my word for it, these dainties are very unsatisfying. Sit down at the table and read the bill of fare, and then I'll describe to you how the dishes taste. Here you are, Hedvig.

HEDVIG. [*Gulping down her tears.*] Thank you. [*She seats herself, but does not read;* GINA *makes signs to her;* HIALMAR *notices it.*]

HIALMAR. [*Pacing up and down the room.*] It's monstrous what absurd things the father of a family is expected to think of; and if he forgets the smallest trifle, he is treated to sour faces at once. Well, well, one gets used to that, too. [*Stops near the stove, by the old man's chair.*] Have you peeped in there this evening, father?

EKDAL. Yes, to be sure I have. She's gone into the basket.

HIALMAR. Ah, she has gone into the basket. Then she's beginning to get used to it.

EKDAL. Yes; just as I prophesied. But you know there are still a few little things . . .

HIALMAR. A few improvements, yes.

EKDAL. They've got to be made, you know.

HIALMAR. Yes, let us have a talk about the improvements, father. Come, let us sit on the sofa.

EKDAL. All right. H'm—think I'll just fill my pipe first. Must clean it out, too. H'm. [*He goes into his room.*]

GINA. [*Smiling to* HIALMAR.] His pipe!

HIALMAR. Oh, yes, yes, Gina; let him alone—the poor, shipwrecked old man. —Yes, these improvements—we had better get them out of hand tomorrow.

GINA. You'll hardly have time tomorrow, Ekdal.

HEDVIG. [*Interposing.*] Oh, yes he will, mother!

GINA. . . . for remember them prints that has to be retouched; they've sent for them time after time.

HIALMAR. There now! those prints again! I shall get them finished all right! Have any new orders come in?

GINA. No, worse luck; tomorrow I have nothing but those two sittings, you know.

HIALMAR. Nothing else? Oh, no, if people won't set about things with a will . . .

GINA. But what more can I do? Don't I advertise in the papers as much as we can afford?

HIALMAR. Yes, the papers, the papers; you see how much good they do. And I suppose no one has been to look at the room either?

GINA. No, not yet.

HIALMAR. That was only to be expected. If people won't keep their eyes open. . . . Nothing can be done without a real effort, Gina!

HEDVIG. [*Going towards him.*] Shall I fetch you the flute, father?

HIALMAR. No; no flute for me; *I* want no pleasures in this world. [*Pacing about.*] Yes, indeed I will work tomorrow; you shall see if I don't. You may be sure I shall work as long as my strength holds out.

GINA. But my dear, good Ekdal, I didn't mean it in that way.

HEDVIG. Father, mayn't I bring in a bottle of beer?

HIALMAR. No, certainly not. I require nothing, nothing . . . [*Comes to a standstill.*] Beer? Was it beer you were talking about?

HEDVIG. [*Cheerfully.*] Yes, father; beautiful, fresh beer.

HIALMAR. Well—since you insist upon it, you may bring in a bottle.

GINA. Yes, do; and we'll be nice and

cosy. [HEDVIG *runs towards the kitchen door.*]

HIALMAR. [*By the stove, stops her, looks at her, puts his arm around her neck and presses her to him.*] Hedvig, Hedvig!

HEDVIG. [*With tears of joy.*] My dear, kind father!

HIALMAR. No, don't call me that. Here have I been feasting at the rich man's table,—battening at the groaning board . . . ! And I couldn't even . . . !

GINA. [*Sitting at the table.*] Oh, nonsense, nonsense, Ekdal.

HIALMAR. It's not nonsense! And yet you mustn't be too hard upon me. You know that I love you for all that.

HEDVIG. [*Throwing her arms round him.*] And we love you, oh so dearly, father!

HIALMAR. And if I am unreasonable once in a while,—why then—you must remember that I am a man beset by a host of cares. There, there! [*Dries his eyes.*] No beer at such a moment as this. Give me the flute. [HEDVIG *runs to the bookcase and fetches it.*] Thanks! That's right. With my flute in my hand and you two at my side . . . ah . . . ! [HEDVIG *seats herself at the table near* GINA; HIALMAR *paces backwards and forwards, pipes up vigorously and plays a Bohemian peasant dance, but in a slow plaintive tempo, and with sentimental expression.* HIALMAR, *breaking off the melody, holds out his left hand to* GINA *and says with emotion.*] Our roof may be poor and humble, Gina; but it is home. And with all my heart I say: here dwells my happiness. [*He begins to play again; almost immediately after, a knocking is heard at the entrance door.*]

GINA. [*Rising.*] Hush, Ekdal,—I think there's some one at the door.

HIALMAR. [*Laying the flute on the bookcase.*] There! Again! [GINA *goes and opens the door.*]

GREGERS WERLE. [*In the passage.*] Excuse me . . .

GINA. [*Starting back slightly.*] Oh!

GREGERS. . . . does not Mr. Ekdal, the photographer, live here?

GINA. Yes, he does.

HIALMAR. [*Going towards the door.*] Gregers! You here after all? Well, come in then.

GREGERS. [*Coming in.*] I told you I would come and look you up.

HIALMAR. But this evening . . . ? Have you left the party?

GREGERS. I have left both the party and my father's house.—Good evening, Mrs. Ekdal. I don't know whether you recognize me?

GINA. Oh, yes; it's not difficult to know young Mr. Werle again.

GREGERS. No, I am like my mother; and no doubt you remember her.

HIALMAR. Left your father's house, did you say?

GREGERS. Yes, I have gone to a hotel.

HIALMAR. Indeed. Well, since you're here, take off your coat and sit down.

GREGERS. Thanks. [*He takes off his overcoat. He is now dressed in a plain grey suit of a countrified cut.*]

HIALMAR. Here, on the sofa. Make yourself comfortable. [GREGERS *seats himself on the sofa;* HIALMAR *takes a chair at the table.*]

GREGERS. [*Looking around him.*] So these are your quarters, Hialmar—this is your home.

HIALMAR. This is the studio, as you see . . .

GINA. But it's the largest of our rooms, so we generally sit here.

HIALMAR. We used to live in a better place; but this flat has one great advantage: there are such capital outer rooms . . .

GINA. And we have a room on the other side of the passage that we can let.

GREGERS. [*To* HIALMAR.] Ah—so you have lodgers, too?

HIALMAR. No, not yet. They're not so easy to find, you see; you have to keep your eyes open. [*To* HEDVIG.] What about the beer, eh? [HEDVIG *nods and goes out into the kitchen.*]

GREGERS. So that is your daughter?

HIALMAR. Yes, that is Hedvig.

GREGERS. And she is your only child?

HIALMAR. Yes, the only one. She is the joy of our lives, and—[*Lowering his voice.*]—at the same time our deepest sorrow, Gregers.

GREGERS. What do you mean?

HIALMAR. She is in serious danger of losing her eyesight.

GREGERS. Becoming blind?

HIALMAR. Yes. Only the first symptoms have appeared as yet, and she may not feel it much for some time. But the doctor has warned us. It is coming, inexorably.

GREGERS. What a terrible misfortune! How do you account for it?

HIALMAR. [*Sighs.*] Hereditary, no doubt.

GREGERS. [*Starting.*] Hereditary?

GINA. Ekdal's mother had weak eyes.

HIALMAR. Yes, so my father says; I can't remember her.

GREGERS. Poor child! And how does she take it?

HIALMAR. Oh, you can imagine we haven't the heart to tell her of it. She dreams of no danger. Gay and careless and chirping like a little bird, she flutters onward into a life of endless night. [*Overcome.*] Oh, it is cruelly hard on me, Gregers. [HEDVIG *brings a tray with beer and glasses, which she sets upon the table.*]

HIALMAR. [*Stroking her hair.*] Thanks, thanks, Hedvig. [HEDVIG *puts her arm around his neck and whispers in his ear.*]

HIALMAR. No, no bread and butter just now. [*Looks up.*] But perhaps you would like some, Gregers.

GREGERS. [*With a gesture of refusal.*] No, no thank you.

HIALMAR. [*Still melancholy.*] Well, you can bring in a little all the same. If you have a crust, that is all I want. And plenty of butter on it, mind. [HEDVIG *nods gaily and goes out into the kitchen again.*]

GREGERS. [*Who has been following her with his eyes.*] She seems quite strong and healthy otherwise.

GINA. Yes. In other ways there's nothing amiss with her, thank goodness.

GREGERS. She promises to be very like you, Mrs. Ekdal. How old is she now?

GINA. Hedvig is close on fourteen; her birthday is the day after tomorrow.

GREGERS. She is pretty tall for her age, then.

GINA. Yes, she's shot up wonderful this last year.

GREGERS. It makes one realize one's own age to see these young people growing up.—How long is it now since you were married?

GINA. We've been married—let me see —just on fifteen years.

GREGERS. Is it so long as that?

GINA. [*Becomes attentive; looks at him.*] Yes, it is indeed.

HIALMAR. Yes, so it is. Fifteen years all but a few months. [*Changing his tone.*] They must have been long years for you, up at the works, Gregers.

GREGERS. They seemed long while I was living them; now they are over, I hardly know how the time has gone. [OLD EKDAL *comes from his room without his pipe, but with his old-fashioned uniform cap on his head; his gait is somewhat unsteady.*]

EKDAL. Come now, Hialmar, let's sit down and have a good talk about this— h'm—what was it again?

HIALMAR. [*Going towards him.*] Father, we have a visitor here—Gregers Werle. —I don't know if you remember him.

EKDAL. [*Looking at* GREGERS, *who has risen.*] Werle? Is that the son? What does he want with me?

HIALMAR. Nothing; it's me he has come to see.

EKDAL. Oh! Then there's nothing wrong?

HIALMAR. No, no, of course not.

EKDAL. [*With a large gesture.*] Not that I'm afraid, you know; but . . .

GREGERS. [*Goes over to him.*] I bring you a greeting from your old hunting-grounds, Lieutenant Ekdal.

EKDAL. Hunting-grounds?

GREGERS. Yes, up in Höidal, about the works, you know.

EKDAL. Oh, up there. Yes, I knew all those places well in the old days.

GREGERS. You were a great sportsman then.

EKDAL. So I was, I don't deny it. You're looking at my uniform cap. I don't ask anybody's leave to wear it in the house. So long as I don't go out in the streets with it . . . [HEDVIG *brings a plate of bread and butter, which she puts upon the table.*]

HIALMAR. Sit down, father, and have a glass of beer. Help yourself, Gregers.

[EKDAL *mutters and stumbles over to the sofa.* GREGERS *seats himself on the chair nearest to him,* HIALMAR *on the other side of* GREGERS. GINA *sits a little way from the table, sewing;* HEDVIG *stands beside her father.*]

GREGERS. Can you remember, Lieutenant Ekdal, how Hialmar and I used to come up and visit you in the summer and at Christmas?

EKDAL. Did you? No, no, no; I don't remember it. But sure enough I've been a tidy bit of a sportsman in my day. I've shot bears, too. I've shot nine of 'em, no less.

GREGERS. [*Looking sympathetically at him.*] And now you never get any shooting?

EKDAL. Can't just say that, sir. Get a shot now and then perhaps. Of course not in the old way. For the woods you see—the woods, the woods . . . ! [*Drinks.*] Are the woods fine up there now?

GREGERS. Not so fine as in your time. They have been thinned a good deal.

EKDAL. Thinned? [*More softly, and as if afraid.*] It's dangerous work that. Bad things come of it. The woods revenge themselves.

HIALMAR. [*Filling up his glass.*] Come—a little more, father.

GREGERS. How can a man like you—such a man for the open air—live in the midst of a stuffy town, boxed within four walls?

EKDAL. [*Laughs quietly and glances at* HIALMAR.] Oh, it's not bad here. Not at all so bad.

GREGERS. But don't you miss all the things that used to be a part of your very being—the cool sweeping breezes, the free life in the woods and on the uplands, among beasts and birds . . . ?

EKDAL. [*Smiling.*] Hialmar, shall we let him see it?

HIALMAR. [*Hastily and a little embarrassed.*] Oh, no, no, father; not this evening.

GREGERS. What does he want to show me?

HIALMAR. Oh, it's only something—you can see it another time.

GREGERS. [*Continues, to the old man.*] You see I have been thinking, Lieutenant Ekdal, that you should come up with me to the works; I am sure to be going back soon. No doubt you could get some copying there, too. And here, you have nothing on earth to interest you—nothing to liven you up.

EKDAL. [*Stares in astonishment at him.*] Have *I* nothing on earth to . . . !

GREGERS. Of course you have Hialmar; but then he has his own family. And a man like you, who has always had such a passion for what is free and wild . . .

EKDAL. [*Thumps the table.*] Hialmar, he shall see it!

HIALMAR. Oh, do you think it's worth while, father? It's all dark.

EKDAL. Nonsense; it's moonlight. [*Rises.*] He shall see it, I tell you. Let me pass! Come and help me, Hialmar.

HEDVIG. Oh, yes, do, father!

HIALMAR. [*Rising.*] Very well then.

GREGERS. [*To* GINA.] What is it?

GINA. Oh, nothing so very wonderful, after all. [EKDAL *and* HIALMAR *have gone to the back wall and are each pushing back a side of the sliding door;* HEDVIG *helps the old man;* GREGERS *remains standing by the sofa;* GINA *sits still and sews. Through the open doorway a large, deep irregular garret is seen with odd nooks and corners; a couple of stove-pipes running through it, from rooms below. There are skylights through which clear moonbeams shine in on some parts of the great room; others lie in deep shadow.*]

EKDAL. [*To* GREGERS.] You may come close up if you like.

GREGERS. [*Going over to them.*] Why, what is it?

EKDAL. Look for yourself. H'm.

HIALMAR. [*Somewhat embarrassed.*] This belongs to father, you understand.

GREGERS. [*At the door, looks into the garret.*] Why, you keep poultry, Lieutenant Ekdal.

EKDAL. Should think we did keep poultry. They've gone to roost now. But you should just see our fowls by daylight, sir!

HEDVIG. And there's a . . .

EKDAL. Sh—sh! don't say anything about it yet.

GREGERS. And you have pigeons, too, I see.

EKDAL. Oh, yes, haven't we just got pigeons! They have their nest-boxes up there under the roof-tree; for pigeons like to roost high, you see.

HIALMAR. They aren't all common pigeons.

EKDAL. Common! Should think not indeed! We have tumblers and a pair of pouters, too. But come here! Can you see that hutch down there by the wall?

GREGERS. Yes; what do you use it for?

EKDAL. That's where the rabbits sleep, sir.

GREGERS. Dear me; so you have rabbits, too?

EKDAL. Yes, you may take my word for it, we have rabbits! He wants to know if we have rabbits, Hialmar! H'm! But now comes the thing, let me tell you! Here we have it! Move away, Hedvig. Stand here; that's right,—and now look down there.—Don't you see a basket with straw in it?

GREGERS. Yes. And I can see a fowl lying in the basket.

EKDAL. H'm—"a fowl" . . .

GREGERS. Isn't it a duck?

EKDAL. [Hurt.] Why, of course it's a duck.

HIALMAR. But what kind of duck, do you think?

HEDVIG. It's not just a common duck . . .

EKDAL. Sh!

GREGERS. And it's not a Muscovy duck either.

EKDAL. No, Mr.—Werle; it's not a Muscovy duck; for it's a wild duck!

GREGERS. Is it really? A wild duck?

EKDAL. Yes, that's what it is. That "fowl" as you call it—is the wild duck. It's our wild duck, sir.

HEDVIG. My wild duck. It belongs to me.

GREGERS. And can it live up here in the garret? Does it thrive?

EKDAL. Of course it has a trough of water to splash about in, you know.

HIALMAR. Fresh water every other day.

GINA. [Turning towards HIALMAR.] But my dear Ekdal, it's getting icy cold here.

EKDAL. H'm, we had better shut up then. It's as well not to disturb their night's rest, too. Close up, Hedvig. [HIALMAR and HEDVIG push the garret doors together.]

EKDAL. Another time you shall see her properly. [Seats himself in the armchair by the stove.] Oh, they're curious things, these wild ducks. I can tell you.

GREGERS. How did you manage to catch it, Lieutenant Ekdal?

EKDAL. I didn't catch it. There's a certain man in this town whom we have to thank for it.

GREGERS. [Starts slightly.] That man was not my father, was he?

EKDAL. You've hit it. Your father and no one else. H'm.

HIALMAR. Strange that you should guess that, Gregers.

GREGERS. You were telling me that you owed so many things to my father; and so I thought perhaps . . .

GINA. But we didn't get the duck from Mr. Werle himself . . .

EKDAL. It's Hakon Werle we have to thank for her, all the same, Gina. [To GREGERS.] He was shooting from a boat, you see, and he brought her down. But your father's sight is not very good now. H'm; she was only wounded.

GREGERS. Ah! She got a couple of slugs in her body, I suppose.

HIALMAR. Yes, two or three.

HEDVIG. She was hit under the wing, so that she couldn't fly.

GREGERS. And I suppose she dived to the bottom, eh?

EKDAL. [Sleepily, in a thick voice.] Of course. Always do that, wild ducks do. They shoot to the bottom as deep as they can get, sir—and bite themselves fast in the tangle and seaweed—and all the devil's own mess that grows down there. And they never come up again.

GREGERS. But your wild duck came up again, Lieutenant Ekdal.

EKDAL. He had such an amazingly clever dog, your father had. And that dog—he dived in after the duck and fetched her up again.

GREGERS. [Who has turned to HIALMAR.] And then she was sent to you here?

HIALMAR. Not at once; at first your father took her home. But she wouldn't thrive there; so Pettersen was told to put an end to her . . .

EKDAL. [Half asleep.] H'm—yes—Pettersen—that ass . . .

HIALMAR. [Speaking more softly.] That

was how we got her, you see; for father knows Pettersen a little; and when he heard about the wild duck he got him to hand her over to us.

GREGERS. And now she thrives as well as possible in the garret there?

HIALMAR. Yes, wonderfully well. She has got fat. You see, she has lived in there so long now that she has forgotten her natural wild life; and it all depends on that.

GREGERS. You are right there, Hialmar. Be sure you never let her get a glimpse of the sky and the sea. . . . But I mustn't stay any longer; I think your father is asleep.

HIALMAR. Oh, as for that . . .

GREGERS. But, by-the-bye—you said you had a room to let—a spare room?

HIALMAR. Yes; what then? Do you know of anybody . . . ?

GREGERS. Can I have that room?

HIALMAR. You?

GINA. Oh, no, Mr. Werle, you . . .

GREGERS. May I have the room? If so, I'll take possession first thing tomorrow morning.

HIALMAR. Yes, with the greatest pleasure . . .

GINA. But, Mr. Werle, I'm sure it's not at all the sort of room for you.

HIALMAR. Why, Gina! how can you say that?

GINA. Why, because the room's neither large enough nor light enough, and . . .

GREGERS. That really doesn't matter, Mrs. Ekdal.

HIALMAR. I call it quite a nice room, and not at all badly furnished either.

GINA. But remember the pair of them underneath.

GREGERS. What pair?

GINA. Well, there's one as has been a tutor . . .

HIALMAR. That's Molvik—Mr. Molvik, B.A.

GINA. And then there's a doctor, by the name of Relling.

GREGERS. Relling? I know him a little; he practised for a time up in Höidal.

GINA. They're a regular rackety pair, they are. As often as not, they're out on the loose in the evenings; and then they come home at all hours, and they're not always just . . .

GREGERS. One soon gets used to that sort of thing. I daresay I shall be like the wild duck . . .

GINA. H'm; I think you ought to sleep upon it first, anyway.

GREGERS. You seem very unwilling to have me in the house, Mrs. Ekdal.

GINA. Oh, no! What makes you think that?

HIALMAR. Well, you really behave strangely about it, Gina. [To GREGERS.] Then I suppose you intend to remain in the town for the present?

GREGERS. [Putting on his overcoat.] Yes, now I intend to remain here.

HIALMAR. And yet not at your father's? What do you propose to do, then?

GREGERS. Ah, if I only knew that, Hialmar, I shouldn't be so badly off! But when one has the misfortune to be called Gregers—! "Gregers"—and then "Werle" after it; did you ever hear anything so hideous?

HIALMAR. Oh, I don't think so at all.

GREGERS. Ugh! Bah! I feel I should like to spit upon the fellow that answers to such a name. But when a man is once for all doomed to be Gregers—Werle in this world, as I am . . .

HIALMAR. [Laughs.] Ha, ha! If you weren't Gregers Werle, what would you like to be?

GREGERS. If I should choose, I should like best to be a clever dog.

GINA. A dog!

HEDVIG. [Involuntarily.] Oh, no!

GREGERS. Yes, an amazingly clever dog; one that goes to the bottom after wild ducks when they dive and bite themselves fast in tangle and sea-weed, down among the ooze.

HIALMAR. Upon my word now, Gregers—I don't in the least know what you're driving at.

GREGERS. Oh, well, you might not be much the wiser if you did. It's understood, then, that I move in early tomorrow morning. [To GINA.] I won't give you any trouble; I do everything for myself. [To HIALMAR.] We can talk about the rest tomorrow.—Good-night, Mrs. Ekdal. [Nods to HEDVIG.] Good-night.

GINA. Good-night, Mr. Werle.

HEDVIG. Good-night.

HIALMAR. [*Who has lighted a candle.*] Wait a moment; I must show you a light; the stairs are sure to be dark. [GREGERS *and* HIALMAR *go out by the passage door.*]

GINA. [*Looking straight before her, with her sewing in her lap.*] Wasn't that queer-like talk about wanting to be a dog?

HEDVIG. Do you know, mother—I believe he meant something quite different by that.

GINA. Why, what should he mean?

HEDVIG. Oh, I don't know; but it seemed to me he meant something different from what he said—all the time.

GINA. Do you think so? Yes, it was sort of queer.

HIALMAR. [*Comes back.*] The lamp was still burning. [*Puts out the candle and sets it down.*] Ah, now one can get a mouthful of food at last. [*Begins to eat the bread and butter.*] Well, you see, Gina—if only you keep your eyes open . . .

GINA. How, keep your eyes open . . . ?

HIALMAR. Why, haven't we at last had the luck to get the room let? And just think—to a person like Gregers—a good old friend.

GINA. Well, I don't know what to say about it.

HEDVIG. Oh, mother, you'll see; it'll be such fun!

HIALMAR. You're very strange. You were so bent upon getting the room let before; and now you don't like it.

GINA. Yes, I do, Ekdal; if it had only been to some one else . . . But what do you suppose Mr. Werle will say?

HIALMAR. Old Werle? It doesn't concern him.

GINA. But surely you can see that there's something amiss between them again, or the young man wouldn't be leaving home. You know very well those two can't get on with each other.

HIALMAR. Very likely not, but . . .

GINA. And now Mr. Werle may fancy it's you that has egged him on . . .

HIALMAR. Let him fancy it, then! Mr. Werle has done a great deal for me; far be it from me to deny it. But that doesn't make me everlastingly dependent upon him.

GINA. But, my dear Ekdal, maybe grandfather'll suffer for it. He may lose the little bit of work he gets from Graberg.

HIALMAR. I could almost say: so much the better! Is it not humiliating for a man like me to see his grey-haired father treated as a pariah? But now I believe the fulness of time is at hand. [*Takes a fresh piece of bread and butter.*] As sure as I have a mission in life, I mean to fulfil it now!

HEDVIG. Oh, yes, father, do!

GINA. Hush! Don't wake him!

HIALMAR. [*More softly.*] I will fulfil it, I say. The day shall come when . . . And that is why I say it's a good thing we have let the room; for that makes me more independent. The man who has a mission in life must be independent. [*By the armchair, with emotion.*] Poor old white-haired father! Rely on your Hialmar. He has broad shoulders—strong shoulders, at any rate. You shall yet wake up some fine day and . . . [*To* GINA.] Do you not believe it?

GINA. [*Rising.*] Yes, of course I do; but in the meantime suppose we see about getting him to bed.

HIALMAR. Yes, come. [*They take hold of the old man carefully.*]

THE CURTAIN FALLS

ACT THREE

HIALMAR EKDAL's studio. It is morning: the daylight shines through the large window in the slanting roof; the curtain is drawn back.

HIALMAR is sitting at the table, busy retouching a photograph; several others lie before him. Presently GINA, wearing her hat and cloak, enters by the passage door; she has a covered basket on her arm.

HIALMAR. Back already, Gina?

GINA. Oh, yes, one can't let the grass grow under one's feet. [Sets her basket on a chair and takes off her things.]

HIALMAR. Did you look in at Gregers' room?

GINA. Yes, that I did. It's a rare sight, I can tell you; he's made a pretty mess to start off with.

HIALMAR. How so?

GINA. He was determined to do everything for himself, he said; so he sets to work to light the stove, and what must he do but screw down the damper till the whole room is full of smoke. Ugh! There was a smell fit to . . .

HIALMAR. Well, really!

GINA. But that's not the worst of it; for then he thinks he'll put out the fire, and goes and empties his water-jug into the stove and so makes the whole floor one filthy puddle.

HIALMAR. How annoying!

GINA. I've got the porter's wife to clear up after him, pig that he is! But the room won't be fit to live in till the afternoon.

HIALMAR. What's he doing with himself in the meantime?

GINA. He said he was going out for a little while.

HIALMAR. I looked in upon him, too, for a moment—after you had gone.

GINA. So I heard. You've asked him to lunch.

HIALMAR. Just to a little bit of early lunch, you know. It's his first day—we can hardly do less. You've got something in the house, I suppose?

GINA. I shall have to find something or other.

HIALMAR. And don't cut it too fine, for I fancy Relling and Molvik are coming up, too. I just happened to meet Relling on the stairs, you see; so I had to . . .

GINA. Oh, are we to have those two as well?

HIALMAR. Good Lord—a couple more or less can't make any difference.

OLD EKDAL. [Opens his door and looks in.] I say, Hialmar . . . [Sees GINA.] Oh!

GINA. Do you want anything, grandfather?

EKDAL. Oh, no, it doesn't matter. H'm! [Retires again.]

GINA. [Takes up the basket.] Be sure you see that he doesn't go out.

HIALMAR. All right, all right. And, Gina, a little herring-salad wouldn't be a bad idea; Relling and Molvik were out on the loose again last night.

GINA. If only they don't come before I'm ready for them . . .

HIALMAR. No, of course they won't; take your own time.

GINA. Very well; and meanwhile you can be working a bit.

HIALMAR. Well, I am working! I am working as hard as I can!

GINA. Then you'll have that job off your hands, you see. [She goes out to the kitchen with her basket. HIALMAR sits for a time pencilling away at the photograph, in an indolent and listless manner.]

EKDAL. [Peeps in, looks round the studio and says softly.] Are you busy?

HIALMAR. Yes, I'm toiling at these wretched pictures . . .

EKDAL. Well, well, never mind,—since you're so busy—h'm! [He goes out again; the door stands open.]

HIALMAR. [Continues for some time in silence; then he lays down his brush and goes over to the door.] Are you busy, father?

EKDAL. [In a grumbling tone, within.] If you're busy, I'm busy, too. H'm!

HIALMAR. Oh, very well, then. [Goes to his work again.]

EKDAL. [Presently, coming to the door again.] H'm; I say, Hialmar, I'm not so very busy, you know.

HIALMAR. I thought you were writing.

EKDAL. Oh, the devil take it! can't Graberg wait a day or two? After all, it's not a matter of life and death.

HIALMAR. No; and you're not his slave either.

EKDAL. And about that other business in there . . .

HIALMAR. Just what I was thinking of. Do you want to go in? Shall I open the door for you?

EKDAL. Well, it wouldn't be a bad notion.

HIALMAR. [*Rises.*] Then we'd have that off our hands.

EKDAL. Yes, exactly. It's got to be ready first thing tomorrow. It is tomorrow, isn't it? H'm?

HIALMAR. Yes, of course it's tomorrow. [*HIALMAR and EKDAL push aside each his half of the sliding door. The morning sun is shining in through the skylights; some doves are flying about; others sit cooing, upon the perches; the hens are heard clucking now and then, further back in the garret.*]

HIALMAR. There; now you can get to work, father.

EKDAL. [*Goes in.*] Aren't you coming, too?

HIALMAR. Well, really, do you know . . . ; I almost think . . . [*Sees GINA at the kitchen door.*] I? No; I haven't time; I must work.—But now for our new contrivance . . . [*He pulls a cord, a curtain slips down inside, the lower part consisting of a piece of old sailcloth, the upper part of a stretched fishing net. The floor of the garret is thus no longer visible.* HIALMAR *goes to the table.*] So! Now, perhaps I can sit in peace for a little while.

GINA. Is he rampaging in there again?

HIALMAR. Would you rather have had him slip down to Madam Eriksen's? [*Seats himself.*] Do you want anything? You know you said . . .

GINA. I only wanted to ask if you think we can lay the table for lunch here?

HIALMAR. Yes; we have no early appointment, I suppose?

GINA. No, I expect no one today except those two sweethearts that are to be taken together.

HIALMAR. Why the deuce couldn't they be taken together another day!

GINA. Don't you know, I told them to come in the afternoon, when you are having your nap.

HIALMAR. Oh, that's capital. Very well, let us have lunch here then.

GINA. All right; but there's no hurry about laying the cloth; you can have the table for a good while yet.

HIALMAR. Do you think I am not sticking at my work? I'm at it as hard as I can!

GINA. Then you'll be free later on, you know. [*Goes out into the kitchen again. Short pause.*]

EKDAL. [*In the garret doorway, behind the net.*] Hialmar!

HIALMAR. Well?

EKDAL. Afraid we shall have to move the water-trough, after all.

HIALMAR. What else have I been saying all along?

EKDAL. H'm—h'm—h'm. [*Goes away from the door again.* HIALMAR *goes on working a little; glances towards the garret and half rises.* HEDVIG *comes in from the kitchen.*]

HIALMAR. [*Sits down again hurriedly.*] What do you want?

HEDVIG. I only wanted to come in beside you, father.

HIALMAR. [*After a pause.*] What makes you go prying around like that? Perhaps you are told off to watch me?

HEDVIG. No, no.

HIALMAR. What is your mother doing out there?

HEDVIG. Oh, mother's in the middle of making the herring-salad. [*Goes to the table.*] Isn't there any little thing I could help you with, father?

HIALMAR. Oh, no. It is right that I should bear the whole burden—so long as my strength holds out. Set your mind at rest, Hedvig; if only your father keeps his health . . .

HEDVIG. Oh, no, father! You mustn't talk in that horrid way. [*She wanders about a little, stops by the doorway and looks into the garret.*]

HIALMAR. Tell me, what is he doing?

HEDVIG. I think he's making a new path to the water-trough.

HIALMAR. He can never manage that by himself! And here am I doomed to sit . . . !

HEDVIG. [*Goes to him.*] Let me take the brush, father; I can do it, quite well.

HIALMAR. Oh, nonsense; you will only hurt your eyes.

HEDVIG. Not a bit. Give me the brush.

HIALMAR. [*Rising.*] Well, it won't take more than a minute or two.

HEDVIG. Pooh, what harm can it do then? [*Takes the brush.*] There! [*Seats herself.*] I can begin upon this one.

HIALMAR. But mind you don't hurt

your eyes! Do you hear? *I* won't be answerable; you do it on your own responsibility—understand that.

HEDVIG. [*Retouching.*] Yes, yes, I understand.

HIALMAR. You are quite clever at it, Hedvig. Only a minute or two, you know. [*He slips through by the edge of the curtain into the garret.* HEDVIG *sits at her work.* HIALMAR *and* EKDAL *are heard disputing inside.*]

HIALMAR. [*Appears behind the net.*] I say, Hedvig—give me those pincers that are lying on the shelf. And the chisel. [*Turns away inside.*] Now you shall see, father. Just let me show you first what I mean! [HEDVIG *has fetched the required tools from the shelf and hands them to him through the net.*]

HIALMAR. Ah, thanks. I didn't come a moment too soon. [*Goes back from the curtain again; they are heard carpentering and talking inside.* HEDVIG *stands looking in at them. A moment later there is a knock at the passage door; she does not notice it.*]

GREGERS WERLE. [*Bareheaded, in indoor dress, enters and stops near the door.*] H'm . . . !

HEDVIG. [*Turns and goes towards him.*] Good morning. Please come in.

GREGERS. Thank you. [*Looking towards the garret.*] You seem to have workpeople in the house.

HEDVIG. No, it is only father and grandfather. I'll tell them you are here.

GREGERS. No, no, don't do that; I would rather wait a little. [*Seats himself on the sofa.*]

HEDVIG. It looks so untidy here . . . [*Begins to clear away the photographs.*]

GREGERS. Oh, don't take them away. Are those prints that have to be finished off?

HEDVIG. Yes, they are a few I was helping father with.

GREGERS. Please don't let me disturb you.

HEDVIG. Oh, no. [*She gathers the things to her and sits down to work;* GREGERS *looks at her, meanwhile, in silence.*]

GREGERS. Did the wild duck sleep well last night?

HEDVIG. Yes, I think so, thanks.

GREGERS. [*Turning towards the garret.*] It looks quite different by day from what it did last night in the moonlight.

HEDVIG. Yes, it changes ever so much. It looks different in the morning and in the afternoon; and it's different on rainy days from what it is in fine weather.

GREGERS. Have you noticed that?

HEDVIG. Yes, how could I help it?

GREGERS. Are you, too, fond of being in there with the wild duck?

HEDVIG. Yes, when I can manage it . . .

GREGERS. But I suppose you haven't much spare time; you go to school, no doubt.

HEDVIG. No, not now; father is afraid of my hurting my eyes.

GREGERS. Oh; then he reads with you himself?

HEDVIG. Father has promised to read with me; but he has never had time yet.

GREGERS. Then is there nobody else to give you a little help?

HEDVIG. Yes, there is Mr. Molvik; but he is not always exactly—quite . . .

GREGERS. Sober?

HEDVIG. Yes, I suppose that's it!

GREGERS. Why, then you must have any amount of time on your hands. And in there I suppose it is a sort of world by itself?

HEDVIG. Oh, yes, quite. And there are such lots of wonderful things.

GREGERS. Indeed?

HEDVIG. Yes, there are big cupboards full of books; and a great many of the books have pictures in them.

GREGERS. Aha!

HEDVIG. And there's an old bureau with drawers and flaps, and a big clock with figures that go out and in. But the clock isn't going now.

GREGERS. So time has come to a standstill in there—in the wild duck's domain.

HEDVIG. Yes. And then there's an old paint-box and things of that sort; and all the books.

GREGERS. And you read the books, I suppose?

HEDVIG. Oh, yes, when I get the chance. Most of them are English though, and I don't understand English. But then I look at the pictures.—There is one great big book called "Harrison's History of London."[1] It must be a hundred years old; and there are such heaps of pictures in it. At the beginning there is Death with an hour-glass and a woman. I think that is horrid. But then there are all the other pictures of churches and castles and streets and great ships sailing on the sea.

GREGERS. But tell me, where did all those wonderful things come from?

HEDVIG. Oh, an old sea captain once lived here, and he brought them home with him. They used to call him "The Flying Dutchman." That was curious, because he wasn't a Dutchman at all.

GREGERS. Was he not?

HEDVIG. No. But at last he was drowned at sea; and so he left all those things behind him.

GREGERS. Tell me now—when you are sitting in there looking at the pictures, don't you wish you could travel and see the real world for yourself?

HEDVIG. Oh, no! I mean always to stay at home and help father and mother.

GREGERS. To retouch photographs?

HEDVIG. No, not only that. I should love above everything to learn to engrave pictures like those in the English books.

GREGERS. H'm. What does your father say to that?

HEDVIG. I don't think father likes it; father is strange about such things. Only think, he talks of my learning basket-making and straw-plaiting! But I don't think that would be much good.

GREGERS. Oh, no, I don't think so either.

HEDVIG. But father was right in saying that if I had learnt basket-making I could have made the new basket for the wild duck.

GREGERS. So you could; and it was you that ought to have done it, wasn't it?

HEDVIG. Yes, for it's my wild duck.

GREGERS. Of course it is.

HEDVIG. Yes, it belongs to me. But I lend it to father and grandfather as often as they please.

GREGERS. Indeed? What do they do with it?

HEDVIG. Oh, they look after it, and build places for it, and so on.

GREGERS. I see; for no doubt the wild duck is by far the most distinguished inhabitant of the garret?

HEDVIG. Yes, indeed she is; for she is a real wild fowl, you know. And then she is so much to be pitied; she has no one to care for, poor thing.

GREGERS. She has no family, as the rabbits have . . .

HEDVIG. No. The hens, too, many of them, were chickens together; but she has been taken right away from all her friends. And then there is so much that is strange about the wild duck. Nobody knows her, and nobody knows where she came from either.

GREGERS. And she has been down in the depths of the sea.

HEDVIG. [With a quick glance at him, represses a smile and asks.] Why do you say "the depths of the sea"?

GREGERS. What else should I say?

HEDVIG. You could say "the bottom of the sea."[2]

GREGERS. Oh, mayn't I just as well say the depths of the sea?

HEDVIG. Yes; but it sounds so strange to me when other people speak of the depths of the sea.

GREGERS. Why so? Tell me why?

HEDVIG. No, I won't; it's so stupid.

GREGERS. Oh, no, I am sure it's not. Do tell me why you smiled.

HEDVIG. Well, this is the reason: whenever I come to realize suddenly—in a flash—what is in there, it always seems to me that the whole room and everything in it should be called "the depths of the sea."—But that is so stupid.

GREGERS. You mustn't say that.

HEDVIG. Oh, yes, for you know it is only a garret.

GREGERS. [Looks fixedly at her.] Are you so sure of that?

HEDVIG. [Astonished.] That it's a garret?

GREGERS. Are you quite certain of it? [HEDVIG is silent, and looks at him open-

[1] A New and Universal History of the Cities of London and Westminster, by Walter Harrison. London, 1775, folio.

[2] Gregers here uses the old-fashioned expression "havsens bund," while Hedvig would have him use the more commonplace "havets bund" or "havbunden."

mouthed. GINA *comes in from the kitchen with the table things.* GREGERS *rises.*] I have come in upon you too early.

GINA. Oh, you must be somewhere; and we're nearly ready now, anyway. Clear the table, Hedvig. [HEDVIG *clears away her things; she and* GINA *lay the cloth during what follows.* GREGERS *seats himself in the armchair and turns over an album.*]

GREGERS. I hear you can retouch, Mrs. Ekdal.

GINA. [*With a side glance.*] Yes, I can.

GREGERS. That was exceedingly lucky.

GINA. How—lucky?

GREGERS. Since Ekdal took to photography, I mean.

HEDVIG. Mother can take photographs, too.

GINA. Oh, yes; I was bound to learn that.

GREGERS. So it is really you that carry on the business, I suppose?

GINA. Yes, when Ekdal hasn't time himself . . .

GREGERS. He is a great deal taken up with his old father, I daresay.

GINA. Yes; and then you can't expect a man like Ekdal to do nothing but take car-de-visits of Dick, Tom and Harry.

GREGERS. I quite agree with you; but having once gone in for the thing . . .

GINA. You can surely understand, Mr. Werle, that Ekdal's not like one of your common photographers.

GREGERS. Of course not; but still . . . [*A shot is fired within the garret.*]

GREGERS. [*Starting up.*] What's that?

GINA. Ugh! now they're firing again!

GREGERS. Have they firearms in there?

HEDVIG. They are out shooting.

GREGERS. What! [*At the door of the garret.*] Are you shooting, Hialmar?

HIALMAR. [*Inside the net.*] Are you there? I didn't know; I was so taken up . . . [*To* HEDVIG.] Why did you not let us know? [*Comes into the studio.*]

GREGERS. Do you go shooting in the garret?

HIALMAR. [*Showing a double-barrelled pistol.*] Oh, only with this thing.

GINA. Yes, you and grandfather will do yourselves a mischief some day with that there pigstol.

HIALMAR. [*With irritation.*] I believe I have told you that this kind of firearm is called a pistol.

GINA. Oh, that doesn't make it much better, that I can see.

GREGERS. So you have become a sportsman, too, Hialmar?

HIALMAR. Only a little rabbit-shooting now and then. Mostly to please father, you understand.

GINA. Men are strange beings; they must always have something to pervert theirselves with.

HIALMAR. [*Snappishly.*] Just so; we must always have something to divert ourselves with.

GINA. Yes, that's just what I say.

HIALMAR. H'm. [*To* GREGERS.] You see the garret is fortunately so situated that no one can hear us shooting. [*Lays the pistol on the top shelf of the bookcase.*] Don't touch the pistol, Hedvig! One of the barrels is loaded; remember that.

GREGERS. [*Looking through the net.*] You have a fowling-piece, too, I see.

HIALMAR. That is father's old gun. It's of no use now; something has gone wrong with the lock. But it's fun to have it all the same; for we can take it to pieces now and then, and clean and grease it, and screw it together again.—Of course, it's mostly father that fiddle-faddles with all that sort of thing.

HEDVIG. [*Beside* GREGERS.] Now you can see the wild duck properly.

GREGERS. I was just looking at her. One of her wings seems to me to droop a bit.

HEDVIG. Well, no wonder; her wing was broken, you know.

GREGERS. And she trails one foot a little. Isn't that so?

HIALMAR. Perhaps a very little bit.

HEDVIG. Yes, it was by that foot the dog took hold of her.

HIALMAR. But otherwise she hasn't the least thing the matter with her; and that is simply marvellous for a creature that has a charge of shot in her body and has been between a dog's teeth . . .

GREGERS. [*With a glance at* HEDVIG.] . . . and that has lain in the depths of the sea—so long.

HEDVIG. [*Smiling.*] Yes.

GINA. [*Laying the table.*] That blessed

wild duck! What a lot of fuss you do make over her.

HIALMAR. H'm;—will lunch soon be ready?

GINA. Yes, directly. Hedvig, you must come and help me now. [GINA *and* HEDVIG *go out into the kitchen.*]

HIALMAR. [*In a low voice.*] I think you had better not stand there looking in at father; he doesn't like it. [GREGERS *moves away from the garret door.*] Besides, I may as well shut up before the others come. [*Claps his hands to drive the fowls back.*] Shh-shh, in with you! [*Draws up the curtain and pulls the doors together.*] All the contrivances are my own invention. It's really quite amusing to have things of this sort to potter with and to put to rights when they get out of order. And it's absolutely necessary, too; for Gina objects to having rabbits and fowls in the studio.

GREGERS. To be sure; and I suppose the studio is your wife's special department?

HIALMAR. As a rule, I leave the every-day details of business to her; for then I can take refuge in the parlour and give my mind to more important things.

GREGERS. What things may they be, Hialmar?

HIALMAR. I wonder you have not asked that question sooner. But perhaps you haven't heard of the invention?

GREGERS. The invention? No.

HIALMAR. Really? Have you not? Oh, no, out there in the wilds . . .

GREGERS. So you have invented something, have you?

HIALMAR. It is not quite completed yet; but I am working at it. You can easily imagine that when I resolved to devote myself to photography, it wasn't simply with the idea of taking likenesses of all sorts of commonplace people.

GREGERS. No; your wife was saying the same thing just now.

HIALMAR. I swore that if I consecrated my powers to this handicraft, I would so exalt it that it should become both an art and a science. And to that end I determined to make this great invention.

GREGERS. And what is the nature of the invention? What purpose does it serve?

HIALMAR. Oh, my dear fellow, you mustn't ask for details yet. It takes time, you see. And you must not think that my motive is vanity. It is not for my own sake that I am working. Oh, no; it is my life's mission that stands before me night and day.

GREGERS. What is your life's mission?

HIALMAR. Do you forget the old man with the silver hair?

GREGERS. Your poor father? Well, but what can you do for him?

HIALMAR. I can raise up his self-respect from the dead, by restoring the name of Ekdal to honour and dignity.

GREGERS. Then that is your life's mission?

HIALMAR. Yes. I will rescue the ship-wrecked man. For shipwrecked he was, by the very first blast of the storm. Even while those terrible investigations were going on, he was no longer himself. That pistol there—the one we use to shoot rabbits with—has played its part in the tragedy of the house of Ekdal.

GREGERS. The pistol? Indeed?

HIALMAR. When the sentence of imprisonment was passed—he had the pistol in his hand . . .

GREGERS. Had he . . . ?

HIALMAR. Yes; but he dared not use it. His courage failed him. So broken, so demoralized was he even then! Oh, can you understand it? He, a soldier; he, who had shot nine bears, and who was descended from two lieutenant-colonels—one after the other, of course. Can you understand it, Gregers?

GREGERS. Yes, I understand it well enough.

HIALMAR. I cannot. And once more the pistol played a part in the history of our house. When he had put on the grey clothes and was under lock and key—oh, that was a terrible time for me, I can tell you. I kept the blinds drawn down over both my windows. When I peeped out, I saw the sun shining as if nothing had happened. I could not understand it. I saw people going along the street, laughing and talking about indifferent things. I could not understand it. It seemed to me that the whole of existence must be at a standstill—as if under an eclipse.

GREGERS. I felt that, too, when my mother died.

HIALMAR. It was in such an hour that Hialmar Ekdal pointed the pistol at his own breast.

GREGERS. You, too, thought of . . . !

HIALMAR. Yes.

GREGERS. But you did not fire?

HIALMAR. No. At the decisive moment I won the victory over myself. I remained in life. But I can assure you it takes some courage to choose life under circumstances like those.

GREGERS. Well, that depends on how you look at it.

HIALMAR. Yes, indeed, it takes courage. But I am glad I was firm; for now I shall soon perfect my invention; and Dr. Relling thinks, as I do myself, that father may be allowed to wear his uniform again. I will demand that as my sole reward.

GREGERS. So that is what he meant about his uniform . . . ?

HIALMAR. Yes, that is what he most yearns for. You can't think how my heart bleeds for him. Every time we celebrate any little family festival—Gina's and my wedding-day, or whatever it may be—in comes the old man in the lieutenant's uniform of happier days. But if he only hears a knock at the door—for he daren't show himself to strangers, you know—he hurries back to his room again as fast as his old legs can carry him. Oh, it's heart-rending for a son to see such things!

GREGERS. How long do you think it will take you to finish your invention?

HIALMAR. Come now, you mustn't expect me to enter into particulars like that. An invention is not a thing completely under one's own control. It depends largely on inspiration—on intuition—and it is almost impossible to predict when the inspiration may come.

GREGERS. But it's advancing?

HIALMAR. Yes, certainly, it is advancing. I turn it over in my mind every day; I am full of it. Every afternoon, when I have had my dinner, I shut myself up in the parlour, where I can ponder undisturbed. But I can't be goaded to it; it's not a bit of good; Relling says so, too.

GREGERS. And you don't think that all that business in the garret draws you off and distracts you too much?

HIALMAR. No, no, no; quite the contrary. You mustn't say that. I cannot be everlastingly absorbed in the same laborious train of thought. I must have something alongside of it to fill up the time of waiting. The inspiration, the intuition, you see—when it comes, it comes, and there's an end of it.

GREGERS. My dear Hialmar, I almost think you have something of the wild duck in you.

HIALMAR. Something of the wild duck? How do you mean?

GREGERS. You have dived down and bitten yourself fast in the undergrowth.

HIALMAR. Are you alluding to the well-nigh fatal shot that has broken my father's wing—and mine, too?

GREGERS. Not exactly to that. I don't say that your wing has been broken; but you have strayed into a poisonous marsh, Hialmar; an insidious disease has taken hold of you, and you have sunk down to die in the dark.

HIALMAR. I? To die in the dark? Look here, Gregers, you must really leave off talking such nonsense.

GREGERS. Don't be afraid; I shall find a way to help you up again. I, too, have a mission in life now; I found it yesterday.

HIALMAR. That's all very well; but you will please leave me out of it. I can assure you that—apart from my very natural melancholy, of course—I am as contented as any one can wish to be.

GREGERS. Your contentment is an effect of the marsh poison.

HIALMAR. Now, my dear Gregers, pray do not go on about disease and poison; I am not used to that sort of talk. In my house nobody ever speaks to me about unpleasant things.

GREGERS. Ah, that I can easily believe.

HIALMAR. It's not good for me, you see. And there are no marsh poisons here, as you express it. The poor photographer's roof is lowly, I know—and my circumstances are narrow. But I am an inventor, and I am the breadwinner of a family. That exalts me above my mean surroundings.—Ah, here comes lunch! [GINA *and* HEDVIG *bring bottles of ale, a decanter of brandy, glasses, etc. At the same time,* RELLING *and* MOLVIK *enter from the passage; they are both without hat or overcoat.* MOLVIK *is dressed in black.*]

GINA. [*Placing the things upon the table.*] Ah, you two have come in the nick of time.

RELLING. Molvik got it into his head that he could smell herring-salad, and then there was no holding him.—Good morning again, Ekdal.

HIALMAR. Gregers, let me introduce you to Mr. Molvik. Doctor . . . Oh, you know Relling, don't you?

GREGERS. Yes, slightly.

RELLING. Oh, Mr. Werle, junior! Yes, we two have had one or two little skirmishes up at the Höidal works. You've just moved in?

GREGERS. I moved in this morning.

RELLING. Molvik and I live right under you; so you haven't far to go for the doctor and the clergyman, if you should need anything in that line.

GREGERS. Thanks, it's not quite unlikely; for yesterday we were thirteen at table.

HIALMAR. Oh, come now, don't let us get upon unpleasant subjects again!

RELLING. You may make your mind easy, Ekdal; I'll be hanged if the finger of fate points to you.

HIALMAR. I should hope not, for the sake of my family. But let us sit down now, and eat and drink and be merry.

GREGERS. Shall we not wait for your father?

HIALMAR. No, his lunch will be taken in to him later. Come along! [*The men seat themselves at table, and eat and drink.* GINA *and* HEDVIG *go in and out and wait upon them.*]

RELLING. Molvik was frightfully screwed yesterday, Mrs. Ekdal.

GINA. Really? Yesterday again?

RELLING. Didn't you hear him when I brought him home last night?

GINA. No, I can't say I did.

RELLING. That was a good thing, for Molvik was disgusting last night.

GINA. Is that true, Molvik?

MOLVIK. Let us draw a veil over last night's proceedings. That sort of thing is totally foreign to my better self.

RELLING. [*To* GREGERS.] It comes over

him like a sort of possession, and then I have to go out on the loose with him. Mr. Molvik is dæmonic, you see.

GREGERS. Dæmonic?

RELLING. Molvik is dæmonic, yes.

GREGERS. H'm.

RELLING. And dæmonic natures are not made to walk straight through the world; they must meander a little now and then.—Well, so you still stick up there at those horrible grimy works?

GREGERS. I have stuck there until now.

RELLING. And did you ever manage to collect that claim you went about presenting?

GREGERS. Claim? [*Understands him.*] Ah, I see.

HIALMAR. Have you been presenting claims, Gregers?

GREGERS. Oh, nonsense.

RELLING. Faith, but he has, though! He went around to all the cottars' cabins presenting something he called "the claim of the ideal."

GREGERS. I was young then.

RELLING. You're right; you were very young. And as for the claim of the ideal—you never got it honoured while *I* was up there.

GREGERS. Nor since either.

RELLING. Ah, then you've learnt to knock a little discount off, I expect.

GREGERS. Never, when I have a true man to deal with.

HIALMAR. No, I should think not, indeed. A little butter, Gina.

RELLING. And a slice of bacon for Molvik.

MOLVIK. Ugh, not bacon! [*A knock at the garret door.*]

HIALMAR. Open the door, Hedvig; father wants to come out. [HEDVIG *goes and opens the door a little way;* EKDAL *enters with a fresh rabbit-skin; she closes the door after him.*]

EKDAL. Good morning, gentlemen! Good sport today. Shot a big one.

HIALMAR. And you've gone and skinned it without waiting for me . . . !

EKDAL. Salted it, too. It's good tender meat, is rabbit; it's sweet; it tastes like sugar. Good appetite to you, gentlemen. [*Goes into his room.*]

MOLVIK. [*Rising.*] Excuse me . . . ; I

can't . . . ; I must get downstairs immediately . . .

RELLING. Drink some soda water, man!

MOLVIK. [*Hurrying away.*] Ugh—ugh!
[*Goes out by the passage door.*]

RELLING. [*To* HIALMAR.] Let us drain a
glass to the old hunter.   .

HIALMAR. [*Clinks glasses with him.*] To
the undaunted sportsman who has looked
death in the face!

RELLING. To the grey-haired . . .
[*Drinks.*] By-the-bye, is his hair grey or
white?

HIALMAR. Something between the two,
I fancy; for that matter, he has very few
hairs left of any colour.

RELLING. Well, well, one can get
through the world with a wig. After all,
you are a happy man, Ekdal; you have
your noble mission to labour for . . .

HIALMAR. And I do labour, I can tell
you.

RELLING. And then you have your excellent wife, shuffling quietly in and out
in her felt slippers, and that see-saw walk
of hers, and making everything cosy and
comfortable about you.

HIALMAR. Yes, Gina—[*Nods to her.*]—
you are a good helpmate on the path of
life.

GINA. Oh, don't sit there cricketizing
me.

RELLING. And your Hedvig, too, Ekdal!

HIALMAR. [*Affected.*] The child, yes!
The child before everything! Hedvig,
come here to me. [*Strokes her hair.*]
What day is it tomorrow, eh?

HEDVIG. [*Shaking him.*] Oh, no, you're
not to say anything, father.

HIALMAR. It cuts me to the heart when
I think what a poor affair it will be; only
a little festivity in the garret . . .

HEDVIG. Oh, but that's just what I like!

RELLING. Just you wait till the wonderful invention sees the light, Hedvig!

HIALMAR. Yes, indeed—then you shall
see . . . ! Hedvig, I have resolved to
make your future secure. You shall live
in comfort all your days. I will demand—
something or other—on your behalf. That
shall be the poor inventor's sole reward.

HEDVIG. [*Whispering, with her arms
round his neck.*] Oh, you dear, kind
father!

RELLING. [*To* GREGERS.] Come now,
don't you find it pleasant, for once in a
way, to sit at a well-spread table in a
happy family circle?

HIALMAR. Ah, yes, I really prize these
social hours.

GREGERS. For my part, I don't thrive
in marsh vapours.

RELLING. Marsh vapours?

HIALMAR. Oh, don't begin with that
stuff again!

GINA. Goodness knows there's no
marsh vapours in this house, Mr. Werle;
I give the place a good airing every
blessed day.

GREGERS. [*Leaves the table.*] No airing
you can give will drive out the taint I
mean.

HIALMAR. Taint!

GINA. Yes, what do you say to that,
Ekdal!

RELLING. Excuse me—may it not be you
yourself that have brought the taint from
those mines up there?

GREGERS. It is like you to call what I
bring into this house a taint.

RELLING. [*Goes up to him.*] Look here,
Mr. Werle, junior: I have a strong suspicion that you are still carrying about that
"claim of the ideal" large as life, in your
coat-tail pocket.

GREGERS. I carry it in my breast.

RELLING. Well, wherever you carry it, I
advise you not to come dunning us with
it here, so long as *I* am on the premises.

GREGERS. And if I do so nonetheless?

RELLING. Then you'll go head-foremost
down the stairs; now I've warned you.

HIALMAR. [*Rising.*] Oh, but Relling
. . . !

GREGERS. Yes, you may turn me out
. . .

GINA. [*Interposing between them.*] We
can't have that, Relling. But I must say,
Mr. Werle, it ill becomes you to talk
about vapours and taints, after all the
mess you made with your stove. [*A
knock at the passage door.*]

HEDVIG. Mother, there's somebody
knocking.

HIALMAR. There now, we're going to
have a whole lot of people!

GINA. I'll go . . . [*Goes over and opens
the door, starts, and draws back.*] Oh—

oh, dear! [WERLE, *in a fur coat, advances one step into the room.*]

WERLE. Excuse me; but I think my son is staying here.

GINA. [*With a gulp.*] Yes.

HIALMAR. [*Approaching him.*] Won't you do us the honour to . . . ?

WERLE. Thank you, I merely wish to speak to my son.

GREGERS. What is it? Here I am.

WERLE. I want a few words with you, in your room.

GREGERS. In my room? Very well . . . [*About to go.*]

GINA. No, no, your room's not in a fit state . . .

WERLE. Well then, out in the passage here; I want to have a few words with you alone.

HIALMAR. You can have them here, sir. Come into the parlour, Relling. [HIALMAR *and* RELLING *go off to the right.* GINA *takes* HEDVIG *with her into the kitchen.*]

GREGERS. [*After a short pause.*] Well, now we are alone.

WERLE. From something you let fall last evening, and from your coming to lodge with the Ekdals, I can't help inferring that you intend to make yourself unpleasant to me, in one way or another.

GREGERS. I intend to open Hialmar Ekdal's eyes. He shall see his position as it really is—that is all.

WERLE. Is that the mission in life you spoke of yesterday?

GREGERS. Yes. You have left me no other.

WERLE. Is it I, then, that crippled your mind, Gregers?

GREGERS. You have crippled my whole life. I am not thinking of all that about mother . . . But it's thanks to you that I am continually haunted and harassed by a guilty conscience.

WERLE. Indeed! It is your conscience that troubles you, is it?

GREGERS. I ought to have taken a stand against you when the trap was set for Lieutenant Ekdal. I ought to have cautioned him; for I had a misgiving as to what was in the wind.

WERLE. Yes, that was the time to have spoken.

GREGERS. I did not dare to, I was so cowed and spiritless. I was mortally afraid of you—not only then, but long afterwards.

WERLE. You have got over that fear now, it appears.

GREGERS. Yes, fortunately. The wrong done to old Ekdal, both by me and by —others, can never be undone; but Hialmar I can rescue from all the falsehood and deception that are bringing him to ruin.

WERLE. Do you think that will be doing him a kindness?

GREGERS. I have not the least doubt of it.

WERLE. You think our worthy photographer is the sort of man to appreciate such friendly offices?

GREGERS. Yes, I do.

WERLE. H'm—we shall see.

GREGERS. Besides, if I am to go on living, I must try to find some cure for my sick conscience.

WERLE. It will never be sound. Your conscience has been sickly from childhood. That is a legacy from your mother, Gregers—the only one she left you.

GREGERS. [*With a scornful half-smile.*] Have you not yet forgiven her for the mistake you made in supposing she would bring you a fortune?

WERLE. Don't let us wander from the point.—Then you hold to your purpose of setting young Ekdal upon what you imagine to be the right scent?

GREGERS. Yes, that is my fixed resolve.

WERLE. Well, in that case I might have spared myself this visit; for, of course, it is useless to ask whether you will return home with me?

GREGERS. Quite useless.

WERLE. And I suppose you won't enter the firm either?

GREGERS. No.

WERLE. Very good. But as I am thinking of marrying again, your share in the property will fall to you at once.[3]

GREGER. [*Quickly.*] No, I do not want that.

[3] By Norwegian law, before a widower can marry again, a certain proportion of his property must be settled on his children by his former marriage.

WERLE. You don't want it?

GREGERS. No, I dare not take it, for conscience' sake.

WERLE. [*After a pause.*] Are you going up to the works again?

GREGERS. No; I consider myself released from your service.

WERLE. But what are you going to do?

GREGERS. Only to fulfill my mission; nothing more.

WERLE. Well, but afterwards? What are you going to live upon?

GREGERS. I have laid by a little out of my salary.

WERLE. How long will that last?

GREGERS. I think it will last my time.

WERLE. What do you mean?

GREGERS. I shall answer no more questions.

WERLE. Good-bye then, Gregers.

GREGERS. Good-bye. [WERLE *goes.*]

HIALMAR. [*Peeping in.*] He's gone, isn't he?

GREGERS. Yes. [HIALMAR *and* RELLING *enter; also* GINA *and* HEDVIG *from the kitchen.*]

RELLING. That luncheon-party was a failure.

GREGERS. Put on your coat, Hialmar; I want you to come for a long walk with me.

HIALMAR. With pleasure. What was it your father wanted? Had it anything to do with me?

GREGERS. Come along. We must have a talk. I'll go and put on my overcoat. [*Goes out by the passage door.*]

GINA. You shouldn't go out with him, Ekdal.

RELLING. No, don't you do it. Stay where you are.

HIALMAR. [*Gets his hat and overcoat.*] Oh, nonsense! When a friend of my youth feels impelled to open his mind to me in private . . .

RELLING. But devil take it—don't you see that the fellow's mad, cracked, demented!

GINA. There, what did I tell you! His mother before him had crazy fits like that sometimes.

HIALMAR. The more need for a friend's watchful eye. [*To* GINA.] Be sure you have dinner ready in good time. Good-bye for the present. [*Goes out by the passage door.*]

RELLING. It's a thousand pities the fellow didn't go to hell through one of the Höidal mines.

GINA. Good Lord! what makes you say that?

RELLING. [*Muttering.*] Oh, I have my own reasons.

GINA. Do you think young Werle is really mad?

RELLING. No, worse luck; he's no madder than most other people. But one disease he has certainly got in his system.

GINA. What is it that's the matter with him?

RELLING. Well, I'll tell you, Mrs. Ekdal. He is suffering from an acute attack of integrity.

GINA. Integrity?

HEDVIG. Is that a kind of disease?

RELLING. Yes, it's a national disease; but it only appears sporadically. [*Nods to* GINA.] Thanks for your hospitality. [*He goes out by the passage door.*]

GINA. [*Moving restlessly to and fro.*] Ugh, that Gregers Werle—he was always a wretched creature.

HEDVIG. [*Standing by the table and looking searchingly at her.*] I think all this is very strange.

THE CURTAIN FALLS

ACT FOUR

HIALMAR EKDAL's studio. A photograph has just been taken; a camera with the cloth over it, a pedestal, two chairs, a folding table, etc., are standing out in the room. Afternoon light; the sun is going down; a little later it begins to grow dusk.

GINA stands in the passage doorway,

with a little box and a wet glass plate in her hand, and is speaking to somebody outside.

GINA. Yes, certainly. When I make a promise I keep it. The first dozen shall be ready on Monday. Good afternoon. [*Someone is heard going downstairs.* GINA *shuts the door, slips the plate into the box and puts it into the covered camera.*]

HEDVIG. [*Comes in from the kitchen.*] Are they gone?

GINA. [*Tidying up.*] Yes, thank goodness, I've got rid of them at last.

HEDVIG. But can you imagine why father hasn't come home yet?

GINA. Are you sure he's not down in Relling's room?

HEDVIG. No, he's not; I ran down the kitchen stair just now and asked.

GINA. And his dinner standing and getting cold, too.

HEDVIG. Yes, I can't understand it. Father's always so careful to be home to dinner!

GINA. Oh, he'll be here directly, you'll see.

HEDVIG. I wish he would come; everything seems so queer today.

GINA. [*Calls out.*] There he is! [HIALMAR EKDAL *comes in at the passage door.*]

HEDVIG. [*Going to him.*] Father! Oh, what a time we've been waiting for you!

GINA. [*Glancing sidelong at him.*] You've been out a long time, Ekdal.

HIALMAR. [*Without looking at her.*] Rather long, yes. [*He takes off his overcoat;* GINA *and* HEDVIG *go to help him; he motions them away.*]

GINA. Perhaps you've had dinner with Werle?

HIALMAR. [*Hanging up his coat.*] No.

GINA. [*Going towards the kitchen door.*] Then I'll bring some in for you.

HIALMAR. No; let the dinner alone. I want nothing to eat.

HEDVIG. [*Going nearer to him.*] Are you not well, father?

HIALMAR. Well? Oh, yes, well enough. We have had a tiring walk, Gregers and I.

GINA. You didn't ought to have gone so far, Ekdal; you're not used to it.

HIALMAR. H'm; there's many a thing a man must get used to in this world. [*Wanders about the room.*] Has any one been here whilst I was out?

GINA. Nobody but the two sweethearts.

HIALMAR. No new orders?

GINA. No, not today.

HEDVIG. There will be some tomorrow, father, you'll see.

HIALMAR. I hope there will; for tomorrow I am going to set to work in real earnest.

HEDVIG. Tomorrow! Don't you remember what day it is tomorrow?

HIALMAR. Oh, yes, by-the-bye. . . . Well, the day after, then. Henceforth I mean to do everything myself; I shall take all the work into my own hands.

GINA. Why, what can be the good of that, Ekdal? It'll only make your life a burden to you. I can manage the photography all right; and you can go on working at your invention.

HEDVIG. And think of the wild duck, father,—and all the hens and rabbits and . . . !

HIALMAR. Don't talk to me of all that trash! From tomorrow I will never set foot in the garret again.

HEDVIG. Oh, but father, you promised that we should have a little party . . .

HIALMAR. H'm, true. Well, then, from the day after tomorrow. I should almost like to wring that cursed wild duck's neck!

HEDVIG. [*Shrieks.*] The wild duck!

GINA. Well, I never!

HEDVIG. [*Shaking him.*] Oh, no, father; you know it's my wild duck!

HIALMAR. That is why I don't do it. I haven't the heart to—for your sake, Hedvig. But in my inmost soul I feel that I ought to do it. I ought not to tolerate under my roof a creature that has been through those hands.

GINA. Why, good gracious, even if grandfather did get it from that poor creature, Pettersen . . .

HIALMAR. [*Wandering about.*] There are certain claims—what shall I call them? —let me say claims of the ideal—certain obligations, which a man cannot disregard without injury to his soul.

HEDVIG. [*Going after him.*] But think of the wild duck,—the poor wild duck!

HIALMAR. [*Stops.*] I tell you I will spare it—for your sake. Not a hair of its head shall be—I mean, it shall be spared. There are greater problems than that to be dealt with. But you should go out a little now, Hedvig, as usual; it is getting dusk enough for you now.

HEDVIG. No, I don't care about going out now.

HIALMAR. Yes, do; it seems to me your eyes are blinking a great deal; all these vapours in here are bad for you. The air is heavy under this roof.

HEDVIG. Very well, then, I'll run down the kitchen stair and go for a little walk. My cloak and hat?—oh, they're in my own room. Father—be sure you don't do the wild duck any harm whilst I'm out.

HIALMAR. Not a feather of its head shall be touched. [*Draws her to him.*] You and I, Hedvig—we two . . . ! Well, go along. [HEDVIG *nods to her parents and goes out through the kitchen.*]

HIALMAR. [*Walks about without looking up.*] Gina.

GINA. Yes?

HIALMAR. From tomorrow—or, say, from the day after tomorrow—I should like to keep the household account-book myself.

GINA. Do you want to keep the accounts, too, now?

HIALMAR. Yes; or to check the receipts at any rate.

GINA. Lord help us! that's soon done.

HIALMAR. One would hardly think so; at any rate, you seem to make the money go a very long way. [*Stops and looks at her.*] How do you manage it?

GINA. It's because me and Hedvig, we need so little.

HIALMAR. Is it the case that father is very liberally paid for the copying he does for Mr. Werle?

GINA. I don't know as he gets anything out of the way. I don't know the rates for that sort of work.

HIALMAR. Well, what does he get, about? Let me hear!

GINA. Oh, it varies; I daresay it'll come to about as much as he costs us, with a little pocket-money over.

HIALMAR. As much as he costs us! And you have never told me this before!

GINA. No, how could I tell you? It pleased you so much to think he got everything from you.

HIALMAR. And he gets it from Mr. Werle.

GINA. Oh, well, he has plenty and to spare, he has.

HIALMAR. Light the lamp for me, please!

GINA. [*Lighting the lamp.*] And, of course, we don't know as it's Mr. Werle himself; it may be Graberg . . .

HIALMAR. Why attempt such an evasion?

GINA. I don't know; I only thought . . .

HIALMAR. H'm.

GINA. It wasn't me that got grandfather that copying. It was Bertha, when she used to come about us.

HIALMAR. It seems to me your voice is trembling.

GINA. [*Putting the lamp-shade on.*] Is it?

HIALMAR. And your hands are shaking, are they not?

GINA. [*Firmly.*] Come right out with it, Ekdal. What has he been saying about me?

HIALMAR. Is it true—can it be true that —that there was an—an understanding between you and Mr. Werle, while you were in service there?

GINA. That's not true. Not at that time. Mr. Werle did come after me, that's a fact. And his wife thought there was something in it, and then she made such a hocus-pocus and hurly-burly, and she hustled me and bustled me about so, that I left her service.

HIALMAR. But afterwards, then?

GINA. Well, then I went home. And mother—well, she wasn't the woman you took her for, Ekdal; she kept on worrying and worrying at me about one thing and another—for Mr. Werle was a widower by that time.

HIALMAR. Well, and then?

GINA. I suppose you've got to know it. He gave me no peace until he'd had his way.

HIALMAR. [*Striking his hands together.*] And this is the mother of my child! How could you hide this from me?

GINA. Yes, it was wrong of me; I ought

certainly to have told you long ago.

HIALMAR. You should have told me at the very first;—then I should have known the sort of woman you were.

GINA. But would you have married me all the same?

HIALMAR. How can you dream that I would?

GINA. That's just why I didn't dare tell you anything, then. For I'd come to care for you so much, you see; and I couldn't go and make myself utterly miserable . . .

HIALMAR. [*Walks about.*] And this is my Hedvig's mother. And to know that all I see before me—[*Kicks a chair.*]—all that I call my home—I owe to a favoured predecessor! Oh, that scoundrel Werle!

GINA. Do you repent of the fourteen—the fifteen years we've lived together?

HIALMAR. [*Placing himself in front of her.*] Have you not every day, every hour, repented of the spider's-web of deceit you have spun around me? Answer me that! How could you help writhing with penitence and remorse?

GINA. Oh, my dear Ekdal, I've had all I could do to look after the house and get through the day's work . . .

HIALMAR. Then you never think of reviewing your past?

GINA. No; Heaven knows I'd almost forgotten those old stories.

HIALMAR. Oh, this dull, callous contentment! To me there is something revolting about it. Think of it—never so much as a twinge of remorse!

GINA. But tell me, Ekdal—what would have become of you if you hadn't had a wife like me?

HIALMAR. Like you . . . !

GINA. Yes; for you know I've always been a bit more practical and wide-awake than you. Of course I'm a year or two older.

HIALMAR. What would have become of me!

GINA. You'd got into all sorts of bad ways when first you met me; that you can't deny.

HIALMAR. "Bad ways" do you call them? Little do you know what a man goes through when he is in grief and despair—especially a man of my fiery temperament.

GINA. Well, well, that may be so. And I've no reason to crow over you, neither; for you turned a moral of a husband, that you did, as soon as ever you had a house and home of your own.—And now we'd got everything so nice and cosy about us; and me and Hedvig was just thinking we'd soon be able to let ourselves go a bit, in the way of both food and clothes.

HIALMAR. In the swamp of deceit, yes.

GINA. I wish to goodness that detestable thing had never set his foot inside our doors!

HIALMAR. And I, too, thought my home such a pleasant one. That was a delusion. Where shall I now find the elasticity of spirit to bring my invention into the world of reality? Perhaps it will die with me; and then it will be your past, Gina, that will have killed it.

GINA. [*Nearly crying.*] You mustn't say such things, Ekdal. Me, that has only wanted to do the best I could for you, all my days!

HIALMAR. I ask you, what becomes of the breadwinner's dream? When I used to lie in there on the sofa and brood over my invention, I had a clear enough presentiment that it would sap my vitality to the last drop. I felt even then that the day when I held the patent in my hand—that day—would bring my—release. And then it was my dream that you should live on after me, the dead inventor's well-to-do widow.

GINA. [*Drying her tears.*] No, you mustn't talk like that, Ekdal. May the Lord never let me see the day I am left a widow!

HIALMAR. Oh, the whole dream has vanished. It is all over now. All over! [GREGERS WERLE *opens the passage door cautiously and looks in.*]

GREGERS. May I come in?

HIALMAR. Yes, come in.

GREGERS. [*Comes forward, his face beaming with satisfaction, and holds out both his hands to them.*] Well, dear friends . . . ! [*Looks from one to the other and whispers to* HIALMAR.] Have you not done it yet?

HIALMAR. [*Aloud.*] It is done.

GREGERS. It is?

HIALMAR. I have passed through the bitterest moments of my life.

GREGERS. But also, I trust, the most ennobling.

HIALMAR. Well, at any rate, we have got through it for the present.

GINA. God forgive you, Mr. Werle.

GREGERS. [*In great surprise.*] But I don't understand this.

HIALMAR. What don't you understand?

GREGERS. After so great a crisis—a crisis that is to be the starting-point of an entirely new life—of a communion founded on truth and free from all taint of deception . . .

HIALMAR. Yes, yes, I know; I know that quite well.

GREGERS. I confidently expected, when I entered the room, to find the light of transfiguration shining upon me from both husband and wife. And now I see nothing but dulness, oppression, gloom . . .

GINA. Oh, is that it? [*Takes off the lamp-shade.*]

GREGERS. You will not understand me, Mrs. Ekdal. Ah, well, you, I suppose, need time to. . . . But you, Hialmar? Surely you feel a new consecration after the great crisis.

HIALMAR. Yes, of course I do. That is— in a sort of way.

GREGERS. For surely nothing in the world can compare with the joy of forgiving one who has erred and raising her up to oneself in love.

HIALMAR. Do you think a man can so easily throw off the bitter cup I have drained?

GREGERS. No, not a common man, perhaps. But a man like you . . . !

HIALMAR. Good God! I know that well enough. But you must keep me up to it, Gregers. It takes time, you know.

GREGERS. You have much of the wild duck in you, Hialmar. [RELLING *has come in at the passage door.*]

RELLING. Oho! is the wild duck to the fore again?

HIALMAR. Yes; Mr. Werle's wing-broken victim.

RELLING. Mr. Werle's . . . ? So it's him you are talking about?

HIALMAR. Him and—ourselves.

RELLING. [*In an undertone to* GREGERS.] May the devil fly away with you!

HIALMAR. What is that you are saying?

RELLING. Only uttering a heartfelt wish that this quack-salver would take himself off. If he stays here, he is quite equal to making an utter mess of life, for both of you.

GREGERS. These two will not make a mess of life, Mr. Relling. Of course I won't speak of Hialmar—him we know. But she, too, in her innermost heart, has certainly something loyal and sincere . . .

GINA. [*Almost crying.*] You might have let me alone for what I was, then.

RELLING. [*To* GREGERS.] Is it rude to ask what you really want in this house?

GREGERS. To lay the foundations of a true marriage.

RELLING. So you don't think Ekdal's marriage is good enough as it is?

GREGERS. No doubt it is as good a marriage as most others, worse luck. But a true marriage it has yet to become.

HIALMAR. You have never had eyes for the claims of the ideal, Relling.

RELLING. Rubbish, my boy!—but excuse me, Mr. Werle: how many—in round numbers—how many true marriages have you seen in the course of your life?

GREGERS. Scarcely a single one.

RELLING. Nor I either.

GREGERS. But I have seen innumerable marriages of the opposite kind. And it has been my fate to see at close quarters what ruin such a marriage can work in two human souls.

HIALMAR. A man's whole moral basis may give away beneath his feet; that is the terrible part of it.

RELLING. Well, I can't say I've ever been exactly married, so I don't pretend to speak with authority. But this I know, that the child enters into the marriage problem. And you must leave the child in peace.

HIALMAR. Oh—Hedvig! my poor Hedvig!

RELLING. Yes, you must be good enough to keep Hedvig outside of all this. You two are grown-up people; you are free, in God's name, to make what mess and muddle you please of your life. But you must deal cautiously with Hedvig, I tell you; else you may do her a great injury.

HIALMAR. An injury!

RELLING. Yes, or she may do herself an injury—and perhaps others, too.

GINA. How can you know that, Relling?

HIALMAR. Her sight is in no immediate danger, is it?

RELLING. I am not talking about her sight. Hedvig is at a critical age. She may be getting all sorts of mischief into her head.

GINA. That's true—I've noticed it already! She's taken to carrying on with the fire, out in the kitchen. She calls it playing at house-on-fire. I'm often scared for fear she really sets fire to the house.

RELLING. You see; I thought as much.

GREGERS. [To RELLING.] But how do you account for that?

RELLING. [Sullenly.] Her constitution's changing, sir.

HIALMAR. So long as the child has me . . . ! So long as I am above ground . . . ! [A knock at the door.]

GINA. Hush, Ekdal; there's some one in the passage. [Calls out.] Come in! [MRS. SÖRBY, in walking dress, comes in.]

MRS. SÖRBY. Good evening.

GINA. [Going towards her.] Is it really you, Bertha?

MRS. SÖRBY. Yes, of course it is. But I'm disturbing you, I'm afraid?

HIALMAR. No, not at all; an emissary from that house . . .

MRS. SÖRBY. [To GINA.] To tell the truth, I hoped your men-folk would be out at this time. I just ran up to have a little chat with you, and to say good-bye.

GINA. Good-bye? Are you going away, then?

MRS. SÖRBY. Yes, tomorrow morning,—up to Höidal. Mr. Werle started this afternoon. [Lightly to GREGERS.] He asked me to say good-bye for him.

GINA. Only fancy . . . !

HIALMAR. So Mr. Werle has gone? And now you are going after him?

MRS. SÖRBY. Yes, what do you say to that, Ekdal?

HIALMAR. I say: beware!

GREGERS. I must explain the situation. My father and Mrs. Sörby are going to be married.

HIALMAR. Going to be married!

GINA. Oh, Bertha! So it's come to that at last!

RELLING. [His voice quivering a little.] This is surely not true?

MRS. SÖRBY. Yes, my dear Relling, it's true enough.

RELLING. You are going to marry again?

MRS. SÖRBY. Yes, it looks like it. Werle has got a special license, and we are going to be married quite quietly, up at the works.

GREGERS. Then I must wish you all happiness, like a dutiful stepson.

MRS. SÖRBY. Thank you very much—if you mean what you say. I certainly hope it will lead to happiness, both for Werle and for me.

RELLING. You have every reason to hope that. Mr. Werle never gets drunk—so far as I know; and I don't suppose he's in the habit of thrashing his wives, like the late lamented horse-doctor.

MRS. SÖRBY. Come now, let Sörby rest in peace. He had his good points, too.

RELLING. Mr. Werle has better ones, I have no doubt.

MRS. SÖRBY. He hasn't frittered away all that was good in him, at any rate. The man who does that must take the consequences.

RELLING. I shall go out with Molvik this evening.

MRS. SÖRBY. You mustn't do that, Relling. Don't do it—for my sake.

RELLING. There's nothing else for it. [To HIALMAR.] If you're going with us, come along.

GINA. No, thank you. Ekdal doesn't go in for that sort of dissertation.

HIALMAR. [Half aloud, in vexation.] Oh, do hold your tongue!

RELLING. Good-bye, Mrs.—Werle. [Goes out through the passage door.]

GREGERS. [To MRS. SÖRBY.] You seem to know Dr. Relling pretty intimately.

MRS. SÖRBY. Yes, we have known each other for many years. At one time it seemed as if things might have gone further between us.

GREGERS. It was surely lucky for you that they did not.

MRS. SÖRBY. You may well say that. But I have always been wary of acting on impulse. A woman can't afford absolutely to throw herself away.

GREGERS. Are you not in the least afraid that I may let my father know about this old friendship?

MRS. SÖRBY. Why, of course, I have told him all about it myself.

GREGERS. Indeed?

MRS. SÖRBY. Your father knows every single thing that can, with any truth, be said about me. I have told him all; it was the first thing I did when I saw what was in his mind.

GREGERS. Then you have been franker than most people, I think.

MRS. SÖRBY. I have always been frank. We women find that the best policy.

HIALMAR. What do you say to that, Gina?

GINA. Oh, we're not all alike, us women aren't. Some are made one way, some another.

MRS. SÖRBY. Well, for my part, Gina, I believe it's wisest to do as I've done. And Werle has no secrets either, on his side. That's really the great bond between us, you see. Now he can talk to me as openly as a child. He has never had the chance to do that before. Fancy a man like him, full of health and vigour, passing his whole youth and the best years of his life in listening to nothing but penitential sermons! And very often the sermons had for their text the most imaginary offenses —at least so I understand.

GINA. That's true enough.

GREGERS. If you ladies are going to follow up this topic, I had better withdraw.

MRS. SÖRBY. You can stay as far as that's concerned. I shan't say a word more. But I wanted you to know that I had done nothing secretly or in an underhand way. I may seem to have come in for a great piece of luck; and so I have, in a sense. But after all, I don't think I am getting any more than I am giving. I shall stand by him always, and I can tend and care for him as no one else can, now that he is getting helpless.

HIALMAR. Getting helpless?

GREGERS. [To MRS. SÖRBY.] Hush, don't speak of that here.

MRS. SÖRBY. There is no disguising it any longer, however much he would like to. He is going blind.

HIALMAR. [Starts.] Going blind? That's strange. He, too, going blind!

GINA. Lots of people do.

MRS. SÖRBY. And you can imagine what that means to a business man. Well, I shall try as well as I can to make my eyes take the place of his. But I mustn't stay any longer; I have such heaps of things to do.—Oh, by-the-bye, Ekdal, I was to tell you that if there is anything Werle can do for you, you must just apply to Graberg.

GREGERS. That offer I am sure Hialmar Ekdal will decline with thanks.

MRS. SÖRBY. Indeed? I don't think he used to be so . . .

GINA. No, Bertha, Ekdal doesn't need anything from Mr. Werle now.

HIALMAR. [Slowly, and with emphasis.] Will you present my compliments to your future husband and say that I intend very shortly to call upon Mr. Graberg . . .

GREGERS. What! You don't really mean that?

HIALMAR. To call upon Mr. Graberg, I say, and obtain an account of the sum I owe his principal. I will pay that debt of honour—ha ha ha! a debt of honour, let us call it! In any case, I will pay the whole with five per cent. interest.

GINA. But, my dear Ekdal, God knows we haven't got the money to do it.

HIALMAR. Be good enough to tell your future husband that I am working assiduously at my invention. Please tell him that what sustains me in this laborious task is the wish to free myself from a torturing burden of debt. That is my reason for proceeding with the invention. The entire profits shall be devoted to releasing me from my pecuniary obligations to your future husband.

MRS. SÖRBY. Something has happened here.

HIALMAR. Yes, you are right.

MRS. SÖRBY. Well, good-bye. I had something else to speak to you about, Gina; but it must keep till another time. Good-bye. [HIALMAR and GREGERS bow *silently.* GINA *follows* MRS. SÖRBY *to the door.*]

HIALMAR. Not beyond the threshold, Gina! [MRS. SÖRBY *goes;* GINA *shuts the door after her.*]

HIALMAR. There now Gregers, I have got that burden of debt off my mind.

GREGERS. You soon will, at all events.

HIALMAR. I think my attitude may be called correct.

GREGERS. You are the man I have always taken you for.

HIALMAR. In certain cases, it is impossible to disregard the claim of the ideal. Yet, as the breadwinner of a family, I cannot but writhe and groan under it. I can tell you it is no joke for a man without capital to attempt the repayment of a long-standing obligation, over which, so to speak, the dust of oblivion had gathered. But it cannot be helped: the Man in me demands his rights.

GREGERS. [*Laying his hand on* HIALMAR'S *shoulder.*] My dear Hialmar—was it not a good thing I came?

HIALMAR. Yes.

GREGERS. Are you not glad to have had your true position made clear to you?

HIALMAR. [*Somewhat impatiently.*] Yes, of course I am. But there is one thing that is revolting to my sense of justice.

GREGERS. And what is that?

HIALMAR. It is that—but I don't know whether I ought to express myself so unreservedly about your father.

GREGERS. Say what you please, so far as I am concerned.

HIALMAR. Well, then, is it not exasperating to think that it is not I, but he, who will realize the true marriage?

GREGERS. How can you say such a thing?

HIALMAR. Because it is clearly the case. Isn't the marriage between your father and Mrs. Sörby founded upon complete confidence, upon entire and unreserved candour on both sides? They hide nothing from each other, they keep no secrets in the background; their relation is based, if I may put it so, on mutual confession and absolution.

GREGERS. Well, what then?

HIALMAR. Well, is not that the whole

thing? Did you not yourself say that this was precisely the difficulty that had to be overcome in order to found a true marriage?

GREGERS. But this is a totally different matter, Hialmar. You surely don't compare either yourself or your wife with those two . . . ? Oh, you understand me well enough.

HIALMAR. Say what you like, there is something in all this that hurts and offends my sense of justice. It really looks as if there were no just providence to rule the world.

GINA. Oh, no, Ekdal; for God's sake don't say such things.

GREGERS. H'm; don't let us get upon those questions.

HIALMAR. And yet, after all, I cannot but recognize the guiding finger of fate. He is going blind.

GINA. Oh, you can't be sure of that.

HIALMAR. There is no doubt about it. At all events there ought not to be; for in that very fact lies the righteous retribution. He has hoodwinked a confiding fellow creature in days gone by . . .

GREGERS. I fear he has hoodwinked many.

HIALMAR. And now comes inexorable, mysterious Fate and demands Werle's own eyes.

GINA. Oh, how dare you say such dreadful things! You make me quite scared.

HIALMAR. It is profitable, now and then, to plunge deep into the night side of existence. [HEDVIG, *in her hat and cloak, comes in by the passage door. She is pleasurably excited and out of breath.*]

GINA. Are you back already?

HEDVIG. Yes, I didn't care to go any farther. It was a good thing, too; for I've just met some one at the door.

HIALMAR. It must have been that Mrs. Sörby.

HEDVIG. Yes.

HIALMAR. [*Walks up and down.*] I hope you have seen her for the last time. [*Silence.* HEDVIG, *discouraged, looks first at one and then at the other, trying to divine their frame of mind.*]

HEDVIG. [*Approaching, coaxingly.*] Father.

HIALMAR. Well—what is it, Hedvig?

HEDVIG. Mrs. Sörby had something with her for me.

HIALMAR. [*Stops.*] For you?

HEDVIG. Yes, something for tomorrow.

GINA. Bertha has always given you some little thing on your birthday.

HIALMAR. What is it?

HEDVIG. Oh, you mustn't see it now. Mother is to give it to me tomorrow morning before I'm up.

HIALMAR. What is all this hocus-pocus that I am to be in the dark about!

HEDVIG. [*Quickly.*] Oh, no, you may see it if you like. It's a big letter. [*Takes the letter out of her cloak pocket.*]

HIALMAR. A letter, too?

HEDVIG. Yes, it is only a letter. The rest will come afterwards, I suppose. But fancy—a letter! I've never had a letter before. And there's "Miss" written upon it. [*Reads.*] "Miss Hedvig Ekdal." Only fancy—that's me!

HIALMAR. Let me see that letter.

HEDVIG. [*Hands it to him.*] There it is.

HIALMAR. That is Mr. Werle's hand.

GINA. Are you sure of that, Ekdal?

HIALMAR. Look for yourself.

GINA. Oh, what do *I* know about such-like things?

HIALMAR. Hedvig, may I open the letter —and read it?

HEDVIG. Yes, of course you may, if you want to.

GINA. No, not tonight, Ekdal; it's to be kept till tomorrow.

HEDVIG. [*Softly.*] Oh can't you let him read it! It's sure to be something good; and then father will be glad, and everything will be nice again.

HIALMAR. I may open it, then?

HEDVIG. Yes, do, father. I'm so anxious to know what it is.

HIALMAR. Well and good. [*Opens the letter, takes out a paper, reads it through and appears bewildered.*] What is this . . . !

GINA. What does it say?

HEDVIG. Oh, yes, father—tell us!

HIALMAR. Be quiet. [*Reads it through again; he has turned pale, but says with self-control.*] It is a deed of gift, Hedvig.

HEDVIG. Is it? What sort of gift am I to have?

HIALMAR. Read for yourself. [HEDVIG *goes over and reads for a time by the lamp.* HIALMAR *speaks half-aloud, clenching his hands.*] The eyes! The eyes—and then that letter!

HEDVIG. [*Leaves off reading.*] Yes, but it seems to me that it's grandfather that's to have it.

HIALMAR. [*Takes letter from her.*] Gina —can you understand this?

GINA. I know nothing whatever about it; tell me what's the matter.

HIALMAR. Mr. Werle writes to Hedvig that her old grandfather need not trouble himself any longer with the copying, but that he can henceforth draw on the office for a hundred crowns a month . . .

GREGERS. Aha!

HEDVIG. A hundred crowns, mother! I read that.

GINA. What a good thing for grandfather!

HIALMAR. . . . a hundred crowns a month so long as he needs it—that means, of course, so long as he lives.

GINA. Well, so he's provided for, poor dear.

HIALMAR. But there is more to come. You didn't read that, Hedvig. Afterwards this gift is to pass on to you.

HEDVIG. To me! The whole of it?

HIALMAR. He says that the same amount is assured to you for the whole of your life. Do you hear that, Gina?

GINA. Yes, I hear.

HEDVIG. Fancy—all that money for me! [*Shakes him.*] Father, father, aren't you glad . . . ?

HIALMAR. [*Eluding her.*] Glad! [*Walks about.*] Oh what vistas—what perspectives open up before me! It is Hedvig, Hedvig that he showers these benefactions upon!

GINA. Yes, because it's Hedvig's birthday . . .

HEDVIG. And you'll get it all the same, father! You know quite well I shall give all the money to you and mother.

HIALMAR. To mother, yes! There we have it.

GREGERS. Hialmar, this is a trap he is setting for you.

HIALMAR. Do you think it's another trap?

GREGERS. When he was here this morning he said: Hialmar Ekdal is not the man you imagine him to be.

HIALMAR. Not the man . . . !

GREGERS. That you shall see, he said.

HIALMAR. He meant you should see that I would let myself be bought off . . . !

HEDVIG. Oh, mother, what does all this mean?

GINA. Go and take off your things. [HEDVIG *goes out by the kitchen door, half-crying.*]

GREGERS. Yes, Hialmar—now is the time to show who was right, he or I.

HIALMAR. [*Slowly tears the paper across, lays both pieces on the table and says.*] Here is my answer.

GREGERS. Just what I expected.

HIALMAR. [*Goes over to* GINA, *who stands by the stove, and says in a low voice.*] Now please make a clean breast of it. If the connection between you and him was quite over when you—came to care for me, as you call it—why did he place us in a position to marry?

GINA. I suppose he thought as he could come and go in our house.

HIALMAR. Only that? Was not he afraid of a possible contingency?

GINA. I don't know what you mean.

HIALMAR. I want to know whether—your child has the right to live under my roof.

GINA. [*Draws herself up; her eyes flash.*] You ask that!

HIALMAR. You shall answer me this one question: Does Hedvig belong to me—or . . . ? Well!

GINA. [*Looking at him with cold defiance.*] I don't know.

HIALMAR. [*Quivering a little.*] You don't know!

GINA. How should *I* know. A creature like me . . .

HIALMAR. [*Quietly turning away from her.*] Then I have nothing more to do in this house.

GREGERS. Take care, Hialmar! Think what you are doing!

HIALMAR. [*Puts on his overcoat.*] In this case, there is nothing for a man like me to think twice about.

GREGERS. Yes, indeed, there are endless things to be considered. You three must be together if you are to attain the true frame of mind for self-sacrifice and forgiveness.

HIALMAR. I don't want to attain it. Never, never! *My* hat! [*Takes his hat.*] My home has fallen in ruins about me. [*Bursts into tears.*] Gregers, I have no child!

HEDVIG. [*Who has opened the kitchen door.*] What is that you're saying? [*Coming to him.*] Father, father!

GINA. There, you see!

HIALMAR. Don't come near me, Hedvig! Keep far away. I cannot bear to see you. Oh! those eyes . . . ! Good-bye. [*Makes for the door.*]

HEDVIG. [*Clinging close to him and screaming loudly.*] No! no! Don't leave me!

GINA. [*Cries out.*] Look at the child, Ekdal! Look at the child!

HIALMAR. I will not! I cannot! I must get out—away from all this! [*He tears himself away from* HEDVIG *and goes out by the passage door.*]

HEDVIG. [*With despairing eyes.*] He is going away from us, mother! He is going away from us! He will never come back again!

GINA. Don't cry, Hedvig. Father's sure to come back again!

HEDVIG. [*Throws herself sobbing on the sofa.*] No, no, he'll never come home to us any more.

GREGERS. Do you believe I meant all for the best, Mrs. Ekdal?

GINA. Yes, I daresay you did; but God forgive you, all the same.

HEDVIG. [*Lying on the sofa.*] Oh, this will kill me! What have I done to him? Mother, you must fetch him home again!

GINA. Yes, yes, yes; only be quiet, and I'll go out and look for him. [*Puts on her outdoor things.*] Perhaps he's gone in to Relling's. But you mustn't lie there and cry. Promise me!

HEDVIG. [*Weeping convulsively.*] Yes, I'll stop, I'll stop; if only father comes back!

GREGERS. [*To* GINA, *who is going.*] After all, had you not better leave him to fight out his bitter fight to the end?

GINA. Oh, he can do that afterwards. First of all, we must get the child quieted. [*Goes out by the passage door.*]

HEDVIG. [*Sits up and dries her tears.*] Now you must tell me what all this means. Why doesn't father want me any more?

GREGERS. You mustn't ask that till you are a big girl—quite grown-up.

HEDVIG. [*Sobs.*] But I can't go on being as miserable as this till I'm grown-up.—I think I know what it is.—Perhaps I'm not really father's child.

GREGERS. [*Uneasily.*] How could that be?

HEDVIG. Mother might have found me. And perhaps father has just got to know it; I've read of such things.

GREGERS. Well, but if it were so . . .

HEDVIG. I think he might be just as fond of me for all that. Yes, fonder almost. We got the wild duck in a present, you know, and I love it so dearly all the same.

GREGERS. [*Turning the conversation.*] Ah, the wild duck, by-the-bye! Let us talk about the wild duck a little, Hedvig.

HEDVIG. The poor wild duck! He doesn't want to see it any more either. Only think, he wanted to wring its neck!

GREGERS. Oh, he won't do that.

HEDVIG. No; but he said he would like to. And I think it was horrid of father to say it; for I pray for the wild duck every night and ask that it may be preserved from death and all that is evil.

GREGERS. [*Looking at her.*] Do you say your prayers every night?

HEDVIG. Yes.

GREGERS. Who taught you to do that?

HEDVIG. I myself; one time when father was very ill, and had leeches on his neck and said that death was staring him in the face.

GREGERS. Well?

HEDVIG. Then I prayed for him as I lay in bed; and since then I have always kept it up.

GREGERS. And now you pray for the wild duck, too?

HEDVIG. I thought it was best to bring in the wild duck; for she was so weakly at first.

GREGERS. Do you pray in the morning, too?

HEDVIG. No, of course not.

GREGERS. Why not in the morning as well?

HEDVIG. In the morning it's light, you know, and there's nothing in particular to be afraid of.

GREGERS. And your father was going to wring the neck of the wild duck that you love so dearly?

HEDVIG. No; he said he ought to wring its neck, but he would spare it for my sake; and that was kind of father.

GREGERS. [*Coming a little nearer.*] But suppose you were to sacrifice the wild duck of your own free will for his sake.

HEDVIG. [*Rising.*] The wild duck!

GREGERS. Suppose you were to make a free-will offering, for his sake, of the dearest treasure you have in the world!

HEDVIG. Do you think that would do any good?

GREGERS. Try it, Hedvig.

HEDVIG. [*Softly, with flashing eyes.*] Yes, I will try it.

GREGERS. Have you really the courage for it, do you think?

HEDVIG. I'll ask grandfather to shoot the wild duck for me.

GREGERS. Yes, do. But not a word to your mother about it.

HEDVIG. Why not?

GREGERS. She doesn't understand us.

HEDVIG. The wild duck! I'll try it to-morrow morning. [GINA *comes in by the passage door.*]

HEDVIG. [*Going towards her.*] Did you find him, mother?

GINA. No, but I heard as he had called and taken Relling with him.

GREGERS. Are you sure of that?

GINA. Yes, the porter's wife said so. Molvik went with them, too, she said.

GREGERS. This evening, when his mind so sorely needs to wrestle in solitude . . . !

GINA. [*Takes off her things.*] Yes, men are strange creatures, so they are. The Lord only knows where Relling has dragged him to! I ran over to Madam Eriksen's, but they weren't there.

HEDVIG. [*Struggling to keep back her tears.*] Oh, if he should never come home any more!

GREGERS. He will come home again. I

shall have news to give him tomorrow; and then you shall see how he comes home. You may rely upon that, Hedvig, and sleep in peace. Good-night. [*He goes out by the passage door.*]

HEDVIG. [*Throws herself sobbing on* GINA's *neck.*] Mother, mother!

GINA. [*Pats her shoulder and sighs.*] Ah, yes; Relling was right, he was. That's what comes of it when crazy creatures go about presenting the claims of the—what-you-may-call-it.

THE CURTAIN FALLS

ACT FIVE

HIALMAR EKDAL's studio. Cold, grey morning light. Wet snow lies upon the large panes of the sloping roof-window.

GINA comes from the kitchen with an apron and bib on, and carrying a dusting-brush and a duster; she goes towards the sitting-room door. At the same moment HEDVIG comes hurriedly in from the passage.

GINA. [*Stops.*] Well?

HEDVIG. Oh, mother, I almost think he's down at Relling's . . .

GINA. There, you see!

HEDVIG. . . . because the porter's wife says she could hear that Relling had two people with him when he came home last night.

GINA. That's just what I thought.

HEDVIG. But it's no use his being there, if he won't come up to us.

GINA. I'll go down and speak to him at all events. [OLD EKDAL, *in dressing-gown and slippers, and with a lighted pipe, appears at the door of his room.*]

EKDAL. Hialmar . . . Isn't Hialmar at home?

GINA. No, he's gone out.

EKDAL. So early? And in such a tearing snowstorm? Well, well; just as he pleases; I can take my morning walk alone. [*He slides the garret door aside;* HEDVIG *helps him; he goes in; she closes it after him.*]

HEDVIG. [*In an undertone.*] Only think, mother, when poor grandfather hears that father is going to leave us.

GINA. Oh, nonsense; grandfather mustn't hear anything about it. It was a heaven's mercy he wasn't at home yesterday in all that hurly-burly.

HEDVIG. Yes, but . . . [GREGERS *comes in by the passage door.*]

GREGERS. Well, have you any news of him?

GINA. They say he's down at Relling's.

GREGERS. At Relling's! Has he really been out with those creatures?

GINA. Yes, like enough.

GREGERS. When he ought to have been yearning for solitude, to collect and clear his thoughts . . .

GINA. Yes, you may well say so. [RELLING *enters from the passage.*]

HEDVIG. [*Going to him.*] Is father in your room?

GINA. [*At the same time.*] Is he there?

RELLING. Yes, to be sure he is.

HEDVIG. And you never let us know!

RELLING. Yes, I'm a brute. But in the first place I had to look after the other brute; I mean our dæmonic friend, of course; and then I fell so dead asleep that . . .

GINA. What does Ekdal say today?

RELLING. He says nothing whatever.

HEDVIG. Doesn't he speak?

RELLING. Not a blessed word.

GREGERS. No, no; I can understand that very well.

GINA. But what's he doing then?

RELLING. He's lying on the sofa, snoring.

GINA. Oh, is he? Yes, Ekdal's a rare one to snore.

HEDVIG. Asleep? Can he sleep?

RELLING. Well it certainly looks like it.

GREGERS. No wonder, after the spiritual conflict that has rent him . . .

GINA. And then he's never been used to gadding about out of doors at night.

HEDVIG. Perhaps it's a good thing that he's getting sleep, mother.

GINA. Of course it is; and we must take care we don't wake him up too early. Thank you, Relling. I must get the house cleaned up a bit now, and then . . . Come and help me, Hedvig. [GINA and HEDVIG go into the sitting-room.]

GREGERS. [Turning to RELLING.] What is your explanation of the spiritual tumult that is now going on in Hialmar Ekdal?

RELLING. Devil a bit of a spiritual tumult have I noticed in him.

GREGERS. What! Not at such a crisis, when his whole life has been placed on a new foundation . . . ? How can you think that such an individuality as Hialmar's . . . ?

RELLING. Oh, individuality—he! If he ever had any tendency to the abnormal developments you call individuality, I can assure you it was rooted out of him while he was still in his teens.

GREGERS. That would be strange indeed, —considering the loving care with which he was brought up.

RELLING. By those two high-flown, hysterical maiden aunts, you mean?

GREGERS. Let me tell you that they were women who never forgot the claim of the ideal—but of course you will only jeer at me again.

RELLING. No, I'm in no humour for that. I know all about those ladies; for he has ladled out no end of rhetoric on the subject of his "two soul-mothers." But I don't think he has much to thank them for. Ekdal's misfortune is that in his own circle he has always been looked upon as a shining light . . .

GREGERS. Not without reason, surely. Look at the depth of his mind!

RELLING. I have never discovered it. That his father believed in it I don't so much wonder; the old lieutenant has been an ass all his days.

GREGERS. He has had a child-like mind all his days; that is what you cannot understand.

RELLING. Well, so be it. But then, when our dear, sweet Hialmar went to college, he at once passed for the great light of the future amongst his comrades, too! He was handsome, the rascal—red and white —a shop-girl's dream of manly beauty; and with his superficially emotional temperament, and his sympathetic voice and his talent for declaiming other people's verses and other people's thoughts . . .

GREGERS. [Indignantly.] Is it Hialmar Ekdal you are talking about in this strain?

RELLING. Yes, with your permission; I am simply giving you an inside view of the idol you are grovelling before.

GREGERS. I should hardly have thought I was quite stone blind.

RELLING. Yes, you are—or not far from it. You are a sick man, too, you see.

GREGERS. You are right there.

RELLING. Yes. Yours is a complicated case. First of all there is that plaguy integrity-fever; and then—what's worse—you are always in a delirium of hero-worship; you must always have something to adore, outside yourself.

GREGERS. Yes, I must certainly seek it outside myself.

RELLING. But you make such shocking mistakes about every new phœnix you think you have discovered. Here again you have come to a cotter's cabin with your claim of the ideal; and the people of the house are insolvent.

GREGERS. If you don't think better than that of Hialmar Ekdal, what pleasure can you find in being everlastingly with him?

RELLING. Well, you see, I'm supposed to to be a sort of a doctor—save the mark! I can't but give a hand to the poor sick folk who live under the same roof with me.

GREGERS. Oh, indeed! Hialmar Ekdal is sick, too, is he!

RELLING. Most people are, worse luck.

GREGERS. And what remedy are you applying in Hialmar's case?

RELLING. My usual one. I am cultivating the life-illusion[1] in him.

GREGERS. Life—illusion? I didn't catch what you said.

RELLING. Yes, I said illusion. For illusion, you know, is the stimulating principle.

GREGERS. May I ask with what illusion Hialmar is inoculated?

---

1 "Livslögnen," literally "the life-lie."

RELLING. No, thank you; I don't betray professional secrets to quack-salvers. You would probably go and muddle his case still more than you have already. But my method is infallible. I have applied it to Molvik as well. I have made him "dæmonic." That's the blister I have to put on his neck.

GREGERS. Is he not really dæmonic, then?

RELLING. What the devil do you mean by dæmonic! It's only a piece of gibberish I've invented to keep up a spark of life in him. But for that, the poor harmless creature would have succumbed to self-contempt and despair many a long year ago. And then the old lieutenant! But he has hit upon his own cure, you see.

GREGERS. Lieutenant Ekdal? What of him?

RELLING. Just think of the old bear-hunter shutting himself up in that dark garret to shoot rabbits! I tell you there is not a happier sportsman in the world than that old man pottering about in there among all that rubbish. The four or five withered Christmas trees he has saved up are the same to him as the whole great fresh Höidal forest; the cock and the hens are big game-birds in the fir-tops; and the rabbits that flop about the garret floor are the bears he has to battle with— the mighty hunter of the mountains!

GREGERS. Poor unfortunate old man! Yes: he has indeed had to narrow the ideals of his youth.

RELLING. While I think of it, Mr. Werle, junior—don't use that foreign word: ideals. We have the excellent native word: lies.

GREGERS. Do you think the two things are related?

RELLING. Yes, just about as closely as typhus and putrid fever.

GREGERS. Dr. Relling, I shall not give up the struggle until I have rescued Hialmar from your clutches!

RELLING. So much the worse for him. Rob the average man of his life-illusion, and you rob him of his happiness at the same stroke. [To HEDVIG, who comes in from the sitting-room.] Well, little wild-duck-mother, I'm just going down to see whether papa is still lying meditating upon that wonderful invention of his. [Goes out by passage door.]

GREGERS. [Approaches HEDVIG.] I can see by your face that you have not yet done it.

HEDVIG. What? Oh, that about the wild duck! No.

GREGERS. I suppose your courage failed when the time came.

HEDVIG. No, that wasn't it. But when I awoke this morning and remembered what we had been talking about, it seemed so strange.

GREGERS. Strange?

HEDVIG. Yes, I don't know . . . Yesterday evening, at the moment, I thought there was something so delightful about it; but since I have slept and thought of it again, it somehow doesn't seem worth while.

GREGERS. Ah, I thought you could not have grown up quite unharmed in this house.

HEDVIG. I don't care about that, if only father would come up . . .

GREGERS. Oh, if only your eyes had been opened to that which gives life it's value —if you possessed the true, joyous, fearless spirit of sacrifice, you would soon see how he would come up to you.—But I believe in you still, Hedvig. [He goes out by the passage door. HEDVIG wanders about the room for a time; she is on the point of going into the kitchen when a knock is heard at the garret door. HEDVIG goes over and opens it a little; OLD EKDAL comes out; she pushes the door to again.]

EKDAL. H'm, it's not much fun to take one's morning walk alone.

HEDVIG. Wouldn't you like to go shooting, grandfather?

EKDAL. It's not the weather for it today. It's so dark there, you can scarcely see where you're going.

HEDVIG. Do you never want to shoot anything besides the rabbits?

EKDAL. Do you think the rabbits aren't good enough?

HEDVIG. Yes, but what about the wild duck?

EKDAL. Ho-ho! are you afraid I shall shoot your wild duck? Never in the world. Never.

HEDVIG. No, I suppose you couldn't;

they say it's very difficult to shoot wild ducks.

EKDAL. Couldn't! Should rather think I could.

HEDVIG. How would you set about it, grandfather?—I don't mean with my wild duck, but with others?

EKDAL. I should take care to shoot them in the breast, you know; that's the surest place. And then you must shoot against the feathers, you see—not the way of the feathers.

HEDVIG. Do they die then, grandfather?

EKDAL. Yes, they die right enough—when you shoot properly. Well, I must go and brush up a bit. H'm—understand—h'm. [*Goes into his room.* HEDVIG *waits a little, glances towards the sitting-room door, goes over to the book-case, stands on tiptoe, takes the double-barrelled pistol down from the shelf and looks at it.* GINA, *with brush and duster, comes from the sitting-room.* HEDVIG *hastily lays down the pistol, unobserved.*]

GINA. Don't stand raking amongst father's things, Hedvig.

HEDVIG. [*Goes away from the book-case.*] I was only going to tidy up a little.

GINA. You'd better go into the kitchen and see if the coffee's keeping hot; I'll take his breakfast on a tray, when I go down to him. [HEDVIG *goes out.* GINA *begins to sweep and clean up the studio. Presently the passage door is opened with hesitation, and* HIALMAR EKDAL *looks in. He has on his overcoat, but not his hat; he is unwashed, and his hair is dishevelled and unkempt. His eyes are dull and heavy.* GINA, *standing with the brush in her hand and looking at him.*] Oh, there now, Ekdal—so you've come after all!

HIALMAR. [*Comes in and answers in a toneless voice.*] I come—only to depart again immediately.

GINA. Yes, yes, I suppose so. But, Lord help us! what a sight you are!

HIALMAR. A sight?

GINA. And your nice winter coat, too! Well, that's done for.

HEDVIG. [*At the kitchen door.*] Mother, hadn't I better . . . ? [*Sees* HIALMAR, *gives a loud scream of joy and runs to him.*] Oh, father, father!

HIALMAR. [*Turns away and makes a ges-ture of repulsion.*] Away, away, away! [*To* GINA.] Keep her away from me, I say!

GINA. [*In a low tone.*] Go into the sitting-room, Hedvig. [HEDVIG *does so without a word.*]

HIALMAR. [*Fussily pulls out the table-drawer.*] I must have my books with me. Where are my books?

GINA. Which books?

HIALMAR. My scientific books, of course; the technical magazines I require for my invention.

GINA. [*Searches in the bookcase.*] Is it these here paper-covered ones?

HIALMAR. Yes, of course.

GINA. [*Lays a heap of magazines on the table.*] Shan't I get Hedvig to cut them for you?

HIALMAR. I don't require to have them cut for me. [*Short silence.*]

GINA. Then you're still set on leaving us, Ekdal?

HIALMAR. [*Rummaging amongst the books.*] Yes, that is a matter of course, I should think.

GINA. Well, well.

HIALMAR. [*Vehemently.*] How can I live here, to be stabbed to the heart every hour of the day?

GINA. God forgive you for thinking such vile things of me.

HIALMAR. Prove . . . !

GINA. I think it's you as has got to prove.

HIALMAR. After a past like yours? There are certain claims—I may almost call them claims of the ideal . . .

GINA. But what about grandfather? What's to become of him, poor dear!

HIALMAR. I know my duty; my helpless father will come with me. I am going out into the town to make arrangements . . . H'm— [*Hesitatingly.*]—has any one found my hat on the stairs?

GINA. No. Have you lost your hat?

HIALMAR. Of course I had it on when I came in last night; there's no doubt about that; but I couldn't find it this morning.

GINA. Lord help us! where have you been to with those two ne'er-do-wells?

HIALMAR. Oh, don't bother me about trifles. Do you suppose I am in the mood to remember details?

GINA. If only you haven't caught cold, Ekdal . . . [*Goes out into the kitchen.*]

HIALMAR. [*Talks to himself in a low tone of irritation, whilst he empties the table-drawer.*] You're a scoundrel, Relling!—You're a low fellow!—Ah, you shameless tempter!—I wish I could get some one to stick a knife into you! [*He lays some old letters on one side, finds the torn document of yesterday, takes it up and looks at the pieces; puts it down hurriedly as* GINA *enters.*]

GINA. [*Sets a tray with coffee, etc., on the table.*] Here's a drop of something hot, if you'd fancy it. And there's some bread and butter and a snack of salt meat.

HIALMAR. [*Glancing at the tray.*] Salt meat? Never under this roof! It's true I have not had a mouthful of solid food for nearly twenty-four hours; but no matter.—My memoranda! The commencement of my autobiography! What has become of my diary, and all my important papers? [*Opens the sitting-room door but draws back.*] She is there, too!

GINA. Good Lord! the child must be somewhere!

HIALMAR. Come out. [*He makes room,* HEDVIG *comes, scared, into the studio.*]

HIALMAR. [*With his hand upon the door-handle, says to* GINA.] In these, the last moments I spend in my former home, I wish to be spared from interlopers . . . [*Goes into the room.*]

HEDVIG. [*With a bound towards her mother, asks softly, trembling.*] Does that mean me?

GINA. Stay out in the kitchen, Hedvig; or, no—you'd best go into your own room. [*Speaks to* HIALMAR *as she goes in to him.*] Wait a bit, Ekdal; don't rummage so in the drawers; I know where everything is.

HEDVIG. [*Stands a moment immovable, in terror and perplexity, biting her lips to keep back the tears; then she clenches her hands convulsively and says softly.*] The wild duck. [*She steals over and takes the pistol from the shelf, opens the garret door a little way, creeps in and draws the door to after her.* HIALMAR *and* GINA *can be heard disputing in the sitting-room.*]

HIALMAR. [*Comes in with some manuscript books and old loose papers, which he lays upon the table.*] That portmanteau is of no use! There are a thousand and one things I must drag with me.

GINA. [*Following with the portmanteau.*] Why not leave all the rest for the present and only take a shirt and a pair of woollen drawers with you?

HIALMAR. Whew!—all these exhausting preparations . . . ! [*Pulls off his overcoat and throws it upon the sofa.*]

GINA. And there's the coffee getting cold.

HIALMAR. H'm. [*Drinks a mouthful without thinking of it and then another.*]

GINA. [*Dusting the backs of the chairs.*] A nice job you'll have to find such another big garret for the rabbits.

HIALMAR. What! Am I to drag all those rabbits with me, too?

GINA. You don't suppose grandfather can get on without his rabbits.

HIALMAR. He must just get used to doing without them. Have not *I* to sacrifice very much greater things than rabbits!

GINA. [*Dusting the bookcase.*] Shall I put the flute in the portmanteau for you?

HIALMAR. No. No flute for me. But give me the pistol!

GINA. Do you want to take the pistol with you?

HIALMAR. Yes. My loaded pistol.

GINA. [*Searching for it.*] It's gone. He must have taken it in with him.

HIALMAR. Is he in the garret?

GINA. Yes, of course he's in the garret.

HIALMAR. H'm—poor lonely old man. [*He takes a piece of bread and butter, eats it and finishes his cup of coffee.*]

GINA. If we hadn't have let that room, you could have moved in there.

HIALMAR. And continued to live under the same roof with . . . ! Never,—never!

GINA. But couldn't you put up with the sitting-room for a day or two? You could have it all to yourself.

HIALMAR. Never within these walls!

GINA. Well, then, down with Relling and Molvik.

HIALMAR. Don't mention those wretches' names to me! The very thought of them almost takes away my appetite.—Oh, no, I must go out into the storm and the snow-drift,—go from house to house and seek shelter for my father and my-self.

GINA. But you've got no hat, Ekdal! You've been and lost your hat, you know.

HIALMAR. Oh, those two brutes, those slaves of all the vices! A hat must be pro-cured. [*Takes another piece of bread and butter.*] Some arrangements must be made. For I have no mind to throw away my life, either. [*Looks for something on the tray.*]

GINA. What are you looking for?

HIALMAR. Butter.

GINA. I'll get some at once. [*Goes into the kitchen.*]

HIALMAR. [*Calls after her.*] Oh, it doesn't matter; dry bread is good enough for me.

GINA. [*Brings a dish of butter.*] Look here; this is fresh churned. [*She pours out another cup of coffee for him; he seats himself on the sofa, spreads more butter on the already buttered bread and eats and drinks awhile in silence.*]

HIALMAR. Could I, without being sub-ject to intrusion—intrusion of any sort—could I live in the sitting-room there for a day or two?

GINA. Yes, to be sure you could, if you only would.

HIALMAR. For I see no possibility of getting all father's things out in such a hurry.

GINA. And, besides, you've surely got to tell him first as you don't mean to live with us others no more.

HIALMAR. [*Pushes away his coffee cup.*] Yes, there is that, too; I shall have to lay bare the whole tangled story to him . . . I must turn matters over; I must have breathing-time; I cannot take all these burdens on my shoulders in a single day.

GINA. No, especially in such horrible weather as it is outside.

HIALMAR. [*Touching* WERLE'S *letter.*] I see that paper is still lying about here.

GINA. Yes, *I* haven't touched it.

HIALMAR. So far as I am concerned it is mere waste paper . . .

GINA. Well, *I* have certainly no notion of making any use of it.

HIALMAR. . . . but we had better not let it get lost all the same;—in all the upset when I move, it might easily . . .

GINA. I'll take good care of it, Ekdal.

HIALMAR. The donation is in the first instance made to father, and it rests with him to accept or decline it.

GINA. [*Sighs.*] Yes, poor old father . . .

HIALMAR. To make quite safe . . . Where shall I find some gum?

GINA. [*Goes to the bookcase.*] Here's the gum-pot.

HIALMAR. And a brush?

GINA. The brush is here, too. [*Brings him the things.*]

HIALMAR. [*Takes a pair of scissors.*] Just a strip of paper at the back . . . [*Clips and gums.*] Far be it from me to lay hands upon what is not my own—and least of all upon what belongs to a desti-tute old man—and to—the other as well.—There now. Let it lie there for a time; and when it is dry, take it away. I wish never to see that document again. Never! [GREGERS WERLE *enters from the passage.*]

GREGERS. [*Somewhat surprised.*] What, —are you sitting here, Hialmar?

HIALMAR. [*Rises hurriedly.*] I had sunk down from fatigue.

GREGERS. You have been having break-fast, I see.

HIALMAR. The body sometimes makes its claims felt, too.

GREGERS. What have you decided to do?

HIALMAR. For a man like me, there is only one course possible. I am just put-ting my most important things together. But it takes time, you know.

GINA. [*With a touch of impatience.*] Am I to get the room ready for you, or am I to pack your portmanteau?

HIALMAR. [*After a glance of annoy-ance at* GREGERS.] Pack—and get the room ready!

GINA. [*Takes the portmanteau.*] Very well; then I'll put in the shirt and the other things. [*Goes into the sitting-room and draws the door to after her.*]

GREGERS. [*After a short silence.*] I never dreamed that this would be the end of it. Do you really feel it a necessity to leave house and home?

HIALMAR. [*Wanders about restlessly.*] What would you have me do?—I am not fitted to bear unhappiness, Gregers. I must feel secure and at peace in my surroundings.

GREGERS. But can you not feel that here? Just try it. I should have thought you had firm ground to build upon now —if only you start afresh. And remember, you have your invention to live for.

HIALMAR. Oh, don't talk about my invention. It's perhaps still in the dim distance.

GREGERS. Indeed!

HIALMAR. Why, great heavens, what would you have me invent? Other people have invented almost everything already. It becomes more and more difficult every day . . .

GREGERS. And you have devoted so much labour to it.

HIALMAR. It was that blackguard Relling that urged me to it.

GREGERS. Relling?

HIALMAR. Yes, it was he that first made me realize my aptitude for making some notable discovery in photography.

GREGERS. Aha—it was Relling!

HIALMAR. Oh, I have been so truly happy over it! Not so much for the sake of the invention itself, as because Hedvig believed in it—believed in it with a child's whole eagerness of faith.—At least, I have been fool enough to go and imagine that she believed in it.

GREGERS. Can you really think Hedvig has been false to you?

HIALMAR. I can think anything now. It is Hedvig that stands in my way. She will blot out the sunlight from my whole life.

GREGERS. Hedvig! Is it Hedvig you are talking of? How should she blot out your sunlight?

HIALMAR. [Without answering.] How unutterably I have loved that child! How unutterably happy I have felt every time I came home to my humble room, and she flew to meet me, with her sweet little blinking eyes. Oh, confiding fool that I have been! I loved her unutterably;—and I yielded myself up to the dream, the delusion, that she loved me unutterably in return.

GREGERS. Do you call that a delusion?

HIALMAR. How should I know? I can get nothing out of Gina; and besides, she is totally blind to the ideal side of these complications. But to you I feel impelled to open my mind, Gregers. I cannot shake off this frightful doubt—perhaps Hedvig has never really and honestly loved me.

GREGERS. What would you say if she were to give you a proof of her love? [Listens.] What's that? I thought I heard the wild duck . . . ?

HIALMAR. It's the wild duck quacking. Father's in the garret.

GREGERS. Is he? [His face lights up with joy.] I say, you may yet have proof that your poor misunderstood Hedvig loves you!

HIALMAR. Oh, what proof can she give me? I dare not believe in any assurance from that quarter.

GREGERS. Hedvig does not know what deceit means.

HIALMAR. Oh, Gregers, that is just what I cannot be sure of. Who knows what Gina and that Mrs. Sörby may many a time have sat here whispering and tattling about? And Hedvig usually has her ears open, I can tell you. Perhaps the deed of gift was not such a surprise to her, after all. In fact, I'm not sure but that I noticed something of the sort.

GREGERS. What spirit is this that has taken possession of you?

HIALMAR. I have had my eyes opened. Just you notice;—you'll see, the deed of gift is only a beginning. Mrs. Sörby has always been a good deal taken up with Hedvig; and now she has the power to do whatever she likes for the child. They can take her from me whenever they please.

GREGERS. Hedvig will never, never leave you.

HIALMAR. Don't be so sure of that. If only they beckon to her and throw out a golden bait . . . ! And, oh! I have loved her so unspeakably! I would have counted it my highest happiness to take her tenderly by the hand and lead her, as one leads a timid child through a great dark empty room!—I am cruelly certain now that the poor photographer in his humble attic has never really and truly been anything to her. She has only cunningly contrived to keep on a good footing with him until the time came.

GREGERS. You don't believe that yourself, Hialmar.

HIALMAR. That is just the terrible part of it—I don't know what to believe,—I never can know it. But can you really doubt that it must be as I say? Ho-ho, you have far too much faith in the claim of the ideal, my good Gregers! If those others came, with the glamour of wealth about them, and called to the child:— "Leave him: come to us: here life awaits you . . . !"

GREGERS. [Quickly.] Well, what then?

HIALMAR. If I then asked her: Hedvig, are you willing to renounce that life for me? [Laughs scornfully.] No, thank you! You would soon hear what answer I should get. [A pistol shot is heard from within the garret.]

GREGERS. [Loudly and joyfully.] Hialmar!

HIALMAR. There now; he must needs go shooting, too.

GINA. [Comes in.] Oh, Ekdal, I can hear grandfather blazing away in the garret by hisself.

HIALMAR. I'll look in . . .

GREGERS. [Eagerly, with emotion.] Wait a moment! Do you know what that was?

HIALMAR. Yes, of course I know.

GREGERS. No, you don't know. But I do. That was the proof!

HIALMAR. What proof?

GREGERS. It was a child's free-will offering. She has got your father to shoot the wild duck.

HIALMAR. To shoot the wild duck!

GINA. Oh, think of that . . . !

HIALMAR. What was that for?

GREGERS. She wanted to sacrifice to you her most cherished possession; for then she thought you would surely come to love her again.

HIALMAR. [Tenderly, with emotion.] Oh, poor child!

GINA. What things she does think of!

GREGERS. She only wanted your love again, Hialmar. She could not live without it.

GINA. [Struggling with her tears.] There, you can see for yourself, Ekdal.

HIALMAR. Gina, where is she?

GINA. [Sniffs.] Poor dear, she's sitting out in the kitchen, I dare say.

HIALMAR. [Goes over, tears open the kitchen door and says.] Hedvig, come, come in to me! [Looks around.] No, she's not here.

GINA. Then she must be in her own little room.

HIALMAR. [Without.] No, she's not here either. [Comes in.] She must have gone out.

GINA. Yes, you wouldn't have her anywheres in the house.

HIALMAR. Oh, if she would only come home quickly, so that I can tell her . . . Everything will come right now, Gregers; now I believe we can begin life afresh.

GREGERS. [Quietly.] I knew it; I knew the child would make amends. [OLD EKDAL appears at the door of his room; he is in full uniform and is busy buckling on his sword.]

HIALMAR. [Astonished.] Father! Are you there?

GINA. Have you been firing in your room?

EKDAL. [Resentfully, approaching.] So you go shooting alone, do you, Hialmar?

HIALMAR. [Excited and confused.] Then it wasn't you that fired that shot in the garret?

EKDAL. Me that fired? H'm.

GREGERS. [Calls out to HIALMAR.] She has shot the wild duck herself!

HIALMAR. What can it mean? [Hastens to the garret door, tears it aside, looks in and calls loudly.] Hedvig!

GINA. [Runs to the door.] Good God, what's that!

HIALMAR. [Goes in.] She's lying on the floor!

GREGERS. Hedvig! lying on the floor! [Goes in to HIALMAR.]

GINA. [At the same time.] Hedvig! [Inside the garret.] No, no, no!

EKDAL. Ho-ho! does she go shooting, too, now? [HIALMAR, GINA and GREGERS carry HEDVIG into the studio; in her dangling right hand she holds the pistol fast clasped in her fingers.]

HIALMAR. [Distracted.] The pistol has gone off. She has wounded herself. Call for help! Help!

GINA. [*Runs into the passage and calls down.*] Relling! Relling! Doctor Relling; come up as quick as you can! [HIALMAR *and* GREGERS *lay* HEDVIG *down on the sofa.*]

EKDAL. [*Quietly.*] The woods avenge themselves.

HIALMAR. [*On his knees beside* HEDVIG.] She'll soon come to now. She's coming to . . . ; yes, yes, yes.

GINA. [*Who has come in again.*] Where has she hurt herself? I can't see anything . . . [RELLING *comes hurriedly, and immediately after him* MOLVIK; *the latter without his waistcoat and necktie, and with his coat open.*]

RELLING. What's the matter here?

GINA. They say Hedvig has shot herself.

HIALMAR. Come and help us!

RELLING. Shot herself! [*He pushes the table aside and begins to examine her.*]

HIALMAR. [*Kneeling and looking anxiously up at him.*] It can't be dangerous? Speak, Relling! She is scarcely bleeding at all. It can't be dangerous?

RELLING. How did it happen?

HIALMAR. Oh, we don't know . . .

GINA. She wanted to shoot the wild duck.

RELLING. The wild duck?

HIALMAR. The pistol must have gone off.

RELLING. H'm. Indeed.

EKDAL. The woods avenge themselves. But I'm not afraid, all the same. [*Goes into the garret and closes the door after him.*]

HIALMAR. Well, Relling,—why don't you say something?

RELLING. The ball has entered the breast.

HIALMAR. Yes, but she's coming to!

RELLING. Surely you can see that Hedvig is dead.

GINA. [*Bursts into tears.*] Oh, my child, my child . . .

GREGERS. [*Huskily.*] In the depths of the sea. . . .

HIALMAR. [*Jumps up.*] No, no, she must live! Oh, for God's sake, Relling— only a moment—only just till I can tell her how unspeakably I loved her all the time!

RELLING. The bullet has gone through her heart. Internal hemorrhage. Death must have been instantaneous.

HIALMAR. And I! I hunted her from me like an animal! And she crept terrified into the garret and died for love of me! [*Sobbing.*] I can never atone to her! I can never tell her . . . ! [*Clenches his hands and cries, upwards.*] O thou above . . . ! If thou be indeed! Why hast thou done this thing to me?

GINA. Hush, hush, you mustn't go on that awful way. We had no right to keep her, I suppose.

MOLVIK. The child is not dead, but sleepeth.

RELLING. Bosh!

HIALMAR. [*Becomes calm, goes over to the sofa, folds his arms and looks at* HEDVIG.] There she lies so stiff and still.

RELLING. [*Tries to loosen the pistol.*] She's holding it so tight, so tight.

GINA. No, no, Relling, don't break her fingers; let the pistol be.

HIALMAR. She shall take it with her.

GINA. Yes, let her. But the child mustn't lie here for a show. She shall go to her own room, so she shall. Help me, Ekdal. [HIALMAR *and* GINA *take* HEDVIG *between them.*]

HIALMAR. [*As they are carrying her.*] Oh, Gina, Gina, can you survive this!

GINA. We must help each other to bear it. For now at least she belongs to both of us.

MOLVIK. [*Stretches out his arms and mumbles.*] Blessed be the Lord; to earth thou shalt return; to earth thou shalt return . . .

RELLING. [*Whispers.*] Hold your tongue, you fool; you're drunk. [HIALMAR *and* GINA *carry the body out through the kitchen door.* RELLING *shuts it after them.* MOLVIK *slinks out into the passage.*]

RELLING. [*Goes over to* GREGERS *and says.*] No one shall ever convince me that the pistol went off by accident.

GREGERS. [*Who has stood terrified, with convulsive twitchings.*] Who can say how the dreadful thing happened?

RELLING. The powder has burnt the body of her dress. She must have pressed the pistol right against her breast and fired.

GREGERS. Hedvig has not died in vain. Did you not see how sorrow set free what is noble in him?

RELLING. Most people are ennobled by the actual presence of death. But how long do you suppose this nobility will last in him?

GREGERS. Why should it not endure and increase throughout his life?

RELLING. Before a year is over, little Hedvig will be nothing to him but a pretty theme for declamation.

GREGERS. How dare you say that of Hialmar Ekdal?

RELLING. We will talk of this again, when the grass has first withered on her grave. Then you'll hear him spouting about "the child too early torn from her father's heart"; then you'll see him steep himself in a syrup of sentiment and self-admiration and self-pity. Just you wait!

GREGERS. If you are right and I am wrong, then life is not worth living.

RELLING. Oh, life would be quite tolerable, after all, if only we could be rid of the confounded duns that keep on pestering us, in our poverty, with the claim of the ideal.

GREGERS. [*Looking straight before him.*] In that case, I am glad that my destiny is what is.

RELLING. May I inquire,—what is your destiny?

GREGERS. [*Going.*] To be the thirteenth at table.

RELLING. The devil it is.

THE CURTAIN FALLS

Death comes to summon Everyman in a scene from an outdoor performance of the play given before a cathedral.

Courtesy Friedman-Abeles

Two scenes from the New York production of THE DESPERATE HOURS. *The direct, physical nature of the play's conflict is illustrated in the scene with Paul Newman, Malcolm Brodrick, and Karl Malden.*

BLOOD WEDDING, *a production utilizing black against a stark white set to emphasize the ritualistic nature of Lorca's poetic folk tragedy.*

Laurence Olivier, as an aging Caesar, crowns Vivien Leigh as Cleopatra in a New York production of the Shaw comedy. The kittenish queen is impressed with her new solemnity.

CAESAR AND CLEOPATRA, *Act I, Scene 2, of the Theatre Guild's 1925 production.*

TWELFTH NIGHT, *Act II, Scene 3, in a performance at Ashland, Oregon, on an open-air Elizabethan stage. Malvolio reads his letter while Sir Toby Belch, Sir Andrew Aguecheek, and Fabian watch from above.*

OTHELLO, Act II, Scene 5, at the Ashland, Oregon Shakespearean Festival. Cassio is restrained while Othello glowers, believing him guilty.

OEDIPUS REX, *performed at the Stratford Shakespearean Festival, Ontario, Canada. Using masks, as in the oldest Greek productions, the characters achieve added stature.*

Part
Two

The Major
Modes of
Drama

The world of the play is, we have said, a created world. Plays are made of plots and themes, of characters and settings, but also, we soon realize, of something more. To seek only among the formal elements of a play for a full understanding of the power of drama would be but another case of the trees hiding the forest, of the beams, bricks, and rafters obscuring the structure of which they are but parts. Like all literature, drama depends for its power to attract and move audiences not on its technical virtuosity but on what it says to the minds and emotions of those audiences. Plays that exert a spell over one generation after another endure that critical test of time because they continue to provide insights into our lives. If they did not help us to that essential revaluation of experience, they would not survive. And so, though the dramatic experience, like the experience of life itself, is not separable from the materials and forms that comprise it (save for the purposes of analysis), we must seek through and beyond the formal elements for the inner secret of the drama.

The created world of the play, like all created worlds, has what our actual world so frequently seems to lack—an organizing principle that gives it meaning. A good play must be built of the materials of actual experience or it will seem artificial; but it must also have something more if it is to be other than a mere copy of life and hence without a real vitality of its own. We call this vitalizing principle the playwright's vision. This vision stems from his basic attitudes toward his society and his life. Like those unspoken underlying assumptions which determine the kind of world structure the scientist or the philosopher is likely to imagine, the dramatist's vision controls all the other elements in his play, dictating not only the choice of materials but also their order and arrangement. It is both the initiating spirit and the point of view from which the dramatist sees the events which he shows in his play.

Traditionally, discussions of the drama speak of a comic spirit and a tragic spirit which are sometimes said to move the dramatist to write, sometimes said to inform his work; they also speak of a comic vision and a tragic vision which are said to emerge from that work. Such statements define perhaps as accurately as possible the creative process by which comedy and tragedy come into being. They reveal also that the terms comedy and tragedy are sometimes used in a descriptive sense and sometimes in a normative sense. The introductions to the following comedies and tragedies attempt substantially the same two-fold purpose: to describe how the formal elements of the play are controlled by the dramatist's vision, comic or tragic; and to define and comment on the value of the comic and tragic visions of life contained in the plays.

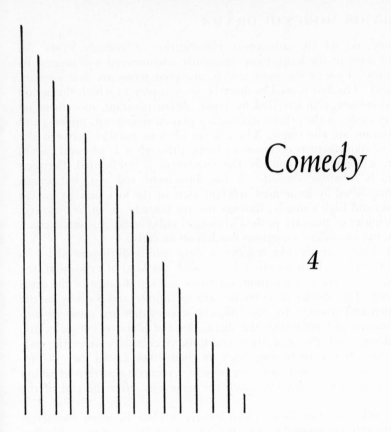

Comedy

4

THE FORM OF COMEDY

It may be true in life that what appears comic to one man will appear tragic to the next. But in the drama such confusion is not possible; a comedy always announces itself, and everybody knows what a comedy is. If a play makes you laugh, and if it has a happy ending, it is a comedy. Define laughter to include the superior smile and the even less pleasant smirk, as well as the hearty guffaw; recognize the ambiguity of "happy"; and the definition, though an obvious oversimplification, has some empiric validity. For we do laugh at most comedies (although also at some things which are not comic), and most comedies do have what seems to be a happy ending: the hero does not die, but gets what he appears to want—the girl. The definition has one value besides its apparent simplicity. It points to two basic approaches in discussing comedy: the analysis of the reaction of the audience, and the analysis of the structure of the play. We can, that is, approach comedy by analyzing its effect on the reader, asking, for example, why he laughs and what he laughs at. (To this question of the psychology of laughter, largely beyond the scope of this book, we will return briefly in a discussion of the comic vision.) Or we can consider how the dramatist handles the elements of story, theme, and character in the various kinds of plays called comedies.

Unfortunately, no wholly satisfactory classification of comedy exists. An enumeration of some of the kinds most frequently encountered will suggest its range and variety. Two of the most widely accepted terms are *low comedy* and *high comedy*. The first is used to describe *farce*, a play in which the action and situation dominate, characterized by rapid, almost constant, movement on stage. A high comedy, at the other extreme, is a play in which wit, raillery, and clever conversation are the staple. There is an obvious parallel between the two; rapidity of movement is common to both, although it is physical movement in farce, while in high comedy the movement is intellectual. Between these extremes is *romantic comedy;* it has movement and wit, but essentially it is distinguished by its amused, tolerant view of the love-play of human beings. And beyond high comedy, moving toward tragedy, is *satiric comedy*, in which the vanities of men are probed in critical indictment; it is intellectual, its wit is sharp, and its raillery sometimes borders on invective.

Whatever its kind, comedy, like tragedy, is most readily distinguished by its plot, by the pattern by which the story is revealed—the kind of exposition, the relative complexity of the complication, the place and significance of the crisis and dénouement. The stories of comedies are as infinite and various as the activities of men and women, for the subjects of comedies are those all-too-common pettinesses and prejudices we share. But the plots of comedies are, generally speaking, much the same; they tend to be circular or concentric, ending up where they began, or turning back on themselves. Often they do not press forward to any real conclusion, but present a recurring pattern of action that can be expected to continue in much the same way after the end of the play.

Since the conflicts in comedies seldom involve a clash between characters wholly or inalterably committed to a particular way of life, no final or binding solution to their problems is necessary. This typical comic pattern contrasts with the linear pattern inherent in tragedy—the pattern that shows men striving to reach eternal goals and failing. The use of a pattern of seemingly random movement enables the comic dramatist to concentrate not on the destiny of man but on those foibles and eccentricities that keep us in our usual turmoil.

The characters and themes of comedies are similarly distinctive, but there is another characteristic which, linked with plot, makes possible the immediate identification of a comedy. It is *tone*—what we feel to be the attitude of the author to his audience. We can feel it in the opening speeches; it is bound up with the wit and the verbal play. It is a feeling we get from the movement on stage. Gently mocking and gently chiding, it is one of the author's chief devices for getting us to listen to him. It is his way of saying, "You and I may not be so important as we think we are, but then neither are we such fools as we think each other to be." It is his way of telling us that frustration is not an inherent quality in life, but one that we in our folly bring to it.

Farce

Because it is almost all action and bustle, farce is the most obvious kind of comedy. Dominated by rapid movement, usually physical and frequently gross, farce affords the best examples of comedy's circular plot. But farce is not wholly a matter of overt physical actions on the level of Abbott and Costello hitting each other with sandbags. Frequently the action arises from some sort of physical incongruity (the small, timid male mated to the large, overbearing wife; the little, frail musician playing the biggest drum, and the fat, husky one playing the tiniest flute). Sometimes it arises from the calm acceptance of the irrational and non-normal in everyday affairs (for example, Charlie Chaplin's famous scene in *The Gold Rush* when, as a starving prospector in Alaska, he patiently cooks and tenderly devours an old shoe). Or it may arise from the intrusion of unexpected behavior into a given situation, as in much of the film comedy of W. C. Fields and the Marx brothers. Consider the slip on the banana skin as the classic farce scene; what is involved beyond the gyrations of the victim is the reduction of false dignity, the punishing of pride by humiliation. By deflating the grandiose, by shocking men out of their presuppositions and stripping them of their pretensions, in its own rough and ready way farce joins the other forms of comedy in restoring that sanity which comes from seeing oneself in a proper perspective.

Because of the immediacy and the spontaneity of its appeal, farce is sometimes compared to melodrama. The comparison is valid in that both types use overt physical action and usually confine themselves to a few obvious situations; but there are significant structural differences which help to reveal something of the mode of comedy. In *The Desperate Hours*, Joseph Hayes spends most of the first two scenes providing the necessary background. In a farce, we usually just walk in on the characters and soon come to know them by seeing them as they are, through a series of actions which all say the same thing. Since such characters are not going anywhere in the sense that characters in a serious play are striving toward some particular end—a desired end which occasions the conflict in the play—characters in a farce will be doing much the same thing when the curtain goes down as when it went up. Where they have come from is not important; only what they do while we are with them matters. Farce, like comedy in general, is not primarily concerned with motive and hence spends little time on exposition. Further, in a melodrama the action is sequential, each event evolving out of the previous one; to break the chain is to destroy the play. But in a farce the bits of action are like spokes of a wheel: they all come out of the same center and are limited by the circumference of the situation, but no necessary logical connection exists among them.

There are elements of farce in most comic plays, notably in those of Aristophanes, Shakespeare, and Molière; and there are some comedies that are almost exclusively farcical. One of the best of the latter, George S. Kaufman and Moss Hart's *You Can't Take It With You*, provides a clear illustration of this circularity of the comic plot. This is one of the depression comedies, so popular in the 1930's, a play about a lower middle class family with few financial resources. An abundant good humor gives them the ability to survive and to love life, and each accepts and even cherishes the eccentricities of the others. The pace of the play is frantic; its action, uninhibited. The Sycamore family is a group of individualists, each of whom blithely goes his own way, doing what he likes best: father makes fireworks in the basement; mother writes novels because someone once delivered a typewriter to the house by mistake; one daughter takes ballet lessons from an impoverished Russian ballet master, Kolenkhov, who always manages to arrive at mealtimes; and a Mr. De Pinna who once came to help father with his fireworks settled down and stayed. Presiding over the family is old Grandpa Vanderhof, with his gentle philosophy of "live and let live."

A single scene from this play will illustrate the nature of farce. At the end of the second act, the Sycamores find themselves the surprised but undaunted hosts of the Kirbys, a wealthy and stuffy family to whose son, Tony, Alice Sycamore has become engaged. The son and daughter have arranged for the two families to meet at dinner—but the Kirbys arrive on the wrong night, finding the Sycamore household at its most disorganized. In addition to the usual commotion, Mrs. Sycamore is painting a picture of Mr. De Pinna, who is posing in the living room in a Roman toga; Grandpa Vanderhof is playing a game of darts; Mr. Sycamore's Erector set (one of his hobbies) is scattered about on the floor; and Gay Wellington, an unsteady actress interested in one of Mrs. Sycamore's plays, has passed out on the couch. Cheerfully ignoring all these unusual activities (or, rather, pretending they are the most natural things in the world—as they are for them), the Sycamores set out to entertain the Kirbys, but their ingenuousness drives their guests to desperation. As the Kirbys rise to leave, the following scene occurs, bringing the act to an end:

KIRBY. It's been very nice to have met you all. . . . Are you coming, Anthony?
TONY. No, Father. I'm not.
KIRBY. I see. . . . Your mother and I will be waiting for you at home. . . . Good night. [*With* MRS. KIRBY *on his arm, he sweeps toward the outer door.*]
[*Before the* KIRBYS *can take more than a step toward the door, however, a new* FIGURE *looms up in the archway. It is a quiet and competent-looking individual with a steely eye, and two more just like him loom up behind him.*]
THE MAN. [*Very quietly.*] Stay right where you are, everybody. [*There is a little scream from* MRS. KIRBY, *an exclamation from* PENNY.] Don't move.
PENNY. Oh, good heavens!
KIRBY. How dare you? Why, what does this mean?
GRANDPA. What *is* all this?
KIRBY. I demand an explanation!
THE MAN. Keep your mouth shut, you! [*He advances slowly into the room, looking the group over. Then he turns to one of his men.*] Which one is it?
ANOTHER MAN. [*Goes over and puts a hand on* ED's *shoulder.*] This is him.
ESSIE. Ed!
ED. [*Terrified.*] Why, what do you mean?
ALICE. Grandpa, what is it?
KIRBY. This is an outrage!
THE MAN. Shut up! [*He turns to* ED.] What's your name?
ED. Edward—Carmichael. I haven't done anything.
THE MAN. You haven't, huh?
GRANDPA. [*Not at all scared.*] This seems rather high-handed to me. What's it all about?
THE MAN. Department of Justice.
PENNY. Oh, my goodness! J-men!
ESSIE. Ed, what have you done?
ED. I haven't done anything.
GRANDPA. What's the boy done, Officer?
ALICE. What is it? What's it all about?
THE MAN. [*Taking his time, and surveying the room.*] That door lead to the cellar?
PENNY. Yes, it does.
PAUL. Yes.

THE MAN. [*Ordering a man to investigate.*] Mac . . . [MAC *goes into the cellar.*] . . . Jim!

JIM. Yes, sir.

THE MAN. Take a look upstairs and see what you find.

JIM. Okay. [JIM *goes upstairs.*]

ED. [*Panicky.*] I haven't done anything!

THE MAN. Come here, you! [*He takes some slips of paper out of his pocket.*] Ever see these before?

ED. [*Gulping.*] They're my—circulars.

THE MAN. You print this stuff, huh?

ED. Yes, sir.

THE MAN. And you put 'em into boxes of candy to get 'em into people's homes.

ESSIE. The Love Dreams!

ED. But I didn't mean anything!

THE MAN. You didn't, huh? [*He reads the circulars.*] "Dynamite the Capitol!" "Dynamite the White House!" "Dynamite the Supreme Court!" "God is the State; the State is God!"

ED. But I didn't mean that. I just like to print. Don't I, Grandpa? [DONALD *returns with the eggs at this point, and stands quietly watching the proceedings.*]

GRANDPA. Now, Officer, the government's in no danger from Ed. Printing is just his hobby, that's all. He prints anything.

THE MAN. He does, eh?

PENNY. I never heard of such nonsense.

KIRBY. I refuse to stay here and— [MR. DE PINNA, *at this point, is shoved through the cellar door by* MAC, *protesting as he comes.*]

DE PINNA. Hey, let me get my pipe, will you? Let me get my pipe.

MAC. Shut up, you! . . . We were right, Chief. They've got enough gunpowder down there to blow up the whole city.

PAUL. But we only use that—

THE MAN. Keep still! . . . Everybody in this house is under arrest.

KIRBY. What's that?

MRS. KIRBY. Oh, good heavens!

GRANDPA. Now look here, Officer—this is all nonsense.

DE PINNA. You'd better let me get my pipe. I left it—

THE MAN. Shut up, all of you!

KOLENKHOV. It seems to me, Officer—

THE MAN. Shut up! [*From the stairs comes the sound of drunken singing—"There was a young lady." etc.* GAY WELLINGTON, *wrapped in* PENNY's *negligee, is being carried down the stairway by a somewhat bewildered* G-MAN.]

THE G-MAN. Keep still, you! Stop that! Stop it!

THE LEADER. [*After* GAY *has been persuaded to quiet down.*] Who's that?

GRANDPA. [*Pretty tired of the whole business.*] That—is my mother.

[*And then, suddenly, we hear from the cellar.* MR. DE PINNA *seems to have been right about his pipe, to judge from the sounds below. It is a whole year's supply of fireworks—bombs, big crackers, little crackers, skyrockets, pin wheels, everything. The house is fairly rocked by the explosion.*]

[*In the room, of course, pandemonium reigns.* MRS. KIRBY *screams; the* G-MAN *drops* GAY *right where he stands and dashes for the cellar, closely followed by* MR. DE PINNA *and* PAUL; PENNY *dashes for her manuscripts and* ED *rushes to save his xylophone.* KOLENKHOV *waves his arms wildly and dashes in all directions at once; everyone is rushing this way and that.*]

[*All except one. The exception, of course, is* GRANDPA, *who takes all things as they come.* GRANDPA *just says, "Well, well, well!"—and sits down. If a lot of people weren't in the way, in fact, you feel he'd like to throw a few darts.*]

CURTAIN

As the excerpt indicates, this play, like other comedies in the same category, is concerned not so much with the problem of *becoming*, of arriving at some goal, some outcome of an action; rather, it relates to the problem of *being*, of living now; and to speak of an ending to this sort of play is something of an anomaly if by "ending" we mean "terminus." Something does come to an end, of course, in *You Can't Take It With You*—namely, the particular bit of action we have been witnessing. But the ending is not, as it is in tragedy, a destination, a finality. We call the ending of a comedy "happy," not because of the prospect of marriage and bliss, but because the characters have been saved from the possible calamities inherent in their follies. Playwrights tend, of course, to use the clinch, and the hint of marriage that makes a union respectable; indeed, each of the comedies in this book, except *Caesar and Cleopatra*, is brought to a satisfactory close by the union of male and female. But such a union is merely a convenient device for stopping the play, and many a dramatist, from Shakespeare to the lowliest scribbler, has been accused of matching off his characters merely to allow the curtain to come down. These dramatists do not necessarily use the happy ending because they believe in the eternal bliss it proffers, but because everyone recognizes it for what it is, a pleasant stop-over on a journey never to be completed. Unlike the end of tragedy, the end of comedy is but the preface to a new beginning.

Finally, much comedy, especially farce, has something of the quality of a record played at double speed. And—to turn to the presence of yet another element in comedy—it is a simple rule of thumb that, to continue the figure, when the record slows down it will make a theme statement. Theme statements in comedies usually point out the inconsistencies and incongruities in our own lives. And the perception of incongruity, the source of wit and the occasion of laughter, is highly significant as a vehicle for the criticism of life. Even more forcefully than sermons can, comedy leads us to evaluate the scene around us critically. Behind the mad action of comedy in general and farce in particular, there is often a simple lesson: enjoy life and your part in it.

The comedies in this book illustrate different solutions to the dramatist's problem of creating situations in which the comic vision may be revealed. The first play, William Saroyan's *The Time of Your Life*, is a joyous and uninhibited comedy, containing strong elements of farce, in which eccentricity becomes a norm; it presents a bizarre set of characters and tries to make a philosophy out of their simple wishes. The second, Bernard Shaw's *Caesar and Cleopatra*, is a more profound character study, its humor subdued but worldly and wise. The last, Shakespeare's *Twelfth Night*, shows a topsy-turvy world in which nothing is what it seems to be, appearance and reality becoming almost hopelessly confused. Despite differences in speech, setting, and story, certain similarities will emerge, similarities which will show the robust and enduring nature of the comic spirit, a spirit that enlightens and entertains man, that forces him to learn through his own laughter.

WILLIAM SAROYAN: *THE TIME OF YOUR LIFE*

A theme or point of view may be made apparent in the pattern of action of a comedy, or it may be stated more explicitly, as it is in *The Time of Your Life*. Without the obvious marks of the serious problem play, Saroyan's philosophical comedy makes the point that without warmth, compassion, and affection, life becomes a sordid affair. It offers an effective and moving criticism of the frustrating tensions and loveless relationships that many of us endure; it brings to life on the stage, in comic terms, a whole attitude toward man, and it suggests for his use a set of values by which he may govern his conduct.

The Time of Your Life is a virtually plotless play; this fact may disturb some readers and spectators, who will keep waiting for something to happen. Some will wait in vain; others will come to realize that the very point of the play depends on the absence of plot in the conventional sense. The play, that is, represents a "slice of life," but not in the sense in which that term is applied to the frequently grim and sordid realistic and naturalistic literature of the twentieth century. Rather, *The Time of Your Life* gives us a glimpse of a variety of characters as they drift in and out of a San Francisco bar, each cherishing his own individuality. The locale could easily be the setting for a tragedy of deprivation and frustration (as it is in Eugene O'Neill's *The Iceman Cometh*). Instead, Saroyan peoples it with warm-hearted beings who are content with little in a material sense and who exult in the sheer joy of living. The play becomes, actually, the dramatization of a philosophical attitude toward man, an attitude that accepts man and all his peculiarities, and which blithely disposes of evil when it appears in the form of those who would corrupt man by depriving him of his individuality and destroying his natural innocence.

Let us anticipate for a moment our reading of the play by summarizing the situation it presents. It is set in Nick's Pacific Street Saloon, Restaurant, and Entertainment Palace (the name disguises a waterfront honky-tonk) at the foot of the Embarcadero in San Francisco. Here, at a center table, sits Joe, young man of indefinite status but considerable means. If there is a central character in the play, it is Joe, who remains here throughout the play, observing and occasionally regulating the action that goes on around him. He takes his pleasure from simple things; he sends his faithful disciple Tom after toys and chewing gum, he distributes money to old men and young boys, he allows a newsboy to take advantage of him by selling him his whole stock of papers, and he encourages a romance between Tom and Kitty Duval, whose worth as a human being he sees underneath her shoddy exterior.

And that is all. People come and go; we see briefly into their lives and get snatches of their stories. Evil intrudes once in the form of the sadistic vice-squad officer, Blick, but he is promptly dispatched by an ancient cowboy who calls himself Kit Carson and who soon weaves the story of the killing of Blick into his other legends of the past. The good, the simple, and the beautiful prevail in the wondrous world of William Saroyan.

Certain problems face the prospective reader of *The Time of Your Life*. More than most plays, this one must be visualized as it is read, for it is a play in which the dialogue by no means tells the whole story. In the San Francisco Saloon in which the action occurs. many characters drift in and out, some remaining on stage throughout most of the play, intent on their own business, but speaking very little. There is Nick, the proprietor, for example—proud of his own place, expansive, affectionate toward all. He is almost constantly present, sometimes serving at the bar, sometimes sitting and reading a newspaper, now and then moving about the stage to wipe off a table or straighten a chair. The picture of normal complacency, he helps by his very presence to establish the tone of the play. Then there is Willie, the marble-game addict, who has almost no dialogue except on the one occasion when he scores a memorable victory over the machine; throughout the reading of the play he must nevertheless be "seen," for he is always there, feeding nickels into the monster. His silent presence—the picture of man grimly determined not to be vanquished by the gorgeous gadgets he has created—adds much to the total atmosphere of the play. Another near-silent character is even more significant. This is the old Arab, who stands at the bar throughout the play, drinking, and now and then muttering one single line: "No foundation. All the way down the line." He functions as a kind of rueful chorus; his one reiterated line is a wistful, poetic comment on the instability of man and his dreams. One must always see him in the background.

There are other important minor characters: the amiable drunk who frequently ambles into the bar, checks the pay-telephone to see if anyone has left any change in it, and strolls out without a word to anyone; Wesley, who sits at the piano, now and then playing a few bars of mournful jazz; and Nick's mother, who bursts in for a moment or so of excited, voluble talk. Each of these characters adds his bit to the total picture of man's life which the play gives. Each is an individual, eccentric by some standards; but, as Saroyan says, each is "living, and letting live . . . following his destiny as he feels it should be followed." If these are "little" people who will never lead armies, make millions of dollars, form corporations, or become successful in the eyes of the world, neither will they wittingly harm anyone else nor invent atomic bombs with which to blow up their fellows.

Apart from the important but easily overlooked presence of such characters, another point that must be kept in mind is that there are often three or four things going on at once on the stage, each of individual importance and all blending to form the composite picture of searching, seeking, living humanity the play offers. Thus, at one point in Act I Joe and Kitty are carrying on a conversation at Joe's table, Nick at the bar is interviewing Harry about a job, and Dudley is making an impassioned plea to his girl friend on the telephone. On other occasions the play may remind one of the climax of a three-ring circus, with frantic activity all over the place. The simultaneity of these events, however, not the nature of the events themselves, is what is significant; the fact that each character pursues his own course, largely unmindful of other events about him, leads to the very meaning of the play. Each character, that is, has achieved a state of grace by being himself; each has escaped from the stresses and fears imposed by the world and has found a happy innocence and an incorruptible purity simply by acting as if every person is naturally good and every manifestation of the human personality is to be cherished.

It is obvious, even from so brief a description, that *The Time of Your Life* is not a conventional comedy. It asks us almost to ignore its action, or rather to take for granted its various bits of action as being part of a formula for living. Curious in its form, it has been called a circus and a carnival, but also, significantly, a hymn and a sermon. It is a play in which an ideal is envisioned in the midst of noisy comedy. In exalting the individual, it insists on his right to do anything he pleases, so long as he hurts no one else. "In the time of your life, live," Saroyan says in the preface; and the effect of the play is to instill a sense of the magic and delight, the sheer ecstasy, of being alive. It urges living mortal man to discover and use all the potentialities of whatever life has been given to him.

The Time of Your Life

By

WILLIAM SAROYAN

THE PLACE: *Nick's Pacific Street Saloon, Restaurant, and Entertainment Palace at the foot of Embarcadero, in San Francisco. A suggestion of room 21 at The New York Hotel, upstairs, around the corner.*

THE TIME: *Afternoon and night of a day in October, 1939.*

In the time of your life, live—so that in that good time there shall be no ugliness or death for yourself or for any life your life touches. Seek goodness everywhere, and when it is found, bring it out of its hiding-place and let it be free and unashamed. Place in matter and in flesh the least of the values, for these are the things that hold death and must pass away. Discover in all things that which shines and is beyond corruption. Encourage virtue in whatever heart it may have been driven into secrecy and sorrow by the shame and terror of the world. Ignore the obvious, for it is unworthy of the clear eye and the kindly heart. Be the inferior of no man, nor of any man be the superior. Remember that every man is a variation of yourself. No man's guilt is not yours, nor is any man's innocence a thing apart. Despise evil and ungodliness, but not men of ungodliness or evil. These, understand. Have no shame in being kindly and gentle, but if the time comes in the time of your life to kill, kill and have no regret. In the time of your life, live—so that in that wondrous time you shall not add to the misery and sorrow of the world, but shall smile to the infinite delight and mystery of it.

ACT ONE

NICK'S is an American place: a San Francisco waterfront honky-tonk.

At a table, JOE: always calm, always quiet, always thinking, always eager, always bored, always superior. His expensive clothes are casually and youthfully

220

worn and give him an almost boyish appearance. He is thinking.

Behind the bar, NICK: a big red-headed young Italian-American with an enormous naked woman tattooed in red on the inside of his right arm. He is studying The Racing Form.

The ARAB, at his place at the end of the bar. He is a lean old man with a rather ferocious old-country mustache, with the ends twisted up. Between the thumb and forefinger of his left hand is the Mohammedan tattoo indicating that he has been to Mecca. He is sipping a glass of beer.

It is about eleven-thirty in the morning. SAM is sweeping out. We see only his back. He disappears into the kitchen. The SAILOR at the bar finishes his drink and leaves, moving thoughtfully, as though he were trying very hard to discover how to live.

The NEWSBOY comes in.

NEWSBOY. [*Cheerfully.*] Good-morning, everybody. [*No answer. To* NICK.] Paper, Mister? [NICK *shakes his head, no. The* NEWSBOY *goes to* JOE.] Paper, Mister? [JOE *shakes his head, no. The* NEWSBOY *walks away, counting papers.*]

JOE. [*Noticing him.*] How many you got?

NEWSBOY. Five. [JOE *gives him a quarter, takes all the papers, glances at the headlines with irritation, throws them away. The* NEWSBOY *watches carefully, then goes.*]

ARAB. [*Picks up paper, looks at headlines, shakes head as if rejecting everything else a man might say about the world.*] No foundation. All the way down the line. [*The* DRUNK *comes in. Walks to the telephone, looks for a nickel in the chute, sits down at* JOE's *table.* NICK *takes the* DRUNK *out. The* DRUNK *returns.*]

DRUNK. [*Champion of the Bill of Rights.*] This is a free country, ain't it? [WILLIE, *the marble-game maniac, explodes through the swinging doors and lifts the forefinger of his right hand comically, indicating one beer. He is a very young man, not more than twenty. He is wearing heavy shoes, a pair of old and dirty corduroys, a light green turtle-neck jersey with a large letter "F" on the*

chest, an oversize two-button tweed coat, and a green hat, with the brim up. NICK *sets out a glass of beer for him, he drinks it, straightens up vigorously saying "Aaah," makes a solemn face, gives* NICK *a one-finger salute of adieu, and begins to leave, refreshed and restored in spirit. He walks by the marble game, halts suddenly, turns, studies the contraption, gestures as if to say, Oh, no. Turns to go, stops, returns to the machine, studies it, takes a handful of small coins out of his pants pocket, lifts a nickel, indicates with a gesture, One game, no more. Puts the nickel in the slot, pushes in the slide, making an interesting noise.*]

NICK. You can't beat that machine.

WILLIE. Oh, yeah? [*The marbles fall, roll, and take their place. He pushes down the lever, placing one marble in position. Takes a very deep breath, walks in a small circle, excited at the beginning of great drama. Stands straight and pious before the contest. Himself vs. the machine. Willie vs. Destiny. His skill and daring vs. the cunning and trickery of the novelty industry of America, and the whole challenging world. He is the last of the American pioneers, with nothing more to fight but the machine, with no other reward than lights going on and off, and six nickels for one. Before him is the last champion, the machine. He is the last challenger, the young man with nothing to do in the world.* WILLIE *grips the knob delicately, studies the situation carefully, draws the knob back, holds it a moment, and then releases it. The first marble rolls out among the hazards, and the contest is on. At the very beginning of the play "The Missouri Waltz" is coming from the phonograph. The music ends here. This is the signal for the beginning of the play.* JOE *suddenly comes out of his reverie. He whistles the way people do who are calling a cab that's about a block away, only he does it quietly.* WILLIE *turns around, but* JOE *gestures for him to return to his work.* NICK *looks up from The Racing Form.*]

JOE. [*Calling.*] Tom. [*To himself.*] Where the hell is he, every time I need him? [*He looks around calmly: the nickel-in-the-slot phonograph in the cor-*

ner; the open public telephone; the stage; the marble-game; the bar; and so on. He calls again, this time very loud.] Hey, Tom.

NICK. [*With morning irritation.*] What do you want?

JOE. [*Without thinking.*] I want the boy to get me a watermelon, that's what *I* want. What do *you* want? Money, or love, or fame, or what? You won't get them studying The Racing Form.

NICK. I like to keep abreast of the times. [TOM *comes hurrying in. He is a great big man of about thirty or so who appears to be much younger because of the childlike expression of his face: handsome, dumb, innocent, troubled, and a little bewildered by everything. He is obviously adult in years, but it seems as if by all rights he should still be a boy. He is defensive as clumsy, self-conscious, overgrown boys are. He is wearing a flashy cheap suit.* JOE *leans back and studies him with casual disapproval.* TOM *slackens his pace and becomes clumsy and embarrassed, waiting for the bawling-out he's pretty sure he's going to get.*]

JOE. [*Objectively, severely, but a little amused.*] Who saved your life?

TOM. [*Sincerely.*] You did, Joe. Thanks.

JOE. [*Interested.*] How'd I do it?

TOM. [*Confused.*] What?

JOE. [*Even more interested.*] How'd I do it?

TOM. Joe, you know how you did it.

JOE. [*Softly.*] I want you to answer me. How'd I save your life? I've forgotten.

TOM. [*Remembering, with a big sorrowful smile.*] You made me eat all that chicken soup three years ago when I was sick and hungry.

JOE. [*Fascinated.*] Chicken soup?

TOM. [*Eagerly.*] Yeah.

JOE. Three years? Is it that long?

TOM. [*Delighted to have the information.*] Yeah, sure. 1937. 1938. 1939. This is 1939, Joe.

JOE. [*Amused.*] Never mind what year it is. Tell me the whole story.

TOM. You took me to the doctor. You gave me money for food and clothes, and

paid my room rent. Aw, Joe, you know all the different things you did. [JOE *nods, turning away from* TOM *after each question.*]

JOE. You in good health now?

TOM. Yeah, Joe.

JOE. You got clothes?

TOM. Yeah, Joe.

JOE. You eat three times a day. Sometimes four?

TOM. Yeah, Joe. Sometimes five.

JOE. You got a place to sleep?

TOM. Yeah, Joe. [JOE *nods. Pauses. Studies* TOM *carefully.*]

JOE. Then, where the hell have you been?

TOM. [*Humbly.*] Joe, I was out in the street listening to the boys. They're talking about the trouble down here on the waterfront.

JOE. [*Sharply.*] I want you to be around when I need you.

TOM. [*Pleased that the bawling-out is over.*] I won't do it again. Joe, one guy out there says there's got to be a revolution before anything will ever be all right.

JOE. [*Impatiently.*] I know all about it. Now, here. Take this money. Go up to the Emporium. You know where the Emporium is?

TOM. Yeah, sure, Joe.

JOE. All right. Take the elevator and go up to the fourth floor. Walk around to the back, to the toy department. Buy me a couple of dollars' worth of toys and bring them here.

TOM. [*Amazed.*] Toys? What kind of toys, Joe?

JOE. Any kind of toys. Little ones that I can put on this table.

TOM. What do you want toys for, Joe?

JOE. [*Mildly angry.*] What?

TOM. All right, all right. You don't have to get sore at *everything*. What'll people think, a big guy like me buying toys?

JOE. *What people?*

TOM. Aw, Joe, you're always making me do crazy things for you, and *I'm* the guy that gets embarrassed. You just sit in this place and make me do all the dirty work.

JOE. [*Looking away.*] Do what I tell you.

TOM. O.K., but I wish I knew why. [*He makes to go.*]

JOE. Wait a minute. Here's a nickel. Put it in the phonograph. Number seven. I want to hear that waltz again.

TOM. Boy, I'm glad *I* don't have to stay and listen to it. Joe, what do you hear in that song anyway? We listen to that song ten times a day. Why can't we hear number six, or two, or nine? There are a lot of other numbers.

JOE. [*Emphatically.*] Put the nickel in the phonograph. [*Pause.*] Sit down and wait till the music's over. Then go get me some toys.

TOM. O.K. O.K.

JOE. [*Loudly.*] Never mind being a martyr about it either. The cause isn't worth it. [TOM *puts the nickel into the machine, with a ritual of impatient and efficient movement which plainly shows his lack of sympathy or enthusiasm. His manner also reveals, however, that his lack of sympathy is spurious and exaggerated. Actually, he is fascinated by the music, but is so confused by it that he pretends he dislikes it. The music begins. It is another variation of "The Missouri Waltz," played dreamily and softly, with perfect orchestral form, and with a theme of weeping in the horns repeated a number of times. At first* TOM *listens with something close to irritation, since he can't understand what is so attractive in the music to* JOE, *and what is so painful and confusing in it to himself. Very soon, however, he is carried away by the melancholy story of grief and nostalgia of the song. He stands, troubled by the poetry and confusion in himself.* JOE, *on the other hand, listens as if he were not listening, indifferent and unmoved. What he's interested in is* TOM. *He turns and glances at* TOM. KITTY DUVAL, *who lives in a room in The New York Hotel, around the corner, comes beyond the swinging doors quietly, and walks slowly to the bar, her reality and rhythm a perfect accompaniment to the sorrowful American music, which is her music, as it is* TOM's, *which the world drove out of her, putting in its place brokenness and all manner of spiritually crippled forms. She seems to understand this, and is angry. Angry with herself, full of hate for the poor world, and full of pity and contempt for its tragic, unbelievable, confounded people. She is a small powerful girl, with that kind of delicate and rugged beauty which no circumstance of evil or ugly reality can destroy. This beauty is that element of the immortal which is in the seed of good and common people, and which is kept alive in some of the female of our kind, no matter how accidentally or pointlessly they may have entered the world.* KITTY DUVAL *is somebody. There is an angry purity, and a fierce pride, in her. In her stance, and way of walking, there is grace and arrogance.* JOE *recognizes her as a great person immediately. She goes to the bar.*]

KITTY. Beer. [NICK *places a glass of beer before her mechanically. She swallows half the drink, and listens to the music again.* TOM *turns and sees her. He becomes dead to everything in the world but her. He stands like a lump, fascinated and undone by his almost religious adoration for her.* JOE *notices* TOM.]

JOE. [*Gently.*] Tom. [TOM *begins to move toward the bar, where* KITTY *is standing. Loudly.*] Tom. [TOM *halts, then turns, and* JOE *motions to him to come over to the table.* TOM *goes over. Quietly.*] Have you got everything straight?

TOM. [*Out of the world.*] What?

JOE. What do you mean, what? I just gave you some instructions.

TOM. [*Pathetically.*] What do you want, Joe?

JOE. I want you to come to your senses. [*He stands up quietly and knocks* TOM's *hat off.* TOM *picks up his hat quickly.*]

TOM. I got it, Joe. I got it. The Emporium. Fourth floor. In the back. The toy department. Two dollars' worth of toys. That you can put on a table.

KITTY. [*To herself.*] Who the hell is he to push a big man like that around?

JOE. I'll expect you back in a half hour. Don't get side-tracked anywhere. Just do what I tell you.

TOM. [*Pleading.*] Joe? Can't I bet four

bits on a horse race? There's a long shot —Precious Time—that's going to win by ten lengths. I got to have money. [JOE *points to the street.* TOM *goes out.* NICK *is combing his hair, looking in the mirror.*]

NICK. I thought you wanted him to get you a watermelon.

JOE. I forgot. [*He watches* KITTY *a moment. To* KITTY, *clearly, slowly, with great compassion.*] What's the dream?

KITTY. [*Moving to* JOE, *coming to.*] What?

JOE. [*Holding the dream for her.*] What's the dream, *now?*

KITTY. [*Coming still closer.*] What dream?

JOE. What dream! The dream you're dreaming.

NICK. Suppose he did bring you a watermelon? What the hell would you do with it?

JOE. [*Irritated.*] I'd put it on this table. I'd look at it. Then I'd eat it. What do you *think* I'd do with it, sell it for a profit?

NICK. How should I know what *you'd* do with *anything?* What I'd like to know is, where do you get your money from? What work do you do?

JOE. [*Looking at* KITTY.] Bring us a bottle of champagne.

KITTY. Champagne?

JOE. [*Simply.*] Would you rather have something else?

KITTY. What's the big idea?

JOE. I thought you might like some champagne. I myself am very fond of it.

KITTY. Yeah, but what's the big idea? You can't push *me* around.

JOE. [*Gently but severely.*] It's not in my nature to be unkind to another human being. I have only contempt for wit. Otherwise I might say something obvious, therefore cruel, and perhaps untrue.

KITTY. You be careful what you think about me.

JOE. [*Slowly, not looking at her.*] I have only the noblest thoughts for both your person and your spirit.

NICK. [*Having listened carefully and not being able to make it out.*] What are you talking about?

KITTY. You shut up. You—

JOE. He owns this place. He's an important man. All kinds of people come to him looking for work. Comedians. Singers. Dancers.

KITTY. I don't care. He can't call me names.

NICK. All right, sister. I know how it is with a two-dollar whore in the morning.

KITTY. [*Furiously.*] Don't you dare call me names. I used to be in burlesque.

NICK. If you were ever in burlesque, I used to be Charlie Chaplin.

KITTY. [*Angry and a little pathetic.*] I *was* in burlesque. I played the burlesque circuit from coast to coast. I've had flowers sent to me by European royalty. I've had dinner with young men of wealth and social position.

NICK. You're dreaming.

KITTY. [*To* JOE.] I *was in burlesque.* Kitty Duval. That was my name. Lifesize photographs of me in costume in front of burlesque theaters all over the country.

JOE. [*Gently, coaxingly.*] I believe you. Have some champagne.

NICK. [*Going to table, with champagne bottle and glasses.*] There he goes again.

JOE. Miss Duval?

KITTY. [*Sincerely, going over.*] That's not my *real* name. That's my *stage* name.

JOE. I'll call you by your stage name.

NICK. [*Pouring.*] All right, sister, make up your mind. Are you going to have champagne with him, or not?

JOE. Pour the lady some wine.

NICK. O.K., Professor. Why you come to this joint instead of one of the high-class dumps uptown is more than I can understand. Why don't you have champagne at the St. Francis? Why don't you drink with a lady?

KITTY. [*Furiously.*] Don't you call me names—you dentist.

JOE. Dentist?

NICK. [*Amazed, loudly.*] What kind of cussing is that? [*Pause. Looking at* KITTY, *then at* JOE, *bewildered.*] This guy doesn't belong here. The only reason I've got champagne is because *he* keeps ordering it all the time. [*To* KITTY.] Don't think you're the only one he drinks champagne with. He drinks with *all* of them. [*Pause.*] He's crazy. Or something.

JOE. [*Confidentially.*] Nick, I think you're going to be all right in a couple of centuries.

NICK. I'm sorry, I don't understand your English. [JOE *lifts his glass.* KITTY *slowly lifts hers, not quite sure of what's going on.*]

JOE. [*Sincerely.*] To the spirit, Kitty Duval.

KITTY. [*Beginning to understand, and very grateful, looking at him.*] Thank you.

JOE. [*Calling.*] Nick.

NICK. Yeah?

JOE. Would you mind putting a nickel in the machine again? Number—

NICK. Seven. I know. I know. I don't mind at all, Your Highness, although, personally, I'm not a lover of music. [*Going to the machine.*] As a matter of fact I think Tchaikowsky was a dope.

JOE. Tchaikowsky? Where'd you ever hear of Tchaikowsky?

NICK. He was a dope.

JOE. Yeah. Why?

NICK. They talked about him on the radio one Sunday morning. He was a sucker. He let a woman drive him crazy.

JOE. I see.

NICK. I stood behind that bar listening to the God-damn stuff and cried like a baby. *None but the lonely heart!* He was a dope.

JOE. What made you cry?

NICK. What?

JOE. [*Sternly.*] What made you cry, Nick?

NICK. [*Angry with himself.*] I don't know.

JOE. I've been underestimating you, Nick. Play number seven.

NICK. They get everybody worked up. They give everybody stuff they shouldn't have. [NICK *puts the nickel into the machine and the Waltz begins again. He listens to the music. Then studies The Racing Form.*]

KITTY. [*To herself, dreaming.*] I like champagne, and everything that goes with it. Big houses with big porches, and big rooms with big windows, and big lawns, and big trees, and flowers growing everywhere, and big shepherd dogs sleeping in the shade.

NICK. I'm going next door to Frankie's to make a bet. I'll be right back.

JOE. Make one for me.

NICK. [*Going to* JOE.] Who do you like?

JOE. [*Giving him money.*] Precious Time.

NICK. Ten dollars? Across the board?

JOE. No. On the nose.

NICK. O.K. [*He goes.* DUDLEY R. BOST-WICK, *as he calls himself, breaks through the swinging doors, and practically flings himself upon the open telephone beside the phonograph.* DUDLEY *is a young man of about twenty-four or twenty-five, ordinary and yet extraordinary. He is smallish, as the saying is, neatly dressed in bargain clothes, overworked and irritated by the routine and dullness and monotony of his life, apparently nobody and nothing, but in reality a great personality. The swindled young man. Educated, but without the least real understanding. A brave, dumb, salmon-spirit struggling for life in weary, stupefied flesh, dueling ferociously with a banal mind which has been only irritated by what it has been taught. He is a great personality because, against all these handicaps, what he wants is simple and basic: a woman. This urgent and violent need, common yet miraculous enough in itself, considering the unhappy environment of the animal, is the force which elevates him from nothingness to greatness. A ridiculous greatness, but in the nature of things beautiful to behold. All that he has been taught, and everything he believes, is phony, and yet he himself is real, almost super-real, because of this indestructible force in himself. His face is ridiculous. His personal rhythm is tense and jittery. His speech is shrill and violent. His gestures are wild. His ego is disjointed and epileptic. And yet deeply he possesses the same wholeness of spirit, and directness of energy, that is in all species of animals. There is little innate or cultivated spirit in him, but there is no absence of innocent animal force. He is a young man who has been taught that he has a chance, as a person, and believes it. As a matter of fact, he hasn't a chance*

*in the world, and should have been told
by somebody, or should not have had his
natural and valuable ignorance spoiled by
education, ruining an otherwise perfectly
good and charming member of the human race. At the telephone he immediately begins to dial furiously, hesitates,
changes his mind, stops dialing, hangs up
furiously, and suddenly begins again. Not
more than half a minute after the fire-
cracker arrival of* DUDLEY R. BOSTWICK,
occurs the polka-and-waltz arrival of
HARRY. HARRY *is another story. He comes
in timidly, turning about uncertainly,
awkward, out of place everywhere, embarrassed and encumbered by the contemporary costume, sick at heart, but
determined to fit in somewhere. His arrival constitutes a dance. His clothes
don't fit. The pants are a little too large.
The coat, which doesn't match, is also a
little too large, and loose. He is a dumb
young fellow, but he has ideas. A philosophy, in fact. His philosophy is simple
and beautiful. The world is sorrowful.
The world needs laughter.* HARRY *is
funny. The world needs* HARRY. HARRY
*will make the world laugh. He has prob-
ably had a year or two of high school.
He has also listened to the boys at the
pool room. He's looking for* NICK. *He
goes to the* ARAB, *and says, "Are you
Nick?" The* ARAB *shakes his head. He
stands at the bar, waiting. He waits very
busily.*]

HARRY. [*As* NICK *returns.*] You Nick?

NICK. [*Very loudly.*] *I am Nick.*

HARRY. [*Acting.*] Can you use a great
comedian?

NICK. [*Behind the bar.*] Who, for instance?

HARRY. [*Almost angry.*] Me.

NICK. You? What's funny about you?
[DUDLEY *at the telephone, is dialing. Because of some defect in the apparatus the
dialing is very loud.*]

DUDLEY. Hello. Sunset 7349? May I
speak to Miss Elsie Mandelspiegel?
[*Pause.*]

HARRY. [*With spirit and noise, dancing.*]
I dance and do gags and stuff.

NICK. In costume? Or are you wearing
your costume?

DUDLEY. All I need is a cigar.

KITTY. [*Continuing the dream of grace.*]
I'd walk out of the house, and stand on
the porch, and look at the trees, and
smell the flowers, and run across the
lawn, and lie down under a tree, and
read a book. [*Pause.*] A book of poems,
maybe.

DUDLEY. [*Very, very clearly.*] Elsie
Mandelspiegel. [*Impatiently.*] She has a
room on the fourth floor. She's a nurse
at the Southern Pacific Hospital. Elsie
Mandelspiegel. She works at night. Elsie.
Yes. [*He begins waiting again.* WESLEY,
*a colored boy, comes to the bar and
stands near* HARRY, *waiting.*]

NICK. Beer?

WESLEY. No, sir. I'd like to talk to you.

NICK. [*To* HARRY.] All right. Get funny.

HARRY. [*Getting funny, an altogether
different person, an actor, with great energy, both in power of voice, and in force
and speed of physical gesture.*] Now, I'm
standing on the corner of Third and
Market. I'm looking around. I'm figuring it out. There it is. Right in front of
me. The whole city. The whole world.
People going by. They're going somewhere. I don't know where, but they're
going. I ain't going *anywhere.* Where
the hell can you go? I'm figuring it out.
All right, I'm a citizen. A fat guy bumps
his stomach into the face of an old lady.
They were in a hurry. Fat and old. *They
bumped.* Boom. I don't know. It may
mean war. *War.* Germany. England.
Russia. I don't know for sure. [*Loudly,
dramatically, he salutes, about faces, presents arms, aims, and fires.*] WAAAAAR.
[*He blows a call to arms.* NICK *gets sick
of this, indicates with a gesture that*
HARRY *should hold it, and goes to* WES-
LEY.]

NICK. What's on your mind?

WESLEY. [*Confused.*] Well—

NICK. Come on. Speak up. Are you hungry, or what?

WESLEY. Honest to God, I ain't hungry.
All I want is a job. I don't want no
charity.

NICK. Well, what can you do, and how
good are you?

WESLEY. I can run errands, clean up,
wash dishes, anything.

DUDLEY. [*On the telephone, very*

eagerly.] Elsie? Elsie, this is Dudley. Elsie, I'll jump in the bay if you don't marry me. Life isn't worth living without you. I can't sleep. I can't think of anything but you. All the time. Day and night and night and day. Elsie, I love you. I love you. What? [*Burning up.*] Is this Sunset 7-3-4-9? [*Pause.*] 7943? [*Calmly, while* WILLIE *begins making a small racket.*] Well, what's your name? *Lorene?* Lorene Smith? I thought you were Elsie Mandelspiegel. What? Dudley. Yeah. Dudley R. Bostwick. Yeah. R. It stands for Raoul, but I never spell it out. I'm pleased to meet *you*, too. What? There's a lot of noise around here. [WILLIE *stops hitting the marble-game.*] Where am I? At Nick's, on Pacific Street. I work at the S. P. I told them I was sick and they gave me the afternoon off. Wait a minute. I'll ask them. I'd like to meet *you*, too. Sure. I'll ask them. [*Turns around to* NICK.] What's this address?

NICK. Number 3 Pacific Street, you cad.

DUDLEY. Cad? You don't know how I've been suffering on account of Elsie. I take things too ceremoniously. I've got to be more lackadaisical. [*Into telephone.*] Hello, Elenore? I mean, Lorene. It's number 3 Pacific Street. Yeah. Sure. I'll wait for you. How'll you know me? You'll *know* me. I'll recognize *you*. Good-by, now. [*He hangs up.*]

HARRY. [*Continuing his monologue, with gestures, movements, and so on.*] I'm standing there. I didn't do anything to anybody. Why should *I* be a soldier? [*Sincerely, insanely.*] BOOOOOOOOOM. *WAR!* O.K. War. *I* retreat. *I* hate war. I move to Sacramento.

NICK. [*Shouting.*] All right, Comedian. Lay off a minute.

HARRY. [*Broken-hearted, going to* WILLIE.] Nobody's got a sense of humor any more. The world's dying for comedy like never before, but nobody knows how to *laugh*.

NICK. [*To* WESLEY.] Do you belong to the union?

WESLEY. What union?

NICK. For the love of Mike, where've you been? Don't you know you can't come into a place and ask for a job and get one and go to work, just like that.

You've got to belong to one of the unions.

WESLEY. I didn't know. I got to have a job. Real soon.

NICK. Well, you've got to belong to a union.

WESLEY. I don't want any favors. All I want is a chance to earn a living.

NICK. Go on into the kitchen and tell Sam to give you some lunch.

WESLEY. Honest, I ain't hungry.

DUDLEY. [*Shouting.*] What I've gone through for Elsie.

HARRY. I've got all kinds of funny ideas in my head to help make the world happy again.

NICK. [*Holding* WESLEY.] No, he isn't hungry. [WESLEY *almost faints from hunger.* NICK *catches him just in time. The* ARAB *and* NICK *go off with* WESLEY *into the kitchen.*]

HARRY. [*To* WILLIE.] See if you think this is funny. It's my own idea. I created this dance myself. It comes after the monologue. [HARRY *begins to dance.* WILLIE *watches a moment, and then goes back to the game. It's a goofy dance, which* HARRY *does with great sorrow, but much energy.*]

DUDLEY. Elsie. Aw, gee, Elsie. What the hell do I want to see Lorene Smith for? Some girl I don't know. [JOE *and* KITTY *have been drinking in silence. There is no sound now except the soft-shoe shuffling of* HARRY, *the Comedian.*]

JOE. What's the dream now, Kitty Duval?

KITTY. [*Dreaming the words and pictures.*] I dream of home. Christ, I always dream of home. I've no *home*. I've no place. But I always dream of all of us together again. We had a farm in Ohio. There was nothing good about it. It was always sad. There was always trouble. But I always dream about it as if I could go back and Papa would be there and Mamma and Louie and my little brother Stephen and my sister Mary. I'm Polish. Duval! My name isn't Duval, it's Koranovsky. Katerina Koranovsky. We lost everything. The house, the farm, the trees, the horses, the cows, the chickens. Papa died. He was old. He was thirteen years older than Mamma. We moved to Chicago. We tried to work. We tried to stay together. Louie got in trouble. The fellows he was with killed him for something. I don't know what. Stephen ran away from home. Seventeen years old. I don't know where he is. Then Mamma died. [*Pause.*] What's the dream? I dream of home. [NICK *comes out of the kitchen with* WESLEY.]

NICK. Here. Sit down here and rest. That'll hold you for a *while*. Why didn't you tell me you were hungry? You all right now?

WESLEY. [*Sitting down in the chair at the piano.*] Yes, I am. Thank you. I didn't know I was *that* hungry.

NICK. Fine. [*To* HARRY *who is dancing.*] Hey. What the hell do you think you're doing?

HARRY. [*Stopping.*] That's my own idea. I'm a natural-born dancer and comedian. [WESLEY *begins slowly, one note, one chord at a time, to play the piano.*]

NICK. You're no good. Why don't you try some other kind of work? Why don't you get a job in a store, selling something? What do you want to be a comedian for?

HARRY. I've got something for the world and they haven't got sense enough to let me give it to them. Nobody knows me.

DUDLEY. *Elsie.* Now I'm waiting for some dame I've never seen before. Lorene Smith. Never saw her in my life. Just happened to get the wrong number. She turns on the personality, and I'm a cooked Indian. Give me a beer, please.

HARRY. Nick, you've got to see my act. It's the greatest thing of its kind in America. All I want is a chance. No salary to begin. Let me try it out tonight. If I don't wow 'em, O.K., I'll go home. If vaudeville wasn't dead, a guy like me would have a chance.

NICK. You're not funny. You're a sad young punk. What the hell do you want to try to be funny for? You'll break everybody's heart. What's there for you to be funny about? You've been poor all your life, haven't you?

HARRY. I've been poor all right, but don't forget that some things count more than some other things.

NICK. What counts more, for instance, than what else, for instance?

HARRY. Talent, for instance, counts more than money, for instance, that's what, and I've got talent. I get new ideas night and day. Everything comes natural to me. I've got style, but it'll take me a little time to round it out. That's all. [*By now* WESLEY *is playing something of his own which is very good and out of the world. He plays about half a minute, after which* HARRY *begins to dance.*]

NICK. [*Watching.*] I run the lousiest dive in Frisco, and a guy arrives and makes me stock up with champagne. The whores come in and holler at me that they're ladies. Talent comes in and begs me for a chance to show itself. Even society people come here once in a while. I don't know what for. Maybe it's liquor. Maybe it's the location. Maybe it's my personality. Maybe it's the crazy personality of the joint. The old honky-tonk. [*Pause.*] Maybe they can't feel at home anywhere else. [*By now* WESLEY *is really playing, and* HARRY *is going through a new routine.* DUDLEY *grows sadder and sadder.*]

KITTY. Please dance with me.

JOE. [*Loudly.*] I never learned to dance.

KITTY. Anybody can dance. Just hold me in your arms.

JOE. I'm very fond of you. I'm *sorry*. I *can't* dance. I wish to God I could.

KITTY. Oh, please.

JOE. Forgive me. I'd like to very much. [KITTY *dances alone.* TOM *comes in with a package. He sees* KITTY *and goes ga-ga again. He comes out of the trance and puts the bundle on the table in front of* JOE.]

JOE. [*Taking the package.*] What'd you get?

TOM. Two dollars' worth of toys. That's what you sent me for. The girl asked me what I wanted with toys. I didn't know what to tell her. [*He stares at* KITTY, *then back at* JOE.] Joe? I've got to have some money. After all you've done for me, I'll do anything in the world for you, but, Joe, you got to give me some money once in a while.

JOE. What do you want it for? [TOM *turns and stares at* KITTY *dancing.*]

JOE. [*Noticing.*] Sure. Here. Here's five. [*Shouting.*] Can you dance?

TOM. [*Proudly.*] I got second prize at the Palomar in Sacramento five years ago.

JOE. [*Loudly, opening package.*] O.K., dance with her.

TOM. You mean *her?*

JOE. [*Loudly.*] I mean Kitty Duval, the burlesque queen. I mean the queen of the world burlesque. Dance with her. She wants to dance.

TOM. [*Worshiping the name Kitty Duval, helplessly.*] Joe, can I tell you something?

JOE. [*He brings out a toy and winds it.*] You don't have to. I know. You love her. You *really* love her. I'm not blind. I know. But take care of yourself. Don't get sick that way again.

NICK. [*Looking at and listening to* WESLEY *with amazement.*] Comes in here and wants to be a dish-washer. Faints from hunger. And then sits down and plays better than Heifetz.

JOE. Heifetz plays the violin.

NICK. All right, don't get careful. He's good, ain't he?

TOM. [*To* KITTY.] Kitty.

JOE. [*He lets the toy go, loudly.*] Don't talk. Just *dance.* [TOM *and* KITTY *dance.* NICK *is at the bar, watching everything.* HARRY *is dancing.* DUDLEY *is grieving into his beer.* LORENE SMITH, *about thirty-seven, very overbearing and funny-looking, comes to the bar.*]

NICK. What'll it be, lady?

LORENE. [*Looking about and scaring all the young men.*] I'm looking for the young man I talked to on the telephone. Dudley R. Bostwick.

DUDLEY. [*Jumping, running to her, stopping, shocked.*] Dudley R. [*Slowly.*] Bostwick? Oh, yeah. He left here ten minutes ago. You mean Dudley Bostwick, that poor man on crutches?

LORENE. Crutches?

DUDLEY. Yeah. Dudley Bostwick. That's what he *said* his name was. He said to tell you not to wait.

LORENE. Well. [*She begins to go, turns around.*] Are you sure *you're* not Dudley Bostwick?

DUDLEY. Who—me? [*Grandly.*] My name is Roger Tenefrancia. I'm a French-Canadian. I never saw the poor fellow before.

LORENE. It seems to me your voice is like the voice I heard over the telephone.

DUDLEY. A coincidence. An accident. A quirk of fate. One of those things. Dismiss the thought. That poor cripple hobbled out of here ten minutes ago.

LORENE. He said he was going to commit suicide. I only wanted to be of help. [*She goes.*]

DUDLEY. Be of help? What kind of help could she be of? [DUDLEY *runs to the telephone in the corner.*] Gee whiz, Elsie. Gee whiz. I'll never leave you again. [*He turns the pages of a little address book.*] Why do I always forget the number? I've tried to get her on the phone a hundred times this week and I still forget the number. She won't come to the phone, but I keep trying anyway. She's out. She's not in. She's working. I get the wrong number. Everything goes haywire. I can't sleep. [*Defiantly.*] She'll come to the phone one of these days. If there's anything to true love at all, she'll come to the phone. Sunset 7349. [*He dials the number, as* JOE *goes on studying the toys. They are one big mechanical toy, whistles, and a music box.* JOE *blows into the whistles, quickly, by way of getting casually acquainted with them.* TOM *and* KITTY *stop dancing.* TOM *stares at her.*]

DUDLEY. Hello. Is this Sunset 7349? May I speak to Elsie? Yes. [*Emphatically, and bitterly.*] No, this is *not* Dudley Bostwick. This is Roger Tenefrancia of Montreal, Canada. I'm a childhood friend of Miss Mandelspiegel. We went to kindergarten together. [*Hand over phone.*] God damn it. [*Into phone.*] Yes. I'll wait, thank you.

TOM. I love you.

KITTY. You want to go to my room? [TOM *can't answer.*] Have you got two dollars?

TOM. [*Shaking his head with confusion.*] I've got *five* dollars, but I *love* you.

KITTY. [*Looking at him.*] You want to spend *all* that money? [TOM *embraces her. They go.* JOE *watches. Goes back to the toy.*]

JOE. Where's the longshoreman, McCarthy?

NICK. He'll be around.

JOE. What do you think he'll have to say today?

NICK. Plenty, as usual. I'm going next door to see who won that third race at Laurel.

JOE. Precious Time won it.

NICK. That's what you think. [*He goes.*]

JOE. [*To himself.*] A horse named McCarthy is running the sixth race today.

DUDLEY. [*On the phone.*] Hello. Hello, Elsie? Elsie? [*His voice weakens; also his limbs.*] My God. She's come to the phone. Elsie, I'm at Nick's on Pacific Street. You've got to come here and talk to me. Hello. Hello, Elsie? [*Amazed.*] Did she hang up? Or was I disconnected? [*He hangs up and goes to bar.* WESLEY *is still playing the piano.* HARRY *is still dancing.* JOE *has wound up the big mechanical toy and is watching it work.* NICK *returns.*]

NICK. [*Watching the toy.*] Say. That's some gadget.

JOE. How much did I win?

NICK. How do you know you *won?*

JOE. Don't be silly. He said Precious Time was going to win by ten lengths, didn't he? He's in love, isn't he?

NICK. O.K. I don't know why, but Precious Time won. You got eighty for ten. How do you do it?

JOE. [*Roaring.*] Faith. Faith. How'd he win?

NICK. By a nose. Look him up in The Racing Form. The slowest, the cheapest, the worst horse in the race, and the worst jockey. What's the matter with my luck?

JOE. How much did you lose?

NICK. Fifty cents.

JOE. You should never gamble.

NICK. Why not?

JOE. You always bet fifty cents. You've got no more faith than a flea, that's why.

HARRY. [*Shouting.*] How do you like this, Nick? [*He is really busy now, all legs and arms.*]

NICK. [*Turning and watching.*] Not bad. Hang around. You can wait table. [*To* WESLEY.] Hey. Wesley. Can you play that again tonight?

WESLEY. [*Turning, but still playing the piano.*] I don't know for sure, Mr. Nick. I can play *something.*

NICK. Good. *You* hang around, too. [*He goes behind the bar. The atmosphere is now one of warm, natural, American ease; every man innocent and good; each doing what he believes he should do, or what he must do. There is deep American naiveté and faith in the behavior of each person. No one is competing with anyone else. No one hates anyone else. Every man is living, and letting live. Each man is following his destiny as he feels it should be followed; or is abandoning it as he feels it must, by now, be abandoned; or is forgetting it for the moment as he feels he should forget it. Although everyone is dead serious, there is unmistakable smiling and humor in the scene; a sense of the human body and spirit emerging from the world-imposed state of stress and fretfulness, fear and awkwardness, to the more natural state of casualness and grace. Each person belongs to the environment, in his own person, as himself:* WESLEY *is playing better than ever.* HARRY *is hoofing better than ever.* NICK *is behind the bar shining glasses.* JOE *is smiling at the toy and studying it.* DUDLEY, *although still troubled is at least calm now and full of melancholy poise.* WILLIE, *at the marble-game, is happy. The* ARAB *is deep in his memories, where he wants to be. Into this scene and atmosphere comes* BLICK. BLICK *is the sort of human being you dislike at sight. He is no different from anybody else physically. His face is an ordinary face. There is nothing obviously wrong with him, and yet you know that it is impossible, even by the most generous expansion of understanding, to accept him as a human being. He is the strong man without strength—strong only among the weak—the weakling who uses force on the weaker.* BLICK *enters casually, as if he were a customer, and immediately* HARRY *begins slowing down.*]

BLICK. [*Oily, and with mock-friendliness.*] Hello, Nick.

NICK. [*Stopping his work and leaning across the bar.*] What do you want to come here for? You're too big a man for a little honky-tonk.

BLICK. [*Flattered.*] Now, Nick.

NICK. Important people never come here. *Here.* Have a drink. [*Whiskey bottle.*]

BLICK. Thanks, I don't drink.

NICK. [*Drinking the drink himself.*] Well, why don't you?

BLICK. I have responsibilities.

NICK. You're head of the lousy Vice Squad. There's no vice here.

BLICK. [*Sharply.*] Street-walkers are working out of this place.

NICK. [*Angry.*] What do you want?

BLICK. [*Loudly.*] I just want you to know that it's got to *stop.* [*The music stops. The mechanical toy runs down. There is absolute silence, and a strange fearfulness and disharmony in the atmosphere now.* HARRY *doesn't know what to do with his hands or feet.* WESLEY'S *arms hang at his sides.* JOE *quietly pushes the toy to one side of the table, eager to study what is happening.* WILLIE *stops playing the marble-game, turns around and begins to wait.* DUDLEY *straightens up very, very vigorously, as if to say: "Nothing can scare me. I know love is the only thing." The* ARAB *is the same as ever, but watchful.* NICK *is arrogantly aloof. There is a moment of this silence and tension, as though* BLICK *were waiting for everybody to acknowledge his presence. He is obviously flattered by the acknowledgment of* HARRY, DUDLEY, WESLEY, *and* WILLIE, *but a little irritated by* NICK'S *aloofness and unfriendliness.*]

NICK. Don't look at me. I can't tell a street-walker from a lady. You married?

BLICK. You're not asking *me* questions. *I'm* telling *you.*

NICK. [*Interrupting.*] You're a man of about forty-five or so. You *ought* to know better.

BLICK. [*Angry.*] Street-walkers are working out of this place.

NICK. [*Beginning to shout.*] Now, don't start any trouble with me. People come here to drink and loaf around. I don't care who they are.

BLICK. Well, I do.

NICK. The only way to find out if a lady is a street-walker is to walk the streets with her, go to bed, and make sure. You wouldn't want to do that. *You'd* like to, of course.

BLICK. Any more of it, and I'll have your joint closed.

NICK. [*Very casually, without ill-will.*] Listen. I've got no use for you, or anybody like you. You're out to change the world from something bad to something worse. Something like yourself.

BLICK. [*Furious pause, and contempt.*] I'll be back tonight. [*He begins to go.*]

NICK. [*Very angry but very calm.*] Do yourself a big favor and don't come back tonight. Send somebody else. I don't like your personality.

BLICK. [*Casually, but with contempt.*] Don't break any laws. I don't like yours, either. [*He looks the place over, and goes. There is a moment of silence. Then* WILLIE *turns and puts a new nickel in the slot and starts a new game.* WESLEY *turns to the piano and rather falteringly begins to play. His heart really isn't in it.* HARRY *walks about, unable to dance.* DUDLEY *lapses into his customary melancholy, at a table.* NICK *whistles a little: suddenly stops.* JOE *winds the toy.*]

JOE. [*Comically.*] Nick. You going to kill that man?

NICK. I'm disgusted.

JOE. Yeah? Why?

NICK. Why should I get worked up over a guy like that? Why should I hate *him*? He's nothing. He's nobody. He's a mouse. But every time he comes into this place I get burned up. He doesn't want to drink. He doesn't want to sit down. He doesn't want to take things easy. Tell me one thing?

JOE. Do my best.

NICK. What's a punk like *that* want to go out and try to change the world for?

JOE. [*Amazed.*] Does he want to change the world, too?

NICK. [*Irritated.*] You know what I mean. What's he want to bother people for? He's *sick*.

JOE. [*Almost to himself, reflecting on the fact that* BLICK *too wants to change the world.*] I guess he wants to change the world at that.

NICK. So I go to work and hate him.

JOE. It's not him, Nick. It's everything.

NICK. Yeah, *I know.* But I've still got no use for him. He's no good. You know what I mean? He hurts little people. [*Confused.*] One of the girls tried to commit suicide on account of him. [*Furiously.*] I'll break his head if he hurts anybody around here. This is *my* joint. [*Afterthought.*] Or anybody's *feelings,* either.

JOE. He may not be so bad, deep down underneath.

NICK. I know all about him. He's no good. [*During this talk* WESLEY *has really begun to play the piano, the toy is rattling again, and little by little* HARRY *has begun to dance.* NICK *has come around the bar, and now, very much like a child —forgetting all his anger—is watching the toy work. He begins to smile at everything: turns and listens to* WESLEY: *watches* HARRY: *nods at the* ARAB: *shakes his head at* DUDLEY: *and gestures amiably about* WILLIE. *It's his joint all right. It's a good, low-down, honky-tonk American place that lets people alone.*]

NICK. I've got a good joint. There's nothing wrong here. Hey. Comedian. Stick to the dancing tonight. I think you're O.K. Wesley? Do some more of that tonight. That's fine!

HARRY. Thanks, Nick. Gosh, I'm on my way at last. [*On telephone.*] Hello, Ma? Is that you, Ma? Harry. I got the job. [*He hangs up and walks around, smiling.*]

NICK. [*Watching the toy all this time.*] Say, that really is something. What is that, anyway? [MARY L. *comes in.*]

JOE. [*Holding it toward* NICK, *and* MARY L.] Nick, this is a toy. A contraption devised by the cunning of man to drive boredom, or grief, or anger out of children. A noble gadget. A gadget, I might say, infinitely nobler than any other I can think of at the moment. [*Everybody gathers around* JOE's *table to look at the toy. The toy stops working.* JOE *winds the music box. Lifts a whistle: blows it, making a very strange, funny and sorrowful sound.*] Delightful. Tragic, but delightful. [WESLEY *plays the music-box theme on the piano.* MARY L. *takes a table.*]

NICK. Joe. That girl, Kitty. What's she mean, calling me a dentist? I wouldn't hurt anybody, let alone a tooth. [NICK *goes to* MARY L.'s *table.* HARRY *imitates the toy. Dances. The piano music comes up, the light dims slowly, while the piano solo continues.*]

CURTAIN

ACT TWO

An hour later. All the people who were at NICK's when the curtain came down are still there. JOE at his table, quietly shuffling and turning a deck of cards, and at the same time watching the face of the WOMAN, and looking at the initials on her handbag, as though they were the symbols of the lost glory of the world. The WOMAN, in turn, very casually regards JOE occasionally. Or rather senses him; has sensed him in fact the whole hour. She is mildly tight on beer, and JOE himself is tight, but as always completely under control; simply sharper. The others are about, at tables, and so on.

JOE. Is it Madge—Laubowitz?

MARY. Is what *what?*

JOE. Is the name Mabel Lepescu?

MARY. What name?

JOE. The name the initials M. L. stand for. The initials on your bag.

MARY. No.

JOE. [*After a long pause, thinking deeply what the name might be, turning a card, looking into the beautiful face of the woman.*] Margie Longworthy?

MARY. [*All this is very natural and sincere, no comedy on the part of the people involved: they are both solemn, being drunk.*] No.

JOE. [*His voice higher-pitched, as though he were growing a little alarmed.*] Midge Laurie? [MARY *shakes her head.*] My initials are J. T.

MARY. [*Pause.*] John?

JOE. No. [*Pause.*] Martha Lancaster?

MARY. No. [*Slight pause.*] Joseph?

JOE. Well, not exactly. That's my first name, but everybody calls me Joe. The last name is the tough one. I'll help you a little. I'm Irish. [*Pause.*] Is it just plain Mary?

MARY. Yes, it is. I'm Irish, too. At least on my father's side. English on my mother's side.

JOE. I'm Irish on both sides. Mary's one of my favorite names. I guess that's why I didn't think of it. I met a girl in Mexico City named Mary once. She was an American from Philadelphia. She got married there. In Mexico City, I mean. While I was *there*. We were in love, too. At least *I* was. You never know about anyone else. They were engaged, you see, and her mother was with her, so they went through with it. Must have been six or seven years ago. She's probably got three or four children by this time.

MARY. Are you still in love with her?

JOE. Well—no. To tell you the truth, I'm not sure. I guess I am. I didn't even know she was engaged until a couple of days before they got married. I thought *I* was going to marry her. I kept thinking all the time about the kind of kids we would be likely to have. My favorite was the third one. The first two were fine. Handsome and fine and intelligent, but that third one was different. Dumb and goofy-looking. I liked *him* a lot. When she told me she was going to be married, I didn't feel so bad about the first two, it was that dumb one.

MARY. [*After a pause of some few seconds.*] What do you do?

JOE. Do? To tell you the truth, nothing.

MARY. Do you always drink a great deal?

JOE. [*Scientifically.*] Not *always*. Only when I'm awake. I sleep seven or eight hours every night, you know.

MARY. How nice. I mean to drink when you're awake.

JOE. [*Thoughtfully.*] It's a privilege.

MARY. Do you really *like* to drink?

JOE. [*Positively.*] As much as I like to breathe.

MARY. [*Beautifully.*] Why?

JOE. [*Dramatically.*] Why do I like to drink? [*Pause.*] Because I don't like to be gypped. Because I don't like to be dead most of the time and just a little alive every once in a long while. [*Pause.*] If I don't drink, I become fascinated by unimportant things—like everybody else. I get busy. Do things. All kinds of little stupid things, for all kinds of little stupid reasons. Proud, selfish, *ordinary* things. I've done them. Now I don't do anything. *I live all the time.* Then I go to sleep. [*Pause.*]

MARY. Do you sleep well?

JOE. [*Taking it for granted.*] Of course.

MARY. [*Quietly, almost with tenderness.*] What are your plans?

JOE. [*Loudly, but also tenderly.*] Plans? I haven't *got* any. *I just get up.*

MARY. [*Beginning to understand everything.*] Oh, yes. Yes, of course. [DUDLEY *puts a nickel in the phonograph.*]

JOE. [*Thoughtfully.*] Why do I drink? [*Pause, while he thinks about it. The thinking appears to be profound and complex, and has the effect of giving his face a very comical and naive expression.*] That question calls for a pretty complicated answer. [*He smiles abstractly.*]

MARY. Oh, I didn't mean—

JOE. [*Swiftly, gallantly.*] No. No. *I* insist. I *know* why. It's just a matter of finding words. Little ones.

MARY. It really doesn't matter.

JOE. [*Seriously.*] Oh, yes, it does. [*Clinically.*] Now, why do I drink? [*Scientifically.*] No. Why does *anybody* drink? [*Working it out.*] Every day has twenty-four hours.

MARY. [*Sadly, but brightly.*] Yes, that's true.

JOE. Twenty-four hours. Out of the twenty-four hours at *least* twenty-three and a half are—my God, I don't know why—dull, dead, boring, empty, and murderous. Minutes on the clock, *not time of living*. It doesn't make any difference who you are or what you do, twenty-three and a half hours of the twenty-four are spent *waiting*.

MARY. Waiting?

JOE. [*Gesturing, loudly.*] And the more you wait, the less there is to wait *for*.

MARY. [*Attentively, beautifully his student.*] Oh?

JOE. [*Continuing.*] That goes on for days and days, and weeks and months and years, and years, and the first thing you know *all* the years are dead. All the minutes are dead. You yourself are dead. There's nothing to wait for any more. Nothing except *minutes* on the *clock*. No time of life. Nothing but minutes, and idiocy. Beautiful, bright, intelligent idiocy. [*Pause.*] Does that answer your question?

MARY. [*Earnestly.*] I'm afraid it does. Thank you. You shouldn't have gone to all the trouble.

JOE. No trouble at all. [*Pause.*] You have children?

MARY. Yes. Two. A son and a daughter.

JOE. [*Delighted.*] How swell. Do they look like you?

MARY. Yes.

JOE. Then why are you sad?

MARY. I was always sad. It's just that after I was married I was allowed to drink.

JOE. [*Eagerly.*] Who are you waiting for?

MARY. No one.

JOE. [*Smiling.*] I'm not waiting for anybody, either.

MARY. My husband, of course.

JOE. Oh, sure.

MARY. He's a lawyer.

JOE. [*Standing, leaning on the table.*] He's a great guy. I like him. I'm very fond of him.

MARY. [*Listening.*] You have responsibilities?

JOE. [*Loudly.*] One, and *thousands*. As a matter of fact, I feel responsible to everybody. At least to everybody I meet. I've been trying for three years to find out if it's possible to live what I think is a civilized life. I mean a life that can't hurt any other life.

MARY. You're famous?

JOE. Very. Utterly unknown, but very famous. Would you like to dance?

MARY. All right.

JOE. [*Loudly.*] I'm *sorry*. I don't dance. I didn't think you'd like to.

MARY. To tell you the truth, I don't like to dance at all.

JOE. [*Proudly—commentator.*] I can hardly walk.

MARY. You mean you're tight?

JOE. [*Smiling.*] No. I mean *all* the time.

MARY. [*Looking at him closely.*] Were you ever in Paris?

JOE. In 1929, and again in 1934.

MARY. What month of 1934?

JOE. Most of April, all of May, and a little of June.

MARY. I was there in November and December that year.

JOE. We were there almost at the same time. You were married?

MARY. Engaged. [*They are silent a moment, looking at one another. Quietly and with great charm.*] Are you *really* in love with me?

JOE. Yes.

MARY. Is it the champagne?

JOE. Yes. Partly, at least. [*He sits down.*]

MARY. If you don't see me again, will you be very unhappy?

JOE. Very.

MARY. [*Getting up.*] I'm so pleased. [JOE *is deeply grieved that she is going. In fact, he is almost panic-stricken about it, getting up in a way that is full of furious sorrow and regret.*] I must go now. Please don't get up. [JOE *is up, staring at her with amazement.*] Good-by.

JOE. [*Simply.*] Good-by. [*The* WOMAN *stands looking at him a moment, then turns and goes.* JOE *stands staring after her for a long time. Just as he is slowly sitting down again, the* NEWSBOY *enters, and goes to* JOE's *table.*]

NEWSBOY. Paper, Mister?

JOE. How many you got this time?

NEWSBOY. Eleven. [JOE *buys them all, looks at the lousy headlines, throws them away. The* NEWSBOY *looks at* JOE, *amazed. He walks over to* NICK *at the bar.*]

NEWSBOY. [*Troubled.*] Hey, Mister, do you own this place?

NICK. [*Casually but emphatically.*] I own this place.

NEWSBOY. Can you use a great lyric tenor?

NICK. [*Almost to himself.*] Great lyric tenor? [*Loudly.*] Who?

NEWSBOY. [*Loud and the least bit angry.*] Me. I'm getting too big to sell papers. I don't want to holler headlines all the time. I want to *sing*. You can use a great lyric tenor, can't you?

NICK. What's lyric about you?

NEWSBOY. [*Voice high-pitched, confused.*] My voice.

NICK. Oh. [*Slight pause, giving in.*] All right, then—sing! [*The* NEWSBOY *breaks into swift and beautiful song: "When Irish Eyes Are Smiling."* NICK *and* JOE *listen carefully:* NICK *with wonder,* JOE *with amazement and delight.*]

NEWSBOY. [*Singing.*]
When Irish eyes are smiling,
Sure 'tis like a morn in Spring.
In the lilt of Irish laughter,
You can hear the angels sing.
When Irish hearts are happy,
All the world seems bright and gay.
But when Irish eyes are smiling—

NICK. [*Loudly, swiftly.*] Are you Irish?

NEWSBOY. [*Speaking swiftly, loudly, a little impatient with the irrelevant question.*] No. I'm Greek. [*He finishes the song, singing louder than ever.*] Sure they steal your heart away. [*He turns to* NICK *dramatically, like a vaudeville singer begging his audience for applause.* NICK *studies the* BOY *eagerly.* JOE *gets to his feet and leans toward the* BOY *and* NICK.]

NICK. Not bad. Let me hear you again about a year from now.

NEWSBOY. [*Thrilled.*] Honest?

NICK. Yeah. Along about November 7th, 1940.

NEWSBOY. [*Happier than ever before in his life, running over to* JOE.] Did you hear it too, Mister?

JOE. Yes, and it's great. What part of Greece?

NEWSBOY. Salonica. Gosh, Mister. Thanks.

JOE. Don't wait a year. Come back with some papers a little later. You're a great singer.

NEWSBOY. [*Thrilled and excited.*] Aw, thanks, Mister. So long. [*Running, to* NICK.] Thanks, Mister. [*He runs out.* JOE *and* NICK *look at the swinging doors.* JOE *sits down.* NICK *laughs.*]

NICK. Joe, people are so wonderful. Look at that kid.

JOE. Of course they're wonderful. Every one of them is wonderful. [MC CARTHY *and* KRUPP *come in, talking.* MC CARTHY *is a big man in work clothes, which make him seem very young. He is wearing black jeans, and a blue workman's shirt. No tie. No hat. He has broad shoulders, a lean intelligent face, thick black hair. In his right back pocket is the longshoreman's hook. His arms are long and hairy. His sleeves are rolled up to just below his elbows. He is a casual man, easy-going in movement, sharp in perception, swift in appreciation of charm or innocence or comedy, and gentle in spirit. His speech is clear and full of warmth. His voice is powerful, but modulated. He enjoys the world, in spite of the mess it is, and he is fond of people, in spite of the mess they are.* KRUPP *is not quite as tall or broad-shouldered as* MC CARTHY. *He is physically encumbered by his uniform, club, pistol, belt, and cap. And he is plainly not at home in the role of policeman. His movement is stiff and unintentionally pompous. He is a naive man, essentially good. His understanding is less than* MC CARTHY's, *but he is honest and he doesn't try to bluff.*]

KRUPP. You don't understand what I mean. Hi-ya, Joe.

JOE. Hello, Krupp.

MC CARTHY. Hi-ya, Joe.

JOE. Hello, McCarthy.

KRUPP. Two beers, Nick. [*To* MC CARTHY.] All I do is carry out orders, carry out orders. I don't know what the idea is behind the order. Who it's for, or who it's against, or why. All I do is carry it out. [NICK *gives them beer.*]

MC CARTHY. You don't read enough.

KRUPP. I do read. I read The Examiner every morning. The Call-Bulletin every night.

MC CARTHY. And carry out orders. What are the orders now?

KRUPP. To keep the peace down here on the waterfront.

MC CARTHY. Keep it for who? [*To* JOE.] Right?

JOE. [*Sorrowfully.*] Right.

KRUPP. How do I know for who? The peace. Just keep it.

MC CARTHY. It's got to be kept for somebody. Who would you suspect it's kept for?

KRUPP. For citizens!

MC CARTHY. I'm a citizen!

KRUPP. All right, I'm keeping it for you.

MC CARTHY. By hitting me over the head with a club? [*To* JOE.] Right?

JOE. [*Melancholy, with remembrance.*] I don't know.

KRUPP. Mac, you know I never hit you over the head with a club.

MC CARTHY. But you will if you're on duty at the time and happen to stand on the opposite side of myself, on duty.

KRUPP. We went to Mission High together. We were always good friends. The only time we ever fought was that time over Alma Haggerty. Did *you* marry Alma Haggerty? [To JOE.] Right?

JOE. Everything's right.

MC CARTHY. No. Did you? [*To* JOE.] Joe, are you with me or against me?

JOE. I'm with everybody. One at a time.

KRUPP. No. And that's just what I mean.

MC CARTHY. You mean neither one of us is going to marry the thing we're fighting for?

KRUPP. *I don't even know what it is.*

MC CARTHY. You don't read enough, I tell you.

KRUPP. Mac, you don't know what you're fighting for, either.

MC CARTHY. It's so simple, it's fantastic.

KRUPP. All right, what are you fighting for?

MC CARTHY. For the rights of the inferior. Right?

JOE. Something like that.

KRUPP. The who?

MC CARTHY. The inferior. The world full of Mahoneys who haven't got what it takes to make monkeys out of everybody else, near by. The men who were created equal. Remember?

KRUPP. Mac, you're not inferior.

MC CARTHY. I'm a longshoreman. And an idealist. I'm a man with too much brawn to be an intellectual, exclusively. I married a small, sensitive, cultured woman so that my kids would be sissies instead of suckers. A strong man with any sensibility has no choice in this world but to be a heel, or a *worker.* I haven't the heart to be a heel, so I'm a worker. I've got a son in high school who's already thinking of being a writer.

KRUPP. I wanted to be a writer once.

JOE. Wonderful. [*He puts down the paper, looks at* KRUPP *and* MC CARTHY.]

MC CARTHY. They *all* wanted to be writers. Every maniac in the world that ever brought about the murder of people through war started out in an attic or a basement writing poetry. It stank. So they got even by becoming important heels. And it's still going on.

KRUPP. Is it really, Joe?

JOE. Look at today's paper.

MC CARTHY. Right now on Telegraph Hill is some punk who is trying to be Shakespeare. Ten years from now he'll be a senator. Or a communist.

KRUPP. Somebody ought to do something about it.

MC CARTHY. [*Mischievously, with laughter in his voice.*] The thing to do is to have more magazines. Hundreds of them. *Thousands.* Print everything they write, so they'll believe they're immortal. That way keep them from going haywire.

KRUPP. Mac, you ought to be a writer yourself.

MC CARTHY. I hate the tribe. They're mischief-makers. Right?

JOE. [*Swiftly.*] Everything's right. Right and wrong.

KRUPP. Then why do you read?

MC CARTHY. [*Laughing.*] It's relaxing. It's soothing. [*Pause.*] The lousiest people born into the world are writers. Language is all right. It's the people who use language that are lousy. [*The* ARAB *has moved a little closer, and is listening carefully. To the* ARAB.] What do you think, Brother?

ARAB. [*After making many faces, thinking very deeply.*] No foundation. All the way down the line. What. What-not. Nothing. I go walk and look at sky. [*He goes.*]

KRUPP. What? What-not? [*To* JOE.] What's that mean?

JOE. [*Slowly, thinking, remembering.*] What? What-not? That means this side, that side. Inhale, exhale. What: birth. What-not: death. The inevitable, the astounding, the magnificent seed of growth and decay in all things. Beginning, and end. That man, in his own way, is a prophet. He is one who, with the help of *beer*, is able to reach that state of deep understanding in which what and what-not, the reasonable and the unreasonable, are *one*.

MC CARTHY. Right.

KRUPP. If you can understand that kind of talk, how can you be a longshoreman?

MC CARTHY. I come from a long line of McCarthys who never married or slept with anything but the most powerful and quarrelsome flesh. [*He drinks beer.*]

KRUPP. I could listen to you two guys for hours, but I'll be damned if I know what the hell you're talking about.

MC CARTHY. The consequence is that all the McCarthys are too great and too strong to be heroes. Only the weak and unsure perform the heroic. They've *got* to. The more heroes you have, the worse the history of the world becomes. Right?

JOE. Go outside and look at it.

KRUPP. You sure can philos—philosoph —Boy, you can talk.

MC CARTHY. I wouldn't talk this way to anyone but a man in uniform, and a man who couldn't understand a word of what I was saying. The party I'm speaking of, my friend, is *YOU*. [*The phone rings.* HARRY *gets up from his table suddenly and begins a new dance.*]

KRUPP. [*Noticing him, with great authority.*] Here. Here. What do you think you're doing?

HARRY. [*Stopping.*] I just got an idea for a new dance. I'm trying it out. Nick. Nick, the phone's ringing.

KRUPP. [*To* MC CARTHY.] Has he got a right to do that?

MC CARTHY. The living have danced from the beginning of time. I might even say, the dance and the life have moved along together, until now we have— [*To* HARRY.] Go into your dance, son, and show us what we have.

HARRY. I haven't got it worked out *completely* yet, but it starts out like this. [*He dances.*]

NICK. [*On phone.*] Nick's Pacific Street Restaurant, Saloon, and Entertainment Palace. Good afternoon. Nick speaking. [*Listens.*] Who? [*Turns around.*] Is there a Dudley Bostwick in the joint? [DUDLEY *jumps to his feet and goes to phone.*]

DUDLEY. [*On phone.*] Hello. Elsie? [*Listens.*] You're coming down? [*Elated. To the saloon.*] She's coming down. [*Pause.*] No. I won't drink. Aw, gosh, Elsie. [*He hangs up, looks about him strangely, as if he were just born, walks around touching things, putting chairs in place, and so on.*]

MC CARTHY. [*To* HARRY.] Splendid. Splendid.

HARRY. Then I go into this little routine. [*He demonstrates.*]

KRUPP. Is that good, Mac?

MC CARTHY. It's awful, but it's honest and ambitious, like everything else in this great country.

HARRY. Then I work along into this. [*He demonstrates.*] And *this* is where I *really* get going. [*He finishes the dance.*]

MC CARTHY. Excellent. A most satisfying demonstration of the present state of the American body and soul. Son, you're a genius.

HARRY. [*Delighted, shaking hands with* MC CARTHY.] I go on in front of an audience for the first time in my life tonight.

MC CARTHY. They'll be delighted. Where'd you learn to dance?

HARRY. Never took a lesson in my life. I'm a natural-born dancer. And *comedian*, too.

MC CARTHY. [*Astounded.*] You can make people *laugh*?

HARRY. [*Dumbly.*] I can be funny, but they won't laugh.

MC CARTHY. That's odd. Why not?

HARRY. I don't know. They just won't laugh.

MC CARTHY. Would you care to be funny now?

HARRY. I'd like to try out a new monologue I've been thinking about.

MC CARTHY. Please do. I promise you if it's funny I shall *roar* with laughter.

HARRY. This is it. [*Goes into the act, with much energy.*] I'm up at Sharkey's on Turk Street. It's a quarter to nine, daylight saving. Wednesday, the eleventh. What I've got is a headache and a 1918 nickel. What I *want* is a cup of coffee. If I buy a cup of coffee with the nickel, I've got to walk home. I've got an eight-ball problem. George the Greek is shooting a game of snooker with Pedro the Filipino. *I'm in rags.* They're wearing thirty-five dollar suits, made to order. I haven't got a cigarette. They're smoking Bobby Burns panatelas. I'm thinking it over, like I always do. George the Greek is in a tough spot. If I buy a cup of coffee, I'll want another cup. What happens? My *ear* aches! My ear. George the Greek takes the cue. Chalks it. Studies the table. Touches the cueball delicately. Tick. What happens? He makes the three-ball! What do I do? I get confused. *I go out and buy a morning paper.* What the hell do I want with a morning paper? What I *want* is a cup of coffee, and a good used car. I go out and buy a morning paper. Thursday, the twelfth. Maybe the headline's about *me*. I take a quick look. *No. The headline is not about me.* It's about Hitler. Seven thousand miles away. I'm here. Who the hell is Hitler? Who's behind the eight-ball? I turn around. *Everybody's behind the eight-ball!* [*Pause.* KRUPP *moves toward* HARRY *as if to make an important arrest.* HARRY *moves to the swinging doors.* MC CARTHY *stops* KRUPP.]

MC CARTHY. [*To* HARRY.] It's the funniest thing I've ever heard. Or *seen*, for that matter.

HARRY. [*Coming back to* MC CARTHY.] Then, why don't you laugh?

MC CARTHY. I don't know, *yet*.

HARRY. I'm always getting funny ideas that nobody will laugh at.

MC CARTHY. [*Thoughtfully.*] It may be that you've stumbled headlong into a new kind of comedy.

HARRY. Well, what good is it if it doesn't make anybody laugh?

MC CARTHY. There are *kinds* of laughter, son. I must say, in all truth, that I *am* laughing, although not *out loud*.

HARRY. I want to *hear* people laugh. *Out loud.* That's why I keep thinking of funny things to say.

MC CARTHY. Well. They may catch on in time. Let's go, Krupp. So long, Joe. [MC CARTHY *and* KRUPP *go.*]

JOE. So long. [*After a moment's pause.*] Hey, Nick.

NICK. Yeah.

JOE. Bet McCarthy in the last race.

NICK. You're crazy. That horse is a double-crossing, no-good—

JOE. Bet everything you've got on McCarthy.

NICK. I'm not betting a nickel on him. *You* bet everything you've got on McCarthy.

JOE. I don't need money.

NICK. What makes you think McCarthy's going to win?

JOE. McCarthy's name's McCarthy, isn't it?

NICK. Yeah. So what?

JOE. The *horse* named McCarthy is going to win, *that's all*. Today.

NICK. Why?

JOE. You do what I tell you, and everything will be all right.

NICK. McCarthy likes to talk, that's all. [*Pause.*] Where's Tom?

JOE. He'll be around. He'll be miserable, but he'll be around. Five or ten minutes more.

NICK. You don't believe that Kitty, do you? About being in burlesque?

JOE. [*Very clearly.*] I believe dreams sooner than statistics.

NICK. [*Remembering.*] She sure is somebody. Called me a dentist. [TOM, *turning about, confused, troubled, comes in, and hurries to* JOE's *table.*]

JOE. What's the matter?

TOM. Here's your five, Joe. I'm in trouble again.

JOE. If it's not organic, it'll cure itself. If it is organic, science will cure it. What is it, organic or non-organic?

TOM. Joe, I don't know— [*He seems to be completely broken down.*]

JOE. What's eating you? I want you to go on an errand for me.

TOM. It's Kitty.

JOE. What about her?

TOM. She's up in her room, crying.

JOE. Crying?

TOM. Yeah, she's been crying for over an hour. I been talking to her all this time, but she won't stop.

JOE. What's she crying about?

TOM. I don't know. I couldn't understand anything. She kept crying and telling me about a big house and collie dogs all around and flowers and one of her brothers dead and the other one lost somewhere. Joe, I can't stand Kitty crying.

JOE. You want to marry the girl?

TOM. [Nodding.] Yeah.

JOE. [Curious and sincere.] Why?

TOM. I don't know why, exactly, Joe. [Pause.] Joe, I don't like to think of Kitty out in the streets. I guess I love her, that's all.

JOE. She's a nice girl.

TOM. She's like an angel. She's not like those other street-walkers.

JOE. [Swiftly.] Here. Take all this money and run next door to Frankie's and bet it on the nose of McCarthy.

TOM. [Swiftly.] All this money, Joe? McCarthy?

JOE. Yeah. Hurry.

TOM. [Going.] Ah, Joe. If McCarthy wins we'll be rich.

JOE. Get going, will you? [TOM runs out and nearly knocks over the ARAB coming back in. NICK fills him a beer without a word.]

ARAB. No foundation, anywhere. Whole world. No foundation. All the way down the line.

NICK. [Angry.] McCarthy! Just because you got a little lucky this morning, you have to go to work and throw away eighty bucks.

JOE. He wants to marry her.

NICK. Suppose she doesn't want to marry him?

JOE. [Amazed.] Oh, yeah. [Thinking.] Now, why wouldn't she want to marry a nice guy like Tom?

NICK. She's been in burlesque. She's had flowers sent to her by European royalty. She's dined with young men of quality and social position. She's above Tom. [TOM comes running in.]

TOM. [Disgusted.] They were running when I got there. Frankie wouldn't take the bet. McCarthy didn't get a call till the stretch. I thought we were going to save all this money. Then McCarthy won by two lengths.

JOE. What'd he pay, fifteen to one?

TOM. Better, but Frankie wouldn't take the bet.

NICK. [Throwing a dish towel across the room.] Well, for the love of Mike.

JOE. Give me the money.

TOM. [Giving back the money.] We would have had about a thousand five hundred dollars.

JOE. [Bored, casually, inventing.] Go up to Schwabacher-Frey and get me the biggest Rand-McNally map of the nations of Europe they've got. On your way back stop at one of the pawn shops on Third Street, and buy me a good revolver and some cartridges.

TOM. She's up in her room crying, Joe.

JOE. Go get me those things.

NICK. What are you going to do, study the map, and then go out and shoot somebody?

JOE. I want to read the names of some European towns and rivers and valleys and mountains.

NICK. What do you want with the revolver?

JOE. I want to study it. I'm interested in things. Here's twenty dollars, Tom. Now go get them things.

TOM. A big map of Europe. And a revolver.

JOE. Get a good one. Tell the man you don't know anything about firearms and you're trusting him not to fool you. Don't pay more than ten dollars.

TOM. Joe, you got something on your mind. Don't go fool with a revolver.

JOE. Be sure it's a good one.

TOM. Joe.

JOE. [Irritated.] What, Tom?

TOM. Joe, what do you send me out for crazy things for all the time?

JOE. [Angry.] They're not crazy, Tom. Now, get going.

TOM. What about Kitty, Joe?

JOE. Let her cry. It'll do her good.

TOM. If she comes in here while I'm gone, talk to her, will you, Joe? Tell her about me.

JOE. O.K. Get going. Don't load that gun. Just buy it and bring it here.

TOM. [*Going.*] You won't catch me loading any gun.

JOE. Wait a minute. Take these toys away.

TOM. Where'll I take them?

JOE. Give them to some kid. [*Pause.*] No. Take them up to Kitty. Toys stopped me from crying once. That's the reason I had you buy them. I wanted to see if I could find out *why* they stopped me from crying. I remember they seemed awfully stupid at the time.

TOM. Shall I, Joe? Take them up to Kitty? Do you think they'd stop *her* from crying?

JOE. They might. You get curious about the way they work and you forget whatever it is you're remembering that's making you cry. That's what they're for.

TOM. Yeah. Sure. The girl at the store asked me what I wanted with toys. I'll take them up to Kitty. [*Tragically.*] She's like a little girl. [*He goes.*]

WESLEY. Mr. Nick, can I play the piano again?

NICK. Sure. Practice all you like—until I tell you to stop.

WESLEY. You going to pay me for playing the piano?

NICK. Sure. I'll give you enough to get by on.

WESLEY. [*Amazed and delighted.*] Get money for playing the piano? [*He goes to the piano and begins to play quietly. HARRY goes up on the little stage and listens to the music. After a while he begins a soft-shoe dance.*]

NICK. What were you crying about?

JOE. My mother.

NICK. What about her?

JOE. She was dead. I stopped crying when they gave me the toys. [*NICK's MOTHER, a little old woman of sixty or so, dressed plainly in black, her face shining, comes in briskly, chattering loudly in Italian, gesturing. NICK is delighted to see her.*]

NICK'S MOTHER. [*In Italian.*] Everything all right, Nickie?

NICK. [*In Italian.*] Sure, Mamma. [*NICK'S MOTHER leaves as gaily and as noisily as she came, after half a minute of loud Italian family talk.*]

JOE. Who was that?

NICK. [*To* JOE, *proudly and a little sadly.*] My mother. [*Still looking at the swinging doors.*]

JOE. What'd she say?

NICK. Nothing. Just wanted to see me. [*Pause.*] What do you want with that gun?

JOE. I study things, Nick. [*An old man who looks as if he might have been Kit Carson at one time walks in importantly, moves about, and finally stands at* JOE'S *table.*]

KIT CARSON. Murphy's the name. Just an old trapper. Mind if I sit down?

JOE. Be delighted. What'll you drink?

KIT CARSON. [*Sitting down.*] Beer. Same as I've been drinking. And thanks.

JOE. [*To* NICK.] Glass of beer, Nick. [*NICK brings the beer to the table,* KIT CARSON *swallows it in one swig, wipes his big white mustache with the back of his right hand.*]

KIT CARSON. [*Moving in.*] I don't suppose you ever fell in love with a midget weighing thirty-nine pounds?

JOE. [*Studying the man.*] Can't say I have, but have another beer.

KIT CARSON. [*Intimately.*] Thanks, thanks. Down in Gallup, twenty years ago. Fellow by the name of Rufus Jenkins came to town with six white horses and two black ones. Said he wanted a man to break the horses for him because his left leg was wood and he couldn't do it. Had a meeting at Parker's Mercantile Store and finally came to blows, me and Henry Walpal. Bashed his head with a brass cuspidor and ran away to Mexico, but he didn't die. Couldn't speak a word. Took up with a cattle-breeder named Diego, educated in California. Spoke the language better than you and me. Said, Your job, Murph, is to feed them prize bulls. I said, Fine, what'll I feed them? He said, Hay, lettuce, salt, beer, and aspirin. Came to blows two days later over an accordion he claimed

I stole. I had *borrowed* it. During the fight I busted it over his head; ruined one of the finest accordions I ever saw. Grabbed a horse and rode back across the border. Texas. Got to talking with a fellow who looked honest. Turned out to be a Ranger who was looking for me.

JOE. Yeah. You were saying, a thirty-nine-pound midget.

KIT CARSON. Will I ever forget that lady? Will I ever get over that amazon of small proportions?

JOE. Will you?

KIT CARSON. If I live to be sixty.

JOE. *Sixty?* You look more than sixty now.

KIT CARSON. That's trouble showing in my face. Trouble and complications. I was fifty-eight three months ago.

JOE. That accounts for it, then. Go ahead, tell me more.

KIT CARSON. Told the Texas Ranger my name was Rothstein, mining engineer from Pennsylvania, looking for something worth while. Mentioned two places in Houston. Nearly lost an eye early one morning, going down the stairs. Ran into a six-footer with an iron claw where his right hand was supposed to be. Said, You broke up my home. Told him I was a stranger in Houston. The girls gathered at the top of the stairs to see a fight. Seven of them. Six feet and an iron claw. That's bad on the nerves. Kicked him in the mouth when he swung for my head with the claw. Would have lost an eye except for quick thinking. He rolled into the gutter and pulled a gun. Fired seven times. I was back upstairs. Left the place an hour later, dressed in silk and feathers, with a hat swung around over my face. Saw him standing on the corner, waiting. Said, Care for a wiggle? Said he didn't. I went on down the street and left town. I don't suppose you ever had to put a dress on to save your skin, did you?

JOE. No, and I never fell in love with a midget weighing thirty-nine pounds. Have another beer?

KIT CARSON. Thanks. [*Swallows glass of beer.*] Ever try to herd cattle on a bicycle?

JOE. No. I never got around to that.

KIT CARSON. Left Houston with sixty cents in my pocket, gift of a girl named Lucinda. Walked fourteen miles in fourteen hours. Big house with barb-wire all around, and big dogs. One thing I never could get around. Walked past the gate, anyway, from hunger and thirst. Dogs jumped up and came for me. Walked right into them, growing older every second. Went up to the door and knocked. Big negress opened the door, closed it quick. Said, On your way, white trash. Knocked again. Said, On your way. Again. On your way. Again. This time the old man himself opened the door, ninety, if he was a day. Sawed-off shotgun, too. Said, I ain't looking for trouble, Father. I'm hungry and thirsty, name's Cavanaugh. Took me in and made mint juleps for the two of us. Said, Living here alone, Father? Said, Drink and ask no questions. Maybe I am and maybe I ain't. You saw the lady. Draw your own conclusions. I'd heard of that, but didn't wink out of tact. If I told you that old Southern gentleman was my grandfather, you wouldn't believe me, would you?

JOE. I might.

KIT CARSON. Well, it so happens he wasn't. Would have been romantic if he had been, though.

JOE. Where did you herd cattle on a bicycle?

KIT CARSON. Toledo, Ohio, 1918.

JOE. Toledo, Ohio? They don't herd cattle in Toledo.

KIT CARSON. They don't anymore. They did in 1918. One fellow did, leastaways. Bookkeeper named Sam Gold. Straight from the East Side, New York. Sombrero, lariats, Bull Durham, two head of cattle and two bicycles. Called his place The Gold Bar Ranch, two acres, just outside the city limits. That was the year of the War, you'll remember.

JOE. Yeah, I remember, but how about herding them two cows on a bicycle? How'd you do it?

KIT CARSON. Easiest thing in the world. Rode no hands. Had to, otherwise couldn't lasso the cows. Worked for Sam Gold till the cows ran away. Bicycles scared them. They went into Toledo. Never saw hide nor hair of them again. Advertised in every paper, but never got them back. Broke his heart. Sold both bikes and returned to New York. Took four aces from a deck of red cards and walked to town. Poker. Fellow in the game named Chuck Collins, liked to gamble. Told him with a smile I didn't suppose he'd care to bet a hundred dollars I wouldn't hold four aces the next hand. Called it. My cards were red on the blank side. The other cards were blue. Plumb forgot all about it. Showed him four aces. Ace of spades, ace of clubs, ace of diamonds, ace of hearts. I'll remember them four cards if I live to be sixty. Would have been killed on the spot except for the hurricane that year.

JOE. Hurricane?

KIT CARSON. You haven't forgotten the Toledo hurricane of 1918, have you?

JOE. No. There was no hurricane in Toledo in 1918, or any other year.

KIT CARSON. For the love of God, then what do you suppose that commotion was? And how come I came to in Chicago, dream-walking down State Street?

JOE. I guess they scared you.

KIT CARSON. No, that wasn't it. You go back to the papers of November 1918, and I think you'll find there was a hurricane in Toledo. I remember sitting on the roof of a two-story house, floating northwest.

JOE. [Seriously.] Northwest?

KIT CARSON. Now, son, don't tell me *you* don't believe me, either?

JOE. [Pause. Very seriously, energetically and sharply.] Of course I believe you. Living is an art. It's not bookkeeping. It takes a lot of rehearsing for a man to get to be himself.

KIT CARSON. [Thoughtfully, smiling, and amazed.] You're the first man I've ever met who believes me.

JOE. [Seriously.] Have another beer. [TOM comes in with the Rand-McNally book, the revolver, and the box of cartridges. KIT goes to bar.]

JOE. [To TOM.] Did you give her the toys?

TOM. Yeah, I gave them to her.

JOE. Did she stop crying?

TOM. No. She started crying harder than ever.

JOE. That's funny. I wonder why.

TOM. Joe, if I was a minute earlier, Frankie would have taken the bet and now we'd have about a thousand five hundred dollars. How much of it would you have given me, Joe?

JOE. If she'd marry you—*all* of it.

TOM. Would you, Joe?

JOE. [Opening packages, examining book first, and revolver next.] Sure. In this realm there's only one subject, and you're it. It's my duty to see that my subject is happy.

TOM. Joe, do you think we'll ever have eighty dollars for a race sometime again when there's a fifteen-to-one shot that we like, weather good, track fast, they get off to a good start, our horse doesn't get a call till the stretch, we think we're going to lose all that money, and then it wins, by a nose?

JOE. I didn't quite get that.

TOM. You know what I mean.

JOE. You mean the impossible. No, Tom, we won't. We were just a little late, that's all.

TOM. We might, Joe.

JOE. It's not likely.

TOM. Then how am I ever going to make enough money to marry her?

JOE. I don't know, Tom. Maybe you aren't.

TOM. Joe, I got to marry Kitty. [Shaking his head.] You ought to see the crazy room she lives in.

JOE. What kind of a room is it?

TOM. It's little. It crowds you in. It's bad, Joe. Kitty don't belong in a place like that.

JOE. You want to take her away from there?

TOM. Yeah. I want her to live in a house where there's room enough to live. Kitty ought to have a garden, or something.

JOE. You want to take care of her?

TOM. Yeah, sure, Joe. I ought to take care of somebody good that makes me feel like *I'm* somebody.

JOE. That means you'll have to get a job. What can you do?

TOM. I finished high school, but I don't know what I can do.

JOE. Sometimes when you think about it, what do you think you'd like to do?

TOM. Just sit around like you, Joe, and have somebody run errands for me and drink champagne and take things easy and never be broke and never worry about money.

JOE. That's a noble ambition.

NICK. [*To* JOE.] How do you do it?

JOE. I really don't know, but I think you've got to have the full co-operation of the Good Lord.

NICK. I can't understand the way you talk.

TOM. Joe, shall I go back and see if I can get her to stop crying?

JOE. Give me a hand and I'll go with you.

TOM. [*Amazed.*] What! You're going to get up already?

JOE. She's crying, isn't she?

TOM. She's crying. Worse than ever now.

JOE. I thought the toys would stop her.

TOM. I've seen you sit in one place from four in the morning till two the next morning.

JOE. At my best, Tom, I don't travel by foot. That's all. Come on. Give me a hand. I'll find some way to stop her from crying.

TOM. [*Helping* JOE.] Joe, I never did tell you. You're a different kind of a guy.

JOE. [*Swiftly, a little angry.*] Don't be silly. I don't understand things. I'm trying to understand them. [JOE *is a little drunk. They go out together. The lights go down slowly, while* WESLEY *plays the piano, and come up slowly on . . .*]

ACT THREE

A cheap bed in NICK's to indicate room 21 of The New York Hotel, upstairs, around the corner from NICK's. The bed can be at the center of NICK's, or up on the little stage. Everything in NICK's is the same, except that all the people are silent, immobile and in darkness, except WESLEY who is playing the piano softly and sadly. KITTY DUVAL, in a dress she has carried around with her from the early days in Ohio, is seated on the bed, tying a ribbon in her hair. She looks at herself in a hand mirror. She is deeply grieved at the change she sees in herself. She takes off the ribbon, angry and hurt. She lifts a book from the bed and tries to read. She begins to sob again. She picks up an old picture of herself and looks at it. Sobs harder than ever, falling on the bed and burying her face. There is a knock, as if at the door.

KITTY. [*Sobbing.*] Who is it?

TOM's VOICE. Kitty, it's me. Tom. Me and Joe. [JOE, *followed by* TOM, *comes to the bed quietly.* JOE *is holding a rather large toy carousel.* JOE *studies* KITTY *a moment. He sets the toy carousel on the floor, at the foot of* KITTY's *bed.*]

TOM. [*Standing over* KITTY *and bending down close to her.*] Don't cry any more, Kitty.

KITTY. [*Not looking, sobbing.*] I don't like this life. [JOE *starts the carousel which makes a strange, sorrowful, tinkling music. The music begins slowly, becomes swift, gradually slows down, and ends.* JOE *himself is interested in the toy, watches and listens to it carefully.*]

TOM. [*Eagerly.*] Kitty. Joe got up from his chair at Nick's just to get you a toy and come here. This one makes music. We rode all over town in a cab to get it. Listen. [KITTY *sits up slowly, listening, while* TOM *watches her. Everything happens slowly and somberly.* KITTY *notices the photograph of herself when she was a little girl. Lifts it, and looks at it again.*]

TOM. [*Looking.*] Who's that little girl, Kitty?

KITTY. That's me. When I was seven.

TOM. [*Looking, smiling.*] Gee, you're pretty, Kitty. [JOE *reaches up for the photograph, which* TOM *hands to him.* TOM *returns to* KITTY *whom he finds as pretty now as she was at seven.* JOE *studies the photograph.* KITTY *looks up at* TOM. *There is no doubt that they really love one another.* JOE *looks up at them.*]

KITTY. Tom?

TOM. [*Eagerly.*] Yeah, Kitty.

KITTY. Tom, when you were a little boy what did you want to be?

TOM. [*A little bewildered, but eager to please her.*] What, Kitty?

KITTY. Do you remember when you were a little boy?

TOM. [*Thoughtfully.*] Yeah, I remember sometimes, Kitty.

KITTY. What did you want to be?

TOM. [*Looks at* JOE. JOE *holds* TOM's *eyes a moment. Then* TOM *is able to speak.*] Sometimes I wanted to be a locomotive engineer. Sometimes I wanted to be a policeman.

KITTY. I wanted to be a great actress. [*She looks up into* TOM's *face.*] Tom, didn't you ever want to be a doctor?

TOM. [*Looks at* JOE. JOE *holds* TOM's *eyes again, encouraging* TOM *by his serious expression to go on talking.*] Yeah, now I remember. Sure, Kitty. I wanted to be a doctor—once.

KITTY. [*Smiling sadly.*] I'm so glad. Because I wanted to be an actress and have a young doctor come to the theater and see me and fall in love with me and send me flowers. [JOE *pantomimes to* TOM, *demanding that he go on talking.*]

TOM. I would do that, Kitty.

KITTY. I wouldn't know who it was and then one day I'd see him in the street and fall in love with him. I wouldn't know *he* was the one who was in love with me. I'd think about him all the time. I'd dream about him. I'd dream of being near him the rest of my life. I'd dream of having children that looked like him. I wouldn't be an actress all the time. Only until I found him and fell in love with him. After that we'd take a train and go to beautiful cities and see the wonderful people everywhere and give money to the poor and whenever people were sick he'd go to them and make them well again. [TOM *looks at* JOE, *bewildered, confused, and full of sorrow.* KITTY *is deep in memory, almost in a trance.*]

JOE. [*Gently.*] Talk to her, Tom. Be the wonderful young doctor she dreamed about and never found. Go ahead. Correct the errors of the world.

TOM. Joe. [*Pathetically.*] I don't know what to say. [*There is rowdy singing in the hall. A loud young* VOICE *sings: "Sailing, sailing, over the bounding main."*]

VOICE. Kitty. Oh, Kitty! [KITTY *stirs, shocked, coming out of the trance.*] Where the hell are you? Oh, Kitty. [TOM *jumps up, furiously.*]

WOMAN'S VOICE. [*In the hall.*] Who are you looking for, Sailor Boy?

VOICE. The most beautiful lay in the world.

WOMAN'S VOICE. Don't go any further.

VOICE. [*With impersonal contempt.*] You? No. Not you. Kitty. You stink.

WOMAN'S VOICE. [*Rasping, angry.*] Don't you dare talk to me that way. You pickpocket.

VOICE. [*Still impersonal, but louder.*] Oh, I see. Want to get tough, hey? Close the door. Go hide.

WOMAN'S VOICE. You pickpocket. All of you. [*The door slams.*]

VOICE. [*Roaring with laughter which is very sad.*] Oh—Kitty. Room 21. Where the hell is that room?

TOM. [*To* JOE.] Joe, I'll kill him.

KITTY. [*Fully herself again, terribly frightened.*] Who is it? [*She looks long and steadily at* TOM *and* JOE. TOM *is standing, excited and angry.* JOE *is completely at ease, his expression full of pity.* KITTY *buries her face in the bed.*]

JOE. [*Gently.*] Tom. Just take him away.

VOICE. Here it is. Number 21. Three naturals. Heaven. My blue heaven. The west, a nest, and you. Just Molly and me. [*Tragically.*] Ah, to hell with everything. [*A young* SAILOR, *a good-looking boy of no more than twenty or so, who is only drunk and lonely, comes to the bed, singing sadly.*]

SAILOR. Hi-ya, Kitty. [*Pause.*] Oh. Visitors. Sorry. A thousand apologies. [*To* KITTY.] I'll come back later.

TOM. [*Taking him by the shoulders, furiously.*] If you do, I'll kill you. [JOE *holds* TOM. TOM *pushes the frightened boy away.*]

JOE. [*Somberly.*] Tom. You stay here with Kitty. I'm going down to Union Square to hire an automobile. I'll be back in a few minutes. We'll ride out to the ocean and watch the sun go down. Then we'll ride down the Great Highway to Half Moon Bay. We'll have supper down there, and you and Kitty can dance.

TOM. [*Stupefied, unable to express his amazement and gratitude.*] Joe, you mean you're going to go on an errand for *me?* You mean you're not going to send me?

JOE. That's right. [*He gestures toward* KITTY, *indicating that* TOM *shall talk to her, protect the innocence in her which is in so much danger when* TOM *isn't near, which* TOM *loves so deeply.* JOE *leaves.* TOM *studies* KITTY, *his face becoming childlike and somber. He sets the carousel into motion, listens, watching* KITTY, *who lifts herself slowly, looking only at* TOM. TOM *lifts the turning carousel and moves it slowly toward* KITTY, *as though the toy were his heart. The piano music comes up loudly and the lights go down, while* HARRY *is heard dancing swiftly.*]

BLACKOUT

ACT FOUR

A little later.

WESLEY, the colored boy, is at the piano.

HARRY is on the little stage, dancing.

NICK is behind the bar.

The ARAB is in his place.

KIT CARSON is asleep on his folded arms.

The DRUNKARD comes in. Goes to the telephone for the nickel that might be in the return-chute. NICK comes to take him out. He gestures for NICK to hold on a minute. Then produces a half dollar. NICK goes behind the bar to serve the DRUNKARD whiskey.

THE DRUNKARD. To the old, God bless them. [*Another.*] To the new, God love them. [*Another.*] To—children and small animals, like little dogs that don't bite. [*Another. Loudly.*] To reforestation. [*Searches for money. Finds some.*] To— President Taft. [*He goes out. The telephone rings.*]

KIT CARSON. [*Jumping up, fighting.*] Come on, *all* of you, if you're looking for trouble. I never asked for quarter and I always gave it.

NICK. [*Reproachfully.*] Hey, Kit Carson.

DUDLEY. [*On the phone.*] Hello. Who?

Nick? Yes. He's here. [*To* NICK.] It's for you. I think it's important.

NICK. [*Going to the phone.*] Important! *What's* important?

DUDLEY. He sounded like big-shot.

NICK. Big *what?* [*To* WESLEY *and* HARRY.] Hey, you. Quiet. I want to hear this important stuff. [WESLEY *stops playing the piano.* HARRY *stops dancing.* KIT CARSON *comes close to* NICK.]

KIT CARSON. If there's anything I can do, name it. I'll do it for you. I'm fifty-eight years old; been through three wars; married four times; the father of countless children whose *names* I don't even know. I've got no money. I live from hand to mouth. But if there's anything I can do, name it. I'll do it.

NICK. [*Patiently.*] Listen, Pop. For a moment, please sit down and go back to sleep—*for me.*

KIT CARSON. I can do that, too. [*He sits down, folds his arms, and puts his head into them. But not for long. As* NICK *begins to talk, he listens carefully, gets to his feet, and then begins to express in pantomime the moods of each of* NICK's *remarks.*]

NICK. [*On phone.*] Yeah? [*Pause.*] Who? Oh, I see. [*Listens.*] Why don't you leave them alone? [*Listens.*] The church-people? Well, to hell with the church-people. I'm a Catholic myself. [*Listens.*] All right. I'll send them away. I'll tell them to lay low for a couple of days. Yeah, I know how it is. [NICK's *daughter* ANNA *comes in shyly, looking at her father, and stands unnoticed by the piano.*] What? [*Very angry.*] Listen. I don't like that Blick. He was here this morning, and I told him not to come back. I'll keep the girls out of here. You keep Blick out of here. [*Listens.*] I know his brother-in-law is important, but I don't want him to come down here. He looks for trouble everywhere, and he always finds it. I don't break any laws. I've got a dive in the lousiest part of town. Five years nobody's been robbed, murdered or gypped. I leave people alone. Your swanky joints uptown make trouble for you every night. [NICK *gestures to* WESLEY—*keeps listening on the phone—puts his hand over the mouthpiece. To* WESLEY *and* HARRY.] Start playing again. My ears have got a headache. Go into your dance, son. [WESLEY *begins to play again.* HARRY *begins to dance.* NICK, *into mouthpiece.*] Yeah. I'll keep them out. Just see that Blick doesn't come around and start something. [*Pause.*] O.K. [*He hangs up.*]

KIT CARSON. Trouble coming?

NICK. That lousy Vice Squad again. It's that gorilla Blick.

KIT CARSON. Anybody at all. You can count on me. What kind of a gorilla is this gorilla Blick?

NICK. Very dignified. Toenails on his fingers.

ANNA. [*To* KIT CARSON, *with great, warm, beautiful pride, pointing at* NICK.] That's my father.

KIT CARSON. [*Leaping with amazement at the beautiful voice, the wondrous face, the magnificent event.*] Well, bless your heart, child. Bless your lovely heart. I had a little daughter point me out in a crowd once.

NICK. [*Surprised.*] Anna. What the hell are you doing here? Get back home where you belong and help Grandma cook me some supper. [ANNA *smiles at her father, understanding him, knowing*

that his words are words of love. She turns and goes, looking at him all the way out, as much as to say that she would cook for him the rest of her life. NICK *stares at the swinging doors.* KIT CARSON *moves toward them, two or three steps.* ANNA *pushes open one of the doors and peeks in, to look at her father again. She waves to him. Turns and runs.* NICK *is very sad. He doesn't know what to do. He gets a glass and a bottle. Pours himself a drink. Swallows some. It isn't enough, so he pours more and swallows the whole drink. To himself.*] My beautiful, beautiful baby. Anna, she is you again. [*He brings out a handkerchief, touches his eyes, and blows his nose.* KIT CARSON *moves close to* NICK, *watching* NICK's *face.* NICK *looks at him. Loudly, almost making* KIT *jump.*] You're broke, aren't you?

KIT CARSON. Always. Always.

NICK. All right. Go into the kitchen and give Sam a hand. Eat some food and when you come back you can have a couple of beers.

KIT CARSON. [*Studying* NICK.] Anything at all. I know a good man when I see one. [*He goes.* ELSIE MANDELSPIEGEL *comes into* NICK's. *She is a beautiful, dark girl, with a sorrowful, wise, dreaming face, almost on the verge of tears, and full of pity. There is an aura of dream about her. She moves softly and gently, as if everything around her were unreal and pathetic.* DUDLEY *doesn't notice her for a moment or two. When he does finally see her, he is so amazed, he can barely move or speak. Her presence has the effect of changing him completely. He gets up from his chair, as if in a trance, and walks toward her, smiling sadly.*]

ELSIE. [*Looking at him.*] Hello, Dudley.

DUDLEY. [*Broken-hearted.*] Elsie.

ELSIE. I'm sorry. [*Explaining.*] So many people are sick. Last night a little boy died. I love you, but—[*She gestures, trying to indicate how hopeless love is. They sit down.*]

DUDLEY. [*Staring at her, stunned and quieted.*] Elsie. You'll never know how glad I am to see you. Just to see you. [*Pathetically.*] I was afraid I'd never see you again. It was driving me crazy. I didn't want to live. Honest. [*He shakes his head mournfully, with dumb and beautiful affection.* TWO STREETWALKERS *come in, and pause near* DUDLEY, *at the bar.*] I know. You told me before, but I can't help it, Elsie. I love you.

ELSIE. [*Quietly, somberly, gently, with great compassion.*] I know you love me, and I love you, but don't you see love is impossible in this world?

DUDLEY. Maybe it isn't, Elsie.

ELSIE. Love is for birds. They have wings to fly away on when it's time for flying. For tigers in the jungle because they don't know their end. We know *our* end. Every night I watch over poor, dying men. I hear them breathing, crying, talking in their sleep. Crying for air and water and love, for mother and field and sunlight. We can never know love or greatness. We *should* know both.

DUDLEY. [*Deeply moved by her words.*] Elsie, I love you.

ELSIE. You want to live. *I* want to live, too, but where? Where can we escape our poor world?

DUDLEY. Elsie, we'll find a place.

ELSIE. [*Smiling at him.*] All right. We'll try again. We'll go together to a room in a cheap hotel, and dream that the world is beautiful, and that living is full of love and greatness. But in the morning, can we forget debts, and duties, and the cost of ridiculous things?

DUDLEY. [*With blind faith.*] Sure, we can, Elsie.

ELSIE. All right, Dudley. Of course. Come on. The time for the new pathetic war has come. Let's hurry, before they dress you, stand you in line, hand you a gun, and have you kill and be killed. [ELSIE *looks at him gently, and takes his hand.* DUDLEY *embraces her shyly, as if he might hurt her. They go, as if they were a couple of young animals. There is a moment of silence. One of the* STREET-WALKERS *bursts out laughing.*]

KILLER. Nick, what the hell kind of a joint are you running?

NICK. Well, it's not out of the world. It's on a street in a city, and people come and go. They bring whatever they've got with them and they say what they must say.

THE OTHER STREETWALKER. It's floozies like her that raise hell with our racket.

NICK. [*Remembering.*] Oh, yeah. Finnegan telephoned.

KILLER. That mouse in elephant's body?

THE OTHER STREETWALKER. What the hell does *he* want?

NICK. Spend your time at the movies for the next couple of days.

KILLER. They're all lousy. [*Mocking.*] All about love.

NICK. Lousy or not lousy, for a couple of days the flat-foots are going to be romancing you, so stay out of here, and lay low.

KILLER. I always was a pushover for a man in uniform, with a badge, a club and a gun. [KRUPP *comes into the place. The girls put down their drinks.*]

NICK. O.K., get going. [*The* GIRLS *begin to leave and meet* KRUPP.]

THE OTHER STREETWALKER. We was just going.

KILLER. We was formerly models at Magnin's. [*They go.*]

KRUPP. [*At the bar.*] The strike isn't enough, so they've got to put us on the tails of the girls, too. I don't know. I wish to God I was back in the Sunset holding the hands of kids going home from school, where I belong. I don't like trouble. Give me a beer. [NICK *gives him a beer. He drinks some.*] Right now, McCarthy, my best friend, is with sixty strikers who want to stop the finks who are going to try to unload the *Mary Luckenbach* tonight. Why the hell McCarthy ever became a longshoreman instead of a professor of some kind is something I'll never know.

NICK. Cowboys and Indians, cops and robbers, longshoremen and finks.

KRUPP. They're all guys who are trying to be happy; trying to make a living; support a family; bring up children; enjoy sleep. Go to a movie; take a drive on Sunday. They're all good guys, so out of nowhere comes trouble. All they want is a chance to get out of debt and relax in front of a radio while Amos and Andy go through their act. What the hell do they always want to make trouble for? I been thinking everything over, Nick, and you know what I think?

NICK. No. What?

KRUPP. I think we're all crazy. It came to me while I was on my way to Pier 27. All of a sudden it hit me like a ton of bricks. A thing like that never happened to me before. Here we are in this wonderful world, full of all the wonderful things—here we are—all of us, and look at us. Just look at us. We're crazy. We're nuts. We've got everything, but we always feel lousy and dissatisfied just the same.

NICK. Of course we're crazy. Even so, we've got to go on living together. [*He waves at the people in his joint.*]

KRUPP. There's no hope. I don't suppose it's right for an officer of the law to feel the way I feel, but, by God, right or not right, that's how I feel. Why are we all so lousy? This is a good world. It's wonderful to get up in the morning and go out for a little walk and smell the trees and see the streets and the kids going to school and the clouds in the sky. It's wonderful just to be able to move around and whistle a song if you feel like it, or maybe try to sing one. This is a nice world. So why do they make all the trouble?

NICK. I don't know. Why?

KRUPP. We're crazy, that's why. We're no good any more. All the corruption everywhere. The poor kids selling themselves. A couple of years ago they were in grammar school. Everybody trying to get a lot of money in a hurry. Everybody betting the horses. Nobody going quietly for a little walk to the ocean. Nobody taking things easy and not wanting to make some kind of a killing. Nick, I'm going to quit being a cop. Let somebody else keep law and order. The stuff I hear about at headquarters. I'm thirty-seven years old, and I still can't get used to it. The only trouble is, the wife'll raise hell.

NICK. Ah, the wife.

KRUPP. She's a wonderful woman, Nick. We've got two of the swellest boys in the world. Twelve and seven years old. [*The* ARAB *gets up and moves closer to listen.*]

NICK. I didn't know that.

KRUPP. Sure. But what'll I do? I've wanted to quit for seven years. I wanted to quit the day they began putting me through the school. I didn't quit. What'll I do if I quit? Where's money going to be coming in from?

NICK. That's one of the reasons we're all crazy. We don't know where it's going to be coming in from, except from wherever it happens to be coming in from at the time, which we don't usually like.

KRUPP. Every once in a while I catch myself being mean, hating people just because they're down and out, broke and hungry, sick or drunk. And then when I'm with the stuffed shirts at headquarters, all of a sudden I'm nice to them, trying to make an impression. On who? People I don't like. And I feel disgusted. [*With finality.*] I'm going to quit. That's all. Quit. Out. I'm going to give them back the uniform and the gadgets that go with it. I don't want any part of it. This is a good world. What do they want to make all the trouble for all the time?

ARAB. [*Quietly, gently, with great understanding.*] No foundation. All the way down the line.

KRUPP. What?

ARAB. No foundation. No foundation.

KRUPP. I'll say there's no foundation.

ARAB. All the way down the line.

KRUPP. [*To* NICK.] Is that all he ever says?

NICK. That's all he's been saying *this* week.

KRUPP. What is he, anyway?

NICK. He's an Arab, or something like that.

KRUPP. No, I mean what's he do for a living?

NICK. [*To* ARAB.] What do you do for a living, brother?

ARAB. Work. Work all my life. All my life, work. From small boy to old man, work. In old country, work. In new country, work. In New York. Pittsburgh. Detroit. Chicago. Imperial Valley. San Francisco. Work. No beg. Work. For what? Nothing. Three boys in old country. Twenty years, not see. Lost. Dead. Who knows? What. What-not. No foundation. All the way down the line.

KRUPP. What'd he say last week?

NICK. Didn't say anything. Played the harmonica.

ARAB. Old country song, I play. [*He*

brings a harmonica from his back pocket.]

KRUPP. Seems like a nice guy.

NICK. Nicest guy in the world.

KRUPP. [*Bitterly.*] But crazy. Just like all the rest of us. Stark raving mad. [WESLEY *and* HARRY *long ago stopped playing and dancing. They sat at a table together and talked for a while; then began playing casino or rummy. When the* ARAB *begins his solo on the harmonica, they stop their game to listen.*]

WESLEY. You hear that?

HARRY. That's *something*.

WESLEY. That's crying. That's crying.

HARRY. I want to make people laugh.

WESLEY. That's deep, deep crying. That's crying a long time ago. That's crying a thousand years ago. Some place five thousand miles away.

HARRY. Do you think you can play to that?

WESLEY. I want to *sing* to that, but I can't *sing*.

HARRY. You try and play to that. I'll try to dance. [WESLEY *goes to the piano, and after closer listening, he begins to accompany the harmonica solo.* HARRY *goes to the little stage and after a few efforts begins to dance to the song. This keeps up quietly for some time.* KRUPP *and* NICK *have been silent, and deeply moved.*]

KRUPP. [*Softly.*] Well, anyhow, Nick.

NICK. Hmmmmmmmm?

KRUPP. What I said. Forget it.

NICK. Sure.

KRUPP. It gets me down once in a while.

NICK. No harm in talking.

KRUPP. [*The* POLICEMAN *again, loudly.*] Keep the girls out of here.

NICK. [*Loud and friendly.*] Take it easy. [*The music and dancing are now at their height.*]

CURTAIN

ACT FIVE

That evening. Fog-horns are heard throughout the scene. A man in evening clothes and a top hat, and his woman, also in evening clothes, are entering.

WILLIE is still at the marble game. NICK is behind the bar. JOE is at his table, looking at the book of maps of the countries of Europe. The box containing the revolver and the box containing the cartridges are on the table, beside his glass. He is at peace, his hat tilted back on his head, a calm expression on his face. TOM is leaning against the bar, dreaming of love and KITTY. The ARAB is gone. WESLEY and HARRY are gone. KIT CARSON is watching the boy at the marble game.

LADY. Oh, come on, please. [*The gentleman follows miserably. The* SOCIETY MAN *and* WIFE *take a table.* NICK *gives them a menu. Outside, in the street, the Salvation Army people are playing a song. Big drum, tambourines, cornet and* singing. They are singing "The Blood of the Lamb." The music and words come into the place faintly and comically. This is followed by an old sinner testifying. It is the* DRUNKARD. *His words are not intelligible, but his message is unmistakable. He is saved. He wants to sin no more. And so on.*]

DRUNKARD. [*Testifying, unmistakably drunk.*] Brothers and sisters. I was a sinner. I chewed tobacco and chased women. Oh, I sinned, brothers and sisters. And then I was saved. Saved by the Salvation Army, God forgive me.

JOE. Let's see now. Here's a city. Pribor. Czechoslovakia. Little, lovely, lonely Czechoslovakia. I wonder what kind of a place Pribor was? [*Calling.*] Pribor! Pribor! [TOM *leaps.*]

LADY. What's the matter with him?

MAN. [*Crossing his legs, as if he ought to go to the men's room.*] Drunk.

TOM. Who you calling, Joe?

JOE. Pribor.

TOM. Who's Pribor?

JOE. He's a Czech. And a Slav. A Czechoslovakian.

LADY. How interesting.

MAN. [*Uncrosses legs.*] He's drunk.

JOE. Tom, Pribor's a city in Czechoslovakia.

TOM. Oh. [*Pause.*] You sure were nice to her, Joe.

JOE. Kitty Duval? She's one of the finest people in the world.

TOM. It sure was nice of you to hire an automobile and take us for a drive along the ocean front and down to Half Moon Bay.

JOE. Those three hours were the most delightful, the most somber, and the most beautiful I have ever known.

TOM. Why, Joe?

JOE. Why? I'm a student. [*Lifting his voice.*] Tom. [*Quietly.*] I'm a student. I study all things. All. All. And when my study reveals something of beauty in a place or in a person where by all rights only ugliness or death should be revealed, then I know how full of goodness this life is. And that's a good thing to know. That's a truth I shall always seek to verify.

LADY. Are you *sure* he's drunk?

MAN. [*Crossing his legs.*] He's either drunk, or just naturally crazy.

TOM. Joe?

JOE. Yeah.

TOM. You won't get sore or anything?

JOE. [*Impatiently.*] What is it, Tom?

TOM. Joe, where do you get all that money? You paid for the automobile. You paid for supper and the two bottles of champagne at the Half Moon Bay Restaurant. You moved Kitty out of the New York Hotel around the corner to the St. Francis Hotel on Powell Street. I saw you pay her rent. I saw you give her money for new clothes. Where do you get all that money, Joe? Three years now and I've never asked.

JOE. [*Looking at* TOM *sorrowfully, a little irritated, not so much with* TOM *as with the world and himself, his own superiority. He speaks clearly, slowly and solemnly.*] Now don't be a fool, Tom. Listen carefully. If anybody's got any money—to hoard or to throw away—you can be sure he stole it from other people. Not from rich people who can spare it, but from poor people who can't. From their lives and from their dreams. I'm no exception. I *earned* the money I throw away. I stole it like everybody else does. I hurt people to get it. Loafing around this way, I *still* earn money. The money itself earns *more*. I *still* hurt people. I don't know who they are, or where they are. If I did, I'd feel worse than I do. I've got a Christian conscience in a world that's got no conscience at all. The world's trying to get some sort of a *social* conscience, but it's having a devil of a time trying to do *that*. I've got money. I'll always have money, as long as this world stays the way it is. I don't work. I don't make anything. [*He sips.*] I drink. I worked when I was a kid. I worked *hard*. I mean hard, Tom. People are supposed to enjoy living. I got tired. [*He lifts the gun and looks at it while he talks.*] I decided to get even on the world. Well, you can't enjoy living unless you work. Unless you do something. I don't do anything. I don't *want* to do anything any more. There isn't anything I can do that won't make me feel embarrassed. Because I can't do simple, good things. I haven't the patience. And I'm too smart. Money is the guiltiest thing in the world. It stinks. Now, don't ever bother me about it again.

TOM. I didn't mean to make you feel bad, Joe.

JOE. [*Slowly.*] Here. Take this gun out in the street and give it to some worthy hold-up man.

LADY. What's he saying?

MAN. [*Uncrosses legs.*] You wanted to visit a honky-tonk. Well, *this* is a honky-tonk. [*To the world.*] Married twenty-eight years and she's still looking for adventure.

TOM. How should I know who's a hold-up man?

JOE. Take it away. Give it to somebody.

TOM. [*Bewildered.*] Do I *have* to *give* it to somebody?

JOE. Of course.

TOM. Can't I take it back and get some of our money?

JOE. Don't talk like a business man. Look around and find somebody who appears to be in need of a gun and give it to him. It's a good gun, isn't it?

TOM. The man said it was, but how can I tell who needs a gun?

JOE. Tom, you've seen good people who needed guns, haven't you?

TOM. I don't remember. Joe, I might give it to the wrong kind of guy. He might do something crazy.

JOE. All right. I'll find somebody myself. [TOM *rises.*] Here's some money. Go get me this week's *Life, Liberty, Time,* and six or seven packages of chewing gum.

TOM. [*Swiftly, in order to remember each item.*] *Life, Liberty, Time,* and six or seven packages of chewing gum?

JOE. That's right.

TOM. All that chewing gum? What kind?

JOE. Any kind. Mix 'em up. All kinds.

TOM. Licorice, too?

JOE. Licorice, by all means.

TOM. Juicy Fruit?

JOE. Juicy Fruit.

TOM. Tutti-frutti?

JOE. Is there such a gum?

TOM. I think so.

JOE. All right. Tutti-frutti, too. Get *all* the kinds. Get as many kinds as they're selling.

TOM. *Life, Liberty, Time,* and all the different kinds of gum. [*He begins to go.*]

JOE. [*Calling after him loudly.*] Get some jelly beans too. All the different colors.

TOM. All right, Joe.

JOE. And the longest panatela cigar you can find. Six of them.

TOM. Panatela. I got it.

JOE. Give a news-kid a dollar.

TOM. O.K., Joe.

JOE. Give some old man a dollar.

TOM. O.K., Joe.

JOE. Give them Salvation Army people in the street a couple of dollars and ask them to sing that song that goes—[*He sings loudly.*]

Let the lower lights be burning, send

a gleam across the wave.

TOM. [*Swiftly.*]

Let the lower lights be burning, send

a gleam across the wave.

JOE. That's it. [*He goes on with the song, very loudly and religiously.*]

Some poor, dying, struggling seaman,

you may rescue, you may save.

[*Halts.*]

TOM. O.K., Joe. I got it. *Life, Liberty, Time,* all the kinds of gum they're selling, jelly beans, six panatela cigars, a dollar for a news-kid, a dollar for an old man, two dollars for the Salvation Army. [*Going.*]

Let the lower lights be burning, send

a gleam across the wave.

JOE. That's it.

LADY. He's absolutely insane.

MAN. [*Wearily crossing legs.*] You asked me to take you to a honky-tonk, instead of to the Mark Hopkins. You're *here* in a honky-tonk. I can't help it if he's crazy. Do you want to go back to where people *aren't* crazy?

LADY. No, not just yet.

MAN. Well, all right then. Don't be telling me every minute that he's crazy.

LADY. You needn't be huffy about it. [MAN *refuses to answer, uncrosses legs. When* JOE *began to sing,* KIT CARSON *turned away from the marble game and listened. While the man and woman are arguing he comes over to* JOE's *table.*]

KIT CARSON. Presbyterian?

JOE. I attended a Presbyterian Sunday School.

KIT CARSON. Fond of singing?

JOE. On occasion. Have a drink?

KIT CARSON. Thanks.

JOE. Get a glass and sit down. [KIT CARSON *gets a glass from* NICK, *returns to the table, sits down,* JOE *pours him a drink, they touch glasses just as the Salvation Army people begin to fulfill the request. They sip some champagne, and at the proper moment begin to sing the song together, sipping champagne, raising hell with the tune, swinging it, and so on. The* SOCIETY LADY *joins them, and is stopped by her* HUSBAND.] Always was fond of that song. Used to sing it at the top of my voice. Never saved a seaman in my life.

KIT CARSON. [*Flirting with the* SOCIETY LADY *who loves it.*] I saved a seaman once. Well, he wasn't exactly a seaman. He was a darky named Wellington. Heavy-set sort of a fellow. Nice personality, but no friends to speak of. Not until I came along, at any rate. In New Orleans. In the summer of the year 1899. No. Ninety-eight. I was a lot younger of course, and had no mustache, but was regarded by many people as a man of means.

JOE. Know anything about guns?

KIT CARSON. [*Flirting.*] All there is to know. Didn't fight the Ojibways for nothing. Up there in the Lake Takalooca Country, in Michigan. [*Remembering.*] Along about in 1881 or two. Fought 'em right up to the shore of the Lake. Made 'em swim for Canada. One fellow in particular, an Indian named Harry Daisy.

JOE. [*Opening the box containing the revolver.*] What sort of a gun would you say this is? Any good?

KIT CARSON. [*At sight of gun, leaping.*] Yep. That looks like a pretty nice hunk of shooting iron. That's a six-shooter. Shot a man with a six-shooter once. Got him through the palm of his right hand. Lifted his arm to wave to a friend. Thought it was a bird. Fellow named, I believe, Carroway. Larrimore Carroway.

JOE. Know how to work one of these things? [*He offers* KIT CARSON *the revolver, which is old and enormous.*]

KIT CARSON. [*Laughing at the absurd question.*] Know how to work it? Hand me that little gun, son, and I'll show you all about it. [JOE *hands* KIT *the revolver. Importantly.*] Let's see now. This is probably a new kind of six-shooter. After my time. Haven't nicked an Indian in years. I believe this here place is supposed to move out. [*He fools around and gets the barrel out for loading.*] That's it. There it is.

JOE. Look all right?

KIT CARSON. It's a good gun. You've got a good gun there, son. I'll explain it to you. You see these holes? Well, that's where you put the cartridges.

JOE. [*Taking some cartridges out of the box.*] Here. Show me how it's done.

KIT CARSON. [*A little impatiently.*]

Well, son, you take 'em one by one and put 'em in the holes, like this. There's one. Two. Three. Four. Five. Six. Then you get the barrel back in place. Then cock it. Then all you got to do is aim and fire. [*He points the gun at the* LADY *and* GENTLEMAN *who scream and stand up, scaring* KIT CARSON *into paralysis. The gun is loaded, but uncocked.*]

JOE. It's all set?

KIT CARSON. Ready to kill.

JOE. Let me hold it. [KIT *hands* JOE *the gun. The* LADY *and* GENTLEMAN *watch, in terror.*]

KIT CARSON. Careful, now, son. Don't cock it. Many a man's lost an eye fooling with a loaded gun. Fellow I used to know named Danny Donovan lost a nose. Ruined his whole life. Hold it firm. Squeeze the trigger. Don't snap it. Spoils your aim.

JOE. Thanks. Let's see if I can unload it. [*He begins to unload it.*]

KIT CARSON. Of course you can. [JOE *unloads the revolver, looks at it very closely, puts the cartridges back into the box.*]

JOE. [*Looking at gun.*] I'm mighty grateful to you. Always wanted to see one of those things close up. Is it really a good one?

KIT CARSON. It's a beaut, son.

JOE. [*Aims the empty gun at a bottle on the bar.*] Bang!

WILLIE. [*At the marble game, as the machine groans.*] Oh, Boy! [*Loudly, triumphantly.*] There you are, Nick. Thought I couldn't do it, hey? *Now,* watch. [*The machine begins to make a special kind of noise. Lights go on and off. Some red, some green. A bell rings loudly six times.*] One. Two. Three. Four. Five. Six. [*An American flag jumps up.* WILLIE *comes to attention. Salutes.*] Oh, boy, what a beautiful country. [*A loud music-box version of the song "America."* JOE, KIT, *and the* LADY *get to their feet. Singing.* "My country, 'tis of thee, sweet land of liberty, of thee I sing." *Everything quiets down. The flag goes back into the machine.* WILLIE *is thrilled, amazed, delighted.* EVERYBODY *has watched the performance of the defeated machine from wherever he happened to*

be when the performance began. WIL-
LIE, *looking around at everybody, as if
they had all been on the side of the machine.*] O.K. How's that? I knew I could
do it. [*To* NICK.] Six nickels. [NICK *hands
him six nickels.* WILLIE *goes over to* JOE
and KIT.] Took me a little while, but I
finally did it. It's scientific, really. With a
little skill a man can make a modest living beating the marble games. Not that
that's what I want to do. I just don't like
the idea of anything getting the best of
me. A machine or anything else. Myself,
I'm the kind of a guy who makes up his
mind to do something, and then goes to
work and does it. There's no other way
a man can be a success at anything. [*Indicating the letter "F" on his sweater.*]
See that letter? That don't stand for
some little-bitty high school somewhere.
That stands for *me.* Faroughli. Willie
Faroughli. I'm an Assyrian. We've got a
civilization six or seven centuries old, I
think. Somewhere along in there. Ever
hear of Osman? Harold Osman? He's an
Assyrian, too. He's got an orchestra down
in Fresno. [*He goes to the* LADY *and*
GENTLEMAN.] I've never seen you before
in my life, but I can tell from the clothes
you wear and the company you keep
[*Graciously indicating the* LADY.] that
you're a man who looks every problem
straight in the eye, and then goes to work
and *solves* it. I'm that way myself. Well.
[*He smiles beautifully, takes the* GENTLE-
MAN's *hand furiously.*] It's been wonderful talking to a nicer type of people for
a change. Well. I'll be seeing you. So
long. [*He turns, takes two steps, returns
to the table. Very politely and seriously.*]
Good-by, lady. You've got a good man
there. Take good care of him. [WILLIE
goes, saluting JOE *and the world.*]

KIT CARSON. [*To* JOE.] By God, for a
while there I didn't think that young
Assyrian was going to do it. That fellow's got something. [TOM *comes back
with the magazines and other stuff.*]

JOE. Get it all?

TOM. Yeah. I had a little trouble finding the jelly beans.

JOE. Let's take a look at them.

TOM. These are the jelly beans. [JOE
puts his hand into the cellophane bag and

*takes out a handful of the jelly beans,
looks at them, smiles, and tosses a couple
into his mouth.*]

JOE. Same as ever. Have some. [*He
offers the bag to* KIT.]

KIT CARSON. [*Flirting.*] Thanks! I remember the first time I ever ate jelly
beans. I was six, or at the most seven.
Must have been in [*Slowly.*] eighteen
—seventy-seven. Seven or eight. Balti-
more.

JOE. Have some, Tom. [*Tom takes
some.*]

TOM. Thanks, Joe.

JOE. Let's have some of that chewing
gum. [*He dumps all the packages of gum
out of the bag onto the table.*]

KIT CARSON. [*Flirting.*] Me and a boy
named Clark. Quinton Clark. Became a
Senator.

JOE. Yeah. Tutti-frutti, all right. [*He
opens a package and folds all five pieces
into his mouth.*] Always wanted to see
how many I could chew at one time.
Tell you what, Tom. I'll bet I can chew
more at one time than you can.

TOM. [*Delighted.*] All right. [*They
both begin to fold gum into their
mouths.*]

KIT CARSON. I'll referee. Now, one at a
time. How many you got?

JOE. Six.

KIT CARSON. All right. Let Tom catch
up with you.

JOE. [*While* TOM's *catching up.*] Did
you give a dollar to a news-kid?

TOM. Yeah, sure.

JOE. What'd he say?

TOM. Thanks.

JOE. What sort of a kid was he?

TOM. Little, dark kid. I guess he's
Italian.

JOE. Did he seem pleased?

TOM. Yeah.

JOE. That's good. Did you give a dollar
to an old man?

TOM. Yeah.

JOE. Was he pleased?

TOM. Yeah.

JOE. Good. How many you got in your
mouth?

TOM. Six.

JOE. All right. I got six, too. [*Folds one
more in his mouth.* TOM *folds one too.*]

KIT CARSON. Seven. Seven each. [*They each fold one more into their mouths, very solemnly, chewing them into the main hunk of gum.*] Eight. Nine. Ten.

JOE. [*Delighted.*] Always wanted to do this. [*He picks up one of the magazines.*] Let's see what's going on in the world. [*He turns the pages and keeps folding gum into his mouth and chewing.*]

KIT CARSON. Eleven. Twelve. [KIT *continues to count while* JOE *and* TOM *continue the contest. In spite of what they are doing, each is very serious.*]

TOM. Joe, what'd you want to move Kitty into the St. Francis Hotel for?

JOE. She's a better woman than any of them tramp society dames that hang around that lobby.

TOM. Yeah, but do you think she'll feel at home up there?

JOE. Maybe not at first, but after a couple of days she'll be all right. A nice big room. A bed for sleeping in. Good clothes. Good food. She'll be all right, Tom.

TOM. I hope so. Don't you think she'll get lonely up there with nobody to talk to?

JOE. [*Looking at* TOM *sharply, almost with admiration, pleased but severe.*] There's nobody *anywhere* for *her* to talk to—except *you.*

TOM. [*Amazed and delighted.*] Me, Joe?

JOE. [*While* TOM *and* KIT CARSON *listen carefully,* KIT *with great appreciation.*] Yes, you. By the grace of God, you're the other half of that girl. Not the angry woman that swaggers into this waterfront dive and shouts because the world has kicked her around. *Anybody* can have *her.* You belong to the little kid in Ohio who once dreamed of living. Not with her carcass, for *money*, so she can have food and clothes, and pay rent. With *all* of her. I put her in that hotel, so she can have a chance to gather herself together again. She can't do that in the New York Hotel. You saw what happens there. There's nobody anywhere for her to talk to, except you. They all make her talk like a whore. After a while, she'll *believe* them. Then she won't be able to remember. She'll get lonely. Sure. People can

get lonely for *misery*, even. I want her to go on being lonely for *you*, so she can come together again the way she was meant to be from the beginning. Loneliness is good for people. Right now it's the only thing for Kitty. Any more licorice?

TOM. [*Dazed.*] What? Licorice? [*Looking around busily.*] I guess we've chewed all the licorice in. We still got Clove, Peppermint, Doublemint, Beechnut, Teaberry, and Juicy Fruit.

JOE. Licorice used to be my favorite. Don't worry about her, Tom, she'll be all right. You really want to marry her, don't you?

TOM. [*Nodding.*] Honest to God, Joe. [*Pathetically.*] Only, I haven't got any money.

JOE. Couldn't you be a prize-fighter or something like that?

TOM. Naaaah. I couldn't hit a man if I wasn't sore at him. He'd have to do something that made me hate him.

JOE. You've got to figure out something to do that you won't mind doing very much.

TOM. I wish I could, Joe.

JOE. [*Thinking deeply, suddenly.*] Tom, would you be embarrassed driving a truck?

TOM. [*Hit by a thunderbolt.*] Joe, I never thought of that. I'd like that. Travel. Highways. Little towns. Coffee and hot cakes. Beautiful valleys and mountains and streams and trees and daybreak and sunset.

JOE. There *is* poetry in it, at that.

TOM. Joe, that's just the kind of work I *should* do. Just sit there and travel, and look, and smile, and bust out laughing. Could Kitty go with me, sometimes?

JOE. I don't know. Get me the phone book. Can you drive a truck?

TOM. Joe, you know I can drive a truck, or any kind of thing with a motor and wheels. [TOM *takes* JOE *the phone book.* JOE *turns the pages.*]

JOE. [*Looking.*] Here! Here it is. Tuxedo 7900. Here's a nickel. Get me that number. [TOM *goes to telephone, dials the number.*]

TOM. Hello.

JOE. Ask for Mr. Keith.

TOM. [*Mouth and language full of gum.*] I'd like to talk to Mr. Keith. [*Pause.*] Mr. Keith.

JOE. Take that gum out of your mouth for a minute. [TOM *removes the gum.*]

TOM. Mr. Keith. Yeah. That's right. Hello, Mr. Keith?

JOE. Tell him to hold the line.

TOM. Hold the line, please.

JOE. Give me a hand, Tom. [TOM *helps* JOE *to the telephone. At phone, wad of gum in fingers delicately.*] Keith? Joe. Yeah. Fine. Forget it. [*Pause.*] Have you got a place for a good driver? [*Pause.*] I don't think so. [*To* TOM.] You haven't got a driver's license, have you?

TOM. [*Worried.*] No. But I can get one, Joe.

JOE. [*At phone.*] No, but he can get one easy enough. To hell with the union. He'll join later. All right, call him a Vice-President and say he drives for relaxation. Sure. What do you mean? Tonight? I don't know why not. San Diego? All right, let him start driving without a license. What the hell's the difference? Yeah. Sure. Look him over. Yeah. I'll send him right over. Right. [*He hangs up.*] Thanks. [*To telephone.*]

TOM. Am I going to get the job?

JOE. He wants to take a look at you.

TOM. Do I look all right, Joe?

JOE. [*Looking at him carefully.*] Hold up your head. Stick out your chest. How do you feel? [TOM *does these things.*]

TOM. Fine.

JOE. You *look* fine, too. [JOE *takes his wad of gum out of his mouth and wraps Liberty magazine around it.*]

JOE. You win, Tom. Now, look. [*He bites off the tip of a very long panatela cigar, lights it, and hands one to* TOM, *and another to* KIT.] Have yourselves a pleasant smoke. Here. [*He hands two more to* TOM.] Give those slummers one each. [*He indicates the* SOCIETY LADY *and* GENTLEMAN. TOM *goes over and without a word gives a cigar each to the* MAN *and the* LADY. *The* MAN *is offended; he smells and tosses aside his cigar. The* WOMAN *looks at her cigar a moment, then puts the cigar in her mouth.*]

MAN. What do you think you're doing?

LADY. Really, dear. I'd like to.

MAN. Oh, this is too much.

LADY. I'd *really*, really like to, dear. [*She laughs, puts the cigar in her mouth. Turns to* KIT. *He spits out tip. She does the same.*]

MAN. [*Loudly.*] The mother of five grown men, and she's still looking for *romance*. [*Shouts as* KIT *lights her cigar.*] No. I forbid it.

JOE. [*Shouting.*] What's the matter with you? Why don't you leave her alone? What are you always pushing your women around for? [*Almost without a pause.*] Now, look, Tom. [*The* LADY *puts the lighted cigar in her mouth, and begins to smoke, feeling wonderful.*] Here's ten bucks.

TOM. Ten bucks?

JOE. He may want you to get into a truck and begin driving to San Diego tonight.

TOM. Joe, I got to tell Kitty.

JOE. I'll tell her.

TOM. Joe, take care of her.

JOE. She'll be all right. Stop worrying about her. She's at the St. Francis Hotel. Now, look. Take a cab to Townsend and Fourth. You'll see the big sign. Keith Motor Transport Company. He'll be waiting for you.

TOM. O.K., Joe. [*Trying hard.*] Thanks, Joe.

JOE. Don't be silly. Get going. [TOM *goes.* LADY *starts puffing on cigar. As* TOM *goes,* WESLEY *and* HARRY *come in together.*]

NICK. Where the hell have you been? We've got to have some entertainment around here. Can't you see them fine people from uptown? [*He points at the* SO-CIETY LADY *and* GENTLEMAN.]

WESLEY. You said to come back at ten for the second show.

NICK. Did I say that?

WESLEY. Yes, sir, Mr. Nick, that's exactly what you said.

HARRY. Was the first show all right?

NICK. That wasn't a show. There was no one here to see it. How can it be a show when no one sees it? People are afraid to come down to the waterfront.

HARRY. Yeah. We were just down to Pier 27. One of the longshoremen and a cop had a fight and the cop hit him over the head with a blackjack. We saw it happen, didn't we?

WESLEY. Yes, sir, we was standing there looking when it happened.

NICK. [*A little worried.*] Anything else happen?

WESLEY. They was all talking.

HARRY. A man in a big car came up and said there was going to be a meeting right away and they hoped to satisfy everybody and stop the strike.

WESLEY. Right away. *Tonight.*

NICK. Well, it's about time. Them poor cops are liable to get nervous and—shoot somebody. [*To* HARRY, *suddenly.*] Come back here. I want you to tend bar for a while. I'm going to take a walk over to the pier.

HARRY. Yes, sir.

NICK. [*To the* SOCIETY LADY *and* GENTLEMAN.] You society people made up your minds yet?

LADY. Have you champagne?

NICK. [*Indicating* JOE.] What do you think he's pouring out of that bottle, water or something?

LADY. Have you a chill bottle?

NICK. I've got a dozen of them chilled. He's been drinking champagne here all day and all night for a month now.

LADY. May we have a bottle?

NICK. It's six dollars.

LADY. I think we can manage.

MAN. I don't know. I *know* I don't know. [NICK *takes off his coat and helps* HARRY *into it.* HARRY *takes a bottle of champagne and two glasses to the* LADY *and* GENTLEMAN, *dancing, collects six dollars, and goes back behind the bar, dancing.* NICK *gets his coat and hat.*]

NICK. [*To* WESLEY.] Rattle the keys a little son. Rattle the keys.

WESLEY. Yes, sir, Mr. Nick. [NICK *is on his way out. The* ARAB *enters.*]

NICK. Hi-ya, *Mahmed.*

ARAB. No foundation.

NICK. All the way down the line. [*He goes.* WESLEY *is at the piano, playing quietly. The* ARAB *swallows a glass of beer, takes out his harmonica, and begins to play.* WESLEY *fits his playing to the Arab's.* KITTY DUVAL, *strangely beautiful, in new clothes, comes in. She walks shyly,* as if she were embarrassed by the fine clothes, as if she had no right to wear them. The LADY and GENTLEMAN are very impressed. HARRY looks at her with amazement. JOE is reading Time magazine. KITTY goes to his table. JOE looks up from the magazine, without the least amazement.]

JOE. Hello, Kitty.

KITTY. Hello, Joe.

JOE. It's nice seeing you again.

KITTY. I came in a cab.

JOE. You been crying again? [KITTY *can't answer. To* HARRY.] Bring a glass. [HARRY *comes over with a glass.* JOE *pours* KITTY *a drink.*]

KITTY. I've got to talk to you.

JOE. Have a drink.

KITTY. I've never been in burlesque. We were just poor.

JOE. Sit down, Kitty.

KITTY. [*Sits down.*] I tried other things.

JOE. Here's to you, Katerina Koranovsky. Here's to you. And Tom.

KITTY. [*Sorrowfully.*] Where *is* Tom?

JOE. He's getting a job tonight driving a truck. He'll be back in a couple of days.

KITTY. [*Sadly.*] I told him I'd marry him.

JOE. He wanted to see you and say good-by.

KITTY. He's too good for me. He's like a little boy. [*Wearily.*] I'm— Too many things have happened to me.

JOE. Kitty Duval, you're one of the few truly innocent people I have ever known. He'll be back in a couple of days. Go back to the hotel and wait for him.

KITTY. That's what I mean. I can't stand being alone. I'm no good. I tried very hard. I don't know what it is. I miss— [*She gestures.*]

JOE. [*Gently.*] Do you really want to come back here, Kitty?

KITTY. I don't know. I'm not sure. Everything *smells* different. I don't know how to feel, or what to think. [*Gesturing pathetically.*] I know I don't belong there. It's what I've wanted all my life, but it's too *late.* I try to be happy about it, but all I can do is remember everything and cry.

JOE. I don't know what to tell you, Kitty. I didn't mean to hurt you.

KITTY. You haven't hurt me. You're the only person who's ever been good to me. I've never known anybody like you. I'm not sure about love any more, but I know I love you, and I know I love Tom.

JOE. I love you too, Kitty Duval.

KITTY. He'll want babies. I know he will. I know *I* will, too. Of course I will. I can't—[*She shakes her head.*]

JOE. Tom's a baby himself. You'll be very happy together. He wants you to ride with him in the truck. Tom's good for you. You're good for Tom.

KITTY. [*Like a child.*] Do you want me to go back and wait for him?

JOE. I can't *tell* you what to do. I think it would be a good idea, though.

KITTY. I wish I could tell you how it makes me feel to be alone. It's almost worse.

JOE. It might take a whole week, Kitty. [*He looks at her sharply, at the arrival of an idea.*] Didn't you speak of reading a book? A book of poems?

KITTY. I didn't know what I was saying.

JOE. [*Trying to get up.*] Of course you knew. I think you'll like poetry. Wait here a minute, Kitty. I'll go see if I can find some books.

KITTY. All right, Joe. [*He walks out of the place, trying very hard not to wobble. Fog-horn. Music. The* NEWSBOY *comes in. Looks for* JOE. *Is broken-hearted because* JOE *is gone.*]

NEWSBOY. [*To* SOCIETY GENTLEMAN.] Paper?

MAN. [*Angry.*] No. [*The* NEWSBOY *goes to the* ARAB.]

NEWSBOY. Paper, Mister?

ARAB. [*Irritated.*] No foundation.

NEWSBOY. What?

ARAB. [*Very angry.*] No foundation. [*The* NEWSBOY *starts out, turns, looks at the* ARAB, *shakes head.*]

NEWSBOY. No foundation? How do you figure? [BLICK *and* TWO COPS *enter.*]

NEWSBOY. [*To* BLICK.] Paper, Mister? [BLICK *pushes him aside. The* NEWSBOY *goes.*]

BLICK. [*Walking authoritatively about the place, to* HARRY.] Where's Nick?

HARRY. He went for a walk.

BLICK. Who are you?

HARRY. Harry.

BLICK. [*To the* ARAB *and* WESLEY.] Hey, you. Shut up. [*The* ARAB *stops playing the harmonica,* WESLEY *the piano.*]

BLICK. [*Studies* KITTY.] What's your name, sister?

KITTY. [*Looking at him.*] Kitty Duval. What's it to you? [KITTY'S *voice is now like it was at the beginning of the play: tough, independent, bitter and hard.*]

BLICK. [*Angry.*] Don't give me any of your gutter lip. Just answer my questions.

KITTY. You go to hell, you.

BLICK. [*Coming over, enraged.*] Where do you live?

KITTY. The New York Hotel. Room 21.

BLICK. Where do you work?

KITTY. I'm not working just now. I'm looking for work.

BLICK. What kind of work? [KITTY *can't answer.*] What kind of work? [KITTY *can't answer. Furiously.*] WHAT KIND OF WORK? [KIT CARSON *comes over.*]

KIT CARSON. You can't talk to a lady that way in *my* presence. [BLICK *turns and stares at* KIT. *The* COPS *begin to move from the bar.*]

BLICK. [*To the* COPS.] It's all right, boys. I'll take care of this. [*To* KIT.] *What'd you say?*

KIT CARSON. You got no right to hurt people. Who are you? [BLICK, *without a word, takes* KIT *to the street. Sounds of a blow and a groan.* BLICK *returns, breathing hard.*]

BLICK. [*To the* COPS.] O.K., boys. You can go now. Take care of him. Put him on his feet and tell him to behave himself from now on. [*To* KITTY *again.*] Now answer my question. What kind of work?

KITTY. [*Quietly.*] I'm a whore you son of a bitch. You know what kind of work I do. And I know what kind you do.

MAN. [*Shocked and really hurt.*] Excuse me, officer, but it seems to me that your attitude—

BLICK. Shut up.

MAN. [*Quietly.*] —is making the poor child say things that are not true.

BLICK. Shut up, I said.

LADY. Well. [*To the* MAN.] Are you going to stand for such insolence?

BLICK. [*To* MAN, *who is standing.*] Are you?

MAN. [*Taking the* WOMAN'S *arm.*] I'll get a divorce. I'll start life all over again. [*Pushing the* WOMAN.] Come on. Get the hell out of here! [*The* MAN *hurries his* WOMAN *out of the place,* BLICK *watching them go.*]

BLICK. [*To* KITTY.] Now. Let's begin again, and see that you tell the truth. What's your name?

KITTY. Kitty Duval.

BLICK. Where do you live?

KITTY. Until this evening I lived at the New York Hotel. Room 21. This evening I moved to the St. Francis Hotel.

BLICK. Oh. To the St. Francis Hotel. Nice place. Where do you work?

KITTY. I'm looking for work.

BLICK. What kind of work do you do?

KITTY. I'm an actress.

BLICK. I see. What movies have I seen you in?

KITTY. I've worked in burlesque.

BLICK. You're a liar. [WESLEY *stands, worried and full of dumb resentment.*]

KITTY. [*Pathetically, as at the beginning of the play.*] It's the truth.

BLICK. What are you doing here?

KITTY. I came to see if I could get a job here.

BLICK. Doing what?

KITTY. Singing—and—dancing.

BLICK. You can't sing or dance. What are you lying for?

KITTY. I can. I sang and danced in burlesque all over the country.

BLICK. You're a liar.

KITTY. I said lines, too.

BLICK. So you danced in burlesque?

KITTY. Yes.

BLICK. All right. Let's see what you did.

KITTY. I can't. There's no music, and I haven't got the right clothes.

BLICK. There's music. [*To* WESLEY.] Put a nickel in that phonograph. [WESLEY *can't move.*] Come on. Put a nickel in that phonograph. [WESLEY *does so. To* KITTY.] All right. Get up on that stage and do a hot little burlesque number. [KITTY *stands. Walks slowly to the stage, but is unable to move.* JOE *comes in, holding three books.*] Get going, now. Let's see you dance the way you did in

burlesque, all over the country. [KITTY *tries to do a burlesque dance. It is beautiful in a tragic way.*]

BLICK. All right, start taking them off! [KITTY *removes her hat and starts to remove her jacket.* JOE *moves closer to the stage, amazed.*]

JOE. [*Hurrying to* KITTY.] Get down from there. [*He takes* KITTY *into his arms. She is crying. To* BLICK.] What the hell do you think you're doing?

WESLEY. [*Like a little boy, very angry.*] It's that man, Blick. *He* made her take off her clothes. He beat up the old man, too. [BLICK *pushes* WESLEY *off, as* TOM *enters.* BLICK *begins beating up* WESLEY.]

TOM. What's the matter, Joe? What's happened?

JOE. Is the truck out there?

TOM. Yeah, but what's happened? Kitty's crying again!

JOE. You driving to San Diego?

TOM. Yeah, Joe. But what's he doing to that poor colored boy?

JOE. Get going. Here's some money. Everything's O.K. [*To* KITTY.] Dress in the truck. Take these books.

WESLEY'S VOICE. You can't hurt me. You'll get yours. You wait and see.

TOM. Joe, he's hurting that boy. I'll kill him!

JOE. [*Pushing* TOM.] Get out of here! Get married in San Diego. I'll see you when you get back. [TOM *and* KITTY *go.* NICK *enters and stands at the lower end of bar.* JOE *takes the revolver out of his pocket. Looks at it.*] I've always wanted to kill somebody, but I never knew who it should be. [*He cocks the revolver, stands real straight, holds it in front of him firmly and walks to the door. He stands a moment watching* BLICK, *aims very carefully, and pulls trigger. There is no shot.* NICK *runs over and grabs the gun, and takes* JOE *aside.*]

NICK. What the hell do you think you're doing?

JOE. [*Casually, but angry.*] That dumb Tom. Buys a six-shooter that won't even shoot once. [JOE *sits down, dead to the world.* BLICK *comes out, panting for breath.* NICK *looks at him. He speaks slowly.*]

NICK. Blick! I told you to stay out of

here! Now get out of here. [*He takes* BLICK *by the collar, tightening his grip as he speaks, and pushing him out.*] If you come back again, I'm going to take you in that room where you've been beating up that colored boy, and I'm going to murder you—slowly—with my hands. Beat it! [*He pushes* BLICK *out. To* HARRY.] Go take care of the colored boy. [HARRY *runs out.* WILLIE *returns and doesn't sense that anything is changed.* WILLIE *puts another nickel into the machine, but he does so very violently. The consequence of this violence is that the flag comes up again.* WILLIE, *amazed, stands at attention and salutes. The flag goes down. He shakes his head.*]

WILLIE. [*Thoughtfully.*] As far as I'm concerned, this is the *only* country in the world. If you ask me, *nuts* to Europe! [*He is about to push the slide in again when the flag comes up again. Furiously, to* NICK, *while he salutes and stands at attention, pleadingly.*] Hey, Nick. This machine is out of order.

NICK. [*Somberly.*] Give it a whack on the side. [WILLIE *does so. A hell of a whack. The result is the flag comes up and down, and* WILLIE *keeps saluting.*]

WILLIE. [*Saluting.*] Hey, Nick. Something's wrong. [*The machine quiets down abruptly.* WILLIE *very stealthily slides a new nickel in, and starts a new game. From a distance two pistol shots are heard, each carefully timed.* NICK *runs out. The* NEWSBOY *enters, crosses to* JOE's *table, senses something is wrong.*]

NEWSBOY. [*Softly.*] Paper, Mister? [JOE *can't hear him. The* NEWSBOY *backs away, studies* JOE, *wishes he could cheer* JOE *up. Notices the phonograph, goes to it, and puts a coin in it, hoping music will make* JOE *happier. The* NEWSBOY *sits down. Watches* JOE. *The music begins.* "The Missouri Waltz." *The* DRUNKARD *comes in and walks around. Then sits down.* NICK *comes back.*]

NICK. [*Delighted.*] Joe, Blick's dead! Somebody just shot him, and none of the cops are trying to find out who. [JOE *doesn't hear.* NICK *steps back, studying* JOE. *Shouting.*] Joe.

JOE. [*Looking up.*] What?

NICK. Blick's dead.

JOE. Blick? Dead? Good! That Goddamn gun wouldn't go off. I *told* Tom to get a good one.

NICK. [*Picking up gun and looking at it.*] Joe, you wanted to kill that guy! [HARRY *returns.* JOE *puts the gun in his coat pocket.*] I'm going to buy you a bottle of champagne. [NICK *goes to bar.* JOE *rises, takes hat from rack, puts coat on. The* NEWSBOY *jumps up, helps* JOE *with coat.*]

NICK. What's the matter, Joe?

JOE. Nothing. Nothing.

NICK. How about the champagne?

JOE. Thanks. [*Going.*]

NICK. It's not eleven yet. Where you going, Joe?

JOE. I don't know. Nowhere.

NICK. Will I see you tomorrow?

JOE. I don't know. I don't think so. [KIT CARSON *enters, walks to* JOE. JOE *and* KIT *look at one another knowingly.*]

JOE. Somebody just shot a man. How are you feeling?

KIT. Never felt better in my life. [*Loudly, bragging, but somber.*] I shot a man once. In San Francisco. Shot him two times. In 1939, I think it was. In October. Fellow named Blick or Glick or something like that. Couldn't stand the way he talked to ladies. Went up to my room and got my old pearl-handled revolver and waited for him on Pacific Street. Saw him walking, and let him have it, two times. Had to throw the beautiful revolver into the Bay. [HARRY, NICK, *the* ARAB *and the* DRUNKARD *close in around him.* JOE *searches his pockets, brings out the revolver, puts it in* KIT's *hand, looks at him with great admiration and affection.* JOE *walks slowly to the stairs leading to the street, turns and waves.* KIT, *and then one by one everybody else, waves, and the marble game goes into its beautiful American routine again: flag, lights, and music. The play ends.*]

CURTAIN

BERNARD SHAW: *CAESAR AND CLEOPATRA*

In Shaw's *Caesar and Cleopatra* the comedy derives primarily from character conflict, and thus the play requires a different approach from that made to the other comedies in the book. Although, as we have seen, comedies are known primarily by the pattern of their action, they also acquire some of their special qualities from the kinds of characters we meet in them. A review of some of the types of characters already encountered will prepare for the more elaborate characterization, the more profound insight into human nature, offered by the Shaw comedy.

The characters in comedies are as infinite as those in life, but they may for convenience be classified in three groups. Some are the ordinary people (like Tony Kirby and Alice Sycamore), who have little to distinguish them as characters or as people, but who, though undistinguished, are nevertheless frequently found at the center of a play because they are the ones caught in the situations that give the comedy substance. Neither flat nor stock, they are also certainly not well-rounded. We know only their surface, and only one side of that surface, because we see them only as they go by on the merry-go-round. They are never quite strong enough to stop the action.

Then there are the so-called comic types, usually caricatures of *humour* characters, in which one quality or trait dominates, often exaggerated until it becomes ridiculous. Kolenkhov, the Russian ballet instructor, and the G-man in *You Can't Take It With You;* most of the people who wander in and out of Nick's bar in *The Time of Your Life;* Britannus in *Caesar and Cleopatra*—these are all comic types. Such characters are flat, created by emphasizing one eccentricity, one foible, one folly, until the character *becomes* his abnormality. Sir Andrew Aguecheek in *Twelfth Night* is one of the classic comic types. Such characters individually, and as a group, remind us how usual abnormality is in our own lives and how insignificant our idiosyncrasies really are when weighed against the meaningful social relations we cherish. Without such characters, there would be no comedies.

The third kind of character peculiar to comedy is exemplified by Grandpa Vanderhof in *You Can't Take It With You,* by Joe in *The Time of Your Life,* and by the Caesar that Shaw created in *Caesar and Cleopatra.* Two qualities mark him. First, he is master of the scene in which he appears. Though an integral part of it—frequently, like Joe, a kind of puppet master—he seems to be insulated from its madness and confusion. Viewed in terms of the plot, he may be said to make the play go, to provide its motive force. Thus the Sycamore household runs on Grandfather's vision, to say nothing of his cash; Joe creates a life for Tom and Kitty; and it is Caesar's attempt to educate Cleopatra that Shaw tells about.

Secondly, viewed as a character with attributes of his own, this comic visionary belongs neither with the ordinary people whose lives he directs nor among the comic types for whom he is a kind of touchstone. His essential quality is a childlike, almost saintly, directness. Like the children in the old Hans Christian Andersen fairy tale, he sees—and makes us see—that the deluded Emperor has no clothes on. He is never bewildered by the multiplicity of the scene, nor confused by the masks others wear. Above all, he is the asker of simple questions, those that bring us up short and make us examine the whole foundation of our lives. Of the excited person who rushes by shouting, "We must!" he quietly asks, "Why must we?" The answer, found in the play in which such a character appears, usually reveals that it is our vanities and prejudices, disguised as inviolable social conventions, that keep us running in darkness instead of walking in the light. Such characters as Grandpa, Joe, and Caesar show us by their positive affirmations what the comic types reveal by their negative rejections—that all too frequently it is man's own shadow that clouds his light.

The comic seer may sometimes be as flat a character as any comic type. Like Joe in *The Time of Your Life*, he may so obviously be the spokesman for the dramatist as to approach that special type, the sentimental visionary. But so long as the playwright uses him primarily to move the scene, this danger can be avoided. One of the dramatist's key problems is here revealed, however; he must maintain adequate characterization in a context which prevents sustained analysis or revelation. Shaw solves the problem in *Caesar and Cleopatra* by making Caesar both the *subject* and the *motive force* of the play. In so doing, he illustrates the limits of characterization in a comedy.

In addition to being a comedy of character, *Caesar and Cleopatra* is also, as Shaw subtitles it, a history. But it is important to realize that, although the story consists of a series of quasi-historical events, the plot is essentially comic. True, Caesar comes, Caesar conquers, Caesar leaves; but there is more than a merely chronological sequence in these events. True, Caesar educates Cleopatra, and effects a change in her; but though much is changed, infinitely more remains the same. As the closing scene with Caesar, Cleopatra, and Rufio suggests, life in Egypt will be essentially the same after Caesar leaves as it was before he came. In the Egypt he leaves, as in the world it symbolizes, the same mad race for power will go on when his steadying influence is withdrawn. The play does follow Caesar as he walks through the world, but its concern is with what he sees, with what Cleopatra learns from him, not with where he is going. Its subject is not Caesar's destiny or Cleopatra's, but the human folly his presence reveals.

It is the existence of certain qualities in Caesar's character that brings forth this display of folly. Shaw insists in his notes to the play that he attributes to Caesar only one major quality, originality. As he says, "Originality gives a man an air of frankness, generosity, and magnanimity by enabling him to estimate the value of truth, money, or success in any particular instance quite independently of convention and moral generalization." It is this air of frankness, generosity, and magnanimity that confounds the power-corrupted world of the Egyptian court, and the earnest moralizing of Rufio and Britannus as well. But though witty paradoxes may suffice to reveal the follies of British society—for this is Shaw's actual subject—they cannot in themselves create a character, other than the comic type of the wit. And Shaw meant Caesar to be much more than a wit.

In creating a character like Caesar, in attempting to provide full characterization in comedy, Shaw finds it necessary to put his seer into enough situations to insure a cumulative effect from the many examples of folly his presence reveals. Hence the shifting scene and the three-pronged attack in the play: Cleopatra not as the tragic heroine but as the silly girl who must learn about power; Britannus as the prototype of pious British morality; the Egyptian court as the corrupt world. Shaw imposes on his story a pattern that moves Caesar rapidly back and forth among these elements, each change of scene heralding the revelation of some new folly.

Shaw's other problem is the need to provide Caesar with enough opportunity for *self*-revelation. But Caesar's only consistent characteristic—aside from those deeds of frankness, generosity, and magnanimity that are displayed to reflect the folly of others—emerges in the constant references to his age. If we must characterize Caesar by his own words, we will know him as a man conscious and fearful that he is past his prime. Obviously this one trait is not enough to produce a well-rounded character, but it suffices to make clear that the relationship between Caesar and Cleopatra is much different from that of Shakespeare's Antony and Cleopatra.

Like all dilemmas, this problem of making Caesar real has no solution; stating it, however, serves to indicate some of the limits of characterization in comedy. The Caesar that emerges in this play is a man with as many brilliant sides as the problems he encounters, but with little depth. Even in the climactic scene at the end of Act IV, following the significantly non-comic action of Pothinus' murder, Caesar is still but the reflector of our follies. The comparison to Christ reveals society's problems, not Caesar's torments. And the aforementioned closing scene, built around Rufio's parable, shows, again, that Caesar's character is not Shaw's primary concern.

A study of character on a notable scale, *Caesar and Cleopatra*, finally, illuminates one significant attribute of comedy and reveals how it forever differs from tragedy. Although Shaw tries everywhere in this play, as the stage directions indicate, to make us see Caesar as alternately proud and fearful, haughty and compassionate, vain and selfless—possessing, in other words, all the emotional extremes a man may have—he can never wholly succeed. For the very nature of comedy, as contrasted with tragedy, requires that its characters be treated externally. One reason why tragedies seem more meaningful and significant than comedies is that comedies are always more concerned with the actions than with the motives of characters. The man who is seen *doing* is usually not heard *meditating*. In tragedy we witness the weighing of the motives of the soul, but in comedy we observe the actions of the personality. Hence in comedies the characters are exhibited in groups and through their social actions. The masks we wear as we move through society are the real subjects of comedies, and the characters of comedies are those masks, not the souls and spirits they hide.

Caesar and Cleopatra

by

BERNARD SHAW

CÆSAR

CLEOPATRA

FTATATEETA

POTHINUS

THEODOTUS

PTOLEMY

ACHILLAS

RUFIO

BRITANNUS

LUCIUS SEPTIMIUS

APOLLODORUS

IRAS

CHARMIAN

BELZANOR

PERSIAN

CENTURION

SENTINEL

RA

BEL AFFRIS

NUBIAN SENTINEL

COURTIERS, SOLDIERS, SLAVES,

LADIES, *et al.*

PROLOGUE

In the doorway of the temple of RA *in Memphis. Deep gloom. An august personage with a hawk's head is mysteriously visible by his own light in the darkness within the temple. He surveys the modern audience with great contempt; and finally speaks the following words to them.*

Peace! Be silent and hearken unto me, ye quaint little islanders. Give ear, ye men with white paper on your breasts and nothing written thereon (to signify the innocency of your minds). Hear me, ye women who adorn yourselves alluringly and conceal your thoughts from your men, leading them to believe that ye deem them wondrous strong and masterful whilst in truth ye hold them in your hearts as children without judgment. Look upon my hawk's head; and know that I am Ra, who was once in Egypt a mighty god. Ye cannot kneel nor prostrate yourselves; for ye are packed in rows without freedom to move, obstructing one another's vision; neither do any of ye regard it as seemly to do aught until ye see all the rest do so too; wherefore it commonly happens that in great emergencies ye do nothing, though each telleth his fellow that something must be done. I ask you not for worship, but for silence. Let not your men speak nor your women cough; for I am come to draw you back two thousand years over the graves of sixty generations. Ye poor posterity, think not that ye are the first. Other fools before ye have seen the sun rise and set, and the moon change her shape and her hour. As they were so ye are; and yet not so great; for the pyramids my people built stand to this day; whilst the dustheaps on which ye slave, and which ye call empires, scatter in the wind even as ye pile your dead sons' bodies on them to make yet more dust.

Hearken to me then, oh ye compulsorily educated ones. Know that even as there is an old England and a new, and ye stand perplexed between the twain; so in the

263

days when I was worshipped was there an old Rome and a new, and men standing perplexed between them. And the old Rome was poor and little, and greedy and fierce, and evil in many ways; but because its mind was little and its work was simple, it knew its own mind and did its own work; and the gods pitied it and helped it and strengthened it and shielded it; for the gods are patient with littleness. Then the old Rome, like the beggar on horseback, presumed on the favor of the gods, and said, "Lo! there is neither riches nor greatness in our littleness: the road to riches and greatness is through robbery of the poor and slaughter of the weak." So they robbed their own poor until they became great masters of that art, and knew by what laws it could be made to appear seemly and honest. And when they had squeezed their own poor dry, they robbed the poor of other lands, and added those lands to Rome until there came a new Rome, rich and huge. And I, Ra, laughed; for the minds of the Romans remained the same size whilst their dominion spread over the earth.

Now mark me, that ye may understand what ye are presently to see. Whilst the Romans still stood between the old Rome and the new, there arose among them a mighty soldier: Pompey the Great. And the way of the soldier is the way of death; but the way of the gods is the way of life; and so it comes that a god at the end of his way is wise and a soldier at the end of his way is a fool. So Pompey held by the old Rome, in which only soldiers could become great; but the gods turned to the new Rome, in which any man with wit enough could become what he would. And Pompey's friend Julius Cæsar was on the side of the gods; for he saw that Rome had passed beyond the control of the little old Romans. This Cæsar was a great talker and a politician: he bought men with words and with gold, even as ye are bought. And when they would not be satisfied with words and gold, and demanded also the glories of war, Cæsar in his middle age turned his hand to that trade; and they that were against him when he sought their welfare, bowed down before him when he became a slayer and a conqueror; for such is the nature of you mortals. And as for Pompey, the gods grew tired of his triumphs and his airs of being himself a god; for he talked of law and duty and other matters that concerned not a mere human worm. And the gods smiled on Cæsar; for he lived the life they had given him boldly, and was not forever rebuking us for our indecent ways of creation, and hiding our handiwork as a shameful thing. Ye know well what I mean; for this is one of your own sins.

And thus it fell out between the old Rome and the new, that Cæsar said, "Unless I break the law of old Rome, I cannot take my share in ruling her; and the gift of ruling that the gods gave me will perish without fruit." But Pompey said, "The law is above all; and if thou break it thou shalt die." Then said Cæsar, "I will break it: kill me who can." And he broke it. And Pompey went for him, as ye say, with a great army to slay him and uphold the old Rome. So Cæsar fled across the Adriatic sea; for the high gods had a lesson to teach him, which lesson they shall also teach you in due time if ye continue to forget them and to worship that cad among gods, Mammon. Therefore before they raised Cæsar to be master of the world, they were minded to throw him down into the dust, even beneath the feet of Pompey, and blacken his face before the nations. And Pompey they raised higher than ever, he and his laws and his high mind that aped the gods, so that his fall might be the more terrible. And Pompey followed Cæsar, and overcame him with all the majesty of old Rome, and stood over him and over the whole world even as ye stand over it with your fleet that covers thirty miles of the sea. And when Cæsar was brought down to utter nothingness, he made a last stand to die honorably, and did not despair; for he said, "Against me there is Pompey, and the old Rome, and the law and the legions: all, all against me; but high above these are the gods; and Pompey is a fool." And the gods laughed and approved; and on the field of Pharsalia the impossible came to pass; the blood and iron ye pin your faith on fell before the spirit of man; for the spirit of man is the will of the gods; and Pompey's power crumbled in his hand, even as the power of imperial Spain crumbled when it was set against your fathers in the days when England was little, and knew her own mind, and had a mind to know instead of a circulation of newspapers. Wherefore look to it, lest some little people whom ye would enslave rise up and become in the hand of God the scourge of your boastings and your injustices and your lusts and stupidities.

And now, would ye know the end of Pompey, or will ye sleep while a god speaks? Heed my words well; for Pompey went where ye are gone, even to Egypt, where there was a Roman occupation even as there was but now a British one. And Cæsar pursued Pompey to Egypt: a Roman fleeing, and a Roman pursuing: dog eating dog. And the Egyptians said, "Lo: these Romans which have lent money to our kings and levied a distraint upon us with their arms, call for ever upon us to be loyal to them by betraying our own country to them. But now behold two Romes! Pompey's Rome and Cæsar's Rome! To which of the twain shall we pretend to be loyal?" So they turned in their perplexity to a soldier that had once served Pompey, and that knew the way of Rome and was full of her lusts. And they said to him, "Lo: in thy country dog eats dog; and both dogs are coming to eat us: what counsel hast thou to give us?" And this soldier, whose name was Lucius Septimius, and whom ye shall presently see before ye, replied, "Ye shall diligently consider which is the bigger dog of the two; and ye shall kill the other dog for his sake and thereby earn his favor." And the Egyptians said, "Thy counsel is expedient; but if we kill a man outside the law we set ourselves in the place of the gods; and this we dare not do. But thou, being a Roman, art accustomed to this kind of killing; for thou hast imperial instincts. Wilt thou therefore kill the lesser dog for us?" And he said, "I will; for I have made my home in Egypt; and I desire consideration and influence among you." And they said, "We knew well thou wouldst not do it for nothing: thou shalt have thy reward." Now when Pompey came, he came alone in a little galley, putting his trust in the law and the constitution. And it was plain to the people of Egypt that Pompey was now but a very small dog. So when he set his foot on the shore he was greeted by his old comrade Lucius Septimius, who welcomed him with one hand and with the other smote off his head, and kept it as it were a pickled cabbage to make a present to Cæsar. And mankind shuddered; but the gods laughed; for Septimius was but a knife that Pompey had sharpened; and when it turned against his own throat they said that Pompey had better have made Septimius a ploughman than so brave and ready-handed a slayer. Therefore again I bid you beware, ye who would all be Pompeys if ye dared; for war is a wolf that may come to your own door.

Are ye impatient with me? Do ye crave for a story of an unchaste woman? Hath the name of Cleopatra tempted ye hither? Ye foolish ones; Cleopatra is as yet but a child that is whipped by her nurse. And what I am about to shew you for the good of your souls is how Cæsar, seeking Pompey in Egypt, found Cleopatra; and how he received that present of a pickled cabbage that was once the head of Pompey; and what things happened between the old Cæsar and the child queen before he left Egypt and battled his way back to Rome to be slain there as Pompey was slain, by men in whom the spirit of Pompey still lived. All this ye shall see; and ye shall marvel, after your ignorant manner, that men twenty centuries ago were already just such as you, and spoke and lived as ye speak and live, no worse and no better, no wiser and no sillier. And the two thousand years that have past are to me, the god Ra, but a moment; nor is this day any other than the day in which Cæsar set foot in the land of my people. And now I leave you; for ye are a dull folk, and instruction is wasted on you; and I had not spoken so much but that it is in the nature of a god to struggle for ever with the dust and the darkness, and to drag from them, by the force of his longing for the divine, more life and more light. Settle ye therefore in your seats and keep silent; for ye are about to hear a man speak, and a great man he was, as ye count greatness. And fear not that I shall speak to you again: the rest of the story must ye learn from them that lived it. Farewell; and do not presume to applaud me. [*The temple vanishes in utter darkness.*]

AN ALTERNATIVE TO THE PROLOGUE

An October night on the Syrian border of Egypt towards the end of XXXIII Dynasty, in the year 706 by Roman computation, afterwards reckoned by Christian computation as 48 B.C. A great radiance of silver fire, the dawn of a moonlit night, is rising in the east. The stars and the cloudless sky are our own contemporaries, nineteen and a half centuries younger than we know them; but you would not guess that from their appearance. Below them are two notable drawbacks of civilization: a palace, and soldiers. The palace, an old, low, Syrian building of whitened mud, is not so ugly as Buckingham Palace; and the officers in the courtyard are more highly civilized than modern English officers: for example, they do not dig up the corpses of their dead enemies and mutilate them, as we dug up Cromwell and the Mahdi. They are in two groups: one intent on the gambling of their captain Belzanor, a warrior of fifty, who, with his spear on the ground beside his knee, is stooping to throw dice with a sly-looking young Persian recruit; the other gathered about a guardsman who has just finished telling a naughty story (still current in English barracks) at which they are laughing uproariously. They are about a dozen in number, all highly aristocratic young Egyptian guardsmen, handsomely equipped with weapons and armor, very unEnglish in point of not being ashamed of and uncomfortable in their professional dress; on the contrary, rather ostentatiously and arrogantly warlike, as valuing themselves on their military caste.

Belzanor is a typical veteran, tough and wilful; prompt, capable and crafty where brute force will serve; helpless and boyish when it will not: an active sergeant, an incompetent general, a deplorable dictator. Would, if influentially connected, be employed in the two last capacities by a modern European State on the strength of his success in the first. Is rather to be pitied just now in view of the fact that Julius Cæsar is invading his country. Not knowing this, is intent on his game with the Persian, whom, as a foreigner, he considers quite capable of cheating him.

His subalterns are mostly handsome young fellows whose interest in the game and the story symbolize with tolerable completeness the main interests in life of which they are conscious. Their spears are leaning against the walls, or lying on the ground ready to their hands. The corner of the courtyard forms a triangle of which one side is the front of the palace, with a doorway, the other a wall with a gateway. The story-tellers are on the palace side: the gamblers, on the gateway side. Close to the gateway, against the wall, is a stone block high enough to enable a Nubian sentinel, standing on it, to look over the wall. The yard is lighted by a torch stuck in the wall. As the laughter from the group round the storyteller dies away, the kneeling Persian, winning the throw, snatches up the stake from the ground.

BELZANOR. By Apis, Persian, thy gods are good to thee.

THE PERSIAN. Try yet again, O captain. Double or quits!

BELZANOR. No more. I am not in the vein.

THE SENTINEL. [Poising his javelin as he peers over the wall.] Stand. Who goes there? [They all start, listening. A strange VOICE replies from without.]

VOICE. The bearer of evil tidings.

BELZANOR. [Calling to the sentry.] Pass him.

THE SENTINEL. [Grounding his javelin.] Draw near, O bearer of evil tidings.

BELZANOR. [Pocketing the dice and picking up his spear.] Let us receive this man with honor. He bears evil tidings. [The GUARDSMEN seize their spears and gather about the gate, leaving a way *through for the newcomer.*]

PERSIAN. [*Rising from his knee.*] Are evil tidings, then, so honorable?

BELZANOR. O barbarous Persian, hear my instruction. In Egypt the bearer of good tidings is sacrificed to the gods as a thank offering; but no god will accept the blood of the messenger of evil. When we have good tidings, we are careful to send them in the mouth of the cheapest slave we can find. Evil tidings are borne by young noblemen who desire to bring themselves into notice. [*They join the rest at the gate.*]

THE SENTINEL. Pass. O young captain; and bow the head in the House of the Queen.

VOICE. Go anoint thy javelin with fat of swine, O Blackamoor: for before morning the Romans will make thee eat it to the very butt. [*The owner of the* VOICE, *a fairhaired dandy, dressed in a different fashion from that affected by the* GUARDSMEN, *but no less extravagantly, comes through the gateway laughing. He is somewhat battlestained; and his left forearm, bandaged, comes through a torn sleeve. In his right hand he carries a Roman sword in its sheath. He swaggers down the courtyard, the* PERSIAN *on his right,* BELZANOR *on his left, and the* GUARDSMEN *crowding down behind him.*]

BELZANOR. Who are thou that laughest in the House of Cleopatra the Queen, and in the teeth of Belzanor, the captain of her guard?

THE NEW COMER. I am Bel Affris, descended from the gods.

BELZANOR. [*Ceremoniously.*] Hail, cousin!

ALL. [*Except the* PERSIAN.] Hail, cousin!

PERSIAN. All the Queen's guards are descended from the gods, O stranger, save myself. I am Persian, and descended from many kings.

BEL AFFRIS. [*To the* GUARDSMEN.] Hail, cousins! [*To the* PERSIAN, *condescendingly.*] Hail, mortal!

BELZANOR. You have been in battle, Bel Affris; and you are a soldier among soldiers. You will not let the Queen's women have the first of your tidings.

BEL AFFRIS. I have no tidings, except that we shall have our throats cut presently, women, soldiers, and all.

PERSIAN. [*To* BELZANOR.] I told you so.

THE SENTINEL. [*Who has been listening.*] Woe, alas!

BEL AFFRIS. [*Calling to him.*] Peace, peace, poor Ethiop: destiny is with the gods who painted thee black. [*To* BELZANOR.] What has this mortal [*Indicating the* PERSIAN.] told you?

BELZANOR. He says that the Roman Julius Cæsar, who has landed on our shores with a handful of followers, will make himself master of Egypt. He is afraid of the Roman soldiers. [*The* GUARDSMEN *laugh with boisterous scorn.*] Peasants, brought up to scare crows and follow the plough! Sons of smiths and millers and tanners! And we nobles, consecrated to arms, descended from the gods!

PERSIAN. Belzanor: the gods are not always good to their poor relations.

BELZANOR. [*Hotly, to the* PERSIAN.] Man to man, are we worse than the slaves of Cæsar?

BEL AFFRIS. [*Stepping between them.*] Listen, cousin. Man to man, we Egyptians are as gods above the Romans.

THE GUARDSMEN. [*Exultantly.*] Aha!

BEL AFFRIS. But this Cæsar does not pit man against man: he throws a legion at you where you are weakest as he throws a stone from a catapult; and that legion is as a man with one head, a thousand arms, and no religion. I have fought against them; and I know.

BELZANOR. [*Derisively.*] Were you frightened, cousin? [*The* GUARDSMEN *roar with laughter, their eyes sparkling at the wit of their captain.*]

BEL AFFRIS. No, cousin; but I was beaten. They were frightened (perhaps); but they scattered us like chaff. [*The* GUARDSMEN, *much damped, utter a growl of contemptuous disgust.*]

BELZANOR. Could you not die?

BEL AFFRIS. No: that was too easy to be worthy of a descendant of the gods. Besides, there was no time: all was over in a moment. The attack came just where we least expected it.

BELZANOR. That shews that the Romans are cowards.

BEL AFFRIS. They care nothing about cowardice, these Romans: they fight to win. The pride and honor of war are nothing to them.

PERSIAN. Tell us the tale of the battle. What befell?

THE GUARDSMEN. [*Gathering eagerly round* BEL AFFRIS.] Ay: the tale of the battle.

BEL AFFRIS. Know then, that I am a novice in the guard of the temple of Ra in Memphis, serving neither Cleopatra nor her brother Ptolemy, but only the high gods. We went a journey to inquire of Ptolemy why he had driven Cleopatra into Syria, and how we of Egypt should deal with the Roman Pompey, newly come to our shores after his defeat by Cæsar at Pharsalia. What, think ye, did we learn? Even that Cæsar is coming also in hot pursuit of his foe, and that Ptolemy has slain Pompey, whose severed head he holds in readiness to present to the conqueror. [*Sensation among the* GUARDSMEN.] Nay, more: we found that Cæsar is already come; for we had not made half a day's journey on our way back when we came upon a city rabble flying from his legions, whose landing they had gone out to withstand.

BELZANOR. And ye, the temple guard! did ye not withstand these legions?

BEL AFFRIS. What man could, that we did. But there came the sound of a trumpet whose voice was as the cursing of a black mountain. Then saw we a moving wall of shields coming towards us. You know how the heart burns when you charge a fortified wall; but how if the fortified wall were to charge you?

THE PERSIAN. [*Exulting in having told them so.*] Did I not say it?

BEL AFFRIS. When the wall came nigh, it changed into a line of men—common fellows enough, with helmets, leather tunics, and breastplates. Every man of them flung his javelin: the one that came my way drove through my shield as through a papyrus—lo there! [*He points to the bandage on his left arm.*] and would have gone through my neck had I not stooped. They were charging at the double then, and were upon us with short swords almost as soon as their javelins. When a man is close to you with such a sword, you can do nothing with our weapons: they are all too long.

THE PERSIAN. What did you do?

BEL AFFRIS. Doubled my fist and smote my Roman on the sharpness of his jaw. He was but mortal after all: he lay down in a stupor; and I took his sword and laid it on. [*Drawing the sword.*] Lo! a Roman sword with Roman blood on it!

THE GUARDSMEN. [*Approvingly.*] Good! [*They take the sword and hand it round, examining it curiously.*]

THE PERSIAN. And your men?

BEL AFFRIS. Fled. Scattered like sheep.

BELZANOR. [*Furiously.*] The cowardly slaves! Leaving the descendants of the gods to be butchered!

BEL AFFRIS. [*With acid coolness.*] The descendants of the gods did not stay to be butchered, cousin. The battle was not to the strong; but the race was to the swift. The Romans who have no chariots, sent a cloud of horsemen in pursuit, and slew multitudes. Then our high priest's captain rallied a dozen descendants of the gods and exhorted us to die fighting. I said to myself: surely it is safer to stand than to lose my breath and be stabbed in the back; so I joined our captain and stood. Then the Romans treated us with respect; for no man attacks a lion when the field is full of sheep, except for the pride and honor of war, of which these Romans know nothing. So we escaped with our lives; and I am come to warn you that you must open your gates to Cæsar; for his advance guard is scarce an hour behind me; and not an Egyptian warrior is left standing between you and his legions.

THE SENTINEL. Woe, alas! [*He throws down his javelin and flies into the palace.*]

BELZANOR. Nail him to the door, quick! [*The* GUARDSMEN *rush for him with their spears; but he is too quick for them.*] Now this news will run through the palace like fire through stubble.

BEL AFFRIS. What shall we do to save the women from the Romans?

BELZANOR. Why not kill them?

PERSIAN. Because we should have to pay blood money for some of them. Better let the Romans kill them: it is cheaper.

BELZANOR. [*Awestruck at his brain power.*] O subtle one! O serpent!

BEL AFFRIS. But your Queen?

BELZANOR. True: we must carry off Cleopatra.

BEL AFFRIS. Will ye not await her command?

BELZANOR. Command! a girl of sixteen! Not we. At Memphis ye deem her a Queen: here we know better. I will take her on the crupper of my horse. When we soldiers have carried her out of Cæsar's reach, then the priests and the nurses and the rest of them can pretend she is a Queen again, and put their commands into her mouth.

PERSIAN. Listen to me, Belzanor.

BELZANOR. Speak, O subtle beyond thy years.

THE PERSIAN. Cleopatra's brother Ptolemy is at war with her. Let us sell her to him.

THE GUARDSMEN. O subtle one! O serpent!

BELZANOR. We dare not. We are descended from the gods; but Cleopatra is descended from the river Nile; and the lands of our fathers will grow no grain if the Nile rises not to water them. Without our father's gifts we should live the lives of dogs.

PERSIAN. It is true: the Queen's guard cannot live on its pay. But hear me further, O ye kinsmen of Osiris.

THE GUARDSMEN. Speak, O subtle one. Hear the serpent begotten!

PERSIAN. Have I heretofore spoken truly to you of Cæsar, when you thought I mocked you?

GUARDSMEN. Truly, truly.

BELZANOR. [*Reluctantly admitting it.*] So Bel Affris says.

PERSIAN. Hear more of him, then. This Cæsar is a great lover of women: he makes them his friends and counsellors.

BELZANOR. Faugh! This rule of women will be the ruin of Egypt.

THE PERSIAN. Let it rather be the ruin of Rome! Cæsar grows old now: he is past fifty and full of labors and battles. He is too old for the young women; and the old women are too wise to worship him.

BEL AFFRIS. Take heed, Persian. Cæsar is by this time almost within earshot.

PERSIAN. Cleopatra is not yet a woman: neither is she wise. But she already troubles men's wisdom.

BELZANOR. Ay: that is because she is descended from the river Nile and a black kitten of the sacred White Cat. What then?

PERSIAN. Why, sell her secretly to Ptolemy, and then offer ourselves to Cæsar as volunteers to fight for the overthrow of her brother and the rescue of our Queen, the Great Granddaughter of the Nile.

THE GUARDSMEN. O serpent!

PERSIAN. He will listen to us if we come with her picture in our mouths. He will conquer and kill her brother, and reign in Egypt with Cleopatra for his Queen. And we shall be her guard.

GUARDSMEN. O subtlest of all the serpents! O admiration! O wisdom!

BEL AFFRIS. He will also have arrived before you have done talking, O word spinner.

BELZANOR. That is true. [*An affrighted uproar in the palace interrupts him.*] Quick: the flight has begun: guard the door. [*They rush to the door and form a cordon before it with their spears. A mob of women-servants and nurses surges out. Those in front recoil from the spears, screaming to those behind to keep back.* BELZANOR's *voice dominates the disturbance as he shouts.*] Back there. In again, unprofitable cattle.

THE GUARDSMEN. Back, unprofitable cattle.

BELZANOR. Send us out Ftatateeta, the Queen's chief nurse.

THE WOMEN. [*Calling into the palace.*] Ftatateeta, Ftatateeta. Come, come. Speak to Belzanor.

A WOMAN. Oh, keep back. You are thrusting me on the spearheads. [*A huge grim woman, her face covered with a network of tiny wrinkles, and her eyes old, large, and wise; sinewy handed, very tall, very strong; with the mouth of a bloodhound and the jaws of a bulldog, appears on the threshold. She is dressed like a person of consequence in the palace, and confronts the* GUARDSMEN *insolently.*]

FTATATEETA. Make way for the Queen's chief nurse.

BELZANOR. [*With solemn arrogance.*] Ftatateeta: I am Belzanor, the captain of the Queen's guard, descended from the gods.

FTATATEETA. [*Retorting his arrogance with interest.*] Belzanor: I am Ftatateeta, the Queen's chief nurse; and your divine ancestors were proud to be painted on the wall in the pyramids of the kings whom my fathers served. [*The women laugh triumphantly.*]

BELZANOR. [*With grim humor.*] Ftatateeta: daughter of a long-tongued, swivel-eyed chameleon, the Romans are at hand. [*A cry of terror from* THE WOMEN: *they would fly but for the spears.*] Not even the descendants of the gods can resist them; for they have each man seven arms, each carrying seven spears. The blood in their veins is boiling quicksilver; and their wives become mothers in three hours, and are slain and eaten the next day. [*A shudder of horror from* THE WOMEN. FTATATEETA, *despising them and scorning the soldiers, pushes her way through the crowd and confronts the spear points undismayed.*]

FTATATEETA. Then fly and save yourselves, O cowardly sons of the cheap clay gods that are sold to fish porters; and leave us to shift for ourselves.

BELZANOR. Not until you have first done our bidding, O terror of manhood. Bring out Cleopatra the Queen to us; and then go whither you will.

FTATATEETA. [*With a derisive laugh.*] Now I know why the gods have taken her out of our hands. [*The* GUARDSMEN *start and look at one another.*] Know, thou foolish soldier, that the Queen has been missing since an hour past sundown.

BELZANOR. [*Furiously.*] Hag: you have hidden her to sell to Cæsar or her brother. [*He grasps her by the left wrist, and drags her, helped by a few of the guard, to the middle of the courtyard, where, as they fling her on her knees, he draws a murderous looking knife.*] Where is she? Where is she? or—[*He threatens to cut her throat.*]

FTATATEETA. [*Savagely.*] Touch me, dog; and the Nile will not rise on your fields for seven times seven years of famine.

BELZANOR. [*Frightened, but desperate.*] I will sacrifice: I will pay. Or stay. [*To the* PERSIAN.] You, O subtle one: your father's lands lie far from the Nile. Slay her.

PERSIAN. [*Threatening her with his knife.*] Persia has but one god; yet he loves the blood of old women. Where is Cleopatra?

FTATATEETA. Persian: as Osiris lives, I do not know. I chid her for bringing evil days upon us by talking to the sacred cats of the priests, and carrying them in her arms. I told her she would be left alone here when the Romans came as a punishment for her disobedience. And now she is gone—run away—hidden. I speak the truth. I call Osiris to witness—

THE WOMEN. [*Protesting officiously.*] She speaks the truth, Belzanor.

BELZANOR. You have frightened the child: she is hiding. Search—quick—into the palace—search every corner. [*The* GUARDS, *led by* BELZANOR, *shoulder their way into the palace through the flying crowd of women, who escape through the courtyard gate.*]

FTATATEETA. [*Screaming.*] Sacrilege! Men in the Queen's chambers! Sa— [*Her voice dies away as the Persian puts his knife to her throat.*]

BEL AFFRIS. [*Laying a hand on* FTATATEETA's *left shoulder.*] Forbear her yet a moment, Persian. [*To* FTATATEETA, *very significantly.*] Mother: your gods are asleep or away hunting; and the sword is at your throat. Bring us to where the Queen is hid, and you shall live.

FTATATEETA. [*Contemptuously.*] Who shall stay the sword in the hand of a fool, if the high gods put it there? Listen to me, ye young men without understanding. Cleopatra fears me; but she fears the Romans more. There is but one power greater in her eyes than the wrath of the Queen's nurse and the cruelty of Cæsar; and that is the power of the Sphinx that sits in the desert watching the way to the sea. What she would have it know, she tells into the ears of the sacred cats; and on her birthday she sacrifices to it and decks it with poppies.

Go ye therefore into the desert and seek Cleopatra in the shadow of the Sphinx; and on your heads see to it that no harm comes to her.

BEL AFFRIS. [*To the* PERSIAN.] May we believe this, O subtle one?

PERSIAN. Which way come the Romans?

BEL AFFRIS. Over the desert, from the sea, by this very Sphinx.

PERSIAN. [*To* FTATATEETA.] O mother of guile! O aspic's tongue! You have made up this tale so that we two may go into the desert and perish on the spears of the Romans. [*Lifting his knife.*] Taste death.

FTATATEETA. Not from thee, baby. [*She snatches his ankle from under him and flies stooping along the palace wall, vanishing in the darkness within its precinct.* BEL AFFRIS *roars with laughter as the* PERSIAN *tumbles. The* GUARDSMEN *rush out of the palace with* BELZANOR *and a mob of fugitives, mostly carrying bundles.*]

PERSIAN. Have you found Cleopatra?

BELZANOR. She is gone. We have searched every corner.

THE NUBIAN SENTINEL. [*Appearing at the door of the palace.*] Woe! Alas! Fly, fly!

BELZANOR. What is the matter now?

THE NUBIAN SENTINEL. The sacred white cat has been stolen.

ALL. Woe! woe! [*General panic. They all fly with cries of consternation. The torch is thrown down and extinguished in the rush. The noise of the fugitives dies away. Darkness and dead silence.*]

ACT ONE

The same darkness into which the temple of Ra and the Syrian palace vanished. The same silence. Suspense. Then the blackness and stillness break softly into silver mist and strange airs as the windswept harp of Memnon plays at the dawning of the moon. It rises full over the desert; and a vast horizon comes into relief, broken by a huge shape which soon reveals itself in the spreading radiance as a Sphinx pedestalled on the sands. The light still clears, until the upraised eyes of the image are distinguished looking straight forward and upward in infinite fearless vigil, and a mass of color between its great paws defines itself as a heap of red poppies on which a girl lies motionless, her silken vest heaving gently and regularly with the breathing of a dreamless sleeper, and her braided hair glittering in a shaft of moonlight like a bird's wing.

Suddenly there comes from afar a vaguely fearful sound (it might be the bellow of a Minotaur softened by great distance) and Memnon's music stops. Silence: then a few faint high-ringing trumpet notes. Then silence again. Then a man comes from the south with stealing steps, ravished by the mystery of the night, all wonder, and halts, lost in contemplation, opposite the left flank of the Sphinx, whose bosom, with its burden, is hidden from him by its massive shoulder.

THE MAN. Hail, Sphinx: salutation from Julius Cæsar! I have wandered in many lands, seeking the lost regions from which my birth into this world exiled me, and the company of creatures such as I myself. I have found flocks and pastures, men and cities, but no other Cæsar, no air native to me, no man kindred to me, none who can do my day's deed, and think my night's thought. In the little world yonder, Sphinx, my place is as high as yours in this great desert; only I wander, and you sit still; I conquer, and you endure; I work and wonder, you watch and wait; I look up and am dazzled, look down and am darkened, look round and am puzzled, whilst your eyes never turn from looking out—out of the world—to the lost region—the home from which we have strayed. Sphinx, you and

I, strangers to the race of men, are no strangers to one another: have I not been conscious of you and of this place since I was born? Rome is a madman's dream: this is my Reality. These starry lamps of yours I have seen from afar in Gaul, in Britain, in Spain, in Thessaly, signalling great secrets to some eternal sentinel below, whose post I never could find. And here at last is their sentinel—an image of the constant and immortal part of my life, silent, full of thoughts, alone in the silver desert. Sphinx, Sphinx: I have climbed mountains at night to hear in the distance the stealthy footfall of the winds that chase your sands in forbidden play —our invisible children, O Sphinx, laughing in whispers. My way hither was the way of destiny; for I am he of whose genius you are the symbol: part brute, part woman, and part god—nothing of man in me at all. Have I read your riddle, Sphinx?

THE GIRL. [*Who has wakened, and peeped cautiously from her nest to see who is speaking.*] Old gentleman.

CÆSAR. [*Starting violently, and clutching his sword.*] Immortal gods!

THE GIRL. Old gentleman: dont run away.

CÆSAR. [*Stupefied.*] "Old gentleman: dont run away"! ! ! This! to Julius Cæsar!

THE GIRL. [*Urgently.*] Old gentleman.

CÆSAR. Sphinx: you presume on your centuries. I am younger than you, though your voice is but a girl's voice as yet.

THE GIRL. Climb up here, quickly; or the Romans will come and eat you.

CÆSAR. [*Running forward past the Sphinx's shoulder, and seeing her.*] A child at its breast! a divine child!

THE GIRL. Come up quickly. You must get up at its side and creep round.

CÆSAR. [*Amazed.*] Who are you?

THE GIRL. Cleopatra, Queen of Egypt.

CÆSAR. Queen of the Gypsies, you mean.

CLEOPATRA. You must not be disrespectful to me, or the Sphinx will let the Romans eat you. Come up. It is quite cosy here.

CÆSAR. [*To himself.*] What a dream! What a magnificent dream! Only let me

not wake, and I will conquer ten continents to pay for dreaming it out to the end. [*He climbs to the Sphinx's flank, and presently reappears to her on the pedestal, stepping round to its right shoulder.*]

CLEOPATRA. Take care. That's right. Now sit down: you may have its other paw. [*She seats herself comfortably on its left paw.*] It is very powerful and will protect us; but [*Shivering, and with plaintive loneliness.*] it would not take any notice of me or keep me company. I am glad you have come: I was very lonely. Did you happen to see a white cat anywhere?

CÆSAR. [*Sitting slowly down on the right paw in extreme wonderment.*] Have you lost one?

CLEOPATRA. Yes: the sacred white cat: is it not dreadful? I brought him here to sacrifice him to the Sphinx; but when we got a little way from the city a black cat called him, and he jumped out of my arms and ran away to it. Do you think that the black cat can have been my great-great-great-grandmother?

CÆSAR. [*Staring at her.*] Your great-great-great-grandmother! Well, why not? Nothing would surprise me on this night of nights.

CLEOPATRA. I think it must have been. My great-grandmother's great-grandmother was a black kitten of the sacred white cat; and the river Nile made her his seventh wife. That is why my hair is so wavy. And I always want to be let do as I like, no matter whether it is the will of the gods or not: that is because my blood is made with Nile water.

CÆSAR. What are you doing here at this time of night? Do you live here?

CLEOPATRA. Of course not: I am the Queen; and I shall live in the palace at Alexandria when I have killed my brother, who drove me out of it. When I am old enough I shall do just what I like. I shall be able to poison the slaves and see them wriggle, and pretend to Ftatateeta that she is going to be put into the fiery furnace.

CÆSAR. Hm! Meanwhile why are you not at home and in bed?

CLEOPATRA. Because the Romans are

coming to eat us all. You are not at home and in bed either.

CÆSAR. [*With conviction.*] Yes I am. I live in a tent; and I am now in that tent, fast asleep and dreaming. Do you suppose that I believe you are real, you impossible little dream witch?

CLEOPATRA. [*Giggling and leaning trustfully towards him.*] You are a funny old gentleman. I like you.

CÆSAR. Ah, that spoils the dream. Why dont you dream that I am young?

CLEOPATRA. I wish you were; only I think I should be more afraid of you. I like men, especially young men with round strong arms; but I am afraid of them. You are old and rather thin and stringy; but you have a nice voice; and I like to have somebody to talk to, though I think you are a little mad. It is the moon that makes you talk to yourself in that silly way.

CÆSAR. What! you heard that, did you? I was saying my prayers to the great Sphinx.

CLEOPATRA. But this isn't the great Sphinx.

CÆSAR. [*Much disappointed, looking up at the statue.*] What!

CLEOPATRA. This is only a dear little kitten of a Sphinx. Why, the great Sphinx is so big that it has a temple between its paws. This is my pet Sphinx. Tell me: do you think the Romans have any sorcerers who could take us away from the Sphinx by magic?

CÆSAR. Why? Are you afraid of the Romans?

CLEOPATRA. [*Very seriously.*] Oh, they would eat us if they caught us. They are barbarians. Their chief is called Julius Cæsar. His father was a tiger and his mother a burning mountain; and his nose is like an elephant's trunk. [*Cæsar involuntarily rubs his nose.*] They all have long noses, and ivory tusks, and little tails, and seven arms with a hundred arrows in each; and they live on human flesh.

CÆSAR. Would you like me to shew you a real Roman?

CLEOPATRA. [*Terrified.*] No. You are frightening me.

CÆSAR. No matter: this is only a dream—

CLEOPATRA. [*Excitedly.*] It is not a dream: it is not a dream. See, see. [*She plucks a pin from her hair and jabs it repeatedly into his arm.*]

CÆSAR. Ffff—Stop. [*Wrathfully.*] How dare you?

CLEOPATRA. [*Abashed.*] You said you were dreaming. [*Whimpering.*] I only wanted to shew you—

CÆSAR. [*Gently.*] Come, come: dont cry. A queen mustnt cry. [*He rubs his arm, wondering at the reality of the smart.*] Am I awake? [*He strikes his hand against the Sphinx to test its solidity. It feels so real that he begins to be alarmed, and says perplexedly.*] Yes, I— [*Quite panicstricken.*] No: impossible: madness, madness! [*Desperately.*] Back to camp— to camp. [*He rises to spring down from the pedestal.*]

CLEOPATRA. [*Flinging her arms in terror round him.*] No: you shant leave me. No, no, no: dont go. I'm afraid—afraid of the Romans.

CÆSAR. [*As the conviction that he is really awake forces itself on him.*] Cleopatra: can you see my face well?

CLEOPATRA. Yes. It is so white in the moonlight.

CÆSAR. Are you sure it is the moonlight that makes me look whiter than an Egyptian? [*Grimly.*] Do you notice that I have a rather long nose?

CLEOPATRA. [*Recoiling, paralysed by a terrible suspicion.*] Oh!

CÆSAR. It is a Roman nose, Cleopatra.

CLEOPATRA. Ah! [*With a piercing scream she springs up; darts round the left shoulder of the Sphinx; scrambles down to the sand; and falls on her knees in frantic supplication, shrieking.*] Bite him in two, Sphinx: bite him in two. I meant to sacrifice the white cat—I did indeed—I [*Cæsar, who has slipped down from the pedestal, touches her on the shoulder.*] —Ah! [*She buries her head in her arms.*]

CÆSAR. Cleopatra: shall I teach you a way to prevent Cæsar from eating you?

CLEOPATRA. [*Clinging to him piteously.*] Oh do, do, do. I will steal Ftatateeta's jewels and give them to you. I will make the river Nile water your lands twice a year.

CÆSAR. Peace, peace, my child. Your gods are afraid of the Romans: you see the Sphinx dare not bite me, nor prevent me carrying you off to Julius Cæsar.

CLEOPATRA. [*In pleading murmurings.*] You wont, you wont. You said you wouldnt.

CÆSAR. Cæsar never eats women.

CLEOPATRA. [*Springing up full of hope.*] What!

CÆSAR. [*Impressively.*] But he eats girls [*she relapses*] and cats. Now you are a silly little girl; and you are descended from the black kitten. You are both a girl and a cat.

CLEOPATRA. [*Trembling.*] And will he eat me?

CÆSAR. Yes; unless you make him believe that you are a woman.

CLEOPATRA. Oh, you must get a sorcerer to make a woman of me. Are you a sorcerer?

CÆSAR. Perhaps. But it will take a long time; and this very night you must stand face to face with Cæsar in the palace of your fathers.

CLEOPATRA. No, no. I darent.

CÆSAR. Whatever dread may be in your soul—however terrible Cæsar may be to you—you must confront him as a brave woman and a great queen; and you must feel no fear. If your hand shakes: if your voice quavers; then—night and death! [*She moans.*] But if he thinks you worthy to rule, he will set you on the throne by his side and make you the real ruler of Egypt.

CLEOPATRA. [*Despairingly.*] No: he will find me out: he will find me out.

CÆSAR. [*Rather mournfully.*] He is easily deceived by women. Their eyes dazzle him; and he sees them not as they are, but as he wishes them to appear to him.

CLEOPATRA. [*Hopefully.*] Then we will cheat him. I will put on Ftatateeta's headdress; and he will think me quite an old woman.

CÆSAR. If you do that he will eat you at one mouthful.

CLEOPATRA. But I will give him a cake with my magic opal and seven hairs of the white cat baked in it; and—

CÆSAR. [*Abruptly.*] Pah! you are a little fool. He will eat your cake and you too. [*He turns contemptuously from her.*]

CLEOPATRA. [*Running after him and clinging to him.*] Oh please, please! I will do whatever you tell me. I will be good. I will be your slave. [*Again the terrible bellowing note sounds across the desert, now closer at hand. It is the bucina, the Roman war trumpet.*]

CÆSAR. Hark!

CLEOPATRA. [*Trembling.*] What was that?

CÆSAR. Cæsar's voice.

CLEOPATRA. [*Pulling at his hand.*] Let us run away. Come. Oh, come.

CÆSAR. You are safe with me until you stand on your throne to receive Cæsar. Now lead me thither.

CLEOPATRA. [*Only too glad to get away.*] I will, I will. [*Again the bucina.*] Oh come, come, come: the gods are angry. Do you feel the earth shaking?

CÆSAR. It is the tread of Cæsar's legions.

CLEOPATRA. [*Drawing him away.*] This way, quickly. And let us look for the white cat as we go. It is he that has turned you into a Roman.

CÆSAR. Incorrigible, oh, incorrigible! Away! [*He follows her, the bucina sounding louder as they steal across the desert. The moonlight wanes: the horizon again shews black against the sky, broken only by the fantastic silhouette of the Sphinx. The sky itself vanishes in darkness, from which there is no relief until the gleam of a distant torch falls on great Egyptian pillars supporting the roof of a majestic corridor. At the further end of this corridor a Nubian slave appears carrying the torch.* CÆSAR, *still led by* CLEOPATRA, *follows him. They come down the corridor,* CÆSAR, *peering keenly about at the strange architecture, and at the pillar shadows between which, as the passing torch makes them hurry noiselessly backwards, figures of men with wings and hawk's heads, and vast black marble cats, seem to flit in and out of ambush. Further along, the wall turns a corner and makes a spacious transept in which* CÆSAR *sees, on his right, a throne, and behind the throne a door. On each side of the throne is a slender pillar with a lamp on it.*]

CÆSAR. What place is this?

CLEOPATRA. This is where I sit on the throne when I am allowed to wear my crown and robes. [*The slave holds his torch to shew the throne.*]

CÆSAR. Order the slave to light the lamps.

CLEOPATRA. [*Shyly.*] Do you think I may?

CÆSAR. Of course. You are the Queen. [*She hesitates.*] Go on.

CLEOPATRA. [*Timidly, to the slave.*] Light all the lamps.

FTATATEETA. [*Suddenly coming from behind the throne.*] Stop. [*The slave stops. She turns sternly to* CLEOPATRA, *who quails like a naughty child.*] Who is this you have with you; and how dare you order the lamps to be lighted without my permission?* [CLEOPATRA *is dumb with apprehension.*]

CÆSAR. Who is she?

CLEOPATRA. Ftatateeta.

FTATATEETA. [*Arrogantly.*] Chief nurse to—

CÆSAR. [*Cutting her short.*] I speak to the Queen. Be silent. [*To* CLEOPATRA.] Is this how your servants know their places? Send her away; and do you [*to the slave*] do as the Queen has bidden. [*The slave lights the lamps. Meanwhile* CLEOPATRA *stands hesitating, afraid of* FTATATEETA.] You are the Queen: send her away.

CLEOPATRA. [*Cajoling.*] Ftatateeta, dear: you must go away—just for a little.

CÆSAR. You are not commanding her to go away: you are beggng her. You are no Queen. You will be eaten. Farewell. [*He turns to go.*]

CLEOPATRA. [*Clutching him.*] No, no, no. Dont leave me.

CÆSAR. A Roman does not stay with queens who are afraid of their slaves.

CLEOPATRA. I am not afraid. Indeed I am not afraid.

FTATATEETA. We shall see who is afraid here. [*Menacingly.*] Cleopatra—

CÆSAR. On your knees, woman: am I also a child that you dare trifle with me? [*He points to the floor at* CLEOPATRA'S *feet.* FTATATEETA, *half cowed, half savage,*

hesitates. CÆSAR *calls to the* NUBIAN.] Slave. [*The* NUBIAN *comes to him.*] Can you cut off a head? [*The* NUBIAN *nods and grins ecstatically, showing all his teeth.* CÆSAR *takes his sword by the scabbard, ready to offer the hilt to the* NUBIAN, *and turns again to* FTATATEETA, *repeating his gesture.*] Have you remembered yourself, mistress? [FTATATEETA, *crushed, kneels before* CLEOPATRA, *who can hardly believe her eyes.*]

FTATATEETA. [*Hoarsely.*] O Queen, forget not thy servant in the days of thy greatness.

CLEOPATRA. [*Blazing with excitement.*] Go. Begone. Go away. [FTATATEETA *rises with stooped head, and moves backwards towards the door.* CLEOPATRA *watches her submission eagerly, almost clapping her hands, which are trembling. Suddenly she cries.*] Give me something to beat her with. [*She snatches a snake-skin from the throne and dashes after* FTATATEETA, *whirling it like a scourge in the air.* CÆSAR *makes a bound and manages to catch her and hold her while* FTATATEETA *escapes.*]

CÆSAR. You scratch, kitten, do you?

CLEOPATRA. [*Breaking from him.*] I will beat somebody. I will beat him. [*She attacks the slave.*] There, there, there! [*The slave flies for his life up the corridor and vanishes. She throws the snake-skin away and jumps on the step of the throne with her arms waving, crying.*] I am a real Queen at last—a real, real Queen! Cleopatra the Queen! [CÆSAR *shakes his head dubiously, the advantage of the change seeming open to question from the point of view of the general welfare of Egypt. She turns and looks at him exultantly. Then she jumps down from the steps, runs to him, and flings her arms round him rapturously, crying.*] Oh, I love you for making me a Queen.

CÆSAR. But queens love only kings.

CLEOPATRA. I will make all the men I love kings. I will make you a king. I will have many young kings, with round, strong arms; and when I am tired of them I will whip them to death; but you shall always be my king: my nice, kind, wise, good old king.

CÆSAR. Oh, my wrinkles, my wrinkles!

And my child's heart! You will be the most dangerous of all Cæsar's conquests.

CLEOPATRA. [*Appalled.*] Cæsar! I forgot Cæsar. [*Anxiously.*] You will tell him that I am a Queen, will you not?—a real Queen. Listen! [*Stealthily coaxing him.*] let us run away and hide until Cæsar is gone.

CÆSAR. If you fear Cæsar, you are no true queen; and though you were to hide beneath a pyramid, he would go straight to it and lift it with one hand. And then —! [*He chops his teeth together.*]

CLEOPATRA. [*Trembling.*] Oh!

CÆSAR. Be afraid if you dare. [*The note of the bucina resounds again in the distance. She moans with fear.* CÆSAR *exults in it, exclaiming.*] Aha! Cæsar approaches the throne of Cleopatra. Come: take your place. [*He takes her hand and leads her to the throne. She is too downcast to speak.*] Ho, there, Teetatota. How do you call your slaves?

CLEOPATRA. [*Spiritlessly, as she sinks on the throne and cowers there, shaking.*] Clap your hands. [*He claps his hands.* FTATATEETA *returns.*]

CÆSAR. Bring the Queen's robes, and her crown, and her women; and prepare her.

CLEOPATRA. [*Eagerly—recovering herself a little.*] Yes, the crown, Ftatateeta: I shall wear the crown.

FTATATEETA. For whom must the Queen put on her state?

CÆSAR. For a citizen of Rome. A king of kings, Totateeta.

CLEOPATRA. [*Stamping at her.*] How dare you ask questions? Go and do as you are told. [FTATATEETA *goes out with a grim smile.* CLEOPATRA *goes on eagerly, to* CÆSAR.] Cæsar will know that I am a Queen when he sees my crown and robes, will he not?

CÆSAR. No. How shall he know that you are not a slave dressed up in the Queen's ornaments?

CLEOPATRA. You must tell him.

CÆSAR. He will not ask me. He will know Cleopatra by her pride, her courage, her majesty, and her beauty. [*She looks very doubtful.*] Are you trembling?

CLEOPATRA. [*Shivering with dread.*] No, I–I– [*In a very sickly voice.*] No.

[FTATATEETA *and* THREE WOMEN *come in with the regalia.*]

FTATATEETA. Of all the Queen's women, these three alone are left. The rest are fled. [*They begin to deck* CLEOPATRA, *who submits, pale and motionless.*]

CÆSAR. Good, good. Three are enough. Poor Cæsar generally has to dress himself.

FTATATEETA. [*Contemptuously.*] The queen of Egypt is not a Roman barbarian. [*To* CLEOPATRA.] Be brave, my nursling. Hold up your head before this stranger.

CÆSAR. [*Admiring* CLEOPATRA, *and placing the crown on her head.*] Is it sweet or bitter to be a Queen, Cleopatra?

CLEOPATRA. Bitter.

CÆSAR. Cast out fear; and you will conquer Cæsar. Tota: are the Romans at hand?

FTATATEETA. They are at hand; and the guard has fled.

THE WOMEN. [*Wailing subduedly.*] Woe to us! [*The* NUBIAN *comes running down the hall.*]

NUBIAN. The Romans are in the courtyard. [*He bolts through the door. With a shriek, the* WOMEN *fly after him.* FTATATEETA'S *jaw expresses savage resolution: she does not budge.* CLEOPATRA *can hardly restrain herself from following them.* CÆSAR *grips her wrist, and looks steadfastly at her. She stands like a martyr.*]

CÆSAR. The Queen must face Cæsar alone. Answer "So be it."

CLEOPATRA. [*White.*] So be it.

CÆSAR. [*Releasing her.*] Good. [*A tramp and tumult of armed men is heard.* CLEOPATRA'S *terror increases. The bucina sounds close at hand, followed by a formidable clangor of trumpets. This is too much for* CLEOPATRA: *she utters a cry and darts towards the door.* FTATATEETA *stops her ruthlessly.*]

FTATATEETA. You are my nursling. You have said "So be it"; and if you die for it, you must make the Queen's word good. [*She hands* CLEOPATRA *to* CÆSAR, *who takes her back, almost beside herself with apprehension, to the throne.*]

CÆSAR. Now, if you quail–! [*He seats himself on the throne.*]

[*She stands on the step, all but uncon-*

scious, waiting for death. The Roman soldiers troop in tumultuously through the corridor, headed by their ensign with his eagle, and their bucinator, a burly fellow with his instrument coiled round his body, its brazen bell shaped like the head of a howling wolf. When they reach the transept, they stare in amazement at the throne; dress into ordered rank opposite; draw their swords and lift them in the air with a shout of Hail, CÆSAR. CLEOPATRA *turns and stares wildly at* CÆSAR; *grasps the situation; and, with a great sob of relief, falls into his arms.*]

ACT TWO

Alexandria. A hall on the first floor of the Palace, ending in a loggia approached by two steps. Through the arches of the loggia the Mediterranean can be seen, bright in the morning sun. The clean lofty walls, painted with a procession of the Egyptian theocracy, presented in profile as flat ornament, and the absence of mirrors, sham perspectives, stuffy upholstery and textiles, make the place handsome, wholesome, simple and cool, or, as a rich English manufacturer would express it, poor, bare, ridiculous and unhomely. For Tottenham Court Road civilization is to this Egyptian civilization as glass bead and tattoo civilization is to Tottenham Court Road.

The young king PTOLEMY DIONYSUS (aged ten) is at the top of the steps, on his way in through the loggia, led by his guardian POTHINUS, who has him by the hand. The court is assembled to receive him. It is made up of men and women (some of the women being officials) of various complexions and races, mostly Egyptian; some of them, comparatively fair, from lower Egypt, some, much darker, from upper Egypt; with a few Greeks and Jews. Prominent in a group on PTOLEMY's right hand is THEODOTUS, PTOLEMY's tutor. Another group, on PTOLEMY's left, is headed by ACHILLAS, the general of PTOLEMY's troops. THEODOTUS is a little old man, whose features are as cramped and wizened as his limbs, except his tall straight forehead, which occupies more space than all the rest of his face. He maintains an air of magpie keenness and profundity, listening to what the others say with the sarcastic vigilance of a philosopher listening to the exercises of his disciples. ACHILLAS is a tall handsome man of thirty-five, with a fine black beard curled like the coat of a poodle. Apparently not a clever man, but distinguished and dignified. POTHINUS is a vigorous man of fifty, a eunuch, passionate, energetic and quick witted, but of common mind and character; impatient and unable to control his temper. He has fine tawny hair, like fur. PTOLEMY, the King, looks much older than an English boy of ten; but he has the childish air, the habit of being in leading strings, the mixture of impotence and petulance, the appearance of being excessively washed, combed and dressed by other hands, which is exhibited by court-bred princes of all ages.

All receive the King with reverences. He comes down the steps to a chair of state which stands a little to his right, the only seat in the hall. Taking his place before it, he looks nervously for instructions to POTHINUS, who places himself at his left hand.

POTHINUS. The king of Egypt has a word to speak.

THEODOTUS. [*In a squeak which he makes impressive by sheer self-opinionativeness.*] Peace for the King's word!

PTOLEMY. [*Without any vocal inflexions: he is evidently repeating a lesson.*] Take notice of this all of you. I am the first-born son of Auletes the Flute Blower who was your King. My sister Berenice drove him from his throne and reigned in his stead but—but—[*He hesitates.*]—

POTHINUS. [*Stealthily prompting.*]—but the gods would not suffer—

PTOLEMY. Yes—the gods would not suffer—not suffer—[*He stops; then, crestfallen.*] I forgot what the gods would not suffer.

THEODOTUS. Let Pothinus, the King's guardian, speak for the King.

POTHINUS. [*Suppressing his impatience with difficulty.*] The King wished to say that the gods would not suffer the impiety of his sister to go unpunished.

PTOLEMY. [*Hastily.*] Yes: I remember the rest of it. [*He resumes his monotone.*] Therefore the gods sent a stranger one Mark Antony a Roman captain of horsemen across the sands of the desert and he set my father again upon the throne. And my father took Berenice my sister and struck her head off. And now that my father is dead yet another of his daughters my sister Cleopatra would snatch the kingdom from me and reign in my place. But the gods would not suffer—[POTHINUS *coughs admonitorily.*]—the gods—the gods would not suffer—

POTHINUS. [*Prompting.*]—will not maintain—

PTOLEMY. Oh yes—will not maintain such iniquity they will give her head to the axe even as her sister's. But with the help of the witch Ftatateeta she hath cast a spell on the Roman Julius Cæsar to make him uphold her false pretence to rule in Egypt. Take notice then that I will not suffer—that I will not suffer—[*Pettishly, to* POTHINUS.] What is it that I will not suffer?

POTHINUS. [*Suddenly exploding with all the force and emphasis of political passion.*] The King will not suffer a foreigner to take from him the throne of our Egypt. [*A shout of applause.*] Tell the King, Achillas, how many soldiers and horsemen follow the Roman?

THEODOTUS. Let the King's general speak!

ACHILLAS. But two Roman legions, O King. Three thousand soldiers and scarce a thousand horsemen. [*The court breaks into derisive laughter; and a great chattering begins, amid which* RUFIO, *a Roman officer, appears in the loggia. He is a* burly, black-bearded man of middle age, very blunt, prompt and rough, with small clear eyes, and plump nose and cheeks, which, however, like the rest of his flesh, are in ironhard condition.*]

RUFIO. [*From the steps.*] Peace, ho! [*The laughter and chatter cease abruptly.*] Cæsar approaches.

THEODOTUS. [*With much presence of mind.*] The King permits the Roman commander to enter! [CÆSAR, *plainly dressed, but wearing an oak wreath to conceal his baldness, enters from the loggia, attended by* BRITANNUS, *his secretary, a Briton, about forty, tall, solemn, and already slightly bald, with a heavy, drooping, hazel-colored moustache trained so as to lose its ends in a pair of trim whiskers. He is carefully dressed in blue, with portfolio, inkhorn, and reed pen at his girdle. His serious air and sense of the importance of the business in hand is in marked contrast to the kindly interest of* CÆSAR, *who looks at the scene, which is new to him, with the frank curiosity of a child, and then turns to the king's chair:* BRITANNUS *and* RUFIO *posting themselves near the steps at the other side.*]

CÆSAR. [*Looking at* POTHINUS *and* PTOLEMY.] Which is the King? the man or the boy?

POTHINUS. I am Pothinus, the guardian of my lord the King.

CÆSAR. [*Patting* PTOLEMY *kindly on the shoulder.*] So you are the King. Dull work at your age, eh? [*To* POTHINUS.] Your servant, Pothinus. [*He turns away unconcernedly and comes slowly along the middle of the hall, looking from side to side at the courtiers until he reaches* ACHILLAS.] And this gentleman?

THEODOTUS. Achillas, the King's general.

CÆSAR. [*To* ACHILLAS, *very friendly.*] A general, eh? I am a general myself. But I began too old, too old. Health and many victories, Achillas!

ACHILLAS. As the gods will, Cæsar.

CÆSAR. [*Turning to* THEODOTUS.] And you, sir, are—?

THEODOTUS. Theodotus, the King's tutor.

CÆSAR. You teach men how to be kings,

Theodotus. That is very clever of you. [*Looking at the gods on the walls as he turns away from* THEODOTUS *and goes up again to* POTHINUS.] And this place?

POTHINUS. The council chamber of the chancellors of the King's treasury, Cæsar.

CÆSAR. Ah! that reminds me. I want some money.

POTHINUS. The King's treasury is poor, Cæsar.

CÆSAR. Yes: I notice that there is but one chair in it.

RUFIO. [*Shouting gruffly.*] Bring a chair there, some of you, for Cæsar.

PTOLEMY. [*Rising shyly to offer his chair.*] Cæsar—

CÆSAR. [*Kindly.*] No, no, my boy: that is your chair of state. Sit down. [*He makes* PTOLEMY *sit down again. Meanwhile* RUFIO, *looking about him, sees in the nearest corner an image of the god* RA, *represented as a seated man with the head of a hawk. Before the image is a bronze tripod, about as large as a three-legged stool, with a stick of incense burning on it.* RUFIO, *with Roman resourcefulness and indifference to foreign superstitions, promptly seizes the tripod; shakes off the incense; blows away the ash; and dumps it down behind* CÆSAR, *nearly in the middle of the hall.*]

RUFIO. Sit on that, Cæsar. [*A shiver runs through the court, followed by a hissing whisper of* Sacrilege!]

CÆSAR. [*Seating himself.*] Now, Pothinus, to business. I am badly in want of money.

BRITANNUS. [*Disapproving of these informal expressions.*] My master would say that there is a lawful debt due to Rome by Egypt, contracted by the King's deceased father to the Triumvirate; and that it is Cæsar's duty to his country to require immediate payment.

CÆSAR. [*Blandly.*] Ah, I forgot. I have not made my companions known here. Pothinus: this is Britannus, my secretary. He is an islander from the western end of the world, a day's voyage from Gaul. [BRITANNUS *bows stiffly.*] This gentleman is Rufio, my comrade in arms. [RUFIO *nods.*] Pothinus: I want 1,600 talents. [*The courtiers, appalled, murmur loudly, and* THEODOTUS *and* ACHILLAS *appeal mutely to one another against so monstrous a demand.*]

POTHINUS. [*Aghast.*] Forty million sesterces! Impossible. There is not so much money in the King's treasury.

CÆSAR. [*Encouragingly.*] Only sixteen hundred talents, Pothinus. Why count it in sesterces? A sestertius is only worth a loaf of bread.

POTHINUS. And a talent is worth a race-horse. I say it is impossible. We have been at strife here, because the King's sister Cleopatra falsely claims his throne. The King's taxes have not been collected for a whole year.

CÆSAR. Yes they have, Pothinus. My officers have been collecting them all morning. [*Renewed whisper and sensation, not without some stifled laughter, among the courtiers.*]

RUFIO. [*Bluntly.*] You must pay, Pothinus. Why waste words? You are getting off cheaply enough.

POTHINUS. [*Bitterly.*] Is it possible that Cæsar, the conqueror of the world, has time to occupy himself with such a trifle as our taxes?

CÆSAR. My friend: taxes are the chief business of a conqueror of the world.

POTHINUS. Then take warning, Cæsar. This day, the treasures of the temple and the gold of the King's treasury shall be sent to the mint to be melted down for our ransom in the sight of the people. They shall see us sitting under bare walls and drinking from wooden cups. And their wrath be on your head, Cæsar, if you force us to this sacrilege!

CÆSAR. Do not fear, Pothinus: the people know how well wine tastes in wooden cups. In return for your bounty, I will settle this dispute about the throne for you, if you will. What say you?

POTHINUS. If I say no, will that hinder you?

RUFIO. [*Defiantly.*] No.

CÆSAR. You say the matter has been at issue for a year, Pothinus. May I have ten minutes at it?

POTHINUS. You will do your pleasure, doubtless.

CÆSAR. Good! But first, let us have Cleopatra here.

THEODOTUS. She is not in Alexandria: she is fled into Syria.

CÆSAR. I think not. [*To* RUFIO.] Call Totateeta.

RUFIO. [*Calling.*] Ho there, Teetatota. [FTATATEETA *enters the loggia, and stands arrogantly at the top of the step.*]

FTATATEETA. Who pronounces the name of Ftatateeta, the Queen's chief nurse?

CÆSAR. Nobody can pronounce it, Tota, except yourself. Where is your mistress? [CLEOPATRA, *who is hiding behind* FTATATEETA, *peeps out at them, laughing.* CÆSAR *rises.*]

CÆSAR. Will the Queen favor us with her presence for a moment?

CLEOPATRA. [*Pushing* FTATATEETA *aside and standing haughtily on the brink of the steps.*] Am I to behave like a Queen?

CÆSAR. Yes. [CLEOPATRA *immediately comes down to the chair of state; seizes* PTOLEMY; *drags him out of his seat; then takes his place in the chair.* FTATATEETA *seats herself on the step of the loggia, and sits there, watching the scene with sibylline intensity.*]

PTOLEMY. [*Mortified, and struggling with his tears.*] Cæsar: this is how she treats me always. If I am King why is she allowed to take everything from me?

CLEOPATRA. You are not to be King, you little cry-baby. You are to be eaten by the Romans.

CÆSAR. [*Touched by* PTOLEMY's *distress.*] Come here, my boy, and stand by me. [PTOLEMY *goes over to* CÆSAR, *who, resuming his seat on the tripod, takes the boy's hand to encourage him.* CLEOPATRA, *furiously jealous, rises and glares at them.*]

CLEOPATRA. [*With flaming cheeks.*] Take your throne: I dont want it. [*She flings away from the chair, and approaches* PTOLEMY, *who shrinks from her.*] Go this instant and sit down in your place.

CÆSAR. Go, Ptolemy. Always take a throne when it is offered to you.

RUFIO. I hope you will have the good sense to follow your own advice when we return to Rome, Cæsar. [PTOLEMY *slowly goes back to the throne, giving*

CLEOPATRA *a wide berth, in evident fear of her hands. She takes his place beside* CÆSAR.]

CÆSAR. Pothinus—

CLEOPATRA. [*Interrupting him.*] Are you not going to speak to me?

CÆSAR. Be quiet. Open your mouth again before I give you leave; and you shall be eaten.

CLEOPATRA. I am not afraid. A queen must not be afraid. Eat my husband there, if you like: he is afraid.

CÆSAR. [*Starting.*] Your husband! What do you mean?

CLEOPATRA. [*Pointing to* PTOLEMY.] That little thing. [*The two Romans and the Briton stare at one another in amazement.*]

THEODOTUS. Cæsar: you are a stranger here, and not conversant with our laws. The kings and queens of Egypt may not marry except with their own royal blood. Ptolemy and Cleopatra are born king and consort just as they are born brother and sister.

BRITANNUS. [*Shocked.*] Cæsar: this is not proper.

THEODOTUS. [*Outraged.*] How!

CÆSAR. [*Recovering his self-possession.*] Pardon him, Theodotus: he is a barbarian, and thinks that the customs of his tribe and island are the laws of nature.

BRITANNUS. On the contrary, Cæsar, it is these Egyptians who are barbarians; and you do wrong to encourage them. I say it is a scandal.

CÆSAR. Scandal or not, my friend, it opens the gate of peace. [*He addresses* POTHINUS *seriously.*] Pothinus: hear what I propose.

RUFIO. Hear Cæsar there.

CÆSAR. Ptolemy and Cleopatra shall reign jointly in Egypt.

ACHILLAS. What of the King's younger brother and Cleopatra's younger sister?

RUFIO. [*Explaining.*] There is another little Ptolemy, Cæsar: so they tell me.

CÆSAR. Well, the little Ptolemy can marry the other sister; and we will make them both a present of Cyprus.

POTHINUS. [*Impatiently.*] Cyprus is of no use to anybody.

CÆSAR. No matter: you shall have it for the sake of peace.

BRITANNUS. [*Unconsciously anticipating a later statesman.*] Peace with honor, Pothinus.

POTHINUS. [*Mutinously.*] Cæsar: be honest. The money you demand is the price of our freedom. Take it; and leave us to settle our own affairs.

THE BOLDER COURTIERS. [*Encouraged by* POTHINUS's *tone and* CÆSAR's *quietness.*] Yes, yes. Egypt for the Egyptians! [*The conference now becomes an altercation, the Egyptians becoming more and more heated.* CÆSAR *remains unruffled; but* RUFIO *grows fiercer and doggeder, and* BRITANNUS *haughtily indignant.*]

RUFIO. [*Contemptuously.*] Egypt for the Egyptians! Do you forget that there is a Roman army of occupation here, left by Aulus Gabinius when he set up your toy king for you?

ACHILLAS. [*Suddenly asserting himself.*] And now under my command. I am the Roman general here, Cæsar.

CÆSAR. [*Tickled by the humor of the situation.*] And also the Egyptian general, eh?

POTHINUS. [*Triumphantly.*] That is so, Cæsar.

CÆSAR. [*To* ACHILLAS.] So you can make war on the Egyptians in the name of Rome, and on the Romans—on me, if necessary—in the name of Egypt?

ACHILLAS. That is so, Cæsar.

CÆSAR. And which side are you on at present, if I may presume to ask, general?

ACHILLAS. On the side of the right and of the gods.

CÆSAR. Hm! How many men have you?

ACHILLAS. That will appear when I take the field.

RUFIO. [*Truculently.*] Are your men Romans? If not, it matters not how many there are, provided you are no stronger than 500 to ten.

POTHINUS. It is useless to try to bluff us, Rufio. Cæsar has been defeated before and may be defeated again. A few weeks ago Cæsar was flying for his life before Pompey: a few months hence he may be flying for his life before Cato and Juba of Numidia, the African King.

ACHILLAS. [*Following up* POTHINUS's *speech menacingly.*] What can you do with 4,000 men?

THEODOTUS. [*Following up* ACHILLAS's *speech with a raucous squeak.*] And without money? Away with you.

ALL THE COURTIERS. [*Shouting fiercely and crowding towards* CÆSAR.] Away with you. Egypt for the Egyptians! Be gone. [RUFIO *bites his beard, too angry to speak.* CÆSAR *sits as comfortably as if he were at breakfast, and the cat were clamoring for a piece of Finnan-haddie.*]

CLEOPATRA. Why do you let them talk to you like that, Cæsar? Are you afraid?

CÆSAR. Why, my dear, what they say is quite true.

CLEOPATRA. But if you go away, I shall not be Queen.

CÆSAR. I shall not go away until you are Queen.

POTHINUS. Achillas: if you are not a fool, you will take that girl whilst she is under your hand.

RUFIO. [*Daring them.*] Why not take Cæsar as well, Achillas?

POTHINUS. [*Retorting the defiance with interest.*] Well said, Rufio. Why not?

RUFIO. Try, Achillas. [*Calling.*] Guard there. [*The loggia immediately fills with* CÆSAR's *soldiers, who stand, sword in hand, at the top of the steps, waiting the word to charge from their centurion, who carries a cudgel. For a moment the Egyptians face them proudly: then they retire sullenly to their former places.*]

BRITANNUS. You are Cæsar's prisoners, all of you.

CÆSAR. [*Benevolently.*] Oh no, no, no. By no means. Cæsar's guests, gentlemen.

CLEOPATRA. Wont you cut their heads off?

CÆSAR. What! Cut off your brother's head?

CLEOPATRA. Why not? He would cut off mine, if he got the chance. Wouldnt you, Ptolemy?

PTOLEMY. [*Pale and obstinate.*] I would. I will, too, when I grow up. [CLEOPATRA *is rent by a struggle between her newly-acquired dignity as a queen, and a strong impulse to put out her tongue at him. She takes no part in the scene which follows, but watches it with curiosity and wonder, fidgeting with the restlessness of a child,*] *and sitting down on* CÆSAR's *tripod when he rises.*]

POTHINUS. Cæsar: if you attempt to detain us—

RUFIO. He will succeed, Egyptian: make up your mind to that. We hold the palace, the beach, and the eastern harbor. The road to Rome is open; and you shall travel it if Cæsar chooses.

CÆSAR. [*Courteously.*] I could do no less, Pothinus, to secure the retreat of my own soldiers. I am accountable for every life among them. But you are free to go. So are all here, and in the palace.

RUFIO. [*Aghast at this clemency.*] What! Renegades and all?

CÆSAR. [*Softening the expression.*] Roman army of occupation and all, Rufio.

POTHINUS. [*Bewildered.*] But—but—but—

CÆSAR. Well, my friend?

POTHINUS. You are turning us out of our own palace into the streets; and you tell us with a grand air that we are free to go! It is for you to go.

CÆSAR. Your friends are in the street, Pothinus. You will be safer there.

POTHINUS. This is a trick. I am the king's guardian: I refuse to stir. I stand on my right here. Where is your right?

CÆSAR. It is in Rufio's scabbard, Pothinus. I may not be able to keep it there if you wait too long. [*Sensation.*]

POTHINUS. [*Bitterly.*] And this is Roman justice!

THEODOTUS. But not Roman gratitude, I hope.

CÆSAR. Gratitude! Am I in your debt for any service, gentlemen?

THEODOTUS. Is Cæsar's life of so little account to him that he forgets that we have saved it?

CÆSAR. My life! Is that all?

THEODOTUS. Your life. Your laurels. Your future.

POTHINUS. It is true. I can call a witness to prove that but for us, the Roman army of occupation, led by the greatest soldier in the world, would now have Cæsar at its mercy. [*Calling through the loggia.*] Ho, there, Lucius Septimius [CÆSAR *starts, deeply moved.*] if my voice can reach you, come forth and testify before Cæsar.

CÆSAR. [*Shrinking.*] No, no.

THEODOTUS. Yes, I say. Let the military tribune bear witness. [LUCIUS SEPTIMIUS, *a clean shaven, trim athlete of about 40, with symmetrical features, resolute mouth, and handsome, thin Roman nose, in the dress of a Roman officer, comes in through the loggia and confronts* CÆSAR, *who hides his face with his robe for a moment; then, mastering himself, drops it, and confronts the tribune with dignity.*]

POTHINUS. Bear witness, Lucius Septimius. Cæsar came hither in pursuit of his foe. Did we shelter his foe?

LUCIUS. As Pompey's foot touched the Egyptian shore, his head fell by the stroke of my sword.

THEODOTUS. [*With viperish relish.*] Under the eyes of his wife and child! Remember that, Cæsar! They saw it from the ship he had just left. We have given you a full and sweet measure of vengeance.

CÆSAR. [*With horror.*] Vengeance!

POTHINUS. Our first gift to you, as your galley came into the roadstead, was the head of your rival for the empire of the world. Bear witness, Lucius Septimius: is it not so?

LUCIUS. It is so. With this hand, that slew Pompey, I placed his head at the feet of Cæsar.

CÆSAR. Murderer! So would you have slain Cæsar, had Pompey been victorious at Pharsalia.

LUCIUS. Woe to the vanquished, Cæsar! When I served Pompey, I slew as good men as he, only because he conquered them. His turn came at last.

THEODOTUS. [*Flatteringly.*] The deed was not yours, Cæsar, but ours—nay, mine; for it was done by my counsel. Thanks to us, you keep your reputation for clemency, and have your vengeance too.

CÆSAR. Vengeance! Vengeance!! Oh, if I could stoop to vengeance, what would I not exact from you as the price of this murdered man's blood? [*They shrink back, appalled and disconcerted.*] Was he not my son-in-law, my ancient friend, for 20 years the master of great Rome, for 30 years the compeller of victory? Did not I, as a Roman, share his glory?

Was the Fate that forced us to fight for the mastery of the world, of our making? Am I Julius Cæsar, or am I a wolf, that you fling to me the grey head of the old soldier, the laurelled conqueror, the mighty Roman, treacherously struck down by this callous ruffian, and then claim my gratitude for it! [*To* LUCIUS SEPTIMIUS.] Begone: you fill me with horror.

LUCIUS. [*Cold and undaunted.*] Pshaw! You have seen severed heads before, Cæsar, and severed right hands too, I think; some thousands of them, in Gaul, after you vanquished Vercingetorix. Did you spare him, with all your clemency? Was that vengeance?

CÆSAR. No, by the gods! would that it had been! Vengeance at least is human. No, I say: those severed right hands, and the brave Vercingetorix basely strangled in a vault beneath the Capitol were [*With shuddering satire.*] a wise severity, a necessary protection to the commonwealth, a duty of statesmanship—follies and fictions ten times bloodier than honest vengeance! What a fool was I then! To think that men's lives should be at the mercy of such fools! [*Humbly.*] Lucius Septimius, pardon me: why should the slayer of Vercingetorix rebuke the slayer of Pompey? You are free to go with the rest. Or stay if you will: I will find a place for you in my service.

LUCIUS. The odds are against you, Cæsar. I go. [*He turns to go out through the loggia.*]

RUFIO. [*Full of wrath at seeing his prey escaping.*] That means that he is a Republican.

LUCIUS. [*Turning defiantly on the loggia steps.*] And what are you?

RUFIO. A Cæsarian, like all Cæsar's soldiers.

CÆSAR. [*Courteously.*] Lucius: believe me, Cæsar is no Cæsarian. Were Rome a true republic, then were Cæsar the first of Republicans. But you have made your choice. Farewell.

LUCIUS. Farewell. Come, Achillas, whilst there is yet time. [CÆSAR, *seeing that* RUFIO's *temper threatens to get the worse of him, puts his hand on his shoulder and brings him down the hall out of harm's*

way, BRITANNUS *accompanying them and posting himself on* CÆSAR's *right hand. This movement brings the three in a little group to the place occupied by* ACHILLAS, *who moves haughtily away and joins* THEODOTUS *on the other side.* LUCIUS SEPTIMIUS *goes out through the soldiers in the loggia.* POTHINUS, THEODOTUS *and* ACHILLAS *follow him with the* COURTIERS, *very mistrustful of the* SOLDIERS, *who close up in their rear and go out after them, keeping them moving without much ceremony. The King is left in his chair, piteous, obstinate, with twitching face and fingers. During these movements* RUFIO *maintains an energetic grumbling, as follows.*]

RUFIO. [*As* LUCIUS *departs.*] Do you suppose he would let us go if he had our heads in his hands?

CÆSAR. I have no right to suppose that his ways are any baser than mine.

RUFIO. Psha!

CÆSAR. Rufio: if I take Lucius Septimius for my model, and become exactly like him, ceasing to be Cæsar, will you serve me still?

BRITANNUS. Cæsar: this is not good sense. Your duty to Rome demands that her enemies should be prevented from doing further mischief. [CÆSAR, *whose delight in the moral eye-to-business of his British secretary is inexhaustible, smiles indulgently.*]

RUFIO. It is no use talking to him, Britannus: you may save your breath to cool your porridge. But mark this, Cæsar. Clemency is very well for you; but what is it for your soldiers, who have to fight tomorrow the men you spared yesterday? You may give what orders you please; but I tell you that your next victory will be a massacre, thanks to your clemency. I, for one, will take no prisoners. I will kill my enemies in the field; and then you can preach as much clemency as you please: I shall never have to fight them again. And now, with your leave, I will see these gentry off the premises. [*He turns to go.*]

CÆSAR. [*Turning also and seeing* PTOLEMY.] What! have they left the boy alone! Oh shame, shame!

RUFIO. [*Taking* PTOLEMY's *hand and*

making him rise.] Come, your majesty!

PTOLEMY. [*To* CÆSAR, *drawing away his hand from* RUFIO.] Is he turning me out of my palace?

RUFIO. [*Grimly.*] You are welcome to stay if you wish.

CÆSAR. [*Kindly.*] Go, my boy. I will not harm you; but you will be safer away, among your friends. Here you are in the lion's mouth.

PTOLEMY. [*Turning to go.*] It is not the lion I fear, but [*Looking at* RUFIO.] the jackal. [*He goes out through the loggia.*]

CÆSAR. [*Laughing approvingly.*] Brave boy!

CLEOPATRA. [*Jealous of* CÆSAR's *approbation, calling after* PTOLEMY.] Little silly. You think that very clever.

CÆSAR. Britannus: attend the King. Give him in charge to that Pothinus fellow. [BRITANNUS *goes out after* PTOLEMY.]

RUFIO. [*Pointing to* CLEOPATRA.] And this piece of goods? What is to be done with her? However, I suppose I may leave that to you. [*He goes out through the loggia.*]

CLEOPATRA. [*Flushing suddenly and turning on* CÆSAR.] Did you mean me to go with the rest?

CÆSAR. [*A little preoccupied, goes with a sigh to* PTOLEMY's *chair, whilst she waits for his answer with red cheeks and clenched fists.*] You are free to do just as you please, Cleopatra.

CLEOPATRA. Then you do not care whether I stay or not?

CÆSAR. [*Smiling.*] Of course I had rather you stayed.

CLEOPATRA. Much, much rather?

CÆSAR. [*Nodding.*] Much, much rather.

CLEOPATRA. Then I consent to stay, because I am asked. But I do not want to, mind.

CÆSAR. That is quite understood. [*Calling.*] Totateeta. [FTATATEETA, *still seated, turns her eyes on him with a sinister expression, but does not move.*]

CLEOPATRA. [*With a splutter of laughter.*] Her name is not Totateeta: it is Ftatateeta. [*Calling.*] Ftatateeta. [FTATATEETA *instantly rises and comes to* CLEOPATRA.]

CÆSAR. [*Stumbling over the name.*] Tfatafeeta will forgive the erring tongue

of a Roman. Tota: the Queen will hold her state here in Alexandria. Engage women to attend upon her; and do all that is needful.

FTATATEETA. Am I then the mistress of the Queen's household?

CLEOPATRA. [*Sharply.*] No: *I* am the mistress of the Queen's household. Go and do as you are told, or I will have you thrown into the Nile this very afternoon, to poison the poor crocodiles.

CÆSAR. [*Shocked.*] Oh no, no.

CLEOPATRA. Oh yes, yes. You are very sentimental, Cæsar; but you are clever; and if you do as I tell you, you will soon learn to govern. [CÆSAR, *quite dumbfounded by this impertinence, turns in his chair and stares at her.* FTATATEETA, *smiling grimly, and shewing a splendid set of teeth, goes, leaving them alone together.*]

CÆSAR. Cleopatra: I really think I must eat you, after all.

CLEOPATRA. [*Kneeling beside him and looking at him with eager interest, half real, half affected to shew how intelligent she is.*] You must not talk to me now as if I were a child.

CÆSAR. You have been growing up since the sphinx introduced us the other night; and you think you know more than I do already.

CLEOPATRA. [*Taken down, and anxious to justify herself.*] No: that would be very silly of me: of course I know that. But—[*Suddenly.*] are you angry with me?

CÆSAR. No.

CLEOPATRA. [*Only half believing him.*] Then why are you so thoughtful?

CÆSAR. [*Rising.*] I have work to do, Cleopatra.

CLEOPATRA. [*Drawing back.*] Work! [*Offended.*] You are tired of talking to me; and that is your excuse to get away from me.

CÆSAR. [*Sitting down again to appease her.*] Well, well: another minute. But then—work!

CLEOPATRA. Work! what nonsense! You must remember that you are a king now: I have made you one. Kings dont work.

CÆSAR. Oh! Who told you that, little kitten? Eh?

CLEOPATRA. My father was King of Egypt; and he never worked. But he was a great king, and cut off my sister's head because she rebelled against him and took the throne from him.

CÆSAR. Well; and how did he get his throne back again?

CLEOPATRA. [*Eagerly, her eyes lighting up.*] I will tell you. A beautiful young man, with strong round arms, came over the desert with many horsemen, and slew my sister's husband and gave my father back his throne. [*Wistfully.*] I was only twelve then. Oh, I wish he would come again, now that I am queen. I would make him my husband.

CÆSAR. It might be managed, perhaps; for it was I who sent that beautiful young man to help your father.

CLEOPATRA. [*Enraptured.*] You know him!

CÆSAR. [*Nodding.*] I do.

CLEOPATRA. Has he come with you? [CÆSAR *shakes his head: she is cruelly disappointed.*] Oh, I wish he had, I wish he had. If only I were a little older; so that he might not think me a mere kitten, as you do! But perhaps that is because you are old. He is many many years younger than you, is he not?

CÆSAR. [*As if swallowing a pill.*] He is somewhat younger.

CLEOPATRA. Would he be my husband, do you think, if I asked him?

CÆSAR. Very likely.

CLEOPATRA. But I should not like to ask him. Could you not persuade him to ask me—without knowing that I wanted him to?

CÆSAR. [*Touched by her innocence of the beautiful young man's character.*] My poor child!

CLEOPATRA. Why do you say that as if you were sorry for me? Does he love anyone else?

CÆSAR. I am afraid so.

CLEOPATRA. [*Tearfully.*] Then I shall not be his first love.

CÆSAR. Not quite the first. He is greatly admired by women.

CLEOPATRA. I wish I could be the first. But if he loves me, I will make him kill all the rest. Tell me: is he still beautiful? Do his strong round arms shine in the sun like marble?

CÆSAR. He is in excellent condition— considering how much he eats and drinks.

CLEOPATRA. Oh, you must not say common, earthly things about him; for I love him. He is a god.

CÆSAR. He is a great captain of horsemen, and swifter of foot than any other Roman.

CLEOPATRA. What is his real name?

CÆSAR [*Puzzled.*] His real name?

CLEOPATRA. Yes, I always call him Horus, because Horus is the most beautiful of our gods. But I want to know his real name.

CÆSAR. His name is Mark Antony.

CLEOPATRA. [*Musically.*] Mark Antony, Mark Antony, Mark Antony! What a beautiful name! [*She throws her arms round* CÆSAR's *neck.*] Oh, how I love you for sending him to help my father! Did you love my father very much?

CÆSAR. No, my child; but your father, as you say, never worked. I always work. So when he lost his crown he had to promise me 16,000 talents to get it back for him.

CLEOPATRA. Did he ever pay you?

CÆSAR. Not in full.

CLEOPATRA. He was quite right: it was too dear. The whole world is not worth 16,000 talents.

CÆSAR. That is perhaps true, Cleopatra. Those Egyptians who work paid as much of it as he could drag from them. The rest is still due. But as I most likely shall not get it, I must go back to my work. So you must run away for a little and send my secretary to me.

CLEOPATRA. [*Coaxing.*] No: I want to stay and hear you talk about Mark Antony.

CÆSAR. But if I do not get to work, Pothinus and the rest of them will cut us off from the harbor; and then the way from Rome will be blocked.

CLEOPATRA. No matter: I dont want you to go back to Rome.

CÆSAR. But you want Mark Antony to come from it.

CLEOPATRA. [*Springing up.*] Oh, yes, yes, yes: I forgot. Go quickly and work, Cæsar; and keep the way over the sea open for my Mark Antony. [*She runs out through the loggia, kissing her hand to Mark Antony across the sea.*]

CÆSAR. [*Going briskly up the middle of the hall to the loggia steps.*] Ho, Britannus. [*He is startled by the entry of a wounded Roman* SOLDIER, *who confronts him from the upper step.*] What now?

SOLDIER. [*Pointing to his bandaged head.*] This, Cæsar; and two of my comrades killed in the market place.

CÆSAR. [*Quiet, but attending.*] Ay. Why?

SOLDIER. There is an army come to Alexandria, calling itself the Roman army.

CÆSAR. The Roman army of occupation. Ay?

SOLDIER. Commanded by one Achillas.

CÆSAR. Well?

SOLDIER. The citizens rose against us when the army entered the gates. I was with two others in the market place when the news came. They set upon us. I cut my way out; and here I am.

CÆSAR. Good. I am glad to see you alive. [RUFIO *enters the loggia hastily, passing behind the* SOLDIER *to look out through one of the arches at the quay beneath.*] Rufio: we are besieged.

RUFIO. What! Already?

CÆSAR. Now or tomorrow: what does it matter? We shall be besieged. [BRITANNUS *runs in.*]

BRITANNUS. Cæsar—

CÆSAR. [*Anticipating him.*] Yes: I know. [RUFIO *and* BRITANNUS *come down the hall from the loggia at opposite sides, past* CÆSAR, *who waits for a moment near the step to say to the* SOLDIER.] Comrade: give the word to turn out on the beach and stand by the boats. Get your wound attended to. Go. [*The* SOLDIER *hurries out.* CÆSAR *comes down the hall between* RUFIO *and* BRITANNUS.] Rufio: we have some ships in the west harbor. Burn them.

RUFIO. [*Staring.*] Burn them!!

CÆSAR. Take every boat we have in the east harbor, and seize the Pharos—that island with the lighthouse. Leave half our men behind to hold the beach and the quay outside this palace: that is the way home.

RUFIO. [*Disapproving strongly.*] Are we to give up the city?

CÆSAR. We have not got it, Rufio. This palace we have; and—what is that building next door?

RUFIO. The theatre.

CÆSAR. We will have that too: it commands the strand. For the rest, Egypt for the Egyptians!

RUFIO. Well, you know best, I suppose. Is that all?

CÆSAR. That is all. Are those ships burnt yet?

RUFIO. Be easy: I shall waste no more time. [*He runs out.*]

BRITANNUS. Cæsar: Pothinus demands speech of you. In my opinion he needs a lesson. His manner is most insolent.

CÆSAR. Where is he?

BRITANNUS. He waits without.

CÆSAR. Ho there! admit Pothinus. [POTHINUS *appears in the loggia, and comes down the hall very haughtily to* CÆSAR's *left hand.*]

CÆSAR. Well, Pothinus?

POTHINUS. I have brought you our ultimatum, Cæsar.

CÆSAR. Ultimatum! The door was open: you should have gone out through it before you declared war. You are my prisoner now. [*He goes to the chair and loosens his toga.*]

POTHINUS. [*Scornfully.*] I your prisoner! Do you know that you are in Alexandria, and that King Ptolemy, with an army outnumbering your little troop a hundred to one, is in possession of Alexandria?

CÆSAR. [*Unconcernedly taking off his toga and throwing it on the chair.*] Well, my friend, get out if you can. And tell your friends not to kill any more Romans in the market place. Otherwise my soldiers, who do not share my celebrated clemency, will probably kill you. Britannus: pass the word to the guard; and fetch my armor. [BRITANNUS *runs out.* RUFIO *returns.*] Well?

RUFIO. [*Pointing from the loggia to a cloud of smoke drifting over the harbor.*] See there! [POTHINUS *runs eagerly up the steps to look out.*]

CÆSAR. What, ablaze already! Impossible!

RUFIO. Yes, five good ships, and a barge laden with oil grappled to each. But it is not my doing: the Egyptians have saved me the trouble. They have captured the west harbor.

CÆSAR. [*Anxiously.*] And the east harbor? The lighthouse, Rufio?

RUFIO. [*With a sudden splutter of raging ill usage, coming down to* CÆSAR *and scolding him.*] Can I embark a legion in five minutes? The first cohort is already on the beach. We can do no more. If you want faster work, come and do it yourself.

CÆSAR. [*Soothing him.*] Good, good. Patience, Rufio, patience.

RUFIO. Patience! Who is impatient here, you or I? Would I be here, if I could not oversee them from that balcony?

CÆSAR. Forgive me, Rufio; and [*Anxiously.*] hurry them as much as—[*He is interrupted by an outcry as of an old man in the extremity of misfortune. It draws near rapidly; and* THEODOTUS *rushes in, tearing his hair, and squeaking the most lamentable exclamations.* RUFIO *steps back to stare at him, amazed at his frantic condition.* POTHINUS *turns to listen.*]

THEODOTUS. [*On the steps, with uplifted arms.*] Horror unspeakable! Woe, alas! Help!

RUFIO. What now?

CÆSAR. [*Frowning.*] Who is slain?

THEODOTUS. Slain! Oh, worse than the death of ten thousand men! Loss irreparable to mankind!

RUFIO. What has happened, man?

THEODOTUS. [*Rushing down the hall between them.*] The fire has spread from your ships. The first of the seven wonders of the world perishes. The library of Alexandria is in flames.

RUFIO. Psha! [*Quite relieved, he goes up to the loggia and watches the preparations of the troops on the beach.*]

CÆSAR. Is that all?

THEODOTUS. [*Unable to believe his senses.*] All! Cæsar: will you go down to posterity as a barbarous soldier too ignorant to know the value of books?

CÆSAR. Theodotus: I am an author myself; and I tell you it is better that the Egyptians should live their lives than dream them away with the help of books.

THEODOTUS. [*Kneeling, with genuine literary emotion: the passion of the pedant.*] Cæsar: once in ten generations of men, the world gains an immortal book.

CÆSAR. [*Inflexible.*] If it did not flatter mankind, the common executioner would burn it.

THEODOTUS. Without history, death will lay you beside your meanest soldier.

CÆSAR. Death will do that in any case. I ask no better grave.

THEODOTUS. What is burning there is the memory of mankind.

CÆSAR. A shameful memory. Let it burn.

THEODOTUS. [*Wildly.*] Will you destroy the past?

CÆSAR. Ay, and build the future with its ruins. [THEODOTUS, *in despair, strikes himself on the temples with his fists.*] But harken, Theodotus, teacher of kings: you who valued Pompey's head no more than a shepherd values an onion, and who now kneel to me, with tears in your old eyes, to plead for a few sheepskins scrawled with errors. I cannot spare you a man or a bucket of water just now; but you shall pass freely out of the palace. Now, away with you to Achillas; and borrow his legions to put out the fire. [*He hurries him to the steps.*]

POTHINUS. [*Significantly.*] You understand, Theodotus: I remain a prisoner.

THEODOTUS. A prisoner!

CÆSAR. Will you stay to talk whilst the memory of mankind is burning? [*Calling through the loggia.*] Ho there! Pass Theodotus out. [*To* THEODOTUS.] Away with you.

THEODOTUS. [*To* POTHINUS.] I must go to save the library. [*He hurries out.*]

CÆSAR. Follow him to gate, Pothinus. Bid him urge your people to kill no more of my soldiers, for your sake.

POTHINUS. My life will cost you dear if you take it, Cæsar. [*He goes out after* THEODOTUS. RUFIO, *absorbed in watching the embarkation, does not notice the departure of the two Egyptians.*]

RUFIO. [*Shouting from the loggia to the beach.*] All ready, there?

A CENTURION. [*From below.*] All ready. We wait for Cæsar.

CÆSAR. Tell them Cæsar is coming—the rogues! [*Calling.*] Britannicus. [*This magniloquent version of his secretary's name is one of* CÆSAR's *jokes. In later years it would have meant, quite seriously and officially,* Conqueror of Britain.]

RUFIO. [*Calling down.*] Push off, all except the longboat. Stand by it to embark, Cæsar's guard there. [*He leaves the balcony and comes down into the hall.*] Where are those Egyptians? Is this more clemency? Have you let them go?

CÆSAR. [*Chuckling.*] I have let Theodotus go to save the library. We must respect literature, Rufio.

RUFIO. [*Raging.*] Folly on folly's head! I believe if you could bring back all the dead of Spain, Gaul, and Thessaly to life, you would do it that we might have the trouble of fighting them over again.

CÆSAR. Might not the gods destroy the world if their only thought were to be at peace next year? [RUFIO, *out of all patience, turns away in anger.* CÆSAR *suddenly grips his sleeve, and adds slyly in his ear.*] Besides, my friend: every Egyptian we imprison means imprisoning two Roman soldiers to guard him. Eh?

RUFIO. Agh! I might have known there was some fox's trick behind your fine talking. [*He gets away from* CÆSAR *with an ill-humored shrug, and goes to the balcony for another look at the preparations; finally goes out.*]

CÆSAR. Is Britannus asleep? I sent him for my armor an hour ago. [*Calling.*] Britannicus, thou British islander. Britannicus! [CLEOPATRA *runs in through the loggia with* CÆSAR's *helmet and sword, snatched from* BRITANNUS, *who follows her with a cuirass and greaves. They come down to* CÆSAR, *she to his left hand,* BRITANNUS *to his right.*]

CLEOPATRA. I am going to dress you, Cæsar. Sit down. [*He obeys.*] These Roman helmets are so becoming! [*She takes off his wreath.*] Oh! [*She bursts out laughing at him.*]

CÆSAR. What are you laughing at?

CLEOPATRA. *You're* bald. [*Beginning with a big B, and ending with a splutter.*]

CÆSAR. [*Almost annoyed.*] Cleopatra! [*He rises, for the convenience of* BRITANNUS, *who puts the cuirass on him.*]

CLEOPATRA. So that is why you wear the wreath—to hide it.

BRITANNUS. Peace, Egyptian: they are the bays of the conqueror. [*He buckles the cuirass.*]

CLEOPATRA. Peace, thou: islander! [*To* CÆSAR.] You should rub your head with strong spirits of sugar, Cæsar. That will make it grow.

CÆSAR. [*With a wry face.*] Cleopatra: do you like to be reminded that you are very young?

CLEOPATRA. [*Pouting.*] No.

CÆSAR. [*Sitting down again, and setting out his leg for* BRITANNUS, *who kneels to put on his greaves.*] Neither do I like to be reminded that I am—middle aged. Let me give you ten of my superfluous years. That will make you 26, and leave me only—no matter. Is it a bargain?

CLEOPATRA. Agreed. 26, mind. [*She puts the helmet on him.*] Oh! How nice! You look only about 50 in it!

BRITANNUS. [*Looking up severely at* CLEOPATRA.] You must not speak in this manner to Cæsar.

CLEOPATRA. Is it true that when Cæsar caught you on that island, you were painted all over blue?

BRITANNUS. Blue is the color worn by all Britons of good standing. In war we stain our bodies blue; so that though our enemies may strip us of our clothes and our lives, they cannot strip us of our respectability. [*He rises.*]

CLEOPATRA. [*With* CÆSAR's *sword.*] Let me hang this on. Now you look splendid. Have they made any statues of you in Rome?

CÆSAR. Yes, many statues.

CLEOPATRA. You must send for one and give it to me.

RUFIO. [*Coming back into the loggia, more impatient than ever.*] Now Cæsar: have you done talking? The moment your foot is aboard there will be no holding our men back: the boats will race one another for the lighthouse.

CÆSAR. [*Drawing his sword and trying the edge.*] Is this well set today, Britannicus? At Pharsalia it was as blunt as a barrel-hoop.

BRITANNUS. It will split one of the Egyptian's hairs today, Cæsar. I have set it myself.

CLEOPATRA. [*Suddenly throwing her*

arms in terror round CÆSAR.] Oh, you are not really going into battle to be killed?

CÆSAR. No, Cleopatra. No man goes to battle to be killed.

CLEOPATRA. But they do get killed. My sister's husband was killed in battle. You must not go. Let him go [*Pointing to* RUFIO. *They all laugh at her.*] Oh please, please dont go. What will happen to me if you never come back?

CÆSAR. [*Gravely.*] Are you afraid?

CLEOPATRA. [*Shrinking.*] No.

CÆSAR. [*With quiet authority.*] Go to the balcony; and you shall see us take the Pharos. You must learn to look on battles. Go. [*She goes, downcast, and looks out from the balcony.*] That is well. Now, Rufio. March.

CLEOPATRA. [*Suddenly clapping her hands.*] Oh, you will not be able to go!

CÆSAR. Why? What now?

CLEOPATRA. They are drying up the harbor with buckets—a multitude of soldiers—over there [*Pointing out across the sea to her left.*]—they are dipping up the water.

RUFIO. [*Hastening to look.*] It is true. The Egyptian army! Crawling over the edge of the west harbor like locusts. [*With sudden anger he strides down to* CÆSAR.] This is your accursed clemency, Cæsar. Theodotus has brought them.

CÆSAR. [*Delighted at his own cleverness.*] I meant him to, Rufio. They have come to put out the fire. The library will keep them busy whilst we seize the lighthouse. Eh? [*He rushes out buoyantly through the loggia, followed by* BRITANNUS.]

RUFIO. [*Disgustedly.*] More foxing! Agh! [*He rushes off. A shout from the soldiers announces the appearance of* CÆSAR *below.*]

CENTURION. [*Below.*] All aboard. Give way there. [*Another shout.*]

CLEOPATRA. [*Waving her scarf through the loggia arch.*] Goodbye, goodbye, dear Cæsar. Come back safe. Goodbye!

ACT THREE

The edge of the quay in front of the palace, looking out west over the east harbor of Alexandria to Pharos island, just to the end of which, and connected with it by a narrow mole, is the famous lighthouse, a gigantic square tower of white marble diminishing in size storey by storey to the top, on which stands a cresset beacon. The island is joined to the main land by the Heptastadium, a great mole or causeway five miles long bounding the harbor on the south.

In the middle of the quay a Roman SENTINEL stands on guard, pilum in hand, looking out to the lighthouse with strained attention, his left hand shading his eyes. The pilum is a stout wooden shaft 4½ feet long, with an iron spit about three feet long fixed in it. The SENTINEL is so absorbed that he does not notice the approach from the north end of the quay of four Egyptian market porters carrying rolls of carpet, preceded by FTATATEETA and APOLLODORUS the Sicilian. APOLLODORUS is a dashing young man of about 24, handsome and debonair, dressed with deliberate æstheticism in the most delicate purples and dove greys, with ornaments of bronze, oxydized silver, and stones of jade and agate. His sword, designed as carefully as a medieval cross, has a blued blade shewing through an openwork scabbard of purple leather and filigree. The porters, conducted by FTATATEETA, pass along the quay behind the SENTINEL to the steps of the palace, where they put down their bales and squat on the ground. APOLLODORUS does not pass along with them: he halts, amused by the preoccupation of the SENTINEL.

APOLLODORUS. [*Calling to the* SENTINEL.] Who goes there, eh?

SENTINEL. [*Starting violently and turning with his pilum at the charge, reveal-*

ing himself as a small, wiry, sandy-haired, conscientious young man with an elderly face.] What's this? Stand. Who are you?

APOLLODORUS. I am Apollodorus the Sicilian. Why, man, what are you dreaming of? Since I came through the lines beyond the theatre there, I have brought my caravan past three sentinels, all so busy staring at the lighthouse that not one of them challenged me. Is this Roman discipline?

SENTINEL. We are not here to watch the land but the sea. Cæsar has just landed on the Pharos. [*Looking at* FTATATEETA.] What have you here? Who is this piece of Egyptian crockery?

FTATATEETA. Apollodorus: rebuke this Roman dog; and bid him bridle his tongue in the presence of Ftatateeta, the mistress of the Queen's household.

APOLLODORUS. My friend: this is a great lady, who stands high with Cæsar.

SENTINEL. [*Not at all impressed, pointing to the carpets.*] And what is all this truck?

APOLLODORUS. Carpets for the furnishing of the Queen's apartments in the palace. I have picked them from the best carpets in the world; and the Queen shall choose the best of my choosing.

SENTINEL. So you are the carpet merchant?

APOLLODORUS. [*Hurt.*] My friend: I am a patrician.

SENTINEL. A patrician! A patrician keeping a shop instead of following arms!

APOLLODORUS. I do not keep a shop. Mine is a temple of the arts. I am a worshipper of beauty. My calling is to choose beautiful things for beautiful queens. My motto is Art for Art's sake.

SENTINEL. That is not the password.

APOLLODORUS. It is a universal password.

SENTINEL. I know nothing about universal passwords. Either give me the password for the day or get back to your shop. [FTATATEETA, *roused by his hostile tone, steals towards the edge of the quay with the step of a panther, and gets behind him.*]

APOLLODORUS. How if I do neither?

SENTINEL. Then I will drive this pilum through you.

APOLLODORUS. At your service, my

friend. [*He draws his sword, and springs to his guard with unruffled grace.*]

FTATATEETA. [*Suddenly seizing the* SENTINEL's *arms from behind.*] Thrust your knife into the dog's throat, Apollodorus. [*The chivalrous* APOLLODORUS *laughingly shakes his head; breaks ground away from the* SENTINEL *towards the palace; and lowers his point.*]

SENTINEL. [*Struggling vainly.*] Curse on you! Let me go. Help ho!

FTATATEETA. [*Lifting him from the ground.*] Stab the little Roman reptile. Spit him on your sword. [*A couple of Roman* SOLDIERS, *with a* CENTURION, *come running along the edge of the quay from the north end. They rescue their comrade, and throw off* FTATATEETA, *who is sent reeling away on the left hand of the* SENTINEL.]

CENTURION. [*An unattractive man of fifty, short in his speech and manners, with a vinewood cudgel in his hand.*] How now? What is all this?

FTATATEETA. [*To* APOLLODORUS.] Why did you not stab him? There was time!

APOLLODORUS. Centurion: I am here by order of the Queen to—

CENTURION. [*Interrupting him.*] The Queen! Yes, yes: [*To the* SENTINEL.] pass him in. Pass all these bazaar people in to the Queen, with their goods. But mind you pass no one out that you have not passed in—not even the Queen herself.

SENTINEL. This old woman is dangerous: she is as strong as three men. She wanted the merchant to stab me.

APOLLODORUS. Centurion: I am not a merchant. I am a patrician and a votary of art.

CENTURION. Is the woman your wife?

APOLLODORUS. [*Horrified.*] No, no! [*Correcting himself politely.*] Not that the lady is not a striking figure in her own way. But [*Emphatically.*] she is not my wife.

FTATATEETA. [*To the* CENTURION.] Roman: I am Ftatateeta, the mistress of the Queen's household.

CENTURION. Keep your hands off our men, mistress; or I will have you pitched into the harbor, though you were as strong as ten men. [*To his men.*] To your posts: march! [*He returns with his men the way they came.*]

FTATATEETA. [*Looking malignantly after him.*] We shall see whom Isis loves best: her servant Ftatateeta or a dog of a Roman.

SENTINEL. [*To* APOLLODORUS, *with a wave of his pilum towards the palace.*] Pass in there; and keep your distance. [*Turning to* FTATATEETA.] Come within a yard of me, you old crocodile; and I will give you this [*The pilum.*] in your jaws.

CLEOPATRA. [*Calling from the palace.*] Ftatateeta, Ftatateeta.

FTATATEETA. [*Looking up, scandalized.*] Go from the window, go from the window. There are men here.

CLEOPATRA. I am coming down.

FTATATEETA. [*Distracted.*] No, no. What are you dreaming of? O ye gods, ye gods! Apollodorus: bid your men pick up your bales; and in with me quickly.

APOLLODORUS. Obey the mistress of the Queen's household.

FTATATEETA. [*Impatiently, as the porters stoop to lift the bales.*] Quick, quick: she will be out upon us. [CLEOPATRA *comes from the palace and runs across the quay to* FTATATEETA.] Oh that ever I was born!

CLEOPATRA. [*Eagerly.*] Ftatateeta: I have thought of something. I want a boat —at once.

FTATATEETA. A boat! No, no: you cannot, Apollodorus: speak to the Queen.

APOLLODORUS. [*Gallantly.*] Beautiful queen: I am Apollodorus the Sicilian, your servant, from the bazaar. I have brought you the three most beautiful Persian carpets in the world to choose from.

CLEOPATRA. I have no time for carpets today. Get me a boat.

FTATATEETA. What whim is this? You cannot go on the water except in the royal barge.

APOLLODORUS. Royalty, Ftatateeta, lies not in the barge but in the Queen. [*To* CLEOPATRA.] The touch of your majesty's foot on the gunwale of the meanest boat in the harbor will make it royal. [*He turns to the harbor and calls seaward.*] Ho there, boatman! Pull in to the steps.

CLEOPATRA. Apollodorus: you are my perfect knight; and I will always buy my carpets through you. [APOLLODORUS *bows joyously. An oar appears above the quay; and the* BOATMAN, *a bullet-headed, vivacious, grinning fellow, burnt almost black by the sun, comes up a flight of steps from the water on the* SENTINEL's *right, oar in hand, and waits at the top.*] Can you row, Apollodorus?

APOLLODORUS. My oars shall be your majesty's wings. Whither shall I row my Queen?

CLEOPATRA. To the lighthouse. Come. [*She makes for the steps.*]

SENTINEL. [*Opposing her with his pilum at the charge.*] Stand. You cannot pass.

CLEOPATRA. [*Flushing angrily.*] How dare you? Do you know that I am the Queen?

SENTINEL. I have my orders. You cannot pass.

CLEOPATRA. I will make Cæsar have you killed if you do not obey me.

SENTINEL. He will do worse to me if I disobey my officer. Stand back.

CLEOPATRA. Ftatateeta: strangle him.

SENTINEL. [*Alarmed—looking apprehensively at* FTATATEETA, *and brandishing his pilum.*] Keep off, there.

CLEOPATRA. [*Running to* APOLLODORUS.] Apollodorus: make your slaves help us.

APOLLODORUS. I shall not need their help, lady. [*He draws his sword.*] Now, soldier: choose which weapon you will defend yourself with. Shall it be sword against pilum, or sword against sword?

SENTINEL. Roman against Sicilian, curse you. Take that. [*He hurls his pilum at* APOLLODORUS, *who drops expertly on one knee. The pilum passes whizzing over his head and falls harmless.* APOLLODORUS, *with a cry of triumph, springs up and attacks the* SENTINEL, *who draws his sword and defends himself, crying.*] Ho there, guard. Help! [CLEOPATRA, *half frightened, half delighted, takes refuge near the palace, where the porters are squatting among the bales. The* BOATMAN, *alarmed, hurries down the steps out of harm's way, but stops, with his head just visible above the edge of the quay, to watch the fight. The* SENTINEL *is handicapped by his fear of an attack in the rear from* FTATATEETA. *His swordsmanship, which is of rough and ready sort, is heavily taxed, as he has occasionally to strike at her to keep her off between a blow and a guard with* APOLLODORUS. *The* CENTURION *returns with several* SOLDIERS. APOLLODORUS *springs back towards* CLEOPATRA *as this reinforcement confronts him.*]

CENTURION. [*Coming to the* SENTINEL'S *right hand.*] What is this? What now?

SENTINEL. [*Panting.*] I could do well enough by myself if it werent for the old woman. Keep her off me: that is all the help I need.

CENTURION. Make your report, soldier. What has happened?

FTATATEETA. Centurion: he would have slain the Queen.

SENTINEL. [*Bluntly.*] I would, sooner than let her pass. She wanted to take boat, and go—so she said—to the lighthouse. I stopped her, as I was ordered to; and she set this fellow on me. [*He goes to pick up his pilum and returns to his place with it.*]

CENTURION. [*Turning to* CLEOPATRA.] Cleopatra: I am loth to offend you; but without Cæsar's express order we dare not let you pass beyond the Roman lines.

APOLLODORUS. Well, Centurion; and has not the lighthouse been within the Roman lines since Cæsar landed there?

CLEOPATRA. Yes, yes. Answer that, if you can.

CENTURION. [*To* APOLLODORUS.] As for you, Apollodorus, you may thank the gods that you are not nailed to the palace door with a pilum for your meddling.

APOLLODORUS. [*Urbanely.*] My military friend, I was not born to be slain by so ugly a weapon. When I fall, it will be [*Holding up his sword.*] by this white queen of arms, the only weapon fit for an artist. And now that you are convinced that we do not want to go beyond the lines, let me finish killing your sentinel and depart with the Queen.

CENTURION. [*As the* SENTINEL *makes an angry demonstration.*] Peace there, Cleopatra: I must abide by my orders, and not by the subtleties of this Sicilian. You must withdraw into the palace and examine your carpets there.

CLEOPATRA. [*Pouting.*] I will not: I am the Queen. Cæsar does not speak to me as you do. Have Cæsar's centurions changed manners with his scullions?

CENTURION. [*Sulkily.*] I do my duty. That is enough for me.

APOLLODORUS. Majesty: when a stupid man is doing something he is ashamed of, he always declares that it is his duty.

CENTURION. [*Angry.*] Apollodorus—

APOLLODORUS. [*Interrupting him with defiant elegance.*] I will make amends for that insult with my sword at fitting time and place. Who says artist, says duellist. [*To* CLEOPATRA.] Hear my counsel, star of the east. Until word comes to these soldiers from Cæsar himself, you are a prisoner. Let me go to him with a message from you, and a present; and before the sun has stooped half way to the arms of the sea, I will bring you back Cæsar's order of release.

CENTURION. [*Sneering at him.*] And you will sell the Queen the present, no doubt.

APOLLODORUS. Centurion: the Queen shall have from me, without payment, as the unforced tribute of Sicilian taste to Egyptian beauty, the richest of these carpets for her present to Cæsar.

CLEOPATRA. [*Exultantly, to the* CENTURION.] Now you see what an ignorant common creature you are!

CENTURION. [*Curtly.*] Well, a fool and his wares are soon parted. [*He turns to his* MEN.] Two more men to this post here; and see that no one leaves the palace but this man and his merchandise. If he draws his sword again inside the lines, kill him. To your posts. March. [*He goes out, leaving two auxiliary* SENTINELS *with the other.*]

APOLLODORUS. [*With polite goodfellowship.*] My friends: will you not enter the palace and bury our quarrel in a bowl of wine? [*He takes out his purse, jingling the coins in it.*] The Queen has presents for you all.

SENTINEL. [*Very sulky.*] You heard our orders. Get about your business.

FIRST AUXILIARY. Yes: you ought to know better. Off with you.

SECOND AUXILIARY. [*Looking longingly at the purse—this* SENTINEL *is a hook-*

nosed man, unlike his comrade, who is squab faced.] Do not tantalize a poor man.

APOLLODORUS. [*To* CLEOPATRA.] Pearl of Queens: the centurion is at hand; and the Roman soldier is incorruptible when his officer is looking. I must carry your word to Cæsar.

CLEOPATRA. [*Who has been meditating among the carpets.*] Are these carpets very heavy?

APOLLODORUS. It matters not how heavy. There are plenty of porters.

CLEOPATRA. How do they put the carpets into boats? Do they throw them down?

APOLLODORUS. Not into small boats, majesty. It would sink them.

CLEOPATRA. Not into that man's boat, for instance? [*Pointing to the* BOATMAN.]

APOLLODORUS. No. Too small.

CLEOPATRA. But you can take a carpet to Cæsar in it if I send one?

APOLLODORUS. Assuredly.

CLEOPATRA. And you will have it carried gently down the steps and take great care of it?

APOLLODORUS. Depend on me.

CLEOPATRA. Great, great care?

APOLLODORUS. More than of my own body.

CLEOPATRA. You will promise me not to let the porters drop it or throw it about?

APOLLODORUS. Place the most delicate glass goblet in the palace in the heart of the roll, Queen; and if it be broken, my head shall pay for it.

CLEOPATRA. Good. Come, Ftatateeta. [FTATATEETA *comes to her.* APOLLODORUS *offers to squire them into the palace.*] No, Apollodorus, you must not come. I will choose a carpet for myself. You must wait here. [*She runs into the palace.*]

APOLLODORUS. [*To the* PORTERS.] Follow this lady [*Indicating* FTATATEETA.] and obey her. [*The* PORTERS *rise and take up their bales.*]

FTATATEETA. [*Addressing the* PORTERS *as if they were vermin.*] This way. And take your shoes off before you put your feet on those stairs. [*She goes in, followed by the* PORTERS *with the carpets. Meanwhile* APOLLODORUS *goes to the edge of the quay and looks out over the harbor.*

The SENTINELS *keep their eyes on him malignantly.*]

APOLLODORUS. [*Addressing the* SENTINEL.] My friend—

SENTINEL. [*Rudely.*] Silence there.

FIRST AUXILIARY. Shut your muzzle, you.

SECOND AUXILIARY. [*In a half whisper, glancing apprehensively towards the north end of the quay.*] Cant you wait a bit?

APOLLODORUS. Patience, worthy three-headed donkey. [*They mutter ferociously; but he is not at all intimidated.*] Listen: were you set here to watch me, or to watch the Egyptians?

SENTINEL. We know our duty.

APOLLODORUS. Then why dont you do it? There is something going on over there. [*Pointing southwestward to the mole.*]

SENTINEL. [*Sulkily.*] I do not need to be told what to do by the like of you.

APOLLODORUS. Blockhead. [*He begins shouting.*] Ho there, Centurion. Hoiho!

SENTINEL. Curse your meddling. [*Shouting.*] Hoiho! Alarm! Alarm!

FIRST AND SECOND AUXILIARIES. Alarm! alarm! Hoiho! [*The* CENTURION *comes running in with his* GUARD.]

CENTURION. What now? Has the old woman attacked you again? [*Seeing* APOLLODORUS.] Are you here still?

APOLLODORUS. [*Pointing as before.*] See there. The Egyptians are moving. They are going to recapture the Pharos. They will attack by sea and land: by land along the great mole; by sea from the west harbor. Stir yourselves, my military friends: the hunt is up. [*A clangor of trumpets from several points along the quay.*] Aha! I told you so.

CENTURION. [*Quickly.*] The two extra men pass the alarm to the south posts. One man keep guard here. The rest with me—quick. [*The two* AUXILIARY SENTINELS *run off to the south. The* CENTURION *and his* GUARD *run off northward; and immediately afterwards the bucina sounds. The four* PORTERS *come from the palace carrying a carpet, followed by* FTATATEETA.]

SENTINEL. [*Handling his pilum apprehensively.*] You again! [*The* PORTERS *stop.*]

FTATATEETA. Peace, Roman fellow: you are now single-handed. Apollodorus: this carpet is Cleopatra's present to Cæsar. It has rolled up in it ten precious goblets of the thinnest Iberian crystal, and a hundred eggs of the sacred blue pigeon. On your honor, let not one of them be broken.

APOLLODORUS. On my head be it! [*To the* PORTERS.] Into the boat with them carefully. [*The* PORTERS *carry the carpet to the steps.*]

FIRST PORTER. [*Looking down at the boat.*] Beware what you do, sir. Those eggs of which the lady speaks must weigh more than a pound apiece. This boat is too small for such a load.

BOATMAN. [*Excitedly rushing up the steps.*] Oh thou injurious porter! Oh thou unnatural son of a she-camel! [*To* APOLLODORUS.] My boat, sir, hath often carried five men. Shall it not carry your lordship and a bale of pigeon's eggs? [*To the* PORTER.] Thou mangey dromedary, the gods shall punish thee for this envious wickedness.

FIRST PORTER. [*Stolidly.*] I cannot quit this bale now to beat these; but another day I will lie in wait for thee.

APOLLODORUS. [*Going between them.*] Peace there. If the boat were but a single plank, I would get to Cæsar on it.

FTATATEETA. [*Anxiously.*] In the name of the gods, Apollodorus, run no risks with that bale.

APOLLODORUS. Fear not, thou venerable grotesque: I guess its great worth. [*To the* PORTERS.] Down with it, I say; and gently; or ye shall eat nothing but stick for ten days. [*The* BOATMAN *goes down the steps, followed by the* PORTERS *with the bale:* FTATATEETA *and* APOLLODORUS *watching from the edge.*]

APOLLODORUS. Gently, my sons, my children—[*With sudden alarm.*] gently, ye dogs. Lay it level in the stern—so—tis well.

FTATATEETA. [*Screaming down at one of the* PORTERS.] Do not step on it, do not step on it. Oh thou brute beast!

FIRST PORTER. [*Ascending.*] Be not excited, mistress: all is well.

FTATATEETA. [*Panting.*] All well! Oh, thou hast given my heart a turn! [*She clutches her side, gasping. The four* PORTERS *have now come up and are waiting at the stairhead to be paid.*]

APOLLODORUS. Here, ye hungry ones. [*He gives money to the first* PORTER, *who holds it in his hand to shew to the others. They crowd greedily to see how much it is, quite prepared, after the Eastern fashion, to protest to heaven against their patron's stinginess. But his liberality overpowers them.*]

FIRST PORTER. O bounteous prince!

SECOND PORTER. O lord of the bazaar!

THIRD PORTER. O favored of the gods!

FOURTH PORTER. O father to all the porters of the market.

SENTINEL. [*Enviously, threatening them fiercely with his pilum.*] Hence, dogs: off. Out of this. [*They fly before him northward along the quay.*]

APOLLODORUS. Farewell, Ftatateeta. I shall be at the lighthouse before the Egyptians. [*He descends the steps.*]

FTATATEETA. The gods speed thee and protect my nursling! [*The* SENTRY *returns from chasing the* PORTERS *and looks down at the boat, standing near the stairhead lest* FTATATEETA *should attempt to escape.*]

APOLLODORUS. [*From beneath, as the boat moves off.*] Farewell, valiant pilum pitcher.

SENTINEL. Farewell, shopkeeper.

APOLLODORUS. Ha, ha! Pull, thou brave boatman, pull. Soho-o-o-o-o! [*He begins to sing in barcarolle measure to the rhythm of the oars.*]

My heart, my heart, spread out thy wings:
Shake off thy heavy load of love—
Give me the oars, O son of a snail.

SENTINEL. [*Threatening* FTATATEETA.] Now mistress: back to your henhouse. In with you.

FTATATEETA. [*Falling on her knees and stretching her hands over the waters.*] Gods of the seas, bear her safely to the shore!

SENTINEL. Bear who safely? What do you mean?

FTATATEETA. [*Looking darkly at him.*] Gods of Egypt and of Vengeance, let this Roman fool be beaten like a dog by his captain for suffering her to be taken over the waters.

SENTINEL. Accursed one: is she then in the boat? [*He calls over the sea.*] Hoiho, there, boatman! Hoiho!

APOLLODORUS. [*Singing in the distance.*] My heart, my heart, be whole and free: Love is thine only enemy.

[*Meanwhile* RUFIO, *the morning's fighting done, sits munching dates on a faggot of brushwood outside the door of the lighthouse, which towers gigantic to the clouds on his left. His helmet, full of dates, is between his knees; and a leathern bottle of wine is by his side. Behind him the great stone pedestal of the lighthouse is shut in from the open sea by a low stone parapet, with a couple of steps in the middle to the broad coping. A huge chain with a hook hangs down from the lighthouse crane above his head. Faggots like the one he sits on lie beneath it ready to be drawn up to feed the beacon.* CÆSAR *is standing on the step at the parapet looking out anxiously, evidently ill at ease.* BRITTANNUS *comes out of the lighthouse door.*]

RUFIO. Well, my British islander. Have you been up to the top?

BRITANNUS. I have. I reckon it at 200 feet high.

RUFIO. Anybody up there?

BRITANNUS. One elderly Tyrian to work the crane; and his son, a well conducted youth of 14.

RUFIO. [*Looking at the chain.*] What! An old man and a boy work that! Twenty men, you mean.

BRITANNUS. Two only, I assure you. They have counter-weights, and a machine with boiling water in it which I do not understand: it is not of British design. They use it to haul up barrels of oil and faggots to burn in the brazier on the roof.

RUFIO. But—

BRITANNUS. Excuse me: I came down because there are messengers coming along the mole to us from the island. I must see what their business is. [*He hurries out past the lighthouse.*]

CÆSAR. [*Coming away from the parapet, shivering and out of sorts.*] Rufio: this has been a mad expedition. We shall be beaten. I wish I knew how our men

are getting on with that barricade across the great mole.

RUFIO. [*Angrily.*] Must I leave my food and go starving to bring you a report?

CÆSAR. [*Soothing him nervously.*] No, Rufio, no. Eat, my son, eat. [*He takes another turn,* RUFIO *chewing dates meanwhile.*] The Egyptians cannot be such fools as not to storm the barricade and swoop down on us here before it is finished. It is the first time I have ever run an avoidable risk. I should not have come to Egypt.

RUFIO. An hour ago you were all for victory.

CÆSAR. [*Apologetically.*] Yes: I was a fool—rash, Rufio—boyish.

RUFIO. Boyish! Not a bit of it. Here [*Offering him a handful of dates.*]

CÆSAR. What are these for?

RUFIO. To eat. Thats whats the matter with you. When a mans comes to your age, he runs down before his midday meal. Eat and drink; and then have another look at our chances.

CÆSAR. [*Taking the dates.*] My age! [*He shakes his head and bites a date.*] Yes, Rufio: I am an old man—worn out now —true, quite true. [*He gives way to melancholy contemplation, and eats another date.*] Achillas is still in his prime: Ptolemy is a boy. [*He eats another date, and plucks up a little.*] Well, every dog has his day; and I have had mine: I cannot complain. [*With sudden cheerfulness.*] These dates are not bad, Rufio. [BRITANNUS *returns, greatly excited, with a leathern bag.* CÆSAR *is himself again in a moment.*] What now?

BRITANNUS. [*Triumphantly.*] Our brave Rhodian mariners have captured a treasure. There! [*He throws the bag down at* CÆSAR's *feet.*] Our enemies are delivered into our hands.

CÆSAR. In that bag?

BRITANNUS. Wait till you hear, Cæsar. This bag contains all the letters which have passed between Pompey's party and the army of occupation here.

CÆSAR. Well?

BRITANNUS. [*Impatient of* CÆSAR's *slowness to grasp the situation.*] Well, we shall now know who your foes are. The name of every man who has plotted against you since you crossed the Rubicon may be in these papers, for all we know.

CÆSAR. Put them in the fire.

BRITANNUS. Put them—[*He gasps.*] ! ! !

CÆSAR. In the fire. Would you have me waste the next three years of my life of proscribing and condemning men who will be my friends when I have proved that my friendship is worth more than Pompey's was—than Cato's is. O incorrigible British islander: am I a bull dog, to seek quarrels merely to shew how stubborn my jaws are?

BRITANNUS. But your honor—the honor of Rome—

CÆSAR. I do not make human sacrifices to my honor, as your Druids do. Since you will not burn these, at least I can drown them. [*He picks up the bag and throws it over the parapet into the sea.*]

BRITANNUS. Cæsar: this is mere eccentricity. Are traitors to be allowed to go free for the sake of a paradox?

RUFIO. [*Rising.*] Cæsar: when the islander has finished preaching, call me again. I am going to have a look at the boiling water machine. [*He goes into the lighthouse.*]

BRITANNUS. [*With genuine feeling.*] O Cæsar, my great master, if I could but persuade you to regard life seriously, as men do in my country!

CÆSAR. Do they truly do so, Britannus?

BRITANNUS. Have you not been there? Have you not seen them? What Briton speaks as you do in your moments of levity? What Briton neglects to attend the services at the sacred grove? What Briton wears clothes of many colors as you do, instead of plain blue, as all solid, well esteemed men should? These are moral questions with us.

CÆSAR. Well, well, my friend: some day I shall settle down and have a blue toga, perhaps. Meanwhile, I must get on as best I can in my flippant Roman way. [*APPOLLODORUS comes past the lighthouse.*] What now?

BRITANNUS. [*Turning quickly, and challenging the stranger with official haughtiness.*] What is this? Who are you? How did you come here?

APOLLODORUS. Calm yourself, my

friend: I am not going to eat you. I have come by boat, from Alexandria, with precious gifts for Cæsar.

CÆSAR. From Alexandria!

BRITANNUS. [*Severely.*] This is Cæsar, sir.

RUFIO. [*Appearing at the lighthouse door.*] Whats the matter now?

APOLLODORUS. Hail, great Cæsar! I am Apollodorus the Sicilian, an artist.

BRITANNUS. An artist! Why have they admitted this vagabond?

CÆSAR. Peace, man. Apollodorus is a famous patrician amateur.

BRITANNUS. [*Disconcerted.*] I crave the gentleman's pardon. [*To* CÆSAR.] I understood him to say that he was a professional. [*Somewhat out of countenance, he allows* APOLLODORUS *to approach* CÆSAR, *changing places with him.* RUFIO, *after looking* APOLLODORUS *up and down with marked disparagement, goes to the other side of the platform.*]

CÆSAR. You are welcome, Apollodorus. What is your business?

APOLLODORUS. First, to deliver to you a present from the Queen of Queens.

CÆSAR. Who is that?

APOLLODORUS. Cleopatra of Egypt.

CÆSAR. [*Taking him into his confidence in his most winning manner.*] Apollodorus: this is no time for playing with presents. Pray you, go back to the Queen, and tell her that if all goes well I shall return to the palace this evening.

APOLLODORUS. Cæsar: I cannot return. As I approached the lighthouse, some fool threw a great leathern bag into the sea. It broke the nose of my boat; and I had hardly time to get myself and my charge to the shore before the poor little cockleshell sank.

CÆSAR. I am sorry, Apollodorus. The fool shall be rebuked. Well, well: what have you brought me? The Queen will be hurt if I do not look at it.

RUFIO. Have we time to waste on this trumpery? The Queen is only a child.

CÆSAR. Just so: that is why we must not disappoint her. What is the present, Apollodorus?

APOLLODORUS. Cæsar: it is a Persian carpet—a beauty! And in it are—so I am told—pigeons' eggs and crystal goblets and fragile precious things. I dare not for my head have it carried up that narrow ladder from the causeway.

RUFIO. Swing it up by the crane, then. We will send the eggs to the cook; drink our wine from the goblets; and the carpet will make a bed for Cæsar.

APOLLODORUS. The crane! Cæsar: I have sworn to tender this bale of carpet as I tender my own life.

CÆSAR. [*Cheerfully.*] Then let them swing you up at the same time; and if the chain breaks, you and the pigeons' eggs will perish together. [*He goes to the chain and looks up along it, examining it curiously.*]

APOLLODORUS. [*To* BRITANNUS.] Is Cæsar serious?

BRITANNUS. His manner is frivolous because he is an Italian; but he means what he says.

APOLLODORUS. Serious or not, he spake well. Give me a squad of soldiers to work the crane.

BRITANNUS. Leave the crane to me. Go and await the descent of the chain.

APOLLODORUS. Good. You will presently see me there [*Turning to them all and pointing with an eloquent gesture to the sky above the parapet.*] rising like the sun with my treasure. [*He goes back the way he came.* BRITANNUS *goes into the lighthouse.*]

RUFIO. [*Ill-humoredly.*] Are you really going to wait here for this foolery, Cæsar?

CÆSAR. [*Backing away from the crane as it gives signs of working.*] Why not?

RUFIO. The Egyptians will let you know why not if they have the sense to make a rush from the shore end of the mole before our barricade is finished. And here we are waiting like children to see a carpet full of pigeons' eggs. [*The chain rattles, and is drawn up high enough to clear the parapet. It then swings round out of sight behind the lighthouse.*]

CÆSAR. Fear not, my son Rufio. When the first Egyptian takes his first step along the mole, the alarm will sound; and we two will reach the barricade from our end before the Egyptians reach it from their end—we two, Rufio: I, the old man, and you, his biggest boy. And the old

man will be there first. So peace; and give me some more dates.

APOLLODORUS. [*From the causeway below.*] Soho, haul away. So-ho-o-o-o! [*The chain is drawn up and comes round again from behind the lighthouse.* APOLLODORUS *is swinging in the air with his bale of carpet at the end of it. He breaks into song as he soars above the parapet.*]

Aloft, aloft, behold the blue

That never shone in woman's eyes—

Easy there: stop her. [*He ceases to rise.*] Further round! [*The chain comes forward above the platform.*]

RUFIO. [*Calling up.*] Lower away there. [*The chain and its load begin to descend.*]

APOLLODORUS. [*Calling up.*] Gently—slowly—mind the eggs.

RUFIO. [*Calling up.*] Easy there—slowly—slowly. [APOLLODORUS *and the bale are deposited safely on the flags in the middle of the platform.* RUFIO *and* CÆSAR *help* APOLLODORUS *to cast off the chain from the bale.*]

RUFIO. Haul up. [*The chain rises clear of their heads with a rattle.* BRITANNUS *comes from the lighthouse and helps them to uncord the carpet.*]

APOLLODORUS. [*When the cords are loose.*] Stand off, my friends: let Cæsar see. [*He throws the carpet open.*]

RUFIO. Nothing but a heap of shawls. Where are the pigeons' eggs?

APOLLODORUS. Approach, Cæsar; and search for them among the shawls.

RUFIO. [*Drawing his sword.*] Ha, treachery! Keep back, Cæsar: I saw the shawl move: there is something alive there.

BRITANNUS. [*Drawing his sword.*] It is a serpent.

APOLLODORUS. Dares Cæsar thrust his hand into the sack where the serpent moves?

RUFIO. [*Turning on him.*] Treacherous dog—

CÆSAR. Peace. Put up your swords. Apollodorus: your serpent seems to breathe very regularly. [*He thrusts his hand under the shawls and draws out a bare arm.*] This is a pretty little snake.

RUFIO. [*Drawing out the other arm.*] Let us have the rest of you. [*They pull*

CLEOPATRA *up by the wrists into a sitting position.* BRITANNUS, *scandalized, sheathes his sword with a drive of protest.*]

CLEOPATRA. [*Gasping.*] Oh, I'm smothered. Oh, Cæsar, a man stood on me in the boat; and a great sack of something fell upon me out of the sky; and then the boat sank; and then I was swung up into the air and bumped down.

CÆSAR. [*Petting her as she rises and takes refuge on his breast.*] Well, never mind: here you are safe and sound at last.

RUFIO. Ay; and now that she is here, what are we to do with her?

BRITANNUS. She cannot stay here, Cæsar, without the companionship of some matron.

CLEOPATRA. [*Jealously, to* CÆSAR, *who is obviously perplexed.*] Arnt you glad to see me?

CÆSAR. Yes, yes; I am very glad. But Rufio is very angry; and Britannus is shocked.

CLEOPATRA. [*Contemptuously.*] You can have their heads cut off, can you not?

CÆSAR. They would not be so useful with their heads cut off as they are now, my sea bird.

RUFIO. [*To* CLEOPATRA.] We shall have to go away presently and cut some of your Egyptians' heads off. How will you like being left here with the chance of being captured by that little brother of yours if we are beaten?

CLEOPATRA. But you mustnt leave me alone. Cæsar: you will not leave me alone, will you?

RUFIO. What! not when the trumpet sounds and all our lives depend on Cæsar's being at the barricade before the Egyptians reach it? Eh?

CLEOPATRA. Let them lose their lives: they are only soldiers.

CÆSAR. [*Gravely.*] Cleopatra: when that trumpet sounds, we must take every man his life in his hand, and throw it in the face of Death. And of my soldiers who have trusted me there is not one whose hand I shall not hold more sacred than your head. [CLEOPATRA *is overwhelmed. Her eyes fill with tears.*] Apollodorus: you must take her back to the palace.

APOLLODORUS. Am I a dolphin, Cæsar, to cross the seas with young ladies on my back? My boat is sunk: all yours are either at the barricade or have returned to the city. I will hail one if I can: that is all I can do. [*He goes back to the causeway.*]

CLEOPATRA. [*Struggling with her tears.*] It does not matter. I will not go back. Nobody cares for me.

CÆSAR. Cleopatra—

CLEOPATRA. You want me to be killed.

CÆSAR. [*Still more gravely.*] My poor child: your life matters little here to anyone but yourself. [*She gives way altogether at this, casting herself down on the faggots weeping. Suddenly a great tumult is heard in the distance, bucinas and trumpets sounding through a storm of shouting.* BRITANNUS *rushes to the parapet and looks along the mole.* CÆSAR *and* RUFIO *turn to one another with quick intelligence.*]

CÆSAR. Come, Rufio.

CLEOPATRA. [*Scrambling to her knees and clinging to him.*] No no. Do not leave me, Cæsar. [*He snatches his skirt from her clutch.*] Oh!

BRITANNUS. [*From the parapet.*] Cæsar: we are cut off. The Egyptians have landed from the west harbor between us and the barricade!!!

RUFIO. [*Running to see.*] Curses! It is true. We are caught like rats in a trap.

CÆSAR. [*Ruthfully.*] Rufio, Rufio: my men at the barricade are between the sea party and the shore party. I have murdered them.

RUFIO. [*Coming back from the parapet to* CÆSAR's *right hand.*] Ay: that comes of fooling with this girl here.

APOLLODORUS. [*Coming up quickly from the causeway.*] Look over the parapet, Cæsar.

CÆSAR. We have looked, my friend. We must defend ourselves here.

APOLLODORUS. I have thrown the ladder into the sea. They cannot get in without it.

RUFIO. Ay; and we cannot get out. Have you thought of that?

APOLLODORUS. Not get out! Why not? You have ships in the east harbor.

BRITANNUS. [*Hopefully, at the parapet.*] The Rhodian galleys are standing in towards us already. [CÆSAR *quickly joins* BRITANNUS *at the parapet.*]

RUFIO. [*To* APOLLODORUS, *impatiently.*] And by what road are we to walk to the galleys, pray?

APOLLODORUS. [*With gay, defiant rhetoric.*] By the road that leads everywhere—the diamond path of the sun and moon. Have you never seen a child's shadow play of The Broken Bridge? "Ducks and geese with ease get over"— eh? [*He throws away his cloak and cap, and binds his sword on his back.*]

RUFIO. What are you talking about?

APOLLODORUS. I will shew you. [*Calling to* BRITANNUS.] How far off is the nearest galley?

BRITANNUS. Fifty fathom.

CÆSAR. No, no: they are further off than they seem in this clear air to your British eyes. Nearly quarter of a mile, Apollodorus.

APOLLODORUS. Good. Defend yourselves here until I send you a boat from that galley.

RUFIO. Have you wings, perhaps?

APOLLODORUS. Water wings, soldier. Behold! [*He runs up the steps between* CÆSAR *and* BRITANNUS *to the coping of the parapet; springs into the air; and plunges head foremost into the sea.*]

CÆSAR. [*Like a schoolboy—wildly excited.*] Bravo, bravo! [*Throwing off his cloak.*] By Jupiter, I will do that too.

RUFIO. [*Seizing him.*] You are mad. You shall not.

CÆSAR. Why not? Can I not swim as well as he?

RUFIO. [*Frantic.*] Can an old fool dive and swim like a young one? He is twenty-five and you are fifty.

CÆSAR. [*Breaking loose from* RUFIO.] Old!!!

BRITANNUS. [*Shocked.*] Rufio: you forget yourself.

CÆSAR. I will race you to the galley for a week's pay, father Rufio.

CLEOPATRA. But me! me!! me!!! what is to become of me?

CÆSAR. I will carry you on my back to the galley like a dolphin. Rufio: when you see me rise to the surface, throw her in: I will answer for her. And then in with you after her, both of you.

CLEOPATRA. No, no, NO. I shall be drowned.

BRITANNUS. Caesar: I am a man and a Briton, not a fish. I must have a boat. I cannot swim.

CLEOPATRA. Neither can I.

CÆSAR. [*To* BRITANNUS.] Stay here, then, alone, until I recapture the lighthouse. I will not forget you. Now, Rufio.

RUFIO. You have made up your mind to this folly?

CÆSAR. The Egyptians have made it up for me. What else is there to do? And mind where you jump: I do not want to get your fourteen stone in the small of my back as I come up. [*He runs up the steps and stands on the coping.*]

BRITANNUS. [*Anxiously.*] One last word, Caesar. Do not let yourself be seen in the fashionable part of Alexandria until you have changed your clothes.

CÆSAR. [*Calling over the sea.*] Ho, Apollodorus: [*He points skyward and quotes the barcarolle.*]

The white upon the blue above—

APOLLODORUS. [*Swimming in the distance.*]

Is purple on the green below—

CÆSAR. [*Exultantly.*] Aha! [*He plunges into the sea.*]

CLEOPATRA. [*Running excitedly to the steps.*] Oh, let me see. He will be drowned. [RUFIO *seizes her.*]—Ah—ah— ah—ah! [*He pitches her screaming into the sea.* RUFIO *and* BRITANNUS *roar with laughter.*]

RUFIO. [*Looking down after her.*] He has got her. [*To* BRITANNUS.] Hold the fort, Briton. Caesar will not forget you. [*He springs off.*]

BRITANNUS. [*Running to the steps to watch them as they swim.*] All safe, Rufio?

RUFIO. [*Swimming.*] All safe.

CÆSAR. [*Swimming further off.*] Take refuge up there by the beacon; and pile the fuel on the trap door, Britannus.

BRITANNUS. [*Calling in reply.*] I will first do so, and then commend myself to my country's gods. [*A sound of cheering from the sea.* BRITANNUS *gives full vent to his excitement.*] The boat has reached him: Hip, hip, hip, hurrah!

CLEOPATRA's sousing in the east harbor of Alexandria was in October 48 B.C. In March 47 she is passing the afternoon in her boudoir in the palace, among a bevy of her ladies, listening to a slave girl who is playing the harp in the middle of the room. The harpist's master, an old musician, with a lined face, prominent brows, white beard, moustache and eyebrows twisted and horned at the ends, and a consciously keen and pretentious expression, is squatting on the floor close to her on her right, watching her performance. FTATATEETA is in attendance near the door, in front of a group of female slaves. Except the harp player all are seated: CLEOPATRA in a chair opposite the door on the other side of the room; the rest on the ground. CLEOPATRA's ladies are all young, the most conspicuous being CHARMIAN and IRAS, her favorites. CHARMIAN is a hatchet faced, terra cotta colored little goblin, swift in her movements, and neatly finished at the hands and feet. IRAS is a plump, goodnatured creature, rather fatuous, with a profusion of red hair, and a tendency to giggle on the slightest provocation.

CLEOPATRA. Can I—

FTATATEETA. [Insolently, to the player.] Peace, thou! The Queen speaks. [The player stops.]

CLEOPATRA. [To the old musician.] I want to learn to play the harp with my own hands. Cæsar loves music. Can you teach me?

MUSICIAN. Assuredly I and no one else can teach the queen. Have I not discovered the lost method of the ancient Egyptians, who could make a pyramid tremble by touching a bass string? All the other teachers are quacks: I have exposed them repeatedly.

CLEOPATRA. Good: you shall teach me. How long will it take?

MUSICIAN. Not very long: only four years. Your Majesty must first become proficient in the philosophy of Pythagoras.

CLEOPATRA. Has she [Indicating the slave.] become proficient in the philosophy of Pythagoras?

MUSICIAN. Oh, she is but a slave. She learns as a dog learns.

CLEOPATRA. Well, then, I will learn as a dog learns; for she plays better than you. You shall give me a lesson every day for a fortnight. [The MUSICIAN hastily scrambles to his feet and bows profoundly.] After that, whenever I strike a false note you shall be flogged; and if I strike so many that there is not time to flog you, you shall be thrown into the Nile to feed the crocodiles. Give the girl a piece of gold; and send them away.

MUSICIAN. [Much taken aback.] But true art will not be thus forced.

FTATATEETA. [Pushing him out.] What is this? Answering the Queen, forsooth. Out with you. [He is pushed out by FTATATEETA, the girl following with her harp, amid the laughter of the ladies and slaves.]

CLEOPATRA. Now, can any of you amuse me? Have you any stories or any news?

IRAS. Ftatateeta—

CLEOPATRA. Oh, Ftatateeta, Ftatateeta, always Ftatateeta. Some new tale to set me against her.

IRAS. No: this time Ftatateeta has been virtuous. [All the ladies laugh—not the slaves.] Pothinus has been trying to bribe her to let him speak with you.

CLEOPATRA. [Wrathfully.] Ha! you all sell audiences with me, as if I saw whom you please, and not whom I please. I should like to know how much of her gold piece that harp girl will have to give up before she leaves the palace.

IRAS. We can easily find out that for you. [The ladies laugh.]

CLEOPATRA. [Frowning.] You laugh; but take care, take care. I will find out some day how to make myself served as Cæsar is served.

CHARMIAN. Old hooknose! [They laugh again.]

CLEOPATRA. [Revolted.] Silence. Char-

---

mian: do not you be a silly little Egyptian fool. Do you know why I allow you all to chatter impertinently just as you please, instead of treating you as Ftatateeta would treat you if she were Queen?

CHARMIAN. Because you try to imitate Cæsar in everything; and he lets everybody say what they please to him.

CLEOPATRA. No; but because I asked him one day why he did so; and he said "Let your women talk; and you will learn something from them." What have I to learn from them? I said. "What they are," said he; and oh! you should have seen his eye as he said it. You would have curled up, you shallow things. [*They laugh. She turns fiercely on* IRAS.] At whom are you laughing—at me or at Cæsar?

IRAS. At Cæsar.

CLEOPATRA. If you were not a fool, you would laugh at me; and if you were not a coward you would not be afraid to tell me so. [FTATATEETA *returns.*] Ftatateeta: they tell me that Pothinus has offered you a bribe to admit him to my presence.

FTATATEETA. [*Protesting.*] Now by my father's gods—

CLEOPATRA. [*Cutting her short despotically.*] Have I not told you not to deny things? You would spend the day calling your father's gods to witness to your virtues if I let you. Go take the bribe; and bring in Pothinus. [FTATATEETA *is about to reply.*] Dont answer me. Go. [FTATATEETA *goes out; and* CLEOPATRA *rises and begins to prowl to and fro between her chair and the door, meditating. All rise and stand.*]

IRAS. [*As she reluctantly rises.*] Heigho! I wish Cæsar were back in Rome.

CLEOPATRA. [*Threateningly.*] It will be a bad day for you all when he goes. Oh, if I were not ashamed to let him see that I am as cruel at heart as my father, I would make you repent that speech! Why do you wish him away?

CHARMIAN. He makes you so terribly prosy and serious and learned and philosophical. It is worse than being religious, at our ages. [*The* LADIES *laugh.*]

CLEOPATRA. Cease that endless cackling, will you. Hold your tongues.

CHARMIAN. [*With mock resignation.*] Well, well: we must try to live up to Cæsar. [*They laugh again.* CLEOPATRA *rages silently as she continues to prowl to and fro.* FTATATEETA *comes back with* POTHINUS, *who halts on the threshold.*]

FTATATEETA. [*At the door.*] Pothinus craves the ear of the—

CLEOPATRA. There, there: that will do: let him come in. [*She resumes her seat. All sit down except* POTHINUS, *who advances to the middle of the room.* FTATATEETA *takes her former place.*] Well, Pothinus: what is the latest news from your rebel friends?

POTHINUS. [*Haughtily.*] I am no friend of rebellion. And a prisoner does not receive news.

CLEOPATRA. You are no more a prisoner than I am—than Cæsar is. These six months we have been besieged in this palace by my subjects. You are allowed to walk on the beach among the soldiers. Can I go further myself, or can Cæsar?

POTHINUS. You are but a child, Cleopatra, and do not understand these matters. [*The* LADIES *laugh.* CLEOPATRA *looks inscrutably at him.*]

CHARMIAN. I see you do not know the latest news, Pothinus.

POTHINUS. What is that?

CHARMIAN. That Cleopatra is no longer a child. Shall I tell you how to grow much older, and much, much wiser in one day?

POTHINUS. I should prefer to grow wiser without growing older.

CHARMIAN. Well, go up to the top of the lighthouse; and get somebody to take you by the hair and throw you into the sea. [*The* LADIES *laugh.*]

CLEOPATRA. She is right, Pothinus: you will come to the shore with much conceit washed out of you. [*The* LADIES *laugh.* CLEOPATRA *rises impatiently.*] Begone, all of you. I will speak with Pothinus alone. Drive them out, Ftatateeta. [*They run out laughing.* FTATATEETA *shuts the door on them.*] What are you waiting for?

FTATATEETA. It is not meet that the Queen remain alone with—

CLEOPATRA. [*Interrupting her.*] Ftatateeta: must I sacrifice you to your father's gods to teach you that *I* am Queen of Egypt, and not you?

FTATATEETA. [*Indignantly.*] You are like the rest of them. You want to be what these Romans call a New Woman. [*She goes out, banging the door.*]

CLEOPATRA. [*Sitting down again.*] Now, Pothinus: why did you bribe Ftatateeta to bring you hither?

POTHINUS. [*Studying her gravely.*] Cleopatra: what they tell me is true. You are changed.

CLEOPATRA. Do you speak with Cæsar every day for six months: and you will be changed.

POTHINUS. It is the common talk that you are infatuated with this old man.

CLEOPATRA. Infatuated? What does that mean? Made foolish, is it not? Oh no: I wish I were.

POTHINUS. You wish you were made foolish! How so?

CLEOPATRA. When I was foolish, I did what I liked, except when Ftatateeta beat me; and even then I cheated her and did it by stealth. Now that Cæsar has made me wise, it is no use my liking or disliking: I do what must be done, and have no time to attend to myself. That is not happiness; but it is greatness. If Cæsar were gone, I think I could govern the Egyptians; for what Cæsar is to me, I am to the fools around me.

POTHINUS. [*Looking hard at her.*] Cleopatra: this may be the vanity of youth.

CLEOPATRA. No, no: it is not that I am so clever, but that the others are so stupid.

POTHINUS. [*Musingly.*] Truly, that is the great secret.

CLEOPATRA. Well, now tell me what you came to say?

POTHINUS. [*Embarrassed.*] I! Nothing.

CLEOPATRA. Nothing!

POTHINUS. At least—to beg for my liberty: that is all.

CLEOPATRA. For that you would have knelt to Cæsar. No, Pothinus: you came with some plan that depended on Cleopatra being a little nursery kitten. Now that Cleopatra is a Queen, the plan is upset.

POTHINUS. [*Bowing his head submissively.*] It is so.

CLEOPATRA. [*Exultant.*] Aha!

POTHINUS. [*Raising his eyes keenly to hers.*] Is Cleopatra then indeed a Queen, and no longer Cæsar's prisoner and slave?

CLEOPATRA. Pothinus: we are all Cæsar's slaves—all we in this land of Egypt—whether we will or no. And she who is wise enough to know this will reign when Cæsar departs.

POTHINUS. You harp on Cæsar's departure.

CLEOPATRA. What if I do?

POTHINUS. Does he not love you?

CLEOPATRA. Love me! Pothinus: Cæsar loves no one. Who are those we love? Only those whom we do not hate: all people are strangers and enemies to us except those we love. But it is not so with Cæsar. He has no hatred in him: he makes friends with everyone as he does with dogs and children. His kindness to me is a wonder: neither mother, father, nor nurse have ever taken so much care for me, or thrown open their thoughts to me so freely.

POTHINUS. Well: is not this love?

CLEOPATRA. What! when he will do as much for the first girl he meets on his way back to Rome? Ask his slave, Britannus: he has been just as good to him. Nay, ask his very horse! His kindness is not for anything in me: it is in his own nature.

POTHINUS. But how can you be sure that he does not love you as men love women?

CLEOPATRA. Because I cannot make him jealous. I have tried.

POTHINUS. Hm! Perhaps I should have asked, then, do you love him?

CLEOPATRA. Can one love a god? Besides, I love another Roman: one whom I saw long before Cæsar—no god, but a man—one who can love and hate—one whom I can hurt and who would hurt me.

POTHINUS. Does Cæsar know this?

CLEOPATRA. Yes.

POTHINUS. And he is not angry?

CLEOPATRA. He promises to send him to Egypt to please me!

POTHINUS. I do not understand this man.

CLEOPATRA. [*With superb contempt.*]

You understand Cæsar! How could you? [*Proudly.*] I do—by instinct.

POTHINUS. [*Deferentially, after a moment's thought.*] Your Majesty caused me to be admitted today. What message has the Queen for me?

CLEOPATRA. This. You think that by making my brother king, you will rule in Egypt because you are his guardian and he is a little silly.

POTHINUS. The Queen is pleased to say so.

CLEOPATRA. The Queen is pleased to say this also. That Cæsar will eat up you, and Achillas, and my brother, as a cat eats up mice; and that he will put on this land of Egypt as a shepherd puts on his garment. And when he has done that, he will return to Rome, and leave Cleopatra here as his viceroy.

POTHINUS. [*Breaking out wrathfully.*] That he shall never do. We have a thousand men to his ten; and we will drive him and his beggarly legions into the sea.

CLEOPATRA. [*With scorn, getting up to go.*] You rant like any common fellow. Go, then, and marshal your thousands; and make haste; for Mithridates of Pergamus is at hand with reinforcements for Cæsar. Cæsar has held you at bay with two legions: we shall see what he will do with twenty.

POTHINUS. Cleopatra—

CLEOPATRA. Enough, enough: Cæsar has spoiled me for talking to weak things like you. [*She goes out.* POTHINUS, *with a gesture of rage, is following, when* FTATATEETA *enters and stops him.*]

POTHINUS. Let me go forth from this hateful place.

FTATATEETA. What angers you?

POTHINUS. The curse of all the gods of Egypt be upon her! She sold her country to the Roman, that she may buy it back from him with her kisses.

FTATATEETA. Fool: did she not tell you that she would have Cæsar gone?

POTHINUS. You listened?

FTATATEETA. I took care that some honest woman should be at hand whilst you were with her.

POTHINUS. Now by the gods—

FTATATEETA. Enough of your gods! Cæsar's gods are all powerful here. It is no use you coming to Cleopatra: you are only an Egyptian. She will not listen to any of her own race: she treats us all as children.

POTHINUS. May she perish for it!

FTATATEETA. [*Balefully.*] May your tongue wither for that wish! Go! send for Lucius Septimius, the slayer of Pompey. He is a Roman: may be she will listen to him. Begone!

POTHINUS. [*Darkly.*] I know to whom I must go now.

FTATATEETA. [*Suspiciously.*] To whom, then?

POTHINUS. To a greater Roman than Lucius. And mark this, mistress. You thought, before Cæsar came, that Egypt should presently be ruled by you and your crew in the name of Cleopatra. I set myself against it—

FTATATEETA. [*Interrupting him—wrangling.*] Ay; that it might be ruled by you and your crew in the name of Ptolemy.

POTHINUS. Better me, or even you, than a woman with a Roman heart; and that is what Cleopatra is now become. Whilst I live, she shall never rule. So guide yourself accordingly. [*He goes out.*]

[*It is by this time drawing on to dinner time. The table is laid on the roof of the palace; and thither* RUFIO *is now climbing, ushered by a majestic palace official, wand of office in hand, and followed by a slave carrying an inlaid stool. After many stairs they emerge at last into a massive colonnade on the roof. Light curtains are drawn between the columns on the north and east to soften the westering sun.* THE OFFICIAL *leads* RUFIO *to one of these shaded sections. A cord for pulling the curtains apart hangs down between the pillars.*]

THE OFFICIAL. [*Bowing.*] The Roman commander will await Cæsar here. [*The slave sets down the stool near the southernmost column, and slips out through the curtains.*]

RUFIO. [*Sitting down, a little blown.*] Pouf! That was a climb. How high have we come?

THE OFFICIAL. We are on the palace roof, O Beloved of Victory!

RUFIO. Good! the Beloved of Victory has no more stairs to get up. [*A* SECOND

OFFICIAL *enters from the opposite end, walking backwards.*]

THE SECOND OFFICIAL. Cæsar approaches. [CÆSAR, *fresh from the bath, clad in a new tunic of purple silk, comes in, beaming and festive, followed by two slaves carrying a light couch, which is hardly more than an elaborately designed bench. They place it near the northmost of the two curtained columns. When this is done they slip out through the curtains; and the two* OFFICIALS, *formally bowing, follow them.* RUFIO *rises to receive* CÆSAR.]

CÆSAR. [*Coming over to him.*] Why, Rufio! [*Surveying his dress with an air of admiring astonishment.*] A new baldrick! A new golden pommel to your sword! And you have had your hair cut! But not your beard—? impossible! [*He sniffs at* RUFIO's *beard.*] Yes, perfumed, by Jupiter Olympus!

RUFIO. [*Growling.*] Well: is it to please myself?

CÆSAR. [*Affectionately.*] No, my son Rufio, but to please me—to celebrate my birthday.

RUFIO. [*Contemptuously.*] Your birthday! You always have a birthday when there is a pretty girl to be flattered or an ambassador to be conciliated. We had seven of them in ten months last year.

CÆSAR. [*Contritely.*] It is true, Rufio! I shall never break myself of these petty deceits.

RUFIO. Who is to dine with us—besides Cleopatra?

CÆSAR. Apollodorus the Sicilian.

RUFIO. That popinjay!

CÆSAR. Come! the popinjay is an amusing dog—tells a story; sings a song; and saves us the trouble of flattering the Queen. What does she care for old politicians and camp-fed bears like us? No, Apollodorus is good company, Rufio, good company.

RUFIO. Well, he can swim a bit and fence a bit: he might be worse, if he only knew how to hold his tongue.

CÆSAR. The gods forbid he should ever learn! Oh, this military life! this tedious, brutal life of action! That is the worst of us Romans: we are mere doers and drudgers: a swarm of bees turned into men. Give me a good talker—one with wit and imagination enough to live without continually doing something!

RUFIO. Ay! a nice time he would have of it with you when dinner was over! Have you noticed that I am before my time?

CÆSAR. Aha! I thought that meant something. What is it?

RUFIO. Can we be overheard here?

CÆSAR. Our privacy invites eavesdropping. I can remedy that. [*He claps his hands twice. The curtains are drawn, revealing the roof garden with a banqueting table set across in the middle for four persons, one at each end, and two side by side. The side next* CÆSAR *and* RUFIO *is blocked with golden wine vessels and basins. A gorgeous major-domo is superintending the laying of the table by a staff of slaves. The colonnade goes round the garden at both sides to the further end, where a gap in it, like a great gateway, leaves the view open to the sky beyond the western edge of the roof, except in the middle, where a life size image of* RA, *seated on a huge plinth, towers up, with hawk head and crown of asp and disk. His altar, which stands at his feet, is a single white stone.*] Now everybody can see us, nobody will think of listening to us. [*He sits down on the bench left by the two slaves.*]

RUFIO. [*Sitting down on his stool.*] Pothinus wants to speak to you. I advise you to see him: there is some plotting going on here among the women.

CÆSAR. Who is Pothinus?

RUFIO. The fellow with hair like squirrel's fur—the little King's bear leader, whom you kept prisoner.

CÆSAR. [*Annoyed.*] And has he not escaped?

RUFIO. No.

CÆSAR. [*Rising imperiously.*] Why not? You have been guarding this man instead of watching the enemy. Have I not told you always to let prisoners escape unless there are special orders to the contrary? Are there not enough mouths to be fed without him?

RUFIO. Yes; and if you would have a little sense and let me cut his throat, you would save his rations. Anyhow he wont escape. Three sentries have told him they would put a pilum through him if they saw him again. What more can they do? He prefers to stay and spy on us. So would I if I had to do with generals subject to fits of clemency.

CÆSAR. [*Resuming his seat, argued down.*] Hm! And so he wants to see me.

RUFIO. Ay. I have brought him with me. He is waiting there [*Jerking his thumb over his shouder.*] under guard.

CÆSAR. And you want me to see him?

RUFIO. [*Obstinately.*] I dont want anything. I daresay you will do what you like. Dont put it on to me.

CÆSAR. [*With an air of doing it expressly to indulge* RUFIO.] Well, well: let us have him.

RUFIO. [*Calling.*] Ho there, guard! Release your man and send him up. [*Beckoning.*] Come along! [POTHINUS *enters and stops mistrustfully between the two, looking from one to the other.*]

CÆSAR. [*Graciously.*] Ah, Pothinus! You are welcome. And what is the news this afternoon?

POTHINUS. Cæsar: I come to warn you of a danger, and to make you an offer.

CÆSAR. Never mind the danger. Make the offer.

RUFIO. Never mind the offer. Whats the danger?

POTHINUS. Cæsar: you think that Cleopatra is devoted to you.

CÆSAR. [*Gravely.*] My friend: I already know what I think. Come to your offer.

POTHINUS. I will deal plainly. I know not by what strange gods you have been enabled to defend a palace and a few yards of beach against a city and an army. Since we cut you off from Lake Mareotis, and you dug wells in the salt sea sand and brought up buckets of fresh water from them, we have known that your gods are irresistible, and that you are a worker of miracles. I no longer threaten you—

RUFIO. [*Sarcastically.*] Very handsome of you, indeed.

POTHINUS. So be it: you are the master. Our gods sent the north west winds to keep you in our hands; but you have been too strong for them.

CÆSAR. [*Gently urging him to come to the point.*] Yes, yes, my friend. But what then?

RUFIO. Spit it out, man. What have you to say?

POTHINUS. I have to say that you have a traitress in your camp. Cleopatra—

THE MAJOR-DOMO. [*At the table, announcing.*] The Queen! [CÆSAR *and* RUFIO *rise.*]

RUFIO. [*Aside to* POTHINUS.] You should have spat it out sooner, you fool. Now it is too late. [CLEOPATRA, *in gorgeous raiment, enters in state through the gap in the colonnade, and comes down past the image of* RA *and past the table to* CÆSAR. *Her retinue, headed by* FTATATEETA, *joins the staff at the table.* CÆSAR *gives* CLEOPATRA *his seat, which she takes.*]

CLEOPATRA. [*Quickly, seeing* POTHINUS.] What is he doing here?

CÆSAR. [*Seating himself beside her, in the most amiable of tempers.*] Just going to tell me something about you. You shall hear it. Proceed, Pothinus.

POTHINUS. [*Disconcerted.*] Cæsar— [*He stammers.*]

CÆSAR. Well, out with it.

POTHINUS. What I have to say is for your ear, not for the Queen's.

CLEOPATRA. [*With subdued ferocity.*] There are means of making you speak. Take care.

POTHINUS. [*Defiantly.*] Cæsar does not employ those means.

CÆSAR. My friend: when a man has anything to tell in this world, the difficulty is not to make him tell it, but to prevent him from telling it too often. Let me celebrate my birthday by setting you free. Farewell: we shall not meet again.

CLEOPATRA. [*Angrily.*] Cæsar: this mercy is foolish.

POTHINUS. [*To* CÆSAR.] Will you not give me a private audience? Your life may depend on it. [CÆSAR *rises loftily.*]

RUFIO. [*Aside to* POTHINUS.] Ass! Now we shall have some heroics.

CÆSAR. [*Oratorically.*] Pothinus—

RUFIO. [*Interrupting him.*] Cæsar: the dinner will spoil if you begin preaching your favorite sermon about life and death.

CLEOPATRA. [*Priggishly.*] Peace, Rufio. I desire to hear Cæsar.

RUFIO. [*Bluntly.*] Your Majesty has heard it before. You repeated it to Apollodorus last week; and he thought it was all your own. [CÆSAR's *dignity collapses. Much tickled, he sits down again and looks roguishly at* CLEOPATRA, *who is furious.* RUFIO *calls as before.*] Ho there, guard! Pass the prisoner out. He is released. [*To* POTHINUS.] Now off with you. You have lost your chance.

POTHINUS. [*His temper overcoming his prudence.*] I will speak.

CÆSAR. [*To* CLEOPATRA.] You see. Torture would not have wrung a word from him.

POTHINUS. Cæsar: you have taught Cleopatra the arts by which the Romans govern the world.

CÆSAR. Alas! they cannot even govern themselves. What then?

POTHINUS. What then? Are you so besotted with her beauty that you do not see that she is impatient to reign in Egypt alone, and that her heart is set on your departure?

CLEOPATRA. [*Rising.*] Liar!

CÆSAR. [*Shocked.*] What! Protestations! Contradictions!

CLEOPATRA. [*Ashamed, but trembling with suppressed rage.*] No. I do not deign to contradict. Let him talk. [*She sits down again.*]

POTHINUS. From her own lips I have heard it. You are to be her catspaw: you are to tear the crown from her brother's head and set it on her own, delivering us all into her hand—delivering yourself also. And then Cæsar can return to Rome, or depart through the gate of death, which is nearer and surer.

CÆSAR. [*Calmly.*] Well, my friend; and is not this very natural?

POTHINUS. [*Astonished.*] Natural! Then you do not resent treachery?

CÆSAR. Resent! O thou foolish Egyptian, what have I to do with resentment? Do I resent the wind when it chills me, or the night when it makes me stumble in darkness? Shall I resent youth when it turns from age, and ambition when it turns from servitude? To tell me such a story as this is but to tell me that the sun will rise tomorrow.

CLEOPATRA. [*Unable to contain herself.*] But it is false—false. I swear it.

CÆSAR. It is true, though you swore it a thousand times, and believed all you swore. [*She is convulsed with emotion. To screen her, he rises and takes* POTHINUS *to* RUFIO, *saying.*] Come, Rufio: let us see Pothinus past the guard. I have a word to say to him. [*Aside to them.*] We must give the Queen a moment to recover herself. [*Aloud.*] Come. [*He takes* POTHINUS *and* RUFIO *out with him, conversing with them meanwhile.*] Tell your friends, Pothinus, that they must not think I am opposed to a reasonable settlement of the country's affairs—[*They pass out of hearing.*]

CLEOPATRA. [*In a stifled whisper.*] Ftatateeta, Ftatateeta.

FTATATEETA. [*Hurrying to her from the table and petting her.*] Peace, child: be comforted—

CLEOPATRA. [*Interrupting her.*] Can they hear us?

FTATATEETA. No, dear heart, no.

CLEOPATRA. Listen to me. If he leaves the Palace alive, never see my face again.

FTATATEETA. He? Poth—

CLEOPATRA. [*Striking her on the mouth.*] Strike his life out as I strike his name from your lips. Dash him down from the wall. Break him on the stones. Kill, kill, kill him.

FTATATEETA. [*Shewing all her teeth.*] The dog shall perish.

CLEOPATRA. Fail in this, and you go out from before me for ever.

FTATATEETA. [*Resolutely.*] So be it. You shall not see my face until his eyes are darkened. [CÆSAR *comes back, with* APOLLODORUS, *exquisitely dressed, and* RUFIO.]

CLEOPATRA. [*To* FTATATEETA.] Come soon—soon. [FTATATEETA *turns her meaning eyes for a moment on her mistress; then goes grimly away past* RA *and out.* CLEOPATRA *runs like a gazelle to* CÆSAR.] So you have come back to me, Cæsar. [*Caressingly.*] I thought you were angry. Welcome, Apollodorus. [*She gives him her hand to kiss, with her other arm about* CÆSAR.]

APOLLODORUS. Cleopatra grows more womanly beautiful from week to week.

CLEOPATRA. Truth, Apollodorus?

APOLLODORUS. Far, far short of the truth! Friend Rufio threw a pearl into the sea: Cæsar fished up a diamond.

CÆSAR. Cæsar fished up a touch of rheumatism, my friend. Come: to dinner! to dinner! [*They move towards the table.*]

CLEOPATRA. [*Skipping like a young fawn.*] Yes, to dinner. I have ordered such a dinner for you, Cæsar!

CÆSAR. Ay? What are we to have?

CLEOPATRA. Peacocks' brains.

CÆSAR. [*As if his mouth watered.*] Peacocks' brains, Apollodorus!

APOLLODORUS. Not for me. I prefer nightingales' tongues. [*He goes to one of the two covers set side by side.*]

CLEOPATRA. Roast boar, Rufio!

RUFIO. [*Gluttonously.*] Good! [*He goes to the seat next APOLLODORUS, on his left.*]

CÆSAR. [*Looking at his seat, which is at the end of the table, to RA's left hand.*] What has become of my leathern cushion?

CLEOPATRA. [*At the opposite end.*] I have got new ones for you.

THE MAJOR-DOMO. These cushions, Cæsar, are of Maltese gauze, stuffed with rose leaves.

CÆSAR. Rose leaves! Am I a caterpillar? [*He throws the cushions away and seats himself on the leather mattress underneath.*]

CLEOPATRA. What a shame! My new cushions!

THE MAJOR-DOMO. [*At CÆSAR's elbow.*] What shall we serve to whet Cæsar's appetite?

CÆSAR. What have you got?

THE MAJOR-DOMO. Sea hedgehogs, black and white sea acorns, sea nettles, beccaficoes, purple shellfish—

CÆSAR. Any oysters?

THE MAJOR-DOMO. Assuredly.

CÆSAR. British oysters?

THE MAJOR-DOMO. [*Assenting.*] British oysters, Cæsar.

CÆSAR. Oysters, then. [THE MAJOR-DOMO *signs to a slave at each order; and the slave goes out to execute it.*] I have been in Britain—that western land of romance—the last piece of earth on the edge of the ocean that surrounds the world. I went there in search of its famous pearls. The British pearl was a fable; but in searching for it I found the British oyster.

APOLLODORUS. All posterity will bless you for it. [*To* THE MAJOR-DOMO.] Sea hedgehogs for me.

RUFIO. Is there nothing solid to begin with?

THE MAJOR-DOMO. Fieldfares with asparagus—

CLEOPATRA. [*Interrupting.*] Fattened fowls! have some fattened fowls, Rufio.

RUFIO. Ay, that will do.

CLEOPATRA. [*Greedily.*] Fieldfares for me.

THE MAJOR-DOMO. Cæsar will deign to choose his wine? Sicilian, Lesbian, Chian—

RUFIO. [*Contemptuously.*] All Greek.

APOLLODORUS. Who would drink Roman wine when he could get Greek. Try the Lesbian, Cæsar.

CÆSAR. Bring me my barley water.

RUFIO. [*With intense disgust.*] Ugh! Bring me my Falernian. [*The Falernian is presently brought to him.*]

CLEOPATRA. [*Pouting.*] It is waste of time giving you dinners, Cæsar. My scullions would not condescend to your diet.

CÆSAR. [*Relenting.*] Well, well: let us try the Lesbian. [THE MAJOR-DOMO *fills* CÆSAR's *goblet; then* CLEOPATRA's *and* APOLLODORUS's.] But when I return to Rome, I will make laws against these extravagances. I will even get the laws carried out.

CLEOPATRA. [*Coaxingly.*] Never mind. Today you are to be like other people: idle, luxurious, and kind. [*She stretches her hand to him along the table.*]

CÆSAR. Well, for once I will sacrifice my comfort—[*Kissing her hand.*] there! [*He takes a draught of wine.*] Now are you satisfied?

CLEOPATRA. And you no longer believe that I long for your departure for Rome?

CÆSAR. I no longer believe anything. My brains are asleep. Besides, who knows whether I shall return to Rome?

RUFIO. [*Alarmed.*] How? Eh? What?

CÆSAR. What has Rome to shew me that I have not seen already? One year of Rome is like another, except that I grow older, whilst the crowd in the Appian Way is always the same age.

APOLLODORUS. It is no better here in Egypt. The old men, when they are tired of life, say "We have seen everything except the source of the Nile."

CÆSAR. [*His imagination catching fire.*] And why not see that? Cleopatra: will you come with me and track the flood to its cradle in the heart of the regions of mystery? Shall we leave Rome behind us—Rome, that has achieved greatness only to learn how greatness destroys nations of men who are not great! Shall I make you a new kingdom, and build you a holy city there in the great unknown?

CLEOPATRA. [*Rapturously.*] Yes, yes. You shall.

RUFIO. Ay: now he will conquer Africa with two legions before we come to the roast boar.

APOLLODORUS. Come: no scoffing. This is a noble scheme: in it Cæsar is no longer merely the conquering soldier, but the creative poet-artist. Let us name the holy city, and consecrate it with Lesbian wine.

CÆSAR. Cleopatra shall name it herself.

CLEOPATRA. It shall be called Cæsar's Gift to his Beloved.

APOLLODORUS. No, no. Something vaster than that—something universal, like the starry firmament.

CÆSAR. [*Prosaically.*] Why not simply The Cradle of the Nile?

CLEOPATRA. No: the Nile is my ancestor; and he is a god. Oh! I have thought of something. The Nile shall name it himself. Let us call upon him. [*To* THE MAJOR-DOMO.] Send for him. [*The three men stare at one another; but* THE MAJOR-DOMO *goes out as if he had received the most matter-of-fact order.*] And [*To the retinue.*] away with you all. [*The retinue withdraws, making obeisance. A* PRIEST *enters, carrying a miniature sphinx with a tiny tripod before it. A morsel of incense is smoking in the tripod. The* PRIEST *comes to the table and places the image in the middle of it. The light begins to change to the magenta purple of the Egyptian sunset, as if the god had brought a strange colored shadow with him. The three men are* determined not to be impressed; but they feel curious in spite of themselves.]

CÆSAR. What hocus-pocus is this?

CLEOPATRA. You shall see. And it is not hocus-pocus. To do it properly, we should kill something to please him; but perhaps he will answer Cæsar without that if we spill some wine to him.

APOLLODORUS. [*Turning his head to look up over his shoulder at* RA.] Why not appeal to our hawkheaded friend here?

CLEOPATRA. [*Nervously.*] Sh! He will hear you and be angry.

RUFIO. [*Phlegmatically.*] The source of the Nile is out of his district, I expect.

CLEOPATRA. No: I will have my city named by nobody but my dear little sphinx, because it was in its arms that Cæsar found me asleep. [*She languishes at* CÆSAR *then turns curtly to the* PRIEST.] Go. I am a priestess, and have power to take your charge from you. [*The* PRIEST *makes a reverence and goes out.*] Now let us call on the Nile all together. Perhaps he will rap on the table.

CÆSAR. What! table rapping! Are such superstitions still believed in this year 707 of the Republic?

CLEOPATRA. It is no superstition: our priests learn lots of things from the tables. Is it not so, Apollodorus?

APOLLODORUS. Yes: I profess myself a converted man. When Cleopatra is priestess, Apollodorus is a devotee. Propose the conjuration.

CLEOPATRA. You must say with me "Send us thy voice, Father Nile."

ALL FOUR. [*Holding their glasses together before the idol.*] Send us thy voice, Father Nile. [*The death cry of a man in mortal terror and agony answers them. Appalled, the men set down their glasses, and listen. Silence. The purple deepens in the sky.* CÆSAR, *glancing at* CLEOPATRA, *catches her pouring out her wine before the god, with gleaming eyes, and mute assurances of gratitude and worship.* APOLLODORUS *springs up and runs to the edge of the roof to peer down and listen.*]

CÆSAR. [*Looking piercingly at* CLEOPATRA.] What was that?

CLEOPATRA. [*Petulantly.*] Nothing. They are beating some slave.

CÆSAR. Nothing.

RUFIO. A man with a knife in him, I'll swear.

CÆSAR. [*Rising.*] A murder!

APOLLODORUS. [*At the back, waving his hand for silence.*] S-sh! Silence. Did you hear that?

CÆSAR. Another cry?

APOLLODORUS. [*Returning to the table.*] No, a thud. Something fell on the beach, I think.

RUFIO. [*Grimly, as he rises.*] Something with bones in it, eh?

CÆSAR. [*Shuddering.*] Hush, hush, Rufio. [*He leaves the table and returns to the colonnade:* RUFIO *following at his left elbow, and* APOLLODORUS *at the other side.*]

CLEOPATRA. [*Still in her place at the table.*] Will you leave me, Cæsar? Apollodorus: are you going?

APOLLODORUS. Faith, dearest Queen, my appetite is gone.

CÆSAR. Go down to the courtyard, Apollodorus; and find out what has happened. [APOLLODORUS *nods and goes out, making for the staircase by which* RUFIO *ascended.*]

CLEOPATRA. Your soldiers have killed somebody, perhaps. What does it matter? [*The murmur of a crowd rises from the beach below.* CÆSAR *and* RUFIO *look at one another.*]

CÆSAR. This must be seen to. [*He is about to follow* APOLLODORUS *when* RUFIO *stops him with a hand on his arm as* FTATATEETA *comes back by the far end of the roof, with dragging steps, a drowsy satiety in her eyes and in the corners of the bloodhound lips. For a moment* CÆSAR *suspects that she is drunk with wine. Not so* RUFIO: *he knows well the red vintage that has inebriated her.*]

RUFIO. [*In a low tone.*] There is some mischief between these two.

FTATATEETA. The Queen looks again on the face of her servant. [CLEOPATRA *looks at her for a moment with an exultant reflection of her murderous expression. Then she flings her arms round her; kisses her repeatedly and savagely; and tears off her jewels and heaps them on her. The two men turn from the spectacle to look at one another.* FTATATEETA

drags herself sleepily to the altar; kneels before RA; and remains there in prayer. CÆSAR goes to CLEOPATRA, leaving RUFIO in the colonnade.]

CÆSAR. [*With searching earnestness.*] Cleopatra: what has happened?

CLEOPATRA. [*In mortal dread of him, but with her utmost cajolery.*] Nothing, dearest Cæsar. [*With sickly sweetness, her voice almost failing.*] Nothing. I am innocent. [*She approaches him affectionately.*] Dear Cæsar: are you angry with me? Why do you look at me so? I have been here with you all the time. How can I know what has happened?

CÆSAR. [*Reflectively.*] That is true.

CLEOPATRA. [*Greatly relieved, trying to caress him.*] Of course it is true. [*He does not respond to the caress.*] You know it is true, Rufio. [*The murmur without suddenly swells to a roar and subsides.*]

RUFIO. I shall know presently. [*He makes for the altar in the burly trot that serves him for a stride, and touches* FTATATEETA *on the shoulder.*] Now, mistress: I shall want you. [*He orders her, with a gesture, to go before him.*]

FTATATEETA. [*Rising and glowering at him.*] My place is with the Queen.

CLEOPATRA. She has done no harm, Rufio.

CÆSAR. [*To* RUFIO.] Let her stay.

RUFIO. [*Sitting down on the altar.*] Very well. Then my place is here too; and you can see what is the matter for yourself. The city is in a pretty uproar, it seems.

CÆSAR. [*With grave displeasure.*] Rufio: there is a time for obedience.

RUFIO. And there is a time for obstinacy. [*He folds his arms doggedly.*]

CÆSAR. [*To* CLEOPATRA.] Send her away.

CLEOPATRA. [*Whining in her eagerness to propitiate him.*] Yes, I will. I will do whatever you ask me, Cæsar, always, because I love you. Ftatateeta: go away.

FTATATEETA. The Queen's word is my will. I shall be at hand for the Queen's call. [*She goes out past* RA, *as she came.*]

RUFIO. [*Following her.*] Remember, Cæsar, your bodyguard is also within call. [*He follows her out.* CLEOPATRA, *presuming upon* CÆSAR's *submission to* RUFIO, *leaves the table and sits down on the bench in the colonnade.*]

CLEOPATRA. Why do you allow Rufio to treat you so? You should teach him his place.

CÆSAR. Teach him to be my enemy, and to hide his thoughts from me as you are are now hiding yours?

CLEOPATRA. [*Her fears returning.*] Why do you say that, Cæsar? Indeed, indeed, I am not hiding anything. You are wrong to treat me like this. [*She stifles a sob.*] I am only a child; and you turn into stone because you think some one has been killed. I cannot bear it. [*She purposely breaks down and weeps. He looks at her with profound sadness and complete coldness. She looks up to see what effect she is producing. Seeing that he is unmoved, she sits up, pretending to struggle with her emotion and to put it bravely away.*] But there: I know you hate tears: you shall not be troubled with them. I know you are not angry, but only sad; only I am so silly, I cannot help being hurt when you speak coldly. Of course you are quite right: it is dreadful to think of anyone being killed or even hurt; and I hope nothing really serious has— [*Her voice dies away under his contemptuous penetration.*]

CÆSAR. What has frightened you into this? What have you done? [*A trumpet sounds on the beach below.*] Aha! that sounds like the answer.

CLEOPATRA. [*Sinking back trembling on the bench and covering her face with her hands.*] I have not betrayed you, Cæsar: I swear it.

CÆSAR. I know that. I have not trusted you. [*He turns from her, and is about to go out when* APOLLODORUS *and* BRITANNUS *drag in* LUCIUS SEPTIMIUS *to him.* RUFIO *follows.* CÆSAR *shudders.*] Again, Pompey's murderer!

RUFIO. The town has gone mad, I think. They are for tearing the place down and driving us into the sea straight away. We laid hold of this renegade in clearing them out of the courtyard.

CÆSAR. Release him. [*They let go his arms.*] What has offended the citizens, Lucius Septimius?

LUCIUS. What did you expect, Cæsar? Pothinus was a favorite of theirs.

CÆSAR. What has happened to Pothinus? I set him free, here, not half an hour ago. Did they not pass him out?

LUCIUS. Ay, through the gallery arch sixty feet above ground, with three inches of steel in his ribs. He is as dead as Pompey. We are quits now, as to killing —you and I.

CÆSAR. [*Shocked.*] Assassinated!—our prisoner, our guest! [*He turns reproachfully on* RUFIO.] Rufio—

RUFIO. [*Emphatically—anticipating the question.*] Whoever did it was a wise man and a friend of yours [CLEOPATRA *is greatly emboldened.*] but none of us had a hand in it. So it is no use to frown at me. [CÆSAR *turns and looks at* CLEOPATRA.]

CLEOPATRA. [*Violently—rising.*] He was slain by order of the Queen of Egypt. I am not Julius Cæsar the dreamer, who allows every slave to insult him. Rufio has said I did well: now the others shall judge me too. [*She turns to the others.*] This Pothinus sought to make me conspire with him to betray Cæsar to Achillas and Ptolemy. I refused; and he cursed me and came privily to Cæsar to accuse me of his own treachery. I caught him in the act; and he insulted me—me, the Queen! to my face. Cæsar would not avenge me: he spoke him fair and set him free. Was I right to avenge myself? Speak, Lucius.

LUCIUS. I do not gainsay it. But you will get little thanks from Cæsar for it.

CLEOPATRA. Speak, Apollodorus. Was I wrong?

APOLLODORUS. I have only one word of blame, most beautiful. You should have called upon me, your knight; and in a fair duel I should have slain the slanderer.

CLEOPATRA. [*Passionately.*] I will be judged by your very slave, Cæsar. Britannus: speak. Was I wrong?

BRITANNUS. Were treachery, falsehood, and disloyalty left unpunished, society must become like an arena full of wild beasts, tearing one another to pieces. Cæsar is in the wrong.

CÆSAR. [*With quiet bitterness.*] And so the verdict is against me, it seems.

CLEOPATRA. [*Vehemently.*] Listen to me, Cæsar. If one man in all Alexandria can be found to say that I did wrong, I swear to have myself crucified on the door of the palace by my own slaves.

CÆSAR. If one man in all the world can be found, now or forever, to know that you did wrong, that man will have either to conquer the world as I have, or be crucified by it. [*The uproar in the streets again reaches them.*] Do you hear? These knockers at your gate are also believers in vengeance and in stabbing. You have slain their leader: it is right that they shall slay you. If you doubt it, ask your four counsellors here. And then in the name of that right [*He emphasizes the word with great scorn.*] shall I not slay them for murdering their Queen, and be slain in my turn by their countrymen as the invader of their fatherland? Can Rome do less then than slay these slayers, too, to shew the world how Rome avenges her sons and her honor. And so, to the end of history, murder shall breed murder, always in the name of right and honor and peace, until the gods are tired of blood and create a race that can understand. [*Fierce uproar.* CLEOPATRA *becomes white with terror.*] Hearken, you who must not be insulted. Go near enough to catch their words: you will find them bitterer than the tongue of Pothinus. [*Loftily, wrapping himself up in an impenetrable dignity.*] Let the Queen of Egypt now give her orders for vengeance, and take her measures for defence; for she has renounced Cæsar. [*He turns to go.*]

CLEOPATRA. [*Terrified, running to him and falling on her knees.*] You will not desert me, Cæsar. You will defend the palace.

CÆSAR. You have taken the powers of life and death upon you. I am only a dreamer.

CLEOPATRA. But they will kill me.

CÆSAR. And why not?

CLEOPATRA. In pity—

CÆSAR. Pity! What! has it come to this so suddenly, that nothing can save you now but pity? Did it save Pothinus? [*She rises, wringing her hands, and goes back to the bench in despair.* APOL-

LODORUS *shews his sympathy with her by quietly posting himself behind the bench. The sky has by this time become the most vivid purple, and soon begins to change to a glowing pale orange, against which the colonnade and the great image shew darklier and darklier.*]

RUFIO. Cæsar: enough of preaching. The enemy is at the gate.

CÆSAR. [*Turning on him and giving way to his wrath.*] Ay; and what has held him baffled at the gate all these months? Was it my folly, as you deem it, or your wisdom? In this Egyptian Red Sea of blood, whose hand has held all your heads above the waves? [*Turning on* CLEOPATRA.] And yet, when Cæsar says to such an one, "Friend, go free," you, clinging for your little life to my sword, dare steal out and stab him in the back? And you, soldiers and gentlemen, and honest servants as you forget that you are, applaud this assassination, and say "Cæsar is in the wrong." By the gods, I am tempted to open my hand and let you all sink into the flood.

CLEOPATRA. [*With a ray of cunning hope.*] But, Cæsar, if you do, you will perish yourself. [CÆSAR's *eyes blaze.*]

RUFIO. [*Greatly alarmed.*] Now, by great Jove, you filthy little Egyptian rat, that is the very word to make him walk out alone into the city and leave us here to be cut to pieces. [*Desperately, to* CÆSAR.] Will you desert us because we are a parcel of fools? I mean no harm by killing: I do it as a cat, by instinct. We are all dogs at your heels; but we have served you faithfully.

CÆSAR. [*Relenting.*] Alas, Rufio, my son, my son: as dogs we are like to perish now in the streets.

APOLLODORUS. [*At his post behind* CLEOPATRA's *seat.*] Cæsar: what you say has an Olympian ring in it: it must be right; for it is fine art. But I am still on the side of Cleopatra. If we must die, she shall not want the devotion of a man's heart nor the strength of a man's arm.

CLEOPATRA. [*Sobbing.*] But I dont want to die.

CÆSAR. [*Sadly.*] Oh, ignoble, ignoble!

LUCIUS. [*Coming forward between* CÆSAR *and* CLEOPATRA.] Hearken to me,

CÆSAR. It may be ignoble; but I also mean to live as long as I can.

CÆSAR. Well, my friend, you are likely to outlive Cæsar. Is it any magic of mine, think you, that has kept your army and this whole city at bay for so long? Yesterday, what quarrel had they with me that they should risk their lives against me? But today we have flung them down their hero, murdered; and now every man of them is set upon clearing out this nest of assassins—for such we are and no more. Take courage then; and sharpen your sword. Pompey's head has fallen; and Cæsar's head is ripe.

APOLLODORUS. Does Cæsar despair?

CÆSAR. [*With infinite pride.*] He who has never hoped can never despair. Cæsar, in good or bad fortune, looks his fate in the face.

LUCIUS. Look it in the face, then; and it will smile as it always has on Cæsar.

CÆSAR. [*With involuntary haughtiness.*] Do you presume to encourage me?

LUCIUS. I offer you my services. I will change sides if you will have me.

CÆSAR. [*Suddenly coming down to earth again, and looking sharply at him, divining that there is something behind the offer.*] What! At this point?

LUCIUS. [*Firmly.*] At this point.

RUFIO. Do you suppose Cæsar is mad, to trust you?

LUCIUS. I do not ask him to trust me until he is victorious. I ask for my life, and for a command in Cæsar's army. And since Cæsar is a fair dealer, I will pay in advance.

CÆSAR. Pay! How?

LUCIUS. With a piece of good news for you. [CÆSAR *divines the news in a flash.*]

RUFIO. What news?

CÆSAR. [*With an elate and buoyant energy which makes* CLEOPATRA *sit up and stare.*] What news! What news, did you say, my son Rufio? The relief has arrived: what other news remains for us? Is it not so, Lucius Septimius? Mithridates of Pergamos is on the march.

LUCIUS. He has taken Pelusium.

CÆSAR. [*Delighted.*] Lucius Septimius: you are henceforth my officer. Rufio: the Egyptians must have sent every soldier from the city to prevent Mithridates crossing the Nile. There is nothing in the streets now but mob—mob!

LUCIUS. It is so. Mithridates is marching by the great road to Memphis to cross above the Delta. Achillas will fight him there.

CÆSAR. [*All audacity.*] Achillas shall fight Cæsar there. See, Rufio. [*He runs to the table; snatches a napkin; and draws a plan on it with his finger dipped in wine, whilst* RUFIO *and* LUCIUS SEPTIMIUS *crowd about him to watch, all looking closely, for the light is now almost gone.*] Here is the palace [*Pointing to his plan.*] here is the theatre. You [*To* RUFIO.] take twenty men and pretend to go by that street [*Pointing it out.*]; and whilst they are stoning you, out go the cohorts by this and this. My streets are right, are they, Lucius?

LUCIUS. Ay, that is the fig market—

CÆSAR. [*Too much excited to listen to him.*] I saw them the day we arrived. Good! [*He throws the napkin on the table, and comes down again into the colonnade.*] Away, Britannus: tell Petronius that within an hour half our forces must take ship for the western lake. See to my horse and armor. [BRITANNUS *runs out.*] With the rest, *I* shall march round the lake and up the Nile to meet Mithridates. Away, Lucius; and give the word. [LUCIUS *hurries out after* BRITANNUS.] Apollodorus: lend me your sword and your right arm for this campaign.

APOLLODORUS. Ay, and my heart and life to boot.

CÆSAR. [*Grasping his hand.*] I accept both. [*Mighty handshake.*] Are you ready for work?

APOLLODORUS. Ready for Art—the Art of War. [*He rushes out after* LUCIUS, *totally forgetting* CLEOPATRA.]

RUFIO. Come! this is something like business.

CÆSAR. [*Buoyantly.*] Is it not, my only son? [*He claps his hands. The slaves hurry in to the table.*] No more of this mawkish revelling: away with all this stuff: shut it out of my sight and be off with you. [*The slaves begin to remove the table; and the curtains are drawn, shutting in the colonnade.*] You understand about the streets, Rufio?

RUFIO. Ay, I think I do. I will get through them, at all events. [*The bucina sounds busily in the courtyard beneath.*]

CÆSAR. Come, then: we must talk to the troops and hearten them. You down to the beach: I to the courtyard. [*He makes for the staircase.*]

CLEOPATRA. [*Rising from her seat, where she has been quite neglected all this time, and stretching out her hands timidly to him.*] Cæsar.

CÆSAR. [*Turning.*] Eh?

CLEOPATRA. Have you forgotten me?

CÆSAR. [*Indulgently.*] I am busy now, my child, busy. When I return your affairs shall be settled. Farewell; and be good and patient. [*He goes, preoccupied and quite indifferent. She stands with clenched fists, in speechless rage and humiliation.*]

RUFIO. That game is played and lost, Cleopatra. The woman always gets the worst of it.

CLEOPATRA. [*Haughtily.*] Go. Follow your master.

RUFIO. [*In her ear, with rough familiarity.*] A word first. Tell your executioner that if Pothinus had been properly killed —in the throat—he would not have called out. Your man bungled his work.

CLEOPATRA. [*Enigmatically.*] How do you know it was a man?

RUFIO. [*Startled, and puzzled.*] It was

not you: you were with us when it happened. [*She turns her back scornfully on him. He shakes his head, and draws the curtains to go out. It is now a magnificent moonlit night. The table has been removed.* FTATATEETA *is seen in the light of the moon and stars, again in prayer before the white altar-stone of* RA. RUFIO *starts; closes the curtains again softly; and says in a low voice to* CLEOPATRA.] Was it she? with her own hand?

CLEOPATRA. [*Threateningly.*] Whoever it was, let my enemies beware of her. Look to it, Rufio, you who dare make the Queen of Egypt a fool before Cæsar.

RUFIO. [*Looking grimly at her.*] I will look to it, Cleopatra. [*He nods in confirmation of the promise, and slips out through the curtains, loosening his sword in its sheath as he goes.*]

ROMAN SOLDIERS. [*In the courtyard below.*] Hail, Cæsar! Hail, hail! [CLEOPATRA *listens. The bucina sounds again, followed by several trumpets.*]

CLEOPATRA. [*Wringing her hands and calling.*] Ftatateeta. Ftatateeta. It is dark; and I am alone. Come to me. [*Silence.*] Ftatateeta. [*Louder.*] Ftatateeta. [*Silence. In a panic she snatches the cord and pulls the curtains apart.* FTATATEETA *is lying dead on the altar of* RA, *with her throat cut. Her blood deluges the white stone.*]

* * *

ACT FIVE

High noon. Festival and military pageant on the esplanade before the palace. In the east harbor CÆSAR's galley, so gorgeously decorated that it seems to be rigged with flowers, is alongside the quay, close to the steps APOLLODORUS descended when he embarked with the carpet. A Roman guard is posted there in charge of a gangway, whence a red floorcloth is laid down the middle of the esplanade, turning off to the north opposite the central gate in the palace front, which shuts in the esplanade on the south side. The broad steps of the gate, crowded

with CLEOPATRA's ladies, all in their gayest attire, are like a flower garden. The façade is lined by her guard, officered by the same gallants to whom BEL AFFRIS announced the coming of CÆSAR six months before in the old palace on the Syrian border. The north side is lined by Roman soldiers, with the townsfolk on tiptoe behind them, peering over their heads at the cleared esplanade, in which the officers stroll about, chatting. Among these are BELZANOR and the PERSIAN; also the CENTURION, vinewood cudgel in hand, battle worn, thick-booted, and much outshone, both socially and decoratively, by the Egyptian officers.

APOLLODORUS makes his way through the townsfolk and calls to the officers from behind the Roman line.

APOLLODORUS. Hullo! May I pass?

CENTURION. Pass Apollodorus the Sicilian there! [*The* SOLDIERS *let him through.*]

BELZANOR. Is Cæsar at hand?

APOLLODORUS. Not yet. He is still in the market place. I could not stand any more of the roaring of the soldiers! After half an hour of the enthusiasm of an army, one feels the need of a little sea air.

PERSIAN. Tell us the news. Hath he slain the priests?

APOLLODORUS. Not he. They met him in the market place with ashes on their heads and their gods in their hands. They placed the gods at his feet. The only one that was worth looking at was Apis: a miracle of gold and ivory work. By my advice he offered the chief priest two talents for it.

BELZANOR. [*Appalled.*] Apis the all-knowing for two talents! What said the chief Priest?

APOLLODORUS. He invoked the mercy of Apis, and asked for five.

BELZANOR. Pooh! Why did not Apis cause Cæsar to be vanquished by Achillas? Any fresh news from the war, Apollodorus?

APOLLODORUS. The little King Ptolemy was drowned.

BELZANOR. Drowned! How?

APOLLODORUS. With the rest of them. Cæsar attacked them from three sides at once and swept them into the Nile. Ptolemy's barge sank.

BELZANOR. A marvellous man, this Cæsar! Will he come soon, think you?

APOLLODORUS. He was settling the Jewish question when I left. [*A flourish of trumpets from the north and commotion among the townsfolk announce the approach of* CÆSAR.]

PERSIAN. He has made short work of them. Here he comes. [*He hurries to his post in front of the Egyptian lines.*]

BELZANOR. [*Following him.*] Ho there! Cæsar comes. [*The* SOLDIERS *stand at at-*

tention, and dress their lines. APOLLODORUS *goes to the Egyptian line.*]

CENTURION. [*Hurrying to the gangway guard.*] Attention there! Cæsar comes. [CÆSAR *arrives in state with* RUFIO: BRITANNUS *following. The* SOLDIERS *receive him with enthusiastic shouting.*]

CÆSAR. I see my ship awaits me. The hour of Cæsar's farewell to Egypt has arrived. And now, Rufio, what remains to be done before I go?

RUFIO. [*At his left hand.*] You have not yet appointed a Roman governor for this province.

CÆSAR. [*Looking whimsically at him, but speaking with perfect gravity.*] What say you to Mithridates of Pergamos, my reliever and rescuer, the great son of Eupator?

RUFIO. Why, that you will want him elsewhere. Do you forget that you have some three or four armies to conquer on your way home?

CÆSAR. Indeed! Well, what say you to yourself?

RUFIO. [*Incredulously.*] I! I a governor! What are you dreaming of? Do you not know that I am only the son of a freedman?

CÆSAR. [*Affectionately.*] Has not Cæsar called you his son? [*Calling to the whole assembly.*] Peace awhile there; and hear me.

THE ROMAN SOLDIERS. Hear Cæsar.

CÆSAR. Hear the service, quality, rank and name of the Roman governor. By service, Cæsar's shield; by quality, Cæsar's friend; by rank, a Roman soldier. [THE ROMAN SOLDIERS *give a triumphant shout.*] By name, Rufio. [*They shout again.*]

RUFIO. [*Kissing* CÆSAR's *hand.*] Ay: I am Cæsar's shield; but of what use shall I be when I am no longer on Cæsar's arm? Well, no matter—[*He becomes husky, and turns away to recover himself.*]

CÆSAR. Where is that British Islander of mine?

BRITANNUS. [*Coming forward on* CÆSAR's *right hand.*] Here, Cæsar.

CÆSAR. Who bade you, pray, thrust yourself into the battle of the Delta, uttering the barbarous cries of your native land, and affirming yourself a match for any four of the Egyptians, to whom you applied unseemly epithets?

BRITANNUS. Cæsar: I ask you to excuse the language that escaped me in the heat of the moment.

CÆSAR. And how did you, who cannot swim, cross the canal with us when we stormed the camp?

BRITANNUS. Cæsar: I clung to the tail of your horse.

CÆSAR. These are not the deeds of a slave, Britannicus, but of a free man.

BRITANNUS. Cæsar: I was born free.

CÆSAR. But they call you Cæsar's slave.

BRITANNUS. Only as Cæsar's slave have I found real freedom.

CÆSAR. [*Moved.*] Well said. Ungrateful that I am, I was about to set you free; but now I will not part from you for a million talents. [*He claps him friendlily on the shoulder.* BRITANNUS, *gratified, but a trifle shamefaced, takes his hand and kisses it sheepishly.*]

BELZANOR. [*To the* PERSIAN.] This Roman knows how to make men serve him.

PERSIAN. Ay: men too humble to become dangerous rivals to him.

BELZANOR. O subtle one! O cynic!

CÆSAR. [*Seeing* APOLLODORUS *in the Egyptian corner, and calling to him.*] Apollodorus: I leave the art of Egypt in your charge. Remember: Rome loves art and will encourage it ungrudgingly.

APOLLODORUS. I understand, Cæsar. Rome will produce no art itself; but it will buy up and take away whatever the other nations produce.

CÆSAR. What! Rome produce no art! Is peace not an art? is war not an art? is government not an art? is civilization not an art? All these we give you in exchange for a few ornaments. You will have the best of the bargain. [*Turning to* RUFIO.] And now, what else have I to do before I embark? [*Trying to recollect.*] There is something I cannot remember: what can it be? Well, well: it must remain undone: we must not waste this favorable wind. Farewell, Rufio.

RUFIO. Cæsar: I am loth to let you go to Rome without your shield. There are too many daggers there.

CÆSAR. It matters not: I shall finish my life's work on my way back; and then I shall have lived long enough. Besides: I have always disliked the idea of dying: I had rather be killed. Farewell.

RUFIO. [*With a sigh, raising his hands and giving* CÆSAR *up as incorrigible.*] Farewell. [*They shake hands.*]

CÆSAR. [*Waving his hand to* APOLLODORUS.] Farewell, Apollodorus, and my friends, all of you. Aboard! [*The gangway is run out from the quay to the ship. As* CÆSAR *moves toward it,* CLEOPATRA, *cold and tragic, cunningly dressed in black, without ornaments or decoration of any kind, and thus making a striking figure among the brilliantly dressed bevy of ladies as she passes through it, comes from the palace and stands on the steps.* CÆSAR *does not see her until she speaks.*]

CLEOPATRA. Has Cleopatra no part in this leavetaking?

CÆSAR. [*Enlightened.*] Ah, I knew there was something. [*To* RUFIO.] How could you let me forget her, Rufio? [*Hastening to her.*] Had I gone without seeing you, I should never have forgiven myself. [*He takes her hands, and brings her into the middle of the esplanade. She submits stonily.*] Is this mourning for me?

CLEOPATRA. No.

CÆSAR. [*Remorsefully.*] Ah, that was thoughtless of me! It is for your brother.

CLEOPATRA. No.

CÆSAR. For whom, then?

CLEOPATRA. Ask the Roman governor whom you have left us.

CÆSAR. Rufio?

CLEOPATRA. Yes: Rufio. [*She points at him with deadly scorn.*] He who is to rule here in Cæsar's name, in Cæsar's way, according to Cæsar's boasted laws of life.

CÆSAR. [*Dubiously.*] He is to rule as he can, Cleopatra. He has taken the work upon him, and will do it in his own way.

CLEOPATRA. Not in your way, then?

CÆSAR. [*Puzzled.*] What do you mean by my way?

CLEOPATRA. Without punishment. Without revenge. Without judgment.

CÆSAR. [*Approvingly.*] Ay: that is the right way, the great way, the only possible way in the end. [*To* RUFIO.] Believe it, Rufio, if you can.

RUFIO. Why, I believe it, Cæsar. You have convinced me of it long ago. But look you. You are sailing for Numidia today. Now tell me: if you meet a hungry lion there, you will not punish it for wanting to eat you?

CÆSAR. [*Wondering what he is driving at.*] No.

RUFIO. Nor revenge upon it the blood of those it has already eaten.

CÆSAR. No.

RUFIO. Nor judge it for its guiltiness.

CÆSAR. No.

RUFIO. What, then, will you do to save your life from it?

CÆSAR. [*Promptly.*] Kill it, man, without malice, just as it would kill me. What does this parable of the lion mean?

RUFIO. Why, Cleopatra had a tigress that killed men at her bidding. I thought she might bid it kill you some day. Well, had I not been Cæsar's pupil, what pious things might I not have done to that tigress! I might have punished it. I might have revenged Pothinus on it.

CÆSAR. [*Interjects.*] Pothinus!

RUFIO. [*Continuing.*] I might have judged it. But I put all these follies behind me; and, without malice, only cut its throat. And that is why Cleopatra comes to you in mourning.

CLEOPATRA. [*Vehemently.*] He has shed the blood of my servant Ftatateeta. On your head be it as upon his, Cæsar, if you hold him free of it.

CÆSAR. [*Energetically.*] On my head be it, then; for it was well done. Rufio: had you set yourself in the seat of the judge, and with hateful ceremonies and appeals to the gods handed that woman over to some hired executioner to be slain before the people in the name of justice, never again would I have touched your hand without a shudder. But this was natural slaying: I feel no horror at it. [*RUFIO, satisfied, nods at* CLEOPATRA, *mutely inviting her to mark that.*]

CLEOPATRA. [*Pettish and childish in her impotence.*] No: not when a Roman slays an Egyptian. All the world will now see how unjust and corrupt Cæsar is.

CÆSAR. [*Taking her hands coaxingly.*] Come: do not be angry with me. I am sorry for that poor Totateeta. [*She laughs in spite of herself.*] Aha! you are laughing. Does that mean reconciliation?

CLEOPATRA. [*Angry with herself for laughing.*] No, no, NO!! But it is so ridiculous to hear you call her Totateeta.

CÆSAR. What! As much a child as ever, Cleopatra! Have I not made a woman of you after all?

CLEOPATRA. Oh, it is you who are a great baby: you make me seem silly because you will not behave seriously. But you have treated me badly; and I do not forgive you.

CÆSAR. Bid me farewell.

CLEOPATRA. I will not.

CÆSAR. [*Coaxing.*] I will send you a beautiful present from Rome.

CLEOPATRA. [*Proudly.*] Beauty from Rome to Egypt indeed! What can Rome give me that Egypt cannot give me?

APOLLODORUS. That is true, Cæsar. If the present is to be really beautiful, I shall have to buy it for you in Alexandria.

CÆSAR. You are forgetting the treasures for which Rome is most famous, my friend. You cannot buy them in Alexandria.

APOLLODORUS. What are they, Cæsar?

CÆSAR. Her sons. Come, Cleopatra: forgive me and bid me farewell; and I will send you a man, Roman from head to heel and Roman of the noblest; not old and ripe for the knife; not lean in the arms and cold in the heart; not hiding a bald head under his conqueror's laurels; not stooped with the weight of the world on his shoulders; but brisk and fresh, strong and young, hoping in the morning, fighting in the day, and revelling in the evening. Will you take such an one in exchange for Cæsar?

CLEOPATRA. [*Palpitating.*] His name, his name?

CÆSAR. Shall it be Mark Antony? [*She throws herself into his arms.*]

RUFIO. You are a bad hand at a bargain, mistress, if you will swop Cæsar for Antony.

CÆSAR. So now you are satisfied.

CLEOPATRA. You will not forget.

CÆSAR. I will not forget. Farewell: I do not think we shall meet again. Farewell. [*He kisses her on the forehead. She is much affected and begins to sniff. He embarks.*]

THE ROMAN SOLDIERS. [*As he sets his*

foot on the gangway.] Hail, Cæsar; and farewell! [*He reaches the ship and returns* RUFIO's *wave of the hand.*]

APOLLODORUS. [*To* CLEOPATRA.] No tears, dearest Queen: they stab your servant to the heart. He will return some day.

CLEOPATRA. I hope not. But I cant help crying, all the same. [*She waves her handkerchief to* CÆSAR; *and the ship begins to move.*]

THE ROMAN SOLDIERS. [*Drawing their swords and raising them in the air.*] Hail, Cæsar!

NOTES TO CÆSAR AND CLEOPATRA

Cleopatra's Cure for Baldness

FOR the sake of conciseness in a hurried situation I have made Cleopatra recommend rum. This, I am afraid, is an anachronism: the only real one in the play. To balance it, I give a couple of the remedies she actually believed in. They are quoted by Galen from Cleopatra's book on Cosmetic.

"For bald patches, powder red sulphuret of arsenic and take it up with oak gum, as much as it will bear. Put on a rag and apply, having soaped the place well first. I have mixed the above with a foam of nitre, and it worked well."

Several other receipts follow, ending with: "The following is the best of all, acting for fallen hairs, when applied with oil or pomatum; acts for falling off of eyelashes or for people getting bald all over. It is wonderful. Of domestic mice burnt, one part; of vine rag burnt, one part; of horse's teeth burnt, one part; of bear's grease one; of deer's marrow one; of reed bark one. To be pounded when dry, and mixed with plenty of honey til it gets the consistency of honey; then the bear's grease and marrow to be mixed (when melted), the medicine to be put in a brass flask, and the bald part rubbed til it sprouts."

Concerning these ingredients, my fellow-dramatist Gilbert Murray, who, as a Professor of Greek, has applied to classical antiquity the methods of high scholarship (my own method is pure divination), writes to me as follows: "Some of this I dont understand, and possibly Galen did not, as he quotes your heroine's own language. Foam of nitre is, I think, something like soapsuds. Reed bark is an odd expression. It might mean the outside membrane of a reed: I do not know what it ought to be called. In the burnt mice receipt I take it that you first mixed the solid powders with honey, and then added the grease. I expect Cleopatra preferred it because in most of the others you have to lacerate the skin, prick it, or rub it till it bleeds. I do not know what vine rag is. I translate literally."

Apparent Anachronisms

The only way to write a play which shall convey to the general public an impression of antiquity is to make the characters speak blank verse and abstain from reference to steam, telegraphy, or any of the material conditions of their existence. The more ignorant men are, the more convinced are they that their little parish and their little chapel is an apex to which civilization and philosophy have painfully struggled up the pyramid of time from a desert of savagery. Savagery, they think, became barbarism; barbarism became ancient civilization; ancient civilization became Pauline Christianity; Pauline Christianity became Roman Catholicism; Roman Catholicism became the Dark Ages; and the Dark Ages were finally enlightened by the Protestant instincts of the English race. The whole process is summed up as Progress with a capital P. And any elderly gentleman of Progressive temperament will testify that the improvement since he was a boy is enormous.

Now if we count the generations of Progressive elderly gentlemen since, say, Plato, and add together the successive enormous improvements to which each of them has testified, it will strike us at once as an unaccountable fact that the world, instead of having been improved in 67 generations out of all recognition, presents, on the whole, a rather less dignified appearance in Ibsen's Enemy of the People than in Plato's Republic. And in truth, the period of time covered by history is far too short to allow of any perceptible progress in the popular sense of Evolution of the Human Species. The notion that there has been any such Progress since Cæsar's time (less than 20 centuries) is too absurd for discussion. All the savagery, barbarism, dark ages and the rest of it of which we have any record as existing in the past, exists at the present moment. A British carpenter or stonemason may point out that he gets twice as much money for his labor as his father did in the same trade, and that his suburban house, with its bath, its cottage piano, its drawing room suite, and its album of photographs, would have shamed the plainness of his grandmother's. But the descendants of feudal barons, living in squalid lodgings on a salary of fifteen shillings a week instead of in castles on princely revenues, do not congratulate the world on the change. Such changes, in fact, are not to the point. It has been known, as far back as our records go, that man running wild in the woods is different from man kennelled in a city slum; that a dog seems to understand a shepherd better than a hewer of wood and drawer of water can understand an astronomer; and that breeding, gentle nurture, and luxurious food and shelter will produce a kind of man with whom the common laborer is socially incompatible. The same thing is true of horses and dogs. Now there is clearly room for great changes in the world by increasing the percentage of individuals who are carefully bred and gently nurtured, even to finally making the most of every man and woman born. But that possibility existed in the days of the Hittites as much as it does today. It does not give the slightest real support to the common assumption that the civilized contemporaries of the Hittites were unlike their civilized descendants today.

This would appear the tritest commonplace if it were not that the ordinary citizen's ignorance of the past combines with his idealization of the present to mislead and flatter him. Our latest book on the new railway across Asia describes the dulness of the Siberian farmer and the vulgar pursepride of the Siberian man of business without the least consciousness that the string of contemptuous instances given might have been saved by writing simply "Farmers and provincial plutocrats in Siberia are exactly what they are in England." The latest professor descanting on the civilization of the Western Empire in the fifth century feels bound to assume, in the teeth of his own researches, that the Christian was one sort of animal and the Pagan another. It might as well be assumed as indeed it generally is assumed by implication, that a murder committed with a poisoned arrow is different from a murder committed with a Mauser rifle. All such notions are illusions. Go back to the first syllable of recorded time, and there you will find your Christian and your Pagan, your yokel and your poet, helot and hero, Don Quixote and Sancho, Tamino and Papageno, Newton and bushman unable to count eleven, all alive and contemporaneous, and all convinced that they are the heirs of all the ages and the privileged recipients of THE truth (all others damnable heresies), just as you have them today, flourishing in countries each of which is the bravest and best that ever sprang at Heaven's command from out the azure main.

Again, there is the illusion of "increased command over Nature," meaning that cotton is cheap and that ten miles of country road on a bicycle have replaced four on foot. But even if man's increased command over Nature included any increased command over himself (the only sort of command relevant to his evolution into a higher being), the fact remains that it is only by running away from the increased command over Nature to country places where Nature is still in primitive command over Man that he can recover from the effects of the smoke, the stench, the foul air, the overcrowding, the racket, the ugliness, the dirt which the cheap cotton costs us. If manufacturing activity means Progress, the town must be more advanced than the country; and the field laborers and village artisans of today must be much less changed from servants of Job than the proletariat of modern London from the proletariat of Cæsar's Rome. Yet the cockney proletarian is so inferior to the village laborer that it is only by steady recruiting from the country that London is kept alive. This does not seem as if the change since Job's time were Progress in the popular sense: quite the reverse. The common stock of discoveries in physics has accumulated a little: that is all.

One more illustration. Is the Englishman prepared to admit that the American is his superior as a human being? I ask this question because the scarcity of labor in America relatively to the demand for it has led to a development of machinery there, and a consequent "increase of command over Nature" which makes many of our English methods appear almost medieval to the up-to-date Chicagoan. This means that the American has an advantage over the Englishman of exactly the same nature that the Englishman has over the contemporaries of Cicero. Is the Englishman prepared to draw the same conclusion in both cases? I think not. The American, of course, will draw it cheerfully; but I must then ask him whether, since a modern Negro has a greater "command over Nature" than Washington had, we are also to accept the conclusion, involved in his former one, that humanity has progressed from Washington to the *fin de siècle* Negro.

Finally, I would point out that if life is crowned by its success and devotion in industrial organization and ingenuity, we had better worship the ant and the bee (as moralists urge us to do in our childhood), and humble ourselves before the arrogance of the birds of Aristophanes.

My reason then for ignoring the popular conception of Progress in Cæsar and Cleopatra is that there is no reason to suppose that any Progress has taken place since their time. But even if I shared the popular delusion, I do not see that I could have made any essential difference in the play. I can only imitate humanity as I know it. Nobody knows whether Shakespear thought that ancient Athenian joiners, weavers, or bellows menders were any different from Elizabethan ones; but it is quite certain that he could not have made them so, unless, indeed, he had played the literary man and made Quince say, not "Is all our company here?" but "Bottom: was not that Socrates that passed us at the Piræus with Glaucon and Polemarchus on his way to the house of Kephalus?" And so on.

Cleopatra

Cleopatra was only sixteen when Cæsar went to Egypt; but in Egypt sixteen is a riper age than it is in England. The childishness I have ascribed to her, as far as it is childishness of character and not lack of experience, is not a matter of years. It may be observed in our own climate at the present day in many women of fifty. It is a mistake to suppose that the difference between wisdom and folly has anything to do with the difference between physical age and physical youth. Some women are younger at seventy than most women at seventeen.

It must be borne in mind, too, that Cleopatra was a queen, and was therefore not the typical Greek-cultured, educated Egyptian lady of her time. To represent her by any such type would be as absurd as to represent George IV by a type founded on the attainments of Sir Isaac Newton. It is true that an ordinarily well educated Alexandrian girl of her time would no more have believed bogey stories about the Romans than the daughter of a modern Oxford professor would believe them about the Germans (though, by the way, it is possible to talk great nonsense at Oxford about foreigners when we are at war with them). But I do not feel bound to believe that Cleopatra was well educated. Her father, the illustrious Flute Blower, was not at all a parent of the Oxford professor type. And Cleopatra was a chip of the old block.

Britannus

I find among those who have read this play in manuscript a strong conviction that an ancient Briton could not possibly have been like a modern one. I see no reason to adopt this curious view. It is true that the Roman and Norman conquests must have for a time disturbed the normal British type produced by the climate. But Britannus, born before these events, represents the unadulterated Briton who fought Cæsar and impressed Roman observers much as we should expect the ancestors of Mr. Podsnap to impress the cultivated Italians of their time.

I am told that it is not scientific to treat national character as a product of climate. This only shews the wide difference between common knowledge and the intellectual game called science. We have men of exactly the same stock, and speaking the same language, growing in Great Britain, in Ireland, and in America. The result is three of the most distinctly marked nationalities under the sun. Racial characteristics are quite another matter. The difference between a Jew and a Gentile has nothing to do with the difference between an Englishman and a German. The characteristics of Britannus are local characteristics, not race characteristics. In an ancient Briton they would, I take it, be exaggerated, since modern Britain, disforested, drained, urbanified and consequently cosmopolized, is presumably less characteristically British than Cæsar's Britain.

And again I ask does anyone who, in the light of a competent knowledge of his own age, has studied history from contemporary documents, believe that 67 generations of promiscuous marriage have made any appreciable difference in the human fauna of these isles? Certainly I do not.

Julius Caesar

As to Cæsar himself, I have purposely avoided the usual anachronism of going to Cæsar's books, and concluding that the style is the man. That is only true of authors who have the specific literary genius, and have practised long enough to attain complete self-expression in letters. It is not true even on these conditions in an age when literature is conceived as a game of style, and not as a vehicle of self-expression by the author. Now Cæsar was an amateur stylist writing books of travel and campaign histories in a style so impersonal that the authenticity of the later volumes is disputed. They reveal some of his qualities just as the Voyage of a Naturalist Round the World reveals some of Darwin's, without expressing his private personality. An Englishman reading them would say that Cæsar was a man of great common sense and good taste, meaning thereby a man without originality or moral courage.

In exhibiting Cæsar as a much more various person than the historian of the Gallic wars, I hope I have not been too much imposed on by the dramatic illusion to which all great men owe part of their reputation and some the whole of it. I admit that reputations gained in war are specially questionable. Able civilians taking up the profession of arms, like Cæsar and Cromwell, in middle age, have snatched all its laurels from opponent commanders bred to it, apparently because capable persons engaged in military pursuits are so scarce that the existence of two of them at the same time in the same hemisphere is extremely rare. The capacity of any conqueror is therefore more likely than not to be an illusion produced by the incapacity of his adversary. At all events, Cæsar might have won his battles without being wiser than Charles XII or Nelson or Joan of Arc, who were, like most modern "self-made" millionaires, half-witted geniuses, enjoying the worship accorded by all races to certain forms of insanity. But Cæsar's victories were only advertisements for an eminence that would never have become popular without them. Cæsar is greater off the battle field than on it. Nelson off his quarterdeck was so quaintly out of the question that when his head was injured at the battle of the Nile, and his conduct became for some years openly scandalous, the difference was not important enough to be noticed. It may, however, be said that peace hath her illusory reputations no less than war. And it is certainly true that in civil life mere capacity for work—the power of killing a dozen secretaries under you, so to speak, as a life-or-death courier kills horses—enables men with common ideas and superstitions to distance all competitors in the strife of political ambition. It was this power of work that astonished Cicero as the most prodigious of Cæsar's gifts, as it astonished later observers in Napoleon before it wore him out. How if Cæsar were nothing but a Nelson and a Gladstone combined! a prodigy of vitality without any special quality of mind! nay, with ideas that were worn out before he was born, as Nelson's and Gladstone's were! I have considered that possibility too, and rejected it. I cannot cite all the stories about Cæsar which seem to me to shew that he was genuinely original; but let me at least point out that I have been careful to attribute nothing but originality to him. Originality gives a man an air of frankness, generosity, and magnanimity by enabling him to estimate the value of truth, money, or success in any particular instance quite independently of convention and moral generalization. He therefore will not, in the ordinary Treasury bench fashion, tell a lie which everybody knows to be a lie (and consequently expects him as a matter of good taste to tell). His lies are not found out: they pass for candors. He understands the paradox of money, and gives it away when he can get most for it: in other words, when its value is least, which is just when a common man tries hardest to get it. He knows that the real moment of success is not the moment apparent to the crowd. Hence, in order to produce an impression of complete disinterestedness and magnanimity, he has only to act with entire selfishness; and this is perhaps the only sense in which a man can be said to be *naturally* great. It is in this sense that I have represented Cæsar as great. Having virtue, he has no need of goodness. He is neither forgiving, frank, nor generous, because a man who is too great to resent has nothing to forgive; a man who says things that other people are afraid to say need be no more frank than Bismarck was; and there is no generosity in giving things you do not want to people of whom you intend to make use. This distinction between virtue and goodness is not understood in England: hence the poverty of our drama in heroes. Our stage attempts at them are mere goody-goodies. Goodness, in its popular British sense of self-denial, implies that man is vicious by nature, and that supreme goodness is supreme martyrdom. Not sharing that pious opinion, I have not given countenance to it in any of my plays. In this I follow the precedent of the ancient myths, which represent the hero as vanquishing his enemies, not in fair fight, but with enchanted sword, superequine horse and magical invulnerability, the possession of which, from the vulgar moralistic point of view, robs his exploits of any merit whatever.

As to Cæsar's sense of humor, there is no more reason to assume that he lacked it than to assume that he was deaf or blind. It is said that on the occasion of his assassination by a conspiracy of moralists (it is always your moralist who makes assassination a duty, on the scaffold or off it), he defended himself until the good Brutus struck him, when he exclaimed "What! you too, Brutus!" and disdained further fight. If this be true, he must have been an incorrigible comedian. But even if we waive this story, or accept the traditional sentimental interpretation of it, there is still abundant evidence of his lightheartedness and adventurousness. Indeed it is clear from his whole history that what has been called his ambition was an instinct for exploration. He had much more of Columbus and Franklin in him than of Henry V.

However, nobody need deny Cæsar a share, at least, of the qualities I have attributed to him. All men, much more Julius Cæsars, possess all qualities in some degree. The really interesting question is whether I am right in assuming that the way to produce an impression of greatness is by exhibiting a man, not as mortifying his nature by doing his duty, in the manner which our system of putting little men into great positions (not having enough great men in our influential families to go round) forces us to inculcate, but as simply doing what he naturally wants to do. For this raises the question whether our world has not been wrong in its moral theory for the last 2,500 years or so. It must be a constant puzzle to many of us that the Christian era, so excellent in its intentions, should have been practically such a very discreditable episode in the history of the race. I doubt if this is altogether due to the vulgar and sanguinary sensationalism of our religious legends, with their substitution of gross physical torments and public executions for the passion of humanity. Islam, substituting voluptuousness for torment (a merely superficial difference, it is true) has done no better. It may have been the failure of Christianity to emancipate itself from expiatory theories of moral responsibility, guilt, innocence, reward, punishment, and the rest of it, that baffled its intention of changing the world. But these are bound up in all philosophies of creation as opposed to cosmism. They may therefore be regarded as the price we pay for popular religion.

WILLIAM SHAKESPEARE: *TWELFTH NIGHT*

Shakespeare's *Twelfth Night* creates a world of sufficient scope and magnitude to remind one of life, and of sufficient variety and detail to reinforce one's suspicions that its never-never land of Illyria could, with a few adjustments, be the next county over. True, to Elizabethan audiences the parallel would have been even more easily recognizable, for the world of *Twelfth Night* is a brilliant transcription of the manor-house life of the English countryside in Elizabeth's time. Further, the play abounds in conventional Renaissance love talk; many of the high-flown and seemingly stilted exchanges between Cesario and the Duke, and between Cesario and Olivia, are not much different from the philosophizings about the trials and tribulations of love indulged in by college freshmen today. The language is no longer the language of Plato and the academy, but the truths haven't changed much.

Something of the spirit and mood of Shakespeare's romantic comedy can be deduced from the holiday that gives the play its name. In the calendar of religious observances, Twelfth-night is the evening before January 6, the twelfth day after Christmas and the date of the Feast of the Epiphany (or appearance), the supposed date following the birth of Christ when the star appeared to the wise men of the East. Though religious in origin, the holiday (no longer widely celebrated) has traditionally been anything but grave; rather, it has been a time of feasting and merriment. Indeed, despite its Christian origins, it took on through the years many characteristics of the ancient Roman saturnalia, a pagan festival that came at about the same time of year and permitted organized disorder and general unrestraint. Twelfth-night was a time when men lived under the reign of the Lord of Misrule, a sovereign who was content only when things were upside down.

Whether the play is so entitled because it was written as part of an entertainment for that holiday, or because there is a hint of the title in the old Italian comedy from which Shakespeare drew the story, we cannot tell. But the subtitle, "What You Will," seems to confirm the general impression of disorder we get from the title itself. On the surface, Shakespeare seems to say, "Make of this what you can; see in it what you wish." A closer look, however, makes another interpretation perhaps more plausible. If one remembers the nature of this holiday, the subtitle also seems to suggest that here is a scene in which the characters do what they will, much as we do on Twelfth-night; but as the play shows us, doing what you will, without regard for what you must and should, is a formula for comedy, for misrule, not for life.

Twelfth Night is apparently a romantic love story, told not as a boy-meets-girl tale, but in the older comic pattern of the mistaken identity plot. In fact, unless we soon realize that its conflict is not between the lovers and the barriers to their love, but between the clear view and the clouded view of reality, we are likely to reject this play because of its artificiality. And for good reason, for the story of the love of Orsino for Olivia, of Viola for Orsino, of Olivia for Cesario and then for Sebastian, is pretty silly and hardly worth bothering about. But by plotting this tale as one of mistaken identity, Shakespeare reduces the love nonsense to its proper proportions. Viewed so, the play uses its love mixup to remind us that it is as easy to be misled by one's own disguises as it is to be misled by the external disguises of others. It is, then, a play about self-delusion based on a plot of mistaken identity.

Love is not the only cause of self-delusion, but it is the most easily understood, for man wants most to be loved and he tends to be most vain in judging his achievements in this area. To show how widespread this disease of self-delusion is, Shakespeare makes use of a comic sub-plot. He creates a primary pattern involving Orsino, Olivia, Viola, and Sebastian, and a secondary one using Sir Toby, Sir Andrew, Maria, and Malvolio. Obviously, the patterns will cross, and the ease and skill of the interweaving is a measure of the structural excellence of the comedy. Nothing could do less justice to this play than to view Sir Toby and company merely as a low comedy element used to enliven the romance; for without the non-sense of the great world about them, the nonsense in the kitchen would have little point. It is only by reproducing these patterns of nonsense that Shakespeare forces us to look at them seriously.

If the parallel lines of action of this play are held together by Malvolio, who is involved in both plots and is the most obviously self-deluded character, the play is also unified by the extent to which disguise and self-delusion rule its world. The two lovers, Orsino and Olivia, cannot distinguish between appearance and reality. Orsino, in love with love, fancies himself languishing and pining away because of Olivia's refusal. He reacts, though he does not comprehend his reaction, to the presence of Cesario-Viola. Olivia, in love first with grief and then with the idea of her own independence, has the parallel reaction to Viola masquerading as Cesario. Both Orsino and Olivia change as they are shocked out of a state that has kept their true feelings hidden.

So, too, Viola—whose opening lines, from "What shall I do in Illyria?" to the adoption of the disguise, reveal a rather obvious parallel to Olivia—must adopt a disguise in order to find reality, that is, true love, while Orsino and Olivia must discard their disguises, there being little distinction between physical disguise and self-delusion. Sebastian, who gets only a tourist's-eye-view of these proceedings, is suddenly faced with an unbelievable appearance which turns out astonishingly to be reality.

So too, of course, with the minor characters. Antonio, the sea captain, deludes himself into believing he can be safe in Illyria. Sir Andrew plays out his role as suitor for Olivia's hand; though apparently deluded, and obviously a caricature of the country squire, Sir Andrew is not a dolt or fool, for he has wit enough to realize that he is a player in a scene of masques and revels. Even Sir Toby, Maria, and Feste are reprimanded, though ever so lightly, for having stepped out of place, deluding themselves about their superiority to Malvolio. In this world, as Feste says, "Nothing that is so, is so." In this sentence is summed up the play's (and life's) contradictions; the fool casts a sane eye on his fellow mortals, wonders at their madness, and then shrugs his shoulders in acceptance.

Of Malvolio himself, something more needs to be said, for he is the most fully drawn character in the play. He is, according to Olivia, who values him most highly, a man sick with self-love; but to Maria he is a time-pleaser, an affectioned ass so crammed, as he thinks, with excellences that "it is his grounds of faith that all that look on him love him." Hooked by Maria's bait, Malvolio comes cross-gartered in his midsummer madness to woo the unsuspecting Olivia. He is marked for mad, and the heartless Sir Toby and his crew torment the confused steward unmercifully. Finally released and restored, Malvolio, having no sense of humor, storms off stage vowing revenge.

About Malvolio the play is explicit, for Sir Toby's greatest line, one of the most frequently quoted lines of the play, makes clear that self-love and self-delusion in Malvolio threaten a whole way of life. "Art any more than a steward?" Sir Toby taunts him. "Dost thou think, because thou art virtuous, there shall be no more cakes and ale?" Here self-love involves a presumption above station, a great social vice in Elizabeth I's day; but, even more, it expresses the immature presumption that the world is cast in one's own shadow.

If he spells out the theme for us, Malvolio also leads to the deeper meaning of the play. For if Malvolio is a man who cannot put aside his mask, the world must yet recognize—as the Duke and Olivia make very clear—that he is not to be banished from the world. It is almost as though Shakespeare were saying that this delusion is an element in us individually and among us socially that we might wish to be rid of but cannot wholly blot out. Therefore we must deal with it wisely. And wisely means gently and affectionately.

So the play ends, and once again the meaning of life has been searched for in the comic pattern. Appearances and realities have been reconciled, as much as they ever can be; and Feste the Fool, functioning much as did the Chorus in ancient Greek drama, as a kind of ironic commentator on the action, steps forward to deliver the final jest, full of the playwright's elusive irony:

> A great while ago the world begun . . .
> But that's all one, our play is done.

Twelfth Night

or

What You Will

by

WILLIAM SHAKESPEARE

SCENE: A CITY IN ILLYRIA
AND A SEA-COAST NEAR IT

ORSINO, *Duke of Illyria*
SEBASTIAN, *brother to Viola*
ANTONIO, *a sea captain, friend to Sebastian*
A SEA CAPTAIN, *friend to Viola*
VALENTINE, CURIO, *gentlemen attending
    on the Duke*
SIR TOBY BELCH, *uncle to Olivia*
SIR ANDREW AGUECHEEK
MALVOLIO, *steward to Olivia*
FABIAN, *servant to Olivia*
FESTE, *a clown, servant to Olivia*
OLIVIA
VIOLA
MARIA, *Olivia's woman*
LORDS, PRIESTS, SAILORS, OFFICERS,
    MUSICIANS, *et al.*

ACT ONE

1. *An apartment in the* DUKE'S *palace*

Enter DUKE, CURIO, *and other* LORDS;
    MUSICIANS *attending.*

DUKE. If music be the food of love, play
    on;
Give me excess of it, that, surfeiting,
The appetite may sicken, and so die.
That strain again! it had a dying fall:
O, it came o'er my ear like the sweet
    sound,
That breathes upon a bank of violets,
Stealing and giving odor! Enough; no
    more:
'Tis not so sweet now as it was before.
O spirit of love, how quick and fresh art
    thou!
That, notwithstanding thy capacity
Receiveth as the sea, nought enters there,
Of what validity and pitch soe'er,
But falls into abatement and low price,
Even in a minute! so full of shapes is
    fancy,
That it alone is high fantastical.
CURIO. Will you go hunt, my lord?
DUKE. What, Curio?
CURIO. The hart.
DUKE. Why, so I do, the noblest that I
    have:
O, when mine eyes did see Olivia first,

Methought she purged the air of pesti-
    lence!
That instant was I turn'd into a hart;
And my desires, like fell and cruel
    hounds,
E'er since pursue me.
        [*Enter* VALENTINE.]
How now! what news from her?
VALENTINE. So please my lord, I might
    not be admitted;
But from her handmaid do return this
    answer:
The element itself, till seven years' heat,
Shall not behold her face at ample view;
But, like a cloistress, she will veiled walk
And water once a day her chamber
    round
With eye-offending brine: all this to
    season
A brother's dead love, which she would
    keep fresh
And lasting in her sad remembrance.
DUKE. O, she that hath a heart of that
    fine frame
To pay this debt of love but to a brother,
How will she love, when the rich golden
    shaft
Hath kill'd the flock of all affections else
That live in her; when liver, brain and
    heart,

These sovereign thrones, are all supplied,
and fill'd
Her sweet perfections with one self king!
Away before me to sweet beds of flow-
ers:
Love-thoughts lie rich when canopied
with bowers.
[*Exeunt.*]

2. *The sea-coast*

Enter VIOLA, *a* CAPTAIN, *and* SAILORS.
VIOLA. What country, friends, is this?
CAPTAIN. This is Illyria, lady.
VIOLA. And what should I do in Illyria?
My brother he is in Elysium.
Perchance he is not drown'd: what think
you, sailors?
CAPTAIN. It is perchance that you your-
self were saved.
VIOLA. O my poor brother! and so per-
chance may he be.
CAPTAIN. True, madam: and, to com-
fort you with chance,
Assure yourself, after our ship did split,
When you and those poor number saved
with you
Hung on our driving boat, I saw your
brother,
Most provident in peril, bind himself,
Courage and hope both teaching him the
practice,
To a strong mast that lived upon the sea;
Where, like Arion on the dolphin's back,
I saw him hold acquaintance with the
waves
So long as I could see.
VIOLA. For saying so, there's gold:
Mine own escape unfoldeth to my hope,
Whereto thy speech serves for authority,
The like of him. Know'st thou this coun-
try?
CAPTAIN. Aye, madam, well; for I was
bred and born
Not three hours' travel from this very
place.
VIOLA. Who governs here?
CAPTAIN. A noble Duke, in nature as in
name.
VIOLA. What is his name?
CAPTAIN. Orsino.

VIOLA. Orsino! I have heard my father
name him:
He was a bachelor then.
CAPTAIN. And so is now, or was so very
late;
For but a month ago I went from hence,
And then 'twas fresh in murmur,—as, you
know,
What great ones do the less will prattle
of,—
That he did seek the love of fair Olivia.
VIOLA. What's she?
CAPTAIN. A virtuous maid, the daughter
of a count
That died some twelvemonth since; then
leaving her
In the protection of his son, her brother,
Who shortly also died: for whose dear
love,
They say, she hath abjured the company
And sight of men.
VIOLA. O that I served that lady,
And might not be delivered to the world,
Till I had made mine own occasion mel-
low,
What my estate is!
CAPTAIN. That were hard to compass;
Because she will admit no kind of suit,
No, not the Duke's.
VIOLA. There is a fair behavior in thee,
captain;
And though that nature with a beauteous
wall
Doth oft close in pollution, yet of thee
I will believe thou hast a mind that suits
With this thy fair and outward char-
acter.
I prithee, and I'll pay thee bounteously,
Conceal me what I am, and be my aid
For such disguise as haply shall become
The form of my intent. I'll serve this
Duke:
Thou shalt present me as an eunuch to
him:
It may be worth thy pains; for I can
sing,
And speak to him in many sorts of music,
That will allow me very worth his serv-
ice.
What else may hap to time I will com-
mit;
Only shape thou thy silence to my wit.
CAPTAIN. Be you his eunuch, and your
mute I'll be:

When my tongue blabs, then let mine
eyes not see.

VIOLA. I thank thee: lead me on.

[*Exeunt.*]

3. OLIVIA's *house*

Enter SIR TOBY BELCH *and* MARIA.

SIR TOBY. What a plague means my
niece, to take the death of her brother
thus? I am sure care's an enemy to life.

MARIA. By my troth, Sir Toby, you
must come in earlier o' nights: your
cousin, my lady, takes great exceptions
to your ill hours.

SIR TOBY. Why, let her except, before
excepted.

MARIA. Aye, but you must confine
yourself within the modest limits of
order.

SIR TOBY. Confine! I'll confine myself
no finer than I am: these clothes are
good enough to drink in; and so be these
boots too: an they be not, let them hang
themselves in their own straps.

MARIA. That quaffing and drinking will
undo you: I heard my lady talk of it
yesterday; and of a foolish knight that
you brought in one night here to be her
wooer.

SIR TOBY. Who, Sir Andrew Aguecheek?

MARIA. Aye, he.

SIR TOBY. He's as tall a man as any's in
Illyria.

MARIA. What's that to the purpose?

SIR TOBY. Why, he has three thousand
ducats a year.

MARIA. Aye, but he'll have but a year
in all these ducats; he's a very fool and a
prodigal.

SIR TOBY. Fie, that you'll say so! he
plays o' the viol-de-gamboys, and speaks
three or four languages word for word
without book, and hath all the good gifts
of nature.

MARIA. He hath indeed, almost natural:
for besides that he's a fool, he's a great
quareler: and but that he hath the gift of
a coward to allay the gust he hath in
quarreling, 'tis thought among the pru-

dent he would quickly have the gift of a
grave.

SIR TOBY. By this hand, they are scoundrels and subtractors that say so of him.
Who are they?

MARIA. They that add, moreover, he's
drunk nightly in your company.

SIR TOBY. With drinking healths to my
niece: I'll drink to her as long as there
is a passage in my throat and drink in
Illyria: he's a coward and a coystrill that
will not drink to my niece till his brains
turn o' the toe like a parish-top. What,
wench! Castiliano vulgo; for here comes
Sir Andrew Agueface.

[*Enter* SIR ANDREW AGUECHEEK.]

SIR ANDREW. Sir Toby Belch! how now,
Sir Toby Belch!

SIR TOBY. Sweet Sir Andrew!

SIR ANDREW. Bless you, fair shrew.

MARIA. And you too, sir.

SIR TOBY. Accost, Sir Andrew, accost.

SIR ANDREW. What's that?

SIR TOBY. My niece's chambermaid.

SIR ANDREW. Good Mistress Accost, I
desire better acquaintance.

MARIA. My name is Mary, sir.

SIR ANDREW. Good Mistress Mary Accost,—

SIR TOBY. You mistake, knight: 'accost'
is front her, board her, woo her, assail
her.

SIR ANDREW. By my troth, I would not
undertake her in this company. Is that
the meaning of 'accost'?

MARIA. Fare you well, gentlemen.

SIR TOBY. An thou let part so, Sir Andrew, would thou mightst never draw
sword again.

SIR ANDREW. An you part so, mistress,
I would I might never draw sword again.
Fair lady, do you think you have fools in
hand?

MARIA. Sir, I have not you by the hand.

SIR ANDREW. Marry, but you shall have;
and here's my hand.

MARIA. Now, sir, 'thought is free': I
pray you, bring your hand to the but-
tery-bar and let it drink.

SIR ANDREW. Wherefore, sweetheart?
what's your metaphor?

MARIA. It's dry, sir.

SIR ANDREW. Why, I think so: I am not such an ass but I can keep my hand dry. But what's your jest?

MARIA. A dry jest, sir.

SIR ANDREW. Are you full of them?

MARIA. Aye, sir, I have them at my fingers' ends: marry, now I let go your hand, I am barren. [*Exit.*]

SIR TOBY. O knight, thou lackest a cup of canary: when did I see thee so put down?

SIR ANDREW. Never in your life, I think; unless you see canary put me down. Methinks sometimes I have no more wit than a Christian or an ordinary man has: but I am a great eater of beef and I believe that does harm to my wit.

SIR TOBY. No question.

SIR ANDREW. An I thought that, I'ld forswear it. I'll ride home to-morrow, Sir Toby.

SIR TOBY. Pourquoi, my dear knight?

SIR ANDREW. What is 'pourquoi'? do or not do? I would I had bestowed that time in the tongues that I have in fencing, dancing and bear-baiting: O, had I but followed the arts!

SIR TOBY. Then hadst thou had an excellent head of hair.

SIR ANDREW. Why, would that have mended my hair?

SIR TOBY. Past question; for thou seest it will not curl by nature.

SIR ANDREW. But it becomes me well enough, does 't not?

SIR TOBY. Excellent; it hangs like flax on a distaff; and I hope to see a housewife take thee between her legs and spin it off.

SIR ANDREW. Faith, I'll home to-morrow, Sir Toby: your niece will not be seen; or if she be, it's four to one she'll none of me: the count himself here hard by woos her.

SIR TOBY. She'll none o' the count: she'll not match above her degree, neither in estate, years, nor wit; I have heard her swear 't. Tut, there's life in 't, man.

SIR ANDREW. I'll stay a month longer. I am a fellow o' the strangest mind i' the world; I delight in masques and revels sometimes altogether.

SIR TOBY. Art thou good at these kick-shawses, knight?

SIR ANDREW. As any man in Illyria, whatsoever he be, under the degree of my betters; and yet I will not compare with an old man.

SIR TOBY. What is thy excellence in a galliard, knight?

SIR ANDREW. Faith, I can cut a caper.

SIR TOBY. And I can cut the mutton to 't.

SIR ANDREW. And I think I have the back-trick simply as strong as any man in Illyria.

SIR TOBY. Wherefore are these things hid? wherefore have these gifts a curtain before 'em? are they like to take dust, like Mistress Mall's picture? why dost thou not go to church in a galliard and come home in a coranto? My very walk should be a jig; I would not so much as make water but in a sink-a-pace. What dost thou mean? Is it a world to hide virtues in? I did think, by the excellent constitution of thy leg, it was formed under the star of a galliard.

SIR ANDREW. Aye, 'tis strong, and it does indifferent well in a flame-colored stock. Shall we set about some revels?

SIR TOBY. What shall we do else? were we not born under Taurus?

SIR ANDREW. Taurus! That's sides and heart.

SIR TOBY. No, sir; it is legs and thighs. Let me see thee caper: ha! higher: ha, ha! excellent!

[*Exeunt.*]

4. *The* DUKE's *palace*

Enter VALENTINE, *and* VIOLA *in man's attire.*

VALENTINE. If the Duke continue these favors towards you, Cesario, you are like to be much advanced: he hath known you but three days, and already you are no stranger.

VIOLA. You either fear his humor or my negligence, that you call in question the continuance of his love: is he inconstant, sir, in his favors?

VALENTINE. No, believe me.

VIOLA. I thank you. Here comes the count.

[*Enter* DUKE, CURIO, *and* ATTENDANTS.]

DUKE. Who saw Cesario, ho?

VIOLA. On your attendance, my lord; here.

DUKE. Stand you a while aloof. Cesario,
Thou know'st no less but all; I have un-
      clasp'd
To thee the book even of my secret soul:
Therefore, good youth, address thy gait
      unto her;
Be not denied access, stand at her doors,
And tell them, there thy fixed foot shall
      grow
Till thou have audience.

VIOLA. Sure, my noble lord,
If she be so abandon'd to her sorrow
As it is spoke, she never will admit me.

DUKE. Be clamorous and leap all civil
      bounds
Rather than make unprofited return.

VIOLA. Say I do speak with her, my
      lord, what then?

DUKE. O, then unfold the passion of my
      love,
Surprise her with discourse of my dear
      faith:
It shall become thee well to act my woes;
She will attend it better in thy youth
Then in a nuncio's of more grave aspect.

VIOLA. I think not so, my lord.

DUKE. Dear lad, believe it;
For they shall yet belie thy happy years,
That say thou art a man; Diana's lip
Is not more smooth and rubious; thy
      small pipe
Is as the maiden's organ, shrill and sound;
And all is semblative a woman's part.
I know thy constellation is right apt
For this affair. Some four or five attend
      him;
All, if you will; for I myself am best
When least in company. Prosper well in
      this,
And thou shalt live as freely as thy lord,
To call his fortunes thine.

VIOLA. I'll do my best
To woo your lady: [*Aside.*] yet, a barful
      strife!
Whoe'er I woo, myself would be his
      wife.

[*Exeunt.*]

5. OLIVIA'S *house*

Enter MARIA *and* CLOWN.

MARIA. Nay, either tell me where thou
hast been, or I will not open my lips so
wide as a bristle may enter in way of thy
excuse: my lady will hang thee for thy
absence.

CLOWN. Let her hang me: he that is
well hanged in this world needs to fear
no colors.

MARIA. Make that good.

CLOWN. He shall see none to fear.

MARIA. A good lenten answer: I can tell
thee where that saying was born, of 'I
fear no colors.'

CLOWN. Where, good Mistress Mary?

MARIA. In the wars; and that may you
be bold to say in your foolery.

CLOWN. Well, God give them wisdom
that have it; and those that are fools, let
them use their talents.

MARIA. Yet you will be hanged for
being so long absent; or, to be turned
away, is not that as good as a hanging to
you?

CLOWN. Many a good hanging prevents
a bad marriage; and, for turning away,
let summer bear it out.

MARIA. You are resolute, then?

CLOWN. Not so, neither; but I am resolved on two points.

MARIA. That if one break, the other
will hold; or, if both break, your gaskins
fall.

CLOWN. Apt, in good faith; very apt.
Well, go thy way; if Sir Toby would
leave drinking, thou wert as witty a piece
of Eve's flesh as any in Illyria.

MARIA. Peace, you rogue, no more o'
that. Here comes my lady: make your
excuse wisely, you were best. [*Exit.*]

CLOWN. Wit, an 't be thy will, put me
into good fooling! Those wits, that think
they have thee, do very oft prove fools;
and I, that am sure I lack thee, may pass
for a wise man: for what says Quinapa-
lus? 'Better a witty fool than a foolish
wit.'

[*Enter* LADY OLIVIA *with* MALVOLIO.]
God bless thee, lady.

OLIVIA. Take the fool away.

CLOWN. Do you not hear, fellows? Take away the lady.

OLIVIA. Go to, you're a dry fool; I'll no more of you: besides, you grow dishonest.

CLOWN. Two faults, madonna, that drink and good counsel will amend: for give the dry fool drink, then is the fool not dry: bid the dishonest man mend himself; if he mend, he is no longer dishonest; if he cannot, let the botcher mend him. Any thing that's mended is but patched: virtue that transgresses is but patched with sin; and sin that amends is but patched with virtue. If that this simple syllogism will serve, so; if it will not, what remedy? As there is no true cuckold but calamity, so beauty's a flower. The lady bade take away the fool; therefore I say again, take her away.

OLIVIA. Sir, I bade them take away you.

CLOWN. Misprision in the highest degree! Lady, cucullus non facit monachum; that's as much to say as I wear not motley in my brain. Good madonna, give me leave to prove you a fool.

OLIVIA. Can you do it?

CLOWN. Dexteriously, good madonna.

OLIVIA. Make your proof.

CLOWN. I must catechize you for it, madonna: good my mouse of virtue, answer me.

OLIVIA. Well, sir, for want of other idleness, I'll bide your proof.

CLOWN. Good madonna, why mournest thou?

OLIVIA. Good fool, for my brother's death.

CLOWN. I think his soul is in hell, madonna.

OLIVIA. I know his soul is in heaven, fool.

CLOWN. The more fool, madonna, to mourn for your brother's soul being in heaven. Take away the fool, gentlemen.

OLIVIA. What think you of this fool, Malvolio? doth he not mend?

MALVOLIO. Yes, and shall do till the pangs of death shake him: infirmity, that decays the wise, doth ever make the better fool.

CLOWN. God send you, sir, a speedy infirmity, for the better increasing your folly! Sir Toby will be sworn that I am no fox; but he will not pass his word for two pence that you are no fool.

OLIVIA. How say you to that, Malvolio?

MALVOLIO. I marvel your ladyship takes delight in such a barren rascal: I saw him put down the other day with an ordinary fool that has no more brain than a stone. Look you now, he's out of his guard already; unless you laugh and minister occasion to him, he is gagged. I protest, I take these wise men, that crow so at these set kind of fools, no better than fools' zanies.

OLIVIA. O, you are sick of self-love, Malvolio, and taste with a distempered appetite. To be generous, guiltless and of free dispositon, is to take those things for bird-bolts that you deem cannon-bullets: there is no slander in an allowed fool, though he do nothing but rail; nor no railing in a known discreet man, though he do nothing but reprove.

CLOWN. Now Mercury endue thee with leasing, for thou speakest well of fools!

[Re-enter MARIA.]

MARIA. Madam, there is at the gate a young gentleman much desires to speak with you.

OLIVIA. From the Count Orsino, is it?

MARIA. I know not, madam: 'tis a fair young man, and well attended.

OLIVIA. Who of my people hold him in delay?

MARIA. Sir Toby, madam, your kinsman.

OLIVIA. Fetch him off, I pray you; he speaks nothing but madman: fie on him! [Exit MARIA.] Go you, Malvolio: if it be a suit from the count, I am sick, or not at home; what you will, to dismiss it. [Exit MALVOLIO.] Now you see, sir, how your fooling grows old, and people dislike it.

CLOWN. Thou hast spoke for us, madonna, as if thy eldest son should be a fool; whose skull Jove cram with brains! for,—here he comes,—one of thy kin has a most weak pia mater.

[Enter SIR TOBY.]

OLIVIA. By mine honor, half drunk. What is he at the gate, cousin?

SIR TOBY. A gentleman.

OLIVIA. A gentleman! what gentleman?

SIR TOBY. 'Tis a gentleman here—a

plague o' these pickle-herring! How now, sot!

CLOWN. Good Sir Toby!

OLIVIA. Cousin, cousin, how have you come so early by this lethargy?

SIR TOBY. Lechery! I defy lechery. There's one at the gate.

OLIVIA. Aye, marry, what is he?

SIR TOBY. Let him be the devil, an he will, I care not: give me faith, say I. Well, it's all one. [Exit.]

OLIVIA. What's a drunken man like, fool?

CLOWN. Like a drowned man, a fool and a madman: one draught above heat makes him a fool; the second mads him; and a third drowns him.

OLIVIA. Go thou and seek the crowner, and let him sit o' my coz; for he's in the third degree of drink, he's drowned: go look after him.

CLOWN. He is but mad yet, madonna; and the fool shall look to the madman. [Exit.]

[Re-enter MALVOLIO.]

MALVOLIO. Madam, yond young fellow swears he will speak with you. I told him you were sick; he takes on him to understand so much, and therefore comes to speak with you. I told you you were asleep; he seems to have a foreknowledge of that too, and therefore comes to speak with you. What is to be said to him, lady? he's fortified against any denial.

OLIVIA. Tell him he shall not speak with me.

MALVOLIO. Has been told so; and he says, he'll stand at your door like a sheriff's post, and be the supporter to a bench, but he'll speak with you.

OLIVIA. What kind o' man is he?

MALVOLIO. Why, of mankind.

OLIVIA. What manner of man?

MALVOLIO. Of very ill manner: he'll speak with you, will you or no.

OLIVIA. Of what personage and years is he?

MALVOLIO. Not yet old enough for a man, nor young enough for a boy; as a squash is before 'tis a peascod, or a codling when 'tis almost an apple: 'tis with him in standing water, between boy and man. He is very well-favored and he speaks very shrewishly; one would think

his mother's milk were scarce out of him.

OLIVIA. Let him approach: call in my gentlewoman.

MALVOLIO. Gentlewoman, my lady calls. [Exit.]

[Re-enter MARIA.]

OLIVIA. Give me my veil: come, throw it o'er my face. We'll once more hear Orsino's embassy.

[Enter VIOLA, and ATTENDANTS.]

VIOLA. The honorable lady of the house, which is she?

OLIVIA. Speak to me; I shall answer for her. Your will?

VIOLA. Most radiant, exquisite and unmatchable beauty,—I pray you, tell me if this be the lady of the house, for I never saw her: I would be loath to cast away my speech, for besides that it is excellently well penned, I have taken great pains to con it. Good beauties, let me sustain no scorn; I am very comptible, even to the least sinister usage.

OLIVIA. Whence came you, sir?

VIOLA. I can say little more than I have studied, and that question's out of my part. Good gentle one, give me modest assurance if you be the lady of the house, that I may proceed in my speech.

OLIVIA. Are you a comedian?

VIOLA. No, my profound heart: and yet, by the very fangs of malice I swear, I am not that I play. Are you the lady of the house?

OLIVIA. If I do not usurp myself, I am.

VIOLA. Most certain, if you are she, you do usurp yourself; for what is yours to bestow is not yours to reserve. But this is from my commission: I will on with my speech in your praise, and then show you the heart of my message.

OLIVIA. Come to what is important in 't: I forgive you the praise.

VIOLA. Alas, I took great pains to study it, and 'tis poetical.

OLIVIA. It is the more like to be feigned. I pray you, keep it in. I heard you were saucy at my gates, and allowed your approach rather to wonder at you than to hear you. If you be not mad, be gone; if you have reason, be brief; 'tis not that time of moon with me to make one in so skipping a dialogue.

MARIA. Will you hoist sail, sir? here lies your way.

VIOLA. No, good swabber; I am to hull here a little longer. Some mollification for your giant, sweet lady. Tell me your mind: I am a messenger.

OLIVIA. Sure, you have some hideous matter to deliver, when the courtesy of it is so fearful. Speak your office.

VIOLA. It alone concerns your ear. I bring no overture of war, no taxation of homage: I hold the olive in my hand; my words are as full of peace as matter.

OLIVIA. Yet you began rudely. What are you? what would you?

VIOLA. The rudeness that hath appeared in me have I learned from my entertainment. What I am, and what I would, are as secret as maiden-head; to your ears, divinity, to any other's, profanation.

OLIVIA. Give us the place alone: we will hear this divinity. [*Exeunt* MARIA *and* ATTENDANTS.] Now, sir, what is your text?

VIOLA. Most sweet lady,—

OLIVIA. A comfortable doctrine, and much may be said of it. Where lies your text?

VIOLA. In Orsino's bosom.

OLIVIA. In his bosom! In what chapter of his bosom?

VIOLA. To answer by the method, in the first of his heart.

OLIVIA. O, I have read it: it is heresy. Have you no more to say?

VIOLA. Good madam, let me see your face.

OLIVIA. Have you any commission from your lord to negotiate with my face? You are now out of your text: but we will draw the curtain and show you the picture. Look you, sir, such a one I was this present: is 't not well done? [*Unveiling.*]

VIOLA. Excellently done, if God did all.

OLIVIA. 'Tis in grain, sir; 'twill endure wind and weather.

VIOLA. 'Tis beauty truly blent, whose red and white
Nature's own sweet and cunning hand laid on:
Lady, you are the cruel'st she alive,
If you will lead these graces to the grave
And leave the world no copy.

OLIVIA. O, sir, I will not be so hard-hearted; I will give out divers schedules of my beauty: it shall be inventoried, and every particle and utensil labeled to my will: as, item, two lips indifferent red; item, two gray eyes, with lids to them; item, one neck, one chin, and so forth. Were you sent hither to praise me?

VIOLA. I see you what you are, you are too proud;
But, if you were the devil, you are fair.
My lord and master loves you: O, such love
Could be but recompensed, though you were crown'd
The nonpareil of beauty!

OLIVIA. How does he love me?

VIOLA. With adorations, fertile tears,
With groans that thunder love, with sighs of fire.

OLIVIA. Your lord does know my mind; I cannot love him:
Yet I suppose him virtuous, know him noble,
Of great estate, of fresh and stainless youth;
In voices well divulged, free, learn'd and valiant;
And in dimension and the shape of nature
A gracious person: but yet I cannot love him;
He might have took his answer long ago.

VIOLA. If I did love you in my master's flame,
With such a suffering, such a deadly life,
In your denial I would find no sense;
I would not understand it.

OLIVIA. Why, what would you?

VIOLA. Make me a willow cabin at your gate,
And call upon my soul within the house;
Write loyal cantons of contemned love
And sing them loud even in the dead of night;
Halloo your name to the reverberate hills,
And make the babbling gossip of the air
Cry out 'Olivia!' O, you should not rest
Between the elements of air and earth,
But you should pity me!

OLIVIA. You might do much.
What is your parentage?

VIOLA. Above my fortunes, yet my state is well:
I am a gentleman.

OLIVIA. Get you to your lord;
I cannot love him: let him send no more;
Unless, perchance, you come to me again,
To tell me how he takes it. Fare you well:
I thank you for your pains: spend this for me.

VIOLA. I am no fee'd post, lady; keep your purse:
My master, not myself, lacks recompense.
Love make his heart of flint that you shall love;
And let your fervor, like my master's, be
Placed in contempt! Farewell, fair cruelty. [*Exit.*]

OLIVIA. 'What is your parentage?'
'Above my fortunes, yet my state is well:
I am a gentleman.' I'll be sworn thou art;
Thy tongue, thy face, thy limbs, actions, and spirit,
Do give thee five-fold blazon: not too fast: soft, soft!
Unless the master were the man. How now!
Even so quickly may one catch the plague?
Methinks I feel this youth's perfections
With an invisible and subtle stealth
To creep in at mine eyes. Well, let it be.
What ho, Malvolio!

[*Re-enter* MALVOLIO.]

MALVOLIO. Here, madam, at your service.

OLIVIA. Run after that same peevish messenger,
The county's man: he left this ring behind him,
Would I or not: tell him I'll none of it.
Desire him not to flatter with his lord,
Nor hold him up with hopes; I am not for him:
If that the youth will come this way tomorrow,
I'll give him reasons for 't; hie thee, Malvolio.

MALVOLIO. Madam, I will. [*Exit.*]

OLIVIA. I do I know not what, and fear to find
Mine eye too great a flatterer for my mind.
Fate, show thy force: ourselves we do not owe;
What is decreed must be, and be this so.
[*Exit.*]

ACT TWO

1. *The sea-coast*

Enter ANTONIO *and* SEBASTIAN.

ANTONIO. Will you stay no longer? nor will you not that I go with you?

SEBASTIAN. By your patience, no. My stars shine darkly over me: the malignancy of my fate might perhaps distemper yours; therefore I shall crave of you your leave that I may bear my evils alone: it were a bad recompense for your love, to lay any of them on you.

ANTONIO. Let me yet know of you whither you are bound.

SEBASTIAN. No, sooth, sir: my determinate voyage is mere extravagancy. But I perceive in you so excellent a touch of modesty, that you will not extort from me what I am willing to keep in; therefore it charges me in manners the rather to express myself. You must know of me then, Antonio, my name is Sebastian, which I called Roderigo. My father was that Sebastian of Messaline, whom I know you have heard of. He left behind him myself and a sister, both born in an hour: if the heavens had been pleased, would we had so ended! but you, sir, altered that; for some hour before you took me from the breach of the sea was my sister drowned.

ANTONIO. Alas the day.

SEBASTIAN. A lady, sir, though it was said she much resembled me, was yet of many accounted beautiful: but, though I could not with such estimable wonder overfar believe that, yet thus far I will boldly publish her; she bore a mind that envy could not but call fair. She is drowned already, sir, with salt water, though I seem to drown her remembrance again with more.

ANTONIO. Pardon me, sir, your bad entertainment.

SEBASTIAN. O good Antonio, forgive me your trouble.

ANTONIO. If you will not murder me for my love, let me be your servant.

SEBASTIAN. If you will not undo what you have done, that is, kill him whom you have recovered, desire it not. Fare ye well at once: my bosom is full of kindness, and I am yet so near the manners of my mother, that upon the least occasion more mine eyes will tell tales of me. I am bound to the Count Orsino's court: farewell. [*Exit.*]

ANTONIO. The gentleness of all the gods go with thee!
I have many enemies in Orsino's court,
Else would I very shortly see thee there.
But, come what may, I do adore thee so,
That danger shall seem sport, and I will go. [*Exit.*]

2. *A street*

Enter VIOLA, MALVOLIO *following.*

MALVOLIO. Were not you even now with the Countess Olivia?

VIOLA. Even now, sir; on a moderate pace I have since arrived but hither.

MALVOLIO. She returns this ring to you, sir: you might have saved me my pains, to have taken it away yourself. She adds, moreover, that you should put your lord into a desperate assurance she will none of him: and one thing more, that you be never so hardy to come again in his affairs, unless it be to report your lord's taking of this. Receive it so.

VIOLA. She took the ring of me: I'll none of it.

MALVOLIO. Come, sir, you peevishly threw it to her; and her will is, it should be so returned: if it be worth stooping for, there it lies in your eye; if not, be it his that finds it. [*Exit.*]

VIOLA. I left no ring with her: what means this lady?
Fortune forbid my outside have not charm'd her!

She made good view of me; indeed, so much,
That methought her eyes had lost her tongue,
For she did speak in starts distractedly.
She loves me, sure; the cunning of her passion
Invites me in this churlish messenger.
None of my lord's ring! why, he sent her none.
I am the man: if it be so, as 'tis,
Poor lady, she were better love a dream.
Disguise, I see, thou art a wickedness,
Wherein the pregnant enemy does much.
How easy is it for the proper-false
In women's waxen hearts to set their forms!
Alas, our frailty is the cause, not we!
For such as we are made of, such we be.
How will this fadge? my master loves her dearly;
And I, poor monster, fond as much on him;
And she, mistaken, seems to dote on me.
What will become of this? As I am man,
My state is desperate for my master's love;
As I am woman,—now alas the day!—
What thriftless sighs shall poor Olivia breathe!
O time! thou must untangle this, not I;
It is too hard a knot for me to untie!
[*Exit.*]

3. OLIVIA'S *house*

Enter SIR TOBY *and* SIR ANDREW.

SIR TOBY. Approach, Sir Andrew: not to be abed after midnight is to be up betimes; and 'diluculo surgere,' thou know'st,—

SIR ANDREW. Nay, by my troth, I know not: but I know, to be up late is to be up late.

SIR TOBY. A false conclusion: I hate it as an unfilled can. To be up after midnight and to go to bed then, is early: so that to go to bed after midnight is to go to bed betimes. Does not our life consist of the four elements?

SIR ANDREW. Faith, so they say; but I

think it rather consists of eating and
drinking.

SIR TOBY. Thou 'rt a scholar; let us
therefore eat and drink. Marian, I say! a
stoup of wine!

[*Enter* CLOWN.]

SIR ANDREW. Here comes the fool, i'
faith.

CLOWN. How now, my hearts! did you
never see the picture of 'we three'?

SIR TOBY. Welcome, ass. Now let's have
a catch.

SIR ANDREW. By my troth, the fool has
an excellent breast. I had rather than
forty shillings I had such a leg, and so
sweet a breath to sing, as the fool has. In
sooth, thou wast in very gracious fooling last night, when thou spokest of
Pigrogromitus, of the Vapians passing
the equinoctial of Queubus: 'twas very
good, i' faith. I sent thee sixpence for
thy leman: hadst it?

CLOWN. I did impeticos thy gratillity;
for Malvolio's nose is no whipstock: my
lady has a white hand, and the Myrmi-
dons are no bottle-ale houses.

SIR ANDREW. Excellent! why, this is the
best fooling, when all is done. Now, a
song.

SIR TOBY. Come on; there is sixpence for
you: let's have a song.

SIR ANDREW. There's a testril of me,
too: if one knight give a—

CLOWN. Would you have a love-song,
or a song of good life?

SIR TOBY. A love-song, a love-song.

SIR ANDREW. Aye, aye: I care not for
good life.

CLOWN. [*Sings.*]

O mistress mine, where are you roaming?
O, stay and hear; your true love's coming,
   That can sing both high and low:
Trip no further, pretty sweeting;
Journeys end in lovers meeting,
   Every wise man's son doth know.

SIR ANDREW. Excellent good, i' faith.

SIR TOBY. Good, good.

CLOWN. [*Sings.*]

What is love? 'tis not hereafter;
Present mirth hath present laughter;
   What 's to come is still unsure:
In delay there lies no plenty;
Then come kiss me, sweet and twenty,
   Youth's a stuff will not endure.

SIR ANDREW. A mellifluous voice, as I
am true knight.

SIR TOBY. A contagious breath.

SIR ANDREW. Very sweet and contagious, i' faith.

SIR TOBY. To hear by the nose, it is dul-
cet in contagion. But shall we make the
welkin dance indeed? shall we rouse the
night-owl in a catch that will draw three
souls out of one weaver? shall we do
that?

SIR ANDREW. An you love me, let's do 't.
I am dog at a catch.

CLOWN. By 'r lady, sir, and some dogs
will catch well.

SIR ANDREW. Most certain. Let our
catch be, 'Thou knave.'

CLOWN. 'Hold thy peace, thou knave,'
knight? I shall be constrained in 't to
call thee knave, knight.

SIR ANDREW. 'Tis not the first time I
have constrained one to call me knave.
Begin, fool: it begins 'Hold thy peace.'

CLOWN. I shall never begin if I hold my
peace.

SIR ANDREW. Good, i' faith. Come, begin. [*Catch sung.*]

[*Enter* MARIA.]

MARIA. What a caterwauling do you
keep here! If my lady have not called up
her steward Malvolio and bid him turn
you out of doors, never trust me.

SIR TOBY. My lady's a Cataian, we are
politicians, Malvolio's a Peg-a-Ramsey,
and 'Three merry men be we.' Am not I
consanguineous? am I not of her blood?
Tillyvally. Lady! [*Sings.*] 'There dwelt
a man in Babylon, lady, lady!'

CLOWN. Beshrew me, the knight's in admirable fooling.

SIR ANDREW. Aye, he does well enough
if he be disposed, and so do I too: he
does it with a better grace, but I do it
more natural.

SIR TOBY. [*Sings.*] 'O, the twelfth day of
December,'—

MARIA. For the love o' God, peace!

[*Enter* MALVOLIO.]

MALVOLIO. My masters, are you mad?
or what are you? Have you no wit, manners, nor honesty, but to gabble like tink-
ers at this time of night? Do ye make an
alehouse of my lady's house, that ye
squeak out your coziers' catches without

any mitigation or remorse of voice? Is there no respect of place, persons, nor time in you?

SIR TOBY. We did keep time, sir, in our catches. Sneck up!

MALVOLIO. Sir Toby, I must be round with you. My lady bade me tell you, that, though she harbors you as her kinsman, she's nothing allied to your disorders. If you can separate yourself and your misdemeanors, you are welcome to the house; if not, an it would please you to take leave of her, she is very willing to bid you farewell.

SIR TOBY. 'Farewell, dear heart, since I must needs be gone.'

MARIA. Nay, good Sir Toby.

CLOWN. 'His eyes do show his days are almost done.'

MALVOLIO. Is 't even so?

SIR TOBY. 'But I will never die.'

CLOWN. Sir Toby, there you lie.

MALVOLIO. This is much credit to you.

SIR TOBY. 'Shall I bid him go?'

CLOWN. 'What an if you do?'

SIR TOBY. 'Shall I bid him go, and spare not?'

CLOWN. 'O no, no, no, no, you dare not.'

SIR TOBY. Out o' tune, sir: ye lie. Art any more than a steward? Dost thou think, because thou art virtuous, there shall be no more cakes and ale?

CLOWN. Yes, by Saint Anne, and ginger shall be hot i' the mouth too.

SIR TOBY. Thou 'rt i' the right. Go, sir, rub your chain with crums. A stoup of wine, Maria!

MALVOLIO. Mistress Mary, if you prized my lady's favor at any thing more than contempt you would not give means for this uncivil rule: she shall know of it, by this hand. [Exit.]

MARIA. Go shake your ears.

SIR ANDREW. 'Twere as good a deed as to drink when a man 's a-hungry, to challenge him the field, and then to break promise with him and make a fool of him.

SIR TOBY. Do 't, knight: I'll write thee a challenge; or I'll deliver thy indignation to him by word of mouth.

MARIA. Sweet Sir Toby, be patient for to-night: since the youth of the count's

was to-day with my lady, she is much out of quiet. For Monsieur Malvolio, let me alone with him: if I do not gull him into a nayword, and make him a common recreation, do not think I have wit enough to lie straight in my bed; I know I can do it.

SIR TOBY. Possess us, possess us; tell us something of him.

MARIA. Marry, sir, sometimes he is a kind of puritan.

SIR ANDREW. O, if I thought that, I'ld beat him like a dog!

SIR TOBY. What, for being a puritan? thy exquisite reason, dear knight?

SIR ANDREW. I have no exquisite reason for 't, but I have reason good enough.

MARIA. The devil a puritan that he is, or any thing constantly, but a timepleaser; an affectioned ass, that cons state without book and utters it by great swarths: the best persuaded of himself, so crammed, as he thinks, with excellencies, that it is his grounds of faith that all that look on him love him; and on that vice in him will my revenge find notable cause to work.

SIR TOBY. What wilt thou do?

MARIA. I will drop in his way some obscure epistles of love; wherein, by the color of his beard, the shape of his leg, the manner of his gait, the expressure of his eye, forehead, and complexion, he shall find himself most feelingly personated. I can write very like my lady your niece: on a forgotten matter we can hardly make distinction of our hands.

SIR TOBY. Excellent! I smell a device.

SIR ANDREW. I have 't in my nose too.

SIR TOBY. He shall think, by the letters that thou wilt drop, that they come from my niece, and that she's in love with him.

MARIA. My purpose is, indeed, a horse of that color.

SIR ANDREW. And your horse now would make him an ass.

MARIA. Ass, I doubt not.

SIR ANDREW. O, 'twill be admirable!

MARIA. Sport royal, I warrant you: I know my physic will work with him. I will plant you two, and let the fool make a third, where he shall find the letter: observe his construction of it. For this night,

to bed, and dream on the event. Farewell.
[*Exit.*]

SIR TOBY. Good night, Penthesilea.

SIR ANDREW. Before me, she's a good
wench.

SIR TOBY. She's a beagle, true-bred, and
one that adores me: what o' that?

SIR ANDREW. I was adored once too.

SIR TOBY. Let's to bed, knight. Thou
hadst need send for more money.

SIR ANDREW. If I cannot recover your
niece, I am a foul way out.

SIR TOBY. Send for money, knight; if
thou hast her not i' the end, call me cut.

SIR ANDREW. If I do not, never trust
me, take it how you will.

SIR TOBY. Come, come, I'll go burn
some sack; 'tis too late to go to bed now:
come, knight; come, knight.
[*Exeunt.*]

4. *The* DUKE's *palace*

Enter DUKE, VIOLA, CURIO, *and others.*

DUKE. Give me some music. Now, good
morrow, friends,
Now, good Cesario, but that piece of
song,
That old and antique song we heard last
night:
Methought it did relieve my passion
much,
More than light airs and recollected
terms
Of these most brisk and giddy-paced
times:
Come, but one verse.

CURIO. He is not here, so please your
lordship, that should sing it.

DUKE. Who was it?

CURIO. Feste, the jester, my lord; a fool
that the lady Olivia's father took much
delight in.
He is about the house.

DUKE. Seek him out, and play the tune
the while.
[*Exit* CURIO. *Music plays.*]
Come hither, boy: if ever thou shalt love,
In the sweet pangs of it remember me;
For such as I am all true lovers are,

Unstaid and skittish in all motions else,
Save in the constant image of the creature
That is beloved. How dost thou like this
tune?

VIOLA. It gives a very echo to the seat
Where love is throned.

DUKE. Thou dost speak masterly:
My life upon 't, young though thou art,
thine eye
Hath stay'd upon some favor that it
loves:
Hath it not, boy?

VIOLA. A little, by your favor.

DUKE. What kind of woman is 't?

VIOLA. Of your complexion.

DUKE. She is not worth thee, then.
What years, i' faith?

VIOLA. About your years, my lord.

DUKE. Too old, by heaven: let still the
woman take
An elder than herself; so wears she to
him,
So sways she level in her husband's heart:
For, boy, however we do praise ourselves,
Our fancies are more giddy and unfirm,
More longing, wavering, sooner lost and
worn,
Than women's are.

VIOLA. I think it well, my lord.

DUKE. Then let thy love be younger
than thyself,
Or thy affection cannot hold the bent;
For women are as roses, whose fair
flower
Being once display'd, doth fall that very
hour.

VIOLA. And so they are: alas, that they
are so;
To die, even when they to perfection
grow!
[*Re-enter* CURIO *and* CLOWN.]

DUKE. O, fellow, come, the song we
had last night.
Mark it, Cesario, it is old and plain;
The spinsters and the knitters in the sun
And the free maids that weave their
thread with bones
Do use to chant it: it is silly sooth,
And dallies with the innocence of love,
Like the old age.

CLOWN. Are you ready, sir?

DUKE. Aye; prithee, sing.

SONG

CLOWN. Come away, come away, death,
And in sad cypress let me be laid;
Fly away, fly away, breath;
I am slain by a fair cruel maid.
My shroud of white, stuck all with yew,
O, prepare it!
My part of death, no one so true
Did share it.
Not a flower, not a flower sweet,
On my black coffin let there be strown;
Not a friend, not a friend greet
My poor corpse, where my bones shall
be thrown:
A thousand thousand sighs to save,
Lay me, O, where
Sad true lover never find my grave,
To weep there!

DUKE. There's for thy pains.

CLOWN. No pains, sir; I take pleasure
in singing, sir.

DUKE. I'll pay thy pleasure then.

CLOWN. Truly, sir, and pleasure will be
paid, one time or another.

DUKE. Give me now leave to leave thee.

CLOWN. Now, the melancholy god protect thee; and the tailor make thy doublet
of changeable taffeta, for thy mind is a
very opal. I would have men of such con-
stancy put to sea, that their business
might be every thing and their intent
every where; for that's it that always
makes a good voyage of nothing. Farewell. [Exit.]

DUKE. Let all the rest give place.
[CURIO and ATTENDANTS retire.]
Once more, Cesario,
Get thee to yond same sovereign cruelty:
Tell her, my love, more noble than the
world,
Prizes not quantity of dirty lands;
The parts that fortune hath bestow'd
upon her,
Tell her, I hold as giddily as fortune;
But 'tis that miracle and queen of gems
That nature pranks her in attracts my
soul.

VIOLA. But if she cannot love you, sir?

DUKE. I cannot be so answer'd.

VIOLA. Sooth, but you must.
Say that some lady, as perhaps there is,

Hath for your love as great a pang of
heart
As you have for Olivia: you cannot love
her;
You tell her so; must she not then be
answer'd?

DUKE. There is no woman's sides
Can bide the beating of so strong a pas-
sion
As love doth give my heart; no woman's
heart
So big, to hold so much; they lack re-
tention.
Alas, their love may be call'd appetite,—
No motion of the liver, but the palate,—
That suffer surfeit, cloyment and revolt;
But mine is all as hungry as the sea,
And can digest as much: make no com-
pare
Between that love a woman can bear me
And that I owe Olivia.

VIOLA. Aye, but I know,—

DUKE. What dost thou know?

VIOLA. Too well what love women to
men may owe:
In faith, they are as true of heart as we.
My father had a daughter loved a man,
As it might be, perhaps, were I a woman,
I should your lordship.

DUKE. And what's her history?

VIOLA. A blank, my lord. She never told
her love,
But let concealment, like a worm i' the
bud,
Feed on her damask cheek; she pined in
thought
And with a green and yellow melancholy
She sat like patience on a monument,
Smiling at grief. Was not this love in-
deed?
We men may say more, swear more: but
indeed
Our shows are more than will; for still
we prove
Much in our vows, but little in our love.

DUKE. But died thy sister of her love,
my boy?

VIOLA. I am all the daughters of my
father's house,
And all the brothers too: and yet I know
not.
Sir, shall I to this lady?

DUKE. Aye that's the theme.

To her in haste; give her this jewel; say,
My love can give no place, bide no delay.
[*Exeunt.*]

5. OLIVIA's *garden*

Enter SIR TOBY, SIR ANDREW, *and* FABIAN.

SIR TOBY. Come thy ways, Signior
Fabian.

FABIAN. Nay, I'll come: if I lose a
scruple of this sport, let me be boiled to
death with melancholy.

SIR TOBY. Wouldst thou not be glad to
have the niggardly rascally sheep-biter
come by some notable shame?

FABIAN. I would exult, man: you know,
he brought me out o' favor with my lady
about a bear-baiting here.

SIR TOBY. To anger him we'll have the
bear again and we will fool him black and
blue: shall we not, Sir Andrew?

SIR ANDREW. An we do not, it is pity of
our lives.

SIR TOBY. Here comes the little villain.
[*Enter* MARIA.]
How now, my metal of India!

MARIA. Get ye all three into the box-
tree: Malvolio's coming down this walk:
he has been yonder i' the sun practising
behavior to his own shadow this half
hour: observe him, for the love of mockery; for I know this letter will make a
contemplative idiot of him. Close, in the
name of jesting! Lie thou there [*Throws
down a letter.*] for here comes the trout
that must be caught with tickling. [*Exit.*]
[*Enter* MALVOLIO.]

MALVOLIO. 'Tis but fortune; all is fortune. Maria once told me she did affect me: and I have heard herself come
thus near, that, should she fancy, it
should be one of my complexion. Besides,
she uses me with a more exalted respect
than any one else that follows her. What
should I think on 't?

SIR TOBY. Here's an overweening rogue!

FABIAN. O, peace! Contemplation makes
a rare turkey-cock of him: how he jets
under his advanced plumes!

SIR ANDREW. 'Slight, I could so beat the
rogue!

SIR TOBY. Peace, I say.

MALVOLIO. To be Count Malvolio!

SIR TOBY. Ah, rogue!

SIR ANDREW. Pistol him, pistol him.

SIR TOBY. Peace, peace!

MALVOLIO. There is example for 't; the
lady of the Strachy married the yeoman
of the wardrobe.

SIR ANDREW. Fie on him, Jezebel!

FABIAN. O, peace! now he's deeply in:
look how imagination blows him.

MALVOLIO. Having been three months
married to her, sitting in my state,—

SIR TOBY. O, for a stone-bow, to hit
him in the eye!

MALVOLIO. Calling my officers about
me, in my branched velvet gown; having
come from a day-bed, where I have left
Olivia sleeping,—

SIR TOBY. Fire and brimstone!

FABIAN. O, peace, peace!

MALVOLIO. And then to have the humor
of state; and after a demure travel of regard, telling them I know my place as I
would they should do theirs, to ask for
my kinsman Toby,—

SIR TOBY. Bolts and shackles!

FABIAN. O, peace, peace, peace! now,
now.

MALVOLIO. Seven of my people, with an
obedient start, make out for him: I frown
the while; and perchance wind up my
watch, or play with my—some rich jewel.
Toby approaches; courtesies there to
me,—

SIR TOBY. Shall this fellow live?

FABIAN. Though our silence be drawn
from us with cars, yet peace.

MALVOLIO. I extend my hand to him
thus, quenching my familiar smile with
an austere regard of control,—

SIR TOBY. And does not Toby take you
a blow o' the lips then.

MALVOLIO. Saying, 'Cousin Toby, my
fortunes having cast me on your niece
give me this prerogative of speech,'—

SIR TOBY. What, what?

MALVOLIO. 'You must amend your
drunkenness.'

SIR TOBY. Out, scab!

FABIAN. Nay, patience, or we break the
sinews of our plot.

MALVOLIO. 'Besides, you waste the treasure of your time with a foolish knight,'—

SIR ANDREW. That's me, I warrant you.

MALVOLIO. 'One Sir Andrew,'—

SIR ANDREW. I knew 'twas I; for many do call me fool.

MALVOLIO. What employment have we here? [*Taking up the letter.*]

FABIAN. Now is the woodcock near the gin.

SIR TOBY. O, peace! and the spirit of humors intimate reading aloud to him.

MALVOLIO. By my life, this is my lady's hand: these be her very C's, her U's, and her T's; and thus makes she her great P's. It is, in contempt of question, her hand.

SIR ANDREW. Her C's, her U's and her T's: why that?

MALVOLIO. [*Reads.*] To the unknown beloved, this, and my good wishes:—her very phrases! By your leave, wax. Soft! and the impressure her Lucrece, with which she uses to seal: 'tis my lady. To whom should this be?

FABIAN. This wins, him, liver and all.

MALVOLIO. [*Reads.*]
Jove knows I love:
But who?
Lips, do not move;
No man must know.

'No man must know.' What follows? the numbers altered! 'No man must know:' if this should be thee, Malvolio?

SIR TOBY. Marry, hang thee, brock!

MALVOLIO. [*Reads.*]
I may command where I adore;
But silence, like a Lucrece knife,
With bloodless stroke my heart doth gore:
M, O, A, I, doth sway my life.

FABIAN. A fustian riddle!

SIR TOBY. Excellent wench, say I.

MALVOLIO. 'M, O, A, I, doth sway my life.' Nay, but first, let me see, let me see, let me see.

FABIAN. What dish o' poison has she dressed him!

SIR TOBY. And with what wing the staniel checks at it!

MALVOLIO. 'I may command where I adore.' Why, she may command me: I serve her; she is my lady. Why, this is evident to any formal capacity; there is no obstruction in this: and the end,— what should that alphabetical position portend? If I could make that resemble something in me,— Softly! M, O, A, I,—

SIR TOBY. O, aye, make up that: he is now at a cold scant.

FABIAN. Sowter will cry upon 't for all this, though it be as rank as a fox.

MALVOLIO. M,—Malvolio; M,—why, that begins my name.

FABIAN. Did not I say he would work it out? the cur is excellent at faults.

MALVOLIO. M,—but then there is no consonancy in the sequel; that suffers under probation: A should follow, but O does.

FABIAN. And O shall end, I hope.

SIR TOBY. Aye, or I'll cudgel him, and make him cry O!

MALVOLIO. And then I comes behind.

FABIAN. Aye, an you had any eye behind you, you might see more detraction at your heels than fortunes before you.

MALVOLIO. M, O, A, I; this simulation is not as the former: and yet, to crush this a little, it would bow to me, for every one of these letters are in my name. Soft! here follows prose. [*Reads.*] If this fall into thy hand, revolve. In my stars I am above thee; but be not afraid of greatness: some are born great, some achieve greatness, and some have greatness thrust upon 'em. Thy Fates open their hands; let thy blood and spirit embrace them; and, to inure thyself to what thou art like to be, cast thy humble slough and appear fresh. Be opposite with a kinsman, surly with servants; let thy tongue tang arguments of state; put thyself into the trick of singularity: she thus advises thee that sighs for thee. Remember who commended thy yellow stockings, and wished to see thee ever crossed-gartered: I say, remember. Go to, thou art made, if thou desirest to be so; if not, let me see thee a steward still, the fellow of servants, and not worthy to touch Fortune's fingers. Farewell. She that would alter services with thee,

THE FORTUNATE-UNHAPPY.

Daylight and champain discovers not more; this is open. I will be proud, I will read politic authors, I will baffle Sir Toby, I will wash off gross acquaintance, I will be point-devise the very man. I do not now fool myself, to let imagination jade me; for every reason excites to this, that my lady loves me. She did commend my yellow stockings of late, she did praise my leg being cross-gartered; and in this she manifests herself to my love, and with a kind of injunction drives me to these habits of her liking. I thank my stars I am happy. I will be strange, stout, in yellow stockings, and cross-gartered, even with the swiftness of putting on. Jove and my stars be praised! Here is yet a post-script. [*Reads.*] Thou canst not choose but know who I am. If thou entertainest my love, let it appear in thy smiling; thy smiles become thee well; therefore in my presence still smile, dear my sweet, I prithee.

Jove, I thank thee: I will smile; I will do everything that thou wilt have me. [*Exit.*]

FABIAN. I will not give my part of this sport for a pension of thousands to be paid from the Sophy.

SIR TOBY. I could marry this wench for this device,—

SIR ANDREW. So could I too.

SIR TOBY. And ask no other dowry with her but such another jest.

SIR ANDREW. Nor I neither.

FABIAN. Here comes my noble gull-catcher.

[*Re-enter* MARIA.]

SIR TOBY. Wilt thou set thy foot o' my neck?

SIR ANDREW. Or o' mine either?

SIR TOBY. Shall I play my freedom at tray-trip, and become thy bond-slave?

SIR ANDREW. I' faith, or I either?

SIR TOBY. Why, thou hast put him in such a dream, that when the image of it leaves him he must run mad.

MARIA. Nay, but say true; does it work upon him?

SIR TOBY. Like aqua-vitæ with a midwife.

MARIA. If you will then see the fruits of the sport, mark his first approach before my lady: he will come to her in yellow stockings, and 'tis a color she abhors, and cross-gartered, a fashion she detests; and he will smile upon her, which will now be so unsuitable to her disposition, being addicted to a melancholy as she is, that cannot but turn him into a notable contempt. If you will see it, follow me.

SIR TOBY. To the gates of Tartar, thou most excellent devil of wit!

SIR ANDREW. I'll make one too.

[*Exeunt.*]

ACT THREE

1. OLIVIA's *garden*

Enter VIOLA, *and* CLOWN *with a tabor.*

VIOLA. Save thee, friend, and thy music: dost thou live by thy tabor?

CLOWN. No, sir, I live by the church.

VIOLA. Art thou a churchman?

CLOWN. No such matter, sir: I do live by the church; for I do live at my house, and my house doth stand by the church.

VIOLA. So thou mayst say, the king lies by a beggar, if a beggar dwell near him; or, the church stands by thy tabor, if thy tabor stand by the church.

CLOWN. You have said, sir. To see this age! A sentence is but a cheveril glove to a good wit: how quickly the wrong side may be turned outward!

VIOLA. Nay, that's certain; they that

dally nicely with words may quickly make them wanton.

CLOWN. I would, therefore, my sister had had no name, sir.

VIOLA. Why, man?

CLOWN. Why, sir, her name's a word; and to dally with that word might make my sister wanton. But indeed words are very rascals since bonds disgraced them.

VIOLA. Thy reason, man?

CLOWN. Troth, sir, I can yield you none without words; and words are grown so false, I am loath to prove reason with them.

VIOLA. I warrant thou art a merry fellow and carest for nothing.

CLOWN. Not so, sir, I do care for something; but in my conscience, sir, I do not care for you: if that be to care for nothing, sir, I would it would make you invisible.

VIOLA. Art not thou the Lady Olivia's fool?

CLOWN. No, indeed, sir! the Lady Olivia has no folly: she will keep no fool, sir, till she be married; and fools are as like husbands as pilchards are to herrings; the husband's the bigger: I am indeed not her fool, but her corrupter of words.

VIOLA. I saw thee late at the Count Orsino's.

CLOWN. Foolery, sir, does walk about the orb like the sun, it shines every where. I would be sorry, sir, but the fool should be as oft with your master as with my mistress: I think I saw your wisdom there.

VIOLA. Nay, an thou pass upon me, I'll no more with thee. Hold, there's expenses for thee.

CLOWN. Now Jove, in his next commodity of hair, send thee a beard!

VIOLA. By my troth, I'll tell thee, I am almost sick for one; [*Aside.*] though I would not have it grow on my chin. Is thy lady within?

CLOWN. Would not a pair of these have bred, sir?

VIOLA. Yes, being kept together and put to use.

CLOWN. I would play Lord Pandarus of Phrygia, sir, to bring a Cressida to this Troilus.

VIOLA. I understand you, sir; 'tis well begged.

CLOWN. The matter, I hope, is not great, sir, begging but a beggar: Cressida was a beggar. My lady is within, sir. I will construe to them whence you come; who you are and what you would are out of my welkin, I might say 'element,' but the word is overworn. [*Exit.*]

VIOLA. This fellow is wise enough to play the fool;

And to do that well craves a kind of wit:

He must observe their mood on whom he jests,

The quality of persons, and the time,

And, like the haggard, check at every feather

That comes before his eye. This is a practice

As full of labor as a wise man's art:

For folly that he wisely shows is fit;

But wise men, folly-fall'n, quite taint their wit.

[*Enter* SIR TOBY, *and* SIR ANDREW.]

SIR TOBY. Save you, gentleman.

VIOLA. And you, sir.

SIR ANDREW. Dieu vous garde, monsieur.

VIOLA. Et vous aussi; votre serviteur.

SIR ANDREW. I hope, sir, you are; and I am yours.

SIR TOBY. Will you encounter the house? my niece is desirous you should enter, if your trade be to her.

VIOLA. I am bound to your niece, sir; I mean, she is the list of my voyage.

SIR TOBY. Taste your legs, sir; put them to motion.

VIOLA. My legs do better understand me, sir, than I understand what you mean by bidding me taste my legs.

SIR TOBY. I mean, to go, sir, to enter.

VIOLA. I will answer you with gait and entrance. But we are prevented.

[*Enter* OLIVIA *and* MARIA.]

Most excellent accomplished lady, the heavens rain odors on you!

SIR ANDREW. That youth's a rare courtier: 'Rain odors;' well.

VIOLA. My matter hath no voice, lady, but to your own most pregnant and vouchsafed ear.

SIR ANDREW. 'Odors,' 'pregnant,' and 'vouchsafed:' I'll get 'em all three all ready.

OLIVIA. Let the garden door be shut, and leave me to my hearing. [*Exeunt* SIR TOBY, SIR ANDREW, *and* MARIA.] Give me your hand, sir.

VIOLA. My duty, madam, and most humble service.

OLIVIA. What is your name?

VIOLA. Cesario is your servant's name, fair princess.

OLIVIA. My servant, sir! 'Twas never merry world

Since lowly feigning was call'd compliment:

You're servant to the Count Orsino, youth.

VIOLA. And he is yours, and his must needs be yours:

Your servant's servant is your servant, madam.

OLIVIA. For him, I think not on him: for his thoughts,
Would they were blanks, rather than fill'd with me!

VIOLA. Madam, I come to whet your gentle thoughts
On his behalf.

OLIVIA. O, by your leave, I pray you;
I bade you never speak again of him:
But would you undertake another suit,
I had rather hear you to solicit that
Than music from the spheres.

VIOLA. Dear lady,—

OLIVIA. Give me leave, beseech you. I did send,
After the last enchantment you did here,
A ring in chase of you: so did I abuse
Myself, my servant and, I fear me you:
Under your hard construction must I sit,
To force that on you, in a shameful cunning,
Which you knew none of yours: what might you think?
Have you not set mine honor at the stake
And baited it with all the unmuzzled thoughts
That tyrannous heart can think? To one of your receiving
Enough is shown; a cypress, not a bosom,
Hides my heart. So, let me hear you speak.

VIOLA. I pity you.

OLIVIA. That's a degree to love.

VIOLA. No, not a grize; for 'tis a vulgar proof,
That very oft we pity enemies.

OLIVIA. Why, then, methinks 'tis time to smile again.
O world, how apt the poor are to be proud!
If one should be a prey, how much the better
To fall before the lion than the wolf!
[Clock strikes.]
The clock upbraids me with the waste of time.
Be not afraid, good youth, I will not have you:
And yet, when wit and youth is come to harvest,
Your wife is like to reap a proper man;
There lies your way, due west.

VIOLA. Then westward-ho!
Grace and good disposition attend your ladyship!
You'll nothing, madam, to my lord by me?

OLIVIA. Stay:
I prithee, tell me what thou think'st of me.

VIOLA. That you do think you are not what you are.

OLIVIA. If I think so, I think the same of you.

VIOLA. Then think you right: I am not what I am.

OLIVIA. I would you were as I would have you be!

VIOLA. Would it be better, madam, than I am?
I wish it might, for now I am your fool.

OLIVIA. O, what a deal of scorn looks beautiful
In the contempt and anger of his lip!
A murderous guilt shows not itself more soon
Than love that would seem hid: love's night is noon.
Cesario, by the roses of the spring,
By maidhood, honor, truth and every thing,
I love thee so, that, mauger all thy pride,
Nor wit nor reason can my passion hide.
Do not extort thy reasons from this clause,
For that I woo, thou therefore hast no cause;
But rather reason thus with reason fetter,
Love sought is good, but given unsought is better.

VIOLA. By innocence I swear, and by my youth,
I have one heart, one bosom and one truth,
And that no woman has; nor never none
Shall mistress be of it, save I alone.
And so adieu, good madam: never more
Will I my master's tears to you deplore.

OLIVIA. Yet come again; for thou perhaps mayst move
That heart, which now abhors, to like his love.

[Exeunt.]

2. OLIVIA's *house*

Enter SIR TOBY, SIR ANDREW, *and* FABIAN.

SIR ANDREW. No, faith, I'll not stay a jot longer.

SIR TOBY. Thy reason, dear venom, give thy reason.

FABIAN. You must needs yield your reason, Sir Andrew.

SIR ANDREW. Marry, I saw your niece do more favors to the count's serving-man than ever she bestowed upon me; I saw 't i' the orchard.

SIR TOBY. Did she see thee the while, old boy? tell me that.

SIR ANDREW. As plain as I see you now.

FABIAN. This was a great argument of love in her toward you.

SIR ANDREW. 'Slight, will you make an ass o' me?

FABIAN. I will prove it legitimate, sir, upon the oaths of judgment and reason.

SIR TOBY. And they have been grand-jurymen since before Noah was a sailor.

FABIAN. She did show favor to the youth in your sight only to exasperate you, to awake your dormouse valor, to put fire in your heart, and brimstone in your liver. You should then have accosted her; and with some excellent jests, fire-new from the mint, you should have banged the youth into dumbness. This was looked for at your hand, and this was balked: the double gilt of this opportunity you let time wash off, and you are now sailed into the north of my lady's opinion; where you will hang like an icicle on a Dutchman's beard, unless you do redeem it by some laudable attempt either of valor or policy.

SIR ANDREW. An 't be any way, it must be with valor; for policy I hate: I had as lief be a Brownist as a politician.

SIR TOBY. Why, then, build me thy fortunes upon the basis of valor. Challenge me the count's youth to fight with him; hurt him in eleven places: my niece shall take note of it; and assure thyself, there is no love-broker in the world can more prevail in man's commendation with woman than report of valor.

FABIAN. There is no way but this, Sir Andrew.

SIR ANDREW. Will either of you bear me a challenge to him?

SIR TOBY. Go, write it in a martial hand; be curst and brief; it is no matter how witty, so it be eloquent and full of invention: taunt him with the license of ink: if thou thou'st him some thrice, it shall not be amiss; and as many lies as will lie in thy sheet of paper, although the sheet were big enough for the bed of Ware in England, set 'em down: go, about it. Let there be gall enough in thy ink, though thou write with a goose-pen, no matter: about it.

SIR ANDREW. Where shall I find you?

SIR TOBY. We'll call thee at the cubiculo: go [*Exit* SIR ANDREW.]

FABIAN. This is a dear manakin to you, Sir Toby.

SIR TOBY. I have been dear to him, lad, some two thousand strong, or so.

FABIAN. We shall have a rare letter from him: but you'll not deliver 't?

SIR TOBY. Never trust me, then; and by all means stir on the youth to an answer. I think oxen and wainropes cannot hale them together. For Andrew, if he were opened, and you find so much blood in his liver as will clog the foot of a flea, I'll eat the rest of the anatomy.

FABIAN. And his opposite, the youth, bears in his visage no great presage of cruelty.

[*Enter* MARIA.]

SIR TOBY. Look, where the youngest wren of nine comes.

MARIA. If you desire the spleen, and will laugh yourselves into stitches, follow me. Yond gull Malvolio is turned heathen, a very renegado; for there is no Christian, that means to be saved by believing rightly, can ever believe such impossible passages of grossness. He's in yellow stockings.

SIR TOBY. And cross-gartered?

MARIA. Most villianously; like a pedant that keeps a school i' the church. I have dogged him, like his murderer. He does obey every point of the letter that I dropped to betray him: he does smile his face into more lines than is in the new map with the augmentation of the Indies: you have not seen such thing as 'tis. I can hardly forbear hurling things at him. I know my lady will strike him: if she do, he'll smile and take 't for a great favor.

SIR TOBY. Come, bring us, bring us where he is.

[*Exeunt.*]

3. *A street*

Enter SEBASTIAN *and* ANTONIO.

SEBASTIAN. I would not by my will have troubled you;
But, since you make your pleasure of your pains,
I will no further chide you.

ANTONIO. I could not stay behind you; my desire,
More sharp than filed steel, did spur me forth;
And not all love to see you, though so much
As might have drawn one to a longer voyage,
But jealousy what might befall your travel,
Being skilless in these parts; which to a stranger,
Unguided and unfriended, often prove
Rough and unhospitable: my willing love
The rather by these arguments of fear,
Set forth in your pursuit.

SEBASTIAN. My kind Antonio,
I can no other answer make but thanks,
And thanks; and ever thanks; and oft good turns
Are shuffled off with such uncurrent pay:
But, were my worth as is my conscience firm,
You should find better dealing. What's to do?
Shall we go see the reliques of this town?

ANTONIO. To-morow, sir: best first go see your lodging.

SEBASTIAN. I am not weary, and 'tis long to night:
I pray you, let us satisfy our eyes
With the memorials and the things of fame
That do renown this city.

ANTONIO. Would you'ld pardon me;

I do not without danger walk these streets:
Once, in a sea-fight, 'gainst the count his galleys
I did some service; of such note indeed,
That were I ta'en here it would scarce be answer'd.

SEBASTIAN. Belike you slew great number of his people.

ANTONIO. The offense is not of such a bloody nature;
Albeit the quality of the time and quarrel
Might well have given us bloody argument.
It might have since been answer'd in repaying
What we took from them; which, for traffic's sake,
Most of our city did: only myself stood out;
For which, if I be lapsed in this place,
I shall pay dear.

SEBASTIAN. Do not then walk too open.

ANTONIO. It doth not fit me. Hold, sir, here's my purse.
In the south suburbs, at the Elephant,
Is best to lodge: I will bespeak our diet,
Whiles you beguile the time and feed your knowledge
With viewing of the town: there shall you have me.

SEBASTIAN. Why I your purse?

ANTONIO. Haply your eye shall light upon some toy
You have desire to purchase; and your store,
I think, is not for idle markets, sir.

SEBASTIAN. I'll be your purse-bearer and leave you
For an hour.

ANTONIO. To the Elephant.

SEBASTIAN. I do remember.

[*Exeunt.*]

4. OLIVIA'S *garden*

Enter OLIVIA *and* MARIA.

OLIVIA. I have sent after him: he says he'll come;
How shall I feast him? what bestow of him?

For youth is bought more oft than begg'd
    or borrow'd.
I speak too loud.
Where is Malvolio? he is sad and civil,
And suits well for a servant with my for-
    tunes:
Where is Malvolio?
    MARIA. He's coming, madam; but in
very strange manner. He is, sure, pos-
sessed, madam.
    OLIVIA. Why, what's the matter? does
he rave?
    MARIA. No, madam, he does nothing
but smile: your ladyship were best to
have some guard about you, if he come;
for, sure, the man is tainted in 's wits.
    OLIVIA. Go call him hither. [*Exit* MA-
RIA.] I am as mad as he,
If sad and merry madness equal be.
    [*Re-enter* MARIA, *with* MALVOLIO.]
How now, Malvolio!
    MALVOLIO. Sweet lady, ho, ho.
    OLIVIA. Smilest thou?
I sent for thee upon a sad occasion.
    MALVOLIO. Sad, lady? I could be sad:
this does make some obstruction in the
blood, this cross-gartering; but what of
that? if it please the eye of one, it is with
me as the very true sonnet is, 'Please one,
and please all.'
    OLIVIA. Why, how dost thou, man?
what is the matter with thee?
    MALVOLIO. Not black in my mind,
though yellow in my legs. It did come to
his hands, and commands shall be exe-
cuted: I think we do know the sweet Roman hand.
    OLIVIA. Wilt thou go to bed, Malvolio?
    MALVOLIO. To bed! aye, sweet-heart,
and I'll come to thee.
    OLIVIA. God comfort thee! Why dost
thou smile so and kiss thy hand so oft?
    MARIA. How do you, Malvolio?
    MALVOLIO. At your request! yes; night-
ingales answer daws.
    MARIA. Why appear you with this ri-
diculous boldness before my lady?
    MALVOLIO. 'Be not afraid of greatness:'
'twas well writ.
    OLIVIA. What meanest thou by that,
Malvolio?
    MALVOLIO. 'Some are born great,'—
    OLIVIA. Ha!
    MALVOLIO. 'Some achieve greatness,'—

    OLIVIA. What sayest thou?
    MALVOLIO. 'And some have greatness
thrust upon them.'
    OLIVIA. Heaven restore thee!
    MALVOLIO. 'Remember who com-
mended thy yellow stockings,'—
    OLIVIA. Thy yellow stockings!
    MALVOLIO. 'And wished to see thee
cross-gartered.'
    OLIVIA. Cross-gartered!
    MALVOLIO. 'Go to, thou art made, if
thou desirest to be so;'—
    OLIVIA. Am I made?
    MALVOLIO. 'If not, let me see thee a
servant still.'
    OLIVIA. Why, this is very midsummer
madness.
            [*Enter* SERVANT.]
    SERVANT. Madam, the young gentleman
of the Count Orsino's is returned: I could
hardly entreat him back: he attends your
ladyship's pleasure.
    OLIVIA. I'll come to him. [*Exit* SERVANT.]
Good Maria, let this fellow be looked to.
Where's my cousin Toby? Let some of
my people have a special care of him: I
would not have him miscarry for the half
of my dowry. [*Exeunt* OLIVIA *and* MARIA.]
    MALVOLIO. O, ho! do you come near me
now? no worse man than Sir Toby to
look to me! This concurs directly with
the letter: she sends him on purpose, that
I may appear stubborn to him; for she in-
cites me to that in the letter. 'Cast thy
humble slough,' says she; 'be opposite
with a kinsman, surly with servants; let
thy tongue tang with arguments of state;
put thyself into the trick of singularity;'
and consequently sets down the manner
how; as, a sad face, a reverend carriage, a
slow tongue, in the habit of some sir of
note, and so forth. I have limed her; but
it is Jove's doing, and Jove make me
thankful! And when she went away now,
'Let this fellow be looked to:' fellow!
not Malvolio, nor after my degree, but
fellow. Why, every thing adheres together, that no dram of a scruple, no
scruple of a scruple, no obstacle, no incredulous or unsafe circumstance—What
can be said? Nothing that can be can
come between me and the full prospect
of my hopes. Well, Jove, not I, is the
doer of this, and he is to be thanked.

[*Re-enter* MARIA,
with SIR TOBY *and* FABIAN.]

SIR TOBY. Which way is he, in the name of sanctity? If all the devils of hell be drawn in little, and Legion himself possessed him, yet I'll speak to him.

FABIAN. Here he is, here he is. How is 't with you, sir? how is 't with you, man?

MALVOLIO. Go off; I discard you: let me enjoy my private: go off.

MARIA. Lo, how hollow the fiend speaks within him! did not I tell you? Sir Toby, my lady prays you to have a care of him.

MALVOLIO. Ah, ha! does she so?

SIR TOBY. Go to, go to; peace, peace; we must deal gently with him; let me alone. How do you, Malvolio? how is 't with you? What, man! defy the devil: consider, he's an enemy to mankind.

MALVOLIO. Do you know what you say?

MARIA. La you, an you speak ill of the devil, how he takes it at heart! Pray God, he be not bewitched!

FABIAN. Carry his water to the wise woman.

MARIA. Marry, and it shall be done tomorrow morning, if I live. My lady would not lose him for more than I'll say.

MALVOLIO. How now, mistress!

MARIA. O Lord!

SIR TOBY. Prithee, hold thy peace; this is not the way: do you not see you move him? let me alone with him.

FABIAN. No way but gentleness; gently, gently: the fiend is rough, and will not be roughly used.

SIR TOBY. Why, how now, my bawcock! how dost thou, chuck?

MALVOLIO. Sir!

SIR TOBY. Aye, Biddy, come with me. What, man! 'tis not for gravity to play at cherrypit with Satan: hang him, foul collier!

MARIA. Get him to say his prayers, good Sir Toby, get him to pray.

MALVOLIO. My prayers, minx!

MARIA. No, I warrant you, he will not hear of godliness.

MALVOLIO. Go, hang yourselves all! you are idle shallow things: I am not of your element: you shall know more hereafter. [*Exit.*]

SIR TOBY. Is 't possible?

FABIAN. If this were played upon a stage now, I could condemn it as an improbable fiction.

SIR TOBY. His very genius hath taken the infection of the device, man.

MARIA. Nay, pursue him now, lest the device take air and taint.

FABIAN. Why, we shall make him mad indeed.

MARIA. The house will be the quieter.

SIR TOBY. Come, we'll have him in a dark room and bound. My niece is already in the belief that he's mad: we may carry it thus, for our pleasure and his penance, till our very pastime, tired out of breath, prompt us to have mercy on him: at which time we will bring the device to the bar and crown thee for a finder of madmen. But see, but see.

[*Enter* SIR ANDREW.]

FABIAN. More matter for a May morning.

SIR ANDREW. Here's the challenge, read it: I warrant there's vinegar and pepper in 't.

FABIAN. Is 't so saucy?

SIR ANDREW. Aye, is 't, I warrant him: do but read.

SIR TOBY. Give me. [*Reads.*] Youth, whatsoever thou art, thou art but a scurvy fellow.

FABIAN. Good, and valiant.

SIR TOBY. [*Reads.*] Wonder not, nor admire not in thy mind, why I do call thee so, for I will show thee no reason for 't.

FABIAN. A good note; that keeps you from the blow of the law.

SIR TOBY. [*Reads.*] Thou comest to the lady Olivia, and in my sight she uses thee kindly: but thou liest in thy throat; that is not the matter I challenge thee for.

FABIAN. Very brief, and to exceeding good sense—less.

SIR TOBY. [*Reads.*] I will waylay thee going home; where if it be thy chance to kill me,—

FABIAN. Good.

SIR TOBY. [*Reads.*] Thou killest me like a rogue and a villain.

FABIAN. Still you keep o' the windy side of the law: good.

SIR TOBY. [*Reads.*] Fare thee well; and God have mercy upon one of our souls! He may have mercy upon mine; but my hope is better, and so look to thyself. Thy friend, as thou usest him, and thy sworn enemy, ANDREW AGUECHEEK. If this letter move him not, his legs cannot: I'll give 't him.

MARIA. You may have very fit occasion for 't: he is now in some commerce with my lady, and will by and by depart.

SIR TOBY. Go, Sir Andrew; scout me for him at the corner of the orchard like a bum-baily: so soon as ever thou seest him, draw; and, as thou drawest, swear horrible; for it comes to pass oft that a terrible oath, with a swaggering accent sharply twanged off, gives manhood more approbation than ever proof itself would have earned him. Away!

SIR ANDREW. Nay, let me alone for swearing. [Exit.]

SIR TOBY. Now will not I deliver his letter: for the behavior of the young gentleman gives him out to be of good capacity and breeding; his employment between his lord and my niece confirms no less: therefore this letter, being so excellently ignorant, will breed no terror in the youth: he will find it comes from a clodpole. But, sir, I will deliver his challenge by word of mouth; set upon Aguecheek a notable report of valor; and drive the gentleman, as I know his youth will aptly receive it, into a most hideous opinion of his rage, skill, fury and impetuosity. This will so fright them both, that they will kill one another by the look, like cockatrices.

[Re-enter OLIVIA, with VIOLA.]

FABIAN. Here he comes with your niece: give them way till he take leave, and presently after him.

SIR TOBY. I will meditate the while upon some horrid message for a challenge. [Exeunt SIR TOBY, FABIAN, and MARIA.]

OLIVIA. I have said too much unto a heart of stone,
And laid mine honor too unchary out:
There's something in me that reproves my fault;
But such a headstrong potent fault it is,
That it but mocks reproof.

VIOLA. With the same 'havior that your passion bears
Goes on my master's grief.

OLIVIA. Here, wear this jewel for me, 'tis my picture;

Refuse it not; it hath no tongue to vex you;
And I beseech you come again to-morrow.
What shall you ask of me that I'll deny,
That honor saved may upon asking give?

VIOLA. Nothing but this;—your true love for my master.

OLIVIA. How with mine honor may I give him that
Which I have given to you?

VIOLA. I will acquit you.

OLIVIA. Well, come again to-morrow: fare thee well:
A fiend like thee might bear my soul to hell. [Exit.]

[Re-enter SIR TOBY and FABIAN.]

SIR TOBY. Gentleman, God save thee.

VIOLA. And you, sir.

SIR TOBY. That defense thou hast, betake thee to 't: of what nature the wrongs are thou hast done him, I know not; but thy intercepter, full of despite, bloody as the hunter, attends thee at the orchardend: dismount thy tuck, be yare in thy preparation, for thy assailant is quick, skillful and deadly.

VIOLA. You mistake, sir; I am sure no man hath any quarrel to me: my remembrance is very free and clear from any image of offense done to any man.

SIR TOBY. You'll find it otherwise, I assure you: therefore, if you hold your life at any price, betake you to your guard; for your opposite hath in him what youth, strength, skill and wrath can furnish man withal.

VIOLA. I pray you, sir, what is he?

SIR TOBY. He is knight, dubbed with unhatched rapier and on carpet consideration; but he is a devil in private brawl: souls and bodies hath he divorced three; and his incensement at this moment is so implacable, that satisfaction can be none but by pangs of deaths and sepulcher. Hob, nob, is his word; give 't or take 't.

VIOLA. I will return again into the house and desire some conduct of the lady. I am no fighter. I have heard of some kind of men that put quarrels purposely on others, to taste their valor: belike this is a man of that quirk.

SIR TOBY. Sir, no; his indignation derives itself out of a very competent injury:

therefore, get you on and give him his desire. Back you shall not to the house, unless you undertake that with me which with as much safety you might answer him: therefore, on, or strip your sword stark naked; for meddle you must, that's certain, or forswear to wear iron about you.

VIOLA. This is as uncivil as strange. I beseech you, do me this courteous office, as to know of the knight what my offense to him is: it is something of my negligence, nothing of my purpose.

SIR TOBY. I will do so. Signior Fabian, stay you by this gentleman till my return. [*Exit.*]

VIOLA. Pray you, sir, do you know of this matter?

FABIAN. I know the knight is incensed against you, even to a mortal arbitrement; but nothing of the circumstance more.

VIOLA. I beseech you, what manner of man is he?

FABIAN. Nothing of that wonderful promise, to read him by his form, as you are like to find him in the proof of his valor. He is, indeed, sir, the most skillful, bloody and fatal opposite that you could possibly have found in any part of Illyria. Will you walk towards him? I will make your peace with him if I can.

VIOLA. I shall be much bound to you for't: I am one that had rather go with sir priest than sir knight: I care not who knows so much of my mettle. [*Exeunt.*]

[*Re-enter* SIR TOBY, *with* SIR ANDREW.]

SIR TOBY. Why, man, he's a very devil; I have not seen such a firago. I had a pass with him, rapier, scabbard and all, and he gives me the stuck in with such a mortal motion, that it is inevitable; and on the answer, he pays you as surely as your feet hit the ground they step on. They say he has been fencer to the Sophy.

SIR ANDREW. Pox on't, I'll not meddle with him.

SIR TOBY. Aye, but he will not now be pacified: Fabian can scarce hold him yonder.

SIR ANDREW. Plague on 't, an I thought he had been valiant and so cunning in fence I'ld have seen him damned ere I'ld have challenged him. Let him let the matter slip, and I'll give him my horse, gray Capilet.

SIR TOBY. I'll make the motion: stand here, make a good show on't: this shall end without the perdition of souls. [*Aside.*] Marry, I'll ride your horse as well as I ride you.

[*Re-enter* FABIAN *and* VIOLA.]

[*To* FABIAN.] I have his horse to take up the quarrel: I have persuaded him the youth's a devil.

FABIAN. He is as horribly conceited of him; and pants and looks pale, as if a bear were at his heels.

SIR TOBY. [*To* VIOLA.] There's no remedy, sir; he will fight with you for's oath sake: marry, he hath better bethought him of his quarrel, and he finds that now scarce to be worth talking of: therefore draw, for the supportance of his vow; he protests he will not hurt you.

VIOLA. [*Aside.*] Pray God defend me! A little thing would make me tell them how much I lack of a man.

FABIAN. Give ground, if you see him furious.

SIR TOBY. Come, Sir Andrew, there's no remedy; the gentleman will, for his honor's sake, have one bout with you; he cannot by the duello avoid it: but he has promised me, as he is a gentleman and a soldier, he will not hurt you. Come on; to 't.

SIR ANDREW. Pray God, he keep his oath!

VIOLA. I do assure you, 'tis against my will. [*They draw.*]

[*Enter* ANTONIO.]

ANTONIO. Put up your sword. If this young gentleman
Have done offense, I take the fault on me:
If you offend him, I for him defy you.

SIR TOBY. You, sir! why, what are you?

ANTONIO. One, sir, that for his love dares yet do more
Than you have heard him brag to you he will.

SIR TOBY. Nay, if you be an undertaker, I am for you. [*They draw.*]

[*Enter* OFFICERS.]

FABIAN. O good Sir Toby, hold! here come the officers.

SIR TOBY. I'll be with you anon.

VIOLA. Pray, sir, put your sword up, if you please.

SIR ANDREW. Marry, will I, sir; and, for that I promised you, I'll be as good as my word: he will bear you easily and reins well.

FIRST OFFICER. This is the man; do thy office.

SECOND OFFICER. Antonio, I arrest thee at the suit of Count Orsino.

ANTONIO. You do mistake me, sir.

FIRST OFFICER. No, sir, no jot; I know your favor well,
Though now you have no sea-cap on your head.
Take him away: he knows I know him well.

ANTONIO. I must obey. [*To* VIOLA.] This comes with seeking you:
But there's no remedy; I shall answer it.
What will you do, now my necessity
Makes me to ask you for my purse? It grieves me
Much more for what I cannot do for you
Than what befalls myself. You stand amazed;
But be of comfort.

SECOND OFFICER. Come, sir, away.

ANTONIO. I must entreat of you some of that money.

VIOLA. What money, sir?
For the fair kindness you have show'd me here,
And, part, being prompted by your present trouble,
Out of my lean and low ability
I'll lend you something: my having is not much;
I'll make division of my present with you:
Hold, there's half my coffer.

ANTONIO. Will you deny me now?
Is 't possible that my deserts to you
Can lack persuasion? Do not tempt my misery,
Lest that it make me so unsound a man
As to upbraid you with those kindnesses
That I have done for you.

VIOLA. I know of none;
Nor know I you by voice or any feature:
I hate ingratitude more in a man

Than lying vainness, babbling drunkenness,
Or any taint of vice whose strong corruption
Inhabits our frail blood.

ANTONIO. O heavens themselves!

SECOND OFFICER. Come, sir, I pray you, go.

ANTONIO. Let me speak a little. This youth that you see here
I snatch'd one half out of the jaws of death;
Relieved him with such sanctity of love;
And to his image, which methought did promise
Most venerable worth, did I devotion.

FIRST OFFICER. What's that to us? The time goes by: away!

ANTONIO. But O how vile an idol proves this god!
Thou hast, Sebastian, done good feature shame.
In nature there's no blemish but the mind;
None can be call'd deform'd but the unkind:
Virtue is beauty; but the beauteous evil
Are empty trunks, o'erflourish'd by the devil.

FIRST OFFICER. The man grows mad: away with him!
Come, come, sir.

ANTONIO. Lead me on. [*Exit with* OFFICERS.]

VIOLA. Methinks his words do from such passion fly.
That he believes himself: so do not I.
Prove true, imagination, O prove true,
That I, dear brother, be now ta'en for you!

SIR TOBY. Come hither, knight; come hither, Fabian: we'll whisper o'er a couplet or two of most sage saws.

VIOLA. He named Sebastian: I my brother know
Yet living in my glass; even such and so
In favor was my brother, and he went
Still in this fashion, color, ornament,
For him I imitate: O, if it prove,
Tempests are kind and salt waves fresh in love! [*Exit.*]

SIR TOBY. A very dishonest paltry boy, and more a coward than a hare: his dishonesty appears in leaving his friend here in necessity and denying him; and for his cowardship, ask Fabian.

FABIAN. A coward, a most devout coward, religious in it.

SIR ANDREW. 'Slid, I'll after him again and beat him.

SIR TOBY. Do; cuff him soundly, but never draw thy sword.

SIR ANDREW. An I do not,—[Exit.]

FABIAN. Come, let's see the event.

SIR TOBY. I dare lay any money 'twill be nothing yet.

[Exeunt.]

ACT FOUR

1. Before OLIVIA's house

Enter SEBASTIAN and CLOWN.

CLOWN. Will you make me believe that I am not sent for you?

SEBASTIAN. Go to, go to, thou art a foolish fellow:
Let me be clear of thee.

CLOWN. Well held out, i' faith! No, I do not know you; nor I am not sent to you by my lady, to bid you come speak with her; nor your name is not Master Cesario; nor this is not my nose neither. Nothing that is so is so.

SEBASTIAN. I prithee, vent thy folly somewhere else:
Thou know'st not me.

CLOWN. Vent my folly! he has heard that word of some great man and now applies it to a fool. Vent my folly! I am afraid this great lubber, the world, will prove a cockney. I prithee now, ungird thy strangeness and tell me what I shall vent to my lady: shall I vent to her that thou art coming?

SEBASTIAN. I prithee, foolish Greek, depart from me:
There's money for thee: if you tarry longer,
I shall give worse payment.

CLOWN. By my troth, thou hast an open hand. These wise men that give fools money get themselves a good report—after fourteen years' purchase.

[Enter SIR ANDREW, SIR TOBY, and FABIAN.]

SIR ANDREW. Now, sir, have I met you again? there's for you.

SEBASTIAN. Why, there's for thee, and there, and there. Are all the people mad?

SIR TOBY. Hold, sir, or I'll throw your dagger o'er the house.

CLOWN. This will I tell my lady straight: I would not be in some of your coats for two pence. [Exit.]

SIR TOBY. Come on, sir; hold.

SIR ANDREW. Nay, let him alone: I'll go another way to work with him; I'll have an action of battery against him, if there be any law in Illyria: though I struck him first, yet it's no matter for that.

SEBASTIAN. Let go thy hand.

SIR TOBY. Come, sir, I will not let you go. Come, my young soldier, put up your iron: you are well fleshed; come on.

SEBASTIAN. I will be free from thee. What wouldst thou now?
If thou darest tempt me further, draw thy sword.

SIR TOBY. What, what? Nay, then I must have an ounce or two of this malapert blood from you.

[Enter OLIVIA.]

OLIVIA. Hold, Toby; on thy life, I charge thee, hold!

SIR TOBY. Madam!

OLIVIA. Will it be ever thus? Ungracious wretch,
Fit for the mountains and the barbarous caves,
Where manners ne'er were preach'd! out of my sight!
Be not offended, dear Cesario.
Rudesby, be gone! [Exeunt SIR TOBY, SIR ANDREW, and FABIAN.]
                 I prithee, gentle friend,
Let thy fair wisdom, not thy passion, sway
In this uncivil and unjust extent
Against thy peace. Go with me to my house;

And hear thou there how many fruitless
    pranks
This ruffian hath botch'd up, that thou
    thereby
Mayst smile at this: thou shalt not choose
    but go:
Do not deny. Beshrew his soul for me,
He started one poor heart of mine in
    thee.
  SEBASTIAN. What relish is in this? how
    runs the stream?
Or I am mad, or else this is a dream:
Let fancy still my sense in Lethe steep;
If it be thus to dream, still let me sleep!
  OLIVIA. Nay, come, I prithee: would
    thou'ldst be ruled by me!
  SEBASTIAN. Madam, I will.
  OLIVIA. O, say so, and so be!
            [*Exeunt.*]

2. OLIVIA's *house*

Enter MARIA *and* CLOWN.

  MARIA. Nay, I prithee, put on this gown
and this beard; make him believe thou art
Sir Topas the curate: do it quickly; I'll
call Sir Toby the whilst. [*Exit.*]

  CLOWN. Well, I'll put it on, and I will
dissemble myself in 't; and I would I were
the first that ever dissembled in such a
gown. I am not tall enough to become the
function well, nor lean enough to be
thought a good student; but to be said an
honest man and a good housekeeper goes
as fairly as to say a careful man and a
great scholar. The competitors enter.

    [*Enter* SIR TOBY *and* MARIA.]

  SIR TOBY. Jove bless thee, master Parson.

  CLOWN. Bonos dies, Sir Toby; for, as
the old hermit of Prague, that never saw
pen and ink, very wittily said to a niece
of King Gorboduc, 'That that is;' so I,
being master Parson, am master Parson;
for, what is 'that' but 'that,' and 'is' but
'is'?

  SIR TOBY. To him, Sir Topas.

  CLOWN. What, ho, I say! peace in this
prison!

  SIR TOBY. The knave counterfeits well;
a good knave.

  MALVOLIO. [*Within.*] Who calls there?

  CLOWN. Sir Topas the curate, who
comes to visit Malvolio the lunatic.

  MALVOLIO. Sir Topas, Sir Topas, good
Sir Topas, go to my lady.

  CLOWN. Out, hyperbolical fiend! how
vexest thou this man! talkest thou nothing but of ladies?

  SIR TOBY. Well said, master Parson.

  MALVOLIO. Sir Topas, never was man
thus wronged: good Sir Topas, do not
think I am mad: they have laid me here
in hideous darkness.

  CLOWN. Fie, thou dishonest Satan! I call
thee by the most modest terms; for I am
one of those gentle ones that will use the
devil himself with courtesy: sayest thou
that house is dark?

  MALVOLIO. As hell, Sir Topas.

  CLOWN. Why, it hath bay windows
transparent as barricadoes, and the clear-
stories toward the south north are as lus-
trous as ebony; and yet complainest thou
of obstruction?

  MALVOLIO. I am not mad, Sir Topas: I
say to you, this house is dark.

  CLOWN. Madman, thou errest: I say,
there is no darkness but ignorance; in
which thou art more puzzled than the
Egyptians in their fog.

  MALVOLIO. I say, this house is as dark as
ignorance, though ignorance were as
dark as hell; and I say, there was never
man thus abused. I am no more mad than
you are: make the trial of it in any constant question.

  CLOWN. What is the opinion of Pythagoras concerning wild fowl?

  MALVOLIO. That the soul of our grandam
might haply inhabit a bird.

  CLOWN. What thinkest thou of his
opinion?

  MALVOLIO. I think nobly of the soul,
and no way approve his opinion.

  CLOWN. Fare thee well. Remain thou
still in darkness: thou shalt hold the
opinion of Pythagoras ere I will allow of
thy wits; and fear to kill a woodcock,
lest thou dispossess the soul of thy
grandam. Fare thee well.

  MALVOLIO. Sir Topas, Sir Topas!

  SIR TOBY. My most exquisite Sir Topas!

  CLOWN. Nay, I am for all waters.

  MARIA. Thou mightst have done this
without thy beard and gown: he sees thee
not.

SIR TOBY. To him in thine own voice, and bring me word how thou findest him: I would we were well rid of this knavery. If he may be conveniently delivered, I would he were; for I am now so far in offense with my niece, that I cannot pursue with any safety this sport to the upshot. Come by and by to my chamber. [*Exeunt* SIR TOBY *and* MARIA.]

CLOWN. [*Singing.*] Hey, Robin, jolly Robin,
Tell me how thy lady does.

MALVOLIO. Fool,—

CLOWN. My lady is unkind, perdy.

MALVOLIO. Fool,—

CLOWN. Alas, why is she so?

MALVOLIO. Fool, I say,—

CLOWN. She loves another—Who calls, ha?

MALVOLIO. Good fool, as ever thou wilt deserve well at my hand, help me to a candle, and pen, ink and paper: as I am a gentleman, I will live to be thankful to thee for 't.

CLOWN. Master Malvolio!

MALVOLIO. Aye, good fool.

CLOWN. Alas, sir, how fell you besides your five wits?

MALVOLIO. Fool, there was never man so notoriously abused: I am as well in my wits, fool, as thou art.

CLOWN. But as well? then you are mad indeed, if you be no better in your wits than a fool.

MALVOLIO. They have here propertied me; keep me in darkness, send ministers to me, asses, and do all they can to face me out of my wits.

CLOWN. Advise you what you say; the minister is here. Malvolio, Malvolio, thy wits the heavens restore! endeavor thyself to sleep, and leave thy vain bibble babble.

MALVOLIO. Sir Topas,—

CLOWN. Maintain no words with him, good fellow. Who, I, sir? not I, sir. God be wi' you, good Sir Topas. Marry, amen. I will, sir, I will.

MALVOLIO. Fool, fool, fool, I say,—

CLOWN. Alas, sir, be patient. What say you, sir? I am shent for speaking to you.

MALVOLIO. Good fool, help me to some light and some paper: I tell thee, I am as well in my wits as any man in Illyria.

CLOWN. Well-a-day that you were, sir!

MALVOLIO. By this hand, I am. Good fool, some ink, paper and light; and convey what I will set down to my lady: it shall advantage thee more than ever the bearing of letter did.

CLOWN. I will help you to 't. But tell me true, are you not mad indeed? or do you but counterfeit?

MALVOLIO. Believe me, I am not; I tell thee true.

CLOWN. Nay, I'll ne'er believe a madman till I see his brains. I will fetch you light and paper and ink.

MALVOLIO. Fool, I'll requite it in the highest degree: I prithee, be gone.

CLOWN. [*Singing.*] I am gone, sir,
And anon, sir,
I'll be with you again,
     In a trice,
     Like to the old vice,
Your need to sustain;
Who, with dagger of lath,
In his rage and his wrath,
     Cries, ah, ha! to the devil:
Like a mad lad,
Pare thy nails, dad;
     Adieu, goodman devil.

3. OLIVIA'S *garden*

Enter SEBASTIAN.

SEBASTIAN. This is the air; that is the glorious sun;
This pearl she gave me, I do feel 't and see 't;
And though 'tis wonder that enwraps me thus,
Yet 'tis not madness. Where's Antonio, then?
I could not find him at the Elephant:
Yet there he was; and there I found this credit,
That he did range the town to seek me out.
His counsel now might do me golden service;
For though my soul disputes well with my sense,
That this may be some error, but no madness,

Yet doth this accident and flood of for-
tune
So far exceed all instance, all discourse,
That I am ready to distrust mine eyes
And wrangle with my reason, that per-
suades me
To any other trust but that I am mad,
Or else the lady's mad; yet, if 'twere so,
She could not sway her house, command
her followers,
Take and give back affairs and their dis-
patch
With such a smooth, discreet, and stable
bearing
As I perceive she does: there's some-
thing in 't
That is deceivable. But here the lady
comes.
[*Enter* OLIVIA *and* PRIEST.]
OLIVIA. Blame not this haste of mine. If
you mean well,
Now go with me and with this holy man

Into the chantry by: there, before him,
And underneath that consecrated roof,
Plight me the full assurance of your
faith;
That my most jealous and too doubtful
soul
May live at peace. He shall conceal it
Whiles you are willing it shall come to
note,
What time we will our celebration keep
According to my birth. What do you
say?
SEBASTIAN. I'll follow this good man,
and go with you;
And having sworn truth, ever will be
true.
OLIVIA. Then lead the way, good
father; and heavens so shine,
That they may fairly note this act of
mine!

[*Exeunt.*]

ACT FIVE

1. *Before* OLIVIA's *house*

Enter CLOWN *and* FABIAN.

FABIAN. Now, as thou lovest me, let me
see his letter.
CLOWN. Good Master Fabian, grant me
another request.
FABIAN. Any thing.
CLOWN. Do not desire to see this letter.
FABIAN. This is, to give a dog, and in
recompense desire my dog again.
[*Enter* DUKE, VIOLA, CURIO, *and* LORDS.]
DUKE. Belong you to the Lady Olivia,
friends?
CLOWN. Aye, sir; we are some of her
trappings.
DUKE. I know thee well: how dost thou,
my good fellow?
CLOWN. Truly, sir, the better for my
foes and the worse for my friends.
DUKE. Just the contrary; the better for
thy friends.
CLOWN. No, sir, the worse.
DUKE. How can that be?
CLOWN. Marry, sir, they praise me and
make an ass of me; now my foes tell me

plainly I am an ass: so that by my foes,
sir, I profit in the knowledge of myself;
and by my friends I am abused: so that,
conclusions to be as kisses, if your four
negatives make your two affirmatives,
why then, the worse for my friends, and
the better for my foes.
DUKE. Why, this is excellent.
CLOWN. By my troth, sir, no; though it
please you to be one of my friends.
DUKE. Thou shalt not be the worse for
me: there's gold.
CLOWN. But that it would be double-
dealing, sir, I would you could make it
another.
DUKE. O, you give me ill counsel.
CLOWN. Put your grace in your pocket,
sir, for this once, and let your flesh and
blood obey it.
DUKE. Well, I will be so much a sinner,
to be a double-dealer: there's another.
CLOWN. Primo, secundo, tertio, is a
good play; and the old saying is, the third
pays for all: the triplex, sir, is a good
tripping measure; or the bells of Saint

Bennet, sir, may put you in mind; one, two, three.

DUKE. You can fool no more money out of me at this throw: if you will let your lady know I am here to speak with her, and bring her along with you, it may awake my bounty further.

CLOWN. Marry, sir, lullaby to your bounty till I come again. I go, sir; but I would not have you to think that my desire of having is the sin of covetousness: but, as you say, sir, let your bounty take a nap, I will awake it anon. [*Exit.*]

VIOLA. Here comes the man, sir, that did rescue me.

[*Enter* ANTONIO *and* OFFICERS.]

DUKE. That face of his I do remember well;

Yet, when I saw it last, it was besmear'd
As black as Vulcan in the smoke of war:
A bawbling vessel was he captain of,
For shallow draught and bulk unprizable;
With which such scathful grapple did he make
With the most noble bottom of our fleet,
That very envy and the tongue of loss
Cried fame and honor on him. What's the matter?

FIRST OFFICER. Orsino, this is that Antonio
That took the Phœnix and her fraught from Candy;
And this is he that did the Tiger board,
When your young nephew Titus lost his leg:
Here in the streets, desperate of shame and state,
In private brabble did we apprehend him.

VIOLA. He did me kindness, sir, drew on my side;
But in conclusion put strange speech upon me:
I know not what 'twas but distraction.

DUKE. Notable pirate! thou salt-water thief!
What foolish boldness brought thee to their mercies,
Whom thou, in terms so bloody and so dear,
Hast made thine enemies?

ANTONIO. Orsino, noble sir,
Be pleased that I shake off these names you give me:
Antonio never yet was thief or pirate,

Though I confess, on base and ground enough,
Orsino's enemy. A witchcraft drew me hither:
That most ingrateful boy there by your side,
From the rude sea's enraged and foamy mouth
Did I redeem; a wreck past hope he was:
His life I gave him and did thereto add
My love, without retention or restraint,
All his in dedication; for his sake
Did I expose myself, pure for his love,
Into the danger of this adverse town;
Drew to defend him when he was beset:
Where being apprehended, his false cunning,
Not meaning to partake with me in danger,
Taught him to face me out of his acquaintance,
And grew a twenty years removed thing
While one would wink; denied me mine own purse,
Which I had recommended to his use
Not half an hour before.

VIOLA. How can this be?

DUKE. When came he to this town?

ANTONIO. To-day, my lord; and for three months before,
No interim, not a minute's vacancy,
Both day and night did we keep company.

[*Enter* OLIVIA *and* ATTENDANTS.]

DUKE. Here comes the countess: now heaven walks on earth.
But for thee, fellow; fellow, thy words are madness:
Three months this youth hath tended upon me;
But more of that anon. Take him aside.

OLIVIA. What would my lord, but that he may not have,
Wherein Olivia may seem serviceable?
Cesario, you do not keep promise with me.

VIOLA. Madam!

DUKE. Gracious Olivia,—

OLIVIA. What do you say, Cesario? Good my lord,—

VIOLA. My lord would speak; my duty hushes me.

OLIVIA. If it be aught to the old tune, my lord,

It is as fat and fulsome to mine ear
As howling after music.

DUKE. Still so cruel?

OLIVIA. Still so constant, lord.

DUKE. What, to perverseness? you un-
civil lady,
To whose ingrate and unauspicious altars
My soul the faithfull'st offerings hath
breathed out
That e'er devotion tender'd! What shall
I do?

OLIVIA. Even what it please my lord,
that shall become him.

DUKE. Why should I not, had I the
heart to do it,
Like to the Egyptian thief at point of
death,
Kill what I love?—a savage jealousy
That sometimes savors nobly. But hear
me this:
Since you to non-regardance cast my
faith,
And that I partly know the instrument
That screws me from my true place in
your favor,
Live you the marble-breasted tyrant still;
But this your minion, whom I know you
love,
And whom, by heaven I swear, I tender
dearly,
Him will I tear out of that cruel eye,
Where he sits crowned in his master's
spite.
Come, boy, with me; my thoughts are
ripe in mischief:
I'll sacrifice the lamb that I do love,
To spite a raven's heart within a dove.

VIOLA. And I, most jocund, apt and
willingly,
To do you rest, a thousand deaths would
die.

OLIVIA. Where goes Cesario?

VIOLA. After him I love
More than I love these eyes, more than
my life,
More, by all mores, than e'er I shall love
wife.
If I do feign, you witnesses above
Punish my life for tainting of my love!

OLIVIA. Aye me, detested! how am I be-
guiled!

VIOLA. Who does beguile you? who
does do you wrong?

OLIVIA. Hast thou forgot thyself? is it so
long?
Call forth the holy father.

DUKE. Come, away!

OLIVIA. Whither, my lord? Cesario,
husband, stay.

DUKE. Husband!

OLIVIA. Aye, husband: can he that
deny?

DUKE. Her husband, sirrah!

VIOLA. No, my lord, not I.

OLIVIA. Alas, it is the baseness of thy
fear
That makes thee strangle thy propriety:
Fear not, Cesario; take thy fortunes up;
Be that thou know'st thou art, and then
thou art
As great as that thou fear'st.

[*Enter* PRIEST.]
                O, welcome, father!
Father, I charge thee, by thy reverence,
Here to unfold, though lately we in-
tended
To keep in darkness what occasion now
Reveals before 'tis ripe, what thou dost
know
Hath newly pass'd between this youth
and me.

PRIEST. A contract of eternal bond of
love,
Confirm'd by mutual joinder of your
hands,
Attested by the holy close of lips,
Strengthen'd by interchangement of your
rings;
And all the ceremony of this compact
Seal'd in my function, by my testimony:
Since when, my watch hath told me,
toward my grave
I have travel'd but two hours.

DUKE. O thou dissembling cub! what
wilt thou be
When time hath sow'd a grizzle on thy
case?
Or will not else thy craft so quickly
grow,
That thine own trip shall be thine overthrow?
Farewell, and take her; but direct thy
feet
Where thou and I henceforth may never
meet.

VIOLA. My lord, I do protest—

OLIVIA. O, do not swear!

Hold little faith, though thou hast too
much fear.
[*Enter* SIR ANDREW.]

SIR ANDREW. For the love of God, a
surgeon! Send one presently to Sir Toby.

OLIVIA. What's the matter?

SIR ANDREW. He has broke my head
across and has given Sir Toby a bloody
coxcomb too: for the love of God, your
help! I had rather than forty pound I
were at home.

OLIVIA. Who has done this, Sir Andrew?

SIR ANDREW. The count's gentleman,
one Cesario: we took him for a coward,
but he's the very devil incardinate.

DUKE. My gentleman, Cesario?

SIR ANDREW. 'Od's lifelings, here he is!
You broke my head for nothing; and
that that I did, I was set on to do 't by
Sir Toby.

VIOLA. Why do you speak to me? I
never hurt you:
You drew your sword upon me without
cause;
But I bespake you fair, and hurt you not.

SIR ANDREW. If a bloody coxcomb be a
hurt, you have hurt me: I think you set
nothing by a bloody coxcomb.
[*Enter* SIR TOBY *and* CLOWN.]
Here comes Sir Toby halting; you shall
hear more: but if he had not been in
drink, he would have tickled you other
gates than he did.

DUKE. How now, gentleman! how is't
with you?

SIR TOBY. That's all one: has hurt me,
and there's the end on 't. Sot, didst see
Dick surgeon, sot?

CLOWN. O, he's drunk, Sir Toby, an
hour agone; his eyes were set at eight
i' the morning.

SIR TOBY. Then he's a rogue, and a passy
measures pavin: I hate a drunken rogue.

OLIVIA. Away with him! Who hath
made this havoc with them?

SIR ANDREW. I'll help you, Sir Toby,
because we'll be dressed together.

SIR TOBY. Will you help? an ass-head
and a coxcomb and a knave, a thin-faced
knave, a gull!

OLIVIA. Get him to bed, and let his
hurt be look'd to. [*Exeunt* CLOWN, FA-
BIAN, SIR TOBY *and* SIR ANDREW.]

[*Enter* SEBASTIAN.]

SEBASTIAN. I am sorry, madam, I have
hurt your kinsman;
But, had it been the brother of my blood,
I must have done no less with wit and
safety.
You throw a strange regard upon me,
and by that
I do perceive it hath offended you:
Pardon me, sweet one, even for the vows
We made each other but so late ago.

DUKE. One face, one voice, one habit,
and two persons,
A natural perspective, that is and is not!

SEBASTIAN. *Antonio*, O my dear Antonio!
How have the hours rack'd and tortured
me,
Since I have lost thee!

ANTONIO. Sebastian are you?

SEBASTIAN. Fear'st thou that, Antonio?

ANTONIO. How have you made division
of yourself?
An apple, cleft in two, is not more twin
Than these two creatures. Which is Sebastian?

OLIVIA. Most wonderful!

SEBASTIAN. Do I stand there? I never
had a brother;
Nor can there be that deity in my nature,
Of here and every where. I had a sister,
Whom the blind waves and surges have
devour'd.
Of charity, what kin are you to me?
What countryman? what name? what
parentage?

VIOLA. Of Messaline: Sebastian was
my father;
Such a Sebastian was my brother too,
So went he suited to his watery tomb:
If spirits can assume both form and suit,
You come to fright us.

SEBASTIAN. A spirit I am indeed;
But am in that dimension grossly clad
Which from the womb I did participate.
Were you a woman, as the rest goes
even,
I should my tears let fall upon your
cheek,
And say 'Thrice-welcome, drowned
Viola!'

VIOLA. My father had a mole upon his
brow.

SEBASTIAN. And so had mine.

VIOLA. And died that day when Viola from her birth
Had number'd thirteen years.

SEBASTIAN. O, that record is lively in my soul!
He finished indeed his mortal act
That day that made my sister thirteen years.

VIOLA. If nothing lets to make us happy both
But this my masculine usurp'd attire,
Do not embrace me till each circumstance
Of place, time, fortune, do cohere and jump
That I am Viola: which to confirm,
I'll bring you to a captain in this town,
Where lie my maiden weeds; by whose gentle help
I was preserved to serve this noble count.
All the occurrence of my fortune since
Hath been between this lady and this lord.

SEBASTIAN. [To OLIVIA.] So comes it, lady, you have been mistook:
But nature to her bias drew in that.
You would have been contracted to a maid;
Nor are you therein, by my life, deceived,
You are betroth'd both to a maid and man.

DUKE. Be not amazed; right noble is his blood.
If this be so, as yet the glass seems true,
I shall have share in this most happy wreck.
[To VIOLA.] Boy, thou hast said to me a thousand times
Thou never shouldst love woman like to me.

VIOLA. And all those sayings will I over-swear;
And all those swearings keep as true in soul
As doth that orbed continent the fire
That severs day from night.

DUKE. Give me thy hand;
And let me see thee in thy woman's weeds.

VIOLA. The captain that did bring me first on shore
Hath my maid's garments: he upon some action

Is now in durance, at Malvolio's suit,
A gentleman, and follower of my lady's.

OLIVIA. He shall enlarge him: fetch Malvolio hither:
And yet, alas, now I remember me,
They say, poor gentleman, he's much distract.

[Re-enter CLOWN with a letter and FABIAN.]

A most extracting frenzy of mine own
From my remembrance clearly banish'd his.
How does he, sirrah?

CLOWN. Truly, madam, he holds Belzebub at the stave's end as well as a man in his case may do: has here writ a letter to you; I should have given 't you to-day morning, but as a madman's epistles are no gospels, so it skills not much when they are delivered.

OLIVIA. Open 't and read it.

CLOWN. Look then to be well edified when the fool delivers the madman. [Reads.] By the Lord, madam,—

OLIVIA. How now! art thou mad?

CLOWN. No, madam, I do but read madness: an your ladyship will have it as it ought to be, you must allow Vox.

OLIVIA. Prithee, read i' thy right wits.

CLOWN. So I do, madonna; but to read his right wits is to read thus: therefore perpend, my princess, and give ear.

OLIVIA. [To FABIAN.] Read it you, sirrah.

FABIAN. By the Lord, madam, you wrong me and the world shall know it: though you have put me into darkness and given your drunken cousin rule over me, yet have I the benefit of my senses as well as your ladyship. I have your own letter that induced me to the semblance I put on; with the which I doubt not but to do myself much right, or you much shame. Think of me as you please. I leave my duty a little unthought of, and speak out of my injury.

THE MADLY-USED MALVOLIO.

OLIVIA. Did he write this?

CLOWN. Aye, madam.

DUKE. This savors not much of distraction.

OLIVIA. See him deliver'd, Fabian; bring him hither. [Exit FABIAN.]

My lord, so please you, these things
further thought on,
To think me as well a sister as a wife,
One day shall crown the alliance on 't,
so please you,
Here at my house and at my proper cost.

DUKE. Madam, I am most apt to em-
brace your offer.
[*To* VIOLA.] Your master quits you; and
for your service done him,
So much against the mettle of your sex,
So far beneath your soft and tender
breeding,
And since you call'd me master for so
long,
Here is my hand: you shall from this
time be
Your master's mistress.

OLIVIA. A sister! you are she.
[*Re-enter* FABIAN, *with* MALVOLIO.]
DUKE. Is this the madman?

OLIVIA. Aye, my lord, this same.
How now, Malvolio!

MALVOLIO. Madam, you have done me
wrong,
Notorious wrong.

OLIVIA. Have I, Malvolio? no.

MALVOLIO. Lady, you have. Pray you,
peruse that letter.
You must not now deny it is your hand:
Write from it, if you can, in hand or
phrase;
Or say 'tis not your seal, not your in-
vention:
You can say none of this: well, grant it
then
And tell me, in the modesty of honor,
Why you have given me such clear lights
of favor,
Bade me come smiling and cross-garter'd
to you,
To put on yellow stockings and to frown
Upon Sir Toby and the lighter people;
And, acting this in an obedient hope,
Why have you suffer'd me to be im-
prison'd,
Kept in a dark house, visited by the
priest,
And made the most notorious geck and
gull
That e'er invention play'd on? tell me
why.

OLIVIA. Alas, Malvolio, this is not my
writing,

Though, I confess, much like the char-
acter:
But out of question 'tis Maria's hand.
And now I do bethink me, it was she
First told me thou wast mad; then cam-
est in smiling,
And in such forms which here were
presupposed
Upon thee in the letter. Prithee, be con-
tent:
This practice hath most shrewdly pass'd
upon thee;
But when we know the grounds and
authors of it,
Thou shalt be both the plaintiff and the
judge
Of thine own cause.

FABIAN. Good madam, hear me speak,
And let no quarrel nor no brawl to come
Taint the condition of this present hour,
Which I have wonder'd at. In hope it
shall not,
Most freely I confess, myself and Toby
Set this device against Malvolio here,
Upon some stubborn and uncourteous
parts
We had conceived against him: Maria
writ
The letter at Sir Toby's great impor-
tance;
In recompense whereof he hath married
her.
How with a sportful malice it was
follow'd
May rather pluck on laughter than re-
venge;
If that the injuries be justly weigh'd
That have on both sides pass'd.

OLIVIA. Alas, poor fool, how have they
baffled thee!

CLOWN. Why, 'some are born great,
some achieve greatness, and some have
greatness thrown upon them.' I was one,
sir, in this interlude; one Sir Topas, sir;
but that's all one. 'By the Lord, fool, I
am not mad.' But do you remember?
'Madam, why laugh you at such a barren rascal? an you smile not, he's
gagged:' and thus the whirligig of time
brings in his revenges.

MALVOLIO. I'll be revenged on the
whole pack of you. [*Exit.*]

OLIVIA. He hath been most notoriously
abused.

DUKE. Pursue him, and entreat him to
a peace:
He hath not told us of the captain yet:
When that is known, and golden time
convents,
A solemn combination shall be made
Of our dear souls. Meantime, sweet sis-
ter,
We will not part from hence. Cesario,
come;
For so you shall be, while you are a
man;
But when in other habits you are seen,
Orsino's mistress and his fancy's queen.
[*Exeunt all, except* CLOWN.]
CLOWN. [*Sings.*]
When that I was and a little tiny boy,
  With hey, ho, the wind and the rain,
A foolish thing was but a toy,
  For the rain it raineth every day.
But when I came to man's estate,
  With hey, ho, the wind and the rain,
'Gainst knaves and thieves men shut their
  gate,
  For the rain it raineth every day.
But when I came, alas! to wive,
  With hey, ho, the wind and the rain,
By swaggering could I never thrive,
  For the rain it raineth every day.
But when I came unto my beds,
  With hey, ho, the wind and the rain,
With toss-pots still had drunken heads,
  For the rain it raineth every day.
A great while ago the world begun,
  With hey, ho, the wind and the rain,
But that's all one, our play is done,
  And we'll strive to please you every
  day.
                                    [*Exit.*]

THE COMIC VISION

Neither the comic nor the tragic dramatist has available the direct statements and discursive arguments used by preachers and philosophers to persuade their fellowmen. Thus, to ask what a play means, solely in terms of its machinery, its plot or theme or characters, is to forget that, for art, the meaning lies in the total communicated experience; only if the play creates an experience does it communicate a meaning—in the same way that one knows only what one lives. As it peers searchingly into human nature in order to expose, in a variety of moods ranging from contempt to compassion, the foibles and vanities of men, the droll, pathetic, and ludicrous things they do, comedy suggests the values that ought to rule men's lives. If it succeeds in creating a world that appears real on the stage, it will help the reader learn more about the world he actually lives in.

The comic vision that builds the dramatist's world is closely related to the layman's sense of humor. Both have a unique quality that sets them apart from all other virtues. Neither attribute is listed among the traditional four natural virtues (prudence, fortitude, temperance, and justice) nor among the three Christian virtues (faith, hope, and charity), all of which are essentially personal virtues. But among the social virtues few are more highly valued than a sense of humor, and that fact in itself yields a key to understanding the comic spirit and the dramatic comedy that grows out of it. For above all else, comedies are the social—indeed, the civilizing—form of literature. Paradoxically, they exalt the group in order to preserve the individual.

A sense of humor, like the comic vision which underlies a play, develops out of the perspective of maturity; comedy is, after all, an adult and sophisticated thing. The sense of humor is a social quality that recognizes communication among human beings as the ultimate cohesive force in society. Consider, for example, any group at the moment of a clash of personalities or prejudices, or a more significant clash of principles. As the dispute grows, the group may seem to be generating forces that will eventually tear it apart. The more heated each person becomes, the more loudly he shouts and the less he communicates. Everyone speaks but no one listens, until, as the noise dissolves into silence— just before the tension breaks the group—someone with a sense of humor opportunely says or does something which refocuses the group's view of the situation. The new perspective is accompanied by laughter, the laughter of relief and the laughter of triumph. But it is not a matter of individual triumph so much as it is the realization, first, that the group will survive the idiosyncrasies of its members, and, second, that there is a communal good not incompatible with the individual ends so violently and uncompromisingly sought just a moment ago.

Like the man with a sense of humor, the dramatist with the comic vision looks into the human situation and decides that all is not hopeless; though apparently hopelessly entangled in frustrations created by his own foibles and errors, man is not in reality doomed to defeat. By emphasizing the wonder and the possibility of fruitful *being*, comedies free man from the pain of brooding about *becoming*, a burden that so frequently makes the human condition seem intolerable. While tragedy places the reader at the heart of the situation, comedy does not; it removes him to a distance from which he can look at the absurdities of characters who sometimes turn out to be very like himself. The experience may chasten him, but it does not defeat him. Thus comedy on the stage, like the sense of humor in the individual, helps us to see that life is livable, and so it becomes a road to survival for the group and, even more significantly, for the individuals who constitute that group.

Thus is the comic vision revealed in some of its forms. Comedy does not plumb the same depths that tragedy does; nevertheless, the comic vision is at least the equal of pity and terror as the liberator of souls. For the comic dramatist has long known what the modern psychologist is just discovering—how easily our masks can become our shrouds.

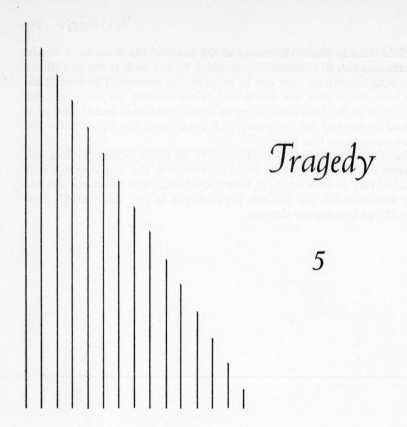

Tragedy

5

What is a tragedy? Can we say, as we did of a comedy, that everyone knows what a tragedy is? Many people are doubtless prepared to answer affirmatively, on the assumption, not uncommon, that any piece of writing that ends unhappily is tragic; if this were so, we would already have encountered tragedy in *The Wild Duck*. Such an assumption—that *unhappy* and *tragic* are somehow equivalent adjectives—is an understandable one. For everyday usage has progressively taken away from *tragic*, as a word, most of its precision of meaning, with the consequence that we glibly describe as tragic everything from a natural disaster to the loss of a child in an automobile accident. That such events are unhappy ones, or pathetic ones, is of course beyond question. But they are not tragic, and cannot be so described by anyone determined to use the word exactly. Fortunately, where the term applies to literature, and especially to dramatic literature, some degree of precision is recoverable, and such precision is essential to our discussion of the second of the drama's major modes.

Once again, it may be useful to begin with the apparently obvious. A tragedy originates in its author's commitment to a tragic vision of life—not an easy phrase to define, as the divergent views of critics from Aristotle to our own day make manifest. To begin with, we are concerned with a tragic *vision*, and this word clearly points to an encompassing view of man's situation. Obviously, then, the writer seeking to dramatize a tragic vision will be engaged in interpreting Life—and here the capital L is warranted, since behind the individuals he sets in motion will loom conditions of human existence that he sees as fundamental and unchanging. This does not mean that the tragic dramatist is a systematic philosopher, in the sense of one who categorizes thought and behavior; within single tragedies—Shakespeare's *King Lear* is an apt example—there is ample room for conflicting and even contradictory ideas. None the less, above and beyond whatever contradictions we may discern, tragedy does disclose a darkened view of human destiny that transcends inconsistencies, and that directs the dramatist's choice of conflict, development of character, and structural procedures. One conclusion is therefore already available to us: in tragedy the element of theme will be conspicuous and significant.

Significant also—as a consequence—will be the choice of a specific conflict to embody the tragic dramatist's vision. The forces engaged in struggle will be large-scaled, and the issue of the struggle will be vital both to the characters directly involved and to mankind as well. *Everyman* may well come to mind at this point; the medieval Morality Play is not, of course, based on a tragic vision, but it is based on a potentially tragic conflict between the kinds of ultimate values that tragedy deals in. *Othello*, as will be seen, presents us with a conflict between (and within) individuals moved by reason and passion. King Oedipus opposes, and is destroyed by, a universal law he never fully comprehends. Willy Loman makes his final (and perhaps futile) gesture because of his need to transcend the mediocrity of the world he finally suspects himself of representing. Tragedy thus involves us in conflicts which are never merely those of a Theban king, a Venetian general, or an American salesman.

Yet conflict—even conflict capable of universal reference—is not, as we already know, the special property of tragedy; there is a comic vision as well as a tragic. What are the properties of the tragic view of life, then, that make the conflict between, let us say, Othello and Iago, distinct from that between Malvolio and Sir Toby? One of these properties has been mentioned already, though only in passing. The tragic view is a darkened view of life. It looks toward ultimate questions which the human condition seems to beg, and to which, possibly, there can be no affirmative answers; it is concerned, not with man's being, but with his becoming—not with the question of whether the social fabric is mended, but with the question of whether man may preserve his values and yet avoid annihilation. To the question of man's becoming there have, of course, been answers—every religion aims to offer them—but none has satisfied all men, and none has been free from skeptical attack. This failure of any religion to earn universal acceptance is perhaps one cogent reason for the darkness of the tragic dramatist's view. But there is another and more important reason.

Whatever age the tragic dramatist has lived in, he has been acutely sensitive to evil and painfully aware of its omnipresence. He has looked about him and seen the guilty brought to account, but he has also seen the innocent struck down with the guilty: Oedipus' children condemned with their father, Lady Macduff and her children preceding Macbeth into destruction, Othello suffering a fate less harsh in degree, but not in kind, than Iago's. This blindness of Fate's—blindness to any distinction between its victims—is a significant clue to the tragic vision. In the light of such examples as these, the writer of tragedy sees the universe as indifferent to man, sees divine justice as a justice so withdrawn from, and so indifferent to, the plight of the individual that indifference is sometimes translated into malignity. Thus Gloucester, in *King Lear*, cries out that

> As flies to wanton boys, are we to the gods,
> They kill us for their sport.

And in his tragedy, *The Duchess of Malfi*, Webster echoes:

> We are merely the stars' tennis-balls, struck and bandied
> Which way please them.

It should be noted, in passing, that these are hardly Christian sentiments; indeed, great tragedy is never compatible with Christianity, since it rejects as inadequate the answers that formalized religion makes to ultimate questions. Yet we must acknowledge at once that Gloucester's statement does not define the tragic vision. If it did so, that vision would be, not darkened, but black. Such is not the case, however, for the harsh destinies of Oedipus' children or of Lady Macduff's are not at the center of the dramatist's view in either play; these "innocents" are destroyed, but their destruction is a by-product, as it were, of the central action. Our focus, and the writer's, remains fixed on the protagonist, on the tragic hero, and in *him* we find such qualities as compensate for the bleakness of the tragic universe.

Of the principal ingredients listed by Clifford Leech[1] as indispensable to the tragic vision, two have now been touched on: a sense of the indifference or the remoteness of the gods (or of God), and an acute awareness of the existence and power of evil. The third ingredient is an enduring faith in Man. Man, by no choice of his own, inhabits a universe only fitfully under his control—a fact never more apparent, perhaps, than in the middle of the twentieth century. He appears to be a creature uniquely endowed to enjoy the fruits of his world; he is gifted with reason, even with a degree of wisdom. And yet he is constantly subject not only to the uncertain winds of chance, but to fundamental instabilities in his own nature, instabilities which, moreover, are inevitably reflected in the society he constructs. His endowments are weighed in the balance with the claims of a justice so remote as to be unintelligible to him, and his endowments are ultimately found wanting. In the unequal struggle, he goes down to defeat. Yet if his endowments are inadequate to a full understanding of—or the control of—his universe, they must never be taken as negligible. If they are not divine, they are at least unique. For man alone is able at the same time to endure his fate and to comprehend it. Comprehending it, he can at last hurl his defiance heroically in its teeth. Do your worst, Shakespeare's Marc Antony seems to say: "I am Antony yet!" On the very threshold of defeat, in the face of death, the tragic hero triumphantly proclaims his individual humanity. Then he is destroyed; but only then. And before the moment of destruction arrives he has demonstrated, as tragic hero, a moving capacity for endurance and a no less moving capacity for expanding awareness. These are the qualities that fit him for his role: he is both the supreme representative of, and the supreme spokesman for, his race.

[1] Clifford Leech, *Shakespeare's Tragedies and other studies in XVII Century Drama* (1950). We are indebted especially to the essays "Implications of Tragedy" and "The Tragic Picture."

The fact of his representativeness, however, requires a further comment. From what has been said of him to this point, it might well be thought that the tragic hero is a faultless individual, a man so near perfection as to escape the obligations of humanity. He is, on the contrary, distinctly fallible, and he represents us both in his weaknesses, which are our own, and in his strengths, which transcend ours. Lacking such strengths, he could not symbolize the greatness we believe ourselves capable of; lacking the weaknesses of common humanity, he would be divorced from us, and could not be our representative. In his awareness, his courage and endurance, he surpasses us, but his imperfections frame him as a human being. As Aristotle recognized, the hero is a man "better than we are," but he must not be pre-eminently great.

But this adjective *great* is ambiguous, especially in the tragic context, since it can point both to greatness of soul and to greatness conceived as power and position. Greatness of soul, joined to human fallibility, has been recognized as an inherent attribute of the hero in every age. But greatness in the other sense—as rank or position—was also assumed as requisite by Aristotle in ancient Greece, by Boethius and Chaucer in feudal times—so long, in fact, as the aristocratic ideal prevailed. This critical assumption reflected the practice of tragic dramatists in Athens as in Elizabethan London; but it also reflected, more fundamentally, the social structures that produced the dramatists themselves: as a matter of course, the hero in Sophocles or in Shakespeare is king, or prince, the head of a great house, or at least, as in *Othello*, an eminent man in a position of power. But what of the tragic hero in a modern democratic society? This problem has been, as we might expect, a major crux in contemporary criticism; it is one we must deal with directly in connection with the clearly non-aristocratic Leonardo (in Lorca's play) and Willy Loman in *Death of a Salesman*. It must suffice at the moment that we recognize that rank, as such—social, political, economic—is non-essential to tragedy, and that to focus our attention on it, to take it as the starting place for defining the tragic hero, is to deflect our attention from what is essential: greatness of soul. In any case, a second conclusion, with respect to tragedy in general, may now be postulated: in tragic drama, the element of character, like that of theme, will occupy a position of the highest importance.

Since the hero's ultimate destruction is inherent in his fallibility, the forces in tragedy are not equal. Yet they are nearly enough equal to produce high tension, closely enough matched, thanks to his greatness, to cause us to hope that the hero may somehow escape his destiny. And this illusory sense of balance in the tragic forces is reflected in another aspect of tragedy; this has to do with the special kind of response that we make to a tragic play. Aristotle, dealing with this troublesome problem in ancient Athens, described our response as *catharsis*, a purging of the conflicting emotions aroused by tragedy, the emotions of pity and fear. But it may be suggested that this description, to which writers about tragedy have acceded for many centuries, had particular relevance to the special social, political, and religious milieu of Greek drama, and only limited relevance elsewhere. In our own age, dramatic critics (Professor Leech among them) have tended to define our ultimate response as an established equilibrium. On the one hand is the terror roused in us by the bleakness of the tragic universe, and by the inevitability of the hero's fate—this last point is to be discussed momentarily. On the other hand is the quality of soul with which the hero reacts to his universe and his fate, a quality we have already described as composed of endurance and comprehension. The equilibrium established between a sombre fate and a heroic defiance moves us to the profoundest kind of contemplation because, when it is achieved in great tragedy, we see that death and spiritual triumph are for a moment co-existent.

A final aspect of tragedy remains to be discussed in our brief summary of its components. If we are to judge from the practice of its creators from Aeschylus to Arthur Miller, tragic writers are committed to causation: every act has its inescapable consequences, and these consequences are often more terrible than the events that produced them. So it is with *Othello*. So it is with another of Shakespeare's mature tragedies, *King Lear*. Lear's combined arrogance and bad judgment lead inevitably to his own death and that of Cordelia, the one daughter who loves him; to underscore the inevitability of terrible effects issuing from evil causes, Shakespeare—in the same drama—draws a parallel relation between the begetting of the bastard, Edmond, and the horrible blinding of Gloucester. An evil act is committed, and at once sets in motion a chain of events which the individual is powerless to interrupt. Act begets act, effect follows cause, and there can be no break in the chain until catastrophe calls a halt. Inevitability is thus an essential part of any tragic structure. The universe operates implacably and indifferently on its axis of causation; determinism characterizes tragic action, whether that determinism emanates, as in *Oedipus*, from a mandate of the gods, or, as in *Othello*, from governing and uncontrollable traits of character.

And yet, if determinism is the atmosphere we seem to breathe in a tragic play, the dramatist must nevertheless manage to make us feel that his characters are in some way autonomous, possessed of some measure of free will. Were we not allowed to convince ourselves of the "freedom" of the hero's decisions, he would strike us as a mere mechanical contrivance, a puppet or an automaton; and automatons can rouse in us neither pride nor profound sympathy. The dramatist's solution to this problem has been to show us the tragic hero frequently exercising his "free will" in apparently minor matters such as may confront him in day-to-day life; the hero is presented with a realism adequate to our acceptance of him as lifelike, and that likeness to life helps persuade us that he is an autonomous agent. The effect of such presentation is that, owing to the more or less routine decisions we have watched him make, we come to accept as autonomous also, at the play's crisis, decisions which actually stem from that blindness or obsession in the hero that embodies dramatically the deterministic principle. At the moment of crisis, when our emotional response is immediate, we accept the fatal choice as a free one; a moment's reflection reveals it to have been inevitable.

For we bring to the tragic drama, after all, a kind of double-vision, prepared to see or read on two levels, almost simultaneously. On the one level are those everyday matters that tie the hero to us in a common humanity: Othello promoting Cassio instead of Iago, Oedipus dispatching Creon to the Delphic oracle, Lorca's Bride consenting to marry the Bridegroom. But on the other level are those actions and choices which, even when the choices are bad ones, provide the hero with his symbolic stature: Othello kneeling with Iago in sworn brotherhood, Oedipus resolving on the punishment of Creon, the Bride choosing to elope with Leonardo. These are, in each case, critical actions; they are, even, as we know, actions *determined* by the situations and the traits of character involved. Yet the preparation for them has been such that we accept them, at the moment, as free acts of the participants. We know, at least from the crisis onward, that Oedipus is damned; we certainly know after Act III that Desdemona is doomed; yet in both dramas we continue to the last to hope that the protagonists may escape.

The nature of the tragic hero, and of the conflict he is engaged in, has one further important effect, a structural one. The hero is marked by the fact that he is becoming, not being. He is in pursuit of unattainable goals. Because his goals are unattainable, and because he is subject, in his pursuit, to the logic of cause and effect, he is struck down. But it is the journey he goes on that we watch; it is never a long one, and its end is—if we look closely—frequently in sight; every detour he takes only leads him back, finally, to a point further along the road to destruction. Tragedy, therefore, driving its hero toward ultimate ends, is built on a linear plot, as opposed to the circular plot of comedy. This kind of plot, according to Aristotle so fundamental to the mode itself, derives from the dramatist's concept of life; it is conditioned by the nature of the tragic hero and his relation to the human community.

SOPHOCLES: *OEDIPUS REX*

Oedipus Rex[2] is, in the purest meaning of the adjective, a terrible story. Its chain of events, embracing murder, incest, suicide, and self-mutilation, catches us in a vortex of terror—and, as Aristotle tells us, the offering of such an experience is one of the properties of tragedy. But it must be remembered that this story was in no sense Sophocles' invention; it was, rather, an inheritance from earlier writers, who, in telling the tale, were simply exploiting for dramatic purposes one of the most ancient of Greek heroic legends. This fact is of the greatest importance, for it indicates past question that Sophocles, turning once again to this familiar material, was attracted to it by aims other than suspense or melodramatic excitement. The latter characteristic of the tale, as we of the twentieth century first encounter it, must have been almost totally lacking for the drama's Greek audiences, who, after all, knew the outcome of the action before they entered the theater. Indeed, it would be difficult to find a clearer instance than this of a dramatist's using an existing story to accommodate a statement about the nature of life.

It therefore becomes our responsibility, if we are to realize the tragic grandeur of *Oedipus,* to arrive at an understanding of this larger view of the author's. Our authority, as with all such problems, is the play itself as Sophocles

---

[2] The title of Sophocles' play in the Greek was *Oedipus Tyrannos*. The term *tyrannos* is most closely translated as "king," but several ideas included in the original term no longer appear in our modern word. *Tyrannos* referred not to a ruler who had inherited power but to one who had seized it, or been awarded it. But unlike our modern "tyrant," the Greek term did not include the idea of despotically administered power; rather, it was usually used for benevolent, competent, self-made rulers. Such a ruler was Oedipus. It should be remembered that the title we use is only one among several possibilities.

wrote it; but since no dramatist writes in a social and intellectual vacuum, it may be helpful to glance briefly at a pair of ideas about the human situation which Sophocles shared with his contemporaries.

The dramatist was probably born in 496 B.C.; he died ninety years later. In the preceding generation the pre-eminent writer of tragedy had been Aeschylus, in whose austere dramas the presiding deity was a Zeus capable of direct intervention in the lives of men. The Aeschylean Zeus could control man's destiny almost as completely as the puppeteer that of his puppet. But in Sophocles' time this belief in the direct intervention of the gods in human affairs had been radically modified. The presiding deity in *Oedipus* is Apollo, and while Apollo predicts, he does not impel. In the Sophoclean universe men are not presented as puppets; they seem to act as they do in their own right. As a messenger says, at the end of *Oedipus*, "The greatest griefs are those we cause ourselves."

Nevertheless, the messenger's comment does not indicate that men are altogether free agents. Though not subject to direct control by the gods, men are subject to the universal *logos*, a law of order which is ineluctably obeyed. Sophocles, that is, discerned a rational pattern in that universe of which man is a small part, and that pattern is evidenced in the *logos*. The difficulty—and the frequent source of tragedy—lies in the inadequacy of man's finite reason; he cannot see the larger pattern; the *logos* is revealed to him only in intermittent flashes of insight; and humanity is therefore tragically susceptible to violating the *logos* unknowingly.

A second concept central to the Sophoclean universe resides in the opposition between what the Greeks called *diké* and *adikia*. Starting with the idea of the *logos*, the divine pattern, and conceiving that pattern as law for the universe, they came to the idea of *diké* as the human or social state of being in harmony with that larger, rational pattern which governs the universe, no matter how imperfectly comprehended by man. *Adikia*, then, is the human act which does violence to this rational and hence beneficent law, and is clearly aberration and wrong-doing.

But something more is involved in these terms. *Diké* not only defines the state of harmony; it also implies the constant tendency of things to return to that state. Implicit in the term is a corrective, retributive process, the inevitable eradication of the evil results of *adikia*, the redressing of the balance. It is this concept that provides the framework for Sophocles' use of the ancient story. If the re-establishment of *diké* is inevitable, so too *adikia*, however disguised or obscured in the mists of time, must ultimately manifest itself outwardly. Unlike us, Sophocles (and indeed most peoples until our own times) saw the external physical universe as but the reflection of the moral universe. Until it is recognized and eradicated through appropriate retribution, therefore, *adikia* is likely to fester in the body politic and finally to work to the surface in public disaster. Implicit in *diké*, therefore, is also the idea of a washing out, the cleansing of the stain with which the wrong act has soiled and, as it were, affronted the rational nature of the universe.

Hence the plague which besets Thebes is in the last analysis a scourge properly laid at the feet of Oedipus. His unknowing, his "innocent" crime, in killing his father and marrying his mother, ultimately manifests itself in a devastating threat to the lives of all his people.

The plot of *Oedipus*, as H. D. F. Kitto has noted, is of a type common among the Greek dramatists: "something unpleasant is predicted, the persons concerned try to avert it and think themselves safe, but in some natural though surprising fashion the prediction is fulfilled."[3] Sophocles adapts to this "prediction-fulfilled" plot the ancient Theban materials. As a consequence of the Delphic prediction, the hero, as an infant, was cast out by his father, Laius,[4] and ordered killed. But the shepherd charged with carrying out the execution took pity on the child, giving him for safe-keeping into the hands of a Corinthian who, first, cut the bonds that maimed the infant's feet, and, second, carried him to the court of Polybus, King of Corinth. In time Oedipus reached manhood as adoptive son of the childless Polybus. But the absence of resemblance to his supposed father drove Oedipus himself to the Delphic Oracle, where the dread prediction was repeated. Fearing that if he returned to Corinth, he would bring disaster on his putative parents, he set out for other lands; but on the way he encountered Laius, whom he slew in a cross-roads scuffle. Now, Laius had been, himself, on a pilgrimage to the Oracle to ask how he might rid his city of the dreadful monster, the Sphinx, who, having taken a stand near the city gates, throttled and devoured every Theban who failed to answer the riddle put to him. Oedipus, approaching Thebes in his wanderings, solved the riddle and saved the city, and as a consequence was in a position to woo and marry Laius' widow, the Queen Jocasta. Of the true identity of Laius and Jocasta, as of his own early history, Oedipus was of course initially ignorant; and the period covered by his ignorance coincides with the antecedent action in Sophocles' dramatic scheme.

By the time the drama opens, Jocasta has borne her son's children, and the city of which that son is now king has been visited with a devastating plague. From the moment the enacted story begins, we are confronted with what is still recognized as the *locus classicus* of *dramatic irony*. What had motivated Oedipus' journey to Thebes? The urgent necessity to separate himself permanently from Polybus. But en route he slew Laius, and, as Sophocles begins his action, Oedipus learns that the plague afflicting his city will be lifted only with the punishment of Laius' murderer. So it is that, when the hero condemns the still unknown criminal, we perceive the terrible irony in his action: his unwitting self-condemnation.

As the climax nears, further ironies are perceived. Following the ambiguous but profoundly unsettling revelations of Teiresias, the blind soothsayer who reluctantly supplies the clues to the past action, Jocasta prays to Apollo for deliverance from the accursed plague and for a calmed and serene Oedipus. Within an hour she has hanged herself. Between these two events, the Corinthian messenger—the same man who, years before, conveyed the royal infant to Polybus—arrives from Corinth with the news of Polybus' death and the decision of his subjects to crown Oedipus as his successor. Oedipus takes this as evidence that, Polybus having died a natural death, his doom has been lifted; but upon further

---

[3] H. D. F. Kitto, *Greek Tragedy* (Garden City: Doubleday & Company, Anchor Edition, 1954), p. 142. The editors are indebted to Kitto's detailed analysis for many ideas vital to their interpretation of Sophocles' drama.

[4] In our discussion of *Oedipus Rex* we have chosen to use the conventional, Anglicized spellings of certain names: Jocasta, Laius, Polybus. In the version of the play that follows, however, translators Fitts and Fitzgerald have endeavored to approximate the original Greek sound: Iocaste, Laïos, Polybos.

questioning the messenger also reveals Oedipus' adoptive status. Little by little the truth of the past is recovered. With the forced testimony of the humane shepherd who long ago refused to kill the maimed infant, the terrible picture is complete. The hero, whose earlier solution of the Sphinx's riddle has led him to believe no obscurity is beyond his powers of penetration, is propelled into catastrophe. Jocasta, an hour after sacrificing to Apollo, receives the god's appalling answer, and destroys herself. Oedipus, blinded by the same terrible truth, puts out his eyes and goes into sightless exile. For the enormity of his crime, death is an inadequate punishment.

But what, in all this horror, has happened to "justice"? Why is so awful a punishment visited upon a man who has acted, if precipitately, at least in apparent good faith? Surely the fate of Oedipus is chargeable to a malign and irresponsible deity. Such a conclusion might have been drawn from the story, but not by Sophocles. It must be remembered that the dramatist's god predicts, but does not impel. Oedipus was not forced into killing his father; the act was his own impetuous response to the angry impetuosity of his father's charioteer. Apollo is not to be blamed for the incestuous marriage with a Queen who must have been nearly twice the hero's age; this, again, was a "free" act of the hero.

But the author's purpose is not to moralize by showing how the gods punish impetuosity or unsavory ambition. Rather, Sophocles' vision is rooted in his faith in the *logos*, "obeyed law." This law has been violated, even though unwittingly; *adikia* must be wiped out, and here *diké* has as its agents Teiresias, Creon, the Corinthian messenger, the old shepherd, and Oedipus' own insatiable thirst for the whole truth. What, then, is the King's crime? Of what is he guilty?

This question has long been troublesome. In our own time the answers have been various. Some critics, for example, hold that Oedipus is guilty of pride of intellect, originating in his solution of the Sphinx's riddle, and thus regard the play as a critique of rationalism. Others interpret Sophocles' aim as one of demonstrating to his people, through a horrible example, the extraordinary power of the gods over the destinies of men. Both answers are inadequate. Critics subscribing to the first must finally slight the fact that Oedipus does not know his true identity when he commits the criminal acts on which the tragedy hinges; what produces the plague is not the king's obvious enough pride, but the earlier murder and incest, and these are essentially another issue. And answers of the second sort, which see the play as a salutary object lesson to forgetful men, plausible as they seem at first, simply do not have Sophocles' warrant. Nowhere in *Oedipus* is there any statement pointing to such a conclusion —even though there is an appropriate setting, in the final choral passages, for the making of such a statement. Further, to accept any such answer is to deny what the dramatist seems at some pains to make us believe, namely, that despite the prediction, Oedipus, Jocasta, Teiresias, the Messenger, and the Shepherd all act as autonomous persons.

What emerges, then, is a view of this tragedy which sees the question of whether Oedipus is guilty of deliberate crime as almost irrelevant—except insofar as we must acknowledge that his overweening pride merits punishment, if only for his treatment of Creon and the blind prophet. But the center of Sophocles' thought in this play is found in the inescapable fact that *adikia* has been committed, however "innocently"; and in the belief that aberration must be

corrected and the rational order of the universe re-established. Oedipus consequently suffers, and the true innocents, his children, are made to suffer along
with the guilty. *Oedipus* leads to one conclusion only: This is the way life is.
The larger and controlling pattern we cannot see whole; the *logos* by which it
operates in the affairs of men is seen only indistinctly and understood only partially. But it must in the end prevail, and in its prevalence it may well cut across
individual human lives.

Why is life thus? This ultimate question Sophocles does not attempt to answer here; he is content to make a statement of the human condition.

Yet, if this is the true "meaning" of his tragedy, how can we understand
Aristotle's selection of it above all others as a model for tragic poets to follow?
Where, specifically, is there provision for what the Greeks demanded of their
tragedies—*catharsis?* Does it lie merely in Oedipus' desperate embrace of his
destiny? Can this acceptance purge for us the emotions of terror and pity
which the play has roused? Hardly. As Kitto has pointed out, "When you are
knocked flat, you must accept it; and if you cannot get up again, you must be
resigned."

Nevertheless, catharsis is offered by this tragedy—a fact empirically demonstrated in the continuing power of the play to move us profoundly. Catharsis
arises from two aspects of the drama not yet considered. One of these is the
perfection of the play's form, which, in its controlled use of every detail to
forward the author's vision, is at once a reflection and an affirmation of the
universal *logos;* and the *logos*, avowing the rational order of the universe, stands
for the forces of good, even though our finite reason is too limited to comprehend their working out. Secondly, against this larger force we measure finally
the stature of the hero as a human being. In his travail Oedipus has been heroic.
One of the first things we learn of him is that he has answered the Sphinx's
riddle: to the question, "What is it that walks on four legs in the morning, on
two at noon, and on three in the evening?" Oedipus has rightly answered,
"Man." The particular appropriateness of this part of the old myth to Sophocles'
aims is apparent, since the drama we read shows us man encountering that which
is more than man. And what Sophocles says about man—what Oedipus learns
from his travail—is that man is not the measure of all things. Driven to discover
who he is, Oedipus brings down death and destruction on his world in the very
process of discovery. Yet it is this self-destruction that cleanses Thebes because,
re-establishing *diké*, it honors that *logos* which is finally beyond our comprehension.

And here is the key to the claim that the tragedy makes on us. It is not
through terror and pity alone that *Oedipus* purges us of base emotions; ultimately, it is in the weighing of man's soul that we find release. Oedipus, parricide, lover of his mother, brother of his children, over-proud ruler, a man
blindest in his clearest visions, yet achieves magnificent stature. Greatness of
soul is the final measure of man. And greatness of soul, despite his pride, despite
his ambition and impetuosity, is the crowning attribute of the Theban king.

Oedipus Rex

by

SOPHOCLES

translated by

Dudley Fitts *and* Robert Fitzgerald

Characters

OEDIPUS
A PRIEST
CREON
TEIRESIAS
IOCASTE
MESSENGER
SHEPHERD OF LAIOS
SECOND MESSENGER
CHORUS OF THEBAN ELDERS

THE SCENE. *Before the palace of Oedipus, King of Thebes. A central door and two lateral doors open onto a platform which runs the length of the façade. On the platform, right and left, are altars; and three steps lead down into the* orchestra, *or chorus-ground.*

The steps are crowded by suppliants who have brought branches and chaplets of olive leaves and who lie in various attitudes of despair. OEDIPUS enters.

OEDIPUS. My children, generations of the living
In the line of Kadmos, nursed at his ancient hearth:
Why have you strewn yourselves before these altars
In supplication, with your boughs and garlands?
The breath of incense rises from the city
With a sound of prayer and lamentation.
        Children,
I would not have you speak through messengers,
And therefore I have come myself to hear you—
I, Oedipus, who bear the famous name.
[*To a* PRIEST.] You, there, since you are eldest in the company,
Speak for them all, tell me what preys upon you,
Whether you come in dread, or crave some blessing:
Tell me, and never doubt that I will help you

In every way I can; I should be heartless
Were I not moved to find you suppliant here.
    PRIEST. Great Oedipus, O powerful King of Thebes!
You see how all the ages of our people
Cling to your altar steps: here are boys
Who can barely stand alone, and here are priests
By weight of age, as I am a priest of God,
And young men chosen from those yet unmarried;
As for the others, all that multitude,
They wait with olive chaplets in the squares,
At the two shrines of Pallas, and where Apollo
Speaks in the glowing embers.
        Your own eyes
Must tell you: Thebes is in her extremity
And can not lift her head from the surge of death.
A rust consumes the buds and fruits of the earth;
The herds are sick; children die unborn,
And labor is vain. The god of plague and pyre

374

Raids like detestable lightning through the city,
And all the house of Kadmos is laid waste,
All emptied, and all darkened: Death alone
Battens upon the misery of Thebes.
　You are not one of the immortal gods, we know;
Yet we have come to you to make our prayer
As to the man of all men best in adversity
And wisest in the ways of God. You saved us
From the Sphinx, that flinty singer, and the tribute
We paid to her so long; yet you were never
Better informed than we, nor could we teach you:
It was some god breathed in you to set us free.
　Therefore, O mighty King, we turn to you:
Find us our safety, find us a remedy,
Whether by counsel of the gods or men.
A king of wisdom tested in the past
Can act in a time of troubles, and act well.
Noblest of men, restore
Life to your city! Think how all men call you
Liberator for your triumph long ago;
Ah, when your years of kingship are remembered,
Let them not say *We rose, but later fell*—
Keep the State from going down in the storm!
Once, years ago, with happy augury,
You brought us fortune; be the same again!
No man questions your power to rule the land:
But rule over men, not over a dead city!
Ships are only hulls, citadels are nothing,
When no life moves in the empty passageways.
　OEDIPUS. Poor children! You may be sure I know
All that you longed for in your coming here.
I know that you are deathly sick; and yet,

Sick as you are, not one is as sick as I.
Each of you suffers in himself alone
His anguish, not another's; but my spirit
Groans for the city, for myself, for you.
　I was not sleeping, you are not waking me.
No, I have been in tears for a long while
And in my restless thought walked many ways.
In all my search, I found one helpful course,
And that I have taken: I have sent Creon,
Son of Menoikeus, brother of the Queen,
To Delphi, Apollo's place of revelation,
To learn there, if he can,
What act or pledge of mine may save the city.
I have counted the days, and now, this very day,
I am troubled, for he has overstayed his time.
What is he doing? He has been gone too long.
Yet whenever he comes back, I should do ill
To scant whatever hint the god may give.
　PRIEST. It is a timely promise. At this instant
They tell me Creon is here.
　OEDIPUS.　　　　　O Lord Apollo!
May his news be fair as his face is radiant!
　PRIEST. It could not be otherwise: he is crowned with bay,
The chaplet is thick with berries.
　OEDIPUS.　　　　We shall soon know;
He is near enough to hear us now.
　　　　　[*Enter* CREON.]
　　　　　　　　　　　O Prince:
Brother: son of Menoikeus:
What answer do you bring us from the god?
　CREON. It is favorable. I can tell you, great afflictions
Will turn out well, if they are taken well.
　OEDIPUS. What was the oracle? These vague words
Leave me still hanging between hope and fear.
　CREON. Is it your pleasure to hear me with all these

Gathered around us? I am prepared to speak,
But should we not go in?

OEDIPUS.   Let them all hear it.
It is for them I suffer, more than for myself.

CREON. Then I will tell you what I heard at Delphi.
In plain words
The god commands us to expel from the land of Thebes
An old defilement that it seems we shelter.
It is a deathly thing, beyond expiation.
We must not let it feed upon us longer.

OEDIPUS. What defilement? How shall we rid ourselves of it?

CREON. By exile or death, blood for blood. It was
Murder that brought the plague-wind on the city.

OEDIPUS. Murder of whom? Surely the god has named him?

CREON. My lord: long ago Laïos was our king,
Before you came to govern us.

OEDIPUS.   I know;
I learned of him from others; I never saw him.

CREON. He was murdered; and Apollo commands us now
To take revenge upon whoever killed him.

OEDIPUS. Upon whom? Where are they? Where shall we find a clue
To solve that crime, after so many years?

CREON. Here in this land, he said. If we make enquiry,
We may touch things that otherwise escape us.

OEDIPUS. Tell me: Was Laïos murdered in his house,
Or in the fields, or in some foreign country?

CREON. He said he planned to make a pilgrimage.
                    He did not come home again.

OEDIPUS. And was there no one,
No witness, no companion, to tell what happened?

CREON. They were all killed but one, and he got away
So frightened that he could remember one thing only.

OEDIPUS. What was that one thing?
One may be the key
To everything, if we resolve to use it.

CREON. He said that a band of highwaymen attacked them,
Outnumbered them, and overwhelmed the King.

OEDIPUS. Strange, that a highwayman should be so daring—
Unless some faction here bribed him to do it.

CREON. We thought of that. But after Laïos' death
New troubles arose and we had no avenger.

OEDIPUS. What troubles could prevent your hunting down the killers?

CREON. The riddling Sphinx's song
Made us deaf to all mysteries but her own.

OEDIPUS. Then once more I must bring what is dark to light.
It is most fitting that Apollo shows,
As you do, this compunction for the dead.
You shall see how I stand by you, as I should,
To avenge the city and the city's god,
And not as though it were for some distant friend,
But for my own sake, to be rid of evil.
Whoever killed King Laïos might—who knows?—
Decide at any moment to kill me as well.
By avenging the murdered king I protect myself.
Come, then, my children: leave the altar steps,
Lift up your olive boughs!
                    One of you go
And summon the people of Kadmos to gather here.
I will do all that I can; you may tell them that. [*Exit a* PAGE.]
So, with the help of God,
We shall be saved—or else indeed we are lost.

PRIEST. Let us rise, children. It was for this we came,
And now the King has promised it himself.
Phoibos has sent us an oracle; may he descend

Himself to save us and drive out the plague.

[*Exeunt* OEDIPUS *and* CREON *into the palace by the central door. The* PRIEST *and the* SUPPLIANTS *disperse R and L. After a short pause the* CHORUS *enters the orchestra.*]

CHORUS. What is the god singing in his profound
Delphi of gold and shadow?
What oracle for Thebes, the sunwhipped city?
Fear unjoints me, the roots of my heart tremble.
Now I remember, O Healer, your power, and wonder:
Will you send doom like a sudden cloud, or weave it
Like nightfall of the past?
Ah no: be merciful, issue of holy sound:
Dearest to our expectancy: be tender!
Let me pray to Athenê, the immortal daughter of Zeus,
And to Artemis her sister
Who keeps her famous throne in the market ring,
And to Apollo, bowman at the far butts of heaven—
O gods, descend! Like three streams leap against
The fires of our grief, the fires of darkness;
Be swift to bring us rest!
As in the old time from the brilliant house
Of air you stepped to save us, come again!
Now our afflictions have no end,
Now all our stricken host lies down
And no man fights off death with his mind;
The noble plowland bears no grain,
And groaning mothers can not bear—
See, how our lives like birds take wing,
Like sparks that fly when a fire soars,
To the shore of the god of evening.
The plague burns on, it is pitiless,
Though pallid children laden with death
Lie unwept in the stony ways,
And old gray women by every path
Flock to the strand about the altars
There to strike their breasts and cry

Worship of Zeus in wailing prayers:
Be kind, God's golden child!
There are no swords in this attack by fire,
No shields, but we are ringed with cries.
Send the besieger plunging from our homes
Into the vast sea-room of the Atlantic
Or into the waves that foam eastward of Thrace—
For the day ravages what the night spares—
Destroy our enemy, lord of the thunder!
Let him be riven by lightning from heaven!
Phoibos Apollo, stretch the sun's bowstring,
That golden cord, until it sing for us,
Flashing arrows in heaven!
                    Artemis, Huntress,
Race with flaring lights upon our mountains!
O scarlet god, O golden-banded brow,
O Theban Bacchos in a storm of Maenads,
[*Enter* OEDIPUS, *from the palace.*]
Whirl upon Death, that all the Undying hate!
Come with blinding cressets, come in joy!

OEDIPUS. Is this your prayer? It may be answered. Come,
Listen to me, act as the crisis demands,
And you shall have relief from all these evils.
Until now I was a stranger to this tale,
As I had been a stranger to the crime.
Could I track down the murderer without a clue?
But now, friends,
As one who became a citizen after the murder,
I make this proclamation to all Thebans:
If any man knows by whose hand Laïos, son of Labdakos,
Met his death, I direct that man to tell me everything,
No matter what he fears for having so long withheld it.
Let it stand as promised that no further trouble
Will come to him, but he may leave the land in safety.

Moreover: If anyone knows the murderer to be foreign,
Let him not keep silent: he shall have his reward from me.
However, if he does conceal it; if any man
Fearing for his friend or for himself disobeys this edict,
Hear what I propose to do:
I solemnly forbid the people of this country,
Where power and throne are mine, ever to receive that man
Or speak to him, no matter who he is, or let him
Join in sacrifice, lustration, or in prayer.
I decree that he be driven from every house,
Being, as he is, corruption itself to us: the Delphic
Voice of Zeus has pronounced this revelation.
Thus I associate myself with the oracle
And take the side of the murdered king.
As for the criminal, I pray to God—
Whether it be a lurking thief, or one of a number—
I pray that that man's life be consumed in evil and wretchedness.
And as for me, this curse applies no less
If it should turn out that the culprit is my guest here,
Sharing my hearth.
You have heard the penalty.
I lay it on you now to attend to this
For my sake, for Apollo's, for the sick
Sterile city that heaven has abandoned.
Suppose the oracle had given you no command:
Should this defilement go uncleansed for ever?
You should have found the murderer: your king,
A noble king, had been destroyed!
Now I,
Having the power that he held before me,
Having his bed, begetting children there
Upon his wife, as he would have, had he lived—
Their son would have been my children's brother,
If Laïos had had luck in fatherhood!
(But surely ill luck rushed upon his reign)—
I say I take the son's part, just as though
I were his son, to press the fight for him
And see it won! I'll find the hand that brought
Death to Labdakos' and Polydoros' child,
Heir of Kadmos' and Agenor's line.
And as for those who fail me,
May the gods deny them the fruit of the earth,
Fruit of the womb, and may they rot utterly!
Let them be wretched as we are wretched, and worse!
For you, for loyal Thebans, and for all
Who find my actions right, I pray the favor
Of justice, and of all the immortal gods.

CHORAGOS. Since I am under oath, my lord, I swear
I did not do the murder, I can not name
The murderer. Might not the oracle
That has ordained the search tell where to find him?

OEDIPUS. An honest question. But no man in the world
Can make the gods do more than the gods will.

CHORAGOS. There is one last expedient—
OEDIPUS.   Tell me what it is.
Though it seem slight, you must not hold it back.

CHORAGOS. A lord clairvoyant to the lord Apollo,
As we all know, is the skilled Teiresias.
One might learn much about this from him, Oedipus.

OEDIPUS. I am not wasting time:
Creon spoke of this, and I have sent for him—
Twice, in fact; it is strange that he is not here.

CHORAGOS. The other matter—that old report—seems useless.

OEDIPUS. Tell me. I am interested in all reports.

CHORAGOS. The King was said to have been killed by highwaymen.

OEDIPUS. I know. But we have no witnesses to that.

CHORAGOS. If the killer can feel a particle of dread,

Your curse will bring him out of hiding!

OEDIPUS.   No.

The man who dared that act will fear no curse.

[*Enter the blind seer* TEIRESIAS, *led by a* PAGE.]

CHORAGOS. But there is one man who may detect the criminal.

This is Teiresias, this is the holy prophet

In whom, alone of all men, truth was born.

OEDIPUS. Teiresias: seer: student of mysteries,

Of all that's taught and all that no man tells,

Secrets of Heaven and secrets of the earth:

Blind though you are, you know the city lies

Sick with plague; and from this plague, my lord,

We find that you alone can guard or save us.

Possibly you did not hear the messengers?

Apollo, when we sent to him,

Sent us back word that this great pestilence

Would lift, but only if we established clearly

The identity of those who murdered Laïos.

They must be killed or exiled.

Can you use

Birdflight or any art of divination

To purify yourself, and Thebes, and me

From this contagion? We are in your hands.

There is no fairer duty

Than that of helping others in distress.

TEIRESIAS. How dreadful knowledge of the truth can be

When there's no help in truth! I knew this well,

But did not act on it: else I should not have come.

OEDIPUS. What is troubling you? Why are your eyes so cold?

TEIRESIAS. Let me go home. Bear your own fate, and I'll

Bear mine. It is better so: trust what I say.

OEDIPUS. What you say is ungracious and unhelpful

To your native country. Do not refuse to speak.

TEIRESIAS. When it comes to speech, your own is neither temperate

Nor opportune. I wish to be more prudent.

OEDIPUS. In God's name, we all beg you—

TEIRESIAS.   You are all ignorant.

No; I will never tell you what I know.

Now it is my misery; then, it would be yours.

OEDIPUS. What! You do know something, and will not tell us?

You would betray us all and wreck the State?

TEIRESIAS. I do not intend to torture myself, or you.

Why persist in asking? You will not persuade me.

OEDIPUS. What a wicked old man you are! You'd try a stone's

Patience! Out with it! Have you no feeling at all?

TEIRESIAS. You call me unfeeling. If you could only see

The nature of your own feelings . . .

OEDIPUS.   Why,

Who would not feel as I do? Who could endure

Your arrogance toward the city?

TEIRESIAS.   What does it matter!

Whether I speak or not, it is bound to come.

OEDIPUS. Then, if "it" is bound to come, you are bound to tell me.

TEIRESIAS. No, I will not go on. Rage as you please.

OEDIPUS. Rage? Why not!

And I'll tell you what I think:

You planned it, you had it done, you all but

Killed him with your own hands: if you had eyes,

I'd say the crime was yours, and yours alone.

TEIRESIAS. So? I charge you, then,

Abide by the proclamation you have made:

From this day forth

Never speak again to these men or to me;

You yourself are the pollution of this
country.

OEDIPUS. You dare say that! Can you
possibly think you have
Some way of going free, after such insolence?

TEIRESIAS. I have gone free. It is the
truth sustains me.

OEDIPUS. Who taught you shameless-
ness? It was not your craft.

TEIRESIAS. You did. You made me
speak. I did not want to.

OEDIPUS. Speak what? Let me hear it
again more clearly.

TEIRESIAS. Was it not clear before? Are
you tempting me?

OEDIPUS. I did not understand it. Say it
again.

TEIRESIAS. I say that you are the murderer whom you seek.

OEDIPUS. Now twice you have spat out
infamy. You'll pay for it!

TEIRESIAS. Would you care for more?
Do you wish to be really angry?

OEDIPUS. Say what you will. Whatever
you say is worthless.

TEIRESIAS. I say that you live in hideous
love with her
Who is nearest you in blood. You are
blind to the evil.

OEDIPUS. It seems you can go on mouth-
ing like this for ever.

TEIRESIAS. I can, if there is power in
truth.

OEDIPUS.   There is:
But not for you, not for you,
You sightless, witless, senseless, mad old
man!

TEIRESIAS. You are the madman. There
is no one here
Who will not curse you soon, as you
curse me.

OEDIPUS. You child of endless night!
You can not hurt me
Or any other man who sees the sun.

TEIRESIAS. True: it is not from me your
fate will come.
That lies within Apollo's competence,
As it is his concern.

OEDIPUS.   Tell me:
Are you speaking for Creon, or for yourself?

TEIRESIAS. Creon is no threat. You
weave your own doom.

OEDIPUS. Wealth, power, craft of states-
manship!
Kingly position, everywhere admired!
What savage envy is stored up against
these,
If Creon, whom I trusted, Creon my
friend,
For this great office which the city once
Put in my hands unsought—if for this
power
Creon desires in secret to destroy me!

He has bought this decrepit fortune-
teller, this
Collector of dirty pennies, this prophet
fraud—
Why, he is no more clairvoyant than I
am!
                                    Tell us:
Has your mystic mummery ever ap-
proached the truth?
When that hellcat the Sphinx was per-
forming here,
What help were you to these people?
Her magic was not for the first man who
came along:
It demanded a real exorcist. Your birds—
What good were they? or the gods, for
the matter of that?
But I came by,
Oedipus, the simple man, who knows
nothing—
I thought it out for myself, no birds
helped me!
And this is the man you think you can
destroy,
That you may be close to Creon when
he's king!
Well, you and your friend Creon, it
seems to me,
Will suffer most. If you were not an old
man,
You would have paid already for your
plot.

CHORAGOS. We can not see that his
words or yours
Have been spoken except in anger, Oedi-
pus,
And of anger we have no need. How can
God's will
Be accomplished best? That is what most
concerns us.

TEIRESIAS. You are a king. But where
argument's concerned
I am your man, as much a king as you.

I am not your servant, but Apollo's.
I have no need of Creon to speak for me.
  Listen to me. You mock my blindness,
    do you?
But I say that you, with both your eyes,
    are blind:
You can not see the wretchedness of
    your life,
Nor in whose house you live, no, nor
    with whom.
Who are your father and mother? Can
    you tell me?
You do not even know the blind wrongs
That you have done them, on earth and
    in the world below.
But the double lash of your parents'
    curse will whip you
Out of this land some day, with only
    night
Upon your precious eyes.
Your cries then—where will they not be
    heard?
What fastness of Kithairon will not echo
    them?
And that bridal-descant of yours—you'll
    know it then,
The song they sang when you came here
    to Thebes
And found your misguided berthing.
All this, and more, that you can not guess
    at now,
Will bring you to yourself among your
    children.

  Be angry, then. Curse Creon. Curse my
    words.
I tell you, no man that walks upon the
    earth
Shall be rooted out more horribly than
    you.

  OEDIPUS. Am I to bear this from him?
    —Damnation
Take you! Out of this place! Out of my
    sight!

  TEIRESIAS. I would not have come at all
    if you had not asked me.

  OEDIPUS. Could I have told that you'd
    talk nonsense, that
You'd come here to make a fool of your-
    self, and of me?

  TEIRESIAS. A fool? Your parents thought
    me sane enough.

  OEDIPUS. My parents again!—Wait: who
    were my parents?

  TEIRESIAS. This day will give you a
father, and break your heart.

  OEDIPUS. Your infantile riddles! Your
    damned abracadabra!

  TEIRESIAS. You were a great man once
    at solving riddles.

  OEDIPUS. Mock me with that if you
    like; you will find it true.

  TEIRESIAS. It was true enough. It
    brought about your ruin.

  OEDIPUS. But if it saved this town?

  TEIRESIAS. [To the PAGE.] Boy, give me
    your hand.

  OEDIPUS. Yes, boy; lead him away.
                    —While you are here
We can do nothing. Go; leave us in
    peace.

  TEIRESIAS. I will go when I have said
    what I have to say.
How can you hurt me? And I tell you
    again:
The man you have been looking for all
    this time,
The damned man, the murderer of Laïos,
That man is in Thebes. To your mind he
    is foreign-born,
But it will soon be shown that he is a
    Theban,
A revelation that will fail to please.
                            A blind man,
Who has his eyes now; a penniless man,
    who is rich now;
And he will go tapping the strange earth
    with his staff.
To the children with whom he lives now
    he will be
Brother and father—the very same; to her
Who bore him, son and husband—the
    very same
Who came to his father's bed, wet with
    his father's blood.

  Enough. Go think that over.
If later you find error in what I have
    said,
You may say that I have no skill in
    prophecy.

  [Exit TEIRESIAS, led by his PAGE.
  OEDIPUS goes into the palace.]

  CHORUS. The Delphic stone of prophe-
    cies
Remembers ancient regicide
And a still bloody hand.
That killer's hour of flight has come.
He must be stronger than riderless

Coursers of untiring wind,
For the son of Zeus armed with his
    father's thunder
Leaps in lightning after him;
And the Furies follow him, the sad
    Furies.

Holy Parnassos' peak of snow
Flashes and blinds that secret man,
That all shall hunt him down:
Though he may roam the forest shade
Like a bull gone wild from pasture
To rage through glooms of stone.
Doom comes down on him; flight will
    not avail him;
For the world's heart calls him desolate,
And the immortal Furies follow, for ever
    follow.

But now a wilder thing is heard
From the old man skilled at hearing Fate
    in the wingbeat of a bird.
Bewildered as a blown bird, my soul
    hovers and can not find
Foothold in this debate, or any reason or
    rest of mind.

But no man ever brought—none can
    bring
Proof of strife between Thebes' royal
    house,
Labdakos' line, and the son of Polybos;
And never until now has any man
    brought word
Of Laïos' dark death staining Oedipus
    the King.

Divine Zeus and Apollo hold
Perfect intelligence alone of all tales ever
    told;
And well though this diviner works, he
    works in his own night;
No man can judge that rough unknown
    or trust in second sight,
For wisdom changes hands among the
    wise.
Shall I believe my great lord criminal
At a raging word that a blind old man let
    fall?
I saw him, when the carrion woman
    faced him of old,
Prove his heroic mind! These evil words
    are lies.

CREON. Men of Thebes:
I am told that heavy accusations
Have been brought against me by King
    Oedipus.

I am not the kind of man to bear this
    tamely.
If in these present difficulties
He holds me accountable for any harm
    to him
Through anything I have said or done—
    why, then,
I do not value life in this dishonor.
It is not as though this rumor touched
    upon
Some private indiscretion. The matter is
    grave.
The fact is that I am being called disloyal
To the State, to my fellow citizens, to
    my friends.

CHORAGOS. He may have spoken in
    anger, not from his mind.

CREON. But did you not hear him say I
    was the one
Who seduced the old prophet into lying?

CHORAGOS. The thing was said; I do not
    know how seriously.

CREON. But you were watching him!
    Were his eyes steady?
Did he look like a man in his right mind?

CHORAGOS.   I do not know.
I can not judge the behavior of great
    men.
But here is the King himself.

                [Enter OEDIPUS.]
OEDIPUS.   So you dared come back.
Why? How brazen of you to come to
    my house,
You murderer!
                Do you think I do not know
That you plotted to kill me, plotted to
    steal my throne?
Tell me, in God's name: am I coward, a
    fool,
That you should dream you could ac-
    complish this?
A fool who could not see your slippery
    game?
A coward, not to fight back when I saw
    it?
You are the fool, Creon, are you not?
    hoping
Without support or friends to get a
    throne?
Thrones may be won or bought: you
    could do neither.

CREON. Now listen to me. You have
    talked; let me talk, too.

You can not judge unless you know the facts.

OEDIPUS. You speak well: there is one fact; but I find it hard
To learn from the deadliest enemy I have.

CREON. That above all I must dispute with you.

OEDIPUS. That above all I will not hear you deny.

CREON. If you think there is anything good in being stubborn
Against all reason, then I say you are wrong.

OEDIPUS. If you think a man can sin against his own kind
And not be punished for it, I say you are mad.

CREON. I agree. But tell me: what have I done to you?

OEDIPUS. You advised me to send for that wizard, did you not?

CREON. I did. I should do it again.

OEDIPUS.   Very well. Now tell me:
How long has it been since Laïos—

CREON.   What of Laïos?

OEDIPUS. Since he vanished in that onset by the road?

CREON. It was long ago, a long time.

OEDIPUS.   And this prophet,
Was he practicing here then?

CREON. He was; and with honor, as now.

OEDIPUS. Did he speak of me at that time?

CREON.   He never did;
At least, not when I was present.

OEDIPUS.   But . . . the enquiry?
I suppose you held one?

CREON. We did, but we learned nothing.

OEDIPUS. Why did the prophet not speak against me then?

CREON. I do not know; and I am the kind of man
Who holds his tongue when he has no facts to go on.

OEDIPUS. There's one fact that you know, and you could tell it.

CREON. What fact is that? If I know it, you shall have it.

OEDIPUS. If he were not involved with you, he could not say
That it was I who murdered Laïos.

CREON. If he says that, you are the one that knows it!—
But now it is my turn to question you.

OEDIPUS. Put your questions. I am no murderer.

CREON. First, then: You married my sister?

OEDIPUS.   I married your sister.

CREON. And you rule the kingdom equally with her?

OEDIPUS. Everything that she wants she has from me.

CREON. And I am the third, equal to both of you?

OEDIPUS. That is why I call you a bad friend.

CREON. No. Reason it out, as I have done.
Think of this first: Would any sane man prefer
Power, with all a king's anxieties,
To that same power and the grace of sleep?
Certainly not I.
I have never longed for the king's power
—only his rights.
Would any wise man differ from me in this?
As matters stand, I have my way in everything
With your consent, and no responsibilities.
If I were king, I should be a slave to policy.
How could I desire a scepter more
Than what is now mine—untroubled influence?
No, I have not gone mad; I need no honors,
Except those with the perquisites I have now.
I am welcome everywhere; every man salutes me,
And those who want your favor seek my ear,
Since I know how to manage what they ask.
Should I exchange this ease for that anxiety?
Besides, no sober mind is treasonable.
I hate anarchy
And never would deal with any man who likes it.

Test what I have said. Go to the priestess
At Delphi, ask if I quoted her correctly.
And as for this other thing: if I am found
Guilty of treason with Teiresias,
Then sentence me to death! You have my word
It is a sentence I should cast my vote for—
But not without evidence!
                        You do wrong
When you take good men for bad, bad men for good.
A true friend thrown aside—why, life itself
Is not more precious!
              In time you will know this well:
For time, and time alone, will show the just man,
Though scoundrels are discovered in a day.

CHORAGOS. This is well said, and a prudent man would ponder it.
Judgments too quickly formed are dangerous.

OEDIPUS. But is he not quick in his duplicity?
And shall I not be quick to parry him?
Would you have me stand still, hold my peace, and let
This man win everything, through my inaction?

CREON. And you want—what is it, then? To banish me?

OEDIPUS. No, not exile. It is your death I want,
So that all the world may see what treason means.

CREON. You will persist, then? You will not believe me?

OEDIPUS. How can I believe you?

CREON.   Then you are a fool.

OEDIPUS. To save myself?

CREON.   In justice, think of me.

OEDIPUS. You are evil incarnate.

CREON. But suppose that you are wrong?

OEDIPUS. Still I must rule.

CREON.   But not if you rule badly.

OEDIPUS. O city, city!

CREON.   It is my city, too!

CHORAGOS. Now, my lords, be still. I see the Queen,

Iocastê, coming from her palace chambers;
And it is time she came, for the sake of you both.
This dreadful quarrel can be resolved through her.

                    [Enter IOCASTE.]

IOCASTE. Poor foolish men, what wicked din is this?
With Thebes sick to death, is it not shameful
That you should rake some private quarrel up?
[To OEDIPUS.] Come into the house.
              —And you, Creon, go now:
Let us have no more of this tumult over nothing.

CREON. Nothing? No, sister: what your husband plans for me
Is one of two great evils: exile or death.

OEDIPUS. He is right.
Why, woman I have caught him squarely
Plotting against my life.

CREON.   No! Let me die
Accurst if ever I have wished you harm!

IOCASTE. Ah, believe it, Oedipus!
In the name of the gods, respect this oath of his
For my sake, for the sake of these people here!

CHORAGOS. Open your mind to her, my lord. Be ruled by her, I beg you!

OEDIPUS. What would you have me do?

CHORAGOS. Respect Creon's word. He has never spoken like a fool,
And now he has sworn an oath.

OEDIPUS.   You know what you ask?

CHORAGOS.   I do.

OEDIPUS.   Speak on, then.

CHORAGOS. A friend so sworn should not be baited so,
In blind malice, and without final proof.

OEDIPUS. You are aware, I hope, that what you say
Means death for me, or exile at the least.

CHORAGOS. No, I swear by Helios, first in Heaven!
May I die friendless and accurst,
The worst of deaths, if ever I meant that!
    It is the withering fields
        That hurt my sick heart:
    Must we bear all these ills,
        And now your bad blood as well?

OEDIPUS. Then let him go. And let me die, if I must,
Or be driven by him in shame from the land of Thebes.
It is your unhappiness, and not his talk,
That touches me.
                              As for him—
Wherever he is, I will hate him as long as I live.
    CREON. Ugly in yielding, as you were ugly in rage!
Natures like yours chiefly torment themselves.
    OEDIPUS. Can you not go? Can you not leave me?
    CREON.   I can.
You do not know me; but the city knows me,
And in its eyes I am just, if not in yours.
    [*Exit* CREON.]
    CHORAGOS. Lady Iocastê, did you not ask the King to go to his chambers?
    IOCASTE. First tell me what has happened.
    CHORAGOS. There was suspicion without evidence; yet it rankled
As even false charges will.
    IOCASTE.   On both sides?
    CHORAGOS.   On both.
    IOCASTE.   But what was said?
    CHORAGOS. Oh let it rest, let it be done with!
Have we not suffered enough?
    OEDIPUS. You see to what your decency has brought you:
You have made difficulties where my heart saw none.
    CHORAGOS. Oedipus, it is not once only I have told you—
You must know I should count myself unwise
To the point of madness, should I now forsake you—
    You, under whose hand,
        In the storm of another time,
    Our dear land sailed out free.
        But now stand fast at the helm!
    IOCASTE. In God's name, Oedipus, inform your wife as well:
Why are you so set in this hard anger?
    OEDIPUS. I will tell you, for none of these men deserves
My confidence as you do. It is Creon's work,

His treachery, his plotting against me.
    IOCASTE. Go on, if you can make this clear to me.
    OEDIPUS. He charges me with the murder of Laïos.
    IOCASTE. Has he some knowledge? Or does he speak from hearsay?
    OEDIPUS. He would not commit himself to such a charge,
But he has brought in that damnable soothsayer
To tell his story.
    IOCASTE.   Set your mind at rest.
If it is a question of soothsayers, I tell you
That you will find no man whose craft gives knowledge
Of the unknowable.
                              Here is my proof:
    An oracle was reported to Laïos once
(I will not say from Phoibos himself, but from
His appointed ministers, at any rate)
That his doom would be death at the hands of his own son—
His son, born of his flesh and of mine!
    Now, you remember the story: Laïos was killed
By marauding strangers where three highways meet;
But his child had not been three days in this world
Before the King had pierced the baby's ankles
And had him left to die on a lonely mountain.
    Thus, Apollo never caused that child
To kill his father, and it was not Laïos' fate
To die at the hands of his son, as he had feared.
This is what prophets and prophecies are worth!
Have no dread of them.
                              It is God himself
Who can show us what he wills, in his own way.
    OEDIPUS. How strange a shadowy memory crossed my mind,
Just now while you were speaking; it chilled my heart.
    IOCASTE. What do you mean? What memory do you speak of?

OEDIPUS. If I understand you, Laïos was killed
At a place where three roads meet.

IOCASTE.   So it was said;
We have no later story.

OEDIPUS.   Where did it happen?

IOCASTE. Phokis, it is called: at a place where the Theban Way
Divides into the roads toward Delphi and Daulia.

OEDIPUS. When?

IOCASTE. We had the news not long before you came
And proved the right to your succession here.

OEDIPUS. Ah, what net has God been weaving for me?

IOCASTE. Oedipus! Why does this trouble you?

OEDIPUS.   Do not ask me yet.
First, tell me how Laïos looked, and tell me
How old he was.

IOCASTE.
            He was tall, his hair just touched
With white; his form was not unlike your own.

OEDIPUS. I think that I myself may be accurst
By my own ignorant edict.

IOCASTE.   You speak strangely.
It makes me tremble to look at you, my King.

OEDIPUS. I am not sure that the blind man can not see.
But I should know better if you were to tell me—

IOCASTE. Anything—though I dread to hear you ask it.

OEDIPUS. Was the King lightly escorted, or did he ride
With a large company, as a ruler should?

IOCASTE. There were five men with him in all: one was a herald;
And a single chariot, which he was driving.

OEDIPUS. Alas, that makes it plain enough!
                    But who—
Who told you how it happened?

IOCASTE.   A household servant,
The only one to escape.

OEDIPUS.   And is he still
A servant of ours?

IOCASTE.
            No; for when he came back at last
And found you enthroned in the place of the dead king,
He came to me, touched my hand with his, and begged
That I would send him away to the frontier district
Where only the shepherds go—
As far away from the city as I could send him.
I granted his prayer; for although the man was a slave,
He had earned more than this favor at my hands.

OEDIPUS. Can he be called back quickly?

IOCASTE.   Easily.
But why?

OEDIPUS.
            I have taken too much upon myself
Without enquiry; therefore I wish to consult him.

IOCASTE. Then he shall come.
                    But am I not one also
To whom you might confide these fears of yours?

OEDIPUS. That is your right; it will not be denied you,
Now least of all; for I have reached a pitch
Of wild foreboding. Is there anyone
To whom I should sooner speak?
Polybos of Corinth is my father.
My mother is a Dorian: Meropê.
I grew up chief among the men of Corinth
Until a strange thing happened—
Not worth my passion, it may be, but strange.
    At a feast, a drunken man maundering in his cups
Cries out that I am not my father's son!
I contained myself that night, though I felt anger
And a sinking heart. The next day I visited
My father and mother, and questioned them. They stormed,
Calling it all the slanderous rant of a fool;
And this relieved me. Yet the suspicion
Remained always aching in my mind;
I knew there was talk; I could not rest;

And finally, saying nothing to my parents,
I went to the shrine at Delphi.
The god dismissed my question without reply;
He spoke of other things.
                  Some were clear,
Full of wretchedness, dreadful, unbearable:
As, that I should lie with my own mother, breed
Children from whom all men would turn their eyes;
And that I should be my father's murderer.
    I heard all this, and fled. And from that day
Corinth to me was only in the stars
Descending in that quarter of the sky,
As I wandered farther and farther on my way
To a land where I should never see the evil
Sung by the oracle. And I came to this country
Where, so you say, King Laïos was killed.
    I will tell you all that happened there, my lady.
There were three highways
Coming together at a place I passed;
And there a herald came towards me, and a chariot
Drawn by horses, with a man such as you describe
Seated in it. The groom leading the horses
Forced me off the road at his lord's command;
But as this charioteer lurched over towards me
I struck him in my rage. The old man saw me
And brought his double goad down upon my head
As I came abreast.
              He was paid back, and more!
Swinging my club in this right hand I knocked him
Out of his car, and he rolled on the ground.
                  I killed him.
I killed them all.

Now if that stranger and Laïos were—kin,
Where is a man more miserable than I?
More hated by the gods? Citizen and alien alike
Must never shelter me or speak to me—
I must be shunned by all.
                  And I myself
Pronounced this malediction upon myself!
    Think of it: I have touched you with these hands,
These hands that killed your husband. What defilement!
    Am I all evil, then? It must be so,
Since I must flee from Thebes, yet never again
See my own countrymen, my own country,
For fear of joining my mother in marriage
And killing Polybos, my father.
                      Ah,
If I was created so, born to this fate,
Who could deny the savagery of God?
    O holy majesty of heavenly powers!
May I never see that day! Never!
Rather let me vanish from the race of men
Than know the abomination destined me!
    CHORAGOS. We too, my lord, have felt dismay at this.
But there is hope: you have yet to hear the shepherd.
    OEDIPUS. Indeed, I fear no other hope is left me.
    IOCASTE. What do you hope from him when he comes?
    OEDIPUS.   This much:
If his account of the murder tallies with yours,
Then I am cleared.
    IOCASTE.   What was it that I said
Of such importance?
    OEDIPUS. Why, "marauders," you said,
Killed the King, according to this man's story.
If he maintains that still, if there were several,
Clearly the guilt is not mine: I was alone.
But if he says one man, singlehanded, did it,
Then the evidence all points to me.

IOCASTE. You may be sure that he said there were several;
And can he call back that story now? He can not.
The whole city heard it as plainly as I.
But suppose he alters some detail of it:
He can not ever show that Laïos' death
Fulfilled the oracle: for Apollo said
My child was doomed to kill him; and my child—
Poor baby!—it was my child that died first.
No. From now on, where oracles are concerned,
I would not waste a second thought on any.

OEDIPUS. You may be right.
                But come: let someone go
For the shepherd at once. This matter must be settled.

IOCASTE. I will send for him.
I would not wish to cross you in anything,
And surely not in this.—Let us go in.

[*Exeunt into the palace, the* CHORUS *remaining.*]

CHORUS. Let me be reverent in the ways of right,
Lowly the paths I journey on;
Let all my words and actions keep
The laws of the pure universe
From highest Heaven handed down.
For Heaven is their bright nurse,
Those generations of the realms of light;
Ah, never of mortal kind were they begot,
Nor are they slaves of memory, lost in sleep:
Their Father is greater than Time and ages not.

The tyrant is a child of Pride
Who drinks from his great sickening cup
Recklessness and vanity,
Until from his high crest headlong
He plummets to the dust of hope.
That strong man is not strong.
But let no fair ambition be denied;
May God protect the wrestler for the State
In government, in comely policy,
Who will fear God, and on His ordinance wait.

Haughtiness and the high hand of disdain

Tempt and outrage God's holy law;
And any mortal who dares hold
No immortal Power in awe
Will be caught up in a net of pain:
The price for which his levity is sold.
Let each man take due earnings, then,
And keep his hands from holy things,
And from blasphemy stand apart—
Else the crackling blast of heaven
Blows on his head, and on his desperate heart;
Though fools will honor impious men,
In their cities no tragic poet sings.

Shall we lose faith in Delphi's obscurities,
We who have heard the world's core
Discredited, and the sacred wood
Of Zeus at Elis praised no more?
The deeds and the strange prophecies
Must make a pattern yet to be understood.
Zeus, if indeed you are lord of all,
Throned in light over night and day,
Mirror this in your endless mind:
Our masters call the oracle
Words on the wind, and the Delphic vision blind!
Their hearts no longer know Apollo,
And reverence for the gods has died away.

[*Enter* IOCASTE.]

IOCASTE. Princes of Thebes, it has occurred to me
To visit the altars of the gods, bearing
These branches as a suppliant, and this incense.
Our King is not himself: his noble soul
Is overwrought with fantasies of dread,
Else he would consider
The new prophecies in the light of the old.
He will listen to any voice that speaks disaster,
And my advice goes for nothing.

[*She approaches the altar.*]
                To you, then, Apollo,
Lycean lord, since you are nearest, I turn in prayer.
Receive these offerings, and grant us deliverance
From defilement. Our hearts are heavy with fear
When we see our leader distracted, as helpless sailors

Are terrified by the confusion of their
  helmsman.

[*Enter* MESSENGER.]

MESSENGER. Friends, no doubt you can
  direct me:
Where shall I find the house of Oedipus,
Or, better still, where is the King himself?

CHORAGOS. It is this very place, stranger;
  he is inside.
This is his wife and mother of his children.

MESSENGER. I wish her happiness in a
  happy house,
Blest in all the fulfillment of her marriage.

IOCASTE. I wish as much for you: your
  courtesy
Deserves a like good fortune. But now,
  tell me:
Why have you come? What have you to
  say to us?

MESSENGER. Good news, my lady, for
  your house and your husband.

IOCASTE. What news? Who sent you
  here?

MESSENGER.   I am from Corinth.
The news I bring ought to mean joy for
  you,
Though it may be you will find some
  grief in it.

IOCASTE. What is it? How can it touch
  us in both ways?

MESSENGER. The people of Corinth,
  they say,
Intend to call Oedipus to be their king.

IOCASTE. But old Polybos—is he not
  reigning still?

MESSENGER. No. Death holds him in his
  sepulchre.

IOCASTE. What are you saying? Polybos is dead?

MESSENGER. If I am not telling the
  truth, may I die myself.

IOCASTE. [*To a* MAIDSERVANT.] Go in,
  go quickly; tell this to your master.
O riddlers of God's will, where are
  you now!
This was the man whom Oedipus, long
  ago,
Feared so, fled so, in dread of destroying
  him—
But it was another fate by which he
  died.

[*Enter* OEDIPUS, *from palace.*]

OEDIPUS. Dearest Iocastê, why have you
  sent for me?

IOCASTE. Listen to what this man says,
  and then tell me
What has become of the solemn prophecies.

OEDIPUS. Who is this man? What is his
  news for me?

IOCASTE. He has come from Corinth
  to announce your father's death!

OEDIPUS. Is it true, stranger? Tell me
  in your own words.

MESSENGER. I can not say it more
  clearly: the King is dead.

OEDIPUS. Was it by treason? Or by an
  attack of illness?

MESSENGER. A little thing brings old
  men to their rest.

OEDIPUS. It was sickness, then?

MESSENGER.   Yes, and his many years.

OEDIPUS. Ah!
Why should a man respect the Pythian
  hearth, or
Give heed to the birds that jangle above
  his head?
They prophesied that I should kill
  Polybos,
Kill my own father; but he is dead and
  buried,
And I am here—I never touched him,
  never,
Unless he died of grief for my departure,
And thus, in a sense, through me. No.
  Polybos
Has packed the oracles off with him
  underground.
They are empty words.

IOCASTE.   Had I not told you so?

OEDIPUS. You had; it was my faint
  heart that betrayed me.

IOCASTE. From now on never think of
  those things again.

OEDIPUS. And yet—must I not fear my
  mother's bed?

IOCASTE. Why should anyone in this
  world be afraid,
Since Fate rules us and nothing can be
  foreseen?
A man should live only for the present
  day.
  Have no more fear of sleeping with
  your mother:

How many men, in dreams, have lain
    with their mothers!
No reasonable man is troubled by such
    things.
    OEDIPUS. That is true; only—
If only my mother were not still alive!
But she is alive. I can not help my dread.
    IOCASTE. Yet this news of your father's
    death is wonderful.
    OEDIPUS. Wonderful. But I fear the liv-
    ing woman.
    MESSENGER. Tell me, who is this
    woman that you fear?
    OEDIPUS. It is Meropê, man; the wife
    of King Polybos.
    MESSENGER. Meropê? Why should you
    be afraid of her?
    OEDIPUS. An oracle of the gods, a
    dreadful saying.
    MESSENGER. Can you tell me about it
    or are you sworn to silence?
    OEDIPUS. I can tell you, and I will.
Apollo said through his prophet that I
    was the man
Who should marry his own mother, shed
    his father's blood
With his own hands. And so, for all
    these years
I have kept clear of Corinth, and no
    harm has come—
Though it would have been sweet to see
    my parents again.
    MESSENGER. And is this the fear that
    drove you out of Corinth?
    OEDIPUS. Would you have me kill my
    father?
    MESSENGER.   As for that
You must be reassured by the news I
    gave you.
    OEDIPUS. If you could reassure me, I
    would reward you.
    MESSENGER. I had that in mind, I will
    confess: I thought
I could count on you when you returned
    to Corinth.
    OEDIPUS. No: I will never go near my
    parents again.
    MESSENGER. Ah, son, you still do not
    know what you are doing—
    OEDIPUS. What do you mean? In the
    name of God tell me!
    MESSENGER. —If these are your reasons
    for not going home.

    OEDIPUS. I tell you, I fear the oracle
    may come true.
    MESSENGER. And guilt may come upon
    you through your parents?
    OEDIPUS. That is the dread that is al-
    ways in my heart.
    MESSENGER. Can you not see that all
    your fears are groundless?
    OEDIPUS. How can you say that? They
    are my parents, surely?
    MESSENGER. Polybos was not your
    father.
    OEDIPUS.   Not my father?
    MESSENGER. No more your father than
    the man speaking to you.
    OEDIPUS. But you are nothing to me!
    MESSENGER.   Neither was he.
    OEDIPUS. Then why did he call me son?
    MESSENGER.   I will tell you:
Long ago he had you from my hands,
    as a gift.
    OEDIPUS. Then how could he love me
    so, if I was not his?
    MESSENGER. He had no children, and
    his heart turned to you.
    OEDIPUS. What of you? Did you buy
    me? Did you find me by chance?
    MESSENGER. I came upon you in the
    crooked pass of Kithairon.
    OEDIPUS. And what were you doing
    there?
    MESSENGER.   Tending my flocks.
    OEDIPUS. A wandering shepherd?
    MESSENGER.
        But your savior, son, that day.
    OEDIPUS. From what did you save me?
    MESSENGER.
        Your ankles should tell you that.
    OEDIPUS. Ah, stranger, why do you
    speak of that childhood pain?
    MESSENGER. I cut the bonds that tied
    your ankles together.
    OEDIPUS. I have had the mark as long
    as I can remember.
    MESSENGER. That was why you were
    given the name you bear.
    OEDIPUS. God! Was it my father or my
    mother who did it?
Tell me!
    MESSENGER. I do not know. The man
    who gave you to me
Can tell you better than I.
    OEDIPUS. It was not you that found me,
    but another?

MESSENGER. It was another shepherd gave you to me.

OEDIPUS. Who was he? Can you tell me who he was?

MESSENGER. I think he was said to be one of Laïos' people.

OEDIPUS. You mean the Laïos who was king here years ago?

MESSENGER. Yes; King Laïos; and the man was one of his herdsmen.

OEDIPUS. Is he still alive? Can I see him?

MESSENGER.   These men here Know best about such things.

OEDIPUS.   Does anyone here Know this shepherd that he is talking about?

Have you seen him in the fields, or in the town?

If you have, tell me. It is time things were made plain.

CHORAGOS. I think the man he means is that same shepherd

You have already asked to see. Iocastê perhaps

Could tell you something.

OEDIPUS.   Do you know anything About him, Lady? Is he the man we have summoned?

Is that the man this shepherd means?

IOCASTE.   Why think of him? Forget this herdsman. Forget it all.

This talk is a waste of time.

OEDIPUS.   How can you say that, When the clues to my true birth are in my hands?

IOCASTE. For God's love, let us have no more questioning!

Is your life nothing to you?

My own is pain enough for me to bear.

OEDIPUS. You need not worry. Suppose my mother a slave,

And born of slaves: no baseness can touch you.

IOCASTE. Listen to me, I beg you: do not do this thing!

OEDIPUS. I will not listen; the truth must be made known.

IOCASTE. Everything that I say is for your own good!

OEDIPUS.   My own good Snaps my patience, then; I want none of it.

IOCASTE. You are fatally wrong! May you never learn who you are!

OEDIPUS. Go, one of you, and bring the shepherd here.

Let us leave this woman to brag of her royal name.

IOCASTE. Ah, miserable!

That is the only word I have for you now.

That is the only word I can ever have.

[Exit into the palace.]

CHORAGOS. Why has she left us, Oedipus? Why has she gone

In such a passion of sorrow? I fear this silence:

Something dreadful may come of it.

OEDIPUS.   Let it come! However base my birth, I must know about it.

The Queen, like a woman, is perhaps ashamed

To think of my low origin. But I

Am a child of Luck; I can not be dishonored.

Luck is my mother; the passing months, my brothers,

Have seen me rich and poor.

        If this is so, How could I wish that I were someone else?

How could I not be glad to know my birth?

CHORUS. If ever the coming time were known

To my heart's pondering,

Kithairon, now by Heaven I see the torches

At the festival of the next full moon,

And see the dance, and hear the choir sing

A grace to your gentle shade:

Mountain where Oedipus was found,

O mountain guard of a noble race!

May the god who heals us lend his aid,

And let that glory come to pass

For our king's cradling-ground.

        Of the nymphs that flower beyond the years,

Who bore you, royal child,

To Pan of the hills or the timberline Apollo,

Cold in delight where the upland clears,

Or Hermês for whom Kyllenê's heights are piled?

Or flushed as evening cloud,
Great Dionysos, roamer of mountains,
He—was it he who found you there,
And caught you up in his own proud
Arms from the sweet god-ravisher
Who laughed by the Muses' fountains?

OEDIPUS. Sirs: though I do not know
the man,
I think I see him coming, this shepherd
we want:
He is old, like our friend here, and the
men
Bringing him seem to be servants of my
house.
But you can tell, if you have ever seen
him.

[*Enter* SHEPHERD *escorted by servants.*]

CHORAGOS. I know him, he was Laïos'
man. You can trust him.

OEDIPUS. Tell me first, you from
Corinth: is this the shepherd
We were discussing?

MESSENGER.   This is the very man.

OEDIPUS. [*To* SHEPHERD.] Come here.
No, look at me. You must answer
Everything I ask.—You belonged to
Laïos?

SHEPHERD. Yes: born his slave, brought
up in his house.

OEDIPUS. Tell me: what kind of work
did you do for him?

SHEPHERD. I was a shepherd of his, most
of my life.

OEDIPUS. Where mainly did you go for
pasturage?

SHEPHERD. Sometimes Kithairon, sometimes the hills near-by.

OEDIPUS. Do you remember ever seeing this man out there?

SHEPHERD. What would he be doing
there? This man?

OEDIPUS. This man standing here. Have
you ever seen him before?

SHEPHERD. No. At least, not to my
recollection.

MESSENGER. And that is not strange, my
lord. But I'll refresh
His memory: he must remember when
we two
Spent three whole seasons together,
March to September,
On Kithairon or thereabouts. He had
two flocks;

I had one. Each autumn I'd drive mine
home
And he would go back with his to Laïos'
sheepfold.—
Is this not true, just as I have described
it?

SHEPHERD. True, yes; but it was all so
long ago.

MESSENGER. Well, then: do you remember, back in those days,
That you gave me a baby boy to bring
up as my own?

SHEPHERD. What if I did? What are
you trying to say?

MESSENGER. King Oedipus was once
that little child.

SHEPHERD. Damn you, hold your
tongue!

OEDIPUS.   No more of that!
It is your tongue needs watching, not
this man's.

SHEPHERD. My King, my Master, what
is it I have done wrong?

OEDIPUS. You have not answered his
question about the boy.

SHEPHERD. He does not know . . .
He is only making trouble . . .

OEDIPUS. Come, speak plainly, or it will
go hard with you.

SHEPHERD. In God's name, do not torture an old man!

OEDIPUS. Come here, one of you; bind
his arms behind him.

SHEPHERD. Unhappy king! What more
do you wish to learn?

OEDIPUS. Did you give this man the
child he speaks of?

SHEPHERD.   I did.
And I would to God I had died that
very day.

OEDIPUS. You will die now unless you
speak the truth.

SHEPHERD. Yet if I speak the truth, I
am worse than dead.

OEDIPUS. Very well; since you insist
upon delaying—

SHEPHERD. No! I have told you already
that I gave him the boy.

OEDIPUS. Where did you get him?
From your house? From somewhere
else?

SHEPHERD. Not from mine, no. A man
gave him to me.

OEDIPUS. Is that man here? Do you know whose slave he was?

SHEPHERD. For God's love, my King, do not ask me any more!

OEDIPUS. You are a dead man if I have to ask you again.

SHEPHERD. Then . . . Then the child was from the palace of Laïos.

OEDIPUS. A slave child? or a child of his own line?

SHEPHERD. Ah, I am on the brink of dreadful speech!

OEDIPUS. And I of dreadful hearing. Yet I must hear.

SHEPHERD. If you must be told, then . . . They said it was Laïos' child; But it is your wife who can tell you about that.

OEDIPUS. My wife!—Did she give it to you?

SHEPHERD.   My lord, she did.

OEDIPUS. Do you know why?

SHEPHERD.   I was told to get rid of it.

OEDIPUS. An unspeakable mother!

SHEPHERD.

There had been prophecies . . .

OEDIPUS. Tell me.

SHEPHERD. It was said that the boy would kill his own father.

OEDIPUS. Then why did you give him over to this old man?

SHEPHERD. I pitied the baby, my King, And I thought that this man would take him far away To his own country.

He saved him—but for what a fate! For if you are what this man says you are, No man living is more wretched than Oedipus.

OEDIPUS. Ah God! It was true! All the prophecies! —Now, O Light, may I look on you for the last time! I, Oedipus, Oedipus, damned in his birth, in his marriage damned, Damned in the blood he shed with his own hand!

[He rushes into the palace.]

CHORUS. Alas for the seed of men.

What measure shall I give these generations
That breathe on the void and are void
And exist and do not exist?
Who bears more weight of joy
Than mass of sunlight shifting in images,
Or who shall make his thoughts stay on
That down time drifts away?
Your splendor is all fallen.
O naked brow of wrath and tears,
O change of Oedipus!
I who saw your days call no man blest—
Your great days like ghósts góne.

That mind was a strong bow.
Deep, how deep you drew it then,
    hard archer,
At a dim fearful range,
And brought dear glory down!
You overcame the stranger—
The virgin with her hooking lion claws—
And though death sang, stood like a
    tower
To make pale Thebes take heart.
Fortress against our sorrow!
Divine king, giver of laws,
Majestic Oedipus!
No prince in Thebes had ever such renown,
No prince won such grace of power.
And now of all men ever known
Most pitiful is this man's story:
His fortunes are most changed, his state
Fallen to a low slave's
Ground under bitter fate.

O Oedipus, most royal one!
The great door that expelled you to the
    light
Gave at night—ah, gave night to your
    glory:
As to the father, to the fathering son.
All understood too late.
How could that queen whom Laïos
    won,
The garden that he harrowed at his
    height,
Be silent when that act was done?
But all eyes fail before time's eye,
All actions come to justice there.
Though never willed, though far down
    the deep past,
Your bed, your dread sirings,
Are brought to book at last.
    Child by Laïos doomed to die,

Then doomed to lose that fortunate little
    death,
Would God you never took breath in
    this air
That with my wailing lips I take to cry:
For I weep the world's outcast.
Blind I was, and can not tell why;
Asleep, for you had given ease of breath;
A fool, while the false years went by.

[*Enter, from the palace*, SECOND
    MESSENGER.]

SECOND MESSENGER. Elders of Thebes,
    most honored in this land,
What horrors are yours to see and hear,
    what weight
Of sorrow to be endured, if, true to
    your birth,
You venerate the line of Labdakos!
I think neither Istros nor Phasis, those
    great rivers,
Could purify this place of the corruption
It shelters now, or soon must bring to
    light—
Evil not done unconsciously, but willed.
    The greatest griefs are those we cause
    ourselves.
    CHORAGOS. Surely, friend, we have grief
    enough already;
What new sorrow do you mean?
    SECOND MESSENGER. The Queen is dead.
    CHORAGOS. Iocastê? Dead? But at whose
    hand?
    SECOND MESSENGER.   Her own.
The full horror of what happened you
    can not know,
For you did not see it; but I, who did,
    will tell you
As clearly as I can how she met her
    death.
    When she had left us,
In passionate silence, passing through the
    court,
She ran to her apartment in the house,
Her hair clutched by the fingers of both
    hands.
She closed the doors behind her; then,
    by that bed
Where long ago the fatal son was con-
    ceived—
That son who should bring about his
    father's death—
We heard her call upon Laïos, dead so
    many years,

And heard her wail for the double fruit
    of her marriage,
A husband by her husband, children by
    her child.
    Exactly how she died I do not know:
For Oedipus burst in moaning and would
    not let us
Keep vigil to the end: it was by him
As he stormed about the room that our
    eyes were caught.
From one to another of us he went, beg-
    ging a sword,
Cursing the wife who was not his wife,
    the mother
Whose womb had carried his own chil-
    dren and himself.
I do not know: it was none of us aided
    him,
But surely one of the gods was in con-
    trol!
For with a dreadful cry
He hurled his weight, as though
    wrenched out of himself,
At the twin doors: the bolts gave, and
    he rushed in.
And there we saw her hanging, her body
    swaying
From the cruel cord she had noosed
    about her neck.
A great sob broke from him, heartbreak-
    ing to hear,
As he loosed the rope and lowered her
    to the ground.
    I would blot out from my mind what
    happened next!
For the King ripped from her gown the
    golden brooches
That were her ornament, and raised
    them, and plunged them down
Straight into his own eyeballs, crying,
    "No more,
No more shall you look on the misery
    about me,
The horrors of my own doing! Too long
    you have known
The faces of those whom I should never
    have seen,
Too long been blind to those for whom
    I was searching!
From this hour, go in darkness!" And as
    he spoke,
He struck at his eyes—not once, but
    many times;
And the blood spattered his beard,

Bursting from his ruined sockets like red
hail.
So from the unhappiness of two this
evil has sprung,
A curse on the man and woman alike.
The old
Happiness of the house of Labdakos
Was happiness enough: where is it to-
day?
It is all wailing and ruin, disgrace, death
—all
The misery of mankind that has a name—
And it is wholly and for ever theirs.

CHORAGOS. Is he in agony still? Is there
no rest for him?

SECOND MESSENGER. He is calling for
someone to lead him to the gates
So that all the children of Kadmos may
look upon
His father's murderer, his mother's—no,
I can not say it!
And then he will leave Thebes,
Self-exiled, in order that the curse
Which he himself pronounced may de-
part from the house.
He is weak, and there is none to lead
him,
So terrible is his suffering.
But you will see:
Look, the doors are opening; in a mo-
ment
You will see a thing that would crush a
heart of stone.

[*The central door is opened;*
OEDIPUS, *blinded, is led in.*]

CHORAGOS. Dreadful indeed for men to
see.
Never have my own eyes
Looked on a sight so full of fear.
Oedipus!
What madness came upon you, what
daemon
Leaped on your life with heavier
Punishment than a mortal man can bear?
No: I can not even
Look at you, poor ruined one.
And I would speak, question, ponder,
If I were able. No.
You make me shudder.

OEDIPUS. God. God.
Is there a sorrow greater?
Where shall I find harbor in this world?
My voice is hurled far on a dark wind.
What has God done to me?

CHORAGOS. Too terrible to think of, or
to see.

OEDIPUS. O cloud of night,
Never to be turned away: night coming
on,
I can not tell how: night like a shroud!
My fair winds brought me here.
O God. Again
The pain of the spikes where I had sight,
The flooding pain
Of memory, never to be gouged out.

CHORAGOS. This is not strange.
You suffer it all twice over, remorse in
pain,
Pain in remorse.

OEDIPUS. Ah dear friend
Are you faithful even yet, you alone?
Are you still standing near me, will you
stay here,
Patient, to care for the blind?
The blind man!
Yet even blind I know who it is attends
me,
By the voice's tone—
Though my new darkness hide the com-
forter.

CHORAGOS. Oh fearful act!
What god was it drove you to rake black
Night across your eyes?

OEDIPUS. Apollo. Apollo. Dear
Children, the god was Apollo.
He brought my sick, sick fate upon me.
But the blinding hand was my own!
How could I bear to see
When all my sight was horror every-
where?

CHORAGOS. Everywhere; that is true.

OEDIPUS. And now what is left?
Images? Love? A greeting even,
Sweet to the senses? Is there anything?
Ah, no, friends: lead me away.
Lead me away from Thebes.
Lead the great wreck
And hell of Oedipus, whom the gods
hate.

CHORAGOS. Your fate is clear, you are
not blind to that.
Would God you had never found it out!

OEDIPUS. Death take the man who un-
bound
My feet on that hillside
And delivered me from death to life!
What life?
If only I had died,

This weight of monstrous doom
Could not have dragged me and my
  darlings down.
CHORAGOS. I would have wished the
  same.
OEDIPUS. Oh never to have come here
With my father's blood upon me! Never
To have been the man they call his
  mother's husband!
Oh accurst! Oh child of evil,
To have entered that wretched bed—
    the selfsame one!
More primal than sin itself, this fell to
  me.
CHORAGOS. I do not know how I can
  answer you.
You were better dead than alive and
  blind.
OEDIPUS. Do not counsel me any more.
This punishment
That I have laid upon myself is just.
If I had eyes,
I do not know how I could bear the sight
Of my father, when I came to the house
  of Death,
Or my mother: for I have sinned against
  them both
So vilely that I could not make my peace
By strangling my own life.
        Or do you think my children,
Born as they were born, would be sweet
  to my eyes?
Ah never, never! Nor this town with its
  high walls,
Nor the holy images of the gods.
        For I,
Thrice miserable!—Oedipus, noblest of
  all the line
Of Kadmos, have condemned myself to
  enjoy
These things no more, by my own male-
  diction
Expelling that man whom the gods de-
  clared
To be a defilement in the house of Laïos.
After exposing the rankness of my own
  guilt,
How could I look men frankly in the
  eyes?
No, I swear it,
If I could have stifled my hearing at its
  source,
I would have done it and made all this
  body

A tight cell of misery, blank to light and
  sound:
So I should have been safe in a dark
  agony
Beyond all recollection.
                    Ah Kithairon!
Why did you shelter me? When I was
  cast upon you,
Why did I not die? Then I should never
Have shown the world my execrable
  birth.
  Ah Polybos! Corinth, city that I be-
  lieved
The ancient seat of my ancestors: how
  fair
I seemed, your child! And all the while
  this evil
Was cancerous within me!
                    For I am sick
In my daily life, sick in my origin.
  O three roads, dark ravine, woodland
  and way
Where three roads met: you, drinking
  my father's blood,
My own blood, spilled by my own hand:
  can you remember
The unspeakable things I did there, and
  the things
I went on from there to do?
                O marriage, marriage!
The act that engendered me, and again
  the act
Performed by the son in the same bed—
                    Ah, the net
Of incest, mingling fathers, brothers,
  sons,
With brides, wives, mothers: the last evil
That can be known by men: no tongue
  can say
How evil!
    No. For the love of God, conceal me
Somewhere far from Thebes; or kill me;
  or hurl me
Into the sea, away from men's eyes for
  ever.
  Come, lead me. You need not fear to
  touch me.
Of all men, I alone can bear this guilt.
            [Enter CREON.]
  CHORAGOS. We are not the ones to de-
  cide; but Creon here
May fitly judge of what you ask. He
  only
Is left to protect the city in your place.

OEDIPUS. Alas, how can I speak to him?
What right have I
To beg his courtesy whom I have deeply
wronged?

CREON. I have not come to mock you,
Oedipus,
Or to reproach you, either.
[To ATTENDANTS.]—You, standing there:
If you have lost all respect for man's
dignity,
At least respect the flame of Lord Helios:
Do not allow this pollution to show it-
self
Openly here, an affront to the earth
And Heaven's rain and the light of day.
No, take him
Into the house as quickly as you can.
For it is proper
That only the close kindred see his grief.

OEDIPUS. I pray you in God's name,
since your courtesy
Ignores my dark expectation, visiting
With mercy this man of all men most
execrable:
Give me what I ask—for your good, not
for mine.

CREON. And what is it that you would
have me do?

OEDIPUS. Drive me out of this country
as quickly as may be
To a place where no human voice can
ever greet me.

CREON. I should have done that before
now—only,
God's will had not been wholly revealed
to me.

OEDIPUS. But his command is plain: the
parricide
Must be destroyed. I am that evil man.

CREON. That is the sense of it, yes; but
as things are,
We had best discover clearly what is to
be done.

OEDIPUS. You would learn more about
a man like me?

CREON. You are ready now to listen to
the god.

OEDIPUS. I will listen. But it is to you
That I must turn for help. I beg you,
hear me.
The woman in there—
Give her whatever funeral you think
proper:

She is your sister.
                —But let me go, Creon!
Let me purge my father's Thebes of the
pollution
Of my living here, and go out to the wild
hills,
To Kithairon, that has won such fame
with me,
The tomb my mother and father ap-
pointed for me,
And let me die there, as they willed I
should.
And yet I know
Death will not ever come to me through
sickness
Or in any natural way: I have been pre-
served
For some unthinkable fate. But let that
be.
   As for my sons, you need not care for
them.
They are men, they will find some way
to live.
But my poor daughters, who have shared
my table,
Who never before have been parted
from their father—
Take care of them, Creon; do this for
me.
And will you let me touch them with
my hands
A last time, and let us weep together?
Be kind, my lord,
Great prince, be kind!
                Could I but touch them,
They would be mine again, as when I
had my eyes.
[Enter ANTIGONE and ISMENE, attended.]
Ah, God!
Is it my dearest children I hear weeping?
Has Creon pitied me and sent my daugh-
ters?

CREON. Yes, Oedipus: I knew that they
were dear to you
In the old days, and know you must love
them still.

OEDIPUS. May God bless you for this
—and be a friendlier
Guardian to you than he has been to me!
Children, where are you?
Come quickly to my hands: they are
your brother's—
Hands that have brought your father's
once clear eyes

To this way of seeing—
                    Ah dearest ones,
I had neither sight nor knowledge then,
    your father
By the woman who was the source of
    his own life!
And I weep for you—having no strength
    to see you—,
I weep for you when I think of the bit-
    terness
That men will visit upon you all your
    lives.
What homes, what festivals can you at-
    tend
Without being forced to depart again in
    tears?
And when you come to marriageable age,
Where is the man, my daughters, who
    would dare
Risk the bane that lies on all my chil-
    dren?
Is there any evil wanting? Your father
    killed
His father; sowed the womb of her who
    bore him;
Engendered you at the fount of his own
    existence!
That is what they will say of you.
                    Then, whom
Can you ever marry? There are no
    bridegrooms for you,
And your lives must wither away in
    sterile dreaming.
O Creon, son of Menoikeus!
You are the only father my daughters
    have,
Since we, their parents, are both of us
    gone for ever.
They are your own blood: you will not
    let them
Fall into beggary and loneliness;
You will keep them from the miseries
    that are mine!
Take pity on them; see, they are only
    children,
Friendless except for you. Promise me
    this,
Great Prince, and give me your hand in
    token of it. [CREON *clasps his right
    hand.*]

Children:
I could say much, if you could under-
    stand me,
But as it is, I have only this prayer for
    you:
Live where you can, be as happy as you
    can—
Happier, please God, than God has made
    your father!
CREON. Enough. You have wept enough.
    Now go within.
OEDIPUS. I must; but it is hard.
CREON.   Time eases all things.
OEDIPUS. But you must promise—
CREON.   Say what you desire.
OEDIPUS. Send me from Thebes!
CREON.   God grant that I may!
OEDIPUS. But since God hates me . . .
CREON.   No, he will grant your wish.
OEDIPUS. You promise?
CREON. I can not speak beyond my
    knowledge.
OEDIPUS. Then lead me in.
CREON. Come now, and leave your
    children.
OEDIPUS. No! Do not take them from
    me!
CREON.   Think no longer
That you are in command here, but
    rather think
How, when you were, you served your
    own destruction.
    [*Exeunt into the house all but
    the* CHORUS; *the* CHORAGOS *chants
    directly to the audience.*]
    CHORAGOS. Men of Thebes: look upon
    Oedipus.
This is the king who solved the famous
    riddle
And towered up, most powerful of men.
No mortal eyes but looked on him with
    envy,
Yet in the end ruin swept over him.
    Let every man in mankind's frailty
Consider his last day; and let none
Presume on his good fortune until he find
Life, at his death, a memory without
    pain.

WILLIAM SHAKESPEARE: *OTHELLO*

The universe in which Oedipus moves seems not merely indifferent but fundamentally inimical to man. The world of Othello seems so, too. But neither really is. Both worlds are, rather, heroic; and our mistaken impression of them comes simply from the fact that in the worlds of heroes there is no place for radical weakness. Allowance is made for human fallibility; but heroes cannot be forgiven, because their errors are such that, once committed, they lead to inescapable destruction.

Oedipus, as we have seen, suffers ultimately from his belief in his power to solve all problems, to seek out and establish the truth. As we watch this search, undertaken, at first, in good faith as a virtuous act, we see Oedipus' vice—his pride—overpower him and drive him to disaster. For Sophocles' chorus the lesson is clear:

Dwellers in our native Thebes, behold, this is Oedipus, who knew the famed riddle, and was a man most mighty: on whose fortunes what citizen did not gaze with envy? Behold into what a stormy sea of dread trouble he hath come!
Therefore, while our eyes wait to see the destined final day, we must call no man happy who is of mortal race, until he hath crossed life's border, free from pain.[5]

As epitomized in those lines, the conflict in Sophocles' drama is clearly the uneven one between the logos—the ordained order—and man's presumption, Oedipus' sin of pride. But the idea of such a conflict was foreign to Othello's and Shakespeare's Christian world. The primary concern of Elizabethan tragedy was not man's failure to comprehend the universal order of which he was part, but rather man's inability to rule himself. By Shakespeare's time the site of tragic conflict had shifted to men's minds, and the source of the conflict had become the eternal struggle, within man, between his reason and his passions—between, as the Elizabethans so frequently repeated, that part of him he shared with God's angels and that part he shared with the beasts of the field. The dominant element in Elizabethan tragedy is therefore character.

And among Shakespeare's plays, *Othello* is pre-eminent as a study of human character. Its theme is an old one: the corruption of human reason by jealousy, a base human passion seen in many forms here, but centrally in its most destructive form, sexual jealousy. So powerfully are we made to feel the workings of sexual jealousy that the hero's downfall holds no surprises for us; no tragic outcome could conceivably strike us as more clearly inevitable. Given these characters in this situation—man being what he is—the progress to catastrophe is from the first irreversible. What has engaged Shakespeare's interest is the tragic process by which jealousy can destroy Othello and Desdemona and ultimately Iago himself, but the evils Shakespeare sees, he sees as issuing directly out of the characters. Yet it is only his poetry and his profound probing of Othello's soul that gain acceptance for what would otherwise seem an implausible story.

A brief comment on the story and the play's structure may therefore appropriately precede our discussion of the characterization. The story is a

[5] Translated by R. C. Jebb. From *The Tragedies of Sophocles* by R. C. Jebb. By permission of The Macmillan Company, publishers.

simple one: a great general is persuaded, by a displaced subordinate, of his wife's infidelity; having killed his wife, the remorseful general then commits suicide, and the subordinate is apprehended and punished. To use this story for his purposes, Shakespeare was driven to extensive sub-plotting, involving minor characters who can move freely within the general's world, but who are so wrapped up in their own jealous suits that they can be easily manipulated. Thus the first two acts are given over to the actions of Iago and Roderigo and Iago and Cassio, and to the frame-story involving the fortunes of Venice at war with the Turks. One function of these actions is certainly to establish, as we shall see in a moment, not only Iago's but also Othello's and Desdemona's characters. But their essential function is to create the situation in which it is possible for Iago, having once opened Othello's soul to corruption by planting the seed of jealousy, to confirm his insinuations by providing "ocular proof."

Because so much plot preparation is necessary, there is little emotional involvement before the actual crisis scene itself (III, iii). But once we see Iago tempting Othello, once the conflict is, so to speak, internalized—no longer between Iago and Othello, but between Othello's reason and the passionate jealousy Iago blows ever hotter—we are drawn into the maelstrom. The play rushes to its catastrophe. This headlong development is one cause of the emotional exhaustion of *Othello*'s audiences, for the terrible intensity of the oath-swearing is maintained without break until the murder itself. Partly because of this emotional intensity (and partly because it has been adequately motivated) we hardly think to question the rapid shift in Othello's character. Seeing him no longer rational, we are not likely to ask why he does not discuss this matter rationally with Desdemona. We know the catastrophe to be inevitable; Shakespeare has shown us the people involved.

Few of Shakespeare's heroes are drawn with bolder strokes than the Moor. Noble of birth and bearing, unquestioned of courage, of indubitable integrity, Othello is a warrior, at home on the field, perhaps in the council chamber, but, though a successful suitor, ill at ease in the drawing-room or boudoir. He is also, in dangerous areas, naive; his life has been given so fully to military considerations that he is without those kinds of experience which would help him to recognize and combat the machinations of Iago. Much is often made of Othello's simplicity, and this quality, suggestive also of his directness, is part of the Moor's nature; it even endows his very egoism with an individual and redeeming tone, as one can appreciate from the frank account, to the Venetian senators, of his courtship. Further, like Shakespeare's Brutus, Othello is essentially humorless, and like many humorless men who are likely to unite this quality with a complacent view of themselves, he is not notably sensitive in his relationships with others. Like Brutus, secure in the knowledge of his own integrity and high-mindedness, he is blind to the corruption of integrity in others, and so makes, with Iago, the same class of fatal error that Brutus makes with Cassius. He cannot see into the minds of Iago and Desdemona, perhaps principally because it would not occur to him to be drawn into such questionings.

Most significantly, Othello is passionate. He is a black Moor, and the importance of his color is simply that it would have emphasized for the Elizabethan audience his greater tendency—his greater susceptibility—to passionate action. Though the discipline of his military career has taught him a tight control over his passions, they are ever-present, and, once roused, they are of a sweeping nature which makes recovery of control a doubtful issue. He is, as Bradley noted, all of one piece. Where he trusts, he trusts absolutely; where he loves, his love is unqualified; when he acts on indignation, as he has "in Aleppo once," he acts impetuously, without hesitation; and so, when he is jealous, his jealousy proves uncontrollable.

This is Othello, Moor of Venice, who wins and then kills the gentle Desdemona. Such a portrait makes clear why Desdemona is attracted to him, and also why Iago, once determined on the hero's destruction, finds in Othello such malleable material. Desdemona is less complex. We first see her reading her father the Renaissance lesson of duty, to father and to husband. She is forthright, even bold, and her instinctive recognition of greatness in Othello discloses a vital aspect of her character. Indeed, she shares with Othello that special quality of simplicity, and its attendant strength, that marks them both apart from "chamberers" and courtiers. Yet she is everything that is softly feminine, and in her inexperience of the world's ways she exceeds even Othello. Facing his wrath, she assumes her own fault, but cannot understand it; she has no resources beyond grief and bewilderment. Overwhelmed, Desdemona suffers passively, and we suffer with her. But unlike her, we catch the irony of Emilia's discourse concerning the price the world puts on virtue—her answer to the willow song.

We come to know Othello and Desdemona as we come to know most characters in plays. We watch them in action, and others tell us about them. But Shakespeare had available another device. This is the soliloquy, lines spoken by a character directly to the audience, and its purpose is to reveal the mind of the character without the usual involvement in action. In the course of the opening expository lines of the play, between Iago and Roderigo, we learn about Iago's "just cause" against the Moor; we also learn something of his mode of action:

> For when my outward action does demonstrate
> The native act and figure of my heart
> In complement extern, 'tis not long after
> But I will wear my heart upon my sleeve
> For daws to peck at. I am not what I am.
> (I, i, 61-65)

From this point on, in a series of soliloquies, Iago keeps us posted as to the developing action, his motives, and his attitudes (I, iii, 389f; II, i, 292f; II, iii, 389f). Important for keeping the audience abreast of the involved action, the soliloquies also serve to characterize Othello—the Moor is "frank and open," "of a constant, loving noble nature"—and, most of all, to reveal Iago himself.

Like Othello's, Iago's reason has also been unseated, but not by passion. In Iago reason resigns its governing place to naked will; reason is not for him a way of life, but merely an instrument. It is Iago's coldness, his calculated manipulation of Roderigo and Cassio, his relentless probing and torturing of Othello, that repel us. Will is the center of his character. His avowed creed is absolute egoism. If he has struck some readers as inhuman, this is because Shakespeare saw him as embodying the egoistic principle. His perverted consecration of himself to his own selfish ends, which leads him to regard the rest of the race (obsequious servants aside) as unmitigated fools, cuts him off from his own kind. Nothing illustrates more clearly his detachment from his kind than Iago's particular response to the theme of sexual jealousy. He announces that the world suspects Othello of improper relations with Emilia—he suspects Cassio, too; but Shakespeare makes clear that, even if grounded in fact, the suspicion could not disturb Iago greatly. He is intoxicated with the scent of power, and no other human feeling can touch him.

If we ask, then, what motivates Iago's actions, one answer is clear. He is a man of extraordinary capacities. In his egoism he is restive under the limitations of a subservient position; if his will is to be effective, it must be a will to power. Iago, moreover, is a man of reckless courage, one who finds in danger that special savor of life that calls forth his maximum capabilities. Yet in the past his will has lacked an opening; to issue in action it requires the exciting force of an affront to the principles by which he lives. And this exciting force develops when Othello affronts Iago by favoring Cassio for promotion. Insignificant in itself, since Iago is never shown as conspicuously ambitious for office, this promotion nevertheless gives him the occasion he requires. Telling himself that he hates the Moor for it, he can now proceed, his "reasons" established, to enjoy his growing dominion over the great General.

Men who toy with other men fascinate us even though they also repel us. Yet, however Iago may fascinate us as we watch him at work, he does not satisfy us for long. For the poetry of the play is all Othello's. Elizabethan drama, being poetic drama, forces us to realize how much of a play's meaning is locked up in its language. Iago's early line, "I am not what I am," warns us that *Othello* is a drama about appearance and reality. But from the very beginning the play's language contrasts black and white, light and dark, wit and witchcraft, ignorance and wisdom, reason and passion; these are the terms that the characters use to define their world. When, therefore, Othello comes finally to "put out the light, and then put out the light," he has come to see how deeply involved he is in mistaking appearance for reality—that putting out a life is so much more than putting out a light. He rejects the metaphor, but it has already committed him to action, and he must go on.

"It is the cause, it is the cause," Othello cries, justifying himself as he moves to darken his universe with murder: "a huge eclipse of sun and moon." What makes him great? He was great to begin with, a noble, frank, open, generous Moor, a warrior, preserver of Venice, a man of many virtues. His suffering does not make him great; like his suicide, it only reveals his greatness to us. From the moment when he first realizes that his "blood begins [his] safer guides to rule" to the final anguished realization that "I have no wife," we share his torment as he searches hopelessly for certainty. His greatness, like Oedipus', lies in the knowing search. Committed to the cause of virtue, he reveals to us the depths of torment man can endure in its cause. If we say then, "But what a waste!" we are but describing the world of tragedy.

Othello

by

WILLIAM SHAKESPEARE

Characters

OTHELLO, *the Moor*

BRABANTIO, *Father of Desdemona*

CASSIO, *an honorable Lieutenant*

IAGO, *a villain, 'ancient' or standard-bearer and third in command to Othello*

RODERIGO, *a gulled gentleman*

DUKE OF VENICE

SENATORS

MONTANO, *Governor of Cyprus*

GENTLEMEN OF CYPRUS

LODOVICO *and* GRATIANO, *two noble Venetians, relative and brother, respectively, of Brabantio*

DESDEMONA, *wife of Othello and daughter of Brabantio*

EMILIA, *wife to Iago*

BIANCA, *a courtesan*

MESSENGERS, SAILORS, CLOWN, HERALD, OFFICERS, MUSICIANS, AND ATTENDANTS

SCENE: ACT I, AT VENICE; ACTS II–V, AT A SEA-PORT (FAMAGOSTA) IN CYPRUS

ACT ONE

1. *Venice, a street*

Enter RODERIGO *and* IAGO.

RODERIGO. Tush! Never tell me! I take it much unkindly
That thou, Iago, who hast had my purse
As if the strings were thine, shouldst know of this.

IAGO. 'Sblood, but you will not hear me!
If ever I did dream of such a matter,
Abhor me.

RODERIGO. Thou told'st me thou didst hold him in thy hate.

IAGO. Despise me if I do not. Three great ones of the city,
In personal suit to make me his lieutenant,
Off-capp'd to him; and, by the faith of man
(I know my price), I am worth no worse a place.
But he, as loving his own pride and purposes,
Evades them with a bombast circumstance
Horribly stuff'd with epithets of war;
And, in conclusion,
Nonsuits my mediators; for, 'Certes,' says he,
'I have already chose my officer.'
And what was he?
Forsooth, a great arithmetician,
One Michael Cassio, a Florentine
(A fellow almost damn'd in a fair wife),
That never set a squadron in the field,
Nor the division of a battle knows
More than a spinster,—unless the bookish theoric,

Wherein the toged consuls can pro-
pose
As masterly as he. Mere prattle, without
practice,
Is all his soldiership; but he, sir, had the
election,
And I (of whom his eyes had seen the
proof
At Rhodes, at Cyprus, and on other
grounds
Christian and heathen) must be be-lee'd
and calm'd
By Debitor-and-Creditor. This coun-
ter-caster,
He, in good time, must his lieutenant be,
And I—God bless the mark!—his Moor-
ship's ancient.
   RODERIGO. By heaven, I rather would
   have been his hangman.
   IAGO. Why, there's no remedy. 'Tis the
   curse of service.
Preferment goes by letter and affection,
And not by old gradation, where each
second
Stood heir to the first. Now, sir, be
judge yourself,
Whether I in any just term am affin'd
To love the Moor.
   RODERIGO. I would not follow him then.
   IAGO. O sir, content you.
I follow him to serve my turn upon him;
We cannot be all masters, nor all masters
Cannot be truly follow'd. You shall mark
Many a duteous and knee-crooking
knave,
That (doting on his own obsequious
bondage)
Wears out his time much like his mas-
ter's ass,
For nought but provender, and when he's
old,—cashier'd!
Whip me such honest knaves. Others
there are
Who, trimm'd in forms and visages of
duty,
Keep yet their hearts attending on them-
selves,
And throwing but shows of service on
their lords,
Do well thrive by 'em, and when they
have lin'd their coats

Do themselves homage. Those fellows
have some soul,
And such a one do I profess myself. For,
sir,
It is as sure as you are Roderigo,
Were I the Moor, I would not be Iago.
In following him, I follow but myself;
Heaven is my judge, not I for love and
duty,
But seeming so for my peculiar end.
For when my outward action does dem-
onstrate
The native act and figure of my heart
In complement extern, 'tis not long
after
But I will wear my heart upon my sleeve
For daws to peck at. I am not what I am.
   RODERIGO. What a full fortune does the
   thick-lips owe,
If he can carry't thus!
   IAGO.   Call up her father.
Rouse him, make after him, poison his
delight,
Proclaim him in the street, incense her
kinsmen,
And though he in a fertile climate dwell,
Plague him with flies; though that his joy
be joy,
Yet throw such chances of vexation on't
As it may lose some color.
   RODERIGO. Here is her father's house.
   I'll call aloud.
   IAGO. Do; with like timorous accent
   and dire yell
As when (by night and negligence) the
fire
Is spied in populous cities.
   RODERIGO. What, ho, Brabantio! Signior
   Brabantio, ho!
   IAGO. Awake! what, ho, Brabantio!
   thieves! thieves! thieves!
Look to your house, your daughter, and
your bags!
Thieves! thieves!
   [BRABANTIO at a window, above.]
   BRABANTIO. What is the reason of this
   terrible summons?
What is the matter there?
   RODERIGO. Signior, is all your family
   within?
   IAGO. Are your doors lock'd?

BRABANTIO.
            Why, wherefore ask you this?
IAGO. 'Zounds, sir, you're robb'd!—
For shame, put on your gown!—
Your heart is burst, you have lost half
    your soul.
Even now, now, very now, an old black
    ram
Is tupping your white ewe. Arise, arise!
Awake the snorting citizens with the
    bell,
Or else the devil will make a grandsire
    of you.
Arise, I say.
    BRABANTIO. What! have you lost your
        wits?
    RODERIGO. Most reverend signior, do
        you know my voice?
    BRABANTIO. Not I. What are you?
    RODERIGO. My name is Roderigo.
    BRABANTIO.   The worser welcome!
I have charg'd thee not to haunt about
    my doors.
In honest plainness thou hast heard me
    say
My daughter is not for thee; and now, in
    madness,
Being full of supper and distempering
    draughts,
Upon malicious bravery dost thou come
To start my quiet.
    RODERIGO. Sir, sir, sir!
    BRABANTIO.
            But thou must needs be sure,
My spirit and my place have in them
    power
To make this bitter to thee.
    RODERIGO.   Patience, good sir.
    BRABANTIO. What tell'st thou me of
        robbing? This is Venice.
My house is not a grange.
    RODERIGO.   Most grave Brabantio,
In simple and pure soul I come to you.
    IAGO. 'Zounds, sir, you are one of those
that will not serve God if the devil bid
you. Because we come to do you service
you think we are ruffians, you'll have
your daughter covered with a Barbary
horse; you'll have your nephews neigh
to you; you'll have coursers for cousins
and jennets for germans.

    BRABANTIO. What profane wretch art
thou?
    IAGO. I am one, sir, that come to tell
you, your daughter and the Moor are
now making the beast with two backs.
    BRABANTIO. Thou art a villain.
    IAGO.   You are—a senator.
    BRABANTIO. This thou shalt answer. I
        know thee, Roderigo.
    RODERIGO. Sir, I will answer anything.
        But, I beseech you,
If't be your pleasure and most wise con-
    sent
(As partly, I find, it is) that your fair
    daughter,
At this odd-even and dull watch o' th'
    night,
Transported with no worse nor better
    guard
But with a knave of common hire, a
    gondolier,
To the gross clasps of a lascivious Moor—
If this be known to you, and your allow-
    ance,
We then have done you bold and saucy
    wrongs.
But if you know not this, my manners
    tell me
We have your wrong rebuke. Do not
    believe
That, from the sense of all civility,
I thus would play and trifle with your
    reverence.
Your daughter (if you have not given
    her leave,
I say again) hath made a gross revolt,
Tying her duty, beauty, wit and fortunes
In an extravagant and wheeling stranger
Of here and everywhere. Straight satisfy
    yourself.
If she be in her chamber or your house,
Let loose on me the justice of the state
For thus deluding you.
    BRABANTIO.   Strike on the tinder, ho!
Give me a taper! call up all my people!
This accident is not unlike my dream.
Belief of it oppresses me already.
Light, I say! light! [*Exit.*]
    IAGO.   Farewell, for I must leave you.
It seems not meet nor wholesome to my
    place

To be produc'd (as, if I say, I shall)
Against the Moor; for I do know the
    state
(However this may gall him with some
    check)
Cannot with safety cast him; for he's
    embark'd
With such loud reason to the Cyprus
    wars,
Which even now stand in act, that, for
    their souls,
Another of his fathom they have not
To lead their business. In which regard,
Though I do hate him as I do hell's pains,
Yet for necessity of present life,
I must show out a flag and sign of love,
Which is indeed but sign. That you shall
    surely find him,
Lead to the Sagittary the raised search,
And there will I be with him. So, fare-
well. [*Exit.*]

[*Enter below* BRABANTIO *in his night
gown, and* SERVANTS *with torches.*]

BRABANTIO. It is too true an evil. Gone
    she is,
And what's to come of my despised
    time
Is nought but bitterness. Now, Roderigo,
Where didst thou see her? O unhappy
    girl!
With the Moor, sayst thou? Who would
    be a father!
How didst thou know 'twas she? O, she
    deceives me
Past thought. What said she to you? Get
    mo tapers!
Raise all my kindred! Are they married,
    think you?
RODERIGO. Truly, I think they are.
BRABANTIO. O heaven! How got she
    out? O treason of the blood!
Fathers, from hence trust not your
    daughters' minds
By what you see them act. Is there not
    charms
By which the property of youth and
    maidhood
May be abus'd? Have you not read,
    Roderigo,
Of some such thing?

RODERIGO.   Yes, sir, I have indeed.
BRABANTIO. Call up my brother. O,
    would you had had her!
Some one way, some another! Do you
    know
Where we may apprehend her and the
    Moor?
RODERIGO. I think I can discover him, if
    you please
To get good guard and go along with
    me.
BRABANTIO. Pray, lead me on. At every
    house I'll call;
I may command at most. Get weapons,
    ho!
And raise some special officers of night.
On, good Roderigo. I'll deserve your
    pains.

[*Exeunt.*]

2. *Another street, before the Sagittary*

Enter OTHELLO, IAGO, *and* ATTENDANTS
with torches.

IAGO. Though in the trade of war I
    have slain men,
Yet do I hold it very stuff o' th' con-
    science
To do no contriv'd murder. I lack
    iniquity
Sometimes to do me service. Nine or ten
    times
I had thought t' have yerk'd him here
    under the ribs.
OTHELLO. 'Tis better as it is.
IAGO.   Nay, but he prated,
And spoke such scurvy and provoking
    terms
Against your Honor
That with the little godliness I have
I did full hard forbear him. But, I pray,
    sir,
Are you fast married? Be assur'd of this,
That the magnifico is much belov'd,
And hath in his effect a voice potential
As double as the duke's. He will di-
    vorce you,
Or put upon you what restraint and
    grievance

The law, with all his might to enforce it
    on,
Will give him cable.

OTHELLO.   Let him do his spite.
My services which I have done the Si-
    gnory
Shall out-tongue his complaints. 'Tis yet
    to know
(Which when I know that boasting is an
    honor
I shall promulgate), I fetch my life and
    being
From men of royal siege, and my de-
    merits
May speak unbonneted to as proud a
    fortune
As this that I have reach'd. For know,
    Iago,
But that I love the gentle Desdemona,
I would not my unhoused free condi-
    tion
Put into circumscription and confine
For the sea's worth. But, look! what
    lights come yond?
IAGO. Those are the raised father and
    his friends.
You were best go in.
OTHELLO.   Not I. I must be found.
My parts, my title, and my perfect
    soul
Shall manifest me rightly. Is it they?
IAGO. By Janus, I think no.

[*Enter* CASSIO *with lights*, OFFICERS
            and torches.]

OTHELLO. The servants of the duke, and
    my lieutenant.
The goodness of the night upon you,
    friends!
What is the news?
CASSIO.
        The duke does greet you, general,
And he requires your haste-post-haste
    appearance,
Even on the instant.
OTHELLO.
            What's the matter, think you?
CASSIO. Something from Cyprus, as I
    may divine.
It is a business of some heat. The galleys
Have sent a dozen sequent messengers

This very night at one another's heels,
And many of the consuls, rais'd and met,
Are at the duke's already. You have been
    hotly call'd for;
When being not at your lodging to be
    found,
The Senate sent above three several
    quests
To search you out.
OTHELLO. 'Tis well I'm found by you.
I will but spend a word here in the house,
And go with you.

        [*Enters the Sagittary*.]

CASSIO. Ancient, what makes he here?
IAGO. Faith, he to-night hath boarded a
    land carrack.
If it prove lawful prize, he's made for
    ever.
CASSIO. I do not understand.
IAGO.   He's married.
CASSIO.   To who?
IAGO. Marry, to—[*Re-enter* OTHELLO.]
    Come, captain, will you go?
OTHELLO.   Have with you.
CASSIO. Here comes another troop to
    seek for you.
IAGO. It is Brabantio. General, be
    advis'd;
He comes to bad intent.

[*Enter* BRABANTIO, RODERIGO, *and others*,
        with lights and weapons.]

OTHELLO.   Holla! stand there!
RODERIGO. Signior, it is the Moor.
BRABANTIO.   Down with him! Thief!

        [*They draw on both sides*.]

IAGO. You, Roderigo! Come, sir, I am
    for you.
OTHELLO. Keep up your bright swords,
    for the dew will rust 'em.
Good signior, you shall more command
    with years
Than with your weapons.
BRABANTIO. O thou foul thief! Where
    hast thou stow'd my daughter?
Damn'd as thou art, thou hast enchanted
    her;
For I'll refer me to all things of sense,

If she in chains of magic were not bound,
Whether a maid so tender, fair, and
happy,
So opposite to marriage that she shunn'd
The wealthy curled darlings of our na-
tion,
Would ever have (t'incur a general
mock)
Run from her guardage to the sooty
bosom
Of such a thing as thou—to fear, not to
delight.
Judge me the world, if 'tis not gross in
sense
That thou hast practis'd on her with foul
charms,
Abus'd her delicate youth with drugs or
minerals
That weaken motion. I'll have't disputed
on.
'Tis probable, and palpable to thinking.
I therefore apprehend and do attach thee
For an abuser of the world, a practiser
Of arts inhibited and out of warrant.
Lay hold upon him. If he do resist,
Subdue him at his peril.

OTHELLO.   Hold your hands,
Both you of my inclining and the rest.
Were it my cue to fight, I should have
known it
Without a prompter. Where will you
that I go
To answer this your charge?

BRABANTIO.   To prison, till fit time
Of law and course of direct session
Call thee to answer.

OTHELLO.   What if I do obey?
How may the duke be therewith satis-
fied,
Whose messengers are here about my
side
Upon some present business of the state
To bring me to him?

OFFICER. 'Tis true, most worthy signior.
The duke's in council, and your noble
self,
I am sure, is sent for.

BRABANTIO. How? The duke in council!
In this time of the night! Bring him
away.

Mine's not an idle cause. The duke himself,
Or any of my brothers of the state,
Cannot but feel this wrong as 'twere
their own;
For if such actions may have passage
free,
Bondslaves and pagans shall our states-
men be.
                                    [Exeunt.]

3. The Doge's palace

Enter DUKE and SENATORS, set at a table
with lights and ATTENDANTS.

DUKE. There is no composition in these
news
That gives them credit.

FIRST SENATOR.
            Indeed, they are disproportion'd.
My letters say a hundred and seven
galleys.

DUKE. And mine, a hundred forty.

SECOND SENATOR.
                    And mine, two hundred.
But though they jump not on a just
account
(As in these cases, where the aim reports,
'Tis oft with difference), yet do they all
confirm
A Turkish fleet, and bearing up to Cyprus.

DUKE. Nay, it is possible enough to
judgment.
I do not so secure me in the error,
But the main article I do approve
In fearful sense.

SAILOR. [Within.] What, ho! what, ho!
what, ho!

OFFICER. A messenger from the galleys.

                    [Enter SAILOR.]

DUKE.   Now! The business?

SAILOR. The Turkish preparation makes
for Rhodes.
So was I bid report here to the state
By Signior Angelo.

DUKE. How say you by this change?

FIRST SENATOR.   This cannot be,
By no assay of reason. 'Tis a pageant
To keep us in false gaze. When we
    consider
Th'importancy of Cyprus to the Turk,
And let ourselves again but understand
That as it more concerns the Turk than
    Rhodes,
So may he with more facile question bear
    it,
For that it stands not in such warlike
    brace,
But altogether lacks th'abilities
That Rhodes is dress'd in—if we make
    thought of this,
We must not think the Turk is so un-
    skilful
To leave that latest which concerns him
    first,
Neglecting an attempt of ease and gain
To wake and wage a danger profitless.
DUKE. Nay, in all confidence, he's not
    for Rhodes.
OFFICER. Here is more news.

[*Enter a* MESSENGER.]

MESSENGER. The Ottomites, reverend
    and gracious,
Steering with due course toward the isle
    of Rhodes,
Have there injointed them with an after
    fleet.
FIRST SENATOR. Ay, so I thought. How
    many, as you guess?
MESSENGER. Of thirty sail; and now
    they do re-stem
Their backward course, bearing with
    frank appearance
Their purposes toward Cyprus. Signior
    Montano,
Your trusty and most valiant servitor,
With his free duty recommends you
    thus,
And prays you to believe him.
DUKE. 'Tis certain then, for Cyprus.
Marcus Luccicos is not here in town?
FIRST SENATOR. He's now in Florence.
DUKE. Write from us: wish him post-
    post-haste dispatch.
FIRST SENATOR. Here comes Brabantio
    and the valiant Moor.

[*Enter* BRABANTIO, OTHELLO, CASSIO,
    IAGO, RODERIGO, *and* OFFICERS.]

DUKE. Valiant Othello, we must straight
    employ you
Against the general enemy Ottoman.
[*To* BRABANTIO.] I did not see you. Wel-
    come, gentle signior;
We lack'd your counsel and your help
    to-night.
BRABANTIO. So did I yours. Good your
    Grace, pardon me.
Neither my place nor aught I heard of
    business
Hath rais'd me from my bed, nor doth
    the general care
Take hold on me, for my particular grief
Is of so floodgate and o'erbearing na-
    ture
That it engluts and swallows other sor-
    rows
And it is still itself.
DUKE.   Why, what's the matter?
BRABANTIO. My daughter! O my daugh-
    ter!
ALL.   Dead?
BRABANTIO.   Ay, to me.
She is abus'd, stol'n from me, and cor-
    rupted
By spells and medicines bought of
    mountebanks;
For nature so preposterously to err
Being not deficient, blind, or lame of
    sense,
Sans witchcraft could not.
DUKE. Whoe'er he be that in this foul
    proceeding
Hath thus beguil'd your daughter of her-
    self
And you of her, the bloody book of
    law
You shall yourself read in the bitter let-
    ter
After your own sense; yea, though our
    proper son
Stood in your action.
BRABANTIO.
                  Humbly I thank your Grace.
Here is the man, this Moor; whom now,
    it seems,
Your special mandate for the state affairs

Hath hither brought.

ALL.   We are very sorry for't.

DUKE.   [*To* OTHELLO.] What, in
your own part, can you say to this?

BRABANTIO. Nothing but 'This is so.'

OTHELLO. Most potent, grave, and reverend signiors,

My very noble and approv'd good masters:

That I have ta'en away this old man's
daughter,

It is most true; true, I have married her.

The very head and front of my of-
fending

Hath this extent, no more. Rude am I
in my speech,

And little bless'd with the soft phrase of
peace,

For since these arms of mine had seven
years' pith[106]

Till now some nine moons wasted, they
have us'd

Their dearest action in the tented
field;

And little of this great world can I speak

More than pertains to feats of broil and
battle,

And therefore little shall I grace my
cause

In speaking for myself. Yet, by your gracious patience

I will a round unvarnish'd tale deliver

Of my whole course of love: what drugs,
what charms,

What conjuration, and what mighty
magic,

(For such proceedings am I charg'd
withal)

I won his daughter.

BRABANTIO.   A maiden never bold;

Of spirit so still and quiet, that her motion

Blush'd at herself! And she, in spite of
nature,

Of years, of country, credit, everything,

To fall in love with what she fear'd to
look on!

It is a judgment maim'd and most imper-
fect

That will confess perfection so could err

Against all rules of nature, and must be
driven

To find out practices of cunning hell,

Why this should be. I therefore vouch
again

That with some mixtures powerful o'er
the blood,

Or with some dram conjur'd to this
effect,

He wrought upon her.

DUKE.   To vouch this is no proof,

Without more certain and more overt
test

Than these thin habits and poor likeli-
hoods

Of modern seeming do prefer against
him.

FIRST SENATOR. But, Othello, speak.

Did you by indirect and forced courses

Subdue and poison this young maid's affections?

Or came it by request and such fair question

As soul to soul affordeth?

OTHELLO.   I do beseech you,

Send for the lady to the Sagittary,

And let her speak of me before her
father.

If you do find me foul in her report,

The trust, the office I do hold of you

Not only take away, but let your sentence

Even fall upon my life.

DUKE.   Fetch Desdemona hither.

[*Exit two or three.*]

OTHELLO. Ancient, conduct them. You
best know the place.

[*Exit* IAGO.]

And till she come, as truly as to heaven

I do confess the vices of my blood,

So justly to your grave ears I'll present

How I did thrive in this fair lady's love,

And she in mine.

DUKE. Say it, Othello.

OTHELLO. Her father lov'd me; oft invited me,

Still question'd me the story of my life

From year to year, the battles, sieges,
fortunes

That I have pass'd.

I ran it through, even from my boyish
   days
To th' very moment that he bade me tell
   it.
Wherein I spake of most disastrous
   chances,
Of moving accidents by flood and field,
Of hair-breadth 'scapes i' th' imminent
   deadly breach,
Of being taken by the insolent foe
And sold to slavery, of my redemption
   thence
And portance in my traveller's his-
   tory.
Wherein of antres vast and deserts
   idle,
Rough quarries, rocks and hills whose
   heads touch heaven,
It was my hint to speak (such was the
   process),
And of the Cannibals that each other eat,
The Anthropophagi, and men whose
   heads
Do grow beneath their shoulders. This
   to hear
Would Desdemona seriously incline;
But still the house-affairs would draw
   her thence,
Which ever as she could with haste dis-
   patch
She'd come again, and with a greedy ear
Devour up my discourse. Which I ob-
   serving,
Took once a pliant hour and found
   good means
To draw from her a prayer of earnest
   heart
That I would all my pilgrimage dilate,
Whereof by parcels she had something
   heard,
But not intentively. I did consent;
And often did beguile her of her tears,
When I did speak of some distressful
   stroke
That my youth suffer'd. My story being
   done,
She gave me for my pains a world of
   sighs.
She swore, i' faith, 'twas strange, 'twas
   passing strange;
'Twas pitiful, 'twas wondrous pitiful.

She wish'd she had not heard it, yet she
   wish'd
That heaven had made her such a man.
   She thank'd me,
And bade me, if I had a friend that lov'd
   her,
I should but teach him how to tell my
   story,
And that would woo her. Upon this hint
   I spake.
She lov'd me for the dangers I had pass'd,
And I lov'd her that she did pity them.
This only is the witchcraft I have us'd.
Here comes the lady; let her witness it.

[*Enter* DESDEMONA, IAGO, *and the rest.*]

DUKE. I think this tale would win my
   daughter too.
Good Brabantio,
Take up this mangled matter at the
   best.
Men do their broken weapons rather use
Than their bare hands.
   BRABANTIO. I pray you, hear her speak.
If she confess that she was half the
   wooer,
Destruction on my head, if my bad
   blame
Light on the man! Come hither, gentle
   mistress.
Do you perceive in all this noble com-
   pany
Where most you owe obedience?
   DESDEMONA.   My noble father,
I do perceive here a divided duty.
To you I am bound for life and educa-
   tion.
My life and education both do learn
   me
How to respect you: you are the lord
   of duty,
I am hitherto your daughter. But here's
   my husband;
And so much duty as my mother show'd
To you, preferring you before her father,
So much I challenge that I may profess
Due to the Moor my lord.
   BRABANTIO.
            God be with you! I have done.
Please it your Grace, on to the state af-
   fairs.

I had rather to adopt a child than get
it.
Come hither, Moor:
I here do give thee that with all my heart
Which, but thou hast already, with all
my heart
I would keep from thee. For your sake,
jewel,
I am glad at soul I have no other child,
For thy escape would teach me tyranny,
To hang clogs on 'em. I have done, my
lord.
DUKE. Let me speak like yourself and
lay a sentence,
Which, as a grise or step, may help
these lovers
Into your favor.
When remedies are past, the griefs are
ended
By seeing the worst, which late on hopes
depended.
To mourn a mischief that is past and
gone
Is the next way to draw more mischief
on.
What cannot be preserv'd when Fortune
takes,
Patience her injury a mockery makes.
The robb'd that smiles steals something
from the thief;
He robs himself that spends a bootless
grief.
BRABANTIO. So let the Turk of Cyprus
us beguile,
We lose it not so long as we can smile.
He bears the sentence well that nothing
bears
But the free comfort which from thence
he hears;
But he bears both the sentence and the
sorrow
That, to pay grief, must of poor patience
borrow.
These sentences, to sugar, or to gall,
Being strong on both sides, are equivocal:
But words are words; I never yet did
hear
That the bruis'd heart was pierced
through the ear.
Beseech you, now to the affairs of state.
DUKE. The Turk with a most mighty

preparation makes for Cyprus. Othello,
the fortitude of the place is best known
to you; and though we have there a sub-
stitute of most allowed sufficiency, yet
opinion, a sovereign mistress of effects,
throws a more safer voice on you. You
must therefore be content to slubber
the gloss of your new fortunes with this
more stubborn and boisterous expedition.
OTHELLO. The tyrant custom, most
grave senators,
Hath made the flinty and steel couch of
war
My thrice-driven bed of down. I do
agnize
A natural and prompt alacrity
I find in hardness, and do undertake
These present wars against the Otto-
mites.
Most humbly therefore bending to your
state,
I crave fit disposition for my wife,
Due reference of place and exhibi-
tion,
With such accommodation and besort
As levels with her breeding.
DUKE.   If you please,
Be't at her father's.
BRABANTIO.   I'll not have it so.
OTHELLO. Nor I.
DESDEMONA.
                Nor I. I would not there reside,
To put my father in impatient thoughts
By being in his eye. Most gracious duke,
To my unfolding lend your prosper-
ous ear,
And let me find a charter in your
voice
T'assist my simpleness.
DUKE.   What would you? Speak.
DESDEMONA. That I did love the Moor
to live with him,
My downright violence and storm of
fortunes
May trumpet to the world. My heart's
subdu'd
Even to the very quality of my lord.
I saw Othello's visage in his mind,
And to his honors and his valiant parts
Did I my soul and fortunes consecrate.
So that, dear lords, if I be left behind,

A moth of peace, and he go to the war,
The rites for which I love him are bereft
    me,
And I a heavy interim shall support
By his dear absence. Let me go with him.
    OTHELLO. Your voices, lords! Beseech
    you, let her will
Have a free way. I therefore beg it not
To please the palate of my appetite,
Nor to comply with heat the young af-
    fects
In my distinct and proper satisfaction,
But to be free and bounteous to her
    mind;
And heaven defend your good souls that
    you think
I will your serious and great business
    scant
For she is with me. No, when light-
    wing'd toys
Of feather'd Cupid seel with wanton
    dulness
My speculative and offic'd instruments,
That my disports corrupt and taint my
    business,
Let housewives make a skillet of my
    helm,
And all indign and base adversities
Make head against my estimation!
    DUKE. Be it as you shall privately de-
    termine,
Either for her stay or going. Th' affair
    cries haste,
And speed must answer. You must hence
    to-night.
    DESDEMONA. To-night, my lord?
    DUKE.   This night.
    OTHELLO.   With all my heart.
    DUKE. At ten i' the morning here we'll
    meet again.
Othello, leave some officer behind,
And he shall our commission bring to
    you;
With such things else of quality or re-
    spect
As doth concern you.
    OTHELLO.
            Please your Grace, my ancient.
A man he is of honesty and trust.
To his conveyance I assign my wife,

With what else needful your good Grace
    shall think
To be sent after me.
    DUKE.   Let it be so.
Good night to everyone. [To BRABANTIO.]
    And, noble signior,
If virtue no delighted beauty lack,
Your son-in-law is far more fair than
    black.
    FIRST SENATOR. Adieu, brave Moor! use
    Desdemona well.
    BRABANTIO. Look to her, Moor, if thou
    hast eyes to see:
She has deceiv'd her father, and may
    thee.
    OTHELLO. My life upon her faith!

[Exeunt DUKE, SENATORS, OFFICERS,
            and others.]

                                Honest Iago,
My Desdemona must I leave to thee:
I prithee, let thy wife attend on her;
And bring her after in the best advan-
    tage.—
Come, Desdemona; I have but an hour
Of love, of worldly matters and direc-
    tion
To spend with thee. We must obey the
    time.

[Exeunt MOOR and DESDEMONA.]

    RODERIGO. Iago!
    IAGO. What sayst thou, noble heart?
    RODERIGO. What will I do, think'st
thou?
    IAGO. Why, go to bed, and sleep.
    RODERIGO. I will incontinently drown
myself.
    IAGO. Well, if thou dost, I shall never
love thee after it. Why, thou silly gentleman?
    RODERIGO. It is silliness to live when to
live is a torment; and then have we a
prescription to die when death is our
physician.
    IAGO. O, villainous! I ha' looked upon
the world for four times seven years, and
since I could distinguish between a benefit and an injury, I never found a man
that knew how to love himself. Ere I
would say I would drown myself for the

love of a guinea-hen, I would change my humanity with a baboon.

RODERIGO. What should I do? I confess it is my shame to be so fond, but it is not in my virtue to amend it.

IAGO. Virtue! a fig! 'Tis in ourselves that we are thus or thus. Our bodies are gardens, to the which our wills are gardeners; so that if we will plant nettles or sow lettuce, set hyssop and weed up thyme, supply it with one gender of herbs or distract it with many, either to have it sterile with idleness or manured with industry, why, the power and corrigible authority of this lies in our wills. If the balance of our lives had not one scale of reason to poise another of sensuality, the blood and baseness of our natures would conduct us to most preposterous conclusions. But we have reason to cool our raging motions, our carnal stings, our unbitted lusts, whereof I take this that you call love to be a sect or scion.

RODERIGO. It cannot be.

IAGO. It is merely a lust of the blood and a permission of the will. Come, be a man. Drown thyself? Drown cats and blind puppies. I profess me thy friend, and I confess me knit to thy deserving with cables of perdurable toughness. I could never better stead thee than now. Put money in thy purse. Follow these wars; defeat thy favor with an usurped beard. I say, put money in thy purse. It cannot be that Desdemona should long continue her love unto the Moor,—put money in thy purse,—nor he his to her. It was a violent commencement, and thou shalt see an answerable sequestration. Put but money in thy purse. These Moors are changeable in their wills. Fill thy purse with money. The food that to him now is as luscious as locusts, shall be to him shortly as acerb as the coloquintida. She must change for youth. When she is sated with his body, she will find the error of her choice. She must have change, she must. Therefore put money in thy purse. If thou wilt needs damn thyself, do it a more delicate way than drowning. Make all the money thou canst. If sanctimony and a frail vow betwixt an erring barbarian and a super-subtle Venetian be not too hard for my wits and all the tribe of hell, thou shalt enjoy her: therefore make money. A pox o' drowning! 'tis clean out of the way. Seek thou rather to be hanged in compassing thy joy than to be drowned and go without her.

RODERIGO. Wilt thou be fast to my hopes if I depend on the issue?

IAGO. Thou art sure of me. Go, make money. I have told thee often, and I tell thee again and again, I hate the Moor. My cause is hearted: thine hath no less reason. Let us be conjunctive in our revenge against him. If thou canst cuckold him, thou dost thyself a pleasure, me a sport. There are many events in the womb of time which will be delivered. Traverse! go! provide thy money! We will have more of this to-morrow. Adieu.

RODERIGO. Where shall we meet i' th' morning?

IAGO. At my lodging.

RODERIGO. I'll be with thee betimes.

IAGO. Go to; farewell. Do you hear, Roderigo?

RODERIGO. What say you?

IAGO. No more of drowning, do you hear?

RODERIGO. I am chang'd. I'll sell all my land.

IAGO. Go to; farewell. Put money enough in your purse. [*Exit* RODERIGO.]
Thus do I ever make my fool my purse;
For I mine own gain'd knowledge should profane,
If I would time expend with such a snipe
But for my sport and profit. I hate the Moor,
And it is thought abroad that 'twixt my sheets
He's done my office. I know not if't be true,
But I, for mere suspicion in that kind,
Will do as if for surety. He holds me well.
The better shall my purpose work on him.

Cassio's a proper man. Let me see
now.—
To get his place, and to plume up my
will
In double knavery: how? how? Let's
see.—
After some time t'abuse Othello's ear
That he is too familiar with his wife.
He has a person and a smooth dispose
To be suspected, fram'd to make women
false;

The Moor a free and open nature too,
That thinks men honest that but seem to
be so,
And will as tenderly be led by th' nose
As asses are.
I hav't! it is engender'd! Hell and night
Must bring this monstrous birth to the
world's light.
[Exit.]

ACT TWO

1. *Famagosta, capital of Cyprus,
an open place near the quay*

Enter MONTANO, *Governor of Cyprus,
with two other* GENTLEMEN.

MONTANO: What from the cape can
you discern at sea?
FIRST GENTLEMAN. Nothing at all. It is
a high-wrought flood;
I cannot 'twixt the heaven and the main
Descry a sail.
MONTANO. Methinks the wind does
speak aloud at land;
A fuller blast ne'er shook our battle-
ments.
If it hath ruffian'd so upon the sea,
What ribs of oak, when mountains melt
on them,
Can hold the mortise? What shall we
hear of this?
SECOND GENTLEMAN. A segregation of
the Turkish fleet;
For do but stand upon the foaming shore,
The chidden billow seems to pelt the
clouds;
The wind-shak'd surge, with high and
monstrous mane,
Seems to cast water on the burning bear
And quench the guards of th' ever-fixed
pole.
I never did like molestation view
On the enchafed flood.

MONTANO.   If that the Turkish fleet
Be not enshelter'd and embay'd, they are
drown'd.
It is impossible they bear it out.

[Enter a third GENTLEMAN.]

THIRD GENTLEMAN. News, lads! our
wars are done.
The desperate tempest hath so bang'd the
Turks
That their designment halts. A noble
ship of Venice
Hath seen a grievous wrack and suffer-
ance
On most part of their fleet.
MONTANO. How! is this true?
THIRD GENTLEMAN.
                    The ship is here put in,
LA VERONESA. Michael Cassio,
Lieutenant to the warlike Moor Othello,
Is come on shore; the Moor himself at
sea,
And is in full commission here for Cy-
prus.
MONTANO. I am glad on't; 'tis a worthy
governor.
THIRD GENTLEMAN. But this same Cassio,
though he speak of comfort
Touching the Turkish loss, yet he looks
sadly
And prays the Moor be safe, for they
were parted

With foul and violent tempest.
MONTANO.   Pray heaven he be;
For I have serv'd him, and the man com-
mands
Like a full soldier. Let's to the seaside,
ho!
As well to see the vessel that's come in
As to throw out our eyes for brave
Othello,
Even till we make the main and th' aerial
blue
An indistinct regard.
THIRD GENTLEMAN.   Come, let's do so;
For every minute is expectancy
Of more arrivance.

[Enter CASSIO.]

CASSIO. Thanks to the valiant of this
warlike isle,
That so approve the Moor! And let the
heavens
Give him defence against the elements,
For I have lost him on a dangerous sea.
MONTANO. Is he well shipp'd?
CASSIO. His bark is stoutly timber'd, and
his pilot
Of very expert and approv'd allow-
ance.
Therefore my hopes, not surfeited to
death,
Stand in bold cure.
MESSENGER. *[Within.]* A sail!—a sail!
—a sail!

[Enter a MESSENGER.]

CASSIO. What noise?
MESSENGER. The town is empty. On
the brow o' th' sea
Stand ranks of people, and they cry, 'A
Sail!'
CASSIO. My hopes do shape him for the
governor.

[A shot.]

SECOND GENTLEMAN. They do discharge
the shot of courtesy.
Our friends, at least.
CASSIO.   I pray you, sir, go forth,
And give us truth who 'tis that is arriv'd.
SECOND GENTLEMAN. I shall. *[Exit.]*

MONTANO. But, good lieutenant, is your
general wiv'd?
CASSIO. Most fortunately. He hath
achiev'd a maid
That paragons description and wild
fame;
One that excels the quirks of blazoning
pens,
And in th' essential vesture of creation
Does tire the ingener.

[Enter SECOND GENTLEMAN.]

                Now, who has put in?
SECOND GENTLEMAN. 'Tis one Iago, an-
cient to the general.
CASSIO. He's had most favorable and
happy speed.
Tempests themselves, high seas, and
howling winds,
The gutter'd rocks, and congregated
sands,
Traitors ensteep'd to clog the guiltless
keel,
As having sense of beauty, do omit
Their mortal natures, letting go safely
by
The divine Desdemona.
MONTANO.   What is she?
CASSIO. She that I spoke of, our great
captain's captain,
Left in the conduct of the bold Iago,
Whose footing here anticipates our
thoughts
A sennight's speed. Great Jove, Othello
guard,
And swell his sail with thine own power-
ful breath,
That he may bless this bay with his tall
ship,
Make love's quick pants in Desdemona's
arms,
Give renew'd fire to our extinced
spirits,
And bring all Cyprus comfort!

*[Enter DESDEMONA, IAGO, EMILIA, and
RODERIGO, with ATTENDANTS.]*

                        O! behold,
The riches of the ship is come ashore.
Ye men of Cyprus, let her have your
knees.

Hail to thee, lady! and the grace of
heaven,
Before, behind thee, and on every hand,
Enwheel thee round!
DESDEMONA.
        I thank you, valiant Cassio.
What tidings can you tell me of my
lord?
CASSIO. He is not yet arriv'd; nor know
I aught
But that he's well, and will be shortly
here.
DESDEMONA. O, but I fear! How lost
you company?

[*Cry within*: 'A sail!—a sail!']

CASSIO. The great contention of the sea
and skies
Parted our fellowship. But hark! a sail.
[*Guns heard.*]
SECOND GENTLEMAN. They give their
greeting to the citadel:
This likewise is a friend.
CASSIO. See for the news! [*Exit* SECOND
GENTLEMAN.]
Good ancient, you are welcome. [*Kisses*
EMILIA.] Welcome, mistress.
Let it not gall your patience, good Iago,
That I extend my manners. 'Tis my
breeding
That gives me this bold show of cour-
tesy.
IAGO. Sir, would she give you so much
of her lips
As of her tongue she oft bestows on me,
You'd have enough.
DESDEMONA.   Alas, she has no speech.
IAGO. In faith, too much.
I find it still when I have list to sleep.
Marry, before your ladyship, I grant,
She puts her tongue a little in her heart,
And chides with thinking.
EMILIA. You have little cause to say so.
IAGO. Come on, come on! You are pic-
tures out o' doors,
Bells in your parlors, wild cats in your
kitchens,
Saints in your injuries, devils being of-
fended,
Players in your housewifery, and house-
wives in your beds.

DESDEMONA. O fie upon thee, slanderer!
IAGO. Nay, it is true, or else I am a
Turk.
You rise to play and go to bed to work.
EMILIA. You shall not write my praise.
IAGO.   No, let me not.
DESDEMONA. What wouldst thou write
of me, if thou shouldst praise me?
IAGO. O gentle lady, do not put me to't,
For I am nothing if not critical.
DESDEMONA. Come on; assay. There's
one gone to the harbor?
IAGO. Ay, madam.
DESDEMONA. I am not merry, but I do
beguile
The thing I am by seeming otherwise.
Come, how wouldst thou praise me?
IAGO. I am about it, but indeed my in-
vention comes from my pate as bird-
lime does from frieze. It plucks out
brains and all. But my muse labors, and
thus she is deliver'd.
If she be fair and wise.—Fairness and
wit:
The one's for use, the other useth it.
DESDEMONA. Well prais'd! How if she
be black and witty?
IAGO. If she be black, and thereto have
a wit,
She'll find a white that shall her blackness fit.
DESDEMONA. Worse and worse.
EMILIA. How if fair and foolish?
IAGO. She never yet was foolish that
was fair,
For even her folly help'd her to an
heir.
DESDEMONA. These are old fond paradoxes to make fools laugh i' th' alehouse.
What miserable praise hast thou for her
that's foul and foolish?
IAGO. There's none so foul and foolish
thereunto
But does foul pranks which fair and
wise ones do.
DESDEMONA. O heavy ignorance that
praises the worst best! But what praise
couldst thou bestow on a deserving
woman indeed? one that, in the authority
of her merits, did justly put on the
vouch of very malice itself?

IAGO. She that was ever fair and never proud,
Had tongue at will and yet was never loud;
Never lack'd gold and yet went never gay,
Fled from her wish and yet said 'Now I may';
She that being anger'd, her revenge being nigh,
Bade her wrong stay and her displeasure fly;
She that in wisdom never was so frail
To change the cod's head for the salmon's tail;
She that could think and ne'er disclose her mind,
See suitors following and not look behind:
She was a wight, if ever such wights were,—

DESDEMONA. To do what?

IAGO. To suckle fools and chronicle small beer.

DESDEMONA. O most lame and impotent conclusion! Do not learn of him, Emilia, though he be thy husband. How say you, Cassio? Is he not a most profane and liberal counsellor?

CASSIO. He speaks home, madam. You may relish him more in the soldier than in the scholar.

IAGO. [*Aside.*] He takes her by the palm. Ay, well said, whisper! With as little a web as this will I ensnare as great a fly as Cassio. Ay, smile upon her, do! I will gyve thee in thine own courtship. [CASSIO *speaks to* DESDEMONA *in pantomime.*] You say true, 'tis so, indeed. If such tricks as these strip you out of your lieutenantry, it had been better you had not kissed your three fingers so oft, which now again you are most apt to play the sir in. Very good! well kissed! an excellent courtesy! 'tis so, indeed. Yet again your fingers to your lips? would they were clysterpipes for your sake! [*Trumpets within.*] The Moor! I know his trumpet.

CASSIO. 'Tis truly so.

DESDEMONA. Let's meet him and receive him.

CASSIO. Lo, where he comes!

[*Enter* OTHELLO *and* ATTENDANTS.]

OTHELLO. O my fair warrior!

DESDEMONA.   My dear Othello!

OTHELLO. It gives me wonder great as my content
To see you here before me. O my soul's joy,
If after every tempest come such calms,
May the winds blow till they have waken'd death!
And let the laboring bark climb hills of seas
Olympus-high, and duck again as low
As hell's from heaven! If it were now to die,
'Twere now to be most happy, for I fear
My soul hath her content so absolute
That not another comfort like to this
Succeeds in unknown fate.

DESDEMONA.   The heavens forbid
But that our loves and comforts should increase
Even as our days do grow.

OTHELLO. Amen to that, sweet powers!
I cannot speak enough of this content.
It stops me here. It is too much of joy;
And this; and this, the greatest discords be
That e'er our hearts shall make! [*They kiss.*]

IAGO. [*Aside.*] O! you are well tun'd now,
But I'll set down the pegs that make this music,
As honest as I am.

OTHELLO.   Come, let us to the castle.—
News, friends! Our wars are done. The Turks are drown'd.
How does my old acquaintance of this isle?—
Honey, you shall be well desir'd in Cyprus;
I have found great love amongst them. O my sweet,
I prattle out of fashion, and I dote

In mine own comforts. I prithee, good Iago,
Go to the bay and disembark my coffers.
Bring thou the master to the citadel;
He is a good one, and his worthiness
Does challenge much respect. Come, Desdemona!
Once more, well met at Cyprus!

[*Exit* OTHELLO *and* DESDEMONA *with all except* IAGO *and* RODERIGO.]

IAGO. [*To* RODERIGO.] Do thou meet me presently at the harbor. Come hither. If thou be'st valiant (as they say base men being in love have then a nobility in their natures more than is native to them), list me. The lieutenant to-night watches on the court of guard. First, I must tell thee this: Desdemona is directly in love with him.

RODERIGO. With him? Why, 'tis not possible.

IAGO. Lay thy finger thus, and let thy soul be instructed. Mark me with what violence she first loved the Moor but for bragging and telling her fantastical lies. And will she love him still for prating? Let not thy discreet heart think it. Her eye must be fed; and what delight shall she have to look on the devil? When the blood is made dull with the act of sport, there should be, again to inflame it, and to give satiety a fresh appetite, loveliness in favor, sympathy in years, manners, and beauties; all which the Moor is defective in. Now, for want of these required conveniences, her delicate tenderness will find itself abused, begin to heave the gorge, disrelish and abhor the Moor. Very nature will instruct her in it, and compel her to some second choice. Now, sir, this granted (as it is a most pregnant and unforced position), who stands so eminently in the degree of this fortune as Cassio does? A knave very voluble, no farder conscionable than in putting on the mere form of civil and humane seeming for the better compassing of his salt and hidden affections? Why, none; why, none. A subtle, slippery knave, a finder-out of occasions, that has an eye can stamp and counterfeit advantages, though true advantage never present itself. A devilish knave! Besides, the knave is handsome, young, and hath all those requisites in him that folly and green minds look after. A pestilent complete knave! and the woman has found him already.

RODERIGO. I cannot believe that in her. She's full of most bless'd condition.

IAGO. Bless'd fig's end! The wine she drinks is made of grapes. If she had been bless'd, she would never have loved the Moor. Bless'd pudding! Didst thou not see her paddle with the palm of his hand? Didst not mark that?

RODERIGO. Yes, that I did; but that was but courtesy.

IAGO. Lechery, by this hand! an index and obscure prologue to the history of lust and foul thoughts. They met so near with their lips that their breaths embraced together. Villainous thoughts, Roderigo! When these mutualities so marshal the way, hard at hand comes the master and main exercise, the incorporate conclusion. Pish! But, sir, be you ruled by me: I have brought you from Venice. Watch you to-night. For your command, I'll lay't upon you. Cassio knows you not. I'll not be far from you. Do you find some occasion to anger Cassio, either by speaking too loud, or tainting his discipline, or from what other cause you please which the time shall more favorably minister.

RODERIGO. Well.

IAGO. Sir, he is rash and very sudden in choler, and haply with his truncheon may strike at you. Provoke him that he may, for even out of that will I cause these of Cyprus to mutiny, whose qualification shall come into no true taste again but by the displanting of Cassio. So shall you have a shorter journey to your desires by the means I shall then have to prefer them, and the impediment most profitably removed without the which there were no expectation of our prosperity.

RODERIGO. I will do this, if you can bring it to any opportunity.

IAGO. I warrant thee. Meet me by and by at the citadel. I must fetch his necessaries ashore. Farewell.

RODERIGO. Adieu. [*Exit.*]

IAGO. That Cassio loves her, I do well believe't;
That she loves him, 'tis apt, and of great credit.
The Moor (howbeit that I endure him not)
Is of a constant, noble, loving nature;
And I dare think he'll prove to Desdemona
A most dear husband. Now, I do love her too,—
Not out of absolute lust (though peradventure
I stand accountant for as great a sin),
But partly led to diet my revenge,
For that I do suspect the lusty Moor
Hath leap'd into my seat; the thought whereof
Doth like a poisonous mineral gnaw my inwards.
And nothing can nor shall content my soul
Till I am even'd with him, wife for wife,—
Or failing so, yet that I put the Moor
At least into a jealousy so strong
That judgment cannot cure. Which thing to do,
If this poor trash of Venice, whom I thrash
For his quick hunting, stand the putting-on,
I'll have our Michael Cassio on the hip,
Abuse him to the Moor in the rank garb
(For I fear Cassio with my night-cap too),
Make the Moor thank me, love me, and reward me
For making him egregiously an ass
And practising upon his peace and quiet
Even to madness. 'Tis here, but yet confus'd:

Knavery's plain face is never seen till us'd.

[*Exit.*]

2. *A street*

Enter Othello's HERALD, *with a proclamation.*

HERALD. It is Othello's pleasure, our noble and valiant general, that, upon certain tidings now arrived, importing the mere perdition of the Turkish fleet, every man put himself into triumph; some to dance, some to make bonfires, each man to what sport and revels his addiction leads him; for, besides these beneficial news, it is the celebration of his nuptial. So much was his pleasure should be proclaimed. All offices are open, and there is full liberty of feasting from this present hour of five till the bell have tolled eleven. Heaven bless the isle of Cyprus and our noble general Othello! [*Exit.*]

3. *A hall in the Citadel*

Enter OTHELLO, DESDEMONA, CASSIO, *and* ATTENDANTS.

OTHELLO. Good Michael, look you to the guard to-night.
Let's teach ourselves that honorable stop,
Not to outsport discretion.

CASSIO. Iago hath direction what to do;
But, notwithstanding, with my personal eye
Will I look to't.

OTHELLO. Iago is most honest.
Michael, good night. To-morrow with your earliest
Let me have speech with you. [*To* DESDEMONA.] Come, my dear love.
The purchase made, the fruits are to ensue;
The profit's yet to come 'twixt me and you.

Good night. [*Exeunt* OTHELLO *and* DESDE-
MONA *and* ATTENDANTS.]

[*Enter* IAGO.]

CASSIO. Welcome, Iago; we must to the
watch.

IAGO. Not this hour, lieutenant; 'tis not
yet ten o'clock. Our general cast us
thus early for the love of his Desdemona,
—who let us not therefore blame. He
hath not yet made wanton the night with
her, and she is sport for Jove.

CASSIO. She's a most exquisite lady.

IAGO. And, I'll warrant her, full of
game.

CASSIO. Indeed, she is a most fresh and
delicate creature.

IAGO. What an eye she has! Methinks
it sounds a parley of provocation.

CASSIO. An inviting eye, and yet methinks right modest.

IAGO. And when she speaks, is it not an
alarum to love?

CASSIO. She is indeed perfection.

IAGO. Well, happiness to their sheets!
Come, lieutenant, I have a stoup of wine,
and here without are a brace of Cyprus
gallants that would fain have a measure
to the health of black Othello.

CASSIO. Not to-night, good Iago. I have
very poor and unhappy brains for drinking. I could well wish courtesy would
invent some other custom of entertainment.

IAGO. O they are our friends. But one
cup. I'll drink for you.

CASSIO. I have drunk but one cup tonight, and that was craftily qualified
too, and, behold, what innovation it
makes here. I am unfortunate in the infirmity, and dare not task my weakness
with any more.

IAGO. What, man! 'tis a night of revels.
The gallants desire it.

CASSIO. Where are they?

IAGO. Here at the door. I pray you, call
them in.

CASSIO. I'll do't; but it dislikes me.

IAGO. If I can fasten but one cup upon
him,

With that which he hath drunk to-night
already,
He'll be as full of quarrel and offence
As my young mistress' dog. Now, my
sick fool Roderigo,
Whom love hath turn'd almost the
wrong side out,
To Desdemona hath to-night carous'd
Potations pottle-deep; and he's to
watch.
Three lads of Cyprus, noble swelling
spirits,
That hold their honors in a wary dis-
tance,
The very elements of this warlike isle,
Have I to-night fluster'd with flowing
cups,
And they watch too. Now, 'mongst this
flock of drunkards,
Am I to put our Cassio in some action
That may offend the isle. But here they
come.
If consequence do but approve my
dream,
My boat sails freely, both with wind and
stream.

[*Enter* CASSIO, MONTANO, *and* GENTLE-
MEN, BOYS *following with wine.*]

CASSIO. 'Fore God, they have given me
a rouse already.

MONTANO. Good faith, a little one. Not
past a pint, as I am a soldier.

IAGO. Some wine, ho! [*Sings.*]
And let me the canikin clink, clink;
And let me the canikin clink.
  A soldier's a man;
  O man's life's but a span;
Why then let a soldier drink.
  Some wine, boys!

CASSIO. 'Fore God, an excellent song.

IAGO. I learned it in England, where indeed they are most potent in potting.
Your Dane, your German, and your
swag-bellied Hollander,—drink, ho!—are
nothing to your English.

CASSIO. Is your Englishman so exquisite
in his drinking?

IAGO. Why, he drinks you with facility
your Dane dead drunk. He sweats not
to overthrow your Almain. He gives

your Hollander a vomit ere the next pottle can be filled.

CASSIO. To the health of our general!

MONTANO. I am for it, lieutenant; and I'll do you justice.

IAGO. O sweet England! [*Sings.*]
King Stephen was and—a worthy peer,
  His breeches cost him but a crown.
He held them sixpence all too dear,
  With that he call'd the tailor lown.
He was a wight of high renown,
  And thou art but of low degree.
'Tis pride that pulls the country down,
  Then take thine owd cloak about
    thee.
    Some wine, ho!

CASSIO. 'Fore God, this is a more exquisite song than the other.

IAGO. Will you hear't again?

CASSIO. No; for I hold him to be unworthy of his place that does those things. Well, God's above all; and there be souls must be saved, and there be souls must not be saved.

IAGO. It's true, good lieutenant.

CASSIO. For mine own part,—no offence to the general, nor any man of quality, —I hope to be saved.

IAGO. And so do I too, lieutenant.

CASSIO. Ay; but, by your leave, not before me. The lieutenant is to be saved before the ancient. Let's have no more of this; let's to our affairs. God forgive us our sins! Gentlemen, let's look to our business. Do not think, gentlemen, I am drunk. This is my ancient; this is my right hand, and this is my left hand. I am not drunk now. I can stand well enough, and I speak well enough.

GENTLEMEN. Excellent well.

CASSIO. Why, very well, then. You must not think then that I am drunk. [*Exit.*]

MONTANO. To the platform, masters. Come, let's set the watch.

IAGO. You see this fellow that is gone before.
He is a soldier fit to stand by Cæsar
And give direction; and do but see his
    vice.
'Tis to his virtue a just equinox,
The one as long as th' other. 'Tis pity of
    him.
I fear the trust Othello puts him in,
On some odd time of his infirmity,
Will shake this island.

MONTANO.   But is he often thus?

IAGO. 'Tis evermore the prologue to his
    sleep:
He'll watch the horologe a double set,
If drink rock not his cradle.

MONTANO.   It were well
The general were put in mind of it.
Perhaps he sees it not, or his good nature
Prizes the virtue that appears in Cassio,
And looks not on his evils. Is not this
    true?

[*Enter* RODERIGO.]

IAGO. [*Aside to him.*] How now, Roderigo?
I pray you, after the lieutenant. Go!
    [*Exit* RODERIGO.]

MONTANO. And 'tis great pity that the
    noble Moor
Should hazard such a place as his own
    second
With one of an ingraft infirmity.
It were an honest action to say
So to the Moor.

IAGO.   Not I, for this fair island:
I do love Cassio well, and would do
    much
    [*Cry within:* 'Help! Help!']
To cure him of this evil. But hark! what
    noise?
    [*Enter* CASSIO, *driving in* RODERIGO.]

CASSIO. Zounds! You rogue, you rascal!

MONTANO. What's the matter, lieutenant?

CASSIO. A knave teach me my duty! I'll beat the knave into a twiggen bottle.

RODERIGO. Beat me?

CASSIO. Dost thou prate, rogue? [*Striking* RODERIGO.]

MONTANO. [*Staying him.*] Nay, good lieutenant. I pray you, sir, hold your hand.

CASSIO. Let me go, sir, or I'll knock you o'er the mazzard.

MONTANO. Come, come; you're drunk.

CASSIO. Drunk! [*They fight.*]

IAGO. [*Aside to* RODERIGO.] Away, I say!
Go out, and cry a mutiny. [*Exit*
RODERIGO.]

Nay, good lieutenant! God's will, gentlemen!

Help, ho! Lieutenant! Sir Montano! sir!

Help, masters! Here's a goodly watch indeed!

[*A bell rung.*]

Who's that that rings the bell? *Diablo*,
ho!

The town will rise. God's will! lieutenant, hold!

You will be sham'd for ever.

[*Enter* OTHELLO *and* GENTLEMEN
with weapons.]

OTHELLO.   What is the matter here?

MONTANO. Zounds! I bleed still. I am
hurt to the death.

OTHELLO. Hold, for your lives!

IAGO. Hold, hold, lieutenant! Sir Montano! gentlemen!

Have you forgot all sense of place and
duty?

Hold! the general speaks to you; hold
for shame!

OTHELLO. Why, how now, ho! from
whence arises this?

Are we turn'd Turks, and to ourselves do
that

Which heaven has forbid the Ottomites?

For Christian shame put by this barbarous brawl.

He that stirs next to carve for his own
rage

Holds his soul light; he dies upon his motion.

Silence that dreadful bell! it frights the
isle

From her propriety. What's the matter masters?

Honest Iago, that looks dead with grieving,

Speak, who began this? On thy love, I
charge thee.

IAGO. I do not know. Friends all but
now, even now,

In quarter and in terms like bride and
groom

Devesting them for bed; and then, but
now

(As if some planet had unwitted men)

Swords out, and tilting one at other's
breast,

In opposition bloody. I cannot speak

Any beginning to this peevish odds,

And would in action glorious I had lost

These legs that brought me to a part of
it!

OTHELLO. How came it, Michael, you
were thus forgot?

CASSIO. I pray you, pardon me; I cannot speak.

OTHELLO. Worthy Montano, you were
wont be civil.

The gravity and stillness of your youth

The world hath noted, and your name is
great

In mouths of wisest censure. What's the
matter,

That you unlace your reputation thus

And spend your rich opinion for the
name

Of a night-brawler? give me answer to't.

MONTANO. Worthy Othello, I am hurt
to danger.

Your officer, Iago, can inform you

(While I spare speech, which something now offends me)

Of all that I do know; nor know I aught

By me that's said or done amiss this night,

Unless self-charity be sometime a vice,

And to defend ourselves it be a sin

When violence assails us.

OTHELLO.   Now, by heaven,

My blood begins my safer guides to rule,

And passion, having my best judgment
collied,

Assays to lead the way. Zounds! If I stir,

Or do but lift this arm, the best of you

Shall sink in my rebuke. Give me to
know

How this foul rout began, who set it
on;

And he that is approv'd in this offence,

Though he had twinn'd with me—both
at a birth—

Shall lose me. What! in a town of war,

Yet wild, the people's hearts brimful of
　　fear,
To manage private and domestic quar-
　　rels
In night, and on the court and guard of
　　safety!
'Tis monstrous. Iago, who began't?
　MONTANO. If partially affin'd, or leagu'd
　　in office,
Thou dost deliver more or less than
　　truth,
Thou art no soldier.
　　　IAGO.　　　　Touch me not so near.
I had rather have this tongue cut from
　　my mouth
Than it should do offence to Michael
　　Cassio;
Yet I persuade myself, to speak the truth
Shall nothing wrong him. Thus it is, gen-
　　eral.
Montano and myself being in speech,
There comes a fellow crying out for help,
And Cassio following him with de-
　　termin'd sword
To execute upon him. Sir, this gentle-
　　man
Steps in to Cassio, and entreats his
　　pause.
Myself the crying fellow did pursue,
Lest by his clamor (as it so fell out)
The town might fall in fright. He, swift
　　of foot,
Outran my purpose, and I return'd the
　　rather
For that I heard the clink and fall of
　　swords,
And Cassio high in oath, which till to-
　　night
I ne'er might say before. When I came
　　back
(For this was brief), I found them close
　　together,
At blow and thrust, even as again they
　　were
When you yourself did part them.
More of this matter can I not report,
But men are men; the best sometimes
　　forget.
Though Cassio did some little wrong to
　　him,

As men in rage strike those that wish
　　them best,
Yet surely Cassio, I believe, receiv'd
From him that fled some strange in-
　　dignity,
Which patience could not pass.
　OTHELLO.　　　　　　　I know, Iago,
Thy honesty and love doth mince this
　　matter,
Making it light to Cassio. Cassio, I love
　　thee;
But never more be officer of mine—

[*Enter* DESDEMONA, *with others.*]

Look, if my gentle love be not rais'd
　　up!—
[*To* CASSIO.] I'll make thee an example.
　DESDEMONA.　　　　What's the matter?
　OTHELLO. All's well now, sweeting.
　　Come away to bed.—
Sir, for your hurts, myself will be your
　　surgeon.
Lead him off. [MONTANO *is led off.*]
Iago, look with care about the town,
And silence those whom this vile brawl
　　distracted.
Come, Desdemona; 'tis the soldiers' life,
To have their balmy slumbers wak'd with
　　strife.

[*Exeunt.* MOOR, DESDEMONA, *and*
ATTENDANTS.]

　IAGO. What! are you hurt, lieutenant?
　CASSIO. Ay, past all surgery.
　IAGO. Marry, God forbid!
　CASSIO. Reputation, reputation, reputation! O! I have lost my reputation. I
have lost the immortal part of myself,
and what remains is bestial. My reputation, Iago, my reputation!
　IAGO. As I am an honest man, I thought
you had received some bodily wound.
There is more sense in that than in reputation. Reputation is an idle and most
false imposition, oft got without merit,
and lost without deserving. You have
lost no reputation at all, unless you re-
pute yourself such a loser. What, man!
there are ways to recover the general
again. You are but now cast in his
mood (a punishment more in policy

than in malice), even so as one would beat his offenceless dog to affright an imperious lion. Sue to him again, and he is yours.

CASSIO. I will rather sue to be despised than to deceive so good a commander with so slight, so drunken, and so indiscreet an officer. Drunk! and speak parrot! and squabble, swagger, swear, and discourse fustian with one's own shadow! O thou invisible spirit of wine! if thou hast no name to be known by, let us call thee devil!

IAGO. What was he that you followed with your sword? What had he done to you?

CASSIO. I know not.

IAGO. Is't possible?

CASSIO. I remember a mass of things, but nothing distinctly; a quarrel, but nothing wherefore. O God! that men should put an enemy in their mouths to steal away their brains; that we should, with joy, revel, pleasure, and applause, transform ourselves into beasts.

IAGO. Why, but you are now well enough. How came you thus recovered?

CASSIO. It hath pleased the devil drunkenness to give place to the devil wrath. One unperfectness shows me another, to make me frankly despise myself.

IAGO. Come, you are too severe a moraler. As the time, the place, and the condition of this country stands, I could heartily wish this had not so befallen, but since it is as it is, mend it for your own good.

CASSIO. I will ask him for my place again. He shall tell me I am a drunkard. Had I as many mouths as Hydra, such an answer would stop them all. To be now a sensible man, by and by a fool, and presently a beast! O strange! Every inordinate cup is unblessed and the ingredient is a devil.

IAGO. Come, come; good wine is a good familiar creature if it be well used. Exclaim no more against it. And, good lieutenant, I think you think I love you.

CASSIO. I have well approved it, sir. I drunk!

IAGO. You or any man living may be drunk at some time. I'll tell you what you shall do. Our general's wife is now the general. I may say so in this respect, for that he has devoted and given up himself to the contemplation, mark, and denotement of her parts and graces. Confess yourself freely to her; importune her help to put you in your place again. She is of so free, so kind, so apt, so blessed a disposition, that she holds it a vice in her goodness not to do more than she is requested. This broken joint between you and her husband entreat her to splinter, and my fortunes against any lay worth naming, this crack of your love shall grow stronger than it was before.

CASSIO. You advise me well.

IAGO. I protest, in the sincerity of love and honest kindness.

CASSIO. I think it freely; and betimes in the morning will I beseech the virtuous Desdemona to undertake for me. I am desperate of my fortunes if they check me here.

IAGO. You are in the right. Good night, lieutenant; I must to the watch.

CASSIO. Good night, honest Iago! [*Exit* CASSIO.]

IAGO. And what's he, then, that says I
    play the villain,
When this advice is free I give and
    honest,
Probal to thinking and indeed the
    course
To win the Moor again? For 'tis most
    easy
Th' inclining Desdemona to subdue
In any honest suit; she's fram'd as fruit-
    ful
As the free elements. And then for her
To win the Moor,—were't to renounce
    his baptism,
All seals and symbols of redeemed sin,
His soul is so enfetter'd to her love,
That she may make, unmake, do what
    she list,
Even as her appetite shall play the god
With his weak function. How am I,
    then, a villain

To counsel Cassio to this parallel course
Directly to his good? Divinity of hell!
When devils will their blackest sins put on,
They do suggest at first with heavenly shows,
As I do now; for while this honest fool
Plies Desdemona to repair his fortunes,
And she for him pleads strongly to the Moor,
I'll pour this pestilence into his ear
That she repeals him for her body's lust;
And, by how much she strives to do him good,
She shall undo her credit with the Moor.
So will I turn her virtue into pitch,
And out of her own goodness make the net
That shall enmesh them all. [*Enter* RODERIGO.] How now, Roderigo?

RODERIGO. I do follow here in the chase, not like a hound that hunts, but one that fills up the cry. My money is almost spent; I have been tonight exceedingly well cudgelled; and I think the issue will be, I shall have so much experience for my pains; and so, with no money at all and a little more wit, return again to Venice.

IAGO. How poor are they that have not patience! What wound did ever heal but by degrees?
Thou know'st we work by wit and not by witchcraft,
And wit depends on dilatory time.
Does't not go well? Cassio has beaten thee,
And thou by that small hurt hast cashiered Cassio.
Though other things grow fair against the sun,
Yet fruits that blossom first will first be ripe.
Content thyself awhile. By the mass, 'tis morning;
Pleasure and action make the hours seem short.
Retire thee; go where thou art billeted.
Away, I say; thou shalt know more hereafter.
Nay, get thee gone. [*Exit* RODERIGO.]
Two things are to be done:
My wife must move for Cassio to her mistress—
I'll set her on—;
Myself awhile to draw the Moor apart,
And bring him jump when he may Cassio find
Soliciting his wife. Ay, that's the way.
Dull not device by coldness and delay.

[*Exit.*]

ACT THREE

1. *Before the Citadel*

Enter CASSIO *with* MUSICIANS.

CASSIO. Masters, play here, I will content your pains.
Something that's brief, and bid 'Good morrow, general.'

[*They play, and enter the* CLOWN.]

CLOWN. Why, masters, ha' your instruments been at Naples, that they speak i' th' nose thus?

MUSICIAN. How, sir? how?

CLOWN. Are these, I pray, called wind-instruments?

MUSICIAN. Ay, marry, are they, sir.

CLOWN. O! thereby hangs a tail.

MUSICIAN. Whereby hangs a tale, sir?

CLOWN. Marry, sir, by many a wind-instrument that I know. But, masters, here's money for you; and the general so likes your music that he desires you, for love's sake, to make no more noise with it.

MUSICIAN. Well, sir, we will not.

CLOWN. If you have any music that may not be heard, to't again; but (as they say) to hear music the general does not greatly care.

MUSICIAN. We ha' none such, sir.

CLOWN. Then put up your pipes in your bag, for I'll away. Go; vanish into air; away! [*Exeunt* MUSICIANS.]

CASSIO. Dost thou hear, my honest friend?

CLOWN. No, I hear not your honest friend; I hear you.

CASSIO. Prithee, keep up thy quillets. There's a poor piece of gold for thee. If the gentlewoman that attends the general's wife be stirring, tell her there's one Cassio entreats her a little favor of speech. Wilt thou do this?

CLOWN. She is stirring, sir. If she will stir hither, I shall seem to notify unto her.

CASSIO. Do, good my friend. [*Exit* CLOWN.]

[*Enter* IAGO.]

                    In happy time, Iago.

IAGO. You ha' not been a-bed, then?

CASSIO. Why, no. The day had broke Before we parted. I ha' made bold, Iago, To send in to your wife. My suit to her Is that she will to virtuous Desdemona Procure me some access.

IAGO.   I'll send her to you presently, And I'll devise a mean to draw the Moor Out of the way, that your converse and business May be more free.

CASSIO. I humbly thank you for't. [*Exit* IAGO.] I never knew A Florentine more kind and honest.

[*Enter* EMILIA.]

EMILIA. Good morrow, good lieutenant. I am sorry For your displeasure; but all will soon be well. The general and his wife are talking of it And she speaks for you stoutly. The Moor replies

That he you hurt is of great fame in Cyprus And great affinity, and that in wholesome wisdom He might not but refuse you; but he protests he loves you, And needs no other suitor but his likings To take the saf'st occasion by the front To bring you in again.

CASSIO.   Yet, I beseech you, If you think fit, or that it may be done, Give me advantage of some brief discourse With Desdemona alone.

EMILIA.   Pray you, come in. I will bestow you where you shall have time To speak your bosom freely.

CASSIO.   I am much bound to you. [*Exeunt.*]

2. *A Room in the Citadel*

Enter OTHELLO, IAGO, *and other* GENTLEMEN.

OTHELLO. These letters give, Iago, to the pilot, And by him do my duties to the Senate. That done, I will be walking on the works; Repair there to me.

IAGO.   Well, my good lord, I'll do't.

OTHELLO. This fortification, gentlemen, shall we see't?

GENTLEMEN. We wait upon your lordship.

          [*Exeunt.*]

3. *The garden of the Citadel*

Enter DESDEMONA, CASSIO, *and* EMILIA.

DESDEMONA. Be thou assur'd, good Cassio, I will do All my abilities in thy behalf.

EMILIA. Good madam, do. I know it grieves my husband,

As if the case were his.

DESDEMONA. O that's an honest fellow!
Do not doubt, Cassio,
But I will have my lord and you again
As friendly as you were.

CASSIO.   Bounteous madam,
Whatever shall become of Michael Cassio,
He's never anything but your true servant.

DESDEMONA. O, sir, I thank you. You
do love my lord.
You have known him long; and be you
well assur'd
He shall in strangeness stand no farther
off
Than in a politic distance.

CASSIO.   Ay, but, lady,
That policy may either last so long,
Or feed upon such nice and waterish
diet,
Or breed itself so out of circumstances,
That, I being absent and my place supplied,
My general will forget my love and
service.

DESDEMONA. Do not doubt that. Before
Emilia here
I give thee warrant of thy place. Assure thee,
If I do vow a friendship, I'll perform it
To the last article. My lord shall never
rest;
I'll watch him tame, and talk him out
of patience;
His bed shall seem a school, his board a
shrift;
I'll intermingle everything he does
With Cassio's suit. Therefore be merry,
Cassio;
For thy solicitor shall rather die
Than give thy cause away.

[Enter OTHELLO and IAGO at a distance.]

EMILIA. Madam, here comes my lord.

CASSIO. Madam, I'll take my leave.

DESDEMONA. Why, stay, and hear me
speak.

CASSIO. Madam, not now. I am very ill
at ease,
Unfit for mine own purposes.

DESDEMONA. Well, do your discretion.

[Exit CASSIO.]

IAGO. Ha! I like not that.

OTHELLO.   What dost thou say?

IAGO. Nothing, my lord; or if—I know
not what.

OTHELLO. Was not that Cassio parted
from my wife?

IAGO. Cassio, my lord? No, sure, I cannot think it,
That he would steal away so guilty-like,
Seeing you coming.

OTHELLO.   I do believe 'twas he.

DESDEMONA. How now, my lord!
I have been talking with a suitor here.
A man that languishes in your displeasure.

OTHELLO. Who is't you mean?

DESDEMONA. Why, your lieutenant,
Cassio. Good my lord,
If I have any grace or power to move
you,
His present reconciliation take;
For if he be not one that truly loves you,
That errs in ignorance and not in cunning,
I have no judgment in an honest face.
I prithee call him back.

OTHELLO.   Went he hence now?

DESDEMONA. Yes, faith; so humbled,
That he has left part of his griefs with
me.
I suffer with him. Good love, call him
back.

OTHELLO. Not now, sweet Desdemon.
Some other time.

DESDEMONA. But shall't be shortly?

OTHELLO.   The sooner, sweet, for you.

DESDEMONA. Shall't be to-night at supper?

OTHELLO.   No, not to-night.

DESDEMONA. To-morrow dinner then?

OTHELLO.   I shall not dine at home.
I meet the captains at the citadel.

DESDEMONA. Why then, to-morrow
night, or Tuesday morn;
On Tuesday noon, or night; on Wednesday morn.
I prithee name the time, but let it not
Exceed three days. I' faith, he's penitent;
And yet his trespass, in our common
reason

(Save that they say, the wars must make
    examples
Out of their best), is not almost a fault
T' incur a private check. When shall he
    come?
Tell me, Othello. I wonder in my soul,
What you could ask me that I should
    deny,
Or stand so mammering on. What?
    Michael Cassio,
That came a-wooing with you, and so
    many a time,
When I have spoke of you dispraisingly,
Hath ta'en your part; to have so much to
    do
To bring him in! By 'r Lady, I could
    do much—
  OTHELLO. Prithee, no more! Let him
    come when he will.
I will deny thee nothing.
  DESDEMONA.   Why, this is not a boon.
'Tis as I should entreat you wear your
    gloves,
Or feed on nourishing dishes, or keep
    you warm,
Or sue to you to do a peculiar profit
To your own person. Nay, when I have
    a suit
Wherein I mean to touch your love in-
    deed,
It shall be full of poise and difficulty,
And fearful to be granted.
  OTHELLO.   I will deny thee nothing.
Whereon, I do beseech thee, grant me
    this,
To leave me but a little to myself.
  DESDEMONA. Shall I deny you? No.
    Farewell, my lord.
  OTHELLO. Farewell, my Desdemona. I'll
    come to thee straight.
  DESDEMONA. Emilia, come. Be it as
    your fancies teach you.
Whate'er you be, I am obedient.

    [*Exeunt* DESDEMONA *and* EMILIA.]

  OTHELLO. Excellent wretch! Perdition
    catch my soul
But I do love thee! and when I love thee
    not,
Chaos is come again.
  IAGO. My noble lord,—

  OTHELLO.   What dost thou say, Iago?
  IAGO. Did Michael Cassio, when you
    woo'd my lady,
Know of your love?
  OTHELLO. He did, from first to last.
    Why dost thou ask?
  IAGO. But for a satisfaction of my
    thought.
No further harm.
  OTHELLO.   Why of thy thought, Iago?
  IAGO. I did not think he had been ac-
    quainted with her.
  OTHELLO. O yes; and went between us
    very oft.
  IAGO. Indeed?
  OTHELLO. Indeed? ay, indeed. Discern'st
    thou aught in that?
Is he not honest?
  IAGO.   Honest, my lord?
  OTHELLO.   Honest? ay, honest.
  IAGO. My lord, for aught I know.
  OTHELLO. What dost thou think?
  IAGO.   Think, my lord?
  OTHELLO.   Think, my lord?
By heaven, he echoes me,
As if there were some monster in his
    thought
Too hideous to be shown.—Thou didst
    mean something.
I heard thee say but now, thou lik'st not
    that,
When Cassio left my wife. What didst
    not like?
And when I told thee he was of my
    counsel
In my whole course of wooing thou
    criedst, 'Indeed?'
And didst contract and purse thy brow
    together,
As if thou then hadst shut up in thy
    brain
Some horrible conceit. If thou dost love
    me,
Show me thy thought.
  IAGO. My lord, you know I love you.
  OTHELLO.   I think thou dost;
And, for I know thou'rt full of love
    and honesty,
And weigh'st thy words before thou
    give 'em breath,

Therefore these stops of thine fright me
    the more;
For such things in a false disloyal knave
Are tricks of custom, but in a man
    that's just
They are close delations, working from
    the heart
That passion cannot rule.

    IAGO.   For Michael Cassio,
I dare be sworn I think that he is honest.

    OTHELLO. I think so too.

    IAGO.   Men should be what they seem;
Or those that be not, would they might
    seem none!

    OTHELLO. Certain, men should be what
    they seem.

    IAGO. Why then, I think Cassio's an
    honest man.

    OTHELLO. Nay, yet there's more in this.
I pray thee, speak to me as to thy think-
    ings,
As thou dost ruminate, and give thy
    worst of thoughts
The worst of words.

    IAGO.   Good my lord, pardon me;
Though I am bound to every act of
    duty,
I am not bound to that all slaves are free
    to.
Utter my thoughts? Why, say they are
    vile and false;
As where's that palace whereinto foul
    things
Sometimes intrude not? who has a breast
    so pure
But some uncleanly apprehensions
Keep leets and law-days, and in session
    sit
With meditations lawful?

    OTHELLO. Thou dost conspire against
    thy friend, Iago,
If thou but think'st him wrong'd, and
    mak'st his ear
A stranger to thy thoughts.

    IAGO.   I do beseech you,
Though I perchance am vicious in my
    guess
(As, I confess, it is my nature's plague
To spy into abuses, and oft my jealousy
Shapes faults that are not)—I entreat you
    then,

From one that so imperfectly conjects,
You'ld take no notice nor build yourself
    a trouble
Out of my scattering and unsure ob-
    servance.
It were not for your quiet nor your good,
Nor for my manhood, honesty, or wis-
    dom,
To let you know my thoughts.

    OTHELLO.   What dost thou mean?

    IAGO. Good name in man, and woman,
    dear my lord,
Is the immediate jewel of our souls.
Who steals my purse steals trash. 'Tis
    something, nothing;
'Twas mine, 'tis his, and has been slave to
    thousands;
But he that filches from me my good
    name
Robs me of that which not enriches him,
And makes me poor indeed.

    OTHELLO. By heaven, I'll know thy
    thought.

    IAGO. You cannot, if my heart were in
    your hand;
Nor shall not, whilst 'tis in my custody.

    OTHELLO. Ha!

    IAGO. O beware, my lord, of jealousy!
It is the green-ey'd monster which doth
    mock
The meat it feeds on. That cuckold lives
    in bliss
Who, certain of his fate, loves not his
    wronger;
But, O, what damned minutes tells he
    o'er
Who dotes, yet doubts; suspects, yet
    strongly loves!

    OTHELLO. O misery!

    IAGO. Poor and content is rich, and rich
    enough,
But riches fineless is as poor as winter
To him that ever fears he shall be poor.
Good God, the souls of all my tribe
    defend
From jealousy.

    OTHELLO. Why, why is this?
Think'st thou I'd make a life of jealousy,
To follow still the changes of the moon
With fresh suspicions? No; to be once
    in doubt

Is once to be resolv'd. Exchange me for
a goat
When I shall turn the business of my
soul
To such exsufflicate and blown sur-
mises,
Matching thy inference. 'Tis not to make
me jealous
To say my wife is fair, feeds well, loves
company,
Is free of speech, sings, plays, and dances
well.
Where virtue is, these are more virtuous.
Nor from mine own weak merits will I
draw
The smallest fear or doubt of her re-
volt;
For she had eyes and chose me. No, Iago.
I'll see before I doubt; when I doubt,
prove;
And, on the proof, there is no more but
this:
Away at once with love or jealousy!
  IAGO. I am glad of this; for now I shall
have reason
To show the love and duty that I bear
you
With franker spirit. Therefore (as I am
bound)
Receive it from me—I speak not yet of
proof.
Look to your wife. Observe her well
with Cassio.
Wear your eye thus, not jealous nor se-
cure.
I would not have your free and noble
nature
Out of self-bounty be abus'd. Look
to't!
I know our country disposition well;
In Venice they do let God see the pranks
They dare not show their husbands.
Their best conscience
Is not to leave undone, but keep un-
known.
  OTHELLO. Dost thou say so?
  IAGO. She did deceive her father,
marrying you:
And when she seem'd to shake and fear
your looks,
She lov'd them most.

  OTHELLO.   And so she did.
  IAGO.   Why,
go to, then.
She that so young could give out such a
seeming,
To seel her father's eyes up close as
oak,—
He thought 'twas witchcraft—but I am
much to blame.
I humbly do beseech you of your pardon
For too much loving you.
  OTHELLO. I am bound to thee for ever.
  IAGO. I see, this hath a little dash'd your
spirits.
  OTHELLO. Not a jot, not a jot.
  IAGO.   I' faith, I fear it has.
I hope you will consider what is spoke
Comes from my love. But I do see you're
mov'd.
I am to pray you not to strain my speech
To grosser issues nor to larger reach
Than to suspicion.
  OTHELLO. I will not.
  IAGO.   Should you do so, my lord,
My speech should fall into such vile suc-
cess
As my thoughts aim not at. Cassio's my
trusty friend—
My lord, I see you're mov'd.
  OTHELLO.   No, not much mov'd.
I do not think but Desdemona's honest.
  IAGO. Long live she so! and long live
you to think so!
  OTHELLO. And, yet, how nature erring
from itself,—
  IAGO. Ay, there's the point: as (to be
bold with you)
Not to affect many proposed matches
Of her own clime, complexion, and de-
gree,
Whereto, we see, in all things nature
tends—
Foh! one may smell, in such a will, most
rank,
Foul disproportion, thoughts unnatural.
But pardon me; I do not in position
Distinctly speak of her, though I may
fear
Her will, recoiling to her better judg-
ment,

May fall to match you with her country forms
And happily repent.

OTHELLO.   Farewell, farewell.
If more thou dost perceive, let me know more.
Set on thy wife to observe. Leave me, Iago.

IAGO. My lord, I take my leave. [*Going.*]

OTHELLO. Why did I marry? This honest creature, doubtless,
Sees and knows more, much more, than he unfolds.

IAGO. [*Returning.*] My lord, I would I might entreat your honor
To scan this thing no further; leave it to time.
Though it be fit that Cassio have his place
(For sure he fills it up with great ability),
Yet if you please to hold him off awhile,
You shall by that perceive him and his means.
Note if your lady strain his entertainment
With any strong or vehement importunity;
Much will be seen in that. In the mean time,
Let me be thought too busy in my fears,
As worthy cause I have to fear I am,
And hold her free, I do beseech your honor.

OTHELLO. Fear not my government.

IAGO. I once more take my leave.

OTHELLO. This fellow's of exceeding honesty,
And knows all qualities, with a learned spirit,
Of human dealing. If I do prove her haggard,
Though that her jesses were my dear heartstrings,
I'd whistle her off and let her down the wind,
To prey at fortune. Haply, for I am black,
And have not those soft parts of conversation

That chamberers have, or for I am declin'd
Into the vale of years (yet that's not much)—
She's gone, I am abus'd, and my relief
Must be to loathe her. O curse of marriage!
That we can call these delicate creatures ours,
And not their appetites. I had rather be a toad,
And live upon the vapor of a dungeon,
Than keep a corner in the thing I love
For others' uses. Yet, 'tis the plague of great ones;
Prerogativ'd are they less than the base.
'Tis destiny unshunnable, like death:
Even then this forked plague is fated to us
When we do quicken.
                    Look, where she comes!
If she be false, O then heaven mocks itself.
I'll not believe't.

[*Enter* DESDEMONA *and* EMILIA.]

DESDEMONA. How now, my dear Othello?
Your dinner and the generous islanders
By you invited do attend your presence.

OTHELLO. I am to blame.

DESDEMONA.
                    Why is your speech so faint?
Are you not well?

OTHELLO. I have a pain upon my forehead here.

DESDEMONA. Faith, that's with watching; 'twill away again.
Let me but bind your head; within this hour
It will be well.

OTHELLO. Your napkin is too little.

[*He puts the handkerchief from him, and it drops.*]

Let it alone. Come, I'll go in with you.

DESDEMONA. I am very sorry that you are not well.

[*Exeunt* OTHELLO *and* DESDEMONA.]

EMILIA. I am glad I have found this napkin.
This was her first remembrance from the Moor.
My wayward husband hath a hundred times
Woo'd me to steal it, but she so loves the token
(For he conjur'd her she should ever keep it)
That she reserves it evermore about her
To kiss and talk to. I'll have the work ta'en out,
And give't Iago.
What he will do with it heaven knows, not I.
I nothing know, but for his fantasy—

[Enter IAGO.]

IAGO. How now! what do you here alone?

EMILIA. Do not you chide. I have a thing for you.

IAGO. A thing for me? It is a common thing—

EMILIA. Ha?

IAGO. To have a foolish wife.

EMILIA. O, is that all? What will you give me now
For that same handkerchief?

IAGO.   What handkerchief?

EMILIA. What handkerchief?
Why, that the Moor first gave to Desdemona;
That which so often you did bid me steal.

IAGO. Hast stol'n it from her?

EMILIA. No, faith. She let it drop by negligence,
And, to th' advantage, I, being here, took't up.
Look, here it is.

IAGO.   A good wench! give it me.

EMILIA. What will you do with't, that you have been so earnest
To have me filch it?

IAGO. Why, what's that to you? *[Snatches it.]*

EMILIA. If it be not for some purpose of import,

Give me't again. Poor lady, she'll run mad
When she shall lack it.

IAGO. Be not acknown on't. I have use for it.

Go, leave me. *[Exit EMILIA.]*
I will in Cassio's lodging lose this napkin,
And let him find it. Trifles light as air
Are to the jealous confirmations strong
As proofs of holy writ; this may do something.
The Moor already changes with my poison,
Dangerous conceits are in their natures poison.
Which at the first are scarce found to distaste,
But, with a little act upon the blood,
Burn like the mines of sulphur. I did say so.
Look, where he comes! *[Enter OTHELLO.]*
Not poppy, nor mandragora,
Nor all the drowsy syrups of the world,
Shall ever medicine thee to that sweet sleep
Which thou ow'dst yesterday.

OTHELLO.   Ha! ha! false to me?

IAGO. Why, how now, general? No more of that.

OTHELLO. Avaunt! be gone! Thou hast set me on the rack.
I swear 'tis better to be much abus'd
Than but to know't a little.

IAGO.   How now, my lord?

OTHELLO. What sense had I of her stol'n hours of lust?
I saw't not, thought it not, it harm'd not me.
I slept the next night well, was free and merry;
I found not Cassio's kisses on her lips.
He that is robb'd, not wanting what is stol'n,
Let him not know't and he's not robb'd at all.

IAGO. I am sorry to hear this.

OTHELLO. I had been happy if the general camp,
Pioneers and all, had tasted her sweet body,

So I had nothing known. O, now for
    ever
Farewell the tranquil mind! farewell
    content!
Farewell the plumed troops and the big
    wars
That make ambition virtue! O, farewell!
Farewell the neighing steed, and the
    shrill trump,
The spirit-stirring drum, th' ear-piercing
    fife,
The royal banner, and all quality,
Pride, pomp, and circumstance of
    glorious war!
And, O ye mortal engines, whose rude
    throats
Th' immortal Jove's great clamor coun-
    terfeit,
Farewell! Othello's occupation's gone!
    IAGO. Is't possible, my lord?
    OTHELLO. Villain, be sure thou prove
    my love a whore,
Be sure of it! Give me the ocular proof;
Or by the worth of man's eternal soul,
Thou hadst been better have been born
    a dog
Than answer my wak'd wrath.
    IAGO.   Is't come to this?
    OTHELLO. Make me to see't; or, at the
    least, so prove it
That the probation bear no hinge nor
    loop
To hang a doubt on, or woe upon thy
    life!
    IAGO. My noble lord,—
    OTHELLO. If thou dost slander her and
    torture me,
Never pray more. Abandon all remorse;
On horror's head horrors accumulate;
Do deeds to make heaven weep, all earth
    amaz'd;
For nothing canst thou to damnation add
Greater than that.
    IAGO.   O grace! O heaven defend me!
Are you a man? Have you a soul or
    sense?
God be wi' you! Take mine office. O
    wretched fool!
That liv'st to make thine honesty a vice.
O monstrous world! Take note, take
    note, O world,

To be direct and honest is not safe.
I thank you for this profit, and from
    hence
I'll love no friend, sith love breeds such
    offence.
    OTHELLO. Nay, stay. Thou shouldst be
    honest.
    IAGO. I should be wise, for honesty's a
    fool,
And loses that it works for.
    OTHELLO.   By the world,
I think my wife be honest and think she
    is not;
I think that thou art just and think thou
    are not.
I'll have some proof. Her name, that was
    as fresh
As Dian's visage, is now begrim'd and
    black
As mine own face. If there be cords or
    knives,
Poison or fire or suffocating streams,
I'll not endure it. Would I were satisfied!
    IAGO. I see, sir, you are eaten up with
    passion.
I do repent me that I put it to you.
You would be satisfied?
    OTHELLO.   Would? Nay, I will!
    IAGO. And may; but how? How satis-
    fied, my lord?
Would you, the supervisor, grossly gape
    on,
Behold her topp'd?
    OTHELLO.   Death and damnation! O!
    IAGO. It were a tedious difficulty, I
    think,
To bring them to that prospect. Damn
    them, then,
If ever mortal eyes do see them bolster
More than their own. What then? how
    then?
What shall I say? Where's satisfaction?
It is impossible you should see this,
Were they as prime as goats, as hot as
    monkeys,
As salt as wolves in pride, and fools as
    gross
As ignorance made drunk. But yet, I say,
If imputation, and strong circumstances,
Which lead directly to the door of truth,

Will give you satisfaction, you may
have't.

OTHELLO. Give me a living reason
she's disloyal.

IAGO. I do not like the office;
But sith I am enter'd in this cause so far
(Prick'd to't by foolish honesty and
love),
I will go on. I lay with Cassio lately;
And, being troubled with a raging tooth,
I could not sleep.
There are a kind of men so loose of soul
That in their sleeps will mutter their
affairs.
One of this kind is Cassio.
In sleep I heard him say, 'Sweet Desde-
mona,
Let us be wary, let us hide our loves!'
And then, sir, would he gripe and wring
my hand,
Cry out 'Sweet creature!' and then kiss
me hard,
As if he pluck'd up kisses by the roots
That grew upon my lips; then laid his leg
Over my thigh, and sigh'd, and kiss'd;
and then
Cried, 'Cursed fate, that gave thee to the
Moor!'

OTHELLO. O monstrous! monstrous!

IAGO. Nay, this was but his dream.

OTHELLO. But this denoted a foregone
conclusion.

IAGO. 'Tis a shrewd doubt, though it
be but a dream;
And this may help to thicken other
proofs
That do demonstrate thinly.

OTHELLO. I'll tear her all to pieces!

IAGO. Nay, but be wise. Yet we see
nothing done;
She may be honest yet. Tell me but this:
Have you not sometimes seen a handkerchief
Spotted with strawberries in your wife's
hand?

OTHELLO. I gave her such a one. 'Twas
my first gift.

IAGO. I know not that; but such a handkerchief
(I am sure it was your wife's) did I today

See Cassio wipe his beard with.

OTHELLO.   If't be that,—

IAGO. If it be that, or any that was hers,
It speaks against her with the other
proofs.

OTHELLO. O that the slave had forty
thousand lives!
One is too poor, too weak, for my re-
venge.
Now do I see 'tis true. Look here, Iago;
All my fond love thus do I blow to
heaven.
'Tis gone.
Arise, black vengeance, from thy hol-
low cell!
Yield up, O love, thy crown and
hearted throne
To tyrannous hate. Swell, bosom, with
thy fraught,
For 'tis of aspics' tongues!

IAGO.   Pray, be content.

OTHELLO. O blood! Iago, blood!

IAGO. Patience, I say. Your mind, perhaps, may change.

OTHELLO. Never Iago. Like to the
Pontic sea,
Whose icy current and compulsive
course
Ne'er feels retiring ebb, but keeps due on
To the Propontic and the Hellespont,
Even so my bloody thoughts, with vio-
lent pace,
Shall ne'er look back, ne'er ebb to
humble love,
Till that a capable and wide revenge
Swallow them up. [*He kneels.*] Now, by
yond marble heaven,
In the due reverence of a sacred vow
I here engage my words.

IAGO.   Do not rise yet.
[*Kneels.*] Witness, you ever-burning
lights above!
You elements that clip us round about!
Witness that here Iago doth give up
The execution of his wit, hands, heart,
To wrong'd Othello's service! Let him
command,
And to obey shall be in me remorse,
What bloody work soever. [*They rise.*]

OTHELLO.   I greet thy love,

Not with vain thanks, but with accept-
ance bounteous,
And will upon the instant put thee
to't.
Within these three days let me hear thee
say
That Cassio's not alive.
   IAGO. My friend is dead; 'tis done as
you request.
But let her live.
   OTHELLO. Damn her, lewd minx! O,
damn her!
Come, go with me apart. I will withdraw
To furnish me with some swift means of
death
For the fair devil. Now art thou my lieu-
tenant.
   IAGO. I am your own for ever.
                              [*Exeunt.*]

4. *Before the Citadel*

Enter DESDEMONA, EMILIA, *and the* CLOWN.
   DESDEMONA. Do you know, sirrah,
where Lieutenant Cassio lies?
   CLOWN. I dare not say he lies anywhere.
   DESDEMONA. Why, man?
   CLOWN. He is a soldier, and for one to
say a soldier lies is stabbing.
   DESDEMONA. Go to! Where lodges he?
   CLOWN. To tell you where he lodges is
to tell you where I lie.
   DESDEMONA. Can anything be made of
this?
   CLOWN. I know not where he lodges,
and for me to devise a lodging, and say
he lies here or he lies there, were to lie in
mine own throat.
   DESDEMONA. Can you inquire him out,
and be edified by report?
   CLOWN. I will catechize the world for
him; that is, make questions, and by them
answer.
   DESDEMONA. Seek him. Bid him come
hither; tell him I have moved my lord in
his behalf, and hope all will be well.
   CLOWN. To do this is within the compass of man's wit, and therefore I will attempt the doing it. [*Exit* CLOWN.]

   DESDEMONA. Where should I lose that
handkerchief, Emilia?
   EMILIA. I know not, madam.
   DESDEMONA. Believe me, I had rather
have lost my purse
Full of cruzadoes; and but my noble
Moor
Is true of mind, and made of no such
baseness
As jealous creatures are, it were enough
To put him to ill thinking.
   EMILIA.   Is he not jealous?
   DESDEMONA. Who, he? I think the sun
where he was born
Drew all such humors from him.
   EMILIA.   Look where he comes!
   DESDEMONA. I will not leave him now
till Cassio
Be call'd to him. [*Enter* OTHELLO.] How
is't with you, my lord?
   OTHELLO. Well, my good lady. [*Aside.*]
O hardness to dissemble!—
How do you, Desdemona?
   DESDEMONA.   Well, my good lord.
   OTHELLO. Give me your hand. This
hand is moist, my lady.
   DESDEMONA. It yet has felt no age nor
known no sorrow.
   OTHELLO. This argues fruitfulness and
liberal heart:
Hot, hot, and moist. This hand of yours
requires
A sequester from liberty, fasting and
prayer,
Much castigation, exercise devout;
For here's a young and sweating devil
here
That commonly rebels. 'Tis a good hand,
A frank one.
   DESDEMONA. You may, indeed, say so,
For 'twas that hand that gave away my
heart.
   OTHELLO. A liberal hand! The hearts of
old gave hands,
But our new heraldry is hands not
hearts.
   DESDEMONA. I cannot speak of this.
Come now, your promise.
   OTHELLO. What promise, chuck?
   DESDEMONA. I have sent to bid Cassio
come speak with you.

OTHELLO. I have a salt and sorry rheum offends me.
Lend me thy handkerchief.
DESDEMONA. Here, my lord.
OTHELLO. That which I gave you.
DESDEMONA. I have it not about me.
OTHELLO. Not?
DESDEMONA. No, 'faith, my lord.
OTHELLO. That is a fault.
That handkerchief
Did an Egyptian to my mother give.
She was a charmer and could almost read
The thoughts of people. She told her, while she kept it,
'Twould make her amiable and subdue my father
Entirely to her love, but if she lost it
Or made a gift of it, my father's eye
Should hold her loathly, and his spirits should hunt
After new fancies. She dying gave it me;
And bid me, when my fate would have me wive,
To give it her. I did so,—and take heed on't;
Make it a darling like your precious eye.
To lose or give't away were such perdition
As nothing else could match.
DESDEMONA. Is't possible?
OTHELLO. 'Tis true. There's magic in the web of it.
A sibyl, that had number'd in the world
The sun to course two hundred compasses,
In her prophetic fury sew'd the work.
The worms were hallow'd that did breed the silk,
And it was dy'd in mummy which the skilful
Conserv'd of maidens' hearts.
DESDEMONA. I' faith? is't true?
OTHELLO. Most veritable; therefore look to't well.
DESDEMONA. Then would to God that I had never seen it!
OTHELLO. Ha? wherefore?
DESDEMONA. Why do you speak so startingly and rash?

OTHELLO. Is't lost? is't gone? Speak! Is 't out o' the way?
DESDEMONA. Heaven bless us!
OTHELLO. Say you?
DESDEMONA. It is not lost: but what an if it were?
OTHELLO. How!
DESDEMONA. I say, it is not lost.
OTHELLO. Fetch't, let me see't.
DESDEMONA. Why, so I can, sir, but I will not now.
This is a trick to put me from my suit.
Pray you, let Cassio be receiv'd again.
OTHELLO. Fetch me that handkerchief.
My mind misgives.
DESDEMONA. Come, come;
You'll never meet a more sufficient man.
OTHELLO. The handkerchief!
DESDEMONA. I pray, talk me of Cassio.
OTHELLO. The handkerchief!
DESDEMONA. A man that all his time
Hath founded his good fortunes on your love,
Shar'd dangers with you,—
OTHELLO. The handkerchief!
DESDEMONA. I' faith, you are to blame.
OTHELLO. Zounds! [Exit OTHELLO.]
EMILIA. Is not this man jealous?
DESDEMONA. I ne'er saw this before.
Sure, there's some wonder in this handkerchief.
I am most unhappy in the loss of it.
EMILIA. 'Tis not a year or two shows us a man.
They are all but stomachs, and we all but food.
They eat us hungerly, and when they are full
They belch us. Look you! Cassio and my husband.

[Enter IAGO and CASSIO.]

IAGO. There is no other way; 'tis she must do't.
And, lo, the happiness! Go and importune her.
DESDEMONA. How now, good Cassio? what's the news with you?
CASSIO. Madam, my former suit. I do beseech you

That by your virtuous means I may
again
Exist, and be a member of his love
Whom I with all the office of my heart
Entirely honor. I would not be delay'd.
If my offence be of such mortal kind
That nor my service past, nor present
sorrows,
Nor purpos'd merit in futurity,
Can ransom me into his love again,
But to know so must be my benefit.
So shall I clothe me in a forc'd content,
And shut myself up in some other course
To fortune's alms.
    DESDEMONA.   Alas, thrice-gentle Cassio,
My advocation is not now in tune.
My lord is not my lord; nor should I
know him,
Were he in favor as in humor alter'd.
So help me every spirit sanctified,
As I have spoken for you all my best
And stood within the blank of his dis-
pleasure
For my free speech. You must awhile be
patient.
What I can do I will, and more I will
Than for myself I dare. Let that suffice
you.
    IAGO. Is my lord angry?
    EMILIA.   He went hence but now,
And certainly in strange unquietness.
    IAGO. Can he be angry? I have seen the
cannon,
When it hath blown his ranks into the
air,
And, like the devil, from his very arm
Puff'd his own brother,—and can he be
angry?
Something of moment then. I will go
meet him;
There's matter in't indeed, if he be
angry.
    DESDEMONA. I prithee, do so. [*Exit*
IAGO.]
                Something, sure, of state,
Either from Venice, or some unhatch'd
practice
Made demonstrable here in Cyprus to
him,
Hath puddled his clear spirit; and in
such cases

Men's natures wrangle with inferior
things,
Though great ones are their object. 'Tis
even so;
For let our finger ache, and it endues
Our other healthful members ev'n to that
sense
Of pain. Nay, we must think men are not
gods,
Nor of them look for such observancy
As fits the bridal. Beshrew me much,
Emilia,
I was (unhandsome warrior as I am)
Arraigning his unkindness with my soul;
But now I find I had suborn'd the wit-
ness,
And he's indicted falsely.
    EMILIA. Pray heaven it be state-matters,
as you think,
And no conception, nor no jealous toy
Concerning you.
    DESDEMONA. Alas the day! I never gave
him cause.
    EMILIA. But jealous souls will not be
answer'd so.
They are not ever jealous for the cause,
But jealous for they are jealous. 'Tis a
monster
Begot upon itself, born on itself.
    DESDEMONA. Heaven keep that monster
from Othello's mind!
    EMILIA. Lady, amen.
    DESDEMONA. I will go seek him. Cassio,
walk hereabout.
If I do find him fit, I'll move your suit
And seek to effect it to my uttermost.
    CASSIO. I humbly thank your ladyship.

[*Exeunt* DESDEMONA *and* EMILIA.
Enter BIANCA.]

    BIANCA. 'Save you, friend Cassio!
    CASSIO. What make you from home?
How is it with you, my most fair Bianca?
I' faith, sweet love, I was coming to your
house.
    BIANCA. And I was going to your lodg-
ing, Cassio.
What! keep a week away? seven days
and nights?
Eight score eight hours? and lovers'
absent hours,

More tedious than the dial eight score
    times?
O weary reckoning!
    CASSIO.   Pardon me, Bianca,
I have this while with leaden thoughts
    been press'd,
But I shall, in a more continuate time,
Strike off this score of absence. Sweet
    Bianca, [*Giving her* DESDEMONA'S
    handkerchief.]
Take me this work out.
    BIANCA.   O Cassio! whence came this?
This is some token from a newer friend;
To the felt absence now I feel a cause;
Is't come to this? Well, well.
    CASSIO.   Go to, woman!
Throw your vile guesses in the devil's
    teeth,
From whence you have them. You are
    jealous now
That this is from some mistress, some
    remembrance.
No, by my faith, Bianca.
    BIANCA.   Why, whose is it?

CASSIO. I know not, sweet. I found it in
    my chamber.
I like the work well. Ere it be demanded
(As like enough it will), I'd have it
    copied.
Take it and do't; and leave me for this
    time.
    BIANCA. Leave you? wherefore?
    CASSIO. I do attend here on the gen-
    eral,
And think it no addition nor my wish
To have him see me woman'd.
    BIANCA.   Why, I pray you?
    CASSIO. Not that I love you not.
    BIANCA.   But that you do not love me.
I pray you, bring me on the way a little
And say if I shall see you soon at night.
    CASSIO. 'Tis but a little way that I can
    bring you,
For I attend here; but I'll see you soon.
    BIANCA. 'Tis very good. I must be cir-
    cumstanc'd.
                    [*Exeunt.*]

ACT FOUR

1. *Before the Citadel*

Enter OTHELLO *and* IAGO.
    IAGO. Will you think so?
    OTHELLO.   Think so, Iago!
    IAGO.   What!
To kiss in private?
    OTHELLO.   An unauthoriz'd kiss.
    IAGO. Or to be naked with her friend
    abed
An hour or more, not meaning any harm?
    OTHELLO. Naked abed, Iago, and not
    mean harm?
It is hypocrisy against the devil.
They that mean virtuously, and yet do
    so,
The devil their virtue tempts, and they
    tempt heaven.
    IAGO. So they do nothing, 'tis a venial
    slip.

But if I give my wife a handkerchief,—
    OTHELLO. What then?
    IAGO. Why, then, 'tis hers, my lord;
    and, being hers,
She may, I think, bestow't on any man.
    OTHELLO. She is protectress of her
    honor too.
May she give that?
    IAGO. Her honor is an essence that's not
    seen.
They have it very oft that have it not;
But for the handkerchief,—
    OTHELLO. By heaven, I would most
    gladly have forgot it.
Thou said'st (O it comes o'er my memory
As doth the raven o'er the infected
    house,
Boding to all) he had my handkerchief.
    IAGO. Ay, what of that?

OTHELLO.   That's not so good now.

IAGO.   What
If I had said I had seen him do you
    wrong?
Or heard him say (as knaves be such
    abroad,
Who having, by their own importunate
    suit
Or voluntary dotage of some mistress,
Convinced or supplied them, cannot
    choose
But they must blab)—

OTHELLO.   Hath he said anything?

IAGO. He hath, my lord; but be you
    well assur'd,
No more than he'll unswear.

OTHELLO.   What hath he said?

IAGO. Faith, that he did—I know not
    what he did.

OTHELLO. What? what?

IAGO. Lie—

OTHELLO. With her?

IAGO. With her, on her—what you will.

OTHELLO. Lie with her! lie on her! We
say, lie on her, when they belie her. Lie
with her? Zounds, that's fulsome! Handkerchief!—confessions!—handkerchief! To
confess and be hanged for his labor. First,
to be hanged, and then to confess: I
tremble at it. Nature would not invest
herself in such shadowing passion without some instruction. It is not words
that shake me thus. Pish! Noses, ears, and
lips. Is't possible?—Confess!—Handkerchief!—O devil! [*Falls in a trance.*]

IAGO. Work on,
My medicine, work! Thus credulous
    fools are caught;
And many worthy and chaste dames
    even thus,
All guiltless, meet reproach. What, ho!
    my lord!
My lord, I say! Othello!
[*Enter* CASSIO.] How now, Cassio!

CASSIO. What's the matter?

IAGO. My lord is fallen into an epilepsy.
This is his second fit; he had one yester-
    day.

CASSIO. Rub him about the temples.

IAGO.   No, forbear.
The lethargy must have his quiet course.
If not he foams at mouth, and by and by
Breaks out to savage madness. Look! he
    stirs.
Do you withdraw yourself a little while,
He will recover straight. When he is
    gone,
I would on great occasion speak with
    you. [*Exit* CASSIO.]
How is it, general? Have you not hurt
    your head?

OTHELLO. Dost thou mock me?

IAGO.   I mock you! no, by heaven.
Would you would bear your fortunes
    like a man!

OTHELLO. A horned man's a monster
    and a beast.

IAGO. There's many a beast then, in a
    populous city,
And many a civil monster.

OTHELLO. Did he confess?

IAGO.   Good sir, be a man.
Think every bearded fellow that's but
    yok'd
May draw with you. There's millions
    now alive
That nightly lie in those unproper beds
Which they dare swear peculiar. Your
    case is better.
O, 'tis the spite of hell, the fiend's arch-
    mock,
To lip a wanton in a secure couch,
And to suppose her chaste. No, let me
    know;
And knowing what I am, I know what
    she shall be.

OTHELLO. O, thou art wise, 'tis certain.

IAGO.   Stand you awhile apart;
Confine yourself but in a patient list.
Whilst you were here o'erwhelmed with
    your grief
(A passion most unsuiting such a man),
Cassio came hither. I shifted him away,
And laid good 'scuse upon your ec-
    stasy;
Bade him anon return and here speak
    with me,
The which he promis'd. Do but encave
    yourself,
And mark the fleers, the gibes, and nota-
    ble scorns

That dwell in every region of his face;
For I will make him tell the tale anew,
Where, how, how oft, how long ago,
 and when
He has, and is again to cope your wife.
I say, but mark his gesture. Marry, pa-
 tience;
Or I shall say you're all in all in spleen,
And nothing of a man.
 OTHELLO. Dost thou hear, Iago?
I will be found most cunning in my pa-
 tience,
But—dost thou hear?—most bloody.
 IAGO. That's not amiss;
But yet keep time in all. Will you with-
 draw? [OTHELLO *goes apart.*]
Now will I question Cassio of Bianca,
A housewife that by selling her desires
Buys herself bread and clothes. It is a
 creature
That dotes on Cassio (as 'tis the strum-
 pet's plague
To beguile many and be beguil'd by
 one).
He, when he hears of her, cannot refrain
From the excess of laughter. Here he
 comes.

[*Enter* CASSIO.]

As he shall smile, Othello shall go mad;
And his unbookish jealousy must con-
 strue
Poor Cassio's smiles, gestures, and light
 behavior
Quite in the wrong. [*Aloud.*] How do
 you now, lieutenant?
 CASSIO. The worser that you give me
 the addition
Whose want even kills me.
 IAGO. Ply Desdemona well, and you are
 sure on't.
[*Speaking lower.*] Now, if this suit lay
 in Bianca's power,
How quickly should you speed!
 CASSIO. Alas! poor caitiff!
 OTHELLO. Look how he laughs already!
 IAGO. I never knew a woman love man
 so.
 CASSIO. Alas! poor rogue! I think, i'
 faith, she loves me.

OTHELLO. Now he denies it faintly, and
 laughs it out.
IAGO. Do you hear, Cassio?
OTHELLO. Now he importunes him
To tell it o'er. Go to! well said, well said.
IAGO. She gives it out that you shall
 marry her.
Do you intend it?
 CASSIO. Ha, ha, ha!
OTHELLO. Do you triumph, Roman? Do
you triumph?
 CASSIO. I marry her! what? a cus-
tomer? I prithee, bear some charity to
my wit; do not think it so unwhole-
some. Ha, ha, ha!
 OTHELLO. So, so, so, so. Laugh that
wins!
 IAGO. Faith, the cry goes you shall
marry her.
 CASSIO. Prithee, say true.
 IAGO. I am a very villain else.
 OTHELLO. Have you scored me? Well!
 CASSIO. This is the monkey's own giving out. She is persuaded I will marry
her, out of her own love and flattery,
not out of my promise.
 OTHELLO. Iago beckons me. Now he begins the story.
 CASSIO. She was here even now; she
haunts me in every place. I was t'other
day talking on the sea bank with certain
Venetians, and thither comes the bau-
ble, and falls me thus about my neck—
 OTHELLO. Crying, 'O dear Cassio!' as it
were. His gesture imports it.
 CASSIO. So hangs and lolls and weeps
upon me; so hales and pulls me. Ha, ha,
ha!
 OTHELLO. Now he tells how she plucked
him to my chamber. O, I see that nose of
yours, but not that dog I shall throw it
to.
 CASSIO. Well, I must leave her company.
 IAGO. Before me! look where she
comes!
 CASSIO. 'Tis such another fitchew!
marry, a perfumed one! [*Enter* BIANCA.]
What do you mean by this haunting of
me?
 BIANCA. Let the devil and his dam

haunt you! What did you mean by that same handkerchief you gave me even now? I was a fine fool to take it. I must take out the work? A likely piece of work, that you should find it in your chamber and not know who left it there! This is some minx's token, and I must take out the work! There, give it your hobbyhorse, wheresoever you had it. I'll take out no work on't.

CASSIO. How now, my sweet Bianca? how now? how now?

OTHELLO. By heaven, that should be my handkerchief!

BIANCA. An you'll come to supper to-night, you may. An you will not, come when you are next prepared for.

IAGO. After her! after her!

CASSIO. Faith, I must. She'll rail i' the street else.

IAGO. Will you sup there?

CASSIO. Faith, I intend so.

IAGO. Well, I may chance to see you, for I would very fain speak with you.

CASSIO. Prithee, come; will you?

IAGO. Go to! Say no more. [*Exit* CAS-SIO.]

OTHELLO. [*Advancing.*] How shall I murder him, Iago?

IAGO. Did you perceive how he laughed at his vice?

OTHELLO. O Iago!

IAGO. And did you see the handker-chief?

OTHELLO. Was that mine?

IAGO. Yours, by this hand. And to see how he prizes the foolish woman your wife! She gave it him, and he hath given it his whore.

OTHELLO. I would have him nine years a-killing. A fine woman! a fair woman! a sweet woman!

IAGO. Nay, you must forget that.

OTHELLO. Ay, let her rot and perish, and be damned to-night, for she shall not live. No, my heart is turned to stone. I strike it, and it hurts my hand. O, the world has not a sweeter creature. She might lie by an emperor's side and command him tasks.

IAGO. Nay, that's not your way.

OTHELLO. Hang her! I do but say what she is. So delicate with her needle! An admirable musician! O, she will sing the savageness out of a bear. Of so high and plenteous wit and invention!

IAGO. She's the worse for all this.

OTHELLO. O, a thousand, a thousand times. And then, of so gentle a condi-tion!

IAGO. Ay, too gentle.

OTHELLO. Nay, that's certain. But yet the pity of it, Iago! O, Iago, the pity of it, Iago!

IAGO. If you be so fond over her in-iquity, give her patent to offend; for, if it touches not you, it comes near nobody.

OTHELLO. I will chop her into messes. Cuckold me—

IAGO. O, 'tis foul in her.

OTHELLO. With mine officer!

IAGO. That's fouler.

OTHELLO. Get me some poison, Iago, this night. I'll not expostulate with her, lest her body and beauty unprovide my mind again. This night, Iago.

IAGO. Do it not with poison. Strangle her in her bed, even the bed she hath contaminated.

OTHELLO. Good, good. The justice of it pleases. Very good.

IAGO. And for Cassio, let me be his undertaker.
You shall hear more by midnight.

OTHELLO. Excellent good. [*A trumpet.*] What trumpet is that same?

IAGO. Something from Venice, sure. 'Tis Lodovico,
Come from the duke; and see, your wife is with him.

[*Enter* LODOVICO, DESDEMONA, *and* AT-TENDANTS.]

LODOVICO. God save you, worthy gen-eral!

OTHELLO.   With all my heart, sir.

LODOVICO. The duke and senators of Venice greet you. [*Gives him a letter.*]

OTHELLO. I kiss the instrument of their pleasures. [*Opens the letter and reads.*]

DESDEMONA. And what's the news, good cousin Lodovico?

IAGO. I am very glad to see you, signior. Welcome to Cyprus.

LODOVICO. I thank you. How does Lieutenant Cassio?

IAGO. Lives, sir.

DESDEMONA. Cousin, there's fall'n between him and my lord
An unkind breach, but you shall make all well.

OTHELLO. Are you sure of that?

DESDEMONA. My lord?

OTHELLO. [Reads.] 'This fail you not to do, as you will'—

LODOVICO. He did not call. He's busy in the paper.
Is there division 'twixt thy lord and Cassio?

DESDEMONA. A most unhappy one. I would do much
T'atone them for the love I bear to Cassio.

OTHELLO. Fire and brimstone!

DESDEMONA.   My lord?

OTHELLO.   Are you wise?

DESDEMONA. What! is he angry?

LODOVICO.
              May be the letter mov'd him;
For, as I think, they do command him home,
Deputing Cassio in his government.

DESDEMONA. By my troth, I am glad on't.

OTHELLO.   Indeed?

DESDEMONA.   My lord?

OTHELLO. I am glad to see you mad.

DESDEMONA.   How, sweet Othello?

OTHELLO. Devil! [Strikes her.]

DESDEMONA.   I have not deserved this.

LODOVICO. My lord, this would not be believ'd in Venice,
Though I should swear I saw't. 'Tis very much.
Make her amends, she weeps.

OTHELLO.   O devil, devil!
If that the earth could teem with women's tears,
Each drop she falls would prove a crocodile.
Out of my sight!

DESDEMONA. [Going.] I will not stay to offend you.

LODOVICO. Truly, an obedient lady!
I do beseech your lordship, call her back.

OTHELLO. Mistress!

DESDEMONA.   My lord?

OTHELLO.
              What would you with her, sir?

LODOVICO. Who, I, my lord?

OTHELLO. Ay, you did wish that I would make her turn.
Sir, she can turn, and turn, and yet go on,
And turn again. And she can weep, sir, weep;
And she's obedient, as you say, obedient,
Very obedient.—Proceed you in your tears.—
Concerning this, sir,—O well painted passion!—
I am commanded here—Get you away;
I'll send for you anon.—Sir, I obey the mandate,
And will return to Venice.—Hence! avaunt! [Exit DESDEMONA.]
Cassio shall have my place. And, sir, tonight,
I do entreat that we may sup together.
You are welcome, sir, to Cyprus.—Goats and monkeys! [Exit.]

LODOVICO. Is this the noble Moor whom our full senate
Call all-in-all sufficient? Is this the nature
Whom passion could not shake, whose solid virtue
The shot of accident nor dart of chance
Could neither graze nor pierce?

IAGO.   He is much chang'd.

LODOVICO. Are his wits safe? is he not light of brain?

IAGO. He's that he is. I may not breathe my censure.
What he might be (if what he might he is not)
I would to heaven he were!

LODOVICO.   What! strike his wife!

IAGO. Faith, that was not so well; yet would I knew
That stroke would prove the worst!

LODOVICO.   Is it his use?
Or did the letters work upon his blood,

And new-create this fault?

IAGO.   Alas, alas!
It is not honesty in me to speak
What I have seen and known. You shall
    observe him,
And his own courses will denote him so
That I may save my speech. Do but go
    after
And mark how he continues.

LODOVICO. I am sorry that I am deceiv'd
    in him.
                                              [*Exeunt.*]

2. *A room in the Citadel*

Enter OTHELLO *and* EMILIA.

OTHELLO. You have seen nothing, then?

EMILIA. Nor ever heard, nor ever did
    suspect.

OTHELLO. Yes, you have seen Cassio and
    she together.

EMILIA. But then I saw no harm, and
    then I heard
Each syllable that breath made up be-
    tween 'em.

OTHELLO. What! did they never whis-
    per?

EMILIA.   Never, my lord.

OTHELLO. Nor send you out o' the way?

EMILIA.   Never.

OTHELLO. To fetch her fan, her gloves,
    her mask, nor nothing?

EMILIA. Never, my lord.

OTHELLO. That's strange.

EMILIA. I durst, my lord, to wager she
    is honest,
Lay down my soul at stake. If you think
    other,
Remove your thought. It doth abuse
    your bosom.
If any wretch have put this in your head,
Let heaven requite it with the serpent's
    curse!
For if she be not honest, chaste, and true,
There's no man happy; the purest of
    their wives
Is foul as slander.

OTHELLO.   Bid her come hither. Go.
    [*Exit* EMILIA.]
She says enough; yet she's a simple
    bawd
That cannot say as much. This is a subtle
    whore,
A closet lock and key of villainous
    secrets;
And yet she'll kneel and pray. I have
    seen her do't.

[*Enter* DESDEMONA *and* EMILIA.]

DESDEMONA. My lord, what is your
    will?

OTHELLO.   Pray, chuck, come hither.

DESDEMONA. What is your pleasure?

OTHELLO.   Let me see your eyes;
Look in my face.

DESDEMONA. What horrible fancy's
    this?

OTHELLO. [*To* EMILIA.] Some of your
    function, mistress.
Leave procreants alone and shut the
    door;
Cough or cry 'hem' if anybody come.
Your mystery, your mystery. Nay, dis-
    patch. [*Exit* EMILIA.]

DESDEMONA. Upon my knees, what does
    your speech import?
I understand a fury in your words
But not the words.

OTHELLO. Why, what art thou?

DESDEMONA.
            Your wife, my lord; your true
And loyal wife.

OTHELLO. Come, swear it, damn thy-
    self;
Lest, being like one of heaven, the devils
    themselves
Should fear to seize thee. Therefore be
    double damn'd.
Swear thou art honest.

DESDEMONA.
                    Heaven doth truly know it.

OTHELLO. Heaven truly knows that
    thou art false as hell.

DESDEMONA. To whom, my lord? with
    whom? how am I false?

OTHELLO. Ah! Desdemon! Away, away,
    away!

DESDEMONA. Alas, the heavy day! Why
do you weep?
Am I the motive of these tears, my lord?
If haply you my father do suspect
An instrument of this your calling back,
Lay not your blame on me. If you have
lost him,
Why, I have lost him too.
OTHELLO.   Had it pleas'd heaven
To try me with affliction, had they rain'd
All kinds of sores and shames on my bare
head,
Steep'd me in poverty to the very lips,
Given to captivity me and my utmost
hopes,
I should have found in some part of my
soul
A drop of patience. But, alas!, to make
me
A fixed figure for the time of scorn
To point his slow unmoving fingers at!
Yet could I bear that too. Well! very
well!
But there, where I have garner'd up my
heart,
Where either I must live or bear no life;
The fountain from the which my current
runs
Or else dries up: to be discarded thence,
Or keep it as a cistern for foul toads
To knot and gender in! Turn thy com-
plexion there,
Patience, thou young and rose-lipp'd
cherubin.
I here look grim as hell!
  DESDEMONA. I hope my noble lord es-
teems me honest.
  OTHELLO. O, ay. As summer flies are
in the shambles,
That quicken even with blowing.
O thou black weed, why art so lovely
fair?
Thou smell'st so sweet that the sense
aches at thee.
Would thou hadst ne'er been born!
  DESDEMONA. Alas, what ignorant sin
have I committed?
  OTHELLO. Was this fair paper, this most
goodly book,
Made to write 'whore' on? What com-
mitted?

Committed! O thou public commoner!
I should make very forges of my cheeks,
That would to cinders burn up modesty,
Did I but speak thy deeds. What com-
mitted?
Heaven stops the nose at it and the moon
winks,
The bawdy wind that kisses all it meets
Is hush'd within the hollow mine of
earth,
And will not hear't. What committed?
Impudent strumpet!
  DESDEMONA.
          By heaven, you do me wrong.
  OTHELLO. Are not you a strumpet?
  DESDEMONA.   No, as I am a Christian.
If to preserve this vessel for my lord
From any other foul unlawful touch
Be not to be a strumpet, I am none.
  OTHELLO. What! not a whore?
  DESDEMONA.   No, as I shall be sav'd.
  OTHELLO. Is't possible?
  DESDEMONA. O heaven, forgiveness!
  OTHELLO.   I cry you mercy, then.
I took you for that cunning whore of
Venice
That married with Othello. You, mis-
tress,
That have the office opposite to Saint
Peter,
And keep the gate of hell!

            [*Enter* EMILIA.]
                You, you, ay, you!
We have done our course. There's
money for your pains.
I pray you, turn the key and keep our
counsel. [*Exit.*]
  EMILIA. Alas! what does this gentle-
man conceive?
How do you, madam? how do you, my
good lady?
  DESDEMONA. Faith, half asleep.
  EMILIA. Good madam, what's the mat-
ter with my lord?
  DESDEMONA. With who?
  EMILIA.   Why, with my lord, madam.
  DESDEMONA. Who is thy lord?
  EMILIA.   He that is yours, sweet lady.
  DESDEMONA. I have none; do not talk
to me, Emilia;

I cannot weep, nor answer have I none,
But what should go by water. Prithee,
    to-night
Lay on my bed our wedding sheets. Re-
    member;
And call thy husband hither.
EMILIA.   Here is a change indeed!
    [*Exit.*]
DESDEMONA. 'Tis meet I should be us'd
    so, very meet.
How have I been behav'd, that he might
    stick
The small'st opinion on my greatest
    abuse?

[*Enter* IAGO *and* EMILIA.]

IAGO. What is your pleasure, madam?
    How is't with you?
DESDEMONA. I cannot tell. Those that do
    teach young babes
Do it with gentle means and easy tasks.
He might have chid me so, for, in good
    faith,
I am a child to chiding.
IAGO. What is the matter, lady?
EMILIA. Alas! Iago, my lord hath so
    bewhor'd her,
Thrown such despite and heavy terms
    upon her,
As true hearts cannot bear.
DESDEMONA. Am I that name, Iago?
IAGO.   What name, fair lady?
DESDEMONA. Such as she says my lord
    did say I was.
EMILIA. He call'd her whore. A beggar
    in his drink
Could not have laid such terms upon his
    callet.
IAGO. Why did he so?
DESDEMONA. I do not know. I am sure I
    am none such.
IAGO. Do not weep, do not weep. Alas
    the day!
EMILIA. Has she forsook so many noble
    matches,
Her father, and her country, and her
    friends,
To be call'd whore? Would it not make
    one weep?
DESDEMONA. It is my wretched fortune.

IAGO.   Beshrew him for't!
How comes this trick upon him?
DESDEMONA.   Nay, heaven doth know.
EMILIA. I will be hang'd if some eternal
    villain, some busy and insinuating
    rogue,
Some cogging, cozening slave, to get
    some office
Have not devis'd this slander. I'll be
    hang'd else.
IAGO. Fie! there is no such man. It is
    impossible.
DESDEMONA. If any such there be,
    heaven pardon him!
EMILIA. A halter pardon him, and hell
    gnaw his bones!
Why should he call her whore? who
    keeps her company?
What place? what time? what form?
    what likelihood?
The Moor's abus'd by some outrageous
    knave,
Some base notorious knave, some scurvy
    fellow.
O heaven! that such companions
    thou'dst unfold,
And put in every honest hand a whip
To lash the rascal naked through the
    world,
Even from the east to the west!
IAGO.   Speak within doors.
EMILIA. O, fie upon him! Some such
    squire he was
That turn'd your wit the seamy side
    without,
And made you to suspect me with the
    Moor.
IAGO. You are a fool. Go to!
DESDEMONA.   O good Iago,
What shall I do to win my lord again?
Good friend, go to him; for, by this light
    of heaven,
I know not how I lost him. Here I kneel.
If e'er my will did trespass 'gainst his
    love,
Either in discourse of thought or actual
    deed,
Or that mine eyes, mine ears, or any
    sense
Delighted them in any other form;

Or that I do not yet, and ever did,
And ever will (though he do shake me
off
To beggarly divorcement) love him
dearly,
Comfort forswear me! Unkindness may
do much;
And his unkindness may defeat my life,
But never taint my love. I cannot say
'whore.'
It does abhor me now I speak the word;
To do the act that might th' addition
earn
Not the world's mass of vanity could
make me.

IAGO. I pray you be content. 'Tis but
his humor.
The business of the state does him offence
And he does chide with you.

DESDEMONA. If 'twere no other,—
[*Trumpets within.*]

IAGO.   'Tis but so, I warr'nt you.
Hark how these instruments summon
you to supper,
And the great messengers of Venice
stay.
Go in, and weep not. All things shall be
well. [*Exeunt women.*]

[*Enter* RODERIGO.]

How now, Roderigo?

RODERIGO. I do not find that thou deal'st
justly with me.

IAGO. What in the contrary?

RODERIGO. Every day thou daffest me
with some device, Iago; and rather, as it
seems to me, thou keepest from me all
conveniency, than suppliest me with
the least advantage of hope. I will indeed no longer endure it, nor am I yet
persuaded to put up in peace what already I have foolishly suffered.

IAGO. Will you hear me, Roderigo?

RODERIGO. Faith, I have heard too much,
for your words and performance are no
kin together.

IAGO. You charge me most unjustly.

RODERIGO. With nought but truth. I
have wasted myself out of my means.
The jewels you have had from me to

deliver to Desdemona would half have
corrupted a votarist. You have told me
she has received them, and returned me
expectations and comforts of sudden respect and acquaintance, but I find none.

IAGO. Well, go to! Very well.

RODERIGO. Very well? go to? I cannot
go to, man; nor 'tis not very well. By
this hand, I say 'tis very scurvy, and begin to find myself fopped in it.

IAGO. Very well.

RODERIGO. I tell you 'tis not very well. I
will make myself known to Desdemona.
If she will return me my jewels, I will
give over my suit and repent my unlawful solicitation. If not, assure yourself I
will seek satisfaction of you.

IAGO. You have said now?

RODERIGO. Ay, and said nothing but
what I protest intendment of doing.

IAGO. Why, now I see there's mettle
in thee, and even from this instant do
build on thee a better opinion than ever
before. Give me thy hand, Roderigo.
Thou hast taken against me a most just
exception; but yet, I protest, I have dealt
most directly in thy affair.

RODERIGO. It hath not appeared.

IAGO. I grant indeed it hath not appeared, and your suspicion is not without
wit and judgment. But, Roderigo, if thou
hast that within thee indeed, which I
have greater reason to believe now than
ever (I mean purpose, courage, and
valor), this night show it. If thou the
next night following enjoyest not Desdemona, take me from this world with
treachery and devise engines for my
life.

RODERIGO. Well, what is it? is it within
reason and compass?

IAGO. Sir, there is especial commission
come from Venice to depute Cassio in
Othello's place.

RODERIGO. Is that true? Why, then
Othello and Desdemona return again to
Venice.

IAGO. O, no! he goes into Mauritania,
and takes away with him the fair Desdemona, unless his abode be lingered here

by some accident; wherein none can be so determinate as the removing of Cassio.

RODERIGO. How do you mean, removing of him?

IAGO. Why, by making him uncapable of Othello's place. Knocking out his brains.

RODERIGO. And that you would have me to do!

IAGO. Ay; if you dare do yourself a profit and right. He sups to-night with a harlotry, and thither will I go to him. He knows not yet of his honorable fortune. If you will watch his going thence (which I will fashion to fall out between twelve and one), you may take him at your pleasure. I will be near to second your attempt, and he shall fall between us. Come, stand not amazed at it, but go along with me. I will show you such a necessity in his death that you shall think yourself bound to put it on him. It is now high supper-time, and the night grows to waste. About it.

RODERIGO. I will hear further reason for this.

IAGO. And you shall be satisfied.

[*Exeunt.*]

3. *State bedroom in the Citadel*

Enter OTHELLO, LODOVICO, DESDEMONA, EMILIA, *and* ATTENDANTS.

LODOVICO. I do beseech you, sir, trouble yourself no further.

OTHELLO. O pardon me; 'twill do me good to walk.

LODOVICO. Madam, good night. I humbly thank your ladyship.

DESDEMONA. Your honor is most welcome.

OTHELLO.   Will you walk, sir?—
O! Desdemona.

DESDEMONA. My lord?

OTHELLO. Get you to bed o' the instant. I will be returned forthwith.
Dispatch your attendant there. Look it be done.

DESDEMONA. I will, my lord.

[*Exit* OTHELLO, *with* LODOVICO *and* ATTENDANTS.]

EMILIA. How goes it now? He looks gentler than he did.

DESDEMONA. He says he will return incontinent.
He hath commanded me to go to bed,
And bade me to dismiss you.

EMILIA.   Dismiss me!

DESDEMONA. It was his bidding. Therefore, good Emilia,
Give me my nightly wearing, and adieu.
We must not now displease him.

EMILIA. I would you had never seen him.

DESDEMONA. So would not I. My love doth so approve him,
That even his stubbornness, his checks and frowns,—
Prithee, unpin me,—have grace and favor in them.

EMILIA. I have laid those sheets you bade me on the bed.

DESDEMONA. All's one. Good faith! how foolish are our minds!
If I do die before thee, prithee, shroud me
In one of those same sheets.

EMILIA.   Come, come, you talk!

DESDEMONA. My mother had a maid call'd Barbary:
She was in love, and he she lov'd prov'd mad
And did forsake her. She had a song of 'willow';
An old thing 'twas, but it express'd her fortune,
And she died singing it. That song to-night
Will not go from my mind. I have much to do
But to go hang my head all at one side,
And sing it like poor Barbary. Prithee, dispatch.

EMILIA. Shall I go fetch your nightgown?

DESDEMONA.   No, unpin me here.
This Lodovico is a proper man.

EMILIA. A very handsome man.

DESDEMONA. He speaks well.

EMILIA. I know a lady in Venice would have walked barefoot to Palestine for a touch of his nether lip.

DESDEMONA. [*Sings.*] The poor soul sat sighing by a sycamore tree,—
Sing all a green willow.
Her hand on her bosom, her head on her knee,—
Sing willow, willow, willow.
The fresh streams ran by her, and murmur'd her moans.
Sing willow, willow, willow.
Her salt tears fell from her, and soften'd the stones.
Sing willow, willow, willow.
Lay by these.—
Willow, willow.
Prithee, hie thee; he'll come anon.
Sing all a green willow must be my garland.
Let nobody blame him, his scorn I approve,—
Nay, that's not next. Hark! who is it that knocks?

EMILIA. It is the wind.

DESDEMONA. I call'd my love false love; but what said he then?
Sing willow, willow, willow.
If I court mo women, you'll couch with mo men.
Now get thee gone. Good night. Mine eyes do itch;
Does that bode weeping?

EMILIA. 'Tis neither here nor there.

DESDEMONA. I have heard it said so. O these men, these men!
Dost thou in conscience think (tell me, Emilia)
That there be women do abuse their husbands
In such gross kind?

EMILIA. There be some such, no question.

DESDEMONA. Wouldst thou do such a deed for all the world?

EMILIA. Why, would not you?

DESDEMONA. No, by this heavenly light!

EMILIA. Nor I neither by this heavenly light. I might do't as well i' th' dark.

DESDEMONA. Wouldst thou do such a deed for all the world?

EMILIA. The world is a huge thing. It is a great price for a small vice.

DESDEMONA. Good troth, I think thou wouldst not.

EMILIA. By my troth, I think I should, and undo't when I had done it. Marry, I would not do such a thing for a joint-ring, nor for measures of lawn, nor for gowns, petticoats, nor caps, nor any petty exhibition. But for the whole world? Ud's pity! who would not make her husband a cuckold to make him a monarch? I should venture purgatory for't.

DESDEMONA. Beshrew me, if I would do such a wrong
For the whole world.

EMILIA. Why, the wrong is but a wrong i' the world; and having the world for your labor, 'tis a wrong in your own world, and you might quickly make it right.

DESDEMONA. I do not think there is any such woman.

EMILIA. Yes, a dozen; and as many to the vantage, as would store the world they played for.
But I do think it is their husbands' faults
If wives do fall. Say that they slack their duties,
And pour our treasures into foreign laps,
Or else break out in peevish jealousies,
Throwing restraint upon us; or say they strike us,
Or scant our former having in despite;
Why, we have galls, and though we have some grace,
Yet have we some revenge. Let husbands know
Their wives have sense like them. They see and smell,
And have their palates both for sweet and sour,
As husbands have. What is it that they do
When they change us for others? Is it sport?

I think it is. And doth affection breed it?
I think it doth. Is't frailty that thus errs?
It is so too. And have not we affections,
Desires for sport, and frailty as men have?
Then, let them use us well; else let them know,
The ills we do, their ills instruct us so.
DESDEMONA. Good night, good night!
God me such usage send,
Not to pick bad from bad, but by bad mend!
[Exeunt.]

ACT FIVE

1. *A street near Bianca's lodging*

Enter IAGO *and* RODERIGO.
IAGO. Here, stand behind this bulk.
Straight will he come.
Wear thy good rapier bare, and put it home.
Quick, quick. Fear nothing; I'll be at thy elbow.
It makes us, or it mars us. Think of that,
And fix most firm thy resolution.
RODERIGO. Be near at hand. I may miscarry in't.
IAGO. Here, at thy hand. Be bold, and take thy stand. [Retires.]
RODERIGO. I have no great devotion to the deed;
And yet he has given me satisfying reasons.
'Tis but a man gone. Forth, my sword! he dies.
IAGO. I have rubb'd this young quat almost to the sense,
And he grows angry. Now, whether he kill Cassio,
Or Cassio him, or each do kill the other,
Every way makes my gain. Live Roderigo,
He calls me to a restitution large
Of gold and jewels that I bobb'd from him,
As gifts to Desdemona.
It must not be. If Cassio do remain,
He has a daily beauty in his life
That makes me ugly; and, besides, the Moor
May unfold me to him. There stand I in peril.
No, he must die. Be it so! I hear him coming.

[Enter CASSIO.]

RODERIGO. I know his gait; 'tis he. Villain, thou diest! [Makes a pass at CASSIO.]
CASSIO. That thrust had been my enemy indeed
But that my coat is better than thou think'st.
I will make proof of thine. [Draws, and wounds RODERIGO.]
RODERIGO.   O! I am slain!

[IAGO from behind wounds CASSIO in the leg, and exit.]

CASSIO. I am maim'd for ever! Light, ho! murder! murder! [Falls.]

[Enter OTHELLO.]

OTHELLO. The voice of Cassio. Iago keeps his word.
RODERIGO. O villain that I am!
OTHELLO.   Hark! 'Tis even so.
CASSIO. O, help, ho! light! a surgeon!
OTHELLO. 'Tis he. O brave Iago, honest and just,
That hast such noble sense of thy friend's wrong!
Thou teachest me. Minion, your dear lies dead,
And your fate hies apace. Strumpet, I come!

Forth of my heart those charms, thine eyes, are blotted.
Thy bed, lust-stain'd, shall with lust's blood be spotted. [*Exit* OTHELLO.]

[*Enter* LODOVICO *and* GRATIANO.]

CASSIO. What ho! no watch? no passage? murder! murder!
GRATIANO. 'Tis some mischance. The cry is very direful.
CASSIO. O, help!
LODOVICO. Hark!
RODERIGO. O wretched villain!
LODOVICO. Two or three groan. It is a heavy night;
These may be counterfeits. Let's think't unsafe
To come in to the cry without more help.
RODERIGO. Nobody come? then shall I bleed to death.
LODOVICO. Hark!

[*Enter* IAGO, *with a light.*]

GRATIANO. Here's one comes in his shirt, with light and weapons.
IAGO. Who's there? Whose noise is this that cries on murder?
LODOVICO. We do not know.
IAGO. Did not you hear a cry?
CASSIO. Here, here! For heaven's sake, help me.
IAGO. What's the matter?
GRATIANO. This is Othello's ancient, as I take it.
LODOVICO. The same indeed. A very valiant fellow.
IAGO. What are you here that cry so grievously?
CASSIO. Iago? O, I am spoil'd, undone by villains!
Give me some help.
IAGO. O my lieutenant! what villains have done this?
CASSIO. I think that one of them is hereabout,
And cannot make away.
IAGO. O treacherous villains!
[*To* LODOVICO *and* GRATIANO.] What are you there? Come in, and give some help.

RODERIGO. O help me here!
CASSIO. That's one of them.
IAGO. O murderous slave! O villain!
[*Stabs* RODERIGO.]
RODERIGO. O damn'd Iago! O inhuman dog!
IAGO. Kill men i' the dark! Where be those bloody thieves?
How silent is this town! Ho! murder! murder!
What may you be? are you of good or evil?
LODOVICO. As you shall prove us, praise us.
IAGO. Signior Lodovico?
LODOVICO. He, sir.
IAGO. I cry you mercy. Here's Cassio hurt by villains.
GRATIANO. Cassio?
IAGO. How is it, brother?
CASSIO. My leg is cut in two.
IAGO. Marry, heaven forbid!
Light, gentlemen. I'll bind it with my shirt.

[*Enter* BIANCA.]

BIANCA. What is the matter, ho? who is't that cried?
IAGO. Who is't that cried!
BIANCA. O my dear Cassio! O my sweet Cassio!
Cassio! Cassio!
IAGO. O notable strumpet! Cassio, may you suspect
Who they should be that thus have mangled you?
CASSIO. No.
GRATIANO. I am sorry to find you thus. I have been to seek you.
IAGO. Lend me a garter. So. O for a chair,
To bear him easily hence!
BIANCA. Alas! he faints! O Cassio, Cassio, Cassio!
IAGO. Gentlemen all, I do suspect this trash
To bear a part in this.
Patience awhile, good Cassio. Come, come.
Lend me a light. Know we this face, or no?

Alas! my friend and my dear country-
man,
Roderigo? no: yes, sure. O heaven!
Roderigo.
GRATIANO. What? of Venice?
IAGO. Even he, sir. Did you know him?
GRATIANO.   Know him? ay.
IAGO. Signior Gratiano? I cry you
gentle pardon.
These bloody accidents must excuse my
manners,
That so neglected you.
    GRATIANO.   I am glad to see you.
IAGO. How do you, Cassio? O, a chair,
a chair!
    GRATIANO. Roderigo! [*A chair brought
in.*]
    IAGO. He. 'Tis he.—O! that's well said;
the chair.
Some good man bear him carefully from
hence.
I'll fetch the general's surgeon. [*To
BIANCA.*] For you, mistress,
Save you your labor. He that lies slain
here, Cassio,
Was my dear friend. What malice was
betwixt you?
    CASSIO. None in the world; nor do I
know the man.
    IAGO. [*To BIANCA.*] What! look you
pale? O, bear him out o' the air.
[*CASSIO borne off.*]
Stay you, good gentlemen. Look you
pale, mistress?—
Do you perceive the gastness of her
eye?—
Nay, if you stare, we shall hear more
anon.—
Behold her well; I pray you, look upon
her.
Do you see, gentlemen? nay, guiltiness
Will speak though tongues were out of
use.

[*Enter EMILIA.*]

    EMILIA. 'Las! what's the matter? what's
the matter, husband?
    IAGO. Cassio has here been set on in the
dark
By Roderigo and fellows that are 'scap'd.
He's almost slain, and Roderigo dead.

    EMILIA. Alas, good gentleman! alas,
good Cassio!
    IAGO. This is the fruit of whoring. Pray,
Emilia,
Go know of Cassio where he supp'd to-
night.—
What! do you shake at that?
    BIANCA. He supp'd at my house, but I
therefore shake not.
    IAGO. O, did he so? I charge you, go
with me.
    EMILIA. Fie, fie upon thee, strumpet!
    BIANCA. I am no strumpet, but of life
as honest
As you that thus abuse me.
    EMILIA.   As I! foh! fie upon thee!
    IAGO. Kind gentlemen, let's go see poor
Cassio dress'd.
Come, mistress, you must tell's another
tale.
Emilia, run you to the citadel,
And tell my lord and lady what has
happ'd.
Will you go on afore? [*Aside.*] This is
the night
That either makes me or fordoes me
quite.

[*Exeunt.*]

2. *State bedroom in the Citadel*

Enter OTHELLO *with a light, and* DESDE-
MONA *in her bed.*

    OTHELLO. It is the cause, it is the cause,
my soul.
Let me not name it to you, you chaste
stars!
It is the cause. Yet I'll not shed her blood,
Nor scar that whiter skin of hers than
snow,
And smooth as monumental alabaster.
Yet she must die, else she'll betray more
men.
Put out the light, and then put out the
light.
If I quench thee, thou flaming minister,
I can again thy former light restore,
Should I repent me; but once put out
thy light,

Thou cunning'st pattern of excelling na-
ture,
I know not where is that Promethean
heat
That can thy light relume. When I have
pluck'd thy rose,
I cannot give it vital growth again.
It needs must wither. I'll smell it on the
tree. [*He kisses her.*]
O balmy breath, that doth almost per-
suade
Justice to break her sword! One more,
one more.
Be thus when thou art dead, and I will
kill thee
And love thee after. Once more, and
this the last!
So sweet was ne'er so fatal. I must weep,
But they are cruel tears. This sorrow's
heavenly,
It strikes where it doth love. She wakes.

DESDEMONA. Who's there? Othello?
OTHELLO.   Ay, Desdemona.
DESDEMONA. Will you come to bed,
my lord?
OTHELLO. Have you pray'd to-night,
Desdemon?
DESDEMONA.   Ay, my lord.
OTHELLO. If you bethink yourself of
any crime
Unreconcil'd as yet to heaven and
grace,
Solicit for it straight.
DESDEMONA. Alas, my lord, what may
you mean by that?
OTHELLO. Well, do it, and be brief. I
will walk by.
I would not kill thy unprepared spirit.
No (heaven forfend!), I would not kill
thy soul.
DESDEMONA. Talk you of killing?
OTHELLO.   Ay, I do.
DESDEMONA.   Then heaven
Have mercy on me!
OTHELLO.   Amen! with all my heart.
DESDEMONA. If you say so, I hope you
will not kill me.
OTHELLO. Humh!
DESDEMONA. And yet I fear you; for
you are fatal then

When your eyes roll so. Why I should
fear I know not,
Since guiltiness I know not; but yet I
feel I fear.
OTHELLO. Think on thy sins.
DESDEMONA.
              They are loves I bear to you.
OTHELLO. Ay, and for that thou diest.
DESDEMONA. That death's unnatural that
kills for loving.
Alas, why gnaw you so your nether lip?
Some bloody passion shakes your very
frame.
These are portents, but yet, I hope, I
hope,
They do not point on me.
OTHELLO.   Peace, and be still!
DESDEMONA. I will so. What's the mat-
ter?
OTHELLO. That handkerchief which I
so lov'd and gave thee
Thou gav'st to Cassio.
DESDEMONA.   No, by my life and soul!
Send for the man and ask him.
OTHELLO.   Sweet soul, take heed,
Take heed of perjury. Thou'rt on thy
death-bed.
DESDEMONA. Ay, but not yet to die.
OTHELLO.   Yes, presently.
Therefore confess thee freely of thy
sin;
For to deny each article with oath
Cannot remove nor choke the strong
conception
That I do groan withal. Thou art to die.
DESDEMONA. Then Lord have mercy on
me!
OTHELLO.   I say, amen.
DESDEMONA. And have you mercy too!
I never did
Offend you in my life; never lov'd
Cassio
But with such general warranty of
heaven
As I might love. I never gave him token.
OTHELLO. By heaven, I saw my hand-
kerchief in his hand.
O perjur'd woman! thou dost stone my
heart,
And mak'st me call what I intend to do
A murder, which I thought a sacrifice.

I saw the handkerchief.

DESDEMONA.   He found it then.
I never gave it him. Send for him hither;
Let him confess a truth.

OTHELLO.   He has confess'd.

DESDEMONA. What, my lord?

OTHELLO. That he hath us'd thee.

DESDEMONA.   How? unlawfully?

OTHELLO. Ay.

DESDEMONA. He will not say so.

OTHELLO.   No; his mouth is stopp'd.
Honest Iago hath ta'en order for't.

DESDEMONA. O! my fear interprets.
    What! is he dead?

OTHELLO. Had all his hairs been lives,
    my great revenge
Had stomach for them all.

DESDEMONA. Alas, he is betray'd and
    I undone!

OTHELLO. O strumpet! Weep'st thou
    for him to my face?

DESDEMONA. O, banish me, my lord, but
    kill me not!

OTHELLO. Down, strumpet!

DESDEMONA. Kill me to-morrow; let me
    live to-night!

OTHELLO. Nay, an you strive,—

DESDEMONA. But half an hour!

OTHELLO.
            Being done, there is no pause.

DESDEMONA. But while I say one prayer!

OTHELLO.
            It is too late. [*He stifles her.*]

EMILIA. [*Calls within.*] My lord, my
    lord! what, ho! my lord, my lord!

OTHELLO. What noise is this? Not dead?
    not yet quite dead?
I that am cruel am yet merciful;
I would not have thee linger in thy pain.
So, so.

EMILIA. [*Within.*] What, ho! my lord,
    my lord!

OTHELLO.   Who's there?

EMILIA. [*Within.*] O! good my lord,
    I'ld speak a word with you.

OTHELLO. Yes; 'tis Emilia.—By and by.—
She's dead.
'Tis like she comes to speak of Cassio's
death.
The noise was high. Ha! no more mov-
ing?

Still as the grave. Shall she come in?
    Were't good?
I think she stirs again: no. What's the
    best?
If she come in, she'll sure speak to my
    wife:
My wife! my wife! what wife? I have
    no wife:
O, insupportable! O heavy hour!
Methinks it should be now a huge eclipse
Of sun and moon, and that the affrighted
    globe
Should yawn at alteration.

EMILIA. [*Within.*]   I do beseech you
That I may speak with you, O good my
    lord.

OTHELLO. I had forgot thee. O, come in,
    Emilia!—
Soft, by and by.—Let me the curtains
    draw.—
Where art thou? [*Unlocks the door.*]

[*Enter* EMILIA.]

    What's the matter with thee now?

EMILIA. O! my good lord, yonder's foul
    murders done.

OTHELLO. What! now?

EMILIA.   But now, my lord.

OTHELLO. It is the very error of the
    moon.
She comes more near the earth than she
    was wont,
And makes men mad.

EMILIA. Cassio, my lord, has kill'd a
    young Venetian
Call'd Roderigo.

OTHELLO.   Roderigo kill'd!
And Cassio kill'd!

EMILIA.   No, Cassio is not kill'd.

OTHELLO. Not Cassio kill'd! then mur-
    der's out of tune,
And sweet revenge grows harsh.

DESDEMONA. O falsely, falsely mur-
    der'd.

EMILIA.   O Lord! what cry is that?

OTHELLO. That? what?

EMILIA. Out and alas! it is my lady's
    voice.
Help! Help, ho! help! O lady, speak
    again!

Sweet Desdemona! O sweet mistress, speak!

DESDEMONA. A guiltless death I die.

EMILIA. O! who has done this deed?

DESDEMONA. Nobody. I myself. Farewell!

Commend me to my kind lord. O farewell! [*She dies.*]

OTHELLO. Why, how should she be murder'd?

EMILIA.   Alas, who knows?

OTHELLO. You heard her say herself it was not I.

EMILIA. She said so. I must needs report a truth.

OTHELLO. She's like a liar gone to burning hell.

'Twas I that kill'd her.

EMILIA.   O the more angel she,
And you the blacker devil.

OTHELLO. She turn'd to folly, and she was a whore.

EMILIA. Thou dost belie her, and thou art a devil.

OTHELLO. She was false as water.

EMILIA.   Thou art rash as fire to say

That she was false. O she was heavenly true.

OTHELLO. Cassio did top her. Ask thy husband else.

O I were damn'd beneath all depth in hell

But that I did proceed upon just grounds
To this extremity. Thy husband knew it all.

EMILIA. My husband?

OTHELLO. Thy husband.

EMILIA. That she was false to wedlock?

OTHELLO. Ay, with Cassio. Nay, had she been true,

If heaven would make me such another world

Of one entire and perfect chrysolite,
I'd not have sold her for it.

EMILIA. My husband?

OTHELLO.

               Ay, 'twas he that told me first.
An honest man he is, and hates the slime

That sticks on filthy deeds.

EMILIA.   My husband?

OTHELLO. What needs this iterance, woman? I say thy husband.

EMILIA. O mistress! villainy hath made mocks with love.

My husband say that she was false?

OTHELLO.   He, woman.

I say, thy husband; dost understand the word?

My friend, thy husband, honest, honest Iago.

EMILIA. If he say so, may his pernicious soul

Rot half a grain a day! He lies to the heart.

She was too fond of her most filthy bargain.

OTHELLO. Ha!

EMILIA. Do thy worst.

This deed of thine is no more worthy heaven

Than thou wast worthy her.

OTHELLO.   Peace! you were best.

EMILIA. Thou hast not half the power to do me harm

As I have to be hurt. O gull! O dolt!

As ignorant as dirt! Thou hast done a deed,—

I care not for thy sword. I'll make thee known,

Though I lost twenty lives. Help! help, ho! help!

The Moor has kill'd my mistress! Murder! murder!

[*Enter* MONTANO, GRATIANO, IAGO, *and others.*]

MONTANO. What is the matter? How now, general?

EMILIA. O, are you come, Iago? You have done well,

That men must lay their murders on your neck.

GRATIANO. What is the matter?

EMILIA. Disprove this villain if thou be'st a man:

He says thou told'st him that his wife was false.

I know thou didst not. Thou'rt not such a villain.

Speak, for my heart is full.

IAGO. I told him what I thought, and told no more

Than what he found himself was apt and true.

EMILIA. But did you ever tell him she was false?

IAGO. I did.

EMILIA. You told a lie, an odious damned lie;

Upon my soul, a lie, a wicked lie.

She false with Cassio! Did you say with Cassio?

IAGO. With Cassio, mistress. Go to, charm your tongue.

EMILIA. I will not charm my tongue; I am bound to speak.

My mistress here lies murder'd in her bed.

ALL. O heavens forfend!

EMILIA. And your reports have set the murder on.

OTHELLO. Nay, stare not, masters. It is true indeed.

GRATIANO. 'Tis a strange truth.

MONTANO. O monstrous act!

EMILIA. Villainy! villainy! villainy!

I think upon't, I think, I smell't. O villainy!

I thought so then. I'll kill myself for grief.

O villainy, villainy!

IAGO. What! are you mad? I charge you, get you home.

EMILIA. Good gentlemen, let me have leave to speak.

'Tis proper I obey him, but not now.

Perchance, Iago, I will ne'er go home.

OTHELLO. Oh! Oh! Oh! [OTHELLO *falls on the bed.*]

EMILIA. Nay, lay thee down and roar,

For thou hast kill'd the sweetest innocent

That e'er did lift up eye.

OTHELLO. O! she was foul.

I scarce did know you, uncle. There lies your niece,

Whose breath, indeed, these hands have newly stopp'd.

I know this act shows terrible and grim.

GRATIANO. Poor Desdemon, I am glad thy father's dead.

Thy match was mortal to him, and pure grief

Shore his old thread a-twain. Did he live now,

This sight would make him do a desperate turn,

Yea, curse his better angel from his side,

And fall to reprobation.

OTHELLO. 'Tis pitiful; but yet Iago knows

That she with Cassio hath the act of shame

A thousand times committed. Cassio confess'd it;

And she did gratify his amorous works

With the recognizance and pledge of love

Which I first gave her. I saw it in his hand.

It was a handkerchief, an antique token

My father gave my mother.

EMILIA. O God! O heavenly God!

IAGO. Zounds! hold your peace.

EMILIA. 'Twill out, 'twill out! I hold my peace, sir? No!

No, I will speak as liberal as the north.

Let heaven and men and devils, let them all,

All, all, cry shame against me, yet I'll speak.

IAGO. Be wise, and get you home.

EMILIA.

I will not. [IAGO *threatens* EMILIA.]

GRATIANO. Fie!

Your sword upon a woman?

EMILIA. O thou dull Moor! that handkerchief thou speak'st of

I found by fortune and did give my husband,

For often with a solemn earnestness

(More than, indeed, belong'd to such a trifle)

He begg'd of me to steal it.

IAGO. Villainous whore!

EMILIA. She give it Cassio? No, alas! I found it,

And I did give't my husband.

IAGO. Filth, thou liest!

EMILIA. By heaven, I do not. I do not, gentlemen.

O murderous coxcomb! what should such a fool

Do with so good a wife?

OTHELLO.
    Are there no stones in heaven

But what serves for the thunder? Precious villain!

[*The* MOOR *runs at* IAGO. IAGO *kills his wife.*]

GRATIANO. The woman falls. Sure, he has kill'd his wife.

[*Exit* IAGO.]

EMILIA. Ay, ay. O lay me by my mistress' side.

GRATIANO. He's gone, but his wife's kill'd.

MONTANO. 'Tis a notorious villain. [*To* GRATIANO.] Take you this weapon,

Which I have here recover'd from the Moor.

Come, guard the door without. Let him not pass,

But kill him rather. I'll after that same villain,

For 'tis a damned slave. [*Exeunt* MONTANO *and* GRATIANO.]

OTHELLO.   I am not valiant neither,

But every puny whipster gets my sword.

But why should honor outlive honesty?

Let it go all.

EMILIA. What did thy song bode, lady?

Hark, canst thou hear me? I will play the swan,

And die in music. [*Sings.*] Willow, willow, willow.

Moor, she was chaste. She lov'd thee, cruel Moor.

So come my soul to bliss as I speak true.

So speaking as I think, I die, I die. [*She dies.*]

OTHELLO. I have another weapon in this chamber.

It is a sword of Spain, the ice brook's temper.

O here it is.—Uncle, I must come forth.

GRATIANO. [*Within.*] If thou attempt it, it will cost thee dear.

Thou hast no weapon, and perforce must suffer.

OTHELLO. Look in upon me then, and speak to me,

Or, naked as I am, I will assault thee.

[*Enter* GRATIANO.]

GRATIANO. What is the matter?

OTHELLO.   Behold! I have a weapon.

A better never did itself sustain

Upon a soldier's thigh. I have seen the day

That with this little arm and this good sword

I have made my way through more impediments

Than twenty times your stop. But O vain boast!

Who can control his fate? 'Tis not so now.

Be not afraid, though you do see me weapon'd.

Here is my journey's end, here is my butt

And very sea-mark of my utmost sail.

Do you go back dismay'd? 'Tis a lost fear.

Man but a rush against Othello's breast,

And he retires. Where should Othello go?—

Now, how dost thou look now? O illstarr'd wench!

Pale as thy smock! When we shall meet at compt,

This look of thine will hurl my soul from heaven,

And fiends will snatch at it. Cold, cold, my girl,

Even like thy chastity.

O cursed, cursed slave! Whip me, ye devils,

From the possession of this heavenly sight!

Blow me about in winds! roast me in sulphur!

Wash me in steep-down gulfs of liquid fire!

O Desdemona! Desdemona! dead!

O! O! O!

[*Enter* LODOVICO, MONTANO, IAGO *as a prisoner, and* OFFICERS, CASSIO *in a chair.*]

LODOVICO. Where is this rash and most unfortunate man?

OTHELLO. That's he that was Othello. Here I am.

LODOVICO. Where is that viper? bring the villain forth.

OTHELLO. I look down towards his feet, but that's a fable.

If that thou be'st a devil, I cannot kill thee. [*Wounds* IAGO.]

LODOVICO. Wring his sword from him.

IAGO.   I bleed, sir, but not kill'd.

OTHELLO. I am not sorry neither. I'd have thee live,

For in my sense 'tis happiness to die.

LODOVICO. O thou Othello that wert once so good,

Fall'n in the practice of a damned slave,

What shall be said to thee?

OTHELLO.   Why, anything:

An honorable murderer, if you will;

For nought did I in hate, but all in honor.

LODOVICO. This wretch hath part confess'd his villainy.

Did you and he consent in Cassio's death?

OTHELLO. Ay.

CASSIO. Dear general, I did never give you cause.

OTHELLO. I do believe it, and I ask you pardon.

Will you, I pray, demand that demi-devil

Why he hath thus ensnar'd my soul and body.

IAGO. Demand me nothing. What you know, you know:

From this time forth I never will speak word.

LODOVICO. What! not to pray?

GRATIANO.

          Torments will ope your lips.

OTHELLO. Well, thou dost best.

LODOVICO. Sir, you shall understand what hath befall'n,

Which, as I think, you know not. Here is a letter

Found in the pocket of the slain Roderigo,

And here another. The one of them imports

The death of Cassio to be undertook

By Roderigo.

OTHELLO. O villain!

CASSIO.

          Most heathenish and most gross!

LODOVICO. Now here's another discontented paper,

Found in his pocket too; and this, it seems,

Roderigo meant t' have sent this damned villain,

But that, belike, Iago in the interim

Came in and satisfied him.

OTHELLO.   O the pernicious caitiff!

How came you, Cassio, by that handkerchief

That was my wife's?

CASSIO.   I found it in my chamber;

And he himself confess'd it even now

That there he dropp'd it for a special purpose

Which wrought to his desire.

OTHELLO.   O fool! fool! fool!

CASSIO. There is besides in Roderigo's letter

How he upbraids Iago that he made him

Brave me upon the watch, whereon it came

That I was cast: and even but now he spake

(After long seeming dead): Iago hurt him,

Iago set him on.

LODOVICO. You must forsake this room and go with us.

Your power and your command is taken off,

And Cassio rules in Cyprus. For this slave,

If there be any cunning cruelty

That can torment him much and hold him long,

It shall be his. You shall close prisoner rest,

Till that the nature of your fault be known

To the Venetian state. Come, bring him away.

OTHELLO. Soft you! A word or two before you go.

I have done the state some service, and
    they know't;
No more of that. I pray you, in your
    letters,
When you shall these unlucky deeds re-
    late,
Speak of them as they are. Nothing ex-
    tenuate,
Nor set down aught in malice. Then must
    you speak
Of one that lov'd not wisely but too well;
Of one not easily jealous, but, being
    wrought,
Perplex'd in the extreme; of one whose
    hand
(Like the base Indian) threw a pearl
    away
Richer than all his tribe; of one whose
    subdu'd eyes,
Albeit unused to the melting mood,
Drops tears as fast as the Arabian trees
Their medicinal gum. Set you down this;
And say besides, that in Aleppo once,
Where a malignant and a turban'd Turk
Beat a Venetian and traduc'd the state,
I took by the throat the circumcised dog,
And smote him thus. [*He stabs himself.*]

LODOVICO. O bloody period!
GRATIANO.
        All that's spoke is marr'd.
OTHELLO. I kiss'd thee ere I kill'd thee.
    No way but this,
Killing myself to die upon a kiss. [*He
    dies.*]
CASSIO. This did I fear, but thought he
    had no weapon;
For he was great of heart.
LODOVICO. [*To* IAGO.] O Spartan dog,
More fell than anguish, hunger, or the
    sea,
Look on the tragic loading of this bed!
This is thy work. The object poisons
    sight;
Let it be hid. Gratiano, keep the house,
And seize upon the fortunes of the Moor,
For they succeed to you. To you, lord
    governor,
Remains the censure of this hellish villain,
The time, the place, the torture. O, en-
    force it!
Myself will straight aboard, and to the
    state
This heavy act with heavy heart relate.
    [*Exeunt omnes.*]

FEDERICO GARCIA LORCA: *BLOOD WEDDING*

When the reader of the modern Spanish folk-tragedy, *Blood Wedding*, encounters nameless characters who are more obviously symbols than they are flesh-and-blood persons, when he finds that much of the play is written in verse, and when he finds that Death is personified and the Moon speaks as a messenger of Death, he may think himself far removed from the modern world. It may come as a surprise, then, to learn that the central incident in *Blood Wedding*—a tragedy resulting from a conventional love triangle—had a mundane origin in a contemporary newspaper report.

The very fact that this is so invites several major questions regarding the methods and resources of the dramatist; Lorca's solutions to these problems underlie this striking and unique modern tragedy. In this respect, a telling comparison can be made between the Lorca play and Joseph Hayes's *The Desperate Hours*. The Hayes play, too, is based on an actual occurrence of the sort one may read about frequently in the newspapers—the kind of gamble made by desperate men anxious to avoid society's justice and willing to sacrifice other lives to do so. In his treatment of such an incident, Hayes was content to tell his story pretty much as it did occur, or may have occurred; his action develops along lines that are conventional for this type of suspense melodrama, his characters are the familiar and expected ones, and the dialogue they utter is the typical speech we would expect to hear from them if we encountered them in day-to-day life.

The Hayes play is a success on this literal level because of the skill with which it weaves together its rather commonplace elements. But the author of *Blood Wedding* had more ambitious plans, and used his materials—again, materials suggested by life—in a quite different way, with the result that his play, although exhibiting influences of his particular time and place, aspires to a kind of universality that a more literal, journalistic account of its events would not attempt.

This is not to say that the author deliberately ignored the temporal and the mundane. Few recent writers have, in fact, been more actively involved in the affairs of their time than has Federico Garcia Lorca. He was deeply committed to the liberal cause during the Spanish Civil War of the 1930's; his works were suppressed by the Franco government; and it is generally supposed that his death, in 1936, was a political murder carried out by the Fascist Falangists.

Lorca's three folk-tragedies, however—the other two are *Yerma* and *The House of Bernarda Alba*—do not reflect his personal sentiments on politics or reform; but they are none the less deeply rooted in the customs of Lorca's native land and reflect brilliantly the particular intensity of life which seems to issue out of the Spanish soil. Proceeding in *Blood Wedding* not as a social reformer but as a man of the theater seeking the universal in the particular, Lorca realized that, through the formalization of characters and action, and the employment of language more elevated and more lyrical than his peasant characters could possibly use in real life, he could raise a sordid love affair and its violent action to the level of genuine tragedy, with its chastening and purifying consequences.

461

Lorca's treatment of his materials is the first aspect of *Blood Wedding* that demands attention. The dramatist was not concerned only with transcribing for the stage a tabloid report of an incident that had caught his attention. He did, in fact, transform the story in such a way as to take it almost completely out of the realm of realism. Perhaps his most obvious departure occurs in his approach to character. Only one person in the play, Leonardo, has a name; the others are identified by person or relationship. These characters, who bear such designations as "The Bride," "The Mother," and "The Bridegroom," may remind the reader of the disembodied voices who spoke to him in *Everyman*. And, as in that Morality Play, the namelessness of these characters has the similar effect of lifting them above the commonplace and identifying them as enduring human types, rather than reducing them to lifeless abstractions.

Certain other characters are used in a different and more clearly symbolic fashion. These are the Three Woodcutters, the Moon, and the Beggar Woman, who appear in Act III. At this point in the play, the tragic love affair is rushing toward its violent conclusion; in a climactic scene, Lorca introduces a group of symbolic characters who comment on the action (much as did the Greek chorus) and assist in establishing its meaning. Three Woodcutters appear in a dim, misty forest. At first glance they might pass as Spanish peasants, but their speech and behavior soon characterize them as being other than earthly creatures. They are, in fact, the Fates, and their dialogue generalizes on the impending doom of the unsanctified lovers. Like the Fates, they do not moralize or condemn; they merely state what must ensue, given the nature of man. "You have to follow your passion," says one; another adds, "You have to follow the path of your blood." Recognizing the motives that impel the fleeing lovers, they make this further point:

SECOND WOODCUTTER. But blood that sees the light of day is drunk up by the earth.
FIRST WOODCUTTER. What of it? Better dead with the blood drained away than alive with it rotting.

The Fates thus underscore the inevitability of the outcome. The lovers—like most men and women—are slaves to their own natural passions, and will find it impossible, as the Second Woodcutter acknowledges, to "break through the circle" of vengeful hate their own passions have aroused. In such a dilemma, the Fates claim, it is best to live with maximum intensity, even though such intensity condemns one, in the end, to nothing but ruin and death.

The brief scene with the Fates is interrupted by the entrance of another symbolic figure—a fourth Woodcutter, this one young and with a white face. He is the Moon, and the Moon here is the messenger of Death. His appearance properly summons Death to the scene, and when she appears (as a Beggar Woman, slyly requesting all men to give themselves to her), she commands the destined outcome. "White sheets/wait on the floor of the bedroom/for heavy bodies with torn throats," she says grimly; and then she tells the Moon: "Light up the waistcoat and open the buttons; the knives will know the path after that." Her lines bring us to the culmination of the action and recall the foreboding expressed by the Mother at the very beginning of the play, when, remembering the death by violence of her husband and one of her sons, she says, "Knives, knives. Cursed be all knives, and the scoundrel who invented them."

As if to openly assert that Lorca's symbolic characters are there to give a poetic extension to his meaning, the Beggar Woman thus acknowledges, by her command, that she is herself merely a projection of something already present in the human characters, whose "knives know the path," whose destiny is certain to lead them to her door. Death is thus not only a character in the play; like the passions, she represents an experience to be endured by each of the participants in the tragedy. She is a part of Nature, the terminus of the passions which rule these doomed representatives of man.

Apart from this symbolic use of characters, the most striking feature of *Blood Wedding* is its lyrical language. Poetry is not used throughout the play, but makes its appearance in three major scenes. On each occasion, its use is carefully controlled for a specific purpose, in conformity with the dramatist's over-all intention.

Its first significant appearance is in the wedding scene (II, i). In its imagery and its restrained but obvious passion, Lorca's love poetry in this scene may remind one of the Song of Solomon. It is warm, lyrical, and sensuous, portending the fulfillment of physical desire. Then, when the Woodcutters appear and Death waits for the lovers (III, i), verse is used again, but there is a marked difference in tone as the Moon anticipates Death:

> But this night there will be
> red blood for my cheeks,

and later, like a refrain,

> . . . this night there will be
> sweet blood for my cheeks.

Here the verse conveys a sense of terror, almost horror, as the Moon and then Death gloat over the prospect of the blood that is about to be shed.

Verse is used again in the final scene (III, ii). By this time, the action has been concluded; the last scene does not advance the story, but rather serves as a muted and generally elegiac comment on the previous action. Here too, Lorca's use of poetry is justified by the purpose it serves. The Mother has lost her last son; she is now beyond grief, beyond caring that the Bride has preserved her meaningless honor. Even grief is here expressed in formal and traditional terms; Lorca's poetic lines reveal the depth of the characters' feelings, underneath their restrained behavior and their carefully controlled speech.

The three scenes in which Lorca uses verse have certain traits in common, thus providing some clues to his intention and to the response he expects from us. These scenes are the crucial ones, not only in terms of plot development, but also in that they most fully bring to the fore the passions that give rise both to the potential joy and to the ultimate terror these characters experience. In the first of the poetic scenes, it is the fulfillment of love that is experienced; in the second, the threat of death; and in the third, the grief that follows death. Thus Lorca calls upon the assistance of verse in crucial scenes when he has a high, intense emotion to express, indicating his awareness that, by this means, he can gain a certain dignity, an elevation, which would be less likely in prose, or at least in the prose that these characters would normally speak.

One other element these scenes have in common is that each one turns on an occurrence in the life of man for which, out of the necessity to memorialize the significance certain moments have for him, he has devised some sort of formal ritual. A ritual, a ceremony which follows an established pattern, both intensifies and makes bearable man's most supremely felt moments—those occupied with love, death, and grief. Thus, to heighten the impression that grave matters are involved, that these significant moments impend, Lorca not only uses verse, but deliberately chooses that kind of verse which moves with the formal accents of the ritual and captures the religious tone of such occasions.

These non-realistic conventions may seem unusual to the present-day reader conditioned to expect journalistic realism, but they are among the oldest devices of drama. Lorca's use of them ties him less to the twentieth-century "Expressionists" (discussed under "The Elements in Balance") than to the long tradition of dramatists dating back to Sophocles who saw the drama not as a copy of life but as an elevated and formalized means of reflecting on some of its problems. But more important than debates over the propriety of verse in an age that seems unwilling to listen to it, or the use of formalized characters in a time that asks for realism, is an inquiry into the nature of the finished product, to discover the source of its power.

As with other tragedies, an explanation of the play's effect on us may reside in the particular view of life which underlies the action of the play, and in the nature of the characters whose actions bring that view to light. Lorca, by making his characters epitomes of love, jealousy, and revenge, elevates them to universal forces, and so enlarges their human significance. Here, surely, is one source of the play's strength; the characters, by the very fact that they lack individual names but are nevertheless so powerfully motivated, remind us almost of the primitive instincts of man at work, terrifying but awesome. These are the instincts, the play reminds us, not of this particular person or that one, but of Man; and this is what happens when those instincts break through all the restraints imposed by society, by church, and by reason, to precipitate catastrophe. It is perhaps the very size of this conflict which gives it its power; and it is a measure of the success of the dramatist that he has been able to contain his brutal and violent story within a rigidly controlled and formalized framework.

NOTE: *This edition of* Blood Wedding *has been scrupulously revised by Margarita Xirgu in accordance with the original manuscript of Federico Garcia Lorca and contains his latest revisions.*

Blood Wedding

by

FEDERICO GARCIA LORCA

translated by

James Graham-Luján

and

Richard L. O'Connell

Characters

THE MOTHER
THE BRIDE
THE MOTHER-IN-LAW
LEONARDO'S WIFE
THE SERVANT WOMAN
THE NEIGHBOR WOMAN
YOUNG GIRLS
LEONARDO
THE BRIDEGROOM
THE BRIDE'S FATHER
THE MOON
DEATH [*as a Beggar Woman*]
WOODCUTTERS
YOUNG MEN

ACT ONE

1.

A room painted yellow.

BRIDEGROOM. [*Entering.*] Mother.

MOTHER. What?

BRIDEGROOM. I'm going.

MOTHER. Where?

BRIDEGROOM. To the vineyard. [*He starts to go.*]

MOTHER. Wait.

BRIDEGROOM. You want something?

MOTHER. Your breakfast, son.

BRIDEGROOM. Forget it. I'll eat grapes. Give me the knife.

MOTHER. What for?

BRIDEGROOM. [*Laughing.*] To cut the grapes with.

MOTHER. [*Muttering as she looks for the knife.*] Knives, knives. Cursed be all knives, and the scoundrel who invented them.

BRIDEGROOM. Let's talk about something else.

MOTHER. And guns and pistols and the smallest little knife—and even hoes and pitchforks.

BRIDEGROOM. All right.

MOTHER. Everything that can slice a man's body. A handsome man, full of young life, who goes out to the vineyards or to his own olive groves—his own because he's inherited them . . .

BRIDEGROOM. [*Lowering his head.*] Be quiet.

MOTHER. . . . and then that man doesn't come back. Or if he does come back it's only for someone to cover him over with a palm leaf or a plate of rock salt so he won't bloat. I don't know how you dare carry a knife on your body—or how I let this serpent [*She takes a knife from a kitchen chest.*] stay in the chest.

BRIDEGROOM. Have you had your say?

MOTHER. If I lived to be a hundred I'd talk of nothing else. First your father; to me he smelled like a carnation and I had him for barely three years. Then your brother. Oh, is it right—how can it be—that a small thing like a knife or a pistol can finish off a man—a bull of a man? No, I'll never be quiet. The months pass and the hopelessness of it stings in my eyes and even to the roots of my hair.

BRIDEGROOM. [*Forcefully.*] Let's quit this talk!

MOTHER. No. No. Let's not quit this talk. Can anyone bring me your father back? Or your brother? Then there's the jail. What do they mean, jail? They eat there, smoke there, play music there! My dead men choking with weeds, silent, turning to dust. Two men like two beautiful flowers. The killers in jail, carefree, looking at the mountains.

BRIDEGROOM. Do you want me to go kill them?

MOTHER. No . . . If I talk about it it's because . . . Oh, how can I help talking

465

about it, seeing you go out that door?
It's . . . I don't like you to carry a knife.
It's just that . . . that I wish you
wouldn't go out to the fields.

BRIDEGROOM. [*Laughing.*] Oh, come
now!

MOTHER. I'd like it if you were a
woman. Then you wouldn't be going out
to the arroyo now and we'd both of us
embroider flounces and little woolly
dogs.

BRIDEGROOM. [*He puts his arm around
his mother and laughs.*] Mother, what if
I should take you with me to the vineyards?

MOTHER. What would an old lady do
in the vineyards? Were you going to put
me down under the young vines?

BRIDEGROOM. [*Lifting her in his arms.*]
Old lady, old lady—you little old, little
old lady!

MOTHER. Your father, he used to take
me. That's the way with men of good
stock; good blood. Your grandfather left
a son on every corner. That's what I like.
Men, men; wheat, wheat.

BRIDEGROOM. And I, Mother?

MOTHER. You, what?

BRIDEGROOM. Do I need to tell you
again?

MOTHER. [*Seriously.*] Oh!

BRIDEGROOM. Do you think it's bad?

MOTHER. No.

BRIDEGROOM. Well, then?

MOTHER. I don't really know. Like this,
suddenly, it always surprises me. I know
the girl is good. Isn't she? Well behaved.
Hard working. Kneads her bread, sews
her skirts, but even so when I say her
name I feel as though someone had hit
me on the forehead with a rock.

BRIDEGROOM. Foolishness.

MOTHER. More than foolishness. I'll be
left alone. Now only you are left me—I
hate to see you go.

BRIDEGROOM. But you'll come with us.

MOTHER. No. I can't leave your father
and brother here alone. I have to go to
them every morning and if I go away
it's possible one of the Félix family, one
of the killers, might die—and they'd bury
him next to ours. And that'll never happen! Oh, no! That'll never happen! Because I'd dig them out with my nails and,
all by myself, crush them against the
wall.

BRIDEGROOM. [*Sternly.*] There you go
again.

MOTHER. Forgive me. [*Pause.*] How
long have you known her?

BRIDEGROOM. Three years. I've been
able to buy the vineyard.

MOTHER. Three years. She used to have
another sweetheart, didn't she?

BRIDEGROOM. I don't know. I don't
think so. Girls have to look at what
they'll marry.

MOTHER. Yes. I looked at nobody. I
looked at your father, and when they
killed him I looked at the wall in front
of me. One woman with one man, and
that's all.

BRIDEGROOM. You know my girl's good.

MOTHER. I don't doubt it. All the same,
I'm sorry not to have known what her
mother was like.

BRIDEGROOM. What difference does it
make now?

MOTHER. [*Looking at him.*] Son.

BRIDEGROOM. What is it?

MOTHER. That's true! You're right!
When do you want me to ask for her?

BRIDEGROOM. [*Happily.*] Does Sunday
seem all right to you?

MOTHER. [*Seriously.*] I'll take her the
bronze earrings, they're very old—and
you buy her . . .

BRIDEGROOM. You know more about
that . . .

MOTHER. . . . you buy her some openwork stockings—and for you, two suits
—three! I have no one but you now!

BRIDEGROOM. I'm going. Tomorrow I'll
go see her.

MOTHER. Yes, yes—and see if you can
make me happy with six grandchildren—
or as many as you want, since your
father didn't live to give them to me.

BRIDEGROOM. The first-born for you!

MOTHER. Yes, but have some girls. I
want to embroider and make lace, and be
at peace.

BRIDEGROOM. I'm sure you'll love my
wife.

MOTHER. I'll love her. [*She starts to
kiss him but changes her mind.*] Go on.
You're too big now for kisses. Give them

to your wife. [*Pause. To herself.*] When she is your wife.

BRIDEGROOM. I'm going.

MOTHER. And that land around the little mill—work it over. You've not taken good care of it.

BRIDEGROOM. You're right. I will.

MOTHER. God keep you. [*The* SON *goes out. The* MOTHER *remains seated—her back to the door. A* NEIGHBOR WOMAN *with a 'kerchief on her head appears in the door.*] Come in.

NEIGHBOR. How are you?

MOTHER. Just as you see me.

NEIGHBOR. I came down to the store and stopped in to see you. We live so far away!

MOTHER. It's twenty years since I've been up to the top of the street.

NEIGHBOR. You're looking well.

MOTHER. You think so?

NEIGHBOR. Things happen. Two days ago they brought in my neighbor's son with both arms sliced off by the machine. [*She sits down.*]

MOTHER. Rafael?

NEIGHBOR. Yes. And there you have him. Many times I've thought your son and mine are better off where they are—sleeping, resting—not running the risk of being left helpless.

MOTHER. Hush. That's all just something thought up—but no consolation.

NEIGHBOR. [*Sighing.*] Ay!

MOTHER. [*Sighing.*] Ay! [*Pause.*]

NEIGHBOR. [*Sadly.*] Where's your son?

MOTHER. He went out.

NEIGHBOR. He finally bought the vineyard!

MOTHER. He was lucky.

NEIGHBOR. Now he'll get married.

MOTHER. [*As though reminded of something, she draws her chair near* THE NEIGHBOR.*] Listen.

NEIGHBOR. [*In a confidential manner.*] Yes. What is it?

MOTHER. You know my son's sweetheart?

NEIGHBOR. A good girl!

MOTHER. Yes, but . . .

NEIGHBOR. But who knows her really well? There's nobody. She lives out there alone with her father—so far away—fifteen miles from the nearest house. But she's a good girl. Used to being alone.

MOTHER. And her mother?

NEIGHBOR. Her mother I *did* know. Beautiful. Her face glowed like a saint's—but *I* never liked her. She didn't love her husband.

MOTHER. [*Sternly.*] Well, what a lot of things certain people know!

NEIGHBOR. I'm sorry. I didn't mean to offend—but it's true. Now, whether she was decent or not nobody said. That wasn't discussed. She was haughty.

MOTHER. There you go again!

NEIGHBOR. You asked me.

MOTHER. I wish no one knew anything about them—either the live one or the dead one—that they were like two thistles no one even names but cuts off at the right moment.

NEIGHBOR. You're right. Your son is worth a lot.

MOTHER. Yes—a lot. That's why I look after him. They told me the girl had a sweetheart some time ago.

NEIGHBOR. She was about fifteen. He's been married two years now—to a cousin of hers, as a matter of fact. But nobody remembers about their engagement.

MOTHER. How do you remember it?

NEIGHBOR. Oh, what questions you ask!

MOTHER. We like to know all about the things that hurt us. Who was the boy?

NEIGHBOR. Leonardo.

MOTHER. What Leonardo?

NEIGHBOR. Leonardo Félix.

MOTHER. Félix!

NEIGHBOR. Yes, but—how is Leonardo to blame for anything? He was eight years old when those things happened.

MOTHER. That's true. But I hear that name—Félix—and it's all the same. [*Muttering.*] Félix, a slimy mouthful. [*She spits.*] It makes me spit—spit so I won't kill!

NEIGHBOR. Control yourself. What good will it do?

MOTHER. No good. But you see how it is.

NEIGHBOR. Don't get in the way of your son's happiness. Don't say anything to him. You're old. So am I. It's time for you and me to keep quiet.

MOTHER. I'll say nothing to him.

NEIGHBOR. [*Kissing her.*] Nothing.

MOTHER. [*Calmly.*] Such things . . . !

NEIGHBOR. I'm going. My men will soon be coming in from the fields.

MOTHER. Have you ever known such a hot sun?

NEIGHBOR. The children carrying water out to the reapers are black with it. Goodbye, woman.

MOTHER. Goodbye. [*The* MOTHER *starts toward the door at the left. Halfway there she stops and slowly crosses herself.*]

CURTAIN

2.

A room painted rose with copperware and wreaths of common flowers. In the center of the room is a table with a tablecloth. It is morning.

Leonardo's MOTHER-IN-LAW sits in one corner holding a child in her arms and rocking it. His WIFE is in the other corner mending stockings.

MOTHER-IN-LAW. Lullaby, my baby
once there was a big horse
who didn't like water.
The water was black there
under the branches.
When it reached the bridge
it stopped and it sang.
Who can say, my baby,
what the stream holds
with its long tail
in its green parlor?

WIFE. [*Softly.*] Carnation, sleep and dream,
the horse won't drink from the stream.

MOTHER-IN-LAW. My rose, asleep now lie,
the horse is starting to cry.
His poor hooves were bleeding,
his long mane was frozen,
and deep in his eyes
stuck a silvery dagger.
Down he went to the river,
Oh, down he went down!
And his blood was running,
Oh, more than the water.

WIFE. Carnation, sleep and dream,
the horse won't drink from the stream.

MOTHER-IN-LAW. My rose, asleep now lie,
the horse is starting to cry.

WIFE. He never did touch
the dank river shore
though his muzzle was warm
and with silvery flies.
So, to the hard mountains
he could only whinny
just when the dead stream
covered his throat.
Ay-y-y, for the big horse
who didn't like water!
Ay-y-y, for the snow-wound
big horse of the dawn!

MOTHER-IN-LAW. Don't come in! Stop him
and close up the window
with branches of dreams
and a dream of branches.

WIFE. My baby is sleeping.

MOTHER-IN-LAW. My baby is quiet.

WIFE. Look, horse, my baby
has him a pillow.

MOTHER-IN-LAW. His cradle is metal.

WIFE. His quilt a fine fabric.

MOTHER-IN-LAW. Lullaby, my baby.

WIFE. Ay-y-y, for the big horse
who didn't like water!

MOTHER-IN-LAW. Don't come near, don't come in!
Go away to the mountains
and through the grey valleys,
that's where your mare is.

WIFE. [*Looking at the baby.*] My baby is sleeping.

MOTHER-IN-LAW. My baby is resting.

WIFE. [*Softly.*] Carnation, sleep and dream,
The horse won't drink from the stream.

MOTHER-IN-LAW. [*Getting up, very softly.*] My rose, asleep now lie
for the horse is starting to cry.

[*She carries the child out.* LEONARDO *enters.*]

LEONARDO. Where's the baby?

WIFE. He's sleeping.

LEONARDO. Yesterday he wasn't well. He cried during the night.

WIFE. Today he's like a dahlia. And you? Were you at the blacksmith's?

LEONARDO. I've just come from there. Would you believe it? For more than two months he's been putting new shoes on the horse and they're always coming off. As far as I can see he pulls them off on the stones.

WIFE. Couldn't it just be that you use him so much?

LEONARDO. No. I almost never use him.

WIFE. Yesterday the neighbors told me they'd seen you on the far side of the plains.

LEONARDO. Who said that?

WIFE. The women who gather capers. It certainly surprised me. Was it you?

LEONARDO. No. What would I be doing there, in that wasteland?

WIFE. That's what I said. But the horse was streaming sweat.

LEONARDO. Did you see him?

WIFE. No. Mother did.

LEONARDO. Is she with the baby?

WIFE. Yes. Do you want some lemonade?

LEONARDO. With good cold water.

WIFE. And then you didn't come to eat!

LEONARDO. I was with the wheat weighers. They always hold me up.

WIFE. [*Very tenderly, while she makes the lemonade.*] Did they pay you a good price?

LEONARDO. Fair.

WIFE. I need a new dress and the baby a bonnet with ribbons.

LEONARDO. [*Getting up.*] I'm going to take a look at him.

WIFE. Be careful. He's asleep.

MOTHER-IN-LAW. [*Coming in.*] Well! Who's been racing the horse that way? He's down there, worn out, his eyes popping from their sockets as though he'd come from the ends of the earth.

LEONARDO. [*Acidly.*] I have.

MOTHER-IN-LAW. Oh, excuse me! He's your horse.

WIFE. [*Timidly.*] He was at the wheat buyers.

MOTHER-IN-LAW. He can burst for all of me! [*She sits down. Pause.*]

WIFE. Your drink. Is it cold?

LEONARDO. Yes.

WIFE. Did you hear they're going to ask for my cousin?

LEONARDO. When?

WIFE. Tomorrow. The wedding will be within a month. I hope they're going to invite us.

LEONARDO. [*Gravely.*] I don't know.

MOTHER-IN-LAW. His mother, I think, wasn't very happy about the match.

LEONARDO. Well, she may be right. She's a girl to be careful with.

WIFE. I don't like to have you thinking bad things about a good girl.

MOTHER-IN-LAW. [*Meaningfully.*] If he does, it's because he knows her. Didn't you know he courted her for three years?

LEONARDO. But I left her. [*To his* WIFE.] Are you going to cry now? Quit that! [*He brusquely pulls her hands away from her face.*] Let's go see the baby. [*They go in with their arms around each other. A* GIRL *appears. She is happy. She enters running.*]

GIRL. Señora.

MOTHER-IN-LAW. What is it?

GIRL. The groom came to the store and he's bought the best of everything they had.

MOTHER-IN-LAW. Was he alone?

GIRL. No. With his mother. Stern, tall. [*She imitates her.*] And such extravagance!

MOTHER-IN-LAW. They have money.

GIRL. And they bought some openwork stockings! Oh, such stockings! A woman's dream of stockings! Look: a swallow here, [*She points to her ankle.*] a ship here, [*She points to her calf.*] and here, [*She points to her thigh.*] a rose!

MOTHER-IN-LAW. Child!

GIRL. A rose with the seeds and the stem! Oh! All in silk.

MOTHER-IN-LAW. Two rich families are being brought together.

[LEONARDO *and his* WIFE *appear.*]

GIRL. I came to tell you what they're buying.

LEONARDO. [*Loudly.*] We don't care.

WIFE. Leave her alone.

MOTHER-IN-LAW. Leonardo, it's not that important.

GIRL. Please excuse me. [*She leaves, weeping.*]

MOTHER-IN-LAW. Why do you always have to make trouble with people?

LEONARDO. I didn't ask for your opinion. [*He sits down.*]

MOTHER-IN-LAW. Very well. [*Pause.*]

WIFE. [*To* LEONARDO.] What's the matter with you? What idea've you got boiling there inside your head? Don't leave me like this, not knowing anything.

LEONARDO. Stop that.

WIFE. No. I want you to look at me and tell me.

LEONARDO. Let me alone. [*He rises.*]

WIFE. Where are you going, love?

LEONARDO. [*Sharply.*] Can't you shut up?

MOTHER-IN-LAW. [*Energetically, to her daughter.*] Be quiet! [LEONARDO *goes out.*] The baby! [*She goes into the bedroom and comes out again with the baby in her arms. The* WIFE *has remained standing, unmoving.*]

MOTHER-IN-LAW. His poor hooves were
  bleeding,
his long mane was frozen,
and deep in his eyes
stuck a silvery dagger.
Down he went to the river,
Oh, down he went down!
And his blood was running,
Oh, more than the water.

WIFE. [*Turning slowly, as though
  dreaming.*] Carnation, sleep and
  dream,
the horse is drinking from the stream.

MOTHER-IN-LAW. My rose, asleep now
  lie
the horse is starting to cry.

WIFE. Lullaby, my baby.

MOTHER-IN-LAW. Ay-y-y, for the big
  horse
who didn't like water!

WIFE. [*Dramatically.*] Don't come
  near, don't come in!
Go away to the mountains!
Ay-y-y, for the snow-wound,
big horse of the dawn!

MOTHER-IN-LAW. [*Weeping.*] My baby
  is sleeping . . .

WIFE. [*Weeping, as she slowly moves
  closer.*] My baby is resting . . .

MOTHER-IN-LAW. Carnation, sleep and
  dream,
the horse won't drink from the stream.

WIFE. [*Weeping, and leaning on the

table.*] My rose, asleep now lie,
the horse is starting to cry.

CURTAIN

3.

Interior of the cave where the BRIDE lives. At the back is a cross of large rose colored flowers. The round doors have lace curtains with rose colored ties. Around the walls, which are of a white and hard material, are round fans, blue jars, and little mirrors.

SERVANT. Come right in . . . [*She is very affable, full of humble hypocrisy. The* BRIDEGROOM *and his* MOTHER *enter. The* MOTHER *is dressed in black satin and wears a lace mantilla; the* BRIDEGROOM *in black corduroy with a great golden chain.*] Won't you sit down? They'll be right here. [*She leaves. The* MOTHER *and* SON *are left sitting motionless as statues. Long pause.*]

MOTHER. Did you wear the watch?

BRIDEGROOM. Yes. [*He takes it out and looks at it.*]

MOTHER. We have to be back on time. How far away these people live!

BRIDEGROOM. But this is good land.

MOTHER. Good; but much too lonesome. A four hour trip and not one house, not one tree.

BRIDEGROOM. This is the wasteland.

MOTHER. Your father would have covered it with trees.

BRIDEGROOM. Without water?

MOTHER. He would have found some. In the three years we were married he planted ten cherry trees, [*Remembering.*] those three walnut trees by the mill, a whole vineyard and a plant called Jupiter which had scarlet flowers—but it dried up. [*Pause.*]

BRIDEGROOM. [*Referring to the* BRIDE.] She must be dressing. [*The* BRIDE'S FATHER *enters. He is very old, with shining white hair. His head is bowed. The* MOTHER *and the* BRIDEGROOM *rise. They shake hands in silence.*]

FATHER. Was it a long trip?

MOTHER. Four hours. [*They sit down.*]

FATHER. You must have come the longest way.

MOTHER. I'm too old to come along the cliffs by the river.

BRIDEGROOM. She gets dizzy. [*Pause.*]

FATHER. A good hemp harvest.

BRIDEGROOM. A really good one.

FATHER. When I was young this land didn't even grow hemp. We've had to punish it, even weep over it, to make it give us anything useful.

MOTHER. But now it does. Don't complain. I'm not here to ask you for anything.

FATHER. [*Smiling.*] You're richer than I. Your vineyards are worth a fortune. Each young vine a silver coin. But—do you know?—what bothers me is that our lands are separated. I like to have everything together. One thorn I have in my heart, and that's the little orchard there, stuck in between my fields—and they won't sell it to me for all the gold in the world.

BRIDEGROOM. That's the way it always is.

FATHER. If we could just take twenty teams of oxen and move your vineyards over here, and put them down on that hillside, how happy I'd be!

MOTHER. But why?

FATHER. What's mine is hers and what's yours is his. That's why. Just to see it all together. How beautiful it is to bring things together!

BRIDEGROOM. And it would be less work.

MOTHER. When I die, you could sell ours and buy here, right alongside.

FATHER. Sell, sell? Bah! Buy, my friend, buy everything. If I had had sons I would have bought all this mountainside right up to the part with the stream. It's not good land, but strong arms can make it good, and since no people pass by, they don't steal your fruit and you can sleep in peace. [*Pause.*]

MOTHER. You know what I'm here for.

FATHER. Yes.

MOTHER. And?

FATHER. It seems all right to me. They have talked it over.

MOTHER. My son has money and knows how to manage it.

FATHER. My daughter too.

MOTHER. My son is handsome. He's never known a woman. His good name cleaner than a sheet spread out in the sun.

FATHER. No need to tell you about my daughter. At three, when the morning star shines, she prepares the bread. She never talks: soft as wool, she embroiders all kinds of fancy work and she can cut a strong cord with her teeth.

MOTHER. God bless her house.

FATHER. May God bless it. [*The* SERVANT *appears with two trays. One with drinks and the other with sweets.*]

MOTHER. [*To the* SON.] When would you like the wedding?

BRIDEGROOM. Next Thursday.

FATHER. The day on which she'll be exactly twenty-two years old.

MOTHER. Twenty-two! My oldest son would be that age if he were alive. Warm and manly as he was, he'd be living now if men hadn't invented knives.

FATHER. One mustn't think about that.

MOTHER. Every minute. Always a hand on your breast.

FATHER. Thursday, then? Is that right?

BRIDEGROOM. That's right.

FATHER. You and I and the bridal couple will go in a carriage to the church which is very far from here; the wedding party on the carts and horses they'll bring with them.

MOTHER. Agreed. [*The* SERVANT *passes through.*]

FATHER. Tell her she may come in now. [*To the* MOTHER.] I shall be much pleased if you like her.

[*The* BRIDE *appears. Her hands fall in a modest pose and her head is bowed.*]

MOTHER. Come here. Are you happy?

BRIDE. Yes, señora.

FATHER. You shouldn't be so solemn. After all, she's going to be your mother.

BRIDE. I'm happy. I've said "yes" because I wanted to.

MOTHER. Naturally. [*She takes her by the chin.*] Look at me.

FATHER. She resembles my wife in every way.

MOTHER. Yes? What a beautiful glance! Do you know what it is to be married, child?

BRIDE. [*Seriously.*] I do.

MOTHER. A man, some children and a wall two yards thick for everything else.

BRIDEGROOM. Is anything else needed?

MOTHER. No. Just that you all live— that's it! Live long!

BRIDE. I'll know how to keep my word.

MOTHER. Here are some gifts for you.

BRIDE. Thank you.

FATHER. Shall we have something?

MOTHER. Nothing for me. [*To the* SON.] But you?

BRIDEGROOM. Yes, thank you. [*He takes one sweet, the* BRIDE *another.*]

FATHER. [*To the* BRIDEGROOM.] Wine?

MOTHER. He doesn't touch it.

FATHER. All the better. [*Pause. All are standing.*]

BRIDEGROOM. [*To the* BRIDE.] I'll come tomorrow.

BRIDE. What time?

BRIDEGROOM. Five.

BRIDE. I'll be waiting for you.

BRIDEGROOM. When I leave your side I feel a great emptiness, and something like a knot in my throat.

BRIDE. When you are my husband you won't have it any more.

BRIDEGROOM. That's what I tell myself.

MOTHER. Come. The sun doesn't wait. [*To the* FATHER.] Are we agreed on everything?

FATHER. Agreed.

MOTHER. [*To the* SERVANT.] Goodbye, woman.

SERVANT. God go with you!

[*The* MOTHER *kisses the* BRIDE *and they begin to leave in silence.*]

MOTHER. [*At the door.*] Goodbye, daughter. [*The* BRIDE *answers with her hand.*]

FATHER. I'll go out with you. [*They leave.*]

SERVANT. I'm bursting to see the presents.

BRIDE. [*Sharply.*] Stop that!

SERVANT. Oh, child, show them to me.

BRIDE. I don't want to.

SERVANT. At least the stockings. They say they're all open work. Please!

BRIDE. I said no.

SERVANT. Well, my Lord. All right then. It looks as if you didn't want to get married.

BRIDE. [*Biting her hand in anger.*] Ay-y-y!

SERVANT. Child, child! What's the matter with you? Are you sorry to give up your queen's life? Don't think of bitter things. Have you any reason to? None. Let's look at the presents. [*She takes the box.*]

BRIDE. [*Holding her by the wrists.*] Let go.

SERVANT. Ay-y-y, girl!

BRIDE. Let go, I said.

SERVANT. You're stronger than a man.

BRIDE. Haven't I done a man's work? I wish I were.

SERVANT. Don't talk like that.

BRIDE. Quiet, I said. Let's talk about something else.

[*The light is fading from the stage. Long pause.*]

SERVANT. Did you hear a horse last night?

BRIDE. What time?

SERVANT. Three.

BRIDE. It might have been a stray horse —from the herd.

SERVANT. No. It carried a rider.

BRIDE. How do you know?

SERVANT. Because I saw him. He was standing by your window. It shocked me greatly.

BRIDE. Maybe it was my fiancé. Sometimes he comes by at that time.

SERVANT. No.

BRIDE. You saw him?

SERVANT. Yes.

BRIDE. Who was it?

SERVANT. It was Leonardo.

BRIDE. [*Strongly.*] Liar! You liar! Why should he come here?

SERVANT. He came.

BRIDE. Shut up! Shut your cursed mouth.

[*The sound of a horse is heard.*]

SERVANT. [*At the window.*] Look. Lean out. Was it Leonardo?

BRIDE. It was!

QUICK CURTAIN

ACT TWO

1.

The entrance hall of the BRIDE's house. A large door in the back. It is night. The BRIDE enters wearing ruffled white petticoats full of laces and embroidered bands, and a sleeveless white bodice. The SERVANT is dressed the same way.

SERVANT. I'll finish combing your hair out here.

BRIDE. It's too warm to stay in there.

SERVANT. In this country it doesn't even cool off at dawn. [*The* BRIDE *sits on a low chair and looks into a little hand mirror. The* SERVANT *combs her hair.*]

BRIDE. My mother came from a place with lots of trees—from a fertile country.

SERVANT. And she was so happy!

BRIDE. But she wasted away here.

SERVANT. Fate.

BRIDE. As we're all wasting away here. The very walls give off heat. Ay-y-y! Don't pull so hard.

SERVANT. I'm only trying to fix this wave better. I want it to fall over your forehead. [*The* BRIDE *looks at herself in the mirror.*] How beautiful you are! Ay-y-y! [*She kisses her passionately.*]

BRIDE. [*Seriously.*] Keep right on combing.

SERVANT. [*Combing.*] Oh, lucky you— going to put your arms around a man; and kiss him; and feel his weight.

BRIDE. Hush.

SERVANT. And the best part will be when you'll wake up and you'll feel him at your side and when he caresses your shoulders with his breath, like a little nightingale's feather.

BRIDE. [*Sternly.*] Will you be quiet.

SERVANT. But, child! What *is* a wedding? A wedding is just that and nothing more. Is it the sweets—or the bouquets of flowers? No. It's a shining bed and a man and a woman.

BRIDE. But you shouldn't talk about it.

SERVANT. Oh, *that's* something else again. But fun enough too.

BRIDE. Or bitter enough.

SERVANT. I'm going to put the orange blossoms on from here to here, so the wreath will shine out on top of your hair. [*She tries on the sprigs of orange blossom.*]

BRIDE. [*Looking at herself in the mirror.*] Give it to me. [*She takes the wreath, looks at it and lets her head fall in discouragement.*]

SERVANT. Now what's the matter?

BRIDE. Leave me alone.

SERVANT. This is no time for you to start feeling sad. [*Encouragingly.*] Give me the wreath. [*The* BRIDE *takes the wreath and hurls it away.*] Child! You're just asking God to punish you, throwing the wreath on the floor like that. Raise your head! Don't you want to get married? Say it. You can still withdraw. [*The* BRIDE *rises.*]

BRIDE. Storm clouds. A chill wind that cuts through my heart. Who hasn't felt it?

SERVANT. You love your sweetheart, don't you?

BRIDE. I love him.

SERVANT. Yes, yes. I'm sure you do.

BRIDE. But this is a very serious step.

SERVANT. You've got to take it.

BRIDE. I've already given my word.

SERVANT. I'll put on the wreath.

BRIDE. [*She sits down.*] Hurry. They should be arriving by now.

SERVANT. They've already been at least two hours on the way.

BRIDE. How far is it from here to the church?

SERVANT. Five leagues by the stream, but twice that by the road. [*The* BRIDE *rises and* THE SERVANT *grows excited as she looks at her.*]

SERVANT. Awake, O Bride, awaken,
On your wedding morning waken!
The world's rivers may all
Bear along your bridal Crown!

BRIDE. [*Smiling.*] Come now.

SERVANT. [*Enthusiastically kissing her and dancing around her.*] Awake,
with the fresh bouquet
of flowering laurel.
Awake,
by the trunk and branch
of the laurels!

[*The banging of the front door latch is heard.*]

BRIDE. Open the door! That must be the first guests. [*She leaves. The* SERVANT *opens the door.*]

SERVANT. [*In astonishment.*] You!

LEONARDO. Yes, me. Good morning.

SERVANT. The first one!

LEONARDO. Wasn't I invited?

SERVANT. Yes.

LEONARDO. That's why I'm here.

SERVANT. Where's your wife?

LEONARDO. I came on my horse. She's coming by the road.

SERVANT. Didn't you meet anyone?

LEONARDO. I *passed* them on my horse.

SERVANT. You're going to kill that horse with so much racing.

LEONARDO. When he dies, he's dead! [*Pause.*]

SERVANT. Sit down. Nobody's up yet.

LEONARDO. Where's the bride?

SERVANT. I'm just on my way to dress her.

LEONARDO. The bride! She ought to be happy!

SERVANT. [*Changing the subject.*] How's the baby?

LEONARDO. What baby?

SERVANT. Your son.

LEONARDO. [*Remembering, as though in a dream.*] Ah!

SERVANT. Are they bringing him?

LEONARDO. No.

[*Pause.* VOICES *sing distantly.*]

VOICES. Awake, O Bride, awaken,
On your wedding morning waken!

LEONARDO. Awake, O Bride, awaken,
On your wedding morning waken!

SERVANT. It's the guests. They're still quite a way off.

LEONARDO. The bride's going to wear a big wreath, isn't she? But it ought not to be so large. One a little smaller would look better on her. Has the groom already brought her the orange blossom that must be worn on the breast?

BRIDE. [*Appearing, still in petticoats and wearing the wreath.*] He brought it.

SERVANT. [*Sternly.*] Don't come out like that.

BRIDE. What does it matter? [*Seriously.*] Why do you ask if they brought the orange blossom? Do you have something in mind?

LEONARDO. Nothing. What would I have in mind? [*Drawing near her.*] You, you know me; you know I don't. Tell me so. What have I ever meant to you? Open your memory, refresh it. But two oxen and an ugly little hut are almost nothing. That's the thorn.

BRIDE. What have you come here to do?

LEONARDO. To see your wedding.

BRIDE. Just as I saw yours!

LEONARDO. Tied up by you, done with your two hands. Oh, they can kill me but they can't spit on me. But even money, which shines so much, spits sometimes.

BRIDE. Liar!

LEONARDO. I don't want to talk. I'm hot-blooded and I don't want to shout so all these hills will hear me.

BRIDE. My shouts would be louder.

SERVANT. You'll have to stop talking like this. [*To the* BRIDE.] You don't have to talk about what's past. [*The* SERVANT *looks around uneasily at the doors.*]

BRIDE. She's right. I shouldn't even talk to you. But it offends me to the soul that you come here to watch me, and spy on my wedding, and ask about the orange blossom with something on your mind. Go and wait for your wife at the door.

LEONARDO. But, can't you and I even talk?

SERVANT. [*With rage.*] No! No, you can't talk.

LEONARDO. Ever since I got married I've been thinking night and day about whose fault it was, and every time I think about it, out comes a new fault to eat up the old one; but always there's a fault left!

BRIDE. A man with a horse knows a lot of things and can do a lot to ride rough-shod over a girl stuck out in the desert. But I have my pride. And that's why

I'm getting married. I'll lock myself in with my husband and then I'll have to love him above everyone else.

LEONARDO. Pride won't help you a bit. [*He draws near to her.*]

BRIDE. Don't come near me!

LEONARDO. To burn with desire and keep quiet about it is the greatest punishment we can bring on ourselves. What good was pride to me—and not seeing you, and letting you lie awake night after night? No good! It only served to bring the fire down on me! You think that time heals and walls hide things, but it isn't true, it isn't true! When things get that deep inside you there isn't anybody can change them.

BRIDE. [*Trembling.*] I can't listen to you. I can't listen to your voice. It's as though I'd drunk a bottle of anise and fallen asleep wrapped in a quilt of roses. It pulls me along, and I know I'm drowning—but I go on down.

SERVANT. [*Seizing* LEONARDO *by the lapels.*] You've got to go right now!

LEONARDO. This is the last time I'll ever talk to her. Don't you be afraid of anything.

BRIDE. And I know I'm crazy and I know my breast rots with longing; but here I am—calmed by hearing him, by just seeing him move his arms.

LEONARDO. I'd never be at peace if I didn't tell you these things. I got married. Now you get married.

SERVANT. But she *is* getting married!

[*Voices are heard singing, nearer.*]

VOICES. Awake, O Bride, awaken,
On your wedding morning waken!

BRIDE. Awake, O Bride, awaken, [*She goes out, running toward her room.*]

SERVANT. The people are here now. [*To* LEONARDO.] Don't you come near her again.

LEONARDO. Don't worry. [*He goes out to the left. Day begins to break.*]

FIRST GIRL. [*Entering.*] Awake, O Bride, awaken,
the morning you're to marry;
sing round and dance round;
balconies a wreath must carry.

VOICES. Bride, awaken!

SERVANT. [*Creating enthusiasm.*]
Awake,

with the green bouquet
of love in flower.
Awake,
by the trunk and the branch
of the laurels!

SECOND GIRL. [*Entering.*] Awake,
with her long hair,
snowy sleeping gown,
patent leather boots with silver—
her forehead jasmines crown.

SERVANT. Oh, shepherdess,
the moon begins to shine!

FIRST GIRL. Oh, gallant,
leave your hat beneath the vine!

FIRST YOUNG MAN. [*Entering, holding his hat on high.*] Bride, awaken,
for over the fields
the wedding draws nigh
with trays heaped with dahlias
and cakes piled high.

VOICES. Bride, awaken!

SECOND GIRL. The bride
has set her white wreath in place
and the groom
ties it on with a golden lace.

SERVANT. By the orange tree,
sleepless the bride will be.

THIRD GIRL. [*Entering.*] By the citron
vine,
gifts from the groom will shine.

[*Three* GUESTS *come in.*]

FIRST YOUTH. Dove, awaken!
In the dawn
shadowy bells are shaken.

GUEST. The bride, the white bride
today a maiden,
tomorrow a wife.

FIRST GIRL. Dark one, come down
trailing the train of your silken gown.

GUEST. Little dark one, come down,
cold morning wears a dewy crown.

FIRST GUEST. Awaken, wife, awake,
orange blossoms the breezes shake.

SERVANT. A tree I would embroider her
with garnet sashes wound,
And on each sash a cupid,
with "Long Live" all around.

VOICES. Bride, awaken.

FIRST YOUTH. The morning you're to
marry!

GUEST. The morning you're to marry
how elegant you'll seem;
worthy, mountain flower,
of a captain's dream.

FATHER. [*Entering.*] A captain's wife
the groom will marry.
He comes with his oxen the treasure to
carry!
THIRD GIRL. The groom
is like a flower of gold.
When he walks,
blossoms at his feet unfold.
SERVANT. Oh, my lucky girl!
SECOND YOUTH. Bride, awaken.
SERVANT. Oh, my elegant girl!
FIRST GIRL. Through the windows
hear the wedding shout.
SECOND GIRL. Let the bride come out.
FIRST GIRL. Come out, come out!
SERVANT. Let the bells
ring and ring out clear!
FIRST YOUTH. For here she comes!
For now she's near!
SERVANT. Like a bull, the wedding
is arising here!

[*The* BRIDE *appears. She wears a black
dress in the style of 1900, with a bustle
and large train covered with pleated
gauzes and heavy laces. Upon her hair,
brushed in a wave over her forehead, she
wears an orange blossom wreath. Guitars
sound. The* GIRLS *kiss the* BRIDE.]

THIRD GIRL. What scent did you put on
your hair?
BRIDE. [*Laughing.*] None at all.
SECOND GIRL. [*Looking at her dress.*]
This cloth is what you can't get.
FIRST YOUTH. Here's the groom!
BRIDEGROOM. Salud!
FIRST GIRL. [*Putting a flower behind his
ear.*] The groom
is like a flower of gold.
SECOND GIRL. Quiet breezes
from his eyes unfold.

[*The* GROOM *goes to the* BRIDE.]

BRIDE. Why did you put on those
shoes?
BRIDEGROOM. They're gayer than the
black ones.
LEONARDO'S WIFE. [*Entering and kissing the* BRIDE.] Salud! [*They all speak
excitedly.*]
LEONARDO. [*Entering as one who performs a duty.*] The morning you're
to marry
We give you a wreath to wear.
LEONARDO'S WIFE. So the fields may be
made happy

with the dew dropped from your hair!
MOTHER. [*To the* FATHER.] Are those
people here, too?
FATHER. They're part of the family.
Today is a day of forgiveness!
MOTHER. I'll put up with it, but I don't
forgive.
BRIDEGROOM. With your wreath, it's a
joy to look at you!
BRIDE. Let's go to the church quickly.
BRIDEGROOM. Are you in a hurry?
BRIDE. Yes. I want to be your wife
right now so that I can be with you
alone, not hearing any voice but yours.
BRIDEGROOM. That's what I want!
BRIDE. And not seeing any eyes but
yours. And for you to hug me so hard,
that even though my dead mother should
call me, I wouldn't be able to draw away
from you.
BRIDEGROOM. My arms are strong. I'll
hug you for forty years without stopping.
BRIDE. [*Taking his arm, dramatically.*]
Forever!
FATHER. Quick now! Round up the
teams and carts! The sun's already out.
MOTHER. And go along carefully! Let's
hope nothing goes wrong. [*The great
door in the background opens.*]
SERVANT. [*Weeping.*] As you set out
from your house,
oh, maiden white,
remember you leave shining
with a star's light.
FIRST GIRL. Clean of body, clean of
clothes
from her home to church she goes. [*They
start leaving.*]
SECOND GIRL. Now you leave your home
for the church!
SERVANT. The wind sets flowers
on the sands.
THIRD GIRL. Ah, the white maid!
SERVANT. Dark winds are the lace
of her mantilla.

[*They leave. Guitars, castanets and
tambourines are heard.* LEONARDO *and his*
WIFE *are left alone.*]

WIFE. Let's go.
LEONARDO. Where?
WIFE. To the church. But not on your
horse. You're coming with me.
LEONARDO. In the cart?

WIFE. Is there anything else?

LEONARDO. I'm not the kind of man to ride in a cart.

WIFE. Nor I the wife to go to a wedding without her husband. I can't stand any more of this!

LEONARDO. Neither can I!

WIFE. And why do you look at me that way? With a thorn in each eye.

LEONARDO. Let's go!

WIFE. I don't know what's happening. But I think, and I don't want to think. One thing I do know. I'm already cast off by you. But I have a son. And another coming. And so it goes. My mother's fate was the same. Well, I'm not moving from here.

[VOICES *outside.*]

VOICES. As you set out from your home and to the church go remember you leave shining with a star's glow.

WIFE. [*Weeping.*] Remember you leave shining
with a star's glow!
I left my house like that too. They could have stuffed the whole countryside in my mouth. I was that trusting.

LEONARDO. [*Rising.*] Let's go!

WIFE. But you with me!

LEONARDO. Yes. [*Pause.*] Start moving! [*They leave.*]

VOICES. As you set out from your home and to the church go, remember you leave shining with a star's glow.

SLOW CURTAIN

2.

The exterior of the BRIDE's Cave Home, in white gray and cold blue tones. Large cactus trees. Shadowy and silver tones. Panoramas of light tan tablelands, everything hard like a landscape in popular ceramics.

SERVANT. [*Arranging glasses and trays on a table.*] A-turning,
the wheel was a-turning
and the water was flowing,
for the wedding night comes.
May the branches part
and the moon be arrayed
at her white balcony rail.
[*In a loud voice.*] Set out the tablecloths!
[*In a pathetic voice.*] A-singing,
bride and groom were singing
and the water was flowing
for their wedding night comes.
Oh, rime-frost, flash!—
and almonds bitter
fill with honey!
[*In a loud voice.*] Get the wine ready!
[*In a poetic tone.*] Elegant girl,
most elegant in the world,
see the way the water is flowing,
for your wedding night comes.
Hold your skirts close in
under the bridegroom's wing
and never leave your house,
for the Bridegroom is a dove
with his breast a firebrand
and the fields wait for the whisper
of spurting blood.
A-turning
the wheel was a-turning
and the water was flowing
and your wedding night comes.
Oh, water, sparkle!

MOTHER. [*Entering.*] At last.

FATHER. Are we the first ones?

SERVANT. No. Leonardo and his wife arrived a while ago. They drove like demons. His wife got here dead with fright. They made the trip as though they'd come on horseback.

FATHER. That one's looking for trouble. He's not of good blood.

MOTHER. What blood would you expect him to have? His whole family's blood. It comes down from his great grandfather, who started in killing, and it goes on down through the whole evil breed of knife wielding and false smiling men.

FATHER. Let's leave it at that!

SERVANT. But how can she leave it at that?

MOTHER. It hurts me to the tips of my veins. On the forehead of all of them I see only the hand with which they killed what was mine. Can you really see me? Don't I seem mad to you? Well, it's the madness of not having shrieked out all my breast needs to. Always in my breast there's a shriek standing tiptoe that I have to beat down and hold in under my shawls. But the dead are carried off and one has to keep still. And then, people find fault. [*She removes her shawl.*]

FATHER. Today's not the day for you to be remembering these things.

MOTHER. When the talk turns on it, I have to speak. And more so today. Because today I'm left alone in my house.

FATHER. But with the expectation of having someone with you.

MOTHER. That's my hope: grandchildren. [*They sit down.*]

FATHER. I want them to have a lot of them. This land needs hands that aren't hired. There's a battle to be waged against weeds, the thistles, the big rocks that come from one doesn't know where. And those hands have to be the owner's, who chastises and dominates, who makes the seeds grow. Lots of sons are needed.

MOTHER. And some daughters! Men are like the wind! They're forced to handle weapons. Girls never go out into the street.

FATHER. [*Happily.*] I think they'll have both.

MOTHER. My son will cover her well. He's of good seed. His father could have had many sons with me.

FATHER. What I'd like is to have all this happen in a day. So that right away they'd have two or three boys.

MOTHER. But it's not like that. It takes a long time. That's why it's so terrible to see one's own blood spilled out on the ground. A fountain that spurts for a minute, but costs us years. When I got to my son, he lay fallen in the middle of the street. I wet my hands with his blood and licked them with my tongue—because it was my blood. You don't know what that's like. In a glass and topaze shrine I'd put the earth moistened by his blood.

FATHER. Now you must hope. My daughter is wide-hipped and your son is strong.

MOTHER. That's why I'm hoping. [*They rise.*]

FATHER. Get the wheat trays ready!

SERVANT. They're all ready.

LEONARDO'S WIFE. [*Entering.*] May it be for the best!

MOTHER. Thank you.

LEONARDO. Is there going to be a celebration?

FATHER. A small one. People can't stay long.

SERVANT. Here they are!

[*Guests begin entering in gay groups. The* BRIDE *and* GROOM *come in arm-in-arm.* LEONARDO *leaves.*]

BRIDEGROOM. There's never been a wedding with so many people!

BRIDE. [*Sullen.*] Never.

FATHER. It was brilliant.

MOTHER. Whole branches of families came.

BRIDEGROOM. People who never went out of the house.

MOTHER. Your father sowed well, and now you're reaping it.

BRIDEGROOM. There were cousins of mine whom I no longer knew.

MOTHER. All the people from the seacoast.

BRIDEGROOM. [*Happily.*] They were frightened of the horses. [*They talk.*]

MOTHER. [*To the* BRIDE.] What are you thinking about?

BRIDE. I'm not thinking about anything.

MOTHER. Your blessings weigh heavily. [*Guitars are heard.*]

BRIDE. Like lead.

MOTHER. [*Stern.*] But they shouldn't weigh so. Happy as a dove you ought to be.

BRIDE. Are you staying here tonight?

MOTHER. No. My house is empty.

BRIDE. You ought to stay!

FATHER. [*To the* MOTHER.] Look at the dance they're forming. Dances of the far away seashore.

[LEONARDO *enters and sits down. His* WIFE *stands rigidly behind him.*]

MOTHER. They're my husband's cousins. Stiff as stones at dancing.

FATHER. It makes me happy to watch them. What a change for this house! [*He leaves.*]

BRIDEGROOM. [*To the* BRIDE.] Did you like the orange blossom?

BRIDE. [*Looking at him fixedly.*] Yes.

BRIDEGROOM. It's all of wax. It will last forever. I'd like you to have had them all over your dress.

BRIDE. No need of that. [LEONARDO *goes off to the right.*]

FIRST GIRL. Let's go and take out your pins.

BRIDE. [*To the* GROOM.] I'll be right back.

LEONARDO'S WIFE. I hope you'll be happy with my cousin!

BRIDEGROOM. I'm sure I will.

LEONARDO'S WIFE. The two of you here; never going out; building a home. I wish I could live far away like this, too!

BRIDEGROOM. Why don't you buy land? The mountainside is cheap and children grow up better.

LEONARDO'S WIFE. We don't have any money. And at the rate we're going . . . !

BRIDEGROOM. Your husband is a good worker.

LEONARDO'S WIFE. Yes, but he likes to fly around too much; from one thing to another. He's not a patient man.

SERVANT. Aren't you having anything? I'm going to wrap up some wine cakes for your mother. She likes them so much.

BRIDEGROOM. Put up three dozen for her.

LEONARDO'S WIFE. No, no. A half-dozen's enough for her!

BRIDEGROOM. But today's a day!

LEONARDO'S WIFE. [*To the* SERVANT.] Where's Leonardo?

BRIDEGROOM. He must be with the guests.

LEONARDO'S WIFE. I'm going to go see. [*She leaves.*]

SERVANT. [*Looking off at the dance.*] That's beautiful there.

BRIDEGROOM. Aren't you dancing?

SERVANT. No one will ask me.

[*Two* GIRLS *pass across the back of the stage; during this whole scene the background should be an animated crossing of figures.*]

BRIDEGROOM. [*Happily.*] They just don't know anything. Lively old girls like you dance better than the young ones.

SERVANT. Well! Are you tossing me a compliment, boy? What a family yours is! Men among men! As a little girl I saw your grandfather's wedding. What a figure! It seemed as if a mountain were getting married.

BRIDEGROOM. I'm not as tall.

SERVANT. But there's the same twinkle in your eye. Where's the girl?

BRIDEGROOM. Taking off her wreath.

SERVANT. Ah! Look. For midnight, since you won't be sleeping, I have prepared ham for you, and some large glasses of old wine. On the lower shelf of the cupboard. In case you need it.

BRIDEGROOM. [*Smiling.*] I won't be eating at midnight.

SERVANT. [*Slyly.*] If not you, maybe the bride. [*She leaves.*]

FIRST YOUTH. [*Entering.*] You've got to come have a drink with us!

BRIDEGROOM. I'm waiting for the bride.

SECOND YOUTH. You'll have her at dawn!

FIRST YOUTH. That's when it's best!

SECOND YOUTH. Just for a minute.

BRIDEGROOM. Let's go.

[*They leave. Great excitement is heard. The* BRIDE *enters. From the opposite side two* GIRLS *come running to meet her.*]

FIRST GIRL. To whom did you give the first pin; me or this one?

BRIDE. I don't remember.

FIRST GIRL. To me, you gave it to me here.

SECOND GIRL. To me, in front of the altar.

BRIDE. [*Uneasily, with a great inner struggle.*] I don't know anything about it.

FIRST GIRL. It's just that I wish you'd . . .

BRIDE. [*Interrupting.*] Nor do I care. I have a lot to think about.

SECOND GIRL. Your pardon.

[LEONARDO *crosses at the rear of the stage.*]

BRIDE. [*She sees* LEONARDO.] And this is an upsetting time.

FIRST GIRL. We wouldn't know anything about that!

BRIDE. You'll know about it when your time comes. This step is a very hard one to take.

FIRST GIRL. Has she offended you?

BRIDE. No. You must pardon me.

SECOND GIRL. What for? But *both* the pins are good for getting married, aren't they?

BRIDE. Both of them.

FIRST GIRL. Maybe now one will get married before the other.

BRIDE. Are you so eager?

SECOND GIRL. [*Shyly.*] Yes.

BRIDE. Why?

FIRST GIRL. Well . . . [*She embraces the* SECOND GIRL. *Both go running off.*]

[*The* GROOM *comes in very slowly and embraces the* BRIDE *from behind.*]

BRIDE. [*In sudden fright.*] Let go of me!

BRIDEGROOM. Are you frightened of me?

BRIDE. Ay-y-y! It's you?

BRIDEGROOM. Who else would it be? [*Pause.*] Your father or me.

BRIDE. That's true!

BRIDEGROOM. Of course, your father would have hugged you more gently.

BRIDE. [*Darkly.*] Of course!

BRIDEGROOM. [*Embracing her strongly and a little bit brusquely.*] Because he's old.

BRIDE. [*Curtly.*] Let me go!

BRIDEGROOM. Why? [*He lets her go.*]

BRIDE. Well . . . the people. They can see us.

[*The* SERVANT *crosses at the back of the stage again without looking at the* BRIDE *and* BRIDEGROOM.]

BRIDEGROOM. What of it? It's consecrated now.

BRIDE. Yes, but let me be . . . Later.

BRIDEGROOM. What's the matter with you? You look frightened!

BRIDE. I'm all right. Don't go. [LEONARDO'S WIFE *enters.*]

LEONARDO'S WIFE. I don't mean to intrude . . .

BRIDEGROOM. What is it?

LEONARDO'S WIFE. Did my husband come through here?

BRIDEGROOM. No.

LEONARDO'S WIFE. Because I can't find him, and his horse isn't in the stable either.

BRIDEGROOM. [*Happily.*] He must be out racing it. [*The* WIFE *leaves, troubled. The* SERVANT *enters.*]

SERVANT. Aren't you two proud and happy with so many good wishes?

BRIDEGROOM. I wish it were over with. The bride is a little tired.

SERVANT. That's no way to act, child.

BRIDE. It's as though I'd been struck on the head.

SERVANT. A bride from these mountains must be strong. [*To the* GROOM.] You're the only one who can cure her, because she's yours. [*She goes running off.*]

BRIDEGROOM. [*Embracing the* BRIDE.] Let's go dance a little. [*He kisses her.*]

BRIDE. [*Worried.*] No. I'd like to stretch out on my bed a little.

BRIDEGROOM. I'll keep you company.

BRIDE. Never! With all these people here? What would they say? Let me be quiet for a moment.

BRIDEGROOM. Whatever you say! But don't be like that tonight!

BRIDE. [*At the door.*] I'll be better tonight.

BRIDEGROOM. That's what I want. [*The* MOTHER *appears.*]

MOTHER. Son.

BRIDEGROOM. Where've you been?

MOTHER. Out there—in all that noise. Are you happy?

BRIDEGROOM. Yes.

MOTHER. Where's your wife?

BRIDEGROOM. Resting a little. It's a bad day for brides!

MOTHER. A bad day? The only good one. To me it was like coming into my own. [*The* SERVANT *enters and goes toward the* BRIDE's *room.*] Like the breaking of new ground; the planting of new trees.

BRIDEGROOM. Are you going to leave?

MOTHER. Yes. I ought to be at home.

BRIDEGROOM. Alone.

MOTHER. Not alone. For my head is full of things: of men, and fights.

BRIDEGROOM. But now the fights are no longer fights. [*The* SERVANT *enters quickly; she disappears at the rear of the stage, running.*]

MOTHER. While you live, you have to fight.

BRIDEGROOM. I'll always obey you!

MOTHER. Try to be loving with your wife, and if you see she's acting foolish or touchy, caress her in a way that will hurt her a little: a strong hug, a bite and then a soft kiss. Not so she'll be angry, but just so she'll feel you're the man, the boss, the one who gives orders. I learned that from your father. And since you don't have him, I have to be the one to tell you about these strong defenses.

BRIDEGROOM. I'll always do as you say.

FATHER. [*Entering.*] Where's my daughter?

BRIDEGROOM. She's inside. [*The* FATHER *goes to look for her.*]

FIRST GIRL. Get the bride and groom! We're going to dance a round!

FIRST YOUTH. [*To the* BRIDEGROOM.] You're going to lead it.

FATHER. [*Entering.*] She's not there.

BRIDEGROOM. No?

FATHER. She must have gone up to the railing.

BRIDEGROOM. I'll go see! [*He leaves. A hubbub of excitement and guitars is heard.*]

FIRST GIRL. They've started it already! [*She leaves.*]

BRIDEGROOM. [*Entering.*] She isn't there.

MOTHER. [*Uneasily.*] Isn't she?

FATHER. But where could she have gone?

SERVANT. [*Entering.*] But where's the girl, where is she?

MOTHER. [*Seriously.*] That we don't know.

[*The* BRIDEGROOM *leaves. Three guests enter.*]

FATHER. [*Dramatically.*] But, isn't she in the dance?

SERVANT. She's not in the dance.

FATHER. [*With a start.*] There are a lot of people. Go look!

SERVANT. I've already looked.

FATHER. [*Tragically.*] Then where is she?

BRIDEGROOM. [*Entering.*] Nowhere. Not anywhere.

MOTHER. [*To the* FATHER.] What does this mean? Where is your daughter? [LEONARDO'S WIFE *enters.*]

LEONARDO'S WIFE. They've run away! They've run away! She and Leonardo. On the horse. With their arms around each other, they rode off like a shooting star!

FATHER. That's not true! Not my daughter!

MOTHER. Yes, your daughter! Spawn of a wicked mother, and he, he too. But now she's my son's wife!

BRIDEGROOM. [*Entering.*] Let's go after them! Who has a horse?

MOTHER. Who has a horse? Right away! Who has a horse? I'll give him all I have—my eyes, my tongue even. . . .

VOICE. Here's one.

MOTHER. [*To the* SON.] Go! After them! [*He leaves with two young men.*] No. Don't go. Those people kill quickly and well . . . but yes, run, and I'll follow!

FATHER. It couldn't be my daughter. Perhaps she's thrown herself in the well.

MOTHER. Decent women throw themselves in water; not that one! But now she's my son's wife. Two groups. There are two groups here. [*They all enter.*] My family and yours. Everyone set out from here. Shake the dust from your heels! We'll go help my son. [*The people separate into two groups.*] For he has his family: his cousins from the sea, and all who came from inland. Out of here! On all roads. The hour of blood has come again. Two groups! You with yours and I with mine. After them! After them!

CURTAIN

ACT THREE

1.

A forest. It is nighttime. Great moist tree trunks. A dark atmosphere. Two violins are heard. Three WOODCUTTERS enter.

FIRST WOODCUTTER. And have they found them?

SECOND WOODCUTTER. No. But they're looking for them everywhere.

THIRD WOODCUTTER. They'll find them.

SECOND WOODCUTTER. Sh-h-h!

THIRD WOODCUTTER. What?

SECOND WOODCUTTER. They seem to be coming closer on all the roads at once.

FIRST WOODCUTTER. When the moon comes out they'll see them.

SECOND WOODCUTTER. They ought to let them go.

FIRST WOODCUTTER. The world is wide. Everybody can live in it.

THIRD WOODCUTTER. But they'll kill them.

SECOND WOODCUTTER. You have to follow your passion. They did right to run away.

FIRST WOODCUTTER. They were deceiving themselves but at the last blood was stronger.

THIRD WOODCUTTER. Blood!

FIRST WOODCUTTER. You have to follow the path of your blood.

SECOND WOODCUTTER. But blood that sees the light of day is drunk up by the earth.

FIRST WOODCUTTER. What of it? Better dead with the blood drained away than alive with it rotting.

THIRD WOODCUTTER. Hush!

FIRST WOODCUTTER. What? Do you hear something?

THIRD WOODCUTTER. I hear the crickets, the frogs, the night's ambush.

FIRST WOODCUTTER. But not the horse.

THIRD WOODCUTTER. No.

FIRST WOODCUTTER. By now he must be loving her.

SECOND WOODCUTTER. Her body for him; his body for her.

THIRD WOODCUTTER. They'll find them and they'll kill them.

FIRST WOODCUTTER. But by then they'll have mingled their bloods. They'll be like two empty jars, like two dry arroyos.

SECOND WOODCUTTER. There are many clouds and it would be easy for the moon not to come out.

THIRD WOODCUTTER. The bridegroom will find them with or without the moon. I saw him set out. Like a raging star. His face the color of ashes. He looked the fate of all his clan.

FIRST WOODCUTTER. His clan of dead men lying in the middle of the street.

SECOND WOODCUTTER. There you have it!

THIRD WOODCUTTER. You think they'll be able to break through the circle?

SECOND WOODCUTTER. It's hard to. There are knives and guns for ten leagues 'round.

THIRD WOODCUTTER. He's riding a good horse.

SECOND WOODCUTTER. But he's carrying a woman.

FIRST WOODCUTTER. We're close by now.

SECOND WOODCUTTER. A tree with forty branches. We'll soon cut it down.

THIRD WOODCUTTER. The moon's coming out now. Let's hurry. [*From the left shines a brightness.*]

FIRST WOODCUTTER. O rising moon! Moon among the great leaves.

SECOND WOODCUTTER. Cover the blood with jasmines!

FIRST WOODCUTTER. O lonely moon! Moon among the great leaves.

SECOND WOODCUTTER. Silver on the bride's face.

THIRD WOODCUTTER. O evil moon! Leave for their love a branch in shadow.

FIRST WOODCUTTER. O sorrowing moon! Leave for their love a branch in shadow.

[*They go out. The* MOON *appears through the shining brightness at the left. The* MOON *is a young woodcutter with a white face. The stage takes on an intense blue radiance.*]

MOON. Round swan in the river
and a cathedral's eye,
false dawn on the leaves,
they'll not escape; these things am I!
Who is hiding? And who sobs
in the thornbrakes of the valley?
The moon sets a knife
abandoned in the air
which being a leaden threat
yearns to be blood's pain.
Let me in! I come freezing
down to walls and windows!
Open roofs, open breasts
where I may warm myself!
I'm cold! My ashes
of somnolent metals
seek the fire's crest
on mountains and streets.
But the snow carries me

upon its mottled back
and pools soak me
in their water, hard and cold.
But this night there will be
red blood for my cheeks,
and for the reeds that cluster
at the wide feet of the wind.
Let there be neither shadow nor bower,
and then they can't get away!
O let me enter a breast
where I may get warm!
A heart for me!
Warm! That will spurt
over the mountains of my chest;
let me come in, oh let me!
    [*To the branches.*] I want no shadows.
    My rays
must get in everywhere,
even among the dark trunks I want
the whisper of gleaming lights,
so that this night there will be
sweet blood for my cheeks,
and for the reeds that cluster
at the wide feet of the wind.
Who is hiding? Out, I say!
No! They will not get away!
I will light up the horse
with a fever bright as diamonds.

[*He disappears among the trunks, and the stage goes back to its dark lighting. An old woman comes out completely covered by thin green cloth. She is barefooted. Her face can barely be seen among the folds. This character does not appear in the cast.*]

BEGGAR WOMAN. That moon's going
away, just when they's near.
They won't get past here. The river's
    whisper
and the whispering tree trunks will muffle
the torn flight of their shrieks.
It has to be here, and soon. I'm worn out.
The coffins are ready, and white sheets
wait on the floor of the bedroom
for heavy bodies with torn throats.
Let not one bird awake, let the breeze,
gathering their moans in her skirt,
fly with them over black tree tops
or bury them in soft mud.
    [*Impatiently.*] Oh, that moon! That
moon!

[*The* MOON *appears. The intense blue light returns.*]

MOON. They're coming. One band

through the ravine and the other along
the river. I'm going to light up the boulders. What do you need?
BEGGAR WOMAN. Nothing.
MOON. The wind blows hard now,
with a double edge.
BEGGAR WOMAN. Light up the waistcoat and open the buttons; the knives will
know the path after that.
MOON. But let them be a long time
    a-dying. So the blood
will slide its delicate hissing between my
    fingers.
Look how my ashen valleys already are
    waking
in longing for this fountain of shuddering gushes!
BEGGAR WOMAN. Let's not let them get
past the arroyo. Silence!
MOON. There they come! [*He goes.
The stage is left dark.*]
BEGGAR WOMAN. Quick! Lots of light!
Do you hear me? They can't get away!
[*The* BRIDEGROOM *and the* FIRST YOUTH
enter. The BEGGAR WOMAN *sits down and
covers herself with her cloak.*]
BRIDEGROOM. This way.
FIRST YOUTH. You won't find them.
BRIDEGROOM. [*Angrily.*] Yes, I'll find
them.
FIRST YOUTH. I think they've taken another path.
BRIDEGROOM. No. Just a moment ago I
felt the galloping.
FIRST YOUTH. It could have been another horse.
BRIDEGROOM. [*Intensely.*] Listen to me.
There's only one horse in the whole
world, and this one's it. Can't you understand that? If you're going to follow me,
follow me without talking.
FIRST YOUTH. It's only that I want
to . . .
BRIDEGROOM. Be quiet. I'm sure of meeting them there. Do you see this arm?
Well, it's not my arm. It's my brother's
arm, and my father's, and that of all the
dead ones in my family. And it has so
much strength that it can pull this tree
up by the roots, if it wants to. And let's
move on, because here I feel the clenched
teeth of all my people in me so that I
can't breathe easily.
BEGGAR WOMAN. [*Whining.*] Ay-y-y!

FIRST YOUTH. Did you hear that?

BRIDEGROOM. You go that way and then circle back.

FIRST YOUTH. This is a hunt.

BRIDEGROOM. A hunt. The greatest hunt there is.

[*The* YOUTH *goes off. The* BRIDEGROOM *goes rapidly to the left and stumbles over* THE BEGGAR WOMAN, DEATH.]

BEGGAR WOMAN. Ay-y-y!

BRIDEGROOM. What do you want?

BEGGAR WOMAN. I'm cold.

BRIDEGROOM. Which way are you going?

BEGGAR WOMAN. [*Always whining like a beggar.*] Over there, far away . . .

BRIDEGROOM. Where are you from?

BEGGAR WOMAN. Over there . . . very far away.

BRIDEGROOM. Have you seen a man and a woman running away on a horse?

BEGGAR WOMAN. [*Awakening.*] Wait a minute . . . [*She looks at him.*] Handsome young man. [*She rises.*] But you'd be much handsomer sleeping.

BRIDEGROOM. Tell me; answer me. Did you see them?

BEGGAR WOMAN. Wait a minute . . . What broad shoulders! How would you like to be laid out on them and not have to walk on the soles of your feet which are so small?

BRIDEGROOM. [*Shaking her.*] I asked you if you saw them! Have they passed through here?

BEGGAR WOMAN. [*Energetically.*] No. They haven't passed; but they're coming from the hill. Don't you hear them?

BRIDEGROOM. No.

BEGGAR WOMAN. Do you know the road?

BRIDEGROOM. I'll go, whatever it's like!

BEGGAR WOMAN. I'll go along with you. I know this country.

BRIDEGROOM. [*Impatiently.*] Well, let's go! Which way?

BEGGAR WOMAN. [*Dramatically.*] This way!

[*They go rapidly out. Two violins, which represent the forest, are heard distantly. The* WOODCUTTERS *return. They have their axes on their shoulders. They move slowly among the tree trunks.*]

FIRST WOODCUTTER. O rising death!

Death among the great leaves.

SECOND WOODCUTTER. Don't open the gush of blood!

FIRST WOODCUTTER. O lonely death!

Death among the dried leaves.

THIRD WOODCUTTER. Don't lay flowers over the wedding!

SECOND WOODCUTTER. O sad death!

Leave for their love a green branch.

FIRST WOODCUTTER. O evil death!

Leave for their love a branch of green!

[*They go out while they are talking.* LEONARDO *and* THE BRIDE *appear.*]

LEONARDO. Hush!

BRIDE. From here I'll go on alone.

You go now! I want you to turn back.

LEONARDO. Hush, I said!

BRIDE. With your teeth, with your hands, anyway you can,

take from my clean throat

the metal of this chain,

and let me live forgotten

back there in my house in the ground.

And if you don't want to kill me

as you would kill a tiny snake,

set in my hands, a bride's hands,

the barrel of your shotgun.

Oh, what lamenting, what fire,

sweeps upward through my head!

What glass splinters are stuck in my tongue!

LEONARDO. We've taken the step now; hush!

because they're close behind us,

and I must take you with me.

BRIDE. Then it must be by force!

LEONARDO. By force? Who was it first went down the stairway?

BRIDE. I went down it.

LEONARDO. And who was it put a new bridle on the horse?

BRIDE. I myself did it. It's true.

LEONARDO. And whose were the hands strapped spurs to my boots?

BRIDE. The same hands, these that are yours,

but which when they see you would like to break the blue branches

and sunder the purl of your veins.

I love you! I love you! But leave me!

For if I were able to kill you

I'd wrap you 'round in a shroud

with the edges bordered in violets.

Oh, what lamenting, what fire,

sweeps upward through my head!

LEONARDO. What glass splinters are
stuck in my tongue!
Because I tried to forget you
and put a wall of stone
between your house and mine.
It's true. You remember?
And when I saw you in the distance
I threw sand in my eyes.
But I was riding a horse
and the horse went straight to your door.
And the silver pins of your wedding
turned my red blood black.
And in me our dream was choking
my flesh with its poisoned weeds.
Oh, it isn't my fault—
the fault is the earth's—
and this fragrance that you exhale
from your breasts and your braids.

BRIDE. Oh, how untrue! I want
from you neither bed nor food,
yet there's not a minute each day
that I don't want to be with you,
because you drag me, and I come,
then you tell me to go back
and I follow you,
like chaff blown on the breeze.
I have left a good, honest man,
and all his people,
with the wedding feast half over
and wearing my bridal wreath.
But you are the one will be punished
and that I don't want to happen.
Leave me alone now! You run away!
There is no one who will defend you.

LEONARDO. The birds of early morning
are calling among the trees.
The night is dying
on the stone's ridge.
Let's go to a hidden corner
where I may love you forever,
for to me the people don't matter,
nor the venom they throw on us. [He
embraces her strongly.]

BRIDE. And I'll sleep at your feet,
to watch over your dreams.
Naked, looking over the fields,
as though I were a bitch.
Because that's what I am! Oh, I look at
you
and your beauty sears me.

LEONARDO. Fire is stirred by fire.
The same tiny flame
will kill two wheat heads together.

Let's go!

BRIDE. Where are you taking me?

LEONARDO. Where they cannot come,
these men who surround us.
Where I can look at you!

BRIDE. [Sarcastically.] Carry me with
you from fair to fair,
a shame to clean women,
so that people will see me
with my wedding sheets
on the breeze like banners.

LEONARDO. I, too, would want to leave
you
if I thought as men should.
But wherever you go, I go.
You're the same. Take a step. Try.
Nails of moonlight have fused
my waist and your chains.

[This whole scene is violent, full of
great sensuality.]

BRIDE. Listen!

LEONARDO. They're coming.

BRIDE.   Run!
It's fitting that I should die here,
with water over my feet,
with thorns upon my head.
And fitting the leaves should mourn me,
a woman lost and virgin.

LEONARDO. Be quiet. Now they're appearing.

BRIDE.   Go now!

LEONARDO. Quiet. Don't let them hear
us. [The BRIDE hesitates.]

BRIDE. Both of us!

LEONARDO. [Embracing her.] Any way
you want!
If they separate us, it will be
because I am dead.

BRIDE.   And I dead too.
[They go out in each other's arms.
The MOON appears very slowly. The
stage takes on a strong blue light. The
two violins are heard. Suddenly two
long, ear-splitting shrieks are heard, and
the music of the two violins is cut short.
At the second shriek the BEGGAR WOMAN
appears and stands with her back to the
audience. She opens her cape and stands
in the center of the stage like a great bird
with immense wings. The MOON halts.
The curtain comes down in absolute silence.]

CURTAIN

2.

The Final Scene.

A white dwelling with arches and thick walls. To the right and left, are white stairs. At the back, a great arch and a wall of the same color. The floor also should be shining white. This simple dwelling should have the monumental feeling of a church. There should not be a single gray nor any shadow, not even what is necessary for perspective.

Two GIRLS *dressed in dark blue are winding a red skein.*

FIRST GIRL. Wool, red wool,
what would you make?
SECOND GIRL. Oh, jasmine for dresses,
fine wool like glass.
At four o'clock born,
at ten o'clock dead.
A thread from this wool yarn,
a chain 'round your feet
a knot that will tighten
the bitter white wreath.
LITTLE GIRL. [*Singing.*] Were you at
the wedding?
FIRST GIRL. No.
LITTLE GIRL. Well, neither was I!
What could have happened
'midst the shoots of the vineyards?
What could have happened
'neath the branch of the olive?
What really happened
that no one came back?
Were you at the wedding?
SECOND GIRL. We told you once, no.
LITTLE GIRL. [*Leaving.*] Well, neither
was I!
SECOND GIRL. Wool, red wool,
what would you sing?
FIRST GIRL. Their wounds turning
waxen
balm-myrtle for pain.
Asleep in the morning,
and watching at night.
LITTLE GIRL. [*In the doorway.*] And
then, the thread stumbled
on the flinty stones,
but mountains, blue mountains,
are letting it pass.
Running, running, running,
and finally to come
to stick in a knife blade,

to take back the bread. [*She goes out.*]
SECOND GIRL. Wool, red wool,
what would you tell?
FIRST GIRL. The lover is silent,
crimson the groom,
at the still shoreline
I saw them laid out. [*She stops and looks
at the skein.*]
LITTLE GIRL. [*Appearing in the doorway.*] Running, running, running,
the thread runs to here.
All covered with clay
I feel them draw near.
Bodies stretched stiffly
in ivory sheets!

[*The* WIFE *and* MOTHER-IN-LAW *of*
LEONARDO *appear. They are anguished.*]

FIRST GIRL. Are they coming yet?
MOTHER-IN-LAW. [*Harshly.*] We don't
know.
SECOND GIRL. What can you tell us
about the wedding?
FIRST GIRL. Yes, tell me.
MOTHER-IN-LAW. [*Curtly.*] Nothing.
LEONARDO'S WIFE. I want to go back and
find out all about it.
MOTHER-IN-LAW. [*Sternly.*] You, back
to your house.
Brave and alone in your house.
To grow old and to weep.
But behind closed doors.
Never again. Neither dead nor alive.
We'll nail up our windows
and let rains and nights
fall on the bitter weeds.
LEONARDO'S WIFE. What could have
happened?
MOTHER-IN-LAW. It doesn't matter
what.
Put a veil over your face.
Your children are yours,
that's all. On the bed
put a cross of ashes
where his pillow was. [*They go out.*]
BEGGAR WOMAN. [*At the door.*] A crust
of bread, little girls.
LITTLE GIRL. Go away! [*The* GIRLS
huddle close together.]
BEGGAR WOMAN. Why?
LITTLE GIRL. Because you whine; go
away!
FIRST GIRL. Child!
BEGGAR WOMAN. I might have asked for
your eyes! A cloud

of birds is following me. Will you have one?

LITTLE GIRL. I want to get away from here!

SECOND GIRL. [*To the* BEGGAR WOMAN.] Don't mind her!

FIRST GIRL. Did you come by the road through the arroyo?

BEGGAR WOMAN. I came that way!

FIRST GIRL. [*Timidly.*] Can I ask you something?

BEGGAR WOMAN. I saw them: they'll be here soon; two torrents
still at last, among the great boulders,
two men at the horse's feet.
Two dead men in the night's splendor.
[*With pleasure.*] Dead, yes, dead.

FIRST GIRL. Hush, old woman, hush!

BEGGAR WOMAN. Crushed flowers for eyes, and their teeth
two fistfuls of hard-frozen snow.
Both of them fell, and the Bride returns
with bloodstains on her skirt and hair.
And they come covered with two sheets
carried on the shoulders of two tall boys.
That's how it was; nothing more. What was fitting.
Over the golden flower, dirty sand. [*She goes. The* GIRLS *bow their heads and start going out rhythmically.*]

FIRST GIRL. Dirty sand.

SECOND GIRL. Over the golden flower.

LITTLE GIRL. Over the golden flower
they're bringing the dead from the arroyo.
Dark the one,
dark the other.
What shadowy nightingale flies and weeps
over the golden flower!
[*She goes. The stage is left empty. The* MOTHER *and a* NEIGHBOR WOMAN *appear. The* NEIGHBOR *is weeping.*]

MOTHER. Hush.

NEIGHBOR. I can't.

MOTHER. Hush, I said. [*At the door.*] Is there nobody here? [*She puts her hands to her forehead.*] My son ought to answer me. But now my son is an armful of shrivelled flowers. My son is a fading voice beyond the mountains now. [*With rage, to the* NEIGHBOR.] Will you shut up? I want no wailing in this house. Your tears are only tears from your eyes, but when

I'm alone mine will come—from the soles of my feet, from my roots—burning more than blood.

NEIGHBOR. You come to my house; don't stay here.

MOTHER. I want to be here. Here. In peace. They're all dead now: and at midnight I'll sleep, sleep without terror of guns or knives. Other mothers will go to their windows, lashed by rain, to watch for their sons' faces. But not I. And of my dreams I'll make a cold ivory dove that will carry camellias of white frost to the graveyard. But no; not graveyard, not graveyard: the couch of earth, the bed that shelters them and rocks them in sky. [*A woman dressed in black enters, goes toward the right, and there kneels. To the* NEIGHBOR.] Take your hands from your face. We have terrible days ahead. I want to see no one. The earth and I. My grief and I. And these four walls. Ay-y-y! Ay-y-y! [*She sits down, overcome.*]

NEIGHBOR. Take pity on yourself!

MOTHER. [*Pushing back her hair.*] I must be calm. [*She sits down.*] Because the neighbor women will come and I don't want them to see me so poor. So poor! A woman without even one son to hold to her lips. [*The* BRIDE *appears. She is without her wreath and wears a black shawl.*]

NEIGHBOR. [*With rage, seeing the* BRIDE.] Where are you going?

BRIDE. I'm coming here.

MOTHER. [*To the* NEIGHBOR.] Who is it?

NEIGHBOR. Don't you recognize her?

MOTHER. That's why I asked who it was. Because I don't want to recognize her, so I won't sink my teeth in her throat. You snake! [*She moves wrathfully on the* BRIDE, *then stops. To the* NEIGHBOR.] Look at her! There she is, and she's crying, while I stand here calmly and don't tear her eyes out. I don't understand myself. Can it be I didn't love my son? But, where's his good name? Where is it now? Where is it? [*She beats the* BRIDE *who drops to the floor.*]

NEIGHBOR. For God's sake! [*She tries to separate them.*]

BRIDE. [*To the* NEIGHBOR.] Let her; I came here so she'd kill me and they'd take me away with them. [*To the* MOTHER.] But not with her hands; with grappling hooks, with a sickle—and with force—until they break on my bones. Let her! I want her to know I'm clean, that I may be crazy, but that they can bury me without a single man ever having seen himself in the whiteness of my breasts.

MOTHER. Shut up, shut up; what do I care about that?

BRIDE. Because I ran away with the other one; I ran away! [*With anguish.*] You would have gone, too. I was a woman burning with desire, full of sores inside and out, and your son was a little bit of water from which I hoped for children, land, health; but the other one was a dark river, choked with brush, that brought near me the undertone of its rushes and its whispered song. And I went along with your son who was like a little boy of cold water—and the other sent against me hundreds of birds who got in my way and left white frost on my wounds, my wounds of a poor withered woman, of a girl caressed by fire. I didn't want to; remember that! I didn't want to. Your son was my destiny and I have not betrayed him, but the other one's arm dragged me along like the pull of the sea, like the head toss of a mule, and he would have dragged me always, always, always—even if I were an old woman and all your son's sons held me by the hair! [*A* NEIGHBOR *enters.*]

MOTHER. She is not to blame; nor am I! [*Sarcastically.*] Who is, then? It's a delicate, lazy, sleepless woman who throws away an orange blossom wreath and goes looking for a piece of bed warmed by another woman!

BRIDE. Be still! Be still! Take your revenge on me; here I am! See how soft my throat is; it would be less work for you than cutting a dahlia in your garden. But never that! Clean, clean as a new-born little girl. And strong enough to prove it to you. Light the fire. Let's stick our hands in; you, for your son, I, for my body. *You'll* draw yours out first. [*Another* NEIGHBOR *enters.*]

MOTHER. But what does your good name matter to me? What does your death matter to me? What does anything about anything matter to me? Bless'ed be the wheat stalks, because my sons are under them; bless'ed be the rain, because it wets the face of the dead. Bless'ed be God, who stretches us out together to rest. [*Another* NEIGHBOR *enters.*]

BRIDE. Let me weep with you.

MOTHER. Weep. But at the door.

[*The* GIRL *enters. The* BRIDE *stays at the door. The* MOTHER *is at the center of the stage.*]

LEONARDO'S WIFE. [*Entering and going to the left.*] He was a beautiful horseman,
now he's a heap of snow.
He rode to fairs and mountains
and women's arms.
Now, the night's dark moss
crowns his forehead.

MOTHER. A sunflower to your mother,
a mirror of the earth.
Let them put on your breast
the cross of bitter rosebay;
and over you a sheet
of shining silk;
between your quiet hands
let water form its lament.

WIFE. Ay-y-y, four gallant boys
come with tired shoulders!

BRIDE. Ay-y-y, four gallant boys
carry death on high!

MOTHER. Neighbors.

LITTLE GIRL. [*At the door.*] They're bringing them now.

MOTHER. It's the same thing.
Always the cross, the cross.

WOMEN. Sweet nails,
cross adored,
sweet name
of Christ our Lord.

BRIDE. May the cross protect both the quick and the dead.

MOTHER. Neighbors: with a knife,
with a little knife,
on their appointed day, between two and three,
these two men killed each other for love.
With a knife,
with a tiny knife
that barely fits the hand,
but that slides in clean
through the astonished flesh

and stops at the place
where trembles, enmeshed,
the dark root of a scream,
  BRIDE. And this is a knife,
a tiny knife
that barely fits the hand;
fish without scales, without river,
so that on their appointed day, between
    two and three,
with this knife,
two men are left stiff.

with their lips turning yellow.
  MOTHER. And it barely fits the hand
but it slides in clean
through the astonished flesh
and stops there, at the place
where trembles enmeshed
the dark root of a scream.
[*The* NEIGHBORS, *kneeling on the floor,
sob.*]

CURTAIN

ARTHUR MILLER: *DEATH OF A SALESMAN*

Unlike the dramas by Sophocles, Shakespeare, and Lorca, Arthur Miller's *Death of a Salesman* is a tragedy set in our own times, played out on our own scene, by characters who, however we regard the quality of their thought, speak in our own language and with our own peculiar accents. In one sense, therefore, we cannot claim that the play is foreign to us. For what we lose of *Oedipus* because we are not Athenians, and of *Othello* because we are not Elizabethans, and of *Blood Wedding* by not being Spaniards, that much, at least, is ours because we are Miller's American contemporaries. Even were we to reject his assumptions and deny his conclusions, we would still know the world Miller creates, because the apartment houses that cut off Willy's horizon cut off our own as well, and the three thousand miles from Brooklyn to San Francisco involve more a change of name and site than of setting.

Centering on the quality of the protagonist, most of the comment about this play has argued the question of whether Willy Loman has sufficient stature to be a tragic hero. There is an irony in this debate over the admission of Willy to the company of Oedipus and Othello: few commentators have recognized the significance of the play's structure, of its use of scenes that embody and, at the same time, illustrate the insubstantiality of the salesman's world of the smile and backslap; for the chosen structure indicates that Willy, though no less heroic—no less committed, that is, to his own dreams—is cast in a different mold than that used for the traditional hero. We begin, therefore, with what is most notable about the structure of the play itself, its treatment of time.

As in all tragedies, we first meet the hero a few moments before his end. But Miller's drama does not rely on the usual compressed expository report to acquaint us with the antecedent action necessary to an understanding of the hero's motives. Partly because the advance of modern psychology has made it easy for us to shift from the present to its root-experience in the past and back again, and partly because an illusion of such movement lies within the technical capacity of the modern stage, Miller has chosen actually to show us the scenes which made up the life that now dissolves before us. These he shows us as they exist in Willy's mind, that is, without any clear distinction as to the particular times at which they happened. Thus we come to witness, and not simply to know by report, the younger life of Willy Loman, who, some thirty-five years before, started his pilgrimage to the grave we now stand beside with his wife Linda, and his boys, Biff and Happy. This treatment of time, by putting emphasis on the earlier scenes, reduces the impact of the final suicide. On the other hand, it serves to raise that suicide to the level of sacrifice by linking it with Willy's early dreams.

Into his visualization of the last forty-eight hours of the hero's life, Miller introduces two other kinds of scenes: those involving guidance from Ben, and those involving the nurture of Biff. The first kind are objectifications of Willy's own insecurity, for Willy bows down to the image of Ben's success, finding in Ben's words—as in those of a Delphic oracle—both a guide for action and a reassurance that his own ideas are right. And the second kind of scene shows us Willy bending his son's knee before the idol of success, teaching him the

490

liturgy of the smile, and making him to believe that over the door of heaven is inscribed: "Enter here only the well-liked." These scenes (and that other visualization of the past, the episode of the Woman in Boston), give dimension to the portrait of the protagonist. Without them, the play's theme-statements would be what they are sometimes unwittingly taken to be: sentimental idealizations of a failure. With them, it becomes clear that Willy's failure stems from the quality of his aspirations, and not of his spirit.

There are two theme-statements in the drama. One is Linda Loman's:

I don't say he's a great man. Willy Loman never made a lot of money. His name was never in the paper. He's not the finest character that ever lived. But he's a human being, and a terrible thing is happening to him. So attention must be paid. He's not to be allowed to fall into his grave like an old dog. Attention, attention must be finally paid to such a person.

The second is the epitaph that Charlie reads over his friend, Willy Loman—salesman, sixty-three, suspected suicide:

Nobody dast blame this man. You don't understand: Willy was a salesman. And for a salesman, there is no rock bottom to the life. He don't put a bolt to a nut, he don't tell you the law or give you medicine. He's a man way out there in the blue.

Now, in the first statement, Linda argues that Willy Loman, because he is a man, must have what all men must have: if his name is not to be written in the permanent records of Man, he must at least be able to hear the voices of his children. This minimal certificate of immortality he must have to keep him from oblivion. But Charlie, on the other hand, speaks of Willie as a salesman, not as a human being. There are men, he says, whose lives are built of necessity on nothing more substantial than the smile and the shine, whose satisfactions are no more enduring than dreams of bigger and still bigger orders. A man such as these cannot be blamed for his action if he chooses to die "dramatically" in a last attempt to gain for himself a more substantial place in the memory of men. Some commentators have in effect combined the two theme-statements, asserting that what Miller intended was an indictment of the American system for ruthlessly discarding its faithful servants. For them, Willy symbolizes the failure of the American capitalist ethos, its basic destruction of the humanity of man.

Each of these interpretations—the wife's, the friend's, and the critical view that combines them—points toward the meaning of the play, but each also raises questions that it leaves unanswered. Can we, for example, accept Linda's demand that "attention be paid," knowing as we do the shallowness of Willy's past? Does not this knowledge degrade him below the level of interest? Plain souls like this salesman are of interest to their families and to God; but we need greatness to inspire us. On the other hand, if Miller's concern lay with the tragedy of a salesman in a capitalist world, why did he not show us at least a successful salesman? Willy succeeds only with his batch of cement; he is a carpenter and a planter. But as a salesman he is a failure. Can he then be a valid symbol in an indictment of the capitalist world? Is he more than a symbol of failure?

These questions emphasize the danger, particularly acute in tragedy, of confusing the poetic statement with the whole meaning of the play; life as revealed in tragedy cannot be so easily summed up in a line or two of dialogue. The keys to meaning, on the contrary, are found in the plot, in the characters, and in the conflict that engages them. The conflict Miller chose to communicate his vision is that between Willy as a salesman and Willy as a man. Such a view of the conflict explains and justifies the author's uses of the past; each of the episodes can now be seen as making the same, insistent point: Willy suffers from his attempt to live by his business ethics. He is content to govern all his relationships, including those with his family, by the same standards that prevail when he is on the road. He cannot distinguish—as we do, and as the play insists we do —between the ethics of business (a little happy cheating now and then) and the sterner ethics of life.

Willy is blind to the fundamental contradiction between his progress as a salesman and his self-realization as a man, and his blindness is almost allegorically reflected in his children. Like Willy, Happy lives the life of the business ethic. Like his father, he fails to understand that the smile is no safe-conduct pass through the jungle. Significantly, he is incapable of fruition; he is a philanderer, and wastes himself in a succession of casual, fruitless unions. He has the smell of women on him, in a play in which men cry out to assert their masculinity. Biff, on the other hand, reflects Willy's discontent. He does not understand what troubles him: who his father is. And the episode of the Woman in Boston sets him adrift because the episode is a combined revelation of Willy's key to successful selling and his recurrent attempts to blot out his feelings of inconsequentiality. Biff comes home and is symbolically set free only when he discovers himself as a nobody.

The whole question of Willy's hidden identity is curiously like that in *Oedipus*. The key words—he does not know who he is—point the parallel almost unmistakably. But before we rank the salesman with the king, we need to check one further structural element. From Aristotle to Maxwell Anderson the point of *recognition* has been fundamental in the structure of tragedy. Biff, as we have seen, finally recognizes his situation; he reports that in his flight with the pen, he has suddenly realized the falsity of his life. He discovers his own identity, even though he identifies himself as a nobody. But where is Willy's moment of recognition, and what does it amount to? How much does Willy really see, even after that climactic scene in which Biff, tendering his love, frees both himself and his father? The question we are really asking is whether Willy Loman recognizes anything equal in quality to that which drove Oedipus to his self-mutilation and Othello to his suicide. The answer is both yes and no.

The *impact* of his recognition is of equal quality: it drives him to decisive action. What is different and debased is the quality of the action taken, the solution envisioned. Unable to rise above the commercial values that have defined and limited his life, Willy comes to suicide only as a new answer to his old problem. He is giving Biff something in return for his tendered love; he will trade himself for the money which he still sees as the key to his son's success in life. What is debased is Willy's immature evaluation, and the equally immature response founded on it. It is the response of a man who chooses death, not because life has been made intolerable by a terrible burden of guilt, but because he believes that his death is the purchase price of a security he himself could never find.

But perhaps the best approach to Willy's place among tragic heroes is to ask of his death the same class of question that we ask of the others. Concerning the fall of Oedipus, ruler of Thebes, solver of the Sphinx's riddle, we ask, "Does this fall mean that man is driven by an insatiable desire to know (above all to know himself), but, at the same time, that this desire for self-knowledge leads ultimately to blindness and destruction?" As we witness the fall of Othello, prince of Moors, General of Venice, Governor of Cyprus, we ask, "Does this fall mean that we have in us all that seed of jealousy which, given a dark moment of despair, will germinate and flower into a passion that destroys all reason?" And of the bereavement of the Mother and the slayings of Leonardo and the Bridegroom, are we not forced to ask, "Does this mean that the primitive hunger of the blood must always be satisfied, though it destroy the man, the family, and even the society through which it flows?" But, finally, what are we moved to ask of the death of Willy Loman? To what critical human issue does it point? Or is it merely another depressing episode, and, like his life, without significance? Who is Willy Loman that attention should be paid to him?

To answer that he is three million American salesmen—at least the equal of one Theban king or one Moorish general—is to evade the question. It is also an evasion to say that Willy is a common or Lo-man and hence ineligible to be the hero of a tragedy. The tragic vision is not focussed on the station or status of man, but on the motives of his soul. The stature of Othello and Oedipus and Leonardo comes not from their place but from the intensity of their living. They have had knowledge that life is good; in them a human potential has been reached and, in the face of destruction, their manhood affirmed. It would solve our problem if we could insist that attention be paid to Willy Loman because in his living, whatever his station or work, he had lived, because in his human relations he had soared to what men are capable of. But even where he seems most successful, in the adoration given him by Biff and Happy, we know the shallowness of Willy's achievement; we know the falseness of his aspirations, and how their falsity keeps him from laying any real foundations for their future or his own.

Like Oedipus, Willy does not know who his father is or who his children are. But unlike Oedipus, who has the strength to discover the truth, as well as the strength to destroy himself, Willy has only the weakness of his ignorance. His self-destruction is not, like Othello's, an atonement and redress of balance by a figure who emerges from his torture with dearly bought wisdom; it is the despairing, ill-considered act of immaturity. If we reject Willy, it is because he is only potentially a hero. He never grows to full size, since, though he has something of the heroic spirit, he only vaguely comprehends that his life is without meaning or substance. We reject him because his life, the *unexamined* life, is not worth living. And yet, we cannot wholly reject him: the terror of Miller's vision, and the point at which it joins those of Sophocles and Shakespeare, is that it finally forces us to ask, "Have we created a society fundamentally so inimical to man that, in cutting him off from the sun and the earth, it threatens his very survival?"

Death of a Salesman

by

ARTHUR MILLER

ACT ONE

The theatre is dark and silent. As though out of the air itself a melody is heard, played on a flute; it is a song, small and fine, telling of grass and trees and the horizon. The curtain rises.

At first there is only an angular hulk visible on the stage bathed in the bluish light of evening. Now it takes clearer shape—the line of the gable roof can be seen and a dormer window under it. Two beds become visible on the second floor. It is a house, or rather the anatomical bones of a house showing this upper bedroom, a kitchen on the ground floor, and next to it another bedroom. There are no walls between these rooms, everything can be seen through, just as in memories or in dreams we remember houses and rooms by the scenes we lived through there, by conversations and shouts, and not by the walls that surrounded us.

Behind the house are the towering walls of apartment buildings with here and there a window alight, but not many, for it is well past midnight.

You have often seen this house—in Brooklyn or Cleveland, Chicago or Detroit. Once, years ago, the city was surrounded by what some of its inhabitants thought of as a frontier. Of course there were no Indians around New York then, but there were wild stone cliffs in the Bronx, and in certain parts of Brooklyn dense woods grew, and men who worked all day on Forty-second Street got off at their El station at night and heard the sounds of a squirrel gun going off, the neighing of a horse in pasture, smelled the hopeful smell of grape clusters, and could see their houses unobstructed a long way off. And in the basements of those houses there were shelves filled with preserves—tomatoes especially, tomatoes they had grown on surrounding land that did not belong to them.

Brooklyn was villages in those days, it was little clumps of three or four houses, and a store sometimes miles away where they bought their potatoes in hundred-pound sacks, and in the spring and winter a man needed boots, not rubbers. Brooklyn was gigantic elms and the lushest kind of maples; it was young couples who had brought their small children to escape the prison of the city walls, to recapture a dream of freedom and hopefulness after the first great war.

The anatomy of the house on the stage before us now is like the symbol of that dream, its genesis, its flowering, and—for Willy Loman—its conclusion. This play takes

494

place in the present when the tomato fields are apartment houses, when the view from the bedroom windows has been blinded by brick, when the back yard, which was once limitless and stretched all the way to the school a half mile away, is now precisely defined—just fifteen feet deep and fourteen wide, and dark most of the day. This yard lies between us and the house, and Willy Loman, the salesman, is about to walk into it from the alleyway along-side the house—but before he does, let us have a word about Time in this play.

There is nothing mysterious or difficult about it. Just as you may be sitting and talking to a friend, so does Willy. And then your friend says something that makes a strong connection in your mind with something that happened in your past. And although your friend goes on talking, unaware that your thoughts have moved to another time and place, you exist, you think, you feel and in your imagination you argue, love and fight, in the present and in the past at the same moment.

So it is in this play. There are no "flashbacks" here—we never go backward. It is simply that the past keeps flowing into the present, bringing its scenes and its characters with it—and sometimes we shall see both past and present simultaneously. That is why there are no walls on this stage. For sometimes, in the mind, we move through space without bothering to open doors. Of course when the action is in the present—that is, when Willy's mind is concentrated on what is going on about him at the moment—he and everyone else on the stage do use the doors and behave as though there were walls about them. But as his mind reaches for the past he may walk directly to where he wishes to go, and sometimes he will move out of the kitchen into the back yard by simply stepping "through" the line where a wall would be.

As well, there are times in this play when Willy talks to a person who is really before him, and at the same time with a person who is simply there in his imagination—but a person we too can see. What happens in such cases is simply that the real person talking to him observes that the man is not quite coherent, for Willy, at times, is one of those thousands of men you may see any day in any city—respectably dressed, perfectly ordinary, and talking quietly "to themselves" as they walk along going about their business. In this play we shall see who it is that one of these men is talking to; we shall see that other life in which he simultaneously draws breath, suffers, laughs, triumphs, and fails.

But let us get on. Willy always entered the house through the kitchen door and he does so now, even though the mud streets have long since been paved.

The distant flute is playing still, as Willy Loman crosses the entire stage before us. He is still anonymous to us; the only identification is his sample cases which weigh his shoulders down. He seems tired, and as he comes to a halt at the door to the kitchen and takes out his key, it is clear that he feels he has just barely made it home.

He opens the door and enters the kitchen, sets down the cases, and straightens his painful back. He says something to himself—a kind of sigh, or perhaps, "Oh boy, oh boy." Now he bends again, after rubbing his palms back to circulation, and carries the cases out of the kitchen through a draped doorway at its back.

He is just disappearing through this doorway (leading into the dining room which we cannot see) when something stirs in the bedroom next to the kitchen. A woman is sitting up in the brass bed, having heard a noise in her sleep. She calls out, "Willy?!" We hear Willy's reply from downstairs as he climbs up, "It's all right. I came back."

Linda, his wife, gets out of bed and puts on her robe. She is very concerned, anxious to find out something. And as she puts on her robe the light becomes brighter on this bedroom and we can make her out.

She is about fifty-three years old, she may be large or small, fat or thin, it does not matter. What does matter is that she is a hard woman to know. For she has developed an iron mastery of her objections to her husband. She can be jovial, and most often is, she can also be extremely depressed, but in whatever mood, her eye is upon this man who is about to enter, this Willy Loman, this salesman. For one thing, he may turn upon her in anger, or he may pull her to his breast with a love so desperate as to stun her. But behind his violence and behind his need for her, she has always sensed another Willy, a hovering presence which for thirty-five years she has never been able to predict or understand and which she has come to fear with a fear so deep that a moment ago, in the depths of her sleep, having heard a noise, she knew this presence had returned beforetime. So as she goes to greet him at the bedroom door, she is already preparing herself for a crisis. He comes in now, removing his jacket and tie, and she automatically helps him.

LINDA. What happened? Did something happen, Willy?

WILLY. No. Nothing happened.

LINDA. You didn't smash the car, did you?

WILLY. [With casual irritation.] I said nothing happened. Didn't you hear me?

[Quite possibly this is not at all what he meant to say or the way he meant to say it. For—we can see him clearly now as he sits to remove his shoes—he is a man whose mind is racing, seeking, probing in a depthless night surrounding it. A few moments ago as he was taking his cases out of his car, he was probably thinking how wonderfully safe and warm the sight of LINDA would be. But that was a few moments ago and for WILLY LOMAN at this stage of his life, a moment can die at birth or linger for a very long time; a remark heard years and years ago can return to him now and hold him fast so that he is not aware of happenings around him until the memory of a moment melts, and he flows back into the present.

It was so with the music we heard as the curtain rose and which only now is fading away entirely. It was a song WILLY has been remembering more and more often in recent weeks, a distant, clean melody that plays in his mind, a sound from somewhere beyond his remembering, but a sound that draws a sense of longing out of him and undefined sadness.

But the music is gone now. He is home; LINDA is helping him off with his high-topped shoes, and like a bird which in full flight suddenly swerves and sits on a wire to look around and take stock of things, he begins to classify his thoughts.]

LINDA. Don't you feel well?

WILLY. I'm tired to the death. [The flute has faded away. He sits on the bed beside her, a little numb.] I couldn't make it. I just couldn't make it, Linda.

LINDA. [Very carefully, delicately.] Where were you all day? You look terrible.

WILLY. I got as far as a little above Yonkers. I stopped for a cup of coffee. Maybe it was the coffee.

LINDA. What?

WILLY. [After a pause.] I suddenly couldn't drive any more. The car kept going off onto the shoulder, y'know?

LINDA. [Helpfully.] Oh. Maybe it was the steering again. I don't think Angelo knows the Studebaker.

WILLY. No, it's me, it's me. Suddenly I realize I'm goin' sixty miles an hour and I don't remember the last five minutes. I'm—I can't seem to—keep my mind to it.

LINDA. Maybe it's your glasses. You never went for your new glasses.

WILLY. No, I see everything. I came back ten miles an hour. It took me nearly four hours from Yonkers.

LINDA. [Resigned.] Well, you'll just have to take a rest, Willy, you can't continue this way.

WILLY. I just got back from Florida.

LINDA. But you didn't rest your mind. Your mind is over-active, and the mind is what counts, dear.

WILLY. I'll start out in the morning.

Maybe I'll feel better in the morning. [*She is taking off his shoes.*] These goddam arch supports are killing me.

LINDA. Take an aspirin. Should I get you an aspirin? It'll soothe you.

WILLY. [*With wonder.*] I was driving along, you understand? And I was fine. I was even observing the scenery. You can imagine, me looking at scenery, on the road every week of my life. But it's so beautiful up there, Linda, the trees are so thick, and the sun is warm. I opened the windshield and just let the warm air bathe over me. And then all of a sudden I'm goin' off the road! I'm tellin' ya, I absolutely forgot I was driving. If I'd've gone the other way over the white line I might've killed somebody. So I went on again—and five minutes later I'm dreamin' again, and I nearly—[*He presses two fingers against his eyes.*] I have such thoughts, I have such strange thoughts.

LINDA. Willy, dear. Talk to them again. There's no reason why you can't work in New York.

WILLY. They don't need me in New York. I'm the New England man. I'm vital in New England.

LINDA. But you're sixty years old. They can't expect you to keep traveling every week.

WILLY. I'll have to send a wire to Portland. I'm supposed to see Brown and Morrison tomorrow morning at ten o'clock to show the line. Goddammit, I could sell them! [*He starts putting on his jacket.*]

LINDA. [*Taking the jacket from him.*] Why don't you go down to the place tomorrow and tell Howard you've simply got to work in New York? You're too accommodating, dear.

WILLY. If old man Wagner was alive I'd a been in charge of New York now! That man was a prince, he was a masterful man. But that boy of his, that Howard, he don't appreciate. When I went north the first time, the Wagner Company didn't know where New England was!

LINDA. Why don't you tell those things to Howard, dear?

WILLY. [*Encouraged.*] I will, I definitely will. Is there any cheese?

LINDA. I'll make you a sandwich.

WILLY. No, go to sleep. I'll take some milk. I'll be up right away. The boys in?

LINDA. They're sleeping. Happy took Biff on a date tonight.

WILLY. [*Interested.*] That so?

LINDA. It was so nice to see them shaving together, one behind the other, in the bathroom. And going out together. You notice? The whole house smells of shaving lotion.

WILLY. Figure it out. Work a lifetime to pay off a house. You finally own it, and there's nobody to live in it.

LINDA. Well, dear, life is a casting off. It's always that way.

WILLY. No, no, some people—some people accomplish something. Did Biff say anything after I went this morning?

LINDA. You shouldn't have criticized him, Willy, especially after he just got off the train. You mustn't lose your temper with him.

WILLY. When the hell did I lose my temper? I simply asked him if he was making any money. Is that a criticism?

LINDA. But, dear, how could he make any money?

WILLY. [*Worried and angered.*] There's such an undercurrent in him. He became a moody man. Did he apologize when I left this morning?

LINDA. He was crestfallen, Willy. You know how he admires you. I think if he finds himself, then you'll both be happier and not fight any more.

WILLY. How can he find himself on a farm? Is that a life? A farmhand? In the beginning, when he was young, I thought, well, a young man, it's good for him to tramp around, take a lot of different jobs. But it's more than ten years now and he has yet to make thirty-five dollars a week!

LINDA. He's finding himself, Willy.

WILLY. Not finding yourself at the age of thirty-four is a disgrace!

LINDA. Shh!

WILLY. The trouble is he's lazy, goddammit!

LINDA. Willy, please!

WILLY. Biff is a lazy bum!

LINDA. They're sleeping. Get something to eat. Go on down.

WILLY. Why did he come home? I would like to know what brought him home.

LINDA. I don't know. I think he's still lost, Willy. I think he's very lost.

WILLY. Biff Loman is lost. In the greatest country in the world a young man with such—personal attractiveness, gets lost. And such a hard worker. There's one thing about Biff—he's not lazy.

LINDA. Never.

WILLY. [*With pity and resolve.*] I'll see him in the morning; I'll have a nice talk with him. I'll get him a job selling. He could be big in no time. My God! Remember how they used to follow him around in high school? When he smiled at one of them their faces lit up. When he walked down the street . . . [*He loses himself in reminiscences.*]

LINDA. [*Trying to bring him out of it.*] Willy, dear, I got a new kind of American-type cheese today. It's whipped.

WILLY. Why do you get American when I like Swiss?

LINDA. I just thought you'd like a change—

WILLY. I don't want a change! I want Swiss cheese. Why am I always being contradicted?

LINDA. [*With a covering laugh.*] I thought it would be a surprise.

WILLY. Why don't you open a window in here, for God's sake?

LINDA. [*With infinite patience.*] They're all open, dear.

WILLY. The way they boxed us in here. Bricks and windows, windows and bricks.

LINDA. We should've bought the land next door.

WILLY. The street is lined with cars. There's not a breath of fresh air in the neighborhood. The grass don't grow any more, you can't raise a carrot in the back yard. They should've had a law against apartment houses. Remember those two beautiful elm trees out there? When I and Biff hung the swing between them?

LINDA. Yeah, like being a million miles from the city.

WILLY. They should've arrested the builder for cutting those down. They massacred the neighborhood. [*Lost.*] More and more I think of those days,

Linda. This time of year it was lilac and wisteria. And then the peonies would come out, and the daffodils. What fragrance in this room!

LINDA. Well, after all, people had to move somewhere.

WILLY. No, there's more people now.

LINDA. I don't think there's more people. I think—

WILLY. There's more people! That's what's ruining this country! Population is getting out of control. The competition is maddening! Smell the stink from that apartment house! And another one on the other side . . . How can they whip cheese?

[*Now, as he speaks, a brightness is gradually illuminating the boys' room, which is the room raised six feet above the kitchen. First* BIFF, *the older son, then* HAPPY *sit up slowly in their beds as though they have been awakened by* WILLY's *voice. They listen.*]

LINDA. Go down, try it. And be quiet.

WILLY. [*Turning to* LINDA *guiltily.*] You're not worried about me, are you, sweetheart?

BIFF. What's the matter?

HAPPY. Listen!

LINDA. You've got too much on the ball to worry about.

WILLY. You're my foundation and my support, Linda.

LINDA. Just try to relax, dear. You make mountains out of molehills.

WILLY. I won't fight with him any more. If he wants to go back to Texas, let him go.

LINDA. He'll find his way.

WILLY. Sure. Certain men just don't get started till later in life. Like Thomas Edison, I think. Or B. F. Goodrich. One of them was deaf. [*He starts for the bedroom doorway.*] I'll put my money on Biff.

LINDA. And Willy—if it's warm Sunday we'll drive in the country. And we'll open the windshield, and take lunch.

WILLY. No, the windshields don't open on the new cars.

LINDA. But you opened it today.

WILLY. Me? I didn't. [*He stops.*] Now isn't that peculiar! Isn't that a remarkable—[*He breaks off in amazement and fright as the flute is heard distantly.*]

LINDA. What, darling?

WILLY. That is the most remarkable thing.

LINDA. What, dear?

WILLY. I was thinking of the Chevvy. [*Slight pause.*] Nineteen twenty-eight . . . when I had that red Chevvy— [*Breaks off.*] That funny? I coulda sworn I was driving that Chevvy today.

LINDA. Well, that's nothing. Something must've reminded you.

WILLY. Remarkable. Ts. Remember those days? The way Biff used to simonize that car? The dealer refused to believe there was eighty thousand miles on it. [*He shakes his head.*] Heh! [*To* LINDA.] Close your eyes, I'll be right up. [*He walks out of the bedroom.*]

HAPPY. [*To* BIFF.] Jesus, maybe he smashed up the car again!

LINDA. [*Calling after* WILLY.] Be careful on the stairs, dear! The cheese is on the middle shelf! [*She turns, goes over to the bed, takes his jacket, and goes out of the bedroom.*]

[*Unseen within the house* WILLY *is heard talking to himself—"Eighty thousand miles"—and a little private laugh. Meanwhile in the boys' room where the light has become full,* BIFF *gets out of bed, comes toward us and stands at the edge of the room where it overhangs the kitchen. He listens attentively, trying to pick up what* WILLY *is saying.*

BIFF *is two years older than his brother,* HAPPY—*a well-built young man of thirty-four. But he has that air one sometimes finds in athletes who have outlived their moment of glory—the air of mystification, of frayed self-assurance, even of shame. Of course, for* BIFF *the stands have long since been empty, but he has never been quite able to catch up with the crowd that once was there for him. Like his father,* BIFF *has many dreams; driving, strong, imperative dreams that one day have sent him forth like an eagle across mountains, and the next have withered his hope and left him fearful and terribly lonely.*

His brother, HAPPY, *is also tall and powerfully made, and for him, too, life is not merely what it is, but what it ought to and must be. They are strivers, both, but* HAPPY *has succeeded more, and as troubled and improper as his yearnings may be, they are much more acceptable to society than* BIFF's *because they are less heroically cast. Sexuality is like a visible color on* HAPPY, *or like a scent that many women, despite themselves, have discovered. Like his brother, he is lost, but in a different way, for he has never allowed himself to turn his face toward total defeat. Thus, paradoxically, he is more confused about himself, more hard-skinned, although seemingly more content.*

Now HAPPY, *seeing* BIFF *out of bed, gets out himself and begins to talk to* BIFF, *and he talks to him as though he loves it. And yet everything he says is tentative, as though in his mind he were still the second in importance and* BIFF *the authority. Too, he has succeeded and* BIFF *who flowered so early, has not, and* HAPPY *is eager therefore to defer to him, even guiltily so. There is, in short, love between them.*]

HAPPY. He's going to get his license taken away if he keeps that up. I'm getting nervous about him, y'know, Biff?

BIFF. His eyes are going.

HAPPY. No, I've driven with him. He sees all right. He just doesn't keep his mind on it. I drove into the city with him last week. He stops at a green light and then it turns red and he goes. [*He laughs.*]

BIFF. Maybe he's color-blind.

HAPPY. Pop? Why he's got the finest eye for color in the business. You know that.

BIFF. [*Sitting down on his bed.*] I'm going to sleep.

HAPPY. You're not still sour on Dad, are you, Biff?

BIFF. He's all right, I guess.

WILLY. [*Underneath them, in the living-room.*] Yes, sir, eighty thousand miles —eighty-two thousand!

BIFF. You smoking?

HAPPY. [*Holding out a pack of cigarettes.*] Want one?

BIFF. [*Taking a cigarette.*] I can never sleep when I smell it.

WILLY. What a simonizing job, heh!

HAPPY. [*With deep sentiment.*] Funny, Biff, y'know? Us sleeping in here again? The old beds. [*He pats his bed affectionately.*] All the talk that went across those two beds, huh? Our whole lives.

BIFF. Yeah. Lotta dreams and plans.

HAPPY. [*With a deep and masculine laugh.*] About five hundred women would like to know what was said in this room. [*They share a soft laugh.*]

BIFF. Remember that big Betsy something—what the hell was her name—over on Bushwick Avenue?

HAPPY. [*Combing his hair.*] With the collie dog!

BIFF. That's the one. I got you in there, remember?

HAPPY. Yeah, that was my first time—I think. Boy, there was a pig! [*They laugh, almost crudely.*] You taught me everything I know about women. Don't forget that.

BIFF. I bet you forgot how bashful you used to be. Especially with girls.

HAPPY. Oh, I still am, Biff.

BIFF. Oh, go on.

HAPPY. I just control it, that's all. I think I got less bashful and you got more so. What happened, Biff? Where's the old humor, the old confidence? [*He shakes* BIFF's *knee.* BIFF *gets up and moves restlessly about the room.*] What's the matter?

BIFF. Why does Dad mock me all the time?

HAPPY. He's not mocking you, he—

BIFF. Everything I say there's a twist of mockery on his face. I can't get near him.

HAPPY. He just wants you to make good, that's all. I wanted to talk to you about Dad for a long time, Biff. Something's—happening to him. He—talks to himself.

BIFF. I noticed that this morning. But he always mumbled.

HAPPY. But not so noticeable. It got so embarrassing I sent him to Florida. And you know something? Most of the time he's talking to you.

BIFF. What's he say about me?

HAPPY. I can't make it out.

BIFF. What's he say about me?

HAPPY. I think the fact that you're not settled, that you're still kind of up in the air . . .

BIFF. There's one or two other things depressing him, Happy.

HAPPY. What do you mean?

BIFF. Never mind. Just don't lay it all to me.

HAPPY. But I think if you just got started—I mean—is there any future for you out there?

BIFF. I tell ya, Hap, I don't know what the future is. I don't know—what I'm supposed to want.

HAPPY. What do you mean?

BIFF. Well, I spent six or seven years after high school trying to work myself up. Shipping clerk, salesman, business of one kind or another. And it's a measly manner of existence. To get on that subway on the hot mornings in summer. To devote your whole life to keeping stock, or making phone calls, or selling or buying. To suffer fifty weeks of the year for the sake of a two-week vacation, when all you really desire is to be outdoors, with your shirt off. And always to have to get ahead of the next fella. And still—that's how you build a future.

HAPPY. Well, you really enjoy it on a farm? Are you content out there?

BIFF. [*With rising agitation.*] Hap, I've had twenty or thirty different kinds of jobs since I left home before the war, and it always turns out the same. I just realized it lately. In Nebraska when I herded cattle, and the Dakotas, and Arizona, and now in Texas. It's why I came home now, I guess, because I realized it. This farm I work on, it's spring there now, see? And they've got about fifteen new colts. There's nothing more inspiring or—beautiful than the sight of a mare and a new colt. And it's cool there now, see? Texas is cool now, and it's spring. And whenever spring comes to where I am, I suddenly get the feeling, my God, I'm not gettin' anywhere! What the hell am I doing, playing around with horses, twenty-eight dollars a week! I'm thirty-four years old, I oughta be makin' my future. That's when I come running home. And now, I get here, and I don't know what to do with myself. [*After a pause.*] I've always made a point of not wasting my life, and everytime I come back here I know that all I've done is to waste my life.

HAPPY. You're a poet, you know that, Biff? You're a—you're an idealist!

BIFF. No, I'm mixed up very bad. Maybe I oughta get stuck into something. Maybe that's my trouble. I'm like a boy. I'm not married, I'm not in business, I just—I'm like a boy. Are you content, Hap? You're a success, aren't you? Are you content?

HAPPY. Hell, no!

BIFF. Why? You're making money, aren't you?

HAPPY. [*Moving about with energy, expressiveness.*] All I can do now is wait for the merchandise manager to die. And suppose I get to be merchandise manager? He's a good friend of mine, and he just built a terrific estate on Long Island. And he lived there about two months and sold it, and now he's building another one. He can't enjoy it once it's finished. And I know that's just what I would do. I don't know what the hell I'm workin' for. Sometimes I sit in my apartment—all alone. And I think of the rent I'm paying. And it's crazy. But then, it's what I always wanted. My own apartment, a car, and plenty of women. And still, goddammit, I'm lonely.

BIFF. [*With enthusiasm.*] Listen, why don't you come out West with me?

HAPPY. You and I, heh?

BIFF. Sure, maybe we could buy a ranch. Raise cattle, use our muscles. Men built like we are should be working out in the open.

HAPPY. [*Avidly.*] The Loman Brothers, heh?

BIFF. [*With vast affection.*] Sure, we'd be known all over the counties!

HAPPY. [*Enthralled.*] That's what I dream about, Biff. Sometimes I want to just rip my clothes off in the middle of the store and outbox that goddam merchandise manager. I mean I can outbox, outrun, and outlift anybody in that store, and I have to take orders from those common, petty sons-of-bitches till I can't stand it any more.

BIFF. I'm tellin' you, kid, if you were with me I'd be happy out there.

HAPPY. [*Enthused.*] See, Biff, everybody around me is so false that I'm constantly lowering my ideals . . .

BIFF. Baby, together we'd stand up for one another, we'd have someone to trust.

HAPPY. If I were around you—

BIFF. Hap, the trouble is we weren't brought up to grub for money. I don't know how to do it.

HAPPY. Neither can I!

BIFF. Then let's go!

HAPPY. The only thing is—what can you make out there?

BIFF. But look at your friend. Builds an estate and then hasn't the peace of mind to live in it.

HAPPY. Yeah, but when he walks into the store the waves part in front of him. That's fifty-two thousand dollars a year coming through the revolving door, and I got more in my pinky finger than he's got in his head.

BIFF. Yeah, but you just said—

HAPPY. I gotta show some of those pompous, self-important executives over there that Hap Loman can make the grade. I want to walk into the store the way he walks in. Then I'll go with you, Biff. We'll be together yet, I swear. But take those two we had tonight. Now weren't they gorgeous creatures?

BIFF. Yeah, yeah, most gorgeous I've had in years.

HAPPY. I get that any time I want, Biff. Whenever I feel disgusted. The only trouble is, it gets like bowling or something. I just keep knockin' them over and it doesn't mean anything. You still run around a lot?

BIFF. Naa. I'd like to find a girl—steady, somebody with substance.

HAPPY. That's what I long for.

BIFF. Go on! You'd never come home.

HAPPY. I would! Somebody with character, with resistance! Like Mom, y'know? You're gonna call me a bastard when I tell you this. That girl Charlotte I was with tonight is engaged to be married in five weeks. [*He tries on his new hat.*]

BIFF. No kiddin'!

HAPPY. Sure, the guy's in line for the vice-presidency of the store. I don't know what gets into me, maybe I just have an overdeveloped sense of competition or something, but I went and ruined her, and furthermore I can't get rid of her. And he's the third executive I've done that to. Isn't that a crummy characteristic? And to top it all, I go to their weddings! [*Indignantly, but laughing.*] Like I'm not supposed to take bribes. Manufacturers offer me a hundred-dollar bill now and then to throw an order their way. You know how honest I am, but it's like this girl, see. I hate myself for it. Because I don't want the girl, and, still, I take it and—I love it!

BIFF. Let's go to sleep.

HAPPY. I guess we didn't settle anything, heh?

BIFF. I just got one idea that I think I'm going to try.

HAPPY. What's that?

BIFF. Remember Bill Oliver?

HAPPY. Sure, Oliver is very big now. You want to work for him again?

BIFF. No, but when I quit he said something to me. He put his arm on my shoulder, and he said, "Biff, if you ever need anything, come to me."

HAPPY. I remember that. That sounds good.

BIFF. I think I'll go to see him. If I could get ten thousand or even seven or eight thousand dollars I could buy a beautiful ranch.

HAPPY. I bet he'd back you. 'Cause he thought highly of you, Biff. I mean, they all do. You're well liked, Biff. That's why I say to come back here, and we both have the apartment. And I'm tellin' you, Biff, any babe you want . . .

BIFF. No, with a ranch I could do the work I like and still be something. I just wonder though. I wonder if Oliver still thinks I stole that carton of basketballs.

HAPPY. Oh, he probably forgot that long ago. It's almost ten years. You're too sensitive. Anyway, he didn't really fire you.

BIFF. Well, I think he was going to. I think that's why I quit. I was never sure whether he knew or not. I know he thought the world of me, though. I was the only one he'd let lock up the place.

WILLY. [*Below.*] You gonna wash the engine, Biff?

HAPPY. Shh! [BIFF *looks at* HAPPY, *who is gazing down at the floor, listening.* WILLY, *unseen, is mumbling in the parlor.*]

HAPPY. You hear that? [*They listen.* WILLY *is heard laughing.*]

BIFF. [*Growing angry.*] Doesn't he know Mom can hear that?

WILLY. [*Unseen.*] Don't get your sweater dirty, Biff! [*A look of pain crosses* BIFF's *face.*]

HAPPY. Isn't that terrible? Don't leave again, will you? You'll find a job here. You gotta stick around. I don't know what to do about him, it's getting embarrassing.

WILLY. [*Unseen.*] What a simonizing job!

BIFF. Mom's hearing that!

WILLY. [*Unseen.*] No kiddin', Biff, you got a date? Wonderful!

HAPPY. Go to sleep. But talk to him in the morning, will you?

BIFF. [*Reluctantly getting into bed.*] With her in the house. Brother!

HAPPY. [*Getting into bed.*] I wish you'd have a good talk with him. [*The light on their room begins to fade.*]

BIFF. [*To himself in bed.*] That selfish, stupid . . .

HAPPY. Sh . . . Sleep, Biff.

Their light is out. Well before they have finished speaking, WILLY's *form is dimly seen as he comes into the darkened kitchen below the boys' room. Now light illuminates the kitchen slowly, and we see* WILLY *opening the refrigerator. He searches in there, mumbling to himself, laughing privately at the same time. He gets a bottle of milk and turns and we see now that he is quite different from before. He seems relaxed now as his lips move. His eyes seem to be seeing a vision unknown to us, and his concentration upon this vision is infinitely intense, so much so that as he pours his milk and we begin to make out what he is saying to himself, the whole aspect of the house begins to change before our eyes. A pattern of light seems to be forming all around him—the gaunt walls of the apartment houses are fading into the forms of gigantic old trees, and all around him we discover glittering light-patterns of leaves, until* WILLY LOMAN *now seems surrounded by space, by nature, by the past. And with his vision we hear a new music, fair and sprightly and full of laughter.*

WILLY *seems more and more to be addressing his remarks to a particular kitchen chair which is suffused with its own living light. He is a little gay now, and we can make out what he is saying.*]

WILLY. Just wanna be careful with those girls, Biff, that's all. Don't make any promises. No promises of any kind. Because a girl, y'know, they always believe what you tell 'em, and you're very young, Biff, you're too young to be talking seriously to girls. [*He is totally immersed in himself, smiling faintly.*] Too young entirely, Biff. You want to watch your schooling first. Then when you're all set, there'll be plenty of girls for a boy like you. [*He smiles broadly at the brightened chair.*] That so? The girls pay for you? [*He laughs.*] Boy, you must really be makin' a hit. [*Now* WILLY *is gradually addressing—physically—a point offstage, speaking through the "wall" of the kitchen, and his voice has been rising in volume to that of a normal conversation.*] I been wondering why you polish the car so careful. Ha! Don't leave the hubcaps, boys. Get the chamois to the hubcaps. Happy, use newspaper on the windows, it's the easiest thing. Show him how to do it, Biff! You see, Happy? Pad it up, use it like a pad. That's it, that's it, good work. You're doin' all right, Hap. [*He pauses, then nods in approbation for a few seconds, then looks upward.*] Biff, first thing we gotta do when we get time is clip that big branch over the house. Afraid it's gonna fall in a storm and hit the roof. Tell you what. We get a rope and sling her around, and then we climb up there with a couple of saws and take her down. Soon as you finish the car, boys, I wanna see ya. I got a surprise for you, boys.

BIFF. [*Offstage.*] Whatta ya got, Dad?

WILLY. No, you finish first. Never leave a job till you're finished—remember that. [*Looking toward the "big trees."*] Biff, up in Albany I saw a beautiful hammock. I think I'll buy it next

trip, and we'll hang it right between those two elms. Wouldn't that be something? Just swingin' there under those branches. Boy, that would be . . .

[*From the direction toward which* WILLY *was speaking* YOUNG BIFF *and* YOUNG HAPPY *appear. They come springing onto the stage before the house, looking just as he remembers them.* HAPPY *has a baseball cap askew on his head, wears sneakers and rolled-up pants and an old shirt.* BIFF *wears a sweater with a big block "S" sewed on the chest, and he is carrying a football which he keeps squeezing as though to locate himself in the world. They are both eager, overjoyed at seeing* WILLY, *wishing for him to command them, and* WILLY *is full of power and pleasure as he gazes offstage toward the car.*]

BIFF. [*Pointing in the direction of the car offstage.*] How's that, Pop, professional?

WILLY. Terrific. Terrific job, boys. Good work, Biff.

HAPPY. Where's the surprise, Pop?

WILLY. In the back seat of the car.

HAPPY. Boy! [*He runs off.*]

BIFF. What is it, Dad? Tell me, what'd you buy?

WILLY. [*Laughing, cuffs him.*] Never mind, something I want you to have.

BIFF. [*Turns and starts off.*] What is it, Hap?

HAPPY. [*Offstage.*] It's a punching bag!

BIFF. Oh, Pop!

WILLY. It's got Gene Tunney's signature on it! [HAPPY *runs onstage with a punching bag.*]

BIFF. Gee, how'd you know we wanted a punching bag?

WILLY. Well, it's the finest thing for the timing.

HAPPY. [*Lies down on his back and pedals with his feet.*] I'm losing weight, you notice, Pop?

WILLY. [*To* HAPPY.] Jumping rope is good too.

BIFF. Did you see the new football I got?

WILLY. [*Examining the ball.*] Where'd you get a new ball?

BIFF. The coach told me to practice my passing.

WILLY. That so? And he gave you the ball, heh?

BIFF. Well, I borrowed it from the locker room. [*He laughs confidentially.*]

WILLY. [*Laughing with him at the theft.*] I want you to return that.

HAPPY. I told you he wouldn't like it!

BIFF. [*Angrily.*] Well, I'm bringing it back!

WILLY. [*Stopping the incipient argument, to* HAPPY.] Sure, he's gotta practice with a regulation ball, doesn't he? [*To* BIFF.] Coach'll probably congratulate you on your initiative!

BIFF. Oh, he keeps congratulating my initiative all the time, Pop.

WILLY. That's because he likes you. If somebody else took that ball there'd be an uproar. So what's the report, boys, what's the report?

BIFF. Where'd you go this time, Dad? Gee we were lonesome for you.

WILLY. [*Pleased, puts an arm around each boy and they come down to the stage-edge.*] Lonesome, heh?

BIFF. Missed you every minute.

WILLY. Don't say? Tell you a secret, boys. Don't breathe it to a soul. Someday I'll have my own business, and I'll never have to leave home any more.

HAPPY. Like Uncle Charley, heh?

WILLY. Bigger than Uncle Charley! Because Charley is not—liked. He's liked, but he's not—well liked.

BIFF. Where'd you go this time, Dad?

WILLY. Well, I got on the road, and I went north to Providence. Met the Mayor.

BIFF. The Mayor of Providence!

WILLY. He was sitting in the hotel lobby.

BIFF. What'd he say?

WILLY. He said, "Morning!" And I said, "You got a fine city here, Mayor." And then he had coffee with me. And then I went to Waterbury. Waterbury is a fine city. Big clock city, the famous Waterbury clock. Sold a nice bill there. And then Boston—Boston is the cradle of the Revolution. A fine city. And a couple of other towns in Mass., and on to Portland and Bangor and straight home!

BIFF. Gee, I'd love to go with you sometime, Dad.

WILLY. Soon as summer comes.

HAPPY. Promise?

WILLY. You and Hap and I, and I'll show you all the towns. America is full of beautiful towns and fine, upstanding people. And they know me, boys, they know me up and down New England. The finest people. And when I bring you fellas up, there'll be open sesame for all of us, 'cause one thing, boys: I have friends. I can park my car in any street in New England, and the cops protect it like their own. This summer, heh?

BIFF *and* HAPPY. [*Together.*] Yeah! You bet!

WILLY. We'll take our bathing suits.

HAPPY. We'll carry your bags, Pop!

WILLY. Oh, won't that be something! Me comin' into the Boston stores with you boys carryin' my bags. What a sensation! [BIFF *is prancing around, practicing passing the ball.*] You nervous, Biff, about the game?

BIFF. Not if you're gonna be there.

WILLY. What do they say about you in school, now that they made you captain?

HAPPY. There's a crowd of girls behind him everytime the classes change.

BIFF. [*Taking* WILLY'S *hand.*] This Saturday, Pop, this Saturday—just for you, I'm going to break through for a touchdown.

HAPPY. You're supposed to pass.

BIFF. I'm takin' one play for Pop. You watch me, Pop, and when I take off my helmet, that means I'm breakin' out. Then you watch me crash through that line!

WILLY. [*Kisses* BIFF.] Oh, wait'll I tell this in Boston!

[BERNARD *enters in knickers. He is younger than* BIFF, *earnest and loyal, a worried boy. He lives next door.*]

BERNARD. Biff, where are you? You're supposed to study with me today.

WILLY. Hey, looka Bernard. What're you lookin' so anemic about, Bernard?

BERNARD. He's gotta study, Uncle Willy. He's got Regents next week.

HAPPY. [*Tauntingly, spinning* BERNARD *around.*] Let's box, Bernard!

BERNARD. Biff! [*He gets away from* HAPPY.] Listen, Biff, I heard Mr Birnbaum say that if you don't start studyin' math he's gonna flunk you, and you won't graduate. I heard him!

WILLY. You better study with him, Biff. Go ahead now.

BERNARD. I heard him!

BIFF. Oh, Pop, you didn't see my sneakers! [*He holds up a foot for* WILLY *to look at.*]

WILLY. Hey, that's a beautiful job of printing!

BERNARD. [*Wiping his glasses.*] Just because he printed University of Virginia on his sneakers doesn't mean they've got to graduate him, Uncle Willy!

WILLY. [*Angrily.*] What're you talking about? With scholarships to three universities they're gonna flunk him?

BERNARD. But I heard Mr. Birnbaum say—

WILLY. Don't be a pest, Bernard! [*To his boys.*] What an anemic!

BERNARD. Okay, I'm waiting for you in my house, Biff. [BERNARD *goes off. The* LOMANS *laugh.*]

WILLY. Bernard is not well liked, is he?

BIFF. He's liked, but he's not well liked.

HAPPY. That's right, Pop.

WILLY. That's just what I mean. Bernard can get the best marks in school, y'understand, but when he gets out in the business world, y'understand, you are going to be five times ahead of him. That's why I thank Almighty God you're both built like Adonises. Because the man who makes an appearance in the business world, the man who creates personal interest, is the man who gets ahead. Be liked and you will never want. You take me, for instance. I never have to wait in line to see a buyer. "Willy Loman is here!" That's all they have to know, and I go right through.

BIFF. Did you knock them dead, Pop?

WILLY. Knocked 'em cold in Providence, slaughtered 'em in Boston.

HAPPY. [*On his back, pedaling again.*] I'm losing weight, you notice, Pop?

[LINDA *enters, as of old, a ribbon in her hair, carrying a basket of washing. She, too, is as* WILLY *remembers her. She seems young, even breathless, as she awaits his report of triumphs on the road.*]

LINDA. [*With youthful energy.*] Hello, dear!

WILLY. Sweetheart!

LINDA. How'd the Chevvy run?

WILLY. Chevrolet, Linda, is the greatest car ever built. [*To the boys.*] Since when do you let your mother carry wash up the stairs?

BIFF. Grab hold there, boy!

HAPPY. Where to, Mom?

LINDA. Hang them up on the line. And you better go down to your friends, Biff. The cellar is full of boys. They don't know what to do with themselves.

BIFF. Ah, when Pop comes home they can wait!

WILLY. [*Laughs appreciatively.*] You better go down and tell them what to do, Biff.

BIFF. I think I'll have them sweep out the furnace room.

WILLY. Good work, Biff.

BIFF. [*Goes through the "wall" of the kitchen to a doorway at the back and calls down.*] Fellas! Everybody sweep out the furnace room! I'll be right down!

VOICES. [*From the cellar.*] All right! Okay, Biff.

BIFF. George and Sam and Frank, come out back! We're hangin' up the wash! Come on, Hap, on the double! [*He and* HAPPY *carry out the basket.*]

LINDA. The way they obey him!

WILLY. Well, that's training, the training. I'm tellin' you, I was sellin' thousands and thousands, but I had to come home.

LINDA. Oh, the whole block'll be at that game. Did you sell anything?

WILLY. I did five hundred gross in Providence and seven hundred gross in Boston.

LINDA. No! Wait a minute, I've got a pencil. [*She pulls pencil and paper out of her apron pocket.*] That makes your commission . . . Two hundred—my God! Two hundred and twelve dollars!

WILLY. Well, I didn't figure it yet, but . . .

LINDA. How much did you do?

WILLY. Well, I—I did—about a hundred and eighty gross in Providence. Well, no —it came to—roughly two hundred gross on the whole trip.

LINDA. [*Without hesitation.*] Two hundred gross. That's . . . [*She figures.*]

WILLY. The trouble was that three of the stores were half closed for inventory in Boston. Otherwise I woulda broke records.

LINDA. Well, it makes seventy dollars and some pennies. That's very good.

WILLY. What do we owe?

LINDA. Well, on the first there's sixteen dollars on the refrigerator—

WILLY. Why sixteen?

LINDA. Well, the fan belt broke, so it was a dollar eighty.

WILLY. But it's brand new.

LINDA. Well, the man said that's the way it is. Till they work themselves in, y'know. [*They move through the "wall" into the kitchen.*]

WILLY. I hope we didn't get stuck on that machine.

LINDA. They got the biggest ads of any of them!

WILLY. I know, it's a fine machine. What else?

LINDA. Well, there's nine-sixty for the washing machine. And for the vacuum cleaner there's three and a half due on the fifteenth. Then the roof, you got twenty-one dollars remaining.

WILLY. It don't leak, does it?

LINDA. No, they did a wonderful job. Then you owe Frank for the carburetor.

WILLY. I'm not going to pay that man! That goddam Chevrolet, they ought to prohibit the manufacture of that car!

LINDA. Well, you owe him three and a half. And odds and ends, comes to around a hundred and twenty dollars by the fifteenth.

WILLY. A hundred and twenty dollars! My God, if business don't pick up I don't know what I'm gonna do!

LINDA. Well, next week you'll do better.

WILLY. Oh, I'll knock 'em dead next week. I'll go to Hartford. I'm very well liked in Hartford. You know, the trouble is, Linda, people don't seem to take to me. [*They move through the "wall" of the kitchen onto the forestage.*]

LINDA. Oh, don't be foolish.

WILLY. I know it when I walk in. They seem to laugh at me.

LINDA. Why? Why would they laugh at you? Don't talk that way, Willy. [WILLY *moves to the edge of the stage.* LINDA *goes into the kitchen and starts to darn stockings.*]

WILLY. I don't know the reason for it, but they just pass me by. I'm not noticed.

LINDA. But you're doing wonderful, dear. You're making seventy to a hundred dollars a week.

WILLY. But I gotta be at it ten, twelve hours a day. Other men—I don't know—they do it easier. I don't know why—I can't stop myself—I talk too much. A man oughta come in with a few words. One thing about Charley. He's a man of few words, and they respect him.

LINDA. You don't talk too much, you're just lively.

WILLY. [*Smiling.*] Well, I figure, what the hell, life is short, a couple of jokes. [*To himself.*] I joke too much! [*The smile goes.*]

LINDA. Why? You're—

WILLY. I'm fat. I'm very—foolish to look at, Linda. I didn't tell you, but Christmas time I happened to be calling on F. H. Stewarts, and a salesman I know, as I was going in to see the buyer, I heard him say something about—walrus. And I—I cracked him right across the face. I won't take that. I simply will not take that. But they do laugh at me. I know that.

LINDA. Darling . . .

WILLY. I gotta overcome it. I know I gotta overcome it. I'm not dressing to advantage, maybe.

LINDA. Willy, darling, you're the handsomest man in the world—

WILLY. Oh, no, Linda.

LINDA. To me you are. [*Slight pause.*] The handsomest. [*From the air is heard the laughter of a woman.* WILLY *doesn't turn to it, but it continues through* LINDA's *lines.*] And the boys, Willy. Few men are idolized by their children the way you are.

[*Now music, sly, sensuous and implacable, is heard along with the continuing laughter of a woman.* WILLY *is gripped by it and turns toward a certain dark area beside the house. And there we see now in a new greenish light* THE WOMAN. LINDA *is still in the kitchen mending her stockings, and* WILLY *crosses the whole stage, his mind fixed upon* THE WOMAN *who comes forward now, laughing and primping herself as though she were just finishing dressing. She has never stopped laughing and as* WILLY *approaches her,* LINDA *fades into dimness, as she does in* WILLY's *mind, but does not disappear completely. Indeed, although* WILLY *now is almost within touch of* THE WOMAN *and is looking at her, he is still talking to* LINDA.]

WILLY. [*With great feeling.*] You're the best there is, Linda, you're a pal, you know that? On the road—on the road I want to grab you sometimes and just kiss the life outa you. 'Cause I get so lonely—especially when business is bad and there's nobody to talk to. I get the feeling that I'll never sell anything again, that I won't make a living for you, or a business, a business for the boys. [*He talks through* THE WOMAN's *subsiding laughter;* THE WOMAN *primps at the "mirror."*] There's so much I want to make for—

THE WOMAN. Me? You didn't make me, Willy. I picked you.

WILLY. [*Pleased.*] You picked me?

THE WOMAN. [*Who is quite properlooking,* WILLY's *age.*] I did. I've been sitting at that desk watching all the salesmen go by, day in, day out. But you've got such a sense of humor, and we do have such a good time together, don't we?

WILLY. Sure, sure. [*He takes her in his arms.*] Why do you have to go now?

THE WOMAN. It's two o'clock . . .

WILLY. No, come on in! [*He pulls her.*]

THE WOMAN. . . . my sisters'll be scandalized. When'll you be back?

WILLY. Oh, two weeks about. Will you come up again?

THE WOMAN. Sure thing. You do make me laugh. It's good for me. [*She squeezes his arm, kisses him.*] And I think you're a wonderful man.

WILLY. You picked me, heh?

THE WOMAN. Sure. Because you're so sweet. And such a kidder.

WILLY. Well, I'll see you next time I'm in Boston.

THE WOMAN. I'll put you right through to the buyers.

WILLY. [*Slapping her bottom.*] Right. Well, bottoms up!

THE WOMAN. [*Slaps him gently and laughs.*] You just kill me, Willy. [*He suddenly grabs her and kisses her roughly.*] You kill me. And thanks for the stockings. I love a lot of stockings. Well, good night.

WILLY. Good night. And keep your pores open!

THE WOMAN. Oh, Willy!

[THE WOMAN *bursts out laughing, and* LINDA's *laughter blends in.* THE WOMAN *disappears into the dark. Now the area at the kitchen table brightens.* LINDA *is sitting where she was at the kitchen table, but now he notices that she is mending a pair of her silk stockings.*]

LINDA. You are, Willy. The handsomest man. You've got no reason to feel that—

WILLY. [*Coming out of* THE WOMAN's *dimming area and going over to* LINDA.] I'll make it all up to you, Linda, I'll—

LINDA. There's nothing to make up, dear. You're doing fine, better than—

WILLY. [*Noticing her mending.*] What's that?

LINDA. Just mending my stockings. They're so expensive—

WILLY. [*Angrily, taking them from her.*] I won't have you mending stockings in this house! Now throw them out!

[LINDA *puts the stockings in her pocket.*]

BERNARD. [*Entering on the run.*] Where is he? If he doesn't study!

WILLY. [*Moving to the forestage, with great agitation.*] You'll give him the answers!

BERNARD. I do, but I can't on a Regents! That's a state exam! They're liable to arrest me!

WILLY. Where is he? I'll whip him, I'll whip him!

LINDA. And he'd better give back that football, Willy, it's not nice.

WILLY. Biff! Where is he? Why is he taking everything?

LINDA. He's too rough with the girls, Willy. All the mothers are afraid of him!

WILLY. I'll whip him!

BERNARD. He's driving the car without a license! [THE WOMAN's *laugh is heard.*]

WILLY. Shut up!

LINDA. All the mothers—

WILLY. [*To the sound of this laughter.*] Shut up!

BERNARD. [*Backing quietly away and out.*] Mr. Birnbaum says he's stuck up.

WILLY. Get outa here!

BERNARD. If he doesn't buckle down he'll flunk math! [*He goes off.*]

LINDA. He's right, Willy, you've gotta—

WILLY. [*Exploding at her.*] There's nothing the matter with him! You want him to be a worm like Bernard? He's got spirit, personality . . . [*As he speaks,* LINDA, *almost in tears, exits into the living-room.* WILLY *is alone in the kitchen, wilting and staring. The leaves are gone. It is night again, and the apartment houses look down from behind. He is simply a man talking to himself in his kitchen.*] Loaded with it. Loaded! What is he stealing? He's giving it back, isn't he? Why is he stealing? What did I tell him? I never in my life told him anything but decent things.

[HAPPY *in pajamas has come down the stairs;* WILLY *suddenly becomes aware of* HAPPY's *presence, the grown-man* HAPPY *of today.*]

HAPPY. Let's go now, come on.

WILLY. [*Sitting down at the kitchen table.*] Huh! Why did she have to wax the floors herself? Everytime she waxes the floors she keels over. She knows that!

HAPPY. Shh! Take it easy. What brought you back tonight?

WILLY. I got an awful scare. Nearly hit a kid in Yonkers. God! Why didn't I go to Alaska with my brother Ben that time! Ben! That man was a genius, that man was success incarnate! What a mistake! He begged me to go.

HAPPY. Well, there's no use in—

WILLY. You guys! There was a man started with the clothes on his back and ended up with diamond mines!

HAPPY. Boy, someday I'd like to know how he did it.

WILLY. What's the mystery? The man knew what he wanted and went out and got it! Walked into a jungle, and comes out, the age of twenty-one, and he's rich! The world is an oyster, but you don't crack it open on a mattress!

HAPPY. Pop, I told you I'm gonna retire you for life.

WILLY. You'll retire me for life on seventy goddam dollars a week? And your women and your car and your apartment, and you'll retire me for life! Christ's sake, I couldn't get past Yonkers today! Where are you guys, where are you? The woods are burning! I can't drive a car!

[CHARLEY, *a next-door neighbor, has appeared in the doorway. He is a large man, slow of speech, laconic, immovable. In all he says, despite what he says, there is pity, and now, trepidation. He has a robe over pajamas, slippers on his feet. He enters the kitchen.*]

CHARLEY. Everything all right?

HAPPY. Yeah, Charley, everything's . . .

WILLY. What's the matter?

CHARLEY. I heard some noise. I thought something happened. Can't we do something about the walls? You sneeze in here, and in my house hats blow off.

HAPPY. Let's go to bed, Dad. Come on. [CHARLEY *signals to* HAPPY *to go.*]

WILLY. You go ahead, I'm not tired at the moment.

HAPPY. [*To* WILLY.] Take it easy, huh? [*He exits.*]

WILLY. What're you doin' up?

CHARLEY. [*Sitting down at the kitchen table opposite* WILLY.] Couldn't sleep good. I had a heartburn.

WILLY. Well, you don't know how to eat.

CHARLEY. I eat with my mouth.

WILLY. No, you're ignorant. You gotta know about vitamins and things like that.

CHARLEY. Come on, let's shoot. Tire you out a little.

WILLY. [*Hesitantly.*] All right. You got cards?

CHARLEY. [*Taking a deck from his pocket.*] Yeah, I got them. Some place. What is it with those vitamins?

WILLY. [*Dealing.*] They build up your bones. Chemistry.

CHARLEY. Yeah, but there's no bones in a heartburn.

WILLY. What are you talkin' about? Do you know the first thing about it?

CHARLEY. Don't get insulted.

WILLY. Don't talk about something you don't know anything about. [*They are playing. Pause.*]

CHARLEY. What're you doin' home?

WILLY. A little trouble with the car.

CHARLEY. Oh. [*Pause.*] I'd like to take a trip to California.

WILLY. Don't say.

CHARLEY. You want a job?

WILLY. I got a job, I told you that. [*After a slight pause.*] What the hell are you offering me a job for?

CHARLEY. Don't get insulted.

WILLY. Don't insult me.

CHARLEY. I don't see no sense in it. You don't have to go on this way.

WILLY. I got a good job. [*Slight pause.*] What do you keep comin' in here for?

CHARLEY. You want me to go?

WILLY. [*After a pause, withering.*] I can't understand it. He's going back to Texas again. What the hell is that?

CHARLEY. Let him go.

WILLY. I got nothin' to give him, Charley, I'm clean, I'm clean.

CHARLEY. He won't starve. None a them starve. Forget about him.

WILLY. Then what have I got to remember?

CHARLEY. You take it too hard. To hell with it. When a deposit bottle is broken you don't get your nickel back.

WILLY. That's easy enough for you to say.

CHARLEY. That ain't easy for me to say.

WILLY. Did you see the ceiling I put up in the living-room?

CHARLEY. Yeah, that's a piece of work. To put up a ceiling is a mystery to me. How do you do it?

WILLY. What's the difference?

CHARLEY. Well, talk about it.

WILLY. You gonna put up a ceiling?

CHARLEY. How could I put up a ceiling?

WILLY. Then what the hell are you bothering me for?

CHARLEY. You're insulted again.

WILLY. A man who can't handle tools is not a man. You're disgusting.

CHARLEY. Don't call me disgusting, Willy.

[*Even as* CHARLEY *has spoken his last line a new music is heard, and simultaneously we feel a new presence near*

WILLY. *It comes out of the surrounding darkness—his remembered image of his older brother,* BEN. *And he, too, is as* WILLY *knew him long ago; he carries a valise, he is glancing at his watch and then looking around at this strange place called Brooklyn. He is a stolid man, in his sixties, utterly certain of his destiny, with an aura of far places about him.* CHARLEY, *of course, is aware of nothing but a strange irritableness rising in* WILLY, *an abstracted air which he has observed in* WILLY *many times before.*]

WILLY. I'm getting awfully tired, Ben.

CHARLEY. Good, keep playing; you'll sleep better. Did you call me Ben? [BEN *looks at his watch.*]

WILLY. That's funny. For a second there you reminded me of my brother Ben.

BEN. I only have a few minutes. [*He strolls, inspecting the place.* WILLY *and* CHARLEY *continue playing.*]

CHARLEY. You never heard from him again, heh? Since that time?

WILLY. Didn't Linda tell you? Couple of weeks ago we got a letter from his wife in Africa. He died.

CHARLEY. That so.

BEN. [*Chuckling.*] So this is Brooklyn, eh?

CHARLEY. Maybe you're in for some of his money.

WILLY. Naa, he had seven sons. There's just one opportunity I had with that man . . .

BEN. I must make a train, William. There are several properties I'm looking at in Alaska.

WILLY. Sure, sure! If I'd gone with him to Alaska that time, everything would've been totally different.

CHARLEY. Go on, you'd froze to death up there.

WILLY. What're you talking about?

BEN. Opportunity is tremendous in Alaska, William. Surprised you're not up there.

WILLY. Sure, tremendous.

CHARLEY. Heh?

WILLY. There was the only man I ever met who knew the answers.

CHARLEY. Who?

BEN. How are you all?

WILLY. [*Taking a pot, smiling.*] Fine, fine.

CHARLEY. Pretty sharp tonight.

BEN. Is Mother living with you?

WILLY. No, she died a long time ago.

CHARLEY. Who?

BEN. That's too bad. Fine specimen of a lady, Mother.

WILLY. [*To* CHARLEY.] Heh?

BEN. I'd hoped to see the old girl.

CHARLEY. Who died?

BEN. Heard anything from Father, have you?

WILLY. [*Unnerved.*] What do you mean, who died?

CHARLEY. [*Taking a pot.*] What're you talkin' about?

BEN. [*Looking at his watch.*] William, it's half-past eight!

WILLY. [*As though to dispel his confusion he angrily stops* CHARLEY's *hand.*] That's my build!

CHARLEY. I put the ace—

WILLY. If you don't know how to play the game I'm not gonna throw my money away on you!

CHARLEY. [*Rising.*] It was my ace, for God's sake!

WILLY. I'm through, I'm through!

BEN. When did Mother die?

WILLY. Long ago. Since the beginning you never knew how to play cards.

CHARLEY. [*Picks up the cards and goes to the door.*] All right! Next time I'll bring a deck with five aces.

WILLY. I don't play that kind of game!

CHARLEY. [*Turning to him.*] You ought to be ashamed of yourself!

WILLY. Yeah?

CHARLEY. Yeah! [*He goes out.*]

WILLY. [*Slamming the door after him.*] Ignoramus!

BEN. [*As* WILLY *eagerly comes toward him through the "wall" of the kitchen.*] So you're William.

WILLY. [*Shaking Ben's hand.*] Ben! I've been waiting for you so long! What's the answer? How did you do it?

BEN. Oh, there's a story in that. [LINDA *enters the forestage, as of old, carrying the wash basket.*]

LINDA. Is this Ben?

BEN. [*Gallantly.*] How do you do, my dear.

LINDA. Where've you been all these years? Willy's always wondered why you—

WILLY. [*Pulling* BEN *away from her impatiently.*] Where is Dad? Didn't you follow him? How did you get started?

BEN. Well, I don't know how much you remember.

WILLY. Well, I was just a baby, of course, only three or four years old—

BEN. Three years and eleven months.

WILLY. What a memory, Ben!

BEN. I have many enterprises, William, and I have never kept books.

WILLY. I remember I was sitting under the wagon in—was it Nebraska?

BEN. It was South Dakota, and I gave you a bunch of wild flowers.

WILLY. I remember you walking away down some open road.

BEN. [*Laughing.*] I was going to find Father in Alaska.

WILLY. Where is he?

BEN. At that age I had a very faulty view of geography, William. I discovered after a few days that I was heading due south, so instead of Alaska, I ended up in Africa.

LINDA. Africa!

WILLY. The Gold Coast!

BEN. Principally diamond mines.

LINDA. Diamond mines!

BEN. Yes, my dear. But I've only a few minutes—

WILLY. No! Boys! Boys! [*Young* BIFF *and* HAPPY *appear.*] Listen to this. This is your Uncle Ben, a great man! Tell my boys, Ben!

BEN. Why, boys, when I was seventeen I walked into the jungle, and when I was twenty-one I walked out. [*He laughs.*] And by God I was rich.

WILLY. [*To the boys.*] You see what I been talking about? The greatest things can happen!

BEN. [*Glancing at his watch.*] I have an appointment in Ketchikan Tuesday week.

WILLY. No, Ben! Please tell about Dad. I want my boys to hear. I want them to know the kind of stock they spring from. All I remember is a man with a big beard, and I was in Mamma's lap, sitting around a fire, and some kind of high music.

BEN. His flute. He played the flute.

WILLY. Sure, the flute, that's right! [*New music is heard, a high, rollicking tune.*]

BEN. Father was a very great and a very wild-hearted man. We would start in Boston, and he'd toss the whole family into the wagon, and then he'd drive the team right across the country; through Ohio, and Indiana, Michigan, Illinois, and all the Western states. And we'd stop in the towns and sell the flutes that he'd made on the way. Great inventor, Father. With one gadget he made more in a week than a man like you could make in a lifetime.

WILLY. That's just the way I'm bringing them up, Ben—rugged, well liked, all-around.

BEN. Yeah? [*To* BIFF.] Hit that, boy—hard as you can. [*He pounds his stomach.*]

BIFF. Oh, no, sir!

BEN. [*Taking boxing stance.*] Come on, get to me! [*He laughs.*]

WILLY. Go to it, Biff! Go ahead, show him!

BIFF. Okay! [*He cocks his fists and starts in.*]

LINDA. [*To* WILLY.] Why must he fight, dear?

BEN. [*Sparring with* BIFF.] Good boy! Good boy!

WILLY. How's that, Ben, heh?

HAPPY. Give him the left, Biff!

LINDA. Why are you fighting?

BEN. Good boy! [*Suddenly comes in, trips* BIFF, *and stands over him, the point of his umbrella poised over* BIFF's *eye.*]

LINDA. Look out, Biff!

BIFF. Gee!

BEN. [*Patting* BIFF's *knee.*] Never fight fair with a stranger, boy. You'll never get out of the jungle that way. [*Taking* LINDA's *hand and bowing.*] It was an honor and a pleasure to meet you, Linda.

LINDA. [*Withdrawing her hand coldly, frightened.*] Have a nice—trip.

BEN. [*To* WILLY.] And good luck with your—what do you do?

WILLY. Selling.

BEN. Yes. Well . . . [*He raises his hand in farewell to all.*]

WILLY. No, Ben, I don't want you to think . . . [*He takes* BEN's *arm to show him.*] It's Brooklyn, I know, but we hunt too.

BEN. Really, now.

WILLY. Oh, sure, there's snakes and rabbits and—that's why I moved out here. Why, Biff can fell any one of these trees in no time! Boys! Go right over to where they're building the apartment house and get some sand. We're gonna rebuild the entire front stoop right now! Watch this, Ben!

BIFF. Yes, sir! On the double, Hap!

HAPPY. [*As he and* BIFF *run off.*] I lost weight, Pop, you notice?

[CHARLEY, *as of old, enters in knickers, even before the boys are gone.*]

CHARLEY. Listen, if they steal any more from that building the watchman'll put the cops on them!

LINDA. [*To* WILLY.] Don't let Biff . . .

[BEN *laughs lustily.*]

WILLY. You shoulda seen the lumber they brought home last week. At least a dozen six-by-tens worth all kinds a money.

CHARLEY. Listen, if that watchman—

WILLY. I gave them hell, understand. But I got a couple of fearless characters there.

CHARLEY. Willy, the jails are full of fearless characters.

BEN. [*Clapping* WILLY *on the back, with a laugh at* CHARLEY.] And the stock exchange, friend!

WILLY. [*Joining in* BEN's *laughter.*] Where are the rest of your pants?

CHARLEY. My wife bought them.

WILLY. Now all you need is a golf club and you can go upstairs and go to sleep. [*To* BEN.] Great athlete! Between him and his son Bernard they can't hammer a nail!

BERNARD. [*Rushing in.*] The watchman's chasing Biff!

WILLY. [*Angrily.*] Shut up! He's not stealing anything!

LINDA. [*Alarmed, hurrying off left.*] Where is he? Biff, dear! [*She exits.*]

WILLY. [*Moving toward the left, away*

from BEN.] There's nothing wrong. What's the matter with you?

BEN. Nervy boy. Good!

WILLY. [*Laughing.*] Oh, nerves of iron, that Biff!

CHARLEY. Don't know what it is. My New England man comes back and he's bleedin', they murdered him up there.

WILLY. It's contacts, Charley, I got important contacts!

CHARLEY. [*Sarcastically.*] Glad to hear it, Willy. Come in later, we'll shoot a little casino. I'll take some of your Portland money. [*He laughs at* WILLY *and exits.*]

WILLY. [*Turning to* BEN.] Business is bad, it's murderous. But not for me, of course.

BEN. I'll stop by on my way back to Africa.

WILLY. [*Longingly.*] Can't you stay a few days? You're just what I need, Ben, because I—I have a fine position here, but I—well, Dad left when I was such a baby and I never had a chance to talk to him and I still feel—kind of temporary about myself.

BEN. I'll be late for my train. [*They are at opposite ends of the stage.*]

WILLY. Ben, my boys—can't we talk? They'd go into the jaws of hell for me, see, but I—

BEN. William, you're being first-rate with your boys. Outstanding, manly chaps!

WILLY. [*Hanging on to his words.*] Oh, Ben, that's good to hear! Because sometimes I'm afraid that I'm not teaching them the right kind of—Ben, how should I teach them?

BEN. [*Giving great weight to each word, and with a certain vicious audacity.*] William, when I walked into the jungle, I was seventeen. When I walked out I was twenty-one. And, by God, I was rich! [*He goes off into darkness around the right corner of the house.*]

WILLY. . . . was rich! That's just the spirit I want to imbue them with! To walk into a jungle! I was right! I was right! I was right!

[BEN *is gone. The outlines of the apartment houses take shape, but* WILLY *is still speaking to him as* LINDA, *in night-gown and robe, enters the kitchen, glances around for* WILLY, *then goes to the door of the house, looks out and sees him. Comes down to his left. He looks at her, and she is old.*]

LINDA. Willy, dear? Willy?

WILLY. I was right!

LINDA. Did you have some cheese? [*He can't answer.*] It's very late, darling. Come to bed, heh?

WILLY. [*Looking straight up.*] Gotta break your neck to see a star in this yard.

LINDA. You coming in?

WILLY. Whatever happened to that diamond watch fob? Remember? When Ben came from Africa that time? Didn't he give me a watch fob with a diamond in it?

LINDA. You pawned it, dear. Twelve, thirteen years ago. For Biff's radio correspondence course.

WILLY. Gee, that was a beautiful thing. I'll take a walk.

LINDA. But you're in your slippers.

WILLY. [*Starting to go around the house at the right.*] I was right! I was! [*Half to* LINDA, *as he goes, shaking his head.*] What a man! There was a man worth talking to. I was right!

LINDA. [*Calling after* WILLY.] But in your slippers, Willy! [WILLY *is almost gone when* BIFF, *in his pajamas, comes down the stairs and enters the kitchen.*]

BIFF. What is he doing out there?

LINDA. Sh!

BIFF. God Almighty, Mom, how long has he been doing this?

LINDA. Don't, he'll hear you.

BIFF. What the hell is the matter with him?

LINDA. It'll pass by morning.

BIFF. Shouldn't we do anything?

LINDA. Oh, my dear, you should do a lot of things, but there's nothing to do, so go to sleep. [HAPPY *comes down the stairs and sits on the steps.*]

HAPPY. I never heard him so loud, Mom.

LINDA. Well, come around more often; you'll hear him. [*She sits down at the table and mends the lining of* WILLY's *jacket.*]

BIFF. Why didn't you ever write me about this, Mom?

LINDA. How would I write to you? For over three months you had no address.

BIFF. I was on the move. But you know I thought of you all the time. You know that, don't you, pal?

LINDA. I know, dear, I know. But he likes to have a letter. Just to know that there's still a possibility for better things.

BIFF. He's not like this all the time, is he?

LINDA. It's when you come home he's always the worst.

BIFF. When I come home?

LINDA. When you write you're coming, he's all smiles, and talks about the future, and—he's just wonderful. And then the closer you seem to come, the more shaky he gets, and then, by the time you get here, he's arguing, and he seems angry at you. I think it's just that maybe he can't bring himself to—to open up to you. Why are you so hateful to each other? Why is that?

BIFF. [*Evasively.*] I'm not hateful, Mom.

LINDA. But you no sooner come in the door than you're fighting!

BIFF. I don't know why. I mean to change. I'm tryin', Mom, you understand?

LINDA. Are you home to stay now?

BIFF. I don't know. I want to look around, see what's doin'.

LINDA. Biff, you can't look around all your life, can you?

BIFF. I just can't take hold, Mom. I can't take hold of some kind of a life.

LINDA. Biff, a man is not a bird, to come and go with the springtime.

BIFF. Your hair . . . [*He touches her hair.*] Your hair got so gray.

LINDA. Oh, it's been gray since you were in high school. I just stopped dyeing it, that's all.

BIFF. Dye it again, will ya? I don't want my pal looking old. [*He smiles.*]

LINDA. You're such a boy! You think you can go away for a year and . . . You've got to get it into your head now that one day you'll knock on this door and there'll be strange people here—

BIFF. What are you talking about? You're not even sixty, Mom.

LINDA. But what about your father?

BIFF. [*Lamely.*] Well, I meant him too.

HAPPY. He admires Pop.

LINDA. Biff, dear, if you don't have any feeling for him, then you can't have any feeling for me.

BIFF. Sure I can, Mom.

LINDA. No. You can't just come to see me, because I love him. [*With a threat, but only a threat, of tears.*] He's the dearest man in the world to me, and I won't have anyone making him feel unwanted and low and blue. You've got to make up your mind now, darling, there's no leeway any more. Either he's your father and you pay him that respect, or else you're not to come here. I know he's not easy to get along with—nobody knows that better than me—but . . .

WILLY. [*From the left, with a laugh.*] Hey, hey, Biffo!

BIFF. [*Starting to go out after* WILLY.] What the hell is the matter with him? [HAPPY *stops him.*]

LINDA. Don't—don't go near him!

BIFF. Stop making excuses for him! He always, always wiped the floor with you. Never had an ounce of respect for you.

HAPPY. He's always had respect for—

BIFF. What the hell do you know about it?

HAPPY. [*Surlily.*] Just don't call him crazy!

BIFF. He's got no character— Charley wouldn't do this. Not in his own house —spewing out that vomit from his mind.

HAPPY. Charley never had to cope with what he's got to.

BIFF. People are worse off than Willy Loman. Believe me, I've seen them!

LINDA. Then make Charley your father, Biff. You can't do that, can you? I don't say he's a great man. Willy Loman never made a lot of money. His name was never in the paper. He's not the finest character that ever lived. But he's a human being, and a terrible thing is happening to him. So attention must be paid. He's not to be allowed to fall into his grave like an old dog. Attention, attention must be finally paid to such a person. You called him crazy—

BIFF. I didn't mean—

LINDA. No, a lot of people think he's

lost his—balance. But you don't have to be very smart to know what his trouble is. The man is exhausted.

HAPPY. Sure!

LINDA. A small man can be just as exhausted as a great man. He works for a company thirty-six years this March, opens up unheard-of territories to their trademark, and now in his old age they take his salary away.

HAPPY. [*Indignantly.*] I didn't know that, Mom.

LINDA. You never asked, my dear! Now that you get your spending money someplace else you don't trouble your mind with him.

HAPPY. But I gave you money last—

LINDA. Christmas time, fifty dollars! To fix the hot water it cost ninety-seven fifty! For five weeks he's been on straight commission, like a beginner, an unknown!

BIFF. Those ungrateful bastards!

LINDA. Are they any worse than his sons? When he brought them business, when he was young, they were glad to see him. But now his old friends, the old buyers that loved him so and always found some order to hand him in a pinch —they're all dead, retired. He used to be able to make six, seven calls a day in Boston. Now he takes his valises out of the car and puts them back and takes them out again and he's exhausted. Instead of walking he talks now. He drives seven hundred miles, and when he gets there no one knows him any more, no one welcomes him. And what goes through a man's mind, driving seven hundred miles home without having earned a cent? Why shouldn't he talk to himself? Why? When he has to go to Charley and borrow fifty dollars a week and pretend to me that it's his pay? How long can that go on? How long? You see what I'm sitting here and waiting for? And you tell me he has no character? The man who never worked a day but for your benefit? When does he get the medal for that? Is this his reward—to turn around at the age of sixty-three and find his sons, who he loved better than his life, one a philandering bum—

HAPPY. Mom!

LINDA. That's all you are, my baby! [*To* BIFF.] And you! What happened to the love you had for him? You were such pals! How you used to talk to him on the phone every night! How lonely he was till he could come home to you!

BIFF. All right, Mom. I'll live here in my room, and I'll get a job. I'll keep away from him, that's all.

LINDA. No, Biff. You can't stay here and fight all the time.

BIFF. He threw me out of this house, remember that.

LINDA. Why did he do that? I never knew why.

BIFF. Because I know he's a fake and he doesn't like anybody around who knows!

LINDA. Why a fake? In what way? What do you mean?

BIFF. Just don't lay it all at my feet. It's between me and him—that's all I have to say. I'll chip in from now on. He'll settle for half my pay check. He'll be all right. I'm going to bed. [*He starts for the stairs.*]

LINDA. He won't be all right.

BIFF. [*Turning on the stairs, furiously.*] I hate this city and I'll stay here. Now what do you want?

LINDA. He's dying, Biff. [HAPPY *turns quickly to her, shocked.*]

BIFF. [*After a pause.*] Why is he dying?

LINDA. He's been trying to kill himself.

BIFF. [*With great horror.*] How?

LINDA. I live from day to day.

BIFF. What're you talking about?

LINDA. Remember I wrote you that he smashed up the car again? In February?

BIFF. Well?

LINDA. The insurance inspector came. He said that they have evidence. That all these accidents in the last year—weren't —weren't—accidents.

HAPPY. How can they tell that? That's a lie.

LINDA. It seems there's a woman . . . [*She takes a breath as* BIFF, *sharply but contained.*] What woman?

LINDA. [*Simultaneously.*] . . . and this woman . . .

LINDA. What?

BIFF. Nothing. Go ahead.

LINDA. What did you say?

BIFF. Nothing. I just said what woman?

HAPPY. What about her?

LINDA. Well, it seems she was walking down the road and saw his car. She says that he wasn't driving fast at all, and that he didn't skid. She says he came to that little bridge, and then deliberately smashed into the railing, and it was only the shallowness of the water that saved him.

BIFF. Oh, no, he probably just fell asleep again.

LINDA. I don't think he fell asleep.

BIFF. Why not?

LINDA. Last month . . . [*With great difficulty.*] Oh, boys, it's so hard to say a thing like this! He's just a big stupid man to you, but I tell you there's more good in him than in many other people. [*She chokes, wipes her eyes.*] I was looking for a fuse. The lights blew out, and I went down the cellar. And behind the fuse box—it happened to fall out—was a length of rubber pipe—just short.

HAPPY. No kidding?

LINDA. There's a little attachment on the end of it. I knew right away. And sure enough, on the bottom of the water heater there's a new little nipple on the gas pipe.

HAPPY. [*Angrily.*] That—jerk.

BIFF. Did you have it taken off?

LINDA. I'm—I'm ashamed to. How can I mention it to him? Every day I go down and take away that little rubber pipe. But, when he comes home, I put it back where it was. How can I insult him that way? I don't know what to do. I live from day to day, boys. I tell you, I know every thought in his mind. It sounds so old-fashioned and silly, but I tell you he put his whole life into you and you've turned your backs on him. [*She is bent over in the chair, weeping, her face in her hands.*] Biff, I swear to God! Biff, his life is in your hands!

HAPPY. [*To* BIFF.] How do you like that damned fool!

BIFF. [*Kissing her.*] All right, pal, all right. It's all settled now. I've been remiss. I know that, Mom. But now I'll stay, and I swear to you, I'll apply myself. [*Kneeling in front of her, in a fever of self-reproach.*] It's just—you see, Mom, I don't fit in business. Not that I won't try. I'll try, and I'll make good.

HAPPY. Sure you will. The trouble with you in business was you never tried to please people.

BIFF. I know, I—

HAPPY. Like when you worked for Harrison's. Bob Harrison said you were tops, and then you go and do some damn fool thing like whistling whole songs in the elevator like a comedian.

BIFF. [*Against* HAPPY.] So what? I like to whistle sometimes.

HAPPY. You don't raise a guy to a responsible job who whistles in the elevator!

LINDA. Well, don't argue about it now.

HAPPY. Like when you'd go off and swim in the middle of the day instead of taking the line around.

BIFF. [*His resentment rising.*] Well, don't you run off? You take off sometimes, don't you? On a nice summer day?

HAPPY. Yeah, but I cover myself!

LINDA. Boys!

HAPPY. If I'm going to take a fade the boss can call any number where I'm supposed to be and they'll swear to him that I just left. I'll tell you something that I hate to say, Biff, but in the business world some of them think you're crazy.

BIFF. [*Angered.*] Screw the business world!

HAPPY. All right, screw it! Great, but cover yourself!

LINDA. Hap, Hap!

BIFF. I don't care what they think! They've laughed at Dad for years, and you know why? Because we don't belong in this nuthouse of a city! We should be mixing cement on some open plain, or—or carpenters. A carpenter is allowed to whistle!

[WILLY *walks in from the entrance of the house, at left.*]

WILLY. Even your grandfather was better than a carpenter. [*Pause. They watch him.*] You never grew up. Bernard does not whistle in the elevator, I assure you.

BIFF. [*As though to laugh* WILLY *out of it.*] Yeah, but you do, Pop.

WILLY. I never in my life whistled in

an elevator! And who in the business world thinks I'm crazy?

BIFF. I didn't mean it like that, Pop. Now don't make a whole thing out of it, will ya?

WILLY. Go back to the West! Be a carpenter, a cowboy, enjoy yourself!

LINDA. Willy, he was just saying—

WILLY. I heard what he said!

HAPPY. [*Trying to quiet* WILLY.] Hey, Pop, come on now . . .

WILLY. [*Continuing over* HAPPY's *line.*] They laugh at me, heh? Go to Filene's, go to the Hub, go to Slattery's, Boston. Call out the name Willy Loman and see what happens! Big shot!

BIFF. All right, Pop.

WILLY. Big!

BIFF. All right!

WILLY. Why do you always insult me?

BIFF. I didn't say a word. [*To* LINDA.] Did I say a word?

LINDA. He didn't say anything, Willy.

WILLY. [*Going to the doorway of the living-room.*] All right, good night, good night.

LINDA. Willy, dear, he just decided . . .

WILLY. [*To* BIFF.] If you get tired hanging around tomorrow, paint the ceiling I put up in the living-room.

BIFF. I'm leaving early tomorrow.

HAPPY. He's going to see Bill Oliver, Pop.

WILLY. [*Interestedly.*] Oliver? For what?

BIFF. [*With reserve, but trying, trying.*] He always said he'd stake me. I'd like to go into business, so maybe I can take him up on it.

LINDA. Isn't that wonderful?

WILLY. Don't interrupt. What's wonderful about it? There's fifty men in the City of New York who'd stake him. [*To* BIFF.] Sporting goods?

BIFF. I guess so. I know something about it and—

WILLY. He knows something about it! You know sporting goods better than Spalding, for God's sake! How much is he giving you?

BIFF. I don't know, I didn't even see him yet, but—

WILLY. Then what're you talkin' about?

BIFF. [*Getting angry.*] Well, all I said was I'm gonna see him, that's all!

WILLY. [*Turning away.*] Ah, you're counting your chickens again.

BIFF. [*Starting left for the stairs.*] Oh, Jesus, I'm going to sleep!

WILLY. [*Calling after him.*] Don't curse in this house!

BIFF. [*Turning.*] Since when did you get so clean?

HAPPY. [*Trying to stop them.*] Wait a . . .

WILLY. Don't use that language to me! I won't have it!

HAPPY. [*Grabbing* BIFF, *shouts.*] Wait a minute! I got an idea. I got a feasible idea. Come here, Biff, let's talk this over now, let's talk some sense here. When I was down in Florida last time, I thought of a great idea to sell sporting goods. It just came back to me. You and I, Biff—we have a line, the Loman Line. We train a couple of weeks, and put on a couple of exhibitions, see?

WILLY. That's an idea!

HAPPY. Wait! We form two basketball teams, see? Two water-polo teams. We play each other. It's a million dollars' worth of publicity. Two brothers, see? The Loman Brothers. Displays in the Royal Palms—all the hotels. And banners over the ring and the basketball court: "Loman Brothers." Baby, we could sell sporting goods!

WILLY. That is a one-million-dollar idea!

LINDA. Marvelous!

BIFF. I'm in great shape as far as that's concerned.

HAPPY. And the beauty of it is, Biff, it wouldn't be like a business. We'd be out playin' ball again . . .

BIFF. [*Enthused.*] Yeah, that's . . .

WILLY. Million-dollar . . .

HAPPY. And you wouldn't get fed up with it, Biff. It'd be the family again. There'd be the old honor, and comradeship, and if you wanted to go off for a swim or somethin'—well, you'd do it! Without some smart cooky gettin' up ahead of you!

WILLY. Lick the world! You guys together could absolutely lick the civilized world.

BIFF. I'll see Oliver tomorrow. Hap, if we could work that out . . .

LINDA. Maybe things are beginning to—

WILLY. [*Wildly enthused, to* LINDA.] Stop interrupting! [*To* BIFF.] But don't wear sport jacket and slacks when you see Oliver.

BIFF. No, I'll—

WILLY. A business suit, and talk as little as possible, and don't crack any jokes.

BIFF. He did like me. Always liked me.

LINDA. He loved you!

WILLY. [*To* LINDA.] Will you stop! [*To* BIFF.] Walk in very serious. You are not applying for a boy's job. Money is to pass. Be quiet, fine, and serious. Everybody likes a kidder, but nobody lends him money.

HAPPY. I'll try to get some myself, Biff. I'm sure I can.

WILLY. I see great things for you kids, I think your troubles are over. But remember, start big and you'll end big. Ask for fifteen. How much you gonna ask for?

BIFF. Gee, I don't know—

WILLY. And don't say "Gee." "Gee" is a boy's word. A man walking in for fifteen thousand dollars does not say "Gee!"

BIFF. Ten, I think, would be top though.

WILLY. Don't be so modest. You always started too low. Walk in with a big laugh. Don't look worried. Start off with a couple of your good stories to lighten things up. It's not what you say, it's how you say it—because personality always wins the day.

LINDA. Oliver always thought the highest of him—

WILLY. Will you let me talk?

BIFF. Don't yell at her, Pop, will ya?

WILLY. [*Angrily.*] I was talking, wasn't I?

BIFF. I don't like you yelling at her all the time, and I'm tellin' you, that's all.

WILLY. What're you, takin' over this house?

LINDA. Willy—

WILLY. [*Turning on her.*] Don't take his side all the time, goddammit!

BIFF. [*Furiously.*] Stop yelling at her!

WILLY. [*Suddenly pulling on his cheek, beaten down, guilt ridden.*] Give my best to Bill Oliver—he may remember me. [*He exits through the living-room doorway.*]

LINDA. [*Her voice subdued.*] What'd you have to start that for? [BIFF *turns away.*] You see how sweet he was as soon as you talked hopefully? [*She goes over to* BIFF.] Come up and say good night to him. Don't let him go to bed that way.

HAPPY. Come on, Biff, let's buck him up.

LINDA. Please, dear. Just say good night. It takes so little to make him happy. Come. [*She goes through the living-room doorway, calling upstairs from within the living-room.*] Your pajamas are hanging in the bathroom, Willy!

HAPPY. [*Looking toward where* LINDA *went out.*] What a woman! They broke the mold when they made her. You know that, Biff?

BIFF. He's off salary. My God, working on commission!

HAPPY. Well, let's face it: he's no hotshot selling man. Except that sometimes, you have to admit, he's a sweet personality.

BIFF. [*Deciding.*] Lend me ten bucks, will ya? I want to buy some new ties.

HAPPY. I'll take you to a place I know. Beautiful stuff. Wear one of my striped shirts tomorrow.

BIFF. *She got gray.* Mom got awful old. Gee, I'm gonna go in to Oliver tomorrow and knock him for a—

HAPPY. Come on up. Tell that to Dad. Let's give him a whirl. Come on.

BIFF. [*Steamed up.*] You know, with ten thousand bucks, boy!

HAPPY. [*As they go into the living-room.*] That's the talk, Biff, that's the first time I've heard the old confidence out of you! [*From within the living-room, fading off.*] You're gonna live with me, kid, and any babe you want just say the word . . . [*The last lines are hardly heard. They are mounting the stairs to their parents' bedroom.*]

LINDA. [*Entering her bedroom and ad-*

dressing WILLY, *who is in the bathroom. She is straightening the bed for him.*] Can you do anything about the shower? It drips.

WILLY. [*From the bathroom.*] All of a sudden everything falls to pieces! Goddam plumbing, oughta be sued, those people. I hardly finished putting it in and the thing . . . [*His words rumble off.*]

LINDA. I'm just wondering if Oliver will remember him. You think he might?

WILLY. [*Coming out of the bathroom in his pajamas.*] Remember him? What's the matter with you, you crazy? If he'd've stayed with Oliver he'd be on top by now! Wait'll Oliver gets a look at him. You don't know the average caliber any more. The average young man today— [*He is getting into bed.*]—is got a caliber of zero. Greatest thing in the world for him was to bum around.

[BIFF *and* HAPPY *enter the bedroom. Slight pause.*]

WILLY. [*Stops short, looking at* BIFF.] Glad to hear it, boy.

HAPPY. He wanted to say good night to you, sport.

WILLY. [*To* BIFF.] Yeah. Knock him dead, boy. What'd you want to tell me?

BIFF. Just take it easy, Pop. Good night. [*He turns to go.*]

WILLY. [*Unable to resist.*] And if anything falls off the desk while you're talking to him—like a package or something —don't pick it up. They have office boys for that.

LINDA. I'll make a big breakfast—

WILLY. Will you let me finish? [*To* BIFF.] Tell him you were in the business in the West. Not farm work.

BIFF. All right, Dad.

LINDA. I think everything—

WILLY. [*Going right through her speech.*] And don't undersell yourself. No less than fifteen thousand dollars.

BIFF. [*Unable to bear him.*] Okay. Good night, Mom. [*He starts moving.*]

WILLY. Because you got a greatness in you, Biff, remember that. You got all kinds a greatness . . . [*He lies back, exhausted.* BIFF *walks out.*]

LINDA. [*Calling after* BIFF.] Sleep well, darling!

HAPPY. I'm gonna get married, Mom. I wanted to tell you.

LINDA. Go to sleep, dear.

HAPPY. [*Going.*] I just wanted to tell you.

WILLY. Keep up the good work. [HAPPY *exits.*] God . . . remember that Ebbets Field game? The championship of the city?

LINDA. Just rest. Should I sing to you?

WILLY. Yeah. Sing to me. [LINDA *hums a soft lullaby.*] When that team came out —he was the tallest, remember?

LINDA. Oh, yes. And in gold.

[BIFF *enters the darkened kitchen, takes a cigarette, and leaves the house. He comes downstage into a golden pool of light. He smokes, staring at the night.*]

WILLY. Like a young god. Hercules— something like that. And the sun, the sun all around him. Remember how he waved to me? Right up from the field, with the representatives of three colleges standing by? And the buyers I brought, and the cheers when he came out— Loman, Loman, Loman! God Almighty, he'll be great yet. A star like that, magnificent, can never really fade away! [*The light on* WILLY *is fading. The gas heater begins to glow through the kitchen wall, near the stairs, a blue flame beneath red coils.*]

LINDA. [*Timidly.*] Willy dear, what has he got against you?

WILLY. I'm so tired. Don't talk any more.

[BIFF *slowly returns to the kitchen. He stops, stares toward the heater.*]

LINDA. Will you ask Howard to let you work in New York?

WILLY. First thing in the morning. Everything'll be all right.

[BIFF *reaches behind the heater and draws out a length of rubber tubing. He is horrified and turns his head toward* WILLY'S *room, still dimly lit, from which the strains of* LINDA'S *desperate but monotonous humming rise.*]

WILLY. [*Staring through the window into the moonlight.*] Gee, look at the moon moving between the buildings!

[BIFF *wraps the tubing around his hand and quickly goes up the stairs.*]

CURTAIN

Music is heard, gay and bright. The curtain rises as the music fades away. Willy, in shirt sleeves, is sitting at the kitchen table, sipping coffee, his hat in his lap. Linda is filling his cup when she can.

WILLY. Wonderful coffee. Meal in it-self.

LINDA. Can I make you some eggs?

WILLY. No. Take a breath.

LINDA. You look so rested, dear.

WILLY. I slept like a dead one. First time in months. Imagine, sleeping till ten on a Tuesday morning. Boys left nice and early, heh?

LINDA. They were out of here by eight o'clock.

WILLY. Good work!

LINDA. It was so thrilling to see them leaving together. I can't get over the shaving lotion in this house!

WILLY. [Smiling.] Mmm—

LINDA. Biff was very changed this morning. His whole attitude seemed to be hopeful. He couldn't wait to get downtown to see Oliver.

WILLY. He's heading for a change. There's no question, there simply are certain men that take longer to get—solidified. How did he dress?

LINDA. His blue suit. He's so handsome in that suit. He could be a—anything in that suit! [WILLY gets up from the table. LINDA holds his jacket for him.]

WILLY. There's no question, no ques-tion at all. Gee, on the way home tonight I'd like to buy some seeds.

LINDA. [Laughing.] That'd be wonder-ful. But not enough sun gets back there. Nothing'll grow any more.

WILLY. You wait, kid, before it's all over we're gonna get a little place out in the country, and I'll raise some vege-tables, a couple of chickens . . .

LINDA. You'll do it yet, dear. [WILLY walks out of his jacket. LINDA follows him.]

WILLY. And they'll get married, and come for a weekend. I'd build a little guest house. 'Cause I got so many fine tools, all I'd need would be a little lumber and some peace of mind.

LINDA. [Joyfully.] I sewed the lin-ing . . .

WILLY. I could build two guest houses, so they'd both come. Did he decide how much he's going to ask Oliver for?

LINDA. [Getting him into the jacket.] He didn't mention it, but I imagine ten or fifteen thousand. You going to talk to Howard today?

WILLY. Yeah. I'll put it to him straight and simple. He'll just have to take me off the road.

LINDA. And Willy, don't forget to ask for a little advance, because we've got the insurance premium. It's the grace period now.

WILLY. That's a hundred . . . ?

LINDA. A hundred and eight, sixty-eight. Because we're a little short again.

WILLY. Why are we short?

LINDA. Well, you had the motor job on the car . . .

WILLY. That goddam Studebaker!

LINDA. And you got one more payment on the refrigerator . . .

WILLY. But it just broke again!

LINDA. Well, it's old, dear.

WILLY. I told you we should've bought a well-advertised machine. Charley bought a General Electric and it's twenty years old and it's still good, that son-of-a-bitch.

LINDA. But, Willy—

WILLY. Whoever heard of a Hastings refrigerator? Once in my life I would like to own something outright before it's broken! I'm always in a race with the junkyard! I just finished paying for the car and it's on its last legs. The refrigera-tor consumes belts like a goddam maniac. They time those things. They time them so when you finally paid for them, they're used up.

LINDA. [Buttoning up his jacket as he unbuttons it.] All told, about two hun-dred dollars would carry us, dear. But that includes the last payment on the mortgage. After this payment, Willy, the house belongs to us.

WILLY. It's twenty-five years!

LINDA. Biff was nine years old when we bought it.

WILLY. Well, that's a great thing. To weather a twenty-five year mortgage is—

LINDA. It's an accomplishment.

WILLY. All the cement, the lumber, the reconstruction I put in this house! There ain't a crack to be found in it any more.

LINDA. Well, it served its purpose.

WILLY. What purpose? Some stranger'll come along, move in, and that's that. If only Biff would take this house, and raise a family . . . [*He starts to go.*] Good-by, I'm late.

LINDA. [*Suddenly remembering.*] Oh, I forgot! You're supposed to meet them for dinner.

WILLY. Me?

LINDA. At Frank's Chop House on Forty-eighth near Sixth Avenue.

WILLY. Is that so! How about you?

LINDA. No, just the three of you. They're gonna blow you to a big meal!

WILLY. Don't say! Who thought of that?

LINDA. Biff came to me this morning, Willy, and he said, "Tell Dad, we want to blow him to a big meal." Be there six o'clock. You and your two boys are going to have dinner.

WILLY. Gee whiz! That's really somethin'. I'm gonna knock Howard for a loop, kid. I'll get an advance, and I'll come home with a New York job. Goddammit, now I'm gonna do it!

LINDA. Oh, that's the spirit, Willy!

WILLY. I will never get behind a wheel the rest of my life!

LINDA. It's changing, Willy, I can feel it changing!

WILLY. Beyond a question. G'by, I'm late. [*He starts to go again.*]

LINDA. [*Calling after him as she runs to the kitchen table for a handkerchief.*] You got your glasses?

WILLY. [*Feels for them, then comes back in.*] Yeah, yeah, got my glasses.

LINDA. [*Giving him the handkerchief.*] And a handkerchief.

WILLY. Yeah, handkerchief.

LINDA. And your saccharine?

WILLY. Yeah, my saccharine.

LINDA. Be careful on the subway stairs.

[*She kisses him, and a silk stocking is seen hanging from her hand.* WILLY *notices it.*]

WILLY. Will you stop mending stockings? At least while I'm in the house. It gets me nervous. I can't tell you. Please. [LINDA *hides the stocking in her hand as she follows* WILLY *across the forestage in front of the house.*]

LINDA. Remember, Frank's Chop House.

WILLY. [*Crossing the back yard.*] Maybe beets would grow out there.

LINDA. [*Laughing.*] But you tried so many times.

WILLY. Yeah. Well, don't work hard today. [*He disappears around the left corner of the house.*]

LINDA. Be careful! [*As* WILLY *vanishes,* LINDA *waves to him. Suddenly the phone rings. She runs across the stage and into the kitchen and lifts it.*] Hello? Oh, Biff! I'm so glad you called, I just . . . Yes, sure, I just told him. Yes, he'll be there for dinner at six o'clock, I didn't forget. Listen, I was just dying to tell you. You know that little rubber pipe I told you about? That he connected to the gas heater? I finally decided to go down the cellar this morning and take it away and destroy it. But it's gone! Imagine? He took it away himself, it isn't there! [*She listens.*] When? Oh, then you took it. Oh—nothing, it's just that I'd hoped he'd taken it away himself. Oh, I'm not worried, darling, because this morning he left in such high spirits, it was like the old days! I'm not afraid any more. Did Mr. Oliver see you? . . . Well, you wait there then. And make a nice impression on him, darling. Just don't perspire too much before you see him. And have a nice time with Dad. He may have big news too! . . . That's right, a New York job. And be sweet to him tonight, dear. Be loving to him. Because he's only a little boat looking for a harbor. [*She is trembling with sorrow and joy.*] Oh, that's wonderful, Biff, you'll save his life. Thanks, darling. Just put your arm around him when he comes into the res-

taurant. Give him a smile. That's the boy
. . . Good-by, dear . . . You got your
comb? . . . That's fine. Good-by, Biff
dear.

[*While* LINDA *is speaking, the light on
her is fading. At the same time light is
rising upon a young, fashionably dressed
business man who is appearing on the
right side of the stage close to the audience. He is* HOWARD WAGNER, WILLY'S
*boss, and he is pushing on a small rolling
table on which is a wire recorder. The
light on* LINDA—*and on the entire kitchen
and house—blacks out, leaving* HOWARD
WAGNER *alone on the stage, plugging in
his machine. As we shall see in a moment,
we are in his office, for even now* WILLY
*has stuck his head in and in his most
devil-may-care manner* . . .]

WILLY. Pst! Pst!

HOWARD. Hello, Willy, come in.

WILLY. Like to have a little talk with
you, Howard.

HOWARD. Sorry to keep you waiting.
I'll be with you in a minute.

WILLY. What's that, Howard?

HOWARD. Didn't you ever see one of
these? Wire recorder.

WILLY. Oh. Can we talk a minute?

HOWARD. Records things. Just got delivery yesterday. Been driving me crazy,
the most terrific machine I ever saw in
my life. I was up all night with it.

WILLY. What do you do with it?

HOWARD. I bought it for dictation, but
you can do anything with it. Listen to
this. I had it home last night. Listen to
what I picked up. The first one is my
daughter. Get this. [*He flicks the switch
and "Roll Out the Barrel" is heard being
whistled.*] Listen to that kid whistle.

WILLY. That is lifelike, isn't it?

HOWARD. Seven years old. Get that
tone.

WILLY. Ts, ts. Like to ask a little favor
if you . . . [*The whistling breaks off,
and the voice of* HOWARD'S *daughter is
heard.*]

HIS DAUGHTER. "Now you, Daddy."

HOWARD. She's crazy for me! [*Again
the same song is whistled.*] That's me!
Ha! [*He winks.*]

WILLY. You're very good! [*The whis-

tling breaks off again. The machine runs
silent for a moment.*]

HOWARD. Sh! Get this now, this is my
son.

HIS SON. "The capital of Alabama is
Montgomery; the capital of Arizona is
Phoenix; the capital of Arkansas is Little
Rock; the capital of California is Sacra-
mento . . ." [*And on, and on.*]

HOWARD. [*Holding up five fingers.*]
Five years old, Willy!

WILLY. He'll make an announcer some
day!

HIS SON. [*Continuing.*] "The capital
. . ."

HOWARD. Get that—alphabetical order!
[*The machine breaks off suddenly.*]
Wait a minute. The maid kicked the
plug out.

WILLY. It certainly is a—

HOWARD. Sh, for God's sake!

HIS SON. "It's nine o'clock, Bulova
watch time. So I have to go to sleep."

WILLY. That really is—

HOWARD. Wait a minute! The next is
my wife. [*They wait.*]

HOWARD'S VOICE. "Go on, say something." [*Pause.*] "Well, you gonna talk?"

HIS WIFE. "I can't think of anything."

HOWARD'S VOICE. "Well, talk—it's turning."

HIS WIFE. [*Shyly, beaten.*] "Hello."
[*Silence.*] "Oh, Howard, I can't talk into
this . . ."

HOWARD. [*Snapping the machine off.*]
That was my wife.

WILLY. That is a wonderful machine.
Can we—

HOWARD. I tell you, Willy, I'm gonna
take my camera, and my bandsaw, and all
my hobbies, and out they go. This is the
most fascinating relaxation I ever found.

WILLY. I think I'll get one myself.

HOWARD. Sure, they're only a hundred
and a half. You can't do without it. Supposing you wanna hear Jack Benny, see?
But you can't be at home at that hour. So
you tell the maid to turn the radio on
when Jack Benny comes on, and this
automatically goes on with the radio
. . .

WILLY. And when you come home you
. . .

HOWARD. You can come home twelve

o'clock, one o'clock, any time you like, and you get yourself a Coke and sit yourself down, throw the switch, and there's Jack Benny's program in the middle of the night!

WILLY. I'm definitely going to get one. Because lots of times I'm on the road, and I think to myself, what I must be missing on the radio!

HOWARD. Don't you have a radio in the car?

WILLY. Well, yeah, but who ever thinks of turning it on?

HOWARD. Say, aren't you supposed to be in Boston?

WILLY. That's what I want to talk to you about, Howard. You got a minute? [He draws a chair in from the wing.]

HOWARD. What happened? What're you doing here?

WILLY. Well . . .

HOWARD. You didn't crack up again, did you?

WILLY. Oh, no. No . . .

HOWARD. Geez, you had me worried there for a minute. What's the trouble?

WILLY. Well, tell you the truth, Howard. I've come to the decision that I'd rather not travel any more.

HOWARD. Not travel! Well, what'll you do?

WILLY. Remember, Christmas time, when you had the party here? You said you'd try to think of some spot for me here in town.

HOWARD. With us?

WILLY. Well, sure.

HOWARD. Oh, yeah, yeah. I remember. Well, I couldn't think of anything for you, Willy.

WILLY. I tell ya, Howard. The kids are all grown up, y'know. I don't need much any more. If I could take home—well, sixty-five dollars a week, I could swing it.

HOWARD. Yeah, but Willy, see I—

WILLY. I tell ya why, Howard. Speaking frankly and between the two of us, y'know—I'm just a little tired.

HOWARD. Oh, I could understand that, Willy. But you're a road man, Willy, and we do a road business. We've only got a half-dozen salesmen on the floor here.

WILLY. God knows, Howard, I never asked a favor of any man. But I was with the firm when your father used to carry you in here in his arms.

HOWARD. I know that, Willy, but—

WILLY. Your father came to me the day you were born and asked me what I thought of the name of Howard, may he rest in peace.

HOWARD. I appreciate that, Willy, but there just is no spot here for you. If I had a spot I'd slam you right in, but I just don't have a single solitary spot. [He looks for his lighter. WILLY has picked it up and gives it to him. Pause.]

WILLY. [With increasing anger.] Howard, all I need to set my table is fifty dollars a week.

HOWARD. But where am I going to put you, kid?

WILLY. Look, it isn't a question of whether I can sell merchandise, is it?

HOWARD. No, but it's a business, kid, and everybody's gotta pull his own weight.

WILLY. [Desperately.] Just let me tell you a story, Howard—

HOWARD. 'Cause you gotta admit, business is business.

WILLY. [Angrily.] Business is definitely business, but just listen for a minute. You don't understand this. When I was a boy —eighteen, nineteen—I was already on the road. And there was a question in my mind as to whether selling had a future for me. Because in those days I had a yearning to go to Alaska. See, there were three gold strikes in one month in Alaska, and I felt like going out. Just for the ride, you might say.

HOWARD. [Barely interested.] Don't say.

WILLY. Oh, yeah, my father lived many years in Alaska. He was an adventurous man. We've got quite a little streak of self-reliance in our family. I thought I'd go out with my older brother and try to locate him, and maybe settle in the North with the old man. And I was almost decided to go, when I met a salesman in the Parker House. His name was Dave Singleman. And he was eighty-four years old, and he'd drummed merchandise in thirty-one states. And old Dave, he'd go up to his room, y'understand, put on his green velvet slippers—I'll never forget—and pick up his phone and call the buyers, and without ever leaving his room, at the age of eighty-four, he made his living. And when I saw that, I realized that selling was the greatest career a man could want. 'Cause what could be more satisfying than to be able to go, at the age of eighty-four, into twenty or thirty different cities, and pick up a phone, and be remembered and loved and helped by so many different people? Do you know? when he died—and by the way he died the death of a salesman, in his green velvet slippers in the smoker of the New York, New Haven and Hartford, going into Boston—when he died, hundreds of salesmen and buyers were at his funeral. Things were sad on a lotta trains for months after that. [*He stands up.* HOWARD *has not looked at him.*] In those days there was personality in it, Howard. There was respect, and comradeship, and gratitude in it. Today, it's all cut and dried, and there's no chance for bringing friendship to bear—or personality. You see what I mean? They don't know me any more.

HOWARD. [*Moving away, to the right.*] That's just the thing, Willy.

WILLY. If I had forty dollars a week—that's all I'd need. Forty dollars, Howard.

HOWARD. Kid, I can't take blood from a stone, I—

WILLY. [*Desperation is on him now.*] Howard, the year Al Smith was nominated, your father came to me and—

HOWARD. [*Starting to go off.*] I've got to see some people, kid.

WILLY. [*Stopping him.*] I'm talking about your father! There were promises made across this desk! You mustn't tell me you've got people to see—I put thirty-four years into this firm, Howard, and now I can't pay my insurance! You can't eat the orange and throw the peel away—a man is not a piece of fruit! [*After a pause.*] Now pay attention. Your father —in 1928 I had a big year. I averaged a hundred and seventy dollars a week in commissions.

HOWARD. [*Impatiently.*] Now, Willy, you never averaged—

WILLY. [*Banging his hand on the desk.*] I averaged a hundred and seventy dollars a week in the year of 1928! And your father came to me—or rather, I was in the office here—it was right over this desk —and he put his hand on my shoulder—

HOWARD. [*Getting up.*] You'll have to excuse me, Willy, I gotta see some people. Pull yourself together. [*Going out.*] I'll be back in a little while. [*On* HOWARD'S *exit, the light on his chair grows very bright and strange.*]

WILLY. Pull myself together! What the hell did I say to him? My God, I was yelling at him! How could I! [WILLY *breaks off, staring at the light, which occupies the chair, animating it. He approaches this chair, standing across the desk from it.*] Frank, Frank, don't you remember what you told me that time? How you put your hand on my shoulder, and Frank . . . [*He leans on the desk and as he speaks the dead man's name he accidentally switches on the recorder, and instantly . . .*]

HOWARD'S SON. ". . . of New York is Albany. The capital of Ohio is Cincinnati, the capital of Rhode Island is . . ." [*The recitation continues.*]

WILLY. [*Leaping away with fright, shouting.*] Ha! Howard! Howard! Howard!

HOWARD. [*Rushing in.*] What happened?

WILLY. [*Pointing at the machine, which continues nasally, childishly, with the capital cities.*] Shut it off! Shut it off!

HOWARD. [*Pulling the plug out.*] Look, Willy . . .

WILLY. [*Pressing his hands to his eyes.*] I gotta get myself some coffee. I'll get some coffee . . . [WILLY *starts to walk out.* HOWARD *stops him.*]

HOWARD. [*Rolling up the cord.*] Willy, look . . .

WILLY. I'll go to Boston.

HOWARD. Willy, you can't go to Boston for us.

WILLY. Why can't I go?

HOWARD. I don't want you to represent us. I've been meaning to tell you for a long time now.

WILLY. Howard, are you firing me?

HOWARD. I think you need a good long rest, Willy.

WILLY. Howard—

HOWARD. And when you feel better, come back, and we'll see if we can work something out.

WILLY. But I gotta earn money, Howard. I'm in no position to—

HOWARD. Where are your sons? Why don't your sons give you a hand?

WILLY. They're working on a very big deal.

HOWARD. This is no time for false pride, Willy. You go to your sons and you tell them that you're tired. You've got two great boys, haven't you?

WILLY. Oh, no question, no question, but in the meantime . . .

HOWARD. Then that's that, heh?

WILLY. All right, I'll go to Boston tomorrow.

HOWARD. No, no.

WILLY. I can't throw myself on my sons. I'm not a cripple!

HOWARD. Look, kid, I'm busy this morning.

WILLY. [Grasping HOWARD's arm.] Howard, you've got to let me go to Boston!

HOWARD. [Hard, keeping himself under control.] I've got a line of people to see this morning. Sit down, take five minutes, and pull yourself together, and then go home, will ya? I need the office, Willy. [He starts to go, turns, remembering the recorder, starts to push off the table holding the recorder.] Oh, yeah. Whenever you can this week, stop by and drop off the samples. You'll feel better, Willy, and then come back and we'll talk. Pull yourself together, kid, there's people outside. [HOWARD exits, pushing the table off. WILLY, quickly surrounded by darkness, stares into space, exhausted. Now the music is heard— BEN's music—first distantly, then closer, closer. As WILLY speaks, BEN appears just as WILLY always remembered him—carrying valise and umbrella.]

WILLY. Oh, Ben, how did you do it? What is the answer? Did you wind up the Alaska deal already?

BEN. Doesn't take much time if you know what you're doing. Just a short business trip. Boarding ship in an hour. Wanted to say good-by.

WILLY. Ben, I've got to talk to you.

BEN. [Glancing at his watch.] Haven't the time, William.

WILLY. Ben, nothing's working out. I don't know what to do.

BEN. Now, look here, William. I've bought timberland in Alaska and I need a man to look after things for me.

WILLY. God, timberland! Me and my boys in those grand outdoors!

BEN. You've a new continent at your doorstep, William. Get out of these cities, they're full of talk and time payments and courts of law. Screw on your fists and you can fight for a fortune up there.

WILLY. Yes, yes! Linda, Linda!

[LINDA enters as of old, with the wash. We are again behind the house where WILLY's imagination has taken us.]

LINDA. Oh, you're back?

BEN. I haven't much time.

WILLY. No, wait! Linda, he's got a proposition for me in Alaska.

LINDA. But you've got—[To BEN.] He's got a beautiful job here.

WILLY. But in Alaska, kid, I could—

LINDA. You're doing well enough, Willy!

BEN. [To LINDA.] Enough for what, my dear?

LINDA. [Frightened of BEN and angry at him.] Don't say those things to him! Enough to be happy right here, right now. [To WILLY, while BEN laughs.] Why must everybody conquer the world? You're well liked, and the boys love you, and someday—[To BEN.]— why, old man Wagner told him just the other day that if he keeps it up he'll be a member of the firm, didn't he, Willy?

WILLY. Sure, sure. I am building something with this firm, Ben, and if a man is building something he must be on the right track, mustn't he?

BEN. What are you building? Lay your hand on it. Where is it?

WILLY. [Hesitantly.] That's true, Linda, there's nothing.

LINDA. Why? [To BEN.] There's a man eighty-four years old—

WILLY. That's right, Ben, that's right.

When I look at that man I say, what is there to worry about?

BEN. Bah!

WILLY. It's true, Ben. All he has to do is go into any city, pick up the phone, and he's making his living and you know why?

BEN. [*Picking up his valise.*] I've got to go.

WILLY. [*Holding* BEN *back.*] Look at this boy! [BIFF, *in his high school sweater, enters carrying suitcase.* HAPPY *carries* BIFF's *shoulder guards, gold helmet, and football pants.*]

WILLY. Without a penny to his name, three great universities are begging for him, and from there the sky's the limit, because it's not what you do, Ben. It's who you know and the smile on your face! It's contacts, Ben, contacts! The whole wealth of Alaska passes over the lunch table at the Commodore Hotel, and that's the wonder, the wonder of this country, that a man can end with diamonds here on the basis of being liked! [*He turns to* BIFF.] And that's why when you get out on that field today it's important. Because thousands of people will be rooting for you and loving you. [*To* BEN, *who has again begun to leave.*] And Ben! when he walks into a business office his name will sound out like a bell and all the doors will open to him! I've seen it, Ben, I've seen it a thousand times! You can't feel it with your hand like timber, but it's there!

BEN. Good-by, William.

WILLY. Ben, am I right? Don't you think I'm right? I value your advice.

BEN. There's a new continent at your doorstep, William. You could walk out rich. Rich! [*He is gone.*]

WILLY. We'll do it here, Ben! You hear me? We're gonna do it here! [*Young* BERNARD *rushes in. The gay music of the* BOYS *is heard.*]

BERNARD. Oh, gee, I was afraid you left already!

WILLY. Why? What time is it?

BERNARD. It's half-past one!

WILLY. Well, come on, everybody! Ebbets Field next stop! Where's the pennants? [*He rushes through the "wall"* of the kitchen and out into the living-room.*]

LINDA. [*To* BIFF.] Did you pack fresh underwear?

BIFF. [*Who has been limbering up.*] I want to go!

BERNARD. Biff, I'm carrying your helmet, ain't I?

HAPPY. No, I'm carrying the helmet.

BERNARD. Oh, Biff, you promised me.

HAPPY. I'm carrying the helmet.

BERNARD. How am I going to get in the locker room?

LINDA. Let him carry the shoulder guards. [*She puts her coat and hat on in the kitchen.*]

BERNARD. Can I, Biff? 'Cause I told everybody I'm going to be in the locker room.

HAPPY. In Ebbets Field it's the club-house.

BERNARD. I meant the clubhouse. Biff!

HAPPY. Biff!

BIFF. [*Grandly, after a slight pause.*] Let him carry the shoulder guards.

HAPPY. [*As he gives* BERNARD *the shoulder guards.*] Stay close to us now. [WILLY *rushes in with the pennants.*]

WILLY. [*Handing them out.*] Everybody wave when Biff comes out on the field. [HAPPY *and* BERNARD *run off.*] You set now, boy? [*The music has died away.*]

BIFF. Ready to go, Pop. Every muscle is ready.

WILLY. You realize what this means?

BIFF. That's right, Pop.

WILLY. [*Feeling* BIFF's *muscles.*] You're comin' home this afternoon captain of the All-Scholastic Championship Team of the City of New York.

BIFF. I got it, Pop. And remember, pal, when I take off my helmet, that touchdown is for you.

WILLY. Let's go! [*He is starting out, with his arm around* BIFF, *when* CHARLEY *enters, as of old, in knickers.*] I got no room for you, Charley.

CHARLEY. Room? For what?

WILLY. In the car.

CHARLEY. You goin' for a ride? I wanted to shoot some casino.

WILLY. [*Furiously.*] Casino! [*Incredulously.*] Don't you realize what today is?

LINDA. Oh, he knows, Willy. He's just kidding you.

WILLY. That's nothing to kid about!

CHARLEY. No, Linda, what's goin' on?

LINDA. He's playing in Ebbets Field.

CHARLEY. Baseball in this weather?

WILLY. Don't talk to him. Come on, come on! [*He is pushing them out.*]

CHARLEY. Wait a minute, didn't you hear the news?

WILLY. What?

CHARLEY. Don't you listen to the radio? Ebbets Field just blew up.

WILLY. You go to hell! [CHARLEY *laughs. Pushing them out.*] Come on, come on! We're late.

CHARLEY. [*As they go.*] Knock a homer, Biff, knock a homer!

WILLY. [*The last to leave, turning to* CHARLEY.] I don't think that was funny, Charley. This is the greatest day of his life.

CHARLEY. Willy, when are you going to grow up?

WILLY. Yeah, heh? When this game is over, Charley, you'll be laughing out of the other side of your face. They'll be calling him another Red Grange. Twenty-five thousand a year.

CHARLEY. [*Kidding.*] Is that so?

WILLY. Yeah, that's so.

CHARLEY. Well, then, I'm sorry, Willy. But tell me something.

WILLY. What?

CHARLEY. Who is Red Grange?

WILLY. Put up your hands. Goddam you, put up your hands! [CHARLEY, *chuckling, shakes his head and walks away, around the right corner of the stage.* WILLY *follows him. The music rises to a mocking frenzy.*] Who the hell do you think you are, better than everybody else? You don't know everything, you big, ignorant, stupid . . . Put up your hands!

[WILLY *has followed* CHARLEY *off the stage around the side of the house, yelling at him indignantly. As soon as he disappears a light brightens the opposite side of the stage, where, near the edge, we discover an office table and* BERNARD *sitting at it, whistling quietly to himself. This is the* BERNARD *of today. No longer the anxious boy, he is quite self-pos-sessed, still earnest and modest, but quite manly. He is sitting in* CHARLEY's *outer office waiting for his father. We hear traffic sounds from outside. On the table are two tennis rackets and a leather briefcase. Now a new sound is heard—*WILLY's *shouting voice as though coming from the hallway of this office building.*]

WILLY. [*Heard from the outer hallway.*] What are you walking away for? Don't walk away! If you're going to say something, say it to my face! I know you laugh at me behind my back. You'll laugh out of the other side of your god-dam face after this game. Touchdown! Touchdown! Eighty thousand people! Touchdown! Right between the goal posts. [*Hearing this,* BERNARD *gets up as* JENNY, *his father's secretary, hurries in with deep concern.*]

JENNY. [*Distressed.*] Say, Bernard, will you go out in the hall?

BERNARD. What is that noise? Who is it?

JENNY. Mr. Loman. He just got off the elevator.

BERNARD. [*Getting up.*] Who's he arguing with?

JENNY. Nobody. There's nobody with him. I can't deal with him any more, and your father gets all upset everytime he comes. I've got a lot of typing to do, and your father's waiting to sign it. Will you see him?

WILLY. [*Entering.*] Touchdown! Touch—[*He sees* JENNY.] Jenny, Jenny, good to see you. How're ya? Workin'? Or still honest?

JENNY. Fine. How've you been feeling?

WILLY. Not much any more, Jenny. Ha, ha! [*He is surprised to see the rackets.*]

BERNARD. Hello, Uncle Willy.

WILLY. [*Almost shocked.*] Bernard! Well, look who's here! [*He comes quickly, guiltily, to* BERNARD *and warmly shakes his hand.*]

BERNARD. How are you? Good to see you.

WILLY. What are you doing here?

BERNARD. Oh, just stopped by to see Pop. Get off my feet till my train leaves. I'm going to Washington in a few minutes.

WILLY. Is he in?

BERNARD. Yes, he's in his office with the accountant. Sit down.

WILLY. [*Sitting down.*] What're you going to do in Washington?

BERNARD. Oh, just a case I've got there, Willy.

WILLY. That so? [*Indicating the rackets.*] You going to play tennis there?

BERNARD. I'm staying with a friend who's got a court.

WILLY. Don't say. His own tennis court. Must be fine people, I bet.

BERNARD. They are, very nice. Dad tells me Biff's in town.

WILLY. [*With a big smile.*] Yeah, Biff's in. Working on a very big deal, Bernard.

BERNARD. What's Biff doing?

WILLY. Well, he's been doing very big things in the West. But he decided to establish himself here. Very big. We're having dinner. Did I hear your wife had a boy?

BERNARD. That's right. Our second.

WILLY. Two boys! What do you know!

BERNARD. What kind of a deal has Biff got?

WILLY. Well, Bill Oliver—very big sporting-goods man—he wants Biff very badly. Called him in from the West. Long distance, carte blanche, special deliveries. Your friends have their own private tennis court?

BERNARD. You still with the old firm, Willy?

WILLY. [*After a pause.*] I'm—I'm overjoyed to see how you made the grade, Bernard, overjoyed. It's an encouraging thing to see a young man really—really — Looks very good for Biff—very—[*He breaks off, then.*] Bernard—[*He is so full of emotion, he breaks off again.*]

BERNARD. What is it, Willy?

WILLY. [*Small and alone.*] What— what's the secret?

BERNARD. What secret?

WILLY. How—how did you? Why didn't he ever catch on?

BERNARD. I wouldn't know that, Willy.

WILLY. [*Confidentially, desperately.*] You were his friend, his boyhood friend. There's something I don't understand about it. His life ended after that Ebbets

Field game. From the age of seventeen nothing good ever happened to him.

BERNARD. He never trained himself for anything.

WILLY. But he did, he did. After high school he took so many correspondence courses. Radio mechanics; television; God knows what, and never made the slightest mark.

BERNARD. [*Taking off his glasses.*] Willy, do you want to talk candidly?

WILLY. [*Rising, faces BERNARD.*] I regard you as a very brilliant man, Bernard. I value your advice.

BERNARD. Oh, the hell with the advice, Willy. I couldn't advise you. There's just one thing I've always wanted to ask you. When he was supposed to graduate, and the math teacher flunked him—

WILLY. Oh, that son-of-a-bitch ruined his life.

BERNARD. Yeah, but, Willy, all he had to do was go to summer school and make up that subject.

WILLY. That's right, that's right.

BERNARD. Did you tell him not to go to summer school?

WILLY. Me? I begged him to go. I ordered him to go!

BERNARD. Then why wouldn't he go?

WILLY. Why? Why! Bernard, that question has been trailing me like a ghost for the last fifteen years. He flunked the subject, and laid down and died like a hammer hit him!

BERNARD. Take it easy, kid.

WILLY. Let me talk to you—I got nobody to talk to. Bernard, Bernard, was it my fault? Y'see? It keeps going around in my mind, maybe I did something to him. I got nothing to give him.

BERNARD. Don't take it so hard.

WILLY. Why did he lay down? What is the story there? You were his friend!

BERNARD. Willy, I remember, it was June, and our grades came out. And he'd flunked math.

WILLY. That son-of-a-bitch!

BERNARD. No, it wasn't right then. Biff just got very angry, I remember, and he was ready to enroll in summer school.

WILLY. [*Surprised.*] He was?

BERNARD. He wasn't beaten by it at all. But then, Willy, he disappeared from the block for almost a month. And I got the idea that he'd gone up to New England to see you. Did he have a talk with you then? [WILLY *stares in silence.*] Willy?

WILLY. [*With a strong edge of resentment in his voice.*] Yeah, he came to Boston. What about it?

BERNARD. Well, just that when he came back—I'll never forget this, it always mystifies me. Because I'd thought so well of Biff, even though he'd always taken advantage of me. I loved him, Willy, y'know? And he came back after that month and took his sneakers—remember those sneakers with "University of Virginia" printed on them? He was so proud of those, wore them every day. And he took them down in the cellar, and burned them up in the furnace. We had a fist fight. It lasted at least half an hour. Just the two of us, punching each other down the cellar, and crying right through it. I've often thought of how strange it was that I knew he'd given up his life. What happened in Boston, Willy? [WILLY *looks at him as at an intruder.*] I just bring it up because you asked me.

WILLY. [*Angrily.*] Nothing. What do you mean, "What happened?" What's that got to do with anything?

BERNARD. Well, don't get sore.

WILLY. What are you trying to do, blame it on me? If a boy lays down is that my fault?

BERNARD. Now, Willy, don't get—

WILLY. Well, don't—don't talk to me that way! What does that mean, "What happened?" [CHARLEY *enters. He is in his vest, and he carries a bottle of bourbon.*]

CHARLEY. Hey, you're going to miss that train. [*He waves the bottle.*]

BERNARD. Yeah, I'm going. [*He takes the bottle.*] Thanks, Pop. [*He picks up his rackets and bag.*] Good-by, Willy, and don't worry about it. You know, "If at first you don't succeed . . ."

WILLY. Yes, I believe in that.

BERNARD. But sometimes, Willy, it's better for a man just to walk away.

WILLY. Walk away?

BERNARD. That's right.

WILLY. But if you can't walk away?

BERNARD. [*After a slight pause.*] I guess that's when it's tough. [*Extending his hand.*] Good-by, Willy.

WILLY. [*Shaking* BERNARD'S *hand.*] Good-by, boy.

CHARLEY. [*An arm on* BERNARD'S *shoulder.*] How do you like this kid? Gonna argue a case in front of the Supreme Court.

BERNARD. [*Protesting.*] Pop!

WILLY. [*Genuinely shocked, pained, and happy.*] No! The Supreme Court!

BERNARD. I gotta run. 'By, Dad!

CHARLEY. Knock 'em dead, Bernard! [BERNARD *goes off.*]

WILLY. [*As* CHARLEY *takes out his wallet.*] The Supreme Court! And he didn't even mention it!

CHARLEY. [*Counting out money on the desk.*] He don't have to—he's gonna do it.

WILLY. And you never told him what to do, did you? You never took any interest in him.

CHARLEY. My salvation is that I never took any interest in anything. There's some money—fifty dollars. I got an accountant inside.

WILLY. Charley, look . . . [*With difficulty.*] I got my insurance to pay. If you can manage it—I need a hundred and ten dollars. [CHARLEY *doesn't reply for a moment; merely stops moving.*] I'd draw it from my bank but Linda would know, and I . . .

CHARLEY. Sit down, Willy.

WILLY. [*Moving toward the chair.*] I'm keeping an account of everything, remember. I'll pay every penny back. [*He sits.*]

CHARLEY. Now listen to me, Willy.

WILLY. I want you to know I appreciate . . .

CHARLEY. [*Sitting down on the table.*] Willy, what're you doin'? What the hell is goin' on in your head?

WILLY. Why? I'm simply . . .

CHARLEY. I offered you a job. You can make fifty dollars a week. And I won't send you on the road.

WILLY. I've got a job.

CHARLEY. Without pay? What kind of a job is a job without pay? [*He rises.*] Now, look, kid, enough is enough. I'm no genius but I know when I'm being insulted.

WILLY. Insulted!

CHARLEY. Why don't you want to work for me?

WILLY. What's the matter with you? I've got a job.

CHARLEY. Then what're you walkin' in here every week for?

WILLY. [Getting up.] Well, if you don't want me to walk in here—

CHARLEY. I am offering you a job.

WILLY. I don't want your goddam job!

CHARLEY. When the hell are you going to grow up?

WILLY. [Furiously.] You big ignoramus, if you say that to me again I'll rap you one! I don't care how big you are! [He's ready to fight. Pause.]

CHARLEY. [Kindly, going to him.] How much do you need, Willy?

WILLY. Charley, I'm strapped, I'm strapped. I don't know what to do. I was just fired.

CHARLEY. Howard fired you?

WILLY. That snotnose. Imagine that? I named him. I named him Howard.

CHARLEY. Willy, when're you gonna realize that them things don't mean anything? You named him Howard, but you can't sell that. The only thing you got in this world is what you can sell. And the funny thing is that you're a salesman, and you don't know that.

WILLY. I've always tried to think otherwise, I guess. I always felt that if a man was impressive, and well liked, that nothing—

CHARLEY. Why must everybody like you? Who liked J. P. Morgan? Was he impressive? In a Turkish bath he'd look like a butcher. But with his pockets on he was very well liked. Now listen, Willy, I know you don't like me, and nobody can say I'm in love with you, but I'll give you a job because—just for the hell of it, put it that way. Now what do you say?

WILLY. I—I just can't work for you, Charley.

CHARLEY. What're you, jealous of me?

WILLY. I can't work for you, that's all, don't ask me why.

CHARLEY. [Angered, takes out more bills.] You been jealous of me all your life, you damned fool! Here, pay your insurance. [He puts the money in WILLY's hand.]

WILLY. I'm keeping strict accounts.

CHARLEY. I've got some work to do. Take care of yourself. And pay your insurance.

WILLY. [Moving to the right.] Funny, y'know? After all the highways, and the trains, and the appointments, and the years, you end up worth more dead than alive.

CHARLEY. Willy, nobody's worth nothin' dead. [After a slight pause.] Did you hear what I said? [WILLY stands still, dreaming.]

CHARLEY. Willy!

WILLY. Apologize to Bernard for me when you see him. I didn't mean to argue with him. He's a fine boy. They're all fine boys, and they'll end up big—all of them. Someday they'll all play tennis together. Wish me luck, Charley. He saw Bill Oliver today.

CHARLEY. Good luck.

WILLY. [On the verge of tears.] Charley, you're the only friend I got. Isn't that a remarkable thing? [He goes out.]

CHARLEY. Jesus!

[CHARLEY stares after him a moment and follows. All light blacks out. Suddenly raucous music is heard, and a red glow rises on this forestage area. STANLEY, a young waiter, appears, carrying a table, followed by HAPPY, who is carrying two chairs.]

STANLEY. [Putting the table down.] That's all right, Mr. Loman, I can handle it myself. [He turns and takes the chairs from HAPPY and places them at the table.]

HAPPY. [Glancing around.] Oh, this is better.

STANLEY. Sure, in the front there you're in the middle of all kinds a noise. Whenever you got a party, Mr. Loman, you just tell me and I'll put you back here. Y'know, there's a lotta people they don't like it private, because when they go out they like to see a lotta action around them because they're sick and tired to stay in the house by theirself. But I know you, you ain't from Hackensack. You know what I mean?

HAPPY. [Sitting down.] So how's it coming, Stanley?

STANLEY. Ah, it's a dog's life. I only wish during the war they'd a took me in the Army. I coulda been dead by now.

HAPPY. My brother's back, Stanley.

STANLEY. Oh, he come back, heh? From the Far West.

HAPPY. Yeah, big cattle man, my brother, so treat him right. And my father's coming too.

STANLEY. Oh, your father too!

HAPPY. You got a couple of nice lobsters?

STANLEY. Hundred per cent, big.

HAPPY. I want them with the claws.

STANLEY. Don't worry, I don't give you no mice. [HAPPY laughs.] How about some wine? It'll put a head on the meal.

HAPPY. No. You remember, Stanley, that recipe I brought you from overseas? With the champagne in it?

STANLEY. Oh, yeah, sure. I still got it tacked up yet in the kitchen. But that'll have to cost a buck apiece anyways.

HAPPY. That's all right.

STANLEY. What'd you, hit a number or somethin'?

HAPPY. No, it's a little celebration. My brother is—I think he pulled off a big deal today. I think we're going into business together.

STANLEY. Great! That's the best for you. Because a family business, you know what I mean?—that's the best.

HAPPY. That's what I think.

STANLEY. 'Cause what's the difference? Somebody steals? It's in the family. Know what I mean? [Sotto voce.] Like this bartender here. The boss is goin' crazy what kinda leak he's got in the cash register. You put it in but it don't come out.

HAPPY. [Raising his head.] Sh!

STANLEY. What?

HAPPY. You notice I wasn't lookin' right or left, was I?

STANLEY. No.

HAPPY. And my eyes are closed.

STANLEY. So what's the—?

HAPPY. Strudel's comin'.

STANLEY. [Catching on, looks around.]

Ah, no, there's no—[He breaks off as a furred, lavishly dressed girl enters and sits at the next table. Both follow her with their eyes.]

STANLEY. Geez, how'd ya know?

HAPPY. I got radar or something. [Staring directly at her profile.] Oooooooo . . . Stanley.

STANLEY. I think that's for you, Mr. Loman.

HAPPY. Look at that mouth. Oh, God. And the binoculars.

STANLEY. Geez, you got a life, Mr. Loman.

HAPPY. Wait on her.

STANLEY. [Going to the girl's table.] Would you like a menu, ma'am?

GIRL. I'm expecting someone, but I'd like a—

HAPPY. Why don't you bring her—excuse me, miss, do you mind? I sell champagne, and I'd like you to try my brand. Bring her a champagne, Stanley.

GIRL. That's awfully nice of you.

HAPPY. Don't mention it. It's all company money. [He laughs.]

GIRL. That's a charming product to be selling, isn't it?

HAPPY. Oh, gets to be like everything else. Selling is selling, y'know.

GIRL. I suppose.

HAPPY. You don't happen to sell, do you?

GIRL. No, I don't sell.

HAPPY. Would you object to a compliment from a stranger? You ought to be on a magazine cover.

GIRL. [Looking at him a little archly.] I have been. [STANLEY comes in with a glass of champagne.]

HAPPY. What'd I say before, Stanley? You see? She's a cover girl.

STANLEY. Oh, I could see, I could see.

HAPPY. [To the GIRL.] What magazine?

GIRL. Oh, a lot of them. [She takes the drink.] Thank you.

HAPPY. You know what they say in France, don't you? "Champagne is the drink of the complexion"—Hya, Biff! [BIFF has entered and sits with HAPPY.]

BIFF. Hello, kid. Sorry I'm late.

HAPPY. I just got here. Uh, Miss—?

GIRL. Forsythe.

HAPPY. Miss Forsythe, this is my brother.

BIFF. Is Dad here?

HAPPY. His name is Biff. You might've heard of him. Great football player.

GIRL. Really? What team?

HAPPY. Are you familiar with football?

GIRL. No, I'm afraid I'm not.

HAPPY. Biff is quarterback with the New York Giants.

GIRL. Well, that is nice, isn't it? [*She drinks.*]

HAPPY. Good health.

GIRL. I'm happy to meet you.

HAPPY. That's my name. Hap. It's really Harold, but at West Point they called me Happy.

GIRL. [*Now really impressed.*] Oh, I see. How do you do? [*She turns her profile.*]

BIFF. Isn't Dad coming?

HAPPY. You want her?

BIFF. Oh, I could never make that.

HAPPY. I remember the time that idea would never come into your head. Where's the old confidence, Biff?

BIFF. I just saw Oliver—

HAPPY. Wait a minute. I've got to see that old confidence again. Do you want her? She's on call.

BIFF. Oh, no. [*He turns to look at the GIRL.*]

HAPPY. I'm telling you. Watch this. [*Turning to the GIRL.*] Honey? [*She turns to him.*] Are you busy?

GIRL. Well, I am . . . but I could make a phone call.

HAPPY. Do that, will you, honey? And see if you can get a friend. We'll be here for a while. Biff is one of the greatest football players in the country.

GIRL. [*Standing up.*] Well, I'm certainly happy to meet you.

HAPPY. Come back soon.

GIRL. I'll try.

HAPPY. Don't try, honey, try hard. [*The GIRL exits. STANLEY follows, shaking his head in bewildered admiration.*]

HAPPY. Isn't that a shame now? A beautiful girl like that? That's why I can't get married. There's not a good woman in a thousand. New York is loaded with them, kid!

BIFF. Hap, look—

HAPPY. I told you she was on call!

BIFF. [*Strangely unnerved.*] Cut it out, will ya? I want to say something to you.

HAPPY. Did you see Oliver?

BIFF. I saw him all right. Now look, I want to tell Dad a couple of things and I want you to help me.

HAPPY. What? Is he going to back you?

BIFF. Are you crazy? You're out of your goddam head, you know that?

HAPPY. Why? What happened?

BIFF. [*Breathlessly.*] I did a terrible thing today, Hap. It's been the strangest day I ever went through. I'm all numb, I swear.

HAPPY. You mean he wouldn't see you?

BIFF. Well, I waited six hours for him, see? All day. Kept sending my name in. Even tried to date his secretary so she'd get me to him, but no soap.

HAPPY. Because you're not showin' the old confidence, Biff. He remembered you, didn't he?

BIFF. [*Stopping HAPPY with a gesture.*] Finally, about five o'clock, he comes out. Didn't remember who I was or anything. I felt like such an idiot, Hap.

HAPPY. Did you tell him my Florida idea?

BIFF. He walked away. I saw him for one minute. I got so mad I could've torn the walls down! How the hell did I ever get the idea I was a salesman there? I even believed myself that I'd been a salesman for him! And then he gave me one look and—I realized what a ridiculous lie my whole life has been! We've been talking in a dream for fifteen years. I was a shipping clerk.

HAPPY. What'd you do?

BIFF. [*With great tension and wonder.*] Well, he left, see. And the secretary went out. I was all alone in the waiting-room. I don't know what came over me, Hap. The next thing I know I'm in his office—paneled walls, everything. I can't explain it. I—Hap, I took his fountain pen.

HAPPY. Geez, did he catch you?

BIFF. I ran out. I ran down all eleven flights. I ran and ran and ran.

HAPPY. That was an awful dumb—what'd you do that for?

BIFF. [*Agonized.*] I don't know, I just—wanted to take something, I don't know. You gotta help me, Hap, I'm gonna tell Pop.

HAPPY. You crazy? What for?

BIFF. Hap, he's got to understand that I'm not the man somebody lends that kind of money to. He thinks I've been spiting him all these years and it's eating him up.

HAPPY. That's just it. You tell him something nice.

BIFF. I can't.

HAPPY. Say you got a lunch date with Oliver tomorrow.

BIFF. So what do I do tomorrow?

HAPPY. You leave the house tomorrow and come back at night and say Oliver is thinking it over. And he thinks it over for a couple of weeks, and gradually it fades away and nobody's the worse.

BIFF. But it'll go on forever!

HAPPY. Dad is never so happy as when he's looking forward to something!

[WILLY *enters.*]

HAPPY. Hello, scout!

WILLY. Gee, I haven't been here in years! [STANLEY *has followed* WILLY *in and sets a chair for him.* STANLEY *starts off but* HAPPY *stops him.*]

HAPPY. Stanley! [STANLEY *stands by, waiting for an order.*]

BIFF. [*Going to* WILLY *with guilt, as to an invalid.*] Sit down, Pop. You want a drink?

WILLY. Sure, I don't mind.

BIFF. Let's get a load on.

WILLY. You look worried.

BIFF. N-no. [*To* STANLEY.] Scotch all around. Make it doubles.

STANLEY. Doubles, right. [*He goes.*]

WILLY. You had a couple already, didn't you?

BIFF. Just a couple, yeah.

WILLY. Well, what happened, boy? [*Nodding affirmatively, with a smile.*] Everything go all right?

BIFF. [*Takes a breath, then reaches out and grasps* WILLY's *hand.*] Pal . . . [*He is smiling bravely, and* WILLY *is smiling too.*] I had an experience today.

HAPPY. Terrific, Pop.

WILLY. That so? What happened?

BIFF. [*High, slightly alcoholic, above the earth.*] I'm going to tell you everything from first to last. It's been a strange day. [*Silence. He looks around, composes himself as best he can, but his breath keeps breaking the rhythm of his voice.*] I had to wait quite a while for him, and—

WILLY. Oliver?

BIFF. Yeah, Oliver. All day, as a matter of cold fact. And a lot of—instances—facts, Pop, facts about my life came back to me. Who was it, Pop? Who ever said I was a salesman with Oliver?

WILLY. Well, you were.

BIFF. No, Dad, I was a shipping clerk.

WILLY. But you were practically—

BIFF. [*With determination.*] Dad, I don't know who said it first, but I was never a salesman for Bill Oliver.

WILLY. What're you talking about?

BIFF. Let's hold on to the facts tonight, Pop. We're not going to get anywhere bullin' around. I was a shipping clerk.

WILLY. [*Angrily.*] All right, now listen to me—

BIFF. Why don't you let me finish?

WILLY. I'm not interested in stories about the past or any crap of that kind because the woods are burning, boys, you understand? There's a big blaze going on all around. I was fired today.

BIFF. [*Shocked.*] How could you be?

WILLY. I was fired, and I'm looking for a little good news to tell your mother, because the woman has waited and the woman has suffered. The gist of it is that I haven't got a story left in my head, Biff. So don't give me a lecture about facts and aspects. I am not interested. Now what've you go to say to me? [STANLEY *enters with three drinks. They wait until he leaves.*] Did you see Oliver?

BIFF. Jesus, Dad!

WILLY. You mean you didn't go up there?

HAPPY. Sure he went up there.

BIFF. I did. I—saw him. How could they fire you?

WILLY. [*On the edge of his chair.*] What kind of a welcome did he give you?

BIFF. He won't even let you work on commission?

WILLY. I'm out! [*Driving.*] So tell me, he gave you a warm welcome?

HAPPY. Sure, Pop, sure!

BIFF. [*Driven.*] Well, it was kind of—

WILLY. I was wondering if he'd remember you. [*To* HAPPY.] Imagine, man doesn't see him for ten, twelve years and gives him that kind of a welcome!

HAPPY. Damn right!

BIFF. [*Trying to return to the offensive.*] Pop, look—

WILLY. You know why he remembered you, don't you? Because you impressed him in those days.

BIFF. Let's talk quietly and get this down to the facts, huh?

WILLY. [*As though* BIFF *had been interrupting.*] Well, what happened? It's great news, Biff. Did he take you into his office or'd you talk in the waiting-room?

BIFF. Well, he came in, see, and—

WILLY. [*With a big smile.*] What'd he say? Betcha he threw his arm around you.

BIFF. Well, he kinda—

WILLY. He's a fine man. [*To* HAPPY.] Very hard man to see, y'know.

HAPPY. [*Agreeing.*] Oh, I know.

WILLY. [*To* BIFF.] Is that where you had the drinks?

BIFF. Yeah, he gave me a couple of— no, no!

HAPPY. [*Cutting in.*] He told him my Florida idea.

WILLY. Don't interrupt. [*To* BIFF.] How'd he react to the Florida idea?

BIFF. Dad, will you give me a minute to explain?

WILLY. I've been waiting for you to explain since I sat down here! What happened? He took you into his office and what?

BIFF. Well—I talked. And—and he listened, see.

WILLY. Famous for the way he listens, y'know. What was his answer?

BIFF. His answer was— [*He breaks off, suddenly angry.*] Dad, you're not letting me tell you what I want to tell you!

WILLY. [*Accusing, angered.*] You didn't see him, did you?

BIFF. I did see him!

WILLY. What'd you insult him or something? You insulted him, didn't you?

BIFF. Listen, will you let me out of it, will you just let me out of it!

HAPPY. What the hell!

WILLY. Tell me what happened!

BIFF. [*To* HAPPY.] I can't talk to him!

[*A single, raw trumpet note jars the ear, and instantly the* LOMAN *house which has remained visible behind the little restaurant area, but in relative darkness—the house comes alive as it is, stained with greenish leaves as though seen through the murk of a memory. And while* BIFF *and* HAPPY *are talking with* WILLY *in the restaurant, we glimpse* WILLY'S *thought of young* BERNARD, *dressed in knickers as he used to be, rushing into the kitchen and calling . . .*]

YOUNG BERNARD. [*Frantically.*] Mrs. Loman, Mrs. Loman!

HAPPY. Tell him what happened!

BIFF. [*To* HAPPY.] Shut up and leave me alone!

WILLY. No, no! You had to go and flunk math!

BIFF. What math? What're you talking about?

YOUNG BERNARD. Mrs. Loman, Mrs. Loman!

[LINDA *appears in the house, as of old.*]

WILLY. [*Wildly.*] Math, math, math!

BIFF. Take it easy, Pop!

YOUNG BERNARD. Mrs. Loman!

WILLY. [*Furiously.*] If you hadn't flunked you'd've been set by now!

BIFF. Now, look, I'm gonna tell you what happened, and you're going to listen to me.

YOUNG BERNARD. Mrs. Loman!

BIFF. I waited six hours—

HAPPY. What the hell are you saying?

BIFF. I kept sending in my name but he wouldn't see me. So finally he . . . [*He continues unheard as light fades low on the restaurant, and our total attention is on the house.*]

YOUNG BERNARD. Biff flunked math!

LINDA. No!

YOUNG BERNARD. Birnbaum flunked him! They won't graduate him!

LINDA. But they have to. He's gotta go to the university. Where is he? Biff! Biff!

YOUNG BERNARD. No, he left. He went to Grand Central.

LINDA. Grand— You mean he went to Boston!

YOUNG BERNARD. Is Uncle Willy in Boston?

LINDA. Oh, maybe Willy can talk to the teacher. Oh, the poor, poor boy!

[*The light on* BERNARD *and* LINDA *suddenly snaps out, and we are back in the restaurant where* BIFF, *who has been "talking" throughout this imagined scene, now becomes audible to us. He is holding up a fountain pen, and* WILLY *is staring at him as though desperately trying to focus his mind on what his son is saying.*]

BIFF. . . . so I'm washed up with Oliver, you understand? Are you listening to me?

WILLY. [*At a loss.*] Yeah, sure. If you hadn't flunked—

BIFF. Flunked what? What're you talking about?

WILLY. Don't blame everything on me! I didn't flunk math—you did! What pen?

HAPPY. That was awful dumb, Biff, a pen like that is worth—

WILLY. [*Seeing the pen for the first time.*] You took Oliver's pen?

BIFF. [*Weakening.*] Dad, I just explained it to you.

WILLY. You stole Bill Oliver's fountain pen!

BIFF. I didn't exactly steal it! That's just what I've been explaining to you!

HAPPY. He had it in his hand and just then Oliver walked in, so he got nervous and stuck it in his pocket!

WILLY. My God, Biff!

BIFF. I never intended to do it, Dad!

[*On the heels of* BIFF's *shout we hear, as though out of the air, the phone-distorted voice of a hotel switchboard operator.*]

OPERATOR'S VOICE. Standish Arms, Good evening!

WILLY. [*Shouting wildly into the air.*] I'm not in my room!

BIFF. [*Frightened.*] Dad, what's the matter. [*He and* HAPPY *stand up.*]

OPERATOR. Ringing Mr. Loman for you!

WILLY. I'm not there, stop it!

BIFF. [*Horrified, gets down on one knee before* WILLY.] Dad, I'll make good, I'll make good. [WILLY *tries to get to his feet.* BIFF *holds him down.*] Sit down now.

WILLY. No, you're no good, you're no good for anything.

BIFF. I am, Dad, I'll find something else, you understand? Now don't worry about anything. [*He holds up* WILLY's *face.*] Talk to me, Dad.

OPERATOR. Mr. Loman does not answer. Shall I page him?

WILLY. [*Attempting to stand, as though to rush and silence the Operator.*] No, no, no!

HAPPY. He'll strike something. Pop!

WILLY. No, no . . .

BIFF. [*Desperately, standing over* WILLY.] Pop, listen! Listen to me! I'm telling you something good. Oliver talked to his partner about the Florida idea. You listening? He—he talked to his partner, and he came to me . . . I'm going to be all right, you hear? Dad, listen to me, he said it was just a question of the amount!

WILLY. Then you . . . got it?

HAPPY. He's gonna be terrific, Pop!

WILLY. [*Trying to stand.*] Then you got it, haven't you? You got it! You got it!

BIFF. [*Agonized, holds* WILLY *down.*] No, no. Look, Pop. I'm supposed to have lunch with them tomorrow. I'm just telling you this so you'll know that I can still make an impression, Pop. And I'll make good somewhere, but I can't go tomorrow, see?

WILLY. Why not? You simply—

BIFF. But the pen, Pop!

WILLY. You give it to him and tell him it was an oversight!

HAPPY. Sure, have lunch tomorrow!

BIFF. I can't say that—

WILLY. You were doing a crossword puzzle and accidentally used his pen!

BIFF. Listen, kid, I took those balls years ago, now I walk in with his fountain pen? That clinches it, don't you see? I can't face him like that! I'll try elsewhere.

PAGE'S VOICE. Paging Mr. Loman!

WILLY. Don't you want to be anything?

BIFF. Pop, how can I go back?

WILLY. You don't want to be anything, is that what's behind it?

BIFF. [*Now angry at* WILLY *for not crediting his sympathy.*] Don't take it that way! You think it was easy walking into that office after what I'd done to him? A team of horses couldn't have dragged me back to Bill Oliver!

WILLY. Then why'd you go?

BIFF. Why did I go? Why did I go! Look at you! Look at what's become of you! [WILLY *hears the laughter of* THE WOMAN *and his head turns.*]

WILLY. Biff, you're going to go to that lunch tomorrow, or—

BIFF. I can't go. I've got no appointment!

HAPPY. Biff, for . . . !

WILLY. Are you spiting me?

BIFF. Don't take it that way! Goddammit!

WILLY. [*Strikes* BIFF *and falters away from the table.*] You rotten little louse! Are you spiting me?

THE WOMAN'S VOICE. Someone's at the door, Willy!

BIFF. I'm no good, can't you see what I am?

HAPPY. [*Separating them.*] Hey, you're in a restaurant! Now cut it out, both of you! [*The girls enter.*] Hello, girls, sit down. [*The* WOMAN'S *laughter is heard again.*]

MISS FORSYTHE. I guess we might as well. This is Letta.

THE WOMAN'S VOICE. Willy, are you going to wake up?

BIFF. [*Ignoring* WILLY.] How're ya, miss, sit down. What do you drink?

MISS FORSYTHE. Letta might not be able to stay long.

LETTA. I gotta get up very early tomorrow. I got jury duty. I'm so excited! Were you fellows ever on a jury?

BIFF. No, but I been in front of them! [*The girls laugh.*] This is my father.

LETTA. Isn't he cute? Sit down with us, Pop.

HAPPY. Sit him down, Biff!

BIFF. [*Going to him.*] Come on, slugger, drink us under the table. To hell

with it! Come on, sit down, pal. [*On* BIFF's *last insistence,* WILLY *is about to sit.*]

THE WOMAN'S VOICE. [*Now urgently.*] Willy, are you going to answer the door! [*The* WOMAN'S *call pulls* WILLY *back. He starts left, befuddled.*]

BIFF. Hey, where are you going?

WILLY. Open the door.

BIFF. The door?

WILLY. The washroom . . . the door . . . where's the door?

BIFF. [*Leading* WILLY *to the right.*] Just go straight down. [WILLY *moves right.*]

THE WOMAN'S VOICE. Willy, Willy, are you going to get up, get up, get up, get up? [WILLY *exits right.*]

LETTA. I think it's sweet you bring your daddy along.

MISS FORSYTHE. Oh, he isn't really your father!

BIFF. [*At left, turning to her resentfully.*] Miss Forsythe, you've just seen a prince walk by. A fine, troubled prince. A hard-working, unappreciated prince. A pal, you understand? A good companion. Always for his boys.

LETTA. That's so sweet.

HAPPY. Well, girls, what's the program? We're wasting time. Come on, Biff. Gather round. Where would you like to go?

BIFF. Why don't you do something for him?

HAPPY. Me!

BIFF. Don't you give a damn for him, Hap?

HAPPY. What're you talking about? I'm the one who—

BIFF. I sense it, you don't give a good goddam about him. [*He takes the rolled-up hose from his pocket and puts it on the table in front of* HAPPY.] Look what I found in the cellar, for Christ's sake. How can you bear to let it go on?

HAPPY. Me? Who goes away? Who runs off and—

BIFF. Yeah, but he doesn't mean anything to you. You could help him—I can't! Don't you understand what I'm talking about? He's going to kill himself, don't you know that?

HAPPY. Don't I know it! Me!

BIFF. Hap, help him! Jesus . . . help him . . . Help me, help me, I can't bear to look at his face! [*Ready to weep, he hurries out, up right.*]

HAPPY. [*Starting after him.*] Where are you going?

MISS FORSYTHE. What's he so mad about?

HAPPY. Come on, girls, we'll catch up with him.

MISS FORSYTHE. [*As* HAPPY *pushes her out.*] Say, I don't like that temper of his!

HAPPY. He's just a little overstrung, he'll be all right!

WILLY. [*Off* left, *as* THE WOMAN *laughs.*] Don't answer! Don't answer!

LETTA. Don't you want to tell your father—

HAPPY. No, that's not my father. He's just a guy. Come on, we'll catch Biff, and, honey, we're going to paint this town! Stanley, where's the check! Hey, Stanley!

[*They exit.* STANLEY *looks toward left.*]

STANLEY. [*Calling to* HAPPY *indignantly.*] Mr. Loman! Mr. Loman!

[STANLEY *picks up a chair and follows them off the stage and all light goes out on "the restaurant." Instantly, from the opposite side of the stage,* THE WOMAN *enters laughing, and* WILLY *follows her buttoning up his shirt. She is in a black slip. Raw, sensuous music accompanies their speech, as well as the sound of knocking on a door. Now, on the background immediately around them we notice a pattern of hotel wallpaper, and* WILLY *keeps glancing toward a certain direction as though at the door of a hotel room where the knocking is coming from.*]

WILLY. Will you stop laughing? Will you stop?

THE WOMAN. Aren't you going to answer the door? He'll wake the whole hotel.

WILLY. I'm not expecting anybody.

THE WOMAN. Whyn't you have another drink, honey, and stop being so damn self-centered?

WILLY. I'm so lonely.

THE WOMAN. You know you ruined me, Willy? From now on, whenever you come to the office, I'll see that you go right through to the buyers. No waiting at my desk any more, Willy. You ruined me.

WILLY. That's nice of you to say that.

THE WOMAN. Gee, you are self-centered! Why so sad? You are the saddest, self-centeredest soul I ever did see-saw. [*She laughs. He kisses her.*] Come on inside, drummer boy. It's silly to be dressing in the middle of the night. [*As knocking is heard.*] Aren't you going to answer the door?

WILLY. They're knocking on the wrong door.

THE WOMAN. But I felt the knocking. And he heard us talking in here. Maybe the hotel's on fire!

WILLY. [*His terror rising.*] It's a mistake.

THE WOMAN. Then tell him to go away!

WILLY. There's nobody there.

THE WOMAN. It's getting on my nerves, Willy. There's somebody standing out there and it's getting on my nerves!

WILLY. [*Pushing her away from him.*] All right, stay in the bathroom here, and don't come out. I think there's a law in Massachusetts about it, so don't come out. It may be that new room clerk. He looked very mean. So don't come out. It's a mistake, there's no fire.

[*The knocking is heard again. He takes a few steps away from her, and she vanishes into the wing. The light follows him, and now he is facing young* BIFF, *who carries a suitcase.* BIFF *steps toward him. The music is gone.*]

BIFF. Why didn't you answer?

WILLY. Biff! What are you doing in Boston?

BIFF. Why didn't you answer? I've been knocking for five minutes, I called you on the phone—

WILLY. I just heard you. I was in the bathroom and had the door shut. Did anything happen home?

BIFF. Dad—I let you down.

WILLY. What do you mean?

BIFF. Dad . . .

WILLY. Biffo, what's this about? [*Putting his arm around* BIFF.] Come on, let's go downstairs and get you a malted.

BIFF. Dad, I flunked math.

WILLY. Not for the term?

BIFF. The term. I haven't got enough credits to graduate.

WILLY. You mean to say Bernard wouldn't give you the answers?

BIFF. He did, he tried, but I only got a sixty-one.

WILLY. And they wouldn't give you four points?

BIFF. Birnbaum refused absolutely. I begged him, Pop, but he won't give me those points. You gotta talk to him before they close the school. Because if he saw the kind of man you are, and you just talked to him in your way, I'm sure he'd come through for me. The class came right before practice, see, and I didn't go enough. Would you talk to him? He'd like you, Pop. You know the way you could talk.

WILLY. You're on. We'll drive right back.

BIFF. Oh, Dad, good work! I'm sure he'll change it for you!

WILLY. Go downstairs and tell the clerk I'm checkin' out. Go right down.

BIFF. Yes, sir! See, the reason he hates me, Pop—one day he was late for class so I got up at the blackboard and imitated him. I crossed my eyes and talked with a lithp.

WILLY. [Laughing.] You did? The kids like it?

BIFF. They nearly died laughing!

WILLY. Yeah? What'd you do?

BIFF. The thquare root of thixthy twee is . . . [WILLY bursts out laughing; BIFF joins him.] And in the middle of it he walked in!

[WILLY laughs and THE WOMAN joins in offstage.]

WILLY. [Without hesitation.] Hurry downstairs and—

BIFF. Somebody in there?

WILLY. No, that was next door.

[The WOMAN laughs offstage.]

BIFF. Somebody got in your bathroom!

WILLY. No, it's the next room, there's a party—

THE WOMAN. [Enters, laughing. She lisps this.] Can I come in? There's something in the bathtub, Willy, and it's moving! [WILLY looks at BIFF, who is staring open-mouthed and horrified at THE WOMAN.]

WILLY. Ah—you better go back to your room. They must be finished painting by now. They're painting her room so I let her take a shower here. Go back, go back . . . [He pushes her.]

THE WOMAN. [Resisting.] But I've got to get dressed, Willy, I can't—

WILLY. Get out of here! Go back, go back . . . [Suddenly striving for the ordinary.] This is Miss Francis, Biff, she's a buyer. They're painting her room. Go back, Miss Francis, go back . . .

THE WOMAN. But my clothes, I can't go out naked in the hall!

WILLY. [Pushing her offstage.] Get outa here! Go back, go back! [BIFF slowly sits down on his suitcase as the argument continues offstage.]

THE WOMAN. Where's my stockings? You promised me stockings, Willy!

WILLY. I have no stockings here!

THE WOMAN. You had two boxes of size nine sheers for me, and I want them!

WILLY. Here, for God's sake, will you get outa here!

THE WOMAN. [Enters holding a box of stockings.] I just hope there's nobody in the hall. That's all I hope. [To BIFF.] Are you football or baseball?

BIFF. Football.

THE WOMAN. [Angry, humiliated.] That's me too. G'night. [She snatches her clothes from WILLY, and walks out.]

WILLY. [After a pause.] Well, better get going. I want to get to the school first thing in the morning. Get my suits out of the closet. I'll get my valise. [BIFF doesn't move.] What's the matter? [BIFF remains motionless, tears falling.] She's a buyer. Buys for J. H. Simmons. She lives down the hall—they're painting. You don't imagine—[He breaks off. After a pause.] Now listen, pal, she's just a buyer. She sees merchandise in her room and they have to keep it looking just so . . . [Pause. Assuming command.] All right, get my suits. [BIFF doesn't move.] Now stop crying and do as I say. I gave you an order. Biff, I gave you an order! Is that what you do when I give you an order? How dare you cry! [Putting his arm around BIFF.] Now look, Biff, when you grow up you'll understand about these things. You mustn't—you mustn't overemphasize a thing like this. I'll see Birnbaum first thing in the morning.

BIFF. Never mind.

WILLY. [*Getting down beside* BIFF.] He's going to give you those points. I'll see to it.

BIFF. He wouldn't listen to you.

WILLY. He certainly will listen to me. You need those points for the U. of Virginia.

BIFF. I'm not going there.

WILLY. Heh? If I can't get him to change that mark you'll make it up in summer school. You've got all summer to—

BIFF. [*His weeping breaking from him.*] Dad . . .

WILLY. [*Infected by it.*] Oh, my boy . . .

BIFF. Dad . . .

WILLY. She's nothing to me, Biff. I was lonely, I was terribly lonely.

BIFF. You—you gave her Mama's stockings! [*His tears break through and he rises to go.*]

WILLY. [*Grabbing for* BIFF.] I gave you an order!

BIFF. Don't touch me, you—liar!

WILLY. Apologize for that!

BIFF. You fake! You phony little fake! You fake! [*Overcome, he turns quickly and weeping fully goes out with his suitcase.* WILLY *is left on the floor on his knees.*]

WILLY. I gave you an order! Biff, come back here or I'll beat you! Come back here! I'll whip you!

[WILLY *is on his knees pounding the floor with his fist, and as he calls his unheard commands the light changes around him, the wallpaper design has vanished from his surroundings, and now we see* STANLEY, *the waiter, crossing the stage and approaching him—this man who is on his knees, pounding the floor of the restaurant washroom.* WILLY, *not noticing him yet, is still bellowing his commands . . .*]

WILLY. I gave you an order . . . . ! [*And now, staring up into the waiter's face, he realizes . . . and falls silent,* blank. STANLEY *bends and helps him to his feet as a second waiter appears and watches from a distance.*]

STANLEY. Hey, let's pick it up, pick it up, Mr. Loman. Your boys left with the chippies. They said they'll see you home.

WILLY. But we were supposed to have dinner together. [*Music is heard,* WILLY'S *theme.*]

STANLEY. Can you make it?

WILLY. I'll—sure, I can make it. [*Suddenly concerned about his clothes.*] Do I—I look all right?

STANLEY. Sure, you look all right. [*He flicks a speck off* WILLY'S *lapel.*]

WILLY. Here—here's a dollar.

STANLEY. Oh, your son paid me. It's all right.

WILLY. [*Putting it in* STANLEY'S *hand.*] No, take it. You're a good boy.

STANLEY. Oh, no, you don't have to . . .

WILLY. Here—here's some more, I don't need it any more. [*After a slight pause.*] Tell me—is there a seed store in the neighborhood?

STANLEY. Seeds? You mean like to plant? [*As* WILLY *turns,* STANLEY *slips the money back into his jacket pocket.*]

WILLY. Yes. Carrots, peas . . .

STANLEY. Well, there's hardware stores on Sixth Avenue, but it may be too late now.

WILLY. [*Anxiously.*] Oh, I'd better hurry. I've got to get some seeds. [*He starts off to the right.*] I've got to get some seeds, right away. Nothing's planted. I don't have a thing in the ground. [WILLY *hurries out as the light goes down.* STANLEY *moves over to the right after him, watches him off. The other waiter has been staring at* WILLY.]

STANLEY. [*To the waiter.*] Well, whatta you looking at?

[*The waiter picks up the chairs and moves off right.* STANLEY *takes the table and follows him. The light fades on this area. There is a long pause, the sound of the flute coming over. The light gradually rises on the kitchen, which is empty.* HAPPY *appears at the door of the house, followed by* BIFF. HAPPY *is carrying a large bunch of long-stemmed roses. He enters the kitchen, looks around for*

LINDA. *Not seeing her, he turns to* BIFF, *who is just outside the house door, and makes a gesture with his hands, indicating* "Not here, I guess." *He looks into the living-room and freezes. Inside,* LINDA, *unseen, is seated,* WILLY'S *coat on her lap. She rises ominously and quietly and moves toward* HAPPY, *who backs up into the kitchen, afraid.*]

HAPPY. Hey, what're you doing up? [LINDA *says nothing but moves toward him implacably.*] Where's Pop? [*He keeps backing to the right, and now* LINDA *is in full view in the doorway to the living-room.*] Is he sleeping?

LINDA. Where were you?

HAPPY. [*Trying to laugh it off.*] We met two girls, Mom, very fine types. Here, we brought you some flowers. [*Offering them to her.*] Put them in your room, Ma. [*She knocks them to the floor at* BIFF'S *feet. He has now come inside and closed the door behind him. She stares at* BIFF, *silent.*] Now what'd you do that for? Mom, I want you to have some flowers—

LINDA. [*Cutting* HAPPY *off, violently to* BIFF.] Don't you care whether he lives or dies?

HAPPY. [*Going to the stairs.*] Come upstairs, Biff.

BIFF. [*With a flare of disgust, to* HAPPY.] Go away from me! [*To* LINDA.] What do you mean, lives or dies? Nobody's dying around here, pal.

LINDA. Get out of my sight! Get out of here!

BIFF. I wanna see the boss.

LINDA. You're not going near him!

BIFF. Where is he? [*He moves into the living-room and* LINDA *follows.*]

LINDA. [*Shouting after* BIFF.] You invite him for dinner. He looks forward to it all day—[BIFF *appears in his parents' bedroom, looks around, and exits.*]—and then you desert him there. There's no stranger you'd do that to!

HAPPY. Why? He had a swell time with us. Listen, when I—[LINDA *comes back into the kitchen.*]—desert him I hope I don't outlive the day!

LINDA. Get out of here!

HAPPY. Now look, Mom . . .

LINDA. Did you have to go to women tonight? You and your lousy rotten whores! [BIFF *re-enters the kitchen.*]

HAPPY. Mom, all we did was follow Biff around trying to cheer him up! [*To* BIFF.] Boy, what a night you gave me!

LINDA. Get out of here, both of you, and don't come back! I don't want you tormenting him any more. Go on now, get your things together! [*To* BIFF.] You can sleep in his apartment. [*She starts to pick up the flowers and stops herself.*] Pick up this stuff, I'm not your maid any more. Pick it up, you bum, you! [HAPPY *turns his back to her in refusal.* BIFF *slowly moves over and gets down on his knees, picking up the flowers.*] You're a pair of animals! Not one, not another living soul would have had the cruelty to walk out on that man in a restaurant!

BIFF. [*Not looking at her.*] Is that what he said?

LINDA. He didn't have to say anything. He was so humiliated he nearly limped when he came in.

HAPPY. But, Mom, he had a great time with us—

BIFF. [*Cutting him off violently.*] Shut up! [*Without another word,* HAPPY *goes upstairs.*]

LINDA. You! You didn't even go in to see if he was all right!

BIFF. [*Still on the floor in front of* LINDA, *the flowers in his hand; with self-loathing.*] No. Didn't. Didn't do a damned thing. How do you like that, heh? Left him babbling in a toilet.

LINDA. You louse. You . . .

BIFF. Now you hit it on the nose! [*He gets up, throws the flowers in the waste-basket.*] The scum of the earth, and you're looking at him!

LINDA. Get out of here!

BIFF. I gotta talk to the boss, Mom. Where is he?

LINDA. You're not going near him. Get out of this house!

BIFF. [*With absolute assurance, determination.*] No. We're gonna have an abrupt conversation, him and me.

LINDA. You're not talking to him! [*Hammering is heard from outside the house, off right.* BIFF *turns toward the noise.*]

LINDA. [*Suddenly pleading.*] Will you please leave him alone?

BIFF. What's he doing out there?

LINDA. He's planting the garden!

BIFF. [*Quietly.*] Now? Oh, my God!

[BIFF *moves outside,* LINDA *following. The light dies down on them and comes up on the center of the forestage as* WILLY *walks into it. He is carrying a flashlight, a hoe, and a handful of seed packets. He raps the top of the hoe sharply to fix it firmly, and then moves to the left, measuring off the distance with his foot. He holds the flashlight to look at the seed packets, reading off the instructions. He is in the blue of night in his back yard.*]

WILLY. Carrots . . . quarter-inch apart. Rows . . . one-foot rows. [*He measures it off.*] One foot. [*He puts down a package and measures off.*] Beets. [*He puts down another package and measures again.*] Lettuce. [*He reads the package, puts it down.*] One foot—[*He breaks off as* BEN *appears at the right and moves slowly down to him.*] What a proposition, ts, ts. Terrific, terrific. 'Cause she's suffered, Ben, the woman has suffered. You understand me? A man can't go out the way he came in, Ben, a man has got to add up to something. You can't, you can't—[BEN *moves toward him as though to interrupt.*] You gotta consider, now. Don't answer so quick. Remember, it's a guaranteed twenty-thousand-dollar proposition. Now look, Ben, I want you to go through the ins and outs of this thing with me. I've got nobody to talk to, Ben, and the woman has suffered, you hear me?

BEN. [*Standing still, considering.*] What's the proposition?

WILLY. It's twenty thousand dollars on the barrelhead. Guaranteed, gilt-edged, you understand?

BEN. You don't want to make a fool of yourself. They might not honor the policy.

WILLY. How can they dare refuse? Didn't I work like a coolie to meet every premium on the nose? And now they don't pay off? Impossible!

BEN. It's called a cowardly thing, William.

WILLY. Why? Does it take more guts to stand here the rest of my life ringing up a zero?

BEN. [*Yielding.*] That's a point, William. [*He moves, thinking, turns.*] And twenty thousand—that *is* something one can feel with the hand, it is there.

WILLY. [*Now assured, with rising power.*] Oh, Ben, that's the whole beauty of it! I see it like a diamond, shining in the dark, hard and rough, that I can pick up and touch in my hand. Not like—like an appointment! This would not be another damned-fool appointment, Ben, and it changes all the aspects. Because he thinks I'm nothing, see, and so he spites me. But the funeral—[*Straightening up.*] Ben, that funeral will be massive! They'll come from Maine, Massachusetts, Vermont, New Hampshire! All the old-timers with the strange license plates—that boy will be thunderstruck, Ben, because he never realized—I am known! Rhode Island, New York, New Jersey—I am known, Ben, and he'll see it with his eyes once and for all. He'll see what I am, Ben! He's in for a shock, that boy!

BEN. [*Coming down to the edge of the garden.*] He'll call you a coward.

WILLY. [*Suddenly fearful.*] No, that would be terrible.

BEN. Yes. And a damned fool.

WILLY. No, no, he mustn't, I won't have that! [*He is broken and desperate.*]

BEN. He'll hate you, William. [*The gay music of the Boys is heard.*]

WILLY. Oh, Ben, how do we get back to all the great times? Used to be so full of light, and comradeship, the sleigh-riding in winter, and the ruddiness on his cheeks. And always some kind of good news coming up, always something nice coming up ahead. And never even let me carry the valises in the house, and simonizing, simonizing that little red car! Why, why can't I give him something and not have him hate me?

BEN. Let me think about it. [*He glances at his watch.*] I still have a little time. Remarkable proposition, but you've got to be sure you're not making a fool of yourself. [BEN *drifts off upstage and goes out of sight.* BIFF *comes down from the left.*]

WILLY. [*Suddenly conscious of* BIFF, *turns and looks up at him, then begins picking up the packages of seeds in confusion.*] Where the hell is that seed? [*Indignantly.*] You can't see nothing out here! They boxed in the whole goddam neighborhood!

BIFF. There are people all around here. Don't you realize that?

WILLY. I'm busy. Don't bother me.

BIFF. [*Taking the hoe from* WILLY.] I'm saying good-by to you, Pop. [WILLY *looks at him, silent, unable to move.*] I'm not coming back any more.

WILLY. You're not going to see Oliver tomorrow?

BIFF. I've got no appointment, Dad.

WILLY. He put his arm around you, and you've got no appointment?

BIFF. Pop, get this now, will you? Everytime I've left it's been a fight that sent me out of here. Today I realized something about myself and I tried to explain it to you and I—I think I'm just not smart enough to make any sense out of it for you. To hell with whose fault it is or anything like that. [*He takes* WILLY's *arm.*] Let's just wrap it up, heh? Come on in, we'll tell Mom. [*He gently tries to pull* WILLY *to left.*]

WILLY. [*Frozen, immobile, with guilt in his voice.*] No, I don't want to see her.

BIFF. Come on! [*He pulls again, and* WILLY *tries to pull away.*]

WILLY. [*Highly nervous.*] No, no, I don't want to see her.

BIFF. [*Tries to look into* WILLY's *face, as if to find the answer there.*] Why don't you want to see her?

WILLY. [*More harshly now.*] Don't bother me, will you?

BIFF. What do you mean, you don't want to see her? You don't want them calling you yellow, do you? This isn't your fault; it's me, I'm a bum. Now come inside! [WILLY *strains to get away.*] Did you hear what I said to you? [WILLY *pulls away and quickly goes by himself into the house.* BIFF *follows.*]

LINDA. [*To* WILLY.] Did you plant, dear?

BIFF. [*At the door, to* LINDA.] All right, we had it out. I'm going and I'm not writing any more.

LINDA. [*Going to* WILLY *in the kitchen.*] I think that's the best way, dear. 'Cause there's no use drawing it out, you'll just never get along. [WILLY *doesn't respond.*]

BIFF. People ask where I am and what I'm doing, you don't know, and you don't care. That way it'll be off your mind and you can start brightening up again. All right? That clears it, doesn't it? [WILLY *is silent, and* BIFF *goes to him.*] You gonna wish me luck, scout? [*He extends his hand.*] What do you say?

LINDA. Shake his hand, Willy.

WILLY. [*Turning to her, seething with hurt.*] There's no necessity to mention the pen at all, y'know.

BIFF. [*Gently.*] I've got no appointment, Dad.

WILLY. [*Erupting fiercely.*] He put his arm around . . . ?

BIFF. Dad, you're never going to see what I am, so what's the use of arguing? If I strike oil, I'll send you a check. Meantime forget I'm alive.

WILLY. [*To* LINDA.] Spite, see?

BIFF. Shake hands, Dad.

WILLY. Not my hand.

BIFF. I was hoping not to go this way.

WILLY. Well, this is the way you're going. Good-by. [BIFF *looks at him a moment, then turns sharply and goes to the stairs.*]

WILLY. [*Stops him with.*] May you rot in hell if you leave this house!

BIFF. [*Turning.*] Exactly what is it that you want from me?

WILLY. I want you to know, on the train, in the mountains, in the valleys, wherever you go, that you cut down your life for spite!

BIFF. No, no.

WILLY. Spite, spite, is the word of your undoing! And when you're down and out, remember what did it. When you're rotting somewhere beside the railroad tracks, remember, and don't you dare blame it on me!

BIFF. I'm not blaming it on you!

WILLY. I won't take the rap for this, you hear? [HAPPY *comes down the stairs and stands on the bottom step, watching.*]

BIFF. That's just what I'm telling you!

WILLY. [*Sinking into a chair at the table, with full accusation.*] You're trying to put a knife in me—don't think I don't know what you're doing!

BIFF. All right, phony! Then let's lay it on the line. [*He whips the rubber tube out of his pocket and puts it on the table.*]

HAPPY. You crazy—

LINDA. Biff! [*She moves to grab the hose, but BIFF holds it down with his hand.*]

BIFF. Leave it there! Don't move it!

WILLY. [*Not looking at it.*] What is that?

BIFF. You know goddam well what that is.

WILLY. [*Caged, wanting to escape.*] I never saw that.

BIFF. You saw it. The mice didn't bring it into the cellar! What is this supposed to do, make a hero out of you? This supposed to make me sorry for you?

WILLY. Never heard of it.

BIFF. There'll be no pity for you, you hear it? No pity!

WILLY. [*To LINDA.*] You hear the spite!

BIFF. No, you're going to hear the truth —what you are and what I am!

LINDA. Stop it!

WILLY. Spite!

HAPPY. [*Coming down toward BIFF.*] You cut it now!

BIFF. [*To HAPPY.*] The man don't know who we are! The man is gonna know! [*To WILLY.*] We never told the truth for ten minutes in this house!

HAPPY. We always told the truth!

BIFF. [*Turning on him.*] You big blow, are you the assistant buyer? You're one of the two assistants to the assistant, aren't you?

HAPPY. Well, I'm practically—

BIFF. You're practically full of it! We all are! And I'm through with it. [*To WILLY.*] Now hear this, Willy, this is me.

WILLY. I know you!

BIFF. You know why I had no address for three months? I stole a suit in Kansas City and I was in jail. [*To LINDA, who is sobbing.*] Stop crying. I'm through with it. [*LINDA turns away from them, her hands covering her face.*]

WILLY. I suppose that's my fault!

BIFF. I stole myself out of every good job since high school!

WILLY. And whose fault is that?

BIFF. And I never got anywhere because you blew me so full of hot air I could never stand taking orders from anybody! That's whose fault it is!

WILLY. I hear that!

LINDA. Don't, Biff!

BIFF. It's goddam time you heard that! I had to be boss big shot in two weeks, and I'm through with it!

WILLY. Then hang yourself! For spite, hang yourself!

BIFF. No! Nobody's hanging himself, Willy! I ran down eleven flights with a pen in my hand today. And suddenly I stopped, you hear me? And in the middle of that office building, do you hear this? I stopped in the middle of that building and I saw—the sky. I saw the things that I love in this world. The work and the food and time to sit and smoke. And I looked at the pen and said to myself, what the hell am I grabbing this for? Why am I trying to become what I don't want to be? What am I doing in an office, making a contemptuous, begging fool of myself, when all I want is out there, waiting for me the minute I say I know who I am! Why can't I say that, Willy? [*He tries to make WILLY face him, but WILLY pulls away and moves to the left.*]

WILLY. [*With hatred threateningly.*] The door of your life is wide open!

BIFF. Pop! I'm a dime a dozen, and so are you!

WILLY. [*Turning on him now in an uncontrolled outburst.*] I am not a dime a dozen! I am Willy Loman, and you are Biff Loman! [*BIFF starts for WILLY, but is blocked by HAPPY. In his fury, BIFF seems on the verge of attacking his father.*]

BIFF. I am not a leader of men, Willy, and neither are you! You were never anything but a hard-working drummer who landed in the ash can like all the rest of them! I'm one dollar an hour, Willy! I tried seven states and couldn't raise it. A buck an hour! Do you gather my meaning? I'm not bringing home any prizes any more, and you're going to stop waiting for me to bring them home!

WILLY. [*Directly to* BIFF.] You vengeful, spiteful mut! [BIFF *breaks from* HAPPY. WILLY, *in fright, starts up the stairs.* BIFF *grabs him.*]

BIFF. [*At the peak of his fury.*] Pop, I'm nothing! I'm nothing, Pop. Can't you understand that? There's no spite in it any more. I'm just what I am, that's all. [BIFF's *fury has spent itself, and he breaks down, sobbing, holding on to* WILLY, *who dumbly fumbles for* BIFF's *face.*]

WILLY. [*Astonished.*] What're you doing? What're you doing? [*To* LINDA.] Why is he crying?

BIFF. [*Crying, broken.*] Will you let me go, for Christ's sake? Will you take that phony dream and burn it before something happens? [*Struggling to contain himself, he pulls away and moves to the stairs.*] I'll go in the morning. Put him—put him to bed. [*Exhausted,* BIFF *moves up the stairs to his room.*]

WILLY. [*After a long pause, astonished, elevated.*] Isn't that—isn't that remarkable? Biff—he likes me!

LINDA. He loves you, Willy!

HAPPY. [*Deeply moved.*] Always did, Pop.

WILLY. Oh, Biff! [*Staring wildly.*] He cried! Cried to me. [*He is choking with his love, and now cries out his promise.*] That boy—that boy is going to be magnificent! [BEN *appears in the light just outside the kitchen.*]

BEN. Yes, outstanding, with twenty thousand behind him.

LINDA. [*Sensing the racing of his mind, fearfully, carefully.*] Now come to bed, Willy. It's all settled now.

WILLY. [*Finding it difficult not to rush out of the house.*] Yes, we'll sleep. Come on. Go to sleep, Hap.

BEN. And it does take a great kind of a man to crack the jungle. [*In accents of dread,* BEN's *idyllic music starts up.*]

HAPPY. [*His arm around* LINDA.] I'm getting married, Pop, don't forget it. I'm changing everything. I'm gonna run that department before the year is up. You'll see, Mom. [*He kisses her.*]

BEN. The jungle is dark but full of diamonds, Willy. [WILLY *turns, moves, listening to* BEN.]

LINDA. Be good. You're both good boys, just act that way, that's all.

HAPPY. 'Night, Pop. [*He goes upstairs.*]

LINDA. [*To* WILLY.] Come, dear.

BEN. [*With greater force.*] One must go in to fetch a diamond out.

WILLY. [*To* LINDA, *as he moves slowly along the edge of the kitchen, toward the door.*] I just want to get settled down, Linda. Let me sit alone for a little.

LINDA. [*Almost uttering her fear.*] I want you upstairs.

WILLY. [*Taking her in his arms.*] In a few minutes, Linda. I couldn't sleep right now. Go on, you look awful tired. [*He kisses her.*]

BEN. Not like an appointment at all. A diamond is rough and hard to the touch.

WILLY. Go on now. I'll be right up.

LINDA. I think this is the only way, Willy.

WILLY. Sure, it's the best thing.

BEN. Best thing!

WILLY. The only way. Everything is gonna be—go on, kid, get to bed. You look so tired.

LINDA. Come right up.

WILLY. Two minutes. [LINDA *goes into the living-room, then reappears in her bedroom.* WILLY *moves just outside the kitchen door.*]

WILLY. Loves me. [*Wonderingly.*] Always loved me. Isn't that a remarkable thing? Ben, he'll worship me for it!

BEN. [*With promise.*] It's dark there, but full of diamonds.

WILLY. Can you imagine that magnificence with twenty thousand dollars in his pocket?

LINDA. [*Calling from her room.*] Willy! Come up!

WILLY. [*Calling into the kitchen.*] Yes! Yes. Coming! It's very smart, you realize that, don't you, sweetheart? Even Ben sees it. I gotta go, baby. 'By! 'By! [*Going over to* BEN, *almost dancing.*] Imagine? When the mail comes, he'll be ahead of Bernard again!

BEN. A perfect proposition all around.

WILLY. Did you see how he cried to me? Oh, if I could kiss him, Ben!

BEN. Time, William, time!

WILLY. Oh, Ben, I always knew one way or another we were gonna make it, Biff and I!

BEN. [*Looking at his watch.*] The boat. We'll be late. [*He moves slowly off into the darkness.*]

WILLY. [*Elegiacally, turning to the house.*] Now when you kick off, boy, I want a seventy-yard boot, and get right down the field under the ball, and when you hit, hit low and hit hard, because it's important, boy. [*He swings around and faces the audience.*] There's all kinds of important people in the stands, and the first thing you know . . . [*Suddenly realizing he is alone.*] Ben! Ben, where do I . . . ? [*He makes a sudden movement of search.*] Ben, how do I . . . ?

LINDA. [*Calling from within the house.*] Willy, you coming up?

WILLY. [*Uttering a gasp of fear, whirling about as if to quiet her.*] Sh! [*He turns around as if to find his way; sounds, faces, voices, seem to be swarming in upon him and he flicks at them, crying . . .*] Sh! Sh! [*Suddenly music, faint and high, stops him. It rises in intensity, almost to an unbearable scream. He goes up and down on his toes, and rushes off around the house.*] Shhh!

LINDA. Willy?

[*There is no answer. LINDA waits. BIFF gets up off his bed. He is still in his clothes. HAPPY sits up. BIFF stands listening.*]

LINDA. [*With real fear.*] Willy, answer me! Willy!

[*There is the sound of a car starting and moving away at full speed.*]

LINDA. No!

BIFF. [*Rushing down the stairs.*] Pop!

[*As the car speeds off, the music crashes down in a frenzy of sound, which becomes the soft pulsation of a single cello string. BIFF slowly returns to his bedroom. He and HAPPY gravely don their jackets. LINDA slowly walks out of her room. The music has developed into a dead march. The leaves of day are appearing over everything. CHARLEY and BERNARD, somberly dressed, appear and knock on the kitchen door. BIFF and HAPPY slowly descend the stairs to the kitchen as CHARLEY and BERNARD enter.*]

All stop a moment when LINDA, *in clothes of mourning, bearing a little bunch of roses, comes through the draped doorway into the kitchen. She goes to* CHARLEY *and takes his arm. Now all move toward the audience, through the "wall" of the kitchen. At the limit of the forestage,* LINDA *lays down the flowers, kneels, and sits back on her heels. All stare down at the grave.*]

REQUIEM

CHARLEY. It's getting dark, Linda.

[LINDA *doesn't react. She stares at the grave.*]

BIFF. How about it, Mom? Better get some rest, heh? They'll be closing the gate soon.

[LINDA *makes no move. Pause.*]

HAPPY. [*Deeply angered.*] He had no right to do that. There was no necessity for it. We would've helped him.

CHARLEY. [*Grunting.*] Hmmm.

BIFF. Come along, Mom.

LINDA. Why didn't anybody come?

CHARLEY. It was a very nice funeral.

LINDA. But where are all the people he knew? Maybe they blame him.

CHARLEY. Naa. It's a rough world, Linda. They wouldn't blame him.

LINDA. I can't understand it. At this time especially. First time in thirty-five years we were just about free and clear. He only needed a little salary. He was even finished with the dentist.

CHARLEY. No man only needs a little salary.

LINDA. I can't understand it.

BIFF. There were a lot of nice days. When he'd come home from a trip; or on Sundays, making the stoop; finishing the cellar; putting on the new porch; when he built the extra bathroom; and put up the garage. You know something, Charley, there's more of him in that front stoop than in all the sales he ever made.

CHARLEY. Yeah. He was a happy man with a batch of cement.

LINDA. He was so wonderful with his hands.

BIFF. He had the wrong dreams. All, all, wrong.

HAPPY. [*Almost ready to fight Biff.*] Don't say that!

BIFF. He never knew who he was.

CHARLEY. [*Stopping* HAPPY'S *movement and reply. To* BIFF.] Nobody dast blame this man. You don't understand: Willy was a salesman. And for a salesman, there is no rock bottom to the life. He don't put a bolt to a nut, he don't tell you the law or give you medicine. He's a man way out there in the blue, riding on a smile and a shoeshine. And when they start not smiling back—that's an earthquake. And then you get yourself a couple of spots on your hat, and you're finished. Nobody dast blame this man. A salesman has got to dream, boy. It comes with the territory.

BIFF. Charley, the man didn't know who he was.

HAPPY. [*Infuriated.*] Don't say that!

BIFF. Why don't you come with me, Happy?

HAPPY. I'm not licked that easily. I'm staying right in this city, and I'm gonna beat this racket! [*He looks at* BIFF, *his chin set.*] The Loman Brothers!

BIFF. I know who I am, kid.

HAPPY. All right, boy. I'm gonna show you and everybody else that Willy Loman did not die in vain. He had a good dream. It's the only dream you can have —to come out number-one man. He fought it out here, and this is where I'm gonna win it for him.

BIFF. [*With a hopeless glance at* HAPPY, *bends toward his mother.*] Let's go, Mom.

LINDA. I'll be with you in a minute. Go on, Charley. [*He hesitates.*] I want to, just for a minute. I never had a chance to say good-by.

[CHARLEY *moves away, followed by* HAPPY. BIFF *remains a slight distance up and left of* LINDA. *She sits there, summoning herself. The flute begins, not far away, playing behind her speech.*]

LINDA. Forgive me, dear. I can't cry. I don't know what it is, but I can't cry. I don't understand it. Why did you ever do that? Help me, Willy, I can't cry. It seems to me that you're just on another trip. I keep expecting you. Willy, dear, I can't cry. Why did you do it? I search and search and I search, and I can't understand it, Willy. I made the last payment on the house today. Today, dear. And there'll be nobody home. [*A sob rises in her throat.*] We're free and clear. [*Sobbing more fully, released.*] We're free. [BIFF *comes slowly toward her.*] We're free . . . We're free . . .

[BIFF *lifts her to her feet and moves out up right with her in his arms.* LINDA *sobs quietly.* BERNARD *and* CHARLEY *come together and follow them, followed by* HAPPY. *Only the music of the flute is left on the darkening stage as over the house the hard towers of the apartment buildings rise into sharp focus, and*

THE CURTAIN FALLS

THE TRAGIC VISION

At the start of Chapter Four, we asked the question, what is a tragedy? Subsequently, we considered a good many of the special components of a tragic play—a hero with particular qualifications and with a particular relation to his fellow human beings; a plot conceived as a single line proceeding to a terminus; a dominating vision of life which juxtaposes faith in man with a recognition of evil and awareness of the indifference of the gods. But to list ingredients, however essential, is never to define; if to the question, what is a bicycle? you were to answer, "It is an object composed of two wheels, handle-bars, sprocket, chain, tires, fenders, all attached to a simple frame," you would leave the questioner still in ignorance as to some fundamental aspects of the problem.

There are many ways of approaching definition. Two of these are particularly useful in a consideration of tragedy: analysis and contrast. To begin with the latter, since it is more easily apprehended, there is usually little likelihood that anyone will confuse tragedy and comedy. The mode of *The Time of Your Life* is quite distinct from that of *Othello*, and that of Shaw's *Caesar and Cleopatra* from that of Shakespeare's *Julius Caesar*. These are obvious contrasts. There is, to be sure, a middle ground where the contrast is not so clear, a kind of neutral region, exemplified by Anton Chekhov's play, *The Cherry Orchard*, where comedy and tragedy often seem to overlap; but by and large this first distinction is little likely to cause trouble.

Tragedy and melodrama are by no means so obviously differentiated, however. *The Desperate Hours*, it will be remembered, was identified as a melodrama. Though it has a "happy" ending, Hayes's play presents a situation certainly the opposite of comic. It would be a relatively simple matter to re-write the ending in such a way that the evil Griffin would destroy the good Hilliard. If this change were carried out, would it convert *The Desperate Hours* into a tragedy?

The answer is no. One reason for this answer we have already given in a different context: the emphasis in Hayes's play falls very heavily on action. This emphasis means that he is primarily concerned with telling a story; he is concerned with the particular instance. And the obverse of that statement is that Hayes is *not* concerned with human destiny generally considered: *The Desperate Hours* does not originate in a tragic vision. As a consequence, Hayes has not conceived of Daniel Hilliard as a tragic hero; Hilliard possesses courage, but to what level of comprehension does his experience raise him? To how general an area can we refer his struggle with Glen Griffin? How comparable is this struggle to that between Oedipus and the agents of *diké?* Or that between Othello and his passions?

But the contrast between tragedy and melodrama is most clearly drawn in the matter of structure. That of tragedy is linear, and its linear nature derives from the inevitability of the ultimate end. How inevitable is the end of melodrama—of *The Desperate Hours?* How relentlessly does the principle of causation operate in Hayes's play? The answers to these questions firmly establish the contrast with tragedy; for in melodrama, contrivance often plays as important a part as causation. The melodramatist may, and characteristically does, *reverse* the direction of his action, so that, at the end, he can lift what has seemed an inescapable doom. Because the catastrophe is not inevitable, he manipulates his plot to gain certain story effects; there is not, behind his plot, a controlling and directing vision. For this reason we are justified in calling melodrama a less "serious" type of drama than tragedy, since, obviously, its aims are far less exalted.

So much for what tragedy is not; we must now approach the problem affirmatively. *Oedipus, Othello, Blood Wedding*, and *Death of a Salesman* are all identified as tragedies, and yet they seem, at first, as different as four plays on solemn subjects could well be. The differences between them extend beyond the point of mere contrast in setting (temporal or geographical), beyond the kinds of theaters for which each play was designed. More fundamental are structural distinctions: the difference in time-span covered by the enacted stories of Oedipus and Willy Loman, for example, or the shifting attitude toward the number of characters the dramatist ought to employ to tell his story. The differing nationalities of the authors are themselves important, too, insofar as they suggest the significant role of society in governing the contrasting views of Sophocles and Arthur Miller. As we have seen in considering *Oedipus*, these last-named differences can play an important part in helping us to realize what the dramatist has undertaken to do.

All the same, it is possible to assert that, important as these differences are, they are still superficial; that they are not essential to the tragic vision of life; that they are, on the contrary, chargeable to concepts of tragic drama, and of society, peculiar to special moments in time. Underlying them are characteristics of another sort, however, and these are displayed in common by all four of our tragedies. Turning our attention to these, we should find it possible to evolve a definition of tragedy that will accommodate all four works despite their obvious differences.

It may at first seem a superficial matter that three of our four tragedies carry titles designating, in each instance, the chief figure in the play. In itself this is a surface resemblance, but when we throw into the balance the fact that every one of Shakespeare's tragedies also bears the name of its protagonist as a title, it becomes a resemblance we cannot overlook. It points the way, in fact, to one of the basic concepts of tragedy in all periods. If you were asked what Miller's or Shakespeare's play was "about," you would be likely to begin your answer, "It's about a salesman who . . ." or "It's about a Venetian general who . . ." Such an answer would again demonstrate how central the concept of the individual personality is to the tragic vision. Nevertheless, when we have listed the individualizing characteristics of the hero, and the fateful actions they have led him to undertake, something yet remains that we must account for. That is, the tragic dramatist is centrally concerned with an individual (or with a pair of individuals, as in *Romeo and Juliet*), and the story he tells will be dominated by that individual; but beyond this, tragedy also tends, always, to *exalt* the individual, to show us, with the hero as exemplum, man's capacity to endure and to rise to his highest reach under adversity. No matter how clearly we see the hero as an individual person, we often have difficulty framing him in. And understandably so, since, as a creation of the tragic vision, he is more than a man; he is also a symbol. The characteristics of the man he is point beyond him to something that is greater and more significant than he.

The further fact that tragedy ends with the death of the hero (Oedipus is only an apparent exception to the rule) in no way affects this affirmative tragic statement. There are more kinds of death than one. Physical death, the death of the body, is, to be sure, an awful thing, and in its presence we feel a sense of waste—the waste of a brilliant general, the waste of an imperious but noble king, the waste of human beings larger in stature than most. Yet physical death, the tragic writers assure us, is finally not incompatible with the triumph of the individual suffering it, for in the very moment of his extinction he may (and the tragic hero does) make a spiritual affirmation that cancels out the death of the body. In thus affirming the nobility of the individual, the dramatist also affirms the nobility inherent in the race; exalting the man, he extends his vision to all men, and reconciles the individual with the community.

The mere dominance of a play by an individual character does not, of course, produce tragedy; Shaw's comedy is dominated by Caesar, and Sherwood's fine drama, dominated by Lincoln, is not a tragedy. What counts, therefore, is the writer's attitude toward the individual, seen both as a single man and as a representative of humanity. The hero plays two roles: he is Othello the Moor, but he is also man subject to the rule of his own passions; Willy Loman is one salesman, but he is also a segment of the society which has produced him and is now prepared to abandon him. An important aspect of the tragic dramatist's attitude toward the individual is therefore the representative nature of that individual. But we have seen that this is not all. The writer also recognizes, and affirms, the greatness of which the single man is capable in the face of weaknesses of body or of character, as also in the face of chance and circumstance. Nor is this yet all. For he further acknowledges, and asserts, that man has only a limited control over his destiny, that chance is not subject to his command, and that, too often, the very greatness in him is the consequence of a fatal unbalance. Thus Othello's outgiving frankness, his courage, his integrity, even his innate tenderness, are undermined by qualities of character in himself whose significance he has never appreciated. The balanced man, tragedy declares, is the mediocre man, incapable of greatness. The cost of greatness, then, is often an unbalance which, the elements of chance and circumstance aiding, leads to catastrophe.

The polar aspects of the tragic character—his belief that life is good, but only under circumstances which he is finally unable to control—create the tension that holds us to him. We are attracted in awe by the magnificence of his stature, and repelled in fear by the human taints and flaws that are mirrored in him; we are moved to terror and pity by the apparent inevitability of his doom, and attracted in admiration by his courage and determination never to yield. It is true that, in all tragedies, the conflict that initially captures our attention is the one between protagonist and antagonist—between Oedipus and the agents of diké: Creon, Teiresias, and the shepherd; between Othello and Iago; between Leonardo and the Mother; between Willy Loman and "the system." But we soon realize that what has been dramatized is actually an internal human conflict. The story must therefore be so constructed as to provide the maximum opportunity for the revelation of human motive through action.

To this end, the tragic dramatist adopts the linear plot. And we must never underestimate the importance of plot—the ordering of the events—in tragedy. For, because the tragic plot is linear rather than circular, because we watch a one-way approach to the abyss instead of a trip on the merry-go-round, we soon anticipate what is going to happen to the protagonist. As a result, our attention shifts from the outcome to its causes, and, most of all, to the nature of the man whose journey toward destruction we are witnessing. Were the story's thread not stretched out before us in a straight line, to be picked up at will, we would lack those moments of contemplation in which, searching the hero, we discover the reflection of ourselves.

With all that has been said so far, we would appear to be some distance yet from a definition. Worse still, some of the provisional statements offered seem even to contradict one another: here is an individual who is yet not an individual, an affirmation of life at the point of death, an exalted representative of the race who yet cannot control his destiny. Yet these apparent contradictions can be reconciled—in a paradox; and this paradox presents us finally with the definition we have been seeking. For tragedy is based on the paradox that man, who is so clearly suited to enjoy the fruits of his earth, who is capable of joyousness in the fulfillment of his tasks, who touches sublimity in action as well as in thought, is nevertheless hedged in, is subject, is ultimately subservient, is limited, and must often pay with his life for the possession of those things which make his life meaningful to him. The values he fights and dies for—beauty, love of country, truth and integrity, belief in his gods—are finally measured by a force which his finite mind cannot encompass. Whether this force happens to be defined as the Homeric Necessity, as the will of God, as economic determinism, as Dreiser's "bio-chemistry," or as blind chance, matters not a bit with respect to the *essence* of tragedy. What does matter is that man, with all the benefits of a 2500-year accumulation of philosophical and scientific thought to call on, still confronts ultimate questions to which there is no answer.

Like all paradoxes, this one establishes a tension, and when this tension reaches a level of passionate feeling, the spirit of tragedy is born. There is no reconciling of man's capacities with his manifest destiny. The purchase price of fulfillment is too high for reconciliation. But in paying the price demanded for those things he cherishes, whatever the price in temporal circumstances may happen to be, the hero redeems himself. In paying the price, whether he be Oedipus or Willy Loman, he redeems the dignity of man.

The tragic dramatist is committed to a belief in the worth of the individual, recognizing at the same time, however, that society is composed of individual men. But the individual (and the tragic hero) is subject to limitations in his reach for the realization of his potentialities. These limitations may be the product of "fate," of blind chance, or they may arise in defects of character, often in themselves ultimately beyond the individual's control. In any case, that tension which grows from the gap between his promise and its fulfillment is productive of tragedy. And the spiritual awakening that often accompanies material failure accounts for the great affirmation which tragedy pronounces. Tragic drama, as Arthur Miller has written, is, in fact, more "optimistic" about the condition of man than comedy can ever be. For it conducts man to the highest summits of life and reveals him there fully at home, even in the presence of his own death.